ENCYCLOPEDIA
OF THE
WORLD'S MINORITIES

ENCYCLOPEDIA OF THE WORLD'S MINORITIES

Volume 1
A–F

CARL SKUTSCH, EDITOR
MARTIN RYLE, CONSULTING EDITOR

ROUTLEDGE
NEW YORK AND LONDON

Published in 2005 by
Routledge
Taylor & Francis Group
270 Madison Avenue
New York, NY 10016
www.routledge-ny.com

Published in Great Britain by
Routledge
Taylor & Francis Group
2 Park Square
Milton Park, Abingdon
Oxon OX14 4RN
www.routledge.co.uk

Printed in the United States of America on acid-free paper.

10 9 8 7 6 5 4 3 2 1

Library of Congress Cataloging-in-Publication Data

Encyclopedia of the world's minorities / Carl Skutsch, editor; Martin Ryle, consulting editor.
p. cm.
Includes bibliographical references.
ISBN 1-57958-392-X (alk. paper)
1. Ethnic groups—Encyclopedias. 2. Minorities—Encyclopedias.
I. Skutsch, Carl. II. Ryle, Martin (J. Martin) III. Title.

GN495.4.E63 2005
305.8'003—dc22 2004020324

Advisory Board Members

Table of Contents

List of Entries

Thematic List of Entries

Nations

Topics

Preface

Social and political changes around the world have added an urgency to the study of minorities and minority issues. Globalization, immigration, migration, civil conflict, and ethnic tensions have brought greater public awareness to minority groups and greater academic interest to minority studies. Similarly, the international community's commitment to self-determination, cultural diversity, human differences, and the preservation of traditions has attracted the attention of the public and focused the energies of a worldwide array of scholars working in a range of subject areas.

Reflecting the interdisciplinary and international character of minority studies, the *Encyclopedia of the World's Minorities* includes the work of over 300 contributors from 40 countries specializing in areas as varied as anthropology, cultural studies, ethnography, history, international relations, linguistics, political science, and religion. These scholars work at universities and colleges as well as research centers and organizations around the globe that seek to further our understanding of minority issues and monitor the situation of minority groups. Within this community, the subject is rigorously and often contentiously argued, but the degree of interest and the intensity of debate ultimately testify to its importance. Because the study of minorities involves the difficult issues of rights, justice, equality, dignity, identity, autonomy, political liberties, and cultural freedoms, the discussions in the encyclopedia apply to many areas of public interest and student inquiry.

One of the concepts most vigorously debated by those working in minority studies is the meaning of "minority" itself. This is because the meaning does matter. In the early twentieth century, the African-American political thinker W.E.B. Du Bois declared the color line to be the defining issue of the age. From that time forward the line that demarcates a minority group, acknowledges a minority concern, or defines a minority right has had considerable consequence. The *Encyclopedia of the World's Minorities*, like minority studies itself, attempts not to finalize this definition but to present its histories and complexities.

Traditionally, a minority group has been understood to have an indigenous relationship to an area—what is called an autochthonous relationship—where it is, at a given time, numerically inferior to another group. Such a group is understood to share a cultural characteristic that one member identifies in another. This shared culture may take the form of ethnicity, race, customs, language, or religion; and it receives larger legitimacy by virtue of its long-standing presence in a region. Although this definition functions within limited contexts and is acknowledged throughout the encyclopedia, it is far from universal, because it fails to account for a surplus of historical issues and influences that we confront today.

For example, according to this orthodox definition of minority, a member of an indigenous group may enjoy a legal relationship to a nation that vastly differs from that of an immigrant, a permanent resident, or a migrant worker, all of whom may share the cultural markers of a minority group but have none of the protections. Governments that secure protections, rights, and entitlements—which may include access to employment, political processes, education, health care, the media, and the judicial system—only for recognized minorities may thereby exclude non-indigenous groups from these same privileges. The encyclopedia presents how minority studies discusses the tensions created by conferring legal privileges to indigenous minorities and withholding them from others.

Although numerical inferiority may seem a reasonable, if only intuitive, way to define minority status, it is not sufficient within minority studies. Slavery in the American South, apartheid in South Africa, and the Baathist system in Iraq—where a numerically inferior group dominated a numerically superior group—all serve to remind us that a consideration of cultural and political *non-dominance* must enter our understanding of what minority status means. Numerical superiority of one group often enforces cultural and political dominance over another group, but numbers alone do not adequately define minority or fully describe the relative influence and self-determination one group may enjoy.

In this sense, minority status has come to define a political relationship rather than an inherent or changeless attribute of a people. The discipline does not agree that minority status requires that a people share immutable characteristics that are often associated with race and ethnicity. Religion and language, for example, are not immutable identities, because they can be acquired or change, but they do figure significantly in minorities' self-identification. Recently, some scholars have argued for a definition that accounts for power and equality, in which a minority is any group that has historically been relegated to a status unequal to that of a dominant group, regardless of distinct cultural or ethnic attributes; this definition would include sexual minorities. The encyclopedia brings these issues to light, presents these arguments, and summarizes broader opinion.

The broad opinion might conclude from these debates that the most inclusive definition of a minority or minorities is preferred. Certainly there is truth in this. Nevertheless, for those attempting to create law and public policy that is responsible to an electorate, a pragmatic approach to minority issues is, however flawed, a fundamental but ever-changing reality. For example, principles such as self-determination and cultural autonomy are universally recognized (at least among democratic nations and those creating law and public policy) yet pragmatically circumscribed to prevent instability and secessionist conflicts where coexistence and integration are possible and preferred. Coexistence, intercultural communication, and civil processes are as important to minority studies as independence, difference, and diversity. Incremental progress is also a valued strategy in the discussion of minority issues. On the one hand, national laws regarding minorities are often more restrictive than international proclamations. Thus individual nations, such as the member states of the European Community, while respecting certain basic rights for all, provide substantial protections, politically and culturally, to those minority groups officially recognized by the state. On the other hand, the United Nations uses a very broad definition of minority status and rights—one that may serve groups as they argue and agitate against political facts—but the protections that this definition *guarantees* are unhappily too few. The unhappy compromise is often a reality for the world's minorities.

Organization of the Encyclopedia

Calculations and compromises are necessary in the creation of a work that covers such a large subject. The *Encyclopedia of the World's Minorities* does not contain an entry on every minority group in every nation and region of the world. It presents for the user a thorough resource on minority studies. The information here covers the vast and diverse study of the world's minorities, introducing students to the field and providing an international perspective that enables students to pursue their own interests. To give structure to the scope of such a project, a four-pronged rationale was chosen that creates an accessible architecture for readers of the encyclopedia. This strategy organizes the encyclopedia into four clearly defined entry types: *topics*, *nations*, *groups*, and *biographies*.

Of the 562 entries in the encyclopedia, 75 **Topics entries** introduce students to the broad ideas, concepts, and concerns shared by those working on minority issues. Readers will find definitions and histories of such terms as "Autonomy," "Self-determination," and "Nationalism." Entries of this kind also include organizations and institutions, such as Sinn Féin, the League of Nations, and Minority Rights Group International. These entries help to familiarize students with the language of the discipline and to understand how organizations participate in the field and are discussed within it.

Nations entries (173 in total) describe the history of minorities living within national borders and so explain the political and legal apparatus that states formally create in relation to their minority populations as well as the informal conditions experienced by those groups. In nation entries the reader will find information not only about the dominant group in a country, such as the Swedes in Sweden, but about those other groups that share in the nation-state, such as the Finnish and Saami minorities in Sweden. In this respect, the encyclopedia encourages readers to think outside of categories they commonly associate with the idea of a country—to think of a nation as an assemblage of peoples and cultures rather than as a single, monolithic entity.

Groups entries, composing the largest category with a total of 251 essays, explain the history of peoples living as minorities around the world. These entries discuss whether the group is a single-nation minority or one living in multiple nations, detailing its language, religion, and political and social conditions. Each group entry also contains up-to-date population data garnered from, among other sources such as national censuses, the 2003 *World Factbook* published by the CIA for the United States Government. Group entries are of two kinds: one covers groups who, wherever they are found, live as a minority, such as the Roma (Gypsies); the other covers groups who enjoy a dominant place in a homeland but are found elsewhere as minorities, such as the Japanese. This distinction is important to recognize because the notions of identity and cultural legitimacy are so often linked with a place of origin or with a nation that the situation of stateless peoples is often ignored. Similarly, minorities seeking greater protections have often resorted to nationalism to assert political liberties.

Biographies introduce persons who figure significantly in the history of minority communities and who, through their actions or words, have articulated the larger interests of minority peoples. A total of 62 such entries include Marcus Garvey, Mahatma Gandhi, and Ngugi wa Thiong'o. Biographical entries credit an individual's importance but also reveal how leaders of minority campaigns and struggles influence one another in vastly different parts of the world, showing that a minority group identifies not always only with itself but also with other minority groups as they look to each other for guidance.

Ultimately, an encyclopedia is a wealth of integrated information that maps an area of interest and provides as many access points to that information as possible. In creating this map, the encyclopedia aims to present fact, not opinion. Its entries describe rather than persuade, explain arguments rather than take sides, present rather than resolve areas of contention. The *Encyclopedia of the World's Minorities* contains 562 **signed scholarly essays** about nations, groups, and issues around the world that, written in clear, accessible prose, create a detailed map of a complicated terrain. Each entry includes a selection of **further readings** and **cross-references** (listed in "see also" sections at the end of each entry) to other articles for those readers who wish to explore a topic in greater depth. **Blind entries** serve to guide the reader through the work. A thorough, **analytic index** provides the reader with a critical tool for accessing the work in its entirety.

Creating an encyclopedia is never a solitary undertaking. I would like to extend my appreciation to the editorial board. Their help in formulating the final table of contents was invaluable. I would especially like to thank Martin Ryle, professor of history, emeritus, the University of Virginia, Charlottesville, Virginia. His willingness to review the final manuscript in the closing months of the project was nothing short of heroic. His guidance and commitment to the encyclopedia made its publication possible. Finally, I would like to thank the hundreds of contributors whose work here will further our understanding of the world's minorities.

Notes on Contributors

Rafis Abazov, Harriman Institute, Columbia University, New York, USA.

Jon Abbink, African Studies Centre, Leiden University, The Netherlands.

Marat Akchurin, Bethesda, Maryland, USA.

Shawn Alexander, W.E.B. Du Bois Department of Afro-American Studies, University of Massachusetts at Amherst, USA.

Agron Alibali, Boston, Massachusetts, USA.

Erik Allardt, Department of Sociology, University of Helsinki, Finland.

Mehdi Parvizi Amineh, International Institute for Asian Studies, Leiden, The Netherlands.

Guy Arnold, London, United Kingdom.

Michael Azariadis, Perth, Australia.

Tuncay Babali, Department of Political Science, University of Houston, Texas, USA.

D. Shyam Babu, Rajiv Gandhi Institute for Contemporary Studies, New Delhi, India.

Michael Banton, University of Bristol, United Kingdom.

Abdoulaye Barry, University Gaston Baerger, Saint Louis, Senegal.

Trevor Batrouney, RMIT University, Balwyn, Australia.

Florian Bieber, Nationalism Studies Program, Central European University, Budapest, Hungary.

Charles Boewe, Pittsboro, North Carolina, USA.

Nadia Joanne Britton, Department of Sociological Studies, University of Sheffield, United Kingdom.

Susan Love Brown, Department of Anthropology, Florida Atlantic University, USA.

Anne Brydon, Department of Sociology and Anthropology, Wilfrid Laurier University, Waterloo, Ontario, Canada.

Marcelo Bucheli, Department of History, Stanford University, California, USA.

Debra Buchholtz, Banbury, Oxfordshire, United Kingdom.

Jeff Burke, Religious Studies Program, Lynchburg College, Virginia, USA.

Joan Manuel Cabezas Lopez, University of Barcelona, Catalonia, Spain.

Laura M. Calkins, Vietnam Archive, Texas Tech University, USA.

Gregory R. Campbell, Department of Anthropology, University of Montana at Missoula, USA.

Tim Carmichael, African Studies Center, Michigan State University, USA.

Wendy Carter, USA.

Ellis Cashmore, School of Health, Staffordshire University, Stafford, United Kingdom.

Derek Catsam, Falls Church, Virginia, USA.

Shukai R. Chaudhari, The Nepal Indigenous Development Society, Ratnanagar Tandi, Chitwan, Nepal.

Tan Chee-Beng, Department of Anthropology, The Chinese University of Hong Kong.

James Chin, School of Administrative and Political Studies, University of Papua New Guinea.

Jamsheed Choksy, Middle Eastern Studies Program, Indiana University, USA.

T. Matthew Ciolek, Research School of Asian and Pacific Studies, Australian National University.

Andrew Clark, History Department, University of North Carolina at Wilmington, USA.

Samuel Cohen, Department of English, Lehman College, City University of New York, USA.

Robert O. Collins, Department of History, University of California at Santa Barbara, USA.

Daniele Conversi, Department of Policy Studies, University of Lincolnshire, Lincoln, United Kingdom.

Allan Cooper, Department of Political Science, Otterbein College, Ohio, USA.

Susan Crate, Department of Geography, Miami University, Oxford, Ohio, USA.

Nigel Crawhall, South African San Institute/Indigenous Peoples of Africa Coordinating Committee, Cape Town, South Africa.

Kevin Curow, Bad Homburg, Germany.

Farhad Daftary, Institute of Ismali Studies, London, United Kindgom.

Loring Danforth, Department of Anthropology, Bates College, Maine, USA.

John Davies, Department of Economics, Acadia University, Wolfville, Nova Scotia, Canada.

Darién J. Davis, History Department, Middlebury College, Vermont, USA.

John H. Davis, New York, USA.

Fernand de Varennes, School of Law, Murdoch University, Perth, Australia.

Anne Decoret-Ahiha, Universitè Lyon II, France.

Neil Denslow, Independent Scholar, Dorset, United Kingdom.

Barbara Dilly, Department of Sociology and Anthropology, Creighton University, Nebraska, USA.

Elena Dingu-Kyrklund, Center of Research in International Migration and Ethnic Relations, Stockholm University, Sweden.

Audra Diptee, Department of History, University of Toronto, Ontario, Canada.

Aleksandra Djajic Horváth, Department of History and Civilization, European University Institute, Florence, Italy.

Ivana Djuric, Zagreb, Croatia.

Stephanie Hemelryk Donald, Murdoch University, Perth, Australia.

Yves Dorémieux, Anthropology Department, Center for Mongolian and Siberian Studies, University Paris X, France.

Haley Duschinski, Harvard University, Boston, Massachusetts, USA.

James Eder, Department of Anthropology, Arizona State University, USA.

Fadwa El Guindi, University of Southern California, USA.

Robyn Eversole, Centre for Regional and Rural Development, RMIT University, Hamilton, Victoria, Australia.

Brigit Farley, Department of History, Washington State University, Tri-Cities, USA.

Mariana Ferreira, Anthropology, University of Tennessee, USA.

Peter Finke, Max Planck Institute for Social Anthropology, Halle/Saale, Germany.

Sterling Fluharty, Department of History, University of Oklahoma, USA.

Bernard Formoso, Departement d'ethnologie, Universite Paris X–Nanterre, France.

Germán Freire, University of London, United Kingdom.

Victor Friedman, University of Chicago, Illinois, USA.

Hillel Frisch, Department of Political Studies, Bar-Ilan University, Ramat-Gan, Israel.

Steve Garner, School of Sociology, University of the West of England, Bristol, United Kingdom.

Erika H. Gilson, Princeton University, New Jersey, USA.

Benito Giordano, University of Manchester, United Kingdom.

Martí Grau, Barcelona, Spain.

Joseph Graves, Jr., Glendale, Arizona, USA.

Juan Carlos Gumucio, Department of Cultural Anthropology and Ethnography, Uppsala University, Sweden.

Annette Hamilton, Department of Anthropology, Macquarie University, Sydney, New South Wales, Australia.

Kevin David Harrison, Department of Linguistics, Swarthmore College, Pennsylvania, USA.

Maximilian Hartmuth, University of Vienna, Austria.

Ai Hattori, Alexandria, Virginia, USA.

Angela Haynes, Minority Rights Group, London, United Kingdom.

Dagmar Hellmann-Rajanayagam, Department of Economic and Social Science, University Erlangen-Nuremberg, Germany.

Arthur Helweg, Department of Anthropology, Western Michigan University, USA.

Kristin Henrard, Department of International and Constitutional Law, University of Groningen, The Netherlands.

J. Scott Hill, Richmond, Virginia, USA.

Jeremy Hodes, Kambah, Australia.

Krisadawan Hongladarom, Department of Linguistics, Faculty of Arts, Chulalongkorn University, Bangkok, Thailand.

Tian Hongliang, Department of Anthropology, The Chinese University of Hong Kong.

Michael Houf, Department of History, Texas A&M University–Kingsville, USA.

Jayne Ifekwunigwe, School of Social Sciences, University of East London, United Kingdom.

Rad Ilie, Cluj-Napoca, Romania.

Andrew Irving, London, United Kingdom.

Guillaume Jacques, Paris 7–Denis Diderot University, France.

Amjad Jaimoukha, Jordan Engineers Association, Royal Scientific Society, Amman, Jordan.

Annu Jalais, London School of Economics, United Kingdom.

Laksiri Jayasuriya, Department of Social Work, University of Western Australia.

Richard Jenkins, Migration and Ethnicity Research Center, University of Sheffield, United Kingdom.

Hou Jingrong, The Chinese University of Hong Kong.

Lars Karstedt, Universitat Hamburg, Germany.

Olga Kazmina, Moscow, Russia.

Ime Kerlee, Emory University, Georgia, USA.

Deepa Khosla, Department of Government and Politics, University of Maryland, USA.

Reinhard Klein-Arendt, Institute for African Studies, University of Cologne, Germany.

Laszlo Kocsis, Transylvania, Romania.

Charles C. Kolb, National Endowment for the Humanities, Washington, District of Columbia, USA.

Boris Koltchanov, Riga, Latvia.

Jill E. Korbin, Department of Anthropology, Case Western Reserve University, Ohio, USA.

Chima J. Korieh, Department of History, Central Michigan University, Michigan, USA.

Jørgen Kühl, Aabenraa, Denmark.

Olga Kul'bachevskya, Institute of Ethnology and Anthropology, Russian Academy of Sciences, Moscow, Russia.

P.R. Kumaraswamy, Jawaharlal Nehru University, New Delhi, India.

Yves Laberge, Département de sociologie, Institut Québécois des Hautes Etudes Internationales, Canada.

Andrea Laing-Marshall, Historical Department, Wycliffe College, Toronto, Ontario, Canada.

Laura Laubeova, Prague, Czech Republic.

Benjamin Lawrance, Department of History, Stanford University, California, USA.

Barbara Leigh, Institute for International Studies, Unviersity of Technology, Sydney, New South Wales, Australia.

Keith Leitich, Seattle, Washington, USA.

Rohini Lele, University of Pune, India.

David Leonard, Comparative Ethnic Studies, Washington State University, USA.

Hal Levine, Department of Anthropology, Victoria University of Wellington, New Zealand.

Jerome Lewis, Department of Anthropology, London School of Economics and Political Science, United Kingdom.

Wei Li, Department of Geography, Arizona State University, USA.

Yianna Liatsos, Department of Comparative Literature, Rutgers University, New Jersey, USA.

Peter Limb, Michigan State University, USA.

Pamela Lindell, Sacramento, California, USA.

Michael Lipson, Department of Political Science, Concordia University, Montreal, Quebec, Canada.

Miles Litvinoff, OneWorld International, London, United Kingdom.

Ludomir Lozny, Department of Anthropology, Hunter College, City University of New York, USA.

Leo Lucassen, Department of Social History, University of Amsterdam, The Netherlands.

Tamba M'bayo, Department of History, Michigan State University, USA.

Charles Macdonald, Campus St. Charles, Universite de Provence, Marseille, France.

Sarah Manapa, Biola University, California.

Richard R. Marcus, Department of Political Science, Yale University, Connecticut, USA.

Alexandra Marois.

Oliver Marshall, Centre for Brazilian Studies, Oxford University, United Kingdom.

Marco Martiniello, Belgian National Fund for Scientific Research and University of Liege, Belgium.

Bruce Matthews, Faculty of Arts, Acadia University, Wolfville, Nova Scotia, Canada.

Duncan McCargo, Institute for Politics and International Studies, University of Leeds, United Kingdom.

Pamela McElwee, Department of Anthropology, Yale University, Connecticut, USA.

John McGurk, Claremorris, Mayo, Ireland.

Eugene McLaughlin, Faculty of Social Sciences, The Open University, Milton Keynes, United Kingdom.

Joanne McLean, School of Environmental & Information Sciences, Charles Sturt University, Albury, Australia.

Manuella Meyer, Brown University, Rhode Island, United States.

Jean Michaud, Paris, France.

Paul E. Michelson, Department of History, Huntington College, Indiana, USA.

Alessandro Michelucci, Florence, Italy.

Maged Mikhail, West Covina, California, USA.

Monique Milia-Marie-Luce, Trinité, Martinique.

Ruth Murbach, Département des sciences juridiques, Université du Québec à Montréal, Canada.

Rachel Newcomb, Department of Anthropology, Princeton University, New Jersey, USA.

Beatrice Nicolini, Storia e Istituzioni dell'Africa, Università Cattolica del Sacro Cuore, Milano, Italy.

Stephan Nikolov, Sofia, Bulgaria.

Donnacha Ó Beacháin, Tbilisi, Georgia.

Denise T. Ogden, Penn State University, USA.

Jonathan Okamura, Department of Ethnic Studies, University of Hawaii, USA.

Brendan O'Leary, Convenor of the Government Department, London School of Economics, United Kingdom.

Dennis Papazian, Armenian Research Center, The University of Michigan-Dearborn, USA.

Joshua Pasternak, Routledge, New York, USA.

Doug Pennoyer, School of Intercultural Studies, Biola University, California, USA.

John Edward Phillips, Faculty of Humanities, Hirosaki University, Japan.

Anne Pitsch Santiago, University of Maryland, USA.

Hugh Poulton, London, United Kingdom.

Sabiyha Robin Prince, Columbia, Maryland, USA.

Pavel Puchkov, Moscow, Russia.

Eva Rakel, Amsterdam, The Netherlands.

Riccardo Redaelli, Milano, Italy.

Javaid Rehman, Department of Law, University of Leeds, United Kingdom.

Massimo Repetti, Genova, Liguria, Italy.

Annette Richardson, University of Alberta, Edmonton, Canada.

Edward A. Riedinger, Latin American, Spanish, and Portuguese Collection, Ohio State University Libraries, USA.

Mika Roinila, Department of Geography, State University of New York at New Paltz, USA.

Elisa Roller, Brussels, Belgium.

Victor Roudometof, Department of Social and Political Sciences, University of Cyprus, Nicosia, USA.

Helena Ruotsala, School of Cultural Studies, University of Turku, Finland.

Sue Russell, Biola University, California, USA.

P. Sahadevan, School of International Studies, Jawaharlal Nehru University, New Delhi, India.

Oscar Salemink, Department of Social and Cultural Anthropology, Vrije Universiteit Amsterdam, The Netherlands.

Amandeep Sandhu, Department of Sociology, University of Victoria, British Columbia, Canada.

L. Natalie Sandomirsky, Auburndale, Massachusetts, USA.

Christopher Saunders, Department of Historical Studies, University of Cape Town, Rondebosch, South Africa.

Richard Scaglion, Department of Anthropology, University of Pittsburgh, Pennsylvania, USA.

Antonia Yétúndé Fælárìn Schleicher, National African Language Resource Center, University of Wisconsin, USA.

Ulrike Schuerkens, Paris, France.

Richard Schur, American Studies Department, The University of Kansas, USA.

Murali Shanmugavelan, Communication for Development Programme, Panos Institute, London, United Kingdom.

Marika Sherwood, Oare, Kent, United Kingdom.

Andrei Simic, Department of Anthropology, University of Southern California, USA.

Gregory M. Simon, Department of Anthropology, University of California, San Diego, USA.

Scott Simon, Department of Sociology, University of Ottawa, Ontario, Canada.

Stefaan Smis, Faculty of Law, Vrije Universiteit Brussels, Belgium.

David Norman Smith, Department of Sociology, University of Kansas, USA.

Ingmar Söhrman, Göteborg University, Sweden.

Subhash Sonnad, Department of Sociology, Western Michigan University, USA.

Ernst Spaan, Netherlands Interdisciplinary Demographic Institute, The Hague, The Netherlands.

Sabira Ståhlberg, Varna, Bulgaria.

Erin Stapleton-Corcoran, Chicago, Illinois, USA.

Sian Sullivan, SOAS, London, United Kingdom.

Ingvar Svanberg, Department of East European Studies, Uppsala University, Sweden.

Nicola Tannenbaum, Sociology/Anthropology Department, Lehigh University, Pennsylvania, USA.

George Tarkhan-Mouravi, Tibilisi, Georgia.

Wade Tarzia, Arts & Humanities Division, Naugatuck Valley Community College, Connecticut, USA.

Philip Taylor, Department of Anthropology, The Australian National University, Canberra.

Louis Tenawa, UREDS International, Yaoundé, Cameroon.

Shanthi Thambiah, Gender Studies Program, University of Malaya, Kuala Lumpur, Malaysia.

Ewa M. Thompson, Department of German and Slavic Studies, Rice University, Texas, USA.

Patrick Thornberry, Department of International Relations, Keele University, Newcastle Under Lyme, Staffordshire, United Kingdom.

Lenora Timm, Department of Linguistics, University of California, Davis, USA.

Reeta Chowdhari Tremblay, Department of Political Science, Concordia University, Montreal, Quebec, Canada.

Frances Trix, Ann Arbor, Michigan, USA.

Linda Tie Hua Tsung, Language Center, Hong Kong University of Science & Technology, China.

Greta Uehling, University of Michigan, USA.

Saskia Van Hoyweghen, Antwerpen, Belgium.

Virginie Vate, Paris, France.

Charles Verharen, Department of Philosophy, Howard University, Washington, District of Columbia, USA.

Richard Verrone, The Vietnam Archive, Texas Tech University, USA.

Eduardo J. Ruiz Vieytez, Institute of Human Rights, University of Deusto, Bilbao, Basque Country, Spain.

Iain Walker, Orléans, France.

Charles Westin, Centre for Research in International Migration and Ethnic Relations, Stockholm University, Sweden.

Wim Willems, Institute for Migration and Ethnic Studies, University of Amsterdam, The Netherlands.

Brian Williams, Department of History, University of London, United Kingdom.

Davina Woods, Clever Women Consultants, Melbourne, Victoria, Australia.

Theodore Wright, Niskayuna, New York, USA.

Aborigines

Capsule Summary

Location: the continent and nearby islands of Australia
Total Population: approximately 303,300
Languages: Standard Australian English (80%); Aboriginal English (3%); Aboriginal language not related to English (15%)
Religions: Aboriginal spirituality and/or Christianity

The Aboriginal peoples of Australia are one of the two major Indigenous peoples governed by the Commonwealth and State/Territory governments of the nation-state of Australia. According to the National Aboriginal and Torres Strait Islander survey held by the Australian Bureau of Statistics in 1994, there are approximately 303,300 Aboriginal and Torres Strait Islander people in Australia, the majority of whom are Aboriginal people. The majority of Aboriginal people speak standard Australian English as their first language. Many speak Aboriginal English as a secondary language and a mark of their Aboriginal identity. About 9,000 speak Aboriginal English as their first language. Approximately 15 percent of Aboriginal people speak an Aboriginal language as their first language and about 87 percent of Aboriginal people in Australia have no difficulty with English.

Archaeologists know that Aboriginal people have been in Australia for over 40,000 years, with some archaeologists suggesting that Aboriginal people have been in Australia for approximately 100,000 years. The traditional beliefs of Aboriginal people are that they come from the land itself.

History

Distance and the lack of accurate sea charts lead to mainly accidental and brief encounters with the Dutch, French, and English along the continent's inhospitable western coast. Trade and cultural exchange occurred between the peoples of the Torres Strait Islands and the Aboriginal groups of what is now known as the Cape York Peninsula; the only other regular visitors to the continent have been the Indonesian fishermen from the Dutch-governed port of Macassar at the southern end of the Celebes. The Macassarese visited annually by using the northwest monsoon season between December and February to speed their vessels to points ranging from The Kimberley' to the Gulf of Carpentaria along the northern shore of Australia. They came to fish for trepang (large sea cucumbers) and returned home on the southeast monsoon of March.

It was not until January 1788 that foreigners came to stay. The British established a penal colony at Port Jackson, and thus the invasion of Aboriginal land was commenced.

Invasion

Dispossession and disease were the first tools used by the British to destroy Aboriginal people. Australian history is littered with massacres against Aboriginal people. Cultural markers such as language and religious pursuits were banned and law and authority figures were ignored or ridiculed in an attempt to destroy Aboriginal societies. The establishment of legislation originally within each of the separate colonies and then later in the States and Territories of Australia forced Aboriginal people to live in compounds known as missions or reserves. Their alternative was to accept conditions under which Aboriginal people were denied the right to make contact with their families. On missions and reserves, Aboriginal people were denied the right to education, employment, and living locations of their own choosing. People who were offered certificates to exempt them from living on the reserves and missions were forced to report often and regularly to the local Protector of Aborigines and to prove that they were employed and living away from any contact with other Aboriginal people.

Language

The Aboriginal peoples of Australia have developed a language generically known as Aboriginal English. People from particular areas of Australia use Aboriginal English terms such *Murris*, *Nungas*, *Nyoongas*, *Kooris*, or *Pallawah* to identify themselves as Aboriginal. Through both the classical languages and the contemporary, Aboriginal people maintain their cultural identity as the Indigenous peoples of Australia.

Aboriginal Identity

Aboriginal heritage, self-identification as an Aboriginal person, and acceptance by other members of an Aboriginal community are the ways in which a person is seen as Aboriginal.

Aboriginal Society

Aboriginal people, along with Torres Strait Islanders, make up approximately 3 percent of the overall population of Australia. However, the Aboriginal and Torres Strait Islander peoples of Australia also have the most rapidly growing population within Australia. The majority of Aboriginal and Torres Strait Islander people are less than 10 years old. Aboriginal people have had their traditional authority figures denigrated by the dominant culture and families have been splintered by policies that caused children to be stolen from their families and communities. Addictive drugs, such as opium, were introduced to Aboriginal people early during colonization to keep people from leaving places where they could be used as cheap labor. Missionaries are known to have used tobacco addiction to force people to live on missions, and, in more recent times, alcohol and sniffing substances such as petrol and glue have negatively affected Aboriginal society. However, Aboriginal people comprise many clans, language groups, and communities—many families and extended families. Aboriginal people are working to heal themselves through programs that help them to find family and community, such as Link-Up and organizations that deal with their specific health, legal, and housing issues.

Aboriginal and Torres Strait Islander Commission (ATSIC)

A major step forward in the healing process for Aboriginal people of Australia has been the founding of the Aboriginal and Torres Strait Islander Commission (ATSIC). Established in 1990, ATSIC is the federal government's principal agency for administering to Aboriginal issues. It is also an attempt to give Aboriginal people more control over their lives because it comprises a commission and State-Territory and regional councils of Indigenous Australians elected by Aboriginal and Torres Strait Islander people for a three-year term of office.

The Commission was commenced at about the same time as the federal government held a Royal Commission into Aboriginal deaths in custody, and the process of reconciliation was formally embodied by an Act of the Commonwealth Parliament and the establishment of a Council for Aboriginal Reconciliation. Following closely was the commencement of the Human Rights Commission inquiry into the Separation of Aboriginal Children from their families. The High Court decisions on Mabo and Wik, which forced the Commonwealth government to make landmark legislation in the area of land rights, also occurred in the decade after Australia had entered its third century since the British invasion, which began on January 26, 1788.

Aboriginal Spirituality

Aboriginal spirituality teaches of "Ancestral Beings" who formed the environment, including humans, and dictated the rules upon which Aboriginal traditions are based. Only one group's belief suggests that Aboriginal Ancestral Beings came from anywhere other than Australia; that group's Ancestral Beings are said to have originated from the far north across the sea. Aboriginal Ancestral Beings arose from the land itself and returned to the land in all other Aboriginal belief systems.

Aboriginal people were highly competent in the survival pursuits of hunting, gathering, and preparing food. Thus much time was made available for the consideration of more esoteric pursuits. The spiritual beliefs of Aboriginal peoples are commonly called the Dreaming. Aboriginal people have never been nomadic, as they are often portrayed in Western images and history. Nomadism suggests movement without thought or plan. Aboriginal people moved in clans around their designated country to manage resources and perform ceremonies.

Land Rights

Ancestral Beings guaranteed sustainable management of the environment by giving Aboriginal people the responsibility of custody of the land. However, since the British invasion of 1788, the Indigenous peoples of Australia have had to live under legislation that viewed their land as *terra nullius*, literally meaning "empty land." The High Court decision of June 1993 put an end to this legalized lie and the established a legal footing in the land and sea rights struggle. The High Court decision of June 1993 was the outcome of many years of political lobbying and legal maneuvering on behalf of five plaintiffs representing the Indigenous peoples of the island of Mer in the Torres Strait. One of the plaintiffs was Eddie Mabo, and the High Court decision has become known as the Mabo decision. The Mabo decision was followed in 1996 by the Wik decision where the High Court of Australia ruled that Native Title could coexist with pastoral leases.

Before the High Court challenges of the 1990s, Aboriginal people instigated several other strategies to fight for their rights to own land. The strategies have included going on strike. Aboriginal people of the Pilbara went on strike in 1946, but one of the more well-known cases of refusing to work under appalling, exploitative conditions for less than basic wages from rich and often absent pastoral leaseholders has been the Gurindji walk off from Wave Hill Station in 1966. The leaseholder was Vestey who was paid admirably for the land he freed for the Commonwealth government to lease to the Gurindji.

Urban-based Aboriginal people joined the Land Rights movement by establishing a Tent Embassy on the grounds of what was then Parliament House in Canberra. The Tent Embassy, established in January 1972, drew international attention to the Aboriginal Land Rights movement and gave the world its first view of the Aboriginal flag. A striking black, yellow, and red symbol of people, their land, and hope, the colors of the Aboriginal flag are symbols of Aboriginal qualities in jewelry and other forms of expression by Aboriginal people who see their struggle for identity rights second only to their struggle for land rights.

The Commonwealth Parliament of Australia has moved to a new building, but the Aboriginal Tent Embassy still stands, a tribute to the fact the not all Aboriginal people have rights to land.

The actions of the Gurindji, the Tent Embassy, and other political activities helped to force the Commonwealth government to establish the Northern Territory Land Rights Act of 1976, which would not have been possible if it had not been for the referendum of 1967.

Citizenship

As early as the 1930s, Aboriginal people were organizing themselves into groups such as the Victorian Aboriginal Advancement League, the purpose of which was to focus political activism. However, it was the Federal Council for the Advancement of Aborigines and Torres Strait Islanders (FCAATSI) established in the 1950s that spearheaded the citizenship campaign.

The Freedom Rides of the 1960s, in which busloads of university students including Aboriginal activist, Charlie Perkins, traveled through northern New South Wales to publicize the second class status of Aboriginal people and the blatant racism to which they were subjugated, was but one strategy supported by FCAATSI. FCAATSI also organized petitions and the face-to-face lobbying of politicians.

Until the Referendum held on May 27, 1967, the Commonwealth Government had no rights to legislate on behalf of the Aboriginal people of Australia. This referendum, or "yes" vote, removed the constitutional provision excluding "Aboriginal natives" from being counted in the national census and gave the Commonwealth Government power to legislate over Aboriginal affairs. An impressive 90.77 percent of electors voted to change the Constitution of Australia to recognize Aboriginal people as "equal" citizens.

The passing of the 1967 referendum led to changes such as the control of missions shifting from churches and welfare agencies to community members. Education departments began to take responsibility for the schools, and in most cases this led to improvement in the quality of teaching. Aboriginal people were now able to choose where they lived. Due to high unemployment in rural Australia, many Aboriginal families moved into major cities.

Self-determination

Aboriginal people live in diverse social and economic conditions. Many believe that the right of self-determination is central to addressing the oppressed condition of many Aboriginal people. Self-determination is the capacity of Aboriginal people to end their situation of disadvantage, which they occupy in Australian society. Aboriginal heritage is not a disadvantage; the racism directed against Aboriginal people, both by individuals and institutions, is what causes the disadvantage.

Aboriginal people have been deprived of basic human rights, treated as children, and addicted to dependence on the state for survival. However, the efforts, initiatives, and dedicated work of many Aboriginal people either working as individuals or under the auspices of an Aboriginal organization attest to the fact that Aboriginal people are capable. Aboriginal people are also determined to restore self-esteem, reclaim and maintain culture, and achieve the recognition and rights that are justly theirs.

DAVINA B. WOODS

See also **Assimilation; Mabo, Edward (Torres Strait Islander, Australia); Self-Determination**

Further Reading

Bourke, Colin et al., *Aboriginal Australia—An Introductory Reader in Aboriginal Studies*, Brisbane: University of Queensland Press, 2nd edition, 1998

Brady, Maggie, *Heavy Metal: The Social Meaning of Petrol Sniffing in Australia*, Canberra: Aboriginal Studies Press, 1992

Horton, David, *The Encyclopaedia of Aboriginal Australia*, Canberra: Aboriginal Studies Press for Australian Institute of Aboriginal and Torres Strait Islander Studies, 1994

Johnston, E., Commissioner QC, *Royal Commission Into Aboriginal Deaths In Custody National Report Overview and Recommendations*, Canberra: Australian Government Publishing Service, 1991

Madden, Richard, *National Aboriginal and Torres Strait Islander Survey 1994—Detailed Findings*, Canberra: Australian Bureau of Statistics, Australian Catalogue No. 4190.0, 1994

Nyoongah, M., *Aboriginal Mythology: An A–Z Spanning the History of Aboriginal Mythology from the Earliest Legends to the Present Day*, Glasgow: Thorsons, 1994

Nyoongah, M., *Us Mob—History, Culture, Struggle: An Introduction to Indigenous Australia*, Sydney: Angus & Robertson, 1995

Perkins, et al, *Recognition, Rights and Reform—Report to Government on Native Title Social Justice Measures*, Woden: Aboriginal and Torres Strait Islander Commission, 1995

Roberts, J., *Massacres to Mining—the Colonisation of Aboriginal Australia*, Blackburn: Dove Communications, 1981

Acehnese

Capsule Summary

Location: Northern tip of Sumatra in Indonesia
Language: Acehnese
Religion: Islam

The Acehnese identify themselves as those people who belong to the geographical region known as Aceh. This region is the westernmost designated province of Indonesia at the tip of the island of Sumatra and consists of 53,400 square kilometers (20,826 square miles). Significant numbers of Acehnese are involved in a struggle for their independence from Indonesia. Ethnically the Acehnese are coastal people, whereas the Gayo and Alas inhabit the hinterland. The highland people have their own distinct languages and cultures, but they identify strongly as Acehnese.

History

Trade has always been important for the Acehnese, as is evidenced by historical records. According to Chinese and Indian sources from 500 CE, there was a settlement at the tip of north Sumatra known as P'o-lu that historians agree was probably not far from what is now

Banda Aceh, the modern capital of Aceh. The people made and wore cotton clothing while the ruler wore silk. The king used elephants to pull his wagon. The Chinese annals state that the people were Buddhist then, but Arabic traders came between 846 and 950 CE. When Marco Polo visited in 1292, some of the port cities of what is Aceh in the twenty-first century had already converted to Islam.

For many centuries, the trading port known as Lambri is mentioned in Middle-Eastern, Chinese, European and Indonesian sources and is believed to have been located not far from the present site of Banda Aceh. On the northeast coast there is a jutting landmass that looks like a diamond head. Here the Sultanate of Samudra-Pasè was established and it is believed that this is where Islam first came to the archipelago. Although there is debate over when Islamic beliefs and practices first arrived, the gravestone of the Sultan Malik Al-Saleh, dated 1297, situated in this region attests to the fact that by the thirteenth century, Islam was a significant belief system.

The name Aceh appeared around the beginning of the sixteenth century and was given to the port at the tip of Sumatra. Trade has always been important to Aceh. It was a trading center and haven for those vessels that needed to wait until the winds changed and a center where sailors could replenish their stocks after sailing south from the Bay of Bengal or north through the Straits of Malacca. Aceh also became a center for Islamic learning and teaching as pilgrims from Southeast Asia waited for what became known as the Verandah to Mecca, for the winds to change so that they could undertake the pilgrimage.

The Golden Age of Aceh

The Acehnese look back with pride to the period that began in the sixteenth century and continued into the first half of the seventeenth century. It reached its zenith during the reign of Sultan Iskandar Muda and Sultan Iskandar Thani. Wealth was abundant for those in the palace, and material culture blossomed, invigorated by contacts with the Mughal Empire. The court employed hundreds of artisans, including spinners and weavers, gold and silversmiths, and woodcarvers. The flowering of Islam occurred at the same time. Acehnese writers such as Hamzah Fansuri and Shamsul-Din figured prominently in the Malay Islamic world. Aceh's power extended down the west coast of Sumatra well into what is now West Sumatra. Across the straits, towns on the west coast of the Malay Peninsula were required to pay tribute to the Acehnese Sultan. Trade and Islamic scholarship thrived side by side in this cosmopolitan center.

The Europeans arrived in the area in the fifteenth century. The Portuguese were first; the Dutch, English, and French came later. Initially their interest was trade; they would buy cheap cloth from a port on the Indian subcontinent and exchange it for spices and precious metals, which they would then transport back to Europe. They also handled more expensive textiles suited to the elite taste of the various Southeast Asian court centers. Pidie, on the northeast coast of Aceh, was famous for its silk production, being mentioned in a Sung text and by a Portuguese traveler.

When the Dutch East India Company first came to the region, its influence was most powerful in Java and in certain parts of eastern Indonesia. It set up its headquarters in Batavia, or present-day Jakarta. The Acehnese did not have the same experience of colonization as the Javanese. Aceh was perceived by the Dutch to be a trouble spot, difficult to control. When the Dutch did attempt to take greater control, a war ensued. As part of the Dutch effort to conclude the war, the famous Islamic writer, Christian Snouck Hurgronje, was sent to Aceh. His comprehensive document, *The Acehnese* (1906), still stands as one of the best sources of Acehnese ethnography. Many regard his intervention to have been crucial in determining the eventual success of the Dutch. Indeed, the war against the Dutch by the Acehnese was one of the longest and most bitter of the colonial period. It lasted from 1873 to 1903, and many Acehnese claimed that they never conceded defeat, although the end of Sultanate rule brought the widespread fighting to an end. During this war, the Alas area was estimated to have lost a quarter to a third of its men.

The history of Aceh in the twentieth century has involved increased war and conflict. A dramatic revolt against the Dutch took place in 1942, paving the way for the Japanese arrival. After the end of the war, Indonesia proclaimed its independence in 1945. The Dutch never attempted to reclaim control of this part of Indonesia, finally leaving the country in 1947.

Independence

In the wake of Indonesian independence, the legacy of power held by a number of regional chiefs came to be questioned by many Acehnese. This was successfully resolved by a social revolution that coursed through the late 1940s and early 1950s engineered by the Islamic leader Teungku Mohammad Daud Beureu'eh. Aceh was granted provincial status in 1959 when it was designated a special territory—Daerah Istimewa Aceh—with Professor Haji Ali Hasjmy as its first governor.

War

The Acehnese have lived through many wars. One of their cruelest wars was that of the Indonesian Army against the fighters of the Free Aceh Movement (*Gerakan Aceh Merdeka*). In the name of maintaining national unity, troops from the poorly paid Indonesian Army were sent to Aceh, where they have determined to make their fortune or die. Fighting escalated in the decade following the 1990s; counterinsurgents, informants, and opportunistic thugs have capitalized on the fluid and lawless situation. Rape and sexual torture have been common weapons of war, and rural villagers often have no protection. Thousands have died and have been registered by International Human Rights organizations.

Society

Aceh has rich reserves of oil and liquid natural gas. Other important resources include timber, cloves, coffee, tobacco, sugar, rubber, palm oil, prawns, and forest products. The province has been an important source of revenue for the central Indonesian government over the first decades of the new nation-state.

In the 1960s, the Acehnese population was primarily rural and composed of *mukims* or religious communities consisting of several villages where a small mosque would be the focus of the community. By the end of the twentieth century, the effect of improved transport networks, the growth in air travel, the bureaucratization of Indonesian society extending into health, education, religious administration, police, military, civil administration, public works, industry, and the law had changed the nature of the society. The capital, Banda Aceh had swollen in size. The population was ethnically more diverse and, through many private business links, tied to Singapore, Malaysia, and other cities in Indonesia. At the same time, the Free Aceh Movement continued to grow, fuelled by the violence of the additional Indonesian troops sent to the province and anger at Jakarta's indifference to what Acehnese regard as the plundering of the country's wealth.

Barbara Leigh

See also **Indonesians**

Further Reading

Kell, Tim, *The Roots of the Acehnese Rebellion, 1989–1992*, Ithaca: Cornell Modern Indonesia Project, Publication No.74, 1995

Leigh, Barbara, *Hands of Time: The Crafts of Aceh*, Jakarta: Penerbit Djambatan, 1989

Loeb, Edwin M., *Sumatra: Its History and People*, Singapore: Oxford University Press, 1990, first published 1935 by Verlag des Institut für Volkerkunde der Universitat Wein

Marsden, W., *The History of Sumatra*, 1811, Reprint, Kuala Lumpur: Oxford University Press, 1966

Reid, Anthony, *The Contest for North Sumatra*, Kuala Lumpur: Oxford University Press, 1969

Reid, Anthony, *The Blood of the People*, Kuala Lumpur: Oxford University Press, 1979

Snouck Hurgronje, Christian, *The Acehnese*, translated by A.W.S. O'Sullivan, 2 vols, Leiden/London: E.J. Brill, 1906

Achebe, Chinua (Nigerian)

Philosopher Kwame Anthony Appiah has called Chinua Achebe, the internationally renowned Nigerian novelist, poet, and literary critic,"the founding father of African literature…in the English language." Born Albert Chinualumogu (meaning "may God fight on my behalf") Achebe on November 16, 1930, in Ogidi, southeastern Nigeria, Achebe was raised by devout evangelical Protestant parents who nevertheless instilled in him the traditional values of the native Igbo culture. As Achebe explains in his largely autobiographical series of lectures published as *Home and Exile* (2000), his childhood was shaped by the complex encounter of these two rich religious and cultural forces, the collisions and reconciliations of which are found in many of his nearly 30 books.

Achebe's education brought him from the mission school of Ogidi to the Government College in Umuahia and eventually to the University College at Ibadan, where he received a B.A. with honors in English in 1953. It was in one of his university literature classes that Achebe read British novelist Joyce Cary's *Mister Johnson* (1939), and was infuriated by its derogatory treatment of Africans in general and Nigerians in particular: "*Mister Johnson*... open[ed] my eyes to the fact that my home was under attack." This realization compelled Achebe to write a novel that would more accurately represent the plight of Africans confronting Western values through the colonization of their land. The result was *Things Fall Apart* (1958), his first and most popular novel, which has been translated into over 50 languages and has sold millions of copies worldwide. An essential text in the canon of African literature, *Things Fall Apart* centers on the character of Okonkwo, an Igbo man who struggles to come to terms with the impact of late–nineteenth century British rule in his Nigerian village. Achebe's subsequent four novels—*No Longer at Ease* (1960), *Arrow of God* (1964), *A Man of the People* (1966), and *Anthills of the Savannah* (1987)—also center on protagonists who negotiate the sociopolitical and existential struggles associated with the Westernization of Nigeria and greater Africa. Achebe has also written short stories and children's books, and he won the first Commonwealth Poetry Prize in 1974 for his collection of poetry, *Beware Soul Brother and Other Poems* (1971).

A writer who, early in his career, rejected the Western understanding of autonomous art for a more organic connection between the writer and his or her people, Achebe has become well-known, especially in Nigeria, for his political activism. The politically tumultuous atmosphere of the late 1960s in Nigeria, culminating in the civil conflict of the Biafra war, caused him to campaign actively for the Biafra state—which sought sovereignty from Nigeria—across Europe and North America. He also wrote extensive political commentaries about the political life of Nigeria in the subsequent decades, and, in 1983, he published *The Trouble with Nigeria,* where he expanded on his political critique.

Within African literary circles, Achebe has famously defended the contested employment of the English language over the use of local languages and dialects. In a 1965 essay entitled "English and the African Writer," he argued against the accusation raised by several African authors that African writing in English risks furthering the process of African impoverishment and alienation that began with colonization. He argued rather that the African writer ought to aim to find an English language that is at once universal and particular to his or her subjective experience.

Within international literary circles, Achebe has stirred controversy with his readings of Joseph Conrad's novella *Heart of Darkness* (1902), and Nobel Laureate V.S. Naipaul's novel *A Bend in the River* (1989). In the Chancellor's Lecture at the University of Massachusetts, Amherst he delivered on February 18, 1975, Achebe introduced his well-known critical assessment of Conrad's fictional description of late–nineteenth century Africa. Going against the psychological and allegorical interpretations that *Heart of Darkness* had primarily received up to that point, Achebe offered a literal reading of Conrad's novella, paying close attention to the derogatory depiction of Africans.

Achebe has similarly criticized Naipaul's fictional writing, employing for his argument Naipaul's explicit criticisms of Africa and the greater non-Western world found in lectures and interviews about what he perceives as the contemptible physicality, ignorance, and lack of civility of non-Western peoples. According to Achebe, Naipaul's novel, *A Bend in the River,* which centers on the life of an Indian shopkeeper working in an East African colony, reflects its author's sociopolitical convictions in all their racist and neocolonialist intonations. Achebe's literary criticism is driven by the same conviction that inspired him to write fiction: the need to raise a critical voice against what he considered to be the largely unconscious racism prevalent in Western thinking, and to recall in the minds and hearts of African people the dignity of their traditions and histories.

Achebe's extensive lecturing and teaching across Africa, Europe, and America in the 1970s and 1980s came to a halt after a nearly fatal automobile accident in 1990, which left him confined to a wheelchair. That same year, Achebe was offered the Charles P. Stevenson Jr. Chair in Literature at Bard College, New York, which he still holds.

Biography

Albert Chinualumogu Achebe. Born November 16, 1930, in Ogidi, Nigeria. Received a British education, first at the local mission school of Odigi; Government College in Umuahia, 1944–47; Literary studies at University College in Ibadan, 1948–1953; Broadcasting studies at the British Broadcasting Corporation, 1956; Rockefeller Fellowship, 1960–61;

UNESCO Fellowship, 1963. Talks Producer and then Director of External Broadcasting, Nigerian Broadcasting Corporation, 1954–1966. Senior research fellow at the Institute of African Studies at the University of Nigeria, Nsukka, 1967–1972. Creator and director of Citadel Press, 1967. Member of Colonel Aghanya's BOFF (Biafran Organization of Freedom Fighters) staff, functioning as an "ambassador" of the Biafran people abroad, 1967–69. Chairman of the Biafran National Guidance Committee, 1967–69. Creator and first director of the Frantz Fanon Research Center at Enugu, 1971. Founder and editor of the journal *Okike*, 1971. Editorial advisor and director to Heinemann Educational Books, 1971–72. Creator and editor of the journal *Nsukkascope*, 1971. Visiting professor at the English department of University of Massachusetts, Amherst, 1972–1975. Visiting professor at the University of Connecticut, 1975–1976. Professor of English at the University of Nigeria, Nsukka, 1976–1981. Founding editor of the *Association of Nigerian Authors*, 1981. Deputy national president of the *People's Redemption Party*, 1983. Founder and publisher of the bilingual journal of Ibo life and arts, *Uwa Ndi Igbo*, 1984–present. Professor emeritus at the University of Nigeria, Nsukka, 1985–present. Professor at the University of Massachusetts at Amherest, 1987–1988. Goodwill ambassador for the United Nations Population Fund, 1999. Charles P. Stevenson Jr. Professor of Literature at Bard College, New York, 1990–present. Notable awards: Margaret Wrong Prize, 1959; Nigerian National Trophy for Literature, 1960; Jock Campbell Award for Literature, 1964; Commonwealth Poetry Prize, 1974; Lotus Award for Afro-Asian Writers, 1975; Nigerian National Merit Award, 1979; Campion Medal, 1996; German Booksellers Peace Prize, 2002. Honorary doctorates from more than 30 colleges and universities, the first of which from Dartmouth College, 1972. Member: International Social Prospects Academy (Geneva), Writers and Scholars International (London), Commonwealth Arts Organization, Royal Society of Literature (London), Modern Language Association of America, American Academy and Institute of Arts and Letters, Association of Nigerian Authors, Ghana Association of Writers, among others. He currently divides his time between New York and Nigeria.

Selected Works

Things Fall Apart, 1958
No Longer at Ease, 1960
The Sacrificial Egg and Other Stories, 1962
Arrow of God, 1964
Chike and the River, 1966
A Man of the People, 1966
Beware Soul Brother and Other Poems, 1971
Girls at War and Other Stories, 1972
How the Leopard Got His Claws (children's book), 1972
Christmas in Biafra and Other Poems, 1973
Morning Yet on Creation Day, 1975
The Drum (children's book), 1977
The Flute (children's book), 1977
The Umuahian: A Golden Jubilee Publication (Ed.), 1979
Literature And Society, 1980
The Trouble With Nigeria, 1983
The World of Ogbanje, 1986
Anthills of the Savannah, 1987
The University and the Leadership Factor in Nigerian Politics, 1988
Hopes and Impediments: Selected Essays, 1965–87, 1988
Nigerian Topics, 1989
Beyond Hunger in Africa: Conventional Wisdom and an African Vision, edited by Göran
Hyden, Christopher Magadza, and Achola Pala Okeyo, 1990
Another Africa (with photographer Robert Lyons), 1998
Home and Exile, 2000

YIANNA LIATSOS

See also **Nigeria**

Further Reading

Caroll, David, *Chinua Achebe: Novelist, Poet, Critic*, Basingstoke and London: Macmillan, 1990

Gikandi, Simon, *Reading Chinua Achebe: Language and Ideology in Fiction*, Oxford: James Currey; Portsmouth, New Hampshire: Heinemann; Nairobi: HeienKenya, 1991

Innes, C.L., and Bernth Lindfors, editors, *Critical Perspectives on Chinua Achebe*, Washington, D.C.: Three Continents Press, 1978

Innes, C.L., *Chinua Achebe*, Cambridge: Cambridge University Press, 1990

Killam, G.D., *The Writings of Chinua Achebe*, London: Heinemann Educational Books, 1977

Lindfors, Bernth, editor, *Conversations with Chinua Achebe*, Jackson: University of Mississippi Press, 1997

Lindfors, Bernth, and Bala Kothandaraman, editors, *South Asian Responses to Chinua Achebe*, New Delhi: Prestige Books, 1993

Muoneke, Romanus Okey, *Art, Rebellion and Redemption: A Reading of Chinua Achebe*, New York: Peter Lang, 1994

Ogede, Ode, *Achebe and the Politics of Representation : Form Against Itself, from Colonial Conquest and Occupation to Post-Independence Disillusionment*, Trenton, New Jersey: Africa World Press, 2001

Ohaeto, Ezenwa, *Chinua Achebe: A Biography*, Oxford: James Currey; Bloomington: Indiana University Press, 1997

Ojinmah, Umelo, *Chinua Achebe: New Perspectives*, Ibadan: Spectrum, 1991

Petersen, Kirsten Holst, and Anna Rutherford, editors, *Chinua Achebe: A Celebration*, Portsmouth, New Hampshire: Heinemann ; Sydney, Australia : Dangeroo Press, 1991

Ugah, Ada, *In the Beginning…Chinua Achebe at Work*, Ibadan: Heinemann Educational Books, 1990

Wren, Robert M., *Achebe's World: The Historical and Cultural Context of the Novels of Chinua Achebe*, Washington, D.C.: Three Continents Press, 1980; Great Britain: Longman, 1981

Yankson, Kofi, *Chinua Achebe's Novels: A Socio-Linguistic Perspective*, Obosi, Nigeria: Pacific Publishers, 1990

Adams, Gerry (Northern Ireland Catholic)

Charismatic, divisive, courageous, dishonest, and dangerous are just a few of the terms used over the years to describe Northern Irish political figure Gerry Adams. The source of much of the divided opinion about Adams stems from his involvement with the Irish Republican Army (IRA), a nationalist paramilitary organization, made up of Northern Irish Catholics, that advocates unification with the Republic of Ireland and an end to the British Army's presence in northern Ireland (a presence for which the IRA bears no small responsibility). Since the '1970s, Adams has repeatedly insisted that he was never an IRA member and that Sinn Féin and the IRA have no formal relationship; however, the historical record tells a different story.

Adams was born in Belfast on October 6, 1948. His family had a tradition of republican (i.e., Catholic nationalist) politics. His father had wounded a policeman on a Belfast street in 1942 and had been shot and arrested himself. The junior Adams left school at 17 to work as a bartender. His next job, at Belfast's Duke of York pub, was a gathering place for Belfast's Catholic bohemians and leftists. Even before leaving school, he showed an interest in politics, which may been responsible for his poor academic performance in the latter part of his education. When Adams turned 18, he joined the IRA. In 1969, he was one of the members present at a meeting in Belfast at which it was decided that the group would abandon socialist politics and political methods and instead take up arms against both Protestant paramilitary groups (Loyalists) and the Royal Ulster Constabulary (RUC). This strategy was primarily the result of growing violence, particularly in the cities of Belfast and Derry (or Londonderry), as Catholics began to mount protests to gain full civil rights.

Adams's strategic and tactical skills, as well as his shrewd public relations sensibilities, became almost immediately evident, and he rose quickly in the ranks of the Provisionals (another name for the IRA). The RUC and British intelligence believed that by 1971, Adams was the leader of the IRA unit in his native Ballymurphy neighborhood of west Belfast, a belief that in 1972 resulted in his internment—essentially arrest and imprisonment without trial. He won release later that year to help negotiate the continuation of a brief IRA ceasefire. With the outbreak of more violence, Adams was arrested again in 1973 and had his sentence increased after twice trying to escape from the Long Kesh prison, known as "the Maze." While imprisoned (he was not released until 1977), Adams began to realize that the IRA stood little chance of defeating the British Army. Gingerly at first, he began to reintroduce the idea of political solutions into the IRA lexicon. The degree of success with which this could be accomplished was doubtful because Sinn Féin remained banned from elections and multiparty talks that sought peace for Northern Ireland. The strategy of "Armalite and ballot box" was eventually adopted to indicate that the IRA (and Sinn Féin) would seek political solutions alongside military action (Armalite rifles were the preferred weapon of many IRA men).

Adams's career became more determinedly political with his nomination as Vice President of Sinn Féin in 1978. British and Northern Irish Protestant observers viewed his emerging political role (and his attendant denials of ever being an IRA leader) with the same skepticism that Israelis have showed for Yassar Arafat's pleas for peace. In the eyes of many, including some Catholics both in Ireland and Northern Ireland, Adams had been no better than a terrorist, and his political rebirth and denial of all involvement in the IRA struck many as disingenuous.

It was with some shock that these same observers greeted the news of Adams's election to the New Northern Ireland Assembly (1982–1986). In keeping with Sinn Féin's policy of "active abstentionism," he and the four other elected party members refused to take their seats.

The Northern Irish Parliament at Stormont was dissolved in 1972, and the province has been ruled from Westminster in London since that same year. When Adams won the West Belfast seat on an abstentionist ticket in 1983 (the same year in which he won the presidency of Sinn Féin), he once again refused to take his seat, ostensibly because of the oath of allegiance to the British monarch that all Members of Parliament

(MP's) were required to swear. He modified Sinn Féin's abstentionist policy in 1986 by calling for any elected Sinn Féin candidates to assume their seats on the Irish Parliament, the Dáil. While alienating republican extremists, the move demonstrated Adams's political savvy—he recognized that any progress toward peace (as well as his and other republicans' dreams of a united Ireland) would only come with cooperation from the Republic of Ireland. This change was a result of a growing political friendship with John Hume, then the leader of the Social Democratic and Labor Party (SDLP), the more mainstream and middle-class Catholic political party in Northern Ireland. Hume and Adams had been encouraged to meet by a Belfast priest, Father Alec Reid, who, like Hume, had been a civil rights and peace activist since the late '1960s. Hume and Adams met in secret over an eight-year period between 1985 and 1993 before news of their get-togethers became public, angering each of their respective constituents. Adams also lost his parliamentary seat in 1992 to a candidate from Hume's party.

These apparent setbacks did little to damage his reputation among republicans or his status as a rising force in mainstream Northern Irish politics. He gained more international favor—particularly from Irish-American politicians such as then-President Bill Clinton (who gave Adams a visa allowing him to come to the United States in 1994) and Senator Edward Kennedy—for his role in the IRA ceasefire that began in August 1994. Sinn Féin desperately wanted a role in the proposed multiparty talks for peace and reform that were also to include representatives from the English and Irish governments (as they had in the '1970s and '1980s). For their part, the English were concerned that the ceasefire was a ploy to win Sinn Féin's admittance into the talks; they and Protestant unionists wanted the IRA to decommission all of the group's weapons by the IRA, although an analogous request was not made of Protestant paramilitary groups that had actually been responsible for a slightly higher number of deaths since the advent of the Troubles in 1969.

International pressure (especially from the United States) was exerted on England to maintain talks for peace. Finally, in the spring of 1996, it was announced that England expected Sinn Féin to address only the need to decommission weapons, a development that republicans regarded to be a significant victory, even as political violence remained a barrier to Sinn Féin's participation in further talks. However, Adams's party made a respectable showing in the Elections to the Forum for Peace and Reconciliation that took place on May 30, 1996, winning 17 seats to 21 for the SDLP. The party remained on the outside looking in at the all-party talks in June. Rioting by both Catholics and Protestants took place as July 12th celebrations and marches by loyalists degenerated into violence. Yet Gerry Adams and his chief assistant, Martin McGuinness, were able to stay the hand of the IRA, which next renewed a ceasefire in July 1997. This ceasefire finally gave Adams and Sinn Féin access to the talks, now being directed by former U.S. Senator George Mitchell and led primarily by John Hume and Ulster Unionist Party leader David Trimble.

Adams gave his approval to the extensive reforms of the Good Friday, or Belfast, Agreement signed in April 1998, even though the Agreement contained a formal recognition of the partition of Northern Ireland from the Republic of Ireland. Surprisingly, Adams chose not to accept a position as minister in the new Northern Ireland Executive, even though he retained the presidency of Sinn Féin. Progress since the approval of the Agreement has been slow. Although Catholics have won the civil rights for which they worked so hard, old habits on all sides of the religious and ideological divide have been slow to die. Periodic outbreaks of violence from the ashes of the old Provisional IRS and newly constituted Protestant groups have threatened the province's stability. Yet Adams has seen both the influence of Sinn Féin and his own prestige grow. The party wrested more seats from the SDLP in the 2001 Westminster elections and in Northern Irish elections in 2003.

Through the '1990s and into the current decade, Adams has worked hard to cement a reputation as a writer—he has published several books of fiction, autobiography, and politics—and as a civil rights advocate, meeting with Rosa Parks on one of his many visits to the United States

Biography

Gerard Adams. Born in Belfast, Ireland, October 6, 1948. Educated at St. Mary's Christian Brothers School, left school in 1965.Vice President, Sinn Féin, 1978–1983. President, Sinn Féin, 1983–. Member of Parliament for West Belfast 1983–1992 and 1997–.

Selected Work

A Farther Shore

John H. Davis

See also **Hume, John (Northern Ireland Catholic); Catholics in Northern Ireland; Ireland; Irish Republican Army; Sinn Féin**

Further Reading

Elliott, Sydney, and W.D. Flackes, *Northern Ireland: A Political Directory 1968–1999*, Belfast: Blackstaff Press, 1999

English, Richard, *Armed Struggle: A History of the IRA*, Oxford: Oxford University Press, 2003

Moloney, Ed, *A Secret History of the IRA*, London: Penguin Press, 2002

Sharrock, David, and Mark, Devenport, *Man of War, Man of Peace: The Unauthorised Biography of Gerry Adams*, London: MacMillan, 1997

Adare, *See* **Harari (Adare)**

Afar

Capsule Summary

Location: Africa (Ethiopia, Djibouti, Eritrea)
Total population: 1.5 million
Language: Afar-af
Religon: Islamic

The Afar, formerly called *Danakil*, are a Muslim people living in the hot coastal lowland areas of three countries: Ethiopia, Eritrea, and Djibouti. They were originally a nomadic-pastoralist people. In the first two countries, the Afar are a significant minority in number and strategic location. The Eritrean Afar live in the utmost southeast of the country, and the port city of Assab lies within their traditional territory. In 1869, their land was ceded by the Afar sultan of Rohaita to Italian colonialists seeking a foothold for their expansion on the African continent. In Ethiopia, the Afar form a large autonomous region (the Afar Regional State) within federal Ethiopia. Linguistically, the Afar belong to the Cushitic-speaking group (which also includes Somali and Oromo). In Djibouti they be cannot be called a minority proper. Remarkably, few historical or anthropological studies on the Afar people exist, and many details about their complex social organization, religious life, and current socioeconomic problems remain unclear. The Afar number about 1.5 million people in total.

In the early sixteenth century, the Afar, together with a number of Somali clans around the town of Harar, formed a formidable political-military unit under the leadership of the Somali warlord Ahmed ibn Ibrahim, then the self-appointed Imam (a Muslim leader who claims descent from Muhammad) of the state of Adal. Adal threatened and nearly annihilated the Ethiopian Christian highland empire. After the killing of Ahmed and the dispersal of his army in 1543, the power and influence of this alliance waned, and Adal withered. Both the Afar and Somali retreated into the semi-arid lowlands as camel herders and traders. Although their self-name is Afar, they came to be known by outsiders as "Danakil" or "T'ilt'al." In the centuries that followed, the Afar paid tribute to the highland rulers of Ethiopia.

In nineteenth-century travel literature, the Afar were described as a staunchly independent and ferocious warrior people, wary of outsiders. Customs such as the emasculation of enemies in battle reinforced this image. They raided neighboring groups such as the Issa Somali for livestock, as the latter raided them.

The Afar are predominantly livestock holders (mainly camels, but also goats, sheep, and some cattle) who labor in a harsh environment. Ecological crisis and shrinking pastures in recent decades have forced the Afar to adopt cultivation, migrant labor, and trade to survive. The Ethiopian Afar traditionally engaged in salt trading, found in large quantities in their area, but recently Tigrinya-speaking highlanders have taken over much of this trade.

The Afar are organized in a large number of patrilineal clans, led by elders, and kinship is essential in establishing social relations. Males predominate in all public spheres including politics and economics. Afar society maintains an internal status division in two groups of clans: the "white" Asdoimera and the "red" Asaimera, the latter of whom are more prestigious. A chiefdom structure of sultanates traditionally crosscuts this division and illustrates the hierarchical structure of Afar society. Clans do not form corporate units but are dispersed. Adoption and inclusion of outsiders, even of other peoples like Somalis, occurs regularly.

The present-day geographic area of Afar is extensive. In Ethiopia, it covers the Afar Regional State, which reaches from the Eritrean border almost up to the town of Nazret, some 115 kilometers (71.3 miles) east of Addis Ababa. The Ethiopian Afar number about 1,15 million people. In Eritrea, (with some 200,000 Afar inhabitants) Afar occupy the territory along the coast from the Djibouti border up to the Buri Peninsula. In Djibouti, the northern two-thirds of the country (more than 60 percent) of the state, is Afar land, and the people there number approximately 325,000.

In all three countries, the Afar have long been a distinct minority due to their peripheral geographical, political, and cultural status. Their mobile, pastoral way of life did not lead to a centralized state organization, nor did the Afar effectively integrate into the national polities of Ethiopia and Eritrea (after 1991). In Djibouti, however, Afar form almost half of the population and have since that republic's independence from France in 1977. Afar represent an important constituent in the ethnic balancing in the political system of this state, which also includes the Issa Somali who continue to dominate Djibouti politics.

The Afar are Muslims who follow the Sunni (*Shafi'ite*) tradition. Sufi orders such as the *Qadiriyya* are widespread. Afar religious life combines Islamic precepts with traditional ones from the pre-Islamic past, such as rain sacrifices' on Mt. Ayilu and various forms of divination and folk healing. However, not all the Afar live according to ancestral ways, excluding modernity and industrialization.

Afar have dispersed to towns outside their immediate geographic area, and educated Afar elites have become spokespersons, teachers, and administrators of their own people. On average, the Djibouti Afar probably earn the highest level of education among Afar because of that country's lingering connection with France, the former colonizing country where many Djiboutians go for higher education. In Ethiopia, the ethnofederal structure installed since 1991 has led to an "Afarization" of politics, education, and administration in the Afar autonomous region. In Eritrea's more unitary model of national integration, ethnic differences are not accorded political status. In Djibouti, the dualist structure of power—along Afar and Somali lines in a kind of quota system—is a potentially volatile one that has led to violent uprisings and civil war in the recent past.

The Afar regions are climatically harsh and marginal areas that have not attracted economic investment, and the Afar suffer from recurrent droughts, animal diseases, locust plagues, and a lack of investment in infrastructure, education, and economic development. Since the 1970s, traditional Afar pasture areas have been appropriated by the state for irrigation agriculture practiced by outsiders. Additionally, disputes over pasture lands and other resources have led to increased and frequent, violent conflicts with neighboring groups such as the Issa-Somali, Tigrinya, Karayyu, and Argobba in the past two decades.

In Ethiopia, the Afar formed political resistance organizations in the time of the Derg military dictatorship (1974–1991). One of the most imperative was the Afar Liberation Front, led by Ali Mirah, the exiled Afar sultan from the town of Awssa. In Djibouti, the Afar led the Front for the Restoration of Unity and Democracy (FRUD) guerrilla movement of the 1990s, which is included in the government today after years of armed conflict. Other smaller movements in the area have also emerged, including the Afar Revolutionary Democratic Unity Front (ARDUF), a post-1991 movement that emerged in the Ethiopia-Eritrea border zone. ARDUF desires to unify all Afar in Eritrea and Ethiopia in one Afar homeland (i.e., it aims to unite the Eritrean Afar with the Ethiopian Afar state) and is at odds with both national governments. Perhaps the existence of these insurgent movements demonstrates that the Afar effect on national politics in their respective countries has always been limited.

Jon Abbink

See also **Djibouti; Ethiopia; Eritrea**

Further Reading

Ali, Said, "Resource Use Conflict in the Middle Awash Valley of Ethiopia: The Crisis of Afar Pastoralism," in *Pastoralists, Ethnicity and the State in Ethiopia*, edited by Richard Hogg, London: Haan Publishing, 1997

Chailley, Marcel, *Notes sur les Afar de la Région de Tadjoura,* Paris: Académie des Sciences d'Outre-Mer, 1980
""Maknoun, Gamaledin, "The Decline of Afar Pastoralism," in *Conflict and the Decline of Pastoralism in Africa*, edited by J. Markakis, Houndmills: Macmillan Press, 1993
Morin, Didier, *Le Ginnili: Devin, Poète et Guerrier Afar*, Paris: Edition Peeters, 1991
Morin, Didier, *Poésie Traditionnelle des Afars*, Paris and Louvain, Belgium: Edition Peeters, 1997
Shehim, Kassim, "Ethiopia, Revolution and the Question of Nationalities: The Case of the Afar," *Journal of Modern African Studies,* 23, no. 2 (1985)

Affirmative Action

In a broad sense, affirmative action is one among several *preferential policies* that public administrations use to grant privileges to members of particular groups. In a narrower sense, and particularly as it is understood in the United States, Canada, and Australia, affirmative action is a measure of *compensatory justice*, although its opponents use the pejorative terms of '*reverse*' or '*affirmative discrimination*.' It aims to achieve equal opportunity and stands for temporary programs with specific goals, timetables, and sometimes quotas that help employees, students, and government contractors from minority backgrounds to be made aware of and considered for employment positions, university admissions, and contracts. One of the most controversial issues in the United States, the dilemma of affirmative action, is "If we do not use preferential hiring, we permit discrimination to exist. But preferential hiring is also discrimination. Thus, if we use preferential hiring, we also permit discrimination to exist. The dilemma is that whatever we do, we permit discrimination to exist" (R. Fullwinder 1980, 156).

Preferential policies and affirmative action

Preferential policies are current practice in situations where multiethnic hierarchies cross class cleavages. They can be inclusive or exclusive, aimed at national or local majorities as well as destitute minorities. They are not limited to postcolonial situations or societies whose totalitarian system once chose to co-opt specific groups in the military or state positions. The use of preferential and identity policies is expanding everywhere in the Western world with the internationalization of minorities and the creation of diasporas. The phenomenon of ethnic profiling and differentiation is but one expression of the difficulty to reconcile the plural structures of several states with social and cultural inequalities. One could also say that the great capitalist transformation has neither been able to modify social structures nor to separate cultural, religious, or physical signs from the allegiance to the state. Rather, capitalism modified the meaning of these structures by allowing ethnicity to define who are the Untouchables (*Dalit*) in India, members of '"visible minorities"' in Canada, Jews in the former Soviet Union, and Afro-Americans and Hispanics in the United States. It is nevertheless a fact that less than a third of all contemporary states can pretend that their unity is grounded in a perfect congruence between nation, people, and the state.

In numerous multiethnic societies, one can observe, in several spheres of social organization, that opportunities are monopolized by one particular ethnic group and that some minorities are considered to be intermediaries while latent or manifest discriminations against others endure. Many societies have recognized that members of different groups are unequally represented in certain fields of social life, particularly in employment and education. To remedy (or maintain) such a situation considered unjust (or desirable), they have adopted temporary preferential measures. Such programs are called "*positive discrimination*" in India, "*standardization*" in Sri Lanka, "*policies reflecting the country's federal character*" in Nigeria, "*numerus clausus*" in central Europe and North America between the two World Wars, "*positive action*" or "*affirmative action*" in the United States, Australia, and Canada, "*access to equality*" in Quebec, and in France—to promote women's equal representation among deputies—"*parity*". The targeted groups are as various as these denominations.

Compensatory Justice and Affirmative Action

The concept of affirmative action, in its narrower sense, originated with the recognition that antidiscrimination legislation alone, although useful to make cease behavior based on prejudice, is not enough. The traditional legal approach states that the situation has to be redressed and the victim put into the position he/she would have been in if it were not for the past discrimination. But the idea of affirmative action goes beyond compensation of the individual victim by the "'culprit.'" New information procedures have to ensure that everyone who might be interested knows that a particular position is available and that selection will not be based on factors other than competence and merit. A further step is to take measures on the decision level, which not only guarantees individual equal opportunity but also equal outcome for groups, whose underrepresentation in particular fields is considered to be a consequence, not of individual but 'systemic' discrimination against every member of the group. The controversy about the meanings of equality, about group rights vs. individual rights, and distributive vs. compensatory justice starts at this point.

Formal equality, based on the normative proposition that all subjects are equal, requires ignoring differences between individuals. However, in a world where the natural tendency is to treat those who are different as inferior, to associate difference with inequality and identity with equality, this formal definition is of little use and encourages normalization. It is not able to respect real differences without exploiting them. More complex models have been proposed since Rawls' (1971) fundamental work on distributive justice, such as Walzer's (1983) division of the social world into spheres of justice where differences take various meanings. Many authors contest the neutrality of laws and the belief that we are all the same, governed by the market and the law. The equal distribution of resources cannot be reduced to Rawls' initial position and to equal opportunity for those categorized along criteria such as physical or mental handicap, race, language, gender, sexual orientation, education, class. Particular rights are necessary to redress the perverse effects of preferences.

Affirmative Action in the United States

The term '*positive action*' first appeared in the *Wagner Act* of 1935 to describe an employer's obligation not to harass unionized workers. However, the origin of affirmative action in the United States is generally cited in 1961, with J.F. Kennedy's Executive Order 10925, echoing the growing importance of the Civil Rights movement, which created the Committee on Equal Employment Opportunity and asked federal government contractors to take affirmative action to ascertain that employees were not chosen based on race. Twenty years earlier, however, F.D. Roosevelt—to avoid a march on Washington by black workers from the Brotherhood of Sleeping Car Porters—had to sign another Executive Order (8802) against segregationist hiring practices in defense related industries. An even earlier milestone was the Civil Rights Act of 1866, which already expressed a certain will to provide compensatory justice to the victims of slavery, whereas the Civil Rights Act of 1964 formally outlawed workplace discrimination based on "race, color, religion, sex, or national origin." In the following year, 1965, L.B. Johnson's Executive Order 11246 specified that federal contractors were required to take affirmative action to provide equal opportunity without regard to a person's race, religion, or national origin and to set "good faith goals and timetables" to hire "underutilized," qualified minority group members. Women were added to the protected categories in 1968. The Johnson administration also created the Office of Federal Contract Compliance to design specific programs. It was under the Nixon administration, in 1969, that the first such program, the so-called Philadelphia Plan, required the segregated construction industry in Philadelphia to hire minority members according to clear goals and percentages. Local governments, as well as private businesses, soon followed the federal government's lead.

From the outset of the Civil Rights movement, the field of education was of the highest priority and marked by several court decisions. On the college level, the number of black students began to rise only in the late 1960s, due to affirmative action measures. In1967, colleges and universities receiving federal funds were required to set goals for hiring female and minority faculty. For university students, the 1978 Supreme Court compromise decision in *Regents of the University of California v. Bakke*, established that a university may indeed consider race and ethnic background among other factors for admission purposes. The divided decision also stated, however, that setting aside a specific number of places for minority students without proof of past discrimination was illegal.

Affirmative action remains a controversial issue, illustrating deep tensions between individual and group rights supporters. For many it is still the best means to overcome inequality due to historical discrimination and to fight against conscious or unconscious biases and stereotypes; for others, affirmative action violates individual rights and risks deepening racial divisions in society. Cornell West (1996) considers it a weak response to the "white supremacy" of many fields. The debate surrounding affirmative action has changed considerably over time. In the beginning, both democratic and republican administrations supported it as a "painful way" to create a multiracial society, without people of color and women as second-class citizens. The rise of neoconservatism broke this fragile consensus and created a backlash that started in the 1980s. It transformed the interpretation of equal opportunity to mean that no measure going beyond merit should furthermore be considered. Affirmative action policies came to be seen as "multiracial reverse discrimination," contributing to the low self-esteem of blacks. For many, they were considered programs for less qualified or unqualified women and black people and denounced as "un-American", putting their proponents on the defensive. West's conclusion is clear., "As desirable as those policies are, they will never ameliorate the predicament of poor people of color. More drastic and redistributive measures are needed to address their situation" (West 1996, 33–34). Most analysts agree that the primary beneficiaries of affirmative action have been white women.

Affirmative action may have been justified on the grounds of compensatory justice or as an extension of distributive justice, for utilitarian reasons or because of power relations. In a way, it has politicized the economy and is contested from viewpoints as different as those of the minimal state, of meritocracy, or of the global economy. Whatever the position adopted and the justification given, one cannot deny that affirmative action has a double effect: By eliminating the obstacles to participation of those who are excluded, it confines them to social categories.

RUTH MURBACH

See also **Diaspora; Equal Opportunity; Ethnic Conflict; Gender and Minority Status; Race; Untoucha- bles (Harijans/Dalits/Scheduled Castes)**

Further Reading

Beckwith, F.J., and T.E. Jones, editors, *Affirmative Action: Social Justice or Reverse Discrimination*, Amherst, New York: Prometheus Books, 1997

Cohen, C., *Affirmative Action and Racial Preference: A Debate*, New York: Oxford University Press, 2003

Curry, G.E., \editor, *The Affirmative Action Debate*, Reading, Massachusetts: Addison-Wesley, 1996

Eisaguirre, L., *Affirmative Action*, Contemporary World Issues Series, Santa Barbara, California: ABC-Clio, 1999

Elbaz, M., and R. Murbach, "Preferences, Differences and Sacrifices. Affirmative Action and Legal Pluralism in Canada," in *Le droit soluble*, edited by J.G. Belley, Paris: LGDJ, 1997

Elbaz, M. and R. Murbach, "Affirmative Action and 'Visible Minorities' in Canada: A Generational Issue?" *Revue européenne des migrations internationales*, 9 no. 3(1994)

Fullwinder, R., *The Reverse Discrimination Controversy*, Totowa, New Jersey: Rowman and Littlefield, 1980

Glazer, N., *Affirmative Discrimination. Ethnic Inequality and Public Policy*, New York: Basic Books, 1975

Jacobs, L.A., *Pursuing Equal Opportunities. The Theory and Practice of Egalitarian Justice*, New York: Cambridge University Press, 2004

Rawls, J., *A Theory of Justice,* Cambridge: Harvard University Press, 1971

Rosenfeld, M., *Affirmative Action and Justice*, New Haven: Yale University Press, 1991

Sowell, T., *Preferential Policies*, New York: William Horrow, 1990

Walzer, M., *Spheres of Justice*, New York: Basic Books, 1983

West, C., "Affirmative Action in Context", in *The Affirmative Action Debate*, edited by G.E Curry, Reading, Massachusetts: Addison-Wesley, 1996

Afghanistan

Capsule Summary

Location: Southern Asia, north and west of Pakistan, east of Iran
Total Population: 28,717,213 (July 2003)
Language: Pashtun, Afghan Persian (Dari), Turkic languages (primarily Uzbek and Turkmen), 30 minor languages (including Baluchi and Pashai)
Religions: Sunni Muslim, 84 percent, Shi'a Muslim, 15 percent

Afghanistan is characterized by mountainous deserts, isolated valleys, river basins, and oases. It extends eastward from the Iranian plateau to the Himalayan range. The country, with a strong nomadic tradition, has traditionally based its economy on grazing sheep and goats on the foothills of the Hindu Kush and on subsistence agriculture. Afghanistan is administratively divided in 30 provinces; the people are ethnically, religiously, and linguistically mixed. GDP per capita (purchasing power parity) is $800 (2000). The dominant ethnic group, the Pashtun, is located in the southern part of the country, whereas in the north, ethnic groups are affiliated with the major central Asian divisions. The various ethnic groups in Afghanistan include the Pashtun (44 percent), Tajik (25 percent), Hazara (10 percent), minor ethnic groups such as Aimaks, Turkmen, Baloch, and others (13 percent), and Uzbek (8 percent). The dominant faith is Sunni Islam, with significant Shi'a minorities. The conventional country name today is Afghanistan.

History

Afghanistan has been invaded several times in its history: The object has always been its geographical and strategic position as a key entrance to India from the north, a buffer area between Persia and India, and a strong protection between Russia and India. The Achaemenid Empire of Darius invaded it in 522–330 BCE. Alexander the Great followed as conqueror in 330–327 BCE. Afghanistan was also an important region as part of the Silk Route to China, and from 64 to 220 CE was subjected to the Kushan dynasty. From 224 to 651 CE the country was part of the Sasanian and Hephtalite empires, until the Islamic conquest in 699 CE. From then on, many Muslim dynasties followed, until Genghis Khan's invasion in 1155.

In 1370 the country fell under Timurids, but from 1506 to 1747, it was divided between the Moghul (India) and the Safavid (Persia) empires. From 1747, Ahmed Shah Durrani conquered the whole area, and the relationships with the European powers of the time began, most of all with British presence in India. During the Napoleonic wars, menaced by the French presence in Egypt and by the growing Russian expansion toward Central Asia, Britain developed a new policy (North West Frontier Policy) with the firm object of protecting Indian commercial and political interests. In 1838—1842, the British were defeated in the first Anglo-Afghan war, where only 1 of the 16,000 soldiers of the Army of the Indus, Dr. Brydon, survived, to tell the story. After a long period of political struggle within the Durrani family and with British representatives of the Anglo-Indian Government, the second Anglo-Afghan war broke out between 1878 and 1880, resulting in a second defeat for the British. Nevertheless, the treaty of Gandamak in 1879 guaranteed British control of Afghanistan's foreign affairs. From 1880 to 1901, the Pashtun population was established by Abdur-Rahman in the north, and present boundaries were artificially fixed through a series of international agreements (Durand line of 1893 in eastern Afghanistan). From 1901 to 1919, Habibullah ruled. After the third Anglo-Afghan war, the country became independent from British control on August 10, 1919. For ten years only King Amanullah ruled over Afghanistan. Different ethnic leaders followed in a permanent struggle until 1933, when King Mohammed Zahir Shah came to power. With the partition between India and Pakistan on August 15, 1947, Afghanistan made its first claims on the creation of Pashtunistan. In 1973, following a traditional practice of shifting power in tribal areas of Asia, King Zahir, while he was in Italy, was overthrown by his cousin Daoud through a military coup in 1973.

In 1978, the communist People's Democratic Party of Afghanistan took power through another military coup. However, on December 27, 1979, Soviet troops invaded Afghanistan. Soviet military occupation ended on February 15, 1989. The withdrawal was a consequence of internal struggles within the Soviet Union and of military defeat, a strong confirmation of the Afghan guerrilla spirit to win and fierce feelings for independence. In April 1992, the *Mujahidin* government (fighting for jihad, or holy war) took Kabul, the capital. The fighters identified their leaders locally, and some of these rose to prominence: Jamiat-i-Islami of B. Rabbani; Hisb-e-Islami of Mullah Omar, the *Taliban* (students of religion in *madrasas*, schools) leader; the fierce Tajik Masoud, meaning "lion of the Panshir mountains"—killed on September 9, 2001. In 1994, the Taliban captured Kandahar, then Herat, the famous town historically known as "the key to India", Jalalabad, and finally Kabul. On September 27, 1996 the Talibans imposed their brutal strength. The United Nations (UN) recognized only the B. Rabbani government. Following the September 11, 2001, terrorist attacks in the United States, The Northern Alliance and allied military forces defeated the Talibans. The new president, Hamid Karzai, was elected in June 2002 by the Transitional Islamic State of Afghanistan with a mandate from the Loya Jirga (Grand Assembly) to adopt a constitution and hold nationwide elections. Nevertheless, the country remains divided between tribal factions.

Society

The population of Afghanistan is divided into the following main groups: Afghans; Tadjiks and other Iranians; Turko-Mongolians; Hindu-Kush Indo-Aryans (including Kafirs). The traditional society has always been hierarchical and individualistic; due to nomadic habits, the nuclear family has been dominant and women have been kept isolated from public life.

The economy of Afghanistan is extremely poor, typical of a landlocked country, mainly based on the pastoral nomadic life and livestock raising of its inhabitants. Afghanistan was the biggest producer of opium poppies in 1999, and drug smuggling is one of the major sources of revenue for its many political groups. Its major social and economical tragedy has been the flow of refugees to bordering countries such as Iran and Pakistan: approximately 6 million have escaped, and those who remained still suffer from problems connected to nation's difficulties between 1998 and 2001 and its political uncertainty.

BEATRICE NICOLINI

See also **Iran; Muslims: Shi'a in Sunni Countries; Pakistan; Pashtuns (Pathans)**

Further Reading

Dupree, L., *Afghanistan*, Princeton: Princeton University Press, 1980

Elphinstone, M., *An Account of the Kingdom of Caubul*, 1st edition, 1815; Oxford: Oxford University Press, 1972

Ewans, M., *Afghanistan: A New History*, London: Curzon, 2001

Longworth Dames, M., *Afghanistan, Encyclopaedia of Islam*, Leiden: Brill, 1999, CD-ROM

Marsden, P., *The Taliban: War, Religion and the New Order in Afghanistan*, London: Zed Books, 1998

Rashid, A., *Taliban: Oil, and the New Great Game in Central Asia*, London: Tauris, 2000

Roy, O., *Islam and Resistance in Afghanistan*, Cambridge: Cambridge University Press, 1986

Afghans, *See* **Pashtuns (Pathans)**

Africa: A Continent of Minorities?

Africa encompasses a vast range of different ethnic groups, and in only a very few countries does one ethnic group make up more than 50 percent of the total population. Almost every African country includes major and minor subgroups, whereas across the continent as a whole, at least 1,000 languages can be found, even though some of these are confined to very small, remote ethnic communities.

In addition to these divisions, which have developed over many centuries, the indigenous peoples of Africa have been subjected to two waves of conquest that have profoundly affected racial, religious, and political alignments. The first of these was the spectacular conquest of northern Africa by Muslim Arabs during the seventh, eighth, and ninth centuries that resulted in a wide acceptance of the new religion of Islam, the adoption of the Arabic language, and the assimilation of other cultural and political practices. The second was the European effect that began in the sixteenth century with the slave trade on the west coast, which lasted for 3 centuries and was gradually followed by European colonization, culminating in the so-called "Scramble" for Africa at the end of the nineteenth century. The Europeans brought Christianity to most of the continent that had not already accepted Islam, the widespread use of the English and French languages (and to a lesser extent those of Portugal, Germany, and Italy), and the adoption of Western (colonial) administrative, commercial, and military practices that continued with modifications after independence. The departure of the colonial powers in the 1960s did not mean an end to the European connection; instead, a complex legacy of Afro-European relations that affect many aspects of the continent's cultural and political activities has continued.

Complex, slow-moving migrations across the African continent over many centuries continued until the end of the nineteenth century. The oldest African peoples are the Negrillo (Pygmy) and Khoisan (Bushmen) groups now found only in the Congo forests and desert regions of Namibia and Botswana, respectively. The great majority of Africans, however, belong to the Negroid-Bantu stock. The Sudanese peoples of West Africa are located in the savannah regions that stretch from Cape Verde to Kordofan; they include the darkest peoples in coloring, and their principal groups are the Malinke, Bambara, Sarakhole, Mossi, Songhay, and Hausa. Another main branch of the Bantu peoples are the Guineans, who originally came from the Gulf of Guinea between the Casamance River and Cameroon. Interbreeding between the Sudanese and Guinean peoples has produced a range of widely varying ethnic groups including the Diola, Balante, Soussa, Ashanti, Yoruba, Ewe, and Fon. The population composition of West Africa is exceptionally complex and has changed constantly as a result of migrations. Bantu peoples inhabit most of Central and Southern Africa. Originally they moved out from the core region of Nigeria and central Cameroon and gradually spread southward, crossing the Congo and Bangui rivers eventually to reach Angola. Some also crossed the continent to the east and then turned southward to arrive, after centuries of gradual movement, in Mozambique and the eastern littoral of South Africa, where in the nineteenth century they met the Europeans, Afrikaner, and British, advancing northward from the Cape. It was the arrival of the Bantu peoples in the high veld of South Africa that forced the Khoisan to retreat into the Kalahari and Namib deserts. In the central Congo region, the principal groups are the Bateke, Bangala, Bakongo, Baluba, Balunda, as well as many other smaller divisions. In Southern Africa, the range is enormous and varied: Zambia has 73 ethnic groups with the Bemba, Nyanja, and Tonga composing just under 70 percent of the population; 70 percent of the people of Zimbabwe are Mashona, 16 percent Ndebele. Malawi has an equally mixed population, dominated by the Maravi group, as does Mozambique. The dominant groups in South Africa are the Zulu and Xhosa; the apartheid governments divided the African population into ten main groups for the purpose of assigning them to Bantustans, or Homelands. There are wide variations of feature and skin color, ranging from very dark to very light in all these groups.

The Nilotics, a distinct group to be found in the upper valley of the Nile, are a tall thin people of whom the Dinka of southern Sudan are the most obvious example; other members of this group are the Nuer, Shilluk, and Djour. Their origins are obscure, but they could have been the outcome of interbreeding between the Bantu and Ethiopian peoples. The Caucasoid people from the Horn of Africa include the Ethiopians (or Abyssinians) and Somalis, whose features, which include thin aquiline noses, long faces, and high cheekbones, distinguish them from other African groups. The light-skinned Berbers were the indigenous peoples of the North African Mediterranean coastal regions before the arrival of the Arabs. Subsequently, from about 700 CE onward, many Berbers interbred with the Arabs, although large Berber groups moved into the hills and mountain regions of the Maghrib interior, which acted as a refuge from repeated coastal invasions. The Tuaregs and Moors of the southern Sahara are of Berber stock, as are the original Egyptians and Libyans. These are the principal African groups, but they split further into numerous subdivisions. In Madagascar, the Malagasies are the product of a unique mixture of Negroid or Bantu people from the mainland and Indonesian migrants who came in waves across the Indian Ocean, mainly between the seventh and fifteenth centuries: Their interbreeding has produced the distinctive Merina peoples.

These assorted peoples include many small minorities, and the diversity of a typical African country may be illustrated by reference to a broad grouping such as the Maravi in Malawi which comprises Nyanja, Chewa, Tonga, and Tumbuku peoples, who make up just over 58 percent of that country's population, whereas other groups—the Lomwe, Yao, and Ngoni—account for a additional 38.3 percent of the population.

The continent has witnessed widespread intermingling, much of it having taken place long before the arrival either of the Arabs in North Africa and down the Swahili coast, or of the later Europeans—the Portuguese, Spanish, Dutch, Danes, French, and English. Ethnic complexity can be measured in part by the continent's range of languages. There are an estimated 600 major languages with many subdivisions into additional hundreds of dialects or localized languages, some of which will only be spoken by a few hundred people. Arabic is the principal language of North Africa and the Sahara although Berber predates the coming of the Arabs and is still widely used. Swahili is the most widely spoken language in East Africa; it is a Bantu-based language with Persian, Arabic, and English additions. In West Africa, the most important languages are Hausa, which was spread south by traders from northern Nigeria into Cameroon; Bambara; and Malinke. The Mande languages, Bambara and Malinke, are spoken throughout the Sudan (Sahel) and from Senegal to Côte d'Ivoire. Other major languages in West Africa include Wolof in Senegal, Kanuri in Chad, and Yoruba in western Nigeria. The range of the Bantu languages is so wide and complex that it is difficult to classify them all with any accuracy. The Niger-Congo group of languages is the most extensive on the continent, covering all the divisions and subdivisions of West, Sudanic, and Central Africa. East Africa and the Horn are covered by the Nilo-Saharan family of languages and the Hamitic-Semitic languages, of which Amharic of the Ethiopians is a prime example. In South Africa, the new language of Afrikaans evolved from the Dutch of the first European settlers at the Cape.

European colonialism, especially the division of Africa among the European colonial powers at the end of the nineteenth century, introduced new language dimensions into the continent. The colonial languages—English, French, Portuguese, German, and Italian—became the languages of the elites and the administrations and have continued in these roles since independence. Colonialism also created new problems that could be solved best by the adoption of the foreign language as the lingua franca. Different peoples were brought under colonial control and administered in newly delineated territories for the convenience of the European power; such colonies often included a number of distinct groups, some of major dimensions, that would have been unlikely to come together within the structure of a single territory except under colonial compulsions. Many colonies, often geographically huge, include ethnic groups that are widely different from one another and are sometimes further divided by religion: this, for example, is a notable feature of the Sahel countries, which, without exception, divide north and south in ethnic types and religion.

As nationalism swept through Africa in the 1950s and 1960s, the continent's new leaders faced the daunting task of persuading the many ethnic groups that composed countries, which in most cases were artificial colonial creations, that they were nationals of a single state entity rather than members of older ethnic or tribal groups. In the first flush of post-colonial nationalism this was not too difficult: Being Nigerian, Senegalese, or Kenyan was a way of rejecting colonialism and demonstrating pride in the new nationalism. Nevertheless, ethnic and tribal differences with long histories could not easily be submerged in the new nationalisms, which became a reason, or justification, for the emergence of the one-party state. Partisanship was often feared because a range of parties might attract the different ethnic groups to their ranks and so help to perpetuate tribalism. A further problem arose from the way in which the colonial powers had drawn the boundaries of Africa (30 percent of them were straight lines on the map); these cut through ethnic regions, leaving peoples of the same group divided between two colonies—often colonies of different European powers. The new states that emerged in the 1960s fell into a number of categories with regard to their ethnic composition: first, those with an uneasy division between roughly equal ethnic groups, as in the case of Nigeria; second, those with a clear division that was both racial and religious like that between north and south, which affected Sahel states such as Niger or Sudan; third, states where one tribal group was large enough, potentially, to dominate the rest—the Kikuyu in Kenya or the Bemba in Zambia; fourth, states with a range of ethnic groups, none large enough to achieve a position of dominance, as in Tanzania. A few countries came to independence enjoying an unusual degree of ethnic cohesion, such as Somalia, Botswana, Lesotho, or Swaziland. In addition, there were the half-dozen cases that presented special problems connected with the tribes of white settlement: Algeria, Kenya, Zimbabwe, Angola, and Mozambique, and, above all, South Africa.

Group loyalties constantly transcend the more difficult attractions of nationalist solidarity, as African leaders have discovered; in the worst cases, in some of the apparently unstoppable civil wars that have afflicted the continent since independence. Balancing the claims upon government of different ethnic groups has been a priority occupation of African heads of state. The frequent emergence of one-party states, often under military rule, may be seen as a confession of failure: that the government saw no other way of dealing with countless complex claims upon it than to impose harsh central control. Democracy may become too easily the tool of division rather than the cement of nationalism, or so it has been assumed. Yet there is no easy answer, as the situation in Somalia has proved. Somalia is generally seen as the most ethnically homogeneous country in Africa, but this homogeneity did not prevent its collapse into devastating clan warfare during the late 1980s and 1990s. The situation was worsened by the catastrophically mismanaged United Nations/United States intervention of the early 1990s, which served only to enhance the roles of the clan warlords.

Although it reflects existing realities to refer to Africa as a continent of minorities, this statement only makes sense when it is related to the modern continent of Africa that has been divided into 54 states. This division is the result of European colonialism: As the imperial powers of Europe carved up Africa (mainly during the last 20 years of the nineteenth century in the Scramble for Africa), they delineated their colonies by drawing boundaries between British, French, German, Portuguese and Italian possessions, thus reflecting the political divisions that existed in Europe. Prior to this historical development, the concept of a continent of minorities would hardly have made any sense. The Yoruba of western Nigeria, for example, were a major ethnic group occupying the region they still occupy in modern Nigeria. Prior to the arrival of the British, however, the Yoruba would have been regarded by their neighbors as a powerful people with a long-established system of government who were sometimes a threat to smaller and weaker neighboring groups, which, in their turn, had long occupied the same area or region. Only when the British created the colony of Nigeria and incorporated the Yoruba people within its boundaries did these become a minority within the new state structure. The same argument applies to the rest of the continent. Before the colonial era it might have been seen as a patchwork of ethnic groups, some large and powerful, others small and often dependent upon the goodwill of their neighbors for survival, but each occupying a particular region though these would constantly change, contracting or expanding according to the fortunes of the tribe. In these circumstances, it would have made sense to describe Africa as a continent containing many big and small "nations" that mingled, fought, or conquered each other, a pattern that could be found in most other parts of the world.

Colonialism and the carving up of Africa created a continent of minorities, and it did so by imposing boundaries that rarely accounted for the people on the ground; instead, a single British or French colony might incorporate a dozen groups within the one territorial structure so that most of, if not all, these groups necessarily became minorities within the new colony. Furthermore, a number of colonial boundaries divided tribes and split lands that they had traditionally regarded as their own so that a substantial tribal group was divided into two smaller groups on either side of a colonial boundary, often, moreover, a boundary that differentiated between the territories of rival colonial powers. This was especially true of the colonial divisions in West Africa but applied throughout the continent. A typical example would be the straight line in East Africa that divided the British colony of Kenya from German East Africa (now Tanzania); the Masai, a wide-ranging nomadic people, found that their traditional lands had been partitioned between the British and the Germans, and consequently, they were split into subjects of one or the other colonial power. The fact that they largely ignored this division and continued to move back and forth across the new boundary highlights one of the most important post-colonial problems in Africa: the extent to which divided peoples continue to ignore inherited colonial boundaries.

Almost every African state has to cope with a range of ethnic or tribal divisions, and in only a few does a single ethnic group enjoy a clear majority that allows it to dominate the country as a whole. Many African states such as Cameroon, Congo, Nigeria, Sudan, Zimbabwe, or South Africa may be used to illustrate the complexities of a continent of minorities. Nigeria and South Africa are examined here in detail to illustrate these problems of minorities.

Nigeria's principal ethnic groups consist of the Hausa-Fulani, Yoruba, Ibo, Kanuri, Tiv, Edo, Nupe, Ibibio, and Ijaw, and between them, they account for 80 percent of the population. A proportional breakdown of these groups shows the Hausa as 21.3 percent of the population, Fulani 11.2 percent, Yoruba 21.3 percent, Ibo 18 percent, Ibibio 5.6 percent, Kanuri 4.2 percent, Edo 3.4 percent, Tiv 2.2 percent, Ijaw 1.8 percent, and Nupe 1.2 percent. The three dominant ethnic groups, each of which may claim to be a nation in its own right, are the Hausa-Fulani, Yoruba, and Ibo. Yet within the context of the state of Nigeria each is a minority: between them they account for 71.8 percent of the country's total population and the largest group, the combined Hausa-Fulani at 32.5 percent of the population, remain a minority within the Nigerian state structure. Altogether, there are about 250 ethnic groups in Nigeria, although some of these may number no more than 10,000.

The problems inherent in countries or states composed of a number of distinctive minorities can be appreciated by a brief examination of the colonial and postcolonial history of Nigeria. The British, who conquered Nigeria piecemeal over the latter half of the nineteenth century, began by running the different regions separately. They found old, established systems of government, and much of the colonial structure was devised to run an administration that utilized the existing traditional systems of rule. Only in 1947 did Britain introduce a new constitution that established a federal system based on three regions—Eastern, Western, and Northern—that coincided with the core areas or homelands of the three main ethnic groups—the Ibo, Yoruba, and Hausa-Fulani. By this time in their colonial rule, the British wanted to reconcile the differences between the main groups. In practical political terms, the three groups could be reconciled while the British controlled the political center. The key issue that emerged over the remaining years of British rule (to 1960), as one constitution or adjustment followed another, concerned what would happen to the delicate balance between the main ethnic groups when the British finally withdrew. The tensions between these three groups, which had always been inherent in the colonial invention of Nigeria, soon became apparent at independence. These tensions were further exacerbated by religious differences: the Hausa-Fulani of the north were solidly Muslim, the peoples of the south were Christian or followed traditional beliefs, and the south was fearful of domination by the north. The political parties that emerged prior to independence reflected these suspicions. The Northern Region was dominated by the Northern People's Congress (NPC), which called for a large degree of regional autonomy. The NPC also demanded guarantees for the integrity of Islam in an independent Nigeria and insisted that the North should be allotted 50 percent of the representation in the federal legislature. The Western Region's leading political party, the Action Group (AG), also demanded regional autonomy. Moreover, as the country's principal cocoa-growing area (cocoa was then the main export earner), the Western Region was afraid that its wealth would be used to subsidize less-wealthy regions outside the Yoruba heartland. This fear would recur later when the big oil discoveries transformed the economic prospects of the Eastern Region. In the meantime, the Ibo advocated a strong central government and the distribution of revenues according to need. Regardless, many Ibo were dispersed throughout other parts of Nigeria (far more so than was the case for either the Yoruba or the Hausa-Fulani), which was another reason they favored a strong central administration.

Nigeria became independent on October 1, 1960, and it was not long before the tensions inherent in the new federal system and the power pulls between the three main groups escalated. These tensions were partly about political control: Which group, party, or individual was to obtain most influence and control in the new Nigeria? Yet underlying these normal political tensions were the deeper suspicions arising out of a state structure that had been created by the British for colonial convenience. Without the colonial factor, the three main ethnic groups would never have coalesced into a single state. These tensions were further increased by the religious divide between the Muslim North and the Christian or traditional South.

Because none of the political parties representing the three main groups were able to achieve an absolute majority, one group was bound to be excluded from power should a coalition be formed by the other two, which was what happened in 1960. Subsequently, complex maneuvering between the parties characterized the period from 1960 to 1966 but failed to overcome the divisive faults in the system; the three regions were unable to subordinate their claims for advantage to the nationalist concept of a single Nigeria, and the tensions threatened to pull the country apart. These national rivalries were reflected in the composition of the armed forces, in which a majority of officers at independence were Ibo, a fact that created suspicions on the part of the other groups. These tensions finally came to a head in January 1966 when Ibo officers, most of the young, attempted a coup, killing the Federal Prime Minister, Tafawa Balewa; the Prime Minister of the Northern Region, Sir Ahmadu Bello; the Prime Minister of the Western Region, Chief Akintola; and the Federal Finance Minister, Chief Festus Okotie-Eboh. The immediate result was the establishment of a military government under General Johnson Aguiyi-Ironsi, but in May 1996, Hausa anger at Ibo domination of the government led to reprisals against Ibo in the North that resulted in many deaths. Then, on July 29, General Aguiyi-Ironsi was killed in a coup mounted by northern soldiers; after an interregnum of three days, the chief of staff, Lt Col Yakubu Gowon (later General), who came from the Christian Middle Belt of the country, became military head of state.

At this stage, Ibo outside the Eastern region, and especially the large numbers then in the North, became fearful for their safety and began to return to their homeland. In May 1967, in an attempt to break the North-West-East pattern of distrust and rival tensions, Gowon abolished the three regions and substituted 12 smaller states in their place, but the move came too late to forestall the developing confrontation, with the Ibo now taking the initiative. On May 30, Lt Col Chukwuemeka Odumwegwu Ojukwu, the military commander of the Eastern region, proclaimed an independent Ibo state of Biafra. Civil war followed.

The Ibo were defeated, the state of Biafra ceased to exist, and the integrity of a single Nigeria was maintained following the victory of the Federal Military Government, but the underlying causes of the war, the deep suspicions between the country's three main ethnic groups, had not been eliminated. Over the succeeding 30 years, Nigeria was ruled by the military for all but five of them. Following the death of Sani Abacha in June 1998, Nigeria made its third attempt since the civil war to return to civilian rule, and General Olusegun Obasanjo (the country's military ruler from 1976 to 1979) was elected president and assumed office in May 1999. During his first year in office, he faced mounting religious violence between Muslims and Christians.

Racial conflict and confrontation between different ethnic groups has been a staple of South African history since the arrival of the Dutch at the Cape in the middle of the seventeenth century. Parallel conflicts developed between white and black, white and white, and black and black, and over the years, the conflicts between them encompassed most of the race arguments that later became a familiar aspect of international politics during the latter part of the twentieth century.

As African nationalism swept through the continent in the years following 1945, the whites in South Africa determined to entrench their power and resist nationalist encroachments in their own country. Unlike the British, who could return to Britain if necessary, the Afrikaners had long severed their links with the Netherlands and saw South Africa as their only home. As the nationalists triumphed in one colony after another to the north, the Afrikaners became all the more desperate to maintain white control. The situation in South Africa was further complicated by the presence of two other important race groups: the Cape Coloured community, people of mixed race who, by the 1940s, had been established as a distinct factor in the country's political life for well over a century; and the Asian community, whose first members had been introduced into Natal by the British from India in the first half of the nineteenth century.

The South African whites were not alone in their rearguard action against African nationalism. In the far north of the continent, the *colons* of Algeria were soon to embark upon a bitter war to hold on to their privileged position; in Kenya the Mau Mau rebellion focused attention upon white settler privilege. To the immediate north of South Africa, the Portuguese were about to engage in two hopeless wars to maintain white control in Angola and Mozambique where there were sizeable Portuguese minorities, while in Rhodesia, events were building towards the white rearguard action of Ian Smith and the Rhodesia Front, which proclaimed UDI in 1965. The South African National Party (NP) led the way when, following its election victory of 1948, the government of Dr. Daniel Malan proceeded to apply apartheid laws to every aspect of national life. There had always been race separation in South Africa; now, however, it was to be formalized everywhere by law. These white rearguard actions were each carried out by minorities, although they were minorities that had only recently been established on the continent by the European colonial powers.

Over the next 40 years, in the face of growing world opposition, the National Party held to its course and, as part of its justification for apartheid, tried both to divide and rule and to create the fiction of black independence by its Bantustan, or Homeland, policy. Under this policy, the government, not satisfied with differentiating between the country's four main groups—black, white, Coloured, and Asian—deliberately emphasized tribal differences by subdividing the already disenfranchised blacks into 10 tribal homelands. The former Native Reserves had been based upon the historic homeland areas of different African nations; now these were to be encouraged to develop towards full "self-government." Ten Homelands were created: Transkei, Ciskei, Bophutatswana, Lebowa, Venda, Gazankulu, Qwaqwa, KwaNdebele, KaNgwane, and Kwazulu, although when the Transkei became the first Homeland to achieve "independence" in 1976, the international community refused to recognize it.

By the late 1980s it had become clear, even to hard-line Afrikaner racists, that the system of apartheid could not be maintained. Yet even after the events of 1990—the repeal of the ban against the African National Congress (ANC) and other African political movements and the release of Nelson Mandela—the NP government under F.W. de Klerk still thought to hold the ring by playing off one group against another in the hope of splitting the black majority. This tactic did not work, although Chief Mangosuthu Buthelezi, the Zulu leader, and his Inkatha Freedom Party argued for a strong federal system that would give maximum power to the regions, even though the ANC insisted upon the creation of a strong centralized state.

In 1995, one year after the elections that brought the ANC to power with a majority and for the first time saw all the people of South Africa take part, the breakdown of the country's population was as follows: Black 76.3 percent, White 12.7 percent, Coloured 8.5 percent, Asian 2.5 percent. The black population could be divided as follows: Zulu 22 percent, Xhosa 18 percent, Pedi 9 percent, Sotho 7 percent, Tswana 7 percent, Tsonga 3.5 percent, Swazi 3 percent, and others 6.8 percent.

An analysis of 53 African countries shows that only 25, just under half, possess a dominant group that composes more than 50 percent of the population; even in these cases, the majority group may be substantially divided into subgroups. The question of minorities and how they are integrated within state structures affects the whole continent. In many cases, there have been no conflicts, and tensions between rival ethnic groups have been accepted as the normal strains to be expected in any country between different interest groups. In postindependence, Africa's ethnic confrontations have fallen under several categories, and, all too often, lamentably, these have arisen directly out of the colonial legacy. In countries of white settlement, the colonial legacy has had the most obvious impact, both immediately prior to independence and subsequently. This was the case in Algeria, Kenya, Rhodesia, Angola, and Mozambique. South Africa was in a category of its own for two reasons: It had a much larger proportionate white minority, which had been entrenched for a longer period than in any other state; and it had achieved independence, internationally recognized, under white control in 1931. As a result, it was able to resist the pressures exerted upon the colonial powers by the United Nations after World War II, and it was sufficiently powerful economically to defy the world community until things fell apart internally.

In a second group of countries, ethnic divisions had been emphasized by the colonial powers as a means to divide and rule. This was the case in Nigeria under the British, with consequences that have been discussed above. It was also the case, first under the Germans, and then the Belgians in Burundi and Rwanda, where colonial convenience used the elite Tutsi minority as the instrument of control until the period just prior to independence. Although the Tutsi had been the dominant group before the arrival of the Europeans, the two tribes had learned to live with each other. Subsequently, the repeated massacres and countermassacres in both Burundi and Rwanda from 1959 onward and the appalling Hutu genocide of Tutsi in 1994 in Rwanda had, at least in part, been made more likely as a result of the earlier colonial policies of divide and rule—although that can never be used as a justification for what happened.

Given the complex ethnic mix that covers the African continent. the recent history of bringing together often disparate peoples into unified "colonial" states, and the residual struggles of white minorities to perpetuate their political control, it is unsurprising that Africa has witnessed a number of violent conflicts in the postindependence era, many of which have been based upon these ethnic differences.

GUY ARNOLD

See also **Afrikaners; Algeria; Angola; Burundi; Colonialism; De Klerk, F.W. (Afrikaner); Diola (Joola); Ewe; Fulani; Hausa; Mandela, Nelson (South African); Mossi; Mozambique; Ndebele; Nigeria; Rwanda; South Africa; Tutsi; Yoruba**

Further Reading

Beckwith, C., and M. Van Offelen, *Nomads of Niger*, London: Collins, 1984

Crowder, M., *The Story of Nigeria*, London: Longmans, 4th edition, 1978

de Meideros, F., *Peuples du Golfe du Benin (Aja-Ewe)*. Paris: Karthala, 1984

Doornbos, M., L. Cliffe, and J. Markakis, editors, *Beyond Conflict in the Horn: The Prospects of Peace and Development in Ethiopia, Somalia, Eritrea and Sudan*, Lawrenceville, Kansas: Red Sea Press, 1995

Estermann, C., *Ethnographie du Sud-ouest de l'Angola*, 2 vols, Paris: Academie de Sciences d'Outre-mer, 1984

Fukui, K., and J. Markakis, editors, *Ethnicity and Conflict in the Horn of Africa*, London: James Currey, 1994

Hailey, Lord, *The Republic of South Africa and the High Commission Territories*, London: Oxford University Press, 1963

Harrison Church, R.J., *West Africa*, London: Longman, 2nd edition, 1979

Kanogo, T., *Squatters and the Roots of Mau Mau, 1905–63*, London: James Currey, 1987

Katsuyoski. F., and J. Markakis, editors, *Ethnicity and Conflict in the Horn of Africa*, London: Currey, 1994

Keenan, J,. *The Tuareg*, London: Allen Lane, 1978

Lemarchand, R., *Rwanda and Burundi,* London: Pall Mall, 1970

Maier, Karl, *The House Has Fallen: Nigeria in Crisis*, London: Allen Lane, The Penguin Press, 2001

Ogot, B.A., editor, *Politics and Nationalism in Colonial Kenya*, Nairobi: East African Publishing House, 1972

Post, K.W.J., and M. Vickers, *Structure and Conflict in Nigeria 1960–65*, London: Heinemann, 1973

Prunier, G., *The Rwanda Crisis 1959–1964*: *History of a Genocide*, London: Hurst, 1995

Schapera, L., et al., *Ethnographic Survey of Africa: The Tswana*, London: International African Institute, 1953

Sparks, A., *Tomorrow is Another Country: The Inside Story of South Africa's Road to Change*, New York: Hill and Wang, 1995

Stoneman, C., editor, *Zimbabwe's Prospects: Race, Class, State and Capital*, London: Macmillan, 1988

Thompson, L.M., *History of South Africa,* New Haven: Yale University Press, 1990

Vambe, L., *An Ill-Fated People*: *Zimbabwe Before and After Rhodes*, London: Heinemann, 1972

Whiteman, Kaye, *Chad,* London: Minority Rights Group (Report No. 80), 1988

Wyse, A., *The Krio of Sierra Leone: An Interpretive History*, London: Hurst, 1989

African-American Nationalism and Separatism

African-American nationalist sentiments were developed and nurtured in African self-help societies and religious organizations. African-American nationalist strategies to deal with racism included repatriation and redemption of Africa from colonialism; formation of an African nation in the New World; separatism, or the formation of a nation within a nation; and the formation of a separate nation comprising regions where African Americans would constitute the majority of the population.

African-American nationalism and separatism can be contrasted with the pro-integration stance, which holds that African Americans are American citizens who should be provided with equal protection under the law and should have the opportunity to integrate themselves into every facet of American society. The various strains of nationalist and separatist sentiment have always been a minority view among African Americans. However, these ideas have had a powerful influence on African-American consciousness and political struggle. For example, before the Civil War, both integrationists and nationalists agreed that slavery must be ended and resistance to slavery in all forms must be supported. Some early examples of African-American nationalism were the founding of the Free African Society of Philadelphia by Absalom Jones and Richard Allen in 1787 and the founding of Liberia on the west coast of Africa under the auspices of the American Colonization Society in 1821. As the political crisis over slavery became greater, Henry Highland Garnet called for slave rebellions in 1843; the Colored National Convention of 1848 dealt with emigration to Africa, separatism, and self-help; and the National Emigration Convention stated for a people to be free, they must naturally be their own rulers. Abolitionists strongly disagreed with the emigration movement because they saw it as a way to deport free African Americans. Much of the resistance to slavery, including support for the Underground Railroad, came from free African Americans.

Post-Civil War Nationalism

Several significant African-American nationalist ideas were promulgated after the Civil War. Francis Grimke called for black teachers for black schools in 1885. In 1898, Bishop Henry Turner, of the African Methodist Episcopalians, declared God to be black. Between 1880 and 1913, the idea that there should be separate territories for Africans within the United States gained popularity and support.

Early in the twentieth century, Marcus Garvey and the Universal Negro Improvement Association (UNIA) led the largest African American nationalist movement. Garvey argued for the movement of African Americans back to Africa. UNIA also promoted economic unity programs to build the financial strength of African Americans. One of UNIA's most ambitious ventures was the Black Star Line, which was to be a cruise line devoted exclusively to African-American passengers. At its height, UNIA had millions of African American followers.

Revolutionary Nationalism

Revolutionary nationalism held that a change in the existing social order was necessary to bring about the formation of a black nation. The idea can be traced back to the 1930's and the "Negro Nation" thesis of the American Communist Party. The "Negro Nation" thesis had an important effect on the development of African-American nationalism from the 1920s through the 1950s and was supported by several prominent African-American intellectuals, such as W.E.B. Du Bois. He felt that the hatred and animosity of white Americans toward African Americans made the formation of separate nations the only viable alternative for African-American progress.

The Black Panther Party (BPP) was an example of a revolutionary, nationalist, black political organization. The BPP was originally known as the Black Panther Party for Self-Defense and was founded in Oakland, California, by Huey Newton and Bobby Seale in October 1966. Newton became the Panther's defense minister and Seale its chairman. The BPP advocated black self-defense and social revolution against capitalism. The Panthers believed that only the dismantling of capitalism, imperialism, and racism would allow for a just American society. The Party articulated their goals in a ten-point platform, which demanded, among other things, full employment, exemption of black men from military service, and an end to police brutality.

In the late 1960s, as racial tension increased, the Federal Bureau of Investigation (FBI) blamed the Black Panthers for riots and other incidents of violence. The 'FBI's counterintelligence program was implemented to disrupt efforts to unify black militant groups such as the Student Non-Violent Coordinating Committee, the Black Panthers, and the Nation of Islam. In December 1969, the police killed Fred Hampton and Mark Clark, prominent Chicago Panthers. By the end of the decade, 28 Panthers had been killed and many other members were either in jail or had been forced to leave the United States to avoid arrest. In the 1970s, with many of its leaders debilitated for various reasons and after newspaper reports appeared describing the illicit activities of some party leaders, including extortion schemes directed against Oakland merchants, the BPP ceased to be a political force. Other examples of revolutionary nationalist groups included the Dodge Revolutionary Union Movement (DRUM) and the Republic of New Afrika.

Religious Nationalism: The Nation of Islam and Malcolm X

The most prominent example of an African-American organization driven by religious nationalism is the Nation of Islam, also known as the Black Muslims. Fard Muhammad founded the organization in 1930 as a breakaway group from the Moorish Science Temple, and it was led by Elijah Muhammad after 1933 until his death in 1975.

In the 1960s, the Nation of Islam held that the white man was an incorrigible devil, created by an ancient scientist called Yakub. Integration with whites was impossible. Black Muslims advocated the establishment of a separate African-American homeland in the United States. Elijah Muhammed called for full and complete freedom, equal justice under the law, equality of opportunity, the right to establish a separate state or territory on this continent or elsewhere, and freedom for all believers in Islam now held in federal prisons.

Malcolm X, later known also by the religious name El-Hajj Malik El-Shabazz, is simultaneously one of the best known, most influential, yet least understood African-American nationalists. His development as a black nationalist leader is deeply connected to the Nation of Islam. He adopted a criminal lifestyle as a young man, leading to a conviction and sentencing to prison. While in prison, Malcolm read widely and developed an interest in the Nation of Islam. Released from prison in 1952, Malcolm went to Detroit, Michigan, and joined the Nation of Islam temple. He rose rapidly in the Nation of Islam as a minister and recruiter of new members. Elijah Muhammad appointed him as the chief minister of Harlem's main temple in June 1954. Within five years, Malcolm had become the Nation's most prominent spokesperson.

Between 1955 and 1965, Malcolm X supported the Nation's philosophy and program. He disagreed strongly with the Reverend Martin Luther King, Jr., particularly concerning the tactic of nonviolent resistance. Malcolm X was a great public speaker, and his growing reputation caused tension with the Black Muslim leadership. Elijah Muhammad wanted to maintain the Nation of Islam as a religious self-help movement, while Malcolm X saw it as a political response to racism. Malcolm X also began to reject the racist ideology within the Nation of Islam, including the Yakub theory. In addition, Malcolm was convinced that there was ongoing corruption within the Nation of Islam.

Malcolm X publicly broke with the Nation of Islam on March 8, 1964, and formed his own movement, the Muslim Mosque, Inc. In 1964, Malcolm made a pilgrimage to Mecca, the holy Muslim city in Saudi Arabia. In addition, he also visited several other African and Arab nations. While on this trip, he publicly expressed his own faith as a follower of traditional Islam and renounced the idea that all white men were evil. He became an orthodox Sunni Muslim, or Sunnite, and adopted a religious name, El-Hajj Malik El-Shabazz, meaning the Malcolm (or Malik) who is from the tribe or family of Shabazz and has made the Hajj, or pilgrimage, to Mecca.

When Malcolm X returned to America, he held the first rally of the Organization of Afro-American Unity (OAAU). This group had no direct religious ties, advocated racial solidarity, and strove to unify all black organizations fighting racism. At the same time, Malcolm renounced his previous racism against whites. In contrast to his earlier views, he encouraged blacks to vote, to participate in the political system, and to work with each other and with sympathetic whites and Hispanics to put an end to racial discrimination.

On February 21, 1965, Malcolm X was assassinated while addressing an OAAU rally in New York City. At least two of the three men later convicted of the crime were connected with the Nation of Islam. However, some contend that the federal government played a role in his death.

In the mid 1970s, Wallace D. Muhammad, who succeeded his father Elijah Muhammad, downplayed Black Nationalism, admitted nonblack members, and stressed strict Islamic beliefs and practices. In the late 1970s, however, a dissident faction, led by Louis Farrakhan, assumed the original name Nation of Islam and reasserted the principles of black separatism.

Presently, the Nation of Islam has established accredited schools in more than 45 cities. *The Final Call,* a weekly newspaper originally called *Muhammad Speaks,* has a wide national circulation. The Nation of Islam rehabilitates convicts, drug addicts, and alcoholics through their doing-for-self philosophy. Some estimates place its membership at more than 100,000. In October of 1995, the Nation of Islam played a prominent role in organizing and conceiving "The Million Man March," one of the largest demonstrations ever held in the 'United State's capital.

Cultural Nationalism

Cultural nationalism has been a consistent theme running throughout African-American nationalism and separatism to various degrees. Its main premise is that African Americans must revive African cultural values as an essential step in their liberation. Furthermore, it holds that there are uniquely African culture features, and therefore blacks and whites have separate values, histories, intellectual traditions, and lifestyles. Cultural nationalism was prominent in the emigration movements of the seventeenth and eighteenth centuries. However, as African Americans became more rooted in the United States, it took on the character of a conceptual or aesthetic return, as opposed to an actual physical return to the continent.

One of the most influential cultural nationalist organizations in the 1960s was called US. Ron Karenga founded it in 1965. Based in Southern California, the Watts rebellion and the assassination of Malcolm X were catalysts to its formation. US established itself as a cultural nationalist group, calling for racial unity and for black people to free themselves from white oppression. The key element of this liberation was the embrace of a resurrected African culture. US adhered to Kawaida a quasi-religious system of beliefs and rituals advocating black pride, unity, culture, and self-defense. One of the most significant effects that US provided was Kwanzaa. This holiday was created by US in 1966 and is now observed by millions of African Americans.

Today, the most prominent display of cultural nationalism is the wearing of brightly colored African clothing, such as dashikis; the adaptation of African hairstyles; and the adoption of West African religious practices. Afrocentricity is a contemporary derivative of African-American cultural nationalism.

JOSEPH L. GRAVES, JR.

See also **Afrocentricity; Du Bois, W.E.B.; Garvey, Marcus; Malcolm X (African-American); Nationalism**

Further Reading

Baraka, A., *Kawaida Studies: The New Nationalism*, Chicago: Third World Press, 1972

Bracey, J., A. Meier, E. Rudwick, *Black Nationalism in America*, Indianapolis: Bobbs-Merrill, 1970

Brown, S.D., *Fighting for US: Maulana Karenga, The US Organization, and Black Cultural Nationalism*, New York: New York University Press, 2003

Foner, P., editor, *W.E.B. DuBois Speaks: Speeches and Addresses 1920–1963*, New York: Pathfinder Press, 1970

Gilroy, P., "Black Nationalism: The Sixties and the Nineties." in *Black Popular Culture*, edited by Michele Wallace and Gina Dent, New York: The New Press, 1998

Jacques-Garvey, A., editor, *Philosophy and Opinions of Marcus Garvey*, New York: Atheneum, 1969

Malcolm X, *The Autobiography of Malcolm X, with the Assistance of Alex Haley*, New York: Grove Press, 1966

Okur, N.A., "Asante's Afrocentricity in the Context of African American Nationalism," in *Molefi Kete Asante and Afrocentricity: In Praise and in Criticism*, edited by Dhyana Ziegler, Nashville: James C. Winston Pub., 1995

West, C., "Learning to Think for Ourselves: Malcolm X's Black Nationalism Reconsidered," in *Malcolm X : In Our Own Image*, edited by Joe Wood, New York: St. Martin's Press, 1992

Wilson, W.J., "Revolutionary Nationalism versus Cultural Nationalism Dimensions of the Black Power Movement," *Sociological Focus*, 3, no. 3 (1970)

Africans: Overview

Capsule Summary

Location: Africa
Total population: approximately 861,000,000 (2003)
Languages: Over 2000 indigenous languages; English, French, and Arabic widely spoken
Religion: African traditional religions, Christianity, Islam

Africa is the world's largest continent after Asia. Its distance from Cape Town, South Africa, its southernmost point, to Cairo, Egypt, close to its northern limit, is about 5,000 miles (8,045 kilometers). Across the continent in an east-west direction, the distance from Mogadishu, Somalia in the east to Dakar, Senegal on the Atlantic coast is about 3,000 miles (4,827 kilometers). This massive continent comprises more than 50 nation-states, including island states off its coasts. Although Africa, with an average population density of only about 63 people per square mile, is not as overcrowded as Asia, its high population growth rate is about twice that of the rest of the world. Although about two-thirds of Africans still live in the countryside, there are high rates of rural-urban migration in different parts of the continent. This has resulted in staggering rates of unemployment and overcrowding in urban areas such Lagos, Alexandria, Cairo, Nairobi, and Cape Town.

The oldest human remains and artifacts yet discovered have been found in Africa. For this reason, Africa is regarded as the home of humankind or the "cradle of civilization." Africans thus have been among the pioneers of human culture. During the past millennia, African families and clans settled and expanded in the different ecological environments of the vast continent—rain forest, savannah, and desert. Different groups settling into their lifestyles developed a wide variety of dialects and languages, customs and traditions, and worldviews and values. Over time, the descendants of the original settlers, as well as later migrants, built upon their past to develop cultures that distinguished them from their neighbors. Today, cultural and linguistic diversity runs throughout the continent even though some common elements exist among most ethnic groups. Ethnicity indeed remains an important aspect of identity among Africans. Like other people elsewhere in the world, Africans, many times, have redefined their ethnic identities.

The enormous size of the continent and its geographical variations are reflected in the wide range of cultural traits and economic systems that have developed in a number of areas. In the savannah areas, for example, cattle rearing is the main occupation among the Fulani in West Africa, the Nuer and Dinka in the Sudan, and the Xhosa in South Africa.

Before the colonial period, the ways that Africans provided for their subsistence as well as the ways they handled political and social pressures dictated that they move from place to place. Significantly, the division of Africa during the nineteenth-century European "Scramble," resulting in externally imposed colonial boundaries, brought about radical changes throughout the continent. The whole basis of society was transformed as groups of people previously held together by kinship, kingship, or religious ties were now separated and mixed with other groups with whom they had little in common. With the creation of colonial boundaries, traditional allegiances were replaced with ties to one colonial regime or another. Many Africans resisted European colonialism, often to no avail.

Although Christianity and Islam have influenced many African societies, indigenous religions significantly shaped the lives of most Africans before and after the two monotheistic religions appeared on the continent. Elements of mythology that help explain how the world started, how the first people were created, and the origins of certain societies are central to the belief systems of most Africans. In fact, for most Africans, the major aspects of daily life including political, social, and economic activities cannot be separated from religious beliefs and ritual practices. Although indigenous religions in Africa take a variety of forms, belief in a supreme being, far removed from human activities, is a common phenomenon throughout the continent. Deities and ancestral spirits serve as mediums for reaching a supreme being. Significantly, most Africans blend Christian, Islamic, and African traditional religious practices as they grapple with the demands of their daily existences.

There are over 2,000 different languages spoken in Africa. Because most Africans speak more than one language, barriers to communication are quite often minimal. A number of languages such as Swahili in East Africa or Yoruba in West Africa that dominate some regions, which most people speak as a second language, allows for smoother trade and social contact. Moreover, a large number of these languages are derived from a single source in the distant past. This makes many languages intelligible to even those that are not native speakers. Educated Africans also speak European languages such as English, French, and Portuguese inherited from the colonial past.

Africans have faced a wide range of challenges since the decade of African independence in the 1960s. Declining economies for most countries in Africa means that most Africans are poor; especially those in rural areas in sub-Saharan Africa, where about 60 percent of the population live below the poverty line. Moreover, armed conflicts in various parts of Africa have had a disruptive effective on development programs, thereby exacerbating poverty and displacement, especially in west and central Africa. According to the United Nations High Commissioner for Refugees, 3.2 million of the world's 11.5 million refugees are in Africa. Out of a total population of 20 million internally displaced persons, 12.7 million are in Africa. While there has been a decline in the refugee population in recent years, the number of displaced Africans has increased almost twofold. Although most Africans live in peaceful environments where they go about their daily life without fear, civil wars in recent years have taken their toll on Liberians, Sierra Leoneans, Rwandans, and the Congolese of the Democratic Republic of the Congo (formerly Zaire). During the last two decades, the HIV/AIDS pandemic has afflicted millions of Africans. It is the leading cause of death among Africans.

TAMBA E. M'BAYO

See also **Algeria; Angola; Arabs: North African; Benin; Botswana; Burkina Faso; Burundi; Cameroon; Cape Verde; Christians: Africa; Colonialism; Congo; Congo Republic; Côte d'Ivoire; Egypt; Ethiopia; Fulani; Gabon; Gambia, The; Lesotho; Liberia; Madagascar; Malawi; Mali; Mauritania; Mauritius; Mozambique; Muslims in Africa; Namibia; Nigeria; Rwanda; Senegal; Seychelles; Sierra Leone; Somalia; Somalis; South Africa; Sudan; Suriname; Swaziland; Tanzania; Uganda; Zambia; Zimbabwe**

Further Reading

Fyle, C. Magbaily, *Introduction to the History of African Civilization: Volume I: Precolonial Africa; Volume II: Colonial and Post-Colonial Africa*, Lanham, Maryland: University Press of America, 1999

Gilbert, Erik, and Jonathan T. Reynolds, *Africa in World History: From Prehistory to the Present*, New Jersey: Pearson Education, Inc., 2004

Khapoya, Vincent B., *The African Experience: An Introduction*, New Jersey: Prentice Hall, 1998

Uwechue, Ralph, editor, *Africa Today*, London: Africa Books Ltd., 1996

Africans in Europe

Capsule Summary

Location: Europe
Total population: unknown
Language: local; new immigrants also speak their language of origin
Religion: various

Africans in Europe before 1000 CE

Although there is little documentary evidence, there is no reason not to assume that Africans have lived in Europe since seamen have been able to cross the Mediterranean Sea. The earliest evidence of the African presence can be found in sculptures and paintings: Africans began to appear in European art in Crete from circa1,500 BCE and on the Greek mainland some one thousand years later. Africans appear in the writings of the Greeks and the Romans, who usually referred to them as *Aethiopians*. (Because these Africans were described as having black skin, often flat noses, thick lips, and curled or woolly hair, it seems certain that they were not akin to the mixed race people now living in Africa north of the Sahara.) According to most historians, there were no exhibitions of racial prejudice towards Africans, though both Romans and Greeks were often xenophobic.

The Roman Empire encompassed all of North Africa by the second century CE. According to the historian Michael Grant, "North Africa [was] the homeland of the most remarkable writers in the empire" (Grant 1969, 297). It was the homeland not only of writers but also of an emperor, Septimius Severus (ruled 193–211 CE), who spoke Latin with a Carthaginian accent and who was buried near his outpost in Great Britain.

To conquer its empire and to maintain it, the Romans naturally used troops from one part of the continent to subdue another. Among these troops were Africans, who most likely begat children with native women wherever they were stationed. Upon the expiration of their service, some of these African soldiers, perhaps especially those who had married local women, settled where they were last stationed.

There was also a reverse movement of other "'Romans'" settling in the African section of the empire. More important was the earlier movement of Greeks to Egypt following its conquest by Alexander the Great. Some Greek scholars, such as Pythagoras, went to study there. The Greek historian Herodotus claimed that Greeks had adopted much of their culture from Egyptian settlers. Recent research indicates that many Egyptians were of mixed race.

During the first few hundred years of the Christian era, there were several black popes. Victor I (who determined when Easter should be celebrated, was pope from 189 to 199 CE); Militades, of whom little seems to be known, was pope for only three years, (311–314 CE); and Gelasisus I (492–496 CE) was a scholar and the author of six books, numerous hymns, and prayers. Among the influential Christian scholars of African descent were Tertullian (Quintus Septimus Florens Tertullianus, circa 155–220 CE) and Augustine, later canonized, one of the most important intepreters of Christianity.

There are paintings and sculptures of a black woman holding a child in many European churches, usually referred to as Black Madonnas. Most interpreters believe that these are representations of African goddesses, for example the Egyptian goddess Isis and her son Horus, adopted in the Christian era as a representation of Mary and Jesus. There is at least one African saint, Maurice, usually represented as a soldier in armor. Reputedly an Egyptian legionary commander who did not permit his troops to massacre a Christian uprising, Maurice became known as the Knight of the Holy Lance and was worshipped as early as 460 CE; the cathedral at Magdeburg was dedicated to him in 968. The cult of St. Maurice subsequently spread across medieval Europe, principally along the Rhine River in Switzerland and in northern Italy. Also known as St. Moritz and St. Mauritius, St. Maurice was a significant figure in Germanic iconography.

There is some evidence to indicate that Ireland's African population began with Africans captured by the Vikings and taken there around 860 CE. Evidence suggests that there was trade between Africa and Western Europe, including Ireland, at this time: For example,

Anglo-Saxon beads have been found in East Africa, and Egyptian beads have been found in Ireland.

The Iberian Peninsula (today's Spain and Portugal, then ruled by the Goths) was conquered by the Moors (Arabs and African including Berber Muslims) in 711 CE, but there were perhaps three invasions of Europe by Africans before this time. Some say that the first occurred around 1000 BCE by Africans banished from their African homeland by the king against whom they had revolted. These African settlers were conquered and annihilated by invading Romans some 160 years later. The second invasion occurred about 700 BCE; it was led by Taharaka, identified as the head of an Ethiopian army, who later became king of Egypt. The third invasion was by the Carthaginian general Hannibal (247–183 BCE) who crossed the Alps in 218 BCE to attack Rome. Carthage, an ancient state in North Africa, dominated the western half of the Mediterranean during this time; anthropologists believe that its people, like most coastal Africans, are a mixture of Semites, Africans, and Europeans.

The Moors had begun the jihad (holy war) from Arabia, and the many peoples of northern Africa whom they had conquered en route to the west were incorporated in their invading army. (The Arabs themselves, it is believed, were a mixed people, the descendants of Cushite (Ethiopian) settlers and local peoples.) After the conquest of Spain, the army, led by an African, Gabel (general) Tariq bin Ziad, invaded Gaul (present day France). Charles Martel, the Frankish king of the region around modern Paris, mobilized against the Saracens; by 755 they had all been driven back across the Pyrenees. The Camargue (in southeastern France) remained in Moorish hands until 1140. The Moors remained there, despite constant attacks by the Christians to expel them, for some 700 years. The Moors also captured Sicily in 837 and in 846 invaded Italy, then ruled by the Germans under Otto II, and seized Rome.

1000 to 1500 CE

Moorish rule in Iberia was generally benevolent, except under the Almohades, the fifth dynasty in the twelfth century, who also conquered all of northern Africa as far as Egypt. Jews, Christians, and Moslems were free to practice their faiths. Fused from the mixture of cultures—African, Berber, Arabic, Jewish, and Goth—a creative civilization soon flourished in Al-Andalus (the Muslim Iberian Peninsula). Here, learned manuscripts on all subjects were collected from around the known world and translated into Arabic. Great strides were made in the natural, physical, and military sciences; in medicine; mathematics; city planning (which included public baths, piped water to all streets, and street lighting); and in agriculture and botany. Scholars from around the world studied in Al-Andalus.

When internal upheavals weakened the Arab empire, the Christians began to succeed in their *Reconquista,* or reconquest, of the peninsula. Moors fleeing the Christians crossed the Mediterranean and sought the protection of Morocco's ruler, Yusuf ibn Tashifin, who was of Mandingo origins. Though initially reluctant, Yusuf amassed a vast army, including camel corps; crossed the Straits of Gibraltar (a linguistic corruption of *Gabel Tariq*); and routed the Christians. Yusuf became the Almoravid sultan of Al-Andalus; the Almoravids were a Berber dynasty from the Sahara. Under the Almoravids and their successors, the Almohade, Moorish civilization reached its zenith in wealth, scholarship, and architecture. However, good living reduced Muslim vigilance and the *Reconquista* began anew. Led by King Ferdinand and Queen Isabella, monarchs of the united kingdoms of Castile and Aragon, the Moors were expelled by 1492 and their priceless libraries were burnt to cinders.

Jews and Moors were forced into segregated settlements; those who refused to convert to Christianity or attempted to revolt against the Christians were either enslaved or massacred. Their confiscated wealth permitted Ferdinand and Isabella to begin the exploration and conquest of the world new to Europeans. Eventually all Jews and Muslims, whether converted or not, were expelled. (Later in 1610, Henry IV of France settled 1 million of the expelled people in southern France. Others settled in Holland, Belgium, and Germany.)

Historians have not yet begun to explore the inevitable movement by the Moors into the rest of Western Europe. The curious, the traders, the highly skilled craftsmen, scientists, physicians, architects, geographers, and philosophers must have either investigated opportunities to the north of Al-Andalus or been invited by the royals and nobles to enhance their courts. In Spain, though the very name of the capital city, Madrid, derives from the Arab *majerit,* little research has been done on the African presence and contributions the country.

The Normans re-took Sicily in 1061, established trading relationships with northern Africa, and employed Africans in their armies. Frederick II, for example, not only used such warriors but placed them in his bodyguard. These African guards, together with

African musicians and animal keepers, as well as the Emperor's African personal attendants, formed part of the imperial processions. An African, Johannes Morus, was appointed vizier of the Kingdom of Sicily. (The etymology of the word *moor* is uncertain; it can be traced to the Phoenician term *Mahurin* meaning "Westerners"; from *Mahurin* the ancient Greeks derive *Mauro* meaning "black," the Latin derive *Mauri* meaning "Black African." *Maur, maurus, morus, Mauretania, Morocco*, etc. all derive from the general *Maure*.)

There were Africans in similar positions in other European royal courts, as well as enslaved Africans among the other enslaved peoples. Historians know of one African woman, Salem Casais, from Goa in Songhay, who was married to a noble Toulousian trader/politician in 1413. Aben Ali, a slave servant she had brought with her, became a notable physician.

1500–1800 CE

Scant research has been done to uncover the African presence in Europe at this time. In Britain, written evidence uncovered thus far begins in the early sixteenth century: The records of the royal court of Scotland note the presence of "two blak ledeis," as well as some Moors. By the mid-century, traders were bringing Africans to England, some as slaves (a rarity) and others to learn English so they could act as interpreters. By the sixteenth century there were many Africans living in England, but little is so far known of them. A number of these Africans lived in London where they might have been traders. Equally little is known about the Africans residing in Holland, whose superb portraits were drawn by German artist Albrecht Dürer at the beginning of the century. Some Africans arrived in Britain with a future queen: The retinue of Catherine of Aragon when she came to England as the betrothed of Arthur, Prince of Wales, included Africans. Arthur died, and she eventually became the wife of Henry VIII and bore him a son. The event was celebrated, and it is possible that the black trumpeter on the Great Tournament Roll had arrived with her. Yet another person to sit on the British throne, William of Orange, arrived in England in 1688 with 200 Africans among his troops.

In the fifteenth century, Africans begin to appear in secular Venetian art; given the drawings and paintings of Dürer and Rembrandt, the African presence in Britain was replicated in other seafaring, slave-trading, and then colonizing European countries.

By the seventeenth century Portugal, Britain, Holland, and Denmark were all involved in the trade of enslaved Africans. Some slaves were brought to Europe to be sold or given away as presents to benefactors. Because they were not needed for agricultural labor, they were at first used as ornamental household servants by the rich—and soon as cooks, washerwomen, maids, and valets by the middle class. Some women worked as prostitutes, often catering to the upper classes; others became the mistresses of kings and nobles. For example, both John IV of Portugal and Alessandro de Medici, Duke of Florence had black mothers.

However, not all the enslaved were Africans. For example, the records for the Spanish Cortes for the period 1482–1516 indicate a thriving trade in slaves of many origins in Valencia, among whom there were some 5,400 Africans. Whether they were sold locally or sent abroad is not known. Venice also traded in slaves in the fifteenth century, and their captives included Ethiopians.

In Britain, the legality of slavery soon became a question debated in salons, newspapers, and eventually the courts, which could not reach a decision. Recent research indicates that most Blacks in Britain were free; formal emancipation in the colonies was enacted in 1838. In France, Blacks had to register with the authorities, and, by the late eighteenth century, had to carry their registration papers with them at all times. The same legislation forbade intermarriage, but miscegenation continued. Slavery was ended by the French Revolution in 1794, but was reinstituted by Napoleon some years later, at least in the colonies. In many countries there were laws regarding manumission, and slaves were generally not cruelly treated; the threat of being sent to the colonies was probably sufficient to ensure a slave's ready compliance. When the ever-growing population of free Blacks was seen as a threat, whites took action: For example, most European trade guilds refused to admit qualified Africans, who could thus not become recognized master craftsmen.

Not all Africans in Britain were servants: There were Black shopkeepers, barbers, musicians, entertainers, boxers, actors, dock workers, laundry workers, refuse collectors, soldiers, teachers, and seamen both on merchant vessels (including slavers) and in the navies. In Ireland there are records of an African diving crew doing salvage work from wrecks in 1783. Some African Britons participated in the struggles against slavery, both in print and through addressing public meetings; others were involved in broader political movements. They probably lived, recent research indicates, in every parish in England and Ireland. It is impossible to guess the numbers of Africans residing anywhere in Europe; all scholars know with some degree of certainty is that a greater proportion were men and that there must have been an expanding mixed-race population.

The little research on the dukedoms which became unified as Germany presumes that there were a few residents of African descent; their number was augmented by the arrival of some African-Americans accompanying the Hessian troops returning from the wars in America in 1783–1784.

The major exceptions were Spain and Portugal, where African slaves, who were often maltreated, were used in agriculture. It is therefore probable that the Iberian Black populations formed a much greater proportion of the total population than elsewhere in Europe. For example, historians have determined that in the mid-sixteenth century, about 10 percent of the population of Lisbon and about 7.4 percent of the population of Seville were Black. In Portugal, where in the mid-sixteenth century there were 32,370 slaves and 2,580 'freedmen', the laws that regulated the civil lives of slaves appear to have been roughly equivalent to the status of poor, free Portuguese. In Seville, where certain districts appear to have been much more heavily populated by Blacks, a black city official was in charge of settling problems among Blacks and between Blacks and their masters or city courts. In 1475, Juan de Valadolid, the city official in charge of blacks was appointed to a royal post. Some of the Africans in Western Europe in preeminent cultural positions in the eighteenth century included Juan Latino Ma (1516–1594), who taught at the University of Grenada and was the author of a notable historical work; Anton Wilhelm Amo (circa1700–1748), a scholar of Latin, Greek, Hebrew, French, German, and Dutch who earned a doctorate of philosophy in 1734 at the University of Wittenberg and taught at the universities of Halle and Jena,; and Jacob Eliza Capitein, originally from the Gold Coast, whose thesis from the University of Leyden (1740) argued that slavery was fully compatible with Christian theology and was often the means through which Africans became Christians. In Britain, *A Narrative of the Most Remarkable Particulars in the Life of James Albert Ukawsaw Gronniosaw, An African Prince, Written by Himself* was the first book to be published by an African author (1772). Olaudah Equiano's (circa 1745–1797) autobiography and anti-abolitionist text, *The Interesting Narrative of the Life of Olaudah Equiano, Or Gustavus Vassa, The African. Written by Himself,* published in 1789, went into nine British editions, was translated into Dutch, German, and Russian, and was published in New York in 1791. Ottobah Cugoano's *Thoughts and Sentiments on the Evils of Slavery,* was published in England in 1787 and was quickly translated into French. Though his plays and musical compositions have not been preserved, Ignatius Sancho's autobiography, *Letters of The Late Ignatius Sancho, An African,* was published in 1782.

However, although a few might have become full members of society, most Africans in Europe were not treated as equals. The use of Africans as ornamental household servants, that is, as displays of wealth, spread as far east as Russia. When Peter the Great visited the West in 1690, he returned with several Africans in his entourage. The nobility followed Peter's example. As Russia had abolished chattel slavery in the late eighteenth century, one presumes that these African servants were under the customary lifetime service contracts that had replaced slavery. There might have been fewer objections to the promotion of Blacks in Russia than in the West. For example, a boy bought by a courtier in the slave markets of Constantinople was given as a present to Peter the Great. Baptized as Abram Hannibal (circa 1698–1781), the boy was sent to France to be educated, especially in the art of engineering and military science. On his return, despite many vicissitudes, he was named commandant of the city of Reval in 1743; in 1756, he was appointed major general of the Corps of Engineers, and in 1759, he was the main director of the Ladoga Canal and the Kronstadt and Rogevik construction projects for Empress Elizabeth. His son Ivan became general of naval artillery and a member of the Admiralty College.

In the south of the Russian empire, in the Black Sea area of Abkhazia, there was a settlement of Africans. There are two explanations for their presence: either they had been part of the invading Ottoman forces of the sixteenth century, or they were the descendants of the Colchians, who had settled in that area in the fifth century BCE. According to the ancient Roman scholar Herodotus, these Colchians had black skins and woolly hair. Certainly, the Ottoman armies that conquered and settled in eastern Europe (circa 1326–1606) included African troops, enlisted from the empire's northern African possessions.

It may have been around this time that a community of Africans developed in Montenegro in southeastern Europe. Traders and pirates emanating from port of Ulcinj traded in enslaved Sudanese, whom they also used on their vessels, and gave them away or sold them for use by locals in agriculture and as domestic servants. Apparently the period of servitude in Ulcinj was not permanent, and children were considered free citizens; wives were imported from Sudan and kept in Muslim seclusion; and the men were not allowed to engage in crafts. Enslavement in Montenegro ceased in 1914.

1800–1900

The nineteenth century began with the French and Haitian Revolutions. Among those who participated in the Revolution of 1789 in France was Joseph de Boulogne, the Chevalier de St. George (1745–1799), who led the Black Legion of 100 free Africans. The troop was financed by a group called The Mulattos of Paris. Among the officers in the Legion was Alexander Dumas, son of the Marquis de la Pailleterie, who became a commander in Napoleon's cavalry in Egypt and then a commander in chief in the Army of the Pyrenees. Napoleon employed thousands of Africans and West Indians in his career of conquest in Europe and elsewhere. In the Crimean War (1854–1865) some 40 percent of French troops were Africans and about 6,000 fought in the Franco-Prussian war of 1870–1871; of the over quarter million Africans in the French armies in World War I, some 215,000 fought in Europe. The British, who had employed a few Africans in British regiments since the late eighteenth century, established colonial forces led by white officers. It seems that similar tactics were used the by Dutch government which raised troops in its West African colonies for use in its Indonesian possessions.

In 1836, France declared that all enslaved Africans in France were free and abolished slavery in the colonies. In 1848, the freed colonials were granted French citizenship and representation in the French *Parlement* (Parliament). The resulting increase in the population of Black citizens included students, artists, and professionals. Alexander Dumas (1802–1870), the son of the Napoleonic general, gained international renown as a novelist. Cyril Bissette began to publish the *Revue des Colonies*, probably the first journal published by an African in Europe. In 1848, Bissette was elected as one of two Blacks to represent the Caribbean colonies in the *Parlement*.

Slaves in the British colonies in the Americas were emancipated in the period from 1833 to 1838. Denmark and France emancipated their slaves in 1848, Holland in 1860, and Portugal in 1876. Whether slaves in these 'mother countries had to be formally emancipated has not yet been documented.

Denmark, Britain, Holland, and France all passed antislave trade laws between 1805 and 1818, but many traders, shipbuilders, manufacturers, and insurers found ways to circumvent the laws. The keeping of servants as "decoration" or as status symbols was abandoned. The Black population of the United Kingdom, which had been increased by blacks who had fought for the British in the American War of Independence, probably diminished through intermarriage, only to be slowly augmented by seamen, job hunters, students, and entertainers from the West Indies as well as from North America and West Africa. Among the best known of the entertainers was the African-American Shakespearean actor, Ira Aldridge, who performed throughout Europe. In Russia, General Hannibal's grandson, Alexander Pushkin (1799–1837), poet and novelist of international fame, proudly acknowledged his African ancestry.

Slavery was succeeded by the development of theories of scientific racism, which sought to prove that whites were immutably superior to Blacks. At first, the need for trading partners to some extent overruled this doctrine, as African merchants and traders were welcomed in Europe—and often exploited. Their sons, as well as those of chiefs, were enrolled in European schools. Missionary training establishments increased their intake of Africans. Naturally, with the division of Africa among European powers in 1885, such emigration from the new "'possessions'" to Europe increased.

To reinforce scientific racism to the general population, a considerable proportion of which was illiterate, Africans were imported and displayed in public exposition halls and world's fairs, often with animals as though they were creatures in a zoo. By the end of the nineteenth century in Britain, a variety of racist displays were mounted in the extremely popular empire and colonial exhibitions. The popular press, novelists, and adventure story writers confirmed and reinforced notions of white superiority by depicting blacks as exotic, uncivilized, primitive, and laughable. Throughout much of Europe, such racist depictions of Africans in print were augmented by servile and often repugnant Black figures in advertising as well.

Nevertheless, African-American antislavery campaigners and later those opposed to lynching drew large audiences. For some people it was, and still is, easy to deal with racism elsewhere, as long as they did not have to deal with it at home. Artists, musicians, entertainers, and students continued to arrive and stayed in increasing numbers because European racism was not nearly as codified as it was in the United States, lynching was rare (the first known lynching occurred in Britain in 1919), and opportunities for professional education were absent in Africa and the Caribbean and limited in the North America.

As far as historians know, in Britain there was little social mixing between this professional group and the Black population of lower social status. Thus, for example, there appear to have been no Blacks at the 1900 Pan-African Conference except professionals and university students. Yet there were certainly sizeable Black communities, at least in Europe's major ports. Undoubtedly some of these seamen roamed inland in search of shore work. These Black communities were enlarged after World War I by men from the armed forces who were not returned to the colonies from which they had been recruited.

The century drew to a close with the partitioning of Africa by the European powers in 1885 at the Berlin Conference. The resulting increase in European trade, missionary, and colonizing activities drew more Africans to Europe, and African enclaves developed in many cities, including Berlin and Hamburg. Africans also attempted to establish new trading links. One such link was Ernst Anumu from Togo, who, after being educated in Hamburg, established himself an entrepreneur in 1913. By this time there were a few African traders established in Britain.

Post–World War I

The post-war period was one of great political evolution among Blacks in the European diaspora. Black and African culture flourished in Paris, where the leading luminary of the entertainment world was the African American Josephine Baker, and even anglophone writers such as Claude McKay, a Jamaican, settled in Paris temporarily.

In France, probably the most active Black figure was Dahomean-born Kojo Tovalou Houénou (1887–1925), who founded the *Ligue Universelle de la Défense de la Race Noire* (LUDRN, or Universal League for the Defense of the Black Race) in 1924 and began publishing a journal, *Les Continents,* in the same year. The aims of the *Ligue* included the refutation of scientific racism; the development of "universal brotherhood among all members of the black race"; equality; the "development and evolution of the race"; and either equal rights of citizenship or autonomy. Houénou spoke at the 1924 UNIA convention in New York. A leading member of the LUDRN was René Maran, whose novel *Batouala* won the prestigious Goncourt prize in 1921.

After Houénou's return to West Africa, leadership of the Ligue was assumed by Senegalese Lamine Senghor, an ex–World War I rifleman. The organization's name was changed to the *Comité de Défense de la Race Nègre* (Committee for the Defense of the Negro Race) and a new journal, *La voix des nègres,* was published. Both Hounéou and Senghor had links with Marcus Garvey as well as the Comintern in Moscow, which at that time encouraged anticolonialist efforts. By the end of 1926, the *Comité* had over 300 members. Senghor died of tuberculosis in 1927 after a brief period of imprisonment in southern France. Under the next leader, the Sudanese Garan Kouyaté (died 1942), the organization was renamed the *Ligue de la Défense de la Race Nègre* (LDRN) and became more closely associated with the Comintern and the French Communist Party. Kouyaté worked with the Comintern's International Trade Union Committee of Negro Workers and was on the editorial board of this organization's journal, the *Negro Worker.* The leading figure in both was Trinidad-born George Padmore (1902–1959), then based in Hamburg. The LDRN established important links with African-American writer and social critic W.E.B. Du Bois and the National Association for the Advancement of Colored People (NAACP) in the United States. The LDRN's journal, *Le Cri de Nègres* was quickly banned by the government for, among many other reasons, its socialist overtones. Internal disagreements split the LDRN in 1932: Kouyaté joined the militant *Union des Travailleurs Nègres* (Union of Negro Workers) and continued to publish *Le Cri.* In 1934, he broke with the Comintern, and during World War II, the Fascists executed him. The LDRN, resuscitated in 1934, was fiercely anticommunist, and demanded a "single Negro state, encompassing the whole of black Africa and the Caribbean." In 1937, the French government suppressed the LDRN, despite its change in politics, and exiled its leadership. African students in France formed the *Comité de l'Institut Nègre de Paris* in 1930, but their aims and activities appear not to have been documented.

Two other movements in France at this time exerted worldwide influence: the philosophy of *nègritude* and the work of psychiatrist Frantz Fanon (1925–1961). Nègritude's progenitors were Léopold Senghor (1906–2001), the future president of Senegal, and Aimé Césaire (1913–) of Martinique, poet and future representative in the French *parlement* when Martinque accepted French territorial status. Nègritude proposed the existence and unique quality of the "African personality" to which Senghor later added "African socialism." With other colleagues, the nègritude group published a journal *Présence Africaine*, which, inter alia, opposed cultural assimilation; it is still published today. Fanon, another Martinican, participated in the Algerian struggle for independence and wrote a number of influential books on race and racial theories, which are still in print and much debated.

In Britain there were somewhat similar organizations and publications, although communist affiliation appears to have been less common. However, the two communist-led organizations, the Colonial Defence Association in Cardiff and the Negro Workers Association in London, both attracted working-class membership. Other groups included the African Progress Union formed in 1918 by African and Caribbean professionals, merchants and students; its first president was Liverpool-born photographer John Archer, who was elected mayor of the London borough of Battersea in 1913. Students formed the African Students Union in 1917, then the Union of Students of African Descent, and Nigerian and Gold Coast (modern Ghana) Student unions in the 1920s. In 1925 they were succeeded by the West African Students Union, led by Nigerian Ladipo Solanke (1884–1958), which became a highly political nationalist organization. The League of Coloured People was formed in 1932 under the leadership of Jamaican-born physician Harold Moody (1882–1947). With a membership that was mainly West Indian and professional, it published a newsletter until Moody's death and took an interest in both local and international issues.

Purely political organizing in Britain took a more dramatic route from 1935 onward with the campaigns against the European collaboration with the Italian invasion of Abyssinia from 1935 to 1936. These were led by C.L.R. James (1901–1989), the Trinidad-born historian, intellectual, and activist, and George Padmore, who had settled in London after leaving the Comintern. Together with other West Indian activists such as Ras T. Makoonen (born Peter Griffiths) and Sierra Leonean Moscow-trained I.T.A. Wallace Johnson (1895–1965), they formed the International Friends of Abyssinia, which was transformed into the International African Service Bureau in 1937. They published successively, as finance permitted, *Africa and the World* (1937), *African Sentinel* (1937–1938), and *International African Opinion* (1938–1939) and organized public meetings and petitions until World War II restrictions put an end to all anti-imperialist agitation.

Other newspapers published in Britain were the *African Times* and *Orient Review*, published by Egyptian Dusé Mohamed Ali (1866–1945) from 1912 to 1918, and the *African Telegraph* published by Venezuelan-Trinidadian F.E.M. Hercules and financed by Sierra Leonean John Eldred Taylor.

The situation in Germany differed somewhat. After World War I, France occupied the Rhineland with colonial troops, which resulted in racist propaganda about Africans raping German women. The number of children actually fathered by the African troops is unknown. The eugenicist movement had been powerful in Germany; their philosophies became the core of the Nazi movement. In 1935, Germany passed a law forcing sterilization of all the '"Rhine bastards'"; at least 385 suffered this fate. However, the Nazis did not generally include Africans in their extermination programs; the fate of Black Germans was thus decided by the personal predilections of the Gestapo. The Allied Black POWs, many of whom had suffered racism by their white peers in their units were not subjected to worse treatment in the German camps. Allegations of massacres of Blacks by German troops did, however, surface later.

World War II: Its Aftermath

There is little documentation on how European countries treated their black populations during the war or of the role of Blacks in the war itself. In Britain, the army and the navy maintained a color bar. In Germany, mixed-race marriages were annulled and Blacks were not accepted into the military.

The year 1945 marked not only the end of the war in which hundreds of thousands of Africans, West Indians, and indigenous Blacks had fought for Europe. It was also the year the Pan-African Congress was held in Manchester. The conference was called by the Pan-African Association, an umbrella group formed by Padmore and his colleagues, who included the future premier of independent Kenya, Jomo Kenyatta (1889–1978). The organizers were also helped by the newly arrived (from the United States) Gold Coast student, Kwame Nkrumah (1909–1972), the future president of independent Ghana. Attended by Africans, West Indians, African Americans, and British Blacks, the Congress demanded the end of imperialism, freedom, and equality for all colonized peoples.

The weakening of Britain by World War II and the increase in anti-imperialist struggles led to the relatively peaceful granting of political independence to its colonies, beginning with the Gold Coast in 1957. Some of the French colonies had to fight for their freedom while others accepted territorial or state status within greater France. The Portuguese were only ousted from Mozambique and Angola in the 1970s after bloody wars. Independence, however, was only partial, if not a sham. The colonizing countries ensured that they retained economic control. Control was increased by U.S. hegemony, globalization, and the strictures of the World Bank and the International Monetary Fund (IMF). The resulting impoverishment, coupled with the lack of development during the colonial era, led to ever-increasing emigration to Europe until the imposition of immigration controls. Racial discrimination, sometimes persecution, is rife in Europe; in some countries Black ghettoes crowded with unemployed youths abound in some countries, and lynching is increasing. The white populations deny that there is a centuries-old history of Blacks living in their midst and that hence many have mixed-race ancestry.

Marika Sherwood

See also **Africans: Overview; Césaire, Aimé (Martiniquais); Colonialism; Du Bois, W.E.B. (African-American); Fanon, Frantz Omar (Algerian); James, C.L.R. (Trinidadian); National Association for the Advancement of Colored People (NAACP); Senghor, Leopold (Senegalese)**

Editor's Note: In this article, "Africans" denotes people of African origins and descent. The term "Black" refers to people of African descent domiciled in Europe implying not only color but political status. (In the UK, "Black" often includes peoples of African origin or descent as well as people of Indian subcontinent origin or descent.) The term "Moor" refers to Arabs and Africans, including Berber Muslims, from northwest Africa.

Further Reading

Bernal, Martin, *Black Athena*, London: Vintage, 1991

Blakely, Allison, *Russia and the Negro*, Washington: Howard University Press, 1986

Blakely, Allison, *Blacks in the Dutch World*, Bloomington: Indiana University Press, 1993

Bovill, E.W., T*he Golden Trade of the Moors*, London: Oxford University Press, 1968

Cloy, Shelby T.C., *The Negro in France*, University of Kentucky, 1961

Debrunner, Hans Werner, *Presence and Prestige*, Basel: Afrika Bibliographien, 1979

Fryer, Peter, *Staying Power*, London: Pluto, 1995

Gerzina, Gretchen Holbrook, *Black London: Life before Emancipation*, New Brunswick: Rutgers University Press, 1995

Grant, Michael, *The Ancient Mediterranean*, London: Weidenfeld & Nicolson, 1969

Lusane, Clarence, *Hitler's Black Victims*, New York: Routledge, 2003

Phillips, William D., *Slavery from Roman Times to the Early Transatlantic Trade*, Manchester: University Press, 1985

Pieterse, Jan Nederven, *White on Black*, New Haven: Yale University Press, 1992

Prah, Kwesi Kwaa, *Jacobus Capitein*, Trenton: Africa World Press, 1992

Saunders, A.C de C.M., *A Social History of Black Slaves and Freedmen in Portugal 1441–1555*, Cambridge: Cambridge University Press, 1982

Sertima, Ivan van, *African Presence in Early Europe*, New Brunswick: Transaction Books, 1985

Snowden, Frank M., *Blacks in Antiquity*, Cambridge: Harvard University Press, 1970

Afrikaners

Capsule Summary

Location: South Africa
Population: 2 million
Language: Afrikaans
Religion: Christian (primarily Dutch Reformed)

The minority group that ruled South Africa for most of the twentieth century, the Afrikaners, lost political power in 1994. The group was defined in both racial and linguistic terms: Afrikaners were, and are, whites with Afrikaans as a home language. As Afrikaners always composed the larger part of the white community, as long as the franchise was confined largely or exclusively to whites, they could be sure of political dominance, even though in the 1980s they composed only 7.5 percent of the total population. That proportion fell thereafter, and by 2001 they were only 5 percent of the total population.

In the nineteenth century, the term *Afrikaner* was often used for those whites who regarded themselves to be natives of Africa', that is to say those who identified with, and were usually born in, South Africa rather than Europe. The term was sometimes also used in the same sense for blacks, usually in the variant form *Afrikander.*

The ancestors of those known as Afrikaners in contemporary South Africa were usually called Boers, or Cape Dutch, in the eighteenth and early nineteenth centuries. They were descendants of the setters of largely Dutch, but also French and German extraction, who had arrived at the Cape beginning in 1652. From the late-seventeenth century, the form of Dutch spoken at the Cape developed differences in pronunciation and accidence, and, to a lesser extent, in syntax and vocabulary, from that of Holland. By 1800, the white settlers numbered some twenty thousand, and had been welded into a *volk* (people) with a distinct patois more closely resembling Flemish than Dutch. In time it came to be called *Afrikaans.* Mostly members of the Dutch Reformed Church, they were a relatively close-knit community, with strong family ties and a sense of having a common destiny as people living in Africa, with a special status because of their origins, European culture and color. With the advent of British rule in the early nineteenth century, some prominent Afrikaner families, especially those living in Cape Town, became anglicized. The majority sought to maintain their identity through the Dutch Reformed Church and continued speaking their own language. Others—those who came to be called *Voortrekkers*—fled from British rule into the interior and there developed an idea of being God's chosen people and established independent republics. It was not until the late nineteenth century, in response to a more vigorous form of British imperialism, that those who spoke Afrikaans in the republics and at the Cape developed any sense of being a common people. Even then, Afrikaners were often bitterly divided, often over the best way to preserve Afrikaner identity. One of the worst moments in Afrikaner history occurred at the beginning of the twentieth century, in the conquest of the republics by Britain and then the suffering in the guerrilla phase of the Anglo-Boer war, when 27,000 Afrikaner women and children perished in the concentration camps set up by the British.

Through the twentieth century, Afrikaners formed between 54 and 58 percent of the white population. Whereas in 1880, less than one percent lived in towns, by 1970, over 80 percent lived in small country towns or the large urban centers. An Afrikaner *Broederbond* (band of brothers) was set up as a secret organization in 1918 to further Afrikaner nationalist interests, and gradually the political party representing exclusive Afrikaner nationalism gained more and more support. Great emphasis was laid on the Afrikaner's "civil religion", that is, the notion of a divine calling and a sacred history. The National Party first came to power in 1924 in alliance with an English-speaking party, but in 1948 Afrikaner nationalism triumphed on its own. By then, that nationalism was closely linked with the policy of apartheid, applied from 1948 onward. *Apartheid*, an Afrikaans word meaning "separateness," was a government policy of the white minority government that rigidly classified and racially segregated the people of South Africa. As the National Party consolidated its grip on power, its policy of apartheid came under increasing criticism. The Afrikaner government then sought to broaden its base of support by shifting to a white, rather than Afrikaner, nationalist position. Apartheid itself was modified and in some respects abandoned by the late 1980s. F.W. De Klerk, Afrikaner president from 1989, realized that it was better to negotiate from a position of strength than to hold on to power, and in the early 1990s he sought to protect the position of whites and Afrikaners in the forthcoming new democratic order. The despised apartheid policy was demolished in 1991 when new legislation granted equality to all of South Africa's citizens. Afrikaners lost political power in 1994 but retained most of their material privileges. Most Afrikaners accepted the democratic order and their loss of political power but were critical of the new government and gave their support to opposition parties including the Freedom Front of ex-Defense chief Constand Viljoen. There was fear that the extreme right-wing Afrikaner *Weerstandsbeweging* (Resistance Movement) might use violence against the new government, but it proved a paper tiger. The former ruling National Party looked for new support among nonwhite people who spoke Afrikaans and lost much of its traditional support among whites. In decline, it merged with the English-led Democratic Party to form a Democratic Alliance.

By the late twentieth century, Afrikaans had developed a relatively rich literature, which included many works critical of apartheid; there was no significant pro-apartheid literature in Afrikaans. With the collapse of apartheid, Afrikaans lost status and became one of 11 official languages. Some white Afrikaners sought special constitutional protection for the language in the new political dispensation, while others, having rejected nonwhite Afrikaans-speakers in the apartheid era, rediscovered kinship with them on the basis of a shared language. The great majority, however, continued to regard race and culture as important markers, and confined the term to those regarded as white. Whether a section of Afrikaners will mobilize on an ethnic basis in an attempt to recover political power in the future remains to be seen.

CHRISTOPHER SAUNDERS

See also **Apartheid; De Klerk, F.W. (Afrikaner); South Africa**

Further Reading

Adam, H., and H. Giliomee, *Ethnic Power Mobilised,* Cape Town, 1979

de Klerk, F.W., *The Puritans in Africa,* Cape Town, 1976

du Toit, A., and H. Giliomee, editors, *Afrikaner Political Thought*, vol. I, Cape Town, 1983

February, V., *The Afrikaners of South Africa,* London, 1991

Fisher, J., *The Afrikaners,* London, 1969

le May, G., *The Afrikaners,* Oxford, 1995

Moodie, T.D., *The Rise of Afrikanerdom,* Berkeley, 1975

Afro-Arabs, *See* **Arabs: North African**

Afro-Brazilians

Capsule Summary

Location: Brazil
Total Population: 70 million
Language: Portuguese
Religions: Catholicism, Protestantism, Candomblé, Shangó, and Macumba

Afro-Brazilians, which include *negros* and *afro-mestiços* are a diverse population that has had an effect on every region of Brazil. Brazilian society owes much to the African slaves. Africans and their descendants were not only the major laborers in almost all industries, but they were also the producers of much of Brazilian culture. Moreover, Africans and their descendants have had a major impact on Brazil's cultural productions from food and dance to religion and music. Yet Brazil's political and economic system has systematically marginalized most Afro-Brazilians both politically and economically.

The majority of Africans arrived in Brazil as slaves. Indeed Brazil was the major recipient of African slaves in the Americas, accounting for some 36 percent of the 10 to 15 million slaves brought to the Americas between 1494 and 1860. Many Africans and Afro-Brazilians accommodated to the system of slavery in Brazil, performing a number of skilled and unskilled labors. Others resisted the system through sabotage or by running away to escaped-slave communities, known as *mocambos* or *quilombos.* Still others sought freedom through manumission, but this meant that they were at the mercy of a master. In a few cases, Afro-Brazilians were allowed to rise through the ranks of Brazilian society. Abolition of the slave trade was eventually accomplished in 1888, although by that time the majority of Afro-Brazilians had already been freed. After abolition, Afro-Brazilians and progressive elements of Brazil's white society continued a campaign for social integration and recognition, although they continued to face prejudice and other obstacles.

Middle Class Revolution to Dictatorship

In 1930, Getúlio Vargas ushered in a middle class revolution that would change the political system of the republic created in 1889. One of the first Afro-Brazilian political organizations, the Frente Negra Brasileira, emerged in this period calling for equal treatment and integration into Brazilian national life while encouraging racial pride and competition with whites on all level. By 1936, the Frente had developed into a political party only to be stymied by the emergence of Vargas' dictatorship one year later. When the Estado Novo ended in 1944, new activists emerged with a cautious political participation, but they were ready to raise up banners on behalf of Afro-Brazilians. One such group, the Teatro Experimental do Negro, led by Abdias do Nascimenrto, surfaced in 1944 determined to promote Afro-Brazilian culture while combating racism. The right-wing military coup of 1964 once again stymied Brazilian grassroots and social movements until 1979 when General João Figuieredo presided over the period that would begin the political opening, or return to democracy. From 1979 to 1985, Afro-Brazilian mobilization intensified, culminating in the historical participation of many organizations and individuals in the creation of the new Constitution of 1988. Groups such as the Movimento Negro Unificado (MNU), founded in 1978, emerged in São Paulo and called for national black consciousness. By 1985, more than 400 separate groups had emerged in different regions throughout the country. Many of them participated in the creation of Brazil's progressive 1988 Constitution.

Contemporary Dynamics

After abolition, many Brazilian intellectuals began to explore and foster the myth of Brazil as a social paradise, which would later become known as "racial democracy." Ironically, the strong ideology of *branquemento,* or "whitening," played a significant role in the continued marginalization of blacks and mulattos. Unfortunately, the myth of racial democracy and the idea of whitening remain strong ideologies in Brazil today. On one hand, colonial stereotypes of blacks persist. On the other hand, however, a few Afro-Brazilian have become national icons and universally celebrated. This is especially true in the cultural spheres where Afro-Brazilians such as Pelé and Garrincha in football, Gilberto Gil, Alcione, and Luis Melodia among many others in the music industry enjoy widespread national appeal. Indeed Afro-Brazilian–inspired foods, folklore, and religions transcend any attempts at racial ownership. Religions such as *Candomblé* and *Umbanda* and practices such as *capoiera* are national customs that cut across racial lines. Unfortunately, Afro-Brazilians still face many more social and health obstacles than their white counterparts.

In 1988, the Instituto Brasileiro de Geografia e Estatística (IBGE or Brasilian Institute of National Statistics and Geography) reported that as a general rule, blacks have lower incomes, live in poorer conditions, and die earlier than whites. Afro-Brazilians have a 30 percent higher infant mortality rate and are 50 percent more likely to leave school without learning how to read. Afro-Brazilian women face dire challenges relative to other population groups. In addition to lower earning power regardless of education, Afro-Brazilian women face increased incidence of health problems such as breast cancer and have more hysterectomies. In the media, Afro-Brazilians are most often still to be found in stereotypical roles as maids or servants, or in historical dramas or *novelas* about slavery or the colonial era, or occasionally as dancers musicians or comedians. Several actors such as Ruth de Souza, Lea Garcia, Milton Gonçalves, and Antônio Pitanga follow in the tradition of the great Afro-Brazilian actor Grande Othelo, who as a comic, was able to break into many forums previously unknown to black actors. Young actors such as Taís Araújo, who played the famed Afro-Brazilian historical figure Xica da Silva in a 1990s *novela* of the same name, are slowly beginning to make their mark.

Afro-Brazilians have made significant inroads in the political arena since the 1980s, but their numbers are still out of step with demographic trends. In 1987, Benedita da Silva from the state of Rio de Janeiro became the first black women ever to be elected to Congress. Da Silva represents hope for the future in her defense of blacks and of poor people in Brazil. Other Afro-Brazilian public officials are to be found throughout Brazil's 26 states and the federal district, but none have as much constitutional power and support from the federal authorities as the Fundacão Cultural Palmares for the black community. A product of the 1988 Constitution, this foundation seeks to promote Afro-Brazilian cultural manifestations through studying various activities while aiming to promote racial harmony and deter racial harassment, prejudice, and discrimination. The foundation's most important task to date has been its accreditation of *quilombos*, and in assisting *quilombolos*, the residents of the *quilombos*, in attaining title to their lands.

In the last decade, the Brazilian government has also begun to enforce important anti-discrimination laws and to discuss race relations openly, marking a shift in public practice. Work by human rights organizations and local and regional Afro-Brazilian organizations such as Gelédes in São Paulo have made the plight of Afro-Brazilian more visible. Mass mobilization on a national scale, however, remains elusive. Discrimination against Afro-Brazilians remains endemic, but there are indicators of hope for the future. Afro-Brazilian culture, in particular, remains vibrant and central to the Brazilian experience, and Brazil's challenge is to reconcile its cultural appreciation with its social practices.

DARIÉN J. DAVIS

See also **Brazil; Silva, Benedita da (Afro-Brazilian)**

Further Reading

Andrews, George Reid, *Blacks and Whites in São Paulo, Brazil, 1888–1988*, Madison: University Of Wisconsin Press, 1991

Butler, Kim D., *Freedoms Given Freedoms Won: Afro-Brazilians in Post-Abolition São Paulo and Salvador*, New Brunswick: Rutgers University Press, 1998

Davis, Darién, *Avoiding the Dark: Race and the Forging of National Culture in Modern Brazil,* Alderhsot: Ashgate, 1999

———, *Afro-Brazilians: Time for Recognition*, London: Minority Rights Group, 1999

Hanchard, Michael George, *Orpheus and Power: The Movimento Negro of Rio de Janeiro and São Paulo, Brazil, 1945–1988*, Princeton University Press, 1994

Nascimento, Abdias do, *Mixture or Massacre? Essays on the Genocide of a Black People*, translated by Elisa Larkin Nascimento, New York: Afrodiaspora, 1979

Skidmore, Thomas, *Black into White: Race and Nationality in Brazilian Thought*, New York: Oxford University Press, 1992

Afro-Caribbeans

Capsule Summary

Location: Western Atlantic region, most Caribbean nations are located between the tip of the Florida peninsula and the northern coast of South America
Total Population: Approximately 35 million
Language(s): English, French, Spanish, Dutch, and various dialects of each language
Religion(s): Variants of Christianity to those religions rooted in African cosmologies such as Voodoo, Orisha, and Santeria

The Afro-Caribbean population is a culturally diverse group of people who reside in the many nations of the Caribbean. Latest estimates of the Afro-Caribbean population hover around 35 million. The area defined as the Caribbean typically refers to a narrow chain of islands that lie between the tip of the Florida peninsula and the northern coast of South America. However, the shared historical experience of mainland territories such as Belize, Guyana, French Guiana, and Suriname as well as the northern island of Bermuda means that these nations are often considered Caribbean territory.

The Caribbean was colonized by various European powers. The most successful among these were the

British, French, Spanish, and Dutch. The language of Afro-Caribbean people varies from place to place. They generally speak the languages of former colonial powers as well as a variety of dialects that have been influenced by African linguistic patterns. The religious affiliations of Afro-Caribbean peoples are also varied and range from Christianity to religions grounded in African cosmology such as Voodoo, Orisha, and Santeria. Although most nations of the Caribbean have received political independence from former imperial rulers, there are a number of islands that still remain under imperial rule.

Waves of migration have historically brought people of varied backgrounds to the Caribbean. As a result, the region is racially diverse. The Caribbean, however, is one of the few places in the Western hemisphere where people of African descent are in the numerical majority. This is in stark contrast to blacks living in the United States and in most parts of Latin America. Despite their numerical dominance, however, Afro-Caribbeans have remained a sociological minority until fairly recently, as they slowly achieve the recognition and rights commensurate with their numerical position.

History

The origins of the Afro-Caribbean people are inextricably linked to the development of the transatlantic slave trade, which began in the sixteenth century and continued well in to the nineteenth century. The last known slave ship in the Caribbean arrived in Cuba in the late 1860s. Roughly 3 million of the slaves that crossed the Atlantic ended up in the Caribbean. This is approximately five times greater than the total number of slaves transported to the United States. Although some scholars have argued that there was an African presence in the Americas before the arrival of Columbus, this is a highly debatable and contentious issue. To date, the evidence supporting this line of thinking remains quite limited.

Europe's political expansion into the Americas in the fifteenth century; the consequent demise of the indigenous native population through conquest, disease, and subjugation; and the establishment of extensive agricultural and mineral enterprises led to the enslavement and transportation of approximately 11 to 15 million Africans to the Americas. These Africans were transported across the Atlantic to meet the labor demands of Europeans. Although enslaved Africans were used in a variety of ways in the building of the Americas, the vast majority of Africans in the Caribbean were brought to work on the sugar plantations of the region.

Not all Africans brought to the Caribbean, however, came as slaves. A small but significant number were rescued by the British Navy as it enforced anti–slave trade international agreements between 1808 and 1870. This group of liberated Africans became important in the revitalization of and rejuvenation of African cultural traditions in those territories in which they were landed.

The long history of African enslavement was punctuated by a record of attempts at self-emancipation as they struggled to maintain their humanity in the face of this brutal system of forced labor. The disintegration of the slave system in the Caribbean was a protracted process that began with the Haitian revolution in 1791 and ended with the legal abolition of slavery in Cuba in 1886. The process of slave emancipation in the Caribbean was a complex one. It was influenced by internal factors such as attempts by slaves to secure their own freedom, and in so doing, they helped to undermine the stability and profitability of the system. It was also influenced by external factors such as the changing ideological, economic, and political currents in the metropolitan societies.

Afro-Caribbean Society and Culture

Despite the presence of large numbers of Africans, the Caribbean is a multiracial society. Early in the region's history, Europeans imposed a political and economic order that suited their needs. However, in few colonies did they ever constitute a numerical majority for any period. By the eighteenth century, Africans constituted by far the largest element in the population of the Caribbean. This is despite later waves of migration that brought immigrants from India and China to work on the sugar plantations of the region. Only in some territories (Guyana, Trinidad, Suriname) did the Afro-Caribbean population eventually emerge as a minority.

The long history of colonial rule in the Caribbean has meant that in many ways Caribbean countries continue to be racially divided. The creation of this region meant bringing people of various racial and ethnic backgrounds together. The social hierarchy of the Caribbean was based on skin color. During the period of slavery, whites were at the top of the social ladder, mixed-race persons in the middle, and blacks at the bottom. The introduction of migrants from other parts of the world to some Caribbean countries tended to complicate the biracial nature of Caribbean society. Nonetheless, from early on, colonial officials realized that it was in their interest to create and exploit divisions among ethnic and racial groups. Unfortunately, these divisions have proven difficult to dismantle. As a result, the national unity of various countries in present times is sometimes undermined by racial conflict.

Afro-Caribbean societies are the product of various influences, and because of this, there is much diversity among Afro-Caribbean cultures. The influences of varying imperial powers, in particular the British, French, Spanish, and Dutch, have made the historical experiences of slaves in the Caribbean different from colony to colony. It is the distinct historical experiences throughout the region that have led to the development of diverse Afro-Caribbean cultures and societies.

The African heritage of Afro-Caribbean people, however, has been just as important in shaping the Afro-Caribbean cultures of today. Historians have shown that slaves and other African migrants came from diverse ethnic backgrounds and have often had very distinctive cultural traditions. They were brought from areas within modern Ghana, Nigeria, Senegal, Dahomey, and Angola. Ethnic differences among African slaves have also contributed to the cultural diversity of the region; such diversity is reflected in the food, music, and often religious practices of Afro-Caribbean people.

The inter-cultural mixture of the region is quite complex. For example, whereas Caribbean-based religions such as Voodoo in Haiti, Santeria in Cuba, and Orisha in Trinidad are all grounded in African cosmologies, they have also been influenced by imperial religions such as Catholicism. Language is another area in which the creative interplay of African influences is quite evident. Throughout the region the languages, as popularly spoken, reflect African linguistic forms filtered through European language prisms. These Afro-Euro language creations are as important for vast sections of the population as the formal-official European forms. Although the official language is European, it is the African-influenced language that is popular and is now considered by some to be the national language.

There are also other factors such as the geography of each island, demography, and migration patterns that have influenced the evolution of Afro-Caribbean society and cultures. For example, the mountainous ranges of Jamaica were a place of refuge for escaped slaves known as *maroons*. Two of the most well known maroon communities in Jamaica were located in the Blue Mountains and Cockpit Country. From these and other locations, slaves could not only escape slavery but could attack the oppressive slave system through armed revolts against the ruling plantocracy. Moreover, with the end of slavery in 1838, former slaves had access to available land and could eke out existences based on subsistence farming. On islands with less available land, however, "maroon culture" could not develop. The flat landscape of Barbados, for example, meant that slaves had few places to which they could escape. Moreover, the flat nature of the landscape meant that almost the entire island was under sugar production. As a result, there was little available land for subsistence farming, and long after emancipation, the Afro-Caribbean population of Barbados continued to labor on the sugar plantations of their former masters to survive.

Afro-Caribbean cultures, then, have been influenced by a number of variables. Historical circumstances have led to the creation of distinct, vibrant, rich cultures that vary across Caribbean countries. The end results are various cultural products, including music forms such as reggae and calypso, street festivals such as Carnival and Jonkuno, and the invention of the steel drum.

Political Position

Although in most territories the Afro-Caribbean population constitutes the numerical majority, they have been the sociological minority for most of their history. Racism and color discrimination as a legacy of slavery and colonial rule have meant that numerical predominance never purchased political, economic, or even cultural power until the second half of the twentieth century in some territories. The end of formal slavery ushered in a long period of economic marginalization, political disenfranchisement, and cultural illegitimization. This is true even for Haiti, where freedom and the early end of colonial rule had been gained through revolutionary struggle. With some exceptions (like Haiti), the struggle for political power and economic rights has often had to be at the expense of the recognition of the African cultural origins of the popular masses. The recognition and legitimization of the African derivations in language, religion, and other forms of popular culture has had to await the political changes that swept the region in the post–World War II period, leading to French department status in the French Caribbean and political independence in the Anglo-Caribbean. In the Spanish republics, the struggle for civil and political rights for people of African origin was embroiled in the struggles in the defense for sovereignty against an aggressive American imperialism.

Unfortunately, one of the by-products of colonial rule in the Caribbean is the political fragmentation in the region. The Caribbean has six political traditions: French, British, Spanish, Danish, Dutch, and American. Moreover, the large number of small but politically independent states further increases the levels of parochialism. Afro-Caribbean people generally do not conceptualize their political position from a Pan-Caribbean perspective. It is safe to say that Afro-Caribbean consciousness is informed by a sense of national identity. The multilingual nature of Caribbean society further hinders the development of a Pan-Caribbean political federation.

Although they live in separate political regimes and administrative units, the people of African descent in the region and in the Americas share a common fate that has often prompted the emergence of movements that have transcended these linguistic and administrative barriers by speaking to a common struggle. The emergence of the United Negro Improvement Association (UNIA), led by Jamaican-born Marcus Garvey, is one such movement that sought to create a pan-African consciousness and movement. Although primarily based in the United States among Afro-Americans, the activities of the UNIA resonated throughout the Caribbean among similarly oppressed Afro-Caribbean peoples and contributed to the ongoing struggle for political and social reform. Finally, in the 1970s the Black Power movement of the Caribbean, with its links to the Afro-American struggles for civil rights, contributed to the post-independence struggles for cultural and social decolonization in the Anglo-Caribbean, with its parallel repercussions in the French and Spanish Caribbean.

Caribbean social and political thought has been driven by the writings of a number of Afro-Caribbean intellectuals. Many of these intellectuals have sought to confront the legacy of racism, and as part of the colonial struggle, to redefine the Caribbean and its peoples. They have shown that the Caribbean has not only inherited European traditions, but they have accorded due recognition to the African influences that reshaped those traditions and constructed authentic Caribbean intellectual and cultural products. The world of scholarship would be much poorer without the contributions of a long line of Afro-Caribbean intellectuals that includes J. J. Thomas, Marcus Garvey, Franz Fanon, C. L. R. James, Eric Williams, and Walter Rodney. The world Pan-African congresses, which provided intellectual, political, and economic support for the movement of African independence, had in their front ranks Afro-Caribbean activists such as George Padmore and C. L. R. James. Contemporary literature and literary scholarship owes a considerable debt to Kamau Braithwaite, Derek Walcott, Maryse Conde, Aime Cesaire, and Nicholas Guillen. No less important has been the Rastafari movement, with its reconceptualization of the Christian message and its contribution to the redefinition of self in the region. The history of Afro-Caribbean peoples and their struggle against racism, imperialism, and colonial rule has generated a rich scholarship that forms an important part of modern human history.

Audra Diptee

See also **Césaire, Aimé (Martiniquais); Fanon, Frantz Omar (Algerian); Garvey, Marcus (Jamaican); James, C. L. R. (Trinidadian); Rastafari**

Further Reading

Bolland, Nigel, *Struggles for Freedom: Essays on Slavery, Colonialism and Culture in the Caribbean and Central America*, Belize: The Angelus Press; Kingston, Jamaica: Ian Randle Publishers, 1997

Cooper, Frederick, Thomas Holt, and Rebecca Scott, *Beyond Slavery: Explorations of Race, Slavery, and Citizenship in Post-Emancipation Societies*, Chapel Hill: University of North Carolina Press, 2000

Goslinga, Cornelis, *The Dutch in the Caribbean and in Surinam, 1791–1942*, Assen, Netherlands: Van Gorcum, 1990

Higman, Barry, *Slave Populations of the British Caribbean, 1807–1834*, Baltimore: Johns Hopkins University Press, 1984

Hine, Darlene Clark, and Jacqueline Mcleod, editors, *Crossing Boundaries: Comparative History of Black People in the Diaspora*, Bloomington: Indiana University Press, 1999

Kadish, Doris, editor, *Slavery in the Caribbean Francophone World: Distant Voices, Forgotton Acts, Forged Identities*, Athens: University of Georgia Press, 2000

Knight, Franklin, and Colin Palmer, editors, *The Modern Caribbean*, Chapel Hill: University of North Carolina Press, 1989

Knight, Franklin, *The General History of the Caribbean*, London: Unesco Publishing; Basingstoke: Macmillan Education, 1997

Maingot, Anthony, P.M. Sherlock, and John Parry, *A Short History of the West Indies*, London: MacMillan Caribbean, 1987

Scott, Rebecca, *Slave Emancipation in Cuba: The Transition to Free Labor, 1860–1899*, Princeton, New Jersey: Princeton University Press, 1985

Afro-Cubans

Capsule Summary

Location: Cuba, the largest island in the Caribbean
Total Population: 40–60 percent of the current population of 11 million are reported to be Afro-Cuban, which includes mulattos, negros, and some afro-mestizos
Languages: Spanish (official); English, and Haitian Creole
Religions: Catholicism, Santería, and Protestantism

Afro-Cubans may constitute a majority of the 11 million Cubans today, depending on the definition of Afro-Cuban ethnicity. The Afro-Cuban population is both varied and diverse, although with few exceptions the majority are descendants of African slaves brought to the island to work for the Spaniards in the colonial period. Cuba's Hispanic colonial heritage, which recognized miscegenation and *mestizaje* ("mixing of races" in Spanish), provided a mode of identity that allowed for differences in skin color as well as race. The Hispanic philosophy, which engendered a hierarchical social class with racial overtones, created a complex social system that allowed some Afro-Cubans social mobility. During the nineteenth century Cuban patriots such as Manuel Céspedes, José Martí, Calixto García, and Antonio Maceo utilized a unifying rhetoric of antiracism and freedom to unify Cubans of all colors for the cause of independence from Spain. Yet Cuba was the last Hispanic American country to abolish slavery (in 1886). The tension between patriotic unity and black exclusion has been fundamental to the Afro-Cuban experience since independence from Spain in 1902.

Indeed, in 1902, many Afro-Cubans were denied important political appointments in the Cuban republic despite their efforts in the struggle for independence. Dissatisfaction led to the creation of the Independents of Color, comprising black and mulatto Cubans and eventually evolved into a grassroots political party. Threatened by a new mode of political organization, in 1910 the Cuban senate instituted the Morúa Amendment to Electoral Reform Law, which prohibited the organization of political parties based on one race only. The subsequent racial strife of 1912 pitted the Cuban state against the Independents and their sympathizers, and the latter paid dearly. These measures influenced the way in which blacks would mobilize for the remainder of the twentieth century.

1930s–1959

By the 1930s, many Afro-Cubans had attained prominent positions in Cuban national life. Nicolás Guillén, for example, attained recognition for his poetry. Integrationist Morúa Delgado and president and later dictator of Cuba Fulgencio Batista exerted important influences in the political sphere. The society for Afro-Cuban Studies, led by the anthropologist Fernando Ortiz, the literary movement known as *Negrismo*, which celebrated Cuba's *mulatto* (African and Spanish) origins and Afro-Cuban clubs such as Club Atenas were decidedly mainstream. The mobile Afro-Cuban middle class and their subsequent identification as "'Cuban first'" seemed to indicate that race in and of itself was not a barrier to social mobility and achievement in national life.

From the late 1920s to 1950s, Afro-Cuban advocates promoted an integrated nationalism, avoiding separatist rhetoric. Thus, when Jamaican born Marcus Garvey proposed separation as solution to racial conflict in the Americas and began to organize black immigrant field workers from Haiti and the English-speaking West Indian islands, Cubans hardly took notice. No Cuban public official would dare endorse any type of prejudice, although Cuban nationalism often embraced antiblack sentiments, particularly against black Haitians and other non-Spanish-speaking West Indians. Still, it is important to point out that Afro-Cubans worked closely with other Cubans in shaping Cuban nationalism and raising consciousness. In 1937 a mixed group of progressive individuals founded the National Association against Racist Discrimination. They declared racism illegal, un-Cuban, and a national threat. Many whites and blacks pointed out that without each other they could not edify the national community.

Nevertheless, Afro-Cubans continued to face exclusion from beaches, social clubs, parks, schools, and political parties as late as the 1950s. On the other hand, Cubans insisted that racism was a class problem and that through further education it could be eliminated without creating animosity. In this light, Afro-Cuban attempts to organize exclusively along racial lines continued to meet with opposition. Many Cubans saw such attempts as counterproductive and as negative as white prejudice. When Enrique Andreu attempted to create a Federation of Societies of Color, other Afro-Cubans criticized him. Gustavo Urrutía, for example, claimed that such associations should be formed on the basis of their character and not of their color. For many Cubans, racial affirmation did not mean that blacks should be proud of being of African descent, but rather that they should not feel ashamed of it. Several professional associations also opposed Portuondo Calá's proposition for the foundation of a federation of black organizations. Club Atenas, an Afro-Cuban social and business association, reported that Cuba "takes pride in its goals of fraternity and Cuban affirmation and the promotion of a unified system inspired by the ideas of Juan Gualberto Gómez", a leading *mulatto* nationalist of the nineteenth century. Afro-Cubans did not cease to point out the problems within Cuban society, but more often than not the Afro-Cuban's positive contribution, rather than discrimination, became the focus of discourse on race.

Afro-Cubans played important roles in the 1933 overthrow of the dictator Gerardo Machado. The 1930s and 1940s were decades of national rejuvenation. The abrogation of the Platt Amendment in 1934 had spurred a period of optimism that affected Afro-Cubans as it did other Cubans. Neither nationalism nor political turmoil prohibited black consciousness, rather, it shaped it. Afro-Cuban consciousness emerged, but as a function of Cuban patriotism. Many Afro-Cuban leaders made explicit connections with Cuba's neocolonial position and black poverty. Dr. Mora Gastón y Varona contended that the proletarianization of blacks was part of a larger impoverishment of Cubans in the face of Yankee (American) and other foreign capital usurpation. He saw Cuban wealth in the hand of foreigners. Afro-Cuban leaders saw their role as awakening the consciousness of white Cubans as well as elevating the cultural and economic status of blacks, while stressing racial cooperation in the face of foreign domination.

Cuban Revolution of 1959- Present

While some Afro-Cubans pursued community capitalism before the 1959 Revolution, others believed that capitalism in its present form had exploited both blacks and poor whites. The present system would have to be transformed in order to create a country free of discrimination. Many Afro-Cubans joined the communist party in the hope that the eventual success of communism would eradicate the capitalist-built world system and usher in a period of equality. Nicolás Guillén, Cuba's poet laureate, for example, joined the Communist Party in 1935. Francisco Calderío (Blas Roca) joined the communist party as early as 1929 and was in charge of the party's section in Oriente, a province that was predominantly and traditionally black.

Afro-Cubans saw the contradiction in the rhetoric and participation of the Cuban upper classes that spoke out against racial discrimination while at the same time attending social bourgeois clubs that often denied entrance to Afro-Cubans. Progressive white and black intellectuals around the country stressed the marriage of blacks to the socialist cause as an arm against economic and capitalist oppression. However, even the Afro-Cuban communists at the time attempted to work within the system until Fulgencio Batista's dictatorship turned increasingly oppressive in the late 1950s.

Economic debates had always ranked high on Cuba's Civil Rights agendas after the revolution. Afro-Cubans and progressive whites in Cuba called for continued national integration, rights for Cubans over foreigners and equal opportunity and self-sufficiency. In 1952, the Sociedades de los Negros Cubanos organized a national congress to discuss the role of the Cuban black in culture and society. They resolved to continue to fight discrimination. This was in the same year that General Fulgencio Batista, the mulatto president, began his dictatorship. Batista's policies turned Cubans away from him, however. Corruption, oppression, and limits to freedom mirrored Machado two decades before. Afro-Cubans supported the 1959 Castro-led revolution with its promises of economic, social, and political participation of all. Castro attracted mass support despite his dictatorial status because of his antibias policies and the hope that he offered for the future.

In the 1970s and 1980s Afro-Cubans had made many advances. Education, particularly literacy and health indicators, were at unprecedentedly high levels for all Cubans, but the Revolution had hardly done away with racism. The lack of representation of Afro-Cubans in high position of state and local governments is indicative of this. With the collapse of the Soviet Union in 1989, racial dynamics made a turn for the worst. The government introduced a series of measures to attract foreign currency and prop up the economy, such as legalizing dollars and investing in a multi-million dollar tourist industry. The Cuban exiles who are now able to send money to the island are overwhelmingly white. In addition, hotels and other tourist establishments discriminate openly against Afro-Cubans, as the attempt, as one hotel employee noted, "to put their best foot forward," which for him meant hiring white Cubans who would deal with a tourist population that is overwhelmingly European. For many on the question of race, Cuba has return to policies of the past, only now Afro-Cubans feel betrayed. Nonetheless, Afro-Cuban culture constitutes an essential aspect of Cuban life and it continues to be celebrated universally.

DARIÉN J. DAVIS

See also **Cuba; Garvey, Marcus (Jamaican); Guillen, Nicolas (Cuban)**

Further Reading

Casal, Lourdes, "Race Relations in Contemporary Cuba" *The Position of Blacks in Brazilian and Cuban Society*, London: Minority Rights Group, 1979

Helg, Aline, *Our Rightful Share: The Afro-Cuban Struggle for Equality, 1886—1912*,

Chapel Hill: University of North Carolina Press, 1995

Fernández Robaina, Tomás, *El negro en Cuba*, La Habana, Editorial de Ciencias Sociales, 1990

Peréz Sarduy, Pedro, and Jead Stubbs, editors, *AfroCuba: An Anthology of Cuban Writing on Race, Politics and Culture*, Melbourne, London, and New York: Ocean Press, Latin American Bureau, 1993

Afro-Latin Americans

Capsule Summary

Location: Former Central and South American colonies of Portugal, Spain, and France (presently Latin America: Mexico, Central America, the Caribbean Basin, the Andes, the southern cone, and Brazil)
Total Population: Estimates range from 85 million to over 100 million
Languages: Spanish, Portuguese, French, Creole, Garifuna, Yoruba, and English, among others
Religions: Catholicism, Protestantism, Santeria, Candomblé, Vodum

Afro-Latin Americans refers to the descendants of Africans in the former Central and South American colonies of Portugal, Spain, and France. Afro-Latin Americans are a diverse population that has had an impact on every country in the geographical region known as Latin America, which includes Mexico, Central America, the Caribbean Basin, the Andes, the southern cone, and Brazil.

The majority of modern Afro-Latin Americans are descendants of West African slaves who were forcibly removed from their homelands from the late fifteenth century to the late nineteenth century. Population estimates of Afro-Latin Americans range from 85–100 million, although accurate data on them is often difficult to find. This paucity of information stems, in part, from scant demographic data in many countries and because Afro-Latin Americans are not a monolith. Moreover, how one defines "Afro-Latin American" may vary from country to country. In general, it is safe to conclude that the Afro-Latin American populations have always been undercounted and thus most demographic figures can be used as a minimum. To understand the position of contemporary Afro-Latin Americans, it is important to examine the historical insertion of Africans into Latin American societies.

History

The history of Afro-Latin Americans begins with the conquest of the Americas by Spain and the Portuguese. The first African immigrants came to America largely by way of the Iberian peninsula. In 1455, Pope Nicolás V gave the Portuguese the right to reduce to slavery the inhabitants of the southern coast of Africa since they were (theoretically) enemies of Christ. The Iberians began a modest slave trade in Africans from the Western coasts. The Portuguese, in particular, set up factories or trading posts to trade with local middlemen. African slavery met a steady, but limited, demand in

Europe. Neither Spain nor Portugal could absorb profitably a large number of slaves into their peninsular economies; thus European-African relations did not revolve around the institution of slavery.

The colonization of Latin America took place in two phases: the period of exploration and conquest, and the period of colonization during which Europeans began the transfer of their culture and institutions to the New World. Black participation in the conquest illustrates the flexibility of the Spanish system before colonization, when acquisition of new lands became paramount. Africans served in two major areas: as explorers or skilled aides to the explorers, and as personal servants or slaves. Juan Valiente, for example, a fugitive slave who fought alongside the conquistadors in Chile distinguished himself by his bravery and was granted an encomienda in the 1550s. Blacks Juan Beltrán and Juan Fenández distinguished themselves as brave warriors in the conquest of Chile. Juan Garrido, or Handsome John, participated in the Conquest of Mexico.

Not until circa 1513 did the first Africans arrive from Africa. From 1571 onward, the Spanish provided the Portuguese with grants that allowed them to bring slaves to the islands.

Despite their status as slaves, West Africans were able to transfer many of their cultural traits to the Americas, in a process that the Cuban Fernando Ortiz has called transculturation. Characterized by distinct ethnic groupings with varying religions, customs, and practices from the West African regions we now call Sierra Leone, Benin, Nigeria, Mozambique, and Angola, inhabitants included the Ashanti, the Yoruba, the Ibo, and the Dahomey, all of whom had highly developed civilizations in which religion played a crucial role. Tribes from the Muslim area of North Africa such as the Hausa, the Amalinke, and the Mandingo in addition to tribes from the Central Congo region, such as members of the Bantu-speaking peoples, also influenced culture in the New World. Although fewer slaves came from East Africa, their presence deserves mention.

Slavery varied across the Americas and depended on a variety of local factors. Urban slave labor also differed from life on the plantation, which often had its own set of laws. Black women played important roles under European slavery. Not only were they responsible for the cohesion of the black family, but also for the care of white children. Although exploited, some women of African descent were nonetheless able to gain limited privileges within the system unavailable to their male counterparts. Despite the uneven power relationship between Africans and Europeans, and the treatment of Africans as property, this did not prohibit the Spanish and Portuguese from "pursuing" sexual relations with African women. Miscegenation, or the mixing of the races, inevitably accompanied the development of the New World. Intermixing of Europeans, aborigines, and Africans created a mixed people and facilitated a distinct New World culture though *mestizaje*, or the combining of elements of distinct cultures. Miscegenation, however, engendered a caste system based on skin color which ultimately marginalized blacks, and privileged combinations of European *mestizos* over them. Miscegenation also blurred the distinctions among races and identities which contributed to the diversity among Afro-Latin Americans.

Wars of Independence and National Consolidation

By the end of the eighteenth century, European Enlightenment had produced a new philosophy of Liberalism which called for the equality, liberty, and fraternity of men. These were the supposed tenets of the French Revolution of 1789, which would have a direct impact on Afro-Latin Americans as Latin American nations called for their independence. Only in Haiti, a colony that was overwhelmingly black, did abolition of slavery and independence go hand in hand, however. In other regions, independence preceded abolition in some cases by twenty to thirty years, or in the case of Brazil by more than sixty years. The wars of independence were detrimental to most blacks in Latin America. Blacks and mulattos, slave and free, participated disproportionately in these fights, and thousands died. Blacks such as José Antonio Paez were instrumental in Simón Bolivar's struggles in northern South America. Among the former African slaves who participated in the independence wars were Lieutenant Leonardo Infante, the mulatto general José Laurencio Silva, and the Colombian admiral and popular personality José Prudencio Padilla, founder of the Colombian Navy, who saw battle in Venezuela. In Uruguay the famous "Black Battalion" lent their support to Uruguayan independence. During the Cisplatine War, 1825–1829, Afro-Uruguayans such as Dionisio Oribe and Joaquin Artigas showed valor, as had many others in the creation of the Banda Oriental del Uruguay.

Afro-Latin Americans such as Juan Gualberto Gómez in Cuba, and Patrocinio, Machado de Assis, Luiz Gama, and João da Cruz e Souza in Brazil played important roles in the many abolition movements of the nineteenth century. By the end of the century, however, Afro-Latin Americans were facing competition for jobs by growing numbers of European immigrants, particularly from Europe. Unfortunately, new capitalist investors and industrialists preferred European labor to Afro-Latin Americans because many saw them as representing slavery and backwardness that Latin American elites wanted so badly to escape. Ironically, in Central America economic projects such as the railroads and the Panama Canal depended upon skilled and unskilled cheap laborers from the Caribbean islands, black in their majority. This infusion of immigrants to the isthmus would change national demographics and create a new Afro-Latin American population in Central America while European labor in most other areas of Latin America would help to diminish the relative populations of people of African descent.

1930s to the Present

Before the 1920s, Haiti was one of the few nations that celebrated its African roots. Almost all Haitians are either black or mulatto. Rich cultural traditions from local rhythms such as *méringue* to the Dahomean religion *vodum* attest to Haiti's African roots. Writers such as Jean Price Mars, Jacques Roumain, and René Depestre were renowned orators in the vanguard of Haitian Negritude.

The 1920s marked a new era of black power and consciousness raising. The Jamaican-born Marcus Garvey spoke of decolonization by going back to Africa, but more importantly he encouraged blacks in Central America and the Caribbean to call for a freedom without boundaries. Meanwhile, black women such as the Dominicans Petrolina Gómez, Artagracía Domínguez, and Evelina Rodríquez called for gender equality. A decade later, intellectual activists throughout the region demanded respect and appreciation of the African heritage in the region's cultural patrimony, promoting two distinct, but related cultural movements known as *negrismo* and *negritude*.

Despite its often essentialist rhetoric, the movement dubbed "*Negritude*" was one of the most important cultural revolutions of Black intellectuals in the twentieth century. The promoters of Negritude were intent on exposing the racist attitudes of the Western World that excluded blacks from mainstream society while simultaneously making known the cultural and spiritual gifts that Africans had given Western civilization. Influenced by Marxism and Surrealism in the early decades of the twentieth century, Negritude flourished in the French Caribbean with writers such as Aimé Césaire (Martinique), Leon Damás (French Guiana), and Jacques Roumain (Haiti).

In the late 1920s and 1930s, immigrant, black, mulatto, and *mestizo* masses had begun to swell the major urban centers. The city became the center of national development and cultural production. During this time, writers began to recognize the historical contribution of previously ignored racial sectors to the formation of national identity. Latin Americans began to project positive racial images, celebrating the *mestizaje* of Native, European, and African traits. The Mexican José Vasconcelos noted that miscegenation had created what he called a cosmic race, whereas the Brazilian Gilberto Freyre and the Cuban Elías Entralgo wrote about miscegenation between the European and the African in a positive manner. These views, in part, reflected the twentieth-century nationalists' attempt to view their Latin American identity and development in positive national terms, and not in racial terms. Integration and mixture remained the focus rather than individual rights, however.

The Spanish-speaking Caribbean shows another pattern of cultural proclivity. In the 1920s and 1930s writers such as Nicolás Guillén (Cuba), Luis Pales Mattos (Puerto Rico), and Manuel del Cabral (Dominican Republic) promoted black culture through *mestizaje*. For them, African influences were as important as Spanish. In all three countries, blacks and whites participate in black culture. In Cuba, the movement known as *Negrismo* aimed to celebrate the union of Spanish and African influences in Cuba's mulatto culture. In Cuba, for example, Santeria, an organized Afro-Latin American religion derived from the Yoruba beliefs, remains a vital part of the national landscape. In addition, the vast majority of Cuban popular music is African-derived: the rumba and the son, for example. Puerto Rico and the Dominican Republic illustrate similar dynamics, as do the Caribbean coastal regions of Colombia and Venezuela.

When Marxist parties gained momentum after World War II, many Afro-Latin Americans joined the movement in the hope of changing the fundamental economic system that discriminated against them. In so doing, once again race became secondary to wider problems of class transformation. The 1960 Castro Revolution, for example, spurred the nationalism of racial unity. For Fidel Castro, "*nation*" implied the popular sectors, and he vowed to eliminate both racism and elitism. While, Castro initially had some success, racism continues to be an eroding force in the Cuban society, as it still is in other Latin American countries today. While revolutionary rhetoric stymied autonomous black movements on the left, right-wing military dictatorships that emerged in the 1960s and 1970s prohibited any form of grassroots movements or developments. The political opening of the 1980s, known in many countries as *abertura*, provided a political space that continues to be filled by black movements and community development throughout the region.

Major Afro-Latin American movements also emerged in the 1930s and 1940s in Brazil with the Frente Negra Brasileira founded in Brazil in 1931 and the Teatro Experimental do Negro (T.E.N) in 1946. Under Abdias do Nascimento T.E.N. also forged an Afrocentric aesthetic through art, poetry, and beauty competitions. Afro-Brazilian writers continue to challenge society's assumptions about them. Afro-Brazilians have fought against stereotypical representations which aim, to paraphrase a Brazilian saying, '"to keep blacks in their place'." In her poetry the Afro-Brazilian poetess Elisa Lucinda criticizes the Brazilian commodification of Afro-Brazilian women in her poignant poetry, reminding us that interracial sexual relations, so often celebrated in Brazil, have not necessarily diminished racism.

In Central and South America, (with the exception of Belize, which is a majority black state, and Panama, which has a very large black West Indian population), mass organization and protest among blacks is a relatively new phenomenon. In Panama, West Indian organization dates back to the Marcus Garvey Association for Negro Betterment of the 1920s. Throughout the 1940s, protest continued against West Indian discrimination and exclusion from being accepted as citizens. Visitors to Panama notice the integration of blacks and *antillanos* on all levels of society today. In other areas of Central America, black movements have focused on cultural preservation and political visibility, and not necessarily on protest.

Black political movements played key roles in the intensified nationalism of the 1960s. The coronation of Ras Tafari as King Haile Selassie of Ethiopia led to the creation of the first Rastafarians who had, by the 1960s, increased racial consciousness in the poor sectors of Jamaican society. In the next three decades Rastafarianism would spread throughout the region. Since the 1960s, Afro-Latin American activists and intellectuals have become more visible in national dynamics. This is the case of the Garifuna people of Honduras and the Creoles in Nicaragua. Afro-Costa Rican writers such as Quince Duncan have played key roles in the regions cultural affairs, but mass political organization is a relatively new phenomenon of the 1990s.

Today Afro-Latin Americans, like any ethnic or racial categorization, continue to be nuanced by geography, language, and history and may comprise a variety of social terms—negro, mulatto, *cafuso*, *moreno*, *trigueño*, *antillano*, *prieto*—to name a few. Furthermore, social and personal relations, education, and economic opportunities continue and a host of other variants still play a significant role in determining social standing. The manifestation and national enunciation of an Afro-Latin American identity varies from region to region, vacillating between what Norman Whitten and Arlene Torres call the two major nationalist ideologies of racial culture: *mestizaje* and negritude. The former celebrates racial intermingling while the latter exalts the positive features of blackness.

In Spanish South America, the impact of black mobilization has been most profound in Colombia. In 1990, Colombians voted to replace the antiquated 1886 constitution with a new document that would lay down the foundation for specific ethnic representation in the country's Constituent Assembly. Unfortunately, respected academics such as Víctor Daniel Bonilla who promoted the rights of indigenous people, rallied to deny territorial rights for blacks on the Pacific coast under the same law. Nonetheless, the umbrella organization UNO AFRO (The National Union of African Colombian Organizations) has attempted to coordinate black mobilization all over the country. Other Pacific coast groups such as the Movimiento Nacional Cimarrón (National Maroonage Movement), and the Organización de Barrios Populares y Comunidades Negras de la Costa Pacífica del Chocó (OPABO) have been determined to fight for black rights. In Ecuador, the Association of Ecuadorian Blacks (ASONE) founded in 1988 has pursued similar goals on the Pacific coast.

Uruguay, at the other end of South America, has experienced an explosion in black mobilization since 1990. MUNDO AFRO, Uruguay's largest black umbrella organization, has become increasingly militant in its demands, calling for official recognition, and education and employment opportunities free from discrimination. Other South American countries have not experienced major movements, although organizations such as Peru's Movimiento Pro Derecho Humano del Negro in Peru (The Black Human Rights Peruvian Movement) provide legal assistance to blacks, and battle similar obstacles.

To gain support for their national agendas, many national groups turn to international forums such as the United Nations, the Organization of American States (OAS), and international conferences. Afro-Latin Americans are also increasingly turning to each other for mutual support and for the exchange of ideas, although these exchanges are hampered by economic constraints. Latin American participation has been historically weak in Pan-African congresses for these very reasons. Nonetheless, communication among Afro-Latin American organizations has intensified, as has the dialogue between blacks in the United States and Afro-Latin Americans.

Beginning in the late 1970s, the Congresses on Black Culture in the Americas encouraged international cooperation among black activists and scholars, although the first few conferences were not explicitly political. The Third Congress, held in São Paulo, Brazil in 1982 under the directorship of Abdias do Nascimento began a new political phase with the theme "The African Diaspora: Political Consciousness and African Culture." Since then, increased black consciousness and politicization of black movements has led to a more acute condemnation of racist policies throughout the region. Afro-Latin Americans have attempted to organize extranational activities to forge bonds across borders. In 1994, for example, Uruguay's MUNDO AFRO hosted "The First Seminar on Racism and Xenophobia" in Montevideo, Uruguay in December 1994, with the participation of blacks throughout the Americas, including the United States. More recently, Costa Ricans hosted "The Second Annual Reunion of the Black Family," in 1996 with activists from throughout the region. Others followed in Ecuador and Venezuela. At the United Nations-sponsored regional preparation meeting for the Conference Against Racism, Racial Discrimination, Xenophobia and Other Related Intolerance in Chile in December 2000, Afro-Latin American organizations were well represented.

Black people from Latin America and the Caribbean have participated in major movements throughout the twentieth century. The politics of racial identity, however, continue to pose an obstacle to mass support. Unfortunately, *mestizaje* remains an ideology which denigrates blacks in favor of *mestizos*. In addition, since the vast majority of self-identified blacks come from poor sectors of society, there are significant barriers to mobilization of any kind. Difficulties notwithstanding, many Afro-Latin Americans have courageously opposed oppression and discrimination for centuries. The transculturation experience of the eighteenth and nineteenth centuries has ensured the survival of African customs and practices in Latin America.

DARIÉN J. DAVIS

See also **Brazil; Garifuna; Latin Americans; Negritos; Rastafari; Selassie, Haile (Ethiopian); Uruguay**

Further Reading

Conniff, Michael L., and Thomas J. Davis, *Africans in the Americas: A History of the Black Diaspora*, New York: St. Martin's Press, 1994

Graham, Richard, editor, *The Idea of Race in Latin America*, Austin: University of Texas Press, 1990

Minority Rights, *Invisible No Longer: Afro-Latin Americans Today*, London: Minority Rights Group, 1995

Knight, Franklin, *The African Dimension of Latin American Societies*, New York, Macmillan, 1974

Wade, Peter, *Race and Ethnicity in Latin America*, Chicago: Pluto Press, 1997

Afrocentricity

Afrocentricity is a late twentieth century movement based on two principles: true self-knowledge must be grounded in one's own historical context, and self-knowledge properly pursued yields personal agency moving toward a global community that preserves cultural difference. While the United States African American scholar Molefi K. Asante has given the movement its name and most recent impetus, its roots may be traced through a series of classical twentieth century African thinkers from the likes Frantz Fanon, Cheikh Anta Diop, Alain Locke, and W.E.B. Du Bois all the way back to Frederick Douglass and David Walker in the nineteenth century.

Afrocentricity has received a good deal of critical attention because of its consequences for public education. Contemporary critics like Mary Lefkowitz and Stephen Howe have charged Afrocentric educators with teaching myth as fact to bolster African American students' self-esteem. Such a strategy is illustrated in the following narrative: *Ancient Egyptians were black. They had batteries. They flew gliders. They practiced brain surgery. Egyptian civilization began in sub-Saharan Africa. The Greeks stole Egypt's cultural legacy. Africa was a utopia destroyed by European enslavement and colonization. What is good in the European cultural legacy is African; what is bad is distinctively European. Africans are civilized and Europeans are barbarians.*

Critics of Afrocentricity often confuse the movement with Afrocentrism. W.E.B. Du Bois used the term "Afrocentrism" in the early 1960s in conjunction with his plans for an Encyclopedia Africana to be produced in Ghana. Afrocentrism as a movement exhibits several variations. In its most neutral guise, Afrocentrism is simply a research methodology. Choosing to sympathize with Africans on the African continent or in the African diaspora, proponents of this form of Afrocentrism see the world through Africana eyes and reinterpret world history by filtering it through the viewpoint of African experience. Wilson Moses's *Afrotopia: The Roots of African American Popular History* is perhaps the best example of this form of Afrocentrism in action.

A second kind of Afrocentrism expresses a philosophy of vindicationism that challenges the European tradition of denying the humanity of Africans. A popular variant of vindicationism called "Nile Valley Afrocentrism" claims that the ancient Egyptians were black and that their traditions formed the basis of European civilization. St. Clair Drake's *Black Folk Here and There* furnishes an exhaustive history of Afrocentric vindicationism.

A third kind of Afrocentrism extends beyond vindicationism to a philosophy of black supremacy. Citing environmental, cultural, or genetic reasons for African superiority, proponents of this form of Afrocentrism argue that Africans were not only the first civilized people but have proven themselves to be far more civilized than "barbaric" Europeans could ever hope to be. Because it paints Europeans and their American counterparts as incapable of civilized life, this version of Afrocentrism, vividly depicted by Marimba Ani's *Yurugu*, threatens the very existence of integrated public education.

Mindful of Afrocentrism's potential to drive blacks and whites even further apart, Asante distinguishes his version of Afrocentrism from the other three varieties by calling it "Afrocentricity." Asante first publicizes this term in his *Afrocentricity: The Theory of Social Change* in 1980. The "*Afro*" in "Afrocentricity" reflects a commitment to the idea that all humans are African in origin, the "*centricity*" suggests a commitment to the idea that people must center themselves in their own cultural experiences. African-American students who claim an Africana heritage, for example, must have access to African history from the very beginning of their formal education.

Afrocentricity's centering process arguably leads to a restoration of Africana peoples' agency. However, the same process will work for any group that has lost its natural human agency through enslavement, colonialism, or other less obvious decentering forces. Afrocentricity escapes being the inversion of Eurocentrism because it does not give Africa pride of place. Paradoxically, anyone can be an adherent of the movement if he or she seeks solidarity with everyone else on the globe by way of cultural self-knowledge.

Historical Antecedents

Afrocentric movements constitute a critique of European and American challenges to African humanity. In the Declaration of Independence (1776), Thomas Jefferson famously claimed that all men were created equal. What is implied in this statement is that all white men were created equal. While recognizing slavery's incompatibility with the nation's founding principles, Jefferson also maintained that Africans' obvious inferiority prevented any possibility of their integration into American society as equals. Slavery's abolition, he argued, should be immediately followed by the Africans' return to Africa.

In making such claims, Jefferson anticipated the anti-African sentiments of eighteenth century European philosophers such as Immanuel Kant and Georg Wilhelm Friedrich Hegel. These philosophers—and European society as a whole—could only justify the extremely profitable practice of slavery by dehumanizing Africans. Hegel even went so far as to insist that slavery would bring Africans to full consciousness by increasing their "human" feeling: "Slavery is in and for itself injustice, for the essence of humanity is Freedom; but for this man must be matured" (Hegel, 99). Even some African American thinkers, such as Edward Wilmot Blyden, believed that slavery was part of a divine plan to Christianize Africa.

Such brutal assaults on Africans' humanity gave rise to two distinct responses, prefiguring the vindicationist and black supremacist forms of twentieth century Afrocentrism. One of the earlier thinkers to discuss these issues was the vindicationist David Walker, an African-American who claimed not only that the Egyptians were the founders of the world's first great civilization but also that they were black. In his "Appeal to the Coloured Citizens of the World" of 1829, he described the ancient Egyptians as

> "Africans or coloured people, such as we are—some of them yellow and others dark—a mixture of Ethiopians and the natives of Egypt—about the same as you see the coloured people of the United States at the present day..."

Frederick Douglass also believed that the Egyptians were black. With the deciphering of the Rosetta Stone in the early 1800s—throwing Europe and America into "Egyptomania"—it seemed obvious to Douglass that blacks could not have been subhuman as Hegel and other philosophers claimed. Ironically addressing those who still maintained that nothing glorious could come out of Africa, Douglass said,

> "Egypt is in Africa. Pity that it had not been in Europe, or in Asia, or better still in America! Another unhappy circumstance is, that the ancient Egyptians were not white people; but were, undoubtedly, just about as dark in complexion as many in this country who are considered genuine Negroes..."

Inspired by his vision of a direct connection between ancient Africa and modern America, Douglass advocated integration into American society.

Alexander Crummell and Marcus Garvey took the opposite tack, rejecting assimilation in favor of a return to Africa. Inverting Jefferson's argument about Africans' inferiority, these black supremacists believed in Africans' biological and cultural superiority. In the early twentieth century, Garvey's United Negro Improvement Association laid the groundwork for black supremacist movements that continue to this day. George James' *Stolen Legacy* , for instance, takes its inspiration from Garvey's belief in the African origins of Greek culture. And separatist movements like the Nation of Islam are sympathetic to Garvey's theories about black superiority. The dialectic between assimilation and separatism continues to the present moment.

Afrocentricity's Founders

In the twentieth century, several Afrocentric currents coalesced into the movement now called Afrocentricity. While Molefi Asante is perhaps the best-known proponent, his work builds on that of Cheikh Anta Diop, Frantz Fanon, Alain Locke, and W.E.B. Du Bois. What binds these figures together is their remarkable ability to navigate successfully between the extremes of assimilation and separatism that divided their historical predecessors.

Unlike many of the earlier philosophers on race, these thinkers reject all claims to genetic or cultural superiority and advocate instead a philosophy of universal inclusion. Self-knowledge grounded in each person's individual cultural context is the only route to this universalist philosophy. In Fanon's striking example, African students in former French colonies were once forced to learn about their "ancestors," the Gauls." Under Afrocentricity, African students would first learn about their real (blood) ancestors and only then learn about the ancestors of others—including those of their former colonizers.

Critics like Lefkowitz and Howe ground their arguments in relation to this insistence on self-knowledge, which they claim defines Afrocentrists as separatists. Further, if Afrocentricity is a philosophy of universal inclusion, they demand, why does it particularize itself by invoking the name of Africa? It is true that Afrocentrists are concerned about the survival and flourishing of their own peoples. Diop and Fanon, for instance, hoped to create a continental African unity out of the ashes of colonialism. In addition to their interest in Pan-Africanism, Du Bois and Locke sought an end to segregation in the United States. Asante, the only founder of Afrocentricity still alive, concentrates on post-segregation crises that recall the bleakest hours of Reconstruction.

But Afrocentricity extends far beyond these local concerns to an emphasis on humanity as a whole. In response to critics, most Afrocentrists turn to what has become known as the "Out of Africa" hypothesis—the idea that all humans can trace their cultural and genetic heritage back to Africa. As a trope signifying the whole of humanity by one of its parts, the name "Afrocentricity" urges us to atone for past injustices like slavery and to avoid future sins against human unity.

Diop, for example, in his *Civilization or Barbarism,* notes that modern technology gave Europe the power to enslave or colonize most of the world, while modern philosophers like Hegel provided philosophical justifications of barbaric treatment of non-Europeans. As an alternative to such barbarism, Diop offers a philosophy that brings all people together. Describing humanity's African origins as an accident of geography, Diop does not privilege Africans over any other group of people. Rather, he suggests that we maintain our individual cultural differences yet use our common origins as a foundation for a new global civilization that can stand against barbarism. In this new world community, modern technology can enhance cross-cultural intimacy to unite the world.

And while all of Afrocentricity's founders support close study of Africa's traditions, none of them deny the importance of European cultures—for whites and blacks and all other humans. In fact, most of them were strongly influenced by their exposure to European traditions in Europe itself. Du Bois's ideas about global unity through cultural complementarity were current at the University of Berlin, where he was a student during the late 1800s. Locke's cosmopolitanism was nourished in the company of fellow Rhodes scholars from around the world at Oxford in the early 1900s. Though he was born and raised in the Caribbean, Fanon's French education familiarized him with philosophers ranging from Hegel to Sartre. While Diop was born and raised in West Africa, his explicit references to European classicists and Egyptologists who believed in the African origins of European civilization reflect his many years at the Sorbonne.

Of course, this common background does not mean that these thinkers agree on every point. Their sharpest disagreement focuses on the claims made by Afrocentric historians. Diop and Asante are convinced that the African origin of humanity and civilization has been well established. Du Bois and Locke express reservations about the hypothesis. Fanon challenges it because of its potential to distract African peoples' attention from their most pressing objective: final liberation from enslavement and colonialism. Fanon admits that he would be pleased to learn that Plato had dialogues with ancient African philosophers, but liberation must be centered in the immediate cultural contexts of the oppressed, not in historical hypotheses. Fanon's disagreement with Diop and Asante is a matter of urgent practical judgment rather than philosophical principle. All of Afrocentricity's founders agree that children who claim an Africana heritage must have access to African historical traditions to develop accurate self-knowledge.

In the end, however, whether the "Out of Africa" hypothesis is true is immaterial. Historical speculation and philosophical commitment can exist independently of one another. As a philosophy of universal inclusion, Afrocentricity is indifferent to the results of historical investigation, but not to the method of investigation. Afrocentricity's founders insist that historical claims to self-knowledge be based on research techniques freed from cultural bias—to the degree that is possible.

CHARLES C. VERHAREN

See also **Africans: 1: Overview; African-American Nationalism and Separatism; Du Bois, W.E.B. (African-American); Fanon, Frantz Omar (Algerian); Garvey, Marcus (Jamaican)**

Further Reading

Ani, Marimba, *Yurugu: An African-Centered Critique of European Cultural Thought and Behavior*, Trenton, New Jersey: Africa World Press, 1994

Asante, Molefi K., *Afrocentricity: The Theory of Social Change*, Buffalo, New York: Amulefe, 1980, revised and republished as *Afrocentricity*, Trenton, New Jersey: Africa World Press, 1988

———*Kemet, Afrocentricity and Knowledge*, Trenton, New Jersey: Africa World Press, 1990

———, *The Afrocentric Idea*, Philadelphia: Temple University Press, 1987

Diop, Cheikh Anta, *Civilization or Barbarism: An Authentic Anthropology*, 1981, translated by Y.L.M. Ngemi, Brooklyn, New York: Lawrence Hill Books, 1991

Douglass, Frederick, "The Claims of the Negro Ethnologically Considered," original address delivered at Western Reserve College, July 12, 1854, reprinted in *Life and Writings of Frederick Douglass*, edited by P.S. Foner, New York: International Publishers, 1953

Drake, St. Clair, *Black Folk Here and There: An Essay in History and Anthropology*, 1987, two volumes, Los Angeles: Center for Afro-American Studies, University of California, 1990

Du Bois. W.E.B., *The Education of Black People*, edited by H. Aptheker, New York: Monthly Review Press, 1973

Fanon, F., *Black Skin, White Masks*, 1952, translated by C.L. Markmann, New York: Grove Weidenfeld Press, 1967

Hegel, G.W.F., *The Philosophy of History*, translated by J. Sibree, New York: Dover, 1956

Howe, S., *Afrocentrism: Mythical Pasts and Imagined Homes*, London: Verso, 1998

Lefkowitz, M., *Not Out of Africa: How Afrocentrism Became an Excuse to Teach Myth As History*, New York: Basic Books, 1996

Locke, A., *The Philosophy of Alain Locke*, edited by L. Harris, Philadelphia: Temple University Press, 1989

Moses, W.J., *Afrotopia: The Roots of African American Popular History*, Cambridge: Cambridge University Press, 1998

Walker, David, "Appeal to The Coloured Citizens of the World: Our Wretchedness in Consequence of Slavery," 1829, in *African Intellectual Heritage: A Book of Sources*, edited by M.K. Asante and A.S. Abarry, Philadelphia: Temple University Press, 1996, pp 627–636

Aga Khan (Ismaili)

Aga Khan is an honorific title of Turkic-Mongol-Persian origins meaning "lord and chief," bestowed around 1820 by the Qajar monarch of Iran on the *imam* (or spiritual leader) of the Nizari Ismailis, a minority Shi'a Muslim community. This title has been held on a hereditary basis by the subsequent Ismaili imams, including Prince Karim Aga Khan, the present imam, who succeeded to his spiritual position in 1957.

The Nizari Ismailis, a minority Shi'a Muslim community, have always had an imam who interprets the faith for his followers, numbering 15 million and now scattered in 25 countries of Asia, the Middle East, Africa, Europe, and North America. The Shi'a originally broke from the majority Sunni Muslims over the issue of the successors to Muhammad the prophet. Shi'as believed that Muhammad's successors, or imams, had to be descendants of his family. In the eighth century there was a dispute among the Shi'a over which of two brothers should be imam. The minority followed a brother named Ismail and the thereby became Ismailis. The Aga Khans are supposedly descended from the first Ismail.

Hasan Ali Shah (1804–1881) became the forty-sixth imam of the Nizari Ismailis on the death of his father in 1817. By then, the Nizari Ismaili imams had existed in different parts of Iran for some seven centuries. Around 1820 the Iranian monarch Fath Ali Shah (1797–1834) appointed the youthful Ismaili imam to the governorship of Qom and gave him one of his daughters in marriage, also bestowing upon him the honorific title (*laqab*) of Aga Khan"." Henceforth, Hasan Ali Shah became generally known as Aga Khan Mahallati, because of his royal title and the family's deep roots in the area of Mahallat in central Iran. The title of Aga Khan was inherited by Hasan Ali Shah's successors to the Ismaili imamate.

In 1835, Hasan Ali Shah, Aga Khan I, was appointed to the governorship of Kirman, a major province in Iran. Later, he was dismissed as a result of court intrigues against him, and he was eventually obliged to emigrate from Iran, his ancestral land. In 1841, the Ismaili imam arrived in Afghanistan. Subsequently, after brief stays in Gujarat and Calcutta, Aga Khan I settled permanently in Bombay in 1848.

Aga Khan I had now established extensive contacts with his followers in India, locally known as Khojas. As the spiritual leader of a minority Muslim community, Aga Khan I received the protection of the British establishment in India, where he labored widely to define and delineate the religious identity of his Khoja followers. The latter, it may be noted, had been obliged to disguise themselves for long periods as Sunni or Twelver Shi'a Muslims, in addition to interfacing with Hinduism, as dissimilating measures to safeguard themselves against persecution. It was under such circumstances that the Ismaili imam's authority was challenged by a dissident Khoja group who refused to acknowledge the Ismaili identity of their community. Matters came to a head in 1866 when the dissident Khojas brought their case, designated as the Aga Khan Case, before the Bombay High Court. A detailed judgement was finally rendered against the plaintiffs and in favour of Aga Khan I on all counts. This judgement legally established in British India the status of Aga Khan I's followers as a community of Shi'a Muslims, also recognizing Aga Khan as the spiritual leader of that community and heir in lineal descent to earlier Shi'a imams from the progeny of Ali (d. 661), the first Shi'a imam, and his wife Fatima, the Prophet Muhammad's daughter. Aga Khan I died in 1881 and was buried in the Mazagaon area of Bombay where his impressive mausoleum still stands.

Aga Khan I was succeeded as the spiritual head of the Nizari Ismailis by his son Ali Shah, Aga Khan II. Born in 1830 in Iran, Aga Khan II led the Nizari Ismailis as their forty-seventh imam for only four years, during which time he concentrated his efforts on improving the educational standards of his followers. He died in 1885 and was buried in the family mausoleum in Najaf, Iraq.

Aga Khan II was succeeded by his sole surviving son Sultan Muhammad Shah, Aga Khan III, who led the Nizari Ismailis as their forty-eighth imam for 77 years. Born in Karachi in 1877, Aga Khan III became well known as a Muslim reformer and statesman, owing to his prominent role in Indo-Muslim as well as international affairs. Aga Khan III formulated numerous modernization policies and programs for his followers. At the same time, he made systematic efforts to distinguish the identity of his followers apart from those of the Twelver Shi'ites as well as Sunni Muslims, with whom the Ismailis had mingled for extended periods. The distinctive Nizari Ismaili identity was elaborated in the constitutions that the imam promulgated for his followers in different regions. Aga Khan III worked vigorously to reorganize his Ismaili following into a modern Muslim community with high standards of education, health, and social welfare, also paying particular attention to the emancipation of Ismaili women and their active participation in communal affairs. He founded a network of schools, hospitals, sports clubs, and economic enterprises, also developing new institutional and administrative organizations for his community in the form of a hierarchy of councils.

Meanwhile, the Ismaili imam was increasingly concerned with reform policies that would benefit not only his followers but also other Muslims as well. He campaigned for a variety of educational reforms and became one of the founders of the All-India Muslim League, as well as participating in the discussions that eventually led to the independence of India and Pakistan from British rule. Aga Khan III's involvement in international affairs led to his election in 1937 as president of the League of Nations. As a Muslim leader and reformer, Aga Khan III responded to the challenges of a rapidly changing world and made it possible for his followers to live as a progressive Muslim minority community with a distinct identity in different countries. He died in Geneva in 1957 and was buried at Aswan, overlooking the Nile in Egypt where his ancestors had ruled as the Fatimid caliphs.

Aga Khan III designated his grandson Karim, the elder son of Aly Khan (1911–1960), as his successor to the Ismaili imamate. Born in 1936 in Geneva, Prince Karim al-Husayn, Aga Khan IV, the forty-ninth and current Ismaili imam, was educated at Le Rosey school in Switzerland. He spent his childhood in Kenya and graduated in 1959 from Harvard University with a degree in Islamic history. He became imam in 1957.

Aga Khan IV has substantially expanded the modernization policies of his grandfather, in addition to developing many new programmes for the socioeconomic and educational benefit of his followers and other populations of certain Asian and African countries. To that end, he has created a complex institutional network known as the Aga Khan Development Network (AKDN), which, by the late 1990s, had disbursed around $100 million annually to its nonprofit activities. Many of Aga Khan IV's projects are promoted and financed through the Aga Khan Foundation, established in 1967. Aga Kan IV has launched a variety of projects related to higher education and educational institutions. In 1977, he founded the Institute of Ismaili Studies in London for the promotion of Islamic and Ismaili studies; and the Aga Khan University, with international faculties of medicine, nursing, and education. An affiliated hospital was established in Karachi in 1985. In the economic development field, too, he has launched numerous projects, including industrial ventures and rural development programs.

In his quest to promote a better understanding of Islamic civilization, Aga Khan IV has established a number of innovative programs including those for the preservation of the cultural heritages of Muslim societies. Here, the apex institution is the Aga Khan Trust for Culture, which was set up in 1988 in Geneva to promote awareness of the importance of the built environment in both historic and contemporary contexts, and for encouraging excellence in architecture. The mandate of this institution covers the Aga Khan Award for Architecture, founded in 1977; the Aga Khan Program for Islamic Architecture, established in 1979 at Harvard University and the Massachusetts Institute of Technology in Cambridge, Massachusetts, to educate architects and planners to cater to the needs of modern Muslim societies; and the Historic and public spaces in historic Muslim cities. Aga Khan IV takes a personal interest in the spiritual and secular affairs of his community and supervises the operations of all his institutions from his Secretariat at Aiglemont near Paris.

The Aga Khan manages a worldwide business empire fed by the tithes of his loyal Ismaili followers. The profits from the empire are used to fund charities around the world. The Aga Khan himself is a wealthy man, well known in society circles, and, like his grandfather the Aga Khan III, fond of horse racing. His personal fortune almost certainly exceeds one billion dollars. He is revered by all Ismailis and works to maintain their position as a prosperous minority in many nations. For this reason he eschews political conflicts and refrains from asking his followers to take political sides in their countries of residence.

FARHAD DAFTARY

See also **Ismailis**

Further Reading

Aga Khan III, Sultan Muhammad Shah, *The Memoirs of Aga Khan: World Enough and Time*, London: Cassell and Co., 1954

Aga Khan III, Sultan Muhammad Shah, *Selected Speeches and Writings of Sir Sultan Muhammad Shah*, 2 volumes, edited by K.K. Aziz, London and New York: Kegan Paul International, 1997–98

Daftary, Farhad, *The Ismailis: Their History and Doctrines*, Cambridge: Cambridge University Press, 1990

Daftary, Farhad, *A Short History of the Ismailis: Traditions of a Muslim Community*, Edinburgh: Edinburgh University Press, 1998

Dumasia, Naoroji M., *The Aga Khan and His Ancestors*, Bombay: The Times of India Press, 1939

Frischauer, Willi, *The Aga Khans*, London: Bodley Head, 1970

Fyzee, Asaf A.A., *Cases in the Muhammadan Law of India and Pakistan*, Oxford: Oxford University Press, 1965, pp 504–549

Thobani, Akbarali, *Islam's Quiet Revolutionary: The Story of Aga Khan IV*, New York: Vantage Press, 1993

Ahmadiyas

Capsule Summary

Location: Mostly in Punjab (Pakistan), also spread around the world
Total Population: Approximately 10 million
Language: Punjabi
Religion: Ahmadiya

The Ahmadiya Movement represents a religious community that has its origins in India. The followers of the Ahmadiya (or Ahmadiya) movement are called Ahmadiyas. They are also referred to as *Qadianies* (name derived from the village of Qadian where the founder of the movement, Mirza Ghulam Ahmad, was born) or as the Lahori group. A vast majority of Ahmadiyas are ethnically Punjabis, with Punjabi as their mother language. However, with the spread of the movement at the global level many other ethnic and racial groups have embraced the movement. There are currently estimated to be around 10 million Ahmadiyas worldwide. Pakistan contains the highest number of Ahmadiyas, which are estimated to be around 4 million.

There are differences between orthodox Muslims and the Ahmadiyas over the doctrinal position and stature of Mirza Ghulam Ahmad, the founder of the Ahmadiya belief. The orthodox Muslims claim that Mirza Ghulam Ahmad had proclaimed himself as a prophet, thereby rejecting the fundamental tenet of Islam—*Khatem-e-Nabowat* (a belief in the finality of the Prophet Mohammed). The Ahmadiyas, however, regard Mirza Ghulam Ahmad as a messenger of God or a reformer, but not a prophet. Ahmadiyas also reject the militant version of the Islamic holy war, *jihad*, as propagated from a strict interpretation of Islamic Law, the *Sharia*. Notwithstanding these differences, Ahmadiyas maintain a firm belief in the teachings of Islam, and regard themselves as Muslims. It is this claim to be Muslims that has been a source of friction and led to their discrimination and persecution in Pakistan.

History

Mirza Ghulam Ahmad, the founder of the movement, was born in Eastern Punjab (currently Indian Punjab) in 1835. During his lifetime, Mirza Ghulam Ahmad gained a substantial following. After the partition of India in 1947, a vast majority of the Ahmadiya population in eastern Punjab opted to settle in Pakistan and established their headquarters in Rabwah (West Punjab). They thus migrated en masse to West Punjab. Ahmadiyas, as a small though influential group, had played a significant part in the Pakistan movement. Zaffarullah Khan, an Ahmadiya, was the president of All India Muslim League. The Ahmadiya community represented an educated and a highly articulate community that was eager and competent to deal with various administrative and political challenges facing the new country. Zaffarullah Khan was appointed as Pakistan's first Foreign Minister. There were also a number of key Ahmadiya figures in the political and administrative arena in the years subsequent to Pakistan's establishment. Growing Ahmadiya influence, however, became a source of concern for politicians and religious parties within Pakistan. Demands were voiced that Ahmadiyas be declared *Kafirs* (impostors) and that all Ahmadiyas should be excluded from governmental positions. Religious friction came to peaked in the early part of 1953 with demonstrations and violence against the Ahmadiya community. The government of the day, under the premiership of Khawja Ghulam Ahmad, however, resisted pressure brought by radical parties such as *Jami'at-e-Islami* to have Ahmadiyas declared non-Muslim. The official position was that the Ahmadiyas could not be declared a minority against their own wishes.

Politics, Religion, and Identity

Tension resurfaced in the early 1970s amid renewed demands on the part of Pakistan's clerics to declare Ahmadiyas non-Muslim. During 1974, anti-Ahmadiya riots engulfed the country, claiming 70 lives in Punjab. As a result of persistent political and religious pressure, Zulfiqar Ali Bhutto, the then prime minister, brought the issue before Pakistan's National Assembly. On September 7, 1974, the Assembly, having turned itself into a Special Committee, adopted the Constitution (Second) Amendment Act 1974 which added the Ahmadiyas to the list of Non-Muslims. A new clause to the constitution (Clause 3, Article 260) outlawed the group and stated as follows:

> "A person who does not believe in the absolute and unqualified finality of prophethood of Muhammed (peace be upon him) the last of the prophets, or claims to be a prophet in any sense of the word or of any description whatsoever after Muhammed (peace be upon him), or recognizes such a claimant as a prophet or a religious reformer, is not a Muslim for the purposes of the Constitution or law."

The constitutional amendment dealt a serious blow to the Ahmadiya identity and their claims to being part of the larger Muslim community. On the other hand, the religious orthodoxy having been placated, the years immediately following this constitutional amendment saw minimal assaults on their socioeconomic and legal position as citizens of Pakistan. The "Islamization" period of General Zia-ul-Haq (1977–1988), however, saw the introduction of discriminatory legislation and other administrative practices specifically aimed at persecuting and victimizing the Ahmadiya community. General Zia-ul-Haq introduced a system of a separate electorate for religious minorities and also instituted the anti-Blasphemy laws to target the religious minorities. Under the anti-Blasphemy laws, Ahmadiyas could be prosecuted and punished for having "indirectly or directly posed as a Muslim." A number of criminal proceedings were brought against the Ahmadiyas, for various activities such as offering *Azan* (Islamic call for prayer) or for saying *Assalam-o-Eliakum* (a Muslim form of greeting).

In an environment charged with religious intolerance, various actions challenging the legal validity and constitutionality of the ordinances imposed by General Zia-ul-Haq failed. In *Mujibur Rahman v. Government of Pakistan* the Federal Shariat Court had been asked to exercise its jurisdiction under Article 203D of the Constitution to rule that the ordinances were contrary to the injunctions of the *Quran* and *Sunnah*. The court, however, was of the view that, taking into account the doctrinal differences between Muslims and Ahmadiyas, the Parliament had acted within its authority in declaring the latter as non-Muslims. According to the Court, the Anti-Ahmadiya Ordinance merely restrains Ahmadiyas from "'calling themselves what they are not"'. In upholding the validity of the ordinance, the court also noted that the introduction of this ordinance had been necessary for the maintenance of law and order.

Ahmadiyas live in an environment that is charged with religious extremism. They fear for their own safety and the security of members of their community. There is also substantial evidence of arbitrary detentions and the usage of antiterrorist courts to further victimize the Ahmadiyas. In a number of instances physical attacks have led to the destruction or desecration of Ahmadiya places of worship. There are further reports of several Ahmadiya mosques having been sealed up. At the same time, fundamentalist Muslims threaten to carry out further destruction of mosques, which represent building structures similar to traditional Islamic mosques with minarets and *gumbads*. As a consequence of the prevalent approaches it is not surprising that the Ahmadiya community of Pakistan continues to suffer under the shadow of persecution, discrimination, and social and cultural exclusion. In light of the existing insensitive approach adopted by the present military government, any improvement in the position of the Ahmadiyas appears unlikely.

JAVAID REHMAN

See also **Pakistan; Punjabi**

Further Reading

Boyle, Kevin, and Juliet Sheen, editors, *Freedom of Religion and Belief: A World Report*, London: Routledge, 1997

International Commission of Jurists, *Pakistan: Human Rights After the Martial Law Report of a Mission*, Geneva, 1987

Rehman, Javaid, *The Weakness in the International Protection of Minority Rights,* The Hague: Kluwer Law International, 2000

Rehman, Javaid, "Accommodating Religious Identities in an Islamic State: International Law, Freedom of Religion and the Rights of Religious Minorities," *International Journal on Minority and Group Rights*, 7, no. 2, 2000

Kennedy, Charles H., "Towards the Definition of a Muslim in an Islamic State: The Case of Ahmadiya in Pakistan," in *Religious and Ethnic Minority Politics in South Asia*, edited by Dhirendra Vajpeyi and Yogendra Malik, Glendale: Riverdale Company Publishers, 1989

Ainu

Capsule Summary

Location: Mainly Hokkaido, the northernmost island of Japan
Total Population: 23,767 within the territory of Hokkaido (1999)
Language: Ainu
Religion: Indigenous beliefs

The Ainu are an integrated group of people who now reside mainly on Hokkaido, the northernmost island of Japan. The area of their residence once included the northeast region (Tohoku) of Japan's mainland (Honshu), southern Sakhalin, and the Kurile Islands. It is not clear when the Ainu started living in those areas, and scholars are largely divided into three groups regarding the date of the people's first existence as 10,000 years ago, 5,000 years ago, and 100 years ago. The number of the population has drastically decreased, especially in recent centuries, due to numerous wars with the Japanese, several kinds of diseases, illnesses, and malnutrition, among others. Today, approximately 24,000 Ainu live on Hokkaido alone. Although the Ainu and their culture were considered barbaric and primitive by the Japanese throughout most of history, the newer generations have awakened to their valuable heritage in the past few decades and have fought against social and cultural discrimination in the Japanese-dominated society. The Ainu themselves and the Japanese population have reevaluated Ainu cultural and social traditions and human rights as a minority population since the late 1980s, a decade that marked a revival of mounting interest in the Ainu tradition.

History

Because the Ainu possess no written forms of language, very little is known about their history. However, anthropologists generally consider the Ainu as people described as the *Emishi* or *Ezo* in ancient

Japanese documents such as *the Chronicles of Japan (Nihon Shoki)* and *the Ancient Chronicle (Kojiki)*, although this connection to the Ainu's identity is more of an assumption. It is believed that the Ainu lived in larger parts of northeast Japan including the Tohoku region and Hokkaido from at least the Nara period (710–794) to the Edo period (1600–1868). Ainu also once inhabited the southern Kurile Islands and southern Kamchatka, and a few hundred with Ainu origin are considered to reside in southern Sakhalin even today. In 1884, the Japanese government removed about 100 inhabitants from the northern Kuriles, and at the end of World War II, more Ainu in the southern Kuriles and Sakhalin were taken to Hokkaido when the Japanese evacuated. Documentation records indicate that the last of the Kurile Ainu died in 1941. Today, many Ainu places in northern parts of Japan continue to be a reminder of their ancestors' presence in the past.

The Japanese began recording the life of the Ainu comprehensively during the Edo period. Hokkaido used to be called *Ezo-chi,* or the land of the Ezo, and was put under political supervision of the Japanese *Matsumae-han* (or the Matsumae-clan or -local government). The Ainu and the Japanese of that period shared a trade relationship that ended with the exploitation of wealth and economic independence of the former group. In 1799, the central Edo government incorporated the territory of east Hokkaido under its own ruling because of the economic inequality and security concerns over cases of foreign ships that had more and more frequently appeared near the island. In 1807, the central government additionally absorbed the west side of the territory and launched the first attempt at the assimilation of the Ainu', which was rather more to alleviate the widespread economic gap than to eliminate the Ainu culture. However, the entire land was returned to the Matsumae-han in 1821 with no significant progress. Finally, in 1854, the Edo government once again included Hokkaido within its political sphere. Although it sought further Japanization of the Ainu, including Japanese language education and providence of financial assistance for them, the Edo period ended before producing much achievement.

Three main wars between the Ainu and the Japanese are recorded (1457, 1669, and 1789), although there were 24 other conflicts over this 332-year period. The significance of these battles is that through each event, the Ainu continuingly increased a degree of distrust and suspicion toward the Japanese. In some cases, their fighting ended with massive betrayal by the Japanese side, while in other cases, Japanese victory over the Ainu simply resulted in the death penalty for the leaders and escalated cruel treatment of the Ainu in many aspects of social life.

In 1878, the Ainu were officially categorized as *Kyudo-jin*, former indigenous people, under the Meiji government in Japan. Ainu received this historical move with some humiliation due to the degradation of the people and it accelerated the growing sense of their group identity over decades.

Ethnicity and Society

The Ainu are often cited for their distinguishing physical characteristics that draw a clear line between them and other Mongoloid populations in the neighboring areas. Probably most frequently noted is their body and facial hirsuteness. Some males tend to have abundant hair on the shoulders and back in addition to a fully-grown beard covering a large part of the face. Such abundance, and also waviness, of hair are not at all common among other peoples in the region who are anthropologically described with a lack of or little body hair. Further, the tendency for long-headedness, a deeply depressed nose root, projecting cheekbones, and a broad and heavy lower jaw has been observed.

The Ainu traditional way of living was based on hunting, fishing, and plant-gathering. Naturally, animal and plant products surrounded their living environment. Women wove a coat-like garment called *attush* for men with shredded and softened elm barks and a winter jacket with deerskin. Female Ainu typically wore dyed cotton clothes with colorful accessories. Both males and females would wear shoes and sandals called *keri,* made with salmon skin, deer hide, willow twigs, grape vines, and walnut bark.

Archaeologists believe that the Ainu culture was fully established in the twelfth to thirteenth centuries, when advanced trading with the mainland (Honshu) progressively flourished. The Ainu culture is fused with the influences of the Okhotsk culture brought in from the north and the prehistoric Japanese culture in the south. For example, the Ainu continue to embrace customs and rituals using bears that are common to the Okhotsk culture and share the same types of iron pots and housing models as in the ancient forms of Japanese culture. One of the most remarkable customs unique to the Ainu culture may be tattooing around the mouth of young women. This tattoo was first applied at the onset of puberty and completed at the time of marriage indicating physical and mental maturity as adults.

Among the Ainu's local crafts evolving from long-sustained traditions, some of the most valued include carving, weaving, and indigo dyeing with unique designs of prehistoric prototypes. Although paintings by Japanese artists depicting Ainu culture can be seen in museums, anthropologists confirm that the Ainu culture did not practice painting or drawing as a form of self-representation.

Despite their centuries-long, turbulent history of interaction with the Japanese, Ainu were able to maintain their lifestyle and culture until 1869, a year after the Meiji Restoration, when the new government forcibly introduced Japanese language, names, housing, clothing, food, and other aspects of life on the Ainu population. The Restoration also prohibited the use of Ainu language, tattooing among the female Ainu, earrings for the males, traditional methods of hunting such as with poisoned arrows, and deer hunting without official certificates.

The term "*Ainu*," in their own language, signifies "men" or "people," referring to the group as a whole. Because the Japanese attached such negative connotations to Ainu as a name or group designation in the past, Ainu began utilizing another group name or term, "*Utari*," which means "friends." In time, however, the Ainu name regained importance as cultural identity and awareness among the group advanced, and as Japanese understanding of the Ainu grew.

Since 1972, the government of Hokkaido has conducted five separate research studies on the Ainu population in the region. According to the most recent survey taken in 1999, the total population of the Ainu residing in Hokkaido was 23,767. Approximately 29.5 percent of the workforce is engaged in agriculture and fisheries, and others are employed in smaller businesses. About 30 percent of the population considered their living "difficult" and the number of people who receive financial assistance from the government is about twice that of the average of the entire population in Hokkaido. In addition to this awkward professional and economic situation, education level also indicates that social barriers between the Ainu and the Japanese remain in some form. While 97 percent of Hokkaido residents went to high school in 1999, the rate for the Ainu was 95.2 percent. As for the university entrance rates, the number for the former is 34.5 percent, while the latter remained as low as 16.1 percent.

In 1974, the Hokkaido government established the Utari Welfare Program in cooperation with the national government. This program has emphasized the Ainu's cultural promotion, a spread of understanding among the Japanese, educational advancement, and living stability and economic improvement.

In 1996, an Ainu study group sponsored by the Japanese government published a report on collected facts about the Ainu people, culture, society, and impacts of Japan's historical changes on the population. The group noted that Japanese modernization has destroyed the Ainu's social system and cultural values, especially under the Meiji government, and that the people have continually faced discrimination and poverty, until recent decades. The group also reported that the Utari Welfare Program in Hokkaido was insufficient, at least at that point, in eliminating social and economic gaps between the Ainu and the Japanese, and in further promoting the Ainu culture, although it did acknowledge that their living environment had steadily improved.

In 1997, the Japanese government established a new Law on the Promotion of Ainu Culture and Tradition and the Proliferation of Knowledge. Under this law, the Ainu received recognition as the nation's longest existing ethnic group for the first time in Japan's legal history. The law obliged the national government to protect the rights and social and economic stability among the Ainu population. It also abolished two major Kyodo-jin Protection Laws, which had shackled the Ainu with a range of social and cultural prejudices for many years. This law also led to establishment of the Ainu monetary foundation, national research institute, and policy discussion group, thus guaranteeing the continuing effort to enhance cultural, social, and economic life of the Ainu population. This historic achievement represented growing understanding of the Ainu people and their traditions, as well as struggles since the early 1980s under the leadership of the Hokkaido Utai Association that represented the interests of the Ainu.

Moreover, the Ainu, among others, have benefited from the recent international initiatives of the United Nations and numerous nongovernmental organizations (NGOs) toward wider recognition and more thorough protection of human rights among minority populations worldwide.

Ai Hattori

See also **Japan**

Further Reading

Siddle, Richard, *Race, Resistance and the Ainu of Japan*, New York: Routledge, 1996

De Vos, George A., and William O. Wetherall, *Japan's Minorities: Burakumin, Koreans, Ainu and Okinawans*, London: Minority Rights Group, 1983

Johnson, D.W., *The Ainu of Northeast Asia: A General History*, Idzat International, 1999

Fitzhugh, William W., and Chisato O. Dubreuil, editors, *Ainu: Spirit of a Northern People*, St. Louis: University of Washington Press, 2000

Kayano, Shigeru, *Our Land Was a Forest: An Ainu Memoir*, Boulder, Colorado: Westview Press, 1994

Alawis

Capsule Summary

Location: Northern mountain regions in Syria, northern Lebanon, and southeastern Turkey
Total Population: Around 2.2 million people, of whom 1.6 million live in Syria
Language: Arabic
Religion: Muslim

Alawis are a heterodox Islamic sect and most of the 2.2 million adherents live in Syria, with a smaller number living in northern Lebanon and southeastern Turkey. They constitute around 12 percent of Syria's population and nearly three-fourths of them live in the northwestern Alawi mountains also known as Jabal al-Nasayriyya in the Latakia province.

Little is known about the origin of the community. Some believe Alawis to be the remnants of an ancient Canaanite people who survived in the isolated Syrian mountainous region. Others see them as descendants of people who inhabited the isolated region at the time of Alexander the Great (356–323 BCE). In addition to retaining some ancient Syrian pagan customs, they were influenced by Christianity and Islam. In the Middle Ages they were believed to have adopted the Arabic language and the *Isma'iliyya* sect of Islam. Subsequently Alawis broke off and became a separate sect whose beliefs mostly remained secret, known only to an esoteric circle of the initiate.

Until the French Mandate (1920–1946) Alawis were called Nusayris, after a ninth century theologian named Muhammad ibn Nusayr, a Persian Shi'a leader who proclaimed himself to be *bab* (gate) to the eleventh Shi'a Imam, whom Twelver Shi'as believed had practiced occultism. The sect was brought to northern Syria in the ninth century and later moved to the Latakia mountain range.

An offshoot of the Twelver Shi'a, they believe that Imam Ali—the Prophet's cousin, son-in-law, and the fourth Caliph—was the sole legitimate heir who was deprived of his divine right to inherit the Prophet's position. They portray Ali as bearer of divine essence and hold him in higher esteem than any other prophets mentioned in the Qur'an. The seven pillars of Alawis include the five pillars of the Sunni sect, *jihad* (holy war), and *waliya* (devotion to the Imam Ali family and hatred of his enemies). Although Alawis claim to possess secret knowledge of religion not revealed to others, they do not observe some important Islamic duties such as prayers in mosques, Ramadan fasting, or performing *Hajj* (pilgrimage to Mecca).

Alawis adhere to certain non-Islamic rituals derived from Christianity and Zoroastrianism, and such un-Islamic practices generate resentment and condemnation from the Sunni Muslims. Sheikh al-Islam ibn Taymiyya (1263–1328), an orthodox Sunni Syrian theologian, described Alawis as more dangerous than Christians and called for *jihad* against them.

For centuries, the Alawis struggled to stay afloat in a predominantly Sunni area and their limited internal autonomy under the Ottomans ended in the mid-nineteenth century. Until the twentieth century, the Alawis remained a socially backward, economically deprived, and geographically isolated sect. Sunni Muslims often dismissed them as heretical and anti-Islamic.

Their fortune saw an upward swing with the arrival of the French, who underscored a political separation between the Alawis and Syrians. First the French created an Autonomous District of the Alawis in the Alawi region of the Syrian coast, later renamed the Territory of Alawis (*Territoire des Alaouites*). This arrangement proved temporary, as, owing to the resentment from the Sunni majority, the French eventually incorporated the Alawite entity with the rest of Syria.

The French established religious courts, which institutionalized the Alawis as a branch of Shi'ism and allowed them communal representation in parliament. The emergence of an Alawi entity and separatism were seen as a means of suppressing a national independence movement. For the same reasons, Alawis were recruited in large numbers into the military. The departure of the French in 1946 ended the Alawi autonomy. The Sunni elite who inherited the government swiftly withdrew privileges enjoyed by the community.

The Alawis lack cohesion, and in Syria they comprise four tribes, namely the Kalbiyya, Khayatin, Haddadin, and Matavira. Furthermore, unlike other religious minorities of the Middle East, the Alawis did not forge any special relationship with a Western power. The French interest and involvement in Alawis was primarily motivated to contain nationalist opposition from the Sunni Arabs in Syria.

The Syrian Baa'th party proved attractive for the Alawis, especially for its socialism and secularism; whereas the former offered economic opportunities for poor and rural Alawis, the latter meant lesser prejudicial treatment from the Sunni majority. Consequently, Alawis joined the Baa'th party as well as the military in large numbers and both became the prime instruments of their social mobility. The five-member Military Committee, which brought about the Baa'th revolution on March 8, 1963, comprised only minorities—three Alawis and two Isma'ilis.

In the eyes of the Sunnis, the Alawis broke away from Shi'as nearly a millennium ago and have remained non-Muslim, heretical, and idolatrous. Some Muslims consider Alawis marginal, on the fringes, or even outside of Islam, but in Syria they are recognized, for purposes of personal status jurisdiction, as Shi'a Muslims. This recognition becomes important, as the 1971 Constitution stipulates that the head of state must be a Muslim. In 1974, Imam Musa al-Sadr, an eminent Lebanon-based Twelver Shia theologian, ruled that Alawis of Lebanon (and by extension Syrian Alawis) are a part of the Shi'a school of Islam.

The real transformation of Alawis was marked by the ascendance of Hafiz al-Assad as the first Alawi head of state in 1971. Since then Alawis have consolidated political, economic, and social fortunes. The military-security apparatus, intelligence establishment, special forces, and major combat units have been dominated by the Alawis. Most of the command positions in the elite units of the Syrian army and the supervision of most organs of the state security rest in the hands of the Alawis. They head three out of the four internal security agencies. The co-option of Druze, Ismailis, and rural Sunnis has significantly contributed to the consolidation of the Alawi rule in Syria The smooth transition of power following the death of President Assad in 2000 by his son Bashar was facilitated by the strong support of this coalition.

P.R. Kumaraswamy

See also **Druze, Ismailis, Syria, Zoroastrians**

Further Reading

Eisenstadt, Michael, "Bashar and the Alawite 'Barons'," *Jane's Intelligence Review*, 12, no.8, (August 2000)

Faksh, Mahmud A., "The Alawi Community of Syria: A New Dominant Political Force", *Middle Eastern Studies*, 20, no.2, (April 1984)

Pipes, Daniel, "The Alawi Capture of Power in Syria", *Middle Eastern Studies*, 25, no.4, (October 1989)

Rabinovich, Itamar, "The Compact Minorities of the Syrian state, 1918–45", *Journal of Contemporary History*, 14, no.4, (October 1979)

Yaffe, Gitta, "Suleiman al-Murshid: Beginning of the Alawi leader", *Middle Eastern Studies*, 29, no.4, (October 1993)

Zisser, Eyal, "The Alawis, Lords of Syria: From Ethnic Minority to Ruling Sect", in *Minorities and the State in the Arab World*, edited by Orfa Bengio and Gabriel Ben-Dor, Boulder, Colorado: Lynne Rienner, 1999

Albania

Capsule Summary

Location: southeastern Europe, the Balkans
Total Population: 3,582,205 (July 2003)
Languages: Albanian (Tosk, official dialect), Greek
Religions: Muslim (Sunni, Bektashi), 70 percent; Albanian Orthodox 20 percent; Roman Catholic 10 percent

Albania is a parliamentary republic located in southeastern Europe, bordering the Adriatic Sea and Ionian Sea, between Greece and Serbia and Montenegro. The county gained independence on November 28, 1912 from the Ottoman Empire. It has an area of 28,748 square kilometers and a population of over 3.5 million. Albania's GNP per capita income was $4,400 in 2002. The Albanian language is a separate branch within the larger Indo-European family tree. Albanians are believed to be descendants of the ancient Illyrian-Epirotic tribes, a dichotomy perhaps with roots of the present-day anthropological division into Gegs in the north of the country (Gegëria) and Tosks in the south (Toskënia). Both groups share common ethnical, anthropological, cultural, and customary roots, their differences consisting mainly of dialectal and lifestyle variations.

Albanians represent at least 96 percent of the population of the country. The rest comprise ethnic minority groups, such as the Greek (2 percent), Aromanians or Vlachs (0.6 percent), Roma (0.6 percent), and Southern Slavs (0.6 percent). Albanian is the official language of the country, whereas ethnic minorities speak their own languages. Albanians belong principally to the Sunni, Bektashi, Christian Orthodox, and Catholic religions. Approximately two-thirds of the population is Sunni and Bektashi, and the remaining one-third consists of Christian-Orthodox and Catholic Albanians. The Bektashi religion, a rather liberal and tolerant expression of Islam, predominates in the south of the country. The Sunnis are instead mainly concentrated in the center and partially in the north. Christian-Orthodox Albanians are found in both central and southern Albania, whereas the Catholics live primarily in the north. All mosques and churches were closed in 1967 and religious observances prohibited; in November 1990, Albania began allowing private religious practice.

Albania's current territory coincides with the ancient Southern Illyria and Epirus. The Illyrian-Epirote tribes reached a relatively significant degree of self-rule and civilization, evidenced by a number of archeological findings and present-day vestiges of their unwritten laws. In 168 BCE the Roman army overran their territory and, with time, it became a part of the Roman Empire. The presence of the Roman army and the settlement of Roman colons in Southern Illyria and Epirus eventually created a new Latin component of the population, which may have probably survived to become the present Vlach ethnic group. In 395 CE the country ended up divided along with the Roman Empire itself, although it mostly remained under Byzantium until the Ottoman Turks dominated it. On the other hand, beginning from the sixth century CE, Slav tribes invaded the Balkan Peninsula in significant numbers, thus substantially altering its ethnic composition. The state of Arbëri—the first Albanian state of the Middle Ages—was founded in 1190 and represents the earliest Albanian political entity in which the separate ethnic, linguistic, and customary identity of its people prevailed upon any religious identity or affiliation.

The country changed hands several times between Byzantium and Slavic or Norman conquerors, until it progressively fell under Ottoman Rule after the Battle of Kosovo in 1389. A local prince, Gjergj Kastrioti, also known as Skanderbeg, led the Albanians—between 1444 and 1468—through a successful resistance war against the Ottoman Empire. The impressive series of victorious battles against the otherwise invincible Ottoman armies further reinforced the collective identity of the Albanians, although after Skanderbeg's death the resistance quickly faded.

During the five centuries of Ottoman rule, many Albanians migrated to other countries in Europe. A percentage of those remaining converted from Christianity to Islam, whereas other Christian Albanians became subject to the *millet* system, a religion-based institution that provided a certain degree of self-rule to the non-Muslim subjects of the Ottoman Empire. As a result, the Christian-Orthodox population of

Albania came under the authority of the Greek Orthodox Patriarchate in Istanbul and was compelled to perform religious functions and pursue education solely in the Greek language. In addition, it was around this period that Greek serfs started settling in the farms of Albanian landlords in the present southern Albania, mostly because of a shortage of manpower due to the Ottoman military campaigns.

From its independence in 1912 until 1920, Albania emerged as the stage of a variety of foreign interventions, which led to enormous destruction, loss of life, and other tragic incidents. In December 1920 Albania became a member of the League of the Nations and on October 2, 1921 submitted its Declaration on Minorities, modeled after the Minority Treaties of the League of Nations itself.

At the end of World War II, a Communist government was established under Enver Hoxha in 1946. Communist rule lasted for almost 45 years, during which period the ethnic minorities were treated no differently from the rest of the population, because the Communist persecution and discrimination were solely aimed against "the class enemy" in general, regardless of the ethnic identity. Communist rule ended in 1990 with the establishment of a multiparty system and elections in 1992.

Albania is probably the most homogeneous country in Southeastern Europe. Nevertheless, it has historically been careful to guarantee the protection of the rights of its own minorities; one explanation for this apparent paradox is the presence of significant ethnic-Albanian minorities outside of the borders of the Republic of Albania (i.e., in the Kosovo region of Serbia and Montenegro, in the former Yugoslavia, in the Republic of Macedonia, and in Greece). Some outside ethnic Albanian groups voice union with Albania.

The Greek minority constitutes the largest and the most visible ethnic minority group, with a total number of 70,000 to 80,000, mainly located in about 98 villages in the valleys of Dropulli and Pogoni in the district of Gjirokastër (33 villages), in Delvinë (22 villages), and in Vurgu (44 villages) in the Sarandë area. The Greek minority has maintained its own ethnic, linguistic, religious identity, and tradition, and is relatively integrated into Albanian society.

The Vlachs, numbering at least 10,000, reside in southern and central Albania. Vlachs, who belong to the Christian Orthodox religion, have traditionally lived alongside the Albanian people in several urban and rural areas, including Tirana and Durrës. A major center of the symbiotic Vlach-Albanian culture was the town of Voskopoja in southeastern Albania, which during the eighteenth century boasted a renowned academy, a printing house, and several important religious and artistic monuments. Other groups of Vlachs once lived a nomadic life centered on livestock, but they eventually settled in villages, especially after the social-economical changes in the Albanian countryside brought about by the communist reforms. The Vlach language, Aromanian, is relatively close to present-day Romanian.

Macedonians or Bulgarians are a minority of about 5,000 located primarily in about nine villages alongside the Macedonian-Albanian border in proximity to the Prespa Lakes. They identify themselves as Macedonians.

The Montenegrin minority consists of about 4,000 people. One subgroup of Christian-Orthodox faith once lived in the area of Vrakë of the district of Shkodër in the north, until a large group thereof emigrated in early 1990 to the then-Yugoslav Federation, although about 600 later returned. There are claims of a second subgroup of the Islamic religion, the *Podgoriçans* (originating from Podgorica in Montenegro), whose (either Albanian or Montenegrin) ethnic origin is uncertain. They live mainly in the city of Shkodër and a few adjoining villages.

Other small Southern Slav communities in Albania consist of a few thousand Bosniaks in the Durrës district, Gorans in the Kukës district, and Gollobordans in the Peshkopi district. They belong to the Sunni religion and are relatively assimilated into the surrounding Albanian population.

The Roma and Gypsies are peoples of Asiatic origin who moved to central and southern Albania during the Ottoman Empire. Their claimed number ranges from 20,000 to 30,000 people. The Roma of Albania consists of four principal tribes: Kallbuxhile, Mokçarët, Kartofët, and Cerqarët.

Another important historical minority in Albania used to be the Jews. Although Jewish presence in the area has never been substantial, there are indications that they have arrived in the country since antiquity, and successively during the Middle Ages and World War II. Major Jewish settlements in Albania were the towns of Vlorë and Delvinë, in the southwestern part of the country. The hospitality and protection offered to the Jews by Albania during World War II has been exemplary and almost unique in Europe. As a result, the number of Jews in Albania after World War II was larger than at it was at its beginning, due to the arrival of persecuted Jews from neighboring countries. Repatriation efforts by the government of Israel in the early 1990s led to few Jews remaining in Albania at present. Finally, the Çams constitute a nonlinguistic and atypical minority, which in Albania numbers about 150,000 people, mostly of Muslim religion or affiliation. Originating from the region of Çamëria, in present northwestern Greece, they are nevertheless Albanians as far as ethnic origin, customs, and language are concerned. Formally recognized as an Albanian minority in Greece, Çams were excluded from the Lausanne Convention on the Obligatory Exchange of Population between Greece and Turkey in 1923. In 1944, tens of thousands of Çams of Muslim faith were forcibly displaced from their ancestral homes in Greece. At present they have found temporary shelter in Albania and are still not allowed to return to Greece.

Albania has ratified a number of international treaties and conventions and has adopted constitutional provisions and domestic legislation to ensure full protection of minority rights in the country. Most notably, it ratified the International Covenant for Civil and Political Rights on October 4, 1991, the European Convention on Human Rights and Fundamental Freedoms on October 2, 1996, and the Council of Europe Framework Convention for the Protection of National Minorities on September 28, 1999.

Agron Alibali

See also **Albanians; Greeks; Macedonians; Montenegrins; Roma (Gypsies); Vlachs**

Further Reading

Albanian Helsinki Committee, *On the Status of Minorities in the Republic of Albania*. http://www.ihf-hr.org/albhc.htm

Bërxholli, Arqile, Kristaq Prifti, and Protopapa Sejfi, "The Greek Minority in the Albanian Republic: A Demographic Study," *Nationalities Papers*, Vol. 22, No. 2, (1994)

Swire, Joseph, *Albania: The Rise of a Kingdom*, New York: Arno Press, 1971

Tombrou, Aliki, *Albania: Travelogue No. 4*, Athens, 1996

Winifrith, T.J., *The Vlachs: The History of a Balkan People*, London: Duckworth, 1995

Report Submitted by Albania to the Council of Europe on 26 July 2001 Pursuant to Article 25, Paragraph 1, of the Framework Convention for the Protection of National Minorities, acfc/sr (2001) 5, http://www.humanrights.coe.int/Minorities/Eng/FrameworkConvention/StateReports/Toc.htm

Albanians

Capsule Summary

Location: the western Balkans in southeastern Europe
Total Population: approximately 7 million (including 1.2 million in non-Balkan diaspora)
Language: Albanian
Religions: Muslim, Orthodox Christian, Roman Catholic

The Albanians are an ethnic group of southeastern Europe who live principally on the western side of the Balkan Peninsula. There are approximately 7 million Albanians, and most live in Albania and the immediately surrounding countries, although there are also sizable Albanian diaspora communities in Italy, Turkey, and the United States. Their language, Albanian, is an Indo-European language with no other closely related language. It differs from the Slavic languages of the majority of Albanians' neighbors. Albanians also differ from their neighbors in that they are not of one religion; rather, there are Muslim, Orthodox Christian, and Roman Catholic Albanians. When the Great Powers drew the boundary lines of Albania in the second decade of the twentieth century, half the Albanians were left outside Albania in Montenegro, Serbia, Macedonia, and Greece. Albanians thus became minorities in these surrounding lands, most of which were part of the former Yugoslavia. Through the 1990s, Serbia ruled the Albanians in the region of Kosovo with increasing harshness and police pressure. Fighting broke out in 1998, followed by mass expulsions of Albanians by Serb military in the spring of 1999. NATO intervened and bombed Serbia. When an agreement was signed, most of the Kosovar Albanian refugees returned to Kosovo. With NATO and UN forces occupying Kosovo, the Albanians seek independence while Serbia continues to claim sovereignty. In 2001, neighboring Macedonia also became a place of increased tension as minority Albanians contested more overtly their limited participation in many areas of national life.

History

From a regional perspective, Albanians are far fewer in number than their Slavic neighbors who have coveted lands populated by Albanians, particularly the mineral-rich hinterland of Kosovo and the coastlands on the Adriatic Sea. Albanians' regional status as a minority has been further reinforced by the early twentieth century division of Albanian-populated lands among five countries: Montenegro, Serbia, Macedonia, Greece, and Albania. Albanians have also never had a consistent Great Power sponsor. The Greeks have been supported by Great Britain, the Montenegrins, Serbs, and Bulgarians by the Russians (who are all Orthodox Slavs), and the Serbs also by France. As a people of mixed religion, a majority of whom are Muslim, Albanians have not had the ongoing support of any European nation. What Albanians have had, as minorities in Serbia and Macedonia, is a much higher birthrate than the people who rule them, as well as the growing political will to have more say in how they are governed.

Albanians are among the oldest peoples in southeastern Europe. They trace their ancestry to the ancient Illyrians who are attested to in the western Balkans from the seventh century BCE and during the time of the ancient Greeks. The Romans eventually conquered the Illyrians. The Albanian language shows clear evidence of Latin influence. As the Roman Empire declined, the Byzantine Empire took over the region. Then, in the sixth and seventh centuries, Slavic peoples from the east entered the Balkans in great numbers. They also came under Byzantine rule. The religious history of the Albanians reflects their geographic position between Rome on the west, and Constantinople, later known as Istanbul, on the east. There was a famous trade route between Rome and Constantinople, the Via Ignatia, which went through the middle of what is now Albania. With the division of the Christian Church in the eleventh century, the Albanians (now known by this name), who had been nominally Christianized beginning in the first century, became Roman Catholic to the north of the trade route and Eastern Orthodox to the south of it.

When the Ottoman armies expanded into the Balkans in the fourteenth century, many Albanians fought with their Slav neighbors against the Ottomans. Indeed, in 1389, at the Battle of Kosovo that is seen as marking the beginning of 500 years of Ottoman rule in the Balkans, the Serbian King Lazar had Bosnian, Hungarian, and Albanian battalions on his side fighting the Ottomans. The Albanians continued fighting against the Ottoman armies in the fifteenth century under their leader, Gjergji Kastrioti (1405–1468), also known as Skanderbeg, who became an Albanian national hero. Skanderbeg united the Albanian clans and held off the Ottoman armies for 25 years, but eventually lost to them in 1466.

At this time many families of Albanian notables who had fought with Skanderbeg left Albanian lands for Italy. The King of Naples, whom Skanderbeg had supported, allowed them to settle in seven regions in southern Italy (Campania, Apulia, Molise, Abruzzi, Basilatica, Calabria, and Sicily). These largely Orthodox Christian Albanians became known as the *Arbëresh*, and particularly in Calabria and Sicily maintained their language and many of their traditions to the present. In 1981 there were estimated to be 200,000 Arbëresh in Italy. However, the language is declining in usage as many young people have left southern Italy for work in northern cities. Further, the Arbëresh villages and towns are spread out and there has not been official support of education in Albanian. Italy has thus had an Albanian diaspora community for over five hundred years.

At the same time that Albanian families left for Italy, other Orthodox Christian Albanians fled the Ottomans by moving south to Greece. There they settled in Attica, Boeotia, southern Euboea, and Hydra. They were known as *Arvanitis* and maintained their language until the mid-twentieth century when the government policies of hellenization, as reinforced by public education and insistence that to be Orthodox was to be Greek, mitigated against the continued use of their language, except among the elderly. It is not known how many Arvanidis live in Greece today.

Gradually, during the 500 years of Ottoman rule, many Albanians converted to Islam, particularly from the central regions of what became Albania and

Macedonia, and to the north in Kosovo. As Muslims, people paid lower taxes, they were allowed to carry arms, and they were eligible for employment in the Ottoman administration. Albanians rose to high positions in the Empire including that of grand vizier. They were recognized as excellent soldiers, so much so that the entire palace guard of the last Ottoman sultan was made up of Albanians. Still, not all converted to Islam. By the last Ottoman census in 1910, Albanians were 70 percent Muslim, 20 percent Orthodox Christian, and 10 percent Roman Catholic. It should be noted, however, that Albanians' sense of ethnic identity has frequently overridden religious division.

With the decline of the Ottoman Empire and the growth of Balkan nationalisms in the nineteenth century, the Albanians were the last to free themselves from the Ottomans. The Ottoman state saw the largely Muslim Albanians as their own, yet was unable to defend them from Serbian forces that pushed them out of towns and villages north of Kosovo in the 187'0s. The Ottomans were also unable to protect northern Albanians from having their lands taken by Montenegro; indeed, through Great Power machinations the Ottomans supported the allotting of the northern Albanian port city of Ulqin to Montenegro. In 1878 when Muslim and Christian Albanians came together in the League of Prizren to fight against expropriation of Albanian lands by Slavic states, the Ottomans fought the League. The Ottomans also worked against the education of Albanians in their own language and made writing in Albanian illegal. Further, the very organization of the Ottoman Empire according to the *millet* system that allowed local self-governance on the basis of religion worked against Albanian unity, for it divided them in different millets according to their faith. Geographically the Ottomans divided Albanian lands into four different *vilayets,* or provinces (Janina, Shkodër, Monastir, and Kosovo). The purpose of this was to counter the growing desire of Albanians in the nineteenth century for administrative unity.

Many Albanians emigrated in the last half of the nineteenth century in search of economic security. Muslim Albanians sought work in Istanbul and in Egypt where Mehmet Ali and the following dynasty through King Farouk were of Albanian descent. There remained an Albanian community in Egypt until the time of Nasser in the 1950's. Orthodox Christian Albanians sought work in Europe and the United States. Boston became the center of the Albanian Orthodox in America and remains so to this day. Both groups also traveled to Romania and Bulgaria for work. A small colony remains in Romania.

During the Balkan Wars in 1912 and 1913, the newly independent Balkan nations fought for territory while the Young Turk regime of the Ottomans pursued centralizing policies, and Montenegrins, Serbs, and Greeks all invaded Albanian lands. Albanians were finally moved to declare their own independence from the Ottomans in 1912. The Conference of Ambassadors in London sought to determine boundaries for Albania in late 1912 and 1913, but before their decision was final, World War I began. During the period from 1910 to 1921 there was ongoing warfare in the Balkans and ongoing plans to divide Albanian lands: among Greeks and Serbs, among Italians and Greeks, among Austrians and Italians, among Serbs and Bulgarians. Serbia took over Kosovo–it had been part of the Serbian kingdom in the fourteenth century and Orthodox churches and monasteries remained from that time. Serbia's armies also attempted to secure the coastline in northern Albania for access to the Adriatic. Austria and Italy both opposed this move.

After World War I ended, Greece was persuaded to withdraw from some sections of southern Albania, known to it as the Northern Epirus, where there were and continue to be Greek villages; but it retained control over the southern Epirus where there were Albanian villages of both Muslims and Orthodox Christians. Albanians refer to this southern region as Çameri. Later, during World War II, the invading Italians persuaded some Albanians of Çameri to fight against the Greeks. In retaliation after that war, Muslim Albanian villagers were expelled as traitors en masse, whereas Orthodox Albanian villagers were Hellenized and expected to become Greek.

After World War I the Great Powers refused Serbia's claim to Adriatic coastal access, but they did allow it to retain control of Kosovo, despite the majority of people there being Albanian. The Kosovar Albanians fought this, through diplomacy, to the League of Nations and through guerilla warfare to no avail.

Albanians within Yugoslavia–Minorities in Three Republics

In 1918 the Kingdom of the Serbs, Croats, and Slovenes–the country that later become Yugoslavia–was founded. Albanians lived in compact communities in what had been taken over by this new country in three areas:

Kosovo, which was now part of Serbia and where, undoubtedly, more than the official 64 percent of the population was Albanian; along the western side of southern Serbia (what became Macedonia), including main areas of the city of Skopje; and Montenegro, by the border with Albania. In the interwar period, unlike other minorities in Yugoslavia, Albanians were not recognized as a national minority. Serbia actively repressed the Albanian language by closing down existing schools in the language and imprisoning Albanian language teachers. Through the 1920s and 1930s there were no schools permitted in Albanian and no publications printed in the language in Kosovo.

Throughout this time Serbia engaged in colonization of Kosovo with Serbs. The main purpose was to change the demography of Kosovo. In the early 1920s there were still active guerilla bands of Albanians who had not accepted Serbia's rule and who harassed the newly arrived colonists, but these bands were destroyed by the mid-1920s. Lands were confiscated from the Albanians for the Serbian colonists from the north, numbering around 70,000 and who were deeply resented by the Albanians and, to a lesser extent, by the local Serbs who were culturally closer to the Albanians. To force Albanians to leave Kosovo, there was also harassment via religion. Many mosques were turned into stables. Indeed, many Albanians did emigrate from Kosovo and southern Serbia to Turkey at this time. To further promote this, in 1938 Serbia made an agreement to pay Turkey to take 40,000 families from Kosovo, but World War II intervened and the plan was not carried out.

During World War II the situation temporarily changed. Yugoslavia fell to the Axis powers in less than two weeks. The areas with large Albanian minorities were divided among three of these powers. Bulgaria took much of what later became Macedonia as well as the southeastern part of Kosovo. Germany kept the northeastern part of Kosovo with the valuable Trepça mines. Meanwhile Italy had control of the remaining (main) part of Kosovo and the western side of what became Macedonia. Italy had also taken over Albania itself and had even sent Italian colonists to settle there. It referred to these lands together as "Greater Albania," but in truth the Italians were in command. When Italy capitulated, Germany was in control. In the Albanian minority regions there was little resistance to the Axis powers for several reasons. First, the two main Yugoslav resistance groups, the Çetniks and the Communists, were seen as solidly Slavic and therefore not trusted by the Albanians. In addition, the Çetniks and Communists conducted most of their operations, until the very end of the war, elsewhere in Yugoslavia. Another reason there was little resistance to the Axis by the Albanians was that the Axis powers had immediately set about opening schools in Albanian in the Albanian minority regions. Further, it was during this time that many of the Serbian colonists who had come to Kosovo in the 1920s and 1930s were forced off the lands they had been allotted and expelled from Kosovo.

After World War II, the leader of the communist resistance, Marshall Tito, became head of the new Communist Yugoslavia. For the Albanian minorities there was retribution for not having supported the communist resistance and, in some cases, for having fought against it. This distrust of the Albanians of Kosovo was made worse in 1948 by Yugoslavia's break with the Soviet Union and Albania's continued pro-Soviet policy. Rankovic, the Yugoslav Minister of the Interior until 1966, was seen as strongly anti-Albanian. Albanians were harassed by the Yugoslav Secret Police (UDBA) and accused of harboring weapons and spying for Albania. Their Islamic schools, courts, and Sufi centers were closed down. Emigration of Albanian Muslims, often described as "Turks," although this referred to their Muslim religion and not their ethnicity in most cases, was highly encouraged. It is estimated that over 200,000 Albanians left Kosovo and Macedonia for Turkey in the 195'0s. This was the third wave of Kosovar Albanians to leave Kosovo and Macedonia for Turkey in the twentieth century. The first had come between 1913–1915 when Serbia took control of the region, and the second from 1919–1939. Yet a fourth wave of Albanians from Kosovo would arrive in Turkey in 1999, although most of these would return. Thus, there were four generations of ethnic Albanian immigrants to Turkey from the Balkans in the twentieth century, making Turkey a center for the Albanian diaspora.

The Albanians in Montenegro were also encouraged to leave Montenegro by multiple practices such as discrimination in employment and education. They did leave, but, as many were Roman Catholic, they went first to Italy. From refugee centers in Italy, many Albanians from Montenegro found their way to the United States where they settled largely in New York City and Detroit.

In the late 1960s, Tito initiated a policy of greater decentralization in Yugoslavia, which led to improvement in the political situation of Albanians of Kosovo. Kosovo's status as an Autonomous Province was accorded more authority at the federal level with the 1974 Constitution. What became the University of Pristina, with instruction in both Serbo-Croatian and Albanian, was authorized. Albanians began to be hired in greater numbers in the state apparatus. Indeed, the 1970's were the high point for Albanians in Yugoslavia. At this time the population of Kosovo was approximately 24 percent Serb and Montenegrin, and 72 percent Albanian.

Economic and related demographic changes were still occurring as many Serbs and some Albanians left Kosovo for wealthier parts of Yugoslavia, for western Europe as guest workers, or even for the eastern cities of the United States. At this time the differential between Albanian and Serb birthrates in Kosovo became much greater, due in part to the continued traditional rural ways of many Albanians and their eschewing of birth control for cultural and religious reasons. This demographic change would become highly politicized in the 1980's when nationalisms were enflamed.

After the death of Tito in 1980, conditions for minorities in Yugoslavia declined. The situation of the Albanians quickly worsened after protest demonstrations in Kosovo in 1981 and the subsequent strong reaction of the Yugoslav government. The demonstrations started as a protest over the poor quality of the food for students at the University of Pristina, but within several weeks grew in size and seriousness to demonstrations for Republic status for Kosovo. (The Kosovars had long noted that there were far fewer Montenegrins, 350,000 at that time, and they had their own republic, whereas there were many times more Kosovars, 1.5 million at that time, and they were just an autonomous province.) There were also reported demonstrations for the union of Kosovo with Albania, but these are contested. Some feel there were Serb agitators who fostered this, for most Albanians were aware of the miserable conditions in Hoxha's Albania. In any case, secret police from other regions of Yugoslavia put down the demonstrations by bringing in tanks, shooting demonstrators, and arresting over 2,000 Albanians. In the aftermath many Albanian professionals lost their jobs and many Albanian Party members were expelled.

The 1980's saw the worsening of economic conditions across Europe and the rise of nationalisms in Yugoslavia to the detriment of the "brotherhood and unity" that had been earlier espoused by Tito's Yugoslavia. Serbian nationalism affected the Albanian minorities the most. It drew political power from the alleged victimhood of the now minority Serbs within the largely Albanian Kosovo. Indeed, the Serbs were fewer in number in Kosovo than they had been, but the reasons for this were multiple. Slobodan Milosevic, who earlier had been a Party functionary in the banking sector with no particular interest in Kosovo, rose to power in 1987 on his well-publicized stance to protect the Serbs in Kosovo. They had become the nationalist Serbs' cause célèbre, which served at the same time to foster hatred of the non-Slavic, largely Muslim Albanians. Milosevic became head of the Serbian Communist Party and rapidly maneuvered people who supported him into leadership in Montenegro and Vojvodina. He capitalized on the six hundredth anniversary of the Battle of Kosovo, held in 1989 in Kosovo, as a personal national triumph. At the same time, he worked to take away powers granted to Kosovo in the 1974 Constitution.

Policies of Apartheid Followed by War in Kosovo

Albanians realized what was happening and there were many protests, especially by the miners of the Trepça mines, on several occasions. But Milosevic's forces prevailed and Kosovo lost its earlier autonomous region status and was subsumed directly under Serbian control from Belgrade. Other parts of Yugoslavia also recognized Milosevic's power moves and, rather than come under Serbia's sway, left Yugoslavia. Slovenia, Croatia, and Macedonia declared their independence in 1991, and Bosnian Muslims and Croats (the vote was boycotted by Bosnian Serbs) voted for independence in 1992. Milosevic's attempt to thwart Bosnia's independence led to the Bosnian war of 1992–1995 in which over 200,000 people were killed. The world's eyes were on the conflagration in Bosnia, so it did not notice what was also going on in Kosovo at that time.

Meanwhile, martial law had been declared in Kosovo in 1989 and continued up to the war in 1999. One of the first actions of Belgrade, now directly in control of Kosovo, was to fire Albanians from state-run institutions. As Yugoslavia was a socialist state, almost all institutions were state-run. Thus, in 1990 Albanians who worked for the police were fired and 2,500 Serb police from outside Kosovo were brought in. Albanians who worked for the media, the courts, and health care clinics were also fired. In 1990–1991 Albanian students were forbidden to use the same bathrooms as Serb and Montenegrin students. Albanian teachers were not paid at all during the school year. Then, in the summer of 1991, they were forced to sign a loyalty oath to the regime and were told they must teach the Serbian-language curriculum. When they refused, they were fired. In the fall, Albanian students were blocked from entering the schools. At the same time, all the 1,000 Albanian staff and 27,000 Albanian students at the University of Pristina were expelled. A form of apartheid was thereby established in Kosovo that was in many ways worse than that of South Africa where blacks had at least been allowed their own schools. As for Albanian doctors, by 1993 all of them had also been fired.

The jobs that were taken from Albanians were filled by Serbs, who by then constituted ten percent of the population of Kosovo. Compounding this, the judicial system was co-opted and there were frequent police assaults, raids on homes, arrests, and long prison sentences. The purpose of these practices was to make daily life intolerable for Albanians so they would leave Kosovo. Serbian refugees from the Bosnian conflict were brought to Kosovoo and housed in the now empty Albanian schools. They were to colonize Kosovo when the Albanians left. Indeed, life was most difficult by all accounts. It is estimated that there was an 85 percent unemployment rate among Albanians in what had already been the poorest region of former Yugoslavia. In addition, there was continued violence against the civilian Albanian population with 2,157 physical assaults by police, 3,553 raids on private dwellings, and 2,963 arbitrary arrests reported by Human Rights Watch in 1994 alone. What is remarkable is that during this time Albanians set up their own parallel institutions. When the Serbs closed down the main Albanian newspapers, new independent Albanian ones sprang up. By the spring of 1992, Albanians had set up a parallel school system whose classes met in private homes. This system operated until 1998. Classes had to move from home to home to avoid the police. To pay the teachers, Albanians in Kosovo and in the diaspora taxed themselves. The funds in the diaspora were funneled through banks in New York and Switzerland to the LDK (Democratic League of Kosovo), the main Albanian political party of Kosovo, which turned them over to the Albanian-created government for dispersal. In 1992, Albanians elected their own parliament, and Ibrahim Rugova, literary scholar and president of the Writers' Union, was elected as leader. Rugova and the party he led, the LDK, put forth a policy of nonviolence and civic mindedness. Their assumption was that when the Bosnian war ended, the world would look at their suffering and would work to help them establish their own state.

Yet when the Dayton Accords were signed in 1995, Kosovo was not mentioned. From this time on, Rugova's policy of nonviolence was seen as ineffective and armed resistance among Albanians slowly grew. Still, what became the Kosovar Liberation Army did not gain popular support until after the killing by Serb forces of 51 members of the Jashari family in Drenica in the winter of 1998. Throughout 1998, Serbian paramilitary groups operated along with Serbian police and the Yugoslav military to counter the KLA. The result was a terrorizing of the populace, largely Albanian, but also Serbian, and the destruction of Albanian homes, villages, and food sources. By September of 1998 there were an estimated 300,000 internal refugees in Kosovo. Despite the peace talks in October 1998, and the Rambouillet talks in early 1999, there was a substantial buildup of Serbian military in Kosovo.

When NATO began bombing in March 1999, Milosevic implemented *Operation Horseshoe*, designed to expel large numbers of Albanians from Kosovo. During the eleven weeks of expulsions, 500 Albanian villages were burned and an estimated 10,000 Albanians were killed. As in the Bosnian War, there was significant brutality, particularly from the Serb paramilitary forces. In Kosovo the brutality took such forms as throwing a grenade into a basement full of women and children, burning alive the old and the disabled in their homes, executing villagers, extorting from refugees, raping their daughters, shooting children, and destroying villages and neighborhoods. Individuals were indicted for war crimes in Kosovo by the Hague International Tribunal, including the Yugoslav president, Slobodan Milosevic.

Albanian Society and Emigration

Albanian society is patriarchal and traditionally patrilocal, meaning that when a man and a woman marry they tend to live with the groom's family. For most of history Albanians maintained a clan system that has survived in present times in the northern regions of Montenegro, northern Albania, and parts of Kosovo. The clans are exogamous in that people whose fathers are of the same clan are not allowed to marry. For Albanians of all regions, family ties are strong and extensive. Even in diaspora communities in the United States, many still live in extended families or at least close to other relatives. The tradition is for girls to marry at a relatively young age and children are highly valued.

In Albanian society, guests are treated with great respect. People are rightly proud of their hospitality. This was well demonstrated when over half the Kosovar refugees in both Albania and Macedonia were taken in by local Albanians who received none of the international aid sent to support the refugees. The traditional oral law of Albanians, known as the *Kanun of Lek Dukagjin*, has specific and age-old sections on treatment of guests.

The Kanun also attempts to regulate the old tradition of blood feud, known in Albanian as *hakmarrja,* or "taking what is due." Interestingly, during the forced Serbization of Kosovo in the early 1990s, Albanians worked to reduce the violence among each other and there were mass reconciliations in open-air ceremonies of 2,000 families who had previously feuded with one another.

Albanians have a rich tradition of music, dance, and song, and they value their language very much. As with many immigrants, their culture becomes even more precious far from home. Like the Scots (and there are many similarities with the Scots), Albanians have long had to emigrate to survive. The largest diaspora communities are in Italy, Greece, Turkey, and the United States. With the fall the communist regime of Ramiz Alia in Albania in 1991, many Albanians from Albania traveled to Greece or to Italy in search of work. The new immigrants do not necessarily have much in common with the much older Albanian communities. In the United States, where there are an estimated 500,000 people of Albanian descent, most Albanians live in the New York City area, especially in the northern Bronx, as well as in Detroit, Chicago, and Boston.

Unresolved Tensions in Serbia, Macedonia, and Montenegro

When the Military Technical Agreement was signed by NATO and Serbia on June 10, 1999, the fighting in Kosovo ceased and within two months most of the 800,000 Albanian Kosovar refugees had returned to Kosovo. Kosovar Serbs had also left to avoid the fighting. Not of all of them have since returned and there have been actions against Serbs in Kosovo since the end of the fighting, like the blowing up of a bus containing Serbs returning from Serbia. In the last days of the fighting, Albanian intelligentsia were rounded up and, with other Albanian prisoners, about 4,000 were taken to prisons in Inner Serbia, that is, north of Kosovo. The Military Technical Agreement neglected to mention prisoners. With pressure, most of the prisoners were released within two years, but 400 Albanian Kosovars remained in Serbian prisons as of 2001.

The Agreement also left Kosovo nominally under Serb control, but in fact NATO and UN forces occupied and ruled Kosovo from the end of the fighting. Serbs from different parts of Kosovo congregated in Mitrovica and to the north of it by the Serbian border and refused to let Albanians back into their homes in this area. This district has special import because the Trepça mines, the richest mineral wealth in southeast Europe, are here. Municipal elections were held in the fall of 2000 and Rugova's LDK Party won over the coalition of former leaders from the Kosovo Liberation Army. Albanians look forward to the holding of province-wide elections so that there will be more elected rule in the land. Serbs look forward to Serbia retaining more direct control and the return of more Serbs who left before the fighting. As in the decades of the 1980s and 1990s, there is little communication or mixing between the groups.

In neighboring Macedonia, the situation of the Albanian minority has received less attention than that of the more numerous Kosovars. Yet in terms of percentage of the population of Macedonia, the Albanians there are certainly significant and their situation is precarious. The actual percentage, however, is disputed. The Slavic Macedonians claim that the Albanians make up 24 percent of the population, while the Albanians claim it is closer to 40 percent. The Albanians boycotted the recent censuses of 1991 and 1994 and the results disputed.

Since the founding of the Republic of Macedonia within Yugoslavia after World War II, there has been discrimination against the largely Muslim Albanians in education, government positions, and human rights. The high birthrate of the Albanians, at close to three times the Slavic average, is troublesome for the Slavic Macedonians.

In language issues, Macedonia has at times forced Albanians to slavicize their names, has limited Albanian classes and secondary schools, and has eliminated teacher training schools for Albanian teachers. One continuing issue is the status of the University of Tetovo, established by Albanians in 1994 to provide post-secondary educational opportunities. In 2000 the Macedonian government acknowledged that it would support some post-secondary institutes in Tetovo, but not the university as founded by the Albanians.

Equally important is the lack of representation by Albanians in decision-making positions. In 1994 there were no courts with Albanian chairs, no ethnic Albanians in the Macedonian army's General Staff, and no Albanians in the Ministry of Interior or Foreign Affairs. There were very few police who were Albanian and fewer customs officers. Only 4 percent of the state sector was Albanian, and this was mostly schoolteachers and laborers, not decision-makers. In contrast, reportedly 80 percent of prisoners in Macedonian jails at that time were Albanian.

If Albanians do not get more representation, it is clear that the situation could lead to violence. One fear of Slavic Macedonians is that if the Albanians who live in the western side of the country were to secede, then Bulgaria might take over part of Macedonia. But the demands of the armed Albanians who took over several villages and parts of Tetovo in 2001 were essentially for recognition as equal citizens of Macedonia. As in Kosovo, there is little communication between the two groups, little mixing, and much distrust and hostility.

Finally, in Montenegro, where Albanians numbered around 50,000 in 1998 making up 7 percent of the population, there are still many obstacles for education and advancement. It is estimated that over half of the Albanians of Montenegro have emigrated since 1970. Albanians in Montenegro were pleased when relations between Montenegro and Milosevic's Serbia soured in the late 1990's. Unlike the war with Bosnia, where Montenegro did support Serbia, by the time of the war in Kosovo, Montenegro refused to support Serbia's actions against the Albanians there. The ongoing economic instability of Montenegro, however, is particularly hard on the minority Albanians whose employment situation in Montenegro was bleak before 1990. How the political situation of Montenegro is finally resolved—whether it will remain part of Yugoslavia or whether it will be independent—will undoubtedly affect the Albanians there.

FRANCES TRIX

See also **Albania; Macedonia; Montenegrins; Serbs; Yugoslavia; Yugoslavs (Southern Slavs)**

Further Reading

Elsie, Robert, editor, *Kosovo: In the Heart of the Powder Keg*, Boulder: East European Monographs, No. CDLXXVII, 1997

Federal Writers' Project, *The Albanian Struggle in the Old World and New*, Boston: The Writer, Inc., 1939; New York: AMS Press, 1975

Hall, Derek, *Albania and Albanians*, New York: St. Martin's, 1994

Human Rights Watch, *Yugoslavia: A Village Destroyed, War Crimes in Kosovo*, New York: Human Rights Watch, 1999

———, *Federal Republic of Yugoslavia: Abuses Against Serbs & Roma in the New Kosovo*, New York: Human Rights Watch, 1999

———, *Open Wounds: Human Rights Abuses in Kosovo*, New York: Human Rights Watch, 1994

Malcolm, Noel, *Kosovo: A Short History*, New York: New York University Press, 1998; 2nd edition, 1999

Mead, Alice, *Adem's Cross*, New York: Bantam Doubleday of Dell, 1998

Mertus, Julie, *Kosovo: How Myths and Truths Started a War*, Berkeley: University of California Press, 1999

Poulton, Hugh, *Who Are the Macedonians?*, Bloomington: Indiana University Press, 2000

———. "The Albanians of Macedonia," in *The Southern Balkans: an MRG International Report, 94/4*, edited by MRG Greece, James Pettifer and Hugh Poulton, London: Minority Rights Group International, 1994

Trix, Frances, "Reframing the Forced Migration and Rapid Return of Kosovar Albanians," in *Rethinking Refuge and Displacement: Selected Papers on Refugees and Immigrants (vol. VIII)*, edited by Elzbieta Gozdziak and Dianna Shandy, Arlington, Virginia: American Anthropological Association, 2000

Vickers, Miranda, *Between Albanian and Serb: A Study of Kosovo*, London: Hurst & Co., 1998

Alevis

Capsule Summary

Location: Republic of Turkey
Total Population: approximately 12 million
Languages: Turkish, Kurdish, and Zaza
Religion: Muslim

The Alevi are a religious minority of relatively significant numbers living within the borders of the Turkish republic. While accurate estimates of population size are difficult to discern, the total number is thought to be somewhere between 10–15 million adherents. The group identity of the Alevi is quite complex, as it is fractured along the lines of language, descent, occupational groups, and tribal structure. These internal differences are also reflected in contrasting beliefs and worship practices. The majority of Alevi consider themselves Muslim, although their syncretic interpretation of Islam is often described as unorthodox in relation to the beliefs of Turkey's Sunni majority. There is some tension between these two communities, which has, in the past, sporadically erupted into violent confrontation.

History

The Alevi are widely held to be the descendents of the traditionally nomadic Central Asian Turkoman tribes, whose migration to eastern Anatolia began in the late eleventh century. Eager to escape Mongol oppression, their westward route took them along the shores of the Caspian Sea and through the Islamic lands of Persia. In terms of religion, not all of these tribes had by this time embraced Islam, and those that had had assimilated long-held shamanic beliefs, along with ideas and practices from various faiths with which they had formerly come into contact, including Zoroastrianism, Manicheism, and Christianity.

Circulating amongst the Turkoman tribes in rural Anatolia were the disciples of shaykh Ahmet Yesevi (d. 1167/68), as well as various itinerant dervish groups—known collectively as *kalender*—who together preached a variety of heterodox forms of Islam. Some Anatolian Christian beliefs and practices are also said to have been incorporated into this eclectic framework. Overall, their faith was characterized by *syncretism*, the mingling of beliefs and practices that at one time belonged to separate religious systems. At this time, the transplanted Turkoman tribes did not form a distinct religious community per se, nor did a name exist to describe these heterodox groups as a whole.

Still later, the teachings of Haci Bektaş Veli (d. circa 1295), a dervish from Khorasan who had settled in the central Anatolian village of Sulucakarahöyük (now the town of HaciBektaş Nevşehir province), went some way in providing for a minimal degree of doctrinal and ritual unity. In organizational terms, however, two distinct groups were to evolve. Firstly, there was the formation of a *tarikat* (sufi for "'brotherhood'"), whose primary environment was the *tekke* (dervish lodge). These were often established in either an urban or semi-urban locale. This group, the Bektai, maintained a close, if at times turbulent, relationship with the Ottoman rulers. Additionally, there was a second group who retained their nomadic way of life in the Anatolian countryside. During the sixteenth century, the *kizilbaş,* as this group eventually came to be known, openly opposed the Ottomans by allying themselves with the expansionist Persian Safavid state in their attempt to propagate the doctrine of Twelve-Imam Shi'ism in eastern Anatolia. After the Safavid defeat at Chaldiran, however, the *kizilbaş* fled to the more remote regions of Anatolia in order to escape Ottoman retaliation.

Society and Ethnicity

Traditionally, the *kizilbaş* Alevi have primarily occupied settlements in the central Anatolian provinces of Corum, Yozgat, and Sivas; the eastern provinces of Tunceli, Bingöl, Mara, and Malatya (containing mostly Kurdish Alevi communities); and in the southwest, along a corridor between the coastal provinces of Izmir and Mersin. In general, Alevi villages have remained separate from Sunni villages, whilst in those towns and villages that do have a mixed population; Alevi and Sunni inhabit distinct neighborhoods or *mahalle*. Sealing themselves off both geographically and socially in order to escape the popular prejudices of Sunni society, the Alevi communities have developed an intense in-group focus.

Core elements of the Alevi faith include a pronounced veneration of the first of the Shi'i Imams, Ali Ibn Abi Talib; the hierarchical organization of Holy Lineages; periodic collective ritual gatherings called *cem*, attended by both men and women; the oral, rather than scriptural, communication of religious knowledge; as well as expressive forms of worship incorporating mystical poetry and hymns (*ilahi*), music (especially the playing of a stringed instrument called *saz* or *baglama*), and dance (*semah*).

Beginning in the 1950s, the Alevi found themselves caught in a process of large scale, rural-to-urban migration that signaled an end to their rural isolation. In cities such as Istanbul and Ankara, migrants from the countryside came to establish squatter settlements (*gecekondu*) that, to some degree, has perpetuated the segregational settlement patterns of the village. For the Alevi, the assumption of urban life ultimately triggered a period of socio-religious erosion. In the course of the 1970s, the institution of the *dede*—the traditional spiritual leaders of the Alevi—began to collapse. These figures were unable to respond to the demands of Alevi youth or challenge the appeal of radical political movements such as the "'Turkish Left'", and, in the case of Kurdish Alevis, Kurdish nationalist movements. The Alevi gradually moved from one ideological frame of reference to another and socialism became the central marker of Alevi identity.

Nevertheless, the urban abandonment of the communities' religious self-definition was relatively short-lived. By the end of the 1980s, the Alevi had embarked upon a project of cultural revitalization, once again primarily focused on the religious dimensions of community life. One of the major factors accounting for this transformation was the temporary success of the (Sunni) Islamist political party *Refah Partisi* at both the municipal and national levels. *Refah's* goal of reducing Islam to a single interpretation served as the impetus for promoting conservative Islamic values in public life. Perhaps as a bulwark against assimilation, the Alevi began to fortify their community's boundary through the articulation of religious difference. Various publications attempting to explain what Alevism actually '*is*' have since flourished in a more recent political climate that has, over the last decade, become slightly less hostile to public expressions of religious and ethnic diversity.

Today, Alevism remains engaged in a process of theological and cultural self-exploration. At the vanguard is an educated elite whose task is to restructure Alevism to meet the spiritual demands of the newly urbanized Alevi communities. There are other factors that influence this project as well. Many Alevi, for instance, are mindful of the strategies of the Turkish state, especially in regards to any real or perceived policy of assimilation. The initial unity that seemed to have underpinned the early movement, so focused on recapturing a religiously defined identity, has given way to dissent and factionalization. These divisions are clearly evident in the contrasting discourses of various group representatives. The disaggregation of the urban Alevi community is something that is likely to continue in the future as contrasting schools of thought become further codified.

MICHAEL AZARIADIS

See also **Turkey; Zoroastrianism**

Further Reading

Andrews, Peter A., editor, *Ethnic Groups in the Republic of Turkey*, Weisbaden: Dr Ludwig Reichart, 1989

Ataseven, Ilhan, *The Alevi-Bekta iLegacy: Problems of Acquisition and Explanation*, Lund: Lund Studies in History of Religions, 7, 1997

Kehl-Bodrogi, Krisztina, Barbara Kellner-Heinkele, and Anke Otter-Beaujean, editors, *Syncretistic Religious Communities in the Near East*, Leiden, New York, and Koln: Brill, 1997

Markoff, Irene, "Music, Saints, and Ritual: Sama and the Alevis of Turkey," in *Manifestations of Sainthood in Islam*, edited by G. Martin-Smith and C.W. Ernst, Istanbul: The Isis Press, 1993

Olsson, Tord, Elisabeth Ozdalga, and Catharina Raudvere, editors, *Alevi Identity: Cultural, Religious, and Social Perspectives*, Richmond: Curzon Press, 1998

Özdemir, Adil, and Kenneth Frank, *Visible Islam in Modern Turkey*, Istanbul: Sev Printing and Publishing Co., New York: St. Martin's Press, and London: Macmillan Press, 2000

Shankland, David, "Social Change and Culture: Responses to Modernization in an Alevi Village in Anatolia," in *When History Accelerates: Essays on Rapid Social Change, Complexity, and Creativity*, edited by Chris Hann, London: The Althone Press, 1994

Algeria

Capsule Summary

Country Name: Democratic and Popular Republic of Algeria
Location: North Africa, at the coast of Mediterranean
Total Population: 32,818,500 (July 2003)
Minority Populations: Berbers, 7 million (including Kabyles, Shawiya, Mozabites, and Tuareg), Saharawi 120,000.
Ethnic Groups: Arab-Berber (99%), European (less than 1%)
Languages: Arabic (official), French, Berber dialects
Religions: Sunni Muslim (state religion) (99%), Christian and Jewish (1%)

Algeria (officially the Democratic and Popular Republic of Algeria, Algiers in French) is a republic in North Africa bounded on the north by the Mediterranean Sea, on the east by Tunisia and Libya, on the south by Niger and Mali, and on the west by Mauritania, Western Sahara, and Morocco. With 918,497 square miles (2,378,907 square kilometers), Algeria is the second largest country in Africa after Sudan. With a population of over 32 million, Algeria is one of the fastest growing countries in the world. Its GDP per capita of $5,400 (2002) reflects a thriving oil-based economy. A major port city in Africa, other industries include metallurgy, automotive construction, machine building, and the production of chemicals, tobacco, paper, and cement.

History

The earliest known inhabitants of the area of Algeria were cattle herders and hunters in the Al Hajjar region between 8000 and 2000 BCE, who are presumed to have been tribal Berbers. The territory was invaded by Arabs in the seventh century CE and the Berbers were converted to Islam. Later many Moors who were expelled from Spain in 1492 settled in Algeria. In 1511 the Spanish occupied an island in the city's harbor, but they were driven out when, in 1518, Turkish corsair (pirate) Khay ad-Din (Barbarossa) captured Algeria from the Spanish. The Barbary States, or autonomous provinces of the Turkish Empire in the sixteenth century, included Tripolitania, Tunisia, and Algeria. Under Turkish rule Algeria became the base for Muslim piracy, preying upon Christians in the Mediterranean. The piracy began as part of the military wars against Spain, but in the seventeenth and eighteenth centuries, as Turkish hold on the area grew weaker, the raids became commercial in nature. The booty, ransom, and slaves that resulted from attacks on Mediterranean towns provided valuable revenue for local Muslim rulers. The ruling Turkish official in Algeria, the dey of Algiers, made himself virtually independent of Constantinople in the eighteenth and nineteenth centuries.

The French ended the Ottoman rule over Algeria in 1830 when they captured the port and made the region a French colony. France incorporated Algeria in 1848, subsequently placing the country under military rule under Emperor Napoleon III after a series of intermittent wars with the Arab leader Abdelkader. During World War II Algeria became headquarters for the Allied forces as well as for Charles de Gaulle's provisional French government.

An anti-French uprising in the city in 1954 provided a major spark in the Algerian armed struggle for independence. In the late 1950s, anticolonial resistance continued to stew under Algeria's Front de Liberation Nationale (FLN), and after eight years of guerrilla warfare in which one million Algerians died, the country gained independence July 1, 1962. During the final months before independence was won, the French terrorist Organization of the Secret Army (OAS) bombed the city, damaging industrial and communications facilities. The Front de Liberation Nationale subsequently ruled Algeria as a single-party state until the late 1980s. Its policies of centralization, socialist bureaucracy, leftist revolutionary politics and the practical suppression of Islamic activism unfortunately set the stage for the fundamentalist backlash of the early 1990s.

Algeria has hence faced civil war between Islamists and the military rulers since the beginning of 1990s and a decade of terrorist violence has resulted in more than 100,000 deaths since 1991. The Islamic Salvation Front (*Front Islamique du Salut* or FIS), an illegal political party, was formed in 1989 by Abbassi Madani and Ali Belhadj in opposition to the FLN. It won the first round of the December 1991 balloting, and in response the FLN cancelled the elections. Civil unrest followed and the FIS was banned in March 1992. The Islamic Salvation Army', the party's armed wing, disbanded in January 2000. Whereas some members surrendered under an amnesty program designed to promote national reconciliation, other small numbers of armed militants have persisted in confronting government forces and carrying out isolated attacks on villages and other types of terrorist attacks. Presently, more than 40 political parties, representing a wide segment of the population, are currently active in Algerian national politics. Abdul Aziz Bouteflika was elected president of the republic in November 1999.

Berber Conflicts

In the years post-independence, efforts by nationalist groups to remove all French influence, which to many Algerians represented bitter colonial and cultural domination, grew somewhat contentious. Under colonialism a small population of Gallicized Algerians who worked for the French were Berbers (specifically Kabyles), and recruited in excess of their proportion to the Algerian population. After 1962 the new governmental leaders of the nation set out to craft a new indigenous identity, raising the issue of a national language. Beginning in the late 1960s, the government of President Houari Boumediene decided to pursue a goal of complete Arabization in addition to crucial economic reconstruction. However, the policy of Arabization did not fare well with the Kabyles and other French loyalists who viewed the increasing influence of Arabic as an encroachment on their own status and privileges. Turmoil continued throughout the 1960s with socialist reforms for the redistribution of land organized by the Front de Liberation Nationale. Although the economy was indeed improved by the exploitation of vast deposits of natural gas in the Sahara Desert, unemployment remained high, forcing many Algerians to travel to France in search of employment. There they suffered racism and discrimination. During the 1970s, when more than 70 percent of the workforce was employed on the land, agriculture was neglected in favor of industry and production levels fell.

Militant Kabyle students in particular protested against the increasing Arabization of the education system. In the early 1980s this student movement formed the basis for the Kabyle Cultural Movement. Fighting against the "cultural imperialism" of the Arab-speaking population, the Kabyles demanded the recognition of their dialect as a national language. Kabyle students in Algiers and Tizi Ouzou, the provincial capital of Kabyle, went on strike in the spring of 1980 and this later spread to the larger Kabyle population. While Arabic has gained in the last four decades, the civil services in Algeria are still overwhelmingly dominated by Berbers.

Society and Ethnicity

About 30 percent of the Algerian population is Berber and over the years they have been subjected to suppression and forced assimilation. Berbers, who call themselves *Imazighen*, meaning "noble" or "free-born," include various peoples living in northern Africa west of Tripoli and are not racially homogenous. Concentrated mainly around Kabylia, Chaouia, the Mazb, and the Sahara, Berbers comprise the indigenous inhabitants of the North African littoral.

The antipathy between Berbers and Arabs is ancient, dating as early as circa 700 BCE when the Arabs conquered North Africa. While in modern Algeria the division between Berbers and Arabs no longer as rigid as it once was, this does not mean that there is no discrimination against Berbers. In fact, a large number of Berbers from Algeria have immigrated to France because they have experienced constraints to their freedom of self-expression.

The major ethnic fault line in Algeria lies among Berbers and Arabs. Although both groups follow Islam, they are divided over language. Berbers, who trace their origins to Latin-Christian civilization, speak their indigenous language, French, whereas Arabs speak Arabic. Before the arrival of Arabic-speaking invaders, Berber was the indigenous language; however, over time, Arabic spread to a growing number of the population, with the exception of those in some rural areas where Berber remains the mother tongue. As a Semitic language, Arabic became dominant throughout North Africa with the spread of Islam. Berber, on the other hand, is an Afro-Asiatic language found in the Maghrib.

Several Berber dialect groups are identifiable in modern Algeria (collectively called *tashilheet* or *shila*), with only Kabyle and Chaouia spoken by a substantial number. This chasm of language influences the access of these communities to material resources, especially the jobs in the civil service, which incidentally is the largest employer in Algeria. During colonial rule, the French attempted to prevent solidarity among Berbers and Arabs, and recruited a disproportionate number of Berber civil servants. Although a product of colonial rule, the overrepresentation of Berbers in civil services continues today.

Tuaregs, a nomadic Berber tribe, also exist in Algeria and in the neighboring countries of Mali and Nigeria. As they tend to disregard national boundaries, many have been treated brutally for these violations.

There were about 30,000 Jews in Algeria when the French colonized it, but over the years because of emigration to France and Israel, the Jewish population has diminished to about 400.

AMANDEEP SANDHU

See also **Berbers; Corsicans; Tuareg**

Further Reading

Bennoune, M., *The Making of Contemporary Algeria, 1830–1987*, Cambridge: Cambridge University Press, 1988

Entelis, J.F., and P.C. Naylor, editors, *State and Society in Algeria*, Boulder, Colorado: Westview, 1992

Maghraoui, Abdeslam, "Algeria's Battle of Two Languages," *Middle East Report*, 25, Jan–Feb 1995

Nalli, Brahim, "The Berber Issue in Algeria," in *Algeria: The Revolution Revisited*, edited by R. Shah-Kazemi, London: Islamic World Report, 1997

Roberts, H., *Revolution and Resistance: Algerian Politics and the Kabyle Question*, London: Tauris, 1989

Waltz, Susan E., *Human Rights and Reform: Changing the Face of North African Politics*, Berkeley: University of California Press, 1995

Ali, Muhammad (African-American)

Muhammad Ali exploded into the conscience of Americans in 1964 when he beat "Sonny": Liston in a World Heavyweight Championship fight in Miami. Sports fans were awed by his combination of power and agility, but it was Ali's strutting confidence, which extended to poetry and constant cries of "I am the greatest", along with his racial and political pronouncements outside of the ring that were to make him an important figure in African-American history.

Boxing had been politically and racially significant before Ali as the victories of Jack Johnson and Joe Louis, two previous black Heavyweight Champions, had challenged notions of racial superiority. Louis must be credited with breaking down the color barrier in boxing, but Ali was much more influential as he used his position, charisma, and media attention to promote a wider racial agenda. Although he mainly fought fellow blacks, Ali always found a way to paint his opponents as white. He attacked Liston, the archetypal "bad nigger", for living in a white suburb and he similarly berated Floyd Patterson for having married a white woman. "I'm going to put on him on his back/so that he will start acting black," Ali promised before their 1965 fight.

Ali's political views had been honed by his membership in the controversial Nation of Islam, which he announced the day after he became champion. He also stated that he was changing his name, from Cassius Clay, in accordance with the group's beliefs. The announcement provoked widespread criticism as the Nation was perceived as antiwhite, and Ali followed this line by later refusing to support the civil rights campaign for integration. He did, however, greatly help the Nation spread beyond the northern ghettos of its confines, especially after he became its chief spokesman following the expulsion of Malcolm X'. Ali's victories and antiestablishment actions also provided African-Americans in general with a sense of psychic satisfaction, which was increased by his refusal to serve in the Army. When he was drafted, in 1967, Ali argued that he was entitled to a religious deferment, citing his active role in the Nation of Islam. It was a bold decision, as Ali had been promised a promotional role in the Army that would have spared him from active duty in Vietnam; by refusing it he endangered his entire boxing career. He had already been forced to fight his last five defenses overseas as no American state would grant him a license, and the confiscation of his passport meant that he would be unable to box professionally for the next three-and-a-half years.

Following his refusal, Ali was stripped of his world title and condemned by most white Americans, with few mainstream black leaders willing to defend such a controversial figure. Only established war opponents, like Martin Luther King, and radicals like the Student Non-violence Co-coordinating Committee (SNCC) voiced any support for Ali's stand. However, more conservative black groups did begin to defend Ali once the American public became more widely hostile to the war in Vietnam and as the Nation of Islam began to tone down its antiwhite statements. In 1968, for instance, the W.E.B. Du Bois clubs and the Black Caucus of the National Conference for New Politics joined the more militant CORE, National Black Antiwar, Anti-Draft Union, and SNCC in protesting against a boxing fight designed to fill Ali's heavyweight title.

Ali's stand meant that he was soon in demand as a speaker on American university campuses. He became an icon for student protesters, but it was his influence on black athletes that was perhaps most important. University of California, Los Angeles basketball player Lew Alcindor (Kareem Abdul-Jabbar), Bill Russell, player-coach of the Boston Celtics, and football players including Sid Williams, Walter Beach, and Curtis McClinton had been among the few African-Americans to support Ali from the start. Their actions demonstrated a new militancy amongst Black athletes. Influenced by the 1960s Civil Rights campaigns, they realized that sporting victories were not helping black causes and they had also seen former greats like Jesse Owens and Joe Louis reduced to unfortunate, meager existences. In 1968 this led to the formation of the Olympic Project for Human Rights, which called for an African-American boycott of the Mexico City Olympics. The organization protested racism throughout sport and its number-one demand was the restoration of Ali's world title. Few athletes actually boycotted the games, but Tommie Smith and John Carlos attracted worldwide publicity for their cause by making the Black Power salute as they collected their medals.

The growing activism among athletes and African-Americans in general—coupled with the widespread anti-Vietnam sentiment—led to the United States Supreme Court unanimously agreeing to dismiss the case against Ali in 1971 because of a minor error by the government. This expedient compromise spared Ali prison without, despite what he would claim, recognizing the Nation of Islam as a religious organization. Ali had already been able to resume his boxing career in October 1970 when he beat Jerry Quarry in Georgia. In 1972 he lost to world champion Joe Frazier, but his fame ensured another title fight against George Foreman in 1974. Ali won this classic bout in Kinshasa, Zaire and fought 10 successful defenses before losing to Leon Spinks in February 1978. However, he became the first and only boxer to the win the title three times by winning the rematch in September. By the time of the Spinks fights, Ali was firmly ensconced as an icon in American society; he was the established elder statesman, while Spinks was the brash youngster. This acceptance has continued in his retirement, during which he has remained involved with the Nation of Islam. He has also publicly dealt with the symptoms of "punch drunk" syndrome (a neurological disorder known as Boxer's dementia) and a condition similar to Parkinson's Disease, which was caused bydamage suffered during his boxing career. The disease has forced him to limit his public appearances, but his importance to both African-Americans and to American sport was manifested at the 1996 Atlanta Olympics when he was chosen to light the Olympic flame. For African-Americans, Ali was a symbol of fearless refusal to back down in the face of oppression and white racism.

NEIL DENSLOW

See also **African-American Nationalism and Separatism; Du Bois, W.E.B. (African-American); Malcolm X (African-American)**

Capsule Biography

Cassius Marcellus Clay. Born January 17, 1942 in Louisville, Kentucky. Attended public schools in Louisville. As a Light-Heavyweight, won Golden Gloves Tournament in Chicago and gold medal at the Rome Olympics, 1960; became World Heavyweight Champion, announces his conversion to Islam and changes his name to Muhammad Ali, 1964. Convicted of Draft Evasion and is stripped of his World title, 1967; resumed professional boxing after three-and-a-half-year absence, 1970; U.S. Supreme Court cleared Ali of draft evasion, 1971; regained World title by beating George Foreman, 1974; lost to Leon Spinks but regained title in rematch before retiring, 1976; loses both fights in a short comeback, 1980. Announced that he is suffering from "punch drunk" syndrome (Parkinson's), 1984. Chosen to light the flame at the Atlanta Olympics, 1996; currently lives in Louisville, Kentucky.

Further Reading

Ali, Muhammad, with Richard Durham, *The Greatest: My Own Story*, New York, 1975

Early, Gerald, editor, *The Muhammad Ali Reader*, New York, 1998

Gorn, Elliott J., editor, *Muhammad Ali: The People's Champion*, Urbana, 1995

Hauser, Thomas, with Muhammad Ali, *Muhammad Ali: His Life and Times*, London, 1991

Sammons, Jeffery T., *Beyond the Ring: The Role of Boxing in American Society*, Urbana, 1988

Alsace-Lorraine, *See* **Alsatians**

Alsatians

Capsule Summary

Location: Northeastern France (Alsace-Lorraine), along the western Rhine valley
Total Population: 1,734,145 (1999)
Languages: French, Alsatian
Religions: Catholic (archdiocese of Strasbourg), Lutheran (Église de la Confession d'Augsbourg d'Alsace-Lorraine), Église Réformée d'Alsace (Protestant-Calvinist), Jewish

The Alsatians live in northeastern France, on the German border (the Rhine River), north of Switzerland and south of Luxembourg. Some 1.7 million Alsatians live in the province of Alsace. Their regional language, Alsatian, is an old German dialect that some Germans can more or less understand. There are in fact two distinct dialects in Alsace: one in the south in the Mulhouse region (Haut-Rhinois) and another in the north around Strasbourg (Bas-Rhinois). Both are quite different from the dialect spoken in the neighboring French province, Lorraine (this dialect is called Lorrain), and from dialects spoken in Luxembourg, and Bade-Wurtemberg (in West Germany). People who speak only French would not understand either of the Alsatian dialects, but nowadays most people who have learned Alsatian can also speak French. At the beginning of the twenty-first century, almost all Alsatians spoke French as their first language, and many younger Alsatians had not even learned the Alsatian dialect. But that has not always been the case in past centuries. Alsace—like Lorraine—has often been a part of Germany, although against the will of the majority of Alsatians. In the German language, the province and dialect are named Elsass.

More than half the Alsatian population is Catholic, but four religions are officially recognized in Alsace: Catholicism (Archidiocèse de Strasbourg), Lutheranism (Église de la Confession d'Augsbourg d'Alsace-Lorraine), Église Réformée d'Alsace (Protestant-Calvinism), and Judaism. The Jewish community in Alsace is the second most important in France (after that in the region of Paris) and has had an uninterrupted presence there since the Middle Ages. Today, Alsace is a prosperous province of France and Alsatians are French citizens; but because Alsace was part of Germany during certain periods (sometimes lasting for more than a generation), the region still has, in addition to its unique dialects, a few laws that differ from those in the rest of France, a distinct regional cuisine, and its own customs, which are not to be found either in Germany or in any other part of France. For instance, the French law of 1904 separating church and state was enacted when Alsace was a German possession; therefore, in this regard some French laws do not apply in Alsace, and some old German laws are still enforced in Alsace.

History

Alsace has Celtic origins and was once a part (Germanie) of the Roman Empire. Traces of the first humans in this area, dating back 600,000 years, were found in Hangenbieten, north of Alsace. Julius Caesar's armies invaded Alsace in 58 BCE. Four centuries later, in 357 CE, Germans tried to control Alsace but were defeated by the Roman Emperor. This marked the beginning of countless disputes between the Franks (led by Clovis) and the Alamans (ancestors of the Germans). Alsace had its own king, Rodolphe I of Hapsburg, in 1273; and between 1354 and 1648 it was in some respects an independent country, with free cities. Most of Alsace became a part of France by 1648 under Louis XIV (by the Treaty of Westphalia); but a southern city, Mulhouse, had decided in 1466 to become a part of Switzerland (later, in 1798, nine years after the French Revolution, Mulhouse, with a population of 7,000, did join France). Louis XIV of France is known to have called Alsace its "foreign province"; he insisted that it was important to respect the Alsatians' dialect and customs. By the time of the French Revolution, then, almost all of Alsace was already a part of France; and the Alsatians remained French citizens until the late nineteenth century. In fact, the French national anthem, the "Marseillaise," was originally a war chant composed in Strasbourg in 1792 by Claude Joseph Rouget de Lisle (1760–1836), a French poet who served as a captain in France's "Rhine Army."

In 1870, Germany (actually Prussia and its allies) invaded Alsace and Lorraine, and both provinces became a part of a new enlarged German Reich (by the Treaty of Frankfurt, 1871). In less than a year—before November 1, 1872—more than 158,000 Alsatians (one-tenth of the population) who were opposed to the annexation left the region (renamed Reichland Elsass-Lothringen) for other parts of France, or went to North Africa (French Algeria) and America. During the annexation, the German language was imposed in Alsatian schools and the use of French was forbidden, but Alsatian dialects were tolerated by the German authorities. In November 1918, at the end of World War I, Alsace was liberated and again became part of France. However, after more than a generation (47 years) of German domination, the shift toward French culture seemed brutal, because by then most Alsatians did not understand French. Still, part of the purpose of the Versailles Treaty (1919) was to repair the damages and undo the consequences of the war of 1870 between France and Germany.

In June 1940, after some 20 years of the French regime, Alsace was occupied by the Nazis; this occupation lasted until February 1945. From 1942 onward, almost 100,000 young Alsatians were forced to join the German troops (the *Wehrmacht*) to fight against the Soviet Union; those who protested were executed. During World War II, the French language was once again prohibited in Alsace; the Nazis there forbade even wearing a beret. Many Alsatians perished in concentration camps, especially those who were Jewish. Two death camps were built in Alsace by the Nazis: Schirmeck and Struthof-Natzwiller. In 1944, the Allies bombed Alsatian cities such as Strasbourg and Mulhouse, causing thousands of deaths. In all, some 50,000 Alsatians died during World War II. During and after the war, Alsatians who had been forced to serve with the German troops were often considered collaborators and traitors. In the mid-twentieth century this situation led many French citizens to regard the Alsatians as foreigners; as a result, many Alsatians felt marginalized in their own country.

Citizenship, Identity, and Minority Status

The French historian Numa-Denis Fustel de Coulanges (1830–1889) wrote in 1870 that, although they could be considered a German nation for ethnic, linguistic, and to some extent historical reasons, Alsatians were totally French simply because they wanted to belong to the French civilization that they loved. Many Alsatians were bilingual and fond of both the German and the French heritage and tradition. For centuries, Alsace had a unique regional culture and was a center of gothic art. Its best-known example of gothic architecture is the impressive cathedral of Strasbourg, which took four centuries to build and was finished in 1439; this cathedral has a unique steeple that still remains the highest in Europe. Johannes Gutenberg, the inventor of printing from movable type, lived in Strasbourg from 1434 to 1445. The Reformation had a strong impact on Alsace; and Martin Bucer, who in 1529 tried to forbid Catholic celebrations and imposed Protestantism, was especially influential. Two traditions of Protestantism are still represented in Alsace.

At the beginning of the twenty-first century, Alsatians did not feel that they were a minority, but they realized that they had been treated as foreigners every time they were forced to change their borders and citizenship as a result of wars and political treaties which they themselves did not control. In the nineteenth and twentieth centuries, for instance, such changes of citizenship occurred in Alsace in 1871, 1918, 1940, and 1945; and many Alsatians who were born before 1871 and lived until 1945 (when Alsace was returned to France) changed their citizenship four or five times during their lives, even if they always lived in the same province.

The attachment of many Alsatians to France was perhaps best exemplified in the nostalgic stories of "Hansi" (Jean-Jacques Waltz), a French patriotic writer. In the early twentieth century (during the German regime) Hansi published many books with naive illustrations of traditional Alsatian life as a part of the beloved France. The French novelist Alphonse Daudet (1840–1897) and the Alsatian writer Tomi Ungerer (born in 1931) also wrote nostalgic stories about the disappearance of French culture during the periods when Alsace was German.

Society

Geographically, Alsace is between the plains of the Rhine Valley (on the German border) and the mountains of the Vosges on the west. But its borders and extent have changed over the centuries. German invaders always considered Alsace a true Germanic region that was wrongly located outside their borders; they regarded the Rhine valley not as a fluvial frontier but rather as a link between two similar ethnic groups. Bismarck and Hitler preferred to consider the mountains of the Vosges as a natural border between France and Germany, with Alsace and most of Lorraine on the German side.

Since the middle and late twentieth century, most Alsatians have lived in cities. However, there are many villages, often with typically Alsatian names that in some cases date from the Middle Ages: Colmar, Munster, Guebwiller, Ammerschwihr, Shittigeim, Souffelweyersheim, Thann, Wissembourg, Wittenheim.

The economy of Alsace is diverse but nowadays is centered on industries (notably automobile construction), electricity, new technologies, and the production of potash. Alsace is also renowned for its white wines. Beginning in 1949, Alsace was host to the permanent head of the Council of Europe, located in Strasbourg. Alsatians tend to be strong supporters of the European Union. As of the present writing, some 60,000 people who were officially residents of Alsace had jobs outside France, mostly in nearby Germany and Switzerland.

YVES LABERGE

See also **France; Germany**

Further Reading

Borgé Jacques, and Nicolas Viasnoff, editors, *Archives d'Alsace*. Paris: Éditions Michèle Trinckvel, 1993

Daudet, Alphonse, "La dernière classe: Récit d'un petit Alsacien," in *Contes du lundi*. Paris, Flammarion, 2001; (originally published 1873; there have been many English translations, e.g., "The Last Class: The Story of a Little Alsatian," in *Five Short Stories*, Cambridge, Massachusetts, Harvard Classics Shelf of Fiction, 1917)

Hansi (Jean-Jacques Waltz), *Le paradis tricolore par l'Oncle Hansi*, Paris: Éditions Herscher, 1993, (originally published 1918)

Hoffet, Frédéric, *Psychanalyse de l'Alsace*, Colmar: Éditions Alsatia, 1981, (originally published 1951)

Ungerer, Tomi, *À la guerre comme à la guerre: Dessins et couvenirs d'enfance*. Paris: Médium et École des Loisirs, 2002, (originally published 1991)

Vogler, Bernard, editor, *L'Alsace: Une histoire*, 6th edition Illkirch: Éditions Oberlin, 1995

Altai (Altaians)

Capsule Summary

Location: souther Siberia, Russia; mostly in Altai Republic.
Total Population: 202,900 (in the Altai Republic, 2002)
Minority Population: Altaians (67,000), Talangits (2,600), Teleuts (2,700), Tubalar (1,600), Kumandins (3,100), Chelkans (1,000), Most Teleuts live outside Altai Republic in the Kemerovo Region. Kumandins live both in Altai Republic and Altai Territory.
Languages: Altai, Talangit, Teleut, Tuba, Kumandin, Chelkan.
Religions: Eastern Orthodox Christianity, Burkhanism, Animism.

The Altai Republic, established in 1991 and located in Asia bordering Mongolia, is 35,753 square miles (92,600 square kilometers). Its population of approximately 202,900 people comprises different ethnic groups. The Altaians represent almost one-third (31 percent) of the population, Russians (60 percent), Kazakhs (6 percent), Ukrainians (0.95 percent). The capital city is Gorno-Altaisk.

Altaians are an "official nationality" artificially constructed by the authorities of the former Soviet Union. This community is concentrated in the former Gorno-Altai Autonomous Region (today the Altai Republic). The Altai territory is a mountainous area in southern Siberia bordering on eastern Kazakhstan, China's Xinjiang Uighur Autonomous Region province, and Mongolia. The majority of the Republic's population is Russian; the remainder is so-called Altaian. In reality there was no such ethnic community called Altaians; however, six different Turkic speaking peoples were united under the name: the Altai-kizhi (Altaians proper) including the sub-ethnic group of Maimalar, Talangits (including the remnants of Teles), Teleuts, Tubalar, Chelkans, and Kumandins. These peoples perceive themselves as separate ethnic communities; they speak different languages and, moreover, they differ significantly in terms of in anthropological types and culture. The Altaian history is closely connected with the history of Central Asia and its state formations. The Altaians belong to the Altaian linguistic family of the Kyrgyz-Kypchak subgroup of the eastern branch of the Turkic group. Linguistically, the Altaic peoples are divided into Southern Altaians, who speak the languages of the Northwestern (Kypchak) subgroup, and Northern Altaians, who speak the languages of Northeastern subgroup. Southern Altaians include the Altai-kizhi, Talangits, and Teleuts (the latter can be called "southern" only conditionally because they live more northerly than any other Altaic people). Northern Altaians include the Tubalar, Chelkans, and Kumandins. In 1923 a language based on the Altai-kizhi speaking language with the Cyrillic alphabet was established and elaborated. However, most Northern Altaians do not understand it well.

Ethnographically, the indigenous population is categoriezed into two ethnographic groups—the northern Altaians and the southern Altaians. The northern Altaians are referred to as the Uralic anthropological type formed as a result of the merging of Mongoloid and Caucasoid elements; the southern ones are referred to as Mongoloid Central Asian or south Siberian type.

The Altai-kizhi represent an ethnic minority of the Altai Republic only from a demographic point of view, as they form only a little more than a quarter of its population. In political terms they can hardly be considered an ethnic minority because they hold leading political and social positions in the community. The other ethnic groups that were included in the Altaian "official nationality" are certainly ethnic minorities.

History

Ancient Caucasoid settlements in the Altai region date to the Stone, Bronze, and Iron ages. As early as the fifth century BCE Mongoloids had appeared in Altai and mixed with the local Caucasoid population. In the sixth through eighth centuries BCE Altai was consecutively a part of the Turkic Khanate, the states of ancient Uighurs, and Yeniseian Kirghiz. During that time Turkic-speaking tribes, who had assimilated the population that lived there before, composed the majority of the population of the region. In the thirteenth— eighteenth centuries the Mongols came to dominate in Altai. In general, the Altai-kizhi, Talangits, and Teleuts formed as a result of a mixing of mainly Kypchak Turkic tribes with Mongols, whereas Kumandins, Chelkans, and Tubalar formed from the merging of different Turkic groups (first of all, ancient Uighurs) with Samoyed, Ket, and other Siberian tribes.

By the middle of fifteenth century, as a result of feudal wars, the Altaian population fell under the influence of the western Mongols or the Oirats (also known as the Jungars). Their supremacy lasted until 1756, when the southern Altaians (the Altai-Kizhi, Teleuts, and Telengits) became a part of Russia. The northern Altaians (the Kumandins, the Tubalars, the Tchelkans) had joined Russia much earlier. By the mid eighteenth century the entire territory of the contemporary Altai Republic was incorporated into the Russian Empire. This inclusion protected them from foreign infringements, including attacks from the Chinese Tsin army encroaching from the east. However, after gaining status as a Russian protectorate, the Altaians as well as other peoples of Russia struggled against the existing regime. Working people of Altai took part in the Revolution of 1905–1907.

Soviet power was established in December 1917. From 1922 to 1947 the republic was called Oyrot Autonomous Oblast, and from 1948 to 1990 it was renamed Gorno-Altai Autonomous Oblast. In 1991, after the dissolution of the Soviet Union, the Gorno-Altai Republic was proclaimed as part of the Russian Federation and in 1992 renamed the Altai Republic. In 1997 the Republic adopted its constitution and established Altaian and Russian as the state languages.

Society

The chief traditional occupation of Altai-kizhi and Talangits, as well as of most Teleuts, was nomadic and seminomadic cattle breeding. They raised horses, cattle, sheep, and goats. The Tubalar, Chelkans, Kumandins, and some part of the Teleuts were hunters relying on taiga beasts (hoofed and fur-bearing animals) for their traditional subsistence economy. Some Altaic peoples additionally developed subsistence agriculture, gathering, and to a lesser degree fishing.

The traditional dwelling of the Altai-kizhi and the Talangits was a felt yurt—a circular, domed tent stretched across a collapsible framework—related to the Mongolian type. Northern Altaians and some portion of the Altai-kizhi also built log or bark polygonal yurts with conic bark roofs. Some Altai-kizhi lived in mud huts or semi-mud huts with log or plank walls and birch bark gable roofs. Teleuts, along with representatives of Northern Altaic peoples, lived in conic dwellings made with perches or bark. In later years Altaians constructed large huts with two or four slope roofs influenced by the various surrounding Russian populations.

Traditional garments of all Southern Altaic peoples are quite similar, and the differences between men's and women's garments are insignificant. T traditionally wore long shirts with sleeves, wide breeches, and oriental robes. Both men's and women's street-clothes consisted of long double-breasted sheepskin coats, fur hats, and high boots. Married women wore long sleeveless jackets (*chegedek)* over their coats. Northern Altaians and Teleuts wore linen shirts, short breeches, and single-breasted oriental robes. At present most Altaians wear modern clothes, though traditional garments remain in use.

The traditional food of the Altaians includes soups with mutton or horseflesh, as well as dishes with gopher, marmot, or badger meat, blood pudding, fermented cow's and mare's milk, cream from boiled milk, butter, various kinds of cheese, *talkan* (fried barley flour or crushed and fried barley seeds), edible stems, and roots. The traditional Altaian drink is *aryki,* or milk vodka.

The original Altaians practiced a shamanistic polytheism. One of their deities was Yerlik, the god of the underworld, to whom blood sacrifices were made. Another was Oyrot-Khan, the heroic and wise composite figure constructed from memories of the Jungarian khans. Over time, through migration and settlement changes, the Altaians came into contact with three major world religions—Buddhism, Islam, and Christianity— Initially they resisted the expansion of all three. Presently, Eastern Orthodox Christianity prevails, largely as a result of the establishment in 1829 of an Orthodox mission in the Altai, created as part of the Empire's protectorate. Initially the Orthodox mission pursued enlightened policies, enriching education and respecting the native people, their language, and customs. By the late ninenteenth century, a nascent, ethnocentric Russian nationalism (Russification) led to strict religious doctrine; many Altaians rejected Christianity as a Russian religion. By the beginning of the twentieth century Russian rule had grown increasingly rigid in both church and state. In 1904 the Altaian developed Burkhanism, a monotheistic syncretic religion named after Ak-Burkhan, who believers recognized as the sole god. The new religion was hostile both to the Russians and to the shamans, who were forced to seek protection from the Russian authorities. In the first quarter of the twentieth century the Bolsheviks harshly rallied against and attempted to destroy all religions in Altai. Only the ancient polytheistic beliefs survived, as these could be passed on orally from generation to generation. No Burkhanist texts seem to have survived, and information about the religion has been obtained from the papers of Russian ethnographers who visited Altai and the diaries of Russian missionaries. In recent decades the region has witnessed a revival of both Burkhanism and shamanistic practices, especially among student youth.

Today the overwhelming majority of Kumandins and Chelkans are Russian Orthodox. Tubalar and Teleuts are also mostly Orthodox, though there is a group who practice pagan or shamanistic religions among them. Shamanists prevail among Talangits, but there are also many Orthodox among them. Burkhanism predominates in Altai-Kizhi although there is a considerable group of Orthodox among them.

The interests of Northern Altaian peoples are currently defended by the Association of Northern Ethnoses of Altai.

Pavel Puchkov

See also **Russia; Siberian Indigenous Peoples**

Further Reading

Левин, Максим Григорьевич, и Леонид Павлович Потапов, редакторы, *Народы Сибири,* Москва и Ленинград: Издательство Академии наук СССР, 1956; translated as *Peoples of Siberia,* Levin, Maksim Grigoryevich, and Leonid Pavlovich Potapov, editors, Moscow and Leningrad: USSR Academy of Sciences Press, 1956

Потапов, Леонид Павлович, *Очерки по истории алтайцев,* Москва и Ленинград: Издательство Академии наук СССР, 1953; translated as *Altaians' History Essays,* Potapov, Leonid Pavlovich, Moscow and Leningrad: USSR Academy of Sciences Press, 1953

Потапов, Леонид Павлович, *Этнический состав и происхождение алтайцев,* Ленинград: Издательство Академии наук СССР, 1969; translated as *Ethnic Structure and Origin of Altaians,* Potapov, Leonid Pavlovich, Leningrad: USSR Academy of Science Press, 1969

Тишков, Валерий Александрович, Павел Иванович Пучков и др, редакторы, *Народы и религии мира,* Москва: Издательство "Большая Российская Энциклопедия", 1998; translated as *Peoples and Religions of the World,* Tishkov, Valeri Aleksandrovich, Pavel Ivanovich Puchkov, editors, Moscow: Great Russian Encyclopedia Press, 1998

Токарев, Сергей Александрович, *Этнография народов СССР,* Москва: Издательство Московского университета, 1958; translated as *Ethnography of the Peoples of the USSR,* Tokarev, Sergey Aleksandrovich, Moscow: Moscow University Press, 1958

Толстов, Сергей Павлович, Максим Григорьевич Левин и Николай Николаевич Чебоксаров, редакторы, *Очерки общей этнографии: Азиатская часть СССР,* Москва: Издательство Академии наук СССР, 1960; translated as *General Ethnography Essays: Asian Part of the USSR,* Tolstov, Sergey Pavlovich, Maksim Grigoryevich Levin, and Nikolai Nikolaevich Cheboksarov, editors, Moscow: USSR Academy of Sciences Press, 1960

Grimes, Barbara E., editor, *Ethnologue: Languages of the World,* Dallas, Texas: Summer Institute of Linguistics, Inc.; 13th edition, 1996

Ambedkar, Bhimrao Ramji (Dalit)

The credit of championing the minority causes in India for a sustained period of three decades and facilitating the empowerment of the largest number of minorities through legal channels belongs largely to the figure of Bhimrao Ramji Ambedkar. He challenged many of the assumptions and myths held by the Hindus for more than 3,000 years, in particular the status of the Untouchables, the outcast group into which he was born. He was both a pragmatist and a reflective thinker whose views were affected by his life experiences. A majority of the Hindus, especially the upper caste Hindus, opposed him. However, Ambedkar is today idolized by a large number of minorities in India, and has accomplished the largest mass conversion from one religion to another in modern history as a means of empowerment of the minorities.

Ambedkar was born in the Sakpal family of an "untouchable" caste, that is a *Dalit*, the peoples on the lowest rung of Indian society, shunned and considered morally unclean. He was the last of 14 children. A Brahmin teacher changed the boy's last name (Ambavadekar, his ancestral village) to Ambedkar (the teacher's family name) while he was in school. This represented an act of kindness, as the Dalit (literally meaning "broken people") were identified in part by patronymy. Ambedkar nonetheless routinely suffered the indignities, discriminations, and humiliations heaped on the members of the untouchable caste as a student. He experienced severe prejudice and discrimination even as an adult, although he was able to secure excellent employment due to his credentials as a highly educated individual and in spite of the patronage of the ruler of Baroda state. Nonetheless, although Ambedkar was named as a minister of finance (a Maharaja) in the State of Baroda, the staff he supervised would drop paperwork on his desk rather than hand over the papers and files and therefore avoid "polluting" themselves by touching his hands. Such experiences and discriminatory treatment from the upper caste Hindus and his firm belief in the injustices of the Hindu caste system assuredly motivated Ambedkar as a dedicated social advocate, reformer, and an activist for the Dalit.

Hindus in India are born into the caste (*jat*) system, one of the world's most enduring forms of social stratification. The untouchable caste has been referred to by different names at different times throughout history, although the human rights plight of the Dalit emerged with the rise of Indian nationalism in the twentieth century. They were called Shudras (the lowest of four castes, members of which were occupied in menial labor) for over a thousand years. M.K. Gandhi popularized the term *Harijan,* which meant "God's people," in order to attempt to ameliorate the stigma associated with the lower caste. The term *Scheduled Castes* was another designation that was introduced in the Government of India Act in 1935 by the British. This designation was given constitutional recognition when India gained independence in 1948. Dalit was adopted as the officially sanctioned term in government documents in 1990.

Since the sixth century BCE Jains and Buddhists have tried to do away with the Hindu caste system. Many Hindu religious leaders, political leaders, and mystics from the eleventh century onward tried to introduce reforms in order to improve the social, economic, and educational status of the lower castes. Leaders such as Jyotirao Phule (or Phooley) preceded Ambedkar, but he was the first member of the educated class who was also born in the untouchable community. Ambedkar viewed the caste system as the basis of the evils of the Hindu religion and firmly adhered to that belief. He was recognized as a leader among the untouchables by the 1920s, and in return he thought of himself as the champion of their causes until his death. Revolted by the prejudices and discriminations against the untouchables, the main focus of Ambedkar's work comprised the liberation of the untouchables, the poor, and the disadvantaged, including women and children. The ideology he espoused throughout his leadership focused on liberty, equality, and dignity for the untouchables, goals he was able to achieve in part through his position of education, employment, and political power.

The period including the 1920s and 1930s (leading up to India's independence) marked a pivotal era of the growing Dalit movement. Ambedkar's leadership was characterized by a rejection of previous Dalit liberation, that is, the idea of reintegrating the caste back into the Hindu fold and culture. He replaced this vision by a new image of Dalit culture and the introduction of Dalit politics. Ambedkar's extensive exposure to Western constitutional law at the London School of Economics and Columbia University led him to see constitutional democratic means as the key to activating change and achieving equality. He argued for using political organization as a strategy for liberation, in contrast to the communist ideologies popular at that time (Marxism had had considerable influence among Indian nationalists) that called for a violent overthrow of the upper caste government in power. He rejected Marxism as an agent of change because he believed that the interests of the Dalits and the laboring classes did not always coincide; the Marxists as a group were interested in class divisions and to a large extent ignored the caste issues, and their espousal of violent methods for gaining power did not appeal to Ambedkar. Confrontation, and especially violence, did not fit with his preferred methods and strategies for the betterment of the Dalits.

Ambedkar organized three political parties during his lifetime: the Independent Labor Party (*Swatantra Mazdur Paksh*) in 1936, the Scheduled Caste Federation in 1942, and the Republican Party in 1956. Although only the Republican Party remains today, the histories of these parties testifies to Ambedkar's approach to political means. He believed that social reform could only come through political action and reform and thus concentrated on gaining political safeguards for the scheduled castes. Ambedkar pressed for separate communal electoral reserved seats for the Scheduled Castes at the federal and the state levels, the most important and efficacious way that the untouchables could share political power in India. As part of his plan, in the 1920s he organized demonstrations and marches to allow the untouchables to use water from a public lake, which was open to all other religious groups and even animals. Similarly, he led campaigns to allow untouchables inside the temples in other parts of the Bombay state where they had been physically barred for years.

The Scheduled Castes in different parts of India did not constitute a monolithic group, but rather included over a thousand castes and subcastes with their own hierarchical systems. The Hindu caste system remains so pervasive that, ironically enough, there are some subcastes within the untouchable caste system that do not touch or share food with members of some other untouchable subcastes for fear of pollution. In addition, he was also interested in the labor issues and bettering the position of women.

His efforts in the 1930s to establish separate electorates for the untouchables and build a political party to represent the untouchables unfortunately failed. However, during the 1940s, many of the safeguards forwarded by Ambedkar were included in the newly formed Indian Constitution. These included proportional representation in the central and state legislatures, reservation of a minimum number of jobs in the civil service at different levels for ten years that could be renewed later and the establishment of a commission to watch, investigate, and audit the progress of the scheduled classes (and scheduled tribes). The scheduled castes (and tribes) were also given reserved seats in the educational institutions. Article 17 of the Indian constitution abolished untouchability and prohibited discrimination based on untouchability, although the term was not defined in the Constitution. This was a monumental achievement by any criterion.

True to the declaration he had made 20 years earlier that, though he was born a Hindu, he would not die a Hindu, Ambedkar converted to Buddhism in 1956 and more than 300,000 Dalits followed his lead. Prior to his personal conversion, he had considered other options, including Christianity, as many Dalits had been converted to that religion. He saw in Buddhism, however, a religion based on spirituality, morality, and equality that welcomed the lower castes and women. This choice provided him an effective answer to the flaws and limitations of both Hinduism and Marxism.

Ambedkar's work and career coincided with that of Gandhi's, although the two leaders worked from a different set of assumptions. Gandhi was committed to the complete liberation of the untouchables or *Harijans;* he believed that the lot of the untouchables could be improved through a change of hearts and habits of the upper caste Hindus. Ambedkar vehemently disagreed with this assessment. He argued that the position of the untouchables could never be improved as long as they remained within the domain of Hinduism. The other conflict between Gandhi and Ambedkar was that Gandhi and his followers believed that the most important task facing them was the liberation of the country from the British rule. The tactics against the British were envisioned by Gandhi as a united front in this effort and included the untouchables and the Muslims as well. However, Ambedkar was convinced that the position of the untouchables would deteriorate even further with the independence of India. He was not eager to see the British leave the country and was criticized as a lackey of the British by many nationalists prior to independence in 1947. From the 1930s onwards, Ambedkar called for special concessions such as reservations for the untouchables in the form of reserved seats in the national parliament and state legislatures. When the British declared that they would allocate separate reserve seats, Gandhi fasted in protest; Ambedkar conceded to a compromise in which a larger number of seats were reserved for the depressed classes but as a part of a joint electorate.

Ambedkar worked with the British government in order to achieve his goal of empowerment of the untouchables, and claimed recognition of a separate status for them distinct from that of the Hindus, a claim that many would describe as separatist. His position was largely supported by the British, who believed in the divide and rule policy. His lack of active engagement in the fight for freedom against the British and the perception that he was a tool of the British made him among the most unpopular of Indians at home. Apart from the communist party leaders in India, and leaders of the Muslim league, Ambedkar was the only other major political leader to support the partition of India and the establishment of Pakistan. The political focus in India at that time was on the Hindu-Muslim issue. His ideas were rejected by millions during the time of the fight for independence of India, although he is revered by millions of Dalits today, especially so by the Mahars (his own caste members). His role as a leader and spokesperson who empowered the minorities through constitutional means and the conversion of Dalits to a new faith has significantly enhanced his reputation to the extent that he is now deified by most of his caste members, including those who converted to Buddhism. The increase in the number of statues of Ambedkar, as well as roads and colleges named after him today, probably exceeds that of any other Indian leader.

In retrospect, the overall progress of the Dalits as a group, including the neo-Buddhists (the new coverts to Buddhism), has been slower than expected in the areas of education and economics. Similarly, assimilation with the rest of the Hindus has also been a slow process, in spite of some spectacular exceptions mainly due to reservations of seats for the scheduled classes in many areas. While the conversion of such large numbers to Buddhism had a significant impact on that religion, it is too early to pass judgment on the success of that movement. Some observers see it as a psychological liberation for those who were formerly untouchables, while others feel that most of the converts are unwilling to give up their privileges associated with their former status. The recent communal riots and atrocities against the Dalits are an indication that neither Gandhi nor Ambedkar diagnosed the problem accurately or devised adequate and effective plans for their uplift.

Capsule Biography

Bhimrao Ramji Ambedkar. Born April 14, 1891at Mhow (MHOW) Camp, Bombay Infantry, India. Studied in local public schools in Satara and attended Elphintsone College, University of Bombay, India, B.A. 1912; Columbia University, New York, New York M.A., 1915, Ph.D., 1917, London School of Economics and Political Science, London, M. Sc., 1921, D. Sc., 1923, Gray's Inn, London, Bar-at-Law 1923. Taught at Sydenham College of Commerce and Economics 1918–1920, Testimony before the Southborough Committee on Franchise, 1919; Founder, *Mooknayak,* a weekly newspaper, 1920; Cofounder, Bahishkrit Hitakarini Sabha 1924, Part-time Lecturer at Batliboi's Accountancy training Institute, 1925–1928; founder, editor, *Bahishkrit Bharat* (a biweekly paper) 1927. Acting professor at Government Law College Bombay 1928–1929, principal 1935–1937; Nominated Member for the Depressed Classes to the Bombay Legislative Council, 1927; Organizer of the Mahad Satayagraha, 1927, organized the temple entry movement, Delegate to the Round Table Conference Sessions in 1930, 1931, and 1932. Signatory to the Poona pact with M.K. Gandhi 1932; Founder, Independent Labor Party, 1936; elected as member of the Bombay Legislative Assembly, 1937; served as Labour Member of the Executive Council of Viceroy, 1942–1946; Founder, People's Education Society of Bombay, 1945; Member of the Constituent Assembly of India, 1946–1947; Chair of the Drafting Committee of the Constituent Assembly 1947–1948; Central Cabinet Minister of Law, 1947–1951; converted to Buddhism in 1956. Died in New Delhi, India on December 6, 1956. Awarded honorary degrees from Columbia University, New York, D.L.L. 1952, Osmania University, Hydrabad, India, D. Lit. 1953, Bharat Ratna (Posthumously awarded).

Selected Works

The National Dividend of India: A Historical and Analytical Study, first published as *Evolution of Provincial Finance in British India*, 1925

History of Indian Currency and Banking, first published as *The problem of the Rupee*, 1923; 1947

Pakistan or the Partition of India, first published as *Thoughts on Pakistan*,1940; 2nd edition, 1946

Who Were the Shudras? How They Came to Be the Fourth Varna in the Indo-Aryan Society?, 1946
Mr. Gandhi and the Emancipation of the Untouchables, first published as *The Untouchables and the Indian Constitution*, 1943; 1948
Ranade, Gandhi and Jinnah, 1943
What Congress and Gandhi Have Done to the Untouchables?, 1945
Communal Deadlock and a Way to Solve It, 1945
States and Minorities, 1947
Untouchables: Who Are They and Why They Became Untouchables, New Delhi: Amrit Book Co., 1948
Thoughts on Linguistic States, 1955
Dr. Babasaheb Ambedkar, Writings and Speeches, Volumes I–XIV, Bombay: 1979–1995

SUBHASH R. SONNAD

See also **Gandhi, Mohandas Karamchand (India); Untouchables (Harijans/Dalits/Scheduled Castes)**

Further Reading

Abbasayulu, Y.B., *Scheduled Caste Elite: A Study of Scheduled Caste Elite in Andhra Pradesh*, Hydrabad: Pragati art Printers, 1978
Galanter, Marc, *Competing Equalities: Law and the Backward Classes in India*, Delhi: Oxford University Press, 1984
Gomango, Giridahar, *Constitutional Provision for the Scheduled Castes and the Scheduled Tribes*, Bombay: Himalaya Publishing House, 1992
Gore, M.S., *The Social Context of an Ideology: Ambedkar's Political and Social Thought*, New Delhi: Sage Publications, 1993
Keer, Dhananjay, *Dr. Ambedkar: Life and Mission*, Bombay: Popular Prakashan, Bombay: 3rd edition, 1971
Omvedt, Gail, *Dalits and the Democratic Revolution: Dr. Ambedkar and the Dalit Movement in Colonial India*, New Delhi: Sage Publications, 1994
Sachidananda, *The Harijan Elite: A Study of Their Status, Networks, Mobility and Role in Social Transformation*, Faridabad: Thomson Press (India) Limited, 1977
Shourie, Arun, *Worshipping False Gods: Ambedkar and the Facts Which Have Been Erased*, New Delhi: ASA 1997
Upadhyay, H.C., editor, *Scheduled Castes and Scheduled Tribes in India: A Socioeconomic Profile*, New Delhi: Anmol Publications, 1991
Wadhwa, Kamalesh Kumar, *Minority Safeguards in India: Constitutional Provisions and Their Implementation*, Delhi: Thomson Press (India) limited 1973

American Indian Movement

The American Indian Movement (AIM), an organization of the Native American civil rights movement, was founded in 1968 with the purpose of encouraging self-determination among Native Americans and to establish international recognition of their treaty rights. The AIM emerged from the broader context of ethnic and racial activism during the Civil Rights era in America. AIM was founded on the streets of Minneapolis, Minnesota during a protest to patrol its Indian ghetto to monitor police harassment and abuse. From this original mandate, AIM quickly evolved into a civil rights organization as it expanded the struggle for Native American rights.

Among the many local struggles that AIM members participated in across the country, one major protest event drew national and international attention to American Indian struggles. In 1969 the "Indians of All Tribes" (representing several different tribes) staged an occupation of Alcatraz Island. On November 20, 1969, this symbolic occupation turned into a full-scale occupation that lasted until June 11, 1971. The island was historically used by an indigenous tribal population and later taken by the United States government as a prison, and in particular as disciplinary barracks for Indians in the 1800s and the early 1900s. The "Indians of All Tribes" desired to take back the land and build a university and cultural center. The occupation ended with federal marshals and the FBI forcibly removing unarmed Indians. The underlying goals were to raise consciousness among the American public to the reality of the plight of the Indians and to assert the need for Indian self-determination, a goal that was eventually met with the ending of the government policy of termination of Indian tribes. Dennis Banks, an original founder of AIM, emerged as a major spokesperson during the Alcatraz event. That same year, AIM founded an Indian Health Board in Minneapolis, the first urban-based health care center for American Indians in the nation.

After Alcatraz, AIM founded chapters across the country in many major cities with significant Native American populations in Florida, South Carolina, Tennessee, and Virginia, among others. During this time, some of AIM's most ardent leaders such as Russell Means and John Trudell were recruited into its ranks. Throughout these early years, AIM members expanded their vision for social justice by attacking inequalities on numerous fronts. AIM, for example, occupied abandoned property at the naval air station near Minneapolis to focus attention on Indian education.

In a series of demonstrations, AIM members directly and publicly addressed Native American grievances. In 1970 a legal rights center was founded to assist in alleviating legal issues facing Indian people. On July 4, 1971, AIM members held demonstrations atop Mount Rushmore. On Thanksgiving Day, protesters took over a replica of the Mayflower at Plymouth, Massachusetts, painting Plymouth Rock red. The protestors also used the ship as a public forum to air Native grievances. They assisted the Lac Court Orielles Ojibwa of Wisconsin in taking over a dam controlled by Northern States Power that flooded much of the reservation land. This action led to eventual support by government officials and settlement, returning over 25,000 acres of land to the tribe. The funds provided significant monies and business opportunities to the tribe. Also in 1971, the First National AIM Conference was convened to develop long-range strategies for future directions of the movement. Eighteen AIM chapters attended the meeting.

AIM continued to become directly involved in issues nationwide. In February of 1972, Russell Means led a caravan of about 1,000 people to Gordon, Nebraska, to protest the failure of local authorities to charge two Anglo men in the torture-murder of Raymond Yellow Thunder. AIM also organized a caravan to Washington, D.C., in which the central objective was to present a 20-point solution paper to President Nixon to address Native American grievances on the eve of the 1972 United States presidential election. Called the "Trail of Broken Treaties," 2,000 people from reservations and urban areas across the country arrived in the capital in November. When government officials refused to allow representatives to deliver their 20-point document about treaty rights and self-governance, about 400 AIM members and activists seized the Bureau of Indian Affairs (BIA) headquarters in the Department of Interior building. The six-day occupation only ended after the Nixon administration publicly committed itself to addressing each point. The occupiers left, but not before taking many confidential files that they discovered in BIA offices. The documents revealed many questionable government practices, including land and mineral fraud as well as the forced sterilization of Indian women. AIM came to Washington, D.C., a civil rights organization; it left with the reputation for violent action. This viewpoint was only magnified after the media focused on the vandalism of the Bureau of Indian Affairs offices rather than the issues of indigenous sovereignty.

While AIM members drew national and international attention to Native American issues, they also sought solutions to problems. Realizing that any resolution must be based in a strong cultural and spiritual context, AIM opened several survival schools in Milwaukee and the Twin Cities area. However, in 1973 the federal government abruptly canceled their education grants. Many Indians and supporters believed the withdrawal of funding was a punishment for the Trail of Broken Treaties, although legal action restored them. Within two years, a Federation of Survival Schools was created among 16 schools in the United Sates and Canada. Its purpose was to advocate and cooperate in a culturally based education for American Indian and Native children. That same year, 1975, Housing and Urban Development (HUD) chose AIM to be the primary sponsor of the first Indian-run housing project, called the Little Earth of United Tribes.

AIM leadership was also contacted by Lakota Elders to assist them in solving the pattern of gross corruption within the Bureau of Indian Affairs and the Tribal Council on the Pine Ridge Reservation. The major conflict was between traditional Oglala and the federally sponsored tribal government under Dick Wilson. Traditional Oglala requested support from AIM to defend them against the state of terror carried out by Wilson's tribal government. The conflict led to the 71-day armed confrontation at Wounded Knee, the site of the last great massacre of Native Americans by the United States cavalry in 1890. The occupation began February 28 but the armed stand off involving United States army reserves, FBI agents and other law enforcement, and armed vigilantes, ended May 7 after officials agreed to investigate their complaints. The incident at Wounded Knee became a powerful social point for Indian sovereignty.

After Wounded Knee, the federal government set about systematically destroying the movement by neutralizing leadership through launching a series of criminal charges. Over the eight months of trials, the longest federal trial in United States history, many instances of government misconduct were uncovered by the defense. Eventually most charges were dropped against Russell Means, Dennis Banks, and other movement leaders. On the Pine Ridge reservation, tribal council leader Richard Wilson remained in power despite being out-polled by Russell Means in an election. The Department of Interior upheld the decision to keep Wilson in power; and his vigilantes now began a violent campaign to rid the reservation of any political opposition.

By spring of 1975 armed self-defense was only means of survival for those Oglala persecuted by Wilson's men. In response, AIM members were called back to the reservation and established a base camp at the Jumping Bull property. A force of federal agents, Guardians of the Oglala Nation (GOONS), and BIA police attacked the AIM defensive encampment. Two FBI agents and one AIM member were killed in the gunfight. The FBI brought a force of 250 armed men onto the reservation to capture escaping AIM members. Over the course of the next year, the hostilities on the reservation subsided.

For the killings of the FBI agents, a number of AIM members were tried, and all were acquitted except for Leonard Peltier, who was extradited from Canada in 1977. Peltier was sentenced to two life sentences for the deaths of FBI agents. Despite questionable evidence submitted by the prosecution at the original trial and new evidence that demonstrated that Pelitier's gun did not kill the agents, he remains incarcerated and is considered a political prisoner to many critical of the government's motives and actions.

In 1974 Russell Means founded the International Indian Treaty Council (IITC). Originally formed to charge that the United States government is in violation of an 1868 Treaty, the IITC has evolved into a force for global indigenous issues. Within three years, the IITC arranged the first meeting of Indian peoples from North, South, and Central America before the United Nations Economic and Social Council at the palace of nations in Geneva, Switzerland.

The Longest Walk, in 1978, was the final unified AIM action. Organized by Dennis Banks, the walk began in San Francisco during February. Participants walked across the United States holding a series of public education events to gather local support and participants. By the time of their arrival in Washington D.C. on July 23, the march contained several hundred Native Americans representing more than 80 nations. The participants held a rally on July 25 at the base of the Washington Monument. During the gathering, a manifesto was delivered amplifying the 1972 20-point program. Two days later Congressman Ron Dellems had the piece printed into the congressional record.

Throughout the 1980's and beyond, AIM continued their struggle toward achieving social justice for American Indians. In South Dakota local AIM chapters played an instrumental role in the 1980 Black Hills International Gathering. A year later they founded the Yellow Thunder Camp, a four-year occupation of 880 acres in the Black Hills, South Dakota. AIM members became involved in the Hopi-Navajo land issue by organizing a security camp to protect 10,000 traditional Dine from being forcibly removed from their homes. They assisted the Anishinabe Akeeng Organization in their struggle to regain control of stolen reservation lands. AIM formed the National Coalition on Racism in Sports and Media to confront the media stereotypes about American Indians. AIM remains in the forefront with respect to issues of self-determination, sovereignty, and the improvement of American Indian lives.

Over the course of its existence, the American Indian Movement has gone through a number of alterations in purpose and organizational structure. In the beginning, AIM sought to solve local issues, but quickly evolved into an activist organization to address national and eventually international indigenous issues. During that time however, AIM has gone from a centralized organization to autonomous AIM chapters scattered across various states and into Canada. The dissolving of AIM is the result of several factors. As the political/economic landscape changed, disagreements arose within its ranks over tactics and strategies for continuing the struggle. This factor, combined with governmental efforts to undermine AIM, resulted in charges and countercharges of government collaboration, ethnic fraud, and conspiracy among AIM factions. Despite the internal problems and differing political agendas, each AIM chapter remains committed to achieving indigenous social justice that is rooted in an appropriate spiritual and cultural context.

The legacy of AIM's work has entered into the mainstream of Native North America. On February 27, 1998, the Twenty-fifth Anniversary of Wounded Knee, an Oglala Lakota Nation resolution established that day as a National Day of Liberation. From July 16–19, 1998, the– twenty-fifth Annual Lac Courte Oreilles Honor the Earth Homecoming Celebration to celebrate and honor the people of Lac Courte Oreilles and the American Indian Movement who participated in the July 31, 1971 takeover of the Winter Dam and the Birth of Honor the Earth took place. Several days later, at the Pipe Stone Quarries, Minnesota the American Indian Movement Grand Governing Council convened to commemorate AIM's Thirtieth Anniversary and set the agenda for struggling for American Indian rights and sovereignty. As the American Indian Movement moves through the twenty-first century, it will continue to seek social justice for American Indians and other indigenous peoples.

GREGORY R. CAMPBELL

See also **Indigenous Peoples; International Indian Treaty Council (IITC)**

Further Reading

Churchill, Ward, *Indians Are Us? Culture and Genocide in Native North America*, Monroe: Common Courage Press, 1994

Churchill, Ward, "American Indian Movement," in *Native American in the Twentieth Century: An Encyclopedia*, Mary B. Davis, editor, New York: Garland Publishing, Inc., 1994, pp 37–38

Churchill, Ward, and Jim Vander Wall, *Agents of Repression: The FBI's Secret Wars Against the Black Panther Party and the American Indian Movement*, Boston: South End Press, revised edition, 2002

Deloria, Vine, Jr., *Behind the Trail of Broken Treaties: An American Indian Declaration of Independence*, Austin: University of Texas Press, 2nd edition, 1984

Johansen, Bruce, and Roberto Maestas, *Wasi'shu: The Continuing Indian Wars*, New York: Monthly Review, 1979

Josephy, Alvin M., Jr., *Red Power: The American Indian's Fight for Freedom,* New York: McGraw-Hill, 1971

Americo-Liberians

Capsule Summary

Location: Republic of Liberia, western Africa, bordering the North Atlantic Ocean, between Cote d'Ivoire and Sierra Leone
Total Population: 2.5 percent of Liberia's 3.3 million (July 2003)
Languages: English; Liberian English (Creole form of the language)
Religion: Christian

Americo-Liberians are descendants of free blacks who were repatriated from the United States to Liberia between 1821 and 1847. Today, Americo-Liberians constitute about 2.5 percent of Liberia's total population and are concentrated in Monrovia, the capital, and other coastal cities such as Buchanan, Greenville, Harper, and Robertsport. They speak English and a Creole form the language called Liberian English. Americo-Liberians are overwhelmingly Christian and observe various denominations including Anglican, Baptist, Lutheran, Methodist, and Roman Catholic. Although they constitute only a tiny minority in Liberia, America-Liberians have historically provided most of the country's political and social leadership.

History

The history of Americo-Liberians is rooted in the concern over the existence of free blacks in the United States that grew in the aftermath of the American Revolution in 1776. Many white slave owners regarded freed blacks as a threat to American society because they believed their presence would incite others still in bondage to rise up in revolt. Other whites simply rejected the idea of allowing free blacks to be integrated into American society in the years following the Revolution. The challenge of conceiving a workable colonization scheme emerged with some urgency with the rapid increase of population among free blacks in America. In 1790, free blacks in the United States numbered 59,466, and by 1810 this figure had risen to 186,466.

In a society that was half-slave and half-free, the uneasy existence between free blacks and newly released slaves became a serious concern for the United States government.

In 1816, the American Colonization Society was established by a group of white Americans who pioneered the Liberian colonization scheme. The United States Congress provided $100,000 to assist the society in returning blacks to their ancestral land. The first group left New York on board the *Elizabeth* (a refurbished naval ship) in January 1820. This group of 86 men, women, and children initially landed in Sierra Leone where they hoped to begin a settlement on Sherbro Island. Five months after leaving New York, 12 of the returnees had already died from tropical diseases, such as malaria, against which they had no immunity. A second contingent of blacks from the United States joined the first group in Freetown in March 1821.

The first piece of land for resettlement was secured at Cape Mesurado in April 1822 after United States Naval Captain Robert Field Stockton and the United States government agent, Dr. Eli Ayres, completed negotiations with a local chief in circumstances that still remain unclear. It is believed, however, that the chief concluded the deal at gunpoint and received assorted merchandise in exchange for the land. The settlers named their settlement Monrovia, after ex-President James Monroe and the first president of the Society. In subsequent years more blacks from the United States and African slaves who had been set free by British and United States naval squadrons (intercepted slave ships trying to illegally transport slaves to the Americas) joined them.

Between 1822 and 1847, the settlement was under the control of the American Colonization Society, but the United States government reduced its financial support for the settlers. Four other settlements were established along the coast, which, in 1838, became the Commonwealth of Liberia. The nascent commonwealth faced many difficulties, some of which resulted from poor funding and the absence of a strong economic base. Others grew out of the hostile relationship that developed between the America-Liberians and indigenous Africans who were apprehensive of the prospects of losing their land to the settlers. The Commonwealth also faced external threats, mainly from European traders who were reluctant to recognize the authority of the ACS officials. An attempt by Governor Joseph Jenkins Johnson, an America-Liberian from Virginia, to introduce customs duties in order to raise revenue for the Commonwealth was opposed by European traders. Moreover, by the 1830s, abolitionists began to attack the Society and discredit colonization as a slave-holder's scheme; they viewed the ACS as merely palliative propaganda for the continuation of slavery in the United States.

Independence

Unlike Haiti, the first black republic in the Western Hemisphere, Liberia did not need a revolution to gain its independence. Disputes between Americo-Liberians and the ACS persisted, as it became increasingly clear that the organization could not solve the financial problems of the settlement. Also, the United States government, facing domestic problems of its own over the issue of slavery, showed no interest in adopting Liberia as an official colony despite Britain's insistence that the United States should define its relationship with Liberia. Thus, confronted with increasing pressure from Britain and France over its status in international law, Liberia declared its independence on July 26, 1847. Joseph J. Roberts became its first president. The independent republic modeled its government after that of the United States and adopted a national flag reminiscent of the stars and stripes of the American flag. Ironically, while Britain and France promptly recognized Liberia's independence, it was not until 1862, during Abraham Lincoln's administration, that the United States recognized Liberia's sovereignty.

The True Whig, also known as Liberian Whig Party, was the country's only legal political party for over 100 years, from 1878 to 1980. Throughout the nineteenth century the Americo-Liberian leaders faced both internal and external threats to Liberian independence. Relations between the minority Americo-Liberians and indigenous Liberians for the most part were hostile because of the unequal power relations between the two groups. Post-independence the Liberian government expanded inland in an attempt to establish control over the interior. An interior bureaucracy was set up to exercise control over more than two-thirds of Liberian territory and over three-quarters of its people. This move was seen by most indigenous groups as an attempt to subdue them and deprive them of their land. The system of "indirect rule" adopted by the government was a way to tap the human and material resources of the interior during the last quarter of the nineteenth century when Liberia was experiencing an economic decline. Indigenous groups, especially the Grebo and Kru, resisted the imposition of Liberian authority and the abuses of the system of indirect rule. Between 1871 and 1906 the Americo-Liberian government was forced to obtain loans from Britain to finance its administrative costs. At the same time, it faced British and French attempts to encroach on Liberian territory from their neighboring colonies in Sierra Leone and Cote d'Ivoire, respectively.

At the turn of the twentieth century the Americo-Liberian leadership turned to United States for financial and military aid to deal with its chronic problems and local rebellions by indigenous groups. In 1926, the Liberian government received a $5 million loan from the American Firestone Rubber Company and leased large amounts of land to the company for rubber plantations. A labor scandal erupted in the late 1920s when the government was charged with exporting indigenous Liberians to work on Spanish plantations on the island of Fernando Poo (Bioko), off the coast of Nigeria. This led to the resignation of Vice President Allen Yancy and other government officials who were said to have received payments for authorizing the labor exportation.

When William V.S. Tubman became president of Liberia in 1944, he was determined to improve the economy and integrate the Liberian population. His policies were therefore geared toward providing increased political and economic opportunities for indigenous peoples. His unification policy extended the right to vote and be represented in the national legislature to all indigenous Liberians. At the same time, he ensured that political power remained under the control of a small group of Americo-Liberian families that had ruled Liberia for most of its history.

Tubman died in 1971 and was succeeded by William R. Tolbert, who followed similar policies. With the Liberian economy deteriorating as world demands for rubber and iron ore declined in the 1970s, opposition to Americo-Liberian dominance increased and government officials were accused of corruption and nepotism. In 1979, riots broke out in the streets of Monrovia over a proposed increase in the price of rice. Tolbert's government was toppled the following year in a bloody coup led by an indigenous Liberian, Samuel K. Doe, who established a military regime (the People's Redemption Council). Tolbert and other prominent members of his government were publicly executed, in what apparently was an attempt to put an end to the dominance of Americo-Liberian political power. Doe suspended the constitution and proscribed political parties as he began to consolidate his power. Five members of his People's Redemption Council who had assisted in staging the coup were executed in 1981 on charges of conspiracy. In November 1985, General Quiwonkpa attempted a coup, which was suppressed by troops loyal to the government. Fighting between government troops and the rebels resulted in about 600 deaths. Opposition leaders, among them many prominent Americo-Liberians, were arbitrarily detained and some were forced to flee Liberia.

Doe's repressive rule aggravated the historical power struggle between Americo-Liberians and their indigenous counterparts. But almost a decade of inept government and antidemocratic measures was enough to alienate indigenous and Americo-Liberians alike. In late December 1989, Charles Taylor and his National Patriotic Front of Liberia (NPFL) entered Liberia from neighboring Côte d'Ivoire to begin what would become seven years of bloody conflict between the government and about five rebel factions. The capture and brutal murder of Doe in September 1990 could not persuade the rebels to put down their arms. Nor did the intervention of a multinational West Africa peacekeeping force led by Nigeria. After several short-lived ceasefires and peace initiatives, an interim government was established in August 1996, and a new peace plan was put in place. Taylor and some of the rebel leaders transformed their military movements into political parties. Taylor's victory in the 1997 free and open presidential election and his party's domination in the national legislature meant that the minority Americo-Liberian leadership once again wielded power.

Society, Politics, and Civil War

The minority Americo-Liberian community constitutes only about 2.5 percent of Liberia's total population, but it provides much the country's political and social leadership. Americo-Liberians take great pride in their American heritage, and many families are still able to trace their roots to families in the United States. Wealthy Americo-Liberian parents also send their children to be educated in schools and colleges in the United States. In the past, Americo-Liberians emerged as the country's leaders partly because of their earlier exposure to Western education. This also distanced them from indigenous Liberians who were regarded as uncivilized and unschooled.

Most Americo-Liberians work in the professional sector as civil servants, lawyers, doctors, nurses, engineers, teachers, and journalists. Some serve in the military and other security agencies. Although an increasing number have entered business, most Americo-Liberians traditionally considered commerce an activity for indigenous Liberians and foreign residents. The culture is one that esteems family values in the Judeo-Christian tradition, and men usually marry once and raise a nuclear family, even though they might have mistresses. Although men tend to dominate the family unit, many Americo-Liberian women play important roles in society. Extended families are also valued. It is not uncommon to see married children and their offspring live with their parents until they become financially independent.

TAMBA E. M'BAYO

See also **Liberia; Slavery**

Further Reading

Beyan, Amos, *The American Colonization Society and the Creation of the Liberian State: A Historical Perspective, 1822–1900*, Lanham, Maryland and London: University Press of America, 1991

Dunn, D. Elwood, *Liberia,* Santa Barbara, California and Oxford, England: Clio Press, 1995

Dunn, D. Elwood, and Svend E. Holsoe, *Historical Dictionary of Liberia*, Metuchen, New Jersey and London: The Scarecrow Press, 1985

Sawyer, Amos, *The Emergence of Autocracy in Liberia: Tragedy and Challenge*, San Francisco, California: Institute for Contemporary Studies, 1992

Shick, Tom, *Behold the Promised Land: A History of Afro-American Settler Society in Nineteenth-Century Liberia*, Baltimore, Madison and London: Johns Hopkins University Press, 1980

Sisay, Hassan, *Big Powers and Small Nations: A Case Study of United States-Liberian Relations*, Lanham, Maryland: University Press of America, 1985

Staudenraus, P.J., *The American Colonization Movement 1816–1865*, New York: Columbia University Press, 1961

Amerindians (North America)

Capsule Summary

Location: United States and Canada
Total Population: about 3.5 million
Languages: English, French, and Native languages
Religions: Traditional religions and Christianity

The Amerindian peoples of North America inhabit a diversity of environments across the United States and Canada. This broad category encompasses hundreds of distinct ethnic groups, often called tribes or bands. In the United States they are referred to collectively as Native Americans, American Indians, or Indians. In Canada they are also known as First Nations or First Peoples. They speak more than 200 different languages, besides English and French, and differ from one another in culture and history. There are about 3.5 million people of Native descent north of Mexico. Nearly 2.5 million are in the United States, where they account for 0.9 percent of the population. Less than one million are in Canada, where they make up 3.3 percent of the population. These numbers do not include 1.6 million people of American Indian descent who identified themselves as of mixed race on the 2000 United States census. Nearly 22 percent of the Native people in the United States live in designated areas called reservations. In Canada, more than 29 percent live in similar places, called reserves. The rest reside in towns, cities, and other rural areas. A significant proportion is at least nominally Christian. Despite past attempts by missionaries and government agents to suppress Native religions, most Native peoples maintain traditional beliefs and religious practices, often alongside Christian ones. They also share a sense of affinity, or pan-Indian identity. This stems from their parallel experiences of colonial domination, their unique status, and the challenges they face in common as indigenous minorities.

History

The ancestors of today's Native peoples first entered North America from Siberia via a land bridge across the Bering Strait, by boat, or over the ice. Archaeologists believe they came in several waves beginning 20,000 or more years ago, with the Arctic Inuit last to arrive. By the time Columbus made landfall they had spread throughout the continent. The population in 1492 is a point of dispute. Estimates range from less than 2 million to about 18 million. Europeans looking for souls to save, resources and wealth, labor, and land to settle followed Columbus. They introduced diseases like smallpox and measles, to which the indigenous peoples had no resistance. The centuries of disease, warfare, and forced labor that ensued brought social and cultural upheaval, suffering, and depopulation. Many tribes and communities vanished altogether. Disease alone carried away between 50 percent and 90 percent of the aboriginal population within the area covered by the United States. By the end of the nineteenth century only about 300,000 Indians and Inuits remained in North America. After 1900 their population began to recover.

The British, Spanish, French, Russians, and Dutch vied for control of the continent for more than three centuries. They often recruited Native peoples as allies. For example, Indian fought Indian in the French and Indian War (1754) and the American War of Independence, which ended in 1776. International conflicts also impacted trade and affected them in other ways. The Europeans' means and objectives varied, but wherever they went they exploited, displaced, and killed aboriginal peoples. The peoples they encountered desired their goods, but also resisted their incursions. Sometimes they did so by forming alliances, as in the Pueblo Revolt (1680) and Pontiac's Conspiracy (1763).

With the 1803 Louisiana Purchase, the United States acquired the area between the Mississippi River and the Rocky Mountains from France. This set in motion a wave of settlers intent on fulfilling America's asserted divinely ordained Manifest Destiny to cover the continent. It mattered little that Indians already occupied the regions in question. Territory obtained from Spain (1819) and Mexico (1848) completed the nation's coast-to-coast dominion. Lust for land soon translated into a campaign to civilize and relocate the surviving eastern tribes to Indian Territory west of the Mississippi. The army met any resistance with force, as in the removal of 16,000 Cherokees to Oklahoma in 1838. More than a quarter of them died on what the Cherokees remember as the Trail of Tears.

Banishing the tribes to Indian Territory accomplished little. It caused friction with tribes already there and settlers and prospectors soon followed. With the passage of the Homestead Act in 1862 and completion of the transcontinental railroad after the Civil War what had been a trickle became a flood of settlers. Conflict between Indians and whites erupted across the West. Both sides committed atrocities. The government used a carrot and stick approach to put an end to the violence. Treaties were the carrot, the army the stick. With the army it was business as usual. The treaties, however, offered concessions, food and supplies, money, and services like education and health care in exchange for land and peace. Members of many western tribes and bands accepted reservation life under duress. Some did not and the conflict continued. This was the time of the Great Sioux War. It culminated in Custer's 1876 defeat by Lakota and Cheyenne warriors at the Little Bighorn. The surrender of Geronimo, the Chiricahua Apache raider, in 1886 marked the end of resistance in the Southwest. The army's 1890 massacre of 200 or so Lakota Ghost dancers on Wounded Knee Creek marked the end on the Plains.

The 1887 Dawes Severalty Act inaugurated the modern era in Indian and white relations in the United States. Its intent was to hasten the assimilation of Indians into mainstream society by turning them into land-owning farmers and ranchers and erasing their tribal identities. Instead, it brought poverty and dispossession. In 1887 there were 138 million acres of Indian land in the United States. Only 52 million acres remained in Indian hands when Congress abolished the act in 1934. Canada's First Nations fared slightly better. They had experienced somewhat more benign relations with the Europeans and consequently much less bloodshed. They had also largely escaped dislocation. Nonetheless, by 1923 they retained only 6 million acres of land.

Federal Indian Policy

As did the British before them, the Canadian and American governments made treaties with Native groups. They used these legally binding agreements to obtain land for settlement, create reservations and reserves, and promote assimilation. Differences in what treaties meant to the two governments led to distinct strategies for dealing with what non-Indians termed the "Indian problem." The most important difference had to do with tribal sovereignty, or independence. Canada, then a British colony, viewed its aboriginal peoples as subjects of the Crown. The United States, by making treaties with them, legally recognized tribes as sovereign nations. This gave rise to the semi-sovereign status and special treatment now accorded Indian reservations in the United States. Despite their law-like authority, the treaties invariably got broken, usually to the detriment of the Native peoples. This led to conflict in the eighteenth and nineteenth centuries and decades of litigation and political action in the twentieth century.

The Canadian government used treaties to isolate First Nations peoples on fragments of their homelands. This enabled them to continue their traditional subsistence practices for a time. The outcome was a huge number of small, widely dispersed reserves. The American government used treaties to consolidate bands and tribes on larger reservations. This often entailed relocating them to remote areas not suited to their traditional forms of subsistence. In this way, the government forced them to take up farming or ranching and to rely on annuities and subsidies. Both countries enacted laws and policies designed to undermine Native cultures and hasten assimilation. These originated in a widely held belief that education, conversion to Christianity, individual land ownership, and agriculture would erode tribal identity. Once stripped of their communal identities, Indians would disappear into the national mainstream, or so the logic went.

The twentieth century was a period of ethnic renewal and political struggle for Native peoples across the continent. It was also a time of dramatic policy reversals for those in the United States. Millions of acres of land passed out of Indian hands before John Collier, the Commissioner of Indian Affairs, introduced his New Deal for American Indians in 1933. The Wheeler-Howard Act, or Indian Reorganization Act (IRA), was its cornerstone. The IRA halted the erosion of the Indian land base and encouraged tribal self-government and economic development on the reservations. Collier also ended policies that forced Indians to take part in Christian services and that banned rituals like the Sun Dance and sacramental use of peyote. After World War II, federal policy did an about-face. Renewed interest in assimilation resulted in two initiatives that profoundly impacted tribal life. One encouraged reservation Indians to relocate to urban areas like Chicago and Los Angeles. The other, called termination, withdrew federal support from those tribes deemed ready. Congress terminated about a dozen tribes in all, most with dire consequences. A policy shift in the 1970s restored support for tribal self-determination.

Red Power

Debilitating policies, land claims, threats to tribal resources, and the Civil Rights Movement paved the way for the emergence of the Red Power Movement in the 1960s. The National Indian Youth Council and the American Indian Movement were at its forefront. Three events stand out from this period. The first began in 1969, when a group of Indians reclaimed Alcatraz Island. By the time the peaceful occupation ended a year and a half later, hundreds of Indians had taken part. It left them, and others who watched from a distance, more united and empowered than ever before. The other two events proved as divisive as empowering. Violence marred both. The first occurred in 1972, when the Trail of Broken Treaties caravan traveled to Washington, D.C., to present a list of grievances to federal officials but ended up occupying the Bureau of Indian Affairs building. The second was the long siege at Wounded Knee in 1973.

The violence weakened the Red Power Movement but a cohort of politically astute activists emerged to carry on. They doggedly pursued Native causes in the courts, legislative chambers, mass media, and on the streets. Since the 1970s the United States and Canada have passed major legislation aimed at correcting past wrongs and upholding Native rights. Courts in both countries have been working through long dockets of land claims and other grievances. The struggle continues, however, as Native rights, sovereignty, and tribal resources remain under threat.

Society

Observers once predicted that the Native peoples would vanish, or at least disappear into some cultural melting pot only to reemerge indistinguishable from other North Americans. They were wrong. The continent's indigenous peoples entered the twentieth century diminished in numbers and culturally battered, but they survived and flourished. Today they are everywhere, from the remotest corners of the Arctic to the streets of Manhattan. Some still hunt, trap, and fish, only now using modern technology and business practices. Others farm and ranch where their ancestors once cultivated and hunted. Many work in manufacturing, construction, and the service industries. Some are doctors, lawyers, and educators.

Native peoples still encounter prejudice and discrimination, ignorance, attacks on their sovereignty and resources, and ill-conceived policies. They have disproportionately low per capita incomes and high rates of unemployment, both indicators of their relative poverty. Despair and social problems plague some of their communities. Native peoples across North America draw strength and inspiration from their families, communities, and cultural traditions. They use it to creatively tackle the problems they face. To do so successfully, they must navigate the quagmire of tribal, state and provincial, and national laws, regulations, and bureaucratic structures that constitute Native affairs.

In outward appearance and lifestyle Native peoples resemble other North Americans. Nonetheless they retain a great deal of cultural distinctiveness. This is a source of strength and pride as well as cross-cultural misunderstanding. Family and community ties remain strong, but often reflect forms of social organization alien to outsiders. Political and economic organization can be equally bewildering. Traditional religion remains a vibrant part of most Native communities, either alongside or in competition with Christianity. Religious leaders and elders work together to strengthen community bonds by perpetuating longstanding traditions and offering guidance. College, military service, powwows, and the Native American Church bring together people from different groups. This fosters a sense of pan-Indian identity and an awareness of shared political concerns.

DEBRA BUCHHOLTZ

See also **American Indian Movement (AIM); Indigenous Peoples; International Indian Treaty Council (IITC); Peltier, Leonard**

Further Reading

Berkhofer, Robert F., Jr., *The White Man's Indian: Images of the American Indian from Columbus to the Present*, New York: Alfred A. Knopf, 1978

Deloria, Philip J., and Neal Salisbury, editors, *A Companion to American Indian History*, Oxford and Malden, Massachusetts: Blackwell, 2002

Dickason, Olive Patricia, *Canada's First Nations: A History of Founding Peoples from Earliest Times*, Norman: University of Oklahoma Press, 1992

Dippie, Brian W., *The Vanishing Indian: White Attitudes and U.S. Indian Policy*, Middletown, Connecticut: Wesleyan University Press, 1982

Fixico, Donald L., *Termination and Relocation: Federal Indian Policy, 1945–1960*, Albuquerque: University of New Mexico Press, 1986

Fixico, Donald L., *The Invasion of Indian Country in the Twentieth Century: American Capitalism and Tribal Natural Resources*, Niwot: University Press of Colorado, 1998

Hoxie, Frederick E., *A Final Promise: The Campaign to Assimilate the Indians, 1880–1920*, Lincoln: University of Nebraska Press, 1984; Cambridge, Melbourne, and New York: Cambridge University Press, 1989

Nabokov, Peter, editor, *Native American Testimony: A Chronicle of Indian-White Relations from Prophecy to Present, 1492–1992*, New York: Penguin, 1978; 2nd edition, 1992

Nagel, Joane, *American Indian Ethnic Renewal: Red Power and the Resurgence of Identity and Culture*, New York and Oxford: Oxford University Press, 1996

Thornton, Russell, *American Indian Holocaust and Survival*, Norman and London: University of Oklahoma Press, 1987

Trigger, Bruce G., and Wilcomb E. Washburn, editors, *The Cambridge History of the Native Peoples of the Americas, volume 1, North America, parts 1 and 2*, Cambridge, New York, and Melbourne: Cambridge University Press, 1996

Washburn, Wilcomb E., editor, *Handbook of North American Indians, volume 4: History of Indian-white Relations*, Washington, D.C.: Smithsonian Institution, 1988

Amerindians (South and Central America)

Capsule Summary

Location: Throughout Central and South America.
Total Population: Approximately 40 million.
Languages: Indigenous languages, Spanish, Portuguese, English, and French.
Religions: Indigenous religions and Christianity.

Millions of indigenous peoples live in the cities, towns, rural areas, and remote areas of Central and South America. The proper placement of Mexico in the Americas is a point of dispute. Most people, on the basis of historical and cultural commonalities, consider it part of Central America, although geographical purists, who think in continental terms, put it in North America. This article includes it in Central America. Many scholars lump South and Central America together as Latin America. The combined entity encompasses more than 20 million square kilometers of land. It stretches from north of the equator almost to the Antarctic Circle in the south. Latin America has one of the highest mountain ranges in the world, some of the largest rain forests, and very arid regions. As a result, it is an area of great ecological, biological, cultural, and linguistic diversity. This creates unique challenges and opportunities for those who live there, and for none moreso than the indigenous peoples. Ever since the conquest, Europeans have called those peoples Indians. This is a misleading and overly general racial label that serves only to draw a line between the intruders from the Old World and the very diverse peoples of the New World. It implies a degree of cultural homogeneity that has never existed. To the extent that the so-called Indians now have any sense of a shared identity, it is as oppressed indigenous peoples struggling to overcome difficult conditions rooted in the colonial past.

Twenty-one nation-states and French Guiana, which is an overseas department of France, make up Latin America. Each has its own form of government, national language, and distinct way of dealing with the indigenous peoples within its borders. Accurate and up-to-date population statistics are hard to come by for at least two reasons. First, different countries collect census data in different ways and at different intervals. Second, some countries are reluctant to collect and publish data on their native peoples. Indigenous groups and their defenders tend to produce high estimates; nation-states and development agencies tend to produce low estimates. Self-interest and political considerations are at work in both cases. The best recent estimates date from the 1990s. They put the indigenous population at about 40 million, which is roughly 10 percent of the Latin American total. Indigenous people are a clear majority in Bolivia, where they make up about 55 percent of the population. In Guatemala (44 percent), Peru (45 percent), Ecuador (25 percent), and Mexico (30 percent) they constitute a significant minority. Numerical strength, however, does not automatically translate into political power, social acceptance, or economic well being. As a result, indigenous people are almost invariably the poorest of the poor in their countries. Many people of mixed ethnic heritage do not identify themselves as indigenous and do not live in so-called Indian communities. They appear in most censuses as *mestizos* or *ladinos*.

There are hundreds of culturally distinct groups in South and Central America. Even now, Brazilian officials believe there may be as many as 20 such groups in remote parts of the Amazon Basin that they have yet to contact. The huge number of languages still spoken is just one indicator of the cultural diversity in Latin America. Because of the fine-line distinction between a language and a dialect, there is little agreement as to how many languages currently exist. Most scholars talk in terms of at least 400. Some linguists believe that the indigenous peoples spoke between 550 and 700 different languages in the mid-1990s. They represented 56 different families and included 73 isolates, or languages not related to any other known language. Many had no more than a few hundred speakers and were at risk of dying out. Others had large numbers of speakers. Quechua, the language of the former Incan Empire, is the most widely spoken indigenous language in Latin America. It has an estimated 8.5 million speakers in Peru, Brazil, Bolivia, Argentina, Ecuador, and Columbia. Guaraní is one of the official languages of Paraguay. It has an estimated 3 million speakers. Ke kchí, a Mayan language spoken in Guatemala, and Nahua, a Uto-Aztecan language spoken in Mexico, each have about 1.3 million speakers. Many indigenous people speak more than one language, and most have at least functional use of a national language. Spanish and Portuguese are the most common national languages. English and French also serve in that capacity. Another indicator of the region's cultural diversity is the wide array of traditional religions still in evidence. After centuries of missionary activity, many indigenous people now practice Christianity, mainly Catholicism, often alongside their traditional religions. This has led to the incorporation of elements from one into the other, or what anthropologists call religious syncretism.

Conquest and Colonization

Archaeologists believe that the ancestors of today's indigenous peoples entered the Americas from Asia. They crossed the Bering Strait into what is now Alaska 20,000 or more years ago. Over time they spread across North America into Central America and then South America. Humans have been in the Caribbean basin and on the plains of South America for at least 2,500 years. There is evidence of well-developed societies in the highlands of Mexico, Central America, and the Andes 8,000 years before that. Archaeologists have also found the material remains of even earlier human activity. These remains indicate the presence of agriculture and the emergence of civilizations. Most native peoples explain their origins and histories in a markedly different way from the archaeologists. Some designate specialists to safeguard that knowledge and convey it to others in prescribed contexts and by prescribed means, often through oral history, myths, and rituals. Regardless of how they got there and when, there were millions of people in the Americas by 1492. Estimating aboriginal populations is always a difficult undertaking open to dispute. The most widely accepted attempts to do so put the precontact population of Latin America at between 35 million and 45 million.

There were three types of cultures in Central and South America at the time of the conquest. Nomadic peoples lived in small groups and subsisted by hunting, fishing, and gathering. Sedentary or semisedentary peoples grew at least some of their food. Many of them engaged in what anthropologists call swidden cultivation, referring to the "slash and burn" method they used to prepare the land. Fully sedentary peoples lived in areas that supported high population densities. They engaged in surplus agricultural production. This led to an increase in labor specialization and social differentiation. It also enabled them to build large ceremonial centers. The Aztec, Maya, and Inca civilizations dominated Central America and the Andean area of South America when the Spanish first arrived. The Aztecs were in the central valley of what is now Mexico. They exacted tribute payments, including people to sacrifice, and labor from across a wide swath of the region. The Maya occupied most of present-day Guatemala, Honduras, Belize, and southern Mexico. The Inca, who had created the largest indigenous empire ever known in the Americas, ruled from the valley of Cuzco in Peru. Their political and economic control extended from what is now the northern border of Ecuador to the Maule River in Chile.

After Columbus returned from his first voyage to the Americas, the church granted Spain dominion over the land he had discovered in exchange for Christianizing the people who occupied it. In 1494 Spain and Portugal signed a treaty that gave Portugal a foothold in what is now Brazil. Violence, forced labor, disease, and disruptions of traditional ways of life accompanied their colonization of the New World. These took a huge toll on the indigenous peoples. By the mid-1500s the native peoples had virtually disappeared from the islands of the Caribbean. A Portuguese explorer named Cabral landed in Brazil in 1500. That same year the Spanish entered the mainland of Central America. Within two decades Fernando Cortés had conquered the Aztec and most of the Maya. A smallpox epidemic that greatly weakened them smoothed his way. Smallpox spread south ahead of the *conquistadores* and caused massive death and disruption. It hit Peru by 1527 and aided Francisco Pizarro's conquest of the Inca. Measles, typhus, and influenza followed. A century later, malaria and yellow fever arrived from Africa, and then diphtheria and possibly bubonic plague. By the mid-1600s the population of the area under Spanish control was probably less than 10 percent of what it had been in 1492. Virulent diseases hit the Portuguese areas a bit later, but the results were much the same. It was not until the late seventeenth century that the indigenous population in most parts of Latin America began to recover.

The Spanish quickly established permanent settlements wherever they went. They wasted no time before they introduced European crops and livestock and reorganized indigenous labor to support the colonial economy. By 1570 the colonial administrative structure was firmly in place. Over the next two centuries it changed little. The Spanish used forced labor to develop mining and agriculture for the export market and agriculture, livestock grazing, and textiles for the growing domestic market. They devised various means by which to coerce the native peoples into taking part in the colonial economy. One of the earliest was the *encomienda*. This was a grant of land and indigenous labor to Spanish overlords. In theory at least, the overlords had to protect and Christianize their native wards in return for the wards' labor. Other common means were the rotating labor draft, called *repartimiento*; and the community labor draft, called *mita*. Some of the large estates and mines also used free wage labor, but many did so in such a way that it evolved into a form of debt peonage. Additional tactics included the forced sale of merchandise to poorly paid laborers at inflated prices and mandatory payments of tribute. Both locked indigenous people into the colonial economy by creating debts that they could repay only through wage labor. The Portuguese relied more heavily on slave labor than did the Spanish. They used native slaves, for example, to establish the sugar plantations in Brazil. Eventually, they replaced native slaves with slaves from Africa. The colonial system had a devastating impact on indigenous communities everywhere. Not only did it alter their cultural underpinnings and social structure; it set in motion widespread migration. Some people fled the high tribute payments and insufferable labor conditions. Others were "pushed" out of their home communities and "pulled" into Spanish-dominated towns and cities by the new economic forces.

The church referred to so often in conjunction with the conquest is the Catholic Church. The Protestant missions did not arrive until much later. The Catholic Church played a complex and as yet poorly understood role throughout Latin America; scholars disagree over the exact nature of its role and the extent to which it disrupted indigenous ways of life. However, it appears to have been more critical to the Spanish colonial project than to the Portuguese. The church's main objective was to convert the native peoples to Christianity. But in doing so, it imposed on them not only its own values but also Spanish social practices and political and economic structures. This resulted in the repression of indigenous beliefs and practices and the forcible promotion of Spanish ones. Some scholars, though, have warned against overstating the church's role as an agent of change. They argue that the sudden population collapse caused by epidemic diseases and the continual interaction between native peoples and European newcomers led to far more sweeping changes than the church brought about. Moreover, the church lacked the human resources to provide more than superficial coverage of the vast region during most of the colonial period. In areas with widely scattered native populations, it often joined with the colonial authorities to gather the indigenous peoples in new settlements. This process facilitated their conversion and incorporation into the colonial system but also fostered the spread of disease. The church was clearly an agent of change and assimilation, but it also shielded its wards from what it perceived to be some of the more harmful effects of colonial contact. In particular, it tried to protect them from overly harsh labor demands, corruption, and immorality.

The missionaries and colonial authorities had more power and resources than the native peoples they sought to control and exploit. It would nonetheless be wrong to assume that native peoples were passive victims. They suffered greatly under the repressive conditions imposed by the colonial regime, but like people everywhere they tried to shape the best future they could for themselves and their families. They used both passive and active means to resist colonial domination and the changes it wrought on their ways of life. In many cases, they maintained their traditional beliefs and practices out of sight of the church and the colonial authorities. In other instances, they used more active means to resist. Sometimes they resorted to violent uprisings. Most notable in this regard was the resistance that developed among the badly exploited peoples of the Andes in the eighteenth century. The uprisings began in the 1740s and climaxed in the 1780s under the leadership of José Gabriel de Condorcanqui, who called himself Tupac Amaru II after the great Inca leader. The Spanish eventually put down the rebellion, and it failed to achieve most of its objectives. It did, however, bring about the end of the *repartimiento* system and spurred other important changes in the colonial administrative structure.

Postcolonial situation

Except for a significant number in Mexico, few indigenous people showed much interest in the national independence movements that swept through Latin America between 1808 and 1825. Indeed, the overthrow of the colonial authorities benefited them little, at least for a while. Many of the new governments sought to draw indigenous people into their fledgling nation-states as full citizens equal to all others. This prospect promised to relieve of them of the labor and tribute obligations imposed by the colonial regime, but it also threatened to strip them of what few privileges and protections they had. At the same time, most governments refused to recognize native peoples' communal forms of land ownership. The governments wanted to redistribute all such land to individuals, who would either work it or sell it. Many of the governments, however, lacked the power to implement such changes. Desperate for funds, some retained a form of indigenous tribute for decades. In certain areas, indigenous people found their colonial labor obligations replaced by state-imposed obligations. Scattered uprisings still occurred, just as they had in the colonial period. However, they were now more often offensive initiatives aimed at the recovery of land and other objectives than defensive reactions to specific threats. One noteworthy uprising was the Caste War of the nineteenth century. As a result of this war, nonindigenous people were driven out of large parts of the Yucatan Peninsula.

Demand for Latin American commodities and minerals surged in the last quarter of the nineteenth century. The rapid development and influx of foreign capital it stimulated led to what John Kicza has described as an "atmosphere of disdain toward native peoples and their cultures." This underpinned a renewed attack upon their resources, cultures, and autonomy that continues in many areas to this day. Although not an indigenous uprising per se, the Mexican Revolution, which took place between 1910 and 1920, was a reaction to these developments, at least in part. It included a struggle by indigenous peoples to regain their communally owned lands. Other revolts took place across the continent. The Aymara, for example, staged an uprising in Bolivia in 1952. They succeeded in reclaiming much of their land. In the aftermath, the Bolivian government supported their victory with legis- lation. The unrest spread to the beleaguered indigenous peoples of Peru. The agrarian reforms initiated there in the late 1960s did little to improve their situation. During the next decade, Peru entered a deep and lasting repression. It was out of those conditions that the Maoist Shining Path group emerged. Those same conditions gave rise to an increase in the growing of coca leaf as a cash crop. Coca leaf is processed to become cocaine; consequently, its cultivation has attracted the attention of international (mainly United States) law enforcement agencies.

Indigenous peoples across Latin America continue to face serious threats to their material and cultural survival, and in many cases to their very lives. In some areas, impoverished peasant farmers are moving onto their lands in search of a better life. In other areas, the threat comes from such diverse sources as road building, hydroelectric projects, bio-prospecting, mineral and oil extraction, lumbering, agribusiness, civil war, and tourism. These and other factors are driving indigenous people into urban areas in ever-increasing numbers. They frequently end up in the shantytowns that cling to most Latin American cities. Almost invariably they enter the workforce in the lowest-paid jobs, which tend to be in the service, industrial, and informal sectors. The vast majority of indigenous people, whether in urban or rural areas, are poor. Many are extremely poor. As a result, they often live in inadequate housing with poor sanitation. They also have limited access to education, health care, social services, and legal aid—the very resources they need to break out of poverty. Low levels of education, for example, result in low literacy rates, low wages, and consequently increased poverty. Because of the conditions in which they live, indigenous people are more likely than other people to become ill; but they are less likely to seek medical attention or to be vaccinated.

In recent decades, the indigenous peoples of Latin America have begun to mobilize for political action on many levels, often with the support of concerned outsiders. What began as a grassroots movement has now crossed national borders and united activists from across the continent and beyond. Their aim is to secure their human and indigenous rights, including land rights, and to improve their living conditions. Besides negotiating directly with individual countries, they are taking their cases to the United Nations and other international forums. Although much remains to be accomplished, they are slowly making headway.

Debra Buchholtz

See also **Amerindians: North America; Katari, Tupac (Aymaran); Menchú, Rigoberta (Amerincian); Yanomami**

Further Reading

Adams, Richard E.W., and Murdo J. Macleod, editors, *The Cambridge History of the Native Peoples of the Americas*, Volume 2, *Mesoamerica*, Part 2, Cambridge, New York, Melbourne, and Madrid: Cambridge University Press, 2000

Brysk, Alison, *From Tribal Village to Global Village: Indian Rights and International Relations in Latin America*, Stanford, Calif.: Stanford University Press, 2000

Burkholder, Mark A., and Lyman L. Johnson, *Colonial Latin America*, New York and Oxford: Oxford University Press, 1990; 3rd edition, 1998

Campbell, Lyle, *American Indian Languages: The Historical Linguistics of Native America*, New York and Oxford: Oxford University Press, 1997

Hemming, John, *Die If You Must: Brazilian Indians in the Twentieth Century*, London: Macmillan, 2003

Kicza, John E., editor, *The Indian in Latin American History: Resistance, Resilience, and Acculturation*, Wilmington, Delaware: Scholarly Resources, 1993; revised edition 2000

Salomon, Frank, and Stuart B. Schwartz, editors, *The Cambridge History of the Native Peoples of the Americas*, Volume 3, *South America*, Part 2, Cambridge, New York, Melbourne, and Madrid: Cambridge University Press, 1999

Stenich, Susan, editor, *Endangered Peoples of Latin America: Struggles to Survive and Thrive*, London and Westport, Connecticut: Greenwood Press, 2001

Steward, Julian Haynes, editor, *Handbook of South American Indians*, Bureau of American Ethnology Bulletin 143, Washington, D.C.: U.S. Government Printing Office, 1946–1959

Urban, Greg, and Joel Sherzer, editors, *Nation-States and Indians in Latin America*, Austin: University of Texas Press, 1991

Warren, Kay B., and Jean E. Jackson, editors, *Indigenous Movements, Self-Representation, and the State in Latin America*, Austin: University of Texas Press, 2002

Wauchope, Robert, general editor *Handbook of Middle American Indians*, Austin: University of Texas Press, 1964–1976

Amish

Capsule Summary

Location: United States and Canada
Total Population: over 150,000
Languages: Pennsylvania Dutch, High German, English
Religion: Protestant

The Old Order Amish are an Anabaptist religious isolate. There are currently over 150,000 Old Order Amish living in over 200 settlements in over 20 states of the United States and one Canadian province (Ontario). However, about three-quarters of all Amish live in Ohio, Pennsylvania, and Indiana. The Old Order Amish speak Pennsylvania Dutch within their group, use High German in their church services, and are generally fluent in English.

History

The Amish came into existence when some Mennonites, under the leadership of Jacob Ammann, separated from the Mennonite church in 1693 primarily because, unlike other Mennonites, they believed in a strict adherence to the doctrine of *meidung*, or a total shunning of excommunicated church members. The Amish resided throughout the German-speaking parts of Europe. Due to severe persecution, some Amish migrated to North America between about 1727 and 1860. There are no longer any Amish in Europe.

Amish who felt that the Amish church was becoming too liberal split off from the more liberal majority in 1865. This offshoot minority (consisting of about one-third of all Amish) was given the name Old Order Amish at this time, in recognition of the fact that they wished to retain the old *Ordnung* (order of behavior), or set of orally transmitted rules which govern the behavior of the Amish.

Old Order Amish Society

The primary unit of organization for the Old Order Amish is the congregation, which consists of an average of 30 households with about 150 people living in a church district. The term settlement is used to describe a group of congregations located within the same geographic region which have reasonably similar *Ordnungs*. There is no higher level of church organization above the congregation.

The congregation is led by a bishop, with the assistance of two to three ministers (who are chosen by lot) and one deacon. Bishops are chosen by lot from the group of ministers. Bi-weekly worship services are held in homes. Each church district has its own *Ordnung*, which they reaffirm twice a year during communion. The *Ordnung* consists of both rules that are common to all Old Order Amish and rules that are specific to each congregation. If a member consistently violates the rules of the *Ordnung*, a hierarchy of responses is initiated, with the highest level of response being excommunication in association with *meidung*. At the most extreme, *meidung* requires all members of the congregation (and by extension all Amish) to have absolutely no contact with the shunned individual. However, any shunned person who repents is reincorporated into the community. The severity of the *meidung* has been decreasing in recent years.

The importance of religion in Amish life cannot be overstated; it is embedded in every aspect of Amish life. Phrased differently, a distinction between religious and nonreligious affairs is meaningless for the Amish. Amish life is guided by several key principles, including adult baptism; *Gelassenheit*, or acting with humility and simplicity at all times; a belief that true grace can only be achieved if one lives in isolation from the world; a belief in absolute nonviolence; and a belief that states have no authority in religious matters. Separation from the world is fostered by the utilization of distinctive symbols, such as sixteenth century European peasant clothing, horse and buggy travel, and rejection of electricity from power lines. It is also recognized that separation from the world requires the existence of strong community ties and, in particular, in providing each other with assistance when needed. One of the better known examples of mutual aid is a communal barn raising but, in fact, mutual aid is involved in virtually all aspects of daily life.

The Old Order Amish are often thought of as a static society living the lifestyle of seventeenth or eighteenth century farmers. They are in fact a dynamic society, with a history of selectively incorporating new components, particularly technology which is essential for economic competitiveness, into their cultural system. However, the Amish are selective, refusing to accept anything that they feel might threaten their core beliefs. As one example of the dynamic nature of their society, the Old Order Amish have been undergoing a transition over the past 40 to 50 years from an economic system based primarily on small family-owned farms to one based on wage labor. This transition appears to be primarily due to the joint effects of a rapid rate of population increase in conjunction with an increase in the cost of farm land in the vicinity of the major settlements. The magnitude of this transition varies substantially between settlements. Some Amish wage laborers work primarily with other Amish men, either in Amish-owned shops or in Amish construction crews, but an increasing number of men now work in factories where they have intensive contact with the non-Amish (variously referred to by the Amish as "Yankees" or "English").

Although some Amish have practiced civil disobedience while protesting government policies that they felt infringed on their religious beliefs (such as the military draft), they are otherwise law-abiding citizens. They can be exempt from social security taxes if they are self-employed or work for an Amish employer but otherwise pay the same taxes as all other citizens.

Amish children attend school through the eighth grade. Amish maintain their own schools, but families may choose whether to send their children to public or Amish school. Upon completing school, all boys and many girls enter the workforce. Boys with fathers who farm will often assist with farm work but many boys now work in Amish shops or construction crews. Girls generally work as domestics, in both Amish and non-Amish homes. Sometime in their late teens to early twenties, Amish youth must decide if they will join the Amish church. This is often a difficult time for parents and their children. Currently over 90 percent join the Amish church. Amish people usually marry in their early 20s, and divorce is strictly prohibited. Amish families have an average of 7–8 children.

LAWRENCE P. GREKSA AND JILL E. KORBIN

See also **Christians 1: Overview**

Further Reading

Hostetler, John A., *Amish Society*, Baltimore: Johns Hopkins University Press, 4th edition, 1993

Igou, Brad, editor, *The Amish in Their Own Words: Amish Writings from 25 Years of Family Life Magazine*, Scottdale, PA: Herald Press, 1999

Kraybill, Donald B., 1989, *The Riddle of Amish Culture*, Baltimore: The Johns Hopkins University Press, 1989

Kraybill, Donald B., and Marc A. Olshan, editors, *The Amish Struggle with Modernity*, Hanover: University Press of New England, 1994

Krebs, George M., Joseph F. Donnermeyer, and Marty W. Kreps, *A Quiet Moment in Time*. Sugar Creek, Ohio: Carlisle Press, 1997

Nolt, Steven M., *A History of the Amish*, Intercourse, Pennsylvania: Good Books, 1992

Andhras

Capsule Summary

Location: Andhra Pradesh state, India
Total Population: approximately 65 million
Language: Telugu
Religion: Hinduism

The Andhras, also known as the Telugu, form the predominant ethnic group in Andhra Pradesh, the fifth largest state in India. The state occupies a large portion of the high and arid Deccan Peninsula, sloping down to the low-lying eastern coastal region where the Godavari and Krishna rivers empty into the Bay of Bengal. The Andhra people speak Telugu, the most prevalent members of the Dravidian language family and the official language of the state. Approximately 65 million Andhra people live in Andhra Pradesh, in addition to the Telugu speakers who live in the border areas of surrounding states. The largest Andhra community outside of India is found in Malaysia, where there are approximately 30,000 Telugu speakers.

Smaller diasporic communities live in the former British colonies of Fiji, Guyana, Myanmar, Mauritius, Singapore, and South Africa. Most Andhras are Hindus by religion, although some castes have converted to Christianity and Islam.

History

The land of the Telugu, more than two thousand years ago, was a Buddhist region comprising part of Emperor Ashoka's sprawling Maurya Empire. The weakening of the Mauryan Empire by the first century BCE led to the establishment of an independent Andhra Kingdom that controlled, for a time, much of central India. After the decline of the Andhra dynasty, the region became incorporated into a long line of dynastic succession that held sway for centuries in southern India. The important states exerting their authority during this time included the Pallavas, the Eastern Chalukyas, the Kalingas, and the Cholas. By the fifteenth century, Muslim rulers had established the Bahmani Kingdom and subsequently the Golkonda Sultanate in the northern parts of the Andhra country. These Muslim rulers conquered the southern Hindu Kingdom of Vijayanagara in 1565.

European traders attracted by the rich textile traditions of the Andhra region first arrived in the sixteenth century. The British East India Company vied with French and Dutch trading companies for commercial and political control over this valuable coastal territory, acquiring authority over much of the land from the Golkonda Sultanate in the eighteenth century. While the British Empire administered its rule from the southern port city of Madras, the Nizam of Hyderabad continued to rule the northwest portion of the Andhra-speaking area. Although this princely state was not technically part of the colonial empire, the Nizam accepted the paramountcy (or legitimate supremacy) of British rule, permitting the British to control his state's foreign affairs and defense.

At the time of Partition in 1947, the departing colonial authorities instructed the leaders of the princely states to accede to either India or Pakistan based on the principles of geographical contiguity and the majority religion of the state. Refusing accession to India, the Nizam of Hyderabad attempted instead to establish an independent state. The Nizam's refusal coincided with a communist-led armed rebellion in the Telugu-speaking countryside of Hyderabad, an area known as Telangana. The Indian army entered Hyderabad, and the people of Telangana officially joined India as part of the Madras state in 1949.

In the early years of Indian nationhood, political leaders faced the difficult challenge of carving various states out of the new national territory in accordance with the linguistic, religious, and ethnic affiliations of a diverse citizenry. Representatives of the Andhra community, who had been lobbying for a Telugu-speaking state since the early part of the century, initiated the movement to create a separate Andhra state out of the composite state of Madras. The prime minister of India formed Andhra, the first state established along linguistic lines, in 1953. The state was merged with the Telangana regions of the former princely state of Hyderabad to form Andhra Pradesh in 1956. These two regions shared a common language, but their economic and cultural differences fueled continuing demands for the bifurcation of the state. Despite violent protests in the late 1960s and early 1970s, Andhra Pradesh has remained an integrated state.

The Congress Party controlled state politics in Andhra Pradesh for more than twenty years after Indian independence. In 1982, N.T. Rama Rao, a former Telugu movie idol, founded a regional political party called the Telugu Desam that overwhelmingly won state elections in 1983. The current Chief Minister of the state, N. Chandrabindu Naidu, came to power in 1995 after challenging his father-in-law Rao's position as head of the party. However, the Congress Party continues to control many of the traditional village councils throughout the Andhra countryside.

Economy and Society

The contemporary socioeconomic conditions that frame the lives of the Andhra people illustrate the interlocking of tradition and modernity in postcolonial India. Since the national government began to institute liberalization policies in the early 1990s, individual states have become increasingly important participants in the drive for economic growth. Andhra Pradesh, with a population large enough to rival the world's large nations, embodies many of the complexities and challenges that accompany such attempts at economic reform.

Andhra Pradesh is one of India's largest poor states, and many of its socioeconomic indicators—per capita income, literacy, and infant mortality—are below the national average. The economy of Andhra Pradesh is largely rural in nature, with about 70 percent of the state population pursuing agricultural labor and cultivation as their primary occupation. As social inequalities increase between the rural poor and the urban middle class, life in the countryside continues to be characterized by poverty, indebtedness, and lack of adequate infrastructure. These social conditions heighten the effects of natural disasters, such as the destructive cyclonic storms that periodically ravage the Andhra coast.

In an effort to address the state's socioeconomic problems, Chief Minister Naidu in recent years has instituted an intensive program of development and modernization that aims to integrate the state economies into the global marketplace. Backed by substantial funding from the Work Bank, Naidu has devised an economic strategy that includes the reduction of broad subsidies, the privatization of the power sector, the increase of state revenues, and the improvement of primary education. Through expansion of the computer software industry in Hyderabad, Naidu has succeeded in transforming this capital city into a national center for the development of information technology. However, it remains to be seen whether Naidu's approach to liberal economic reform will alleviate the suffering that millions of Andhra people experience everyday.

HALEY DUSCHINSKI

See also **India**

Further Reading

Dugger, Cynthia, "Even the Poor Pay Heed to the Esoterica of India's Riches," *New York Times,* September 10, 1999

Kakar, Sudhir, *The Colors of Violence: Cultural Identities, Religion, and Violence,* Chicago: University of Chicago Press, 1996

Olsen, Wendy Kay, *Rural Indian Social Relations: A Study of Southern Andhra Pradesh,* Delhi: Oxford University Press, 1996

Talbot, Cynthia, "Inscribing the Other, Inscribing the Self: Hindu-Muslim Identities in Pre-Colonial India," *Comparative Studies in Society and History* 37, no. 4 (1995)

Andorra

Capsule Summary

Country Name: Principality of Andorra
Location: Southwestern Europe, between France and Spain
Total Population: 69,150 (July 2003)
Minority Populations: Andorran (33 percent), Spanish (43 percent), Portuguese (11 percent), French (7 percent)
Languages: Catalan (official), French, Castilian, Portuguese
Religion: Roman Catholic (predominant)

The Principality of Andorra is located in the Pyrenees Mountains, landlocked between France to the north and Spain to the south. Covering an area of 486 km^2 (181 square miles), the micro-state is administratively divided into seven parishes (*parroquies*), the most populous being the country's capital, Andorra la Vella, where a third of the population lives. Catalan is the official language, but Spanish and French are also commonly spoken. The mostly roman catholic citizens of Andorra constitute only a third of the total population (25,511), which is predominantly Spanish (43 percent), with Portuguese (11 percent) and French (7 percent) minorities. Moreover, while there is no legal discrimination against the resident minorities, the law grants many rights and privileges to citizens only.

Andorra's traditional agrarian society underwent profound economic transformations since World War II. Tourism is presently Andorra's primary economic activity. More than 10 million visitors per year brought prosperity to the population, with a GDP per capita of $19,000 (2000), while the future of the country as a tax haven is less certain.

Andorra has a unique political system. It is headed jointly by two princes—the president of France and the Spanish Bishop of Urgell. It became a parliamentary co-principality in 1993, when its first constitution was adopted by popular referendum. In 1993, this feudal system was modified with the titular heads of state retained, but the government transformed into a parliamentary democracy. The Constitution defines it as an independent, democratic, and social constitutional state. The historical origin of this particular political organization reaches back to the ninth century, when Charles the Bald granted count Sunifred of Urgell the valley of Andorra in the county of Urgell. During the following two centuries, the dominion of the bishops of Urgell gradually extended over the valleys and the counts of Urgell yielded their rights over Andorra to them. However, the instability of the region forced the bishop of Urgell to place it under the protection of the Caboet family. When Count of Foix inherited Andorra through marriage, in 1208, his claim initiated a dispute with the Bishop of Urgell that should end only in 1278 and 1288, with the signing of two agreements. These so-called *Partiages* are considered basic documents of Andorra's history. They established equal rights for both parties, fixed the tribute (*quèstia*) to be paid to them in money and in kind, the nomination of *batlles* (judges), the administration of justice and of current affairs, all institutions that survived to the present, however modified. Today, the co-princes have equal powers and are jointly head of the state. The 28 to 42 members of the General Council (parliament) are elected every four years. They elect the six ministers and the head of government who is appointed by the co-princes.

The haunting question of Andorra's statehood—sometimes contested by France when it wanted to join international conventions—has been resolved by its international recognition. Admitted as a full member to the United Nations (1993) and to the Council of Europe (1994), the country has joined a customs union with the European Community (1991) and is a member of the World Trade Organization (1995).

Ruth Murbach

See also **France; Spain; Switzerland**

Further Reading

Jorri Duursma, *Fragmentation and the International Relations of Micro-States: Self-Determination and Statehood*, Cambridge, New York: Cambridge University Press, 1996

Angola

Capsule Summary

Location: Southern Africa, bordering the South Atlantic Ocean, between Namibia and Democratic Republic of the Congo
Total Population: 10,766,471 (July 2003)
Minority Populations: Ovimbundu, Mbundu, Bakongo, Lunda, Chokwe, Nganguela, Nyaneka-Humbe, Ovambo, mestiço, and Portuguese.
Languages: Umbundu, Loanda Mbundu, (Ki)Kongo, Chokwe, Mbwela, Nyemba, other Bantu languages; some Khoisan or Click languages; Portuguese (official)
Religions: Indigenous beliefs (Spiritism or Animism), 47 percent, Roman Catholic 38 percent, Protestant 15 percent (1998)

Angola lies along the southwest coast of Africa and extends into the central southern highlands of the continent. A small enclave of Angola, Cabinda, lies north of the Congo River and is separated from the rest of the country by the delta of the Congo River, occupied by the Democratic Republic of the Congo. Angola's size and shape approximate those of Egypt.

Angola's estimated population of nearly 11 million people is divided into an intricate web of varying ethnic and linguistic groups. However, like almost all peoples of southern Africa, most Angolans speak various dialects or languages of the Bantu family that only occasionally may be mutually intelligible among them.

More than 70 percent of the population settled in the upper western third of the country, where three major ethnic and linguistic groupings concentrate. In the lower half of this area is the largest group, the Ovimbundu, who comprise almost two-fifths of the national population. They speak Umbundu, and their territory stretches up from the Atlantic Ocean into the Benguela Plateau (over 3,000 feet high) and west and south of the Benguela River.

In the mid-section of this western portion of the country, between the Cuanza and Longa Rivers in the south and the Dande River in the north, are the Mbundu, who speak Kimbundu. They comprise about one-fourth of the population and are settled from the coast into the Malanje Plateau, at a lower elevation than the Benguela.

The national capital, Luanda, is located in this region, lying on the coast midway between the Cuanza and Dande Rivers. This city's population, amounting to more than a million, uniquely mixes many of the country's ethnic and linguistic groupings.

Above the Dande River and descending to the Congo River are the Bakongo. They speak (Ki)Kongo and amount to one-sixth of the Angolan population. To the south and east of this western region lies the remaining 30 percent of the population. Varying from less than ten to no more than two percent of the population, these other Bantu-speaking inhabitants are settled in an arc from south to east-northeast, and include the Chokwe, Mbwela, and Nyemba.

There are two non-Bantu speaking groups. In the far southeast are Khoisan (Click) speakers, about two percent of the population, Bush people forced into the region centuries ago by advancing Bantu. Another two percent of the population is *mestiço*, those of mixed African and Portuguese colonial breeding. Speaking primarily Portuguese, most are interspersed through the western half of the country, especially in the capital.

Since the end of the fifteenth century, the Portuguese have been a crucial factor in the development, or lack thereof, of Angola. As the Portuguese made their voyages of discovery during the late 1400s along the coasts of western and eastern Africa, India, the Far East, and Brazil, Angola emerged as a crucial source of slaves. Over the succeeding centuries, the Portuguese lost their empire and therefore resolved to tighten their grip on their remaining African possessions. Angola became especially important for its extensive natural resources of diamonds, iron, and petroleum. After World War II, with independence movements sweeping Africa, an authoritarian Portuguese regime increasingly used military force to hold on to Angola. During the 1960s three independence movements grew in Angola concentrated among the Bakongo, Mbundu, and Ovimbundu.

In 1974 the old regime in Portugal was overthrown, and the following year Angola gained independence. The three independence movements, however, rather than uniting, began a protracted civil war that had devastating continuing consequences. The war was prolonged because each faction received outside aid, reflecting the ideologies of the Cold War, from the former Soviet Union, Cuba, China, the United States, and South Africa. A new *mestiço* minority appeared as the result of Cuban soldiers' offspring with native Angolans. A national unity government was installed in April of 1997, but serious internal fighting resumed in late 1998, leading to hundreds of thousands of people homeless. It is estimated that up to 1.5 million lives may have been lost in fighting over the past quarter century.

Decades of warfare created an economy and society in shambles, with minorities fractured by income, age, education, and health. The gross domestic product of Angola's largely agricultural economy is hardly more than 11 billion dollars, amounting to only $1,000 per capita, with income poorly distributed across classes. Life expectancy is just under 40 years, and the infant mortality rate is almost 200 per 1,000 live births. More than two-fifths of the population are under 14 years of age and over half are 15 to 64. Only three percent of the population is 65 or older. About two-fifths of the population over 15 are literate, and the rate of literacy among males is twice that among females. Many people, especially young males, have lost legs and arms due to land mines. Over two-fifths of the population adhere to spiritist religions; more than one-third is Catholic; and about one-sixth, Protestant. While all religions are a minority, Catholicism at one time held a traditional, official position.

Angola is a society almost totally divided along lines of ethnic, linguistic, economic, political, military, and religious minorities. None of these strands has been able to bond to form a sustaining national majority. The country has wealth that could serve as a great benefit to its inhabitants, but these resources have in practice been a lure resulting in debilitating competition and conflict.

EDWARD A. RIEDINGER

See also **Africa: A Continent of Minorities?; Africans 1: Overview; Colonialism; Imperialism**

Further Reading

Colello, Thomas, editor, *Angola: A Country Study*, Washington, D.C.: Headquarters, United States Army, 1991, and at http://lcweb2.loc.gov/frd/cs/aotoc.html

Birmingham, David, *Frontline Nationalism in Angola and Mozambique*, Trenton, New Jersey: Africa World Press, 1992

Black, Richard, *Angola*, World Bibliographical series, 151, Oxford, England: Clio Press, 1992

Mohanty, Susana, *Political Development and Ethnic Identity in Africa: A Study of Angola Since 1960*, London: Sangam, 1992

Strachan, Beth, and Susan Jean Gowan, *Angola, the Struggle for Power: The Political, Social and Economic Context, 1980–1993: A Select and Annotated Bibliography*, Johannesburg: South African Institute of International Affairs, 1994

Annobonés

Capsule Summary

Location: Annobón and Bioko islands, included in the state of Equatorial Guinea, and also in Malabo (the capital)
Total Population: approximately 3,000
Languages: French and Spanish (official); Annobonés (alternative name: Annobonese, or Fa d'Ambu)
Religion: Christian

The Annobonés are an ethnic group living on Annobón island (also known as Pagalu), a small mountainous island in the Gulf of Guinea; in Bioko island; and in Malabo, the capital city of Equatorial Guinea. These islands are situated south of Sao Tomé island, west of the Gabon coastland, and about 700 kilometers (434 miles) from Malabo. Annobon Island is a small volcanic island covering 18 square kilometers (7 square miles). Most of the estimated 1,900 inhabitants are fisherman specializing in traditional, small-scale tuna fishing and whaling.

Annobonés speak Fa d'Ambu, a Portuguese-based creole language that is closely related to the São Tomense language (spoken on São Tomé Island). It differs from from the Krio spoken on Fernando Po island, the creole (*crioulo*) spoken in Guinea-Bissau, and Kabuverdianu (the language of the Cabo Verde islands). Spanish, however, is the official language used in government and education. Many Annobonés living in Malabo learn the local trade language, Fernando Po creole English. The Annoboné language is deeply connected to the construction of Annoboné identity and provides symbolic bonds that shape ethnic solidarity.

The ethnic structure and composition of the Annobonés is the outcome of different factors, namely the insular nature of their territories, and a particular historical background marked by the influence of Portuguese slave-traders from the fifteenth to the eighteenth centuries and, since 1778, by the Spanish (and, after, Equatorial Guinean) imperialist rule. These geographical and historical conditions generated a differentiated language that shows the specificity of this people.

The Spanish explorer Diego Ramirez de la Diaz first visited Annoboné in 1470 and named it the Island of San Antonio. After 1471, Portuguese traders took slaves from Sao Tomé and Angola, and resettled them on Annobón island. These slaves (called *escravos de resgate* by the Portuguese) were the earliest members of the Annobonés society. The Annobonés' ancestry is inextricably linked to this history, as the heterogeneous origins of the former slaves makes it difficult to conceive of Annobón having an indigenous or ancestral population. A cultural genesis had already begun on the island by 1515–1517. For instance, African women married Europeans, and their children formed a community of *forros* (in Portuguese, "slaves about to be released"), who had a distinct identity and socioeconomic powers. This situation spawned the emergence of a Creole language and a kind of ethnic core of the Annobonés society.

The marginal situation of the Annobonés in relation to the central political powers reinforced a separate ethnic consciousness, which has been characterized by an original Creole speech with a Portuguese-based vocabulary partly influenced by the Spanish. Non-Ceolized Portuguese is presently used as liturgical language. Spanish language is, however, imposed in government and education.

The central but historically tumultuous government of Equatorial Guinea has generally marginalized the Annobonés. In the years after gaining independence from Spain in 1968, many human rights abuses, high levels of emigration, collapse of public structures, and economic decline occurred under the dictatorial regime Francisco Macias Nguema (1968–1979). In September 1968, Macias was elected the first president; in July 1970, he created a single-party state and by May 1971, key portions of the constitution were abrogated. His regime abandoned all government functions except internal security, which was accomplished by terror, leading to the death or exile of up to one-third of the country's population. n 1974, a cholera epidemic plagued Annobon, but Macías refused to allow the Red Cross to aid the ailing population. The Annobonés appealed to Gabon for assistance and, in what critics believed to be a severe punishment, Macías sent troops to the island, killing many civilians. Under his watch the economy crumbled, human rights, education, and religion were repressed, communications with the outside world were eliminated, and the island, along with the rest of Ecquatorial Guinea, suffered tremendous devastation. In 1979, Macias' nephew Teodoro Obiang Nguema Mbasogo, led a successful coup d'etat. Macias was arrested, tried, and executed, and Obiang assumed the presidency.

The island has not fared much better under Obiang's reign; he has continued many of the same actions and political traditions of his uncle, additionally destroying the island's natural environment through the systematic dumping of toxic and radioactive wastes coming from foreign industrial nations. Since 1988, these wastes have been dumped in Annobon according to lucrataive treaties Obiang signed with UK Buckinghampshire and Axim Consortium Group.

The Annoboné economy is presently based primarily on fishing activities, agriculture, and coconut palm recollection, but the terrible ecological damages generated by the government's actions during the last two decades have threatened to destroy the Annobónes' key form of subsistence.

The United States and the United Nations have since become involved in the human rights concerns on Annobon. In August of 1993 a number of Annonbonese youths, protesting economic conditions, held the governor and military commander hostage. Harvests had been exceedingly poor and the authorities had failed to deliver a sufficient supply of food to the island. Local security forces assaulted the youths, killing an innocent bystander, Simplicio Llorente Yaye, and later shot and killed one of the young activists, Manuel Villarrubia, as he attempted to escape. The authorities arrested 21 others, many of whom were not involved in the taking or holding of officials. There were reports of torture committed by security forces of Equatorial Guinea; the Annobonese detainees were tried by a military tribunal for rebellion and supporting Annobon's secession from Equatorial Guinea. Eight were convicted in a one-day trial in September, but they were pardoned in October; the remainder were released without charge but were not returned to Annobon.

JOAN MANUEL CABEZAS LÓPEZ

See also **Guinea**

Further Reading

Castro Antolin, Mariano L. De, *Population of Santa Isabel Island (19th Century)*, Madrid: Spanish Association of Africanists, 1996

Cortés López, José Luís, *Contemporary History of Black Africa*, Madrid: Editorial Mundo Negro, 1999

Hagemeijer, Tjerk, *Babel Island: Créolisation in the Guinean Gulf, in Revista Camoes*, Lisbon: Camoes Institut, 1999

Anti-Semitism

Enmity toward Jews has escalated over the centuries. Originally a local ethnic prejudice in the ancient Middle East, anti-Jewishness developed into a powerful and tenacious global phenomenon. The Nazi Holocaust might seem to have been an extreme that could not be exceeded, but today anti-Jewishness has apparently become an even greater force internationally than ever before. Once primarily religious, this prejudice is now simultaneously religious, racial, economic, and political. *Anti-Semitism* is the term coined, by an extremist agitator in 1879, to capture the novelty and complexity of this ancient yet ultramodern prejudice.

The core meaning of anti-Semitism is what the Germans once conveyed, more directly, by the term *Judenhass*—"hatred of Jews." Yet as Shulamit Volkov (1978) and many others have remarked, anti-Semitism is not just a bias but, rather, a worldview, linked to a constellation of personality traits in those who hold it. Surveys and other types of research have found that anti-Semites hate and fear not only Jews but other ethnic groups, as well as socialists, bankers, and homosexuals. They internalize conventional values and idealize established authority. In the anti-Semitic worldview, Jews are a master explanation or key: the common denominator of all that anti-Semites hate—plutocracy, subversion, deviance, difference—and the enemy of everything that anti-Semites adore: order, tradition, authority. Wherever money or dissent shakes the status quo, anti-Semites see the conspiratorial hand of "the Jews" at work. Today, as capitalism expands exponentially, finance and resistance loom larger than ever. Hence, for the anti-Semite, "the Jewish conspiracy" is ubiquitous and growing.

Anti-Semitism, in other words, is prejudice raised to the second power. What began in antiquity as a routine bias has evolved into what the historian Gavin Langmuir (1990) calls "chimeria": a demonological belief that Jews are master conspirators; secret rulers of a manipulated world; endowed, like the chimeras of Greek and Hittite myth, with fabulous powers drawn from occult sources. Unlike many of the other peoples who have suffered prejudice and discrimination, the Jews suffer because they are thought to rule, and ruin, the entire world. They are the "chosen people" of authoritarians, fundamentalists, and bigots everywhere. This gives anti-Semitism a unique position among contemporary prejudices.

Once, anti-Jewishness was unremarkable. In ancient Israel, when the Israelite ancestors of today's Jews first entered the historical record, they experienced little more than ordinary tension in their relations with such neighboring peoples as the Canaanites and Assyrians. Yet aspects of ancient Judaism did prove relevant to later developments. Perhaps most noteworthy was the monotheistic conviction that Yahweh, the God of the Israelites, is the one and only true God. A teaching of this kind, as Max Weber observed long ago, is intrinsically "disenchanting," prompting deep skepticism about the claims of other faiths. This skepticism contrasted with the syncretic willingness to accept other gods so common among other ancient peoples, giving the Jews a distinctive profile as a people whose devoutness toward Yahweh—and toward the Judaic moral code, the Torah—was equaled by their doubts concerning other deities and other moral systems. Faith in Yahweh spurred disbelief in other gods. Jews became skeptics precisely to the extent that they were also believers.

This skepticism was thrown into bold relief when Christianity sprang from the ferment of ancient Greek and Judaic culture. As messianic claims were made for the new religion, the Jews acquired an exceptional new status as stubborn believers in the Mosaic faith who rejected the new revelation. For the Christian faithful, the Jews now figured as ungrateful elders, who, it was held, had forsaken their covenant with God by "hardening their hearts" against God's risen son. Over the next millennium, as Christianity conquered Europe, the "stiff-necked" Jews remained a persistent and defining negative reference point for Christians—the Chosen People of the Old Testament who had somehow, uncannily, resisted the New Testament gospel.

Popular hostility to Jews remained relatively muted, however, until the commercial revolution of the eleventh century. Until then, medieval life had been mainly quiet, local, and rural, and few large problems had seemed to demand a global explanation. Now, however, bonds of trade and conquest brought a larger world to life for a populace whose worldview until then had been bounded by the village, the cathedral, and the horizon. As customs came unhinged, plagues swept across frontiers, and epic crusades for religious and economic hegemony divided peoples, public opinion sought, and found in the Jews, a pseudo explanation for the world's travails. In most cases, only relatively minor ills were traced to Jewish ill-will; but with the black death of 1349, full-scale anti-Semitic demonology was born. Before then, Jews, like lepers and some women, had been periodically reviled as sorcerers; and increasingly during medieval times, as they were induced to handle money so that Christians could evade its moral taint, they found themselves accused of greed and usury. But now, amid a continent-wide epidemic, they came to be seen as systematic enemies of all Christendom. Expelled from one country after another and hounded by the Inquisition, the Jews were forced to the margins of central and eastern Europe. Confined in some places to prison-like ghettos, in other places to "pales of settlement," the Jews became ghostly outsiders in an increasingly xenophobic world.

The Protestant Reformation added fuel to the fire. Zealotry on all sides led to sectarian violence on an unprecedented scale, culminating in a cycle of religious wars that lasted a century. German Anabaptists and French Calvinists were among the most visible victims of these wars, but there were others as well. And the corrosive intolerance of the times had consequences for Jews, too. Some early figures of the Reformation, like their predecessors and contemporaries among the Inquisitors, saw the Jews as mortal enemies—or indeed immortal enemies, for it was in this period that some people began to find the very survival of the "eternal" and "wandering" Jews unnerving. How could any people have survived such unrelenting hatred for so long? How could they endure after losing God's favor? Were they human at all, or, like the money with which they were increasingly identified, were they imperishable, ever-mobile, and ever-circulating?

When the revolutions of early modernity turned the old world upside down, many of those who were disoriented and dispossessed suspected that malignant subterranean forces were at work. The French Revolution, in particular, was a spur to paranoid conspiracy theory. But it was not clear, to start with, whether any single group would capture the imagination of conspiracy-mongers. For a full century after the outbreak of the French Revolution in 1789, paranoid blame was divided almost equally between Jews, Masons, and such long-vanished forces as the Illuminati; in the United States, the Masons rather than the Jews riveted the attention of the conspiracy-minded until the twentieth century. Ultimately, though, paranoia fastened on the Jews above all others, especially in France, Germany, Russia, Poland, and elsewhere in central and eastern Europe. The Jews' unique history and their status, in folklore and public opinion, as the living incarnation of money and the profit motive made them ideal objects of demonology in the age of capital. In the writings of such early anti-Semites as Toussenel in the 1840s, and later in the even more popular writings of figures such as Drumont and Dühring, the equivalence between Jews and parasitic capitalists (especially bankers) became canonical. Thus was born the modern myth of the Jew as "Bankenstein's monster."

The structure of this myth deserves close attention, since the identification of Jews with finance capital lies at the heart of modern anti-Semitism. Note, to start with, that capital per se is seldom the focus of criticism. On the contrary, anti-Semites tend to admire industrial capitalists as master builders, the born leaders of the community. But bankers, who are viewed as essentially or predominantly Jews, are indicted as predators. The great banking barons of the Rothschild family became, in anti-Semitic fantasy, living emblems of Jews everywhere. Everything negative about capitalism is blamed on Jewish bankers; and everything positive is said to be threatened by the Jews, if not as bankers, then as socialists. The latter claim is another key to the interpretation of modern anti-Semitism. Critics often muse over the apparent illogic of the anti-Semitic claim that Jews are the architects of both proletarian socialism and predatory capitalism. But for anti-Semites, socialism and bank capitalism are just two sides of the Jewish conspiracy against order and tradition. Marx, no less than Rothschild, was a saboteur of justice and prosperity. What anti-Semites want—stability in a world of traditional patriarchal morality and authority—is, they believe, menaced equally by Jewish capitalism and Jewish anticapitalism. The "Jewish conspiracy" grips the world like a vise, from both sides.

This was the claim, put forward by founders of the Nazi Party in Germany, that drew Adolf Hitler to fascism. Assigned by the German authorities to infiltrate potentially dangerous right-wing groups in the aftermath of World War 1, Hitler heard, from the Nazi ideologue Feder, that Jews relied for world domination not only on the "red international" of bolshevism but on the "golden international" of bankocracy. Convinced, Hitler joined the party. Soon it was his party—and like no one before or since, he found ways to convert the anti-Semitic worldview into dynamic mass politics. The roots of this politics extended into the past: to Stöcker's anti-Jewish crusade in Germany in 1879; to the anti-Semitic Dreyfus affair in France, which began in 1894; to Lueger's electoral demagogy in Vienna in the 1890s; and to czarist Russia, where anti-Jewish pogroms were "justified" by the infamous Protocols of the Elders of Zion—a twisted conspiracy fantasy forged by the tsarist secret police. But it was Hitler, far more than his precursors, who learned how to fuse the diverse elements of anti-Semitic mythology. Racial distinctions between non-Jewish "Aryans" and Jewish "Semites," which had become popular in the later nineteenth century, were superimposed on originally religious notions of essential Jewish evil, political antagonism to "Judeo-bolshevism" and "Jewish social democracy," and disdain for the allegedly Jewish parasitism of the banks.

This fusion proved explosive. In the Holocaust, anti-Semitic demonology became genocide. The Nazis, and other fascists in countries under Axis rule during the war (Romania, the Baltics, etc.), annihilated Jews on a prodigious scale. So vast was the slaughter, and so great was the subsequent revulsion in liberal democratic circles, that many people concluded, prematurely, that anti-Semitism had burned itself out in the Nazi apocalypse.

But hidden springs of hatred have slowly become visible once more. The Israelis' policies toward the Palestinians, the international interventionism of the World Bank and the International Monetary Fund since the 1970s, resurgent Islamic fundamentalism, and the colossal power of United States capital markets—all these factors, taken together, have stimulated a revival of demonological anti-Semitism on a geographically wider scale than ever before.

David Norman Smith

See also **Diaspora: Jewish; Genocide; Israel; Palestinian Liberation Organization**

Further Reading

Adorno, Theodor, R. Nevitt Sanford, Else Frenkel-Brunswik, and Daniel Levinson, *The Authoritarian Personality*, New York: Harper, 1950

Altemeyer, Bob, *The Authoritarian Specter*, Cambridge, Massachusetts: Harvard University Press, 1996

Brustein, Wiliam, *Roots of Hate*, New York: Cambridge University Press, 2003

Cohn, Norman, *Warrant for Genocide*, Chico: Scholars Press, 1981, originally published, 1966

Goodman, David, and Masanori Miyazawa, *Jews in the Japanese Mind*, New York: Free Press, 1995

Harris, James, *The People Speak!* Ann Arbor: University of Michigan Press, 1994

Langmuir, Gavin, *History, Religion, and Antisemitism*, Berkeley and Los Angeles: University of California Press, 1990

Massing, Paul, *Rehearsal for Destruction*, New York: Harper, 1949

Neumann, Franz, *Behemoth*, New York: Oxford University Press, 1944

Penslar, Derek, *Shylock's Children*, Berkeley and Los Angeles: University of California Press, 2001

Samuel, Maurice, *The Great Hatred*, Lanham, Maryland: University Press of America, 1988, originally published, 1944

Sartre, Jean-Paul, *Anti-Semite and Jew*, New York: Schocken, 1948

Smith, David Norman, "The Social Construction of Enemies," *Sociological Theory*, 14(3), (1996), pp 203-240

Volkov, Shulamit, "Antisemitism As a Cultural Code," *Leo Baeck Year Book*, 23, 25–46, (1978)

Weber, Max, *Ancient Judaism*, Glencoe, Illinois: Free Press, 1952, originally published, 1917–1919

Wilson, Stephen, *Ideology and Experience*, London and Toronto: Associated University Presses, 1982

Antigua and Barbuda

Capsule Summary

Location: Eastern Caribbean
Total Population: 67,897 (July 2003)
Minority Populations: *Mestiço* majority, small English, Lebanese, and Indian (Asian) minorities
Languages: English and local Creole English
Religions: Christian, (predominantly Anglican with other Protestant, and some Roman Catholic)

Antigua and Barbuda are located in the Caribbean, islands between the Caribbean Sea and the North Atlantic Ocean, east-southeast of Puerto Rico. Antigua and Barbuda has so tiny a national population, hardly that of an American suburb, it may seem redundant to speak of minorities in it. The country consists of three islands—Antigua, Barbuda, and the islet of Redonda, with a total area about three times the size of Washington, D.C. About 90 percent of the population lives on Antigua, the remainder on Barbuda, and Redonda is uninhabated. Although tourism is in decline, the number of visitors annually has reached nearly ten times the national population. Ethnic groups include blacks, British, Portuguese, Lebanese, and Syrian.

The ethnic profile of Antigua and Barbuda is the product of centuries of history. It was originally settled over a period of thousands of years by various successive indigenous groups, comprising Neolithic, Arawak, and Carib peoples (beginning as early as circa 2400 BCE). Early settlements by the Spanish and French were succeeded by the English, who formed a colony in 1667. Christopher Columbus was the first known European to identify the island of Antigua, during his second voyage to the so-called New World in 1493. He named the island for a famous church in the Spanish city of Seville, Santa Maria de Antigua.

Although the Carib natives bitterly fought foreign occupation, they were defeated during the mid-seventeenth century as the English settled Antigua. No indigenous populations remain as a minority in Antigua and Bermuda. The English exploited Antigua for its sugar production and strategic location at the entrance to the Caribbean. As in so much of the New World, the labor for the export of an agricultural product, which was sugar in this case, came from slaves imported from Africa.

The African slave influx peaked during the eighteenth century and established the racial pattern of Antigua and Barbuda that continues to the present. The majority of the population is of African descent.

There are minorities of mixed African and English descent, of English only, and smaller minorities of Portuguese, Arabic, and East Indian descent.

Economic and class profiles have followed this skewed racial pattern. Presently there is a poor black majority and a small white property-owning class. Between these two has emerged a growing but tentative middle class. The racial majority organized itself as a socio-economic element through the union movement that arose in the mid-twentieth century. Vere C. Bird founded the labor party in the British colony during World War II. From this base a native political class arose that led the country to independence from Britain in 1982. However, the independent government has come to resemble the same closed elite organization as the society and economy of the colonial period. The Bird family has become the broker of political and financial power, and has been tainted by numerous allegations and convictions for criminal activity.

The economy of Antigua and Barbuda had sunk in the nineteenth century with the decline of the sugar industry. Only with independence and the growth of tourism did the new native government achieve some economic and social success. By the end of the twentieth century, inhabitants enjoyed a per capita income of approximately $11,000 (2002) per year and a literacy rate of 90 percent.

However, during the last decade of that century tourism began to decline and illegal commerce became an ever-growing pursuit of a criminal minority, often in conjunction with the governing class. Drug trafficking and money laundering increased. Moreover, hurricanes during the period devastated the landscape, creating many homeless and injured.

The socioeconomic profile of the majority in Antigua and Barbuda is relatively somewhat better than the average in the Caribbean. However, as all small populations in countries dependent on providing services to foreign visitors, its position is vulnerable and fragile. It is a member of the Caribbean community of nations known as CARICOM. This was a vehicle during the administration of United States President Ronald Reagan to foster development in the Caribbean through private enterprise investment. This project, known as the Caribbean Basin Initiative, has not been largely effective in its objectives.

Edward A. Riedinger

See also **Afro-Caribbeans**

Further Reading

Berleant-Schiller, Riva, et al., *Antigua and Barbuda*, World Bibliographical Series, 182, Oxford, England: Clio Press, 1995

Coram, Robert, *Caribbean Time Bomb: the United States' Complicity in the Corruption of Antigua*, New York: Morrow, 1993

Dyde, Brian, *A History of Antigua: The Unsuspected Isle*, London: Macmillan Caribbean, 2000

Griffith, Winston H., "CARICOM Countries and the Caribbean Basin Initiative," *Latin American Perspectives*, 17, no. 1, pp 33–54

Lazarus-Black, Mindie, *Legitimate Acts and Illegal Encounters: Law and Society in Antigua and Barbuda*, Washington, D.C.: Smithsonian Institution Press, 1994

Nicholson, Desmond V., *Antigua, Barbuda and Redonda: A Historical Sketch*, St. Johns, Antigua: Antigua and Barbuda Museum, 1991

Anuak

Capsule Summary

Location: Sudan-Ethiopian frontier on the floodplain of the Sobat, Akobo, and Pibor Rivers
Total Population: 200,000
Language: Anuak
Religions: Animist, Christian, Muslim

The Anuak live in the Republic of the Sudan at the foot of the Ethiopian escarpment on the floodplains of the Sobat, Akobo, and Pibor rivers. During the migrations of the Luo in the fifteenth century a group led by Gilo disengaged themselves from the main body of the Luo in the Bahr al-Ghazal to march north and east to the rivers and plains below the Ethiopian escarpment. One clan of the Anuak traveled southwest to Jabal Lafon where they are known as the Pari. Unlike their Dinka and Nuer neighbors their economy depended on sheep, goats, and sorghum rather than cattle. At the end of the nineteenth century the Lau and Jikaing Nuer ravaged Anuakland, inflicting heavy losses, destroying many villages, and the populous Anuak center of Ukaadi on the Akobo River. The Nuer appear to have driven all the way to Ubaa on the Oboth River and the sacred rock of Abula. Although the Nuer withdrew after suffering grave losses of cattle from the tsetse fly along the shady streams of the Ethiopian frontier, at the beginning of the twentieth century the Anuak were near extinction from war with the Nuer and the famine that followed.

They were saved by a technological revolution. Their traditional trade with Ethiopian merchants from Gore in the highland plateau enabled the Anuak to acquire firearms, at first only cast-off muskets, but they produced ivory to purchase more sophisticated rifles and ammunition. The acquisition of firearms, in which the Anuak became proficient, changed the balance of power on the floodplain frontier against the Nuer. The availability and acquisition of shields and spears permitted those influential individuals who controlled the trade in rifles to extend their authority over hitherto small, disparate clans to form a larger political organization. Udiel-wa-Kuat was, at the turn of the century, the first Anuak to obtain firearms followed by Uliimi-war-Agaanya, and Akwei-wa-Cam who, with his riflemen, decimated the Lau and Jikaing Nuer in 1911, capturing several hundred Lau women and children and thousands of cattle. He became the dominant leader among the Anuak by his guns, the strategic location of his capital at Adonga, and his possession of the Royal Emblems handed down during unknown generations from Oshoda, the legendary founder of the Anuak, that conferred upon him the legitimacy to rule. These heirlooms consisted of five necklaces, two thrones, the "Tooth Drum," three spears, and an iron fork whose holder was regarded with veneration.

The Nuer appealed to British authorities of the Anglo-Egyptian Condominium for protection. Authorities were anxious to curtail the Ethiopian arms traffic now flowing to the Anuak, who had acquired some 10,000 guns after Austria had abandoned the Werder rifle to the European and American arms merchants in Ethiopia. A British punitive patrol in 1911 failed to penetrate Adonga, the capital of Akwei-wa-Cam. The following year a powerful column succeeded in driving the Anuak rifle and spear men from the field but only after heavy losses. With the outbreak of World War I in 1914, aggressive military expeditions against the Anuak were replaced by the containment of the Anuak.

After the war British administrators sought to bring peace on the frontier from their post at Akobo by supporting Sham Akwei, the son of Akwei-wa-Cam, the custodian of the Royal Emblems. Their efforts were largely frustrated by the Akobo and Baro rivers that delineated the international boundary between Ethiopia and the Sudan over which the Anuak would pass with abandon to trade with Ethiopian merchants. Neither the British, their Sudanese successors, nor the Ethiopians have ever been able to establish their authority in this isolated frontier. The area became the refuge of Southern Sudanese insurgents in the latter half of the twentieth century. During civil war and famine that has resulted in the death of over two million people throughout the Southern Sudan since 1955, the Anuak have joined the Southern Sudanese insurgents, pro-government militias, and remained isolated in their sanctuary on the Sudan-Ethiopian frontier. Some of the educated elite have joined the Sudanese Diaspora in Europe and North America.

Robert O. Collins

See also **Sudan**

Further Reading

Collins, Robert O., *Land Beyond the Rivers: The Southern Sudan, 1898–1918,* New Haven: Yale University Press, 1971

Collins, Robert O., *Shadows in the Grass: Britain in the Southern Sudan, 1918–1956*, New Haven: Yale University Press, 1983

Evans-Pritchard, Sir E. E., *The Political System of the Anuak of the Anglo-Egyptian Sudan*, London: P. Lund Humphries & Co., 1940

Apartheid

Apartheid, an Afrikaans word meaning "separateness," was a government policy of the white minority government that rigidly classified and racially segregated the people of South Africa in 1948. This reviled apartheid policy was demolished in 1991 when new legislation granted equality to all of South Africa's citizens.

The rise and fall of apartheid must be understood in the context of its historical development. The first people to inhabit present day South Africa were the Khoisan who consisted of the Khoikhoi and the San. They settled in the area during the Iron Age. The Bantus—Zulus and Xhosa—arrived in present-day eastern South Africa around 300 AD. These peoples were the indigenous inhabitants but both groups are now extinct in South Africa. The hugely powerful Dutch East India Company established a supply base at Cape Town in 1652. Shortly thereafter Dutch people settled and became farmers, or Boers (later known as Afrikaners). Free passage by the Dutch East India Company was granted to Germans, French, and Dutch settlers.

Racial segregation began when the whites insisted on land expansion at the expense of the indigenous peoples. Indigenous contact with white culture resulted in smallpox epidemics, outright killings of blacks, and the remaining blacks reduced to servant status. The Dutch took over governing the Cape Town area. They brought their own language. However, the Dutch language eventually evolved into Afrikaans because of the new vocabulary used by the black servants and the slaves who had been brought in by the Dutch East India Company.

The Dutch were eventually displaced by the increasingly powerful English who arrived in the late 1700s to thwart Napoleon's grand schemes of conquest. English domination, prohibition of slavery with the Emancipation Act of 1833 and the superior status of the English language led to considerable tensions between the Boers and the English. The Boers replied to these circumstances by leaving; they went on their Great Trek to find fresh grazing lands. They colonized the Orange Free State in 1854 and the Transvaal in 1857. This time they displaced the indigenous Xhosa. This resulted in a century-long war that the Boers won. The Boers were again aggravated by the British invasions in their states after gold and diamonds were discovered. The huge British population growth derived from *uitlanders.* These were mainly British foreigners who worked in the minerals industries. The Boers greatly resented the strong political and economic influence of the British. The result was the fiercely fought Boer Wars. The Boers, more familiar with the territory and using guerilla warfare, won in 1899. The British won in 1902 due to superior numbers. Peace was ensured by the Peace of Vereeniging that allowed Boers complete control over blacks.

The Orange Free State and the Transvaal won independence from Britain and created The Union of South Africa on May 31, 1910. The territories were efficiently modernized with a centralized administration. A working relationship was created between the Afrikaners, British, and German capitalists, known as Randlords. They were industrialists involved in the mineral industry; they had become wealthy through the labor supplied by the black minority, the blacks earned paltry wages. When blacks complained the Randlords brought in Chinese indentured labor. Segregation was legally sanctioned with increasingly repressive legislation against blacks who lost political rights, were heavily taxed and placed under severe police repression. The Bambatha tax revolt by Zulus in 1906 resulted in 7,000 imprisoned and 4,000 deaths.

Racial segregation existed long before it became known as apartheid. The Native Labor Regulation Act of 1911 regulated employment for blacks, prohibited strikes and curtailed black jobs. The Native Land Act of 1913 required blacks to leave their farms in the Transvaal and the Orange Free State. The Bantu Homelands were established for blacks; these were reserves that consisted of 7 percent of the land yet were extremely overpopulated. The homelands became desolate, overcrowded areas without a chance for economic progress. White women received the right to vote and Afrikaans became the official language.

Several nonwhite organizations were created to counter the racial segregation. The black-based African Political Organization for Coloureds was founded in 1902. The African National Congress was established in 1912. Mahatma Gandhi represented the South African Indian Congress in 1923. He won the Indian population some minor concessions. The Industrial and Commercial Workers Union of South Africa represented labor. However, it held little power because it had no collective bargaining rights. The Union collapsed, not only due to official repression but also to internal discord. In the 1920s more racial policies were enacted to counter the resistance, protests, and the restrictive measures from the minority nonwhites. After the Rand Revolt in 1922 against the government, racial legislation increased. The repressive tactics resulted in rendering these organizations largely moribund and ineffective for the next four decades.

The Mines and Works Act prohibited strikes. The Natives Urban Act of 1923 further exploited nonwhites. They lost their rights to live in urban locations and were forcibly moved to reserves, also called homelands, designated for nonwhites. In 1936 the Native Representation Act cost the blacks the franchise. Jobs were legally segregated and reserved for particular ethnic groups. The Native Representation Act of 1936 elected three whites to represent their interests.

In the1930s education also felt the sting of racial segregation. Only 30 percent of nonwhites received an education in 1939 yet they made up 69 percent of the population. White education received five times more funding than nonwhite education.

Apartheid became official state policy after the surprising and unexpected eight-seat majority win of the election on May 28, 1949 by the Afrikaner National Party (NP). Apartheid was established as a social engineering policy under the leadership of Hendrick Frensch Verwoerd, (1901–1966), a Dutch-born immigrant to South Africa. He had served in various government positions: as senator in 1948, minister of native affairs in 1950, and prime minister from 1958. He was a member of the *Broederbond*, (Brotherbond) the economic and socially elite group of Afrikan nationalists that secretly guided every aspect of government policy. The *Broederbond* adopted Nazi racial policies advocated by one of its members who had studied in Germany. Verwoerd likewise studied in Germany and staunchly believed in *wit baasskap* (white superiority or mastery). He became a fanatical racist who put Nazi racial ideology, apartheid, into practice. Verwoerd rationalized that only the biologically and culturally civilized whites could govern nonwhites who wanted *gelijkstelling* (equality). His attempt to provide each group with its own nation-state, guided by the white minority, ultimately created apartheid.

Apartheid officially became legal with the passage of a number of acts that would rigidly classify the multiracial society of South Africa. The Race Classification Act divided South Africans into four racial categories: whites, Coloreds, Indians, and Blacks; the nonwhite groups were further divided into varying subcategories. The smallest group was the whites who consisted of Afrikaners, English, and Western Europeans. They made up 17 percent of the population in 1948, and some 12 percent of the whites were Boers. Only the whites held the franchise, thus the minority controlled the majority.

The Coloreds were the racially mixed offspring of whites and nonwhites but included major subgroups of Indians and Asians. They were mostly Christian and spoke English and Afrikaans. The white minority never recognized them as equals and considered them closer to the blacks. Indians were classified as the descendants of the slaves and forced labor brought in by both the Dutch East India Company and the British during their time in power. The largest group was the blacks who made up the 70 percent of the population. In this way, the majority became the minority.

Numerous racially restrictive acts were legislated in 1950. The Population Registration Act officially registered all South Africans according to the Race Relations Act. The racial classifications affected all areas of society, created segregation in transportation, government, business, accommodation, entertainment, and facilities. The Group Areas Act of 1950 forcibly removed Coloreds and Indians from white areas to segregated townships. The Interracial Marriage and Immorality Acts forbade interracial sexual relations. The Suppression of Communism Act allowed detention of anyone remotely considered a communist or radical. It allowed detention and arrest of people without legal redress.

More racially motivated acts were passed in 1951. The Bantu Authorities Act established reserves or homelands for blacks. Verwoerd called them Bantustans. Blacks were assigned to these homelands according to their place of origin. Some 3.5 million blacks became citizens of their homeland but lost their South African nationality. Homeland blacks required passports to enter South Africa. The homelands, supposedly independent, were ultimately manipulated by Parliament and entirely dependent on government subsidies. The Separate Representation of Voters Act removed Coloreds off the voters' lists. The Prevention of Illegal Squatting Act allowed the Minister of Native Affairs to remove blacks from public or privately held lands.

The Native Law Amendment Act in 1952 redefined the black categories. The Native Abolition of Passes and Coordination of Documents Act of 1952 forced blacks to carry a pass at all times that restricted their physical movement. The Native Labor (Settlement of Disputes) Act of 1953 prohibited labor strikes by blacks. The Public Safety Act and the Criminal Law Amendment Act granted the government power to declare a state of emergency at its discretion.

Education did not escape racial classification. Direct control over the education of blacks was obtained through the Bantu Education Act of 1953; it abolished African missionary schools. Black education became part of the Ministry of Native Affairs. Blacks were reduced to being trained as semi-skilled labor. Many elementary level black schools were built. Some $180 was spent on educating a white child while $25 was spent on a black child's education. The minority was training the majority for subservient roles in South African society.

The Reservation of Separate Amenities Act segregated all public amenities. The Native Prohibition of Interdict in 1954 disallowed black appeals to the courts against enforced relocation. The 1959 Extension of University Education Act segregated postsecondary education by establishing ethnic universities. Apartheid laws made attendance at African or English schools compulsory.

The Promotion of Bantu Self Government Act of 1959 classified blacks into eight separate ethnic groups. In 1961 the Coloured Persons Communal Reserve Act, the Preservation of Coloured Areas Act, and the Urban Bantu Council Act related to governance. The Terrorism Act allowed for apprehension without trial. It also established the internal security agency known as the Bureau of State Security. Apartheid laws were administered by a huge bureaucracy through the Department of Home Affairs. The bureaucrats ensured harsh punishments to anyone who broke any of the apartheid laws.

South Africa had modernized by the late 1960s. It enjoyed a modern infrastructure. Roads, railways, modern ports, and great prosperity derived from minerals made it a powerful economic power but a power largely based on black labor. Black consciousness appeared by the 1970s. Discontent from apartheid's opponents resulted in numerous riots, shootings, and mass killings. Sharpeville and Soweto, in which blacks were killed, became symbols of white oppression. The ANC and the Inkatha Freedom Party had risen in public prominence and inculcated the ideals of equality in their members. The harsh policies also earned South Africa global condemnation and brought economic sanctions. The government remained defiant regarding apartheid.

The fall of apartheid began in the late 1980s. Prime Minister P.J Botha repealed some of the laws. When F.W. de Klerk came to power, strong measures were taken by the government to quell the dissent. Thousands of blacks were killed. A lengthy state of emergency exacerbated the uncontrollable dissatisfaction. De Klerk ultimately realized that a civil war was looming, that it could only be averted if he abolished apartheid laws. By late 1991 all the apartheid laws were repealed.

In 1994 the first universal elections were held in South Africa. The ANC won the election. Nelson Mandela, the ANC leader who had been imprisoned for nearly 30 years for his advocacy of black rights, became the first black president. The ANC gained more votes in the election in 1999. The social engineering policy of apartheid failed. Repealing the laws did not eradicate the social problems facing South Africa; however, being considered human beings is a first step.

ANNETTE RICHARDSON

See also **Afrikaners; De Klerk, F.W. (Afrikaner); South Africa**

Further Reading

Brogan, Patrick, *The Fighting Never Stopped*, New York: Vinatge Books, 1990

Cronje, Geoffrey, *'nTuiste vir die Nageslag- Die Blywende Oplossing van Suid Afrika se Rassevraagstuk*, Johannesburg: Publicite Handelreklamediens, 1945

Davenport, T.R.H., *South Africa: A Modern History*, Toronto: University of Toronto Press, 4th edition 1991

Elphick, Richard, *Kraal and Castle: Khoikoi and Founding of White South Africa*, New Haven: Yale University Press, 1977

Kenney, Henry, *Architect of Apartheid: H.F. Verwoerd, an Appraisal*, Johannesburg: Jonathan Ball, 1980

Mandela, Nelson, *Long Walk to Freedom*, Boston: Little Brown and Company, 1995

Moster, Noel, *Frontiers: The Epic of South Africa's Creation and the Tragedy of the Xhosa People*, New York: Alfred Knopf, 1992

Omond, Roger, *The Apartheid Handbook: A Guide to South Africa's Everyday Racial Policies*, Harmondsworth, Middlesex, United Kingdom: Penguin Books, 1987

Pakenham Thomas, *The Boer War*, New York: Random House, 1979

Sparks, Allister, *The Mind of South Africa*, New York: Ballantine Books, 1990

Arab-Americans

Capsule Summary

Location: United States
Total Population: approximately 4 million
Languages: Arabic and English
Religions: Muslim and Christian

Arab-American is an ethnic term of reference, increasingly used for self-identity by United States citizens of Arab ancestry and descent. It describes a group of about 4–5 million people who live throughout the United States in big cities and small towns, who are diverse in life-style, social status, economic rank, ethnic and national origin, political opinion, and religious affiliation.

Scholars of Arab-American studies propose three phases of emigration for Muslim and Christian Arabic-speaking people to the United States. The first wave was from the1870s to the 1920s. This wave was mostly by men of rural background from Syria-Lebanon seeking opportunity and prosperity. Many of them traveled to North Dakota, others to Detroit, Michigan, and Ohio.

The second sizeable Arab immigration was from 1948 to 1966; the third phase occurred during 1967 to 1985. The driving force behind immigration of the second and third phases are events of war (1967), occupation of Arab land, and the dispossession and uprootedness of populations, such as the Palestinians and, increasingly, Iraqis. In the 1960s a different immigrant came from the Arab world to the United States who could be characterized as an Egyptian immigrant who is professional, formally educated, and multilingual. These immigrants settled in California, New Jersey, and elsewhere, seeking professional work and a better future for their children.

Much earlier Arab roots in America are being explored on some evidence that Muslims (of Arab origin) preceded the Plymouth Plantation and the Virginia settlements, when, prior to the 1600s, Muslim Arab Spaniards who were expelled from Spain may have made their way to North America. This, if substantiated, would situate Muslim Arabs of Spain among those early settlers of America.

Today, Arab-Americans are one of Michigan's largest, fastest-growing minority populations. Roughly 200,000 Arabs live in Greater Detroit. Syrian Arabs began settling there in 1900 prior to the boom in the automobile industry. These early immigrants tended to find work as peddlers and shopkeepers rather than, as is commonly assumed, industrial workers. Chain migrants from Syria/Lebanon joined relatives and followed co-villagers to find jobs in family-run stores. Significantly, the Ford Rouge Factory employed many Arabs and African-Americans from the South. However, when in the 1970s the industrial sector began to decline, the Arab population continued to steadily increase as thousands more arrived from Lebanon, Palestine, Yemen, and Iraq. Studies report that in 1994 over 5,000 Arab-owned businesses were thriving in greater Detroit.

Dearborn, Michigan today has an unmistakable Arab character to it—from Arabic Street signs to Arabic public schools, to mosques and Eastern churches, Arabic pastry shops and stores. Over 200 Arab-owned businesses exist in the Warren Avenue area alone. This Arab-American community in Detroit is supported by institutions providing social, welfare, cultural, and educational community services of a quality and extent absent from counterpart communities elsewhere in the United States.

The diversity within the Arab-American community is often mistaken for disunity. In fact, Arab-Americans constitute a complex and textured ethnic group whose development followed two parallel paths in the formation of community identity—the cultural and the organizational. The cultural path is one of a slow but steady weaving of an identity out of sharing of heritage and activities. Heritage includes language, a musical tradition, and poetry. Arabic has been the shared language of origin for over 1,400 years and the religious language of 1.2 billion Muslims. It is more than a means to communicate. It is the vehicle transmitting established oral and written traditions, calligraphic and architectural art, public performance and oratory—the source of their ideas and conceptualizations, which both express and shape their social, cultural and sacred world. It is the language of the Muslim scripture, the Qur'an, and thus is both sacred and worldly. To Arab-Americans who feel uprooted from their homeland, Arabic becomes a solace and a primary component of their identity. In their new home, overwhelmed by a dominant culture and national political system, yet unfamiliar with ethnic politics, Arab-Americans often find solace in their language, music, and poetry. It validates their Arabness and temporarily insulates them.

A large presence of Arab-Americans in Southern California does not take the shape of a residential/business community. There is no Arabtown as it were, like Koreatown or Chinatown, nor are there any sustained community services. Unlike Los Angeles, Anaheim shows the emergence of such a community with Brookhurst Street as its hub. Yet there are strong signs of community in Southern California. Communal activities, Arabic press, Arab radio and television, and local activities for members of national Arab organizations exist. Arabs know each other and drive long distances to attend weddings and funerals of community friends and leaders, political events, and fundraising activities.

A recent study carried out by Zogby International for the Arab American Institute sought to identify areas of consensus and difference. It found that despite diversity (in country of origin, religious affiliation, generation, etc.) and their relative newness as a community, there was a greater degree of unity and ethnic pride than can be found in most other United States ethnic groups in the study. The study also shows that, overall, Arab-Americans (United States-born and immigrants) consider the Palestinian-Israeli conflict to be the single most important issue in determining their vote in presidential elections.

Regarding Muslim-Americans, today there are more than 1,250 mosques and Islamic centers throughout the United States, a dramatic growth from 50 mosques in 1950. Islamic life rose to prominence at the beginning of the 1930s. However, with the advent of immigrants in the 1960s with a strong sense of identity, conscious of historical roots, and civilizational background, existing religious institutions from earlier immigrants seemed unsatisfactory. They established new institutions—today there are many day and "Sunday" schools, religious training programs to produce leadership.

Not all Muslims are Arabs, nor are all Arabs Muslims; however, their identities overlap. Arab-Americans' desire and impetus to organize emerged in relation to United States' ethnic/minority identity politics. The need to organize came about as a reaction to the climate the1967 Arab-Israeli War led to in America. "The Arabs" (and stereotyping of Arabs) emerged as outsiders among Americans of other majority ethnicities. No national Arab-American organization had been formed prior to the 1967 war. The Association of Arab American University Graduates (AAUG) was established in 1967, the National Association of Arab Americans (NAAA) in 1972, the American-Arab Anti-Discrimination Committee (ADC) in 1980, and the Arab American Institute (AAI) in 1985. These associations coalesced and mobilized around agendas of lobbying, political education, and protection and defense of Arab-American civil rights. Image construction is central to American ethnic identity politics and combating a negative image of Arabs and Muslims was central to organizational goals. This slowly led to an ethnic awakening. Casey Kasem, the celebrity radio personality, emerged as a representative of Arab-American activism concerned with constructing positive Arab images. He emphasized fame, achievement, wealth, entrepreneurship, hard work, as well as assimilation.

Both Arab and Muslim populations of America finally began to leave visible marks as evinced by the 2001 United States presidential election. Arab-Americans were recognized by the Republican candidate for president and Muslims voted as a bloc for the first time.

Fadwa El Guindi

See also **Muslims in the Americas**

Further Reading

Abraham, Nabeel, and Andrew Shryock, ediors, *Arab Detroit: From Margin to Mainstream*, Detroit: Wayne State University Press, 2000

Abraham, Sameer, and Nabeel Abraham, editors, *The Arab World and Arab Americans*, Detroit: Center for Urban Studies: Wayne State University, 1981

———, *Arabs in the New World: Studies on Arab-American Communities*, Detroit: Center for Urban Studies: Wayne State University, 1983

Abu-Laban, Baha, and Michael Suleiman, *Arab Americans: Continuity and Change*, Belmont, Massachusetts: Association of Arab-American University Graduates, 1989

Aswad, Barbara, and Barbara Bilge, *Family and Gender among American Muslims: Issues Facing Middle Eastern Immigrants and Their Descendants*, Philadelphia: Temple University Press, 1996

Aswad, Barbara, editor, *Arabic Speaking Communities in American Cities*, New York: Center for Migration Studies and AAUG, 1974

Elkholy, Abdo A., *The Arab Moslems in the United States: Religion and Assimilation*, New Haven, Connecticut: College and University Press, 1966

Haddad, Yvonne, and Adair Lummis, *Islamic Values in the United States: A Comparative Study*, New York: Oxford University Press, 1987

Kip, Lornell, and Anne Rasmussen, *Musics of Multicultural America: A Study of Twelve Musical Communities*, New York: Schirmer, 1997

McCarus, Ernest, editor, *The Development of Arab-American Identity*, Ann Arbor: University of Michigan Press, 1984
Naff, Alixa, *Becoming American: The Early Arab Immigrant Experience*, Carbondale: Southern Illinois University Press, 1985
Peters, Cynthia, *Collateral Damage: The "New World" Order at Home and Abroad*, Boston: South End Press, 1992
Wallbridge, Linda, *Without Forgetting the Imam: Lebanese Shi'ism in an American Community*, Detroit: Wayne State University Press, 1997

Arabs: North African

Capsule Summary

Location: Region stretching from Morocco in the west to Egypt in the east
Language: Arabic
Religion: Overwhelmingly Sunni Muslim

Inhabitants of the geographic region stretching from Morocco in the west to Egypt in the east, North African Arabs are a majority population who identify themselves linguistically and ethnically as Arabs. Despite centuries of intermixing with indigenous populations, Arabs trace their ancestry to the Arabic-speaking Semitic tribes who set out from Saudi Arabia in the seventh century to spread the religion of Islam. Geographically, the countries of modern-day North Africa (Maghrib) are Morocco, Algeria, Tunisia, Libya, and Egypt, although Egypt and Libya are often considered part of the Middle East. Politically, religiously, and culturally, Arabs in North Africa share more in common with the Middle East than they do with the African nations bordering to the south.

Arabs first came to North Africa seeking to convert the indigenous population to Islam. Prior to the arrival of the Arabs, Phoenicians, Romans, Vandals, Greeks, and Byzantines had formed small settlements throughout North Africa, but the Arabs were the first to establish a significant long-term presence. Between 642–669, the first wave of Arabs set out to conquer North Africa. Under the Umayyad caliphate in 670, they founded the city of al-Qayrawan in what is now Tunisia. Aided by Berber converts to Islam, the Umayyad caliphate spread its reach throughout all of North Africa by 711. Arab rule did not completely dominate, however, as Berbers periodically rebelled against the invaders and later established their own ruling dynasties.

The indigenous population of North Africa at the time of Arab arrival was largely Berber. Although their origins cannot be definitively determined, Berbers are believed to be a mix of Western Europeans, Sub-Saharan Africans, and northeast Africans. Intermarriage between *Arabs* and *Berbers* has been extensive enough that neither group can claim to be purely Arab or purely Berber. Arab and Berber are linguistic distinctions, as there are several spoken Berber languages that are linguistically distant from Arabic, but the two identities are also assertions of cultural solidarity. Arabs in the region have historically presented themselves as virtuous city dwellers close to the source of Islam, in contrast to the rural, impious Berbers. Contrary historical evidence to these stereotypes, however, abounds, including the existence of religious dynasties founded by Berbers and substantial rural Arab populations.

North African Berbers and Arabs known as "Moors" succeeded in conquering Spain in the eighth century, which they ruled as al-Andalus until 1492, when they were expelled by Spanish Catholics. From the sixteenth century until the nineteenth and twentieth centuries, the region (with the exception of Morocco) was under the control of the Ottoman Empire. After the fall of the Ottoman Empire, colonial powers in North Africa included the French in Morocco (1912–56), Algeria (1830–1962), and Tunisia (1881–1956), Italians in Libya (1911–51), and the British in Egypt (1882–1952). Much of the bureaucratic infrastructure built by the Europeans is still in use today. Independence struggles in all North African countries were based on principles of Arab nationalism. The governments of the Arab North African countries today range from religiously legitimated monarchies (Morocco) to presidencies (Egypt, Tunisia), with leaders generally appointed for life. Despite the nominal presence of parliaments, the regimes are autocratic. Governments are characterized by varying degrees of repression and restrictions on the freedom of expression.

Boasting substantial oil reserves, Algeria and Libya have the wealthiest economies in the region. Other sources of the economy include agriculture (Egypt, Morocco, Tunisia, Algeria), manufacturing (Egypt, Tunisia), tourism (Egypt, Morocco, Tunisia), and mining (Algeria, Morocco, Tunisia). Massive population growth, corruption, and high unemployment rates across the region have led to increased emigration to Europe and widespread popular dissatisfaction with regional governments. Islamist movements have attracted significant support, and local tensions between governments and Islamists remain high. When an Islamic party did well in 1991 Algerian elections, the army seized control of the government and a civil war broke out, resulting in the loss of over 50,000 lives to date.

Although not all Arabs are Muslim, North Africa has no significant presence of Arab Christians. In Egypt, Coptic Christians, representing 8.5 percent of the population, are considered descendants of the ancient Egyptians. Arab North Africa is overwhelmingly Sunni Muslim, with the presence of Sufi mystical brotherhoods as well as local practices that have been syncretized with Islamic customs.

As with many Mediterranean cultures, Arab culture tends to be patriarchal, favoring control of resources by senior males. In rural areas, women play an important role in farming economies, although in the cities, seclusion of middle and upper class women was considered a mark of status until relatively recently. Since gaining independence, most Arab countries in North Africa have promoted the education and entry of women into the public sphere, and across Arab North Africa women are prominent in professions ranging from factory work to civil service. In the past, Arab women played a role in Independence struggles and have formed political, religious, and secular organizations to address issues of women's status. However, the regional average for literacy is 54 percent, the low rate due to high numbers of illiterate women, particularly in rural areas.

The Arabic language, which is today a significant part of the self-definition of Arabs, has maintained its continuity through the preservation of the Qur'an. Although multiple dialects of Arabic exist across North Africa, all North African Arabs speak some form of Arabic. A standardized version of Arabic, used in education and in news media, is recognized across North Africa and the Middle East. Before the rise of Arab nationalism in the nineteenth and twentieth centuries, most Arabic-speakers would have identified themselves not by their language but by other categories such as families, tribes, cities, religions, or empires.

Despite the creation of the Arab League in 1945, Arab nationalist sentiment never resulted in a unified body capable of negotiating with other world powers or solving regional conflicts. The United Nations Arab Human Development report of 2002 argues that Arab countries lag behind other developing regions and must take substantial steps to promote freedom of expression, women's empowerment, and the acquisition and effective use of knowledge.

RACHEL NEWCOMB

See also **Algeria; Berbers; Egypt**

Further Reading

Brett, Michael, and Elizabeth Fentress, *The Berbers*, Cambridge, Massachusetts: Blackwell, 1996

Fernea, Elizabeth Warnock, and Robert Fernea, *The Arab World: Forty Years of Change*, New York: Doubleday, 1997

Hourani, Albert, *A History of the Arab Peoples*, Cambridge, Massachusetts: Harvard University Press, 1991

Lewis, Bernard, *The Arabs in History*, Oxford: Oxford University Press, 1993

Arabs: Palestinians

Capsule Summary

Location: West Bank, Gaza Strip, Jordan, and Israel
Total Population: 1,856,871 in the West Bank and about 1,262,200 in the Gaza Strip (July 2003); about 4.3 million Palestinians live in various countries in the Middle East and elsewhere; 2.3 million of these live in Jordan; about 204,000 live in the United States and 260,000 in various other parts of the world
Language: Arabic
Religions: Mostly Sunni Muslims with a small Christian community

As a *geographical* term, *Palestine* is a region extending inland from the eastern shore of the Mediterranean Sea, but its extent has varied over time and never had precisely defined borders. Today this area is at the heart of the Israeli-Palestinian conflict. Arabs refer to this area as Palestine, (in Arabic, *Filastin*); Jews refer to this area as *Eretz Yisrael* (in Hebrew, "the land of Israel").

With the rise of Islam in the 600s AD came the subsequent Arab military conquest of much of the region. Palestine was the site of the Crusaders' Kingdom of Jerusalem during the the eleventh century. In 1516 the Ottoman Turks occupied Palestine. Palestine did not exist as an administrative unit under the Turks' long reign, which lasted until World War I (approximately 1917). The area that subsequently became Mandatory Palestine was divided into three parts: the southern zone called the *sanjak* (district) of Jerusalem, the northern area as part of the *wilayat* (province) of Beirut and Jerusalem and its suburbs administered directly by Constantinople. (The British Mandate of Palestine comprised this section of territory in the Middle East, formerly belonging to the Ottoman Empire, which the League of Nations gave to the United Kingdom to administer post-World War I.)

In November 1917, when Lord Balfour promised a Jewish national home in Palestine, the Arabs constituted over 90 percent of the population of Palestine. Approved by the League of Nations in July 1922, the Mandate went into effect in September 1923. Incorporating the Balfour's promise, on July 24, 1922, the League of Nation granted the British the mandate over Palestine. Meanwhile, in 1921, the British carved out areas East of the Jordan River and formed the Emirate of Transjordan, which later became the Hashemite Kingdom of Jordan in May 1946.

The Arab inhabitants of Palestine vehemently opposed the idea of a Jewish national home, which involved massive Jewish immigration from the Diaspora. Having failed to resolve an inherently irreconcilable promises to the Jews and Arabs, in 1947 Great Britain handed over the problem of Palestine to the newly formed United Nations (UN), which formed an eleven-member United Nations Special Commission on Palestine (UNSCOP). After weeks of deliberation, the UNSCOP revealed two different proposals for the future of Palestine; the majority favored partition of Palestine and the minority recommended a federal state. The plan called for Jerusalem and Bethlehem as a *corpus separatum* (separate body) under a special international regime. On November 29, 1947, the UN General Assembly voted to partition Palestine.

Under this plan, 45.4 percent of the area went to the Arabs who constituted 70 percent of the population of Palestine, while Jews, who comprised 30 percent of the population and owning just six percent of the land, were given 53.5 percent of the territory. The Jewish state would have a population of 498,000 Jews and 325,000 Arabs, and the Arab Palestine was given 807,000 Arabs and 10,000 Jews. The city of Jerusalem (with a population of 100,000 Jews and 105,000 Arabs) was to be an international trusteeship with free access to holy places.

The state of Israel was proclaimed on May 14, 1948 and Arab armies launched an attack on the infant state leading to the first Arab-Israeli conflict. On September 22, 1948, the Arab Higher Committee met in the Gaza city and proclaimed the formation of an All-Palestine Government recognized by Egypt, Syria, Lebanon, Iraq, Saudia Arabia, and Yemen, but not by Jordan or any non-Arab country. On September 30, Jerusalem Mufti Hajj Amin al-Husseini was elected president, and a cabinet and an 86-member General Assembly were formed. On October 1, 1948, a Palestinian declaration of independence was proclaimed with Jerusalem as its capital and was recognized by Arab states, except the Kingdom of Transjordan, which occupied the West Bank and East Jerusalem. Egypt occupied the Gaza Strip and placed it under military rule. Following the June Arab-Israeli War of 1967 the whole of the West Bank—including East Jerusalem and the Gaza Strip—came under Israeli control.

Political Struggle

The formation in 1964 of the Palestine Liberation Organization (PLO) marked a new beginning in the history of the Palestinians dedicated to the establishment of an independent Palestinian state. Though floated with the backing of the Arab League and with a nominal legislative body of 300 members (the Palestinian National Council, or PNC), by 1968 the PLO had transformed into an independent umbrella organization of the various Palestinian groups. Since 1969, when Yasser Arafat took over as its chairman, it has emerged as the hope and aspirations of the Palestinian struggle. As the Arab states suffered military reversals against Israel in 1967 and 1973, the PLO's popularity grew in the region and elsewhere. The efforts of Arab states to pursue an independent and accommodative policy vis-à-vis Israel have been accompanied by growing acceptance of Palestinian rights by the international community.

Both before and after the June war of 1967 Jordan was a major base for the Palestinians for their operations against Israel. The first major Palestinian guerrilla operation was launched from the PLO base in Karameh in March 1968. The hijacking and blowing up of four international aircrafts by the left-wing Popular Front for the Liberation of Palestine (PFLP) commandos led to a military confrontation between the Jordanian army and the Palestinian guerrillas in Jordan in September 1970. King Hussein was apprehensive that the PLO was seeking to overthrow the Hashemite monarchy and to replace it by a PLO-led government. This civil war between Palestinians and Jordanian officials, commonly referred to as Black September, left about 2,000 Palestinians dead and the expulsion of the PLO leadership and fighters from Jordan.

Even after it lost the West Bank to Israel in the June war and after the PLO's expulsion in 1970, Jordan played a key role in the Palestinian affairs, and Arab financial assistance to the Palestinians was channeled through Amman. This preeminent role was dented in 1974 when the Arab League recognized the PLO as "the sole legitimate representative of the Palestinian people." The Kingdom, however, continued to pay for the upkeep of the various West Bank institutions such as clinics, hospitals, schools, charitable institutions, *shari'a* (sacred law) courts, contributed one-quarter of the budget of the municipalities, and paid salaries to about 9,000 Palestinian officials (including *Waqf* employees, teachers, lawyers and *shari'a* court judges).

Not willing to abandon erstwhile claims, King Hussein was keen to forge a Jordanian-Palestinian federation and in 1984 concluded an agreement to this effect with PLO Chairman Arafat. In the wake of the *intifada* (from Arabic, "shaking off," or the popular name for recent campaigns by the Palestinians against Israel) and the failure of his federal proposal to take off, on July 31, 1988, Hussein severed all legal and administrative links with the West Bank, dissolved the Lower House of the Jordanian parliament, where Palestinians constituted half the membership and, except for *Waqf,* he cancelled salaries given to Palestinian officials. He discontinued the erstwhile practice of granting Jordanian citizenship to Palestinian residence of the occupied territories and introduced the practice of granting only temporary Jordanian passports. While the PLO welcomed the move, it placed severe restrictions on the daily lives of the Palestinians. Even this dissociation did not inhibit Jordan from seeking and securing a special status for the Hashemite Kingdom concerning the future of Jerusalem in its 1994 peace treaty with Israel.

Following the Black September massacre, the Palestinian militias and leadership moved to Lebanon and Beirut became the PLO headquarters. Before long the Palestinians were sucked into the Lebanese civil war (1975–1981), with the Lebanese Muslims perceiving them to be potential allies against the Maronite Christians. In 1981 heavily armed forces of the PLO occupied large areas of southern Lebanon and used it as a base to attack Israel with rockets and artillery. Over the years, the Palestinian presence has dwindled but Lebanon still has a substantial number of Palestinians and most of them reside in the refugee camps.

As regional interests in the Palestinian question waned, an *intifada* or popular uprising erupted in the Gaza Strip in December 1987 and lasted until 1991. What was a spontaneous outburst following the accidental killing of four Palestinians soon transformed into to a mass and protracted protest against Israeli occupation. Initiated by youth, it took the Palestinian leadership by surprise as the local population took control of the situation before the organized leadership in the Diaspora could intervene. Arabs maintaind that the *intifada* occurred in protest of Israel's brutal repression, incluidng extra-judicial killings, mass detentions, house demolitions, indiscriminate torture, and deportations. The popular uprising significantly enhanced the cause of the Palestinians and the idea of a Palestinian state gathered international acceptance.

The gains of Palestinians following the *intifada* were damaged in 1990 when the Palestinians and their leadership supported President Saddam Hussein following the Iraqi invasion of Kuwait, which eventually led to the United States' Gulf War on Iraq and their expulsion from Kuwait in 1991. The Madrid Conference of October 1991 witnessed the rehabilitation of the Palestinians when the PLO agreed to form a joint Jordanian-Palestinian team to seek a negotiated settlement with Israel. By late 1992, Israel engaged in secret negotiation with the PLO (acting as representatives of the Palestinian people), which culminated in the Oslo Accords and the signing of the Declaration of Principles on September 13, 1993.

Afterwards, a series of agreements followed between Israel and the Palestinian leadership aimed at a political settlement between the Jews and Palestinians. The Gaza-Jericho agreement signed in Cairo (May 4, 1994) outlined the first stage of the Palestinian autonomy, including the redeployment of Israeli forces and the establishment of a Palestinian Self-Governing authority. In July 1994, the PLO and Arafat moved to the Gaza Strip from Tunis to administer the Gaza Strip and Jericho. The Taba agreement (September 28, 1995) outlined the second stage of the Palestinian autonomy and divided the occupied territories into three distinct categories; Area A (areas where the Palestinian authority has full civilian jurisdiction and security control); Area B (full Palestinian civil jurisdiction but joint Israeli-Palestinian security control); and Area C (Israel enjoying full civil and overall security control).

In January 1996, a popular vote was held to elect the president of the Palestinian National Authority. Simultaneously, an 88-member Palestinian Legislative Council was elected from 16 electoral districts. The PLC the membership comprised 49 Fatah, 15 independents affiliated with Fatah, 4 independents affiliated with the Islamic movement, 17 independents, and 3 others. (*Fatah*, literally meaning "the victory," is the Palestinian faction founded by Arafat in 1957 committed to gaining full independence for Palestinians.) The Hebron agreement of January 15, 1997, led to Israeli withdrawal from 80 percent of the city while retaining control over a small Jewish enclave and another 35,000 Palestinian residents.

The ongoing and protracted Palestinian-Israeli conflict also saw the emergence of *Hamas* (or *Harakat al-Mouqawama al-Islamiyya*, or in Arabic "Islamic Resistance Movement"), a Palestinian fundamentalist political movement that the United States classifies as a terrorist organization. Founded by Sheikh Ahmad Yassin, this Palestinian outshoot of the Muslim Brotherhood transformed into a political movement following the 1987 *intifada* with the stated goal of ending Israeli occupation of the Palestinian territories. Its charter issued in August 1988 called for a *jihad* (Islamic holy war) against Israel. Since the inauguration of the Oslo process, especially since 1994, Izz Eddin al-Qassem, the military wing of Hamas, has launched a series of violent and brutal terror campaigns inside Israel, often carried out by suicide bombers against public buses. Such campaigns in early 1996 significantly contributed to the election of right-wing Benjamin Netanyahu as Israeli Prime Minister.

The inability of Israel and the Palestinian Authority to reach an agreement on critical issues such as the right of the Palestinian refugees to return to their homeland and the question of Jerusalem were the prime reasons for the failure of the Middle East Peace Summit at Camp David in mid-2000 that involved United States President Bill Clinton, Israeli Prime Minister Ehud Barak, and Palestinian Authority Chairman Arafat. This led to the *al-Aqsa intifada* (or Second Intifada) that erupted in September 2000 with a wave of Palestinian suicide bombings that lasted until 2003. Hundreds of Israelis were killed and thousands seriously wounded. In reprisal Israel sent in the Israel Defence Force to seal off the Gaza Strip and reoccupy the West Bank, which was brought under strict military rule. Israel targeted senior Palestinian militants for assassinations and overall imposed hardships on the Palestinian population. By the end of the conflict over 400 were killed, most of them Palestinians and over 10,000 people injured.

Refugees

The United Nations defines *Palestinian refugees* as "persons whose normal place of residence was Palestine between June 1946 and May 1948" and left the area for any reason connected to the 1948 Arab-Israeli War, including voluntarily and regardless of their place of residence before June 1946. Until the 1980s, the Palestinian problem was considered primarily an issue concerning refugees. Indeed, UN Security Council Resolution 242 of 1967 called for "a just settlement of the refugee problem", a formulation which led to its prolonged rejection by the PLO.

For the Palestinians the formation of the state of Israel was a disaster, and they refer to the development as an-naqba, or "the catastrophe," referring to the events surrounding the establishment of Israel and the resultant dispersion of Palestinians from their homeland. In 1947–48, the population of Palestinian Arabs stood at around 1.3 million. Out of this, about 650,000 remained in their homes following the Arab-Israeli war of 1948–49; 400,000 remained in the West Bank and East Jerusalem occupied by Transjordan; 150,000 in Israel; and another 70,000–100,000 in the Gaza Strip.

The remaining Palestinians numbering around 600,000–650,000 left their homes and became refugees; out of them 200,000 became refugees in the West Bank and a similar number found themselves displaced in Gaza Strip. A further 100,000 moved to Transjordan and 150,000 to Syria.

In December 1948, United Nations General Assembly Resolution 194 recognized the right of Palestinian refugees to return to their homes or to receive compensation, if they chose not to. Unlike other refugees, a separate agency, United Nation Relief and Works Agency for Palestinian Refugees in the Near East (UNRWA) was established in December 1949 to provide emergency assistance to the Palestinians displaced by the Arab-Israeli conflict of 1948–49. With a mandate to provide essential education, health, and relief services to the Palestinian refugees living in camps in Jordan, Lebanon, Syria, and the West Bank and Gaza Strip, it began operating from May 1950 and has continued since then with Gaza as its headquarters.

By 1950 as many as 914,221 refugees were registered with the UNRWA. In 1952, Israel assumed responsibility for the Palestinian refugees who remained inside the state. In 1967, a further 300,000 Palestinians became refugees following the June war, including 175,000 UNRWA-registered refugees who became refugees for a second time. In 2001, there were 3.8 million registered Palestine refugees for which UNRWA provides services out of a total number of about 8 million.

UNRWA provides facilities in 59 recognized refugee camps in Jordan, Lebanon, Syria, the West Bank and the Gaza Strip, the last two of which are considered to be occupied territories. These camps house approximately one-third of all registered Palestinian refugees. Palestinians claim that a sizeable number of the Palestinian refugees in the Diaspora are not registered with the UNRWA because it covers only those whose normal place of residence was Palestine between June 1946 and May 1948 (i.e., those who had lost their homes and means of livelihood as result of the Arab-Israeli conflict of 1948 and had fled to neighboring Arab countries).

At regular intervals during the conflicts Palestinians were expelled from various Arab countries, often owing to political or personal differences between the host country and the PLO and Arafat. For example, in 1995 Libya expelled thousands of Palestinians, and this led to severe entry restrictions by Beirut, which sought to prevent them from coming to Lebanon. Palestinians were also displaced by certain specific actions by Israel. Since 1967, citing security considerations and as a punitive measure, Israel had expelled or deported over 1,700 Palestinian residents of the occupied territories. Following a terrorist incident in December 1992, it had expelled 415 suspected Hamas activists to Marj Az-Zuhur, in southern Lebanon.

While allowing for limited family reunions, Israel had consistently refused to agree to the right of the Palestinian refugees to return. In the past, security considerations and Arab refusal to recognize the existence of the Jewish State were used to justify this position. In the wake of the peace process, Israel cites the demographic dimension of the problem and argues that an unlimited emigration of the refugees would be a national suicide for the Jewish state.

Furthermore, citing its absorption of about 600,000 Jewish refugees from Arab countries in the 1950s Israel argues that a de facto population exchange had indeed taken place. In its view any discussion on the issue of compensation for the Palestinian Arab refugees would have to be weighed against the properties left behind by the Jews in various Arab countries when they emigrated to the newly formed Jewish State. Since the UNRWA never conducted regular census of Palestinian refugees, doubts are raised concerning the accuracy of its refugee figures. The situation of the Palestinian Arab refugees remains one of the world's most enduring refugee problems, and international discussions have yet to reach a definitive conclusion.

The treatment of Palestinian refugees in the Arab world has been different. One of the problems facing the refugees has been the refusal of Arab states to grant residency rights to foreigners. Very often Palestinians receive temporary travel documents whose recognition by outside governments has not been universal.

With the sole exception of Jordan, none of the Arab countries has granted citizenship rights to Palestinians. Most of the Palestinian refugees in the West Bank and Transjordan were given Jordanian citizenship and as a result, about 700,000 Palestinian Arabs, including about 400,000 original inhabitants of the West Bank, became Jordanian citizens. Palestinians served under various Jordanian governments and have occupied important positions in the kingdom. In the Gaza Strip, which was under Egyptian control between 1948 and 1967, the Palestinians refugees were eligible only for temporary Jordanian passports. Most of the Palestinians who work in the Gulf States are Jordanian citizens and this became obvious when 400,000–500,000 Palestinians were expelled from the oil-rich Gulf monarchies as a punishment for the PLO's support for Iraqi President Saddam Hussein during the Kuwait crisis in 1990–91.

Most of the Palestinian refugees who fled to Lebanon in 1948 were Muslim Arabs. The Palestinian Christian refugees were seen as a counterweight to the Lebanese Muslim population and a small number of

Armenians, Greeks, and Circassians. Palestinian Christians were given citizenship by the Maronite presidents. The Palestinian refugees were seen as a security threat and were brought under the tight control of the interior ministry. The refugees lived in 16 camps administered by the UNRWA and these camps often became targets of right-wing Lebanese militias. The refugees are presently prevented from working in the public sector and severe restrictions are in place for private sector employment.

In Syria, the government established a separate administration for their rehabilitation and established six refugees camps located in Damascus, Aleppo, Homs, Hama, and Dar'a. Following the June war of 1967, another wave of Palestinians fled to Syria. Initially the Palestinians were granted employment rights not enjoyed by non-Syrian residents and this included the right to work in civil service. They were also given access to public education up to the university level. They also enjoyed mobility in the economic sector and because of these efforts over 70 percent of the refugees moved out the camps and integrated themselves into the Syrian society. Palestinians enjoy same rights as citizens with the exceptions of the right to vote, hold office, or possess Syrian passports. They are not free to pursue political activities and successive governments have severely restricted their political movements. In the wake of the Oslo process, Damascus has emerged as the prime center for anti-Arafat struggle.

By 1997–98 about 1.8 million lived in West Bank and just over a 1 million in the Gaza Strip. About 4.3 million Palestinians live in various countries in the Middle East and elsewhere. Out of them, 2.3 million live in Jordan; 430,000 in Lebanon; 465,000 in Syria; 48,000 in Egypt; 275,000 in Saudi Arabia; 144,000 in Kuwait and other gulf countries; 75,000 in Libya and Iraq; 5,500 in other Arab countries; 204,000 in the United States; and 260,000 in various other parts of the world. With about 368,000 inhabitants, Gaza remains the largest Palestinian city. The Palestinians who live in the West Bank (including East Jerusalem) and the Gaza Strip constitute about 31 percent of the Palestinian population; 19 percent in the West Bank (including East Jerusalem), and 12 percent in the Gaza Strip; 31 percent in Jordan; 20 percent in Arab countries; 13 percent in Israel; and the rest scattered in various parts of the world.

P.R. Kumaraswamy

See also **Arafat, Yasser (Palestinian); Israel; Jordan; Palestinian Liberation Organization; Refugees**

Further Reading

Khalidi, Rashid, *Palestinian Identity: The Construction of Modern National Consciousness,* New York: Columbia University Press, 1997

Kimmerling, Baruch, and Migdal, Joel S., *Palestinians: The Making of a People,* New York: Free Press, 1993

Morris, Benny, *The Birth of the Palestinian Refugee Problem, 1947–1949,* Cambridge, Massachusetts: Cambridge University Press, 1988

Palumbo, Michael, *The Palestinian Catastrophe: The 1948 Expulsion of a People from Their Homeland,* London: Faber and Faber, 1987

Said, Edward W., *The Question of Palestine,* New York: Times Books, 1980

Wallach, Janet, and John Wallach, *The New Palestinians: The Emerging Generation of Leaders,* Rocklin, California: Prima Publishing, 1992

Arafat, Yasser (Palestinian)

Yasser Arafat is the leader (from 1993 and president (*ra'is*) from 1996) of the Palestinian Authority, chairperson of the Palestine Liberation Organization (PLO, since 1969), and leader of the clandestine gropu Fatah, the largest of the factions within the PLO. As an engineering student in Cairo, along with Khalil al-Wazir and Salah Khalaf, Arafat founded Fatah in 1954.

He attended the Egyptian Military Academy and was active in the *jihad al-Muqaddas* (Holy War) squad. In 1957 during President Gamal Abdel Nasser's campaign against the Muslim Brotherhood, Arafat was expelled from Egypt because of his membership in the organization. He continued his studies at Stuttgart University in West Germany and majored in civil engineering. During 1958–62 he was a civil engineer in Kuwait and then moved to Beirut and Damascus. In 1964, he received commando training from Algerian revolutionaries and the following year he publicly announced the establishment of *Fatah,* whose leadership he had assumed earlier.

On January 1, 1965, *Fatah* launched its first military operations against Israel and Arafat emerged as a leader of the Palestinian struggle for independence. Between 1956 and 1965, he was active in recruiting and organizing Palestinian refugees in the Diaspora. In March 1968, the Palestinian commandos launched a successful raid against Israel in the battle of *Karameh.* Coming against the backdrop of the June 1967 war in which Arab states were routed by Israel, this operation enhanced the prestige of *Fatah* and its leader and in July, ending four years of boycott, *Fatah* attended the fifth session of the Palestine National Council. In February 1969, Arafat assumed leadership of the revamped PLO, which had transformed itself into an umbrella Palestinian organization. Since then he has led the Palestinian struggle for independence. The absence of a territorial base to conduct military operations against Israel and the dispersal of Palestinian refugees in the Middle East states compelled Arafat to depend upon the Arab states for political support, economic largess, and military assistance. However, the relationship has often been troublesome.

In September 1970, Arafat helped organize a civil war in Jordan with the aim of ousting the Hussein regime and replacing it with a PLO-dominated government. This eventually led to the PLO's expulsion from Jordan and ushered in a troubled relationship between Arafat and King Hussein. Despite initial opposition from Jordan, at the Rabat Arab summit in 1974 Arafat was able to secure Arab recognition for the PLO as the sole and legitimate representative of the Palestinian people. The PLO-Jordan tension remained unresolved until February 1985 when Arafat and King Hussein reached an agreement on a Jordanian-Palestinian confederation. This was not well received within the PLO and Arafat made peace with his adversaries in April 1987 by annulling the accord. Following acceptance of the PLO as full member of the Arab League in 1976, Arafat has been officially treated as a head of state in the Arab world and the Third World countries began to follow this pattern in the 1980s.

After the Black September massacre of 1970, Lebanon emerged as the territorial base for Arafat's military operations against Israel. President Anwar Sadat's peace initiatives towards Israel in 1977 alienated Arafat from Egypt. In June 1982, Israel invaded Lebanon with the aim of eliminating Beirut as the base for Palestinian guerrilla operations. Consequently, in December 1983 Arafat and his forces were evacuated from Beirut under an international aegis and were dispersed in various Arab countries and Arafat moved to Tunis along with the PLO headquarters.

By establishing personal contacts with the leadership of the Soviet Union and China, Arafat secured ideological support and military supplies from these countries. A high point of Arafat's diplomacy was his address to the UN General Assembly on November 22, 1974 in securing observer status for the PLO.

The eruption of *intifada* in December 1987 enhanced Arafat's position and led to the November 15, 1988 declaration of the state of Palestine at the Algiers session of the PNC.

In 1990 his support for President Saddam Hussein's linkage between the Kuwait crisis and the Palestinian problem led to the alienation of Arafat from oil-rich countries such as Saudi Arabia and Kuwait and resulted in the expulsion of thousands of Palestinian workers from these countries.

Following the removal of Iraqi occupation of Kuwait, the United States launched a Middle East peace process. Having supported a losing side, Arafat's options were limited and he agreed to the idea of sending a Palestinian delegation to the Madrid peace conference in October 1991 as a joint Jordanian-Palestinian delegation. The absence of progress in the Madrid process led to secret negotiations between Israel and the PLO, facilitated by Norway. On September 9, 1993, Arafat and Prime Minister Yitzhak Rabin exchanged letters of mutual recognition. This led to the signing of the Declaration of Principles and the ushering in of the Oslo process. Following the signing of the Cairo Agreement (May 4, 1994), Arafat entered the Gaza Strip on July 1, 1994 to set up Palestinian autonomy in the Gaza Strip and Jericho. In the wake of the Taba accord of September 1995, Israel withdrew from major Arab population centers.

On numerous occasions assassination attempts have been made against Arafat by Israel and Arab states as well as by rival Palestinian groups, the most prominent being the Israeli air raid on the PLO headquarters in Tunis in August 1988 in which his confidant Khalil al-Wazir was killed. In September 1992, ten Palestinian organizations (including some affiliated with the PLO) met in Damascus and launched an opposition front against the official policy of the PLO. Likewise, following the Oslo accord, Hamas emerged as a major opponent of Arafat as well as of his peace policies towards Israel.

P.R. Kumaraswamy

Capsule Biography

August 4, 1929, born in Cairo as Abd al-Rahman abd al-Rauf Arafat, popularly known as Abu Ammar. 1954, founded *Fatah* in Cairo.1957, expelled from Egypt during Nasser's campaign against Muslim Brotherhood. January 1, 1965, *Fatah*'s first military campaign. February 1969, took over the leadership of the revamped PLO. September 1970, helped organize a civil war in Jordan. 1974, secured Arab recognition for the PLO. November 22, 1974 addressed the UN General Assembly and secured observer status for the PLO. December 1983, evacuated from Beirut following Israeli invasion of Lebanon. February 1985, reached an agreement with King Hussein on a Jordanian-Palestinian confederation. April 1987, annulled the federation accord with Jordan. December 1987, outbreak of *intifada.* November 1, 1988, declared the sate of Palestine at the Algiers session of the PNC. 1990–91, supported Iraqi President Saddam Hussein during the Kuwait crisis and isolated regionally. October 1991, as member of a joint Jordanian-Palestinian delegation attended the Madrid Middle East peace conference in Madrid. 1992, married Suha al-Tawil, journalist and daughter of a prominent Palestinian. September 9, 1993 exchanged letters of mutual recognition with Israeli Prime Minister Yitzhak Rabin. September 13, 1993, signed the Declaration of Principles with Prime Minister Rabin at the White House. May 4, 1994, signed Cairo Agreement. July 1, 1994, entered the Gaza to set up Palestinian autonomy. 1994, shared Nobel peace prize with Rabin and Shimon Peres. January 20, 1996, elected chairman of the Palestinian National Authority and head of the 88-member Palestine Legislative Council.

See also **Arabs: Palestinians; Israel; Palestinian Liberation Organization**

Further Reading

Gowers, Andrew, and Tony Walker, *Behind the Myth: Yasser Arafat and the Palestinian Revolutions,* New York: Olive Branch Press, 1997

Hart, Alan, *Arafat: A Political Biography,* Bloomington: Indiana University Press, 1989

Kiernan, Thomas, *Arafat, the Man and the Myth,* New York: Norton, 1976

Rubin, Barry, *Revolution until Victory? The Politics and History of the PLO,* Cambridge, Massachusetts: Harvard University Press, 1994

Wallach, Janet, and John Wallach, *Arafat in the Eyes of the Beholder,* New York: Carol, 1990

Arakanese

Capsule Summary

Location: Southwestern Burma (Myanmar)
Total Population: Majority are Rakhine Buddhists with 690,000 Rohingya Muslims
Language: A variant of Burmese
Religion: Predominantly Buddhist with significant Muslim followers

The Arakanese are broadly divided into two groups: the majority Rakhine people (Buddhists) and the minority Rohingya (Muslims). They inhabit in the Arakan State (officially renamed Rakhine), one of the seven ethnic minority states of Myanmar (Burma). The country was historically known as Rakhaing but Arakan gained currency among Europeans. The Arakanese live in an area in the coastal region of southern Burma separated by the Arakan mountain range (*Arakan Yoma*) that runs through western Burma between the Irrawaddy River Valley and the coast. It ranges from Cape Negrais in the south to Manipur in India's northeast. Arakanese constitute four percent of the Burmese population.

The Arakanese trace their history to 2666 BCE and they maintain a unique dialect and their own customs. According to the Arakan mythology, the historical Arakan Empire once included the whole of Burma and parts of China and Bengal. An independent Arakan kingdom was supposedly established in the fourth century CE.

The Arakanese were subjected to a series of foreign invasions, including those of the Mongols and

Portuguese, before their eventual conquest by the Burmese kingdom in 1785. Ceded to the British in 1826 under the Treaty of Yandabo, the Arakan state became independent only after the departure of the British in 1948. However, it later became a part of Burma.

Post-independence, the Burmese government maintained that the Rohingya Muslims were recent migrants into Burma and refused to include them in the constitution as an indigenous people, thereby disqualifying them from acquiring citizenship. Rohingyas, too, held a similar view and sought to merge with the eastern part of the newly formed Pakistan. Though Rohingyas were concentrated in the region bordering East Pakistan, the refusal of the Pakistani leadership to entertain their demand led the former to declare themselves to be an Islamic Republic. The Burmese government quickly crushed the movement.

The problem remains intractable, as neither party has modified its stand to facilitate any resolution. Historically, the Rohingyas maintained close socioeconomic relations with the Chittagong region of Bangladesh. Today the problem is punctuated by mutual recriminations: the government charges Rohingyas of insurgency activities and the latter accuse the government of human rights violations (ethnic cleansing).

The problem became regional in 1978 when Burma launched King Dragon Operation against the so-called foreigners who they believed infiltrated northern Arakan. As a result, a large number of Rohingyas took refuge in Bangladesh. While Bangladesh claimed over 250,000 Rohingyas were being sheltered, Burma estimated the figure was 150,000. Following the July 1978 agreement between the two countries, approximately 180,000 Rohingyas returned to Burma. The United Nations High Commissioner for Refugees (UNHCR) got involved in the relief and rehabilitation of the returnees.

However, the Citizenship Act, introduced in 1982, severely restricted the rights of the Rohingyas and made them ineligible for basic social, educational, and health services. Amidst reports of killings and torture, more than 200,000 Rohingyas fled to Bangladesh. By 1992, the figure rose to over 260,000. Following international pressure to stop military operations, the Burmese government initiated the process of allowing the refugees to return home. Under a bilateral agreement concluded in August 1992, Burma agreed to ease earlier restrictions on the Rohingyas: Azam (prayer call) over loudspeakers would be allowed in Muslim majority areas; Rohingyas could move freely from village to village; the refugees in Bangladesh were encouraged to visit their former homes to see the improved conditions; and those Rohingyas who did not posses a citizenship certificate could apply for it after returning home. As a result, in September 1992 refugees began returning and, by 1995, over 150,000 Muslims came back to Burma.

Because of the recurrence of the problem and partly under international pressure, Burma agreed in 1993 to allow the United Nations High Commissioner for Refugees (UNHCR) to maintain a permanent mission in Arakan to facilitate the voluntary repatriation of Rohingyas. However, yet another wave of refugee influx into Bangladesh took place in 1996–1997. In addition to the vexatious issues of citizenship and discrimination, the State Peace and Development Council (formerly State Law and Order Restoration Council) accentuated the trouble by its repressive policies, to include forced labor. Even though most of the refugees returned, a few thousand are still living in Bangladeshi refugee camps.

As in most of the instances, the conflict is between the majority Burmans and the minority ethnic groups. Even Buddhism, practiced by nearly 90 percent of the population, could not be the binding force. For example, the majority Rakhine people, who are Buddhist, are also involved in a separatist struggle against the central government. The groups involved in the conflict with the government are: Rohingya Patriotic Front, the Rohingya Solidarity Organization, the Arakan Liberation Organization, and the Arakan Rohingya Islamic Front.

The feeling among the Burmans that Muslims persecute Rakhine Buddhists in Arakan influenced the government's policy. The ethnic affinity often transcends national borders and becomes intractable. A case in point is the concept of "Greater Mizoram" encompassing the Mizo-inhabited areas of the Indian states of Mizoram, Tripura, Manipur, and Assam as well as the Arakan and Chin states of Burma and parts of Bangladesh. The ethnic linkage has enabled the Mizo insurgents to operate from the Arakan tract.

P.R. Kumaraswamy and D. Shyam Babu

See also **Bangladesh; Buddhists; Muslims in South Asia; Myanmar**

Further Reading

Phayre, Arthur P., *History of Burma*, London: Susil Gupta, 2nd edition, 1967

Smith, Martin, "Burma's Ethnic Minorities: A Central or Peripheral Problem in Regional Context?" in *Burma: The Challenge of Change in a Divided Society*, edited by Peter Carey, London: Macmillan, 1997

The State of the World's Refugees: Fifty Years of Humanitarian Action, "The Plight of the Rohingyas," Oxford: UNHCR, 2000

Thompson, Virginia, and Richard Adloff, *Minority Problems in Southeast Asia*, Stanford, California: Stanford University Press, 1955

Argentina

Capsule Summary

Official Name: *República Argentina* (Argentina Republic)
Location: Southern South America
Total Population: 38,740,807 (July 2003)
Minority Population: Mestizos (14%); Amerindians (1%); Jews (less than 1%); Japanese (less than 1%); Welsh (less than 1%)
Languages: Spanish (official), English, Italian, German, French, Amerindian languages
Religions: Roman Catholics, Jewish, Protestant, Guarani

Argentina is located in the southern part of South America, bordering Bolivia and Paraguay in the north; Brazil and Uruguay in the northeast, and Chile in the west and south. The country has a land area of 2,736,690 square kilometers (1,056,636 square miles) and it is the second largest country in South America after Brazil.

The population of Argentina was estimated at 38,740,807 in 2003. It is predominantly an urban country, with around 86.9 percent of the population living in cities and towns. The country's capital, Buenos Aires, is home for around 2,988,000 people (1996), however, greater Buenos Aires is home to around 13.3 million people (2000) or almost one-third of the country's population. Argentina has one of South America's lowest population growth rates at 1.16 percent and a net migration rate of 0.65 migrant(s) per 1,000 population. It is estimated that its population will reach 41.5 million by 2010. Argentina has a relatively low population density standing at 13 people per square kilometer (33.6 people per square mile) with most of the population concentrating in the northeastern part of the country. However, the areas around Buenos Aires is overcrowded at around 14,000 inhabitants per square kilometer.

Argentina is a presidential democracy. The country declared its independence from Spanish rule in 1816, forming the United Province of South America, which later became known as the Argentine Confederation. According to the Constitution of 1853, Argentina is a federal republic headed by a president with strong executive authority. The revised 1994 Constitution delegated some formerly presidential powers to the legislature. The *Congreso Nacional,* the Parliament, is a bicameral legislative body and consists of the Senate (72 seats) and the Chamber of Deputies (257 seats; one-half of the members elected every two years to four-year terms). Since independence, political life in Argentina has been characterized by political instability and numerous political changes including several military coup d'état and militant confrontations between various political groups. However, the voters' preferences are not necessarily divided according to the ethnic origin or the length of the residence in the country. Despite some existing tensions between recent migrants and those who settled less recently, there has been no political confrontation based on ethnic or racial issues. However, there is a notable cultural and political division between the rural population of inner regions of Argentina and the so-called *portenos* (people of the port), urban multi-ethnic population of Buenos Aires.

Argentina is multiethnic country with a very diverse population. The current ethnic structure was formed during last 150 years as a result of the arrival of large waves of migrants. The Argentines of European origin (mainly Spanish and Italian) make up more than 80 percent of the population. *Mestizo* (mixture between Europeans and indigenous people) and indigenous Amerindians comprise the remaining 15 percent of the population. Around 6.6 million people arrived in Argentina between 1850 and 1940, mainly Spanish and Italian immigrants but also British, German,

French, Russian, Polish, and other immigrants (especially after World War I). During and after World War II there was another wave of migration from war-torn Europe and from neighboring countries. In the 1980s a new wave arrived from Southeast Asia. In the 1990s the latest wave of immigration brought a sizeable number of people from the former Soviet Union and Eastern Europe. Most migrants settled in greater Buenos Aires and other large urban areas. Some migrants prefer to settle as ethnic communities, but they are usually quickly integrated into the Argentine society. Argentina still encourages skilled migration from other parts of the world, although immigration levels remain relatively low.

The Spanish language, which was brought into this region with the arrival of Spanish settlers in 1535, is the official language of the state. It is spoken in several distinct accents and has absorbed words and expressions from other languages including Italian, French, Portuguese, and English. At the beginning of the twentieth century the so-called *lunfardo,* the language of streets and distinct Buenos Aires culture emerged in greater Buenos Aires, absorbing and mixing words from many languages and cultures of people from various cultural and social backgrounds. Most of the immigrants speak their native languages at home or with representatives of their communities (for example, in German farm settlements and cooperatives or in Lebanese shopping districts), however, the second and the following generations usually become fluent in Spanish. Indigenous peoples (Diaguita, Guarani, Pampa Indians, Tehuelche, etc.), who have steadily declined with arrival of European colonizers, speak various native languages and dialects (Tupian linguistic group, Tupi-Guarani, and other distinct languages). However, most of the indigenous population was assimilated by Europeans and often lost their distinct culture and languages.

In Argentina, like in many other South American countries, the majority of the population (around 90 percent) belong to the Roman Catholic Church. Roman Catholicism maintains a strong influence throughout politics and society, and it is constitutionally recognized as the official religion of Argentina. The president and vice president of Argentina are required to be Roman Catholic. However, the Constitution guarantees freedom of worship; thus, Protestants, Jews, Orthodox (Eastern) Christians, and other minorities (around 10 percent of the population) have their own places of worship. Most of the indigenous people who followed various types of shamanistic rituals in the precolonial era were converted to Roman Catholicism in the eighteenth and nineteenth centuries.

Argentina experienced rapid economic growth after World War II, although political instability and military coups negatively affected the economic development of the country. Agriculture and the industrial sector (manufacturing and mining) comprise the two main pillars of the country's economy. Since the early 1990s the government of Argentina has been conducting a policy of economic liberalization, deregulation, and privatization, downsizing the state sector and the state intervention into economic development. Argentina achieved one of the South America's highest GDP per capita, which stood at around $10,500 (2002). However, the income distribution remains extremely uneven. Earnings among the richest segments of population were 25 times greater than those of the poorest groups. According to a World Bank report, the number of individuals living in poverty in Argentina is 13.4 million (36.1 percent of the total population), and of these 3.2 million are extremely poor (8.6 percent of total population). Some studies indicate that the recent migrants and some minority groups, such as indigenous people, remain much poorer than others. In 1998 the United Nations Development Program's Human Development Index (HDI) ranked Argentina 36th, ahead of Uruguay, Brunei, Dominica, Panama, and Venezuela.

RAFIS ABAZOV

See also **Amerindians; Colonialism; Nationalism; Spain**

Further Reading

Baily, L. Samuel, *Immigrants in the Promised Lands: Italians in Buenos Aires & New York City, 1870–1914,* Ithaca, New York: Cornell University Press, 1998

Burdick, Michael, *For God and Fatherland: Religion and Politics in Argentina*, New York, State University of New York Press, 1996

Cavarozzi, Marcelo, *Argentina*, Boulder, Colorado: Westview Press, 1999

Cicerchia, Ricardo, *Historia de la vida privada en Argentina*, Buenos Aires, 1998

Glyn, Williams, *The Welsh in Patagonia: the State and the Ethnic Community*, Cardiff: University of Wales Press, 1991

La migración internacional en la Argentina: Sus características e impacto, Buenos Aires, República Argentina, Ministerio de Economía y Obras y Servicios Públicos, Secretaría de Política Económica, Instituto Nacional de Estadística y Censos, 1995

Lynch, John, *Massacre in the Pampas, 1872: Britain and Argentina in the Age of Migration*, Norman: University of Oklahoma Press, 1998

Monkevicius, Paola, *La comunidad lituana y los festejos nacionales: Algunas consideraciones sobre los "usos del pasado,* En "Tendencias políticas, económicas y geoestratégicas en la Ex Unión Soviética," Centro de Estudios Internacionales para el Desarrollo –CEID-, Buenos Aires, 2000

Pastor, José Manuel Azcona, *Historia de la emigración vasca a Argentina en el siglo XX*, Buenos Aires, Servicio Central de Publicaciones, Gobierno Vasco, 1984

Rock, David, *Argentina, 1516–1987: From Spanish Colonization to Alfonsín*, Berkeley: University of California Press, 1989

Stanganelli, Isabel, *Movimientos migratorios de la ex Unión Soviética en Argentina*, Centro de Estudios Internacionales para el Desarrollo –CEID-, Buenos Aires, 2000

Taylor, Lucy, *Citizenship, Participation and Democracy: Changing Dynamics in Chile and Argentina*, New York: St. Martin's Press, 1998

Armenia

Capsule Summary

Name: Republic of Armenia; independent since September 21, 1991
Location: South Caucasus where Europe and Asia meet
Population: 3.5 million
Ethnic Populations: Armenian (93%), Azeri (1%), Russian (2%), other (mostly Yezidi Kurds, 4%) [2002]
Languages: Armenian (96%), Russian (2%), other (2%).
Religions: Armenian Apostolic (94%), other Christian (4%), Yezidi (Zoroastrian/animist, 2%)

The history of Armenia can be traced back some 3,000 years or more when the proto-Armenians were clearly identifiable on what was traditionally called the Armenian plateau, now called eastern Anatolia or eastern Turkey, and in the South Caucasus. The Armenian language is a part of the Indo-European language family related closely to Proto-Indo-European. Armenia was on the crossroads of international commerce (until the fifteenth century when the age of discovery opened more dependable sea routes) and, consequently, the land became a desired region fought over by contending empires, chiefly the Persian, Roman, Byzantine, Ottoman, Russian, and nomadic invaders. Only the Meliks (kings) of Upper (Mountainous, Nagorno) Karabakh retained armed forces and enjoyed autonomy up until the Russian conquest.

The Armenian King Tirdat accepted Christianity as the state religion early in the fourth century (circa 301– 314 CE). The Church of the Armenians, as the Armenians call it, is autocephalic and headed by the chief patriarch, called the catholicos. It is considered one of the "Lesser Orthodox" churches, a group of anti-Chalcedonian churches.

In the ninth century the Bagratids founded a revitalized Armenian kingdom in western Armenia with its capital at Ani. With the fall of the Bagratid Armenian kingdom to the Seljuk Turks in 1064, relatives of the ruling house established a new Armenian kingdom in Cilicia, in southeast Anatolia. The rulers of the Cilician Armenian kingdom intermarried with the Crusaders, with whom they were allied. Cilicia became an important link between the Italian merchant states and the Orient. The Cilician kingdom fell in 1375, and its last king is buried with the French kings in St. Denis Cathedral near Paris.

The Russians reached the south Caucasus in force in the early 1800s, when they took eastern Armenia from the Persian shahs, leaving western Armenia in Ottoman hands. Western Armenia (today's eastern Turkey) was conquered by the Ottoman Turks between 1514 and 1534. Between 1894 and 1896, the Armenians lost between 100,000–200,000 people in a series of pogroms and massacres under Sultan Abdulhamid II. Then, in 1909, 30,000 Armenians were slaughtered in the former Armenian Cilicia, around the city of Adana. Finally, in 1915–1916, under the cover of World War I, the Young Turk government of the Ottoman Empire butchered some 1.5 million Armenians in the old western Armenian homeland, thus emptying historic Armenia of its last Armenian inhabitants.

The February/March 1917 revolution caused the Russian armies that were fighting in Turkey to disintegrate. Many Armenians fled with the retreating Russians to eastern Armenia. These Armenians, along with native Armenians in the Caucasus, organized a federation with Georgia and Azerbaijan. With the advance of the revitalized Turkish army into the Caucasus in 1918, however, the Transcaucasian Federation dissolved and

Armenia, only some 11,000 square kilometers in size, declared its independence on May 28, 1918 and was left alone to face the advancing Turkish armies. Faced with the problems of security, refugees, war, and famine, Armenia sought an American mandate to sustain the fledgling state and to assist in its reconstruction. President Woodrow Wilson made an appeal to the United States Senate to adopt the mandate, but the Senate, which had grown isolationist, rejected the proposal and left Armenia to survive as best it could.

Meanwhile, the Bolsheviks carried out a coup d'etat against the Provisional Government in October/November 1917 and created a Red Army to consolidate their power and to recapture the territories of the defunct Russian Empire. By 1920, the Armenian Republic, faced by a Turkish army in the west and a Red army in the east, surrendered to the Bolsheviks as the lesser evil. The Bolsheviks then signed a draconian peace with the Turkish Nationalists that left Armenia with only 29,000 square kilometers of territory. Eventually an Armenian Soviet Socialist Republic was established as one of the constituent republics of the soviet Union. The present independent Armenian Republic, with the same boundaries as the former Soviet Republic, occupies only the central eastern edge of historic Armenia.

Soviet Armenia, except for being deprived of Eastern Armenian territory by Turkey, Azerbaijan, and Georgia, began to revitalize. Lenin attempted to pacify the national minorities by a system of "nativization" (*khorenizatsiia*), which encouraged the various peoples to govern their own local republics while remaining loyal to the Soviet central government. Due to Soviet policies, Armenian national consciousness was preserved and strengthened even though Moscow continued to take harsh action against overt nationalists.

Armenian intellectuals living elsewhere in the Soviet Union were encouraged to immigrate to Armenia in order to enrich Armenian cultural life. State support was given to historians, linguists, composers, painters, sculptors, novelists, and poets. The state also supported a university, a conservatory of music, a national theater and opera, and a film studio. Religion and religious practices, however, were discouraged, and the church was suppressed. Armenians enjoyed one of the highest rates of education in the Soviet Union.

Once Josef Stalin solidified his power and introduced rapid industrialization, the five-year plans, and collectivization of agriculture, those who resisted the new order were vigorously suppressed. Furthermore, the great terror that began in the 1930s wiped out almost the entire cadre of top-rank Armenian leaders and intellectuals. By 1939, the purges were over and Stalin had removed any real or possible opposition to his rule. In 1939, Stalin introduced a program of Soviet patriotism, which was a thinly disguised policy of Russianization.

Armenia and Georgia seemed to have been favored by Stalin economically, although he kept strong political control and viciously suppressed any signs of nationalism. Beginning in the 1950s, Georgia and Armenia, due to their climates, topography, development, and facilities, became destinations for Soviet tourists and Diasporan Armenians as well. Otherwise, Armenia experienced Soviet rule much as the other European republics, with economic development and political repression. Armenian cultural and intellectual life, however, managed to grow exponentially.

In the period under Leonid Brezhnev the economy of the entire Soviet Union was undermined by indifference and corruption at all levels. Poor planning and unrestrained growth of industry led to ecological disasters. A movement in the 1980s to save the ecology mutated into a political movement, the Armenian National Movement (ANM), which sought to unify Nagorno-Karabakh with Armenia.

The Azeris were incensed by Armenian demands, and in February 1988, Armenians in Sumgait, a working class suburb of Baku, were massacred, and subsequently in January 1990, another bloody pogrom was carried out in Baku. War broke out between Armenia and Azerbaijan. In 1991, the Soviet Union imploded and Armenia on September 21—along with all the other Soviet republics—became independent. In the first free elections in Armenia since 1919, the ANM won the majority in parliament and Levon Ter-Petrossian, its leader, was elected president. Since then, presidential power has passed into the hands of Robert Kocharian, the former president of Nagorno-Karabakh. The war with Azerbaijan ended with a cease-fire in 1994, but the issue of the political future of Nagorno-Karabakh has yet to be settled. By the end of 1993, virtually all Azeris had emigrated from Armenia due to ongoing ethnic conflicts.

Although Armenia is once more growing economically, it is hindered by a blockade by Azerbaijan in the east and the Republic of Turkey, in sympathy with Azerbaijan, in the west. Nevertheless, Armenia remains the most stable of the three South Caucasus republics.

Under the Soviets, the Armenian economy developed into a major supplier of machine tools, textiles, and other manufactured goods for the various Soviet republics in exchange for raw materials. The fighting with Azerbaijan and the dissolution of the Soviet's centrally directed economic system contributed to severe economic losses in the early 1990s. Since 1991, however, Armenia has been forced to find other means of economic growth, including agricultural production including fruit (namely grapes, vegetables, and livestock). The GDP per capita income in 2002 was $3,600. In the mid-1990s the government embarked on a major International Monetary Fund-sponsored economic program that resulted in positive growth rates in 1995–2003.

Dennis R. Papazian

See also **Armenians; Azerbaijan; Azerbaijani; Russia**

Further Reading

Adalian, Rouben Paul, *Historical Dictionary of Armenia*, Lanham, Maryland: Scarecrow Press, 2002

Bournoutian, George A., *A Concise History of the Armenian People (From Ancient Times to the Present)*, Costa Mesa, California: Mazda Publishers, revised edition, 2003

Chorbajian, Levon, Patrick Donabedian, and Claude Mutafian, *The Caucasian Knot: The History and Geo-Politics of Nagorno-Karabagh*, Atlantic Highlands, New Jersey: Zed Books, 1994

Hewsen, Robert H., *Armenia: A Historical Atlas*, Chicago, Illinois: The University of Chicago Press, 2001

Hovannisian, Richard G., *Armenia on the Road to Independence, 1918*, Berkeley and Los Angeles: University of California Press, 1967

Hovannisian, Richard G., *The Republic of Armenia*, 4 vols, Berkeley and Los Angeles: University of California Press, 1971–1996

Hovannisian, Richard G., editor, *The Armenian People from Ancient to Modern Times*, 2 volumes, New York: St. Martin's Press, 1997

Masih, Joseph, and Robert O. Krikorian, *Armenia: At the Crossroads*, Amsterdam: Harwood Academic Publishers, 1999

Redgate, A.E., *The Armenians*, Oxford and Malden, Massachusetts: Blackwell Publishers, 1998

Walker, Christopher J., *Armenia: The Survival of a Nation*, New York: St. Martin's Press, revised 2nd edition, 1990

Armenians

Capsule Summary

Location: Armenia, Russia, and other former Soviet republics, Middle East, western Europe, United States
Total Population: More than 3 million in Armenia and a few million more throughout the world
Language: Armenian
Religion: Christianity (Armenian Apostolic)

The Armenian people are a Diaspora people, with more Armenians living in other countries than in present-day Armenia itself. There are currently some 3 million people in Armenia, perhaps one and a half million Armenians in Russia, some half million in the other former Soviet republics, perhaps one and a half-million in the United States, and significant numbers in France, England, Sweden, and the Netherlands. There are also remnants of once even larger Diasporas in Egypt, Syria, Lebanon, Jordan, Iraq, and Iran. Few Armenians live in their traditional homeland, which is now a part of Turkey.

The Armenian diasporas are in communication directly and also through contacts in Armenia. Some non-Marxist scholars see nationhood as a construct of ethnicity and a common religion, and they trace back into history three original nations that have survived until this day, namely the Jews, the Armenians, and the Christian Ethiopians. There is a need to explain how a people such as the Armenians have retained a self-identity even though their state has appeared and disappeared several times in history. The Armenians adopted Christianity as their state religion early in the fourth century (circa 301–314), developed their unique alphabet at the beginning of the fifth century (circa 404), engaged in the translation into Armenian of the Bible and all major books in Greek and many in Syriac over the next century, and wrote patriotic histories in what was then the vernacular language. This period is called the Golden Age of Armenian literature.

The translation of the Divine Liturgy (Mass) into what was then the vernacular indicated a society capable of making use of it as a commonality, for the Divine Liturgy was performed in all the churches throughout the land at least once a week and in some places daily. Even now, Armenians of the diaspora consider their first responsibility the building of a church (in which the traditional liturgy and rituals are performed) and then a school. If one travels to any Armenian community anywhere in the world, they would find an Armenian Church performing the same liturgy in the same language as anywhere else in the world. Furthermore, the state religion in the absence of the state became a quasi-state structure binding a far-flung people together. Finally, vernacular Armenian histories identified defining moments of public history. The first was the acceptance of Christianity as the state religion, the second was the building of the mother cathedral, Etchmiadzin, as ordered by Jesus Christ himself, the third was the invention of the Armenian alphabet, which was ascribed to divine inspiration, and the fourth was the battle of Avarayr (451 CE) when the Armenians fought against the overwhelming odds of the Zoroastrian Persian Empire in defense of their freedom to practice Christianity. Finally, for Armenians in the west, a defining moment was the genocide of 1915–1916 carried out by the Young Turk Government of the Ottoman Empire.

The Armenian plateau is located in an area that extends in the west from the headwaters of the Euphrates River eastward to the high lands west of the Caspian Sea. It is a mountainous region with fast flowing rivers, rich valleys, deep cut gorges, and ravines. The mountain chains tend to be located on an east-west axis, thus allowing for movement of trade and invading armies. As in most societies, the vast majority of people were engaged in agriculture. The people were divided into clans, each clan was led by a nobleman (*nakharar*), and each nobleman was assigned a hereditary role at the court of the monarch, such as coronant or leader of the military. Some have compared this structure to the medieval feudal system in Europe. Earliest Armenian culture was related to that of Mesopotamia to the south. In Mesopotamian history, Armenia is generally referred to as the North Country or the land of Ararat.

The Armenians were noted for their export of tin and other minerals, as well as for their horses. With the rise of the Persian Empire, the Armenians became intricately involved in Persian culture, at times sharing the same dynasty, and adopted Zoroastrianism. Although Alexander the Great did not conquer Armenia, it was on the periphery of the Seleucid Empire and slowly adopted Hellenism and the pantheon of Greek gods. It was the Hellenistic ruler Tigran II (95–55 BCE) who built the first Armenian Empire. As the Roman Empire expanded in the east, the Armenians were involved in many wars with Rome, until the land was finally divided between the Persian Empire and the Roman Empire in 387 CE. By this time the Armenians had already accepted Christianity, and soon were to develop their unique alphabet and engage in the translation and writing of books and histories. The alphabet and what was then a unique official religion allowed the Armenians to develop a strong culture that preserved their identity as a people even under foreign rule. Some ancient works in Greek have come down to us only in the Armenian translation. The first work translated, of course, was the Bible. The Armenians wrote original histories, works of geography, science, and philosophy as well.

The Armenians during this period and later were engaged in rug making, the tanning of hides, small-scale production of iron, various crafts, and in east-west trade. The seventh century Arab invasion had its negative as well as positive aspects, but for the first time invaders began to settle in Armenian lands, thus diluting Armenian predominance. The inroads of various Turkic tribes from Central Asia in the eleventh century began the economic and social deterioration of historic Armenia. During this period, many of the Armenian nobility, seeking a more stable environment and encouraged by the Byzantines, moved westward, to southwest Anatolia, to a region called Cilicia. There the Armenians set up a new kingdom, sometimes called Maritime Armenia, because its port cities were transfer points for European goods coming east and eastern goods being sent to the west. The wealth created by manufacturing and trade allowed the Armenians to develop a high culture, religious as well as secular, and to produce literature and artworks of international quality. Especially notable were various illuminated manuscripts. The Armenians of Cilicia mingled with the Crusaders who passed through on their way to the Holy Land, and intermarried with the European nobility. The last king of Armenia, a product of this intermarriage, is buried near Paris in St. Denis Cathedral with the kings of France.

Finally, in the first half of the sixteenth century, western Armenia was conquered by the Ottoman Turks, whereas eastern Armenia fell to a revitalized Persian Empire. Certain Armenians in the Persian Empire, namely those who lived in New Julfa, a suburb of Isfahan, were granted trade monopolies and given special protection by the Shah. These Armenians grew vastly rich and established branches of their trading houses as far east as India and as far west as Russia and Poland in the north and Italy in the south. The Armenians of India were favored by the Mughals and also grew rich, even establishing an endowed college in Calcutta as well as building a dozen churches. The arrival of the British in India was advantageous to the Armenians at first, because the British favored them. Soon, however, the large, joint stock East India Company and others, with which they could not compete, overcame their trading houses. Many of the Armenians of India went farther east to Indochina and Indonesia where they again prospered until the arrival of the large European corporations. It was from these wealthy Armenians of Persia and India that the first Armenian independence movement originated. However, the chief detriment to the Armenians of the east, and to Armenia itself, was the demise of the old trade routes and the establishment of new, cheaper sea routes by the Europeans. Historic Armenia, which once had been at the crossroads of civilizations, now became distant and isolated from the new, dynamic European civilization.

The Armenians who had moved to Russia also prospered, with some even moving into high places within the administrative and military systems. Several noted generals in the czarist armies were of Armenian origin, and several were high administrators, such as Loris-Melikov who was appointed virtual dictator of Russia under Alexander II. The Armenians of the Crimea also prospered and produced an advanced culture.

Armenians in the Ottoman Empire were vastly more numerous because the Empire encompassed the Armenian heartland inhabited largely by peasants in the countryside and artisans and small traders in the towns and cities. Armenian entrepreneurs prospered in Constantinople (present Istanbul) and Smyrna (Izmir), the chief cities of Asia Minor, as well as in Cairo and Alexandria in Egypt. The Ottomans, who were organized into an Islamic theocracy headed by the Sultan-Caliph, established the *millet* system for dealing with non-Muslim Peoples-of-the-Book, namely the Christians and the Jews, who accepted the Bible and therefore were not considered infidels. The *millet* system produced a theocracy within a theocracy. The Armenians, Greeks, and Jews, wherever they might be in the Empire, were placed under the leadership of their respective religious hierarchs. To put it simply, the Armenians were to be ruled by their patriarch, who in turn was responsible to the Sultan-Caliph. This system was rather progressive for its day, when religious minorities of all sorts were being persecuted in Europe. The millet system allowed the Armenians to preserve their church, their culture, and their identity as a people, even though they suffered certain disabilities vis-à-vis the Muslims.

Armenians in the Ottoman Empire were forbidden to bear arms, could not ride horses, had to pay a poll tax, were forced to quarter nomadic Kurds in the winter, and had to give up annually a number of male children who were converted to Islam and enrolled in the Janissary Corps. Furthermore, Armenian testimony was rarely accepted in Muslim courts in which most Muslims brought suits. A few Armenians were Ottomanized, that is, were taken into the ruling class. Several Armenian families of great wealth, called *amiras*, were in charge of such important enterprises as the Ottoman mint, the armory, the famous silk mills, and were the favored architects of the sultans.

As Europe prospered and grew more dynamic, the Ottoman Empire remained static. Its old institutions became anachronistic in the modern world. During the age of imperialism, the European powers cast hungry eyes on Ottoman territory. The British and French (and, later, Italy as well) encroached in North Africa and the Austrians and Russians in Europe and the Russians alone in the Caucasus. The Sultan-Caliphs attempted to resist by modernizing their armies, but in order to do so they borrowed heavily in Europe and consequently had to raise taxes to pay their bourgeoning debt. Because the Ottoman Empire failed to industrialize, the weight of taxation fell on the peasantry, which had already been taxed to the limit. The system was made worse by tax farming, namely by the Sultan giving out for bids the right to collect taxes in a certain province. Those who made bids generally had to borrow the money at usurious rates and consequently raised taxes so high to meet their payments and to produce a profit that the peasants could not possibly pay them. Consequently, the peasants also had to borrow money at usurious rates to meet the growing tax burden. In desperation the peasants would often revolt, and the revolts would then be put down by the central government with irregular troops who carried out massacres. The massacres would attract attention of the European Powers that subsequently demanded reforms in the Empire. While many Armenians in the two major cities were able to prosper, the Armenians in the countryside and in the villages were ground down to abject poverty.

At the beginning of the nineteenth century, American missionaries arrived in the Ottoman Empire and established the largest American mission field in the world. Since it was illegal to convert Muslims, the American missionaries decided to work with the indigenous Christians, chiefly the Armenians, to educate them and make them good examples for the Muslims who they hoped to convert indirectly by this technique. Accordingly, the American missionaries built, over time, five colleges in the areas inhabited by the Armenians, numerous mission stations, schools, orphanages, medical clinics, and Protestant churches. Thus, the Armenians in the interior of Turkey, or western Armenia, were provided with a first-class education by missionaries who had been trained at Harvard, Yale, Oberlin, and other American colleges. Fortunately, or unfortunately, for the Armenians they were taught English as well as American values of democracy, human rights, justice, and a love for education. Indeed, it did raise the level of Armenian Christians above that of the surrounding Muslim society, but rather than persuading the Muslims to convert, it made them envious, jealous, and hostile. The Ottoman government began to look at the Armenians as a potentially troublesome element.

An attempt was made by certain sultans during the nineteenth century to reform the government and produce a constitution—the Tanzimat period. During this time, the Armenians managed to establish a constitution for their own *millet*, granting rights to artisans and intellectuals to help govern the community. Unfortunately, the Tanzimat reforms were stillborn due to the resistance of Muslim clergy and society who refused to accept Christians as equals. The failure of the Tanzimat brought to power Sultan Abdul Hamid II, who both sought to establish a modern bureaucracy as well as to break the backs of the Christian minority in Anatolia, namely the Armenians. Consequently in 1894–1896, a series of massacres was carried out in which 100,000–200,000 Armenians were brutally killed. These massacres raised the ire of the European powers that demanded real reforms. It was due to these massacres that the first significant group of Armenians came to America.

Abdul Hamid II fell into ill repute with his own people. Led by young army officers based at the Third Army Corps headquarters in Salonika, an organization was founded which is generally called the Young Turk Party. They, with the cooperation of the minorities, took power from the Sultan in 1908 and reestablished the constitution of 1876. In 1913, a radical group of Young Turks took power by force and established a dictatorship. It was this dictatorship which led the Ottoman Empire into the disasters of World War I. The dictators were rabid nationalists who wanted to replace the old multiethnic empire with an empire that was purely Turkish, with Anatolia (the original Armenian homeland) as its heartland. Thus, the Armenian Christian minority had to be eliminated. What followed in 1915–1916 has been termed the first genocide of the twentieth century, wherein 1.5 million Armenians were expelled from their homes, massacred, and driven to concentration camps in the Syrian Desert to die of exposure. It was following these massacres that the remnants, mostly women and small children, established themselves in Arab lands, where they were generously received until the advent of modern Arab nationalism and Islamic fundamentalism. Many fled to America where they attempted to rebuild their lives. Substantial help was given to the refugees by the congressionally established Armenian and Syrian Relief organization, later to be known more popularly as Near East Relief. Never before in history had Americans organized and distributed millions of dollars of relief, in this case delivered in general by those same American missionaries who had worked earlier among the Armenians.

Refugees and indigenous Armenian inhabitants of the Caucasus established a small, independent Republic of Armenia in 1918. In 1920, the Republic was taken over by the Red Army, which established a Communist regime. A short time later, Armenia became one of the constituent republics of the Soviet Union. As a Soviet republic it suffered the vicissitudes of living under Stalin and a Communist regime. Fortunately, while the Soviets discouraged nationalism, they encouraged ethnicity. In practice this meant that Armenians were free to develop their language and culture as long as they were subservient to the Soviet system. Thus the Armenians in Armenia were able to establish institutions of higher education, a national opera, a national theater, a national orchestra, music and theater groups, a movie industry, and many museums and libraries, the chief of which is the ancient manuscript library in Yerevan, the capital. Also established were outstanding scientific institutions, a few of which are world famous, and industry, including the production of computer chips and the writing of computer programs. In 1991 the Soviet Union imploded and Armenia, along with all the other constituent republics, became an independent state. At that time a war was going on between the Armenians of Nagorno-Karabakh, aided by Armenia, and the Azeris of Azerbaijan. Nagorno-Karabakh is an Armenian province that was placed under Azerbaijan by Stalin in the 1920s. The people of Nagorno-Karabakh felt that the Azeris were depriving them of their history and culture, and that they were suffering a White Genocide, as compared with a Red Genocide, such as in 1915–1916, which could mean the eventual disappearance of identifiable Armenians in that province.

After pogroms carried out in1988 in Sumgait, a suburb of Baku, and in Kirovabad (now Ganja), in the interior of Azerbaijan, and one carried out in 1990 in Baku, the capital of Azerbaijan, a half million Armenians fled from Azerbaijan to Armenia, Russia, and United States. The situation in landlocked Armenia became dire. An embargo was placed on Armenia by Azerbaijan in the east and the republic of Turkey, in sympathy with Azerbaijan, in the west. The Armenian Diaspora poured millions of dollars into Armenia to help make it viable. Moreover, many Armenians fled either to Russia, various European states, or to the United States where they found jobs and sent money back home to their less fortunate compatriots. Also of significant help was foreign aid extended by the United States.

In the United States the Armenian Diaspora has become the most vital in the world in terms of accomplishments, recognition, wealth, and activities. It is closely followed by the Armenians of France who have produced many artists, intellectuals, and scholars, as well as entrepreneurs. The Armenians in America have built scores of churches, established almost two-dozen day schools, and have organized themselves into many cultural, educational, and politically active groups. The Armenian Diaspora in America, after a generation of financial struggle, has produced businessmen, industrialists, educators, doctors, lawyers, and people in all of the professions. They have attempted, with progressively less success as the generations pass, to retain their Armenian language and culture. They have acculturated and moved from being to feeling Armenian. Nevertheless, second- and third-generation Armenian-Americans have become active in relief and educational work in Armenia. They are also determined to help build high-tech industry in Armenia so that Armenia can once more be self-supporting and prosperous. There is every indication that Armenia and the Armenian Diaspora will remain cohesive, vital, and constructive, and that they will continue to contribute to world science, business, and culture.

DENNIS R. PAPAZIAN

See also **Armenia; Azerbaijan; Azerbaijani; Diaspora**

Further Reading

Bakalian, Anny P., *Armenian-Americans: From Being to Feeling Armenian*, New Brunswick, New Jersey: Transaction Publishers, 1993

Bournoutian, George A., *A Concise History of the Armenian People (From Ancient Times to the Present)*, Costa Mesa, California: Mazda Publishers, revised edition, 2003

Garsoïan, Nina G., "The Problem of Armenian Integration into the Byzantine Empire," in *Studies on the Internal Diaspora of the Byzantine Empire*, edited by Hélène Ahrweiler and Angeliki E. Laiou, Washington, D.C.: Dumbarton Oaks Research Library and Collection, 1998

Hewsen, Robert H., *Armenia: A Historical Atlas*, Chicago, Illinois: The University of Chicago Press, 2001

Hovannisian, Richard G., editor, *The Armenian People from Ancient to Modern Times*, 2 volumes, New York: St. Martin's Press, 1997

Lang, David Marshall, *The Armenians: A People in Exile*, London: George Allen & Unwin, 1981; New edition, London: Unwin Hyman Limited, 1989

Lynch, H.F.B., *Armenia, Travels and Studies*, 2 volumes, London and New York: Longmans, Green and Co., 1901; Reprint, New York: Armenian Prelacy, 1990

Mirak, Robert, *Torn between Two Lands: Armenians in America, 1890 to World War I*, Cambridge: Distributed for The Department of Near Eastern Languages and Civilizations, Harvard University, by Harvard University Press, 1983

Papazian, Dennis, "Armenians in America," *Het Christelijk Osten*, 52, no. 3–4 (2000)

Walker, Christopher J., *Armenia: The Survival of a Nation*, New York: St. Martin's Press, 1980; 2nd edition, 1990

Arvanites

Capsule Summary

Location: Central and Southern Greece
Total Population: Unknown, estimates range up to 10–15 percent of the population
Language: Archaic Albanian dialect (Arbërishte)
Religion: Christian Orthodox

The Arvanítes (or Arbërorë or Arbëresh) are one of the ethnic Albanian groups who settled various Greek lands during the Middle Ages. They live mostly in central and southern Greece and call themselves *Arbërorë* or *Arbëresh*. The Greek term *Arvanites* is related to the root *Arbër*, which in Albanian means, "originating from Arbëria," the medieval designation for present-day Albania.

The Arvanites migrated to Greece from Toskënia, southern Albania in large numbers and several waves, mostly during the fourteenth and fifteenth centuries CE. Other waves of Albanians migrated instead to Italy, especially during the time of the Ottoman occupation of Albania and Greece, forming what is today the Arbëresh community, or the Albanian minority of Italy. Other ethnic Albanian groups in Greece include the Çams, a native Albanian population of Muslim and Christian Orthodox religion from the region of Çamëria—present-day Thesprotia in Northwestern Greece—and the Albanians of Folorina, Kastoria, and Thrace.

The actual number of Arvanites is unknown, as no census has been conducted whereby language spoken at home would determine ethnicity. Unofficial estimates vary considerably ranging from 200,000 to 1.6 million out of a total population of about 11 million, up to approximately 10—15 percent.

The Arvanites are currently located in more than 500 villages in various provinces of Greece. There are about 87 Arvanites villages in the departments of Euboea, 84 in Attica, 70 in Corinth, 60 in Boeotia, 35 in Argolis, 20 in Messenia, 20 in Achaea, and seven in Phtiotis. Other settlements exist in the islands of Andros, Hydra, Poros, Spetsai, Ankistri, and Salamis with a few more in other regions of Greece.

Arvanites speak an archaic Tosk, the southern Albanian dialect. It is called *Arvanitika* by Greeks and is called *Arbërishte* among the Arvanites. This language, heavily influenced by Modern Greek, is still spoken in rural areas, and discussions have emerged as to whether Arvanites should write it in the Greek or Latin alphabet. Historically, there have been limited contacts between Arvanitika or Arbërishte and Albanian, with the exception of the links established after the arrival of Albanian migrants to Greece in the 1990s. The Arvanites, however, understand without any significant difficulty Albanian as spoken by the Arbëresh of Italy as well as by Albanians of Albania.

Arvanitika or Arbërishte does not benefit from legal status in Greece. No teaching of this language is offered at any level of the Greek educational system. The language is in decline due to government policies, public indifference, and to the social changes in the country. Consequently, Arvanitika is considered a language in danger of extinction.

Arvanite customs, family, and cultural traditions are similar to those of Albanians and the Arbëresh of Italy in particular, but their enduring historical interchange with the Greek people—with its positive and negative aspects—has apparently resulted in the creation of a peculiar Arvanite identity. There are claims that this identity is unrelated to Albanian identity; nevertheless, there has been impetus among prominent Arvanites to relate their identity to common Greek/Albanian roots dating back to the Pelasgians, or the earliest non-Indo-European population of ancient Greece and Illyria. The Arvanites, however, generally share a comparable historical, cultural, and linguistic identity with the Arbëresh of Italy who, in turn, are a recognized Albanian minority.

As followers of the Greek Orthodox religion, the Arvanites are not officially recognized as a minority in Greece, despite constituting "a most important element of the population". They contributed substantially to the Greek War of Independence in 1821—1828. Many leaders of the Greek Revolution, including Kundurioti (provisional president of Greece in 1823), Bubulina, Kolokotroni, Miauli, Karaiskaj, and others were Arvanites.

The policy followed by the Modern Greek state toward the Arvanites has been one of assimilation, or Hellenization. One aspect of this policy is the fact that the government has censored the Arvanite language not only in schools, but also in the army and other public places. Various coercive measures, including physical punishment, humiliation, or simple incitation, were applied against its users. The Arvanites are currently one of the endangered linguistic minorities in Europe. Greece has not ratified the Council of Europe Framework Convention for the Protection of National Minorities as well as the European Charter for Regional or Minority Languages.

After 1980 there have been some sporadic and unsustained attempts for a cultural revival among the Arvanites, which include the formation of four cultural associations, the publication of a few books and a bimonthly magazine (*Bessa*), and Christian Orthodox readings and chanting during religious ceremonies at some Arvanite villages. The political climate in Greece in the 1990s in regard to conflicts in the Balkans constituted a significant external factor for the further decline of the cultural life of the Arvanites, resulting in the ceasing of *Bessa* in 1994.

AGRON ALIBALI

See also **Albania; Albanians; Greece**

Further Reading

Bellusci, Antonio, *Ricerche e Studi tra gli Arbërori dell' Ellade, Testi e Documenti*, Centro Ricerche Socio-Culturali "G. Castriota", Cosenza, 1994

Georgacas, Demetrius J., and William A. McDonald, *Place Names of Southwest Peloponnesus, Register and Indexes*, Athens, 1967

Les minorities en Europe, Droits linguistiques et Droits de l'Homme, Avec une carte des langues d'Europe hors texte, Sous la direction de Henri Giordan, Éditions Kimé, 4, rue Saint-Merri, Paris, 1992

Finlay, George, *The History of Greece*, Edinburgh and London: William Blackwood and Sons, 1851

A Handbook of Greece, Vol. I, The Mainland of Old Greece and Certain Neighbouring Islands, July 1918, Naval Staff Intelligence Division, C. B. 837, pp 75—77

Institut de Sociolingüística Catalana, "Euromosaic Report, L'arvanite/L'albanais en Grèce," http://www.uoc.es/euromosaic/web/document/albanes/fr/i2/i2.html.

Jenkins, Romilly, *Byzantium and Byzantinism, Lectures in Memory of Louise Taft Semple*, Ohio: The University of Cincinnati, 1963

Kazazis, Kostas, "Greek and Arvanitika in Corinthia, Balkanistica," *Occasional Papers in Southeast European Studies, III*, Slavica Publishers, Inc., 1976

Salltari, Nikou, *I Zoi Ton Arvaniton Ekoseis Gerou*, Athens: Arvanitiki Vivliografia, 1986

Tsitsipis, Lukas D., *A Linguistic Anthropology of Praxis and Language Shift: Arvanitika (Albanian) and Greek in Contact*, Clarendon Press, Oxford University Press, 1998

Xhufi, Pëllumb, "Albania Greca in the 14th–15th Centuries, A Survey on the Albanian Colonisation in Greece in the Late Middle Ages," *Studia Albanica*, Nr. 1–2, Tirana, 1991, pp 73–108

Asians in Latin America

Capsule Summary

Location: Latin America and the Caribbean
Total Population: 200,000
Languages: Spanish, Portuguese, Hindi, Japanese
Religions: Catholic, Buddhist, Hindu

During the nineteenth and twentieth centuries, immigrants from Asia as well as Europe arrived in Latin America. Their presence modified the economic, cultural, and ethnic configurations of the region. Those who were not indentured, especially in and around the Caribbean area, tended to settle in industrial areas, or regions that exhibited a degree of development. Their arrival set forth one of the dominant themes in the process of national integration in Latin America, that is, the merging of diverse groups in the quest for financial gain. The process is transcultural and global, therefore requiring a global and transcultural perspective in order to understand the situation. In addition, the policies of the host countries had the clear goal of obtaining cheap workers, or in some cases specialized labor, to benefit the national economy by in part increasing industrialization through foreign investment.

There were basically two types of motivation for Asian emigration. Forced emigration, that is, those who were forced to leave their homeland due to economic crises or political oppression. Some had hoped to use their entry into Latin America as a steppingstone to the United States. Many of these, like the Jews, Lebanese, and Chinese in Mexico, had experienced unsuccessful exiles in other countries. The Japanese who went to Chiapas, Mexico, characterize the second type of motivation. They were protected by contracts specifying their economic activities, territorial possessions, and remuneration.

Structural integration of these immigrants into the host society initially started with their place of work. It was here that the host and migrant groups mutually influenced each other's culture. For those who were technologically and professionally well trained, they soon found themselves in a position that well surpassed the social position they occupied at their initial entry. Immigrants who had similar origins but not the technical training or skills were exploited or enslaved. Thus, the position in the receiving community, in some cases, caused divisions in the migrant group between the skilled and unskilled. In other places, where there was only one or the other a unity developed according to origin or occupation. The contributions and influences of Asians in Latin America have been generally overlooked.

With the arrival of Asian and other immigrants over the last two centuries, Asians have been part of the formation of pluralistic societies that have obtained legitimacy on North, Central, and South American soil. As a result, a new definition of power developed for the majority had to abdicate control over minorities, or vice versa, for the liberation forces of Latin America had and have to fight exploitation of the weak by the powerful without ethnic or cultural distinctions. Thus all, including Asians, have assumed an active and responsible role in transforming the societies in which they now live.

One of the transformations has been that the groups from the Old Continent over the past two centuries helped to form pluralistic societies and have gained legitimacy for themselves. The acceptance of the new pluralism has redefined power relationships so that those in power, whether a majority or minority, had to relinquish power to the weak so as to fight and eliminate the exploitation of the weak by the powerful. Thus, the weak, especially minorities, will establish roots in their new abode and take an active and responsible role in transforming the societies in which they live.

Among the most prominent groups include the Asian Indians, Chinese, and Japanese, although Asian-Jews, Arabs, Lebanese, Okinawans, and Nepalese also migrated to Latin America. The notable receiving countries were Cuba, Mexico, Brazil, and the Caribbean area. Peru, Argentina, and Bolivia also received immigrants. Asian Indians went primarily to the Caribbean where they filled the void left by the exodus of blacks from the plantations as a result of the abolition of slavery. These Asian Indians were recruited and worked under an indenture system by which they suffered abuses. Because of owing money at the company store and fines for infraction of rules, they would end up owing more to their employer than they had earned. As a result they would have to sign up for another tour. However the Asian Indians participated in the struggle for freedom in some places and have become a legitimate and viable political entity in others. They number around 100,000.

The Chinese have had a more varied experience. They were brought to Mexico and Cuba to provide cheap labor and/or work on plantations. In the case of Cuba they united with the slaves from Africa to obtain freedom; people tended to consolidate into groups regardless of background. Chinese in Mexico were also recruited for cheap labor, but in northwestern Mexico they formed small businesses, enhanced craft production, and participated in the financial center through their own bank. They also had their own mutual help societies and even their own government that functioned more like a colony than immigrants imported for cheap labor.

The Chinese in Mexico, Cuba, Peru, and Panama illustrate the fact that the immediate causes of migration do not yield similar results; life in their adopted country depends on many factors at their destination. The Chinese, especially in Cuba, had experience at both ends of the skilled/unskilled continuum as well as many positions in between. In the case of the Chinese in northwestern Mexico, they were successful and prosperous—much of which was due to the oil boom in the area. When the oil boom dried up, local Chinese emigrated elsewhere. Also, with the downturn in the economy, an anti-Chinese movement developed, with some Chinese losing their property and assets while others were expelled and yet others simply massacred.

Japanese immigrated to Brazil to work on coffee plantations. They had the opportunity of being socially mobile and in a span of about two generations they rose from being employees to employers and professionals. They maintained enough of their Japanese culture to keep their "Japaneseness" while also borrowing from the culture of their host society also.

Japanese were similar to the Chinese and in some cases like some of the Chinese, they resembled colonials rather than immigrants. They came as a result of a treaty between the Mexican and Japanese governments. The Japanese enjoyed certain guarantees and the right to purchase land. Yet, they also suffered from the hostility and xenophobia of the host society.

The story and understanding of the experiences of Asians in Latin America is an untold story, but it is also a drama that, when told, will shed light on understanding the migration process in general.

ARTHUR HELWEG

See also **Brazil; Cuba; Mexico**

Further Reading

Montiel, Luz M. Martinez, editor, *Asiatic Migrations in Latin America*, Camino al Ajusco: El Colegio de Mexico, 1981

Rustomji-Kerns, Roshni, *Encounters: People of Asian Descent in the Americas*, Lanbam, Boulder, New York, Oxford: Rowman & Littlefield Publishers, Inc., 1999

Bradley, Anita, *Trans-Pacific Relations of Latin America*, New York: Institute of Pacific Relations, 1941

Chang-Rodriguez, E., "Chinese Labor Migration into Latin America in the Nineteenth Century," *Revista de Historia de América*, 46 (December 1958

Martínez Montiel, Luz María, *Asiatic Migrations in Latin America*, México D.F.: El Colegio de México, 1981

Cope, R. Douglas, *The Limits of Racial Domination*, Madison: University of Wisconsin Press, 1994

Moya, Jose C., *Cousins and Strangers*, Berkeley: University of California Press, 1998

Assam, *See* **Assam Movement; Assamese; India**

Assam Movement

The Assam Movement refers to the popular agitation that shook the northeastern Indian state of Assam between 1979 and 1985, when "indigenous" Assamese believed that they were being inundated by "illegal immigrants" as well as reduced to a minority in their own land. Assam is a land-locked northeastern state of India that had a population of 26.63 million in 2001. An inclusive definition for Assamese would refer to all the residents of the state of Assam, whereas an exclusive categorization would restrict the usage to those who can trace their ethnolinguistic lineage to Assam.

A typical "sons of the soil" movement, the Assam movement sought to identify and deport people who illegally entered Assam and settled there. However, for the governments in Guwahati (Assam's capital) and Delhi, identifying—let alone deporting—illegal immigrants had proved to be an uphill task. Indeed, the influx of outsiders into Assam had started during the British rule and those who entered the state after India's independence in 1947 were not all illegal immigrants as many of them came from other parts of India. The agitation was directed, to a large extent, against those who came from East Pakistan, which became Bangladesh in 1971. The bulk of immigrants prior to independence came from East Bengal, which became East Pakistan after partition. Naturally, the movement had acquired a communal color as most of the Bangladeshi immigrants were Muslims and had had repercussions elsewhere in India and strains in Indo-Bangla relations. In a way, the anti-foreigners agitation began with the Indo-Pakistan conflict. In 1965 the state government in Assam, under instructions from the central government, started expelling those they termed infiltrators from East Pakistan.

At times violent, the movement posed the most formidable challenge to state authority both at national and local levels in that it was unrelenting. It enjoyed the support of ethnic Assamese transcending socioeconomic and political divides. The agitation started in 1979 when the All Assam Students Union (AASU) and the Assam Gana Sangram Parishad (AGSP), an umbrella organization of several Assamese political and cultural groups, began mass mobilization demanding for the central government to "identify, disenfranchise and deport" illegal immigrants. According to one estimate by Myron Weiner, excluding immigrants, both legal and illegal, Assam's total population by 1971 census would have been 7.6 million instead of the actual 15 million. Weiner maintains that, when the 1891 census is taken as the base, immigrants and their descendents would (by 1971) number 8.5 million and the locals 6.5 million. Therefore, the sentiments of the Assamese that they were culturally and linguistically outnumbered by aliens could not be countered.

One complication is that unlike the number of Assamese, which decreased over the decades, the number of those declaring Assamese language as their mother tongue increased—from 39 percent in 1931 to 61 percent in 1971. This was interpreted as an attempt by the East Bengali/Bangladeshi Muslim peasant immigrants to assimilate themselves into Assam. The absence of official records as to who entered the state and when emerged as another problem. It would be difficult, either in Assam or in other parts of India, for landless laborers who tend to move from one place to the other in search of employment to prove their domicile.

The decennial census in 1981 could not be carried out in Assam due to violence unleashed by the agitation. This also led to further complications as there was no way to ascertain who or how many people illegally entered Assam between 1971 and 1981. This was a crucial period during which, for the agitators, large-scale influx took place. The electoral process, too, was disrupted and elections could not be held in twelve out of the fourteen constituencies in the state during the 1980 parliamentary elections. As if to highlight the point, those two constituencies where elections were held were located in the immigrant-dominated areas. Similarly, in the elections to the state assembly in 1983 the boycott announced by the agitators was so widespread that it raised questions about the legitimacy of the electoral process itself. Moreover, the ensuing violence claimed the lives of nearly 3,000 people. In Nellie village alone, 1,383 men, women, and children were massacred.

Efforts by the central and state governments to establish order were largely unsuccessful. One reason for the failure was that the ethnic Assamese, the agitators, were the dominant group both in government services and in the state's economy. They were better placed, for example, to call for an economic blockade but at the same time a sympathetic response from the administration had reduced confrontation.

Though the central government initiated negotiations with the agitators in 1980, a formal agreement came about only in August 1985. Both parties agreed that those who came to Assam during 1951–1961 were to be given citizenship and those who entered the state after 1971 were to be identified and deported. The Accord was a compromise for all parties. The agitators who sought the deportation of those who came during 1961–71 were to be content with the disenfranchisement of the latter for only ten years.

The Accord paved the way for fresh elections to the state assembly in 1985 and the formation of a government headed by Asom Gana Parishad (AGP), an offshoot of AASU and AGSP. As a result, whereas the Assam Movement had dissipated the inability of the newly formed government in identifying and deporting those entered Assam after 1971, it left the core issue of the agitation unresolved.

This popular unhappiness over the outcome of the long and violent movement resulted in the birth of other militant outfits like United Liberation Front of Assam (ULFA) and Bodo Security Force (BdSF) which unleashed more violence in Assam.

P.R. Kumaraswamy and D. Shyam Babu

See also **Assamese; Bangladesh; India, Muslims in South Asia**

Further Reading

Baruah, Sanjib, "Immigration, Ethnic Conflict and Political Turmoil-Assam, 1979–1985", *Asian Survey*, 26, no.11 (November 1986)

Baruah, Sanjib, "Politics of Subnationalism: Society Versus State in Assam", in *State and Politics in India*, edited by Partha Chatterjee, New Delhi: Oxford, 1998

Hazarika, Sanjoy, *Strangers of the Mist: Tales of War and Peace from India's Northeast*, New Delhi: Penguin, 1995

Singh, Jaswant, "Assam's Crisis of Citizenship: An Examination of Political Errors", *Asian Survey*, 24, no.10, October 1984

Verghese, B.G., *India's Northeast Resurgent: Ethnicity, Insurgency, Governance, Development*, New Delhi: Konark, 1996

Assamese

Capsule Summary

Location: Northeast India, mostly in the state of Assam
Total population: Approximately 14.6 million (1.3 percent of the country's population)
Language: Assamese
Religions: Hindu, Muslim

The Ahom tribes, who are the descendants of the Assamese, migrated from Myanmar (Burma) into India's northeast region beginning in the thirteenth century. Closely related to Burma's Shan ethnic group, the Assamese are a mongoloid people but their language belongs to the Indo-European family. Their traditional source of livelihood is agriculture and they are plains dwellers. Modern Assam encompasses some 30,300 square miles and borders Bangladesh and Bhutan. The state is known for its tea plantations, but Assam also produces one-sixth of India's petroleum and natural gas.

The Ahom monarchy and aristocracy ruled Assam until the region was annexed by the British empire in 1826. As the British wanted to promote tea cultivation, they encouraged migration from East Bengal to supplement the labor force in the sparsely populated region. Since the early 1900s, some 6.5 million migrants have settled in Assam. Prior to independence these settlers largely assimilated into the Assamese. While the British did temporarily recognize Assamese as a separate language and the medium of instruction in schools, colonial policy favored Bengali speakers who dominated the bureaucratic structures.

The 1947 partition that created India and Pakistan led to a major influx of several hundred thousand Bengali Hindus into Assam. In 1956, in response to demands for a reorganization of the states in the Indian federation, the central government agreed to create new states on a linguistic basis. As a result, four new states were carved out from Assam: Arunachal Pradesh, Meghalaya, Mizoram, and Nagaland. However, Assamese speakers still felt threatened due to further influxes of Bengali speakers and Bengali domination of the public and private sectors and middle-class occupations.

The population in Assam is divided based on language, religion, and tribe. Violent riots between Assamese Hindu and Bengali Hindu speakers arose in 1960 when Assamese was adopted as the sole official state language. While both languages have a common script, disputes have also arisen over which one should be used as the medium of instruction in post-secondary institutions.

The 1971 civil war in Pakistan—which led to India's military intervention and the creation of Bangladesh—exacerbated tensions in Assam as the state was once again the recipient of a major influx of both Hindu and Muslim Bengalis. Assamese speakers feared that they would become a minority in Assam and that political power would be exercised by Bengali immigrants. Developments in the neighboring state of Tripura heightened these fears. In 1947, 93 percent of Tripura's population consisted of tribal peoples; by 1981, the tribals only made up 28.5 percent of that state's population.

Beginning in the late 1970s, the Assamese, led by student organizations such as the All Assam Students Union (AASU), began agitating for the expulsion of Bengalis (some of whom were illegal immigrants who were registered as voters), while also pressing for greater job opportunities in the bureaucracy and professional occupations. Perceptions of neglect by the central government coupled with the state's economic underdevelopment also fueled Assamese discontent. In 1983, in what is referred to as the Nellie massacre, more than 1,000 Bengali speakers were killed.

In 1985, Prime Minister Rajiv Gandhi reached an accord with the AASU. It included a commitment to deport migrants who had arrived in Assam after 1971, the promotion of economic development, and the holding of state elections in December of that year. While a local Assamese party, the Asom Gana Parishad, won the elections, the inability of both the central and state governments to fulfill the requirements of the agreement renewed resentment among the Assamese.

Although it first emerged in 1979, the United Liberation Front of Assam (ULFA), which advocates the secession of Assam, did not receive prominence until about a decade later when it launched a campaign of kidnapping, extortion, and tax collection—in effect, a parallel government in parts of Assam. It also engaged in armed attacks against Bengali immigrants and security forces. In response, the Indian government launched counterinsurgency operations against the militants while also dismissing the state government and imposing federal rule.

Around this time, another armed conflict emerged in Assam, this time between the Assamese and the Bodos, who are tribal peoples that reside in the state's northern plains region. The Bodos, concerned that their own culture and language were under threat by Assamese dominance, sought the creation of a separate Bodoland state within India. Various Bodo organizations have since utilized both conventional and militant activities to press for their demands. Rebel Bodo groups have targeted Assamese and Bengali speakers and the state's apparatus. In 1993, the federal government sought to address Bodo concerns by creating an autonomous Bodo district and local governing council. However, this accord faltered due to a lack of implementation and rebel Bodo groups shortly after resumed their violent campaign.

Since the early 1990s, there has been little change in the situation in Assam. The ULFA, rebel Bodo groups, and militant Bengali Muslims continue to engage in armed attacks against each other's communities and the state's security forces. Other Assamese organizations utilize protests and strikes to press for the expulsion of illegal Bengali immigrants and the promotion of economic rights for Assamese speakers. The Indian government maintains counterinsurgency operations in Assam in an effort to quash the various insurgencies. Human rights abuses are prevalent by the government and the various rebel groups. While the Bodos have held periodic talks with the federal government, little has been achieved so far. In the case of the Assamese, no serious negotiations have occurred due to ULFA demands for sovereignty and Indian rejections of any proposals that would threaten the country's territorial integrity. More than 20,000 have died so far in Assam and the future does not hold much promise for an early resolution to these various conflicts.

DEEPA KHOSLA

See also **Assam Movement; Bangladesh; India; Myanmar**

Further Reading

Baruah, Sanjib, *India against Itself: Assam and the Politics of Nationality*, Philadelphia, Pennsylvania: University of Pennsylvania Press, 1999

Brass, Paul R., *The Politics of India since Independence*, Cambridge and New York: Cambridge University Press, 1990; 2nd edition, 1994

Chattopadhyay, Dilip Kumar, *History of the Assamese Movement since 1947*, Calcutta, India: Minerva Associates Publications, 1990

Chhabra, K.M.L., *Assam Challenge*, New Delhi: Konark Publishers, 1992

Datta, P.S., editor, *Ethnic Movements in Poly-Cultural Assam*, New Delhi: Har-Anand Publications and Vikas Publishing House, 1990

Deka, Meeta, *Social Movements in Assam,* New Delhi: Vikas Publishing House, 1996

Hazarika, Sanjoy, *Rites of Passage: Border Crossings, Imagined Homelands, India's East and Bangladesh*, New Delhi: Penguin Books, 2000

Minorities at Risk Project Website, Center for International Development and Conflict Management, University of Maryland. http://www.bsos.umd.edu/cidcm/mar

Rafiabadi, Hamid Naseem, *Assam from Agitation to Accord*, New Delhi: Genuine Publications and Media, 1988

Assimilation

Assimilation is a process that has impacted on many minority groups throughout history. Assimilation can be forced or voluntary. The force may take the form of legislation that is upheld by military or police services. The force may come as social and economic pressure to conform. The pressure of isolation and rejection is often added, if individuals or groups refuse to assimilate; such assimilation may be seen as voluntary.

Defining Assimilation

Assimilation is a term used to describe the process by which one group of people or individuals of a group are absorbed and/or subjugated to the cultural ways of another, more dominant group. In due course the subordinate group adopts the dominant culture and society of the other group. The ultimate effect of assimilation would be to destroy the suppressed group, unlike integration, where societies evolve and diversify and benefit from the merging and interaction.

Assimilation usually involves a gradual change and takes place in varying degrees; full assimilation occurs when new members of a society become indistinguishable from older members. However, complete assimilation rarely takes place unless the subordinated peoples are relocated and their family units broken.

History and Theory

Assimilation is as old as cultural interaction between groups of peoples. It can be seen as a consequence of imperialism and colonization. Although imperialistic nations within the Asian region also colonized other societies and thus implemented acculturation, an element of the assimilation process, the article will concentrate on the process in European dominated cultures. However, if the reader is interested in assimilation within the Asian context, researching the colonization of Korea by Japan is a good starting point.

During the centuries of European imperialism the monarchs, churches, and governments of countries such as Spain, Portugal, Holland, England, and France invested in expeditions to lands previously little known to them. If the lands were judged of value the Indigenous peoples of these countries were dispossessed and European colonies established. The colonies have become such contemporary nations as India, the Philippines, the United States, Australia, Canada, Mexico, and New Zealand. When considering what to do with the "natives," many European imperialist governments adopted policies to "protect and civilize," policies of forced assimilation.

Literate Europeans influenced by the likes of philosopher and social critic Jean-Jacques Rousseau adopted the vision of the "noble savage" that associated Indigenous people with unspoiled nature. Many of the expeditions to the so-called "new world" were promoted as scientific. Charles Darwin's theories of evolution were being adapted by sociologists to societies; Social Darwinism, with its belief in racist concepts of a hierarchy of the human animal, was spawned. In accordance with the scientific method the experiment placed Indigenous people into a controlled environment called a reserve or mission.

Assimilation and the Aboriginal Peoples of Australia

The experience of the Aboriginal peoples of Australia is a reasonable representation of what occurred in many nations to Indigenous groups.

Missions and Reserves

Colonial governments and church groups established missions and reserves. Missions were places were Aboriginal people were impounded. Often whole language groups and clans were rounded up and marched at gunpoint to the destination chosen by the authorities of the time.

The objective of the missions was to control the original owners/custodians of the land by restricting their movements and making it easier for European colonizers to move in and take over the land. The missions were also controlled environments were the social experiment of assimilation could be implemented. The mission managers had the right to say who could come and go on the properties. If Aboriginal people did not cooperate they would be expelled from living with their families on the compound. In some instances the colonizing government would move people long distances to missions established on islands or other inhospitable places that were hard to escape from.

On the missions, Aboriginal cultural markers such as language, ceremony, and hunting/food gathering practices were outlawed. Aboriginal law and authority was undermined and ridiculed. Groups who may have no common language or who may have been traditionally not allowed to mix with each other or worse, enemies were forced to live on the same small parcel of land.

Many missions were poorly run, with disease killing off whole groups of people who had no immunity to the European diseases of influenza, chicken pox, and the like. Often the people who were appointed to run the mission were without training in health or education. If on a mission staffed by a religious order, people would be taught the new religion and perhaps taught how to read the Bible, but little else. Thus, not allowed to practice their own cultures, Aboriginal people were put into situations with people who may have been able to show them the rudiments of farming or keeping house but very little of the culture into which they were supposed to assimilate.

Separation and Stealing of Children

On some compounds children as young as four years were separated from their parents and placed in dormitories where the children lost contact with their parents and siblings of the opposite gender. Many reports of molestation are recorded and passed on through oral histories.

In other parts of the country forced assimilation meant the forcible removal of children from parents and family and "relocation" to European foster parents, European adoptive parents, or to special "half-caste" or "assimilation" homes located away from the missions.

In 1905, W.E. Roth, the Chief Protector of Aborigines in Queensland, believed that the social status of Aboriginal children he saw as "half-caste" had to be improved. Roth believed that improvement would come about if the so called 'half-caste" children were taken from their communities and raised as European children.

Neville the Protector of Aborigines in Western Australia had a three-point plan. Like his colleague Roth, Neville graded Aboriginal people according to his concept of caste. Such concepts are in contemporary times considered derogatory. However, Neville's three point plan stated that, the "full-bloods" would die out; that the "half-castes" should be removed from their mothers; and that there should be controlled marriages among "half-castes" to encourage intermarriage with the European community.

In 1928, J.W. Bleakley, then Queensland Protector of Aborigines, was asked by the Commonwealth government to report on Aboriginal policy—including the future of "half-castes"—in the Northern Territory. Thereafter "half-castes" were sent to specified institutions around the country, to be "salvaged" because these so-called "protectors" viewed their European blood to be their springboard to civilization and Christendom.

Dr. Cecil Cook, Chief Protector of Aborigines in the Northern Territory, believed that the dominance of colored races and the scarcity of European women to marry with European men would create a position of incalculable future menace to the purity of race in tropical Australia.

The Neville-Bleakley-Cook philosophies became official policy in the Northern Territory in the early 1930s. In the Territory the "mating" of an Aboriginal person with any person other than an Aboriginal was prohibited. Sexual relations among colored aliens with any female of "part" Aboriginal blood was also forbidden.

The Aborigines Protection Board, later the Welfare Board, of the time had a policy of dissociating Aboriginal children from Aboriginal society and cultures. It was the belief of the Board made up of the Protectors of Aborigines from the various states and territories that the act of dissociating children from their families must eventually solve the so-called "Aboriginal problem." The policy of placing Aboriginal children in European homes was seen to be showing the children a superior standard of life, which would pave the way for the assimilation of Aboriginal people into the dominant population.

Dog Tags of Exemption

Certificates were issued to some Aboriginal people to exempt them from restrictive legislation. All Australian States at some time have had legislation exempting from its provision certain Aboriginal people deemed to have been "civilized," in other words, those who were deemed to have sufficiently assimilated. Exemption entitled Aboriginal people to vote, drink alcohol, use hotels, and otherwise exercise the rights enjoyed by other Australians.

Aboriginal people generally refer to the exemption certificates as "dog tags" which illustrates that Aboriginal people generally resented the discrimination implicit in exemption. If I person had a dog tag they were not allowed to interact with other Aboriginal people, not even their immediate family.

Aboriginal Response

In 1990 the Secretariat of the National Aboriginal and Islander Child Care (SNAICC) organization demanded an inquiry into child removal. In August 1991 an Aboriginal media release mentioned this "blank spot" in Australian history and commented on how past policies were continuing to cause damage and trauma felt every day by Aboriginal people.

In 1993–1994, the Australian Archives presented an exhibition in the cities of Sydney, Adelaide, and Canberra as well as in the Northern Territory titled *Between Two Worlds*, a study of the Commonwealth government's removal of Aboriginal "half-caste" children in the Territory from 1918 to the 1960s.

By 1994, Aborigines at the *Going Home* conference in Darwin felt sufficiently confident to begin planning civil lawsuits against governments and missions for the forced removal of children and the break-up of family life.

In May 1995, the Commonwealth Labor government responded to Aboriginal and media pressure by establishing the National Inquiry into the Separation of Aboriginal and Torres Strait Islander Children from their Families. The National Inquiry reported in April 1997. The inquiry was one of 118 official investigations—judicial inquiries, parliamentary committee reports and royal commissions—into aspects of Aboriginal affairs in the twentieth century. It concluded that the Australia government has knowingly committed genocide through the forcible transfer of children, as a matter of official policy, as recently as the 1970s. The forcible removals were intended to assimilate the children in the hope that Aboriginal people would cease to exist as a distinct group within Australian society.

Throughout 1996, the National Inquiry pressed the new Commonwealth conservative government to make a formal submission, as state governments had done. The Commonwealth government continued to stall, thus delaying the release of the inquiries findings, which were published in 1997 and finally released to the public in May 1997. The inquiry summarized that between one in three and one in ten indigenous children were forcibly removed from their families and communities in the period from approximately 1910 until 1970.

The Immigrant Experience

Assimilation is not something that has only been practiced by Europeans against indigenous peoples. In the nineteenth and early twentieth centuries many of the reasonably affluent countries of the so-called New World saw an influx of European immigrants. The United States is a prime example. Rather than allowing migrants to maintain their original cultural characteristics, the dominant English-speaking, Protestant majority indoctrinated the immigrants in the prevailing culture. The immigrant groups adopted the dominant language and ideology. As a result, they did not establish autonomous social groups but rather became assimilated into the new society.

History of United States Immigration

Until about 1860 the population of the United States was relatively homogeneous. The overwhelming number of Americans had their family origins in the British Isles; thus the society of America was significantly Anglo-Saxon Protestant. After the American Civil War (1861–1865) larger numbers of immigrants began to arrive from countries of central and southeastern Europe. People from Italy, the Balkans, Poland, and Russia joined with the Germans, English, and Irish of previous decades in moving to the land of hope and glory. The Europeans who arrived in America post-Civil War, however, were mostly non-English and non-Protestant, which made them different in culture from the peoples who had settled in America since the overthrow of the Native American Tribes who had previously ruled the land.

The immigrants from central and southeastern Europe formed their own neighborhoods and established ethnic societies, clubs, newspapers, and theatres. They formed social enclaves within the larger society of America. However, the English Protestants remained the dominate cultural group within America, retaining a firm hold on the social order by being dominant in the head offices of large corporations, financial institutions, the judiciary system, and education.

Quotas

Mass immigration to the United States slowed from full flow to a drizzle by the establishment of the Immigration Act of 1924. The Act established the national origin system. Quotas were established for each country based on the number of persons of that national origin who were living in the United States in 1920. The Act had the effect of hugely dropping the number of immigrants from southeastern Europe. Under the system put in place by the Immigration Act of 1924, 70 percent of the immigration numbers went to Great Britain, Ireland, and Germany. The quota system was finally abolished in 1968 and a first-come, first-served policy was put in its place. This resulted in an increase in people from Asian countries immigrating to the United States.

Study of Urban Inequality

The term "Ethnics" was coined in the early 1970s to describe Americans other than the Native Americans, African Americans, Spanish-Americans, and Asian Americans and those of the dominant culture. Class came into this social divide as the Ethnics were seen to be predominantly of the middle-class, the dominant culture was also the affluent or upper class, and all others were the poor and working class, with all aspiring to be of the affluent or dominant culture and thus willing to assimilate. The immigrant/economic status and assimilation crossroads are illustrated in the findings of recent research in California.

Immigrants are vital to the continuing prosperity of those countries such as the United States that still call for them to come and join their societies. However, immigrants still have varying opportunities and experiences. Most on entry are channeled towards the city or region in which their skills, whether they be manual laborers or of a higher skill level, are needed.

A study that focused on a survey of more than 4,000 people in Los Angeles County questioned whether or not Los Angeles, as a cosmopolitan city, could continue to survive. It is believed that the racially motivated riots of 1992 encouraged the research. Conducted in 1993 and 1994 under the auspices of the Los Angeles Study of Urban Inequality, it is the only comprehensive report available on race and ethnicity in contemporary Los Angeles. The research provides a unique portrait of how poverty and racial stereotyping affect the everyday lives of people of other then the dominant culture.

The study found that racial and ethnic opposition emerge in the form of pervasive discriminatory practices in the workplace and housing markets. It also found that the geographical concentration of poor people of racial or ethnic origins other than the dominant culture intensifies the grip of poverty and deprivation.

The report states that Spanish-Americans/Latinos resist thinking of themselves in terms of a racial group identity, tending to favor national ancestry-based affiliations, as do Asians. According to the urban inequality survey, African-Americans are indisputably viewed as "least desired" neighbors by all other ethnic-racial groups. Asian immigrants without skills tend to end up in the so-called ethnic economy; in other words, in low-wage jobs in marginal enterprises. It was also found that many people from racial or ethnic groups other than the dominant group work in "secondary" or "ethnic" intensive markets with low pay and no benefits. Poverty and discrimination confine people of racial or ethnic origins other than the dominant group to limited housing and job opportunities.

Conclusion

Elimination of minority groups, which during the twentieth century the practitioners of Nazism and ethnic cleansing pursued, is seen as more violent than assimilation. Although assimilation is less physically violent than elimination, it can be, as attested to by the Australian Royal Commission into Aboriginal Deaths In Custody and the Australian Human Rights Inquiry into the Separation of Aboriginal and Torres Strait Islander Children from their Families, physiologically scaring.

Assimilation is seldom a process of pure suppression. The cultural practices and expressions of indigenous peoples may have adapted, but unless the people themselves were completely eradicated the cultures have never completely disappeared. Each group of immigrants contributes some of its own cultural traits to its new society. In the course of assimilation, the dominant group usually acquires aspects of the minority cultures while imposing its own culture. A society that makes a practice of assimilation usually evolves in the process, and the dominant culture becomes increasingly eclectic. Government and social recognition of the continuing viability of minority societies and identity has been the broad-spectrum call from those subjected to assimilation.

DAVINA B. WOODS

See also **Aborigines; Critical Race Theory; Immigration; Integration; Race; Racism**

Further Reading

Anaya, S. James, *The Native Hawaiian People and International Human Rights Law: Towards a Remedy for Past and Continuing Wrongs*, Volume 28, *Georgia Law Review*, 1994

Armitage, Andrew, *Comparing the Policy of Aboriginal Assimilation: Australia, Canada and New Zealand*, University of British Columbia Press, Canada, 1995

Artucio, A., *Impunity of Perpetrators*, in Netherlands Institute of Human Rights *Seminar on the Right to Restitution, Compensation and Rehabilitation for Victims of Gross Violations of Human Rights and Fundamental Freedoms*, March 11–15, 1992, SIM Special Report, no 12, 1992

Ban, Paul, *The Quest for Legal Recognition of Torres Strait Islander Customary Adoption Practice*, 2, no 60, *Aboriginal Law Bulletin*, 1993

Bobo, Lawrence D., et al., editors, *Prismatic Metropolis—*Inequality in Los Angeles, Los Angles: Russell Sage Foundation, 2001

Horton, David, *The Encyclopaedia of Aboriginal Australia*, Canberra: Aboriginal Studies Press for Australian Institute of Aboriginal and Torres Strait Islander Studies, 1994

Human Rights and Equal Opportunity Commission, *Bringing Tthem Home:* Report of the National Inquiry into the Separation of Aboriginal and Torres Strait Islander Children from Their Families, Sydney, 1997

Johnston, E., Commissioner QC, *Royal Commission into Aboriginal Deaths in Custody National Report Overview and Recommendations*, Canberra: Australian Government Publishing Service, 1991

Tatz, Colin, *Genocide in Australia*, AIATSIS Research Discussion Papers No 8, Canberra: Australian Institute of Aboriginal and Torres Strait Islander Studies, 1999

Assyrians

Capsule Summary

Location: Traditionally centered in Iraq, Iran, and Turkey, more recently in Syria, the United States, Europe, and elsewhere
Total Population: Estimated 350,000–1 million; difficult to determine, as members are scattered and often not counted by governments as a distinct people/group
Language: Syriac, or modern Assyrian, but most will also speak another language, even as a mother tongue, depending on country of residency
Religion: Christian

The modern group known as the Assyrianshas traditionally incorporated those affiliated with the Assyrian Church of the East (or simply the "Church of the East"). At the dawn of Christianity, these people lived in Mesopotamia (an area inside modern-day Iraq), spoke Syriac, and considered themselves descendants of the region's original inhabitants. Tradition contends that there were Syriac-speaking Christians by the second century CE, who subsequently regarded themselves as a religious, versus ethnic, community. These Syriac Christians developed an independent church by the fifth century, and they also accepted the teachings of the bishop Nestorius on the nature of Christ, thereby breaking completely with the Roman Church. It is due to their theological stance that the Assyrians have often been called "Nestorians", a term that many reject today.

From the third to the tenth centuries, although they lived under the rule of other peoples (the Parthians, Romans, Sasanians, and Muslims), the Assyrians generally prospered. They often reached positions of prominence within their societies, produced great works of science, theology, and other disciplines, and sent missions to other lands, even as far as China. During the Mongolian conquests of the fourteenth century, however, the Assyrians fled to the safety of the Kurdistan Mountains in what is today northeastern Turkey and northwestern Iran. After a few centuries, a certain number of them descended to settle in the plains east and south of the mountains. This triangle of northeast Turkey, northwest Iran, and north Iraq remained their homeland until the twentieth century.

After the Mongol invasions, the Assyrians led a more or less peaceful, if isolated and somewhat precarious, existence in their new homelands. The Assyrians were neighbours with various other groups in the regions they inhabited; but traditionally their closest neighbours were the Kurds, with whom they generally enjoyed friendly relations. However, the eighteenth and nineteenth centuries brought changes that soured relations between the Assyrians and their neighbours and local governments. In the decades prior to World War I there were several massacres of Assyrians by Kurdish or Turkish-Kurdish forces. These centuries also saw the rapprochement of the Assyrians and the Western powers and the development of nationalist thinking among the educated Assyrian elite.

The Turkish Ottoman Empire, home of the majority of the Assyrians, joined World War I on the side of the Axis powers, but the Assyrians cooperated with the Allies. As a result, over the course of the war, the Assyrians were first driven out of Ottoman territory and then out of Iran. In what today is Iraq, the British put the Assyrians into refugee camps, and many Assyrian men continued to assist the British as auxiliary troops. The Assyrian losses during the war, from massacre, disease, exposure, and fighting, totaled approximately one-third of their population.

During the war, the Allied powers both implicitly and explicitly gave the Assyrians assurances that they would be given their own homeland, or at least autonomy. At war's end, however, the Assyrians were given nothing. Many Assyrians eventually returned to Iran, with the permission of the government, and others to Turkey, without permission, but the largest portion remained in Iraq.

The relationship between the Assyrians and their governments following the end of World War I has generally been uneasy, though to what degree has depended on the country and its situation. Since the break-up of the Ottoman Empire, Turkey has pursued a policy of radical Turkish nationalism. This policy has placed the Turkish government into conflict with several peoples residing within its borders, including the Kurds and the Assyrians, who resist attempts at cultural homogenization. Iraq, also a country endeavoring to forge a unified national identity, has used the "carrot-and-stick" approach for many of its dissident groups. As regards the Assyrians, they have been officially recognized as a minority population and granted some cultural privileges, but often government measures to guarantee preservation of a culture fall short or are simply not implemented, and any calls for autonomy or national recognition are strongly repressed. Iran has had perhaps the most congenial relationship with the Assyrians, and even after the Islamic Revolution in 1979 they were recognized as a religious minority. However, living in an Islamic republic, especially one that harshly suppresses dissent, has produced a sense of alienation among many Iranian Assyrians. Moreover, as the Assyrians often inhabit regions in these countries where there is violent conflict between the governments and other groups, particularly the Kurds, the Assyrians are often drawn in, willingly and otherwise, and suffer the consequences. For example, during the Iraqi government's brutal campaign against the Kurds in the late 1980s, hundreds of Assyrians were also killed.

Often Assyrians work to gain cultural recognition or rights from the governments under which they live in the Middle East, seeking to become accepted members of their societies. Others actively participate in secessionist movements, particularly in northern Iraq, where some have joined forces with the Kurds in their continuing bid for independence. A frequent response of many Assyrians, however, is emigration. A certain number have settled elsewhere in the Middle East, notably Syria and Lebanon, but most have joined communities across the globe: Europe, North and South America, Australia, and elsewhere. In recent decades, there has emerged among the diaspora communities a renewed passion for cultural preservation, for the gaining of cultural as well as ethnic recognition, and for the advocacy of rights in the Middle East. Among a portion of Assyrians there has also developed a nationalistic-type sentiment, one that includes other Syriac-speaking peoples (Jacobites/Syrian Orthodox, Syrian Catholics, Chaldeans, and Maronites) under the definition of Assyrian. This nationalistic view emphasizes the shared ancestral and language ties of all these groups. In addition to heightening the ethnic sense of Assyrian identity, this nationalistic sentiment often has as one of its goals the renewal of the Assyrian people in the Middle East. Some Assyrians even hold the establishment of a homeland in their traditional territories as a distant dream.

ANDREA LAING-MARSHALL

See also **Armenians; Christians: 1: Overwiew; Iraq; Kurds; Turkey**

Further Reading

Atiya, Aziz, *A History of Eastern Christianity*, London: Methuen & Co., and Notre Dame, Indiana: University of Notre Dame Press, 1968; 2nd edition, Millwood, New York: Kraus Reprint, 1980

Coakley, J.F., "The Church of the East since 1914," *Bulletin of the John Rylands Library*, 78 (1996)

Gervers, Michael, and Ramzi Bikhazi, editors, *Conversion and Continuity: Indigenous Christian Communities in Islamic Lands, Eighth to Eighteenth Centuries*, Toronto, Canada: Pontifical Institute of Mediaeval Studies, 1990

Hill, Henry, "The Assyrians: The Church of the East," in *Light From the East: A Symposium on the Oriental Orthodox and Assyrian Churches*, edited by Henry Hill, Toronto, Canada: Anglican Book Centre, 1988

Johnson, Ronald, "Assyrians," in *Encyclopedia of World Cultures, Vol IX: Africa and the Middle East*, Boston, Massachusetts: GK Hall & Co., 1995

Joseph, John, *The Modern Assyrians of the Middle East: Encounters with Western Christian Missions, Archaeologists, and Colonial Powers*, Studies in Christian Mission, 26, Leiden, Boston, and Köln: Brill, 2000

Le Coz, Raymond, *Histoire de l'Église de l'Orient: Chrétiens d'Irak, d'Iran et de Turquie*, Paris: Éditions du Cerf, 1995

Levinson, David, *Ethnic Groups Worldwide: A Ready Reference Handbook*, Phoenix, Arizona: Oryx Press, 1998

Minority Rights Group International, editor, *World Directory of Minorities*, Chicago, Illinois: St. James Press, 1989; Harlow, Essex: Longman, 1990; 2nd edition, London: Minority Rights Group International, 1997

McCollough, W. Stewart, *A Short History of Syriac Christianity to the Rise of Islam*, Chico, California: Scholars Press, 1982

Yacoub, Joseph, "La diaspora assyro-chaldéenne," *L'Éspace géographique*, 23, no. 1 (1994)

Yacoub, Joseph, "Les Assyro-Chaldéens: Une minorité en voie d'émergence?," *Études internationales*, 21, no. 2 (1990)

Australia

Capsule Summary

Country Name: Commonwealth of Australia
Location: Oceania, continent between the Indian Ocean and the South Pacific Ocean
Total Population: 19,731,984 (July 2003)
Minority Population: 303,300 indigenous Australians
Languages: Standard Australian English, native languages
Religions: Anglican (26.1%), Roman Catholic (26%), other Christian (24.3%), non-Christian (11%), other (12.6%)

The Commonwealth of Australia is an independent state and the smallest continent on the globe, bounded by the Timor and Arafura seas on the north; by the Coral Sea on the northeast; by the Pacific Ocean on the south; and by the Indian Ocean on the south and west. It measures 2,967,909 square miles (7,686,884 square kilometers). Largely desert with many salt lakes and the Great Dividing mountain range along the eastern coast, Australia is divided into six states (New South Wales, Queensland, South Australia, Tasmania, Victoria, Western Australia) and two territories (Australian Capital Territory, Northern Territory). With a Western-style capitalist economy with a per capita GDP on par with the four dominant West European economies ($26,900, 2002), Australia's chief products include wheat, oats, fruit, sugarcane, livestock, wool, gold, silver, uranium, tin, diamonds, oil, iron, and steel. Its economy is based on agriculture (3 percent), industry (26 percent), and services (71 percent) (2001), the latter including tourism.

Multicultural is a term that describes the cultural and linguistic diversity of Australian society. It recognizes that Australia is, and will remain, a culturally diverse country. The terms *multicultural* and *ethnic* entered into common usage in the 1970s. The Australian government since then has always claimed to be committed to a multicultural policy that recognizes the social, cultural, and economic benefits of the nation's diversity and seeks to ensure that it is a positive force for Australia.

However, these ideals did not historically prevail. Australian federation was in part forged in relation to colonial dislike of Asian immigrants. One of the first acts of the new Commonwealth of Australia when it was formed in 1901 was legislation for the restriction of immigration. Australian citizenship itself did not come into being until 1949.

Australian society comprises many peoples. Australian Indigenous peoples, who are generically referred to as Aboriginal and Torres Strait Islanders, are the first peoples of Australia. Although they probably maintained settlements for 40,000 years, they were dispossessed of the land by the British invaders who began colonization of the country in the eighteenth century. The Dutch were the first Europeans to reach the north and west coasts, who named the territory New Holland. British explorer James Cook claimed the eastern territory in 1770; the first English settlement was established in 1788 at Port Jackson in New South Wales (today Sydney).

Many people of Asian heritage live in Australia today, with the first being the Chinese, who came for the Gold Rushes of the 1800s. The Japanese interacted with the peoples of the Torres Strait Islands and the North West of the country when they established pearl industries and thus many of the people living in these areas have Japanese heritage. Afghans came to Australia as the camel drivers for the expeditions carried out by European explorers of the 1800s. Refuges from the two World Wars and those who came to work on labor-intensive projects such as the development of the Snowy Mountain Hydroelectricity scheme mainly derived from European countries outside of the main influence of the British Isles. Refugees and immigrants from the centers of conflict of the late twentieth century such as the Middle East, Vietnam, and Cambodia have expanded the face of Australian society.

White Australia Policy

Contemporary Australia is becoming more aware of the fact that it has a black history that is firmly rooted in the colonialism of the imperialistic British Isles. One of the first acts of its Commonwealth Parliament in 1901 was to pass legislation known as the White Australia Policy. The legislation effectively ceased all non-European immigration into the country leading to a racially insulated European-based society. Representing a widespread sentiment in all of the Australian colonies, the desire for a coordinated immigration bar against non-Europeans was a primary spur in the 1890s toward Australian federation. In fact the slogan "White Australia" was in use by the 1880s and directed primarily against Asians, such as the Chinese and Japanese laborers who were thought to be unassimilable and a threat to the European standard of living. The Act practically excluded Africans as well.

An essential clause of the White Australian Policy, rather than naming particular races or groups for exclusion, provided for a dictation test in any European language to be administered to prospective immigrants. People could be take a test in French, German, or if need be, Lithuanian. The device was amended in 1905 and dictation in any prescribed language could be used to exclude people who were judged as undesirables. Virtually unchanged until the 1950s, the government abandoned the policy in 1958 when entry permits based largely upon economic criteria replaced the dictation test.

During the second half of the 1900s Australia amended its legislation in favor of a nondiscriminatory immigration policy, which meant that anyone from any country could apply to migrate, regardless of his or her ethnic origin, gender, race, or religion. Migration to Australia became dependent on the applicant's ability to meet the migration criteria of the day, which were established to meet Australia's national interest and needs.

Society

Australia became a commonwealth of the British Empire in 1901 and maintains a democratic, federal-state system recognizing the British monarch as sovereign. In 1999 however, Australia celebrated the 50th anniversary of citizenship; prior to 1999, Australians were British subjects. Since 1949, people born in Australia of Australian parents become Australian citizens by birth. Today some 95 percent of the population possesses Australian citizenship, although it was estimated in June 1999 there were still 950,000 people eligible to apply for Australian citizenship. Present-day Australia's ethnic distribution is Caucasian (92 percent), Asian (7 percent), aboriginal and other (1 percent).

Multicultural Policies

The Australian Government of the 1940s and 1950s did not want migrants to form separate enclaves and perpetuate their own culture and identity. Since 1945, almost 5.7 million people have come to Australia as new settlers. In the 50 years of planned postwar migration, Australia has seen agreements reached with Britain, some European countries, and with the International Refugee Organization to encourage migration, including displaced people, from war-torn Europe. At the beginning of the twenty-first century nearly one in four of Australia's 19 million people was born overseas.

In 1979 the Commonwealth Government passed the Australian Institute of Multicultural Affairs Act, which established the Australian Institute of Multicultural Affairs (AIMA), whose objectives included raising awareness of cultural diversity and promoting social cohesion, understanding, and tolerance.

During the late 1980s demographers reported that the Australian population consisted of three groups. These included British and old Australian, counting for 47 percent, and Non-English speaking migrants and their children, counting for 23 percent. The demographers suggested that 30 percent of the Australian population was a mixture of the other two categories. Some observers have concluded from these figures that both assimilation and multiculturalism were being practiced, no matter what government policies may dictate.

On October 30, 1996, the government formally reaffirmed its commitment to racial tolerance. Australia's multicultural policies evolved from the need to address issues raised by the arrival in Australia of large numbers of migrants, many whose first language was not English. This policy drew its rationale from the White Australia policy. The policy effectively excluded non-European immigration.

On June 30, 1997, the Australian government established the National Multicultural Advisory Council (NMAC) to develop a report that recommended a policy and an implementation framework for the next decade, aimed at ensuring that cultural diversity was a unifying force for Australia.

Australia maintains a nondiscriminatory immigration policy, which means that anyone from any country can apply to migrate, regardless of his or her ethnic origin, gender, race, or religion. Migration to Australia is dependent on the applicant's ability to meet the migration criteria of the day, which are established to meet Australia's national interest and needs. There are different criteria for the various categories of migrants, and all migrants must meet Australia's rules on health and character.

The migration programs of the late twentieth century recognized that business globalization has resulted in a major flow of people who often do not intend to stay in Australia permanently. As of June 1998, 23.3 percent of the estimated resident population were born overseas: 6.2 percent of the population was born in the United Kingdom, 12.9 percent was born in Europe and the former Soviet Union, 5.3 percent was born in Asia, 2.3 percent was born in Oceania, 1.2 percent was born in the Middle East and North Africa, and less than 2 percent in other regions. The number of settlers who arrived in Australia between July 1998 and June 1999 totaled 84,143. The Australian resident population was 18.967 million on June 30, 1999, an increase of 236,400 people since June 30, 1998.

On December 9, 1999, the government launched *A New Agenda for Multicultural Australia* in response to *Australian multiculturalism with an eye toward inclusiveness*. To help implement the New Agenda, the Australian government established a broad-based Council for Multicultural Australia (CMA).

Multicultural policies and programs are not to be solely identified with immigration issues and developed for minority ethnic communities. The New Agenda also emphasizes that multicultural policies and programs should be built on the foundation of Australia's democratic system, and emphasize economic and social benefits of Australia's cultural diversity.

DAVINA B. WOODS

See also **Aborigines; Assimilation; Multiculturalism; Torres Strait Islanders; White Australia Policy (1901–1973)**

Further Reading

Bassett, Jan, *The Concise Oxford Dictionary of Australian History*, Melbourne: Oxford University Press, 1986

Dare, Tim, *Australians Making a Great Nation*, Brookvale: Child & Henry Publishing, 1985

Hirst, John, "The Conservative Case for an Australian Republic", *Quadrant*, September 1991

Hirst, John, "A Core Culture is Vital to our Success Story: How Do We Hold Together? By Being Australian," in *The Australian*, February 14, 2001

Horne, Donald, *The Lucky Country*, Ringwood, Victoria: Penguin, 1964

Horne, Donald, editor, *The Coming Republic*, Sydney: Pan Macmillan, 1992

Jupp, J., "How Powerful is the Ethnic Lobby?" edited by G. Hage and R. Couch, *The Future of Australian Multiculturalism*, University of Sydney Jupp, J., "Migration Forum: Noises Off," *Meanjin*, 3/1999

Tacey, David J., *Edge of the Sacred–Ttransformation in Australia*, North Blackburn: Harper Collins Publishers, 1995

Austria

Capsule Summary

Name: Republic of Austria
Total Population: 8,188,207 (July 2003)
Minority Population: 157,000–177,000 persons belonging to national minority groups
Languages: German, Slovenian, Croatian, Hungarian, Czech, Slovak, Turkish, Polish, Serbian, Bosnian, Kurdish, various other immigrant languages
Religions: Roman Catholicism (78%), Protestantism (5%), Islam and other (17%, including Judaism)

Austria is a country with a population of about 8 million and an area of approximately 84,000 square kilometres (52,200 square miles) situated in Central Europe. The capital is Vienna (population 1.6 million). The country's ethnic distribution is German (88 percent), non-nationals (9.3 percent, includes Croatians, Slovenes, Hungarians, Czechs, Slovaks, Roma), naturalized (2 percent, includes those who have lived in Austria at least three generations). The predominantly Catholic country joined the European Union (EU) in 1995. The GDP per capita was $27,900 in 2002. Under centuries of rule by the mighty Hapsburgs, Austria once was the dominant political force in central Europe. The multiethnic kingdom which once stretched from Northern Italy to Romania was reduced to a small parliamentary republic with its current boundaries after its defeat in World War I. Although Austria was the most homogenous of the former kingdom's successor states it had a number of indigenous ethnic minorities, especially in the eastern and southern borderlands.

Referring to minorities, a distinction is made between officially recognized "national minorities" with certain minority rights guaranteed by the constitution, and other groups such as the large immigrant population mostly coming from the former Yugoslavia and Turkey, which does not have the same legal status as the aforementioned groups do. According to the Austrian State Treaty of 1955 the Slovene and Croat minorities in Carinthia, Burgenland, and Styria are expressly recognised. In 1976 a number of national minority groups ("Volksgruppen") with specific rights as to their identity (Croats, Slovenes, Hungarians, Czechs, Slovaks and Roma) were recognized. A report by the European Union of September 2000 commented: "The Austrian legal system protects the existing national minorities in Austria to a greater extent than such a protection exists in many other European Union countries", but criticised that some judgements on linguistic rights have not been fully implemented.

The Croat minority in the province of Burgenland (bordering Hungary and the Slovak Republic) arrived as a result of wars with the Ottoman Empire. Croats had fled north in the sixteenth and seventeenth century to avoid Turkish subjugation and were settled in Burgenland. The popular census of 1991 counted 19,109 people in Burgenland who declared Croatian as their everyday language. The actual number of the minority is believed to be higher. Estimates number approximately 30,000 in Burgenland and another 12,000 in Vienna. At the end of 2000 there were 29 elementary schools in Burgenland where Croat was being taught in addition to German. The Hungarians in Burgenland settled in the territory in the eleventh century in order to fortify the western borders of Hungary. After World War I Burgenland was given to Austria due to its German-speaking majority, leaving Hungarian, Croat, and Roma minorities within the province's borders. Although in 1991 only some 5,000 people in Burgenland and another 9,000 in Vienna declared Hungarian as their everyday language, the actual number of the minority is estimated between 20,000 and 30,000.

The Slovenes in the southern part of the province of Carinthia (Southern Austria) are descendants of the ancient Slavic population that inhabited the southern slopes of the Alps and the Drau/Drava River basin. After both world wars the Yugoslav state, then Austria's neighbor to the south, had aspirations of annexing the part of Carinthia inhabited by the Slovene minority. The Yugoslav invasion of 1918 resulted in a plebiscite in the areas in question in 1920, in which the majority of the region's inhabitants (ironically including a number of Slovenes) chose to remain within the newly formed Austrian state. When Yugoslavia again laid claim to the ethnically mixed borderland after World War II, neither the Allies nor Austria were willing to redraw the borders between the two states. The popular census of 1991 counted 13,962 people in Carinthia who declared Slovenian as their everyday language. Other estimates number about 50,000 throughout Austria, the vast majority living in Carinthia, and to a smaller extent in the neighbouring province of Styria. In Carinthia there were 1,620 children being taught in German and Slovenian in 1998–1999.

Members of the Czech minority are mainly descendents from immigrants who left their homelands in the late nineteenth or early twentieth century to settle in Austria's industrial centers, especially in Vienna. The Austrian capital was said to be the second largest Czech city after the Czech capital, Prague. A large part of this immigrant population quickly assimilated. In 1991, 8,033 persons in Vienna and neighbouring Upper Austria holding Austrian citizenship declared Czech as their everyday language. Contrary to the Czechs, the kindred Slovak minority is an old one. In their traditional areas of settlement—Vienna and the neighbouring province of Lower Austria, which borders the Slovak Republic—the number of Austrian citizens speaking Slovak as their everyday language has been given as only 835 in 1991. The actual number of these minorities is estimated between 15,000 and 20,000 Czechs and 5,000 and 10,000 Slovaks.

The Roma, Sinti, and Lovara, originally being nomadic peoples from Southern Asia, arrived in Austria in the fourteenth century. Their language(s) belong to the Iranian branch of the Indo-European language family. Together with the Jews, the Roma and Sinti were among the ethnic groups that suffered most from the Nazi programs of ethnic extermination. Less than half of the prewar Roma and Sinti population of about 11,000 survived World War II; many were deported to concentration camps. An accurate number of the members of the ethnic group living in Austria is hard to determine, as only a small minority still speaks their ethnic language. Estimates number about 25,000 members. The vast majority comprises Roma; smaller groups are the Sinti and the Lovara. The chief area of settlement is Burgenland, but smaller groups are scattered all over the country.

Althought Austria's Jews are a religious and not a national minority, they constitute an important role in the country's history. While over 185,000 Jews lived on Austrian territory prior to the 1938 Anschluss (the annexation of Austria by Germany), Austrian Jewry had been virtually annihilated during the Holocaust. Almost 70,000 Jews from Austria lost their lives in concentration camps. Only the few of those who survived the Nazis returned to Austria. Accurate figures on the current number of Austrians with a Jewish background are hard to determine because the only statistical information on Jews in Austria is available on a confessional basis. The national census of 1991 stated 7,268 people with "Israelite" confession, the vast majority living in Vienna. Of the estimated 11,000 Jews in Austria, about half are immigrants from the former Soviet Union, including many Jews from Central Asia and the Caucasus. Although not officially recognized as a minority, the Jews are probably the most present of Austria's minority groups in the media and in public.

Of the immigrant groups, (former) nationals of the states of the former Yugoslavia and Turkey form the majority, having come to the country as *Gastarbeiters* (literally "guest workers") in organized immigration waves from the 1960s onward. A large part of the remainder of the immigrant populations comes from Eastern Europe, whereas a smaller portion originates from Africa, the Near East, and other parts of Asia. Between 1950 and 2000 approximately 500,000 immigrants have been granted Austrian citizenship. Currently, foreign citizens constitute almost 10 percent of the republic's population, forming one of the highest rates in the European Union.

Austria, until 2004 at the eastern border of the European Union, also attracts many refugees and asylum-seekers from the east and south. Between 1992 and 1999, in the course of violent conflicts following the break-up of Yugoslavia, more than 100,000 refugees from Bosnia-Herzegovina, Croatia, and Kosovo were accepted, out of which approximately two thirds continued their lives in Austria. According to government estimates, out of 2 million refugees having come to Austria between 1945 and 2000, around 650,000 remained in the country.

MAXIMILIAN HARTMUTH

See also **Croats; Czech Republic; Hungarians; Slovaks; Slovakia; Slovenia**

Further Reading

Henke, Reinhold, editor, *Leben lassen ist nicht genug, Minderheiten in Österreich*, Vienna: Kremayr & Scheriau, 1988
Baumgartner, Gerhard, *6 x Österreich, Geschichte und aktuelle Situation der Volksgruppen*, Klagenfurt: Drava-Verlag, 1995
Bogataj, Mirko, *Die Kärntner Slowenen*, Klagenfurt and Vienna: Hermagoras-Verlag, 1989
Fraenkel, Josef, editor, *The Jews of Austria: Essays on Their Life, History and Destruction*, London: Valentine Mitchell, 1967
Thurner, Erika, *National Socialism and Gypsies in Austria*, Tuscaloosa: University of Alabama Press, 1998
Filla, Wilhelm, "National Minorities in Austria," in *Austria: A Study in Modern Achievement*, edited by Jim Sweeney and Josef Weidenholzer, Aldershot, United Kingdom: Avebury, 1988
Mayerhofer, Claudia, *Dorfzigeuner: Kultur und Geschichte der Burgenland-Roma von der Ersten Republik bis zur Gegenwart*, Vienna: Picus Verlag, 1987

Autonomy

The term *autonomy* derives from the Greek, *autonomia* (*autos*, meaning "self", and *nomos*, meaning "law"). Autonomy is defined as the exercise of the right to self-government; the condition of being autonomous; and independence or freedom of the will. Autonomy of the individual suggests the will of one's actions implying personal freedom as socio-philosophical concept. Autonomy of an organization or group allows such organizations, groups, bodies, or institutions to make their own decisions without influence from other, higher authorities. That implies the capacity of being ruled by one's own statutes, without direct outside control, acting for a specific purpose; such is corporate autonomy. A third kind of autonomy is seen as self-governing communities, as in the condition of being autonomous; self-government, or the right of self-government; independence, whether: **a**. *autonomy of the state*, as an expression of recognized (legislative) authority and legitimacy within and without its territory, also as sovereignty in relationship with other states; **b**. *regional/local autonomy*, related to the politics of devolution by granting legislative power to local governing bodies by the state, thus implicitly yielding a part of its overall power in that region. Specific demands for regional autonomy express prevailing political tensions potentially reflecting separatist tendencies; **c**. *autonomy of groups* and *minorities*, limited to the recognized scope of their classification as a distinct group or minority (e.g., common collective interests and/or cultural, ethnic, religious identity perceived as a distinct sociopolitical feature shared by the members of the community) within a larger political frame and jurisdiction of a state (see 3a) or region (see 3b). Such a classification and the autonomy claim are not unproblematic, even if the separateness in association and self-identification does not involve explicit territorial claims. The concept of autonomy suggests dissociation, in the case of minorities, from a majority and, hence, a claim for distinct rights and differential treatment.

Group autonomy can be an expression of the collective will to preserve the group's identity, but also a quest for self-determination, targeting more than individual human rights granted according to international conventions to the group's members. An autonomous group, such as minority groups sharing a common cultural background, religion, traditions, language, and/or territory often aims to establish, confirm, or exert a certain extent of *political autonomy* meant to substantiate their status as a distinct group.

The demand for *special autonomy*, whether territorial-based political autonomy or administrative autonomy of national minorities or similar groups claiming local autonomy (e.g., the formation or recognition of autonomous counties can be particularly sensitive in the context of a national state) can be perceived by the majority as a hazardous possible threat to the national territory's integrity.

Special autonomy can refer to forms of limited autonomy or self-government granted by a central or regional government to its dependent political units. Historically, that was characteristic for multinational states such as the ancient Roman Empire, the colonial British Empire, as well as the Spanish Colonial Empire. Some illustrative cases in modern times include limited local autonomy such as in Catalonia and the Basque region in Spain; special cases such as Hong Kong, and so forth. Variable degrees of *extended autonomy* (local, administrative, political, economic) granted by federative states in various parts of the world to their subnational divisions—states, cantons, *länder*, autonomous regions, territories, administrative districts, counties—include the United States, Canada, the United Kingdom, Switzerland, Belgium, Germany, the Russian Federation, and India. A superior state power in a central government grants a federalist state a right to limited self-government, creating federalist autonomy.

Political autonomy is a quest for marking the group's determination to preserve or create its differential status by symbolically marking its individuality through local authority or even territorially. Political autonomy derives from a desire to break from a majority group that is often considered oppressive (see the controversial status of Tibet). The autonomy of ethnic groups can be especially problematic when the respective group lacks or has lost its own recognized territory. This can be a major source of conflict, often ending in expressions of violence as a last resort. Lacking a national territory does not preclude national identity and pride, but makes preserving the group's identity more difficult while enhancing the importance of the missing/lacking territory. Some extreme, intricate examples are those of the Kurdish people, spread around as a minority in several countries. The symbolic "return home" of the Jewish people to their promised land, after 2,000 years, is another example of recreation of an ethnic/religious-based national identity, leading community members to share a common identity with particular features. Recreating national identity by reconstructing a national territory also emerges in the case of Palestine. Sometimes, ethnic groups continue to live more or less separately for long periods of time, while at the same time preserving the basic idea of common identity and the distinct quest for autonomy or even independence as a historical condition of their survival (e.g., Cyprus). Another example, the Saami, live spread along territories belonging to several states, but benefit from a particular status, enjoying a kind of limited local self-determination in Sweden. The Balkan conflicts are of a particular type, based on the assumption that various ethnic groups need to secure a territory that shall ensure their survival, corresponding to claims based on historical grounds. A main problem in such a case is to even accept the existence and rights of other populations having inhabited their territory. The case of the former Yugoslavia or other regional claims illustrates this (e.g., Kosovar Albanians, Chechens). Demands of European minorities for autonomy remain a potential source of conflict.

The autonomy of minority groups can thus illustrate various characteristics—those that are ethnically different, but politically autonomous, based on individualism, as allegiance to a group, or based on various criteria (e.g., religious, ethnic, or cultural community); those with economic autonomy (an ethnic minority can be dispersed within another population and still defend itself from assimilation by maintaining a certain amount of economic authority); and those with cultural autonomy (a group can be territorially dispersed but still preserve distinct cultural features, such as religious or linguistic minorities).

ELENA DINGU-KYRKLUND

See also **Albanians; Chechens; Cyprus; Self-Determination; Tibetans**

Further Reading

Romanucci-Ross, Lola, and George DeVos, editors, *Ethnic Identity: Creation, Conflict, and Accomodation*, Walnut Creek, London, New Delhi: Sage-AltaMira Press, 3rd editon, 1995

Fried, C., editor, *Report of the Dahlem Workshop on Minorities: Community and Identity, Berlin 1982*, Berlin: Springer-Verlag, 1983

Castles, Stephen, and Mark J. Miller, *The Age of Migration: International Population Movements in the Modern World*, London-Hong Kong: Macmillan Press, 2nd edition, 1998

Avars

Capsule Summary

Location: Western Russia (Eurasia) in the Volga River region
Total Population: 500,000–1 million
Language: Avar
Religion: Animist

The Avars were an early medieval nomadic people of Eurasia who established a state in the Volga River area of Europe in the early sixth century CE. They migrated from inner central Asia and spoke a Turkic language. Their population was estimated at 500,000–1 million, which was representative of the peoples of that era.

The Avars conquered much of eastern Europe and the Danube basin and established a formidable empire, incorporating eight countries, which lasted for some 300 years. Later they were assimilated by migrating peoples, especially by the Slavs, and vanished despite leaving a lasting mark in Europe's history, their name being also preserved by the denomination of southern Germany, called Bavaria. The Avars formed the second wave of the three main peoples of Eurasian origin, speaking Uralian/Altaian languages that find their home or made the center of their empire in the Carpathian basin and the middle-lower flow of the Danube, and in fact resettled the territories inhabited by their ancestors and direct precursors. These peoples were the Huns (also called Hiung-nus in Chinese), the Avars (Juan-Juans in Chinese) and the Hungarians (Hungarus, Magyars, Ugors, Wengers in European languages). The well documented successive, overlapping settlement of the latter two and the similarity of the archeological findings, the mystery of the exact origins of the Szekely-Hungarians/Seklers led to the highly probable assumption of a double Avar-Magyar (Hungarian) settlement, starting from the sixth and ending in the ninth century. So it can be stated that late descendents of the Avars were assimilated mostly among the Hungarians, and perhaps the people of the tiny Adjar autonomous province of Russia's northern Caucasus region may be linked to them.

History

The precursors of the Avars, the Huns, had formed a great empire in Europe along the Danube basin between 376 and 455 CE. Their headquarters were on the steppes of the lower Danube, in what is today Walachia, in south central Europe between the Danube and the Transylvanian Alps in Romania, and later in the central Tisza region of the great Hungarian plain. The Carpathian basin, especially the great Hungarian plain, became known as Hunnia.

After the dismantling of the Hun Empire, following their great leader Attila's death in 453 CE, the remaining White and Black Huns retreated onto the eastern European (Russian) steppes. According to Székely legends of origin, the remainder of the White Huns traveled to the densely forested region of Transylvania and the eastern Carpathians to avoid total destruction, where they were the ancestors of the Székelys. (The Székely were a Hungarian-speaking ethnic group, historically centered in the Transylvanian town of Székelyudvarhely.) After the Huns' rule ended, the Longobards (or Lombards, a Germanic group that entered the late Roman Empire) and the Gepids, a Germanic group, established their kingdoms in the region.

The Juan-Juan, a confederacy of nomadic tribes on the northern border of China proper, migrated from the steppes of Central Asia from as far as Mongolia to the forested steppe zones on the northern Black Sea coast. There they mingled with the remains of the Huns and other Turkic people before they were known as the Avars. Scholars today believe that an element of the European Avars may have been, at least for a little while, a small part of the Juan-Juan confederacy but that they are not the same people. The Avars were well established in Europe by the 550s, whereas the Juan-Juan still appeared in Chinese sources in the 560s. In 562 the Juan-Juan arrived in the lower Danube region led by their leader Bayan (a Turkish name). The Juan-Juan desired to enter the eastern Roman empire but the emperor refused to settle them so they looked north of the Danube to seize the Carpathian basin, especially the great Hungarian plain, called Pannonia Secunda, a former Roman province and home to the Gepids. The Gepids came to power after 537, settling in the rich area around Belgrade. In 546 the Byzantine Empire joined with the Longobards to defeat the Gepids and expel them from the region. In 567 the Avars finally devastated them in the disastrous Battle of Asfeld.

The Byzantine chronicles recorded the Avar defeat as "Bayan crushing the state of the Gepids" and soon after the Longobards were forced to cede their territory of Pannonia as well. In 568 they had been forced to move to Northern Italy where their territory became known as Lombardia. Originally allies of the Byzantine Empire, the Avars assisted in the fight against the Slavs and the Bulgars in the area between the Volga and Elba rivers. However, as the Avar reach increased, they turned against their chief and powerful rival and attacked Constantinople (today Istanbul) in 619 and 626, the latter ending in a siege. Their failure in the southeast prompted the Avars to turn westwards and try to expand their empire into Italy, but their expedition of 628 proved to be ill fated. This led to prolonged crisis in the Avar Empire from 630 onwards as well as the growth of the Slavic tribes, of whom many inhabited the Avar Empire. Some of these Slavic groups achieved independence with the aid of the Bulgarians, who had also formed an empire in the east. The rise in the Northern Black Sea region (roughly the territory of present-day Ukraine and the lower Volga region) of the Khazar/Kazar Empire pressed the Bulgarians westwards to the lower Danube, where they had mixed with the Slavs and established the Bulgarian czardom. (The Khazars were a semi-nomadic group from from Central Asia who had adopted Judaism and established an independent kingdom in the seventh century.) The expansion of the Khazar Empire, which was one of the most civilized empires of Europe of that time, caused a flood of Onogurs (proto-Hungarians) and various Turkic groups—closely related to the Avars—into the Carpathian basin. Little is known about Kabar/Avars from between the late seventh to late eighth centuries except that most of their neighbours still called them Avars. In 796 the Avars suffered a defeat from the Franks led by Charlemagne (Charles the Great) and their empire was devastated. The end of Avar power came in 829 when the Bulgarians expanded their empire across the Carpathians, into the central and eastern parts of the Avar territory. The Avars were not mentioned in any historical records after the ninth century, and it is doubted that the modern Avars, a pastoral, Muslim people of the Dagestan Republic, are descended from the original Avars.

Society, Language, and Religion

The Avar language was a member of the Turkic family from the Altaian branch of the Uralian/Altaian language group. The Turk, Khazakh, Turkmen, Uzbek, Baskhir, old Mongolian, Tatar, Kirghiz, old or proto-Bulgarian, Hun, Petcheneg, Cuman, Uz, Gagauz, and Yas languages belong(ed) to the Altaian branch, named after the mountain range which served as their ancestral homeland, while the Uralian branch has the Ugor and the Finnish languages as the main groups. The Ugor's most prominent representative is the Hungarian language; smaller related languages like the Hanti, Vogul, and Ostyak are spoken over a vast territory in the Ural mountain region. The Finnish, Estonian, and the small Lapp compose the Finnish branch.

As a relatively common eponym, the word *Avar* has a common root with the Turkish word *avare*, meaning "wanderer" or "vagabond." Linguists thus suggest that terms like *Avar* used for various peoples might have derived from a common Turanian etymology with a meaning similar to "freeman/transcender" along with many similar words from many ancient languages including, for example, Hebrew.

The Avar religion was shamanistic and animist: they believed in many gods, most of them symbolizing the four base elements: the land, water, fire, and air, most notably the Earth, the Sun, the Moon, as well as familiar wild mammals like the wolf, bear, moose, deer, and important predatory birds. These pagan religions have been almost completely wiped out by the aggressive conversion and historical spread of Christianity and Islam.

Tribal unions characterized the Avar society, and many tribes of the empire consisted of related Turkic peoples and Slavs, but they also shared a common core of the steppe culture based mainly on raising horses and cattle. The shaman was the group's spiritual and, sometimes, political leader. The heads of the tribes elected a chief or *khagan*. The Avars were known as horsemen and craftspeople. They lived in a mixed society; many Avar warriors took Slav wives, which led to their partial assimilation following the crushing of the elite. They treated their dead with great respect, especially the warriors who were buried with their horses, harnesses, and weapons.

LASZLO KOCSIS

See also **Turks**

Further Reading

Daim, Falko, editor, *Die Awaren am Rand der byzantinischen Welt: Studien zu Diplomatie, Handel und Technologietransfer im Frühmittelalter,* translated as *The Avars on the Border of the Byzantine World: Diplomacy, Trade and the Transfer of Technology in the Early Middle Ages***,** Innsbruck: Universitätsverlag Wagner, 2000

Aymara

Capsule Summary

Location: South America
Total Population: 1.8 million
Languages: Aymara; Spanish
Religions: Roman Catholic (nominal); others

Aymara refers both to an ethnic group and an aboriginal language found in western South America. Ethnographically, the Aymara are a large, sedentary Indian group native to and currently residing in the Altiplano, particularly the Lake Titicaca basin and plateau of the central Andes in modern Bolivia and Peru, with others inhabiting northern Chile. The northern section of the Titicaca basin is occupied by Quechua-speaking Indians. The Aymara inhabit the *puna* or elevated tableland (averaging 12,000 feet above sea level) situated between the eastern Cordillera of the Andes and the volcanic coastal chain.

Aymara is the language spoken by approximately 1.8 million persons residing in the Titicaca region. The Aymara language is inflexive (there is a subject-object-verb word order) and the tongue is probably related to Quechua, a larger language group native to Bolivia and Peru, but anthropological linguists debate this association. Aymara is closely related linguistically to Jaqaru and Kawaki, and these three languages have recently been classified collectively as members of the Jaqi linguistic family. A majority of ethnic Aymara are also Aymara speakers, but some (particularly men) speak Spanish and one or more other native languages such as Quechua. The Aymara residing in present-day northern Chile number fewer than 50,000, while approximately 300,000 Aymara live in Peru and about 1.3 million Aymara in Bolivia.

The Spanish arrived in western South America in 1535, initially conquering the Inca, but by 1538 Hernando and Gonzalo Pizarro had succeeded in subjugating the Aymara. Some were able to temporarily regain aspects of their aboriginal life/ways, which were distinct from the Inca, but rapid Spanish acculturation, particularly the adoption of new technologies and food sources, coupled with the exploitation of raw materials (especially gold, silver, and tin) resulted in notable cultural change, with native laborers working the mines and agricultural fields. While the economy and subsistence were affected greatly, the social and religious organization of the Aymara was less altered. Dominican and Jesuit friars came in search of converts to Catholicism, but the Aymara maintained a religious dualism with a syncretism of traditional and Catholic beliefs.

The Aymara in the Spanish colonial era were organized into 11 distinct tribes, all of which spoke Aymara, but with some regional dialectic distinctions. These were the Canchi, Caranga, Charca, Colla, Collagua, Collahuaya, Lupaca, Omasuyo, Pacasa, Quillaca, and Ubina. Originally horticulturalists, the Aymara adapted quickly to Spanish agricultural and pastoral practices, using plows and draft animals. The Titicaca region has poor soils and a severe, high-altitude climate, but the native coarse grass provided pasturage for herds of llama and alpaca, which were raised primarily for their wool that was the basis for a native textile industry. Native staple crops included a wide variety of potatoes, oca (Oxalis tuberosa), ullucu (Ullucus tuberosus), quinoa (Chenopodium quinoa), corn (Zea mays or maize), and beans. Net fishing on Lake Titicaca was done from totora-reed rafts. The Spanish introduced wheat, barley, sheep, and cattle to the Aymara, as well as plank boats for fishing. The Spanish colonial agrarian economy necessitated the systematic exploitation of the Aymara in agriculture, in the mines and ore processing facilities, on the coca plantations located in the Amazonian jungle on the east side of the Andes, and as household servants.

The extended family is the basic social unit among the Aymara and consists of a man and his brothers, their wives, sons, and unmarried daughters, living in a cluster of houses within a compound. The primary political unit is the ayllu (comunidad) composed of several extended families, but it resembles little the aboriginal ayllu.

Aymara uprisings against the Spanish began as early as 1629, but a native rebellion began among the Aymara of western Bolivia in 1780, during which the Indians killed a substantial number of Spaniards, and they nearly captured the city of La Paz. The Spanish subdued the Aymara two years later, but insurgencies continued sporadically at a much-diminished level until Peruvian independence from the Spanish was attained in 1821.

Therefore, the contemporary Aymara have passed through three stages of acculturation, initially under the Inca, then under the Spanish during the colonial era, and subsequently during the course of nation-building and modernization. The Inca strengthened local Aymara political dynasties as part of their own imperial system, thusestablishing new religious cults and art styles. The Spanish introduced new domesticated flora and fauna, plow agriculture, iron tools, and European-style technologies for mining and construction. They suppressed native religious practices but effected only a superficial conversion to Christianity. As a result, contemporary Aymara maintain their beliefs in a multi-spirit world; they have numerous categories of magicians, diviners, medicine men, and witches, although they are Christian in their beliefs about the afterworld. Economic acculturation eventually brought changes in Aymara social organization and a decline in the production of traditional arts and crafts.

The overwhelming majority of Aymara live in Bolivia, where the population consists of three major groups: Indians (the indigenous peoples), mestizos (of mixed Indian and European descent), and whites of European (primarily Spanish) descent. With the social, political, and economic reforms that resulted from the Bolivian Revolution of 1952, the Aymara have become increasingly integrated into the mainstream of Bolivian society and many are no longer affiliated with their native communities. The majority of Bolivian Aymara are farmers, miners, and factory or construction workers, but an increasing number have become professionals, and Aymara and Quechua political leaders have been elected to Congress. Victor Hugo Cardenas, an Aymara, served as vice president of Bolivia from 1993 to 1997. Aymara and Quechua are now official languages in Bolivia, along with Spanish, and the government is promoting multicultural and multilingual education and the establishment of indigenous territories in Bolivia's tropical lowlands.

CHARLES C. KOLB

See also **Bolivia; Colonialism; Quechua**

Further Reading

Buechler, Hans C., and Judith-Maria Buechler, *The Bolivian Aymara*, New York: Holt, Rinehart and Winston, 1971

Eagen, James, *The Aymara of South America*, Minneapolis: Lerner, 2002

Hardman, M.J., *The Aymara Language in Its Social and Cultural Context*, Gainesville: University Presses of Florida, 1981

Klein, Herbert S., *A Concise History of Bolivia*, New York: Cambridge University Press, 2002

Llanque, Domingo, *La cultura aymara*, Puno, Peru: IDEA, 1990

Osborne, Harold, *Indians of the Andes: Aymara and Quechua*, London: Routledge and Paul, 1952

Ayta

Capsule Summary

Location: Philippines, provinces of Zambales, Bataan, Pampanga, and Tarlac
Total Population: 35,000 (estimate based on Ayta families displaced by volcano eruption)
Languages: Austronesian, Philippine, Sambal
Religions: Animistic beliefs, some conversion to Christianity

The Ayta (or Aeta) are Philippine Negritos found in small villages and in several resettlement areas throughout the mountain range and coastal foothills of the province of Zambales, and in the nearby provinces of Bataan, Pampanga, and Tarlac. They speak Ayta languages of the Sambal division of the Philippine language tree such as Ambala, Bataan, Mag-anchi, Mag-indi, Abenlen, and are all related to Sambal spoken in Botolan, Zambales.

They were first called "Negrito" or "small blacks" in the traditional anthropological literature. Characterized by short stature, dark skin, and black kinky hair, Ayta are racially distinct from the lowland population; although in the last 50 years a great deal of intermarriage has blurred these physical differences in some places.

History

The history of the Ayta continues to confound anthropologists and archaeologists. One theory suggests that they descended from the original inhabitants of the Philippines who arrived through land bridges that linked the country with the Asian mainland some 30,000 years ago.

Over 50 years ago, anthropologist Robert Fox studied a group of Ayta in the western foothills and grasslands of the Mount Pinatubo area. He noted that they lived in scattered villages of three or four households ranging from 20 to 40 individuals. Houses varied from simple lean-tos on the ground to elevated split bamboo floor houses with bamboo walls and grass roofs. Leadership and decision-making did not go beyond the extended families in these small settlements and there was no area-wide political organization. Arranged marriages were common and men who had the resources to pay the bride price practiced polygamy.

The Pinatubo Ayta used slash and burn horticulture. They cut down and burned off sections of the forest, planted crops, and shifted back and forth between plots after a fallowing period added nutrients back into the soil. Their three main crops were all introduced from the New World—sweet potato, corn, and cassava. Constant cutting and burning and shortened regrowth cycles led to the massive conversion of primary forest to grasslands in the upland plateaus and descending lower slopes in the Mount Pinatubo area by the midpoint of the twentieth century. At the time of Fox's study, the people hunted deer, wild pig, chickens, monkeys, and monitor lizards with the bow and arrow. Bats, birds, and insects were an important supplement to the diet, in addition to a number of plants such as wild and domesticated varieties of bananas, yams, and taro. Loggers eventually contributed to the environmental collapse by logging off both the upland forests and coastal strands.

The Ayta have proven remarkably resistant to cultural and political change. They successfully averted Spain's attempt to resettle them in reservations throughout Spanish rule, and during the early American colonization of the Philippines Ayta preserved their political structure. Nonetheless, in the twentieth century, the decline of the environment, and the loss of lands to encroaching settlers, made life in the mountains and foothills of Mt. Pinatubo increasingly untenable. The Ayta found ways to survive by bartering remaining forest products for food and cash (often at a great loss), or by working as laborers for lowlanders. Some were employed as survival trainers and base guards for the U.S. military bases at Clark Air Force Base in Angeles, Pampanga, and Subic Naval Base in Olongapo, Zambales.

Two events in the early 1990s profoundly affected the Ayta—the return of the American bases to the Philippines with the pullout of American service personnel, and the eruption of Mt. Pinatubo. At the height of the Vietnam War (1961–1973), a number of Ayta were retained by United States armed forces to help train the troops in jungle survival techniques, as well as to guard the perimeter of the bases against intruding thieves bent on stealing equipment and foodstuffs for resale on the black market. The training function continued after the war with reduced numbers of soldiers, and the guard positions were in place as long as the bases remained open. When a hundred-year lease expired, the bases were returned to the Philippines and the United States withdrew all its military personnel. In recent years, some enterprising Ayta have found a new market by demonstrating their aboriginal hunting techniques and survival training skills for busloads of tourists.

The eruption of Mt. Pinatubo in June 1991 produced the greatest change in Ayta lifestyle and subsistence. In March of that year earthquakes were felt in the western side of the mountain and by April a series of explosions opened up several vigorous vents with emissions of ash and steam reaching thousands of feet into the air. In late May these intensified and the ash steadily increased. Most of the Pinatubo Ayta reacted to this progressive intensity and with each successive volcanic activity they moved westward to the coast through Villar and Poonbato toward the coastal town of Botolan. A series of strong explosive eruptions began in the morning of June 12 and, starting near midnight on June 14, the eruptions grew larger and more frequent, resulting in the dramatic and cataclysmic eruptions of June 15. Large quantities of hot ash fell on all the coastal towns of Zambales. Hot lava surged down the mountain slopes and invaded the drainage systems pushing mud and hot rocks over settlements and cultivated land. Most of the people escaped but the volcano wreaked havoc with their lands and wild animals.

The Ayta view Mt. Pinatubo as a sacred place, the habitation of their god, *Apo Namalyari*, the Supreme Being. Many believed that the eruption was the result of human activity around the mountain, like the drilling by the Philippine Oil Company, the clearing of the forest for a road, or the United States Air Force military exercises in the vicinity of the volcano. Tribal spirit mediums suggested that the government and the United States military should provide an animal sacrifice to stop the eruptions.

The June 15 blast sent out seven cubic kilometers of volcanic sediments, killed approximately 300 people, displaced 1.3 million residents, buried 98,600 hectares of farms and damaged some $80 million worth of public and private infrastructure. It left the Ayta homeless and without farming land. Over the next few years their land was further decimated by lahars, massive movements of ash and floods of mud, rendering it unsuitable for cultivation. Then, in August 2001, the Ayta averted another catastrophe, a potential massive flood destined to destroy Botolan and their resettlement area.

Resettlement and Organizations

In 1992 resettlements of Ayta were established in a number of areas in the provinces surrounding Mt. Pinatubo. Scores of people died in temporary tents due to disease and sanitation problems. The Ayta LAKAS organization (Lubos na Alyansa ng mga Katutubong Aeta ng Sambales, or Negrito People's Alliance of Zambales) bought a 7.5-hectare property in Bihawo, Mambog, in Botolan, Zambales, near the government resettlement area. One-hundred and fifty families were allotted 625 square meters of land for planting crops such as bananas, sweet potatoes, and fruit trees (mango and cashew).

Due in part to the earlier achievements of an area-wide literacy program introduced by The Sisters of the Franciscan Missionaries of Mary, in March 2000 four Aytas finished college while 30 completed high school. As part of a community strategy to preserve the Ayta way of life, LAKAS facilitated the building of the School of Indigenous Knowledge and Traditions of the

Ayta Tribe (SIKAT-Ayta). Other active Ayta organizations such as Pagkakaisa ng Aeta ng Pinatubo Philippines(United Pinatubo Aeta of the Philippines) work to promote social justice issues with other indigenous peoples. At the University of the Philippines, the Ayta Studies Center aims to promote and preserve the richness of the culture of the Pinatubo Aytas, which remains threatened by extinction.

F. Douglas Pennoyer

See also **Philippines**

Further Reading

Brosius, J.P., *After Duwagan: Deforestation, Succession and Adaptation in Upland Luzon, Philippines*, Ann Arbor, Michigan: Studies of South and Southeast Asia, no. 2, 1990

Fox, Robert, "The Pinatubo Negritos: Their Useful Plants and Material Culture," *Philippine Journal of Science*, 81, no. 3–4 (1952)

Lubos na Alyansa ng mga Katutubong Ayta ng Sambales (LAKAS), *Eruption and Exodus*, Quezon City, Philippines: Claretian Publications, 1991

Azerbaijan

Capsule Summary

Country Name: Republic of Azerbaijan
Location: Southwestern Asia, bordering the Caspian Sea, between Iran and Russia, with a small European portion north of the Caucasus range
Total population: 7,830,764 (July 2003)
Languages: Azerbaijani (Azeri) (89%), Russian (3%), Armenian (2%), other (6%) [1995]
Religions: Shi'a Muslim (93.4%), Russian Orthodox (2.5%), Armenian Orthodox (2.3%), other (1.8%) [1995]

Azerbaijan is one of the former Soviet Central Asian (CA) states. Azerbaijanis are predominantly Turkic. During the eleventh century CE, the area came to be dominated by Turkic peoples from the Oguz Seljuq migrations, which mixed with the older Iranian inhabitants. The official language of Azerbaijan is Azeri. The total population of Azerbaijan was estimated over 7.8 million in 2003. Azerbaijanis are traditionally Shi'a Muslims, and the country is a multiethnic society, with an absolute majority of Muslims. In 1991, Azerbaijan became independent from the Soviet Union.

Caucasia consist of two regions: the land north of the Greater Caucasus is called Ciscaucasia and to the south of it is Transcaucasia and consists of the Transcaucasian republics of Georgia, Armenia, and Azerbaijan; and several minor administrative units constituted on an ethnic basis. The region harbors more than 50 separate ethnic groups. One of the main ethnic groups of Caucasia is Azeri.

Azerbaijan borders Russia, Georgia, Armenia, Iran, and the Caspian Sea. Its territory includes Nagorno-Karabakh and the geographically detached region of Nakhçivan. The capital of Azerbaijan is Baku (Baki) and the total area of the country is 86,600 square kilometers. The major cities in Azerbaijan, in 1995, were Baku (metro area), with 2.5 million inhabitants; Gäncä (formerly Kirovabad) with 291,000; Sumqayi̱t (Sumgait) 268,000; and Mingä̱cevir (Mingechaur) with 96,000 people.

History

Azerbaijan was, for a long time, the battleground of varieties of great world civilizations including the Persians, Turks, Mongols, Islam, and Christianity. Azerbajian was annexed by the Persian Achaemenid Empire in the second half of the sixth century CE. Iran retained primary political control of present-day Azerbaijan through the early nineteenth century, when Russia conquered the country. The two wars between Persia and Russia (1801–1813 and 1826–1828) ended in Persian defeat, in which Persia accepted sovereignty over all the territory between the Transcaucasia and the Caspian Sea and the current territory of Azerbaijan went to Russia.

After the Bolshevik Revolution, Azerbaijan declared its independence from Russia in 1918. The republic was reconquered by the Red Army in 1920, and was annexed into the Transcaucasian Soviet Federal Socialist Republic (TSFSR) in 1922, which contained Azerbaijan, Georgia, and Armenia. Azerbaijan became a separate Soviet Republic in 1936. Not until September 1989 did Azerbaijan declare its sovereignty. Soviet troops intervened in January 1990, after Azeri militants attacked Armenians in Baku. The escalation in ethnic fighting stemmed from the longstanding conflict between Armenia and Azerbaijan over the sovereignty of Nagorno-Karabakh. In 1990, generally free elections resulted in an overwhelming victory of the Azerbaijan Communist Party (ACP), winning all but 40 of the 350 parliamentary seats. Azerbaijan adopted a declaration of republican sovereignty. However, immediately after the Moscow August 1991 coup, Ayaz Mutalibov, Azerbaijan's president appointed by Moscow, distanced himself from the Communist Party of the Soviet Union (CPSU) and disbanded the ACP, and on August 1991 declared Azerbaijan's independence.

Mutalibov won an unopposed presidential election in September 1991, but was forced from office by popular demonstrations in March 1992. After the Supreme Soviet transferred authority to the National Council, Abulfez Elchibey, a former dissident and leader of Azerbaijan Popular Front (APF), won the June 1992 presidential election. After an armed uprising in June 1993, he was replaced by the former Communist leader, Heydar Aliyev. Aliyev ran as the candidate of the New Azerbaijan Party (NAP), formed by members of the disbanded ACP, and was elected president in October 1993, which was officially reported as a nearly unanimous victory. Aliyev won reelection in October 1998, winning over 75 percent of the votes.

Today Azerbaijan is a presidential republic and governed under a constitution adopted by a referendum in 1995. The president, the head of state, is directly elected for a five-year term, and he appoints the prime minister and the cabinet of ministers. Since October 2003, the president has been Ilham Aliyev, and the prime minister has been Artur Rasizade since November 2003. Legislative power is manifested in the Milli Majlis (National Assembly), composed of 125 members serving five-year terms. Of the 125 seats, 25 are allocated through national popular vote, and 100 go to the winners of district elections. The judiciary consists of a supreme court, which is the country's highest court, and the constitutional court, which acts as the guarantor of the 1995 constitution. Members of both courts are nominated by the president and approved by the Milli Majlis. Azerbaijan has a multi-party system. The main political parties with representation in the Milli Majlis include the NAP, the APF, and the National Independence Party (NIP).

Nagorno-Karabakh War (1992–1994)

One of the main post-Soviet legacies of the Caucasus is ethnic conflict, mainly based on hostile claims to territory during the process of state building, particularly when two emerging states challenge each other's borders. This becomes especially problematic if ethnic populations in a region overlap. One such example is the region of Nagorno-Karabakh, which is viewed by both Azerbaijani and Armenians as a historical patrimony. For this reason, throughout the Soviet period, Nagorno-Karabakh was an autonomous region within the Azerbaijan SSR (Soviet Socialist Republic), primarily inhabited by Armenians. In 1987, the Armenian-dominated regional council requested that the territory be transferred to Armenia, but Moscow rejected this request. On September 11, 1989, the Armenian parliament declared that autonomous Nagorno-Karabakh belonged to Armenia. Armed conflicts triggered a large-scale exodus of Azerbaijanis from Armenia and Armenians from Azerbaijan. In early 1989 some 5,000 Soviet troops were installed in Nagorno-Karabakh, establishing direct control of the region through most of the year. Civil strife erupted between Armenians and Azerbaijanis in 1989–1991, developing to full-scale war in 1992–1993.

By August 1993 Armenian forces in Nagorno-Karabakh, with reinforcements from Armenia, gained control of the enclave as well as some 20 percent of adjacent territory in western Azerbaijan, including a corridor linking the enclave with Armenia. In December 1993 Azerbaijani forces began a renewed offensive in the region, recapturing some areas while suffering heavy casualties. The massive relocation of population had produced an estimated 1 million refugees and displaced persons (primarily Azeri and Armenians) in Azerbaijan alone. Officially, the Armenian government maintains a hands-off position. However Azerbaijan instituted a complete rail, road, and fuel blockade of both Nagorno-Karabakh and Armenia, effectively cutting off fuel supplies and strangling Armenia's economy. Present population estimates in the region are Armenian (76 percent), Azeri (23 percent), in addition to Russian and Kurdish minorities.

Initial cease-fire agreements failed to hold, and fighting continued in Nagorno-Karabakh until May 1994, when both sides agreed again to cease hostilities. Although this cease-fire has remained in effect, ongoing negotiations have failed to achieve a final peace settlement, although some progress has been made. The Organization for Security and Cooperation in Europe (OSCE) continues to mediate the dispute.

Society

Azerbaijan is mostly populated by ethnic Azeris, and this majority group has increased dramatically as a result of recent population shifts. By the mid-1990s the proportion of Azerbaijanis in the total population had increased almost 10 percent since 1989, reaching about 90 percent of the total population. Dagestanis and Russians are the largest minority groups in Azerbaijan, followed by Armenians. In the mid-1990s, Dagestanis represented an estimated 3.2 percent of the population. Russians constituted 2.5 percent of the population, a reduction of about 3 percent since 1989, and Armenians constituted 2 percent (they represented 6 percent before the war). Other ethnic groups include Lezgins, Kurds, and Talysh, and some small communities of Georgians, Ukrainians, and Avars.

Azerbaijan is less developed, in industrial terms, than the other Transcaucasian states. The country contains one of the world's major oil reserves. Its chief industries are petroleum and natural gas, machinery- and equipment-manufacturing, and food processing. Azerbaijan shares all the formidable problems of the former Soviet republics that emerged from the 1991 dissolution in addition to war, political instability, and economic mismanagement in making the transition from a command to a market economy. The conflict in the Nagorno-Karabakh region further exacerbated economic suffering. However, the republic's considerable energy resources are key to its long-term prospects. Real GDP declined about 60 percent from 1991 to 1995. The GDP per capita income was $3,700 in 2002. In 1995 Azerbaijan began a comprehensive economic reform program. Despite the enhanced performance, the size of the economy achieved half the level it had under the Soviet Union. As a result, more than 90 percent of the population still lives in poverty (earning below $89/month). Baku has only recently progressed on economic reform, slowly replacing old economic ties and structures. Trade with the other former Soviet republics and Russia is declining in importance, whereas trade with Turkey, Iran, the UAE, and Europe is growing.

MEHDI PARVIZI AMINEH

See also **Armenia; Armenians; Avars; Azerbaijani; Dagestanis; Georgia; Turkey**

Further Reading

Altstadt, Audry L., The *Azerbaijani Turks: Power and Identity under Russian Rule*, Hoover Series on Nationalities, (Stanford): Hoover Institution Press, 1992

Amineh, Mehdi Parvizi, *Towards the Control of Oil Resources in the Caspian Region,* New York: St. Martin's Press, 1999

Amineh, Mehdi Parvizi, *Die globale kapitalistische Expansion und Iran: Eine Studie der iranischen politichen Ökonomie (1500–1980)*, Munster-Hamburg-London: Lit-Verlag, 1999

Doerfer, Gerhard, "Turkish-Iranian Language Contacts," in *Encyclopaedia Iranica*, 5, edited by Eshan Yarshater, Costa Mesa: Mazda Publishers, 1992

Doerfer, Gerhard, "Azeri Turkish," in *Encyclodaedia Iranica*, 3, edited by Ehsan Yarshater, Costa Mesa: Mazda Publishers, 1989

Haghayeghi, Mehrdad, *Islam and Politics in Central Asia*, New York: St. Martin's Press, 1995

Hambly, Gavin, editor, *Central Asia*, London: Weidenfeld and Nicolson, 1969

Johanson, J., "Iranian Elements in Azeri Turkish," in *Encyclodaedia Iranica*, 3, edited by Ehsan Yarshater, Costa Mesa: Mazda Publishers, 1989

Yarshater, Eshan, "The Iranian Language of Azerbaijan," in *Encyclodaedia Iranica*, 3, edited by Ehsan Yarshater, Costa Mesa: Mazada Publishers, 1989

Wheeler, Geoffrey, *The Modern History of Soviet Central Asia*, London: Weidenfeld and Nicolson, 1964

Azerbaijani

Capsule Summary

Location: South Caucasus region of Europe, mostly in Azerbaijan, and in northwest Iran (East Azerbaijan Province, West Azerbaijan Province, and Ardabil Province)
Total Population: 30–35 million
Language: Azeri
Religion: Shi'a Muslim (predominantly)

The Azerbaijani are an ethnic group in the south Caucasus region and northwest Iran. According to present scholars in the Republic of Azerbaijan there are between 30 and 35 million Azerbaijani, most of whom live in three provinces in northwest Iran: East Azerbaijan Province, West Azerbaijan Province, Ardabil

Province (21 million) and in the Republic of Azerbaijan (7 million). Around 2.5 million Azerbaijani live in Turkey, 1.5 million in the Russian Federation, 1 million in Iraq, 500,000 in Georgia, 42,000 in Ukraine and about 900,000 in Western Europe and the United States.

The Azerbaijani language, Azeri, is a Turkic language. It is not a dialect derived from the Ottoman (or Osmanli), which is spoken in modern Turkey, but much more ancient and richer than standard Ottoman Turkish. Adari was the Iranian language of Azerbaijan before the spread of the Turkish language. Most Azerbaijani are Shi'a Muslim. Between the sixth century BCE until its division between the Persian and Russian empires in 1828 Azerbaijan was mainly part of Persia. After the Bolshevik Revolution in 1917 the northern part of Azerbaijan was integrated into the Soviet Union, but declared its independence in 1991. The southern part of Azerbaijan remains within Iran today.

History

In common usage the name *Azerbaijan* is derived from Atropates, the name of a Persian *satrap* (governor) of the late fourth century BCE. According to another theory it originates in the Persian word *azar* (fire) meaning Azerbaijan is "the land of fire," named for Zoroastrian temples with fires fuelled by the plentiful supply of oil.

The Azerbaijani are a Turkic-speaking ethnic group who trace their origins back to some of the earliest settlements in the territory of the present Republic of Azerbaijan and northwest Iran. The Azerbaijani have lived at the crossroads between Russia, Iran, and Turkey and have thus negotiated multiple and often competing identities as Turks, Iranians, Shi'a Muslims, and Azerbaijani.

From the sixth century BCE the Azerbaijani were primarily ruled by Persian Empires, with significant Turkic influences present from the eleventh century. The gradual weakening of Adari—the Azerbaijani language before Turkish—began with the penetration of Azerbaijan by speakers of Turkish during the time of Mahmud of Gazna (998–1030). But, it was in the Seljuq period (1040–1118) that Turkish tribes started to migrate to Azerbaijan in considerable numbers to settle there. The Turkish population continued to grow, particularly during the rule of the Mongol khans in the thirteenth to mid-fourteenth century and the rulership of Timur (1336–1405) the founder of the Timurid Empire (1370–1506). This development was favored by the Mongol policy of giving land to leading commanders, the presence of the khans themselves in this area, and the migration of Central Asian nomads who accompanied Timur on his campaigns to the west. During the rule of the Persian Safavid Empire, its capital Tabriz (later moved to Isfahan)—the main city of the Azerbaijani provinces in present-day Iran—on several occasions was exposed to attacks from the Ottomans. In 1514, Tabriz was occupied by the forces of Ottoman Sultan Selim (1470–1520). The Safavids had to move their capital to Qazvin in 1555 after further occupation of Tabriz by the Ottomans. Later Tabriz was returned to the Safavids and again occupied by the Ottomans. In 1734 the Persian Shah Nader Afshar (1729–1747) regained Tabriz from the Ottomans.

From the early nineteenth century the Russians exerted intense military, diplomatic, and economic pressure on Azerbaijan. After two wars with the Persian Qajar Empire, in 1828 Azerbaijan was divided between the Russian and the Persian empires according to the Treaty of Turkmanchai. Based on this treaty, what is the present-day Republic of Azerbaijan became part of the Russian Empire and the rest remained within the Persian Empire. The Treaty of Turkmanchai completed the present-day ethnic separation of the Azerbaijani.

Azerbaijani in the Republic of Azerbaijan

The chief language in the Republic of Azerbaijan is Azeri (spoken by 89 percent of the population), but Russian is widely spoken and taught in schools. The predominant religion is the Shi'a sect of Islam. Azerbaijani comprise about 90 percent of the total population in the Republic of Azerbaijan. Other ethnic groups include Dagestani (3.2 percent), Russian (2.5 percent), Armenian (2 percent), and others (2.3 percent, 1998).

Russian rule over northern Azerbaijan from the nineteenth century manifested itself in exploitation as well as technological and educational progress. Western entrepreneurs, Russians, Iranians, and other nonindigenous workers came to the capital city of Baku to work in the petroleum industry and related sectors. In the beginning of the twentieth century the Azerbaijani constituted the poorest sector of the growing population in Baku and were even outnumbered by nonindigenous people.

The Russian Revolution of 1905 brought a political awakening in northern Azerbaijan, with the rise of political associations and a relatively free press.

After the Bolshevik Revolution in 1917 the Soviets established a government centered in Baku. In 1918 an anti-Soviet Azerbaijani National Council proclaimed the Azerbaijani Democratic Republic. The Azerbaijan Republic existed for 23 months, being occupied first by Turkey and later by Great Britain. In 1920 Azerbaijan was incorporated into the Soviet Union and became a Soviet Socialist Republic (SSR) in 1936. In 1991 Azerbaijan for the first time in history became a sovereign nation state.

During the Soviet period (1917–1991) great efforts were made to minimize the role of Islam in Soviet Azerbaijan. After the disintegration of the Soviet Union a great revival of Islam occurred, most visibly in the reopening of mosques that had been closed.

The Soviets introduced universal elementary education in Azerbaijan in 1928. In the same year the Latin alphabet replaced the Arabic alphabet. In 1939 the Cyrillic alphabet was introduced. The literacy rate grew between 1917 and 1959 from about 10 to 97–99 percent. In 1959, eight-year education became compulsory and in 1966 universal secondary education was available, the greatest part in vocational schools. From the late 1950s Russian-language schools for the native population were promoted. In 1991 the Latin script was reintroduced in a modified version.

The marriage rate outside the Muslim communities is very low for men and insignificant for women. Although a great urbanization took place during the Soviet period, kinship ties remain strong and the extended family still plays an important role in personal achievement, professional life, politics, and business.

The rich architectural heritage of the Republic of Azerbaijan reflects the country's multilayered history and diverse outside influences. The Islamic period left the most important imprint on Azerbaijani architecture in the Republic of Azerbaijan, with mosques, minarets, mausoleums, *karavan-sarays* (inns), *madrasas* (Islamic colleges), and fortresses such as the twelfth century Maiden Tower in Baku. The nineteenth century architecture of the oil-boom era is well represented but in bad repair. The architecture of the twentieth century was Soviet, with Stalinist-type grandiose public buildings and monotonous residential blocs.

The Nagorno-Karabakh War (1992–1994)

When the Soviets gained control of Azerbaijan and the other parts in the south Caucasus they established borders that did not take into account the boundaries of the different ethnic groups. Nagorno-Karabakh became an autonomous region within the Azerbaijan SSR in 1923, but was mainly populated by ethnic Armenians. The region (NKAO) occupied the southeastern part of the Lesser Caucasus and covered an area of 4,388 square kilometres. In 1923 Azeris constituted 3 percent of the population of the area; in 1953 their number grew to 13 percent, reaching its peak of 24 percent in 1988. The area of Nakhichevan remained part of Azerbaijan but was isolated from the republic by the region of Zangezur, which became part of Armenia. This complex realignment of borders became the basis for future conflicts. During the Soviet period ethnic Armenians in Nagorno-Karabakh protested against their inclusion in the Azerbaijan SSR, but any tensions between ethnic Armenians and Azerbaijani were contained by the oppressive policy of the Soviets, which was systematically applied to all aspects of economic, political, religious, and cultural life in the oblast. Under Soviet Azerbaijan, Armenian cultural monuments and other forms of expression were altered and even eliminated; authorities closed Armenian schools, and the history of Armenia was removed from secondary school curricula and replaced by the history of Azerbaijan. In all reference textbooks issued by Azerbaijani SSR, Azeris (not Armenians) were cited as the indigenous population of Nagorno-Karabakh.

In light of the mounting tensions and discrimination, in 1989 Armenia declared that the autonomous Nagorno-Karabakh belonged to Armenia. Armed conflicts followed that forced Azerbaijanis to flee Armenia and Armenians to flee Azerbaijan. The war produced about 1 million refugees and displaced persons (primarily Azerbaijani and Armenians) in Azerbaijan alone. In 1991, as a result of the critical situation in Nagorno-Karabakh, the Executive Committee of the Regional Soviet Council declared a state of emergency in the region. On the same day, the Executive Committee appealed to the United Nations and to other state leaders to save the Armenian people from the physical extermination by granting them political asylum.

At the end of 2002, more than 576,000 people remained internally displaced from the western regions of Azerbaijan, who have lived under Armenian occupation since 1993. Additionally, in the same year, about 220,000 Azerbaijani from Armenia were living in refugee-like circumstances in Azerbaijan. Since the cease-fire in 1994 about 70,000 displaced Azerbaijani have returned to regions bordering ethnic Armenian-controlled areas. As Armenian forces continue to control the Nagorno-Karabakh region and its surrounding provinces comprising about 16 percent of Azerbaijan's territory, most displaced persons are not able to return to their home regions. According to a 1995 human rights report issued by the United States department of state, until the May 1994 cease-fire, both sides engaged in "indiscriminate shelling and rocket fire against civilian targets" in both directions along the Armenia-Azerbaijan border and severed trade and transportation links to the other sides, causing severe hardship to civilians in Nagorno-Karabakh, Armenia, and Nakhichevan.

Azerbaijani in Iran

Iran is a multiethnic society in which about 50 percent of the population are of non-Persian origin. The largest minority ethnic group is the Azerbaijani, amounting to about 21 million of approximately 71 million of the total population. Other minorities are Arabs, Baluchis, Turkmen, and others. The main language of Azerbaijani in Iran is Persian, and the Shi'a sect of Islam is the predominant religion.

The Azerbaijani have always held key positions in the Iranian political elite, and also both the Safavid and the Qajar empires were Azerbaijani in origin.

Azerbaijani in Iran played a prominent role during the time of the Constitutional Revolution in Iran [1905–1906]. The constitutionalists aimed at overthrowing the absolutists state form of the Qajar Empire and its social order and replace it with a liberal social order and a state based on a modern parliamentary system.

There was no aspiration among ethnic minorities to establish separate independent states along ethnic lines. One important goal reached by the constitutionalists was the establishment of provincial councils in the Iranian provinces. The role of the Azerbaijani in this context cannot be overestimated. The constitutionalists from Tabriz were pioneers in establishing their own provincial councils. Generally, it can be said that the role of the Azerbaijani in the Constitutional Revolution was so impressive, that from then on the Azerbaijani provinces have been seen as the main centres from which a possible future progressive political change could originate.

In the 1940s the repressive regime of Reza Shah Pahlavi (1921–1941)—particularly against ethnic minorities—as well as the weak central power resultant of Soviet occupation of the Azerbaijani provinces in Iran in 1941 were the precondition for the development of the Soviet-backed ethnic revolts in the Iranian provinces. In mid-1945 Jafar Pishevari founded the *Ferqeh-e demokrat-e azarbaijan* (Azerbaijani Democratic Party) that in late 1945 established its own national congress and declared an Azerbaijani autonomous republic within Iran. During this period the Azerbaijani in Iran gained great cultural freedom manifesting in practising their own language, particularly in publications. The movement in Azerbaijan had a tremendous influence on the ethnic movement in Kurdistan, which also proclaimed an autonomous republic. The central government in Tehran refused to accept the demands of the Azerbaijani and Kurds and reacted with military intervention.

During the period leading up to and including the Iranian Islamic Revolution (1977–1979) Tabriz was an active center participating in the fall of the Pahlavi regime. A great number of Azerbaijani intellectuals, such as Mehdi Bazargan (1907–1995), one of the founders of the Liberation Movement of Iran in 1961, were key figures in the revolution. After the Shah had fled the country in January 1979, new publications appeared in Iran in non-Persian languages such as Azerbaijani, Kurdish, and Armenian. Azerbaijani activists founded the newspaper *Ulduz,* in which they called for their right to use the Azerbaijani language. Soon after the consolidation of the Islamic regime, however, the publication of *Ulduz* was forbidden and it became more difficult to publish books in non-Persian languages.

Varliq (Essence) is the only Azerbaijani-language publication of that period that exists today. This publication's editors clearly stress their national culture, identity, and language as being Azerbaijani while their state identity is Iranian, thus they emphasise that they share a common culture with other Iranians.

During the period of the Islamic Revolution many political organizations were established along ethnic lines. The most important was the *Anjuman-e azarbaijan* (Council of Azerbaijan) founded shortly after the consolidation of the new regime in 1979. In its manifesto it demanded the recognition of the Azerbaijani language and culture, the establishment of schools and mass media in the Turkish language and the right to use Azeri in courts and other governmental offices, like during the Safavid and Qajar periods. It even strove for a confederate relationship with Tehran.

The process of collective identity building accelerated when the theocratic authoritarian nature of the Islamic regime became clear, but in 1982–1983 a severe crackdown of the regime on political opposition occurred. Open expression of ethnic rights was no longer tolerated, and during the Iran-Iraq War(1980–1988) there was no room for political and cultural activity.

The establishment of the Republic of Azerbaijan in 1991 stimulated Azerbaijani in Iran to identify with the Azerbaijani ethnic group but not necessarily with the new state itself. While an increasing expression of Azerbaijani identity can be observed in Iran, since the 1990s few have demanded a secession of the Azerbaijani provinces from Iran and joining the Republic of Azerbaijan. Rather, Azerbaijani ask for more cultural rights within Iran like they did during the Constitutional and the Iranian Islamic Revolutions. The emergence of the Republic, however, has had great influence on the relations between the Republic of Azerbaijan and Iran, and Iran's policy in the Caucasus. Iran fears that the emergence of a strong Republic of Azerbaijan could have a great effect on the increased awareness and expression of identity among its own Azerbaijani population. This fear, for example, has led to Iran's support of Armenia in the conflict over Nagorno-Karabakh.

In 1992 the Iranian government decided to split East Azerbaijan province and create a new province in the Ardabil area. The names Salaban, Sahand, and Ardabil were suggested for this new province. Many Azerbaijani, even those who are part of the ruling elite in Iran and those that have a strong identification with Iran, opposed giving up the name Azerbaijan for this territory. In the end, the government prevailed and in April 1993 the new province was named Ardabil Province.

It is not clear how many Azerbaijani in Iran primarily espouse an Iranian or Azerbaijani identity. In general it can be said that while a number of Azerbaijani in Iran retain a distinctive Azerbaijani identity, many, especially those belonging to the Iranian ruling elite, see themselves primarily as Iranians and Muslims. Since the 1990s a small number of Azerbaijani have actively demanded a political manifestation of their Azerbaijani identity. This, however, is mainly an expression of their disappointment in the Iranian government to live up to its promises of democratisation and more rights for ethnic non-Persians.

EVA RAKEL

See also **Armenia; Armenians; Azerbaijan; Iran**

Further Reading

Amineh, Mehdi Parvizi, *Die globale kapitalistische Expansion und Iran-Eine Studie der iranischen politischen Ökonomie 1500–1980*, Münster, Hamburg, London: Lit Verlag, 1999

Atabaki, Touraj, *Azerbaijan-Ethnicity and Autonomy in Twentieth-Century Iran*, London and New York: British Academy Press, 1993

"Azerbaijan's Policy of Economic, Political and Cultural Discrimination," Office of the Nagorno Karabakh Republic, Washington, D.C., http://www.nkrusa.org/nk_conflict/azerbaijan_discrimination.html

Chorbaijan, Levon, editor, *The Making of Nagorno-Karabakh*, London: Palgrave, 2001

Fawcett, Louise, *Iran and the Cold War: The Azerbaijan Crisis of 1946*, Cambridge: Cambridge University Press, 1992

Van der Leeuw, Charles, *Azerbaijan: A Quest for Identity*, Richmond: Curzon, 1999

Nissman, David, *The Soviet Union and Iranian Azerbaijan: The Uses of Nationalism for Political Penetration*, Boulder: Westview, 1987

Swietochowski, Tadeusz, *Russian Azerbaijan 1905–1920: The Shaping of National Identity in a Muslim Community*, Cambridge: Cambridge University Press, 1985

Yarshater, Ehsan, editor, "Azerbaijan," *Encyclopaedia Iranica*, vol. 3, London: Routledge, and New York: Kegan Paul, 1989

B

Bahamas

Capsule Summary

Country Name: Commonwealth of the Bahamas
Location: Caribbean, chain of islands in the North Atlantic Ocean, southeast of Florida, northeast of Cuba
Total Population: 297,477 (July 2003)
Language: English
Religions: Baptist (32%), Anglican (20%), Roman Catholic (19%), Methodist (6%), Church of God (6%), other Protestant (12%), none or unknown (3%), other (2%)

The Commonwealth of the Bahamas is an archipelago of 700 islands and 2,400 uninhabited cays that extends across 760 miles (1,223 kilometers) from 50 miles off the coast of Florida to the northern coast of Haiti. Only about 50 of the islands are inhabited, and the bulk of the population (about 171,542 or 60 percent) is located in the major city of Nassau on the island of New Providence. The islands are culturally and socially a part of the Caribbean region. About 85 percent of the population is of African descent, while the remaining 15 percent is of European, Asian, or mixed descent. Bahama's population estimates are affected by a high mortality rate due to AIDS, which results in a lower life expectancy, higher infant mortality and death rates, and lower population and growth rates.

Although Haitian immigrants have always been present in the Bahamas, they constitute a substantial ethnic minority within the country with an increasingly problematic existence from the 1950s through the end of the twentieth century. For most of Bahamian history, political and economic powers were vested in the white minority, a situation that changed with the enfranchisement of the black majority in 1964 and the independence of the Bahamas in 1973.

As a member of the Commonwealth of Nations, the Bahamas has a government headed by a prime minister and consisting of two houses, an appointed upper house, or senate, and an elected lower house, the House of Assembly. There are two major political parties. The Progressive Liberal Party was the first political party in the Bahamas and the dominant one from 1968 until 1992 under the leadership of Prime Minister Lynden O. Pindling. The Free National Movement came to power under the leadership of Prime Minister Hubert A. Ingraham in 1992. The head of state is Queen Elizabeth II, who is represented in the Bahamas by the Governor-General. The country has a GDP of $4.59 billion (2002) and a per capita income of $15,300 (2002). The economy depends largely on tourism and offshore banking. Tourism alone accounts for more than 60 percent of the GDP and employs about half of the labor force. Steady growth in tourism, as well as construction booms (new hotels, resorts, and residences), had led to solid GDP growth in recent years, but the decline in the United States economy and the attacks of September 11, 2001, led to reductions in growth in these areas in 2002.

History

The people who originally inhabited the Bahamas between 600 and 1200 CE were called the Taino. Their descendants, the Lucayans, were the people present when Christopher Columbus landed at the island of Gunahaní (today called San Salvador) on October 12, 1492. The Lucayans were an agricultural and fishing people who made stone tools and pottery. Because of the Spanish system of *repartimiento* (the distribution of indigenous peoples for forced labor), many Lucayans were taken as slaves to Hispaniola and Cubagua near Venezuela to work as pearl divers. By the 1530s, because of warfare, disease, and enslavement, the islands were depopulated.

For a while European involvement was sporadic, consisting largely of unsuccessful attempts by the French, English, and Spanish to lay claim. However, in 1648, the Eleutherian Adventurers, a group of Puritan religious dissidents located in Bermuda, established a settlement on the island that became known as Eleuthera. In later years more people from Bermuda found their way to the Bahamas, providing by the 1670s a scant population of 1,000, most of them white and some of them slaves and free blacks. Piracy flourished throughout the islands in the sixteenth century, but it was subdued by 1728 through the concerted action of Woodes Rogers, the first royal governor. A major population boom occurred following the American revolution when, according to Howard Johnson, "between 1783 and 1790, approximately 1,600 whites and 5,700 slaves and free blacks from New York, the Carolinas, and Georgia settled permanently in the Bahamas" (Johnson, *The Bahamas from Slavery to Servitude, 1783–1933,* 1996). A similar influx followed the Haitian revolution, according to Michael Craton and Gail Saunders. From this time on, the islands had a majority black population that was nevertheless subjugated by the white minority.

The white Loyalists attempted to establish the kind of slave-based plantation agriculture familiar to them from their days in the North American colonies and embarked upon the growing of cotton. Slaves were given land on which to grow their own provisions, and most slave owners lived on the island of New Providence, while slaves and overseers minded the plantations on the outer islands of the archipelago. Johnson has noted that Bahamian slaves engaged in agricultural labor worked predominantly according to a task system in which they were given a set number of tasks to perform during a day, after which their time was their own. Slaves who worked in the city engaged in a self-hire system of labor in which they worked for wages and split these with their owners. On the eve of emancipation, there were approximately 10,000 slaves in the Bahamas. The emancipation of slaves in the Bahamas began in 1834 and ended in 1838 after a four-year apprenticeship. Although the former slaves nominally had all of the rights of citizens and all males had the right to vote, a series of measures prevented blacks from full enfranchisement and economic participation.

The boom and bust cycle characteristic of the Bahamas until well into the twentieth century had an effect on the reception received by new immigrants. According to most scholars, all Bahamians exhibited some degree of xenophobia during bad economic times, but new minorities such as Greeks, Lebanese, Jewish, and Chinese immigrants, who remained a tiny percentage of the total population, were often the targets of protective legislation promoted by the merchant oligarchy to fend off competition. Bahamians of African descent had to put up with racial discrimination in the form of segregation and limited access to economic and political opportunities.

In 1953 a racially mixed group of Bahamians formed the Progressive Liberal Party (PLP), the first political party in the Bahamas with the goal of changing the political environment and allowing women to vote and serve in the government. The PLP became the focal point of a rising black nationalism within the Bahamas. In 1956 members of the white minority formed the United Bahamian Party. By 1960 women had gained the vote, and property qualifications had been eliminated. In 1964, the Bahamas was granted internal self-rule, and by 1968 race was no longer an issue in Bahamian elections. The Commonwealth of the Bahamas was created in 1973 as an independent nation.

Upon reaching nationhood and solving most of its problems of racial and political inequities, the Commonwealth of the Bahamas still had to face the problem of illegal immigration that created a sizeable Haitian minority (about four percent of the population). According to Craton and Saunders, the majority of Haitians coming to the Bahamas did so for economic reasons, coming mostly from northern Haiti. Problems of poverty, poor health, and illiteracy, plus the concentration of Haitians in the urban area of Nassau, created ethnic tensions in the islands. In 1995, the Bahamas attempted to come to terms with the problem by repatriating 800 illegal immigrants a month to Haiti, while giving a kind of amnesty to those residing in the Bahamas for more than ten years.

Susan Love Brown

See also **Haiti**

Further Reading

Bethel, E. Clement, *Junkanoo: Festival of the Bahamas*, edited and expanded by Nicolette Bethel, London and Basingstoke: Macmillan Caribbean, 1991

Craton, Michael, *History of the Bahamas*, 3rd edition, Waterloo, Ontario: San Salvador Press, 1986

Craton, Michael, and Gail Saunders, *Islanders in the Stream: A History of the Bahamian People, Volume One: From Aboriginal Times to the End of Slavery*, Athens, Georgia and London: University of Georgia Press, 1992

Craton, Michael, and Gail Saunders, *Islanders in the Stream: A History of the Bahamian People, Volume Two: From the Ending of Slavery to the Twenty-First Century*, Athens, Georgia and London: University of Georgia Press, 1998

Crowley, Daniel J., *I Could Talk Old-Story Good: Creativity in Bahamian Folklore*, Folklore Studies 17, Berkeley, Los Angeles, and London: University of California Press, 1966

Johnson, Howard, *The Bahamas in Slavery and Freedom*, Kingston, Jamaica: Ian Randle, 1991

Johnson, Howard, *The Bahamas from Slavery to Servitude, 1783–1933*, Gainesville: University of Florida Press, 1996

Keegan, William F., *The People Who Discovered Columbus: The Prehistory of the Bahamas*, Gainesville, Florida: University of Florida Press, 1992

Saunders, Gail, *The Bahamian Loyalists and Their Slaves*, London: Macmillan Caribbean, 1983

Saunders, Gail, *The Bahamas: A Family of Islands*, London: Macmillan, 1988

Taylor, Sir Henry, *My Political Memoirs: A Political History of the Bahamas in the 20th Century*, 1988

Bahrain

Capsule Summary

Country Name: Kingdom of Bahrain
Location: Middle East
Total Population: 667,300 (including an estimated 235,100 noncitizens) (2003)
Ethnic Populations: Bahraini (63%), Asian (19%), other Arab (10%), Iranian (8%)
Language: Arabic (official), English, Farsi, Urdu
Religions: Shi'a Muslim (70%), Sunni Muslim (30%)

The Kingdom of Bahrain is located on the Arabian Peninsula in the Middle East, bordering Qatar in the east and Saudi Arabia in the south and west; Iran is across the Persian Gulf to the north. The country has a land area of 711.85 square kilometers (278 square miles), and it is slightly smaller than New York City.

Bahrain's population is predominantly urban, with around 90 percent of the people living in metropolitan areas. The country's capital city, Manama (also Al Manamah), is home to about 150,000 people (2003), or 22 percent of the population. Bahrain has a population growth rate of 1.61 percent. It is estimated that the population could double by the year 2035 if the current birth rate (19.02 births per 1,000 population) and immigration remain at the same level. Bahrain has a high population density, standing at around 937 people per sq km (2,435 people per sq mi).

Bahrain is a constitutional, hereditary monarchy. In this political system, the Emir appoints the cabinet ministers, but some powers also are delegated to the bicameral parliament. The present government's structure was established according to the constitution adopted in December 2000 and was approved by Bahraini voters on February 13 and 14, 2001. The modern political system of the country represents the legacy of Bahrain's history.

The territory that today constitutes Bahrain has experienced a turbulent history. In the sixteenth century it was conquered by the Portuguese. In the early seventeenth century local Arabs revolted and appealed to Persia for help. Iran did help and then established its dominance over Bahrain for nearly 200 years. This explains the fact that the majority of Bahrainis (about 70 percent) are Shi'a Muslims, a greater percentage than in other countries of the Arab Peninsula. In 1783 the al-Khalifa family, a prominent clan from the central Arabian Peninsula, seized power and established its capital in Bahrain. In the nineteenth century Great Britain established its domination over Bahrain, making it one of its important trading outposts in the region. Since 1930, when major oil fields were discovered in Bahrain, the country has become one of the important exporters of oil to international markets. Through a series of negotiations with

Great Britain, the Bahrain authorities peacefully obtained independence on August 15, 1971. The Emir is the head of state, and a significant amount of power is concentrated in his hands. He nominates the Cabinet Ministers, has the right to dissolve the legislature (the monarch did dissolve the National Assembly in 1975) and appoints 40 members of the *Shura* (Council).

Bahrain is a multiethnic country. Representatives of several local Arab tribes, who are ethnically and linguistically close to the Arabs of the Arabian Peninsula, make up about 63 percent of the country's population. The minorities from South and Southeast Asia account for about 16 percent of the total population, the Arabs from other countries account for about 10 percent, and Iranians make up around 8 percent. Various other groups, including western Europeans and Americans, together make up the remaining 3 percent of the population. The current ethnic structure was formed between the 1970s and 1990s, when the government encouraged migration from various parts of the Middle East and various Asian countries, as employees were needed in the booming oil, petrochemical, and service sectors. The United States military base in Bahrain brought a significant community of non-Muslims. However, most of these people are not citizens and have no political rights. There have been significant tensions in Bahrain between the local population and minorities, mainly due to economic turmoil and high unemployment. It was, however, the tensions between the Sunni-dominated political elite and the Shi'a majority that brought significant political turmoil to the country in the 1980s and 1990s.

The Arab language is the official language of the country. However, many communities preserve their native languages, and their members speak Persian, Farsi, Urdu, and some other languages at the family and community levels. The English language is widely used in the business community, and very often it is used in the service (especially tourism), financial, and banking sectors. Bahrain was among the first states in the Arabian Peninsula to establish public education. It has a literacy rate of 98 percent.

In the late 1990s and early 2000s, Bahrain, like neighboring Iran and Saudi Arabia, saw a growing radicalization of various Islamic groups. Islam is the official religion of the country, and the majority of the population (97 percent) is of Muslim background. There is also a very small expatriate community of Christians. Their religious practice is generally tolerated. The radical Islamic groups did play a prominent role in the political unrest of the 1990s. However, the government kept tight control over political developments and of public debates in the country's mass media after the September 11, 2001, terrorist attacks on the United States and the beginning of the United States–led wars in Afghanistan and Iraq.

Bahrain's GDP per capita is relatively modest according to Middle Eastern standards (in purchasing power parity), standing at approximately $15,100 (2002). The unemployment rate, which stands between 15 and 17 percent, remains a major problem for the country. Bahrain relies largely on exports of its petroleum and petrochemical products, but in the 1970s and 1980s it significantly diversified its economy and developed its service sector, including banking, communications, finance, tourism, and light industries. Despite macroeconomic stability and success in structural changes, the economy proved to be vulnerable to external shocks due to the volatility of oil prices in the international market in the late 1990s and early 2000s. In 2003 the UNDP's Human Development Index (HDI) put Bahrain in thirty-seventh place, behind Argentina, Poland, and the Seychelles, but ahead of Hungary, Slovakia, and Uruguay.

RAFIS ABAZOV

See also **Muslims: Shi'a in Sunni Countries; Muslims: Sunni in Shi'a Countries**

Further Reading

Bahrain Monetary Agency, *Bahrain Dinar Digest*, Manama: Bahrain Monetary Agency, 2002

Boyd, Douglas A., *Broadcasting in the Arab World: A Survey of the Electronic Media in the Middle East*, 3rd edition, Ames: Iowa State University Press, 1999

Cordesman, Anthony H., *Bahrain, Oman, Qatar, and the UAE: Challenges of Security*, Boulder, Colorado: Westview Press, 1997

Lienhardt, Peter, *Shaikhdoms of Eastern Arabia*, New York: Palgrave, 2001

Looney, Robert E., *Industrial Development and Diversification of the Arabian Gulf Economies*, Greenwich, Connecticut: JAI Press, 1994

McCoy, Lisa, et al., *Bahrain (Modern Middle East Nations and Their Strategic Place in the World)*, Broomall, Pennsylvania: Mason Crest Publishers, 2003

Said Zahlan, Rosemarie, and Roger Owen, *The Making of the Modern Gulf States: Kuwait, Bahrain, Quatar, the United Arab Emirates and Oman*. Reading, England: Ithaca Press, 1998

Bai

Capsule Summary

Location: Western Yunnan, in southern China, mostly in the Bai Autonomous Zhou (District) of Dali, around Erhai Lake
Total Population: more than 1 million in Yunnan (1.1 million in 1984)
Language: Bai (several dialects)
Religion: Buddhist, Animist

The Bai (or Minjia) people are the second largest minority of Yunnan in southern China, after the Yi people. Like most people of Yunnan, their language is affiliated with the Tibeto-Burman group and remotely related to Chinese. Unlike the Yi minority, which is a heteroclite grouping of very different people (some Yi are in fact closer to the Hani, other are closer to the Lahu), the Bai form a coherent ethnic entity.

Although the Bai no longer play a major role in China and Southeast Asia, they were likely the leading ethnic group of the Nanzhao and the Dali kingdoms, although this opinion is not accepted by all scholars. Since the demise of the Dali kingdom due to the Mongol invasion, the Bai have not enjoyed political independence.

Origins

The affiliation of the Bai language with the Tibeto-Burman group has been contested by some scholars who consider Bai an "aberrant language" and argue that it should be classified in the Sinitic group of languages along with Chinese. Others have even argued it should be classified along with Thai or Hmong. Superficially, Bai lexicon and grammar are more similar to that of Chinese dialects than to other Tibeto-Burman languages. However, it can be rigorously demonstrated that these resemblances are due to a strong and continuous Chinese influence on Bai from the beginning of the Tang Dynasty (610–905) up to the present. Moreover, Bai is possibly related to the Lolo-Burmese branch of Tibeto-Burmese, as common vocabulary items unfound in other branches of Tibeto-Burmese suggest.

The Bai have tenaciously kept their language and resisted complete assimilation, but they could not historically hinder the flow of Chinese influence on their language and their culture. They are considerably more Sinitic (Chinese) than their Tibeto-Burman neighbors. This is most certainly due to the Bai role as elite in the Dali and Nanzhao states. Like the Vietnamese and Koreans, they borrowed Chinese script and modelled Chinese political organization. During the Dali Kingdom, Bai created a writing system based on Chinese characters that is comparable to the Vietnamese and Zhuang characters. These characters are no longer in use, but a few inscriptions from the fourteenth and fifteenth centuries remain and can be deciphered in Bai.

History

We have few texts in the Bai language, and sources are mostly texts written in Chinese by the Bai themselves as well as Chinese historical records. These data, however, are not easy to decipher because the ethnonyms were not used in a consistent way until the Ming dynasty (1368–1644). The Bai are generally identified as the "Bai barbarians" or "Bo people" of the Tang dynasty (618–907 CE), as the characters Bai and Bo (in Tang pronunciation: *Baek* and *Bwok*) might be two transcriptions of the same name. If this is the case, historians might trace the origins of the Bai to antiquity. The name Bo has been known since the third century BCE. It is first cited in the *Lushi Chunqiu* (*Spring and Autumn Annals of Master Lu Buwei*, circa 241 and 238 BCE), and then in Sima Qian's *Records of the Grand Historian of China* (begun in 104 BCE as a sweeping account of Chinese history). The Nanzhao Kingdom (649–902) was a confederation of six tribes that were united in 738 by Piluoge, who was probably a Bai. The Dali Kingdom (937–1253) was founded by Duan Siping (893–944), who was an ethnic Bai and whose family had played a role in the Nanzhao Kingdom. His dynasty lasted until the Mongol invasion by Emperor Mongke.

Society

Several religions are practiced among the Bai. The Bai worship the Benzhu lords, who are superficially similar to the local gods of Chinese popular religion. The

Benzhu, however, are not hierarchically organized, although they may be married and have children. Most Benzhu have a semi-mythical story explaining their origins. In general, they are the spirits of people who perished under special circumstances. The Bai call upon the Benzhu to fulfill wishes (health and wealth), and present them with animal sacrifices.

Buddhism is another important element of Bai culture. The variety of Buddhism that the Bai practice is specific to the group. The priests, known as Azhali (from Sanskrit *acaarya*, "teacher"), are married and transmit traditions and knowledge to their sons. Other married Buddhist practitioners are known in other parts of Asia; some bLama (respected spiritual teachers or gurus) of the rNyingmapa school (the oldest of Tibetan Buddhist sects), for instance, are allowed to marry and grow their hair. However, the Bai variety of Buddhism is totally unrelated to this school; it dates to the Nanzhao Kingdom.

Since the somber days of the Cultural Revolution (1966–1976), Chinese policy toward minorities in Yunnan has become milder and more tolerant. No active measures were taken to assimilate the Bai. However, Bai culture and language are still in danger of being lost as younger generations forget their roots and are absorbed into the Chinese majority.

Some minorities of Yunnan have taken active measures to protect their language. The best example is that of the Yi of Liangshan, who have published traditional texts, textbooks for children, and dictionaries in their language, have created a simplified version of the old Lolo ideographic writing system, and have initiated a bilingual system of education.

According to Chinese sources, Bai-Chinese bilingual education experiments have been attempted in Jianchuan (in the Yunnan province), but the education in Bai is limited to the first three classes. No book is known to have been published in the Bai language, although the Bai maintain a rich oral tradition. Most of Bai's local traditions, however, are still menaced, like the traditional Bai theater, *Chuichuiqiang*.

GUILLAUME JACQUES

See also **Buddhists; China**

Further Reading

Backus, Charles, *Nan-Chao Kingdom and Frontier Policy in Southwestern Frontier*, Cambridge University Press, 1981

Cai, Hua, *Une société sans père ni mari, les Na de Chine*, Paris: Presses universitaires de France, 1997

Dell, Francois, *La langue bai, phonologie et lexique*, Paris: Editions de l'École des hautes études en sciences sociales, 1981

Bakhtyari

Capsule Summary

Location: Western and central Iran
Total Population: approximately 880,000
Language: Bakhtiari subgroup of Iranian
Religion: Muslim

The Bakhtyari (ethnonyms: Bakhtiari, Baktiari, and Bakhtiyari) are a nomadic people indigenous to the rugged Bakhtiari Mountains, a segment of the Zagros Mountains (Lur-e Bozorg), west of Esfahan (Isfahan) and the foothills of the eastern Khuzistan Valley of west central Iran. Occupying an area of about 65,000 square kilometers (25,000 sq miles) consisting of plains and mountains, the vast majority of the Bakhtyari practice transhumant nomadism, that is, migrating with their and herds and flocks in an annual cycle from summer pasture in the high mountains to winter pasture in sheltered valleys and plains. Sheep, goats, cattle, and horses are the primary livestock that are moved from permanent or semi-permanent dwellings in the valleys to the summer mountain pasture where rectangular tents or impermanent brush and wood shelters are used for humans rather than livestock. These annual movements cover more than 150 miles in distance plus significant changes in elevation; they often require up to four weeks each way.

The population in 1980 was estimated at 650,000 but is now thought to number about 880,000—about

1.5 percent of Iran's population in 2000. The vast majority of the Bakhtyari are nomadic pastoralists, although a significant number (estimated at fewer than 50,000) have become sedentary agriculturalists who cultivate wheat and other cereal grains and raise livestock. The nomadic Bakhtiyari obtain agricultural products and goods they cannot themselves produce by bartering or trading with dependent villages. The discovery of oil in Khuzistan Province has resulted in the urbanization of some additional Bakhtiyari in larger villages and cities such as Esfahan after 1996. The largely symbolic Bakhtiari Confederation consists of peoples of diverse ethnic backgrounds including Arabs, Lurs, and Turkmen. A second major confederation, the Qashqai, includes nomadic and non-nomadic peoples in Khuzistan.

The Bakhtiyari speak the Luri dialect of Persian, and their oral and unwritten language belongs to the West Iranian subgroup of Indo-Iranian languages within the Indo-European language family. Many Bakhtiyari men also speak Farsi (Persian), the predominant language of Iran. Both the nomadic and sedentary Bakhtiyari are Shi'ite Muslims and adhere to daily prayers and fasting, among other rituals. Politically the Bakhtiyari were traditionally divided into two main tribal groups composed of multiple clans, the *Char* or *Charah Lang* and the *Haft Lang* ("Four Legs" and "Seven Legs," respectively). Each of these agglomerations of clans (*moieties*) is controlled by a single noble family, which has extensive hereditary political power and owns large herds, flocks, and agricultural lands. The Haft Lang holds the position of *ilkhani* (khan), or paramount leader, for two years, while the leader of the Char Lang serves as his *ilbeg,* or deputy. After two years, the positions are exchanged, with the Char Lang as *ilkhani* and the leader of the Haft Lang as his deputy. Every clan within the two Lang is headed by a *kalantar* who is subservient and loyal to the *ilikhan* and *ilbeg.* Each *kalantar* has substantial privately owned herds and flocks.

Bakhtiyari society is patriarchal, patrilineal, and patrilocal, with extended families as the norm. However, after the 1979 Islamic revolution the traditional ethnic structure and role of the *klantars* were supplanted by the introduction of strict Islamic fundamentalist *mullahs* (honorific title denoting protector or lord) on every tribal level. Bakhtiyari women traditionally enjoyed an unusual degree of freedom in a Muslim society, particularly because of their importance in the national economy as weavers pile carpets with bold patterns and colors, emphasizing yellow.

Bakhtiyari leaders have influenced Iranian politics for over a century and played a significant role in shaping modern Iran (known as Persia until 1935) during the Iranian revolution of 1905–1911. In 1909, led by Haft Lang ilkhani Sardar Asad, Bakhtiyari tribesmen helped the Constitutionalists dethrone Muhammad Ali (1907–1909) by capturing Tehran. Since then many Bakhtiyari have held major political offices in Tehran and have served as provincial governors. From 1921–1924 the Bakhtiyari attempted to create a confederation of southern peoples, but they were defeated by the central government and forced to abandon the effort. As a result, Bakhtiyari influence declined and they took no active part in the 1979 Islamic revolution and play a minor role in present-day Iranian politics.

CHARLES C. KOLB

See also **Iran**

Further Reading

Ember, Melvin, and Carol Ember, editors, *Countries and Their Cultures*, New York: Macmillan Reference, under the auspices of the Human Relations Area Files (Yale University), 2001

Encyclopedia Iranica, Vol. 5, Costa Mesa, California: Mazda, 1990

Famous Players-Lasky Corp., *Grass: A Nation's Battle for Life,* documentary motion picture, Famous Players-Lasky Corp., 1926

Gall, Timothy L., editor, *Worldmark Encyclopedia of Cultures and Daily Life, Volume 3: Asia and Oceania*, Detroit: Gale, 1998

Garthwaite, Gene R., *Khans and Shahs: A Documentary Analysis of the Bakhtiyari in Iran*, Cambridge and New York: Cambridge University Press, 1983

"Iran," in *The CIA World Factbook 2000*

Layard, Austen Henry, *Early Adventures in Persia, Susiana, and Babylonia, Including a Residence among the Bakhtiyari and Other Wild Tribes before the Discovery of Nineveh*, London: John Murray, 1894

Lorimer, David L.R., *The Phonology of the Bakhtiari, Badakshani, and Madaglashi Dialects of Modern Persian, with Vocabularies*, London: Royal Asiatic Society, 1922

Minority Rights Group, *World Directory of Minorities*, directed by Miles Litvinoff, London: Minority Rights Group International, 1997

Ross, Elizabeth Ness MacBean, *A Lady Doctor in Bakhtiari Land*, London: L. Parsons, 1921

Zagarell, Allen, "Regional and Social Borders in the Bakhtiari and Luristan Highlands of Iran," in *Polities and Partitions*, edited by K. Trinkaus, Archaeological Research Report 37, 1987

Balochi, *See* **Baluchis**

Baluchis

Capsule Summary

Location: Baluchistan, vast area west of Asia, lying among Pakistan, Iran, and Afghanistan
Total Population: approximately 4 million (3% of the total population in Pakistan and 2% of the total in Iran)
Languages: Urdu, Farsi, Baluchi, Brahoi
Religion: Sunni Muslim (Hanafi branch)

The Baluchis are ethnically nonhomogeneous. They came originally around the twelfth and thirteenth centuries CE, partly from the northeast of the Iranian plateau, and settled in present Baluchistan. Their language belongs to the Iranian group of Indo-European languages, but the modern form has incorporated elements from Persian, Sindhi, Arabic, and other languages. Baluchis, like most of south central Asian tribal groups, regard themselves as the descendants of a single mythical ancestor, who represents the valor and dignity of their tribal group and lineage. Pakistani Baluchistan, comprising 42 percent of the Baluchistan region, is composed of different ethnic groups, including the Pashtun (known also as Paktuns or Afghans), the Baluch, the Brahois, and the Hindus. The Baluchis represent 3 percent of the total population in Pakistan and 2 percent of the total in Iran.

History

Baluchistan, the land of the Baluch, lies in a central position, at the crossroads of two axes of three macro regions: Asia, Africa, and the Mediterranean Basin. Baluchistan is an extremely inhospitable land, arid and mountainous, with a predominantly nomadic population divided between Pakistan and Iran. Those Baluchis who settled in the northern regions of Baluchistan were characterized by a strong segmentary tribal structure, while those living in the oases with irrigated agriculture developed a socially stratified feudal model. The tribal structure is much looser among the Baluchis than in other tribes of northern central Asia.

Although the Baluchis represent the largest ethnic group, there is a Brahoi minority in the Kalat area, (the Djats), and other Indian elements on the eastern coast, such as the Gichkis, and descendants from African slaves in the Makran coastal region, where the religious sect of the Zikris is concentrated.

Historical sources referring to the strategic position of Baluchistan between the Middle East and India date to the march of Alexander the Great in 325 BCE. The Sassanian dynasty ruled in Baluchistan apparently from the fifth century CE onward. Around 635 to 636 CE, the Brahman dynasty from Sind took power in Baluchistan and determined the boundaries of its possessions. Consequently, soon after the death of the prophet Muhammad, when the Arab invasion took place, Baluchistan must have been in possession of Sind. After the seventh century, Baluchistan fell under the control of a succession of Arab chiefs.

This situation of political external, and essentially nominal, control continued until the birth of the Khanate of Kalat, the kingdom of Kalat located in the northeastern part of Baluchistan. This new political entity was believed to have originated in 1666 CE and marked the beginning of the reign of Mir Ahmad Khan, chief of the Ahmadzai, a tribal section of the Brahoi ethnic group. Exploiting the political vacuum created by the lack of political control over the whole territory, the Brahoi confederation expanded in Makran. At the end of their expansion, Nadir Shah of Persia (1722–47) recognized the Brahoi Ahmadzai as legitimized chiefs and presented them lands in Sind. During the eighteenth century the Khans of Kalat shifted their loyalty, including troops and taxes, from the Persian Shah to the Durrani chiefs of Afghanistan. However, in 1758 Nasir I Khan of Kalat proclaimed his independence from the Afghani rulers. When Nasir I Khan died in 1795, his son, Mahmud Khan, was not able to maintain his father's dominions, and the Khanate fell into a period of political decadence and territorial disruption.

The Baluchis from the coastal regions, a tough people skilled in the use of weaponry and adaptable to climate change and varying environmental conditions, were pushed from the extreme misery of their country toward Persia and toward the coasts of Arabia in search of better life conditions and job opportunities among the local Arab potentates. They offered themselves to the Arab tribes of Oman as soldiers, sailors, palm date cultivators, and bodyguards for pay.

Until the first British explorations around the eighteenth century, Baluchistan was considered as a blank area or *terra incognita* to Westerners, that is, an unknown and empty land on British maps of the epoch. During the eighteenth and nineteenth centuries, the Baluchis were known to the British in India as ferocious freebooters, and they protected and hid the Al Bu Sa'idi dynasty of Oman in their desolate lands. They were mainly employed on the ships of Muscat, one of the main trading ports of Oman, and today the capital of the Sultanate of Oman, or sent on military expeditions into the Omani deserts. It is interesting noting that the Baluchis served not only the Al Bu Sa'idi, but also preceding dynasties of Oman, such as the Ya'rubi, during the sixteenth and seventeenth centuries. Nevertheless, during the first half of the nineteenth century, the permanent bodyguard of the Sultans of Oman was composed of Baluchis; they ignored the political struggles within the Arabian Peninsula, and they naturally obeyed the orders of the Arab princes who paid them. Due to the Arab-Omani expansion along the East African littorals, many Baluchis settled on Zanzibar island, the heart of the Omani African dominions during the nineteenth century, and in many African port towns, where they were called, and are called today, *bulushi* in Kiswahili.

With regard to the history of the northern regions of Baluchistan, during the first Anglo-Afghan war (1838–1842 CE), the strategic position of the Khanate of Kalat along the road toward Afghanistan included local tribal struggles in the British defense policy of the northwest frontiers of British India. The town of Quetta in the northern part of Baluchistan, close to the Afghani border, became a military center administered by the British. The reason for the occupation of Quetta by British forces was the course of military operations during the first Anglo-Afghan war. In 1840 Shah Nawaz Khan of Kalat, faithful to the English authorities, was deposed from the throne, which passed to Nasir Khan II, while the occupation of Kabul continued against increasing opposition and attacks by the local Pashtun tribes. This ended in the disastrous retreat by the British *Army of the Indus*, and the abandoning of Quetta in 1840 CE. Beginning in 1872 CE, borders between Baluchistan, Persia, and Sistan were defined by British representatives, with no attention given to local tribal needs or realities. This artificial intervention produced a long period of tribal revolts, attacks, and plundering (*chupao*). Among the Baluchi tribes there had traditionally been looting and fighting as they remained deeply reluctant to any exercise of power, especially under the form of a centralized state government. In fact, from 1840 to 1876 CE, Quetta was under the dominion of the Khanate of Kalat. The year 1876 CE marked the second British occupation of the city by the escort of Sir Robert Sandeman.

Disorders and revolts had continued until Captain Sandeman, agent to the governor-general in Baluchistan, intervened in 1876 with a treaty with the Khan of Kalat, which gave to the Khanate of Kalat in Baluchistan the status of protected state within the Indian Empire.

Since the treaty of Gandamak, May 26, 1879 CE, between Sandeman and the Khanate of Kalat, many provinces of Baluchistan were officially registered under the Government of British India. Under this administration, which lasted until the independence of India in 1947, the permanent fights for power between the Khans and the local *sardars* (governors-representatives) seriously threatened the application of British indirect rule in Baluchistan. Only at the beginning of the 1940s did Muhammad Ali Jinnah's idea of Pakistan and the succeeding creation of Pakistan make Baluchistan a federal region. Although Quetta remained under the strict control of the British Empire following World War II, the Muslim League of Ali Jinnah, the *Father of Pakistan*, (who sustained its independence from British Baluchistan) and the English political agents differed in their interpretations of the region's administrative status. With the Transfer of Power Act of the August 2, 1947 the government of Pakistan made an agreement with the Khanate of Kalat, which officially became part of the new Pakistani state. Quetta became the administrative capital of Baluchistan in 1948. Baluch nationalism emerged as a strong movement that imagined a state independent from British India, but most of all from the newborn Pakistan of Ali Jinnah, and deeply influenced the political events in Baluchistan. Until the 1970s, Baluchistan did not acquire a constitutional status as did the other Pakistani provinces: Sind, Punjab, Bengal, Northwest Frontier Province. The civil war in 1973 between

Baluchi rebels and the federal army lasted until 1977. The succeeding rule by Zia ul-Haq greatly reduced the political desires for autonomy of the Baluchistan province as a whole. It was the end of the Baluchis' dreams. Benazir Bhutto and Nawaz Sharif gave money and power to the Punjabi ethnic groups, offering space for corruption and drug smuggling from Afghanistan through Baluchistan.

Society

The social organization of the Baluchis is differs greatly from group to group. The importance of a common ancestor within each tribal lineage is one of the chief social features of the Baluchis; in the north, patronymic groups are much stronger than in the southern Makran region. Ethnically, Baluchis lack homogeneity, having intermingled with other ethnic groups: Sindi and Afghan influence the society, for example, in the north, and African slave descendants have influenced it in the southern Makran on the coast. Nevertheless, a gradual process of social absorption gave life to a Baluchi identity that began with the British presence in India. The myth of Baluchi nationalism ended around the 1970s, mainly due to breaks in local tribal alliances and to the destabilizing presence of Afghan refugees at the northern borders of the Baluchistan region. The lack of social homogeneity, combined with the diminishing percentage of Baluchis in Baluchistan, contributed to the social and political instability of the entire region and to the end of its *mythomoteur,* which represented its sociological "red string," and today gives place only to nostalgic memories of a glorious past and to widespread corruption throughout the region.

BEATRICE NICOLINI

See also **Afghanistan, Hindus, Pashtuns (Pathans)**

Further Reading

Dames, M. Longworth, *The Baloch Race. A Historical and Ethnological Sketch*, London: The Royal Asiatic Society, 1904

Frye, R.N., "Baluchistan (Balochistan)," *Encyclopaedia of Islam*, CD-ROM Edition, Leiden: Brill, 1999

Nicolini, B., and R. Redaelli, *Quetta: History and Archives. Note on a Survey of the Archives of Quetta*, Nuova Rivista Storica Fasc. II, 1994

Redaelli, R., *The Father's Bow. The Khanate of Kalat and British India (19th–20th Century),* Florence: Manent, 1997

Piacentini Fiorani, V., and R. Redaelli, editors, *Baluchistan: Terra Incognita. A New Methodological Approach Combining Archaeological, Historical, Anthropological and Architectural Studies*, B.A.R. International Series 1141, Oxford: Archaeopress, 2003

Titus, P., editor, *Marginality and Modernity: Ethnicity and Change in Post-Colonial Baluchistan*, Karachi: Oxford University Press, 1996

Bangladesh

Capsule Summary

Location: South Asia
Total Population: 138,448,210 (July 2003)
Language: Bangla (official), English
Religions: Muslim (88.3%), Hindu (10.5%), others (including Buddhist and Christian) (1.2%)

Bangladesh (formerly East Pakistan) is located in South Asia where it borders India to the west, north, and east, and Burma to the east. The southern part of Bangladesh opens to the Bay of Bengal. The capital city is Dhaka, with an estimated population of 8.58 million. Bangladesh is a young nation that gained independence from Pakistan in December 1971. After World War II, it was a part of India under British colonial rule (known as Bengal, comprised of West Bengal, India, and Bangladesh). The separation in 1947 of British India into the Muslim state of Pakistan (with two sections, West and East) and largely Hindu India was never satisfactorily resolved. A third war between these countries in 1971 resulted in East Pakistan seceding and becoming the separate nation of Bangladesh.

Post-independence Bangladesh has faced a number of grave problems, such as overpopulation, economic woes, political upheavals, and natural calamities, which the government has been unable to successfully resolve. This young and fragile country is now one of the poorest nations in the world, with 35.6 percent of the population living below poverty level (1995–1996). It has only four metropolitan cities and 119 municipalities; thus, the level of urbanization is low at 20 percent, leaving 80 percent of the country's total population to live in rural areas which depend primarily on a poorly developed agriculture for livelihood. Unemployment rates (including underemployment) were estimated at 40 percent in 2002. However, Bangladesh is frequently noted for the extraordinary ethnic and cultural homogeneity of its population. Ethnic and religious minority groups with distinct cultures and traditions add social texture to the entire community of Bangladesh.

Politics and Economy

Bangladesh maintains a presidential government. Its popularly elected president functions as chief of state, although this is often merely a ceremonial position, and an appointed prime minister is the recognized leader. The political system is structured based on the country's 1972 Constitution, which has been amended several times in recent decades. There is also a unicameral parliament known as *Jatiyo Sangsad*, or the House of the People, with 330 seats. Most members are popularly elected, and 30 seats are reserved for women. Authoritarian and military regimes have run Bangladesh almost since its self-rule began in 1971. Current major political parties include the Bangladesh Nationalist Party, the Awami League (People's League), and the Jatiya Party (National Party). More than a few opposition parties exist and periodically form fractious alliances against the party in power.

Bangladesh's GDP was an estimated $238.2 billion in 2002 with a per capita income of $1,800 (2002). The country relies heavily on foreign economic assistance. Bangladesh is an agriculture-based economy with over 60 percent of the entire workforce engaged in some type of agriculture. Bangladesh is the world's largest producer of jute. Other major agricultural products include rice, tea, sugarcane, tobacco, and wheat. Fishing is an important industry as well. Bangladesh also produces beef, dairy products, and poultry. However, about a third of the country floods each year during the monsoon season, hampering economic development.

Society

More than 98 percent of Bangladeshis are Bengalis, and the remainder of the population are Biharis and indigenous tribal peoples. The single major minority group of Bangladeshis, the Biharis, are Urdu-speaking, non-Bengali Muslims. They were originally refugees from Bihar (India's province to the west of Bangladesh) and other parts of northern India. Before Bangladesh's independence, Biharis dominated the upper levels of Bengali society. At the time of the autonomy movement they remained loyal to Pakistan. Hundreds of thousands of Biharis were repatriated to Pakistan after the end of the war between two wings of Pakistan in 1971. Today their numbers are decreasing.

Bangladesh's tribal population is just above 1 percent of the total national population. They mainly live on the Chittagong Hills in southeast and in the regions of Mymensingh, Sylhet, and Rajshahi. The majority of the indigenous population resides in rural areas where many practice shifting cultivation. Most of these tribes are of Sino-Tibetan descent with distinctive Mongoloid physical features, and they speak Tibeto-Burman languages. Their lifestyle differs in social organization, marriage customs, birth and death rituals, food, and other cultural and social customs from other Bangladeshis. They practice Hinduism, Buddhism, Christianity, and other religions.

The four largest tribes in Bangladesh are the Chakmas, Marmas (or Maghs), Tipperas (or Tipras), and Mros (or Moorangs). The most sizable among those groups, the Chakmas, are of mixed origin, although they are culturally closer to Bengalis than any other tribe. The Chakmas as well as the Marmas primarily live in the highland valleys. Most Chakmas are Buddhists, with minorities being Hindus and atheists. The Marmas are of Burmese ancestry, and Burma largely influences their cultural life. Nearly all of the Marmas are Buddhists, while a few others believe in Islam. The Tipperas live in the Chittagong Hills. The northern Tipperas are influenced by Bengali culture. Almost all of them are Hindus. Finally, the Mros, who are considered the original inhabitants of the Chittagong Hills, inhabit the hilltops today. They traditionally have had no written form of their language, although some Mros read and write Burmese and Bangla. Most of them regard themselves as Buddhists, but their religious practices often lack Buddhist characteristics.

Bangladesh's official language is Bangla, which is also sometimes called Bengali. Bangladeshis identify themselves closely with this language. English, a legacy of the colonial period, is still used in urban centers. There are also Bangladeshis who speak Arabic, Persian, and Turkic languages.

Nearly 89 percent of the population is Muslim, which ranks the country as the third largest Islamic population worldwide, following Indonesia and Pakistan. Sunni Islam is dominant among Bangladeshis, although beliefs and practices in rural areas differ to some degree. Yet, there has been no physical strife among different sects. The Eighth Amendment to the 1972 Constitution (promulgated in June 1988) recognizes Islam as the state religion. Hindus are the largest religious minority at 10.5 percent, and other minorities include Buddhists and Christians.

Bangladeshi society holds one of the highest population densities in the world today (about 2,100 people per square mile, or 810 people per square kilometer). The pace of urbanization has been slow for the past three decades and over 80 percent of its population resides in the countryside. Bangladesh remains one of the most rural nations in the Third World. The country suffers from serious problems like malnutrition and poor sanitation, which result in high mortality rates from a variety of diseases. Furthermore, frequent natural disasters, such as coastal cyclones and floods, have tormented Bangladeshis over the years. The national government, with international assistance, continues to tackle those problems in an attempt to reduce unnecessary human losses.

History

The pre-independence history of Bangladesh is intimately related to that of Bengal, which became independent of Delhi in 1341. After several Muslim leaders ruled the territory, the great Mughal Emperor Akbar conquered Bengal in 1576. By the early eighteenth century, Bengal faced British penetration, and in 1775 the British East India Company acquired full control there, as well as in West Bengal, Orissa, and Bihar.

The British divided Bengal into West Bengal and East Bengal in 1905, and this division was maintained until 1911. During the British colonial period, East Bengal was dominated by British leaders and Hindu elites. Hindus controlled a majority of all rural assets, urban real estate, and government and finance-related occupations in East Bengal. In 1947, British India was partitioned into India and Pakistan marking the creation of the latter nation. Pakistan at this time had two wings, one to the west and the other to the east of India. Following this partition, Hindus in East Bengal left the region and Muslims quickly moved in, taking up vacated positions and occupations. The eastern portion consisted of the eastern section of Bengal and the former Sylhet district of Assam; it was called East Bengal until 1955 and East Pakistan later on. The other half of Pakistan in the west was not only over 1,000 miles (1,600 kilometers) from the east wing but also largely different in terms of its history, economy, social system, and geography.

Approximately 56 percent of all Pakistanis lived in the eastern province, and they soon grew discontent over political and economic policies, such as unfair allocation of government investments and funds administered by a national government located in West Pakistan. The result was a riot that broke out in 1968 and 1969, paving the way toward greater autonomy and then eventually to national independence of Bangladesh from Pakistan.

In the general elections held in December 1970, the Awami League, under the trusted leadership of Sheikh Mujibur Rahman (generally known as Sheikh Mujib and also affectionately called the *Bangabandhu*, the "Beloved of Bangladesh"), won all the seats in East Pakistan and thus gained a majority in the Pakistan National Assembly. In response to this unwelcome event, President Muhammad Agha Yahya Khan, who had hoped to prevent political confrontation between East and West Pakistanis, postponed the opening session of the assembly twice.

The clear message sent to East Pakistanis was that the national government, liberally in the hands of West Pakistanis, was seeking to forestall autonomy in the east. Consequently, a series of general strikes and nonpayment of taxes occurred in the east. Civil war broke out on March 25, 1971. The Awami League proclaimed the independence of Bangladesh the next day. During the next months, one million Bengalis are believed to have lost their lives in fighting in the east, and an additional ten million fled to India. On December 6, 1971 India allied with Bangladesh and helped defeat the Pakistani forces in a two-week war from December 3 to December 16. Although the territory of Bangladesh is considerably smaller than that of Pakistan, national independence was thus achieved by the hands of the Bangladeshi people at the cost of tens of thousands of human lives. Sheikh Mujib had been selected president while in prison in West Pakistan. After his release in January 1972, he founded a Bangladesh government and became its first premier. Abu Sayeed Choudhury was chosen as the country's first president.

Bangladesh's relationship with Pakistan remained hostile at the beginning, but tensions had already eased in July 1972, when Pakistan's President Zulfikar Ali

Bhutto and India's Prime Minister Indira Gandhi reached a peaceful settlement. Pakistan officially recognized Bangladesh in February 1974. Bangladesh had earned international acknowledgment by joining the Commonwealth of Nations in 1972 and the United Nations in 1974.

Sheikh Mujib's regime did not last long despite his initial mass support and popularity as the nation's founder. Amid devastating economic and social conditions including high inflation rates and a severe famine, he (as well as most of his family) was assassinated in a military coup in 1975. The young nation was soon to be under the control of Major General Zia ur-Rahman, and for the next two decades a military regime was in power. Zia was killed in a failed coup attempt in 1981 and replaced by Lieutenant General Hussain Mohammad Ershad of the Jatiya Party the following year.

In 1990, Ershad was forced to resign and then jailed because of political corruption. Next to lead the nation was Zia ur-Rahman's widow, Khaleda Zia, from the Bangladesh Nationalist Party. She became prime minister in February 1991, but by 1994 her regime was denounced as corrupt by nearly all the opposition. She resigned in 1996, and following an interim government led by Habibur Rahman, Awami League's Hashina Wazad, a daughter of the nation's memorable first prime minister, came into power.

Bangladesh presently is still a weak nation in a political and economic sense. It continues to face political instability and has yet to sustain steady economic development, manage natural disasters, and improve social conditions. Its impoverished population is often frustrated due to broken political promises and expectations. Yet, even in the midst of persistent social difficulties, Bangladesh remains culturally rich with its unique dynamism of ethnicity, religion, and history.

AI HATTORI

See also **Pakistan**

Further Reading

Baxter, Craig, *Bangladesh: From a Nation to a State,* Boulder, Colorado: Westview Press, 1997

Hashimi, Taj I., *Women and Islam in Bangladesh: Beyond Subjection and Tyranny*, Houndmills (England): Macmillan Press, and New York: St. Martin's Press, 2000

Jahan, Rounaq, editor, *Bangladesh: Promise and Performance*, London and Dhaka: University Press Ltd., 2001

Novak, James J., *Bangladesh: Reflection on the Water*, Bloomington: Indiana University Press, 1993

Sillitoe, Paul, *Indigenous Knowledge Development in Bangladesh: Present and Future*, London: Intermediate Technology, 2000

Sisson, Richard, *War and Secession: Pakistan, India, and the Creation of Bangladesh*, Berkeley: University of California Press, 1990

Bantu

Capsule Summary

Location: Africa, south of a line from the southern Nigeria-Cameroon border to southern Somalia in the east
Total Population: approximately 150 million
Language: Bantu is the largest group of related languages in sub-Saharan Africa (around 600 languages). The most important single one is Swahili as a primary or secondary language (50 million speakers). Bantu groups with more than 1 million members each are the Bemba, Fang, Ganda, Kituba, Lingala, Luba, Nyanja-Chewa, Shona, Sukuma, Umbundu, and Zulu
Religions: Muslim, Christian, traditional African religions

"Bantu" is first and foremost a label invented in the nineteenth century by W.H.I. Bleek, a German linguist, as a term to describe a large group of related languages. The label was formed from the plural of the most common root, *-ntu,* meaning "person" in certain Bantu languages.

Only some of the Bantu cultures and languages have as yet been adequately described. Bantu comprises the largest language family in sub-Saharan Africa, with an estimated 600 languages sharing common linguistic features in their basic vocabulary and grammar. However, they are most often not mutually intelligible, especially when widely separated geographically.

Bantu languages are spoken by over 150 million Africans in an area stretching from the southern Nigeria-Cameroon border in the west to southern Somalia in the east, and extending to South Africa. Many Bantu languages are spoken only by several thousand speakers each, while approximately 50 have over 100,000 speakers each, and over a dozen languages are spoken by over 1 million native speakers. Moreover, some of the latter are used as trade and/or governmental languages in their respective regions, meaning that many speak such languages as a second language.

The largest and most important language in this category is Swahili, spoken by over 50 million people in East Africa as a first or second language. Other languages partly used in school and as national languages are Bemba (Zambia), Fang (Cameroon, Gabon), Ganda (Uganda), Kituba (Congo), Lingala (Congo, Uganda), Luba (Congo), Nyanja-Chewa (Malawi), Shona (Zimbabwe, Mozambique), Sotho (South Africa), Umbundu (Angola), and Zulu (South Africa).

There is no common Bantu culture; the separate cultures may often be similar, but immense variations predominate, such as in their social organization, ranging from the elaborate kingdoms of the Interlacustrine Bantu of Uganda and the Zulu in South Africa to the politically uncentralized peoples of most of the east African savannah. There has never been any shared ethnic consciousness leading to a common identity or "Bantu-ness." Most cultures are based on patrilineal descent, but some, like the Yao in Malawi, are based on matrilineal descent. The traditional economy of Bantu cultures is either mainly pastoralism, or sedentary agriculture, or a combination of agriculture, hunting and gathering, or fishing and river trade.

The origin of the Bantu people is one of the unsolved problems of African historical studies. Traditionally scholars believed that a single ancestor language, whose speakers originated in the southern border region of today's Nigeria and Cameroon, migrated in several waves into their modern homelands a thousand or so years ago. This monogenetic hypothesis is no longer tenable in the light of more recent linguistic findings that indicate today's Bantu cultures are mainly a synthesis of differing origins and contacts with non-Bantu peoples.

It is generally agreed that the roughly one-third of the continent of Africa today occupied by Bantu-speaking peoples was occupied by other groups until approximately 2,000 years ago, mainly Pygmies and Khoisan (Bushmen). However, these soon became minorities within their own regions and were mostly absorbed by the Bantu majority, leaving only traditions surviving locally today. Exceptions to this are Khoisan remnant peoples like the Sandawe and Hadza in Tanzania, while larger Khoisan populations can be found in Namibia and Botswana.

The Bantu form the majority population in most of the countries they are living in today. This does not, however, apply to countries at the northern fringes of the Bantu settlement area, such as Kenya, Uganda, and Cameroon, where they form just one of several distinct larger groups, while they constitute small minorities in Somalia, the Central African Republic, and Nigeria.

In Kenya, the Bantu live mainly in the Highlands and are surrounded by Nilotic peoples to the west (such as the Samburu and Nandi), and by Cushitic peoples to the east (such as the Orma and Somali). Other Bantu live on the coast, among them the Swahili and Mijikenda. Since the Bantu are mainly farmers, while the non-Bantu groups are often pastoralists, though confined to relatively small areas of land the Bantu still form the larger part of the Kenyan population. In Uganda, non-Bantu groups like the Nilotic Acholi and Teso predominate, especially in the north, while the Bantu farmers inhabit the southern half of Uganda. In contact areas in both Kenya and Uganda, latent tension is often present between Bantu farmers and non-Bantu pastoralists competing for fertile grounds.

Cameroon is the home of 286 distinctive African languages. Bantu-speaking peoples (such as the Douala and the Fang) predominate only along the southern coast and in the forested areas. They form 35 to 40 percent of the total population and are of Christian or traditional beliefs. Groups who are subsumed under the label "Semi-Bantu" or "Grassland-Bantu" speak languages that resemble genuine Bantu languages only in certain features. They inhabit the western border and the central mountain region, not having cultural ties to the Bantu of the south.

In Somalia, the so-called Gosha live among a Somali majority in the lower Jubba valley. Amounting today to around 85,000 people, the Gosha are the descendants of Bantu slaves who had been imported by the Somali between 1800 and 1890 from regions further south. Although they are now Muslims, the Somali still despise them because of their farming existence and their origins in slavery. Apart from these, there is a small Swahili enclave on the southern Somali coast at Brava.

In the Central African Republic, the Bantu form a small minority, mainly settled around the border with the Congo (Brazzaville). Out of 69 languages in that region, only 12 are Bantu, of which none has more than 10,000 speakers each. Several may be extinct now, among them Aka, spoken by Pygmy groups of Mongoumba and Lobaye.

Southeastern Nigeria is the home of several peoples speaking Semi-Bantu languages, of which the largest group are the Tiv with 2.2 million members, although it is small compared with the dominant Yoruba, Igbo and Hausa.

In none of the countries discussed are the Bantu populations persecuted by governments or rival groups simply because of their language and culture.

REINHARD KLEIN-ARENDT

See also **Cameroon; Kenya; Nigeria; Somalia; Uganda**

Further Reading

Bryant, Alfred T., *Bantu Origins: The People and Their Language,* Cape Town: Struik, 1963

Hammond-Tooke, W. David, editor, *The Bantu-Speaking Peoples of Southern Africa,* London: Kegan Paul, and Boston: Routledge, 1974

Kuper, Adam, and Pierre van Leynseele, "Social Anthropology and the 'Bantu Expansion,'" *Africa,* 48, no.4 (1978)

Möhlig, Wilhelm J.G., "Stratification in the History of the Bantu Languages," *Sprache und Geschichte in Afrika,* 3 (1981)

Obenga, Théophile H., *Les Bantu. Langues-Peuples-Civilisations,* Paris and Dakar: Présence Africaine, 1985

Barbados

Capsule Summary

Location: Caribbean, island in the North Atlantic Ocean, northeast of Venezuela
Total Population: 280,000 (2004)
Minority Populations: English; Creole
Languages: Bajan; English
Religions: Protestant (67% [Anglican 40%, Pentecostal 8%, Methodist 7%, other 12%]), Roman Catholic (4%), none (17%), other (12%, including Moravian)

The island of Barbados lies 300 miles northeast of Venezuela. It is the easternmost island of the Lesser Antilles. The landscape is marked by layered plains, hills, and mountains, which rise to over a thousand feet in the central part of the island. The island's total size is slightly more than half the area of New York City. The island has ample rainfall, and its tropical climate is tempered by regular tradewinds.

The history of Barbados is essentially that of a plantation society colonized by the English at the beginning of the seventeenth century, producing an export crop that was the product of African slave labor. The name "Barbados" derives from a Portuguese word for "bearded." Portuguese sailors visited the island on their route to Brazil. The name refers to the hanging plants on trees, which are reminiscent of men's beards.

Before the English, the Spanish briefly settled the island, although they eventually abandoned it for larger ones in the Caribbean. An indigenous population occupied the island (Arawak and later Carib) but was decimated by the conquest and diseases of foreign invaders. No indigenous population or language survives on Barbados.

The most profitable export crop the island cultivated after English settlement was sugar. The plantation labor needed to produce it was provided by African slaves. The soil, terrain, and climate were so favorable to sugar production that, by the beginning of the nineteenth century, Barbados had the largest slave population of any island in the Lesser Antilles. The island still has the highest population density in the region. Approximately 90 percent of the population is black, whereas the remainder is divided between white and mixed race mulatto.

Barbados received its independence from Britain in 1966, becoming a member of the organization then known as the British Commonwealth of Nations. Barbadians inherited from Britain a strict sense of class consciousness. Blacks make up the middle and lower classes. High rates of literacy and ample educational opportunities have enhanced competition to rise socially. Nonetheless, the white minority still dominates the business and political affairs of the country. There is a small group of poor whites, descended from indentured servants in the colonial period, who are referred to as "redlegs" and have survived based on subsistence farming and fishing.

An integral part of Barbadian culture remains the tradition of the Anglican (Church of England) religion.

More than a third of the population belongs to this church. It has played a crucial and historic role in developing education on the island from earliest colonial times. Barbados has one of the highest rates of literacy in the Caribbean or, indeed, Latin America. This asset has been a crucial contribution to social ambitions and economic development. Other Protestant religions include the Methodists and Pentecostals, comprising together about a sixth of the population. Another ten percent belongs to a miscellany of Protestant sects. About four percent of the population is Roman Catholic. There is also a small remnant of the Rastifarian sect that originated in Jamaica in the mid-twentieth century.

Barbadians refer to themselves and their culture as "Bajan." This word also describes the dialect of English that Barbadians use. Both standard and Bajan English are interchangeably spoken by the population. Only the former, however, is the official language of the country.

Bajans are a minority population in many countries. The population growth of Barbados is under half of one percent annually, but historically it has had a high birth rate and ever-decreasing mortality rate. Consequently, for more than a century, the island has been unable to provide jobs for its entire population. More than 100,000 Bajans have emigrated from Barbados over the course of the twentieth century.

The Bajans formed the largest group of West Indians who worked on the Panama Canal, and their descendants form part of a Creole colony in the eastern part of Panama. They also emigrated to British Guyana and Cuba. Even greater numbers have emigrated to Great Britain and Canada. At the close of the twentieth century, an estimated 20,000 were living in Canada, primarily in Toronto. In the last half of the century, however, the largest wave of Bajans immigrated to the United States, settling primarily in New York and Florida. More than 50,000 lived in New York City by the year 2000.

The foreign exchange remittances of these emigrants have been an important contribution to the relative prosperity of the island. Barbados had a GDP per capita income of $15,000 in 2002. Historically, the Barbadian economy had relied on sugarcane cultivation, but production in recent years has diversified into manufacturing and tourism.

The terrain of Barbados recalls for many the countryside of England, and the island has often been described as a "Little England." Throughout the Commonwealth, Barbados is known for its star cricket players. However, over the last two generations British cultural sway has diminished, and American influence has steadily risen. American hotel chains, cruise ships, and leisure enterprises dominate the tourism that is such an integral part of the Barbadian economy.

Edward A. Riedinger

See also **Rastafari**

Further Reading

Beckles, Hilary, *A History of Barbados: From Amerindian Settlement to Nation-State*, Cambridge, England: Cambridge University Press, 1990

———, "Independence and the Social Crisis of Nationalism in Barbados," in *Caribbean Freedom: Economy and Society from Emancipation to the Present: A Student Reader*, Princeton, New Jersey: M. Wiener, 1996

Chamberlain, Mary, *Narratives of Exile and Return*, New York: St. Martin's Press, 1997

Gmelch, George, *Double Passage: The Lives of Caribbean Migrants Abroad and Back Home*, Ann Arbor, Michigan: University of Michigan Press, 1992

Gmelch, George, and Sharon Bohn Gmelch, *The Parish behind God's Back: The Changing Culture of Rural Barbados*, Ann Arbor, Michigan: University of Michigan Press, 1997

Greenfield, Sidney M., *English Rustics in Black Skin: A Study of Modern Family Forms in a Pre-industrialized Society*, New Haven, Connecticut: College and University Press, 1966

Howe, Glenford D., and Don D. Marshall, editors, *The Empowering Impulse: The Nationalist Tradition of Barbados*, Barbados: Canoe Press, 2001

Meditz, Sandra W., and Dennis M. Hanratty, editors, "Barbados," in *Islands of the Commonwealth Caribbean, A Regional Study*, Washington, DC: Federal Research Division, Library of Congress, 1989

Potter, Robert B., and Graham M. S. Dann, compilers, *Barbados*, World Bibliographical Series, 76, Oxford, England: Clio Press, 1987

Bariba

Capsule Summary

Location: Northern Benin and adjacent areas of southwestern Nigeria
Total Population: approximately 600,000
Language: Bariba (or Batonum)
Religions: Muslim, Animist, and Christian

The Bariba are an ethnic community inhabiting the Borgu region (North of Benin) and the neighboring areas of Nigeria (Districts of Yashikera, Okuta, Ilesha, and Gwanara). There are approximately 600,000 Bariba, 500,000 of whom live in the territory of Benin. Their language, called Batonum, belongs to the Gur or Voltaic family, geographically centered in Burkina Faso. Moreover, Boko and Mokole speakers are commonly included in the Bariba ethnic group that, better than a homogeneous community, constitutes a complex whole. In this Bariba social structure are also included the Wasangari, formerly a warrior aristocracy of different origins, and the commoners, mainly descendants of Baatombu-speaking peoples. Fulani and Gando ethnic groups also form an integral part of the Bariba society, but remain clearly differentiated due to cultural, economic, and linguistic cleavages.

History

The Bariba people are descendants of different population movements coming, at an undetermined time, from the Voltaic area (in present-day Burkina Faso), but also from the East of the actual Borgu region. Wasangari warriors imposed themselves on the Bariba area progressively from the fourteenth to the eighteenth centuries. In the middle of the nineteenth century, Bussa, Nikki, and Ilo were the most important states ruled by the Wasangari group, but the increasing importance of commercial flows, linked to the strategic position of the Bariba country, caused a drastic shift in the regional political situation.

The former vassal states, because of increasing revenue from the trade route passing through their territories, rebelled and declared their independence. During colonial rule, the arbitrariness of the new administrative borders created a separatist agitation among Nigerian Bariba in the beginning of the twentieth century. Some of these protests were in the form of emigration to Borgu territory under French administration. From the 1950s, the increasing agitation by the Bariba for separation and the declining economic fortune forced the creation of an autonomous Bariba colonial administration in Nigeria. In the Benin part of the Bariba region, there is an increase in ethnic pride reinforced by the artificial nature of the postcolonial African states' boundaries.

Ethnic Structure and Society

The Bariba ethnic community includes a social layer of traditional rulers and warlords called Wasangari, who are perceived as immigrant conquerors. The Wasangari obtained political power while the indigenous chiefs were concerned with religious and symbolic systems, developing a linking function between the newcomers and local divinities. The group of commoners, who are cultivators and hunters, is composed primarily of Baatombu of the lower social category, who came as migrating hunters from the east. It also includes a small number of Mokole of Yoruba origin, as well as Tienga and Boko, both of whom speak Manding languages. Fulani and Gando (descendants of former slaves and war captives) settled in nearby encampments. Autochthones Bariba (named *baaton geo*) are differentiated from the Wasangari in the order of their ritual practices and social roles.

The traditional political influence of Nikki (the senior center of the Bariba culture) includes Boko-speaking districts. On the other hand, Mokole speakers play a prominent role in the political culture of Kandi, another important Bariba city. The Borgu space provides a Bariba-based social background where different groups interact toward cultural integration, highly facilitated by diverse factors: first, the long-term coexistence of these communities; second, the existence of several symbolic objects of veneration. The figure of Kisra, for example, is considered a common mythical ancestor. On the other hand, the Wasangari kings are regarded as kings of the whole Bariba society. Another factor in integration is the *Gaani*, an important annual festival of aristocratic origins that becomes increasingly popular and was extended in all the Bariba territories of the Borgu region.

Bariba Identity

In spite of the irrational division of their territory (the Borgu) among different states, the Bariba people still claim the recognition of a differentiated identity that is tightly rooted in their homeland. By emphasizing language, territory, and common political history as criteria of national definition, the Bariba activists tried to overcome the contrast between the indigenous Bariba and the identity of the Wasangari who came as immigrants. As a logical outcome, the Bariba nation manifests a plural cultural landscape that has endowed into the ethnic structure a high degree of dynamism, enriching their common social capital. The Bariba territory, then, provides an excellent example of differential incorporation of communities into a single identity, because the structure of the resulting society articulates its particular components.

The different social groups possessed complementary functions: jural, political, ritual, sacred, etc. In fact, this complex complementarity is the guarantee for building a cohesive Bariba, especially to the Benin and Nigeria political powers that historically tried to dispossess the Bariba peoples of their own cultural, social, economic, and political instruments. In Benin, the formal adoption of Marxist-Leninist socialism by the Kérékou regime (1974) had forbidden the existence both of traditional chiefs and of the royal festival (*Gaani*), two of the essential pieces of Bariba identity. Local resentments remained widespread in the years of the Marxist regime. Moreover, the project of pushing aside local traditional leaderships fit the policy, promoted by the central state, of directly asserting state authority in rural areas and over agricultural production. In 1981, the resurrection of the *Gaani* represented a significant moment of communion among all Bariba groups coming from all around and still working as a ritual representation that embodies the essence of Bariba history and culture, over and above all differences between traditional status groups.

JOAN MANUEL CABEZAS LÓPEZ

See also **Benin; Nigeria**

Further Reading

Boessen, Elisabeth, Christine Hardung, and Richard Kuba, editors, *Regards sur le Borgou. Pouvoir et altérité dans une région ouest-africaine*, Paris: L'Harmattan, 1998

Kuba, Richard, *Wasangari and Wangara: Borgu and its Neighbours in Historical Perspective*, Hamburg/Münster: Lit Verlag, 1996

Moraes Farias, Paulo F., *Praise Splits the Subjects of Speech: Constructions of Kinship in the Manden and Borgu*, in *Power, Marginality and African Oral Literature*, edited by G. Furniss and L. Gunner, Cambridge: Cambridge University Press, 1995

Bashkir

Capsule Summary

Location: Bashkortostan in Russia; the Russian Federation; Tatarstan; Belarus; Kazakstan; Kyrgyzstan; Latvia; Moldova; Tajikistan; Turkmenistan; Ukraine; Uzbekistan.
Total Population: 1.5 million
Language: Bashkir; Tatar
Religion: Sunni Islam

The traditional culture of the Bashkirs is based on pastoralism, beekeeping, hunting, and agriculture. They raise cattle, sheep, and the world-famous Bashkir breed of horses. They are mentioned in ninth century sources, and they converted to Islam in the tenth century. During the reign of Ivan the Terrible, the area inhabited by the Bashkirs was gradually conquered by the Russians. The Bashkirs, therefore, have a long history as a colonized people within Russia.

Russian colonial rule led to several developments, including the immigration of Russians and Tatars to the area, the recruitment of Baskhkirs to the Russian army, and high taxes that forced the Bashkir pastoralists to adopt a more settled lifestyle. However, at the turn of the twentieth century, most Baskhkirs continued to live as peasants in the rural areas.

After the Russian Revolution in 1917, the Bashkirs enjoyed a brief period of autonomy. When the Bolsheviks finally crushed the White Army, Bashkirs became part of the Soviet Union. Many died during a famine in 1921. As pastoralists and agriculturalists, the Bashkirs were forced into the Soviet collectivization system. They remained mainly a rural population through the twentieth century.

Oil was discovered in 1932, and this caused a rapid industrialization of the Bashkir's native regions. A significant number of workers moved in from other parts of the Soviet Union to work on the oil fields, and the diversity of heavy industries that developed within the region. Although the economy improved, Bashkirs reaped few benefits. Many died during the famine in 1932–33, and large losses were experienced during World War II. The Bashkir population did not reach its pre-Revolution population again until the 1980s.

As in other republics within Russia, national sentiments began to rise at the end of Soviet rule. The Bashkirs proclaimed themselves a sovereign state on October 11, 1990.

The majority of Bashkirs live within the Republic of Bashkortostan, a sovereign republic within the Russian Federation located along the South Urals and the adjacent plains. Its territory covers about 143,600 square kilometers (55,444 square miles), and the population totaled 4.1 million people according to the October 2000 census. Approximately 100 nationalities inhabit Bashkortostan, including the Bashkirs, Russians, Kazan Tatars, Mishar Tatars, Chuvashs, Maris, Ukrainians, and Germans. The indigenous Bashkirs are a minority within their own republic (900,000), comprising some 22 percent of the total population of Bashkortostan. They are outnumbered by the Russians (40 percent) and the Tatars (28 percent).

Bashkirs are also found as ethnic minority groups elsewhere in Russia, with the most significant concentrations in Chelyabinsk (161,200), Orenburg (53,300), Perm (52,300), Sverdlovsk (41,500), Kurgan (17,500) and Tyumen (41,100) regions, as well as in Tatarstan (20,000). They can also be found as diaspora minorities in Belarus (1,300), Kazakstan (22,000), Kyrgyzstan (3,200), Latvia (700), Moldova (600), Tajikistan (5,400), Turkmenistan (2,600), Ukraine (3,700), and Uzbekistan (35,000). Very few Bashkirs live outside the former Soviet Union.

As in most minority areas of the former Union of Soviet Socialist Republics, the culture, religion, and language of the Bashkirs have seen a revival since 1991. The Bashkirs are Sunni Muslims belonging to the Hanafi School. The Bashkir capital, Ufa, was the administrative center for the Muslims of European Russia and Siberia during the Soviet era. Since the early 1990s, the cultural elite and politicians have been engaged in a debate about exactly what the national identity of a sovereign Bashkortostan should be. The main issue in this debate is the question of language, that is, the question of which languages should have official status in Bashkortostan. Most Bashkirs are probably bi- or even trilingual in Tatar and Russian, and the Bashkir language is in a minority within its own republic. It belongs to the northwestern branch of the Turkic languages.

Turkologists differentiate between three dialect groups: the mountain or eastern dialects; the steppe or southwestern dialects; and the northwestern dialects. Although modern Bashkir emerged as a written language in the 1920s, it had only limited use in the Soviet Union. Written Bashkir is based on the mountain dialects. During the first years of its existence, it was written in Arabic. Between 1927 and 1940, it was written with a Latin alphabet, but that was replaced by Cyrillic script in 1940. Approximately 73 percent of the Bashkirs regard Bashkir as their mother tongue, while the rest identify their language as Tatar. Approximately 10 percent reported Russian as their first language.

Bashkir is regarded as one of the endangered languages of the world. However, for the last few years, due to a growing national consciousness among the Bashkirs themselves, a renewed interest in their language and culture has developed. The local authorities have attempted to support and encourage pride in a Bashkir identity through an active language policy, national associations, the school system, media, and literature.

INGVAR SVANBERG

See also **Languages, Disappearing; Russia**

Further Reading

Akiner, Shirin, *Islamic Peoples of the Soviet Union (with an Appendix on the Non-Muslim Turkic Peoples of the Soviet Union)*, London: KPI, 1986

Cornell, Svante, and Ingvar Svanberg, "Russia and Transcaucasia," in *Islam outside the Arab World*, edited by David Westerlund and Ingvar Svanberg, Richmond: Curzon, 1999

Rywkin, Michael, "The Autonomy of Bashkirs," *Central Asian Survey,* 13, no.1, (1994)

Svanberg, Ingvar, "Turkic Ethnobotany and Ethnozoology as Recorded by Johan Peter Falck," *Svenska Linnésällskapets Årsskrift,* 1986–1987 (1987)

Basques

Capsule Summary

Location: northern Spain and southwestern France
Population: approximately 2.5 million
Languages: Basque or Euskara
Religion: Catholic

Basque-speakers called themselves *Euskaldunak* and their country *Euskadi*. Although Euskadi (the Basque Country) is today the official name of one of the 17 Autonomous Communities of the Spanish state, most Basques claim that their country is composed of seven provinces: three of them, Alava (*Araba*), Vizcaya (*Bizkaia*), and Guipú zcoa (*Gipuzkoa*), form the Autonomous Community of Euskadi (officially established in 1980), while Navarre (*Nafarroa*) forms a separate autonomous community (*Comunidad Foral de Navarra*). These four provinces are in Spain. The remaining three provinces are in the French Department of Pyrenees Atlantiques, in the region of Aquitaine: Labourd (*Lapurdi*), Soule (*Zuberoa*) and Basse Navarre (*Baxanabarra* or Low Navarre). Since the Autonomous Community of Euskadi (*Comunidad Autonoma Vasca* - CAV, *Euskal Autonomia Erkidegoa* - EAE, sometimes called *Vascongadas* in the rest of Spain) is deemed to represent only a fraction of the Basque homeland, the more encompassing term *Euskal-Herria* is sometimes preferred to indicate the seven provinces together, although the term was originally devoid of nationalist connotations.

These areas comprise an aggregate area of 20,600 kmq and over 2.5 million inhabitants, 90 percent of whom (2.3 million) live in the four Spanish provinces, while only 200,000 live on the French side. Euskadi Sur (including Navarre) occupies 17,600 kmq, roughly 3.5 percent of Spain's mass land surface with 7 percent of Spain's population.

Basque nationalists call the area located in France *Euskadi Norte* (*Iparralde*) and the area in Spain *Euskadi Sur* (*Hegoaldea*), the latter with 85 percent of the Basque land mass (Navarre counts for over half of that). The Treaty of the Pyrenees in 1659 established the border that dissects the Basque country. Its presence has hindered a shared Basque identity by creating two very different relationships with their respective central governments.

The Basque language, or *Euskara/Euskera*, is Europe's most ancient, with origins shrouded in mystery. Unrelated to any other language, it is the only pre-Indo European tongue still preserved outside the Caucasus—this leads to the claim by most Basques that they are the most ancient surviving ethnic group in Europe. Although the Basques were Christianized relatively late (third–fifth century CE) they produced important religious figures such as St. Ignatius of Loyola and St. Francis Xavier. Around the sixth century they expanded northward into what later became Gascony (roughly "land of the Basques," or Vasconia).

History

The Basques have long been identified as a separate people by foreign travelers and classical writers. Roman historians and Greek geographers, such as Strabo, recorded their existence as early as 7 BCE as "Vasconians." Prehistoric evidences of what were probably the ancestors of today's Basques can be found in caves and archeological sites scattered throughout the region. The Romans never succeeded in subduing them or absorbing their culture, nor did the Visigoths, the Muslims, the Franks, the Normans, or the Spaniards.

The kingdom of Navarre, founded in 824 CE, was the last region of the Iberian Peninsula to come under Spain's direct control (1512). The first known book in Basque appeared afterward in 1545 by the hand of the poet Bernard Dechepare. A New Testament was published in Basque (1571), followed by other books and translations aimed at converting the Basques to Protestantism.

A sense of separate cultural and political identity had existed in the area for centuries. The Jesuit Father Manuel de Larramendi (1690–1766) conceived the Basque provinces as a single unit, over which neither Castile nor France had the right to rule. One hundred years later, the French-Basque chronicler Augustin Chaho (1811–1858) formulated the myth of Aitor, legendary father of the Basques.

The Basque provinces were among the last regions of Spain to maintain their local statutes, the *fueros*.

These charters, agreed to by provincial authorities and the Spanish Crown, exempted the local population from taxation, military service, and other duties. Most of them were codified in the seventeenth and eighteenth centuries, but some dated back to the seventh century. Although local authorities had the right to veto royal edicts, the Crown retained the power to rescind them. With the emergence of a centralized state, the *fueros* were slowly eroded.

During the First Carlist Wars (1833–1839), Catholic traditionalists sided with the Carlists, a Spanish-wide movement which had its stronghold in the Basque provinces, but were crushed. Over 30 years later, a Second Carlist war (1872–1876) resulted in a definitive Basque defeat and in the abolition of the *fueros* (1876). As the provincial assembly *(Diputación)* of Vizcaya refused to collaborate in levying Spanish taxes, Madrid replaced it with a more lenient assembly. The latter managed to wring some concessions from Madrid, and the first *concierto econó mico* was signed in 1878, allowing the Basque Diputaciones to collect their taxes directly. However, the only beneficiaries of this arrangement were the big industrialists who ended up paying a very low share of the tax burden. The Basque industrial oligarchy was heavily represented among Madrid's economic and political élites. The two main branches of this fairly small group were the shipbuilders and the steel magnates, who controlled Spain's high finance. However, the rural areas and small towns felt heavily penalized, as local merchants, professional sectors and the peasants suffered most of the hardships brought about by new industries and taxes.

Following the abolition of the *fueros*, industrialization rapidly swept in, bringing in its wake the destruction of ancient lifestyles. Thus, a relatively insulated and balanced society collided with new, untamed forces. Its response was a neotraditionalist retreat, first in the form of Carlist rebellions, then through the utter defense of the *fueros* and, finally, as an isolationist form of nationalism.

The Birth of Basque Nationalism

More than other nationalist movements, Basque nationalism has been shaped by a single figure, Sabino de Arana y Goiri (1865–1903). Not only did Arana singlehandedly formulate the movement's first political program (1892), he also coined its name (*Euskadi*); defined its geographical extension (the four provinces in Spain and the three French *dé partements*); founded its first political organization (the Basque Nationalist Party or *Partido Nacionalista Vasco,* PNV, in 1893); composed its patriotic anthem (*Gora ta Gora*, in 1895), and designed its flag (the red, white, and green *ikurriñ a*). Finally, the Basque national holiday, *Aberri Eguna* (Day of the Fatherland), celebrates the event of Arana's conversion to nationalism on Easter Sunday 1882.

Arana was born in 1865 in Abando, a borough swallowed up by greater Bilbao during his lifetime. Urban expansion and the destruction of the rural *baserriak* (farmhouses) surrounding Bilbao were powerful reminders of the perverse effects of industrialization throughout Arana's life. His father joined the Carlist uprising in 1872, traveled to England to purchase arms for the rebels and, following defeat, migrated to France as a refugee. The trajectory of the Arana family responded to a common pattern of local élites marginalized by economic development.

Industrialization and Centralism

The quashing of traditional autonomies was the single most important factor in the birth of Basque nationalism. Industrialization was not simply an economic issue; it permeated all levels of society through urbanization and proletarianization. Moreover, since the industrial demand for cheap labor exceeded the local supply, immigrants began to flood the country with dramatic demographic effects. Most of them came from Castile, the land of the "oppressor," and thus were readily identified as oppressor's stooges. The workers' pitiful conditions provided an ideal hunting ground for socialists and class-related doctrines, while early nationalists openly rejected the immigrants. The first general strike in Spanish history occurred in Bilbao (1890) with a mobilization of over 20,000 industrial workers. But, as the newly urbanized Basque youth were quickly forgetting Basque traditions, modernization was seen by many as a fatal infirmity for which Basque nationalism claimed to be the cure. As elsewhere in the modern world, the age of industrialism was also bound to be an age of nationalism (Payne 1975).

In search of a new political ideology, the emerging upper-middle class was soon attracted by the nationalist creed, joining the lower and middle classes. As the 1876 reforms encouraged foreign investment, British capital for mines and furnaces swelled the local oligarchy, contributing further to alienate the lower and middle classes.

The Diffusion of Basque Nationalism (1903–1939)

In the year Arana died (1903), the PNV won two seats in the Vizcayan provincial assembly, and by 1906 Bilbao had a nationalist mayor. A Catholic and nationalist trade union was established in 1911, the *Solidaridad de Obreros Vascos* (SOV, Solidarity of Basque Workers). Spain's neutrality during World War I provided an exceptional stimulus for the expansion of Basque industry, boosting arms manufacture, shipping, and mining. The ensuing wave of economic prosperity brought an electoral triumph for the nationalists, who gained an absolute majority in the Diputació n of Vizcaya (1917). Urbanization and industrialization increased the importance of professionals, tradesmen, bureaucrats, administrators, and other sectors which were providing the nationalist cadres. However, postwar depression and the example of the Bolshevik revolution also led to an increase in labor strife, which in turn nourished a new fear of Communism. As local elites increasingly relied on the central government to quell working-class unrest, the nationalists' electoral power declined in 1919 and 1920.

From Arana's death until 1931, Basque nationalist ideology barely changed, with Arana's nonviolent precepts holding the field. On September 13, 1923, General Miguel Primo de Rivera (1870–1930) declared a dictatorship, forcing the nationalists into clandestine activity. As with most dictatorships, the stronger the repression became, the more the nationalist feelings mounted. At the fall of Primo de Rivera (1930), both Catalan and Basque nationalism emerged with renewed vigor, reinforced by years of secrecy. The dictatorship had helped to unite the different souls of Basque nationalism and mobilize even wider sectors. A Republican convention was held in San Sebastiá n (1930), resulting in a pact to bring down the monarchy and, subsequently, in the creation of a Republican Revolutionary Committee, which became Spain's provisional government by 1931. Basque Republicans and even Carlists joined in full cooperation with their counterparts from other regions (or "historical nationalities": Galicia, Euskadi, Catalonia) in exchange for the recognition of their regional distinctiveness, including the right of self-determination.

In the parliamentary elections of June 1931, a PNV–Carlists coalition won 15 of the 24 seats allocated to the Basque provinces in Madrid's *Cortes* (parliamentary assembly). But as Spain became a Republic, the traditionalist and legitimist Carlists grew increasingly restless in reaction to state-sanctioned secularism. This pushed them into the deadly embrace of the far right. While a Statute of Autonomy was immediately granted to Catalonia (1931), the Basque Country received its statute only in December 1936, shortly before the outbreak of the Civil War.

In the 1933 parliamentary elections, the PNV became the region's largest party, while 84 percent of the voters supported a proposed autonomy statute in a plebiscite held throughout the three provinces, excluding Navarre. It was the highest ever turnout in Spanish history (87 percent) (Payne, 1975: 134). In Madrid, the Right's united cartel achieved a broad victory against the fractured Left (1934). But in February 1936, the Left swept to power again, united under the Popular Front banner. Its government (February–July 1936) carried out a new set of revolutionary reforms in a highly radicalized atmosphere. As an autonomous Basque government was installed the local administration was fully reorganized, transforming the region into the most orderly and least revolutionary part of Republican Spain during the next nine months.

On July 18, 1936, the Spanish garrison in Morocco, under the command of General Francisco Franco (1892–1975), rebelled against the dual threat of socialism and separatism. The Civil War had begun. The Left decreed a general strike, preparing for an armed insurrection.

While in Euskadi the Basque nationalists joined the Socialists and the broader left in a common front against fascism, in Catalonia, the leadership passed to the Anarchist CNT-FAI (*Confederació n Nacional del Trabaj– Federació n Anarquica Iberica*). In November, Hitler and Mussolini recognized Franco's government.

During the Civil War, the Basques supplied the Republicans with some of their most effective troops (the *gudaris*). In 1937, Nazi planes of the Condor Legion bombed the town of Guernica on a market day, slaughtering hundreds of people and razing its historical center to the ground. The event was immortalized in Pablo Picasso's mural *Guernica*, which shocked Parisians when it was first exhibited at the 1937 World's Fair. It was history's first aerial bombardment on a civilian population. The Francoists denied any responsibility, but Basque autonomy lasted just nine months: Bilbao was captured by the Spanish nationalist troops in June 1937. The statute was immediately abrogated and all political parties suppressed.

The Civil War brought about extensive destruction, hundreds of thousands of dead and wounded, with unprecedented population displacements. As the Civil War ended in April 1939, the Francoist era began.

Francoism (1939–1975)

From 1939 to 1945, the Basque Country was subjected to a regime of state terror with no precedent in Basque history and a vindictive campaign to eradicate all signs of Basque identity. In the first years, thousands were imprisoned and hundreds executed under the accusation of promoting separatism, while the number of refugees reached 150,000. A Basque diaspora spread throughout France, Latin America, the United States, and other Western countries. At the same time, the Basque industrial oligarchy sided with the dictatorship, stamping a sinister class mark on state repression.

From 1945 to 1947, in the aftermath of World War II, Basque Republicans tried unsuccessfully to drag the Allies into opposition against the dictatorship. But, with the onset of the Cold War, the United States was lured by the possibility of opening a military base in the peninsula. In 1953, Spain signed a bilateral treaty with the United States and the Basques, together with the democratic opposition, became one of the many victims of the Cold War. The failure of Western democracies, especially Great Britain and the United States, to exert pressures on the regime, led most Basques to conclude that they could not depend on Western assistance. This is one of the crucial factors explaining the birth of a new form of resistance and its slow drift toward terrorism. ETA (*Euzkadi 'ta Askatasuna*, Basque Land and Freedom) was founded on July 31, 1959, emerging from an existing student group (*Ekin*). This was the breakthrough event in modern Basque history. The American betrayal of the Basques is the key ingredient needed to understand why the organization subsequently took a Leftist and even Trotskyist turn. Two other crucial elements were immigration (with its class nature) and ideological diffusion (the leftist vogue spreading over Europe in the 1960s). For years ETA remained a marginal group appealing to a few hundred young activists disillusioned by the lack of impetus of the older generation of mainstream nationalists.

After years of internal debates and splintering, the first premeditated political murder was carried out in 1968. The chosen victim was a well-known police commissioner and alleged torturer, hence a highly symbolic and effective target. The government's swift and ruthless response led to a crescendo of violence and counter-violence, which swelled the rank and file of the armed factions within ETA. While ETA became a clear and tangible threat to the Spanish state, it also justified its actions on the ground that the Spanish state represented a threat to the Basque nation. Its struggle became legitimized as a matter of protecting the security of the Basques against the excesses of a military dictatorship. During several "states of emergency," scores of suspected ETA sympathizers were rounded up, illegally detained, beaten, and intimidated under the accusation of terrorism.

From 1968 on, the level of state repression grew dramatically, and so did ETA's popularity. The most notorious act of ETA was the assassination of Admiral Carrero Blanco (December 1973), the expected successor to Francisco Franco. This act created a spate of international concern and admiration for ETA, as well as a diplomatic focus on the Basque question and a general wave of sympathy for the Basques now universally heralded as defenders of freedom against tyranny, even though this sympathy was entirely conveyed in secret against a wall of radical censorship. At the end, a seemingly all-powerful regime had to come to terms with its own failure to deal with dissent by pure coercion: Its refusal to understand the root causes of terrorism had led to disaster. By the time the dictator died (November 20, 1975) the regime was totally delegitimized, and it collapsed virtually overnight. A new era opened up for Spain.

Transition (1975 to the Present)

Two days after Franco's death, Juan Carlos de Borbó n was crowned King of Spain. The process of democratization that ensued came to be known as the "Transition." (*Transició n*). The King immediately proclaimed a first general amnesty and by 1977 the first general elections were held, leading to the victory of a centrist coalition, with a strong representation of both the left and the various regionalist and nationalist groups. A new Constitution was approved in 1978; it, for the first time, recognized Spain's internal diversity. By 1980 the Basque Country was granted a statute of autonomy, following the Catalan statute (1979). The president of the Basque parliament (*lehendakari*) was allowed to return from his French exile after 43 years. Only after the statute was approved and put into practice did the campaign of ETA's assassinations begin to recede: By 1980 it had reached its peak with over 100 people killed in one year in ETA-related violence.

On February 23, 1981, a plenary session of the Spanish parliament was interrupted by a group of Civil Guards led by Colonel Antonio Tejero, who seized the assembly and held the MPs prisoners for more than one day. They claimed they wanted to defend Spain from separatism and terrorism. A providential intervention by the King prevented the aborted coup from becoming an open military revolt.

The recovery of Basque culture in all its aspects has become a goal inseparable from conflict resolution and the attempt to bring the region back to peace. A promotional campaign was put into action, and a Law of Linguistic Normalization for Euskera was approved by the Basque parliament in 1984, setting the juridical basis for language use in all public domains. Step by step, the official use of Basque has been extended, establishing Basque as the language of instruction, the media, and regional administration.

By the mid 1990s, Basque civil society had begun to mobilize massively against the threat of terrorism. Most nationalist groups, except the radical *Herri Batasuna* (Popular Unity), joined the mass demonstrations that attracted people from all walks of life.

Despite the increasingly sporadic occurrence of ETA's violence, the region has witnessed a continuous decline in armed attacks until ETA's unilateral ceasefire (September 1998–December 1999). However, this historical opportunity was not promptly seized by the Conservative government of Prime Minister José Marí a Aznar Ló pez, who consistently refused to deal with the terrorists—without at the same time being able to provide a credible alternative. The result was that once more violence has come back to plague the stability and prosperity of the region. Spain's transition to democracy has proved highly beneficial to most Basques, yet there remained minorities, increasingly less influential ones, who refused to accept the statute of autonomy, opting for nothing less than complete independence.

Daniele Conversi

Further Reading

Clark, Robert P., *The Basques: The Franco Years and Beyond*, Reno: University of Nevada Press, 1979

Conversi, Daniele, *The Basques, the Catalans, and Spain: Alternative Routes to Nationalist Mobilization*, London: Hurst, 1997; Reno: University of Nevada Press, September 2000

Douglass, William, "Sabino's Sin: Racism and the Founding of Basque Nationalism," in *Ethnonationalism in the Contemporary World: Walker Connor and the Theory of Nationalism*, edited by Daniele Conversi, London: Routledge, 2002

Irvin, Cynthia L., *Militant Nationalism: Between Movement and Party in Ireland and the Basque Country*, Minneapolis: University of Minnesota Press, 1999

Payne, Stanley G., *Basque Nationalism*, Reno: University of Nevada Press, 1975

Payne, Stanley G., "Catalan and Basque Nationalism: Contrasting Patterns," in *Ethnic Challenges to the Modern Nation State*, edited by Shlomo Ben-Ami, Yoav Peled, and Alberto Spektorowski, New York: St. Martin's Press, 2000

Zirakzadeh, Cyrus Ernesto, *A Rebellious People. Basques, Protests, and Politics*, Reno: Nevada University Press, 1991

Zulaika, Joseba, *Basque Violence: Metaphor and Sacrament*, Reno: Nevada University Press, 1988

Zulaika, Joseba, and William A. Douglass, *Terror and Taboo: The Follies, Fables, and Faces of Terrorism*, London: Routledge, 1996

Batak

Capsule Summary

Location: Palawan Island, the Philippines
Total Population: approximately 400
Language: Batak
Religion: Animist

The Batak are one of about 20 culturally and linguistically distinct groups of so-called "Negrito" foraging peoples in the Philippines. They inhabit the forested interior river valleys of the east coast of north central Palawan Island. The Batak speak a language related to the central Visayan group of Philippine languages, and they share important cultural similarities with other indigenous peoples of Palawan. But they are made distinctive by their short stature and other aspects of their physical appearance, by their use of the bow and arrow, and by their extensive reliance on hunting and gathering of forest and riverine resources. At the close of the nineteenth century, before Palawan Island was extensively settled by migrants from elsewhere in the Philippines, the Batak numbered 800–1000 persons. Today they number less than 400 persons, including the offspring of increasingly frequent Batak marriages with others.

History

For centuries the Batak have had important trading links with maritime peoples of the Sulu region, exchanging forest products for manufactured goods and other needs. But Palawan remained on the periphery of the Philippine state, leaving the Batak relatively isolated and undisturbed well into the American colonial period. Since 1900, however, migrants to Palawan have incrementally alienated Batak land and other resources. During the 1930s, the government established a series of coastal plain reservations for the Batak, but these were overrun by a surge of migrants in the 1950s. The Batak have since retreated stepwise to the interior, keeping just ahead of advancing settlers.

Economic Life

The Batak combine forest foraging, collection and sale of forest products, shifting cultivation, and wage labor for lowland Filipino farmers. The principal forest foods collected include wild pig, gliding squirrel, jungle fowl, wild honey, wild yams, wild fruits and greens, fish, mollusks, and crustaceans. Pigs are taken with the spear and hunting dogs or from blinds, with the bow-and-arrow or homemade guns. A variety of traps and snares are also used.

Commercially-valuable forest products exchanged with outside peoples include honey, rattan, and Manila copal (a tree resin used in various industrial processes). Exchange of forest products is the principal means by which the Batak acquire rice, clothing, and other consumer wants. The Batak also produce some rice by shifting cultivation, together with smaller amounts of corn, cassava, and sweet potato. Wage work for neighboring farmers is increasingly important; groups of Batak may hire out for several days at a time to help clear or weed fields, to harvest rice, or to pick coconuts or coffee. Guiding tourists has also become an occasional source of cash income.

Social and Political Life

The Batak live in a series of eight local groups, each identified with a particular river and its watershed. Local group sizes range from 5 to 30 households, and each group has a fixed settlement site located 3–10 km upstream from a coastal lowland Filipino community. But such settlements are not permanently occupied, as economic and social activities may take small groups of individuals or households away from the settlement for days or weeks at a time.

The Batak trace descent through both sides of the family, and their kin terms resemble those of other peoples in the Philippines. All have several names, however, as Batak are ritually prohibited from using the birth names of their affinal kin (in-laws). Divorce and remarriage were common in the past; a *surugiden,* or gathering of the elders, hears and resolves marital disputes. A newly-married couple customarily resides near the wife's parents during the early years of a marriage.

Nuclear family households are the basic economic unit. Labor resources are often pooled and food is often shared, but households are expected to be autonomous and self-reliant. Within households, husbands and wives similarly enjoy considerable freedom of action. Batak have few children, and mean household size is small, about 3.5 persons.

The Batak are strongly egalitarian and independent. Certain older men, by virtue of their kinship ties and personal attributes, emerge as natural leaders and become the focus of day-to-day residential clusters. The opinions of such individuals are respected and influential, but not binding.

Religious Beliefs

The Batak believe their world is inhabited by a variety of nature spirits and supernatural beings, including malevolent *panya'en* and capricious but potentially benevolent *diwata.* Visible only to shamans, these spirit beings inhabit specific trees, rocks, and streams, and are human-like in their actions and desires. *Panya'en* stand in a jealous protective relationship to the various forest and riverine resources utilized by the Batak. Any wasteful or excessive use, intended or not, or even displays of disrespect toward forest animals, may so antagonize a caretaker *panya'en* that it punishes the offending individual with illness or even death. Mediating Batak relationships with supernatural beings are the *babalians,* mediums capable of entering trance states through song or dance in order to appeal to their *diwata* familiars to intercede on behalf of some human enterprise or misfortune, typically illness.

Current Problems

Patron-client ties, linking Batak to outsiders in exploitative and debilitating relations of credit and debt, are a prominent feature of Batak economy. Market wants are growing, but opportunities to earn cash are few, and how to obtain cash while preserving independence is a constant preoccupation. Further, migrant settlers also collect forest products within Batak territory; their often unsustainable collection practices have created serious natural resource management problems. Several non-government organizations (NGOs) are presently assisting the Batak with their livelihood and resource management difficulties, aided by recent government legislation making it easier to secure the ancestral domains of indigenous peoples against further encroachment by outsiders.

JAMES F. EDER

See also **Philippines**

Further Reading

Eder, James F., *On the Road to Tribal Extinction: Depopulation, Deculturation, and Adaptive Well-Being among the Batak of the Philippines,* Berkeley: University of California Press, 1987

Eder, James F., *Batak Resource Management: Belief, Knowledge, and Practice,* Gland, Switzerland: International Union for the Conservation of Nature and Natural Resources and World Wide Fund for Nature, 1997

Venturello, Manuel H., "Manners and Customs of the Tagbanuas and Other Tribes of the Island of Palawan, Philippines," translated by Mrs. Edward Y. Miller, *Smithsonian Museum Collections,* 48 (1907)

Warren, Charles P., *The Batak of Palawan: A Culture in Transition*, Research Series No. 3, Philippine Studies Program, University of Chicago, 1964

Belarus

Capsule Summary

Location: Eastern Europe, between Poland and Russia
Total Population: 10,322,151 (July 2003)
Language: Belarusian, Russian, Polish, and Lithuanian
Religion: Eastern Orthodox (80%), other, including Roman Catholic, Protestant, Jewish, and Muslim, (20%) (1997)

The Republic of Belarus is located in central Europe, bounded by Russia and Latvia in the north, Lithuania on the northwest, Poland on the west, the Ukraine on the south, and Russia on the east. From 1919 to 1991, it was the Belorussian (also spelled Byelorussian) Soviet Socialist Republic, roughly translated as "White Russia." The etymology probably derives from a folk term used in the Middle Ages as a geographic designation of northern territories. Belarus is a large plain about the size of Kansas. Its capital is the city of Minsk (Mensk), the largest and one of the oldest cities in the region.

About 80 percent of the population are Belarussians, and the largest minority groups are Russians, Poles, Ukrainians, Lithuanians, and Jews. Eastern Orthodoxy and Roman Catholicism are the dominant religions. Religious groups with growing numbers of converts more recently have suffered official discouragement and persecution since independence, a policy that was enacted into law in 2002.

Most Belarusians speak two or three languages, including Belarusian and Russian; the latter is more widely used. The Belarusian language belongs to the family of Slavic languages and is close to Russian and Ukrainian. All three languages use the Cyrillic alphabet, with modifications in Ukrainian and Belarusian. There is also a unique version of the Latin-script in Belarusian writing called *Lacinka*. Under communist rule, the Soviet Union dominated the country, but since the fall of the Soviet Union in 1991, Belarusian is again spoken and taught in schools as the national language. To preserve the Belarusian language, a Law on Languages in the Republic of Belarus was passed in 1990, which proclaimed Belarusian the state language. In accordance with a 1995 national referendum the Russian language was given equal status alongside Belarusian. The Law on National Minorities in the Republic of Belarus guarantees the right of each of the ethnic minorities living in the Republic to learn and use its native languages.

History

Since the end of the ninth and the beginning of the tenth centuries CE, Belarusian territories were part of the Kievan Rus kingdom (or Slavs of the Kievan State, the earliest predecessor of modern Ukraine and Russia). For several centuries Byzantine culture, including Orthodox Christianity, its stone architecture and literature, strongly influenced the region. After the destruction of the Kievan Rus in the mid-thirteenth century by the Mongols, the Belarusian territories were incorporated into the Great Lithuanian Duchy. A century later the Duchy formed a union with the Polish Kingdom. These new administrative and political arrangements brought a robust Western European influence to the region, most significantly the Roman Catholic religion. A large Jewish population also settled in Belarus in the fourteenth century. In 1569 the Great Lithuanian Duchy and the Polish Kingdom fused into a multiethnic federal state called the Commonwealth. The state enjoyed a powerful position in Europe for two centuries.

Following the partitions of the Commonwealth in 1772, 1793, and 1795 by Russia, Prussia, and Austria, respectively, the Belarusian territories became a part of the Russian Empire. Tremendous poverty under Russian rule, particularly among Jews, led to mass emigration to the United States in the nineteenth century. The second half of the nineteenth century witnessed the rapid development of capitalism in Belarus.

In the late nineteenth century, western ideas including Marxism were brought into Belarus, and the 1905–1907 Revolution produced the Belarusian national liberation movement. The most significant event in this national awakening process took place in April 1917, when the Congress of the Belarusian National Organizations was held. Its delegates claimed autonomy for Belarus. However, after the October Socialist Revolution in Petersburg succeeded, the Bolsheviks seized power in Belarus. In December 1917, they dissolved the all-Belarussian Congress in Minsk. Regardless of Soviet occupation, the all-Belarussian Congress and the representatives of the political parties declared the Belarussian People's Republic, the first independent Belarusian state on March 25, Ten months later, the Bolsheviks proclaimed the Belarussian Soviet Socialist Republic (BSSR). The new nation-state was formally incorporated into the Soviet Union and remained part of that union until 1991.

On July 27, 1991, the Supreme Soviet of the BSSR adopted the Declaration on State Sovereignty. In August 1991, the Supreme Soviet of the BSSR suspended the Communist Party of Belarus and renamed the country the Republic of Belarus. In December 1991, the Soviet Union was dissolved and Belarus became a cofounder of the Commonwealth of Independent States (CIS).

In March 1994, Belarus adopted a new constitution, creating a presidency and reconstructing the 260-seat Parliament. On July 10, 1994, Alyaksandr Lukashenko was elected the first president of Belarus; he remained in office as recently as mid-2004 (the next elections will be held in 2006). In 1999, the Treaty on the Union of Belarus and Russia was signed, designed to implement greater political and economic integration.

National identity of Belarusians is symbolically linked to two significant moments in the Belarussian history. The national holiday is officially celebrated on July 3, commemorating the day Soviet troops entered Minsk in 1944, liberating the city from Nazi forces. For some Belarusians, March 25 is celebrated as an unofficial Independence Day. The date commemorates the short time period when Belarus broke free from Bolshevik Russia in March 1918, only to be reoccupied in December 1918.

The state symbols of Belarus changed repeatedly throughout the twentieth century. After the referendum in 1995, the state emblem of Belarus was changed to an image of the republic's geographic outline in golden sunrays over the globe, with a five-pointed red star above. A garland of wheat, clover, and flax flowers frames the image. The golden inscription below reads "Republic of Belarus." The new state anthem has lyrics and music that reflect the aspiration of the Belarussian people for freedom and independence, and proclaims their commitment to ideals of humanism, goodness, and justice. Since 1997 a boundary treaty with Ukraine remains unratified over unresolved financial claims, preventing demarcation and encouraging illegal border crossing. Belarus's boundaries with Latvia and Lithuania also remain undemarcated despite financial support from the European Union.

Economy and Politics

The official currency is the rouble (R) (also known as the *zaichik*) divided into 100 k*opecks*. Belarus is an industrial state with developed and diversified agriculture. State-run farms are the chief producers of agrarian goods. Privately owned farms are in development in the twenty-first century. Other key industries include electric power, timber, metallurgy, chemicals and petrochemicals, pulp and paper, building materials, medical, printing, machine-building, microbiology, textiles, and food industries. Belarus's chief trading partners are the other Commonwealth of Independent States (CIS), which it joined in 1991.

The basic law of the Republic is the Constitution of 1994, amended by a referendum in 1996. The population elects the chief of state, the president, for a five-year term. The legislative body, the National Assembly, is composed of the House of Representatives and Council of Republic. The president with the consent of the House of Representatives appoints a Ministerial Council, headed by the Prime Minister. Local Councils with executive and administrative power manage local government. The supreme judicial organ is the Supreme Court, which interprets the constitution.

Society and Culture

Throughout the centuries, Belarusian lands were home to an ethnically and religiously diverse society. Muslims, Jews, Orthodox Christians, Roman Catholics, Uniates and Protestants lived together without major confrontations. Belarusians, Poles, Russians, Jews, Lithuanians, Ukrainians, Tartars, and Gypsies were among the many ethnic groups living in Belarus. Although the twentieth century brought many challenges to this peaceful coexistence, Belarus is in many senses a culture of tolerance. Presently Belarusian ethnic groups include Belarusian (81.2 percent), Russian (11.4 percent), Polish, Ukrainian, and others (7.4 percent). All ethnic groups historically enjoyed equal status, and there is little evidence of hate or ethnically biased crimes. Recently, however, there have been reports of growing anti-Semitism. Approximately 90,000 Jews live in Belarus today (Some estimates cite 120,000, as some people hid their Jewish identities in the past and are now revealing their Jewishness). According to the Anti-Defamation League and the World Jewish Congress, a number of small, anti-Semitic, ultra-nationalist fringe organizations have emerged; these include the Belarussian Liberation Party (BPS), Right Revanche (PR), and the White Legion (the Belarussian version of the Ukrainian paramilitary UNA-UNSO and the Russian National Legion of the NRPR–the Russian National Republican Party). A number of newspapers reputedly regularly print anti-Semitic material. In the 1990s several incidents of vandalism, pamphleteering, and other ethnically motivated acts of hatred prompted human rights groups and the government to investigate minority tensions. Yet in 1997 no legal action was taken by the authorities against the continuing anti-Semitic propaganda, despite the fact that the Belarussian Constitution specifically forbids "incitement to religious or national hatred."

LUDOMIR LOZNY

See also **Belarusians; Poles; Ukranians**

Further Reading

Dawisha, Karen, and Bruce Parrot, editors, *Democratic Changes and Authoritarian Reactions in Russia, Ukraine, Belarus and Moldova*, Cambridge and New York: Cambridge University Press, 1997

Garnett, Sherman W., and Robert Legvold, editors, *Belarus at the Crossroads*, Washington, DC: Carnegie Endowment for International Peace, 1999

Kelly, Robert C., editor, *Belarus, Country Review 1999/2000*, 2000

Novik, Uladzimir, *Belarus: A New Country in Eastern Europe*, Minsk: Independent Publishing Company Technology, 1993

Zaprudnik, Jan, *Belarus: At a Crossroads in History*, Boulder: Westview Press, 1993

Belarusians

Capsule Summary

Location: east central Europe, mostly in the territory of Belarus
Total Population: Approximately 10 million
Language: Belarusian
Religion: Eastern Orthodox Church, Catholic Church

The Belarusians are an ethnic group living in east-central Europe. There are approximately 10 million Belarusians, most of them (approximately 80 percent) living in the Republic of Belarus. The rest of Belarusians live in various regions in Russia, Poland, Lithuania, Canada, and the United States. The Belarusian language, together with Russian and Ukrainian, belongs to the eastern branch of Slavic languages of the Indo-European language family (other Slavic languages are Polish, Slovak, Bulgarian, etc). Belarusians, along with Russians and Ukrainians, unlike neighboring Poles or Slovaks, use the Cyrillic alphabet. The majority of Belarusians belong to the Eastern Orthodox Church, as do the Russians and Ukrainians, and the Orthodox Church was declared the official religion of the state. As a founding member of the Soviet Union, Belarus took part at the historic Belovezh Forest meeting in December 1991 whereby Belarusian President Stanislau Shushkevich, together with Russian and Ukrainian presidents Boris Yeltsin and Leonid Kravchuk, signed a historic document formalizing the dissolution of the Soviet Union.

Early History

Belarusians have a rich history, rooted in the ancient Slavic tribal confederation in the east of Central Europe. Historians believe that Belarusians' ancestors derived from three early Slavic tribes—the *Dregovich, Krivichi, and Radimich*—who settled in the territory of modern Belarus between the sixth and eighth centuries CE. The strategic location between the Kievan Rus (or Slavs of the Kievan State, the earliest predecessor of modern Ukraine and Russia) and Baltic states, and between German and western Slavic states and eastern Slavic kingdoms enriched the Belarusian culture, but at the same time brought numerous wars and turmoil.

The early Slavic tribes settled on the Dvina, Pripyat' and Sozh rivers around the sixth century CE. Gradually they consolidated into early city-states, basing their economy on trade with neighboring states, agriculture, and hunting. By the tenth century these proto-states were absorbed into the powerful Kievan state and were divided into three major principalities, Smolyensk, Polotsk, and Pinsk. Around the same time these previously shamanistic tribes had peacefully accepted Christianity (Eastern Orthodox Church) from missionaries who arrived from Constantinople, the capital of the Byzantine Empire and Eastern Orthodox Church.

The important change came in with the Mongol-Tatar invasion into Eastern Europe in the middle of the thirteenth century. This invasion had a devastating effect as a sizeable part of the population was killed or vanished as a result of it. A number of cities and towns in the territory of the modern Russian Federation and the Ukraine were destroyed. Most of the principalities of the Belarusian territory escaped the devastation inflicted on the Kievan and Moscow Rus, although their political, cultural, and military relations with the eastern Slavic States were weakened for centuries onwards.

In the fourteenth century the Grand Duchy of Lithuania acquired the principalities of the Belarusian territory under favorable conditions: the Belarusian nobility retained their privileges, the Belarusian population could retain their eastern Orthodox Christian religious identity, and their language was used in the state administration. The people could peacefully coexist with representatives of various ethnic groups. The benchmark of this era was humanist scholar Francisk Skaryna's translation and publication of the Bible into the Belarusian language in 1517–1519. Many Belarusian scholars cite the sixteenth century as the Golden Era in the history of the Belarusians, primarily because it was a time of intensive formation and development of the Belarussian nation, growth of the old and new towns and cities, as well as significant cultural achievements.

By the middle of the sixteenth century another important turning point in Belarusian history occurred. With the formation of *Rzech Pospolita,* the union between Lithuania and Poland in 1569, the Belarusians came under increasing pressure from the predominantly Catholic Poles to convert from the Eastern Orthodox Church to Roman Catholicism. Their language subsequently lost its privileged status and gradually diminished to the status of a "peasant language." Some members of the Belarusian nobility were converted to Catholicism and gave up the Belarusian language in favor of Polish; however, a large majority of the population resisted such pressure and regularly revolted against the unpopular rule by escaping to the steppe land.

Bloody wars in Belarusian territory, particularly the wars between Rzech Pospolita and the Moscow Principality, resulted in destruction and weakened Rzech Pospolita. This instability was used by the governments of the three neighboring states. Prussia, Austria, and Russia partitioned Rzech Pospolita in 1772, 1793, and 1795. As a result most of the territory of Belarus came under the Russian Empire's control. The Russian Empire brought positive changes such as ending the policy of cultural assimilation from Poland, although it heavily suppressed cultural and political awakening in the Belarusian society as Russian rule coexisted with the era of industrialization, mass education, and emergence of modern nationalism. The czar's edict of 1840 prohibited the use of the words "Belarus" and "Lithuania;" instead, the name "North-Western Krai (region)" was introduced. The emergence of Russian capitalism in the late nineteenth century aggravated the economic disparity in the Belarusian society, especially in rural areas, and impelled a movement of the population to urban areas in other parts of the Russian Empire and a sizeable emigration to the United States and Canada.

Soviet Rule (1919–1991)

By the beginning of the twentieth century Belarus emerged as a deeply divided society, whose people experienced same difficulties and impoverishment as the rest of the Russian Empire's population, and where freedoms were heavily suppressed. After the Empire had collapsed under the burden of World War I, the political unrest in various parts of the Empire, and the Bolshevik Revolution in Petrograd in 1917, the Belarusian nationalists seized an opportunity and declared the creation of the Belarusian People's (National) Republic in 1918. The Bolsheviks, however, acquired political power in Belarus in 1919 and established the Byelorussian Soviet Socialist Republic, although a significant part of the republic was lost to Poland. In 1939, under a special treaty with Germany, the Soviet Union acquired the so-called Western Byelorussia. World War II arrived in Belarus in 1941 and lasted until 1944. It was the most devastating war in the history of the Belarusians, as the country lost almost a quarter of its population or around two million people. Practically all its industries and major towns and cities were destroyed or burned down, and populations of entire villages and towns were executed. Nazis especially targeted Jews, who had lived in the territory of what is Belarus for centuries (they were mentioned in the Polish Chronicles in the thirteenth and fourteenth centuries) and at the beginning of the war became the second largest ethnic group in the country. A significant portion of their community was executed in the Nazi death camps, especially representatives of large Jewish communities in Kovno, Vitebsk, Grodno, Minsk, and some others. The Belarusian guerrilla (partisan) movement gained the support of the most of the population. The motifs of resistance and suffering were deeply incorporated into Belarusian culture and contemporary folklore, especially into folksongs and laments.

Under Soviet rule the Byelorussian SSR experienced major changes that accompany modernization, industrialization, and urbanization. Mass illiteracy was eradicated with the establishment of modern education and school systems. However, as in other Soviet Union republics, Belarus paid a grave price for these changes: major freedoms were suppressed; and a significant portion of the Belarus political opposition and intelligentsia disappeared during Josef Stalin's brutal purges or ended in Siberian and Central Asian labor camps. The policy of Russification significantly undermined development of the Belarusian culture and language. According to the official report, *Narodnoye Khoziaistvo SSSR v 1989,* only 70.9 percent of the Belarusians in the former USSR declared their native language as the mother tongue (the lowest level among the 15 Soviet republics).

In 1986 one-fourth of Belarus was affected by the nuclear radiation spill from Chernobyl's nuclear power station in the neighboring Ukraine, provoking widespread resentment against the Kremlin leadership.

During the Soviet era Belarus emerged as a multiethnic country. During the first decades of the Soviet rule, the government heavily controlled the population's movement, and some Belarusian social groups were forcibly moved to other parts of the Soviet Union or recruited to work at new industrial and other projects in other Soviet republics. In the 1960s and 1970s the Soviet government relaxed the restrictions and even encouraged migration of skilled workers between the Soviet republics. By 1989, ethnic Belarusians were the fourth largest ethnic minority in the former Soviet Union (after Russians, Ukrainians, and Uzbeks), with 10 million people. Around 7 million Belarusians were living in Belarus, 1.2 million in Russia (the sixth largest minority in the Russian Federation), and approximately 1.8 million in other parts of the Soviet Union. Meanwhile, due to urbanization and other social changes, the population growth in Belarus, as in Russia, Estonia, Latvia, Lithuania, and some other republics, slowed steadily throughout the 1970s and 1980s, prompting labor shortages in some sectors of the economy.

Independence

Gorbachev's policy of *perestroika,* which was launched in 1985, opened the doors for freedom of expression and emergence of various forms of political opposition. The Belarusian nationalist movement gained strength, and its representatives acquired influence in the *Verkhovnyi Sovet,* or Belarusian Parliament. In 1990 the Parliament introduced a Law declaring the Belarusian language the state language in Belarus. In 1991 it changed the Soviet national flag to the flag of the Belarusian People's Republic, which was in turn borrowed from the Grand Duchy of Lithuania. In December 1991 Belarus, as a founding member of the Soviet Union, took part at the historic Belovezh meeting, and Belarusian President Shushkevich, together with the Russian and Ukrainian presidents, signed a historic document formalizing the dissolution of the Soviet Union and the founding of the Commonwealth of Independent States. This action peacefully ended almost 72 years of Soviet rule and almost three centuries of coexistence with the Russians within one state.

Initially Shushkevich's nationalist policy gained some support among the population, as it promoted the Belarusian language, national identity, statehood, and cultural renaissance. However, his policy of distancing from Russia proved to be less popular and, combined with the economic mismanagement and economic difficulties of the independence era, they contributed to the strengthening of hard-line political opposition.

Recent Political Developments

In 1994 the nationalist camp, led by the Belarusian Popular Front, lost its political influence. In 1994 a new politician, Alexander Lukashenko, won 44.8 percent of the votes in the first runoff and 80.1 percent in the second runoff of the presidential elections. Lukashenka's populist political agenda, combined with a heavy-handed approach toward the opposition, have shaped political developments in the Republic since his election. In 1995 he proposed the renunciation of the state flag (derived from the fourteenth century symbol of the Grand Duchy of Lithuania) and replaced it with the slightly revised Belarusian flag of the Soviet era. At the same time, the Russian language was elevated to the status of a state language, along with Belarusian. Lukashenka also called for a closer union with Russia and signed a preliminary Union Treaty with Yeltsin in 1996. Lukashenka also slowed the process of privatization and economic liberalization in Belarus, pointing out the devastating effects of the International Monetary Fund (IMF) and World Bank structural adjustment programs on the economy of the neighboring Ukraine, Russia, and some other former Soviet republics. The political opposition and independent mass media crashed, and some opposition leaders and journalists were forced into exile. In the 1996 referendum President Lukashenka introduced constitutional changes, expanding his executive power and extending his term in office until 2001. Lukashenka comfortably won the presidential elections in September 2001 and his supporters won local elections in March 2003, but many international observers declared these elections not free. Many of Lukashenka's political actions, especially his dealing with the opposition and changes in the legislature and constitution, were widely criticized in the West and in Russia.

Belarusian Society

Belarusian society emerged from the shattered fragments of the Soviet Union as an industrialized country with a diverse and well-educated population. Ethnic Belarusians, who are ethnically and linguistically similar to Russians and Ukrainians, comprise 81 percent of the population. Ethnic Russians make up the largest minority, 11 percent of the population; Poles make up 4.1 percent; Ukrainians, 2.9 percent, and various other groups comprise the remaining 1.0 percent. Although during the Soviet communist era all religions were suppressed, in the post-Soviet era 80 percent of Belarusians claim to be Eastern Orthodox Christians, while less than 20 percent are Roman Catholics, Eastern (Uniate) Catholics, or Protestants. This division is largely due to the effect of the partition for several centuries of the territory of modern Belarus between largely Catholic Poland and Orthodox Christian Russia. Consequently, the eastern part of the country manifests the influence of Russification, and the western parts are often considered strongholds of nationalist forces.

Belarus is a predominantly urban country with around 70 percent of the population living in multi-ethnic cities and towns. However, most of the rural areas are populated predominantly by ethnic Belarusians. The current ethnic structure of the country was formed after World War II, when the Soviet government encouraged migration from various parts of the Soviet Union to the war-torn Belarus. During the Soviet era and following post-independence in 1991 no serious conflicts between ethnic minorities and ethnic Belarusians erupted, most likely due to the fact that all ethnic groups were equally hit by the economic recession and rising unemployment. Between 1991 and 2004 around 110,000 people opted to leave the country permanently, while another 500,000 (from different ethnic backgrounds) moved to the Russian Federation or developed countries as temporary workers.

Rafis Abazov

See also **Belarus**

Further Reading

Balmaceda, Margarita M., et al., editors, *Independent Belarus: Domestic Determinants, Regional Dynamics, and Implications for the West,* Cambridge, Massachusetts: Harvard University Press, 2003

Belarusian Chronicles Home Page. <http://chronicle.home.by/>

Belarusian News Digest Home Page. <http://www.belarus-news.de/>

Chinn, Jeff, and Robert Kaiser, *Russians as the New Minority: Ethnicity and Nationalism in the Soviet Successor States,* Boulder, Colorado: Westview Press, 1996

Entsyklapedyya Historyi Belarusi, Vol. 1–4, Minsk: Entsyclapedyya, 1993–1997

Kipel, Vitaut, and Zora Kipel, editors, *Byelorussian Statehood: Reader and Bibliography,* New York: Byelorussian Institute of Arts and Sciences, 1988

Kolsto, Paul, *Russians in the Former Soviet Republics,* Bloomington: Indiana University Press, 1995

Marples, David, *Belarus: From Soviet Rule to Nuclear Catastrophe,* New York: St. Martin's Press, 1996

Marples, David, *Belarus. A Denationalized Nation,* The Netherlands, Harwood Academic Press, 1999

Mikhnevich, A., halouny redaktar, *Belaruskaia mova: Entsyklapedyia,* Minsk: Belaruskaia entsyklapedyia, 1994

Mikulich, T.M., *Mova i ethnichnaya samasvyadomasts,* Minsk: Nauka i tekhnika, 1996

Pilipenka, M.F., *Vozniknovenie Belorussii: Novaya kontseptsiya,* Minsk: Nauka, 1991

Smith, Graham, et al., editors, *Nation-Building in the Post-Soviet Borderlands: The Politics of National Identities,* Cambridge: Cambridge University Press, 1998

Zaprudnik, Jan, *Belarus: At a Crossroad in History,* Boulder, Colorado: Westview Press, 1992

Zaprudnik, Jan, *Historical Dictionary of Belarus,* Lanham, Maryland,: Scarecrow Press, 1998

Belgium

Capsule Summary

Location: Western Europe, bordering the North Sea, between France and the Netherlands
Total Population: 10,289,088 (July 2003)
Minority Population: Walloons (33%); Italians (2%); Moroccans (1%); Germans (1%)
National Languages: Dutch (official) 60%, French (official) 40%, German (official) less than 1%, legally bilingual (Dutch and French)
Religion: Roman Catholic (75%), Protestant or other (25%, including Muslim and Jewish)

Since its creation as an independent and sovereign state in 1830, the Kingdom of Belgium has been divided. With a population of over 10.2 million, Belgium is at the crossroads of Western Europe and borders France, Germany, Luxembourg, and the Netherlands. Brussels is the national capital.

Belgian national unity has always been problematic: religious, social, and economic cleavages have marked Belgium's political life. Historically a religious divide between Catholics and Protestants has characterized the small country. Moreover, much of its industry is concentrated in the north, contributing to an economic divide along geographic and cultural lines. Additionally, linguistic and cultural divisions have shaped the country and its diverse population.

A federal parliamentary democracy under a constitutional monarch, Belgium is presently divided into three geographic and nearly autonomous political regions, Brussels, Flanders, and Wallonia, which in turn are divided into provinces. The geographic split between the north and south was reinforced by the adoption in 1963 of two national languages, Flemish and French, respectively (German was made a third official, albeit minority, language later). The division opposing the Flemish majority to the Walloons minority rapidly emerged as the most important axis of opposition in recent Belgian politics.

History

Upon gaining independence from the Netherlands, in 1831 Prince Leopold of Saxe-Coburg-Gotha was chosen as king. A final Dutch-Belgian peace treaty was signed in 1839, and the "perpetual neutrality" of Belgium was guaranteed by the major powers at the London Conference of 1838–39. Belgium was among the first European countries to industrialize and soon led the continent in the development of railways, coal mining, and engineering. Under the rule (1865–1909) of Leopold II colonial expansion, notably in the Democratic Republic of Congo (previously Zaïre and before that Belgian Congo), Rwanda and Burundi, occurred. Belgium's neutrality was threatened by German invasions during the two World Wars. Post–World War I under the Treaty of Versailles, Belgium received the strategically important posts of Eupen, Malmédy, and Moresnet, and a mandate over the northwestern corner of the former German East Africa.

After World War II, as an early proponent of a united Europe, Belgium became a member of and the headquarters for the North Atlantic Treaty Organization (NATO) in 1949. In 1960 the Belgian Congo was given its independence, although the subsequent eruption of violence and indigenous rebellions led to economic and political turmoil in the Republic. Rwanda and Burundi, meanwhile, have repeatedly been engulfed by ethnic conflict, most recently and tragically in 1994. Belgian intervention was confined to the evacuation of its own nationals.

Society, Community, and Nationality

Its history is such that Belgium is a country of immigrants. Contrary to other former colonial powers, Belgium decided not to import its labor force from the colonies but relied upon the temporary immigration of foreign workers from southern European countries and North Africa. Until recently, most migrants in Belgium were not citizens; consequently, they had no political rights.

Belgium is both a "multinational" and a "polyethnic" state. The Flemish, Walloons, and the German speakers constitute the chief national groups. Italians, Moroccans, and Turks are among the largest ethnic immigrant groups. Historically, community conflict has been framed as a language issue. The Belgian revolutionaries in the 1830s wanted to impose French as the only national language. The Flemish opposed this project of assimilation. From its origin, the Flemish movement opposed the use of French in Flanders, which was dominated by the French-speaking bourgeoisie. Their struggle aimed at total equality of Flemish and French in the Belgian public space. French-speaking citizens attempted to maintain the predominance of French as long as possible. Then, in 1963, Belgium was divided into four linguistic regions (a French-speaking region, a Flemish-speaking region, a German-speaking region, and the French-Flemish bilingual district of Brussels) by law, which established territoriality. Each region is presently homogenous from a linguistic point of view, and the three national languages are today treated equally.

In 1970, crucial amendments to the Belgian Constitution were passed that began the slow process of federalization of the state. This gradual process of acknowledgment of regional and communitarian autonomies took more than 20 years to complete. Belgium became a federal State in 1993 with three linguistic and cultural entities, namely the Flemish, French, and German communities. The geographic regions (Flanders, Walloonia, and Brussels) differ socially and economically as well. Longstanding conflicts between the Flemish and the Walloons are manifest in these cultural differences as reinforced by the end of the original unitary state. Because ethnicity is not officially recorded, it is difficult to ascertain accurate figures for each ethno-national group. But the number of inhabitants for each part of the country is available: 5,940,000 people live in Flanders, 3,340,000 live in Wallonia, and 960,000 reside in Brussels. Only 70,000 people live in the 10 villages composing the German community.

Since the 1993 Constitution, a series of amendments recognizing the three regions' autonomy have led to the restructuring of the government. Responsibilities are split among the federal, regional, and linguistic communities. These categories include justice, monetary policy, foreign affairs, defense and security, social security (pensions, unemployment benefits, family allowances), public health, national, cultural, and scientific institutions. Among the main responsibilities of the regions are economic policy, employment policy, public transport, housing policy, environmental policy, agriculture, urban planning and external trade. The Communities preside over most cultural matters (television, radio, sport), education, social aid and health policy, familial policy, etc. This federal restructuring has not completely eliminated clashes and conflicts among the various levels of the state.

Since the end of World War I and until the first oil crisis of the early 1970s, Belgium has regularly recruited foreign workers to fill temporary gaps in the labor market. In the 1960s, immigration was also seen as a solution to the demographic decline of the country. However, like many other European governments, Belgium decided to stop any new recruitment of foreign workers in 1974. Since then, new migration patterns emerged (foreign students, asylum seekers, illegal and clandestine immigration) and led to new settlements on Belgian soil. The issue of integration progressively climbed on the political agenda, politicized especially by the Flemish separatist party, Vlaams Blok, at the end of the 1980s.

Today, foreigners and aliens represent 8.8 percent of the total population of the country. More than 300,000 foreigners acquired Belgian citizenship after 1984. This population is not equally spread throughout the country. Immigrants represent 5 percent of the population in Flanders, about 10 percent in Wallonia, and about 28.5 percent in Brussels. Many nationalities are represented, including (in decreasing order) Italians, Moroccans, French, Dutch, Turks, Spaniards, Germans, British, Americans, and Congolese. Most are concentrated in urban areas.

Immigration has deeply changed Belgian society and diversified its cultural and ethnic landscape. For example, Islam is now a practiced religion of the country, which was traditionally dominated by Catholicism. The process of diversification of Belgian society is bound to continue in the age of globalization. Immigrants and ethnics increasingly question by their mere presence the traditional institutional arrangements governing linguistic and cultural pluralism in the country.

Politics and Economy

The recent evolution toward federalization of the State has been accompanied by the rise of ethno-nationalism in Flanders, stimulated chiefly by a rebirth of regionalism in Wallonia and by a resistance toward Belgian patriotism in the newest region, namely Brussels, and also in the German-speaking Belgian community. Under the pressure of separatist movements, the issue of the dismantling of the Belgian State has jumped high on the political agenda. Debates about separatism are no longer taboo. The existence of a Belgian state in the twenty-first century is less taken for granted than ever before in the short history of the Belgian Kingdom.

Political divisions fall into three main groups, each of which is divided into political parties constituted along linguistic lines. Electoral politics have been dominated by coalitions, as none of the four major parties—the Socialists (PS), Christian Social (CVP), Flemish Liberal Democrats (VLD), and Liberal parties (PRL)—have been able to attract sufficient support to establish a government on their own. Several smaller parties significantly influence the outcome of elections (the ecological parties are Ecolo and Agalev, and the extreme right-wing Flemish separatist party is Vlaams Blok).

Belgium's modern, private enterprise economy has historically capitalized on its central geographic location and diversified industrial and commercial base. The country is a member of the European Union and began circulating the euro currency in January 2002. Flemish, Walloons, and Brusselers are bound to commune as partners in the same global economy. On the other hand, they have reached a significant degree of autonomy and they are increasingly "living apart together" in the Belgian State, politically, socially and culturally. Industries such as engineering and metal products, motor vehicle assembly, chemicals, textiles, glass, petroleum, and coal are primarily concentrated in the Flemish north. Agriculture comprises only a tiny portion of its GDP and labor force. With few natural resources, the economy is highly dependent upon exports, making it highly vulnerable to world markets. Roughly three-quarters of its trade is with other European Union countries, and in 2002 the GDP per capita income was $29,200.

MARCO MARTINIELLO

See also **Walloons**

Further Reading

Coenen, Marie-Thérèse, and Rosine Lewin, editors, *La Belgique et ses immigrés*, Bruxelles: Coll. Politique et Histoire, De Boeck Université, 1997

Fitzmaurice, John, *The Politics of Belgium: A Unique Federalism*, London: Hurst, 1996

Lijparhdt, Arend, editor, *Conflict and Coexistence in Belgium. The Dynamics of a Culturally Divided Society*, Berkeley: University of California Press, 1981

Mabille, Xavier, *Histoire politique de la Belgique. Facteurs et acteurs de changement*, Bruxelles: CRISP, 2001

Morelli, Anne, editor, *Histoire des étrangers et de l'immigration en Belgique de la préhistoire à nos jours*, Bruxelles: Editions Vie Ouvrière, 1992

Witte, Els, and Jan Craeybeckx, *La Belgique politique de 1830 à nos jours. Les tensions d'une démocratie bourgeoise*, Bruxelles: Labor, 1987

Belize

Capsule Summary

Location: Central America
Total Population: 266,440 (July 2003)
Minority Populations: Garífuna, Kekchí, Mennonite German, Mopane, Yucateco
Languages: Arawakan, Belize Creole English, English (official), Mayan, Plautdietsch (Low Saxon German), Spanish
Religions: Roman Catholic (49.6%), Protestant (27% [Anglican 5.3%, Methodist 3.5%, Mennonite 4.1%, Seventh-Day Adventist 5.2%, Pentecostal 7.4%, Jehovah's Witnesses 1.5%]), none (9.4%), other (14%) [2000]

Belize is an independent, Central American country bounded on the north by Mexico, on the east by the Caribbean Sea, and on the south and west by Guatemala. With a total area of 22,966 square km (8,867 square miles), Belize is similar in size to the state of New Hampshire and has an extended coast along the Caribbean Sea. The population of Belize, however, is but one-fifth that of New Hampshire. Among the countries of Central America, Belize has the smallest population. The physical, demographic, and economic nature of Belize make it a minority entity in the world.

Belize was initially inhabited by an ancient, relatively advanced Mayan Indian civilization that reached its apex between 250 and 900 CE. The earliest European settlement in the colony occurred circa 1638 by British logwood cutters (logwood was used to produce dyes) from Jamaica (which Great Britain captured from Spain in 1655). The settlement was subjected to numerous attacks from neighboring Spanish settlements (Spain claimed sovereignty over the entire New World except for regions in South America assigned to Portugal) for the next 150 years. The British finally defeated the Spanish opposition in 1798, after which British control over the settlement gradually increased, and in 1871 Belize (British Honduras) was formally declared a British colony. Belize became independent in 1981, continuing its relation with England as a member of the British Commonwealth.

Presently, more than two-thirds of the population is a mixture (*mestizo*, creole) of European, Amerindian, and African lineage. This population is settled through the middle coast and central interior of the country. In the sparsely-settled northwest and southwest corners of the country lie the remaining historic Mayan populations, one-sixth of Belize. Two small colonies of German Mennonites have settled along the northwest and central western frontier borders of Belize with Guatemala. The Spanish-speaking population of Belize, almost a fourth of the country's total, lives in the northern region bordering Mexico. Along the southern coast appear a half-dozen separated groupings of Black Carib Indians, speaking Garífuna, a language related to the Arawak family that once appeared throughout the Caribbean.

Both the English and Spanish languages occur in Belize because the territory was claimed by Spain until the late eighteenth century.

Standard English is the official language of Belize and the one most used by the small minority of those connected to British, European, and American interests. However, a Belizean form of Creole English is spoken also, mainly by the dominant majority of *mestizos* and creoles. The portion of the population that is Mayan speaks the Yucatan form of the language in the north; Mopán in the central western region, and Kekchí in the south. The Mennonite population speaks a form of Low German based principally on dialects from Saxony and Franconia.

The dominant religion is Roman Catholic, to which nearly two-thirds of the Belize population adheres, encompassing much of the mixed and native elements. Those related to, who worked closely with, or aligned themselves with the British colonial administration, adhere to the Anglican religion, slightly more than a tenth of the population. Another tenth of the population adheres to the Methodist and Seventh Day Adventist religions, sects that appeared primarily due to American Protestant missionary efforts. The German Mennonites, a scant percent of the Belizean population, are part of a larger settlement pattern by these people in remote parts of Latin America. There are small enclaves of Chinese, Asian Indians, and Middle Easterners in the cities, generally following their traditional religions.

The *mestizo* and Creole populations resulted from the mixing of Spanish or other Europeans with the native population during the early colonial period and from the local population interbreeding with slaves brought from Africa. During this period the coast of Belize, due to its protective reefs and isolated yet strategic position, provided a haven for pirates. The Mayan populations in Belize represent the furthest eastern and southern extent of this classic native civilization of Mesoamerica, of which they were thriving mercantile and urban elements. The Black Caribs along the southern coast represent the furthest western remnant of Arawak natives. They flourished in the Caribbean but were routed during the last millennium by the more aggressive Carib Indians and then decimated by European diseases following the explorations and settlement of Christopher Columbus and the Spanish.

The plutocratic nature of the Belizean economy makes the population an impoverished minority in its own land. Billionaire foreign businesses control the economy and government, owning banks, the gambling and tourist trades, communications, and the drug traffic. Annual per capita income is well under $3,000. GDP per capita is $4,900 (2002). In this small, essentially private enterprise economy the tourism industry is the number one foreign exchange earner. Other national income comes from the agriculture sector, particularly the export of sugar, bananas, and other tropical fruits. These mainstays of the economy are highly vulnerable to two factors, global markets and weather. Rampant price fluctuations wreak havoc with profits, and massive Caribbean hurricane destruction has obliterated production.

While the bulk of Belize's national income derives from export agriculture, most Belizeans work in low-wage service sector jobs. This sector is especially growing in relation to the tourism industry, particularly hotels and restaurants, as the country develops the attractions of its beaches, coral reefs, and historic and archaeological sites. With a huge foreign debt, the interest on which is paid from national income and taxes, Belize and its inhabitants essentially work to serve the financial and leisure interests of foreigners. They are able to carry out international service functions because there are very low rates of illiteracy through government support of education along with health and welfare. Nevertheless, while as citizens Belizeans form the majority of their country, as economic dependents they are an economic minority in it.

EDWARD A. RIEDINGER

See also **Garifuna**

Further Reading

Annual Studies on Belize Conference, Belize City: Society for the Promotion of Education and Research, 1987

Bolland, O. Nigel, *The Formation of a Colonial Society: Belize, from Conquest to Crown Colony*, Baltimore: Johns Hopkins Press, 1977

Bolland, O. Nigel, *Belize, a New Nation in Central America*, Boulder, Colorado: Westview Press, 1986

A History of Belize: Nation in the Making, 3rd edition, Explorer Series, Belize City: Cubola Productions, 1997

Merrill, Tim, *Guyana and Belize: Country Studies*, 2nd edition, Washington, DC: Federal Research Division, Library of Congress, 1993

Sutherland, Anne, *The Making of Belize, Globalization in the Margins*, Westport, Connecticut: Bergin & Garvey, 1998

Wilk, Richard R., and Mac Chapin, *Ethnic Minorities in Belize: Mopán, Kekchí and Garífuna*, Belize: Spear, 1990

Wright, Peggy, and Brian E. Coutts, compilers, *Belize*, World Bibliographic Series, 21, Oxford, England: Clio Press, 1993

Bengalis

Capsule Summary

Location: Northeastern South Asia; geographical region known as Bengal
Total Population: approximately 210 million
Language: Bengali
Religion: predominantly Muslim and Hindu, some Buddhists

The Bengali people's primary identity is as speakers of the Bengali language who share Bengali culture. Bengali, like most north South Asian languages, belongs to the Indo-Iranian (also called Indo-Aryan) branch of the Indo-European family. The Bengali language has a long literary tradition of which the Bengalis are intensely proud. The Bengal region, approximately 233,000 square kilometers, consists largely of a vast alluvial, deltaic plain laced with the numerous distributaries of the Ganges and Brahmaputra rivers, bounded by the Eastern Himalayas in the north and the Bay of Bengal in the south. The region is divided politically between the nation of Bangladesh (forming 62 percent of the region) and the Indian state of West Bengal (forming the remaining 38 percent of the region) where, according to the last (2001) censuses, approximately 128 million and 70 million Bengalis reside, respectively. Another 12 million Bengalis live in the Indian states of Assam, Tripura, Meghalaya, Orissa, Bihar, Madhya Pradesh, the Andaman Islands, and in the United States, the United Kingdom, Canada, Italy, and France. Bengal was partitioned at the Independence of the Indian subcontinent in 1947, essentially along religious lines. The majority of Bengali Muslims live in Bangladesh and Bengali Hindus in West Bengal.

History

Bengal has found mention as a distinct region in early Hindu texts. Throughout the first millennium CE it was governed by a succession of Buddhist and Hindu rulers. Islam appeared in the region both through conversions initiated by Sufi saints and with Turkish armies, which entered the region in 1204. Bengal had a loose association with the sultanate of Delhi before becoming completely independent in 1341. Muslim rulers asserted their independence despite challenges until 1541, when the region was taken over by Afghans. Dhaka was the capital during much of this period and continued to be so after the city was captured by the Mughal emperor Akbar in 1576. The capital was moved to Murshidabad in 1704; soon after, following Aurangzeb's death in 1707, the Mughal governors of Bengal became virtually independent.

European contact started in 1517 with the Portuguese establishing a settlement in Chittagong. Dutch traders arrived in 1602, the British in 1650, and the French in 1673. The British founded Calcutta in 1690, and British rule began with the administration of part of Bengal in 1757. Lasting until 1947, British rule had a profound impact on Bengali culture and society, especially in Calcutta, which became the premier city of British India and where, after 1835, English was introduced as the medium of higher education. Education and urban life gave rise to a refined class of people (*bhadralok*), many of whom lived off of tenurial rights to rents from agricultural land appropriated by the rulers. Though the intellectual achievements of this essentially upper caste Hindu elite were coupled with efforts at sociocultural and political reform, rural and Muslim Bengalis were inferiorized at the same time. The area now comprising Bangladesh became a hinterland of the commercial and industrial activities of Calcutta, supplying labor and raw materials (notably jute).

Bengal Divided

The tenurial rights and civil service positions obtained by the Calcutta elite increasingly worked to the disadvantage of the Muslim nobility and peasants of eastern Bengal. In the 1920s and 1930s, when the elite-backed Hindu majority were faced with the loss of provincial power, they turned from implicit to increasingly explicit communitarian demands. In 1947, at independence, Bengal was partitioned; the east became part of Pakistan and the west the Indian state of West Bengal.

The partition of Bengal was preceded by and set off a series of religious riots in Calcutta and rural areas of eastern Bengal between Bengalis divided along religious lines. In the wake of partition around 2 million refugees crossed the border between the eastern and western parts of Bengal. The Hindu minorities from eastern Bengal were sent to various camps such as Dandakaranya and Mana in central India.

In the eastern part of Bengal, East Pakistan (as the province was renamed in 1955), resentment and autonomist sentiments grew against the autocratic measures of western Pakistan. Bengalis demanded equal status for their language with Urdu and for greater equality with West Pakistan in civil, economic, and military spheres. In March 1971, negotiations between the two wings broke down, and the army launched a genocidal attack on Bengalis, killing 3 million and making 10 million refugees. Led by Sheikh Mujibur Rahman and helped by India, East Pakistan won independence from West Pakistan in December 1971, and Bangladesh was born.

Today, the major minority groups in Bangladesh are largely lower caste Hindus, the tribal peoples of the Chittagong Hill tracts and the Biharis. Bengali minorities outside Bangladesh and West Bengal are mainly in Tripura and Assam, where Bangladeshi tribal refugees and Bengali Hindus and Muslims from both West Bengal and Bangladesh have sought asylum on political and economic grounds, creating significant tension with the local populations.

Society

Urban elite Bengalis have produced one of South Asia's finest literary traditions, including not only the novel, short story, and poetry, but drama and film. The literary language with which educated speakers are familiar is quite distinct from the everyday language of the majority of Bengalis. The Eastern dialects of Bengali, notably those spoken in the Sylhet and Chittagong districts of Bangladesh, differ quite noticeably from the languages used in the two most important urban centers, Kolkata and Dhaka, respectively the capitals of the West Bengal state and of Bangladesh.

Rural Bengal has an old and well-developed literature, including narrative poetry (*puthi, mangalkavya, pat*), drawn from history, myth, and legend, as well as a very popular itinerant theater (*jatra*). There is also a long tradition of religious music, particularly associated with the more devotional and mystical practices of popular Hinduism (e.g., worship of goddesses Manasa, Sitala, and Kali, and of the gods Satya Narayan, Krishna) and of popular Islam (e.g., the devotional gatherings of various Sufi orders). Hinduism and Islam have been closely connected in Bengal and have given rise to a very important tradition of religious syncretism manifested through Baul, Bhatiyali, Bhaoaiya songs and mixed cults to Bonbibi, Olabibi, Satya Pir and to the shrines of Sufi saints.

ANNU JALAIS

See also **Bangladesh; Canada; India; United Kingdom**

Further Reading

Bandopadhyay, Sekhar, *Caste, Protest and Identity in Colonial India: The Namasudras of Bengal 1872–1947,* Richmond, Surrey, England: Curzon Press, 1997

Chatterjee, Partha, "Agrarian Relations and Communalism in Bengal, 1926–1935," *Subaltern Studies I: Writings on South Asian History and Society*, edited by Ranajit Guha, Delhi: Oxford University Press, 1982

Chatterji, Joya, *Bengal Divided: Hindu Communalism and Partition, 1932–1947,* Cambridge: Cambridge University Press, 1994

Das Gupta, Sanjukta, "Peasant and Tribal Movements in Colonial Bengal: A Historiographic Overview," in *Bengal: Rethinking History*, edited by Sekhar Bandyopadhyay, New Delhi: Manohar, International Centre for Bengal Studies, 2001

Eaton, Richard Maxwell, *The Rise of Islam and the Bengal Frontier 1204–1760,* Berkeley: University of California Press, 1993

Ghosh, Amitav, *The Shadow Lines,* London: Bloomsbury Press, 1988

Inden, Ronald, and Ralph Nicholas, *Kinship in Bengali Culture,* Chicago: Chicago University Press, 1977

Mallick, Ross, *Development, Ethnicity and Human Rights in South Asia*, New Delhi: Sage Publications, 1998

Mallick, Ross, "Refugee Settlement in Forest Reserves: West Bengal Policy Reversal and the Marichjhapi Massacre," *The Journal of Asian Studies*, 58, no. 1 (1999)

Nasrin, Taslima, *Lajja–Shame*, translated from the Bengali by Tutul Gupta, New Delhi: Penguin Books, 1994; original Bengali edition, 1993

Rahman, Md. Mahbubar, and Willem van Schendel, "'I am *Not* a Refugee': Rethinking Partition Migration," *Modern Asian Studies,* 37, no. 3, Cambridge University Press, 2003

Roy, Asim, *The Islamic Syncretistic Tradition in Bengal,* Princeton, New Jersey: Princeton University Press, 1983

Benin

Capsule Summary

Location: West Africa
Total Population: 7,041,490 (2003)
Minority Population: Fon and related (42%), Adja (15.6%), Yoruba (12.1%), Bariba (8.6%), Betammaribé (6.1%), Peul (6.1%), others (10%) (1992 census)
Languages: French (official), Fon and Yoruba (most common vernaculars in south), tribal languages (at least six major ones in north)
Religions: Indigenous beliefs (50%), Christian (30%), Muslim (20%)

Benin is a country in Western Africa, bordering the Bight of Benin, between Nigeria and Togo. Its economic capital is Cotonou, and the administrative capital is Porto Novo. Comprising a total area of 112,620 sq km (43,921.8 sq mi), Benin is approximately the size of the state of Pennsylvania. Its estimated population of just over 7 million reflects the effects of high mortality due to AIDS, which can result in lower life expectancy, higher infant mortality rates, and lower population and growth rates. The country's ethnic distribution is African (99 percent, including 42 ethnic groups, most important being Fon, Adja, Yoruba, Bariba), and Europeans (5,500).

History

An historically native kingdom—one of the most highly organized states of West Africa prior to the arrival of the Portuguese in 1485—Benin exerted significant influence in the seventeenth century when it was known to Europeans as Great Benin.

Before the British took control of Benin in 1897, Tado, former capital of the Adja, presently in Togo, was the likely origin of the indigenous southern Benin peoples. In the early sixteenth century, the Houeda peoples migrated south by the Mono River. They founded a kingdom in Gléhoué, later renamed Ouidah. Later, the Agassou clan, whose ancestors were, according to legend, born of an Adja princess and a panther, followed southeastward after their chief had failed to seize power. They settled in Allada. For several decades, the Agassou dominated the area natives. In the early seventeenth century, fights of succession exploded among heirs to the throne. The eldest remained on the throne while his two brothers left.

Te Agbanlin went eastward and set up his kingdom in Hogbonou, which was renamed Porto Novo circa 1758 by Brazilian sailors. Owing to successive territorial gains and the slave trade, the Goun kingdom grew swiftly. The other brother, Do Aklin, went northward and settled in Guedevi's land near present day Bohicon. His grandson, Aho, conquered his neighbors and imposed his people's supremacy over the natives. Calling himself Huegbadja (1645–1685), Aho founded the Kingdom of Danxome (Dahomey) and its capital, Abomey, built inside surrounding ditches. He created a government with strongly hierarchical institutions. The highly structured political, economic, and religious organization combined with regular aggressive military campaigns ensured the Fon kingdom its power over its neighbors. Raids brought many slaves who were either sold to European and Brazilian slave traders or used as field workers. Nonetheless, Dahomey remained threatened by the Yoruba-Nago. Indeed, the kingdoms of Ifé and Oyo in present day Nigeria had progressively overrun west south and central Benin, before mixing with natives. As a result, numerous kingdoms of Yoruba origin were founded: Itake (Sakete / Pobé), Takon, Ifanhim, Holli and Kétou and Savé, two of the biggest kingdoms of the area. To the west of central Benin, the Tchabé, the Itcha, the Ifé and Manigri people are also from the Yoruba as well as the Mahi and the Sahoué.

The Bariba form the third indigenous group, in Northeast Benin, composing half of the population of this area. They arrived from the East in the thirteenth and fourteenth centuries. Dauntless horsemen, they founded several feudal monarchies organized according to complex relations of vassalage in Kandi, Parakou, Kouandé and Nikki, their kingdom's capital. The Dendi, descendants of the Songhaï empire of Mali, also inhabited Northeast Benin where they arrived in the sixteenth century. The Betammaribe have settled since ancient times in the Atakora Mountains. In the majority of Northwest Benin, they are divided into many subgroups indistinctly named *Somba* by the French. For centuries, several other groups joined them, including the Gourmantche and the Berba; peoples of Mossi origin (the Pila-Pila, the Taneka, the Boulba); and peoples of the Groussi group (the Kabre, the Dompago). The Haussa, native to the furthermost bounds of Niger and Nigeria, have been spreading into Benin for centuries.

When the slave trade was abolished, the kingdom of Dahomey succeeded in transferring economic activity into the sale of palm oil, the output of which was increased by King Guézo and King Glélé. In the late nineteenth century, the British and the French fought for supremacy along the coast. Leaning on rivalries between Abomey and Porto Novo, France conquered the Fon Kingdom in 1892, not without difficulty. At the end of a long war of resistance, King Behanzin (1889–1894) fell from the throne and was sent into exile. Pursuing their advance northward, the French established a colonial protectorate in January 1894; its name, Dahomey, was chosen to commemorate the fierce battles against this kingdom. Benin's boundaries with Togo and Lagos were determined in treaties with Germany and Great Britain in the late nineteenth century, and the county was made an overseas territory of France in 1946.

From independence from France in 1960 until 1972, Benin experienced a period of instability marked by a record number of coups d'état. A succession of military governments ended in 1972 with the rise to power of President (chief of state) Mathieu Kerekou, who established a 17-year-long governmental regime based on Marxist-Leninist principles. In 1975, he changed the name of Dahomey to Benin. A move to representative government began in 1989. As the country was on the verge of rupture, Kerekou accepted, in 1989, the organization of a national conference. Benin's Constitution was ratified in 1990, and Prime Minister Nicephore Soglo won the first free elections in 1991, marking the first successful transfer of power in Africa from a dictatorship to a democracy. Kerekou defeated him in 1996 and was re-elected in 2000, although some irregularities were alleged.

Society and Ethnicity

The multi-ethnic structure of Benin results from a centuries-old continual intermixing of peoples. The Fon, today in the majority, proceed from successive strata of natives, Yoruba, and Adja conquerors. In southern Benin, the Adja-Ewe-Fon group is mainly composed of the Fon, the Goun, the Mina or Guin, the Aïzo and, related to the Adja-Fon, the Popo or Xwela, the Sè, the Ouatchi, and the Houeda.

As a consequence of the multi-ethnic structure, the Vodun religion—the most important animist cult prevailing in Benin—blends elements from the different ethnic groups. The pantheons of all three groups (Mina, Fon, Yoruba) are virtually identical. The Vodun religion is closely connected to the history of the kingdom of Dahomey that integrated and ruled the native gods (Voduns) encountered throughout the conquests. Inter-ethnic Voduns are celebrated alongside purely local Voduns. Christianity, mainly Catholicism, was spread by French missionaries and continues to be practiced mostly in south Benin. Islam is more influential in the North and was brought by the Dendi, the Peul and the Haussa as well as in the southeast, where it is influenced by the Yoruba of Lagos.

Benin's economy, largely based on agriculture (38 percent), industry (15 percent), and services (47 percent), (2002) remains underdeveloped. With a GDP per capita income of $1,100 (2002), Benin's industries include textiles, food processing, chemical production, and construction materials. Economic plans for the country in recent years include the attraction of more foreign investment, increased emphasis on tourism, the development of new food processing systems and agricultural products, and the stimulation of growth in new information and communication technology.

Since independence, Benin's political dynamics have been dominated by ethnic and regional concerns that stem from religious ones. In part, democracy has remained stable as the ruling authorities are obliged to compromise among multi-ethnic factions. The political, social, and religious structure of Benin is thus characterized by a syncretic dynamic that is still working with the regular arrival of new Vodun cults and prophetic religions such as the Celestial Church of Christ.

ANNE DECORET-AHIHA

See also **Yoruba**

Further Reading

Le Bénin, Karthala (Politique africaine), no.59, (October 1995)

Beausoleil Jeanne, editor, *Pour une reconnaissance africaine, Dahomey 1930*, Boulogne-Billancourt: Musée Albert-Kahn, 1996

Cornevin, Robert, *La république populaire du Bénin des origines à nos jours*, Paris: Maisonneuve, 1981

Glélé, Maurice Ahanhanzo, *Le Danxome: Du pouvoir Adja à la nation Fon*, Paris: Nubia, 1974

Herskovits, Jean Malville, *Dahomey, an Ancient West African Kingdom,* Evanston: Northwestern University Press, 1967; New York: Augustin, 1938

Kadya Tall, Emmanuelle, "De la démocratie et des cultes Voduns au Bénin", *Cahiers d'Etudes Africaines*, 137, XXXV-1 (1995)

Medeiros, François, editor, *Peuples du Bénin. Aja-Ewé*, Paris: Karthala, 1984

Berbers

Capsule Summary

Location: Morocco, Algeria, Tunis, Libya, Mali, Niger, Canary Islands, Mauritania, Burkina-Faso, and Egypt
Total population: around 25 million
Language: Berber (alternative name: Tamazight)

The Berber (or Amazigh) peoples live mainly in Northern Africa, throughout the Mediterranean coast, the Sahara region, and the western Sahel (namely, the border region between the Saharan zone and the flat grasslands or savannah). Amazigh history in North

Africa is extensive and diverse. Their ancient ancestors settled in the area just inland of the Mediterranean Sea, east of Egypt. Many ancient Roman, Greek, and Phoenician colonial accounts refer to a group of people collectively known as "Berbera" who lived in northern Africa. Berber is a generic name given to numerous heterogeneous ethnic groups that share similar cultural, political, and economic practices. Before the arrival of Arabs in the seventh century, these areas comprised the Berber world. The Amazigh call their territory or homeland *Tamazgha*.

Today, there are large Berber groups in Morocco (as well as in the Spanish cities of Ceuta and Melilla) and Algeria, important communities in Mali, Niger, and Libya, and smaller groups in Tunis, Mauritania, Burkina-Faso, and Egypt (in the Siwa oasis). The Tuareg (self-named as *Imajaghen*) live in the desert landscapes, and represent one branch of the Berber whole. The Canary Islands, today an autonomous community and historical region of Spain, were originally inhabited by Berbers, and archaeology, topography, music, and customs remain evident in the islands.

It is estimated that there are approximately 20 million speakers of the Berber language, which constitutes a broad group of dialects or languages that can be related based on commonalities. In spite of its broad usage, no country recognizes these strains of indigenous languages. Islamic states north of the Sahara are considered to be Arab cultures using Arabic languages. This conception extends among many Berbers as well, who consider themselves to be Arabs, although ethnic consciousness is also high and increasing among many Berbers, especially in Algeria and Morocco. In Algeria, the Berber population represents around 25 percent of the total (about 7 million). Kabilians, in the West of Alger, represent the most important group, among others including the Shawia (in the Aures Mountains), Mzabit, and Tuareg in the Saharan regions. In Morocco, nearly half of the population is Berber, including three main groups: Tarifit (in the Mediterranean coastland), Tamazigh (in the Atlas Mountains), and Shleuh (southward). Different communities of Berber Hebrews have been situated in the Shleuh areas for hundreds, maybe thousands, of years. The majority of them have since migrated to Israel after 1956.

History

References to the Berbers date to the first millennium BCE, when they inhabited the Sahara and nearly the entire coastal area of the Magrib (such as Northwestern Africa). Indeed, the historian Ibn Khaldun (1332–1395 CE) considered all this area to belong to the Berbers, and named the entire region *mawatin al-Barbar* (the land of the Berber).

Social groups from inland developed a nomadic life based on cattle-raising and complemented herding with trading activities. The Berbers from the coastal regions built a rural, sedentary civilization that provides the human background to the Cartago Phoenician colony (founded circa 814 BCE). Since 40 BCE, the Berber coastland has been under Roman influence, but the Berbers' resistance obstructed Roman aims for further expansion and created a stable borderland (the *limes*) that constituted a viable commercial and cultural zone, connecting the Roman civilization with the Berber world, and even with the societies of sub-Saharan Africa.

The Berber peoples, always strongly attached to their traditions and their egalitarian social organization, offered tenacious resistance to the Arab invasion during the seventh century. At this time Kutama and Sanhadja Berbers occupied the Magribian central area, Masmuda Berbers inhabited the western Magrib, and Luwata and Hawwara Berbers lived in present-day Libya. On the other hand, Christianity (and Judaism to a lesser degree) was widely accepted among the Berbers of the coastal fringe from the fifth century BCE to the sixth century CE. After 704 CE, the entire Magrib region (northwest Africa comprising the Atlas Mountains and the coastlands of Morocco and Algeria and Tunisia) became the western part of the Arab caliphal (Islamic) empire, although probably only 200,000 Arabs invaded the area. Berbers formed the backbone of the Arab armies that eventually conquered Spain. However, the Berbers repeatedly rose against the Arabs, and in the ninth century, for example, they supported the Fatimad dynasty in its conquest of North Africa. The Berbers were able to remain mostly immune to the administrative control of the Arab conquerors, and they adapted Islamic beliefs to their indigenous culture system. An extended period ensued in which Berber support shifted between several sects of Islam as they sought a form of the religion that would best incorporate and align with their traditional values and beliefs. For instance, Berbers followed the Kharijist sect, an egalitarian sect of dissenters who believed that anyone from any class could potentially rule, as in Muslim society. This religious doctrine emerged after a split in the Muslim community: several followers of Caliph Ali, cousin of Prophet Mohamed and his successor, refused to accept a pact with the followers of

Ali's rival (Muawiya). Indeed, the name *Kharijism* comes from the Arabic word *kharadja*, meaning "dissent," "to go away from," or "to leave." The egalitarian framework of the Kharijist sects was closely related to ancient Berber political culture. In fact, Kharijism offered a symbolic system appropriate to resist the oppressive regime of the Omeya caliphs from Damascus (in present-day Syria).

Nonetheless, some Berber groups were progressively "Arabized," especially in the urban areas. The chief reason for the success of Arabization was the dominant character of the Arabic culture, which granted high social and political prestige to the persons or communities who adopted the Arabic language, customs, laws, and values. Berbers eventually converted to Islam with great zeal in large numbers. One of the reasons was likely related to the Islamic focus on language, which included an emphasis on *'ilm* (divine knowledge) that was based on the oral transmisión of wisdom. As Berber was also an exclusively oral language, Islam offered the Amazigh peoples a familar linguistic system within which to embrace animist beliefs. The Berber cultures during the following centuries were increasingly marked by the political dual situation that existed in the Magrib region. The land's administrative center (*Blad Al-Makhzen*) was characterized by a predominantly Arabic culture and a strong urbanized society; and the land of the tribal groups (*Blad As-Siba*), mainly constituted by Berber peoples, remained highly centered in autonomous traditional social systems of beliefs, kinship links, a self-sufficient economy, and minimal political organization.

Succeeding centuries were marked by almost continuous struggles for power in North Africa among the various Berber tribes, between the Berbers and the Arabs, and between both these peoples and Spanish, Portuguese, and Turkish invaders.

Berber Traditional Culture

Many Berber peoples observe saintly cults, dating from prehistory. Evidence of the strong conservatism of the Berber culture is found in the pantheistic belief in the supernatural quality of the mountains, stones, trees, rivers, springs, and wells. Their religious system has existed from ancient times, and was described by Roman historians such as Pliny the Elder (23–79 CE).

Berber culture has maintained a rich oral literature that is still alive in its many communities, including the traditional *kanun* (customs) that governed the social system for centuries. Another important trait of the Berber culture is based on its particular political structure, centered in clanical links that provide the framework for minor but solid political units, which ruled under the recognized authority of an aged person who was the inheritor of the symbolic powers that stemmed from the clan's founders. These political cores functioned by means of an assembly-based system ruled by the family chiefs. The Amazigh political system, combined with the mountainous nature of their homeland landscape, provided literal and figurative shelter that in part explains the enduring character of the Berbers' cultural features.

Oppression Against Berbers

As early as the Islamic Umayyad (Omeya) Empire (659–750 CE), centered in Damascas, Berber societies faced oppression under the yoke of foreign rule. Indeed, under the reign of the Umayyad caliphate severe political measures were established that ensued Berber resistance.The Berbers were considered to be a defeated people who must be brought into submission, even those who were already Islamicized, that is to say, the majority of the Berber peoples. Moreover, thousands of Berber fought in the Islamic wars of conquest, but were not rewarded. Although the Berbers fought discrimination and oppression by remaining fiercely autonomous within their ancestral homelands, by the nineteenth and twentieth centuries the progressive centralization of political power, combined with widespread French and Spanish colonialism in Africa and elsewhere, worsened the situation among Berber communities which fell under ongoing imperialist invasions. At the end of the colonial period in the twentieth century, an Arab-based aristocracy and interest groups remained in power, and these groups negotiated the decolonization process with the metropolitan authorities. In this process Berber historical, cultural, and political rights were completely marginalized; for example, the Arabic and French languages in Morocco and elsewhere received official recognition, but the different Berber dialects remained unrecognized and are presently still not included in the education system and in the chief political and civil institutions.

The Amazigh language has been oppressed in the whole of North Africa by what Berber activists consider ongoing Arab-Islamic nationalism. The language is given little if any presence in the media. The ancient Berber alphabet is forbidden in the public domain. Parents are denied the right to give their children an

Amazigh name. At present Tamazight is written with three alphabets (Arab, Latin, and Tifinagh), which has led to discussions about which form to use in primary education. The Moroccan government prefers the Arab alphabet, while many activists would prefer Berber (Tifinagh) or the European alphabet. Tifinagh is considered important for cultural, historical, and psychological reasons, because it is clearly differentiated from the Arab language and culture. Some historians have argued that Tifinagh has survived thanks to generations of Berber women, who maintained the use of Tamazight letters and symbols in their jewelry-making, textiles, and other traditional handcrafts.

In Morocco, repression of Berber culture emerged acutely during the first years after its independence (1957–1959). The Rif region, in northern Morocco, was the scene of many conflicts in which the Berbers protested their sociopolitical marginalization. The dominant Moroccan political party, the Istiqlal (Independence Party, or PI), deeply rooted in state power structures, preferred military response over political dialogue. In Algeria, since the beginning of independence from France (1962), the Kabylia region (home to Algerian Berbers in the East Atlas mountains) was politically dispossessed of the victory against the French imperialism during the long war for decolonization. In the 1950s, the region played a leading role in the war against French colonialism. Some 60 percent of the rebels who took up arms against the French were Kabyles, and 10,000 of the 14,000 Algerian immigrants who contributed to financing of the National Liberation Front (FLN) were also Kabyles. Post-independence the Kabyles confronted the newly-established Algerian government in the way they had confronted the French. Refusing the drive toward a one-party system and the prominent role of the army, a Kabylian human rights activist, Hocine Ait Ahmed, helped form the opposition party, Socialist Forces Front (FFS) in 1963 in protest of the FLN. The rebellion lasted for two years, after which Hocine Ait Ahmed was captured and then sentenced to death. Tensions between the groups continued and culminated in the so-called Berber (or Kabylian) Spring of April 1980, in what began as a student protest against the suppression of Berber education, language, and human rights, and ended as an important uprising within the Kabyle. The Algerian army responded with aggressive crackdowns against any dissension, student or otherwise, that resulted in the deaths of many Kabylians. Demonstrations, strikes, school boycotts, riots, and arrests have since characterized the oppositional relations between the authorities and the region.

After years of repression, the Amazigh movement in Morocco is presently undergoing a decisive stage in the struggle for recognition of the Moroccan Amazigh identity. Today, Berber activists say the "Arabization" of Morocco has led to discrimination and has marginalized their people. But the government has resisted calls for recognition of Tamazight as an official language of Morocco, fearing that the crusade will spawn a separatist movement. There the political experimentations after 1997 did not guarantee the freedom of the Berber communities: indeed, in June 2001, Moroccan armed forces blocked the meeting of the Berber Manifesto Conference scheduled to take place in Bouznika. The manifesto, written by Berber intellectuals and activists, demanded their national language be considered official and enshrined in the country's constitution. The Moroccan government followed this action with similar interdictions against other Berber meetings all over the Moroccan territory. In schools in predominantly Berber areas, lessons are not taught in Tamazight but in Arabic. Government jobs are off limits to those who speak only Berber, and Tamazight is prohibited in the courts; all legal documents must be translated into Arabic. Berber activists blame Arabization for the high illiteracy rate in Morocco; 56 percent of its citizens cannot read. In spite of this, in October 2001 six private schools started teaching in Tamazight and Arabic, signifying a historic shift in Moroccan attitudes toward the Berber community. This modest but important reform wasmade possible thanks to a government education charter calling for sweeping reforms of the Moroccan education system. The charter was commissioned by the late King Hassan II, who had stated in a televised speech that Tamazight should be taught in schools.

In Algeria, the situation of the Berbers, especially the Kablyian Berbers, remains difficult and conflict-ridden. The year 2001 was marked by ongoing bloody riots between Kablyian activists and Algerian military forces. On October 4 of that year, a protest group arrived in the capital only to be stopped by police. More recently, thousands of Berbers rioted in 1998 over a government decree making Arabic the official language of Algeria and the subsequent assassination of Matoub Lounes, a well-known musician and Berber activist, reputedly by the Armed Islamic Group, a fundamentalist insurgency.

Joan Manuel Cabezas López

See also **Algeria**

Further Reading

Brett, Michael, and Elizabeth Fentress, *The Berbers,* London: Blackwell Publishers, 1998

Hachid, Malika, *Les premièrs Berbers. Entre Meditérranée, Tassili et Nil*, Paris: Éditions Èdisud, 2000

Zartman, I. William, and William Mark Habeeb, editors, *Polity and Society in Contemporary North Africa*, Boulder: Westview, 1993

Bertha

Capsule Summary

Location: Ethiopia, Sudan
Total Population: about 150,000
Languages: Berta, Arabic, Amharic
Religions: Islam, traditional

The Bertha (often spelled Berta) are a people in Western Ethiopia, who since 1992 have formed part of the Beni Shangul-Gumuz Regional State in federal Ethiopia. This state is one of the smallest and economically weakest regional states in Ethiopia, with about half-a-million inhabitants. The Bertha are an indigenous group of peasant farmers in the Ethio-Sudanese border area, remote from the political centers in Ethiopia or Sudan although strongly influenced by them. The Bertha speak a language belonging to the Nilo-Saharan family, which is quite distinct from the Semitic and Cushitic language families that dominate in Ethiopia. The people number about 115,000 in Ethiopia and 35,000 in Sudan. The Bertha are also known as *Jebelawi* (although this refers to one subgroup) or as *Beni Shangul* (the Arabic place-name). Both are somewhat derogatory Sudanese Arabic names. Highland Ethiopians are called the Bertha Shanqilla (also a pejorative term). Scant scholarly or other literature exists on the Bertha people.

History

The Bertha live in the region of Bela Shangul (which is the local name, preferred over Beni Shangul), a multi-ethnic region which is also home to Mao, Gumuz, Shinasha and Koma minorities, in addition to Amhara, Gurage, Tigray and Oromo people who arrived mostly in the past one hundred years. Since 1898 Bela Shangul has been part of Ethiopia. Prior to that date, Bela Shangul was long dominated by the late medieval Funj-Hamej kingdom that emerged in the early sixteenth century and centered in Sennar, Sudan. The region became a popular slave-raiding area for the Funj, Ottoman Turks (ruling in Egypt after 1820), and later for the Sudanese Muslims (e.g., the late nineteenth century Mahdists and others) and a hub of regional trade. In the early twentieth century, highland Ethiopians also arrived to settle and to trade slaves. Because of the Muslim Sudanese raids, many local people migrated or converted to Islam to escape. Apart from slaves, Bela Shangul has been known since antiquity for its gold, panned from the rivers. Gold remains a major source of income for local people, illegal (and untaxed) but condoned by the authorities.

Society

Bertha society was a quasi-feudal, hierarchical society with local rulers (chiefs, called *agur*), a minority elite (called *Wet'awit'*) of mixed Sudanese Muslim immigrants and Islamized local people, and the Bertha population of peasants and craftspeople. The elite distinguished themselves from the common people, who they generally despised. There were several Arabized sheikhdoms in the area (Aqoldi and Khomosha) and a central ruler, or king, based in the town of Asosa (the last one was Sheikh Khojali). Bertha were organized in patrilineal clans, although over time a transition to bilateral descent-reckoning (through both mother and father) has emerged. In present day Bertha society group identity is based on territorial settlement.

Although most Bertha are Muslims, a large group retains their traditional religion, in which a mediatory divination system (*shangur*) dominates with the figure of the diviner (*ngeri*, who was a kind of spiritual leader and "rain master"). Bertha also practiced many other rituals commonly pertaining to land distribution, collective hunting, purification, and the annual harvest. Often they fused Muslim practices with their traditional ones. The name "Bela Shangul" is derived from *shangul*, a sacred ancestral stone carried by the original Bertha clans when they migrated to their present habitat. Currently, Islam is gaining ground at the expense of the traditional faith, and Christianity (Evangelist forms) is expanding.

At present, most Bertha are mixed subsistence farmers involved in livestock raising, beekeeping, coffee cultivation (a cash crop), and petty trade. Contraband trade from and to Sudan also occurs. The exploitation of granite and marble is being considered. The new Regional State administration (since 1992) is underdeveloped as to capacity, but is absorbing more local staff from the Bertha and other local populations.

In the last 50 years, the Bertha social hierarchy has changed drastically, with the prestigious elite groups disinherited and slavery abolished, but the general socio-economic level of the population has not visibly improved. There are still no major investments and the local economy and infrastructure of this small region remain weak with no tax basis. More than 80 percent of the regional state budget comes from the federal Ethiopian authorities.

Political representation of the Bertha in Ethiopia was historically limited due to their marginal position and small numbers. The post-1991 Ethiopian government claims that in the new ethno-federal establishment the Bertha have more self-rule in their own region, but in the Beni Shangul regional state the Bertha are also a minority. The region is also unstable, and corruption persists. In Sudan the Bertha are too small a group to have much impact and are generally looked down upon by northern Sudanese. Due to the ongoing civil war in Sudan, the region also remained isolated from local political arenas.

In the early 1980s a small resistance movement among the Ethiopian Bertha (the Berta Liberation Front) emerged, opposing the military Ethiopian government, but it soon ceased to exist. Later, dissidents established the Benishangul People's Liberation Movement (BPLM). This movement originally opposed the current Ethiopian government, but after a major conflict (1991–92) of the Bertha with the Oromo movement OLF (Oromo Liberation Front), which claimed power in the regional administration, the largest BPLM faction allied itself with the government, whose troops defeated the OLF forces. Another faction associated itself with the Sudanese fundamentalist Muslim party, National Islamic Front, and organized propaganda and armed attacks. In late 1992, BPLM-affiliated people have also violently targeted local highland Ethiopians living in the area (Amhara and others, who form about 25 percent of the total population), leading to the mutilation and death of hundreds of people and the destruction of thousands of homes. In 1996 the dominant BPLM-faction renamed itself the Ethiopian Berta Democratic Organization (an affiliate of the ruling Ethiopian party EPRDF), and claimed to represent the Berta people in the Beni-Shangul regional state. The actual amount of popular support it receives is unknown. In January 2001, the Ethiopian media mentioned "secessionist demands" existing among the Bertha people in the region, probably indicating some dissatisfaction with national government policy.

Jon Abbink

See also **Ethiopia; Sudan**

Further Reading

Triulzi, Alessandro, "Myths and Rituals of the Ethiopian Bertha," in *Peoples and Cultures of the Ethio-Sudan Borderland*, edited by M.L. Bender, East Lansing: African Studies Center, Michigan State University, 1981

———, *Salt, Gold and Legitimacy. Prelude to the History of a No-man's Land: Bela Shangul, Wallaga, Ethiopia (circa 1800–1898)*, Napoli: Istituto Universitario Orientale, 1981

Young, John, "Along Ethiopia's Western Frontier: Gambella and Benishangul in Transition," *Journal of Modern African Studies,* 37, no. 2, 1999

Bhindranwale, Jarnail Sant (India-Sikh)

Jarnail Singh Bhindranwale was the leader of Damdami Taksal, the historic institution founded by Sri Guru Gobind Singh Ji in 1706 as an intellectual center for Sikh studies, orthodoxy, and religious teaching in the Punjab. He became famous in the late 1970s as a religious preacher and later for reviving the demand for a separate Sikh state. At an early age he was selected to join the seminary at Damdami Taksal; he spent seven years learning Sikh scriptures and history. On the death of Kartar Singh, the anointed successor to leader Baba Gurbachan Singh, in 1977, Bhindranwale became the head of the organization. As a proponent of Sikh orthodoxy, Bhindranwale preached that the Sikhs, in keeping with their traditions, should bear weapons and should rid themselves of Brahmanic influences, that is, the religious and social system of orthodox Hinduism.

In order to purify Sikhism from what he perceived as the corrupting influences of Brahmanic practices of caste differentiation, Bhindranwale launched a movement against the heterodox sects of Sikhism. The principal target of Bhindranwale's effort was the Nirankari movement, a nineteenth century Sikh reform movement and heterodox sect that purported to carry on the lineage of Sikh gurus from the death of the tenth guru. When the Nirankaris held their annual convention in Amritsar to coincide with the celebration of the Sikh New Year, *Baisaikhi*, on April 13, 1978, Bhindranwale, along with the Akhand Kirtani Jatha school of followers, assembled a group of 150 people who marched on to the site of the convention, intending to disrupt it.

Nirankaris fired upon the approaching group of protesters, killing 13 of them. This event came to define the texture of politics in the Punjab for the next two decades. Bhindranwale pressed the government to take action against the Nirankaris responsible for the killings. When the courts freed those arrested, Bhindrawale denounced the government and the legal system for colluding with the Nirankaris. Helped by his strident attacks on the government of India, he quickly rose to prominence in Punjab politics. He gained a significant following among the Sikhs who felt alienated from the Indian mainstream.

Bhindranwale's revenge against the Nirankaris was realized on April 24, 1980 when Baba Gurbachan Singh Nirankari, the head of the Nirankari sect, was assassinated in Delhi. Bhindranwale was suspected of conspiracy in his murder. When the authorities tried to arrest Bhindranwale, he shifted his base to the Golden Temple complex in Amritsar, called *Harimandir Sahib*, the central Sikh palace of prayer. He gave himself up voluntarily, but was released due to insufficient evidence.

On September 9, 1981, Lala Jagat Narian, a Hindu press baron from Jullunder whose newspaper coverage was especially critical of Bhindranwale, was assassinated. Bhindranwale was suspected to be behind this murder as well; when authorities attempted to arrest him, he fled and again ensconced himself in the Golden Temple complex only to give himself up on September 20, 1981. When a number of his close associates, including Amrik Singh and Tara Singh, were arrested, Bhindranwale called a meeting of the Sikh community and launched a campaign to secure the release of his associates. Around the same time, Akali Dal, ("the Eternal Party," a popular political party of Sikhs founded in 1934) was engaged in a campaign to stop the Satluj-Yamuna Link canal, a Punjab-Haryana dispute over water supply. Sensing a perceptible fall in support, the Akali Dal decided to shift the location of its campaign to Amritsar, and Bhindranwale agreed to merge his own campaign with the Akali campaign, thus presenting a united opposition to the government.

As a Sikh fundamentalist, Bhindranwale was opposed to modernity and wanted the Sikhs to return to the ways of their own ancestors. He advocated Sikh males wear the traditional dress (*kuccha*) and believed that Sikh women should wear the *salwar-kameez* (a loose, chemise-like garment) over the *sari* and *bindis* (dots placed on the forehead at the site of the Third Eye), both of which he thought of as Hindu symbols. Hinduism for Bhindranwale represented the behemoth of cultural assimilation; fearing that the numerically larger Hindus would assimilate the Sikhs, Bhindranwale sharpened the boundaries between Hinduism and Sikhism through his rhetoric and politics. He dehumanized and criticized Hindus by labeling them as effeminate and by defining them as a nonmarital group.

In the early 1980s Prime Minister Indira Gandhi formed an opportunistic political alliance with Bhindranwale in an effort to control a Sikh secessionist movement in the Punjab region of northwest India. However, their alliance soon deteriorated. Alarmed at the rise in popularity of the highly political Sikh missionary and leader, India's leaders were disturbed by Bhindranwale's proclamation that Sikhs were a sovereign and self-ruling community. On December 15, 1983 Bhindranwale and his supporters entered the Akal Takht (the primary seat of Sikh religious authority and central altar for political assembly) and prepared a network of defensive fortifications inside the temple complex. The group began stockpiling weapons in the complex alongside an increase in violent activities throughout the Punjab. These actions included the burning of a number of railway stations and the murder of a number of Hindus in Punjab. While Bhindranwale never supported the concept of an independent Sikh state, Khalistan, he did not disavow it either. The literal meaning of *Khalistan* is "the sovereign land," which the Sikhs viewed as an egalitarian social system based on the concept of "halemi-raj," meaning "humanitarian and just governance."

Sensing a general separatist drift and perhaps overreacting to the increasing violence, the Prime Minister launched a military operation against Bhindranwale and his followers on July 4, 1984. Operation Blue Star (OBS), a military assault on Amritsar's Golden Temple was designed to flush out Bhindranwale and his supporters. Thousands died in the attack, while thousands more were raped and tortured by police. Several Sikh reference libraries were destroyed across Punjab, in addition to other *gurdwaras* (places of prayer). In the fighting over the next two days, over 2,000 people died in the Golden Temple, including Bhindranwale, who died of gunshot wounds in the basement of the Akal Takht. Within five months, Indira Gandhi was assassinated by two of her Sikh bodyguards in revenge for the OBS. Violent anti-Sikh riots engulfed Delhi at the news of Gandhi's death. Over the next decade Bhindranwale became a highly revered martyr and saint among the Sikh population of the Punjab.

Biography

Jarnail Singh Bhindranwale. Born 1947, Rode, Punjab, India. Studied at Damdami Taksal center for Sikh religious studies, Bhinder Kala, Punjab, 1965–1972; became its head priest in 1971. Elected to head Damdami Taksal 1977. Prominent as extremist leader of Sikh movement. Died in violent siege, Operation Blue Star, in Amritsar, India, 7 June 1984.

AMANDEEP SANDHU

See also **Sikhs; Singh, Tara (Sikh)**

Further Reading

Joshi, Chand, *Bhindranwale: Myth and Reality*, New Delhi: Vikas Publishing, 1984

Kumar, Ram, *The Sikh Unrest and the Indian State,* New Delhi: Ajanta Publisher, 1997

Mahmood, Cynthia, *Fighting for Faith and Nation: Dialogues with Sikh Militants*, Philadelphia: University of Pennsylvania Press, 1996

Singh, Khuswant, *A History of the Sikhs, Volume 2: 1839–1988,* New Delhi: Oxford University Press, 1999

Telford, Hamish, "The Political Economy of Punjab," *Asian Affairs,* 13, no. 11 (1992)

Tully, Mark, and Satish Jacob, *Amritsar: Mrs. Gandhi's Last Battle,* London: Cape, 1985

Bhutan

Capsule Summary

Country Name: Kingdom of Bhutan (also known as Butan or Buten)
Location: Himalayan Mouintain Range, sharing borders with India, China (Tibet) and Nepal
Population: 2,139,549 (July 2003)
Minority population: Bhote (50%), Ethnic Nepolese (35%), Indigenous or migrant tribes (15%)
Languages: Dzongkha (official), Bhotes speak various Tibetan dialects, Nepalese speak various Nepalese dialects
Religions: Lamaistic Buddhist (75%), Indian- and Nepalese-influenced Hinduism (25%)

Bhutan is a small, isolated country in the eastern part of the Himalaya Mountains with an area of 18,150 sq mi (46,538 sq km). It shares borders with India, Nepal, and the Tibetan portion of China. Since the mid-1960s, the country has made radical changes to improve its quality of life and join the international world.

The people of Bhutan originate from three ethnic communities. The Bhutia are the majority, comprising 60 percent of the population; they descend from the Tibetans who immigrated around the ninth century and presently dominate in the northern, central, and western sectors of the country. The Nepalese, the second largest group, comprise a third of the population. They are Hindus, practice the Hindu caste system, speak Nepali, and their immigration and residence patterns are restricted. In fact, discrimination between Nepalese and Tibetan communities discourages assimilation. The people of eastern Bhutan originate from the hill tribes of Assam and Arunachal Pradesh. Known as sharchops, they claim to be the earliest inhabitants and are Indo-Mongolian in their origins. Also, they are less strict about religious customs than the Bhutua.

The tranquility of isolation and being a relatively static society suddenly changed during the reign of King Jigme Dorji Wangchukas (1952–1973). He implemented drastic measures to bring a better quality of life to his people and make the Bhutanese government more representative and sensitive while also maneuvering Bhutan into modern globalization processes. Bhutan's ability to make such rapid changes in a short period is a major issue puzzling social scientists, policymakers, and other interested scholars.

Little is known about Bhutan before the eighth century CE because there is no prior recorded history. It is believed, however, that the region was divided among settlements and village chiefs were continually fighting among themselves. In the eighth century, Sendhu Raja, a king from Rirpochey, invited the Buddhist Guru Rinpochey ("Precious Teacher") to cure him from a fatal disease. Guru Rinpochey subdued the local deities causing the king's illness and than traveled around the country subduing spirits hostile to Buddhism. Thus began the prominence of Buddhism in Bhutan, for Buddhist philosophers and holy men visited, settled and/or established monasteries in the region. Periods of unity and conflict followed.

In 1865, Britain and Bhutan signed the Treaty of Sinchulu, whereby Bhutan received an annual subsidy in exchange for ceding some border land. Under British influence, a monarchy was established in 1907 that minimized British involvement in Bhutanese internal affairs. (This role was assumed by independent India after 1947.) Outside interest came around 1772–73 and 1864–65, when Britain gained control of Bhutan's external affairs in return for a subsidy from the British government. Control of Burma was passed to India at the time India obtained independence. India continued with the subsidy and helped Bhutan develop economically. It was the third king, Jigme Dorji Wanchuk, who cautiously opened the doors to modernization and change in 1960. Bhutan's current ruler, Jigme Sirigyoe Wangchuk, has followed his predecessor's philosophy for economic development.

The magnitude of changes in Bhutan is demonstrated by the illustrative but not exhaustive examples. Before 1960, for instance, people lived in relative isolation, depending on livestock, farms, and the surrounding forest for food, clothing, and other needs. They were secure in their kinsmen and community, but their world was their village endowed with spiritual significance. There were no phones, roads, electricity, or postal services connecting Bhutan with the outside world. Life was hard with an expectancy of 35 years. There were only two hospitals and a handful of dispensaries managed by two trained doctors. Communicable diseases were rampant with a 50 percent death rate at birth or in infancy. Education had no place in family survival.

The current and prominent transformation of Bhutan began cautiously in 1960 but became more intensive starting in 1975, with phenomenal achievements. The economy is no longer dependent entirely on subsistence agriculture, but remains closely aligned with India's through strong trade and monetary links and dependence on India's financial assistance. Benin's products include cement, wood products, processed fruits, alcoholic beverages, and calcium carbide. With a GDP per capita income of $1,300 (2002), the government has made some progress in expanding the nation's productive base and improving social welfare. Hydropower for small modern industry is developing. Since 1980, an additional 5000 hectres of land have been put into intensive cultivation along with a system of agricultural services penetrating into the most inaccessible regions to reach 40,000 farmers in the past five years alone. Bhutan farmers have realized an increased yield of basic grains, some of which are exported. Health care now consists of 28 hospitals, 145 basic health units, and 454 outreach clinics. Improved health services along with improved access to safe water and sanitation have halved the mortality rate and maternity mortality rate. The best indicator of the improvements is in life expectancy, which has reached 66.

Bhutan arguably has been successful where countries with less severe problems have failed to improve their social and political circumstances. First, in spite of periods of extended civil strife, Bhutan has built a society that is unified but tolerates diversity, a success of nation building that has extended over 350 years. During this time it developed a distinct Bhutan identity based on Buddhist beliefs and values with a common language. Also, Bhutan has resisted colonialization since gaining independence from India in 1949. A hereditary monarchy with a vision has been a great asset. Finally, the majority of the country embraces Mahayana Buddhism, which does not stress material rewards but individual development, life, and compassion for others, social harmony and the sanctity of life and nature. Nature, in fact, is perceived as sacred and something to live in harmony with. Unfortunately these social and economic accomplishments have not offset the discontent of the Nepali community. Approximately 100,000 Bhutanese refugees live in Nepal, 90 percent in seven United Nations Office of the High Commissioner for Refugees camps, contributing to strains between the two countries.

Arthur Helweg

See also **Nepal; Nepalese**

Further Reading

Apte, Robert Z., *Three Kingdoms on the Roof of the World: Bhutan, Nepal, and Ladakh*, Berkeley: Paralax Press, 1990

Rustomji, Nari, *Bhutan: The Dragon Kingdom in Crisis*, New York: Oxford University Press, 1978

Savada, Andrea Matles, *Nepal and Bhutan: Country Studies (Area Handbook)*, Washington, DC: Clator's Law Books and Publishing, 1993

Upadhyay, B.N., *From Mountain Kingdom to Public Sector*, Delhi: Devika Publications, 2000

Zeppa, Jamie, *Beyond the Sky and the Earth*, New York: Rivershead Press, 1999

Bihari

Capsule Summary

Location: Bangladesh (formerly East Pakistan)
Total Population: Approximately 250,000
Language: Urdu
Religion: Muslim

The term *Bihari* denotes the community that migrated from the Indian state of Bihar to what was then East Pakistan (subsequently Bangladesh) in the aftermath of the partition of India. During Partition in 1947 there was a mass movement of people between India and Pakistan resulting in the inter-State transfer of approximately 16 million people. Of the 1.3 million Muslims who moved to East Bengal (East Pakistan) 1 million came from the Indian State of Bihar. They came to be known collectively as Biharis. Like the majority of Bengalis, most Biharis are Sunni Muslims. They speak Urdu (as opposed to Bengali) and keenly supported Pakistan's initial efforts to impose the Urdu language on the Bengali people. A majority of Bihari live in camps. They suffer from discrimination, prejudice, and hostility at the hands of the majority Bengalis for their past association with Pakistan and for their desire to resettle in Pakistan.

History

Upon their arrival in East Bengal (East Pakistan) after the creation of the new state, the Biharis were initially welcomed by the indigenous Bengalis. Pakistan was conceived of as an ideological state and established as a safe-haven for all Muslims of South-Asia. A majority of the Biharis settled in Dhaka, Dinajpur, and Rangpur, where they were offered housing and occupational facilities. Skillful, well educated, politically astute, and armed with considerable entrepreneurial skills, the Biharis had little difficulty finding work as traders, clerks, civil service officials, skilled railway or mill workers, doctors, lawyers, and even politicians. Indeed, many were appointed by the Pakistani officials to replace educated Hindus in administrative posts and in the bureaucracy of Pakistan.

In the years that preceded the independence of Pakistan, the Bengalis felt increasingly disillusioned at the assimilation policies of the West Pakistan military and political elite. The imposition of Urdu as the sole official language of East Pakistan became a controversial issue. In the Bengali nationalist campaign which forced the federal government to recognize both Bengali and Urdu as Pakistan's national languages, the

Biharis refused to support the Bengalis. During the military rule of General Ayub Khan (1958–1969) while ethnic Bengalis experienced discrimination and felt deprived of their share in the politics of the State, the Biharis became increasingly unpopular and were seen by Bengalis as symbols of West Pakistani domination. Thus, prior to the Bengali civil war (1971), Biharis were deeply mistrusted by the Bengalis. The Bengalis treated them with contempt for their continued support of West Pakistan's policies and for their apparent disloyalty to the Bengali cause.

Civil War and Independence of Bangladesh

In the first national general elections that took place in Pakistan during December 1970, the Biharis retained their commitment to West Pakistan. They overwhelmingly supported the pro-West Pakistani Muslim League as opposed to the Awami League, which represented the Bengali nationalist movement. The background and continued moral and political support of Biharis alienated them completely from the Bengalis, who soon after the general election began a nationalist movement. The movement developed into a civil war and the demand for complete independence from West Pakistan. During the civil war that ensued for nine months (March—December 1971) the Biharis collaborated with the West Pakistan military in a vain effort to suppress the Bengalis. Two paramilitary organizations led by local Biharis, Al-Shams and Al-Badr, colluded with the Pakistan military to repress the Bengali opposition. The civil war resulted in the extermination of well over one million Bengalis and created nearly 10 million refugees. However, it was not only the Bengalis who were victims of torture and genocide. The civil war also saw tragic atrocities being committed by the Bengalis against Biharis, a situation that degenerated into official acts of violence, genocide, and ethnic cleansing after the secession of East Pakistan into Bangladesh. According to Anthony Mascarenhas

> thousands of families of unfortunate Muslims, many of them refugees from Bihar were mercilessly wiped out. Women were raped and mutilated. Children did not escape the horror: they were either killed alongside their parents, or tortured and mutilated and left facing a life of debilitation, often as orphans. More than 20,000 bodies of non-Bengalis have been found in the main towns of Chittagong, Khulna and Jesore. The real toll may have been as high as 100,000 as thousands of non-Bengalis have vanished without a trace.

After the creation of Bangladesh punitive measures were undertaken against the Biharis. The Acting President's Order 1 of 1972 and Bangladesh Abandoned Property (Control Management and Disposal) Order 1972 were pieces of legislation introduced by the Bangladeshi government to justify the confiscation of Bihari property and businesses. In response to the acts of victimization, an overwhelming majority of Biharis pleaded in desperation for support from Pakistan. They claimed to have retained their Pakistani nationality and wanted to be repatriated to Pakistan. However, only a limited number of Biharis were transferred to Pakistan. By mid 1972 the Biharis within Bangladesh numbered approximately 750,000; they were housed in 66 squalid camps. Some 278,000 were living in camps on the outskirts of Dhaka, and another 250,000 were living around Saidpur in the northwest. By 1974, 108,000 had been allowed to enter Pakistan, a number which had grown by 1981 to 163,000. For those who have remained in the Bihari camps, reconciliation programs have been initiated and Urdu speakers are taught Bengali in an effort to overcome the most obvious obstacle to their acceptance by Bengalis. However, there remain deep psychological barriers to overcome and most Biharis fear further retaliation.

Resettlement of Biharis

Most Biharis would like to resettle in Pakistan and hence have declined to become nationals of Bangladesh. However, Pakistani governments have been extremely reluctant to allow large scale Bihari resettlement into Pakistan for fear of exacerbating the existing ethnic and racial tensions. The concern is that most Biharis would eventually settle in Urban Sindh, already an ethnically volatile region. Despite these concerns, since the 1980s there have been initiatives to resettle Biharis in Pakistan. These initiatives have, however, resulted in few concrete results. In November—December 1982, 4,600 Biharis were settled in Pakistan with a financial package of $1.5 provided by the Gulf countries and supported by the United Nations High Commissioner for Refugees. In July 1988, Pakistan's military ruler, General Zia-ul-Haq, signed an agreement with the World Muslim League providing for the resettlement of almost all Biharis. His assassination in August 1988, however, left the matter in limbo. After the restoration of democracy in Pakistan, the incoming Pakistan Peoples Party (PPP) agreed in principle that "all Pakistanis living abroad by choice or by compulsion had the same rights as citizens of Pakistan". However, the practical implementation of this principle insofar as it concerned the settlement of Biharis proved impossible. The first air flight of Biharis was cancelled in January 1989 after protests by the Sindhi National Alliance and Punjabi-Pakthun Itehad. The Bihari issue contributed immensely to the straining of the relations between the ruling PPP and its coalition partners, ultimately leading to the breakdown of the government.

Some efforts for resolving the Bihari issue were made by PPP's successor, the Pakistan Muslim League, which was led by Nawaz Sharif. According to a joint statement issued by the Pakistani and Bangladeshi governments in August 1992, repatriation of Biharis was to commence in December 1992 with an airlift of 3,000 Biharis. However, once again implementation of such an ambitious program of action proved impossible. Although the settlement procedures were initiated with the first batch of 323 Biharis arriving in Lahore in January 1993 and housed in new Okara in Punjab in the first of the two colonies, further settlements stalled, largely due to opposition from within the ranks of the government as well as from the local population. Opponents feared the political, economic, and cultural ramifications of settlement of a group of such numerical strength would generate serious tensions in the whole of Pakistan.

There has been enormous public pressure that Biharis not be allowed to enter Pakistan. This pressure was evident when the last PPP government (1993–1996) in its effort to win support of the indigenous Sindhis undertook to purge urban Sindh of all illegal immigrants. The government's unwillingness to accept any Biharis developed into a diplomatic row in December 1995 when 288 Bengali-speaking Muslims were deported from Pakistan. More recently, in March 1999 during his visit to Bangladesh, the former Prime Minister Mian Nawaz Sharif, fearful of internal opposition, could not put forward any concrete plans for resolving the Bihari issue. He confined himself to saying that Pakistan was concerned for the Biharis only on humanitarian grounds, and not because it regarded them as citizens of Pakistan. The 250,000–300,000 Biharis who have remained in camps in Bangladesh still face difficulties and discrimination. Although free to settle anywhere in Bangladesh, the Biharis prefer to live in camps for fear of their own safety and security. Their past allegiance to the West Pakistan army has not been forgotten, an issue which is highlighted by attempts to try Gholam Azam and others on charges of war crimes during the Bangladesh war of independence in 1971. Biharis generally describe themselves as "stranded Pakistanis," and some have organized themselves into the Pakistani General Repatriation Committee, which advocates militant action to achieve repatriation. Thus, for instance, in August 1999 members of the Committee demonstrated and led a march toward the Pakistan embassy in Dhaka. Hundreds of people scuffled with the police and a few attempted self immolation in an attempt to pressure the Pakistani government to resettle them in Pakistan.

Camp conditions are extremely poor, and as a recent documentary prepared by the Muhajir Quami Movement (a Pakistani political party) shows, most Biharis live in sub-human conditions. The population of these camps has increased significantly since 1971, but without any provisions to accommodate the inhabitants. Entire families are housed in one room, and often more than one family shares a single room. Food, water, and electricity are scarce. Hygiene conditions are reputedly equally abysmal. There are few provisions for medical facilities; education for the children within these camps is almost nonexistent. Biharis are stateless people, not citizens of India, Pakistan, or Bangladesh. Younger generations of Biharis have known nothing but the camps. The existing political divisions in Pakistan make the prospect of Bihari settlement a forlorn hope. In the present climate it is difficult to suggest a political solution.

Javaid Rehman

See also **Bangladesh, India, Pakistan**

Further Reading

Mascarenhas, Anthony, *The Rape of Bangladesh*, Delhi: Vikas, 1971

Muhajir Quami Movement, Prisoners of Conscience: Stranded Pakistanis in Bangladesh, Documentary Video Recording, 1990

Rehman, Javaid, and Nikhil Roy, "South-Asia," in *World Directory of Minorities,* edited by Miles Litvinoff, Patrick Thornberry, et al, London: Minority Rights Group, 1997

Sen, Sumit, "Stateless Refugees and the Right to Return: The Bihari Refugees of South Asia–Part 1," *International Journal of Refugee Law*, 11, no. 4, (1999)

Sen, Sumit, "Stateless Refugees and the Right to Return: The Bihari Refugees of South Asia–Part II," *International Journal of Refugee Law*, 11, no. 1, (2000)

United States Committee on Refugees, *Fifty Years in Exile: The Bihari Remain in India*, 1998

Whitaker, Ben, et al., The *Biharis of Bangladesh*, London: Minority Rights Group, 1977

Bilin

Capsule Summary

Location: Eritrea
Total Population: about 85,000
Language: Bilin
Religions: Islam, Christianity (Roman Catholic, Orthodox, and Protestant), some traditionalists

The Bilin (singular, Bilina) are an ethnolinguistic minority group in the Ela Bar'ed area of Eritrea, a country with some 4 million inhabitants. They are also known as *Bogos*, but this refers to the area where they live. The Bilin belong to the northernmost branch of the Agaw-speaking people, who inhabited the Ethiopian highlands for ages and pockets of whom still live there, e.g., the Awngi, Qemant, and Khamtanga. The Agaw languages belong to the Central-Cushitic family and the number of those who speak the languages are in decline everywhere. The Bilin are presently about 65 percent Muslim (Sunni) while the rest adhere to Christianity in various denominations, especially Catholics and Orthodox. Religious identity is not a divisive issue in Bilin society due to shared underlying values and customs.

According to their oral traditions, the Bilin migrated north to the Eritrean plateau in the tenth or eleventh century CE. There they mingled with and partly subdued the Tigré pastoralists living in the area. Although since the late nineteenth century the Bilin language and oral traditions were investigated by European scientists (e.g., A. d'Abbadie, C. Conti Rossini and especially L. Reinisch), few recent studies have been made of the society and culture of this people.

Originally the Bilin were mixed farmers, practicing cultivation and keeping livestock on the plateau region around the town of Keren. During the Italian colonial period (since 1890) and especially in the independence struggle with Ethiopia since 1962, many Bilin dispersed to other places, mostly within Eritrea but also to Sudan (as refugees) or to Ethiopia. The result is a mixed pattern of settlement and economic activities, although the majority of Bilin still live in the Keren area, with some 6,000 in the town itself.

The Bilin region historically came to be a crossroads of conflict: it was on the caravan and trade routes from the Red Sea coast to the Nile Valley, increasing in importance after the opening of the Suez Canal in 1867, and in the line of Ottoman Turks in the sixteenth century invading northern Ethiopia-Eritrea. Later, in the late nineteenth century, the Egyptian army moved in. When the Turks became the dominant power on the Red Sea coast after their conquest of Massawa in 1557, the Bilin area was regularly raided for slaves up to the middle of the nineteenth century, and local people were pressured to adopt Islam. These developments illustrate the vulnerable position that the Bilin, with their distinct language and identity, have always had in the wider regional politics of the Horn of Africa. As Egypt became the dominant power in northern Ethiopia-Eritrea after the 1850s, slaving continued. Neighboring Beni Amer Muslims also joined in raiding the Bilin. The Swiss adventurer-explorer W. Munzinger occupied the Bilin area in 1872 as a representative of the Egyptian government of Mohammed' Ali, under whose nominal authority it remained until the late 1880s. The Ethiopian emperor, under whose sovereignty Bilin (then known as Bogos) had always been before foreign invasion, nominally retrieved the area in 1884 under the Hewett Treaty, after two military victories over the Egyptian army, although it took years before the Egyptians cleared out of the Keren area. In 1889, the Italian colonial army occupied the Bilin country and remained there until 1941. Bilin men served in the Italian colonial army in Eritrea and participated in the Fascist invasion of Ethiopia in 1935. Threats to their survival felt in the late nineteenth century urged Bilin to welcome Catholic missionaries and get external assistance.

The Bilin have two "tribal" divisions: the Bet Tärqe Qur and the Bet Taqwe. A third and smaller division, the Bab Janjerin, originally was a later Tigré migrant group that assimilated to the Bilin way of life. The Bilin have a patrilineal kinship structure, and they had nominal clan or lineage chiefs without much power. Bilin society was hierarchical, with an aristocratic elite (the *simgär*, about one fourth of the population, descended from the first Agaw conquerors) and bondsmen or caste groups (the *mäkirukwe*). Between the two strata a patron-client relationship was in force. The elite group controlled the land and its (re)distribution. This structure of inequality, and much of traditional social relations and customary law, was broken by the Eritrean Peoples' Liberation Front (EPLF) when it controlled Bilin country in the 1980s.

Bilin traditionally had a monotheistic faith (with an upper god called *Jar*) combined with a belief in various types of spirits. They also emphasize ancestor veneration. Funerals of important persons are large-scale events of major social and religious significance. The dead are commemorated each year in a collective gathering organized by relatives. It is believed that a proper service to the dead will benefit the living descendants. Other customs and rites of passage around birth, naming, marriage, and expressive culture mark the Bilin as different from the other ethnic groups in Eritrea. They also predominantly marry within their own group. The unwritten Bilin customary law (the *Fatha Mogareh*) was well-developed and complex, but in the twentieth century was overshadowed by Islamic law among the Muslim Bilin and later by state codified law.

In the independence war between the Ethiopian government and Eritrean rebels (of the ELF and EPLF movements) the Bilin country was a major battleground, e.g., in 1997 during the battle of Keren. Many Bilin were victims of violence or became displaced. Bilin economy was severely damaged, and their society and cultural traditions were uprooted and eroded during the long conflict.

Presently, the Bilin are one of the smaller minorities in Eritrea, an independent state since 1991 and officially recognizing nine ethnic groups, or nationalities, and their economy and social life has been recovering from decades of conflict. Within Eritrea the Bilin stand in the shadow of the dominant Tigrinya, Beja and Tigré groups. Their customary law is subservient to Eritrean national law. The Bilin are virtually all bilingual, and indeed their language is in the process of being displaced by Tigré and especially Tigrinya.

Jon Abbink

See also **Eritrea; Ethiopia; Sudan; Tigre**

Further Reading

Abbebe Kifleyesus, "Bilin: Speaker Status Strength and Weakness," *Africa* (Roma), 61, no. 1, 2000

Adhana Mengeste-Ab, "Ancestor Veneration in Blean Culture," in *Proceedings of the VIIIth International Conference of Ethiopian Studies, Addis Ababa 1984*, vol.1, edited by Taddesse Beyene, Huntingdon, United Kingdom: ELM Publications, 1988

———, "Yohannes and Keren," in *Kasa and Kasa. Papers on the Lives, Times and Images of Téwodros II and Yohannes IV (1855–1889)*, edited by Taddese Beyene, et al., Addis Ababa: Institute of Ethiopian Studies, 1990

Ermias, Awet, *Origin and Pattern of Blin Migrations*, Asmara: University of Asmara, 2000

Hamde, Kiflemariam, "Analysis of Some Bilin Proverbs," *Ethiopian Journal of African Studies*, 5, no. 2, 1989

Lamberti, Marcello, "Bilin language," *Encyclopaedia Aethiopica*, vol. 1, edited by Siegbert Uhlig, Wiesbaden: Harrassowitz, 2003

Munzinger, Werner, *Über die Sitten und das Recht der Bogos*, Winterthur, 1859

———, *Ostafrikanische Studien*, Schaffhausen: Hurter, 1864

Neghisti Tesfay, *Traditional Marriage System in the Blean Society*, Addis Ababa: Addis Ababa University, 1983

Smidt, Wolbert, "Bilin Ethnography," in *Encyclopaedia Aethiopica*, vol. 1, edited by Siegbert Uhlig, Wiesbaden: Harrassowitz, 2003

———, "Bilin History," in *Encyclopaedia Aethiopica*, vol. 1, edited by Siegbert Uhlig, Wiesbaden: Harrassowitz, 2003

Bilingualism

The term bilingualism has many different meanings. On an individual level it refers to consecutive or simultaneous learning/acquisition of a second language and involves issues of language competence, performance, ability, proficiency, and achievement. On a societal level it refers to a complex phenomenon of minority and migrants. While it is not possible to separate effects of individual and societal bilingualism, the latter concerns concepts such as diglossia (the existence in a language of a high, or socially prestigious, and a low, or everyday, form) and domain that are helpful in understanding the different ways in which linguistic resources are organized in multilingual communities, including phenomena such as borrowing, interference, and transfer.

Another important distinction is between *ability* (competence) and *use*, sometimes referred to as the difference between degree and function. Bilingualism and multilingualism often involve different degrees of competence in the languages involved. A person may control one language better than another, or a person might have mastered the different languages better for different purposes, using one language for speaking, for example, and another for writing.

The terminology is complex and often overlaps. Apart from the main four language skills, listening, reading, writing, and speaking, also the fifth competence may be distinguished, i.e. cognitive competence as ability to use one or both languages for reasoning and deliberation (also referred to as inner speech used for thinking). Within bilingual ability the following categories may be distinguished: maximal ('native like') and minimal (incipient) bilingualism, balanced bilingualism (dual language proficiency), and semilingualism or double semilingualism, which are all highly controversial terms (Skutnab Kangas, 1984).

Separate from bilingual ability is a person's use of their two languages, referred to as functional bilingualism that concerns the contexts (domains) and targets (people), i.e. when, where, and with who people use their two languages. A distinction needs to be made between functional bilingualism and language background, which is a broader concept, referring to both participative and non-participative experience in language. The latter can be measured by questions such as "what language do your parents, grand parents, speak to each other when you are present?"

Diglossia refers to the coexistence of two forms of the same language in a speech community. Often, one form is the literary or prestige dialect, and the other is a common dialect spoken by most of the population. Sociolinguists may also use the term diglossia to denote bilingualism, the speaking of two or more languages by the members of the same community, as, for example, in New York City, where many members of the Hispanic community speak both Spanish and English, switching from one to the other according to the social situation or the needs of the moment.

There are many different ways and contexts in which children become bilingual, as well as many different outcomes. To date researchers have not agreed on the extent to which the bilingual child's early language systems are merged or separate. Some advocate separation of the two languages either by person or context, and some still assume that bilingualism may be harmful in terms of language interference and mixing. Skutnabb-Kangas has noted two of the most common misconceptions about bilingualism: first, it is always best to teach a child through the medium of the native language; second, the native languages must always be stabilized before instruction through the medium of another can begin. These claims may be true under some circumstances and not others. There seems to be, however, one guiding principle: in order to achieve higher levels of bilingualism, it is better to support via instruction the language which is less likely to develop for other reasons. This strategy has been successfully used by multiethnic schools in the United States. Another myth is that bilingualism itself is the cause of poor achievement at school and accounts for the failure of minority children. Research has shown that socioeconomic class is a crucial variable as bilingualism always develops in a particular social context (Romanine, 1997). Skutnabb-Kangas notes that as far as the role played by education is concerned, we must ask what goals different societies have when they try to make various children bilingual or monolingual. Often children are caught in a vicious circle. Because the schools fail to support their home language, skills in it are often poor. At the same time they do not progress in the new language at school, and are labeled semilingual. Often it is argued that bilingualism impedes development in the second language. Thus the failure of the school to let children develop further in their mother tongue is often used to legitimize further oppression of it (Skutnabb-Kangas, 1984, and Romanine, 1997).

The designation as a bilingual minority depends on the purpose of the categorization. At different times, governments may wish to include or exclude language minorities. Where a single indigenous language exists (e.g. in Ireland or Wales), a government may wish to maximize its counts of bilinguals; a high number may then indicate government success in its indigenous language policy. Vice versa, in a suppressive, assimilationist approach, minority languages and bilinguals may be minimized (e.g. immigrants in England).

Another distinction that needs to be mentioned is between additive and subtractive bilingualism. *Additive bilingualism* is being described as the acquisition of a second language without any loss or weakening of the first language. Current research shows that when students' first language is valued and recognized, the development of the second language is more effective. In reality, however, it is the *subtractive bilingualism* that prevails when the first language has been edged out of the classroom environment. This was the case for many years in South Africa, where Afrikaans (a variant of the Dutch language) had been used as the medium of instruction for a majority of the black students). Similarly, Romanes, the language of Roma/Gypsies, has been suppressed at schools in Central and Eastern Europe. In the United Kingdom this phenomena refers to situations where minority languages such as Urdu, Bengali, or Punjabi are ignored or have inferior status in comparison with the so called world (understand European) languages.

LAURA LAUBEOVA

See also **Assimilation; Languages, Disappearing; Minorities and Language**

Further Reading

Baker, Colin, *Foundation of Bilingual Education and Bilingualism*, Clevedon: Multilingual matters Ltd., 1996

Baker, Colin, and Sylvia Prys Jones, *Encyclopedia of Bilingualism and Bilingual Education, Clevedon:* Multilingual Matters Ltd, 1998

Cummins, Jim, *Bilingualism and Special Education: Issues in Assessment and Pedagogy*, Clevedon: Multilingual Matters, 1984

Romaine, Suzanne, *Bilingualism*, 2nd edition, London: Blackwell Publishers, 1994

Skutnabb-Kangas, Tove, *Bilingualism or Not: The Education of Minorities*, Clevedon: Multilingual Matters, 1984

Skutnabb-Kangas, Tove, *Linguistic Genocide in Education—or Worldwide Diversity and Human Rights?* Lawrence Erlbaum Associates, 2000

Varennes, Fernand de, "*Language, Minorities and Human Rights*," Kluwer Law International, 1996

Wei, Li, The Bilingualism Reader, Taylor & Francis Books Ltd, Routledge, an imprint of Taylor & Francis Books Ltd, 2000

Bolivia

Capsule Summary

Location: South America, southwest of Brazil
Total Population: 8,586,443 (July 2003)
Minority Populations: Quechua, Aymara, *mestizo*, white
Languages: Spanish (official), Quechua (official), Aymara (official), as well as Tupi-Guarani, Chiquito, Plautdietsch (Low German)
Religions: Roman Catholic (95%), remainder: Protestant (Evangelical Methodist), Mormon, Jehovah's Witnesses, Seventh Day Adventist, Pentecostal, Mennonite, Bahai, Jewish

The minority populations of the Republic of Bolivia are a product of the country's geography and historic decisions regarding distribution of population. Bolivia is landlocked, having no direct access to either the Pacific or Atlantic Oceans. Two ranges of the Andes Mountains extend through the southwestern third of the country on northwest-southeast axes. The country has three main regions. The first lies between the western (*Cordillera Occidental*) and eastern mountain ranges (*Cordillera Real* or *Oriental*). Between them extends the *Altiplano*, a high, arid plain bordered on the north by the highest lake in the world, Lake Titicaca, which straddles the border with Peru. The central region contains the semitropical valleys of the *Cordillera Oriental* that extend to the east and north. Descending from these mountains and valleys is the lowland region of *Oriente*, which includes, in the far eastern region, the desert-like Chaco area that extends into Paraguay. Semitropical regions have heavy rainfall, and the mountain valley areas are well-watered and have a temperate climate. The *Altiplano*, however, has little rainfall and reaches altitudes over three miles high that are almost arctic. The Chaco also has little rainfall but high temperatures.

Differences in the Bolivian population accompany the country's wide range of geography, climate, and habitability. The largest, oldest native group is the Aymara, who number nearly two million and comprise about a fourth of the national population. The ancient, advanced Tiahuanaco culture (circa the seventh to eleventh centuries CE) probably preceded the Aymara's homelands. The Aymara are settled in the Altiplano, where the country's capital, La Paz, is presently located. More than five centuries ago the Quechua-speaking Incas, whose empire stretched from Ecuador to Bolivia (also known as Upper Peru), defeated the Aymara. The Incas restricted the Aymara to the Altiplano and surrounded them, occupying the mineral-rich areas of the *Cordillera Real* from north of Lake Titicaca down through today's cities of Cochabamba, Sucre, and Potosi. Quechua speakers amount to almost 3 million inhabitants and over a third of the population.

Both of these native populations were subdued by the Spanish conquerors in the sixteenth century. Bolivia was joined to the Viceroyalty of Buenos Aires in 1776, and struggles continued against the Spanish royalists until the country achieved independence in August 1825. Bolivia was named after independence fighter Simon Bolivar, and much of its subsequent history has consisted of internal strife, as well as a series of nearly 200 coups and counter-coups. Conflicts with border countries Chile, Brazil, and Paraguay, most of them involving land redistribution, continued throughout the twentieth century. Bolivia's civilan government was overthrown in 1964; a new constitution was adopted in 1967, yet civil unrest persisted. Bolivia signed a 1993 agreement with Peru to have access to the Peruvian port of Ilo, alleviating the country's over-100-year landlocked status.

Society and Ethnicity

The Spanish inter-bred with the native populations, producing a Spanish-speaking *mestizo,* or mixed race, that today includes about a fourth of the inhabitants. Approximately ten percent of the population considers itself *blanco,* or white, descended mainly from the Spanish but also from several other European immigrant groups. Nearly half the population of Bolivia speaks Spanish, which together with Aymara and Quechua, comprise the official languages of the country. Many people speak one or more languages. The vast majority of Bolivia's population, therefore, lives in the high plains and around the high mountains, valleys, and lakes of the southwestern third of the country.

Of itself language may not determine one's status in Bolivian society, which is still divided between Indian and non-Indian populations. An Indian, for example, who begins to adopt the habits or dress of the *blanco* or *mestizo*, who is trying to achieve social status, is described as a *cholo*. The term recognizes native ambition but can also be derogatory. An Indian who lives in the interior, knowing nothing of white or *mestizo* ways, is designated a *campesino*, and considered a provincial or "rustic." A crucial event in the political history of Bolivia was the 1952 triumph of the National Revolutionary Movement (*Movimiento Revolucionario Nacional* [MNR]), founded to raise the level of the indigenous population in society. From 1962 to 1984 it was dominated by the military.

Bolivia possesses a variety of quite small minority populations as diverse as is its landscape. Among the Aymara there exist the Qollahuayo (or Callahuaya), a tiny group noted as specialists in folk medicine. The northern and eastern, semitropical lowlands contain most of the smaller Indian groups. In the southern and eastern regions of the country there are about 25,000 speakers of Tupi-Guarani, a language still dominant in Paraguay and at one time spoken throughout Brazil. There are also estimated to be about the same number of speakers of Chiquito in the far eastern portion of the country. There are nearly three dozen other minority language groups in Bolivia with speakers numbering from a few dozen to several hundred or a few thousand.

Scattered through these less populated regions are almost 40,000 Mennonites, part of a larger community of this sect that is settled throughout Latin America. They speak Plautdietsch or Low German. While Roman Catholicism is to some degree the religion of vast majority of the population, many small Evangelical, Pentecostal, and other Protestant sects have grown in the country. Of American origin, they have accompanied the growth of American military influence in Bolivia. American policy has forcefully eradicated *coca* (plant for cocaine) cultivation among native and *mestizo* farmers, not recognizing that this plant possesses numerous indigenous religious, medicinal, and cultural applications. Cultivation of the plant is also of key commercial importance to native farmers.

Bolivia is the poorest country in South America, and this poverty blights the lives of most of its residents. Estimates in 1999 indicated that 70 percent of the population lives below poverty level. Wealth has been concentrated for centuries among a tiny middle class dominated by *blancos* and a few *mestizos*. There has been some economic improvement in recent years, but the GDP per capita income was only $2,500 (2002). Much of the indigenous population is only marginally involved with a money economy. Indians receive the lowest of salaries as miners in the devastating working conditions of various mineral industries. Bolivia made considerable progress in the 1990s toward the development of a market-oriented economy. Successes under President Sanchez De Lozada (1993–97) included the signing of a free trade agreement with Mexico as well as the privatization of the state airline, telephone company, railroad, electric power company, and oil company. Bolivia's industries include mining, smelting, petroleum, food and beverages, tobacco, handicrafts, and clothing, although it remains highly dependent on foreign aid.

Because the live birth rate has improved and the death rate declined, the natural population increase has grown. Over a third of the population is under 14 years of age. Less than five percent of the population is over 64, with elderly males comprising a minority of only 160,000 and elderly females almost 210,000. A minority of less than 20 percent of the population (over 15) is considered illiterate.

EDWARD A. RIEDINGER

Further Reading

Fifer, J. Valerie, *Bolivia*, World Bibliographical Series, 89, Oxford, England: Clio, 2000

Hudson, Rex A., and Dennis M. Hanratty, *Bolivia: A Country Study*, Area Handbook Series, Washington, DC: Federal Research Division, Library of Congress, 1991

Klein, Herbert S., *A Concise History of Bolivia*, Cambridge, England: Cambridge University Press, 2003

———, *Bolivia: The Evolution of a Multi-Ethnic Society*, 2nd edition, Latin American Histories, New York: Oxford University Press, 1992

Lagos, Maria L., *Autonomy and Power: The Dynamics of Class and Culture in Rural Bolivia*, Philadelphia: University of Pennsylvania Press, 1994

Léons, Madeline Barbara, and Harry Sanabria, *Coca, Cocaine, and the Bolivian Reality*, Albany: State University of New York Press, 1997

Lindert, P. van, and Otto Verkoren, *Bolivia: A Guide to the People, Politics and Culture*, translated by John Smith, London: Latin America Bureau, 1994

Morales, Waltraud Q., *A Brief History of Bolivia*, New York: Facts on File, 2003

Paterman, Robert, "Bolivia," in *Cultures of the World*, Marshall Cavendish, 1995

Bonner, Neville Thomas (Aborigine)

Neville Thomas Bonner was the first Australian Aborigine to sit in the Australian Federal Parliament, as a Liberal Party Senator for the State of Queensland, 1971 to 1983. His humble beginnings, along with firsthand experience of poverty, unemployment, and discrimination, hardened his resolve to work within the political system in order to bring change and improved conditions for indigenous Australians. Having a passionate and articulate Aboriginal voice in Federal Parliament helped raise awareness of indigenous people and the issues and challenges confronting them.

He was born in 1922 on Ukerebaagh Island, at the mouth of the Tweed River in northern New South Wales, as his Aboriginal mother had to be out of town before sunset and could not return until sunrise the next day. He never knew his father, an Englishman, who, although married to his mother, returned to England before he was born. His maternal grandfather, Jung Jung (Roger Bell), was the last initiated member of the Jagera Tribe. Orphaned at age nine, Bonner was raised by his grandparents in what he termed "a blacks' camp under the lantana bushes." By age seven he had already been helping the family earn money, by clearing the bush.

Bonner was unable to attend school, for the education system was segregated and there was no mission school nearby. However, his grandmother, who insisted he learn how to read and write, arranged when Bonner was 13 for him to go to the local school, which he did for one year. At 14, following the death of his grandmother, he left school to seek employment, working in a variety of rural jobs on banana plantations, at ringbarking, scrub felling and timber cutting, as a dairy hand, cutting cane, and then as stockman in northwest Queensland where he met his wife, Mona Banfield.

Married in 1943, they moved to her birth place, the Aboriginal settlement of Palm Island, where they and their five sons remained until 1960. Here Bonner became actively involved in community affairs, rising to the highest position open to an Aborigine on the island, that of Assistant Settlement Overseer responsible for the administration of works, with responsibility for 250 workers. The family then moved to Ipswich, where he established a boomerang supply business and became involved with the Colored Welfare Council, which later became the One People of Australia League (OPAL). Mona died in 1969, and he subsequently married Heather Ryan, a director of OPAL, on July 29, 1972.

Bonner joined the Liberal Party in 1967 and was elected chairperson of the Oxley Area Committee in 1969. He was endorsed as a Liberal Party candidate for Queensland in the 1970 half-senate election but failed to win a seat. But after much public debate he was selected by the Liberal Party to fill a casual Senate vacancy in August 1971. In 1974 he was instrumental in ending 77 years of legislative paternalism toward indigenous peoples in Queensland, when he successfully pushed for the Commonwealth Government to introduce overriding legislation to end the abuses of human rights on Queensland Aboriginal and Torres Strait islander Reserves. Bonner also chaired the Senate Select Committee on Aboriginal and Torres Strait Islanders, whose 1976 report, *The Environmental Conditions of Aborigines and Torres Strait Islanders,* saw 82 of its 86 recommendations accepted. He was the first Aborigine to introduce legislation into the Australian Parliament and was also the first back-bencher to introduce a Government Bill, the *Aboriginal Development Commission Bill,* and carry it through all stages.

Elected to the Senate on three occasions, he increasingly advocated for indigenous rights, land rights, and environmental issues such as mining on the Great Barrier Reef, and criticized the Queensland National-Liberal Party government, especially its leader, Premier John Bjelke-Petersen, ensuring that he was relegated to an unwinnable position on the 1983 Queensland Liberal Senate ticket. Left with no choice but to resign from the Liberal Party, he stood unsuccessfully for a Senate seat as an independent. He rejoined the Liberal Party in 1996, and his reconciliation was completed when Prime Minister John Howard bestowed on him life membership in its Queensland Branch.

It was on Palm Island Aboriginal Reserve, remembered by Bonner as "experiencing my private hells," that he forged his political convictions, based on an ideal of interracial cooperation and togetherness. Attacked by some in the Black Power movement for being a moderate, for working within the system, and for belonging to a party on the right of the political spectrum, he always sought reconciliation and nonviolent solutions. Known for his keen sense of humor, dignity, oratory, and self-effacement, he was an inspiration to the many Australians who took heart from the fact that one from such a deprived background could in fact rise to greatness.

Following his parliamentary career he continued to speak out on issues which divide Black and White Australians. Elected a Queensland delegate to the Constitutional Convention, as a member of the *Australians for Constitutional Monarchy* campaigning against an Australian Republic, Bonner argued passionately for the retention of the monarchy. On July 29, 1998, in an historic first, he was invited, as a Jagera elder, the traditional landowners of the Brisbane River district, to open the 49th Queensland Parliament.

Bonner died in 1999, aged 76, after being diagnosed with terminal lung cancer. Mourners at his state funeral included his wife, Heather, some 60 members of his extended family, the Prime Minister, the Premier and Governor of Queensland, and several hundred guests, friends, and members of the public. In 2000, the Commonwealth Government established the Neville Bonner Memorial Fund, contributing $400,000 toward an annual scholarship for an indigenous person studying for an honors degree in political science.

Capsule Biography

Thomas Neville Bonner. Born 28 March 1922 on Ukerebaagh Island, New South Wales, Australia. Education Beaudesert State School, fourth grade. Employment head stockman, 1941–5; assistant settlement overseer, Palm Island; dairy farm manager, Ipswich, 1960–2. Established *Bonnerangs* boomerang manufacturing business, Ipswich, 1966–7. Bridge carpenter, Moreton Shire Council, 1968–71. Board of directors of OPAL, 1965. Queensland President, OPAL, 1967–73. Senator, Australian Senate, 15 August 1971–83. Senate Deputy Chairman of Committees, 1974. Chairman, Joint Committee on Aboriginal Land Rights in the Northern Territory, 1977. Board member, Australian Broadcasting Corporation, 1983–91. Senior official visitor to Queensland state prisons, 1990–7. Member, Griffith University Council, 1992–6. Member, Queensland Land Tribunal, 1992–9. Chairman, Queensland Indigenous Advisory Council, 1997–8. Appointed patron, OPAL, 1980. Patron, World Vision Australia, 1976–90, Ipswich Women's Shelter, Colored Youth Soul Center. Awards: Canberra Australia Day Council Australian of the Year, 1979. Life membership, Young Liberal Movement, Queensland, 1978. Life membership, OPAL, 1979. Order of Australia, 1984. Honorary Doctorate, Griffith University, 1993. Delegate, Australian Constitutional Convention, Canberra, 1998. Life membership, Queensland division of the Liberal Party, 1998. Ipswich Citizen of the Year, 1999. Died in Ipswich, Queensland, 5 February 1999. Buried at Warrill Park Lawn Cemetery, Ipswich.

JEREMY HODES

Selected Works [N.T. Bonner]

Equal World, Equal Share, 1977
For the Love of the Children, 1982

See also **Aborigines; Australia; Torres Strait Islanders**

Further Reading

Burger, Angela, *Neville Bonner: A Biography*, Melbourne: MacMillan, 1979

Turner, Ann, editor, *Black Power in Australia: Bobbi Sykes Versus Senator Neville T. Bonner*, Melbourne: Heinemann, 1975

Bororo

Capsule Summary

Location: Wide bushes of the western African savannah between the Senegambian plain in the West and the Central African republic in the East, mostly in the territories of Guinea, Benin, Mali, Niger, Nigeria, Cameroon, Chad, Central African Republic
Total population in Cameroon: approximately 1,650,000, about 12 percent of the total population
Language: Bororore
Religion: Muslim, animist

The Bororo are people of the Peul subgroup. They are known as "Peul of the bush" (*Ful'bé laddé*) because of their particular attachment to the bush life. The Bororo are spread along the Saharan part of west and central Africa. They are nomadic cattle raisers like in Niger, where they are called *Farfuru,* and in Nigeria. They are also found as sedentary and seminomadic groups, as in Cameroon and the Central African Republic. This life style makes them appear in some lands as a marginal group who are particularly unstable and vulnerable. They are cousins to the Peul', an African people whose origin is unclear; it might be Judea Syrian, Nubian, Arab Berber, or even Indian. The majority of Bororo are Muslim. From a linguistic point of view, Bororore, their language, is an African language similar to Wolof and Serer.

In Cameroon, the Bororo form a tribe made of four main lineages: the Aku, the Wo'dâ'bé, and the Jafuns found in Adamaoua and Grassfields and the Wo'dâ'bé, the Jafun, and the Danêdji found in the North and Far North provinces. Now, they find themselves in small groups in nearly all big agglomerations of the country. In the absence of an official census, statistics of the Mbororo Social and Cultural Development Association (MBOSCUDA) value their national size at a total of 1.65 million, with a great concentration at Sabga, Djakiri, Babanki, Didango, Nkounde, Doumé, Banyo, Betare Oya, Lomta, Poli, Meigaga, Fuguil, Demsa, Koupé Mangouba, and Akwaya.

The Bororo recognize each other by specific anthropometrical characteristics. Slim, thin, Aku and Jafun have curly hair with a small face sometimes covered with hamitic tattoo. They easily differ from their brothers Wo'dâ'bé whose men plait their hair. Their wives wear big earrings and other embellishments on the neck. The Wo'dâ'bé are careless about the cleanliness of their dress. During dry seasons, waves of this lineage from Niger arrive in Cameroon via Nigeria and make a striking appearance, especially in towns where they indulge in the sale of traditional medicines, handicrafts, and other products made of animal skin.

Bororo culture consists of an affinity for nomadism, isolation, and seclusion. The group historically has avoided constraint, adversity, and pressure of any kind, be it natural, social, or sociopolitical. The Bororo reached the Adamaoua highlands (Cameroon) in the late eighteenth century from the Joss highlands and its surroundings in Nigeria. The Jafun came first, then a century later the Danêdji, the "white" named after the white skin of their cows. By 1918 when they arrived in the Bamenda and Foumban regions, they were named Aku. But even before 1570, according to Palmer and Meek (Tardits C, 1981: 240), the Wo'dâ'bé from Bornou (Niger) settled between Gombe (Nigeria) and Benoue (Cameroon). Up to 1930, bororo migrations were noticeable in Cameroon territory. Having moved up to the meridian limit (Ntui, Doume) of the savannah, the Bororo and their herds of cattle faced a natural barrier erected by the equatorial forest unsuited to pastoral activities. This blocked migration resulted in the diminution of pasture areas following the scarcity of lands, the drawing of boundaries between countries, the setting up of administrative units within the national boundaries, and other demographic pressures. The end of their migration forced the creation of new lifestyle patterns. The right to land ownership remains one of the crucial causes of conflicts opposing the Bororos and other ethnic groups and often results in lost lives (in 1991, the Dzeng-Mbiamé (Northwest); in 1993 the Oku (Northwest); in 1996 the Koutaba (West); and in 1997, the Fokwe (West).

As a result of the historical mobility of Bororo groups, their lineages are today scattered nearly nationwide. Their peopling does not illustrate a clear concentration by geographic zones. They regroup in the bush in scattered settlements, in the savanna, or on mountain plains. Dwellings remain grouped in places; but in general there are long distances (three to ten kilometers) between hamlets. The traditional dwelling or *Pouterou* with an old architecture plan is progressively replaced by cabins copied closely from the architectural pattern of their neighbors, the Bantu (brick or breeze block, rooms, windows). Hamlets contain all the houses or *Sare* and are surrounded by edges made of branches, bamboo, and shrubs, which protect agriculture against destructive animals. The *sare* traditional appointment of space is indicative of the tendency to polygamy because one distinguishes immediately at the entrance the chief of the family and his cabin around which there is a harem.

In the course of history, the Bororo society had a strong political and social organization based on small units. It is only recently, with the abandonment of nomadism and of transhumance breeding, that the Bororo became homogeneous and interdependent. At the head of the group, there is the *Ardo*, the leader. He can be appointed by the administrative authority or by the counsel of elders. Ardos of a subregion are headed by a Bororo chief for that territory. As a respected person, an ardo has administrative, financial, and sociocultural duties. Head of judicial staff and head of religious activity, he governs on the basis of peul moral or *Palaku*. The basic social cell is patriarchal. The family is based on marriage through elopment. Traditionally, the treatment of the Bororo woman is different from the Fulbe. She is free to go out to the market, visit relatives, and fetch water or firewood. Social life illustrates today the fact that men spend all their time outdoors, while women are confined to the harem with access forbidden to strangers, particularly men. As an entity of the rural world, the bororo society presently experiences many changes, due to their setting and accumulation of funds gained from their activities. Bororo women bear an average eight children. Eighty percent of this population are less than 30 years old. In contrast, there is a continuous spreading of an upper class style of life, mostly in urban areas near their settlements.

In the bush where the Bororo live, there is a striking absence of medical and educational infrastructures. A Bororo may need to travel 15 to 50 kilometers to reach a school or a hospital, contributing to one of the lowest rates of formal education in the country. Socioeconomic policies and programs created over several decades by different ministries for the integration of these so-called minorities, indigenous people, or marginal populations exist, but are not yet applied, leaving bororo people to wonder for how long they will be treated as second-class citizens.

Louis Tenawa

See also **Cameroon**

Further Reading

Bocquene, H., *Moi, un Bororo*, Paris: Karthala, 1986

El. Fasi, and I. Hrbek, *Histoire générale de l'Afrique/L'Afrique du VII au XII ème siècle,* Unesco/Nea, 1990

Institut Africain International, *Drougth in Africa*, Londres, 1977

Issa A., and Labutut, *Sagesse des peuls nomades*, Yaoundé, clé, 1974

Lacroix, P.F., *Etudes camerounaises: Matériaux pour servir à l'histoire des peuls de l'Adamaoua, Paris:* IFAN, 1952

Tardits, C., *Contribution de la recherche ethnologique à l'histoire des civilisations du Cameroun*, N°551, Paris: CNRS, 1981

Bosnia And Herzegovina

Capsule Summary

Country Name: Republic of Bosnia-Herzegovina
Location: Southeastern Europe, bordering the Adriatic Sea and Croatia
Total Population: 3,989,018 (July 2003)
Language: Croatian, Serbian, Bosnian
Religions: Muslim (40%), Orthodox (31%), Roman Catholic (15%), Protestant (4%), other (10%)

The Republic of Bosnia and Herzegovina is a parliamentary democracy situated in Southeast Europe on the Adriatic Sea and bordered by Croatia, Serbia, and Montenegro. The population of nearly 4 million before the war of 1992–5 comprised Bosniak (44 percent), Serb (31 percent), Croat (17 percent) with 8 percent describing themselves as "Yugoslav" or other ethnicity. As of 2000, the ethnic distribution was Serb (37.1 percent), Bosniak (48 percent), Croat (14.3 percent), and other 0.6 percent. (Bosniak has replaced Muslim as an ethnic term in part to avoid confusion with the religious term Muslim, an adherent to Islam.)

Serbo-Croat (presently classified as three separate languages: Bosnian, Serbian, and Croatian) is the main language shared by all three main groups although many Roma (estimated to number 45,000 before the 1992–5 war) speak Romany as their mother tongue. By religious persuasion the population before the war was estimated to be 40 percent Sunni Muslim, 31 percent Serbian Orthodox, 15 percent Roman Catholic, 4 percent Protestant, and 10 percent "other." However, in 1985 religious observance was only 17 percent, and for most, religious persuasion equates with ethnicity: Bosniaks are Muslims, Croats are Roman Catholic, and Serbs are Orthodox.

Bosnia and Herzegovina ranked next to the Former Yugoslav Republic of Macedonia as the poorest republic in the old Yugoslav federation. Although agriculture (13 percent of the economy) is almost all in private hands, farms are small and inefficient. The Republic relies on foreign imports for much of its food. Its industries include steel, coal, iron ore, lead, zinc, manganese, bauxite, vehicle assembly, textiles, tobacco products, wooden furniture, tank and aircraft assembly, domestic appliances, and oil refining. Since Bosnia's independence from Yugoslavia in 1992, implementation of privatization has been slow, and local entities only reluctantly support national institutions. The bitter interethnic warfare in Bosnia caused production to plummet by 80 percent from 1990 to 1995 and unemployment to soar. The GDP per capita income was $1,900 in 2002.

History

Bosnia and Herzegovina was under the control of the Ottoman Empire from the fifteenth century. Many of the local Slav speakers adopted –Islam, the religion of the new rulers. The empire was divided not along ethnolinguistic lines but by religious affiliation—the *millet* system—and the *millet* became established as the prime focus of identity outside of family and locality, bequeathing a correlation between religion and ethnicity. The nineteenth century saw the gradual disintegration of the Ottoman Empire with the new Serbian state looking to incorporate Bosnia-Hercegovina. However, following the 1875–8 Russo-Turkish War Bosnia-Hercegovina fell under Austro-Hungarian control.

In spite of initial fierce Muslim resistance the Hapsburg government did not dispossess the Bosnian Muslim elites: instead, it coopted them. They quickly saw that their survival depended on maintaining good relations with the central authorities. This strategy continued after the collapse of Austro-Hungary in World War I, and Bosnia-Hercegovina's incorporation into what became Royalist Yugoslavia (1918–1941), with the main Serbo-Croat Muslim political organization, the Yugoslav Muslim Organization, led by Mehmed Spaho, a regular coalition partner. Despite its multi-national character, Royalist Yugoslavia was dominated by the Serbs, who considered the Serbo-Croat-speaking Muslims to be ethnically Serbs, while the Croats viewed them as ethnically Croat.

The collapse of Royalist Yugoslavia in 1941 led to bitter internecine fighting and Bosnia-Herzegovina, which was mostly incorporated into the Croat puppet state set up by the Nazis, was the scene of many of the worst atrocities. Thousands of Serbs were killed by Croat fascists, at times in alliance with Muslims along with many Jews and Roma as well as opposing Croats. The atrocities left deep psychological wounds which would re-open in 1992–5, and tilted the ethnic balance away from the Serbs. In the 1920s they were the largest group with some 830,000 against the second largest population of some 600,000 Muslims who in the post war period became the most numerous group.

Communist Yugoslavia

In order to overcome the rivalry between Serbs and Croats over the Muslim Slavs, Communist Yugoslavia progressively saw them as a separate people, and state policies were enacted to enhance this. The change can be seen in succeeding census terminology. In 1948 they were classified as "indeterminate Muslims"; in 1953 as "indeterminate Yugoslavs"; in 1961 as "Muslims in the ethnic sense"; in 1971 as "Muslims in the sense of nationality"; and finally in 1981 as a separate "nation" of Yugoslavia. The term did not apply to non-Slav groups like the Roma, many of whom were Muslim, the mostly Muslim ethnic Albanians, nor to the solidly Muslim Turks. Also, Bosnia and Herzegovina was one of the state's six constituent republics. In the 1980s intermarriage was about 12 percent (equivalent to Yugoslavia as a whole but less than some other areas), mostly in urban areas. While the concept of Muslims as a separate people was perhaps weak within the lifetime of Yugoslavia, it was immeasurably strengthened by the suffering and hardship of the Bosnian war of 1992–95.

The 1992–1995 War

The elections of December 1990 had seen voting largely on ethnic lines, with the largest party, the Party of Democratic Action (SDA) led by Alija Izetbegovic¢, winning 86 of the 240 seats in both chambers of the assembly. The Serbian Democratic Party (SDS) led by Radovan Karadzic, **won 72,** and the Croatian Democratic Community (HDZ), won 44. The failure of the central Yugoslav organs, now nakedly Serb in orientation and controlled by Serbian President Slobodan Milosevic, to stop Croatia and Slovenia seceding, was followed by attempts to keep control of Serb areas in Bosnia and Herzegovina and elsewhere. Karadzic's SDS set up its own separate assembly and organized a Serbian plebiscite on whether to live in a common Yugoslav state. The Bosnian and Herzegovinian authorities replied with their own referendum on independence. Both referenda overwhelmingly supported the respective conflicting views. In an attempt to avert war, the international community recognized Bosnia and Herzegovina as an independent state, while signaling to the Serbs that the West was unlikely to intervene militarily and imposing an arms embargo, which left the Serbs, who dominated the armed forces, in a militarily advantageous position.

Bitter internecine fighting erupted, and the war descended into barbarity with concentration camps, mass expulsions, murder and rape. Terror was deliberately used against civilians to "solve" by ethnic cleansing the problem of dividing the territory with its previous intricate ethnic mix with the Serbian side bearing the responsibility for the majority and the worst of these outrages, although excesses were carried out by all parties. The Serbs, initially in the ascendancy, announced the creation of a Serbian Republic (RS), which was contiguous with a similar Serbian construct in the Croatian Krajina, both of which had obvious designs to coalesce with Serbia. The RS also included the areas in the east bordering rump Yugoslavia, including Srebrenica, the scene of one of the worst massacres when thousands of Muslim men were slaughtered by Serb forces after the supposed United Nations safe area fell, linked to the western areas by a narrow corridor around Brc°ko. In the southwest where Croats predominated (although numerically more Croats live in other areas of the state) Serbs and Muslims were expelled or fled and the HDZ, with support from Franjo Tudjman's Croatian nationalist government, set up Herceg-Bosna as a Croatian "statelet." Bosnia and Herzegovina appeared to be sandwiched between Milosevic's Serbia and Tudjman's Croatia. The Muslims, now identifying themselves as "Bosniaks," had initially looked to the international community for support, but with the international community apparently acquiescing to Serbian military gains, in 1993 they began to fight back seriously.

However, there were serious divisions within the Muslim camp between Bosnian President Izetbegovic¢ and Fikret Abdic¢, operating from his power base in Velika Kladus°a in the Bihac¢ pocket in the northwestern corner of the republic. In 1994 Abdic¢, who had dealings with both Serb and Croat forces, declared the creation of his own quasi-state, the Autonomous Province of Western Bosnia, and was consequently expelled from the Bosnian government. Bitter inter-Muslim fighting ensued before the defeat of Abdic¢'s "rebels," many of whom fled to Croatia. The personal dimension aside, the Abdic¢ affair can be seen as a conflict between Izetbegovic¢'s position, nominally supported by the international community, for an independent Bosnia-Hercegovina while Abdic¢ appeared prepared to have dealings with Serbia and Croatia, and to countenance remaining in some form of Yugoslavia.

In early 1994 United States pressure was brought to bear on Croatia, which had about 30,000 troops fighting alongside the Bosnian Croats in Bosnia against the Muslims, and as a result on March 2 a Croat-Muslim federation was announced in Washington which ostensibly aimed to end the Croat-Muslim fighting and strengthen the Bosnian government. The war dragged on with international peace proposals being routinely turned down by the Bosnian Serb side even though their gains had left them with thousands of kilometers of indefensible borders vulnerable to counter-attack.

The west finally lost patience with the Bosnian Serbs in 1995, and NATO air power attacked Serb positions. The end of 1995 saw Croatian and Muslim forces pushing the Serbs back in the western half of Bosnia. At this point the United States again stepped in, and the Dayton peace plan was finally signed in late 1995. Some 250,000 had died, over 2 million been displaced, and the country was ruined. The refugee movements (including many Serbs from Krajina to RS) and loss of life, in which the Muslims suffered proportionally more than Serbs or Croats, saw a change in Bosnia and Hercegovina's ethnic population with Serbs again estimated to be the largest group in the state with just over 40 percent.

The Dayton Agreement

The agreement split Bosnia and Hercegovina into two units, 49 percent comprising the RS and 51 percent the Croat-Muslim Federation. Although the agreement called for the return of all refugees ideally to their original homes and stressed that the state was intact and would remain that way, the emerging reality was different. The Serbs, despite paying grudging lip-service at times, regarded the RS entity as their own state. Any Muslim or Croatian refugees who tried to cross the border separating the two units into the RS faced attack and harassment, and communications across the line were virtually nonexistent. Similar problems arose in the south around Mostar. Here, virulently nationalistic Croats turned to Croatia rather than to Sarajevo. Like the Serbs, they did their utmost to obstruct the return of Muslim refugees. To a lesser degree, Muslim authorities in central Bosnia also harassed Croats attempting to return to their homes. Furthermore, within the Federation, the cantonal system created by Dayton contributed to the creation of Bosniak and Croat cantons in some places, and in others to Bosniak and Croat dominated areas within cantons. Almost no community could boast of a mixed Bosniak/Croat population.

Contemporary Situation

The position of chief of state was held by Chairman of the Presidency Dragan Čović from June 2003 to February 2004. A NATO-led Stabilization Force (SFOR) remained in place although troop levels were reduced to approximately 12,000 by the close of 2002. The international community has remained in force in the state keeping the uneasy peace and occasionally arresting suspected war criminals for trial at the international war crimes tribunal in The Hague. Subsequent elections appeared to clearly show that parties which attempted to appeal without recourse to nationalism fared poorly, and the SDA, SDS, and HDZ dominated in their respective ethnic communities. However, the November 2000 elections saw a major change with the nationalist parties gaining less than 50 percent of the vote leading to opposition majorities in the state and Federation parliament lead by the Alliance for Change coalition, and an apparently supportive moderate Serb leader in RS. However, there remained intransigent contrary elements. Attempts to start reconstructing destroyed mosques in RS like the famous sixteenth century Ferhadija one in Banja Luka in May 2001 were postponed due to violent Serb protests. Croatian nationalists' continued work for a Croatian entity centered on Mostar led in early 2001 to the dismissal of a number of leading Croat state officials by the chief international administrator. The possibility of renewed interethnic violence if the international community withdraws is high.

Other, smaller minorities, like the 45,000 or so Roma not belonging to the big three groups, were caught up in the fighting. Indeed the Roma were victims of ethnic cleansing even before hostilities broke out in earnest when in August 1991 some 200 were expelled from Mostar. Further displacement of the Romany population occurred as the Bosnian conflict developed. In Banja Luka, Serb extremists were already pressuring Romany families to leave in 1992. There were also non-Muslim Roma living in Muslim/Bosniak controlled zones, such as Bosnian Kalderash Roma, who feared Muslim domination and fled, as did thousands more, unwilling to take sides. Of the Romany community in Bijeljina which was estimated at between 7,000 and 8,000 before the war, only some 34 reportedly remained in 1998. Many Roma cannot obtain nationality in the Croatian-Muslim Federation as they were not born in Bosnia. Others do not dare to return to homes in areas which are now under the control of a different religious group.

HUGH POULTON

See also **Croats; Croatia; Roma (Gypsies); Yugoslavia; Yugoslavs**

Further Reading

Banac, Ivo, *The National Question in Yugoslavia: Origins, History, Politics,* Ithaca: Cornell University Press, 1984

Donia, Robert J., and John V.A. Fine, Jr., *Bosnia and Hercegovina; A Tradition Betrayed,* London: Hurst, 1994

Magas, Branka, *The Destruction of Yugoslavia: Tracking the Break-up 1980–92,* London: Verso, 1993

Malcolm, Noel, *Bosnia: A Short History,* London: Macmillan 1994

Botswana

Capsule Summary

Location: southern Africa
Total Population: 1,573,267
Ethnic Populations: Tswana (or Setswana) (79%), Kalanga (11%), Basarwa (3%), other, including Kgalagadi and white (7%)
Languages: Setswana, English
Religions: indigenous beliefs (85%), Christian (15%)

A land-locked country, Botswana is bordered by Namibia to the north and west, by Zimbabwe to the northeast, and by South Africa to the south and southeast. The total area is 581,730 sq.km (224,607 sq.miles). The Okavango River, flowing into the northeast of the country, is the largest river system; much of the southern and western part of the country is made up of the Kalahari Desert. The eastern strip is the most fertile and most developed part of the country, and there live 80 percent of the population, and seven of the eight Tswana tribal groups, to which over 80 percent of the population belong. Many Tswana men work in South Africa on contract. The country was chiefly agricultural before independence in September 1966. Substantial diamond deposits were then found, and Botswana is now the largest producer of gem diamonds in the world.

Botswana has maintained one of the world's highest growth rates since independence. Botswana has transformed itself from one of the poorest countries in the world to a middle income country with a per capita GDP of $9,500 in 2002. In addition to diamond mining, tourism, subsistence farming, and cattle raising are other key sectors.

History

As a colonized people, the Tswana occupied a minority status from 1885 vis a vis Britain. In that year a British official proclaimed the annexation of their lands, after their rulers had requested British intervention because they feared the conquest of their lands by the Boers of the South African Republic to the east. Under British rule, the Tswana were protected in their land, and few whites settled in the country. In 1895 the country south of the Molapo River was incorporated into the self-governing Cape Colony, and that north of the river became the High Commission territory of Bechuanaland, ruled directly by Britain. When South Africa was united in 1910, provision was made for a possible inclusion of the High Commission territories at a later date, but because of South Africa's policy of racial segregation this did not happen, and Bechuanaland was led to independence by Britain as the country of Botswana.

Ten years earlier, Seretse Khama, the heir to the chieftainship of the leading Ngwato tribe, had been forced by Britain to renounce the chieftainship because he had married a white woman. This was after pressure had been applied by segregationist South Africa. But in 1961 Khama gained a seat on the legislative council and was appointed the territory's executive. The following year he formed the Bechuanaland (later Botswana) Democratic Party, which attracted the support of many of the colony's influential white settlers. In the first direct election, held in 1965, the BDP won 28 of the 31 seats, and Khama became prime minister. With the advent of independence, he became president of Botswana.

The discovery of diamonds made Botswana one of the success stories of independent Africa and brought relative wealth to its people. Many outside observers hailed the country as the most democratic on the continent. This was despite the dominance of the political system by the BDP, which retained a large majority among the Tswana people in successive elections. Following his death in 1980 Khama, who had played an important role in the Front-line States group that had emerged to counter South Africa, was succeeded as president by Quett Masire, a former minister of finance. Under his leadership, the BDP continued to win sizeable majorities in general elections in 1984, 1989, and 1994. By the mid 1990s there was considerable social and economic discontent, and allegations of corruption in government. In 1998 Masire was succeeded as president by Festus Mogae, another former finance minister. Botswana played a key role in the Southern African Development Community (SADC), the secretariat of which it housed. It sent troops to Lesotho in 1998, when South Africa decided to intervene in that country, and the SADC gave ex-president Masire the task of mediating in the Democratic Republic of the Congo. In the early 2000s, as Zimbabwe's economy collapsed, one of Botswana's greatest fears was that the turmoil there would spread across the border. The government tried to limit the number of refugees arriving from strife-torn Zimbabwe, but allowed thousands of refugees to enter from the Caprivi region of Namibia in 1999/2000, after the collapse of a separatist movement there.

In recent years the Botswana government has come under widespread criticism for the way it has treated its small indigenous minority San (Bushman) and BaKgalagadi population. Thousands of Gana and Gwi people were forcibly moved from the Central Kalahari Game Reserve, on the grounds that their hunting activities were not appropriate in a game park. Some critics alleged that the government's real aim was to clear the reserve of people before diamond mining could take place there, but the government claimed it wanted to relocate the San where they could be provided with social services and have the opportunity to assimilate into mainstream Tswana society.

CHRISTOPHER SAUNDERS

See also **Namibia; South Africa; San (Bushmen)**

Further Reading

Colclough, C., and S. McCarthy, *The Political Economy of Botswana,* London, 1980

Morton, F., et al., *Historical Dictionary of Botswana,* 2nd edition, Metuchen, New Jersey: 1989

Stedman, S.J., *Botswana,* Boulder, Colorado, 1993

Tlou. T., and A. Campbell, *A History of Botswana,* Gaborone, 1984

Brazil

Capsule Summary

Country Name: Federative Republic of Brazil
Location: Eastern South America, bordering the Atlantic Ocean
Total Population: 182,032,604 (July 2003)
Minority Populations: African and/or Indian mixed with Latin European; others of Central European, Middle Eastern, and Japanese descent; several hundred Indian tribes
Languages: Portuguese (official), Spanish, English, French, as well as numerous Indian languages of the Tupi-Guarani, Jê, Arawak, and Carib language families
Religions: Roman Catholic (nominal) (80%); Afro-Brazilian Spiritism, Protestant

The Brazilian population, fifth largest in the word, is concentrated mostly within 100 miles of a 5,000-mile-long coastline where eight of the ten largest cities lie. Over half the country, especially in the area of the Amazon, is unsettled. By far the largest and most populous country in South America, Brazil has overcome more than half a century of military intervention in the governance of the country to pursue industrial and agricultural growth and development. Almost a third of the population is under 14; and only five percent over 65. Brazil's formerly high birth rate has now fallen so that the proportion of children will decline and that of the aged increase. There are almost three million more females in the total population than males.

As many as two million natives may have occupied the land at the time of the country's discovery by the Portuguese in 1500. The dominant group consisted of speakers of Tupi-Guarani, who inhabited tropical rainforest areas that extended from the south central part of the country, up the coast to the mouth of the Amazon, and then through the basin of the river. Smaller groups of Jê-speaking tribes lay in the dry, upland interior beyond the coastal sierra; and Arawak and Carib occupied territories north of the Amazon.

Diseases of Europeans and Africans decimated the native population, who had no immunity to foreign illnesses. The native population today comprises no more than a few hundred thousand, settled mostly in the Amazon. The Indians survive in small groups of at most several hundred, based on distinctions of language and cultural behavior. Although they are protected by the federal government, ranchers and farmers compete for their lands.

Up until a few decades ago unknown tribes were still being discovered in the Amazon. Hardly any Indians now live in isolation. Virtually all have regular contact and communication with white culture. The ethnic distribution in present day Brazil is white (includes Portuguese, German, Italian, Spanish, Polish) 55 percent, mixed white and black 38 percent, black 6 percent, other (includes Japanese, Arab, and Amerindian) 1 percent.

History

Throughout the sixteenth to nineteenth centuries, the Portuguese transported African slaves across the Atlantic and ruled the country. Of the almost 12 million who survived shipment across the Atlantic to the Americas, a third came to Brazil, especially during the Brazilian gold rush era of the eighteenth century. Lacking white women, Brazilian males breeded with Indians, and the resulting black population created an intricate racial mixture. Brazil achieved independence from Portugal on September 7, 1822, and Emperor Pedro I ruled from 1822 to 1831. Despite conflicts with Argentina, Brazil remained relatively peaceful during the reign of Pedro II (1841–1889) and helped overthrow the Argentinian dictatorship of Juan Manuel de Rosas in 1852. Brazil then allied with Argentina and Uruguay in war against Paraguay (1865–1870), deposed Pedro II and adopted a constitution for a federal republic in 1889.

Until the abolition of slavery in 1889, the majority of the Brazilian population was of mixed Portuguese-African ancestry. After the abolition of slavery the needs of a free-labor market attracted millions of immigrants from Italy, Portugal, Spain, and Germany to the rich agricultural lands and burgeoning industrial areas of the southern part of the country.

Brazil settled many of its boundary disputes between 1895 and 1909. Under President Getulio Vargas (1930–1945) the country established constitutions in 1934 and 1937, the latter of which established dictatorial powers. Brazil entered World War II on the side of the Allied Powers in 1942. Vargas was forced to resign in 1945 when a democracy was effected, but he was reelected to a second term in 1951. The capital of Brasília, with an area of 2,245 square miles, was established and construction including a presidential palace, cathedral, and university began in 1956. Brazilian politics in the second half of the twentieth century were characterized by ongoing shifts within the civilian government influenced by numerous political parties including the Brazilian Democratic Movement Party (PMDB), Brazilian Social Democracy Party (PSDB), Brazilian Socialist Party (PSB), Brazilian Progressive Party (PPB), Communist Party of Brazil (PCdoB) and the Democratic Labor Party (PDT).

Society and Ethnicity

The vast majority of the Brazilian population has always been Catholic, being one of the first countries that Jesuit priests evangelized. However, Protestantism, especially Evangelical and Pentecostal sects, has grown rapidly in recent decades, attracting more than 10 percent of the population. The most significant other religion in Brazil is African spiritism, known as *umbanda* or *candomblé*. Though legally repressed and vigorously condemned in the past by the Catholic Church, it has steadily grown and become increasingly respected as the truest expression of Afro-Brazilian culture.

Today, therefore, due to centuries of miscegenation, the majority of the Brazilian population is a varying mixture of white and black races. However, in appearance and according to statistics, more than 50 percent is considered white and a third mulatto. The brown skin of one of mixed race is described as *moreno*. As skin is darker, one is described as *moreno pardo*; and lighter, as *moreno claro*.

Appearances change as one moves through the regions of the country. In the south, from the states of Rio Grande do Sul up to São Paulo, the population appears mostly white; and many inhabitants have Italian, German, Polish, and even Japanese or Arabic surnames. From Rio de Janeiro up through the northeastern state of Bahia and on to the mouth of the Amazon, the area of the old colonial plantations, the population comprises varying shades of white to mulatto. Bahia, the former center of colonial economic and political life, continues today as the focus of Afro-Brazilian culture. The sparsely populated Amazon region is mostly Indian or *mestiço*, a mixture of Indian and white.

Racial and ethnic differences also reflect socioeconomic distinctions. The country has a GDP in terms of purchasing power of approximately $1.376 trillion (2002), but per capita GDP income was only $7,600 in 2002. Brazil's significant and well-developed agricultural, mining, manufacturing, and service sectors result in an economy that outweighs that of all other South American countries and is expanding its presence in world markets. Among developing countries, Brazil has the largest gap between the wealthiest and poorest. The top 10 percent of the population receives almost fifty percent of the national income. The bottom 10 percent receives less than one percent.

For this reason there are large pockets of rural and urban poverty with high rates of infant mortality and homeless children. The infant mortality rate is almost

40 per 1,000 live births, and life expectancy at birth is 63 years (five less for men, five more for women). At the heart of the socioeconomic distortions in Brazil is the fact that it was a slave-owning nation until almost the end of the nineteenth century. A tiny proportion of the population, mostly white and male, owned vast tracts of land cultivating coffee, sugar, tobacco, and cotton for export.

These distortions have caused political imbalances during the twentieth century with governments swinging between authoritarianism and democracy. From 1964 to 1985, a military regime governed Brazil. During 1987–88 a new constitution was written, returning the country to civilian democratic rule. This liberal charter detailed its support of civil and human rights for women, ethnic and racial minorities, those of varying sexual orientations, the aged, children, and the landless. Making reality of these ideals is the fundamental challenge of the Brazilians' future. Nonetheless, the converging region between Argentina, Brazil, and Paraguay remains unstable and problematic as an area for money laundering, smuggling, arms and drug trafficking, and a harbor for Islamic militants.

Edward A. Riedinger

See also **Argentina; Paraguay**

Further Reading

Degler, Carl N., *Neither Black nor White: Slavery and Race Relations in Brazil and the United States*, New York: Macmillan, 1971

Hemming, John, *Amazon Frontier: The Defeat of the Brazilian Indians*, London: Macmillan, 1987

La Cava, Gloria, *Italians in Brazil: The Post–World War II Experience*, New York: P. Lang, 1999

Poppino, Rollie, *Brazil: The Land and People*, New York: Oxford University Press, 1973

Skidmore, Thomas E., *Black into White: Race and Nationality in Brazil and the United States*, Oxford University Press, 1974

Bretons

Capsule Summary

Location: Northwestern France, the Armorican peninsula (historically the coast of Gaul between the Seine and Loire rivers)
Total Population: approximately 3 million
Languages: Breton, French
Religion: Roman Catholic

The Bretons are a distinctive ethnolinguistic group of people, Celtic in origin and tradition, related to the Celts of the British Isles. Their traditional language, Breton or *Brezoneg*, is a member of the Brythonic subgroup of Celtic languages, most closely related to Cornish (now extinct as a mother tongue) and Welsh, and more distantly related to the Goidelic linguistic subgroup (comprising Irish Gaelic, Scots Gaelic and Manx).

The Bretons were part of the Celtic population inhabiting Great Britain at the time of the Roman invasion and occupation (ending in 407 CE). Between the third or fourth and sixth centuries CE, significant numbers of Bretons traversed the English Channel in a series of migrations and began settling in the westernmost peninsula (then known as Armorica) of present day France. By the mid sixth century CE, this territory began to be referred to by historians of the era, writing in Latin, as *Brittania* (and later Brittany). This originally Celtic-speaking population has thus been residing continuously in Brittany for well over 1,500 years.

History

The immigrant Bretons came from southwestern England and Wales, and evidence suggests that the territory they settled in was sparsely inhabited by earlier populations, at least in the northern and western parts of the peninsula; the southern and eastern parts, on the other hand, were more densely inhabited by Gallo-Romans, as strongly suggested by the presence of numerous Latin or Latinized place-names. Scholars are still debating the question of whether the more ancient Continental Celtic language, Gaulish, was still spoken on the peninsula at the time of the Breton migrations, and if Breton, or at least the most southern dialect of it might not be a direct descendant of Gaulish.

The Bretons were Christians; in fact, it is possible that the earliest arrivals were priests, though doubtless there were also soldiers, soon followed by their families. The clergy seems to have played a salient role in the organization of residential and administrative structure around a parish church. Again, place-names offer evidence of this in the numerous villages bearing as the first part of their name the prefix *Plou*—(or a variant), Breton for "parish," often followed by the name of a saint (e.g., *Plouédern,* "parish of St. Edern"); this is still a highly characteristic part of the toponymy of the region today.

The history of the Bretons from the time of their settling into the peninsula until the tenth century is one of more or less continual expansion eastward, engaging increasingly in interaction—military and political—with the similarly expansionist Frankish dynasties (Merovingians and Carolingians). Breton military/political leaders of this era succeeded in extending their domain of influence and control to the present-day city of Rennes, and even beyond. But this was contested repeatedly by the Franks—including Charlemagne himself—who wanted to incorporate the Bretons into the Empire as tribute-payers. The Bretons stubbornly resisted, and much of the eighth and ninth centuries was marked by military campaigns of Frankish forces against the Bretons. In the famous Battle of Ballon in 845, a Breton army led by Nominoë defeated the Frankish army of Charles the Bald. This was the beginning of a brief period of sovereignty for Brittany as first Nominoë and then two male successors ruled the "Kingdom of Brittany" (845–907). The independent regime began to unravel in the early tenth century with renewed assaults by Vikings, who had for many years been another force for the Bretons to contend with. At this time the Nordic invaders utterly devastated Brittany, pillaging and burning parishes and monasteries. The raids wreaked havoc on the store of Breton literary treasures that had been created by monks laboring for generations in their monastic *scriptoria*: taking what manuscripts they could, the monks fled to safer sites in the east.

Viking assaults gradually subsided, and a new Breton leader (Alain Barbetorte, d. 952) sought to restore the kingdom; however, he never enjoyed the prestige or power of his predecessors, and Brittany increasingly was drawn, politically, into the Frankish fold. It entered the Middle Ages as an emerging feudal society, dominated by a landed aristocracy, whose more ambitious members saw their chances for upward political and financial mobility linked to forces outside of Brittany, notably in the ascendant world of the Carolingian Empire. Others maintained a strong sense of Breton identity, which did not die with the official annexation of the Duchy of Brittany to France in 1532. This Act of Union still resonates today with many Bretons, who regard the statue and other images of Brittany's last duchess, Anne, kneeling in submission to the French king, as a profound humiliation. In 1932 Breton nationalists defaced the original statue by detonating a small bomb in it on the occasion of the 400th anniversary of the Franco-Breton union. Throughout the twentieth century Breton activists have sought greater recognition and enhancement of Brittany's economic, political, and sociocultural situation, with a small fraction of them in the interwar years advocating separation from France.

Society, Language, and Economy

Brittany was traditionally a rural society, with the great bulk of its population consisting of peasants, fishermen, and artisans. Until the early twentieth century, the majority of the Breton people spoke Breton as their primary language, only learning French when they attended primary school. (The aristocracy, by contrast, had switched to French centuries earlier.) This pattern of language use changed dramatically after World War II, when adults (who by then were largely bilingual) stopped speaking Breton to their children. The result has been a dramatic decline in the number of Breton-speakers among younger generations, and heroic efforts have been undertaken by language activists to reverse the process of language shift.

In the context of today's France, Brittany constitutes a "region" consisting of four administrative departments—Ile-et-Vilaine, Côtes d'Armor, Finistère, and Morbihan. A fifth department, Loîre-Atlantique—historically and culturally part of the peninsula—was administratively detached from the others in 1941; many Bretons hope to see it reintegrated soon. Brittany's economy was traditionally based on small-scale agriculture, fishing, and light industry; out-migration of the younger work force was endemic during the twentieth century, curtailed only for a while by World War II. Feeling marginalized from the flow of capital and employment initiatives for many generations, Bretons have sometimes applied to their situation the "internal colony" model; however, during the 1960s the French government began channeling additional resources to the region, and, since the 1980s, has been more receptive to promoting its linguistic and cultural heritage. Today Breton agriculture is large-scale and technologized, and the small family farm is disappearing as people seek work in urban centers. Brittany is the premier agricultural producer of France: especially prized are its dairy products, pork, poultry, vegetables, and fruits. Breton seafood, especially its oysters, remains legendary, though this industry has been battered in recent decades by colossal oil-spills from passing tankers.

The development of industrial-scale commercial centers of distribution is a recent, lucrative innovation in the economy, as is the emergence of an impressive telecommunications industry. Last, but not least, tourism has become a major source of employment and revenue, an industry sparked by the attraction of Brittany's magnificent blend of coastal and pastoral scenery and its unique linguistic and cultural heritage.

In spite of their now fuller and more equitable participation in the economic prosperity of France, many Bretons—even if they no longer speak Breton (and the vast majority does not)—retain a strong sense of Breton identity. This is an identity based on a heightened awareness and pride in their history, a renewed appreciation of their traditional forms of music and dance, and a powerful attachment to the diverse and stunning landscapes of the Armorican peninsula.

LENORA TIMM

See also **France**

Further Reading

Ford, Caroline, *Creating the Nation in Provincial France: Religion and Political Identity in Brittany*, Princeton, New Jersey: Princeton University Press, 1993

Galliou, Patrick, and Michael Jones, *The Bretons*, Cambridge, Massachusetts: Basil Blackwell, 1991

Hélias, Pierre Jakez, *The Horse of Pride: Life in a Breton Village*, translated from the French and abridged by June Guicharnaud, New Haven: Yale University Press, 1978

Le Coadic, Ronan, *L'identité bretonne*, Rennes: Terre de Brume, 1998

McDonald, Maryon, *'We are Not French!': Language, Culture, and Identity in Brittany*, New York: Routledge, 1989

Reece, Jack, *The Bretons against France: Ethnic Minority Nationalism in Twentieth-Century Brittany*, Chapel Hill: University of North Carolina Press, 1977

Timm, Lenora, "Ethnic Identity and Minority Language Survival in Brittany," *Language, Ethnicity, and the State*, Vol. 1, edited by Camille O'Reilly, New York: Macmillan, 2001

Brunei

Capsule Summary

Country Name: Negara Brunei Darussalam (Abode of Peace), or State of Brunei Darussalam
Location: Southeast Asia, bordering the South China Sea and Malaysia
Total Population: 358,098 (July 2003)
Ethnic Populations: Malay, which includes Brunei Indigenous communities of Malay, Kedayan, Tutong, Belait, Bisaya, Dusun and Murut (67.6%), other indigenous (Iban, Dayak and Kelabit, 5.9%), Chinese (14.9%), others (11.6%)
Languages: Malay (official); English and Chinese (various dialects)
Religion: Muslim (official, 67%), Buddhist (13%), Christian (10%), indigenous beliefs and other (10%). By law, all Malays are Muslims and Islam is the official religion. The Sultan is head of the Islamic faith in the country

Brunei is an independent sultanate (constitutional monarchy) in Southeast Asia, in the northeast part of Borneo. With an area of 2,226 sq mi (5,765 sq km), Brunei is divided geographically into two parts, each surrounded by the Malaysian state of Sarawak. Brunei is bounded on the north by the South China Sea and the Brunei Bay. The two sections are divided by the Limbang River valley.

History

Before British colonialism in the nineteenth century, the Sultanate of Brunei was a regional power, controlling large parts of Borneo and the Southern Philippine islands. The wealth and power of the Sultanate was based on trade. At various times Brunei was a tributary state of China and the Hindu Majaphit of Java. The extent of the Sultanate's domain was drastically curtailed by the Spanish, Dutch, and British empires. In return for British aid in dealing with regional instability, the sultan handed over Sarawak to the British in 1841. In 1847 the sultanate ceded Labuan (the Malaysian island) to Great Britain and the country was voluntarily made a British protectorate in 1888.

By the late nineteenth century, Brunei had shrunk to about its present size. In 1929 oil was discovered off its coast, but large scale extraction did not begin until after World War II. The Japanese occupied Brunei in 1941 during the war; the country was retaken by Australians in 1945. In the late 1950s, the Brunei People's Party (*Parti Rakyat Brunei*) was established and won elections on a platform of democratic reforms and federation with neighboring states. Unwilling to share power, the Sultan called in Gurkhas and British forces. A state of emergency was declared in 1962 and remains in effect. In the early 1960s, Brunei entered negotiation with Kuala Lumpur to join the Malaysian Federation. However, the negotiations broke down over Brunei's desire to retain control over its oil wealth, and issues pertaining to the status of the Brunei Sultan and in 1963 the country's membership was rejected.

The Gurkhas are still in Brunei today and protect the palace and other key government buildings. Since then, political opposition to the royal household is nonexistent. The country is governed by the 1959 constitution, under which the Sultan is the head of state with full executive authority. There is no notable difference between the state and the Sultan, Hassanal Bolkiah, generally regarded as the richest man in the region. Half of the cabinet comes from the royal family. On January 1, 1984, Brunei became a fully independent state. Since October 1967, the 29th Sultan and Prime Minister has been Haji Hassanal Bolkiah (the monarch is both the chief of state and head of government).

Society

Brunei's economy is small but wealthy, comprising both foreign and domestic entrepreneurship. The country's wealth is based almost entirely on the petroleum industry. The money from oil allows the state to provide its citizens with one of the highest standards of living in Asia. Crude oil and natural gas production account for nearly half of the GDP ($6.5 billion in 2002.). Per capita GDP ($18,600 in 2002) far exceeds most other Third World countries, and substantial income from overseas investment supplements income from domestic production. More than 70 percent of the ethnic Brunei labor force works for the government and another 10–15 percent work for the oil and gas industries, in agriculture, forestry, fishing, and related commercial concerns.

A significant percentage of minorities in Brunei face problems of acquiring citizenship. In 1984 the Sultan tightened citizenship regulations, requiring applicants to have resided in the country for 25 consecutive years and to meet language and cultural qualifications as well. The Sultan declared Brunei an Islamic state, and in 1991 the government began to reinforce the legitimacy of the hereditary monarchy and the observance of traditional and Muslim values by reasserting a national ideology known as the Malayu Islam Beraja (MIB) or "Malay Muslim monarchy". The cumulative effect of these rulings made it difficult for non-Malay and non-Muslims to acquire citizenship. It has also resulted in pressures on the non-Muslim population to convert to Islam and adopt Malay culture. Although Brunei's legal system is based on English common law; for Muslims, Islamic Shari'a law supersedes civil law in a number of areas.

The government in 1993 participated in issuing the Kuala Lumpur Declaration, which affirmed the right of all persons to a wide range of human rights, including freedom of religion. Despite this and constitutional provisions providing for religious freedom, the state routinely restricts the practice of non-Muslim religions by prohibiting proselytizing; occasionally denying entry to foreign clergy or particular priests, bishops, or ministers; banning the importation of religious teaching materials or scriptures such as the Bible; and refusing permission to expand, repair, or build new churches, temples, and shrines. In 1998, the government allowed the Catholic Church to establish the first apostolic prefecture in the country and to install Monsignor Cornelius Sim, a Bruneian of Chinese origin, as the country's first apostolic prefect. The government also routinely censors magazine articles on other faiths, blacking out or removing photographs of crucifixes and other Christian religious symbols. Christians are forced to use shophouses or private homes as churches, deemed illegal under present laws.

In 1998, officials of the Islamic Propagation Center confiscated gold and other precious Buddhist and Christian icons from a number of goldsmiths in the capital, stating that the open display of these items "offended local sensitivities." The items were later returned.

The Ministry of Education has also restricted the teaching of the history of religion or other courses on religion in non-Islamic schools while requiring courses on Islam or the MIB in all schools.

The official policy of the sultanate on minorities is assimilation. Given the omnipresence of the state, the assimilation process of indigenous minorities will take place although the pace is uncertain. In summary there is little hope for minorities in Brunei.

Minorities—Chinese

Ethnic Chinese migrated to Brunei during the British colonial period and they dominate the small non-state commercial sector. Ethnic Chinese are held to be roughly 15 percent of the population. Before independence Chinese in Brunei were British protected persons holding British travel documents but neither British subjects, nor subjects of the Sultan of Brunei. Post-independence, the legal status of many ethnic Chinese became stateless. Only about 9,000 were given full Brunei citizenship. Another few thousand are permanent residents. The rest remain effectively stateless persons. In recent years, Australia has taken some of these stateless persons but a number of them still remain.

After independence, it became much harder for the Chinese to secure citizenship. Reports said that it was easier for a Chinese to obtain permanent residency/citizenship if they converted to Islam and adopted a Malay lifestyle. Chinese Christians face more severe problems as the state is hostile to Christianity (see above). The Chinese who practice traditional religions (Taoism, Buddhism, etc.) face similar problems but to a lesser extent.

Minorities—Dayaks and Other Indigenous Groups

The Ibans formed the largest group of indigenous Dayak tribal groups. They are animistic migratory agricultural cultivators and collectors of jungle products, residing in the forested interior of the country. The Ibans, who constitute roughly 4 percent of the population, are found mostly along the border with Sarawak, a Malaysian state. They still live a traditional lifestyle including living in longhouses along rivers. Over the years the state has tried to convert many to Islam by promising material rewards and financial assistance. Although the Dayaks, as an indigenous group, are left alone by the authorities, there are credible reports that the government frowns upon their traditional beliefs and culture, deeming them to be 'un-Islamic.' The Iban fondness for pork represents a serious irritant to the religious authorities. Overt attempts are being made to convert the younger Dayaks through the schooling system. Converting to Islam for the indigenous population requires them to adopt the Malay culture and language and call themselves "Malays," creating a barrier to conversion.

James Chin

See also **Dayaks; Malays; Malaysia**

Further Reading

Braighlinn, G., *Ideological Innovation under Monarchy: Aspects of Legitimation Activity in Contemporary Brunei,* Amsterdam: VU University Press, 1992

Chin, Ung-Ho, *The Chinese of Southeast Asia,* London: Minority Rights Group, 2000

Gunn, Geoffrey C., *New World Hegemony in the Malay World,* Lawrenceville, New Jersey: Red Sea; London: Turnaround, 2000

Singh, Ranjit, *Brunei 1839–1983: The Problems of Political Survival,* Singapore: Oxford University Press, 1991

State Department, *1999 Country Reports on Human Rights Practices,* Washington DC: Bureau of Democracy, Human Rights, and Labor, 2000

Bubi

Capsule Summary

Location: Bioko Island (included in the Republic of Equatorial Guinea)
Total Population: approximately 40,000–50,000
Language: Bubi
Religions: Roman Catholic, pagan (indigenous)

The Bubi (also called Ediye, Adija, Bombé, Fernandian) are an ethnic group living on the Bioko Island (ancient Fernando Póo) in the Bight of Biafra, about 60 miles southwest of Douala, Cameroon. Bioko's original name, bestowed by a Portuguese sailor in 1472, was Formosa ("the beautiful"). There are 40,000 to 50,000 Bubis, most of who live in their homeland (Bioko), although a large number of them live in Spain, France, and other countries, due to political problems and instability in their country. They speak a Bantu language of the Bubi-Benga family, which is divided into three different dialects: North Bubi, Southeast Bubi and Southwest Bubi. The large number of Bubi subgroups, territorially anchored in ethnic regions, continues to provide cohesion because the differentiations and cleavages that existed within the historical Bubi community are, indeed, the best guarantee for a dynamic and strong society.

Bubi are mainly swidden agriculturalists and fishermen. Practically all Bubis are Catholics, due to the influence of the Spanish colonial rule over Bioko Island and Rio Muni. Both territories, together with Annobón Island, are presently included in the Equatorial Guinea state, independent from Spain since 1968. The government, ruled by dictatorial regimes, oppressed the entire population and, with a higher degree of violence, minority peoples like the Bubi.

History

Linguistic studies suggest the Bubi were among the first Bantu tribes to leave their ancestral homeland (situated in actual Nigeria or Cameroon maybe 5,000 years ago), and migrate southeast, settling on the coast of what is today southern Cameroon or northern Gabon. Approximately 3,000 years ago, another tribe, more warring and numerous, invaded the Bubi's beach homeland, forcing them to leave and migrate to their homeland, the Bioko Island. Living in relative isolation on the island, Bubi formed a unique society, language and religion that was different from their mainland Bantu relatives and left to develop undisturbed. During the eighteenth century even slave-seeking Europeans were intimidated by the Bubi's legendary savagery. The slaughter of an entire English crew by a Batete Bubi tribe in 1810 is among the more dramatic stories of their responses to infiltrators into hard labor and slavery.

Since their settlement in Bioko, the different Bubi groups inhabited the territory in a ring around the island. The names of small villages that today circle the island still preserve the memory of some of those tribes of origin (the Baney, Batate, Baho, Bakake). The Biabba tribe (later the city was named Riabba), is considered the first to arrive. The last groups to arrive included the Batetes and Bokokos. From the fifteenth to the eighteenth centuries, when Europeans initiated the slave trade along the West African coast, any thoughts of an easy landing on Bioko (then called Fernando Póo) were soon dismissed. On Bioko, there were no tribal kings selling off nearby enemy tribesmen.

Society and Culture

In the indigenous Bubi religion, the chief god is Rupe (called Eri on southern parts of the island), a supreme being who created and oversees all. Bubi conceive of three parts to the spirit world: *Labakoppua*, or "heaven and the angels"; *Ommo ich'ori*, or "hell and bad angels"; and *Ommo boeboe*, or "limbo." They believed in the layering or melding of the material and spirit worlds in which the island was shared by the Bubi tribes and a constellation of both good and bad spirits. Bad ones were blamed for diseases, injuries, and unfortunate luck. The coexistence of both spirit and physical worlds on Bioko meant that every distinctive landmark was associated with a Bubi spirit. Rivers, lakes, and mountains were all believed to be points of specific spiritual energy providing a literal and symbolic map for Bubi pagan beliefs.

Bubi Political Situation

Bubi people fought against Spanish attempts to conquer their territory during the end of the nineteenth century. Bubi political activists formed the Bubi Union in the 1960s in order to develop an independence process for their homeland (Bioko Island) that would clearly separate the island from the Rio Muni region of continental Africa, highly dominated by the Fang ethnic groups. However, in 1968 the island of Bioko and the Bubi were included in the same independent state of Equatorial Guinea.

Today Bioko Island is home to the tiny capital city of Malabo (population 35,000), but the island remains controlled by the members of a single Fang clan from the town of Mongomo, in the far east part of the country located on the African mainland (ancient Rio Muni territory). After independence in 1968 Equatorial Guinea was overtaken by a tyrannical president, Francisco Macías Nguema, whose dictatorship was overthrown in a 1979 military coup by his nephew, Teodoro Obiang Nguema Mbasago, the current president. Although the republic has nominally been a constitutional democracy since 1991, the 1996 and 2002 presidential elections were widely seen as being flawed. Although Mbasogo's government is reputedly less violent than his uncle's, he sent in Januarly 1998 Fang-dominated security forces to crush an uprising by a handful of unarmed Bubis. In the days that followed, there were reports of hundreds of arrests and violent interrogations.

JOAN MANUEL CABEZAS LÓPEZ

See also **Annobonés**

Further Reading

Bolekia Boleká, Justo, *Löbëla*, Madrid: Casa de África, 1999
Creus, Jacint, *Equatorial Guinea: The Invention of an Identity*, Vic (Barcelona): Recerques Claretianes, 1994
Nerín, Gustau, *Equatorial Guinea: History in Black and White*, Barcelona: Empúries Editions, 1997
Novoa, José Manuel, *Through the Bubi Magic: Into the Guinean Forests*, Madrid: Vives Editorial, 1991

Buddhists

Capsule Summary

Location: Mainly in Asian countries
Total Population: 359 million worldwide (2003)
Language: Varies
Religion: Buddhism

Buddhists today live in many different countries, predominantly Asian, but in recent years their numbers have spread to the West. Buddhism has been interchangeably described as a religion, philosophy, philosophy-religion, ideology, and a way of life. Although at the core are immutable teachings by the Buddha (Siddhārtha Gautama, circa 563–483 BCE, also known as "the Enlightened One"), Buddhism has developed into numerous schools and sects over a period of 2,500 years. Furthermore, Buddhism has adopted and reshaped its host cultures in Asian countries from India to Japan. Buddhists as a whole comprise the fourth largest religious group of today's world and consist of over 359 million practitioners or believers.

Buddha: The Founder of Buddhism

The Buddha was born as a royal prince circa 563 BCE in Kapilavastu, in northern India and today a part of Nepal. His mother's name was Queen Maya Devi and his fathers was King Suddhodana, the Raja of the Sakya clan in India. He was called Prince Siddhārtha Gautama in his early life and was surrounded by material wealth and luxury. At 16 he married his cousin, Princess Yasodharā, with whom he had a son, Rāhula. He would often wander through the streets of his father,s kingdom, where he encountered the aged, the sick, the infirm, and the dead. These images impressed the young Siddhārtha intently, and he came to believe in the universality of suffering. At the age of 29, he abandoned palace life and became a wandering ascetic, traveling south to the Magadha kingdom in search of truth and enlightenment. After practicing extreme self-mortification for six years, he then meditated under a banyan tree at Bodh Gayā and attained Enlightenment, thereby becoming a Buddha, i.e., "the Awakened" or "the Enlightened." A Buddha is a person who has been released from the cycle of birth and death and liberated from desire and craving. Siddhārtha then taught his doctrine of the "four noble truths" as well as other approaches to life and belief, which came to be called Buddhism, until his death in 483 BCE at the age of 80.

Basic Teachings of Buddhism

The term "Buddhism" derives from *buddhi* (the "intuition"), which is the faculty of *bodhi* ("wisdom," "enlightenment," and "awakening"). The goal of spiritual practice in Buddhism is to attain *nirvana* (or *nibbana* in Pāli), literally meaning "extinction" or "blowing out." A state of supreme Enlightenment, nirvana represents the liberation from *samsara*, the cycle of birth, death, and rebirth, which is believed to be the cause of all suffering. Buddhism conceives of no end to this cycle, which is rather a continuing process of becoming, of mental and spiritual consciousness.

The Buddhist faith encapsulates three sacred ideas called the *Triple Gem:* the Buddha (the Enlightened teacher), the *Dharma* (the truth, hence the teaching of the Buddha) and the *Sangha* (the community of Enlightened individuals, usually monks or followers of the Buddha).

The Buddha left no writings, and for at least 400 years after his death, none of his teachings appeared in written form. Nonetheless, the Buddha's teachings were eventually collected a century after his death and compiled in the *Tipitaka* ("Three Baskets," also known as the *Pāli Canon*), the sacred texts of the school of Theravada Buddhism. These sacred texts cover a wide field of subjects and are made up of exhortations, expositions, and injunctions. The *Tipitaka* was memorized and recited orally by disciples and later transcribed onto three scrolls that were kept in three baskets (*ti-pitaka*). Although it was originally written in Pāli, a middle Prakrit language and the one spoken by Buddha, it was also published in Sanskrit, Tibetan, and Chinese. The *Tipitaka* is composed of three parts: (1) *Vinaya Pitaka* (collection of the Rules of Discipline of the Order, essentially a code of ethics to be obeyed by the early *sangha*, the disciples of Buddha); (2) *Sutta Pitaka*, literally "basket of threads or sermons" (consisted of a collection of numerous philosophical teachings and biographical sketches); and (3) *Abhidhamma Pitaka* (a collection of analytical reflections and teachings of the Reality in relation to metaphysics, psychology and philosophy).

A common theme in these writings and in other Buddhist teachings is the principle of self-salvation. Buddhists are taught to take oneself as one's own refuge rather than relying on external sources of salvation, such as God. Buddhists undergo a ceaseless process of self-perfection, first by realizing causes of suffering and then by obtaining and using the practices described (such as meditation) in order to remove them. These important concepts include meditation, *karma* and *vipaka*. Meditation in varying forms is common to most if not all schools of Buddhism. Although meditation comprises many different practices and even purposes, it is a means of gaining experiential insight into the nature of reality, or communing with the Deity or "Ultimate Reality." Meditation can be religious, spiritual, or simply a means to increase self-awareness, concentration, self-discipline, or equanimity. *Karma* and *vipaka* signify the principle of "action and reaction," in which *karma* means intention or cause (as in "to cause"), accompanied by a separate tenet, v*ipaka*, meaning the result or effect. The dual principles are often misunderstood in the West as cause and effect and originate within the dynamic of *pratitya-samutpada*, or "dependent origination," which suggests that all phenomena are mutually dependent and is used to describe the very nature of existence.

Moreover, by rejecting the concept of given destiny, Buddhism holds that a person's mind and thoughts alone create his or her future circumstances through a chain of interdependent actions and reactions. Therefore, Buddhists strive to perceive circumstances as illusory (to see from within and without) so that the proper functions of mind will not be influenced or swayed.

Similarly, Buddhists perceive that all existences in the world are infinitely interrelated through pairs of opposites. Being and nonbeing, the whole and the constituent parts are irrevocably interrelated. According to the Buddhist concept of "Reality" there is no such thing as separation in any forms of existence based on the laws of *pratitya-samutpada*. Nature functions like a stone thrown into a pond such that the ripples flow outward until they reach an endpoint and then return to their original location. A nurtured awareness of universal wholeness (or oneness) and a sense of connection (or sameness) with others leads to compassion for all existences and everlasting harmony.

The Three Characteristics of Life

Buddhists believe in accordance with Buddha's teaching that all forms of life have three common characteristics: (1) impermanence; (2) suffering; and (3) nonself. These three aspects of life are called the Three Characteristics of Life or the Three Signs of Life (or Being). These terms are merely single translations of Pali words, *anicca*, *dukkha*, and *anatta*. *Anicca* signifies the transitory, impermanent nature of all lives subject to change each moment. Every existing thing is in a flux of ceaseless change and eventually passes away. *Dukkha* is most frequently translated as suffering. This concept covers all possible pains felt emotionally, mentally, or physically, including misery, discomfort, dissatisfaction, incompetence, insufficiency, illnesses, and diseases. *Anatta*, which can be translated into nonself or egolessness, means that there is nothing in existence that holds an immortal soul or any other form of perpetual entity, center, or core. Buddhism teaches that without a concept of self, neither ideas nor outward expression of pride, arrogance, violence, or aggression may arise.

The Four Noble Truths and the Noble Eightfold Path

The Four Noble Truths refer to the noble truth of: (1) suffering; (2) the cause of suffering; (3) the end of suffering; and (4) the path that leads to the end of suffering. Buddhist doctrine holds that life in Reality is rife with suffering from birth to death. Suffering is caused by desire for clinging or craving (*tanha*). Humans are constantly subject to desire sensual satisfaction, often with immediate gratification. Unquenchable thirst for such momentary gratifications of flesh, mind and feelings, which Buddhism maintains are all illusions and produced because of ignorance (*avidya*), results in inescapable suffering. In order to break through the chain or cycle of suffering, it is imperative to overcome ignorance and unnecessary, endless desire. Buddhism offers a way to confront those illusions—the Noble Eightfold Path.

The Noble Eightfold Path signifies: (1) right views; (2) right thoughts and attitude of mind; (3) right speech; (4) right conduct; (5) right livelihood; (6) right effort; (7) right mindfulness; and (8) right concentration and serenity. The Path teaches to avoid two opposite extremes and instead to take the Middle Way. From a "negative" point of view, the Path helps remove the thirst for illusionary satisfaction of desire. From a "positive" point of view, the path leads to a cultivation of compassionate, selfless individuals.

Right Speech, Right Conduct, and Right Livelihood among others are directly linked to the Five Precepts (*pancasila*), which include vows to abstain from: (1) taking (or threatening) life; (2) stealing; (3) sensuality; (4) lying (including speaking of untruths); and (5) intoxication (by alcohol or drug). The interpretation of these Five Precepts can be extrapolated to other ethical teachings. The first rule demands that one control anger and violent thinking; the second calls for the elimination of desire for material possessions; the third the removal of lust for the flesh; the forth demands that one overcome cowardice, and finally the fifth expels unhealthy excitement.

The Four Lofty States of Mind

According to Theravada Buddhism, one is expected to develop *Brahma Viharas*, the "Four Lofty States of Mind," by the time he or she attains the highest level of spirituality. The first is *metta*, "loving kindness," or the embrace of all living beings in the universe. Upon obtaining this benevolence, one lives in peace, free from anger, irritation, and sadness. The second state of mind is *karuna*, "compassion," which is goodwill to free others from suffering. The third is *mudita*, "sympathetic joy," in which happiness grows. The last is *upekkha*, "equanimity," with which one is capable of dealing with any situation in a tranquil, stable state of mind. In order to acquire these states of mind, Buddhists engage in daily meditation.

Meditation

Meditation, or *bhavana*, is a means to cultivate the inner world through intensely focused contemplation. Buddhism mainly teaches two kinds of meditation. One is named *samatha bhavana*, meaning "mental development of inner peace." The first step in this meditation is to recognize the existence of any kind of selfishness and ill will and then to remove it. The second step requires growing universal love and compassion (*metta*). The other kind of meditation is called *vipassana bhavana*, mental development of knowledge and wisdom. Through this meditation, ignorance, another major cause of suffering, is eliminated as one tries to learn the illusionary nature of the Reality and thus free him or herself from suffering.

The Spread of Buddhism

The range of Buddhism in regard to time and space is incredibly vast. It has been 2,500 years since its birth in the sixth century BCE. In its origins Buddhism was one of the most sophisticated moral philosophies of the time. Through its advancement, it developed itself into a religion that included refined ethics, philosophy, psychology, metaphysics, and mysticism. In terms of space, Buddhism spread from India to the easternmost Asian country, Japan. It was not only absorbed into indigenous cultures across Asia, it also reshaped those cultures, including arts and customs, set a moral standard for the people, and contributed to new histories. Because Buddhism possesses no central figure (i.e., God) or authority (i.e., church or temple) it escaped certain restraints or laws that would have disallowed its diversification and spread throughout the east and eventually the west.

Today, Buddhism is usually divided into three (can be two or four depending on the method of classification) major schools, with subdivisions under each of them. The earliest school of Buddhism is the Theravada sect (the "Doctrine of the Elders" or the Southern School of Buddhism). It is presently primarily practiced in Burma (Myanmar), Cambodia, Sri Lanka, and Thailand. Theravadins focus on the Four Noble Truths and the Noble Eightfold Path. The name of the sect implies the meaning of "those supporting the teachings of the elders," which means that the school had conservative tendencies—an attempt to conserve the original teachings of the Buddha. In fact, Theravadans sometimes conflicted with the more liberal Mahāhānghika school that called for a revisionist approach to the early Buddhist doctrine.

A second school is the Mahayana (the "Great Vehicle" or the Northern School of Buddhism), first developed in India in the first century BCE. It includes Tibetan Buddhism (in Tibet and its neighboring Bhutan and Nepal), Zen (most popular in Japan), and Chinese Buddhism. Mahayana developed from the more austere Theravada and is today practiced in China, Japan, Korea and, in lesser numbers, Vietnam and Taiwan. The Mahayana school has been characterized by a greater emphasis on the supernatural and magical, often embodied in the figure of the *bodhisattva* ideal of love and compassion. The *bodhisattva* (*bosatsu* in Japanese, or a person striving for enlightenment) is the one whose life is devoted to mankind, or more specifically, who willingly delays his own Enlightenment for liberation of others. Bodhisattvas reject nirvana and remain on the material plane to assist other believers to achieve enlightenment. Mahayanists also developed the notion of *sunyata* or "emptiness." While Theravadins asserted no existence of a soul through this idea, Mahayanists expanded the concept of sunyata to mean that all existence or phenomena is empty. The Mahayana school generally places less emphasis upon monasticism than the Theravada school, and is also characterized by abundant statue (sculptural) representations of the Buddha figure, a tendency borrowed from the Greco-Roman tradition.

Finally, the Vajrayana (the "Diamond Vehicle") is another major school of Buddhism. This school derived from the Mahayana school in northwest India during circa seventh century and is practiced today in Tibet, Mongolia, Bhutan, China, and Japan. Students in this school focus on studies of sacred texts with a master (or guru), and also through the use of esoteric visualizations, rituals, and mantras (usually a string of syllables in Sanskrit read or spoken in a ritual context). It is known to the west as Tantric Buddhism and also evolved into the school of Shingon Buddhism in Japan.

Contemporary Buddhism

It is estimated that there are approximately 359 million Buddhists in the world today (2000), making Buddhism the fourth largest religious group of the world after Christianity (2 billion), Islam (1.2 billion), and Hinduism (900 million). Until the rise of Communism in China, almost a third of the world population was Buddhist. China had approximately 200 million Buddhists in 1949 before Communism; 100 million in 1955; and only 19,304,632 (about 1.5 percent of the population) in 2003.

According to the *CIA Fact Book 2003*, countries with the highest Buddhist population density today are Thailand (95 percent of the total population or 61,052,012), Cambodia (95 percent, or 12,468,526), Burma (89 percent, or 37,834,377), Japan (84 percent including Shinto, or 106,860,179), Bhutan (75 percent, or 1,604,661), and Sri Lanka (70 percent, or 13,819,707). Buddhists are also found (but as a minority) in Nepal, Bangladesh, Singapore, Indonesia, Laos, Vietnam, Mongolia, China (including Tibet), and South Korea.

Ai Hattori

See also **Bangladesh; Bhutan; Cambodia; China; Hindus; India; Indonesia; Myanmar; Thailand**

Further Reading

Bstan-'dzin-rgya-mtshp (Dalai Lama XIV), *A Simple Path: Basic Buddhist Teachings*, London: Thorsons, 2000

Fowler, Merv, *Buddhism: Beliefs and Practices*, Portland: Sussex Academic Press, 1999

Frederic, Louis, *Buddhism*, New York: Flammarion Iconography Guide, 1995

Harvey, Peter, *An Introduction to Buddhist Ethics: Foundation, Values, and Issues,* New York: Cambridge University Press, 2000

Humphreys, Christmas, *Buddhism: An Introduction and Guide*, New York: Penguin Books, 1990

Leighton, Yaigen Daniel, *Bodhisattva Archetypes: Classic Buddhist Guides to Awaking and Their Modern Expression*, New York: Penguin Arkana, 1998

Lopez, Donald S., *The Story of Buddhism: A Concise Guide to Its History and Teachings*, San Francisco: Harper, 2001

Bulgaria

Capsule Summary

Location: Eastern part of Balkan Peninsula (Southeastern Europe), bordering with Greece, Turkey, Macedonia, rump Yugoslavia, Romania, and Black Sea in the East)
Total Population: 7,537,929 (July 2003)
Ethnic Population: Bulgarian (83.6%), Turk (9.5%), Roma (4.6%), other (2.3%, including Macedonian, Armenian, Tatar, Circassian) (1998)
Languages: Bulgarian, secondary languages closely correspond to ethnic breakdown
Religions: Bulgarian Orthodox (83.8%), Muslim (12.1%), Roman Catholic (1.7%), Jewish (0.1%), Protestant, Gregorian-Armenian, and other (2.3%) (1998)

The Republic of Bulgaria, with an area of 110,993 sq km (42,822 sq mi), shares borders with Greece, the Former Yugoslav Republic of Macedonia, Romania, Serbia, and Montenegro, and Turkey. Its capital is Sofia. The first Slavo-Bulgarian state was founded around the Danube delta, now in Romania, in 680 CE. Passing periods of strength and decay, that first Bulgarian Kingdom once dominated over huge territories of present-day Eastern and Central Europe, but between 1018 and 1185 was under Byzantine domination, and in 1396 fell under Ottoman Turkish domination. Almost five centuries later, in 1878, Bulgaria was liberated after the Russo-Turkish War. According to the Berlin Treaty of 1878 it was divided into two semi-autonomous entities, the principality of Bulgaria and the *vilaya* (province) of Eastern Roumelia, and deprived of some territories, given to neighbor countries or back under the Sultan. The principality was reunified with East Roumelia in 1885, and full independence was proclaimed in 1908, when Prince Ferdinand acquired the title of czar. The Bulgarian Kingdom was mostly at foes with its neighbors, and was among the losers in the two World Wars. In September 1944, Soviet troops entered Bulgaria, and Communist power was established, remaining in effect until 1990.

History

A Turkic tribe of Protobulgarians, led by Khan Asparoukh, came to the Balkan peninsula in theseventh century CE, leaving behind centuries-old military and state traditions in Central Asia. They resided between Danube, Black Sea and Balkan mountains, allied with the Slavic tribes and defeated Byzantine troops, thus compelling the empire to recognize the Slavo-Bulgarian state in 681 CE.

Under Khan Kroum (803–814) Bulgaria acquired large territories, conquering Serdica (present day Sofia), and adjoined in the West Charlemagne's Frankish Empire. Boris I Michael (852–889) accepted Christianity and the Cyrillic alphabet, and his son Simeon (892–927) further consolidated the state, obtaining the title of "Czar of Bulgarians and Byzantines" and strongly sponsoring cultural and spiritual advancement. With the Kievan Prince Svetoslav campaign, Byzantine assaults, and internal riots, the country saw intense decline that led to falling under Byzantine rule (1018–1185 CE). After successful uprising czars Assen, Peter II, and Kaloyan (1187–1207) established the Second Bulgarian state, recovered most territorial possessions, and reversed the crusaders. Under Czar Ivan Assen II (1218–1241) Bulgaria reached the Black, Aegean, and Adriatic Seas, and became a regional power. Later, however, the Bulgarian state was devastated by rebellions and raids and split into three parts to be conquered by the Ottoman Turks. Their rule lasted almost five centuries.

With the Bulgarian Revival at the end of the eighteenth century characterized by struggles for autonomous church and freedom, after the Russo-Turkish War of 1877–78 Bulgaria regained a restricted self-rule. According to the Berlin Treaty, Northern Bulgaria along with Sofia was pronounced a semiautonomous principality. The treaty established Eastern Rumelia, a Turkish province, and the rest of the Bulgarian lands as stated by the 1876 Istanbul Conference of Ambassadors were left under the direct rule of the Sultan or given to neighbor countries. As the Bulgarian dynasty's missed chain of inheritance, only an offspring of the European royal families with their approval could become the Bulgarian head of state. In 1885 the two parts of Bulgaria reunited, which cost the crown of Prince Alexander Batenberg. German Prince Ferdinand Sax-Coburg-Gotta was enthroned under the disapproval of Russia and silent disparagement of the European monarchs. He shaped a strong military force to proclaim full independence in 1908, dubbed himself a czar, and joined an unprecedented all-Balkan alliance against Turkey in the first Balkan War (Fall 1912–May 1913). Dissatisfied by the Bulgarian returns in the end of the war, Czar Ferdinand ordered an offensive against the former allies, which became disastrous for Bulgaria. Bulgaria attempted revenge when World War I ensued on the side of the Central Powers in 1915. Severe devastation followed, and Bulgaria had to cede territories to Romania and Yugoslavia.

Under the rule of Ferdinand's son, Boris III, Bulgaria saw a quarter-century of various regimes, from the populist agrarian rule of Alexander Stamboliyski to the czar's personal governing (from 1934 until his death in 1943), as well as communist conspiracies and terror. The Bulgarian economy recovered enough to be the leading force in the region in 1939 until the start of World War II when the country joined the Axis Powers. In September 1944, Soviet Troops occupied Bulgaria and helped the communist-led guerillas establish a new regime, which soon appeared to be the most obedient toward Moscow among the Communist Bloc.

Post-War and Post-Communist Bulgaria

Bulgarian communists conducted a policy of deliberate and gradual assimilation of the countries' ethnic minorities. The chief minority, the Turks, were returned some of the rights that had been seized in the 1930s, although they remained under strict Communist and secret services control. After the Roma/Gypsies were settled by force and coerced to accept Bulgarian names, the Bulgarian Moslems (Pomaks) were also denied their original names in the late 1960s–early 1970s. In addition, women were deprived of the right to dress traditionally, and many customs, like circumcision were forbidden and criminalized. When the same policies were implemented toward the Turkish minority (mid-1980s), however, the regime faced resistance and international outcry, which accelerated the collapse of communist rule in Bulgaria.

After 1989, like other Central and Eastern European countries, Bulgaria entered a period of democratic changes, and presently it is on the eve of becoming a member of NATO (2004) and the European Union (circa 2007). Though the new Constitution formally forbids political parties on ethnic and confessional basis, ethnic minorities gained representation in the parliament and executive branches, where since 2001 the predominantly Turkish party, Movement for Rights and Freedoms, has been part of the ruling majority.

Society

Bulgaria is home to a range of ethnic groups including native Bulgarians, Turks, Roma, Macedonians, Armenians, Tatars, and Circassians. They practice a variety of religions (Bulgarian Orthodox, Muslim, Roman Catholic, Jewish, Protestant, Gregorian-Armenian, and others), although Bulgarian Orthodox predominates (over 80 percent of the population). The country's economy has struggled post-Communism and presently is divided among agriculture (13.7 percent), industry (28.5 percent), and services (57.9 percent) (2001). Chief industries include electricity, gas and water, tobacco, machinery and equipment, base metals, chemical products, coke, refined petroleum, and nuclear fuel. Export commodities include clothing, footwear, iron and steel, machinery and equipment, and fuels. GDP per capita income was $6,500 in 2002. Bulgaria negotiated a $300 million standby agreement with the International Monetary Fund in 2001 that supported government efforts to overcome high rates of poverty and unemployment.

STEPHAN E. NIKOLOV

See also **Circassians; Roma (Gypsies); Romania; Turks; Yugoslavia**

Further Reading

Chary, Frederick B., *The Bulgarian Jews and the Final Solution 1940–1944*, Pittsburgh: Pittsburgh University Press, 1977

Crampton, Richard, *A Short History of Bulgaria*. Cambridge, United Kingdom, Cambridge University Press, 1987

Eminov, Ali, *Turkish and Other Muslim Minorities in Bulgaria*, London: Hurst and Co., 1997

Kertikov, Kiril, "Ethnonational Issues in Bulgaria (1944–1991)," in *Bulgarian Quarterly*, 1, no. 3 (Winter 1991)

Kertikov, Kiril, "Ethnonational Issues in Bulgaria (1944 1991)", in *Bulgarian Quarterly*, 2, no. 1 (Spring 1991)

Şimşir, Bilal N., The Turks of Bulgaria, London: K. Rustam & Brothers, 1988

Troebst, Stefan, "Nationale Minderheiten,"in Bulgaria: Handbook on Southeast Europe, vol. 6, edited by K. D. Grothusen, Gőtingen, 1990

Burakumin

Capsule Summary

Location: Mostly Honshu, the main island of Japan
Total Population: Estimates range from 1 million to 3 million (no official census exists)
Language: Japanese
Religions: Mainly Buddhism and Shinto, other Japanese

Although often considered a minority group in Japan, the Burakumin (literally translated as "hamlet people" and also called *eta*) are racially identical with other Japanese populations. They are concentrated in a few areas of Japan, namely in parts of Kyushu, the coasts of the Inland Sea, Kobe, Osaka, and Kyoto. Presently there is no official census to provide accurate figures, but estimates count approximately 1 million to 3 million Burakumin living in Japan. The Ainu, the original inhabitants of Japan, sometimes fall under the burakumin umbrella along with prisoners of war, clandestine immigrants, Koreans, Filipinos, and others. The group is estimated to number about 2 percent of the Japanese population or roughly 2 million people.

Questions concerning the Burakumin should not be confused with those of race, ethnicity, or any other categories that are conventionally used to identify a social group. Probably the closest concept in regard to the social categorization of the Burakumin is the caste system in India, in which they can be related to "the untouchables" or the Dalits (literally meaning "broken" people) who suffer discrimination and recrimination. Non-burakumin Japanese historically viewed the burakumin as inherently morally defective. However, Burakumin remain from Japan's feudal system, which no longer exists in modern Japan, and today, the buraku (literally "hamlet") issues tend to steadily disappear thanks to official assimilation policies and projects, efforts in the field of education, and attitudinal changes from generation to generation.

Although one of the most serious considerations facing the Burakumin has been social discrimination in the twentieth century, many Japanese think that this problem is coming to an end. In other words, assimilation, in a positive sense as far as the Burakumin are concerned, has been successful insofar as it has eliminated some of the difficulties of this group in recent decades in Japan.

History

The first usage of the term *Burakumin* dates at least to the late nineteenth century, although it was during the Edo period (1603–1868) when the Burakumin (called the *eta*, "much filth," "much impurity," and the *hinin*, "non-human") emerged as the official lowest members of the caste system and were forced to live in segregated communities. The order of the hierarchy was warrior, farmer, artisan, merchant, *eta-hinin* (*shi-no-ko-sho-eta-hinin*). Burakumin were required to live in ghettos. It is widely agreed today that the first Burakumin were impoverished Japanese who turned to beggary or other lowly occupations that people of the time avoided due to shared Shinto and Buddhist beliefs involving the taking of life (both human and animals). Burakumin discrimination was based on Buddhist prohibitions against killing and Shinto concepts of pollution (hence the connection to *eta* or filth), along with governmental efforts at controlling the population. Buraku Japanese were originally discriminated against because they were also butchers, leatherworkers, and even entertainers.

By the early eighteenth century, feudal laws required that Burakumin wear badges made with leather (considered unclean at that time) and certain clothing and hairstyles. They were forbidden to mingle with different classes or enter such buildings; they were kept to curfews, and prostrated before the higher-class populations. An oft-cited incident that signifies the degree of severe discrimination persistent during those times was when one Burakumin was killed in a brawl in 1859, the court ruled that the murderer was innocent unless he had killed six more Burakumins. In other words, one Burakumin's life was worth only one-seventh of that of any other Japanese.

In 1871, the Meiji government abolished the class system as well as the usage of the derogatory words, *eta* and *hinin*, under the Emancipation Act. They were now given a new status name, "new commoners" (*shin-heimin*). However, no other substantial measures were taken to eliminate the discrimination beyond this act.

Buraku Japanese during the early twentieth century began to organize to fight for their rights. One of the earliest responses to this oppressive reality was a group called the Bisaku Heimin-kai (Bisaku Commoners' Association) formed by young men from a town in Okayama in 1902. Many similar human rights organizations spread throughout Japan in search of improvement in the Burakumin social and economic life and their acceptance in mainstream society. In 1922 Buraku Japanese founded the National Levelers' Association (Zenkoku Suiheisha) in Kyoto whose main objective was to eliminate discrimination. (The name *Suiheisha* derived from *suihei*, meaning horizontal or level, and invoked a call to realize a society that is uniformly even and without discrimination; and *sha*, meaning association.) At the association's founding assembly on March 3, 1922, they adopted the Suiheisha Declaration. This document has been regarded as Japan's first declaration of human rights. The first and largest national organization of its kind, the National Levelers' Association successfully altered Burakumin living condition as well as negative perceptions through other social interventions such as tax and school boycotts, although Buraku struggles continued until 1941.

In response to the Suiheisha Movement and based on ideologies hoisted by the Suiheisha, the national government launched its nationwide assimilation education policy in 1927–1928. However, as the Sino-Japanese War began in 1937, the government began manipulating the notion of assimilation simply to strengthen Japan's military force by solidifying the people and by mobilizing the Buraku Japanese for the war.

After World War II, several key organizations formed to attempt to liberate the Burakumin once again. The first of these was the Buraku Kaiho Zenkoku Iinkai (All-Japan Committee for Buraku Liberation), a politically active organization founded in 1946. It renamed itself as the Buraku Kaiho Domei (Buraku Liberation League) in 1955. The league was joined by socialist and communist parties and pressured the Japanese government into making concessions in the late 1960s which included a Special Measures Law for Assimilation Projects which provided financial aid to Burakumin communities. By the 1960s, however, this leftist organization was confronted by other, more conservative coalitions, and the latter formed a separate group called the Dowa-kai (Society for Integration) in 1960, which soon came to be led by Liberal Democratic politicians. The most recent organization, the Zenkoku Buraku Kaiho Undo (All-Japan Buraku Liberation Movement), was established in 1976 and has remained active since then.

At the same time, many educators became deeply involved with Buraku issues after the end of World War II. Bearing ideals captured in the new democratic peace constitution and the Fundamental Law of Education in mind, they established the Zenkoku Dowa Kyoiku Kenkyu Kyogi-kai (All-Japan Educational Research Conference for Integration) in 1953. By the 1960s, this group of educators accomplished several objectives including substantial guarantees for children's education rights.

In 1968, as part of the continuing efforts to fight prejudice against the Burakumin, the Ministry of Justice prohibited any indication of their class status on registration forms. This regulation prohibited anyone from identifying the Burakumin based on records such as legal, employment, and/or marriage licenses.

Thus, by the late 1990s, signs of decreasing social discrimination against the Burakumin began to appear on statistical data. First, according to recent national government polls, two out of three Burakumin and those related to them said that they never experienced discrimination in 1993. From 1989 to 1999, only one-tenth responded to the survey that they had experienced discrimination at least once. Second, while over 70 percent of the Burakumin over 60 years old today had married another Burakumin within their community, in 1998 the number for those in their 20s was less than 30 percent. In other words, more than 70 percent of the population in the once segregated communities had married outside, thus signifying a shift in thinking in terms of boundaries between Buraku and other members of society.

The Special Measures Law for the 1969 Assimilation Project, one of the most crucial laws that has protected and expanded social rights of the Burakumin in 4,603 buraku districts all over Japan, was invalidated in March 2002. The decision in 1997 to repeal the law suggests that the reality of the Buraku Japanese has changed. As the societal and political boundaries between the various classes erode, the definition of Burakumin has shifted away from its historical implications.

Ai Hattori

See also **Japan; Untouchables (Harijans/Dalits/ Scheduled Castes)**

Further Reading

De Vos, George A., and William O. Wetherall, *Japan's Minorities: Burakumin, Koreans, Ainu and Okinawans*, London: Minority Rights Group, 1983

Kitaguchi, Suehiro, *An Introduction to the Buraku Issue: Questions and Answers*, translated by Alastair McLaughlin, Cuzon Press, 1998

Shimazaki, Toson, *The Broken Commandment*, translated by Kenneth Strong, Tokyo: University of Tokyo, 1977

Sumii, Sue, *River with No Bridge*, translated by Susan Wilkinson, Charles E. Tuttle Co, 1991

Buriats

Capsule Summary

Location: Southern Siberia, mostly in the Republic of Buriatia
Total Population: 417,400 in Russia (1989)
Language: Buriat
Religions: Buddhism, Shamanism, Orthodox Christianity

The Buriats are one of the three indigenous Buddhist peoples of Russia and the largest ethnic minority group in Siberia. Their homeland lies in a Southern Siberian region of steppe, mountains, and fertile valleys around Lake Baikal, the world's deepest lake. The majority lives in the Republic of Buriatia, one of 21 ethnically defined autonomous republics within Russian Federation borders. Buriatia, which is about the same size as Germany, is located east of Lake Baikal and borders Mongolia, a nation ethnically kindred to the Buriats. A third of the republic's population lives in its capital, Ulan-Ude. Buriats also live in the nearby *Ust-Orda-* and *Aga Buriat autonomous districts*. There are also Buriat minorities in Northeastern Mongolia and Inner Mongolia (China).

Although the Buriat Republic had a population of over 1 million in 1989, Buriats formed only 24 percent of the population—70 percent were ethnic Russians. The percentage of Buriats in their own republic is said to have increased significantly during the 1990s, but their percentage might still be smaller than one-third of the republic's total population. The Russian majority lives mostly in the cities. In the Aga Buriat Autonomous District (pop. 77,000) Buriats formed a majority of 55 percent, while in the Ust-Orda Autonomous District they represented only 36 percent of the population of 136,000 (1989). Of all the Buriats living in the territory of the former Soviet Union, 86 percent declared Buriat as their mother tongue in the census of 1989; the remaining spoke Russian. The Buriat language, a subgroup of the Mongolian group of the Altai family, is related to standard Mongolian being spoken in Mongolia. The vertically written Mongolian script has been replaced by Cyrillic during communist rule. A majority of the people are Buddhist, practicing the Tibetan form, Lamaism, while a minority have converted to Orthodox Christianity. In remote areas Shamanistic beliefs have been retained.

The Russian expansion reached Lake Baikal in 1643. Just like many other ethnic groups living in Siberia the indigenous Buriats put up resistance to the Russian forces but were militarily inferior. Also after the conquest several Buriat anti-Russian revolts were suppressed. Nevertheless, the Russian administration first intended not to interfere in the interior affairs of the Buriat people, not even when the majority of the formerly animistic Buriats converted to the Lamaist form of Buddhism under the influence of Tibetan and Mongolian missionaries at the beginning of the eighteenth century. After an Eparchy was founded in Irkutsk in 1731 some Buriats converted to Orthodox Christianity for material incentives, and some were forcibly converted. The majority remained Buddhist; some areas retained Shamanistic beliefs. In 1741 the Lamaist branch of Buddhism was eventually recognized as one of the official religions in Russia and the first Buriat datsan (Buddhist monastery) was built. By 1795 there were about 360,000 persons of non-European origin in Siberia, more than half of them Buriats and Yakuts, the two biggest non-European ethnic groups in the region, compared to about 820,000 Russian settlers.

Similar to the Muslim peoples of Russia the Buriats developed a national consciousness during the nineteenth century. A renaissance of traditional Buriat culture, including its modernization, emerged in response to the threat of Christian missionary agitation and the colonization by Russians and other Slavs. At the beginning of the twentieth century the Buriats protested against the administrative reforms circumscribing their autonomy. Lamaist clergymen and the Buriat elite organized assemblies in Irkutsk and Chita, and a Buriat national duma demanded self-government, an educational system in the Buriat language, and social reforms. Six years after the communist takeover a "Buriat-Mongol Autonomous Soviet Socialist Republic" was formed within the territory as part of the Russian Socialist Federal Soviet Republic (RSFSR) to formally satisfy the Buriats' demand for self-government. Later Joseph Stalin's government separated a number of counties from the Buriat-Mongol ASSR in order to disperse the Buriats. National and religious sentiments were repressed under communist rule. Mongolian script was banned and replaced by Cyrillic. In 1958, "Mongol" was removed from the name of the republic.

Before the Soviet Union's collapse in 1991 the Supreme Soviet of the Buriat ASSR declared state sovereignty of the "Buriat SSR". Buriatia later also dispensed with the label of "Soviet Socialist" from its official name eventually becoming simply "The Republic of Buriatia" in 1992. The republic stated that it had no plans to secede from Russia and that the constitution being drafted would not incorporate full independence for the republic. Moscow acknowledged the republic's right to implement its own educational system consistent with local linguistic and cultural concerns. A "Buriat Cultural Heritage Association" was established with the aim of effecting a Buriat cultural renaissance with links to the wider Mongolian cultural sphere. A constitution of the Republic was adopted by the "People's Khural" (the parliament, elected every four years) in 1994. Leonid Potapov, a former Communist, won 72 percent of the vote in Buriatia's first presidential election. One year later a bilateral treaty with the Russian Federation was signed to determine the competences between the Buriat Republic and the state. Today ethnic Buriats are proportionately overrepresented in the organs of local administration although they constitute only about a quarter of the Republic's population. During the 1990s, the number of ethnic Buriats increased because many Buriats from other parts of the former Soviet Union moved to Buriatia. Conversely, representatives of other ethnic groups (Russians, Belarussians, Ukrainians, Germans) left the area in the 1990s.

Maximilian Hartmuth

See also **Russia; Siberian Indigenous Peoples**

Further Reading

Humphrey, Caroline, "Buryatiya and the Buryats," in *The Nationalities Question in the Post-Soviet States*, edited by Graham Smith, London: Longman, 1996

Moses, Larry W., *The Political Role of Mongol Buddhism*, Indiana University Uralic Altaic Series, 133, Bloomington: Asian Studies Research Institute, Indiana University, 1977

Humphrey, Caroline, "Population Trends, Ethnicity and Religion among the Buryats," in *The Development of Siberia: People and Resources,* Studies in Russia and East Europe, edited by A.Wood and R.A. French, London: Macmillan, 1989

Humphrey, Caroline, *Marx Went Away—but Karl Stayed Behind. Updated Edition of Karl Marx Collective: Economy, Society and Religion in a Siberian Collective Farm*, Ann Arbor: The University of Michigan Press, 1998

Krader, Lawrence, "Shamanism: Theory and History in Buryat Society," in *Shamanism in Siberia*, edited by V. Dioszegi and M. Hoppal, Budapest: Akademiai Kiado, 1978

Smith, Graham, editor, *The Nationalities Question in the Soviet Union*, London: Longman, 1990

Burkina Faso

Capsule Summary

Location: Western Africa
Total Population: 13,228,460 (July 2003)
Minority Populations: Mossi, Gurunsi, Senufo, Lobi, Busansi, Samo, Marka, Diola
Languages: French (official); Mòoré, the Mossi language spoken by a majority of the population; Diola and Fulfulde, also recognized as national languages
Religions: Indigenous beliefs (40%), Muslim (50%), Christian (mainly Roman Catholic) (10%)

Burkina Faso, formerly Upper Volta and a French colony, is a landlocked country in Western Africa, bordered by Mali to the west and north, Niger and Benin to the east, and Togo, Ghana, and the Ivory Coast (Côte d'Ivoire) to the south. Its over 13 million inhabitants are concentrated on the central plateau around the capital city Ouagadougou, while northern provinces are sparsely populated. With an area of 105,869 square miles (274,201 square kilometers), Burkina Faso is slightly larger than the state of Colorado.

Agriculture accounts for half the gross national product and provides nine tenths of jobs. However, Burkina Faso has few natural resources, fragile soil, and a highly unequal distribution of income. Periodic severe droughts cause the annual migration of almost one third of the workforce to the Côte d'Ivoire and

Ghana. The population, with a per capita GDP purchasing power parity $1,100 (2002), is among the poorest in the region.

Over 60 ethnic groups, each speaking its own language, inhabit the country. Largest is the Gur (Voltaic) group with five main subgroups: Mossi (including Gurma and Yarse), Gurunsi, Senufo, Bobo, and Lobi. Next is the Mande group, with four subgroups: Diola, Samo, Marka, and Busansi. In addition there are Hausa traders, Fulani herders, and the Bella, servants of the Tuareg. French is the official language; Mòoré, the language of the Mossi, is spoken by a majority of the population; Diola is the language of commerce, and Fulfulde is also widely spoken.

About one eighth of the population is Christian (Roman Catholic). The majority is roughly equally divided between Islam and traditional religions.

Burkina Faso is a parliamentary republic. Executive power is vested in an elected president, who appoints a prime minister. Legislative power is entrusted to an elected bicameral parliament. The judicial system is patterned on French law. The current constitution was approved in 1991 and provides for a multiparty system.

History

Bobo, Lobi, and Gurunsi were the first known inhabitants of the region. In about 1300, horsemen began arriving from the south and founded the Gurma and Mossi kingdoms. The most powerful was the Mossi empire of Ouagadougou, which, with its cavalry, held back Songhai and Fulani invasions; Islam arrived late in the region. Mossi chiefs maintained friendly trade relations with the Diola, Hausa, and Ashanti keeping commerce flowing throughout the area well into the nineteenth century. Their authority has been remarkably stable, and some old dynasties still rule.

The area, deep in the interior of the African continent, attracted little attention from Europeans until after the Berlin Conference (1884–85), when Great Britain and France competed for it. The French were not interested in Burkina Faso's meager resources, but projected that it could provide needed workers for the profitable Côte d'Ivoire's factories and plantations. Wogbo, the chief of Ouagadougou, refused the French offer of protectorate. The French defeated him in the late 1880s and burned down his capital.

In 1898 Great Britain agreed to French domination of what was then called Upper Volta. In 1904 this colony was incorporated into the Upper Senegal-Niger colony. The French replaced recalcitrant Mossi chiefs with compliant ones and imposed the *indigénat*, a system that created a small elite with citizenship privileges and officially instituted an inferior status for the masses, guaranteeing French administrators all real power. Forced labor, taxation, compulsory military service, and compulsory cultivation of cash crops made life hard for the Burkinabe. There were revolts, and thousands emigrated to the British Gold Coast. The situation did not improve when France made Upper Volta a separate colony. Droughts and famines led the French to dismantle the colony (1932) and attach most of it to the Côte d'Ivoire.

In 1947, however, upon the request of Mossi chiefs, anxious to regain their prominence, and in recompense to the thousands of Burkinabe who had fought in De Gaulle's Free France forces, France reconstituted Upper Volta. Independence came in 1960, bringing about overt political factionalism. Ethnic minorities, faced by the preponderance of Mossi, fought to gain some measure of power. Moreover, civilian governments were repeatedly overthrown by the military.

In November 1982, noncommissioned officers rebelled and installed Major Jean-Baptiste Ouedraogo as president. Soon, the radical faction of Ouedraogo's government seized power and set up a National Revolutionary Council (CNR) with Flight Commander Thomas Sankara as head of state. Vowing to fight neocolonialism and imperialism, Sankara viewed Marxism as the way to improve the Burkinabe's lot. He demanded integrity in government and renamed the country Burkina Faso, "land of upright people." He advocated women's liberation, appointed women to ministerial posts, campaigned against female circumcision, and suggested changes in family law. He improved living conditions by building schools, providing health services, and increasing food production. Though Sankara did lighten the burden of the masses, his noncompromising attitude made him many enemies among the country's traditionally powerful: Mossi chiefs saw their status threatened; labor unions resented his opposition to strikes; the military felt dispossessed. Used to taking action when they disapproved of the government, they assassinated Sankara (1987). His friend Blaise Compaoré succeeded him.

Compaoré took power at the head of a triumvirate called the Popular Front (FP), which promised to adhere to Sankara's principles while "rectifying" his revolution. The FP advocated self-sufficiency in food, better relations with neighboring conservative states and the West, with Mossi authorities, the army, and the business community. The government formed a new umbrella party, the Organization for Popular Democracy/Labor Movement (ODP/MT) and drafted a new constitution, allowing for multiparty elections. Since then, political parties in Burkina Faso have proliferated, but the ODP/MT has continued to dominate national elections.

Growing debts forced Compaoré to agree to a World Bank structural adjustment program (1991). The austerity measures required provoked strikes, but the government's continued adherence to World Bank reforms made Burkina Faso eligible for debt relief. In rural areas, where most inhabitants still live, soil conservation measures are beginning to pay off. A measure of ethnic and religious tolerance has avoided civil wars and allowed the arts, film in particular, to flourish. However, the Burkinabe are still extremely poor, and recent xenophobia in the Côte d'Ivoire has deprived them of the possibility of supplementing their families' income by working there seasonally as they used to. Recently Burkina Faso border regions have become a staging area for Liberia and Côte d'Ivoire rebels and an asylum for refugees caught in regional fighting; the Ivorian Government accuses Burkina Faso of supporting Ivorian rebels.

L. Natalie Sandomirsky

See also **Côte d'Ivoire**

Further Reading

Anderson, Samantha, editor and translator, *Thomas Sakara Speaks: The Burkina Faso Revolution, 1983–87,* New York: Pathfinder Press, 1989

Benoit, Michel, *The Mossi of Upper Volta: the Political Development of a Sudanese People,* Stanford CA: Stanford University Press, 1964

———, *African Urban Life: The Transformation of Ouagadougou,* Princeton: Princeton University Press, 1974

Guion, Jean R., *Blaise Compaoré, réalisme et intégrité: Portrait de l'homme de la rectification au Burkina Faso,* [Blaise Compaoré, Realism and Integrity: Portrait of the Man behind Rectification in Burkina Faso], Paris: Berger-Levrault, 1991

Jaffré, Bruno, *Burkina Faso: Les années Sankara de la révolution à la rectification,* [Burkina Faso: The Sankara Years from Revolution to Rectification], Paris: L'Harmattan, 1989

Kohler, Jean-Marie, *Activités agricoles et changements sociaux dans l'Ouest Mossi, Haute Volta,* [Agricultural Activities and Social Changes in the Mossi West, Upper Volta], Paris: Orstom, 1971

McFarland, Daniel M., *Historical Dictionary of the Upper Volta,* Lanham, Maryland: Scarecrow Press, 1998

Skinner, Elliott P., *The Mossi of Burkina Faso: Chiefs, Politicians and Soldiers,* Prospect Heights, Illinois: Waveland Press, 1989

Skinner, Elliott P., *The Mossi of the Upper Volta; the Political Development of a Sudanese People,* Stanford, California: Stanford University Press, 1964

Burma, *See* **Myanmar**

Burundi

Capsule Summary

Location: East-Central Africa, the wider region is often called the Great Lakes region
Total Population: 6,096,156 (July 2003)
Ethnic Populations: Hutu (Bantu) 85%, Tutsi (Hamitic) 14%, Twa (Pygmy) 1%, Europeans 3,000, South Asians
Languages: Kirundi (official), French (official), Swahili (along Lake Tanganyika and in the Bujumbura area)
Religions: Christian (67%, [Roman Catholic 62%, Protestant 5%]), indigenous beliefs (23%), Muslim (10%)

The Republic of Burundi is a small, densely populated, land locked country in East-Central Africa bounded on the northeast by Lake Tanganyika, on the north by Rwanda, on the east and south by Tanzania, and on the west by the Democratic Republic of Congo. Its area is 10,759 square miles (27,866 square kilometers), and its capital city is Bujumbura. Its population of over six million is affected by high mortality due to AIDS, resulting in lower life expectancy, higher infant mortality and death rates, and lower population and growth rates.

History

Burundi was inhabited for several centuries by the indigenous Hutu and Tutsi. Rwanda and Burundi were integrated into German East Africa in 1899. In 1916, Ruanda-Urundi became a mandate territory under Belgian rule. Burundi was not really an artificial colonial creation since it had been a kingdom for centuries. The so-called ethnic groups of Burundi, namely Hutu, Tutsi, and Twa, (representing respectively 80 to 85 percent, 14 to 19 percent, and 1 percent of the population) are not ethnic groups in the anthropological sense of the word. The ethnic labels are at most indicators of (former) economic activity. Hutu have traditionally been farmers, while Tutsi were pastoralists, and the Twa pygmies hunters and gatherers. Otherwise, the country forms a remarkable cultural and historical unity. All groups share the same language (Kirundi) and cultural practices, and have always lived side by side, often intermarrying. There are no separate Hutu and Tutsi territories. While the King (*Mwami*) and the royal class (*ganwa*) are often identified as Tutsi, they constituted a special class ruling over both Hutu and Tutsi. Ordinary Tutsi have never had more claims to political power than Hutu. However, the Belgians favored ruling through a Tutsi elite and have hence contributed to the development of ethnic consciousness. At the time of independence (July 1, 1962, from United Nations trusteeship under Belgian administration), however, the struggle for power was not between Hutu and Tutsi but between different royal clans each mobilizing between Hutu and Tutsi.

After independence, Burundi initially remained a constitutional monarchy. However, the events in neighboring Rwanda (namely the abolition of the monarchy, the Hutu "social revolution" and massacres of the Tutsi population) had a destabilizing effect on Burundi. In the first years after independence, several governments held office based on equal representation of Hutu and Tutsi, and political instability was on the increase. The first years of independence were rife with political assassinations. When a group of Hutu *gendarmes* engaged in a coup attempt in October 1965, nearly the whole political Hutu elite was wiped out in subsequent acts of repression. Lt. Gen. Michel Micombero took power in 1966 and established the First Republic. It marked the abolition of the monarchy and the start of the supremacy of the Tutsi from Bururi (the south). The monarchy had been the last political institution with which all sections of the population could identify.

When in April 1972 exiled Hutu killed 2,000 to 3,000 Tutsi, military repression was severe. At least 100,000 Hutu were killed (if not 200,000) and a further 300,000 fled the country. Micombero was deposed in a military coup by Col. Jean-Baptiste Bagaza in 1976. In 1987, Major Jean Pierre Buyoya, deposed Bagaza in a military coup but cautiously embarked on a process of liberalization and democratization, leading up to the 1993 general elections. The election was won by FRODEBU (*Front démocratique du Burundi*), and Melchior Ndadaye (a Hutu) became president. A demographic majority finally became a political majority. Only a few months later, Ndadaye was killed, leading to large-scale ethnic violence throughout the country. Both Hutu and Tutsi were victims of this violence. The new President Cyprien Ntariyamira perished with Rwandan President Habyarimana in the fatal plane crash in Kigali in April 1994 that marked the start of the genocide in Rwanda. In 1996, the army staged a new coup, returning Buyoya to power. In the meantime, both sides in the conflict have fragmented. Among both Hutu and Tutsi there exist groups adopting extreme and more moderate positions alike.

While much stress is often placed upon ethnicity as an explanation for the conflict in Burundi, it is crucial to understand that ethnic differences are not the root cause of conflict. While it is true that Hutu, Tutsi, and Twa have historically never been discrete categories for social and political action, through violence they have since become social realities. Each group fears extermination by the other. Hutu fear repression and violation of their rights by a state dominated by a Tutsi minority, while Tutsi fear extermination in the event of a Hutu majority gaining access to the state. These fears have a large mobilizing potential among ordinary people, while conflict remains in essence a struggle for political (and economic) power between members of a small elite class.

The issue of minorities in Burundi is thus an ambiguous one. Hutus represent the majority in a demographic sense, while Tutsis and Twas are numerical minorities. However, an ethnic minority (i.e., the Tutsi) has dominated the political, economic, and military scene for decades. Both Hutu and Tutsi have been the target of ethnic purification. Hence, from the perspective of rights, it is not always clear to which group the status of victim of the minority/majority cleavage is best applied. It could be argued that the Twa, although hardly ever mentioned, are the most excluded, impoverished, and discriminated-against ethnic group in Burundi. They are not only socially but also economically marginalized. In the context of land pressure and deforestation, they have lost their traditional subsistence base and rights to the little land that remains.

While Buyoya's second coup in 1996 resulted in a trade embargo enforced by neighboring countries, he did move slowly toward negotiations with the opposition. Only in 1998 did the Arusha negotiations start, first mediated by former Tanzanian President Julius Kambarage Nyerere and, since his death in 2000, by former South African President Nelson Mandela. The most important challenge facing the negotiations is to work out an institutional framework simultaneously guaranteeing the protection of the numerical minority (i.e., the Tutsi) and representing the rights of the political minority (i.e., the Hutu). Unfortunately, localized violence continues despite the United Nations' peacekeeping efforts. Tutsi, Hutu, and other conflicting ethnic groups, associated political rebels, armed gangs, and various government forces continue fighting in the Great Lakes region, transcending the boundaries of Burundi, Democratic Republic of the Congo, Rwanda, and Uganda to gain control over populated and natural resource areas.

Society

Burundi is a resource-poor country with an economy that is predominantly agricultural. Roughly 90 percent of the population is dependent on subsistence agriculture that includes coffee, cotton, tea, corn, sorghum, sweet potatoes, bananas, manioc (tapioca); beef, milk, and hides. Coffee and tea are the only significant cash crops, accounting for 90 percent of foreign exchange earnings. Due to the high population density (on average 245 persons/sq km, (95 persons/sq mi) making it the second most densely populated country in Africa), demographic pressure on land remains the major economic, but also political, challenge. Industrial activity is virtually nonexistent, and the country does not posses any mineral wealth of current economic importance. The GDP per capita income was only $500 in 2002. Burundi has also not been without (often extremely violent) conflict since its independence in 1962. These factors in combination with the regional trade embargo imposed upon Burundi from the mid 1990s, and the significant decline of international assistance since that period, explain why the World Bank ranks it among the poorest countries in the world. Doubts about the prospects for sustainable peace continue to impede development. Only one in two children attends school, and approximately one in ten adults has HIV/AIDS.

Saskia Van Hoyweghen

See also **Twa, Tutsi, Rwanda**

Further Reading

Lemarchand, René, *Burundi: Ethnocide as Discourse and Practice*, Cambridge: Woodrow Wilson Center and Cambridge University Press, 1994

Lewis, Jerome, *The Batwa Pygmies of the Great Lakes Region*, London: Minority Rights Group International, 2000

Reyntjens, Filip, *Burundi: Prospects for Peace*, London: Minority Rights Group International, 2000

Van Hoyweghen, Saskia, "De ontaarding van de logica van de democratische meerderheid en minderheid. Het etnische geweld in Burundi," *Noord-Zuid Cahier*, 22, no. 4 (1997)

C

Cambodia

Concise Summary

Name: Cambodia or Kampuchea
Total Population: 13,124,764 (July 2003)
Minority Populations: Khmer (90%); Vietnamese (5%); Chinese (1%); other including Cham Muslim, Thai, Khmer Loeu (4%)
Languages: Khmer (official [95%]), French, English, Vietnamese, Chinese, Cham
Religions: Theravada Buddhist (95%), other (5% [Islam, Animism, Christianity])

A republic in Southeast Asia, Cambodia is located on an important cultural crossroads and is home to a great variety of people. Cambodia is bounded on the north by Thailand and Laos, on the east and southeast by Vietnam, on the southwest by the Gulf Thailand, and on the west and northwest by Thailand. With an area of 69,898 square miles (181,036 square kilometers), its capital is Phnom Penh.

Cambodia is predominantly agricultural, a country of rice paddies, abundant fresh water resources, wooded mountains, and serene Buddhist temples. Although profound transformations have occurred during its consolidation as a modern nation state since it declared independence from France in November 1953, it has remained a place of considerable ethnic diversity. However, it has also known extreme violence and has been riven by conflicts at the heart of which were questions of race, ethnic diversity, and historical memory.

History

The Cambodian state emerged in the latter half of the first millennium CE. Its agricultural society was based on hydrological control of the Mekong lowlands for wet rice cultivation. Influenced by Indian culture and distinguished by a religious and ritual system centering on the institution of the king, its most famous achievement was the temple complex of Angkor Wat.

In the latter half of the second millennium, Cambodia became the victim first of Thai and Vietnamese expansionism and then of French colonization. During the thirteenth century, Buddhism spread, and the country was attacked by Annamese and Siamese city-states, becoming alternately the province of Annam or Siam. In 1863, Cambodia became a French protectorate. During World War II, the Japanese occupied the country along with much of Indochina. Cambodia became fully independent in 1954 and joined the United Nations in 1955. Its borders were the scene of fighting during the Vietnam War, and its civilian government was overthrown by the military in March 1970. The northeast and eastern areas were subsequently occupied by the North Vietnamese and penetrated by the United States and South Vietnamese forces. The dictator Pol Pot came to power in 1975 instituting a regime of terror that lead to mass slaughter of the population. Over 1 million displaced people died from execution or enforced hardships. A 1978 Vietnamese invasion drove the Cambodian communists, known as the Khmer Rouge, into the countryside and touched off almost 20 years of fighting. Elections sponsored by the United Nations in 1993 helped restore some stability as did the rapid diminishment of the Khmer Rouge in the mid-1990s. A coalition government formed after national elections in 1998.

Society, Ethnicity, and Minorities

Much of the story of ethnic minorities in Cambodia can be understood in reference to the history of a state which has consolidated at the expense of other social and political formations but which has itself been the recipient of migration from other areas and subject to domination and division by other states. Ethnic identity in Cambodia is a result of these processes. To call oneself Khmer today means more than just to speak the Khmer language or to have Khmer parents, although these are important markers of identity. It means very often to have internalised images of Khmer ethnicity fashioned by a succession of state projects and to identify with certain symbols held up by the state as indigenous.

There are many residents of Cambodia who do not so identify or are not accepted as Khmer but are regarded as ethnic minorities or foreigners. These comprise two main types: those who have been living in the area contemporaneously with the growth and consolidation of the Khmer state and who have found themselves now within its borders, and those who have settled in or migrated to Cambodia and have not adopted a Khmer ethnic identity. The most significant of these groups will be described before addressing recent historical developments.

The residents of the mountainous regions of Cambodia are referred to as Khmer Loeu, literally the "upper Khmer." The larger of these groups are the Jarai, Kreungbrou, Tampuan, Stieng, Kuay and Mnong but there are more than two-dozen groups in all. They are located in the mountainous regions of Ratanakiri, Mondulkiri and Koh Kong provinces. While culturally, linguistically, and economically distinct in many ways, they have long traded with the lowland people and were sometimes raided for slaves. More recently they came into direct contact with the state and lowlanders through rubber plantations, infrastructure and development projects, revolutionary and military activities, hydro-electricity projects, and tourism. Attempts have long been made to assimilate them to the lowland way of life by settling them in permanent settlements and introducing Khmer institutions.

The ethnic Cham (also known as Cham Muslims or Khmer Islam) comprise those who trace their origins from the kingdom of Champa as refugees from the Vietnamese takeover of that kingdom. They are a long-term resident minority of Cambodia and historically have been relatively well accepted by other groups. Most speak Cham, a Malayo-Polynesian language, but they are a multi-lingual group and many speak Malay, Khmer, and Arabic along with European languages. They intermarried with Malay descendants in Cambodia and some regard their origins not as Cham but as Malay. They follow Islam and live in the vicinity of mosques.

Ethnic Chinese people have lived in Cambodia for a long period of time. Most of them are from the Chinese region of Teochiu. The Chinese are generally associated with entrepreneurial activities and have served as the backbone of the trade economy under a series of regimes, from precolonial times to the present. The majority live in urban areas. They have frequently intermarried with the ethnic Khmer majority.

The ethnic Vietnamese in Cambodia work in fishing, agriculture, trade transport, and services. They are concentrated in the central and southeastern regions of the country. Of all the ethnic minorities, their relationship with the ethnic Khmer is the most tense. The enmity many ethnic Khmer feel towards them is associated with the historical annexation of the Mekong delta by the Vietnamese and their perceived political and economic domination in subsequent eras. When the Vietnamese intervened in the 1980s to oust the Khmer Rouge, they were not only seen as liberators of a repressive regime but were the focus of renewed tensions and suspicion. There are also a number of ethnic Thai in Cambodia, who have historical links with Cambodia's other powerful neighbor. Although ethnic conflicts had flared under the Lon Nol government from 1970–75, the situation of Cambodia's ethnic minorities became disastrous when the Khmer Rouge came to power in 1975. Their ultra-nationalist, genocidal policies resulted in mass deaths and tore through the fabric of Cambodian society. Aiming to "purify" the Khmer nation, the Khmer Rouge targeted those who were of urban or educated backgrounds, influenced by foreign culture, or from the ethnic minorities. Discriminated against due to perceived differences of culture, race, and class, many members of Cambodia's ethnic minorities were executed or died in disastrous policies of social engineering.

In the wake of the Vietnamese invasion and withdrawal and the decline of the Khmer Rouge, the country has returned to peace and has painstakingly begun to rebuild. The political transition to democracy was overseen by the United Nations. The economy is growing, favoring many members of the urban-based ethnic minorities. However, "development" has impacted heavily on the environment and the subsistence lifestyles of many minority groups, and it has been accompanied by severe social problems such as AIDS and prostitution.

Economy

Regional economic crisis, civil violence, and political infighting in the late 1990s severely slowed Cambodia's economy. After 1999, some progress was made on economic reforms and growth. The country had a GDP of $20.42 billion and a GDP per capita income of $1,600 in 2002. Eighty percent of the labor force is employed in agriculture with other industries including tourism, garments, rice milling, fishing, wood and wood products, rubber, cement, gem mining, and textiles. Tourism was Cambodia's fastest growing industry before the September 11, 2001 terrorist attacks in the United States. The population is hampered by lack of education, productive skills, and infrastructure, as well as widespread poverty, especially in rural areas.

Philip Taylor

See also **Khmer; Vietnam; Vietnamese**

Further Reading

Chandler, David, *A History of Cambodia*, Colorado: Westview Press, 1992

Ebihara, May, Carol A. Mortland, and Judy Ledgerwood, editors, *Cambodian Culture since 1975: Homeland and Exile*, Ithaca: Cornell University Press, 1994

International Centre for Ethnic Studies, *Minorities in Cambodia*, London: Minority Rights Group International, 1995

Kiernan, Ben, *The Pol Pot Regime: Race, Power and Genocide in Cambodia under the Khmer Rouge, 1975–79*, New Haven and London: Yale University Press, 1995

Martin, Marie Alexandrine, *Cambodia: A Shattered Society*, Berkley: University of California Press, 1994

Cameroon

Capsule Summary:

Location: West-Central Africa along the Atlantic Coast.
Population: 15,746,179 (July 2003)
Ethnic Population: Cameroon Highlanders (31%), Equatorial Bantu (19%), Kirdi (11%), Fulani (10%), Northwestern Bantu (8%), Eastern Nigritic (7%), other African (13%), non-African (less than 1%)
Languages: French (80%) and English (20%), Pidgin English, 250 indigenous languages
Religion: Indigenous beliefs (40%), Christian (40%), Muslim (20%)

The Republic of Cameroon in West Africa is bordered on the north and northeast by Chad, on the East by the Central African Republic, on the south by the Republic of Congo, Gabon, and Equatorial Guinea, on the southwest by the Bight of Biafra, and on the west and northwest by Nigeria. With an area of 183,591 square miles (475,501 square kilometers), Cameroon is an extremely diverse country. Its historical, cultural, and environmental diversity have led many to call it "Africa in miniature." The languages spoken derive from 24 language families reflecting the mélange of cultures and histories from West and Central Africa. In addition to more than 250 local languages, many people speak one or both of the two official languages, French or English. More than two million people also speak Cameroonian Pidgin English, which has been evolving for more than 300 years. The country is home to more than 250 ethnic groups: Cameroon Highlanders, Equatorial Bantu, Kirdi, Fulani, Northwestern Bantu, Eastern Negritic, other African, and non-African.

History

Although hunter-gatherer groups often called *pygmies* are thought to be the original ancient inhabitants of Cameroon, the region shares its ancient history with other groups. In fact, many archaeologists believe the origin of Bantu groups, which have expanded into most of central and southern Africa, originated in what is present day Cameroon. During the first millennium CE, the Sao Civilization and the Kanem-Bornu Empire grew and exerted its political and cultural influence in the region. The ancient trans-Saharan trade connected the area to North Africa and the rest of the old world. In the late fifteenth century, the Portuguese entered the estuaries of Cameroon and met the Douala peoples, beginning the ever-growing transatlantic trade of goods and slaves.

By the eighteenth century, Fulani groups who had converted to Islam began leading *jihad* or holy war in Northern Cameroon. This movement connected Northern Cameroon to the Sokoto Empire based in Northern Nigeria. Many indigenous groups accepted Fulani rule and culture, while others migrated to more isolated locations to preserve their autonomy. Whether autonomous or not, most of these groups and others in the Western Highlands were subjected to recurrent Fulani cavalry raids for slaves and or tribute.

From the south, the transatlantic slave trade dramatically affected Cameroon. Trade networks which brought the slaves to the coast in Nigeria and Cameroon created alliances and feuds among the many ethnic groups that were either trading slaves or being captured. Guns and whiskey in exchange for slaves transformed all who were involved in this decidedly dark era of history.

Although the British had many links to Cameroon, in 1884, the Germans obtained treaties from coastal peoples and then fought for and subjugated the people living in what they called *Kamerun*. During World War I, in 1916, the League of Nations mandated that France and Britain govern East and West Cameroon respectively.

In 1960 East Cameroon gained its independence, one year before West Cameroon's independence. The two states united in 1961 under a federal system of government led by President Ahmadou Ahidjo. In 1972, Ahidjo changed the constitution making the federation a unitary republic. As a result the English-speaking West Cameroon lost much of its legal autonomy, leading to a disparity between the peoples of both the East and West regions. A preponderance of Western Cameroonians believed that the primarily francophone government did little to represent their interests.

In 1982, Ahidjo resigned due to health reasons and appointed the Prime Minister Paul Biya as President, who has led the country ever since. Throughout Biya's regime, many steps have been made to promote democratization. Political parties and independent newspapers were legalized in the early 1990s. More recently, the airways have opened somewhat to radio and television. However, today these institutions still report closings and harassment when openly critiquing the current regime. Militants from various political parties also report human rights abuses by the current regime. Despite Cameroon's multiparty system, the President still wields a preponderance of power. Yet Cameroon nonetheless stands out in the region as a peaceful and stable country. The next presidential election will be held in October 2004. The ruling Cameroon People's Democratic Party (CPDM) and major opposition parties including the Social Democratic Front (SDF), the Union of the Population in Cameroon (UPN), National Union for Democracy and Progress (NUDP), and the Cameroon Democratic Union (CDU) will compete for the presidency. However, many believe that the elections will follow the fate of earlier elections, likely resulting in the reelection of Biya for another seven-year term. The last legislative and municipal elections in June 2002 were shrouded in widespread allegations of election fraud, further centralizing CPDM control with 73 percent of the legislature and CPDM municipal authorities in areas previously controlled by opposition parties.

Society and Ethnicity

Cameroon is divided into three regions: the Muslim north, dominated by Fulani dynasties and the numerous Kirdi or non-Muslim minority groups; the Cameroon highlands or Grassfields with highly structured and hierarchical kingdoms and nomadic Fulani herders; and the southern forest zone with its many independent Bantu groups and a small number of Pygmy groups.

In the north, the term *Kirdi* means "pagan," a label used by the Fulani to describe the diverse ethnic groups of the northern provinces. The Fulani dominate the region. The Fulani also have traditional control over many Kirdi groups that had weak political systems and were unable to resist the expansion of the Fulbe empire in the eighteenth century. Some of the more important of these Kirdi groups are the Gbaya, Duru, Kapsiki, and Mandara. In the extreme north there are many small enclaves of Choa Arabs.

The western highlands or Grassfields region is home to dozens of complex paramount chiefdoms with kings (called Fons) and sub-chiefs ruling over their largely agricultural communities. The Northwest Province, an English-speaking area, includes groups such as the

Kom, Bamum, Nso, Bali, Bafut, Wimbum, and Oku. The West Province is similar culturally to the Northwest, but is francophone and is home to the many independent kingdoms often grouped together as Bamileke. The Bamileke have primarily been successful farmers, growing maize, yams, peanuts, and some livestock. As a result, they control much of the economy in Cameroon. Although this makes them a powerful minority group, the Bamileke and other groups from the Grassfields have been targets of animosity. The Grassfields encompasses three subgroups of peoples: Bamileke, Bamum (Bamoun), and Bamenda Tikar. Within these complexes exist numerous smaller ethnic groups which are loosely affiliated with one another and share many historical and political similarities while retaining separate identities. In the last century, many small groups of semi-nomadic Fulani herders have moved into the highlands to graze their cattle. As a result, there have been numerous farmer-herder conflicts in the region.

In the southern forest belt of Cameroon, most ethnic groups were classified as Bantu-speaking groups. The Beti, which encompasses many related groups, is the dominant group around the capital city of Yaounde. The Bassa, Douala, Fang, and Maka are some of the other major Bantu groups in this region.

The *Bagyeli, Baka,* and *Bakola* are three terms labeling former Pygmy groups in the southern regions of Cameroon. These groups are among the most disenfranchised and threatened minority groups in Cameroon. Batwa groups are considered the original inhabitants of the Central African rainforests and traditionally lived by gathering fruits, nuts, honey, and other forest products, along with hunting. Throughout central Africa, they have little political or economic power and are often discriminated against. The fact that they tend to be among the shortest people in the world emphasizes their difference and makes it more difficult to blend in with the dominant Bantu culture of most of southern Cameroon.

Southwest Cameroon is the mountainous forest belt bordering Nigeria. In this province there are mostly Bantu groups as well as the Bakweri, Bakossi, Balong, and Mbo. However, several groups including the Efik, Ejagham, and Banyang have additional influences from the cultures of Nigeria, differentiating them from other groups.

In addition to these traditional inhabitants outlined above, Cameroon has a number of immigrants from a variety of countries. Among them, the Ibos and other groups from eastern Nigeria are the most numerous. Many foreign nationals from France, Lebanon, India, China and other countries have moved to Cameroon to pursue trade, religious, humanitarian or development work and now make up slightly less than 1 percent of the population.

Despite its oligarchic structure, Cameroon has generally enjoyed stability, which has permitted the development of agriculture, roads, railways, and a petroleum industry. Relative stability, in addition to favorable agricultural traditions and oil resources, have allowed Cameroon's economy to exceed that of many other underdeveloped African nations. Its export commodities include crude oil and petroleum products, lumber, cocoa beans, aluminum, coffee, and cotton. Cameroon's GDP per capita income was an estimated $1,700 in 2002. The GDP's composition by sector in 2001 was agriculture (46 percent); industry (21 percent), and services (33 percent).

J. Scott Hill

***See also* Fulani; Nigeria**

Further Reading

Burnham, P.C., *The Politics of Cultural Difference in Northern Cameroon*, Washington, D.C.: Smithsonian Institution Press, 1996

DeLancey, Mark, *Historical Dictionary of the Republic of Cameroon*, Lanham, Maryland.: Scarecrow Press, 2000

DeLancey, Mark, Cameroon [Electronic Resource]. World Bibliographical Series; V. 63. Boulder, CO: Netlibrary, 2000

Grimes, Barbara, editor; and Joseph Grimes, consulting editor, *Ethnologue: Languages of the World*, 14th Ed. Dallas, TX: SIL International. Also on web at: www.ethnologue.com, 1996

Konings, Piet and Francis B. Nyamnjoh, *Negotiating an Anglophone Identity: A Study of the Politics of Recognition and Representation in Cameroon*, Boston: Brill, 2003

Canada

Capsule Summary:

Location: Northern North America, bordering the North Atlantic Ocean on the east, North Pacific Ocean on the west, the Arctic Ocean on the north, and the coterminous United States to the south.
Total Population: 32,207,113 (July 2003)
Minority Populations: French (22.8%); German (3.4%); Italian (2.8%); Chinese (2.2%); Amerindian and Inuit (1.7%); Ukrainian (1.5%); Dutch (1.3%) (1991)
Languages: English (59.3%, official), French (23.2%, official), other (17.5%)
Religions: Roman Catholic (45.2%); Protestant (mainly United Church and Anglican, 36.4%), Eastern Orthodox (1.9%); Jewish (1.2%); Muslim (0.9%); Buddhist (0.6%); Hindu (0.6%); non-religious (12.5%); other (0.7%).

Canada is the second largest country in the world in area after Russia, but is also one of the most sparsely populated. Approximately 85 percent of the population is concentrated within 300 km (186 miles) of the U.S. border. Canada's total area, including the Canadian share of the Great Lakes and adjacent islands, is 3,851,809 square miles (9,976,185 square kilometers). Canada is bounded on the north by the Arctic Ocean, on the east by the Atlantic Ocean, on the south by 12 states of the United States, and on the west by the Pacific Ocean and the U.S. state of Alaska. Canada has over 30 million inhabitants, and most of the population live in urban areas (78 percent in 1996). Due to its high ethnic diversity it is referred to as an ethnic mosaic.

Canada is a federal multiparty parliamentary state with two legislative houses, the Senate and the House of Commons. The formal Chief of State is the British Monarch represented by the Governor General. Actual power is held by the government led by the Prime Minister.

The country is divided into the ten provinces of Alberta, British Columbia, Manitoba, New Brunswick, Newfoundland, Nova Scotia, Ontario, Prince Edward Island, Québec, and Saskatchewan along with three territories, the Northwest Territories, the Yukon Territory, and Nunavut. The third territory was created only in 1999. The national capital of Canada is Ottawa.

History

Canada's history has been shaped by the complex interactions among its diverse inhabitants—indigenous peoples, the French, the British, and other immigrants from around the world. Scholars estimate that Canada was populated about 10,000 years ago. When the first European settlers arrived in the early seventeenth century, the 200,000 indigenous inhabitants were divided into several distinct nations and spoke about 50 different languages. Prior to the conquest of New France by the British in 1760, Canada's European population was virtually all of French origin. Around 1820, the British began outnumbering the French. Between 1820 and 1850, immigrants arrived primarily from the United Kingdom, but immigrants from all over the world, including China, were attracted to the West Coast of Canada by the gold rush of the second half of 19th century.

By 1871, the total population of Canada was 3,485,761: the proportion of Canadians of French origin had declined to 31 percent, the British had increased to 61 percent, with a much smaller German population of about 6 percent. In the early twentieth century, emigration to Canada was aggressively promoted by government emissaries throughout northern Europe, and by 1951, the proportion of Canadians of British origin had declined to 48 percent. Those of French origin were still at 31 percent largely due to an exceptionally high birth rate.

Since confederation in 1867, Canada has become steadily less linked with Great Britain and more influenced by the United States. French separatism continued to be a major concern during the latter half of the twentieth century. From the late 1960s, the Parti Québécois pressed for separation; during the 1980s and 1990s various constitutional reform programs, intended to provide greater autonomy for Quebec, failed to gain approval.

The official Canadian policy of multiculturalism was shaped amid controversy to counter the implications of *biculturalism* as used in the terms of reference of the Royal Commission on Bilingualism and Biculturalism, a commission appointed in 1963 by the federal government to examine the claims of French Canadians for an equal partnership in Canadian society.

In 1988, Parliament adopted the *Canadian Multiculturalism Act*, designed "to preserve and enhance the multicultural heritage of Canadians while working to achieve the equality of all Canadians" through a variety of programs. This law speaks not only of values of equality of opportunity and of participation, but also of partnership, justice and fairness, acceptance and respect. In 1996 Canada officially recognized that all previous policies towards the aboriginal people (First Nations) had been wrong and called for remedy and ending of the centuries-long neglect, abuse, and oppression by the government.

Ethnicity and Minority Issues

According to the 1996 census, less than 30 percent of all Canadians reported only British (17 percent), only French (10 percent) or only Aboriginal (2 percent) origins. In contrast, 26 percent reported having only origins other than British, French, Aboriginal or Canadian, and another 26 percent reported multiple ethnic origins. The most frequently reported ethnic origins other than British, French, or Canadian were, in descending order: German, Italian, Aboriginal, Ukrainian, Chinese, Dutch, East Indian, Polish, Portuguese, Jewish, Black, Filipino, Greek, Hungarian, and Vietnamese. Ethnic diversity varies significantly from region to region, with the most diverse being western Canada.

Canada uses the concept of *visible minorities* to refer to ethnic groups most likely to suffer from prejudice, intolerance, or inequity. Visible minorities are defined as individuals who are non-white in color and non-Caucasian by race (i.e., not of European origin). Aboriginals are not always included in this definition, for instance, in the Employment Equity Act. According to the Census data in 1996, more than 10 percent of the total Canadian population reported belonging to a visible minority; the three most numerous non-Aboriginal visible minority groups were, in descending order, Chinese, South Asian, and Black.

French has been spoken in Canada without interruption for about 400 years, but only in 1970 did it become an official language of the federal institutions, with the adoption of the *Official Languages Act* in 1969. It became an official language of the country in 1981 with the adoption of the *Canadian Charter of Rights and Freedoms*. According to the census data, 31 percent of Canadians could conduct a conversation in French, but only 23 percent spoke French most often at home. Almost 90 percent of *francophones* (French speaking persons, as opposed to Anglophones, English speakers, and Allophones, speakers of a language other than French or English), live in Québec. Outside Québec, the largest Francophone minority is found in Ontario, but the relative weight of the smaller Acadian population of New Brunswick is greater, almost a third of the provincial population. "Acadians" are the descendants of the French who settled in Acadia, now known as the Maritime Provinces. Most were deported and their properties seized by the British between 1755 and 1760.

There are almost 5 million Allophones, or people with a mother tongue other than English or French, in Canada: apart from the Northwest Territories and Nunavut where Aboriginal languages are widespread, the proportion is highest in British Columbia, Ontario, and Manitoba and lowest in the Atlantic Provinces. The most spoken languages other than English or French are Chinese (includes Mandarin and Cantonese), Italian and German, with each of these three languages being spoken by over 2 percent of the Canadian population. In some regions, other languages rank among the most spoken, such as the Aboriginal languages, Spanish, Punjabi, Arabic, Ukrainian, and Dutch. Chinese is by far the most frequently reported home language other than English or French. Indigenous peoples belong predominantly to the Algonquian linguistic group; other representative linguistic groups are the Iroquoian, Salishan, Athapaskan, and Inuit.

More than 85 percent of Canada's population claim affiliation in some degree with either the Roman Catholic or a Protestant church. The major Protestant churches are the United Church of Canada, the Anglican Church of Canada, and the Lutheran Church. The balance of the population adhere to the Jewish, Eastern Orthodox, and other faiths, or have no affiliation. In Quebec, more than 80 percent of the population is Roman Catholic, and New Brunswick also has a Roman Catholic majority. The other provinces have Protestant majorities.

Economy

Canada maintains a market-oriented economy, closely resembling that of the United States, with high living standards and high-tech industry. Since World War II, Canada's primarily rural economy has transformed into one based in manufacturing, mining, and other commercial services. The 1989 U.S.-Canada Free Trade Agreement (FTA) and the 1994 North American Free Trade Agreement (NAFTA) spurred a significant increase in trade and economic integration with the U.S. The GDP per capita income in 2002 was $29,300, with a 16.4 million labor force occupying the following sectors: services 74 percent, manufacturing 15 percent, construction 5 percent, agriculture 3 percent, other 3 percent.

LAURA LAUBEOVA

See also **Bilingualism; French; Inuit; Quebecois**

Further Reading

Mata, Fernando and Adsett, Margaret, *Multiculturalism, Immigration and Racism: Selected Public Opinion Poll Findings in Canada, 1991–96*, Ottawa: Department of Canadian Heritage, Multiculturalism, 1997

Kymlicka, Will, *Finding our Way: Rethinking Ethnocultural Relations in Canada*, Toronto: Oxford University Press, 1998

Pendakur, Ravi and Hennebry, Jenna, *Multicultural Canada: a Demographic Overview*, Ottawa: Strategic Research and Business Planning, Multiculturalism, Department of Canadian Heritage, 1998

Royal Commission on Aboriginal Peoples, *Report of the Royal Commission on Aboriginal Peoples*, Ottawa: the Commission, 1996

Kottak, Conrad, Kozaitis, Kathryn, *On Being Different. Diversity and Multiculturalism in the North American Mainstream*, Ann Arbor: McGraw-Hill Publishing Company, 1998

Canadian Heritage, *Multicultural Program, Respect, Equality, Diversity, Program Guidelines,* July 1998

Cape Verde

Capsule Summary

Location: Western Africa; a group of 15 islands in the North Atlantic Ocean, 300 miles west of Senegal
Total Population: 412,137 (July 2003)
Minority Populations: Creole (mulatto, 71%), African (28%), European (1%)
Languages: Portuguese, Crioulo (a blend of Portuguese and West African words)
Religions: Roman Catholic (infused with indigenous beliefs); Protestant (mostly Church of the Nazarene), African Spiritism

The Portuguese came upon the mountainous, volcanic islands of Cape Verde in the late fifteenth century during their pioneer voyages of discovery down the African coast. About the size of Rhode Island, the archipelago is shaped like the wings of a butterfly and comprises 1557 square miles (4033 square kilometers). The windward islands curve northwestward while the leeward islands arch southwest. Among the latter is the island of Fogo, which has a still active volcano. Uninhabited at the time of their discovery, the archipelago came to be referred to as *Cabo Verde* (Green Cape) because its forested slopes offered wood and timber supplies for passing ships. Denuded by overcutting of trees and without any regular rainfall, the islands now have a bare, desert-like appearance. Sand winds from the Sahara blow incessantly over the area.

First settled in 1462 subsequent to a 1460 visit by Portuguese navigator Diogo Gomes, the islands were the object of fighting between the English and French for several centuries, although Portugal maintained control. Its strategic location made Cape Verde a significant coaling and resupply stop for whaling and transatlantic shipping. Its status changed from one of a Portuguese colony to an overseas province in 1951. Cape Verde became independent in July 1975, and the republic has enjoyed political stability since then.

Dominating the commerce in African slaves for several centuries, the Portuguese used the islands as a prosperous entrepôt for this trade. Most of the population of Cabo Verde is thereby of mixed race due to inter-breeding between the Portuguese and Africans. The mixed-race offspring, known as mulattos or Creoles, comprise almost one-fourth the population. A fourth of the population is African and one percent, European.

Just as race is mixed so also are language, culture, and religion. The population speaks Portuguese and Crioulo, a mixture of Portuguese and West African words. About 300,000 Cape Verdeans use Crioulo. This language also has more than a 100,000 speakers in the West African countries of Senegal and Guinea-Bissau. There are probably also many thousands of speakers in the Europe and the United States due to the emigration of Cape Verdeans to these regions. The financial remittances these emigrants send back to Cape Verde contribute a significant amount to the nation's income. Through performances and recordings in Europe and the Americas, the Cape Verdean singer, Cesaria Évora, has been a singular force in introducing the Crioulo language and culture to people around the world.

Cape Verde became the oldest, most thoroughly creolized society of the Portuguese empire. The educated elite of this society served as civil servants in the administration of other Portuguese colonies. Through these agents, the empire falsely convinced itself that it carried out a civilizing mission through cultural assimilation.

The dominant cultural feature of Cape Verde is Catholicism, implanted from the beginning of Portuguese colonization. The earliest African converts, however, combined Catholic forms of worship with their native spiritist traditions. Many of their descendants continue such hybrid religious practices. As with Catholicism throughout the former Portuguese empire in Africa and Brazil, African natives created numerous Afro-Catholic syncretic cults, which were vigorously opposed and repressed by the Church. In recent times a small Protestant minority has grown in Cape Verde, mainly the Nazarene sect, resulting from American missionary activity.

Impoverished since the end of the slave trade, Cape Verde now has a gross domestic product that amounted in 2002 to an estimated $600 million, with a GDP per capita annual income of just $1,400. Suffering from drought and with few natural resources, the economy of the island is mostly service-oriented, especially for repair and refueling of ocean-going vessels. Neither agriculture nor fishing are fully exploited to their potential. Agriculture is poor and unable to serve the needs of the country, yet most of the population is rural; over 80 percent of Cape Verde's food supply is imported. Smuggling and drug traffic contribute to national income. The population growth rate is less than one percent annually, with just over one percent of the population emigrating each year. Cape Verdeans have settled throughout the rim of Atlantic Basin nations, a small contingent of trans-cultural representatives over the continents of Africa, Europe, and the Americas.

EDWARD A. RIEDINGER

See also **Creole (mixed-origin minorities); Portugal**

Further Reading

Baptista, Marlyse, *The Syntax of Cape Verdean Creole: The Sotavento Varieties*, Linguistik aktuell, vol. 54, Amsterdam: John Benjamins Publisher, 2002

Carreira, António, *The People of the Cape Verde Islands: Exploitation and Emigration*, translated from Portuguese by Christopher Fyfe, London: Archon Books, 1982

Chabal, Patrick, and David Birmingham, *A History of Postcolonial Lusophone Africa*, Bloomington: Indiana University Press, 2002

Halter, Marilyn, *Between Race and Ethnicity: Cape Verdean American Immigrants, 1860–1965*, Urbana: University of Illinois Press, 1993

Lobban, Richard, *Cape Verde: Crioulo Colony to Independent Nation*, Boulder: Westview Press, 1995

Lobhan, Richard, and Marlene Lopes, *Historical Dictionary of the Republic of Cape Verde*, Methuchen, New Jersey: Scarecrow Press, 1995

Shaw, Caroline S., compiler, *Cape Verde*, World Bibliographical Series, vol. 123, Oxford, England: Clio Press, 1991

Caste and Minority Status, *See* **Untouchables (Harijans/Dalits/Scheduled castes)**

Catalans

Capsule Summary:

Location: Mediterranean region of Europe, mostly in the Spanish autonomous community of Catalunya or Catalonia (located in northeastern Spain) and southern part of France

Total Population: approximately 6 million (in Spanish Catalonia)
Language: Catalan and Spanish
Religion: mostly Roman Catholic

The Catalans are an ethnic group living primarily in the Spanish autonomous community of Catalonia although there an estimated 200,000 Catalans in North Catalonia (Department of Pyrénées-Orientales) in the south of France. The Catalan language is also spoken by about 20,000 people out of a total of 40,000 inhabitants in the city of Alghero in the North-West of Sardinia in Italy.

In 800 CE, Charlemagne's army conquered part of the present-day Catalan territory from the Moors occupying the Iberian peninsula, and thus Catalonia was born, comprised of the counties of Gerona, Ampurias, Barcelona-Ausona and Urgell-Cerdanya. By the ninth century, Catalonia had become an independent nation, and in 1137 entered into a confederal union with the neighboring kingdom of Aragón. During the subsequent two centuries, Catalonia enjoyed both a substantial degree of institutional autonomy and rapid economic development. The Crown of Aragón managed to expand territorially to include Valencia, the Balearic islands, and Murcia, and its realm of dominance spread to many areas of the Mediterranean, including Sardinia, Sicily, Naples, and the Greek cities of Athens and Neopatria. This period has often been described as Catalonia's Golden Age.

In 1479, the Union of the Crowns of Ferdinand and Isabella, the Catholic Kings, unified Aragón and the Spanish kingdom of Castille. In the century that followed, Catalonia remained marginalized from the rest of Spain's imperial ambitions. It was able to retain many of the privileges and a substantial measure of autonomy it had enjoyed under the Crown of Aragón. Nevertheless this ended in 1640, when the Catalans revolted in the Segadors rebellion due to increasing pressure from Castille to contribute financially to the Spanish empire—along with the simultaneous decline of Aragón's traditional hegemony in the Mediterranean. This event would subsequently lead to the War of Spanish Succession against Castille, which Catalonia entered in 1705. Catalonia was eventually abandoned by its Dutch and English allies, leading to the capture of Barcelona by the Bourbon troops on September 11, 1714.

Catalonia's defeat by the Castillian forces was followed by a period in which its autonomy became increasingly curtailed by the central government. Following the introduction of the Decree of Nova Planta of 1714, most administrative matters were centralized. The central government began to exert greater control over economic, political, and social matters, many of which had traditionally fallen under the domain of the Catalan authorities. The historic Catalan institutions of the Generalitat and the Consell de Cent were abolished and Catalonia lost the Mediterranean territories of Menorca, Sicily, Sardinia and Naples. A special tax for Catalans, the cadastre, was introduced, much to the discontent of Catalonia's emerging bourgeoisie.

Despite its decline in political influence following the dismantling of its autonomous institutions and decreasing leverage in the Mediterranean basin during the nineteenth century, Catalonia became one of the centers of Spain's industrialization. While the rest of Spain continued to suffer from inherent poverty, corruption, and the inefficient administration of the Bourbon dynasty, the Catalans (along with the Basques in northern Spain) continued to enjoy growing economic prosperity. The Cátalans' successful economy and their modern, outward-looking views contrasted sharply with their limited participation, like the Basques, in the Spanish political process. This lack of incorporation into the political process and the refusal of Catalan society to assimilate the imposed homogenizing cultural, economic, and political policies contributed to many Catalans' sense of differentiation. This system of imposed cultural, economic, and political assimilation was later reintroduced during both the Primo de Rivera dictatorship (1923–1930) and the Franco regime (1939–1975), generating a backlash of nationalist sentiment and simultaneous demands for democratization and autonomy. With the death of General Francisco Franco in 1975, two of the first events in the Spanish transition to democracy were the restoration of the Catalan government (*Generalitat*) in 1977 and the 1978 Spanish Constitution which laid out special provisions for Spain's newly created 17 autonomous communities.

The Catalan language is part of the group of western neo-Latin languages that include Spanish, Portuguese, and French. It is spoken in a large area (68,000 square km., 26,520 square miles) in the east of Spain, including Catalonia, the Balearic Islands, Valencia, the Franja (the area in Aragon bordering on Catalonia) other municipalities in Murcia that border on Valencia, and Andorra, as well as in the south of France (North Catalonia—the Department of Pyrénées Orientales) and in the Sardinian city of l'Alguer (Alghero). The language, including a variety of dialects, is spoken over an area with a population of 10 million.

Between the tenth and eleventh centuries, Catalan was already a fully formed language, clearly distinguishable from its Latin origins, but it appeared for the first time in written form in the twelfth century. In the eighteenth century, King Philip V abolished all the government institutions then existing in Catalonia and implemented Spanish laws. During the nineteenth century however, all things Catalan—economic, social and political—enjoyed a revival, known as the *Renaixença* (Renaissance). During the first 30 years of the twentieth century, Catalonia went through a period of political fervor, culminating in the recovery of a degree of political power in the Generalitat during the 1930s and the restoration of Catalan as an official language during the Second Republic (1931–1939). During the Franco regime, the use of Catalan in public was forbidden and the language retreated into the home. With the restoration of Catalan autonomy, the language issue has been central in legislation, in party politics, and as a cohesive force in Catalan society.

The use of Catalan has also increased dramatically with legislation promoting its use. According to the 1996 census, 95 percent of the population of Catalonia understand Catalan, and about 79 percent can speak it. Catalonia's Statute of Autonomy states that both Castilian and Catalan are official languages, but that Catalan is that country's own language. The Catalan government's comprehensive language policy is regulated by legislation in 1983 and 1998.

Elisa Roller

Further Reading

Balcells, Albert, *Catalan Nationalism*, edited by Geoffrey J. Walker, London: Macmillan Press Ltd, 1996

Conversi, Daniele, *The Basques, the Catalans and Spain: Alternative Routes to Nationalist Mobilization,* London: Hurst & Company, 1997

Díez Medrano, Juan, *Divided Nations: Class, Politics, and Nationalism in the Basque Country and Catalonia,* Ithaca: Cornell University Press, 1995

Guibernau, Montserrat, "Images of Catalonia," *Nations and Nationalism,* 3, no. 1 (1997)

Guibernau, Montserrat, *Nations without States: Political Communities in a Global Age,* Blackwell Publishers, Malden Massachusetts, 1999

Keating, Michael, *Nations against the State: The New Politics of Nationalism in Quebec, Catalonia and Scotland,* London: Macmillan, 1996; 2nd edition, 2001

Mar-Molinero, Clare, and Angel Smith, editors, *Nationalism and the Nation in the Iberian Peninsula: Competing and Conflicting Identities*, Oxford: Berg, 1996

Catalonia, *See* **Catalans**

Catholics in Northern Ireland

Capsule Summary

Location: British Province of Northern Ireland, northern part of the island of Ireland
Total Population: approximately 737,473 out of a total of 1,685,267 (Census of April 29, 2001)
Language: English
Religion: Roman Catholic

The Catholics of Northern Ireland are an ethnic group living in the British province of the same name in the northeast corner of Ireland. The area officially came into existence in 1920 when the rest of Ireland won independence from England. The six counties of Armagh, Antrim, Derry/Londonderry, Down, Fermanagh, and Tyrone—all with significant Protestant populations mostly of English and Scottish descent—were separated from the rest of newly independent Ireland and remained under British rule. Today, the Catholic population continues to grow, while that of the Protestants has more or less stabilized, leading some demographers to project a Catholic majority within the next few decades. At the last census in 2001, Catholics comprised 43.76 percent of the population. Northern Irish Catholics speak English. Although some have taken to learning the Irish tongue of Gaelic (primarily for Irish nationalist reasons), the language is not spoken in Northern Ireland. After decades of turmoil and violence, both the political fate and status of the region remain open questions as both Catholics and Protestants labor to make a more lasting success of recent attempts at self government, as well as religious and political toleration.

History

The six counties that comprise present-day Northern Ireland are part of the nine-county region of Ulster, the northernmost of the four regions that comprise Ireland. Although Ulster and Northern Ireland are often used synonymously, their historical borders are different: Ulster traditionally includes the counties of Cavan, Donegal, and Monaghan, which are part of the Republic of Ireland, not Northern Ireland. In this essay, "Ulster" will be used until the partition of the region is discussed.

Difficulties existed between the Irish population and English and Scottish settlers in Ulster even in the centuries before religious conflicts worked to more solidly ground previous differences over culture, language, farming methods, and political organization (to name but a few). Yet it is undeniable that the attempts to introduce Protestantism into Ireland in the sixteenth century began to exacerbate older conflicts. In the sixteenth and early seventeenth centuries, England's policy had been one of accommodation and acculturation—Irish lords co-existed with English, but the government hoped that what they perceived were naturally superior English ways would eventually predominate. After a failed uprising in 1601, however, more aggressive policies were gradually put in place.

The system of plantation, whereby arable land was granted to English Protestants and Scottish Presbyterians, became common practice. Due to its having been the center of the unsuccessful rebellion, the plantation system was concentrated in Ulster. Its success in the early decades of the seventeenth century marks the line at which significant cultural and religious conflicts begin to divide the region. One complicating factor was the growing presence of Presbyterians or Scottish Covenanters in the region. Often persecuted with as much if not more vehemence than Catholics, Presbyterians felt understandably uneasy, even as Puritansim was gaining popularity in England.

Yet to the newer English and Scottish settlers, their Irish neighbors remained a mostly uncivilized, barbarous people practicing an especially eccentric version of what they already regarded as an irrational and dangerous faith. Gone, it seems, were the days when adventurers and emigrants embraced Celtic ways, as had been the case from the first Anglo-Norman invasion in 1166. Imported in large numbers, the new settlers also seemed to arrive more determined than their forebears to retain their identity as Protestant subjects of the English crown, a standing helped by an earlier parliamentary decision that allowed expanded representation for the settler community.

Years of uprisings and rebellions followed, with the worst occurring in 1641 and 1689. The defeat of the Catholic king of England, James II, by the forces of the Dutch prince, William of Orange, on July 12, 1689 at the Battle of the Boyne firmly established the reputation of England as a militantly Protestant nation and of Ireland as a rebelliously Catholic one. The celebration of July 12 by groups of marching Protestant Unionists known as Orangemen, those desiring political ties with England, would be the occasion for much subsequent violence, especially due to the Orangemen's insistence on parading through Catholic neighborhoods.

In the nineteenth century, agitation for Home Rule (or some form of independence) gripped Ireland during the years of gradual stability following the end of the Potato Famine (1845–50). Many Irish would have been content with full Catholic emancipation—some restrictions on Catholics remained in place despite gradual progress earlier in the century—and a more or less independent Irish Parliament in Dublin. Others wanted complete independence from England on the American model and went so far as to recommend that Gaelic replace English as the national language. The phrase "Sinn Fein," which roughly translates as "we ourselves" (though it is sometimes written as, "ourselves alone") first makes its appearance in these debates. Ulster Protestants were not taken with either alternative as they feared the erosion of their rights in any national incarnation that would be dominated by Catholics.

The British government's three Home Rule initiatives in 1886, 1893, and 1912 were answered with a resurgence of militant Protestantism that was increasingly known as Orangeism. For example, on September 12, 1918, 200,000 men and a larger number of women signed a petition citing their unqualified opposition to any form of Home Rule or Irish independence. In the face of such sterling protests, the possibility of severing part or all of Ulster was first broached during debates about the future of Ireland.

The outbreak of World War I forestalled the debate and put off the possibility of armed protest by Ulster Protestants. However, an insurrection was being planned in Dublin by a small, disparate group of Catholic trade unionists, teachers, and writers impatient with parliamentary maneuverings and weary of endless talk of Home Rule with few tangible results. Between April 24 and 29 in 1916, slightly more than 1,200 rebels occupied the Dublin post office and declared an Irish Republic. The Easter Rising, as it would be called, was strategically a curious event. The rebellion was quickly put down in part because it lacked popular support and in part because no thought seems to have gone in to creating a plan that would have resulted in anything but defeat. England regarded it as an attempt to "stab the Empire in the back" during wartime and responded with brutal actions by military police. This, and the subsequent execution of the sixteen surviving planners, endowed an initially unpopular act with the air of martyrdom. The executed were soon given new life in W.B. Yeats's elegiac poem "Easter, 1916." The mythology that grew up around the Easter Rising would loom large for Ulster Catholics in the years of "The Troubles" that began in 1969.

By the end of World War I, Irish Catholics were frustrated with the lack of progress toward independence and stopped negotiating with the British government. Most of the country then fell into war with England. The Government of Ireland Act, passed in 1920, allowed the six counties that would soon form Northern Ireland to call their own parliament in Belfast. Most observers at the time did not expect this partition arrangement to last.

Between 1919 and 1924, much of Ireland was engulfed by violence. International pressure and a military stalemate between the British military and Irish guerilla forces finally dragged the parties to the negotiating table. The Anglo-Irish treaty was signed and ratified on January 7, 1922. It called for six counties in Ulster to remain apart from the newly formed Republic of Ireland. Both sides thought that Ulster Protestants would soon allow their parliament to be absorbed by that of Dublin or London, though most Ulster Protestants were proud that they had held on to their independence and saw no hurry to unify with Dublin. This settlement also made Catholics in the state of Northern Ireland a numerical minority (430,000 to 820,000 Protestants).

Just as Protestant Unionists did whatever they could to stymie Irish independence, Ulster Catholics now sought to make Northern Ireland ungovernable. Yet the Catholics enjoyed few economic, political, or military resources. In the violence that followed during the early 1920s, many disloyalists were expelled from the country. More than 100 Catholics were killed, 11,000 made unemployed, and 23,000 made homeless. In addition, more than 4,500 businesses were burned, robbed, or ruined. In 1922, at the height of the violence, the Special Powers Act was passed by the Northern Irish Parliament. It gave security forces the power to arrest people without a warrant, detain without charges or trial, search homes without warrants, prohibit meetings and processions, and whip and hang offenders. Most of this work was carried out by the paramilitary Ulster Special Constabulary, a group whose origins can be traced back to the Home-Rule-disrupting Ulster Volunteer Force, certain vigilante groups, and the Ulster Protestant Association, a loyalist group responsible for several Catholic murders.

By 1926, it was clear that Northern Ireland had no intentions of unifying with Ireland and wanted independence from Britain. In 1932, the Northern Irish Parliament opened at Stormont in Belfast. Election districts had been gerrymandered to ensure Protestant majorities. Anti-Catholic discrimination was openly practiced in public employment. State-sponsored holidays and festivals commemorated events such as King William's victory at the Battle of the Boyne on July 12, events that were explicitly pro-Protestant and anti-Catholic. In the years following 1921, Catholics dealt with the situation by fostering a culture of their own, creating their own newspapers, and sponsoring their own sports and social clubs. The Northern Irish government helped to subsidize Catholic parochial schools. While this was generally viewed favorably, it had the unfortunate effect of preventing children of different religious backgrounds from mixing.

As early as the 1950s, Protestant politicians saw that population trends indicated that there would be a Catholic majority in Northern Ireland at some point. Terence O'Neil became Northern Ireland's prime minister in 1963 and was determined to "persuade Catholics in Northern Ireland that they have a place within the United Kingdom." Yet many Catholics, inspired by the American Civil Rights Movement, saw O'Neil's attempts at conciliation as a superficial gesture to placate them with small gifts while avoiding the more pressing and serious issues of election redistricting, employment, and economic modernization. The city of Derry/Londonderry, for example, had seen its economy slowly but successfully stagnated, if not destroyed, over the years by Protestant city leaders committed to maintaining their electoral majority and keeping Catholics in poverty. In 1967, the Northern Irish Civil Rights Association tried a new tactic. Rather than focus on the traditional theme of Irish nationalism, they insisted on "British rights for British citizens." A series of peaceful protests in 1968 and 1969 were broken up by baton-wielding members of the Royal Ulster Constabulary (RUC). Broadcast images of the first of these derailed marches gave the world outside Northern Ireland a first-hand look at the violent methods routinely utilized by the successor organization to the Ulster Special Constabulary while bringing the plight of Northern Irish Catholics to the attention of large numbers of people. On January 1, 1969, a "long march" from Belfast to Derry was broken up by violent Protestant mobs at the Burntollet Bridge near the outskirts of Derry. The mob included an embarrassing number of off-duty policemen. When the marchers finally reached the city, rioting broke out in Catholic neighborhoods. While the violence only strengthened the resolve of Catholic protesters, most Protestants continued to believe that "British rights for British citizens" was simply a cover for a nationalist, republican movement. The "long march" marked the end of the O'Neil government and the beginning of the long period of violence in Northern Ireland known as The Troubles.

Civil rights protests continued, especially in Belfast and Derry, with more and more frequent outbreaks of violence, thanks in part to Protestants and the RUC, both of whom refused to believe that the marches throughout Northern Ireland represented anything short of nationalist insurrection. In August 1969, British troops were called in to help quell Catholic rioters in Derry whom the RUC and Protestant paramilitaries could not contain. It was the most violence that Northern Ireland had seen since the 1920s, and the British army soon became a familiar sight in the most explosive areas of Northern Ireland.

The homes of nationalists had been burned by the RUC during the Derry riots, and large numbers of people had been displaced. The Irish Republican Army abandoned its socialist politics and resumed its status as the self-styled "people's army" in the aftermath of the violence. The group stepped up its campaign for an end to British Rule and for unification with the Republic of Ireland, itself still the home of hundreds of IRA members. Its growth was rapid. Though it consisted mainly of working-class Catholics who were often poorly educated and unemployed, the IRA attracted enough men with organizational and paramilitary skills to present a growing threat by 1971. British intelligence found it impossible to break the organization in spite of countless home searches, stops and seizures, and other methods designed to weaken the group. The IRA began to wield enormous power and influence in poorer urban Catholic neighborhoods, where they were soon countered by an array of loyalist organizations in poor urban Protestant neighborhoods.

The majority of Catholics still rejected violence and had no truck with the IRA. Unfortunately, however, the events of Sunday, January 30, 1972 led many Catholics to embrace, if not violence, then at least the belief that non-violence was useless and ineffective. A civil rights march through Derry ended in a small-scale riot when several younger people refused to disperse at the orders of the RUC. An elite parachute unit of the British army was summoned to help end the riot. Believing that they were facing an IRA insurgency, British soldiers fired on the crowd, killing 13 unarmed protesters–but not one IRA member.

Bloody Sunday became the single most effective recruiting tool the IRA would ever know. The growing numbers of IRA "volunteers," as the group termed its members, allowed them to step up their campaign of violent protest against the Protestant majority and allied British government. Sensitive to the reality that Catholics, as a minority perceived to be subversively desiring independence from Britain, were far less sympathetic to the British public, the British army concentrated their efforts on the IRA and let most Protestant paramilitary organizations operate with little interference. However, there were arrests and convictions of major and minor figures on both sides.

Most observers in Ireland, as well as some in Britain, felt by early 1972 that Northern Ireland's government was an abject failure based on its unwillingness to extend civil rights to Catholics and its inability to stem the tide of sectarian violence. The burgeoning voice of the Social Democratic and Labor Party (SDLP), Northern Ireland's only Catholic political party of consequence, kept the issues of employment, economics, and civil rights at the forefront of its claim that Stormont should be abolished. In March 1972, the British government seemed to be in agreement—it dissolved the Northern Irish government and replaced it with direct rule from London. Loyalists were outraged at what they considered a selling-out by the British, which led to more violence on the Protestant side.

More than one year after the fall of Stormont, an attempt was made to restore Northern Irish rule of the state. At a civil-service training center in Sunningdale in December 1973, representatives from the Irish and British governments and the Northern Irish political parties met for the first time in an effort to create a new government based on proportional representation, thus ensuring a greater voice for Northern Irish Catholics in the state's political system. A power-sharing executive would be created with substantial involvement by the Ulster Unionist Party (UUP) and the SDLP, who would send six ministers to serve in positions roughly analogous to American cabinet secretaries, in the day-to-day running of the state. The British also admitted that expanded cooperation in governmental matters between Northern Ireland and the Republic of Ireland needed to take place.

Despite the banning of the IRA's political party, Sinn Fein, and initial efforts by moderate Protestants to start a new government on Sunningdale's model, most Protestants rejected these proposals. Abetted by loyalist paramilitaries and led by the newly formed anti-Catholic Democratic Ulster Party (DUP), workers called for a general strike in spring 1974 and then threatened a flood of raw sewage should the new government begin to implement its programs. Loyalist paramilitaries also killed 33 people in Dublin and Monaghan (both in the Republic) by car bombs, the largest single-day death toll in Northern Ireland's tortured history. Faced with so much Protestant resistance, England resumed direct rule. UUP head Brian Faulkner asked the British government to intervene to prevent the strike, but he was refused. Many historians regard Sunningdale as one of the great near misses in a series of efforts to stabilize Northern Ireland. Every subsequent plan for peace and electoral and governmental reform has essentially revisited the proposals set forth at Sunningdale.

After the resumption of British rule, the violence continued, especially in Belfast and Derry, following a brief flirtation with a truce and ceasefire by the IRA. While the IRA continued to view itself as a revolutionary army dedicated to the unification of Ireland, by 1976 the British government saw them as a criminal organization that used terrorist tactics. Any IRA member sent to prison regarded himself as a political prisoner, while the British government regarded them as common criminals convicted of violent offenses.

The election of a Conservative government with Margaret Thatcher as prime minister in 1979 saw a resumption of cooperative efforts between the Irish and British governments to bring peace to Northern Ireland. It also saw increased British rhetoric about the IRA's status as an organization of terrorist criminals. Demanding that they be regarded as political prisoners, several inmates at Long Kesh prison, known as the Maze, began on a hunger strike in 1980 and again in 1981. Thatcher refused to treat anyone convicted of violent, politically related crimes as a political prisoner. The situation attracted international attention, helped by sympathy for the IRA's cause among many Irish-Catholic Americans, and the prisoners received substantial compassion from the international community.

Bobby Sands became the public face of the Maze hunger strikers. He had joined the IRA after his family had been forced to move out of a Belfast neighborhood due to threats and harassment from loyalist groups. His conviction was for the relatively non-violent crime of arms possession. He spent much of his time in prison composing poetry and writing in his journal. Sinn Fein nominated him *in absentia* for a suddenly opened seat in Parliament, which he won—a symbolic gesture, as Northern Ireland was still ruled by the British Parliament at Westminster. The British government was unyielding, despite considerable embarrassment about the plight of the prisoners. 66 days into his strike, Sands died on May 5, 1981. His death led to the worst round of rioting since the early 1970s, and more than 100,000 people attended his funeral.

By October, most of the demands of the Northern Irish Catholic prisoners had been met, and the hunger strikes ended. Sentiment generated by the strikes led to a revival for the IRA's political wing, Sinn Fein. The IRA itself adopted a new tactic, seeking the fulfillment of its goals by way of "Armalite and the ballot box," Armalite being a reference to the light, flexible rifles smuggled to Ireland by American sympathizers primarily during the 1970s. The growing popularity of Sinn Fein and the impossibility of political careers for the rank and file of the SDLP sufficiently frightened Dublin and London enough to try once more to make peace and provide a political voice for Northern Ireland's Catholics.

Discussions at the New Ireland Forum between 1983–4 led to the British and Irish governments coming together in a series of secret meetings. As had been the case at Sunningdale, both sides showed a willingness to compromise on matters that had previously been thorny. In the Anglo-Irish Agreement, the British government agreed that the Irish government would have to play a critical role in any efforts to govern Northern Ireland, while the Irish assented to the idea that no drastic political changes could take in the state without the consent of a majority of the people in Northern Ireland. Further, the Irish government agreed to remove a passage in its Constitution that called for the ultimate addition of Northern Ireland to the Republic. This represented a critical step forward.

There were more incidents of violence following the Anglo-Irish Agreement, but the people of Northern Ireland seemed to be growing weary of the seemingly endless cycle of destruction by the beginning of the 1990s. The rapid growth of the Irish economy created a ripple effect of increased prosperity for Northern Irish Catholics and Protestants and thus contributed to the idea that violence was simply never going to succeed. In addition, England was tired of pouring endless millions of tax pounds into a region that seemed unable to let go of violence. Although it had not repudiated armed struggle, the IRA was making increased calls for mainstream recognition of Sinn Fein. They were also claiming that violence would only be used for specific, tactical gains. Gerry Adams and Martin McGuiness were leaders who had been frustrated by the inability of the IRA to score any political gains from 1969 through the early 1990s. Adams publicly rejected what he called "politics of the gun" and seemed to embrace more traditional, deliberative means via the desire to see Sinn Fein become an influential force in Northern Irish politics. Although Sinn Fein would be in competition with his party for Northern Irish Catholic votes, SDLP leader John Hume, a veteran of Catholic politics since before Sunningdale, seized the moment and met with Adams several times between the late 1980s and 1993.

The British and Irish governments reiterated the ideas of the Anglo-Irish Agreement in a joint declaration from Downing Street on December 15, 1993. By granting the controversial Adams a visa so that he could visit the U.S., Bill Clinton showed a willingness to enter the fray of Northern Irish politics with or without British approval. In this new atmosphere of hope, the IRA called for a complete cease-fire in August 1994 and in October, loyalist groups reciprocated. Protestant Unionists, led by the head of the UUP, David Trimble, wanted assurances that the IRA would destroy all of their weapons. The dialogue continued. In November 1995, another joint statement from Dublin and London suggested that all-party talks about the creation of a self-governing Northern Ireland could only progress if decommissioning began to take place. Former American Senator George Mitchell—like Clinton, of Irish descent—chaired a three-member international committee set up specifically to examine the logistics of weapons decommissioning. Unionists and the British government were upset by the Mitchell Commission's report, delivered in January 1996, which stated clearly that forestalling further all-party talks while waiting for weapons to be destroyed or made useless was unrealistic. The report further advised that talks move forward simultaneously with arms decommissioning.

The IRA were furious that British Prime Minister John Major had not set a firm date for elections to a new Northern Irish Parliament or done more personally to advance talks They were also unhappy that fewer people were calling for Protestant paramilitaries to turn in or destroy their weapons. Thus, the IRA ended the ceasefire on February 9, 1996 by first issuing a press release and then exploding a bomb near London's Canary Wharf. Two dead, more than 100 injured, and £85 million worth of damage were the immediate result. Yet the violence that followed was far more contained on both the Protestant and Catholic side than had previously been the case. Great international—especially American—pressure was exerted on England to keep pushing for peace. On February 29, 1996, elections were announced, and another round of talks was scheduled to begin on June 10, 1996. Furthermore, it was stipulated that following the elections Sinn Fein would have to only address the *need* to decommission IRA weapons. Republicans regarded these decisions as a major victory for their cause, even as political violence remained a barrier to participation in the June talks.

This did not stop Sinn Féin from making a respectable stand in Elections to the Forum for Peace and Reconciliation that took place on May 30, 1996. Of the Unionist parties, the UUP won 30 seats, the DUP 24. The SDLP won the majority of Catholic votes, winning 21 seats, but Sinn Fein followed closely behind with 17. Yet Sinn Fein was still excluded from the all-party talks in June. Rioting by both Catholics and Protestants took place as July 12 celebrations and marches by loyalists degenerated into violence. Yet Gerry Adams and Martin McGuiness were able to stay the hand of the IRA. In spite of lower levels of violence and an existing blueprint for power sharing that had not changed dramatically since 1973, the talks progressed slowly. In the meantime, John Major's Conservative government was replaced by Tony Blair's Labour administration in May 1997. Blair made resolution of the Northern Irish situation one of his top priorities. He scheduled new talks for September 1997 and May 1998. An IRA ceasefire that began in July 1997 enabled Sinn Fein to participate, which led to the DUP walking out of the talks. UUP leader David Trimble was able to quiet similarly angry members of his own party. Although Sinn Fein won a seat at the table, the bulk of the negotiations were dominated by John Hume of the SDLP and Trimble. For most Catholics, civil rights and justice within Northern Ireland remained more important than the nationalist goals of Sinn Fein.

The Good Friday Agreement, sometimes called the Belfast Agreement, was finally reached on April 10, 1998. Among other measures, it called for electoral reform, anti-discrimination laws, job-creation plans, and the comprehensive reorganization of the RUC, which Catholics had long suspected of collusion with loyalist paramilitaries along with a host of other anti-Catholic biases, including its own hiring policies. Although John Hume and David Trimble would share the 1998 Nobel Peace Prize, the consensus was that the SDLP had emerged with more of what it sought than any other party. Witheringly described as "Sunningdale for slow learners" by senior SDLP member Seamus Mallon, the Good Friday Agreement represented the first real steps toward peace and access to political power for Catholics since the partition of Ireland in 1922.

More than five years later, Northern Ireland's Catholics still struggle for recognition of their cultural identity. In contrast to the image created by unionists and loyalists, most are not republicans seeking unity with the rest of Ireland. Indeed, Sinn Fein's recent growth in popularity has more to do with that party's greater understanding of the needs of its constituents than in any flowering of the nationalism promoted by the party in the 1970s and 1980s. It remains to be seen whether the slow, not-always-steady pace of the post-Good Friday Agreement years will win them a lasting presence in the fate of their state.

JOHN H. DAVIS

See also **Ireland; Irish; Northern Ireland; Hume, John (Northern Ireland Catholic); Ireland; Irish Republican Army; Sinn Féin; Trimble, David (Northern Ireland); United Kingdom**

Further Reading

Bardon, Jonathan, *A History of Ulster,* Belfast: Blackstaff Press, 2001

Conroy, John, *Belfast Diary: War as a Way of Life,* Boston: Beacon Press, 1995

Elliott, Marianne, *Catholics of Ulster: A History,* New York: Basic Books, 2001

Foster, Roy, *Modern Ireland: 1600–1972*, Oxford: Oxford University Press, 1991

Holland, Jack, *Hope Against History: The Course of Conflict in Northern Ireland,* New York: Henry Holt & Company, 1999

McKittrick, David, and David McVea, *Making Sense of the Troubles: The Story of the Conflict in Northern Ireland,* Chicago: New Amsterdam Books 2002

Mulholland, Marc, *The Longest War: Northern Ireland's Troubled History,* Oxford: Oxford University Press, 2002

Pringle, Peter, and Philip Jacobson, *Those Are Real Bullets: Bloody Sunday, Derry, 1972,* New York: Grove Press, 2001

Césaire, Aimé Ferdinand (Martiniquais)

Poet, playwright, and statesman, Aimé Ferdinand Césaire was a key figure of the black anti-colonialist movement in the mid-twentieth century. He spent eight years in Paris, between1932 and 1939, where he gained insight into himself and his countrymen by discovering his African heritage. His experiences and contacts during this time inspired his writings and political activities. In Paris, Césaire developed his anti-colonialist beliefs and found a compelling imagery in surrealism and surrealist literature.

A brilliant student, he had received a solid foundation in Western culture in his native Martinique. Once in Paris, he enrolled at the Lycée Louis-le-Grand as a post-graduate to prepare for admission to the Ecole Normale Supérieure (Higher Normal School). Césaire befriended other black students, most notably Léopold Sédar Senghor, from whom he learned about the African world. Césaire repeatedly emphasized the importance of this encounter, which he described as having revealed to him the essence of his own being. He understood why he felt alienated in Martinique: the myth of assimilation, long propounded by the French, had deprived Martinican blacks of their ancestral roots, leaving them worse off than Africans who had at least remained in contact with their land and culture.

With Senghor, Louis Gontran Damas, and other like-minded students, Césaire founded a journal called *L'Etudiant Noir* (The Black Student). In its March 1935 issue, he published an essay against assimilation, in which he coined the term "Negritude." The term was meant to reclaim the nobility of the black heritage and to fight against the psychological exploitation of blacks. For Césaire, Negritude did not connote racism in reverse, since he believed that the identity he sought could be reconciled with universality. Negritude did not suggest that blacks were superior to other people, simply that their cultures deserved to be placed on equal footing with those of the white colonizers

In 1939 he returned to Martinique. With René Ménil, Georges Gratiant and others, he launched a journal called *Tropiques* (1941–45). The *Tropiques* editors broke with the tradition of assimilation, with the imitation of Parnassian and Symbolist French poetry which characterized Martinican writing at the time, and strove to share with their readers what they had learned about Africa. The very fact of asserting their negritude was revolutionary. Since in Martinique race and class were one and the same—blacks constituted the proletariat oppressed by the white bourgeoisie—the social message of *Tropiques* threatened the status quo. The editors and the journal projected a cosmopolitan anti-colonial stance and advanced a vision of freedom achieved by reconnecting with pre-colonial Africa and by relying both on Marxism to bring about an egalitarian society and on surrealism to open minds and hearts. Surrealism, Césaire explained, freed him from traditional forms of language and from rational expression, and enabled him to conjure ardent unconscious forces. The mutual attraction between Césaire and Parisian surrealists was also due to their common opposition to colonialism, capitalism, the clergy, and bourgeois society.

Césaire turned to poetry because he believed in its utopian powers. Poetry, "welling up from the depth of his being with volcanic force," was for him the essential mode of expression . In his first volume of poems, *Cahier d'un retour au pays natal* (Return to a Native Land,1939), he exhorted Martinican blacks to find true freedom in a return to their origins, pointing out that political independence is insufficient without cultural independence and that achieving the latter required a painful search for truth in one's own soul. Césaire claimed to speak for all silently suffering oppressed peoples. The *Cahier* voices Césaires rebellion against Western values, assimilation, and his own people's unwillingness to face the fact that, far from encouraging true assimilation, France continued to deny Martinican blacks even the most elementary equality.

Césaire developed the themes of the *Cahier* in subsequent collections of poems. He also exploited the medium of theater, especially plays, within his oeuvre. He believed theatre, an oral means of communication, could reach larger audiences, and its visual elements gave words impetus. In *Toussaint l'Ouverture* (1962), Césaire told the epic saga of Toussaint Breda (later known as Toussaint l'Ouverture), the self-taught revolutionary who liberated Haiti from France during the Haitian Revolution (1974–1804). In *The Tragedy of King Christophe* (1963) Césaire chastised megalomaniac, tyrannical African post-independence leaders.

But writing alone proved to be an insufficient mode of action for Césaire, and he thus turned to politics. He was elected mayor of Fort-de-France in 1945 and soon thereafter deputy to the French National Assembly on the French Communist Party ticket. Césaire endeavored to obtain a change in the status of the Antilles from colonies to departments of France, but after departmentalization had been granted, he realized that in itself it did not guarantee equal rights. He understood that demanding independence was unrealistic, but continued to call for greater autonomy. After resigning from the French Communist Party over philosophical beliefs and strategies in 1956 he founded the Parti Progressiste Martiniquais (Martinican Progressive Party) and worked tirelessly to sensitize and educate his people in order to some day enable them have their own nation.

Césaire expounded his political creed in *Discours sur le colonialisme* (Discourse on Colonialism, 1950), a treatise in which he exploded the myth that white European colonizers maintained a mission of cultural and religious civilization. He described the impact of colonialism on the colonized, and most importantly, Césaire treated the figure of the colonizer who, by inflicting torture, violence, and race hatred, had degraded himself and endangered his own civilization. Césaire pointed out that the Western bourgeoisie had awoken in horror when faced with Nazi atrocities during World War II, but never recognized that before being the victim of Nazism it had been its accomplice. Césaire's caustic study of colonialism was much more than the study of a historical period.

Though philosophically opposed to doctrinaire movements, Césaire had joined the Communist Party in France because he saw Communism as opposing capitalism, imperialism, and the enslavement of blacks. He viewed the Soviet Union as anti-racist, anti-fascist, a defender of the downtrodden, a spokesperson for independence for colonies. He found the Marxist interpretation of history tempting for its liberalizing and revolutionary potential. However, after the Soviet invasion of Hungary, Césaire wrote an open letter of resignation in 1956 to Maurice Thorez, Secretary General of the French Communist Party. Racism, he wrote, cannot be subordinated to the class struggle. Universal emancipation regardless of class conflict was primarily and urgently needed.

To be fully appreciated, Césaire's ideological and political contributions must be viewed within their historical framework; his artistic contribution to French-language literature, however, is timeless and remains outstanding.

L. NATALIE SANDOMIRSKY

Biography

Aimé Ferdinand Césaire. Born June 26, 1913 in Basse-Pointe, Martinique. Studied at Lycée Schoelcher in Fort-De France, Martinique; Lycée Louis-le-Grand in Paris, 1932–35; Ecole Normale Supérieure in Paris, 1935–38. Married Martinican Suzanne Roussi. Returned to Martinique, 1939. Taught at Lycée Schoelcher, 1939–45. Co-founded review *Tropiques, 1941–45.* Elected Mayor, Fort-de-France, 1945. Joined French Communist Party, 1946. Deputy to French National Assembly, 1946–93. Resigned from Communist Party, 1956. Founded Parti Progressiste Martiniquais, 1958. Resides in Fort-de France, Martinique.

Selected Works

Cahier d'un retour au pays natal, in *Volontés* (1939), [*Return to a Native Land,* translated by Emil Snyder, 1968], *Tropiques 1941–45 collection complète,* 1978
Les Armes miraculeuses [Miraculous Weapons], 1946
Soleil cou coupé [Beheaded Sun], 1948
Corps perdu, (1949). [Lost Body, translated by Clayton Eshleman and Annette Smith, illustrated by Pablo Picasso, 1986]
Discours sur le colonialisme, 1950; 3rd edition, 1955, [Discourse on Colonialism, translated by Joan Pinkham, 1972]
Et les chiens se taisaient 1956
Lettre à Maurice Thorez [Letter to Maurice Thorez], 1956
Ferrements, 1960
Cadastre: Poèmes, 1961, [Cadastre: Poems, translated by Emil Snyder and Sanford Upson, 1973]
Toussaint l'Ouverture: la Révolution française et le problème colonial, 1960
La Tragédie du roi Christophe, 1963 [The Tragedy of King Christophe, translated by Ralph Manheim, 1969]
Une Saison au Congo, 1967 [A Season in the Congo, translated by Ralph Manheim, 1969]
Une Tempête, d'après la tempête de Shakespeare: Adaptation pour un théâtre nègre. 1969 [A Tempest, translated by Richard Miller, 1986]
Moi, Laminaire, 1982
Aimé Césaire: The Collected Poetry, translated by Clayton Eshleman and Annette Smith, 1983
Lyric and Dramatic Poetry, 1946–83 by Aimé Césaire, translated by Clayton Eshleman and Annette Smith, 1990

***See also* Afro-Caribbeans; Negritude; Senghor, Leopold (Senegalese)**

Further Reading

Condé, Maryse, *Cahier d'un retour au pays natal: Césaire: Analyse critique* [Notebook of a Return to the Native Country: Césaire: Critical Analysis], Paris: Hatier, 1978
Confiant, Raphaël, *Une Traversée paradoxale du siècle* [A Paradoxical Crossing of the Century], Paris: Stock, 1991
Davis, Gregson, *Aimé Césaire,* Cambridge and New York: Cambridge University Press, 1997
Hountondji, Victor, *Cahier d'Aimé Césaire: Evénement littéraire et facteur de revolution* [Aimé Césaire's Notebook: Literary Event and Catalyst of Revolution], Paris: L'Harmattan, 1993
Kesteloot, Lilyane, *Aimé Césaire,* Paris: Seghers, 1993
Moutoussamy, Ernest, *Aimé Césaire; Député à L'Assemblée National, 1945–1993* [Aimé Césaire; Deputy to the National Assembly, 1945–1993], Paris: L'Harmattan, 1993
Ngal, Mbwil a Mpaang, *Aimé Césaire: Un homme à la recherche d'une patrie* [Aimé Césaire: A Man in Search of a Fatherland], Paris: Présence Africaine, 1994
Pallister, Janis L., *Aimé Césaire,* New York: Twayne Publishers/Maxwell Macmillan International, 1991
Toumson, Roger, and Simone Henry-Valmore, *Aime Césaire, le nègre inconsolé* [Aimé Césaire, The Disconsolate Negro], Paris: Syros, 1994

Ceylon, *See* **Sri lanka**

See **Sri lanka**

Cham

Capsule Summary

Location: Cambodia, Vietnam, Malaysia, Thailand, Indonesia, China, Philippines, United States, Australia, France
Total Population: unknown
Language: Cham
Religion: Islam, Hinduism, Animism, ancestor worship

The Cham live as a minority in Cambodia, Vietnam, and a number of other countries within and beyond Southeast Asia. To a greater or lesser extent the Cham trace descent to the former kingdom of Champa, located in what is now central Vietnam. Over the long period beginning in the eleventh century CE and ending early in the nineteenth during which Champa was annexed by the Vietnamese, some of the Cham were absorbed and many assimilated by the expanding Vietnamese state. Others scattered far and wide, to regions with which Champa had entertained trade and cultural relations. Their descendants are found in Cambodia, where around 200,000 live, as well as Malaysia, Thailand, Indonesia, Hainan Island, and the Philippines. In some cases, this migration led to a reduction in identification with the kingdom of Champa and, in interaction with their new surroundings, the emergence of new conceptions of self.

The majority of Cham live in what are among the poorest nations in the world. In Vietnam, they number around 100,000 and are to be found in relatively poor and remote areas such as the mountains, the central coastal plain and beside the Cambodian border, although a small number live in Ho Chi Minh City. Agriculture and fishing have long been the staple subsistence activities in both Vietnam and Cambodia, yet the Cham also engage in handicraft production and commerce. Some Cham engage in cross-border trade. Up in the hills of Vietnam, a number of Cham work as shifting cultivators although the government has tried to impose a sedentary way of life on them.

Cham is a Malayo-Polynesian language, which has continued to be enriched by exposure to a variety of local languages. Most Cham also speak the dominant language of the country in which they reside: Vietnamese, Khmer, Malay, English, etc. Many Cham are multilingual, a capacity reflecting their complex history of migration and intercultural contacts in recent centuries. In central Vietnam the Cham language is written using a script derived from Sanskrit, the Cham in the Mekong delta use an Arabic script. Some speak and write Arabic.

The former kingdom of Champa entered the historical record in 192 CE. In its heyday, the kingdom was militarily and economically powerful largely due to its people's mastery of the sea. Champa engaged in trade relations with the seaboard nations of Southeast Asia and had significant relations with China. It was well known for its Hinduized culture, a legacy of contacts with India that was manifest in a propensity for religious depictions of gods such as Vishnu and Ganesh; these were popular among Cham carvers although their cult was mediated through Southeast Asian conceptions. Yet Champa was also influenced by and served as a regional relay for the transmission of Islam, Mahayana Buddhism, and Chinese culture. It maintained a tributary relationship with the societies of the uplands and with the predecessor states to Cambodia and Laos. With Vietnam it had a long, violent, and ultimately fatal relationship.

A number of the Cham who presently live in central Vietnam follow what is sometimes referred to as the Hindu or Brahman religion, in which Indian religious elements are woven into the ritual propitiation of nature, ancestors, former rulers, and protector deities such as the mother goddess Po Inu Nagar. Many Cham in the central coast also follow Islam, which first arrived in the region in the ninth century and blossomed in the eleventh. The Islam of these people, known as the Bani, is mixed with magical practices, worship of powerful spirits, and propitiation of the souls of former kings. In comparison with the Sunni Islam observed elsewhere in Southeast Asia, its codes are relatively relaxed. For example,

Cham Bani avoid eating pork but some do drink alcohol. The most important and effervescent festival for the Cham of central Vietnam is Kate, venerating the ancient Cham royalty and gods. The Cham also have rich traditions of dance, music, costume, and poetry.

The biggest migration of Cham was to Cambodia, where they came into contact with Muslims, many of Malay descent, who lived and traded in the Mekong delta. At a later point, a small number of these resettled back across the border in Vietnam. Sunni Islam, albeit a localized version blended with some Buddhist and magical practices, emerged as the dominant focus of this group's identity, to the point that many describe their ethnicity not as Cham but as "Muslim", or "Khmer Islam." Islam is the key cultural focus for this group. People reside around mosques. The religious festivals of Ramadam, El Fitri, and the Haj are the most important festivals of the year. The link with the Cham kingdom is further broken in that many of these people also consider themselves of Malay descent and emphasize linguistic and cultural differences from the Cham to the North.

For several centuries the Cham found that Cambodia provided a refuge from the expanding Vietnamese state. In comparison with the ethnic Vietnamese and Chinese population in Cambodia, the Cham have been seen as closer to an indigenous minority. Few follow the dominant Theravada Buddhist religion, yet they maintain good relations with the nation's ethnic Khmer majority. However, this condition of acceptance was drastically suspended when Pol Pot came to power in 1975. The genocidal Khmer Rouge regime, which fell in 1979, persecuted the Cham on the basis of perceived class distinctions, as well as on religious and ethnic differences. Although accepted as an ethnic minority within Vietnam, the Cham remain on the cultural, linguistic, religious and political periphery of the Vietnamese nation. In the devastating wake of the wars in Indochina, many Cham fled as refugees to North America, Europe and elsewhere, where, outnumbered by more prominent groups of Indochinese origin, they comprise a minority within a minority.

PHILIP TAYLOR

See also **Cambodia; Khmer; Vietnam**

Further Reading

International Centre for Ethnic Studies, *Minorities in Cambodia*, London: Minority Rights Group International, 1995

Kiernan, Ben, *The Pol Pot Regime: Race, Power and Genocide in Cambodia under the Khmer Rouge, 1975–79*, New Haven and London: Yale University Press, 1995

Scupin, Raymond, "Historical Ethnographic, and Contemporary Political Analyses of the Muslims of Kampuchea and Vietnam," *Sojourn*, 10, no. 2 (1995)

Thurgood, Graham, *From Ancient Cham to Modern Dialects: Two Thousand Years of Language Contact and Change Honolulu*: University of Hawaii Press, 1999

Chávez, César (Mexican-American)

The American labor leader César Chávez is best known as the founder of the United Farm Workers of America, the first union in agricultural labor history to successfully organize migrant farm workers. In addition, Chávez is remembered for improving the lives of tens of thousands of migrant workers in the United States, especially Mexican and Chicanos (American with Mexican ancestry). His commitment inspired many throughout the world to join the movement for social change. In his quest for social justice, Chávez was dedicated to non-violence, volunteerism, public action, solidarity/unity, and respect for all cultures and lifestyles.

A third generation Mexican-American, César Estrada Chávez was born on March 31, 1927 near Yuma, Arizona to Librado and Juana Estrada Chávez. The Chávez family settled in the North Gila Valley on a farm homesteaded during the 1880s by Chávez's grandfather, Cesario Chávez. At age 10, after his family lost the farm in the Great Depression, Chávez became a migrant worker. In 1942, Chávez's father was hurt in an automobile accident and was unable to work. To help support his family, as was typical of migrant workers in those days, Chávez quit school after completing the eighth grade to work full time in the fields. He traveled across the southwest where he experienced firsthand the injustices felt by migrant workers. Although Chávez only had an eighth grade education, he was self-taught in many areas including philosophy, economics, and the history of labor unions.

In 1944, Chávez began a two-year stint in the U.S. Navy. It was in the Navy that he realized that other nationalities also suffered discrimination. In 1948, Chávez married Helen Fabela, whom he met while working in the vineyards of California. The family settled in Sal Si Puedes ("Get Out if You Can"), a barrio in East San Jose, California. Helen supported César by believing in his movement, taking care of their eight children and working in the fields to support the family while César organized the farm workers. In 1952, César joined the Community Service Organization (CSO), a Latino Civil Rights Group. He served as national director of the CSO in the late 1950 and early 1960s.

Still concerned with the plight of the migrant worker, in 1962, César began the National Farm Workers Association (NFWA), the first farm workers union, which was the precursor to the United Farm Workers (UFW) union. The NFWA flag contained a black eagle on a red background and the organization adopted "Viva la Causa" (long live our cause) as the official motto. In later years the flag was kept as the emblem of the UFW.

Chávez's personal slogan was "Si Se Puede" (Yes we can). This slogan later became that of the UFW. In the 1960s and 1970s, Chávez challenged some of the country's biggest agribusiness firms in the U.S. Inspired by Mohandas Gandhi and St. Francis of Assisi, Chávez advocated non-violent tactics for the union such as the use of strikes, boycotts, and pickets. In 1966, the National Farm Workers Association joined with the Agricultural Workers Organizing Committee to form the United Farm Workers Organizing Committee (UFWOC), which was later renamed the United Farm Workers (UFW). The UFW was chartered by the AFL-CIO and Chávez was appointed president.

A major event occurred in 1965, when Filipino workers in the Agricultural Workers Organizing Committee (AWOC), the other major union, went on strike against grape growers in Delano, California. The NFWA voted to support this strike and Chávez took a lead role in the strike against California grape pickers in demand for higher wages. At that time, farm workers were among the lowest paid workers in America. The strike, internationally known as The Great Delano Grape Strike, turned into a national boycott of grapes that lasted five years. During this period, many of the strikers including Chávez were jailed.

By 1970, most of the table grape growers signed contracts with the UFW. These contracts brought union protection to about 10,000 workers employed by 26 growers. In addition, the contracts established grievance procedures and a joint union-management committee to enforce state safety regulations regarding the use of pesticides in the vineyards. In 1973, due to another labor dispute, César called for a worldwide grape boycott. The success of the boycott forced growers to support the 1975 Agricultural Labor Relations Act. This was the first law governing farm labor organizing in the continental U.S. The law provided for secret ballot elections, the right to boycott, voting rights for migrant seasonal workers and control over the timing of elections.

Future boycotts, including one of the lettuce industry, followed. Throughout the boycotts, despite harassment and violence against union members, César stood by his non-violence stance.

During his fight for "La Causa" (the cause), César fasted many times. In 1968, he undertook a 25 day water-only fast which was repeated in 1972 for 24 days, and in 1988 for 36 days. He used fasting as a non-violent means to attract attention to the suffering of farm workers and their children, and the dangers of pesticides. Chávez knew that farm workers wanted to resort to violent means, but pleaded with them to continue non-violent forms of protest. He convinced many of his followers that through persistence, hard work, and a willingness to sacrifice, union members would earn respect from the community.

Chávez's life was not without controversy. Many farmers felt the union leader nearly destroyed their businesses with his protest tactics. In addition, some members of the UFW thought he went too far in promoting the cause. After his death, it was also revealed that Chávez and the UFW had been under investigation in 1965 by the Federal Bureau of Investigation for alleged communist ties. An academic review of the FBI documents proved the allegations were unwarranted. Despite these controversies, time has dissipated the opposition to Chávez as scholarships, monuments, libraries, parks, legislation, and awards have been named after him.

Never making more than $6,000 a year, Chávez never profited materially in his civil rights pursuits. At the ages of 66, César Chávez died in his sleep on April 23, 1993 in San Luis, Arizona, near where he grew up. On April 29, 1993, more than 50,000 mourners honored Chávez at a funeral procession in Delano, California. He is laid to rest at the UFW headquarters, La Paz, in Keene, California. On August 8, 1994, President Bill Clinton posthumously awarded him the Medal of Freedom, the United States's highest civilian honor. On September 2, 1994, California Governor Pete Wilson, signed the César Chávez holiday bill, designating Chávez's birthday, March 31, as a state holiday. This made Chávez the fist union leader in U.S. history to be celebrated with a paid holiday. On April 23, 2003, the tenth anniversary of his death, the United States Post Office issued a commemorative stamp to honor him.

Chávez is remembered not only for helping migrant workers, but for being an advocate for human decency. He believed that once social change begins, it cannot be reversed. Education and instilling pride were the answers to removing the oppression faced by migrant farm workers.

Biography

César Estrada Chávez. Born March 31, 1927 near Yuma, Arizona. Attended more than 30 elementary schools in the Southwest; highest level achieved was 8th grade. Served in the Navy 1944–45 Worked at Saul Alinsky's Community Service Organization, 1952–62, lastly as national director. Began the National Farm Workers Association in 1962 which was the precursor to the United Farm Workers (UFW) union. Under Chávez's leadership, in 1966, the National Farm Workers Association joined with the Agricultural Workers Organizing Committee to form the United Farm Workers Organizing Committee (UFWOC), which was later renamed the United Farm Workers (UFW). Mexican President, Salinas de Gortari, awards Chávez the Aguila Azteca, the highest Mexican civilian award, 12 November 1990. Died in San Luis, Arizona, April 23, 1993. President Bill Clinton awards the U.S. Medal of Freedom posthumously to Chávez, August 8, 1994. California Governor, Pete Wilson, signs the César Chávez holiday bill, designating March 31 as a state holiday, September 2, 1994. On the tenth anniversary of his death, April 23, 2003, the United States Post Office issued a commemorative stamp to honor Chávez.

Selected Works

Levy, Jacques E., *César Chávez: Autobiography of La Causa*, New York: W.W. Norton & Company, 1975.

The Words of César Chávez (Richard J Jensen and John C. Hammerback (editors), Texas A&M University Press, 2002.

DENISE T. OGDEN

See also **Mexican-Americans**

Further Reading

Dalton, Frederick J., *The Moral Vision of César Chávez*, Orbis Books, 2003

del Castillo, Richard Griswold, and Richard A. Garcia, *César Chávez: A Triumph of Spirit*, Norman: University of Oklahoma Press, 1995

Ferriss, Susan, and Ricardo Sandoval, *The Fight in the Fields: César Chávez and the Farmworkers Movement*, New York: Hartcourt Brace, 1998

Fusco, Paul, *La Causa : The California Grape Strike,* New York: Collier Books, 1970

Horwitz, George D., and Paul Frusco, La Causa: The California Grape Strike, New York: The Macmillan Company, 1970

Matthiessen, Peter, *Sal Si Puedes: César Chávez and the New American Revolution*, New York: Random House, 1969

Ross, Fred, *Conquering Goliath: César Chávez at the Beginning.* Detroit, Michigan: Wayne State University Press, 1989

Taylor, Ronald B., *Chávez and the Farm Workers*, Boston, Massachusetts: Beacon Press, 1975

Chechens

Capsule Summary

Location: North Caucasus region of Europe, mostly in the territory of Chechnya
Total Population: approximately 1 million
Language: Chechen
Religion: Muslim

The Chechens are an ethnic group living in the North Caucasus region. There are approximately 1 million Chechens, most of who live in the territory of Chechnya. Their language, Chechen, belongs to the Nakh subfamily of the North Caucasian language group.

Chechen, like the other Caucasian languages (e.g., Abkhaz and Georgian), belongs to no other language family and is linguistically separate from the Turkic and Indo-European languages spoken by other neighboring ethnic groups.

Most Chechens are Muslims. Chechnya was a part of the Soviet Union, but after the Soviet Union's collapse the Chechens declared their independence. Russia refused to accept this declaration, and Chechnya has been the site of fighting between Chechens and Russians since 1994. Legally, the international community considers Chechnya part of Russia, and thus Chechens are a minority culture within the Russian Federation.

History

"It is just as hard to subjugate the Chechens and other peoples of this region as to level the Caucasian mountains. This is not something to achieve with bayonets but rather with time and enlightenment. The fighting may bring great personal benefits to General Yermolov, but none whatsoever to Russia." These words, written by Russian General Mikhail Orlov in 1820, seem likely to have been echoed by many Russian officers serving in the more recent Chechen campaign of 1999-2000. Replace nineteenth-century General Alexei Yermolov with twentieth-century Russian President Vladimir Putin, and the echo of history would be complete. From their first encounter with the invading Russians until the current conflicts, the Chechens have been engaged in a centuries-long war for independence.

The Chechens have existed as a people since at least the time of the Romans. They were converted to Islam during the Arab invasions of the seventh century, unlike many of the other Caucasus peoples who remained with the Eastern Orthodox Christian Church. The Chechens' tribal-based society maintained its cultural traditions throughout the many conquests—Roman, Arab, Turkish, and Mongol—that the region endured. From all reports, they were a proud and independent people.

In the early eighteenth century, the Russian Empire began expanding into the Caucasus. In 1818, the Russians built a fort in the region that became the nucleus of Grozny, Chechnya's modern capital city. Despite these Russian efforts, the Chechens and other neighboring peoples maintained an active rebellion for more than 25 years. In this fighting, they were led by the *imam* Shamil, a dedicated Muslim holy warrior who became a Chechen symbol of resistance, a kind of Chechen George Washington—although he was ethnically not a Chechen but a member of a related ethnic group. The Russians captured his towns and forts but were unable to corner his guerilla fighters. It was only with his surrender in 1859 that the Russians were able to completely subdue the region.

After the collapse of the old Russian Empire in 1917, the Chechens tried to break away and establish their independence, but the newly created Soviet Union forced Chechnya to become an autonomous *oblast* (province) in the new Soviet state. The autonomy was purely nominal, and the Chechens remained as repressed under the Communists as they had been under the emperors.

In 1944, during World War II, Josef Stalin accused the Chechens of cooperating with the invading Germans; he dissolved the republic and deported the entire Chechen population to Kazakhstan in central Asia. Many Chechens died during this forced relocation. In 1957, with the coming to power of Soviet leader Nikita Khrushchev, the Chechens were allowed to return, and their autonomous republic was reestablished.

Independence

After the collapse of the Soviet Union, Chechnya demanded its independence. Led by a former Soviet general, Dzhokhar Dudayav, Chechens seized control of their country and held new elections in which Dudayav was chosen president. In November 1991, Dudayav officially declared Chechnya an independent nation.

Russia, however, refused to accept Chechnya's declaration. In the days of the Soviet Union, Russia's leaders pointed out, Chechnya had always been a subsidiary republic under the control of Russia. When Russia left the Soviet Union, it legally took Chechnya with it. Although the Russian argument was legally sound, it ignored the reality that most Chechens wanted nothing to do with Russia, and it was clear that Russia was not motivated primarily by its faith in legalisms. Chechnya has oil and gas reserves that make it a tempting target. In addition, Russia had other restive minorities; if the Chechens were allowed to leave freely, other parts of Russia might try to break away. To hold Russia together, Russian leaders felt that they had to make an example of Chechnya.

For two years, there was a standoff. Russia denied Chechnya's de jure independence but accepted its de facto existence. Occupied by other problems—such as the war in Bosnia—the rest of the world paid little attention to Chechnya. No nation was willing to court

Russia's disapproval and officially acknowledge Chechnya's existence as an independent nation.

War with Russia

In December 1994, tired of Chechnya's refusal to accept Russian authority, Russia's president, Boris Yeltsin, ordered an invasion of the country. Forty thousand troops, backed by helicopters and tanks and later reinforced by additional divisions, invaded Chechnya and in eight weeks fought their way to Grozny, the Chechen capital. Although Chechnya was a nation of 1 million and Russia a nation of 140 million, it took additional months for the Russians to occupy the northern plains of Chechnya. Even so, the Chechens continued to fight as Dudayav led his troops in their strongholds in the hills of the south.

The fighting continued for two years, during which Dudayav was killed by a Russian missile. In July 1996, the Russians declared Chechnya to have been successfully conquered. Then, in August 1996, Aslan Maskhadov, Dudayav's replacement, led a surprise counterattack that retook Grozny and reinvigorated the Chechens' will to fight. Discouraged by the failure of two years of fighting, the Russians agreed to a temporary peace. They withdrew from Chechnya in January 1997. They did not, however, agree to Chechen independence: this was only a temporary withdrawal.

Maskhadov was elected president of Chechnya, but Chechen problems continued. Maskhadov was unable to control a country that had been damaged by two years of confusion and two more years of bloody war. Each local Chechen leader saw himself as a law unto himself and refused to cooperate with the president if it did not suit his interests. As a result, Chechnya operated as a place without law, where patriot guerilla leaders operated as gangsters. Some Chechen leaders operated protection rackets; others resorted to kidnapping to raise money. With legal unemployment at 80 percent, crime was one of the few options open to Chechens wanting to support their families.

With banditry a part of the government, Chechnya was unable to pull itself together enough to face the Russians. Maskhadov was not even able to stop Chechens from carrying out cross-border raids into Russia for the purpose of kidnapping people and holding them for ransom. This activity naturally alienated the Russians, even those who had wanted peace with Chechnya.

In September 1999, a number of bombs went off in crowded Moscow buildings, killing more than 300 civilians. Chechen guerillas or gangsters—the difference sometimes seemed unclear—were blamed. Russia's new prime minister, Vladimir Putin, ordered a new invasion. Putin proclaimed that his army would "wipe the terrorists out wherever we find them, even if they are sitting on the toilet." Russians were eager for revenge, and Putin's popularity increased dramatically.

By early 2000, most of Chechnya was again under Russian control, but as yet the Chechens have refused to surrender. Fighting continues as guerillas hide in the countryside, occasionally ambushing isolated Russian columns. The fighting has been bitter. An issue of *Kommersant-Vlast,* a Moscow weekly, described what Russian troops did to a Chechen woman sniper captured in the battle for Grozny. They tied her legs to a pair of light armored cars and tore her in half. Chechens have been similarly cruel, torturing the few prisoners whom they capture—most are killed.

Tens of thousands of Chechens have died since the wars for Chechen independence began. More than 100,000 have become refugees. The city of Grozny is a moonscape of rubble, with almost none of its original buildings intact. The Chechens still seem determined to resist, and Russia still seems determined to defeat them. If the latter succeeds, it may be at the cost of destroying the Chechens as a people.

Society

Chechnya's economy used to be centered on petroleum and natural gas production. The city of Grozny was also a manufacturing center. Since the fighting, Chechnya's economy has been in shambles.

Although most Chechens are Muslims, their loyalty to Islamic tradition was eroded by the many years under Soviet control. That loyalty, however, was not destroyed, and Islam remains an important element in Chechen culture. In Chechnya, Islam was linked to the tradition of Sufism, or mystical Islam. Many early Chechen leaders, including the imam Shamil, were brothers in a Sufi order. Even after the Soviets closed down Chechnya's mosques, Sufis continued to meet in one another's homes. With the collapse of the Soviet Union, the mosques reopened, but Islam has still not recovered its former place in Chechen lives. Some Chechen fighters wear green headbands, symbolizing their loyalty to Islam, but, with few Muslim clerics active in the country, most Chechens are fairly ignorant of all the obligations of being a Muslim.

Geographically, Chechnya is divided between the plains of the north, where Grozny is located, and the rough hills and mountains of the south. During their long history, the Chechens living in the mountains, partially isolated from neighbors and overlords alike, tended to be very loyal to their own villages and communities. Like other mountain peoples such as the Scots, the Chechens were organized in extended families, making the primary social unit the clan (*teip* in Chechen), of which there are more than 150 in Chechnya. Traditionally, Chechens were loyal to family, clan, faith, and country, in about that order. Modern Chechens are not as clannish as their ancestors, but tradition and the pressure of Russian invasions have kept this spirit alive.

Chechen society has a long tradition of close proximity to violence. Blood feuds, sometimes involving entire clans, were a traditional way of solving conflicts. Some of these feuds still sputtered into the twentieth century. For this reason, many Chechens, particularly those of the mountainous south, were very accustomed to carrying and using weapons. This made them formidable enemies during their conflicts with Russia. Chechens of the southern hills were much more comfortable with weapons than the scared young Russian conscripts they faced in battle. The ugly result of this violent aspect of Chechen culture is a long tradition of banditry, kidnapping, and murder.

One legacy of the Chechen tradition of violence is the prominent place Chechens have had in Russia's criminal organizations. Chechen mafias, often organized around clan loyalties, operated during the time of the Soviet Union and became particularly prominent after its collapse. Chechen gangs operated in all the Russian cities, particularly in Moscow, and were blamed for the 1999 explosions in Moscow apartment buildings. With Chechnya's declaration of independence, the line between Chechen gangster boss and Chechen guerilla patriot has not always been clear.

As in many traditional societies, Chechen women do not have equal status with men. Men serve as political leaders, dominate the family unit, and hold most of the important economic positions in society. Local village leaders are almost always men, and military leaders are always men, although women do sometimes serve as soldiers. This was not always the case. During the Soviet years, women received nearly equal opportunities for education and advancement as men. However, with the militarization of Chechnya after the conflicts with Russia, women have been increasingly pushed into the background.

CARL SKUTSCH

See also **Bosnia-Herzegovina; Russia**

Further Reading

Gail, Carlotta, and Thomas de Waal, *Chechnya: Calamity in the Caucasus,* New York: New York University Press, 1998

Human Rights Watch, *Russia/Chechnya: A Legacy of Abuse,* New York: Human Rights Watch, 1997

Lieven, Anatol, *Chechnya: Tombstone of Russian Power,* New Haven, Connecticut: Yale University Press, 1998

Chechnya, *See* **Chechens**

Chile

Capsule Summary

Location: Southern South America, bordering the South Pacific Ocean, between Argentina and Peru
Population: 15,665,216 (July 2003)
Ethnic Population: White and white-Amerindian (95%), Amerindian (3%), other (2%)
Language: Spanish
Religion: Roman Catholic (89%), Protestant (11%), Jewish (negligible percentage)

The Republic of Chile in Southern South America is bordered by Argentina, Bolivia, and Peru. To the west is the Pacific Ocean and to the east, the Andes Mountains. Its geographical area measures 292,257 square miles (756,946 square kilometers) and includes Easter Island (Isla de Pascua) and Isla Sala y Gomez.

History

At the beginning of the fifteenth century, what is now central Chile was populated by groups of Mapuche or Araucanians. In the south, to the valley of the Maipo river, the territory had become a part of the Inca empire. The Western conquest of Chile began in 1540 with the arrival of an Spanish expedition under the leadership of Pedro de Valdivia. Suppressing the initial native resistance, Santiago and several other towns and settlements were founded, even in the densely populated territory south of the Bio-Bio river. In 1553, in reaction to the harsh and oppressive conditions imposed by the conquistadores, the Mapuche raised in armed rebellion, beginning a long conflict that resulted after some decades in the retreat of the Spaniards. Independence was maintained throughout the colonial period and well into the republican era.

After a prolonged conflict, Chile obtained its independence from Spain in 1818. Political instability and even anarchy marked the first republican years until a consolidation of the state was achieved under the leadership of Diego Portales. Colonization was encouraged and by 1850 the southern part of Mapuche territory had been occupied at the same time that the colonization of Magallanes was under way. In the War of the Pacific against Bolivia and Peru, from 1879 to 1883, Chile obtained the northern provinces of Antofagasta and Tarapaca. The occupation of Araucania, the core area of Mapuche territory, was completed by 1882.

Political power has traditionally been concentrated in the presidency, with a short period of congressional regime after the civil war of 1891. Recent history in the country is marked by the 1973 military coup against the socialist regime of President Salvador Allende, the 17 years of military dictatorship under General Augusto Pinochet, and the long and difficult transition of a return to democracy. Human rights abuses surfaced during Pinochet's repressive regime (1973-1990) in the hands of the armed and intelligence forces. Thousands of Chileans were reportedly murdered or disappeared, taken to concentration camps and tortured; hundreds of thousands were arrested or had to seek exile abroad.

Free elections held in 1989 resulted in a return to civilian government, and since 1990 President Ricardo Lagos Escobar has governed Chile. However, political decision making has by tradition been strongly centralized in the capital of Santiago, which together with a traditional reliance in the concept of the unitary state, has led to widespread opposition to the recent demands for special rights and even autonomy from ethnic groups, particularly the Mapuche.

Indigenous Populations

The Fueguians inhabited the vast area of islands and channels to the north of the Strait of Magellan and Tierra del Fuego. After the extinction of the Chono and the Ona, only small groups of Kaweshkar and Yamana remain. Of about 100 Kaweshkar, some 20 are still living near places of traditional settlement. The majority of some 75 Yamana reside in Navarino Island. Although these two groups spoke different languages, their traditional way of life was very similar. The barch canoe was the indispensable means of transportation between temporary settlements in search for marine food and edible plants. Their very simple material life was in sharp contrast to the varied and profound spiritual values, conveyed in languages rich in expressive possibilities and manifested in various myths and ceremonies.

By far the largest indigenous population in the country is the Mapuche, with almost 930,000 people according to the census of 1992. A majority of Mapuche live in the lowland areas, but 338,000 live in the south-central regions where three regional ethnic subdivisions are found,: the Pewenche who reside in the Andean valleys of the Upper Bio-Bio river basin; the Williche, in the southern area (Los Lagos or Region X) and the Lafquenche, who inhabit the coastal sector of Araucania (Region IX). Although a major segment of the population, the Mapuche have very limited access to political influence, even at the municipal level.

The rural Mapuche population of today, scattered in hundreds of settlements called *comunidades*, subsists with farming as the main occupation. The recollection of seeds from Araucaria pines is an important economic activity among the Pewenche. Social organization does not differ today significantly from the rest of the population, but elements of traditional religion persist. Although belonging to various Christian churches, thousands assemble in regularly held traditional ceremonies such as the *guillatun*. The celebration of the new year at the winter solstice, called the *We Tripantu*, is taking root again and shamans, called *machi*, are active in many areas, even among urban Mapuche. An increased social and political awareness has resulted in militant efforts to obtain the return of ancestral lands and growing demands for political autonomy.

As Easter Island belongs to Chile, mention must be made of its Polynesian population, the Rapa-Nui. Of a total of 21,850 individuals, the vast majority live in different parts of the country and about 5 percent still reside on Easter Island. There as elsewhere in Polynesia, what remains of traditional culture confronts the pressures of modernization and the demands of tourism.

In Northern Chile, some 10,000 Kunza or Atacama live in villages along the river Loa, where in some places pre-Hispanic irrigation channels are still in use. Here, Catholic saint-worship, as in the cult of San Pedro de Atacama, combines with reverence for the divine Pachamama, or Mother Earth. The native language is, however, a total loss.

For the traditional Aymara pastoral economy in the Andean plateau of Tarapaca, as in neighboring regions in Bolivia, llama herds have been the most important asset. At lower altitudes, the cultivation of crops like quinoa and potato has been the main economic activity. Water, however, has become a scarce commodity after its diversion to the cities of the coast. Partly as a result of this, less than 5 percent of the 48,500 Aymara still live in villages within historical settlement areas like Putre, Colchane, and Camiña.

Many people belonging to ethnic groups have become integrated in Chilean society and are today active in all kinds of professions and activities. At the same time, a majority live in unfavorable conditions in cities and rural communities. While in the midst of a process of modernization, it can be seen how the Aymara, Atacama, and Mapuche share important cultural traits, constituting a prolongation of Andine culture that reaches all the way to the rainy forests of southern beeches and Chiloé.

Chile's market-oriented economy is characterized by a high level of foreign trade. The 2002 GDP of $156.1 billion and a per capita income of $10,100 represented a downturn from the period between 1991 and 1997 when the country's real growth in GDP measured 8 percent. Chile's industries include copper, other minerals, foodstuffs, fish processing, iron and steel, wood and wood products, transport equipment, cement, and textiles. Chile is also a key country for the trans-shipment of cocaine destined for the United States and Europe; economic prosperity and increasing trade have made Chile more attractive to traffickers seeking to launder drug profits.

JUAN-CARLOS GUMUCIO

See also **Bolivia**

Further Reading

Chapman, Anne, *Drama and Power in a Hunting Society: The Selknam of Tierra del Fuego*, Cambridge: Cambridge University Press, 1982

Hidalgo, Jorge, et al., *Culturas de Chile, Etnografia. Sociedades Indígenas Contemporáneas y su Ideologia*, Santiago de Chile: Editorial Andrés Bello, 1996

Stuchlik, Milan, *Life on a Half Share, Mechanisms of Social Recruitment among the Mapuche of Southern Chile*, London: Hurst & Co., 1979

Chin

Capsule Summary

Location: Southernmost part of the mountain range separating Burma (Myanmar) from India.
Total Population: 1.5 million (estimation, 2003)
Language: Tibeto-Burman languages
Religion: Mostly Christian

Recognized by the United Nations as an "indigenous people," the Chin are a Mongoloid group of tribes inhabiting the southern portions of the mountain range that separates northwestern Burma from India. The presence of the Chin in Burma dates back to the twelfth century, and for the most part, they have led an independent life. Two centuries of internecine wars and feuds ended in the late nineteenth century, following the British expedition into and annexation of the Chin Hills to prevent raids on Burma's plains.

The hereditary chiefs exercise political control over the traditionally self-sufficient Chin villages. Speaking Tibeto-Burmese languages, the Chin share cultural and linguistic traits of Kuki, Lushai, and Lakher peoples who live in the region covering Burma and India's northeast. Though they have come under the influence of Christian missionaries, the Chin also practice traditional religions, worshiping numerous deities and spirits.

In 1955, Pawi-Lakher Regional Council was formed in India's northeast to safeguard the minority interests of the Pawis (Lai or Chin). Though they gained some autonomy following the independence of India and Burma, their position has been threatened by their economic dependence upon their neighbors.

At the time of Burma's independence, the national leadership promised to create a federal and secular polity wherein minorities would be able to lead an autonomous life within Burma. However, with the assassination of Aun Sang in 1948 and, more particularly, following the military coup in 1961, the hopes of the minorities for a liberal Burma faded. The subsequent moves by the central authorities toward greater "Burmanization" and the fact that Buddhism was made the state religion created further hurdles for reconciliation.

Under the Burmese Constitution of 1947, the Chin area was made a special division that eventually became a state in 1974. Though it was an improvement over the earlier arrangement, the actual impact was minimal with the Chin continuing to suffer from neglect and marginalization. The Chin State is one of the seven ethnic minority states of Burma. Besides the Chin State, the Chin people are also comprised of Kuki, Hmar, and Mizos or Lushai tribes in India. "The Chin" is a generic expression in that more than 40 different subgroups are included in this category in Burma.

The centralized politics of Burma led to the fleeing of some Chin into India and Thailand while others resorted to armed resistance for independence. The State Law and Order Restoration Council (SLORC), which came to power in 1988, imposed a host of repressive measures against the Chin, including ill treatment and forced relocation. While thousands of dissidents went into exile, poverty and deprivation compelled many Chin youth to join the Burmese army.

Around 40,000 to 50,000 Chin from Burma live and work illegally in the Indian state of Mizoram and have become the target for anti-foreigner agitation of some students. Though some Chin have been living in Mizoram since the 1960s, the refugee influx began only after 1988. Since 1994, nearly 10,000 Chin were forcibly repatriated to Burma.

The suspected cooperation between members of the CNF and various insurgent groups in northeast India forced the Indian government to take a tough stand on the issue. In fact, the armies of India and Burma even conducted joint operations in 1995 against the Chin. The absence of formal refugee status complicates the already precarious position of the Chin in India. As a result, they have formed the Chin Students Union (CSU) and the Chin Refugee Committee (CRC) as a means of highlighting their plight.

Compared to other ethnic minorities, the Chin are relatively peaceful although not without animosities with the majority Burmans. The uneasy relationship between the Chin and the central government deteriorated with the advent of SLORC. In addition to the regime's failure to correct any of the past mistakes in dealing with the minorities, the SLORC's extreme repression proved to be more damaging to the minorities such as Chin and Rohingyas. For example, measures like forced labor and forced migration of their population increased their alienation.

The simultaneous ethnic turmoil in India's northeast and Burma's northwest has at times created strains in Indo-Burmese ties as most of the tribes involved share many commonalties.

The main economic activity is agriculture at subsistence level. The mostly inaccessible and unfriendly mountainous terrain remains a formidable barrier not only for their economic advancement but also for their integration with the majority. In 1988, the Chin National Front joined the ten-member National Democratic Front which was set up in 1975 to fight for the creation of a federal Burma as envisaged in 1947. One reason for the failure of these joint efforts of ethic minorities has been the policy of the central government, especially under the SLORC and its present form—the State Development and Peace Council (SDPC)—to deal with each group separately.

The crackdown against pro-democracy activists in 1988 led to the formation of the Chin National Front (CNF), an insurgent group whose ranks are mostly drawn from students. Along with other ethnic Burmese, they share distrust and antipathy toward the military regime. Their efforts to secure the support of the Mizos in northeast India were partially successful. Despite their ethno-linguistic affinity with the Chin, the Mizos did not go beyond extending moral support to the Chin insurgency.

P.R. Kumaraswamy and D. Shyam Babu

See also **Buddhists; India; Myanmar**

Further Reading:

Phayre, Arthur P., *History of Burma*, London: Susil Gupta, 2nd edition, 1967
Rajah, Ananda, "Ethnicity and Civil War in Burma: Where is the Rationality," in *Burma: Prospects for a Democratic Future*, edited by Robert I Rotberg, Washington, DC: Brookings, 1998
Smith, Martin, "Burma's Ethnic Minorities: A Central or Peripheral Problem in Regional Context?" in *Burma: The Challenge of Change in a Divided Society*, edited by Peter Carey, London: Macmillan, 1997
Smith, Martin, *Burma: Insurgency and the Politics of Burma*, London: Zed, 1991
Smith, Martin, *Ethnic Groups in Burma*, London: Anti-Slavery International, 1994
Thompson, Virginia, and Richard Adloff, *Minority Problems in Southeast Asia*, Stanford, Californai: Stanford University Press, 1955

China

Capsule Summary

Country Name: The People's Republic of China
Location: Eastern Asia, bordering the East China Sea, Korea Bay, Yellow Sea, and South China Sea, between North Korea and Vietnam
Total Population: 1,286,975,468 (July 2003)
Minority Population: 160,000,000
Ethnic Populations: Han Chinese (91.9%), Zhuang, Uygur, Hui, Yi, Tibetan, Miao, Manchu, Mongol, Buyi, Korean, and other nationalities (8.1%)
Languages: Standard Chinese or Mandarin (Putonghua, based on the Beijing dialect), Yue (Cantonese), Wu (Shanghaiese), Minbei (Fuzhou), Minnan (Hokkien-Taiwanese), Xiang, Gan, Hakka dialects, minority languages
Religions: Daoist (Taoist), Buddhist, Muslim (1%–2%), Christian (3%–4%), although the country is officially atheist

The People's Republic of China (PRC) is the world's most populous country, with over 1.28 billion citizens, 160 million of which are officially minorities. The largest minority groups (with figures in millions from the 2000 census) are Zhuang (16.2), Manchu (10.7), Hui (i.e., Muslim Chinese, 9.8), Miao (7.4), Uyghurs (8.4), Yi (7.8), Tujia (8.0), Mongols (5.8), and Tibetans (5.4). Administratively, China is comprised of 23 provinces, including, according to the Chinese government, Taiwan, along with five municipalities. Minorities occupy most of China's border areas, largely in five minority Autonomous Regions and close to 200 minority Autonomous Counties. A Communist country, China occupies an area of 3,700,000 square miles (9,583,000 square kilometers) making it slightly smaller than the United States.

On the island of Taiwan (historically a part of China and known as the Republic of China), the 20 different Austronesian minority groups constitute less than 2 percent of Taiwan's population, with a population totalling 433,689 in 2002.

Though minorities constitute only 8.4 percent of the current population of the People's Republic of China, they played an important role in China's emergence as a nation-state. As they also occupy 60 percent of China's landmass in strategic peripheral areas, minorities are crucial to China's future.

The ethnic majority in China, the Han Chinese, represents over 80 percent of the population. The non-Han peoples of China are known as Minority Nationalities (*shaoshu minzu* • • • •), a concept based on the Stalinist notion of *nacional"nost"*: a group with a common language, territory, socioeconomic basis, and psychological makeup. The latter criterion was in practice defined so broadly as to include customs and even ancestry. In addition to the majority Han Chinese, today 55 minority nationalities enjoy official recognition.

Not all of China's minorities have received official recognition; some distinct ethnic groups have been lumped together under one nationality. Though some scholars have argued that non-dominant Han groups should also be considered minorities, in both China and Taiwan the term *minority* refers exclusively to groups other than the Han Chinese.

Chinese attitudes towards non-Han peoples have been strongly dichotomized over the centuries. These views have evolved from an empire-vs.-barbarians dichotomy to a paternalistic more/less-advanced division of China's citizens. Official policy maintains that each ethnic group should have the right to develop its own culture and language, though integration remains a key goal. The degree of national integration of minorities varies widely. Some groups, such as the Zhuang and Koreans, are well integrated; others, such as the Tibetans and Uyghurs, retain a strong sense of separate cultural identity.

History: Imperial China, Han and Non-Han relations

The majority Han Chinese civilization has a 4000-year history as attested in the so-called oracle bone inscriptions. Though non-Han peoples do not have such early written records, archaeological and linguistic evidence of cultural contact suggest that a variety of human groups lived within the territory that is today China.

Chinese civilization originated along the lowest reaches of the Yellow River and expanded to the north and west to the Loess plateau, and south to the coasts. From the earliest Shang dynasty (eighteenth–twelfth centuries BCE) to the end of the imperial system in 1911, Chinese imperial strength and the size of its territory expanded and shrank along with the fortunes of the Empire. Until around 1000 CE, non-Han peoples of the region were quite autonomous. During times when the Han Chinese dynasties were weak, non-Han peoples raided and even sometimes conquered the Chinese territories. These non-Chinese peoples often partially adopted Han Chinese titles such as emperor, dress, and even language, but they required all citizens to submit to some of their own practices, such as the obligatory queue—hair braid—for men during the Manchu Qing dynasty. Most of these non-Han dynasties were short-lived, but not all: the last, the Manchu Qing dynasty, lasted from 1644 until 1911. Other significant foreign (minority) dynasties included the Hsiung-nu, a Central Asian steppe people, who ruled northern China between 311–589, and the Mongol Yuan dynasty from 1280–1368 CE. Both the Mongol Yuan and the Manchu Qing dynasties significantly expanded Chinese territory and also resulted in an ever-more multicultural empire. The five major civilizations within the Chinese territory were implicitly recognized in the turn-of-the-eighteenth century publication the Pentaglot Dictionary (•••••) written in Manchu, Tibetan, Mongolian, Uyghur, and Chinese.

Those peoples on the periphery of the empire whose language and culture differed from that of the ruling group were considered barbarians. Ironically, even foreign dynasty rulers such as Manchus and Mongols were not immune to such views. Written records generally termed the peoples to the north and west *hu* • (which we may call "northern barbarian"), while those to the south were known as *Yi* • or *Man* • "Southern Barbarians"; indigenous peoples of Taiwan were often termed *Dong Di* •• or *Dong Fan* ••, "Eastern Savages."

Premodern Chinese Nationalism and non-Han groups

Starting in the mid-nineteenth century, Chinese nationalistic identity coalesced around the concept of a Han nationality, whose population spoke Sinitic languages (i.e., Chinese dialects). The equation of Chinese with Han provided another good reason to overthrow the foreign Manchu Qing dynasty at the end of the nineteenth century. After the 1911 Revolution by Chinese Nationalists, Sun Yat-Sen used *minzu* in the sense of "nation-state," thus extending the notion of Chinese nationality, called *Zhonghua minzu,* to include all major groups within the Chinese territory. Many historians consider this broadened definition simply due to territorial considerations.

The phrase *shaoshu minzu*, meaning "minority nationality," was first used by the Nationalist leader Sun Yat-sen in 1924, and took on a more prominent role in the inclusive rhetoric of the Communist Party during the Civil War in the 1930s and 1940s. Though the Communist message was overtly egalitarian to recruit all peoples, minority nationalities were consistently referred to in paternalistic terms: the Party would help *ruoxiao minzu*, "weak and small nationalities," and *luohou minzu*, "backward nationalities." Such terms reflect the social Darwinist thinking that prevailed at the time, which implicitly advocated the cultural assimilation of ethnic groups into the "more advanced" Han state.

The term *xiongdi minzu* "brother nationality" was also introduced and is still used today. In the compound word *xiongdi* (literally "elder brother-younger brother"), it is clear that by "elder brother" the "more civilized" Hans are meant, while the "younger brothers" are all other peoples. Though this Han chauvinism has been denounced since the Communist Revolution, the Han people are expected to assist the minorities in economic, social, and cultural development.

The Communist Revolution and Nationality Identification

Since October 1, 1949 the government has been a Socialist People's Republic, founded by Mao Zedong. Policy on minorities during the 1950s was strongly influenced both by Soviet nationality policies as well as Russian ethnographic theories. The PRC Common Programme, the interim constitution, of 1949 is egalitarian, asserting that all nationalities were equal, and that nationalities each had the "freedom to develop their dialects and languages, and to preserve or reform their traditional customs, and religious beliefs" (Articles 50 & 53). In theory, then, the Han is but one of many ethnic groups, each of whose culture and language should be respected. The People's Republic of China initiated a two-pronged process to identify formal and official Nationalities and reinforce this concept into the public consciousness. First, teams of linguists were sent out all over China to investigate the status of ethnolinguistic groups; second, any group considering itself to be a Nationality was encouraged to petition for formal recognition. Already by 1955, more than 400 groups had applied for recognition, 200 alone in the southwestern Yunnan province. In the subsequent two years, the Central government's State Ethnic Affairs Commission formally declared 55 Nationalities, using the Stalinist Criteria for Nationalities to evaluate data from the research teams. Political considerations were a factor in many decisions as well. Only one group, the Tibeto-Burman Jinuo of Yunnan, has since successfully petitioned (in 1979) to be added to the list. Many others, lumped together under one overarching Nationality name, have tried unsuccessfully to gain official recognition as individual groups.

Some scholars outside China have suggested that some Han Chinese subgroups constitute minorities, particularly the Yue speakers (of which Canton is a part) and the Hakkas. Both meet most of the criteria for Nationality status, having a unique territory, identity, and language varieties unintelligible to speakers of the Standard Language. Yet Hakkas and Yue speakers share the Chinese writing system and consider themselves Chinese, so they are classified as Han; to classify them as separate groups would directly counter the aims of the unified modern Chinese nation-state.

Regional Political Autonomy

The Central Government established areas with over 30 percent Minority Nationalities as autonomous organs of self-government. The National Minority Regional Autonomy Law adopted in 1984 provides specific guidelines for minority regional autonomy through the People's Congress and Governments. These included five Autonomous Regions: Inner Mongolia, founded on May 1, 1947; Xinjiang Uygur, October 1, 1955; Guangxi Zhuang, March 15, 1958; Ningxia Hui, October 25, 1958; and Tibet, September 1, 1965. There are also 30 Autonomous Prefectures and 120 Autonomous Counties, including three "banners", in addition to more than 1,300 Autonomous Townships. Typically, the chair or vice-chair of the People's Congress Standing Committee in each Autonomous area is a member of the eponymous Minority Nationality; minority-cadre representation in the national People's Congress was over 14 percent in 2003, a significant rise from 6.6 percent in 1990.

National Minority Autonomous Area governments are by law empowered to enact legislation appropriate to local political, economic, and cultural conditions; enact local holidays; independently control local revenue, and manage infrastructural and social-welfare projects. Despite this, in practice, the control of the Central Government and of the Han Nationality is strongly felt in minority Autonomous areas. Though the Autonomous Area Committee Chair is usually a member of the Autonomous Area Nationality (e.g., a Tibetan in Tibet), the vice-chair tends to wield real power, and he is invariably Han Chinese. To maintain the integrity of the state, the Central Government in Beijing frequently issues directives to Autonomous area governments.

Between 1979 and 1989, China encouraged increased autonomy in designated minority areas and allowed a cultural and religious revival in Han and minority areas alike. This trend towards openness came to an end, however, when the central government decided that cultural, religious and especially political expression was becoming a threat to the unity of the Chinese state. This resulted not only in the 1989 suppression of pro-democracy demonstrators in Tiananmen Square, but also the arrests of alleged separatists in minority Autonomous Regions in the 1990s. Martial law-like conditions were imposed in Tibet and Xinjiang from 1997 onwards as a means of stemming violent protests from separatists. Furthermore, controls on religious expression (see the later section on Religion) were re-introduced for all citizens of China. Still, it can be argued that this hardened minority policy is relatively unchanged since 1949. The government's message to the minorities is clear: as long as you play by our rules and support the Chinese state, we will help you develop and integrate.

To facilitate this development, China has enacted two types of preferential policies towards its National Minorities: university entrance quotas and family policies.

Preferential Policies for National Minorities: Education

China has made great strides in its goal of a universal nine years of education for its citizens, but the introduction of school fees in the 1990s meant that the poorest families no longer could afford to send their children to school. This has affected a disproportionate number of minorities. Still, the number of National Minority schoolchildren and teachers has steadily increased since the 1950s. Ideally, pupils are taught in their native language and Chinese from primary school onwards. In practice, minority-language education is offered only in areas with significant minority populations, and then only if the language has an official writing system: Korean, Uyghur, Tibetan, Mongolian, Yi, and Dai. Even if largely symbolic, this support of minority-language education by the central government far exceeded that of the former Soviet government for its minority languages. It has, in addition, supplied the national minority autonomous areas with large quantities of financial aid and material resources. As a result, the percentage of minority students at tertiary institutions increased between 1978–1992, declining from the mid-1990s onwards after the imposition of university fees.

Nonetheless, interest in bilingual education has waned in recent years, as many minority parents see economic advantages in having their children learn Chinese from an early age. At the tertiary level, minority-region universities have reduced minority-language courses or abandoned them altogether (e.g., Xinjiang University in 2002). Previously, minorities studying in the minority language would attend an extra "preparatory" year of university, but only receive credit for four years; moreover, these students had difficulty finding employment upon graduation.

At the tertiary level, China recognized early on the need to train minority cadres, teachers, and technicians. In 2001, the *Law on Regional Autonomy* was amended to improve recruitment of National Minorities to government positions. From the 1950s, the central government, under the State Ethnic Affairs Commission, established institutes of tertiary education specifically for National Minorities: the Central Nationalities Institute (now University) in Beijing, established in 1951, and twelve regional Nationalities Institutes. These institutions are less prestigious than the national universities.

Despite preferential admissions standards, minorities are underrepresented in the national universities (6 percent at Beijing University, for example). Nonetheless, the use of strategies such as, for example, preferential quotas in Inner Mongolia and differential exam requirements in Xinjiang, was a significant equalizing factor in education, allowing 187,000 minority students to attend postsecondary institutions in 1995–96. The central government views the postsecondary education of minorities as an integral part of the overall economic and cultural development of minority regions: those sent to national universities as ethnic minority classes (*minzu ban*), as well as a number of those at Nationalities Institutes, are required to sign contracts pledging to return to their home region.

Preferential Policies: Family Planning

Preferential policies on marriage and family planning vary from region to region in China. Generally, minorities may marry two years earlier than Han Chinese, for whom the minimum age is 20 for males and 18 for females. Though China implemented a one-child-per-family policy in 1980 to stem its explosive population growth, officially recognized minorities are partially exempt. Those in urban areas have been allowed two children (or three if both are girls or one is disabled); those in rural areas, generally three. In contrast, the Han Chinese are allowed two in rural areas. Violations of these limits result in monetary penalties, which are decided locally. A first violation might cost 1000 *yuan* ($120)—two months' income for the average citizen—whereas a second violation could cost up to ten times that amount. Nonetheless, larger families are common in remote rural areas, due to the need for farm hands and a general preference for male children.

Religion

The dominant religions of China are Daoism, Buddhism, and folk religion. For many minorities, professing a religious belief distinct from that of the Han has been a vital means of maintaining identity.

The PRC government discouraged religion but did not ban it outright, except during the disastrous period of the Cultural Revolution from 1966–78. During that time, most places of worship, whether Buddhist monasteries, Daoist temples, Muslim mosques or Christian churches, were closed or destroyed, and the clergy forced into labor. From 1978 to the early 1990s, religious observance was quietly renewed and expanded by many ethnic groups including the Han; a number of temples, monasteries, mosques, and churches were built or refurbished during this period. From the mid-1990s on, however, increasing political restrictions in minority areas have been accompanied by increasing censure of religion by the central government. Party members have never been allowed to openly practice religion.

Chinese minorities represent a wide spectrum of religious beliefs:

Islam. With 20 million adherents in China, Islam is the largest minority religion. Besides the Chinese-speaking Hui, most are speakers of Turkic languages in western China: Uyghurs, Kazakhs, Kirghiz, Tatar, Uzbek, Salar, some Mongolic groups (Baonan and Dongxiang), and the so-called Tajiks (more accurately Sarikoli and Wakhi).

Buddhism. Most Buddhist minorities, around 1.3 million, are Lamaists (i.e., Tibetan Buddhists). They are overwhelmingly Tibeto-Burman, including Tibetans, Naxi, Mosuo (officially classified as Naxi) and the Mongolic peoples, including Mongols, Dagurs, and the Eastern Yugur. The Dai are primarily Hinayana Buddhists.

Folk Religion. Many ethnic groups have animist practices, at least historically; most of the Altaic peoples, including Turkic, Mongolic, and Manchu-Tungusic speakers, have a long history of employing trance mediums. Those groups still preserving more active animist and shamanist practices include the Mongolic Dagur and Monguor (Tu), the Tungusic Ewenki and Orochen, the Hani, the Naxi, the Mosuo, and some Austronesian groups on Taiwan. In addition, most all minorities within the Chinese cultural sphere of influence practice ancestor worship, including Muslim Chinese.

Polytheism. Polytheism is attributed to a number of minority groups in southwestern and southern China, including the Yao, Yi, Zhuang, and Hani Nationalities. Often, polytheism is comprised of a syncretic system of worship, which includes local elements, Chinese religious elements, and external religious elements. For example, the Hani groups, Tibeto-Burman peoples of Yunnan and Guizhou provinces, are subject to an number of spirits of natural topography and the weather, of heaven and earth, and of the underworld. While Buddhism and Daoism interpreted as Chinese polytheism, have made some inroad, Christianity has had little impact in these regions.

Christianity. Christianity was introduced in waves from the ninth century onwards, although it was adopted by only a few minority group members in China. Presbyterian and Catholic missionaries on Taiwan in the nineteenth century, however, managed to convert up to 70 percent of the indigenous peoples there. In the PRC, Catholic communication with the Vatican is frowned upon.

Judaism. The oldest Jewish community was in Kaifeng, Henan province, where a synagogue and a sizeable population flourished from at least the twelfth century CE until the synagogue's demolition in 1860. These Jews were overwhelmingly assimilated. During the nineteenth century, smaller immigrant Jewish communities existed in Shanghai and Harbin. During the mid-1980s, intellectuals who knew themselves to be descended from Jews near Kaifeng contemplated petitioning for recognition as a Minority Nationality. Such a move was not viewed favorably by the PRC government, and today Chinese Jews, some of whom are relearning traditions of their ancestors, are generally discouraged from publicly discussing their heritage.

Minorities by Geographic Region

National minorities are concentrated on China's peripheries, except for the Muslim Chinese Hui and to a lesser extent the Manchus, who are found throughout China although concentrated in the Northwest and Northeast.

The minorities of North China are traditionally pastoral nomads with hierarchically structured societies. Historically, due to their nomadic life and powers of archery, these nomads regularly established vast but short-lived empires. These included the forerunners of the modern northern Chinese minorities, such as the Huns, Kitan, Jurchen, Mongols, and Manchus.

The Northeast: Manchuria

Northeastern China, which includes Heilongjiang, Jilin, and Liaoning provinces, is part of a temperate forest and taiga ecology that today is a farming area. The western part of Manchuria falls today within the Inner Mongolian region. Though the area today is heavily settled by Han agriculturalists and plays host to China's Rust Belt, it is home to some 20–30 groups and subgroups, many of them Tungusic. The largest of these is the Manchu group (*Manju*, in Chinese *Man*), who ruled China as the foreign Qing dynasty from 1644–1911. By the end of that dynasty, most Manchus were so well integrated into Chinese society that they rapidly lost their language. Today, the Manchu language is virtually extinct, except for a handful of speakers in Manchuria and, significantly, a group who were sent from 1763 to 1765 to western Jungaria, which today is located in the Yili Valley of Xinjiang and known as the Sibe (Ch. *Xibo*, population188,824 in 2000). Though almost all Manchus today speak Chinese, the number of Manchus in the country has soared to 10.7 million in 2000, as people recognize the benefits of preferential minority policies.

The remaining minority population consists of small pockets of Tungusic and Mongolic peoples. The Tungusic groups, who were traditionally reindeer herders, consist of five groups: the Nanay (*Hezhen*, population 4640), including the Nanay, Kili, Ulcha, and Orok groups; the Evenki, including the Orochen (*Elunchun*, population 8196), the Solon (*Ewenke*, population 30,505), and the Negidal groups; and the Udege, including the Oroch, Taz, and Kyakalas. Many of these had extended contact with Mongolic peoples concentrated in western Manchuria: the Khamnigan, Buryat, and Bargut Mongols, as well as Dagur. All of the latter Mongolic speakers except the Dagur (*Dawuer*, 132,394) are officially classified as one Mongolian group *(Menggu*). Up to 900 Khakas (i.e., South Siberian Turkic) are found in Manchuria, although speakers of the language number less than a dozen. Nearly two million Koreans inhabit Manchuria and have limited schooling and media available in their language.

Northern Inner Asia: Inner Mongolia

Mongolic peoples today are found from Outer Mongolia in the north, through Inner Mongolia to the Ordos area of the Yellow River, and westwards to the Jungarian Basin. From the twentieth century onwards, Mongolic peoples have found themselves on two sides of an international border, in China and also in Mongolia, which declared independence in 1921, became the People's Republic of Mongolia in 1924 and had strong ties to the Union of Soviet Socialist Republics (USSR) until democratization in 1989. After 1950, the pastoral Mongolic population became largely sedentarized with the massive influx of Han Chinese farmers, who came to outnumber Mongols 5:1 in most areas. Officially, the arid steppe plateau of the Inner Mongolian Autonomous Region is populated by Mongols (*`Menggu*) including Buryat and Bargu in the northeast, Oyrat in the west and Xinjiang, Alaa in the northwest, Chakhar in central regions, and Khorchin in the south. Desertification due to farming and demographic pressure is a major issue.

Western Inner Asia: Xinjiang

Xinjiang, the New Dominion, or Eastern Turkestan, has long been a crossroads of civilizations due to its oases midway along the arid Silk Route. The 13 recognized Nationalities of the Xinjiang Uygur Autonomous Region are predominantly Turkic peoples. The nomadic or historically nomadic groups including the Kazakh (population 1.25 million in 2000, the Kirghiz (160,000), and the Mongol (Kalmyk Oyrat, 110,000), inhabit the central and northern mountain areas around the Jungarian Basin. The agriculturalists including Uyghur, Uzbek (12,000), and now Han and Muslim Chinese (Hui) inhabit the oases ringing the Tarim Basin in the south, as well as the Yili valley in the west. As in Inner Mongolia, the immigration of Han Chinese in the last 50 years has resulted in a changed demographic, with 38.7 percent of the population of 18 million being Han Chinese, 46.5 percent Uyghur and 14.8 percent other, not including at least one million Chinese troops and approximately 100,000 itinerant laborers. Shortages of arable land and especially water due to this immigration have resulted in widespread unease with Chinese rule, which occasionally turns violent. The PRC's concern that Uyghur separatists will threaten China's territorial integrity has resulted in intensified restrictions on religious organizations, alleging that some are linked with terrorists and Islamic fundamentalists. The vast territory is populated by a number of smaller groups, including Tuvans (who are officially Mongols) in the far north, modern Manchu speakers known as Sibe in the west, and Iranic peoples (Sarikoli and Wakhi) in the southwest, as well as small populations of Russians, Tatars, and Ainus (Abdal who speak a Uyghur-Iranic jargon).

Southern Inner Asia: Greater Tibet

The area that is culturally and geographically Tibetan includes the Tibet Autonomous Region (TAR), western Sichuan, southern Gansu, and Qinghai provinces. It is an arid high plateau populated by nomadic herders and sedentary barley and wheat farmers. Predominant among all ethnic groups of the plateau are varieties of Tibetan Buddhism, which often coexist with folk religions and, along the northern periphery, Islam. The Tibetans proper (Ch. *Zang*) comprise three major dialect-cultural areas: Amdo region in the northeast (population 850,000), Central region near Dbusgtsang, including Lhasa, (1.1 million as of 1990), and Khams region in the east and north (1.5 million as of 1994). The designation *Zang* also includes a number of other unrecognized Tibeto-Burman groups, such as the Atuence, Groma, Nyarong, Gyarong, Deng, Lhomi, Panang, Tseku, and Tinan Lahul. Han immigration to the TAR has not been nearly has dramatic as elsewhere, though the Han population there as of 2000 had increased to 5.9 percent of the population, excluding itinerant merchants and laborers.

On the eastern periphery of the greater region are a number of largely pastoralist Tibeto-Burman speakers, such as the Qiang (Sichuan, population 306,000); Moinba (TAR, Ch. *Menba*, 8923); Lhoba (TAR, 2965) Bogar (southeastern TAR, 3000, classified as Lhoba), and the Nu (northwestern Yunnan, 28,759). One rather newly discovered group, the Guichong of Sichuan, remains unclassified.

Amdo (Northeastern) Tibet also includes other groups whose languages and cultures are heavily influenced by the Amdo Tibetans, such as the Muslim Mongolic-speaking Baonan, the Santa (Ch. *Dongxiang*), the Enger/Shera Yugur (Ch. *Dongbu Yugu*), the Monguor (Ch. *Tu*), and the Turkic-speaking Sari Yugur (Ch. *Xibu Yugu*).

The Southwest

The Chinese Southwest, including Yunnan, Sichuan, Guizhou, and Guangxi provinces, is one of the most ethnically diverse of China. Many Tibeto-Burman peoples live in this area as well as representatives of the major ethnic groups of Southeast Asia: Tai-Kadai, Mon-Khmer, Hmong-Mien, and many numerically smaller groups. The most populous minority groups include the Yi, Miao, Yao, and Zhuang. The area is mountainous, temperate in the north and tropical in the south. Ethnic tourism is popular here, despite the extreme poverty in the southeast of this area.

Tibeto-Burman peoples

The Yi Nationality, a branch of Tibeto-Burman, encompasses a number of ethnic groups and up to 20 languages, which can be broadly classified into six ethnolinguistic regions: the northern standard in Sichuan (Xide); the Nuosu of the Sichuan-Yunnan border; those dialects in central Yunnan (Lipo, Dayao and Nanhua); southeastern Yi in Yunnan (Ahi, Axi, and Sani); southern (Dian-Qian) in Yunnan and Guizhou; and those dialects in western Yunnan (Dongshan and Xishan). Yis today are still aware of their caste origins, which entailed a hierarchy of the aristocratic Black Yi, the former Han-slave White Yi, and recent former slaves.

Independent agriculturalist Nationalities who speak an Yi-group Tibeto-Burman language include the Hani and Lisu. The diverse Hani, known as Akha in Thailand, have a population of 1.44 million as of 2000, including three regional dialects: Ha-Ai, Bi-Kaw, and Hao-Bai. The Lisu, comprising the Anung and Chenung, have a population of 634,912 and live in Yunnan and Sichuan.

The Tibeto-Burman Naxi of northwestern Yunnan, (population 308,839 as of 2000), boast a unique ideographic writing system. The Mosuo (classified as Naxi) practice matrilineal descent and "walking marriage."

A separate branch of the Tibet-Burman languages is represented by Qiang (autonym *Rma*, population 306,072 as of 2000), spoken from northwestern Sichuan to Yunnan. Both pastoralists and agriculturalists, the Qiang have maintained close contact with the Han and Zhuang. The Tibeto-Burman Prmi (Ch. *Pumi*), who live near the Mosuo, number 33,600 and were long considered a branch of the Qiang peoples; they comprise three ethnolinguistic groups: Phzomi, Phzome, Tshomi. These pastoral peoples inhabit northwestern Yunnan and practice both Tibetan Buddhism and polytheism.

The Lahu (453,705, including Na, Ni, Shehleh) are another major subgroup of Tibeto-Burman in Yunnan.

The Bai of Yunnan and Guizhou (population 1.86 million) are difficult to classify, and the three dialects of Dali, Jianchuan, and Bijiang may be separate languages. They are likely a branch of Tibeto-Burman and have had close contact with the Han.

Peoples of the Kachin subgroup include the Achang Nationality (population 27,708) along with the closely related Jingpo (132,143, subgroup Guari and the unrelated Zaiwa) and Drung (*Delong,* 7,426) Nationalities. The Gyarong peoples of northwestern Sichuan, who number at least 230,000 and include the Horpa, Jiarong, Shangzhai, and Guanyinqiao, are officially Tibetan.

One unclassified Himalyish Tibeto-Burman group are the Baima of Yunnan (population 110,000 as of 1995). Finally, on the eastern edge of this region, in Guizhou, Hunan, and Hubei, are the agriculturalist Tujia. This group, though large, is largely assimilated to Han culture.

Tai-Kadai (Zhuang-Dong) peoples

The eponymous Tai (Ch. *Dai*) is a huge group (population 1.16 million) comprising three subgroups: Dailu, Daina, and Daija. They inhabit tropical river valleys and are rice farmers. The northeasternmost extension of Tai culture is represented by the Kam (Ch. *Dong*, population 2.96 million) in Guizhou and Guangxi. Closely related independent Nationalities in Guangxi and Guizhou include the agriculturalist Maonan (population 107,166), Mulam (*Mulao*, population 207,352), and Shui (Sui, population 406,902), and Gelao (580,000). Other unrecognized Tai-Kadai groups include the Buyang (officially Zhuang), Cun (officially Han), and Then (officially Buyi).

China's largest Nationality, which includes the subgroups Gubei and Guibian, is the Zhuang, who live principally in the Guangxi Zhuang Autonomous Region. The Buyi, whose language is closely related to northern Zhuang, are classified as a separate Nationality and found primarily in southern Guizhou.

Mon-Khmer peoples

Most of the Mon-Khmer peoples, part of the larger Austroasiatic family, are farmers. In Yunnan, the Blang (population 91,882) enjoy official recognition and are Theravada Buddhists; other officially recognized Yunnan frontier peoples include the De'ang (Benlong, population 17,935), and the Va (Ch. *Wa* including A-wa, Amok, population 400,000).

Hmong-Mien (Miao-Yao) peoples

The Miao Nationality is closely related to the Hmongs of Southeast Asia, found in Guizhou, Sichuan and Guangxi. Chinese military campaigns against the Miao in the eighteenth and nineteenth centuries resulted in 70 or more subgroups; within China alone, there are seven major ethnolinguistic groups with mutually unintelligible languages: Central (*Chuanqiandian*), Black, Red, White, Azure, Flower, Grass. A closely related group is the Gelao (Guizhou, 580,000)

Yao (population 2.6 million) is another umbrella term for four distinct ethnolinguistic groups; the Biao Min, Kim Mun, Mien, and Yao Min. Yao also includes the Tai-Kadai Yerong people. Mixed hunting, foraging, and agriculture has resulted in their being spread throughout Guangxi, Hunan, Guangdong, Guizhou, and Yunnan.

The Grass Miao (*Cao Miao, Mjiuniang*) and the Tea Mountain Yao (*Chashan Yao, Lakkja*), though classed as Miao-Yao, are linguistically Tai-Kadai speakers.

The Southeast

Though the Southeast is one of the most populous areas of China, the non-Han minority population is scant. The main exceptions are the peoples of Hainan island and the She Nationality in Fujian, Zhejiang, and Guangxi (population 700,000); the latter are related to the Miao but now speak Chinese.

Hainan Island, off the coast of Guangdong province, became a province in 1988. It is home to the Li (1.25 million) including the Jiamao and Hlai, Tai-Kadai languages who are agriculturalists living in tropical forest mountains at the center of Hainan island (Bendi, Qi, Ha languages). Also represented are the Lingao (Ongbe, 500,000) and the Chamic Tsat people (population 4,500). The latter are Muslims, officially of the Hui Nationality.

Taiwan

Taiwan's indigenous peoples, numbering 433,689 in 2002, are Austronesian and boast a 12,000-year history on the island. Though all indigenous peoples on Taiwan are known in the PRC as the Gaoshan Nationality, they comprise the following official indigenous groups: Atayal, Saisiyat, Bunun, Tsou, Paiwan, Rukai, Puyuma, Ami, Shao (newly classified in 2002), and Yami. At least eleven assimilated groups who once lived on the western plains of Taiwan have been subsumed under the cover term *Pingpu*. Those dwelling in the mountains or east coast have better resisted assimilation.

The indigenous peoples of Taiwan (ROC) were formerly called *shanbao* • • "mountain compatriots," but this pejorative term was replaced in 1994 by *yuanzhumin* (• • •), "indigenous peoples." The National Assembly also passed Additional Articles to the ROC Constitution which accorded indigenous people equal legal status, the right to political participation, and "...assistance and encouragement for their education, cultural preservation, social welfare, and business undertakings."

In 1996, the national government established the Council of Aboriginal Affairs; minority rights to participate in educational policies and reforms were guaranteed in the Aboriginal Education Act of 1998. Nine seats in the Legislature are reserved for indigenous peoples. Finally, an aboriginal school of ethnology, the College of Indigenous Studies at Donghuan University, was recently established.

Economy

In late 1978, the Chinese leadership began transititoning the economy from a Soviet-style, centrally planned economy to a more market-oriented system. Whereas the economy operates within strict Communist control, the economic influence of non-state organizations and individual citizens has been steadily increasing. By increasing the authority granted to local officials and small-scale enterprises, China gradually opened its market economy in areas of manufacturing and services, thereby initiating foreign investment and trade.

China had in 2002 a GDP of $5,989 trillion with a per capita income of $4,700. The GDP's composition by sector in 2001 was 15.2 percent agriculture, 51.2 percent industry and construction, and 33.6 percent services. Industries include iron and steel, coal, machine building, armaments, textiles and apparel, petroleum, cement, chemical fertilizers, footwear, toys, food processing, automobiles, consumer electronics, and telecommunications.

The poorest areas of China are Tibet, Gansu, southern Xinjiang, and Guangxi—all largely minority areas. Half of the counties officially listed as the poorest in China are in minority areas; fully 80 percent of those without adequate food and clothing are in minorities. The standard of living for most minorities rose in the 1990s: the average annual income in Autonomous Minority Areas rose from 2,040 to 6,822 *yuan* (402 to 1,653 *yuan* in rural areas, not adjusted for inflation). However, inequalities widened, with the average income of largely Han cities in minority areas being generally six times that of largely minority towns and rural areas (e.g., in Xinjiang, 8,846 *yuan* in the Han oil town of Karamay vs. 1,223 *yuan* in Kashgar).

Some minority areas are rich in natural resources, such as Xinjiang's oil, natural gas, and minerals) or Manchuria's coal. Though local people have indirectly benefited from the infrastructural development such as railroad and highway construction associated with the extraction of these resources, most of the jobs are given to non-minorities, particularly at the management level. The low population density of minority areas is seen as another resource and has lead to the optional subsidized migration and mandatory resettlement of millions of Chinese to Yunnan, Tibet, Xinjiang, and Inner Mongolia. Since 2000, China has actively implemented a plan to develop the Western Regions: Shaanxi, Sichuan, Guizhou, Yunnan, Qinghai, Gansu, and the five Autonomous Regions.

Since the early 1980s, ethnotourism has been an increasingly important part of the minority area economies. The mystiques of the Silk Road, Genghis Khan, and Tibetan Buddhism have drawn overseas and Chinese tourists alike to Xinjiang, Inner Mongolia, and Tibet, respectively. Between 1990–1999, income from foreign tourists rose from 12 to 85.8 million dollars.

AREIENNE DWYER

See also **Buddhists; Korea; Koreans; Mongols; Mongolia; Tibetans**

Further Reading

Barfield, Thomas, *The Perilous Frontier*, Cambridge, Massachusetts: Blackwell, 1989

Brown, Melissa J., editor, *Negotiating Ethnicities in China and Taiwan,* Berkeley: Center for East Asian Studies, 1996

Dreyer, June T., *China's Forty Millions: Minority Nationalities and National Integration in the People's Republic of China*, Harvard University Press, 1976

Fei Xiaotong (Fei Hsiao Tung), *Toward's a People's Anthropology*, Beijing: New World Press, 1981

Goldstein, Melvyn C., *A History of Modern Tibet: The Demise of the Lamaist State*, Berkeley: University of California Press, 1989

Harrell, Stevan, editor, *Cultural Encounters on China's Ethnic Frontiers,* Seattle: University of Washington Press, 1995

Harrell, Stevan, *Ways of Being Ethnic in Southwest China*, Seattle: University of Washington Press, 2001

Heberer, Thomas, *China and Its National Minorities: Autonomy or Assimilation*? M.E. Sharp, 1989

Jachid, Sechen, and Paul Hyer, *Mongolia's Culture and Society,* Boulder: Westview Press, 1979

Janhunen, Juha, *Manchuria: An Ethnic History*, Helsinki: Finno-Ugrian Society, 1996

Mackerras, Colin, *China's Miinorities Integration and Modernization in the Twentieth Century*, Oxford, 1994

Mackerras, Colin, *China's Ethnic Miinorities and Globalisation*, RoutledgeCurzon, 2003

Sautman, Barry, Preferential Policies for Ethnic Minorities in China: The Case of Xinjiang. *Nationalism and Ethnic Politics Special Issue* Spring/Summer Vol 4:1–2: 86–113, 1998

Chinese in Australia

Concise Summary

Location: Australia
Total Population: Unknown, estimated to be over 500 000
Language: English, Cantonese, Mandarin
Religion: Christian, Buddhist

The Chinese have a long and varied history in Australia, dating back to colonial times. Their migration to Australia was due to two distinct factors that occurred over one hundred years apart. Although the target of Australia's discriminatory immigration policies in the early to mid-twentieth century, ongoing Chinese migration to Australia from Hong Kong and other Southeast Asian countries is ensuring the maintenance of a vibrant and dynamic Australian Chinese community.

History

The first organized Chinese group came to Australia as a direct result of the cessation of convict transportation to New South Wales in 1840. The group consisted of 100 men and 20 boys, all peasants from around Canton. These workers were considered to be "temperate, frugal, hard working and law-abiding." A steady stream of Chinese were brought into the country as the supply of cheap convict labor dwindled. The discovery of gold in 1851 led to many of them seeking their fortune on the goldfields. In 1854, there were 2,341 Chinese in Victoria, rising to over 30,000 by 1857 and 38,258 in the Australian colonies in 1861. Their presence led to resentment from European miners who objected to their numbers, their isolation from the rest of the community, their mining methods, their ability to successfully work what were considered unproductive fields, and the fact that they were not European. This resentment erupted into outright hostility in 1860–61, with the worst incident occurring at Lambing Flat in New South Wales, where several thousand Chinese were driven out by a mob of European miners. Similar resentments flared on the Palmer River goldfield in Queensland, where by 1876 some 17,000 Chinese were working. Chinese emigration to Queensland was halted the following year by the introduction of a £10 poll tax on all Chinese entering the colony. By 1887, all the Australian colonies had restrictive Chinese immigration policies.

One of the first laws passed by the new Commonwealth of Australia after its formation in 1901 was the Immigration Restriction Act, designed to keep the Chinese and other non-Europeans out of the country and which resulted in few Chinese entering into Australia until after World War II. This, along with Chinese immigrants returning to China after making their fortunes, resulted in their population declining from a high of 50,000 in 1888, to 17,000 in 1921 and 10,800 in 1933. This population consisted of two distinct groups: the majority were single men working in a variety of rural and urban laboring jobs, including market gardening where they dominated the supply of fresh vegetables in Australian towns. A smaller group consisted of successful Chinese professionals and businessmen, many of whom had married European women.

Postwar Migration

The abandonment of the White Australia Policy (1901–1973) led to a new influx of Chinese immigration, bolstered by several thousand Chinese from Papua New Guinea after that country received independence in 1975, as well as significant numbers of ethnic Chinese from Vietnam following the end of the Vietnam War. These migrants came in search of political and personal security, and, starting in the 1980s, because of family reunions. By 1986 the Chinese population had increased to some 200,000, with 20 percent Australian born, 20 percent from Indochina, 15 percent from Malaysia, 15 percent from China, 13 percent from Honk Kong, and the remainder from Indonesia, East Timor, Singapore, and Papua New Guinea.

A 1985 decision to allow overseas fee paying students into Australia saw large numbers coming from the People's Republic of China (PRC). After the Tiananmen Square crackdown in 1989, Chinese students were allowed to apply for permanent residence, with almost 37,000 taking up this offer by 1996. The 1990s saw an influx of Hong Kong professionals and managers, concerned about the post-1997 handover of their colony to China. Many of these were "astronauts," a term used to describe those families who live in Australia while the husbands continue to reside and work in Hong Kong. By 1999 there were living in Australia 156,000 people born in China and 62,000 born in Hong Kong. 86 percent of all Chinese Australians now live in Sydney, Melbourne, and Brisbane, where there are substantial "Chinatowns."

Society

In 1991, 25 percent of Chinese speakers in Australia described themselves as Christian, with nearly half of those being Catholics, while 13 percent were Buddhist, mainly those from Vietnam and Malaysia. The rest, including the majority of those born in the Peoples Republic of China, claimed no religion. There are presently several Chinese language daily and weekly newspapers published in Sydney and distributed nationally, along with a large number of Chinese associations and organizations catering for specific groups and their interests.

The Chinese are now the second largest non-English speaking ethnic group in Australia, after the Italian community. This has led to widespread community concern over the high level of Asian immigration to Australia. It is unfortunate that this resentment has been successfully exploited by right-wing political groups, most noticeably Pauline Hanson and her One Nation party. Despite this the Chinese have been successful in business, public life, and the professions, especially in the medical field. Among Australians, Chinese food is popular, as are martial arts and traditional Chinese medicine such as acupuncture.

JEREMY HODES

See also **Australia; China; White Australia Policy (1901–1973)**

Further Reading

"Chinese in Australia," in *The Australian Encyclopedia*, 6th edition, Sydney: Australian Geographic, 1996

Choi, C.Y, *Chinese Migration and Settlement in Australia*, Sydney: Sydney University Press, 1975

Inglis, Christine, "Australia," in *The Encyclopedia of Chinese Overseas*, edited by Lynn Pan, Singapore: Archipelago Press, 1998

Rolls, Eric, *Citizens: Flowers and the Wide Sea; Continuing the Epic Story of China's Centuries-old Relationship with Australia*, Brisbane: University of Queensland Press, 1996

Rolls, Eric, *Sojourners: The Epic Story of China's Ccenturies-old Relationship with Australia: Flowers and the Wide Sea*, Brisbane: University of Queensland Press, 1992

Shen, Yuanfang, *Dragon Seed in the Antipodes: Chinese-Australian Autobiographies*, Melbourne: Melbourne University Press, 2001

Chinese-Americans

Capsule Summary:

Location: United States
Total Population: 2,865,232 [as of April 1, 2000.] The number includes mixed-race Chinese numbering 432,647, and Taiwanese (one race, 118,048 and mixed-race, 26,747); Chinese Americans represent (1.02%) of total population in the United States
Main Language: Cantonese (various dialects), English, Mandarin, Taiwanese/Minnan
Religion: Buddhism; Christianity; Islam; Taoism

Chinese-Americans include both foreign-born Chinese and American-born Chinese of various generations who live in the United States. The Chinese were one of the earliest immigrant groups to settle on the American West Coast. Like other racial minorities, they were victims of racial discrimination and scapegoating during periods of economic hardship. They faced prejudice, violence, exclusion, and deportation, and many were forced to retreat to their own social and spatial world—inner-city Chinatowns. The circumstances for Chinese-Americans in the United States changed considerably with the passage of the Immigration and Naturalization Act of 1965. The heterogeneity of contemporary Chinese-Americans reflects their countries of origin, educational attainment, language ability, occupational status, income, and housing tenure, as well as political and ethnic identity. As a result of the changes in population composition, Chinese-American settlement forms and society likewise have changed a great deal over time. Chinese-Americans have made important contributions to the U.S. economy and society.

History

Chinese people began migrating to the United States in large numbers after 1850. In addition to population pressures and natural disasters, heavy taxation, corruption, and oppression by the Qing Dynasty during the nineteenth century caused food shortages, social unrest, and rebellion in China. Many people, especially peasants from the Pearl River Delta area of southern Guangdong Province, boarded boats in a search of survival abroad. Pulled by the Gold Rush and better opportunities in the United States, many of these early Chinese immigrants came as sojourners, hoping to find their fortune, support their families, and eventually return to China. Most were young males who settled on the West Coast, particularly California. These Chinese were recruited to meet the demand for labor for the economic development of the western United States. They worked as manual laborers in mine fields and railway construction sites, or in farming, fishing, and manufacturing. In 1880, the Chinese population of the United States reached 105,000. In California alone, the Chinese accounted for 10 percent of the total population and one quarter of the labor force.

The combination of social tensions and economic competition provoked hatred toward the Chinese. The economic situation worsened after intense stock market speculations in 1872 and a severe drought in 1876, which caused massive business failures and the loss of jobs nationwide. These factors and labor unrest contributed to anti-Chinese violence in several Western states, where arguments that Chinese were inassimilable were deployed by employers and politicians to direct the anger of white laborers against the Chinese. Anti-Chinese sentiment also reflected a deep-rooted racist attitude towards nonwhites by whites claiming superiority over "yellow inferiority." Anti-Chinese sentiment was articulated in federal law with the Page Act, signed on March 3, 1875, which restricted Chinese female immigration on the assumption that most were prostitutes and prevented wives from reuniting with their husbands. On May 6 1882, nationwide anti-Chinese sentiment prompted Congress to pass the Chinese Exclusion Act, the first and the only federal law to exclude a group of people solely based on their race and class. This act barred skilled and unskilled Chinese labor from entering the United States for a period of ten years and prohibited Chinese from becoming naturalized citizens. The Chinese Exclusion Act was revised or renewed in the subsequent years, until 1904 when it was extended indefinitely. A total of 15 anti-Chinese laws were enacted by Congress between 1882 and 1913.

As a result of these restrictive immigration policies, the total Chinese population in the United States fell to less than 62,000 in 1920. Desperate to circumvent the exclusion laws, many Chinese came in the early twentieth century as "paper-sons." Following the 1906 San Francisco earthquake and fire that destroyed official documents, including birth certificates, Chinese seized the opportunity to claim U.S. citizenship via an American birthright or American-born parents. In response, the United States set up a detention center on Angel Island, just offshore in the San Francisco Bay, to ferret out those entering under false pretenses. During 1910–1940, about 50,000 Chinese were confined for weeks, months, or even years, and repeatedly interrogated to determine their fates.

Under the shadow of exclusion and violence, the Chinese changed their economic strategies, residential patterns, and geographical locations in order to cope with the harsh conditions imposed by the host society. They eliminated occupations that directly competed with white labor and turned to businesses that required less capital to start. Thus, Chinese laundries and restaurants constituted the two primary Chinese-owned businesses through World War II. The Chinese left small towns and rural areas and established communities in large cities designed to stimulate social cohesion and ethnic solidarity; these "Chinatowns" dominated Chinese settlement until the 1960s. Chinatowns usually were located in depressed downtown areas, where immigrants lived, worked, and sought to protect themselves from discrimination in American society. Many Chinese opted to leave the hostile West for other parts of the country, including large East Coast cities, where the Chinese population increased and many Chinatowns formed. Chinese exclusion dramatically affected the Chinese-American community. Chinese men were prevented from bringing their wives to the United States and the anti-miscegenation laws forbade lasting relationships with white women, resulting in an extremely unbalanced sex ratio. Chinatowns were communities of male relatives and friends. This demographic situation in turn contributed to Chinatowns' social problems, such as gambling and prostitution. The Chinese were confined within their own world, and traditional Chinese family- and district-based organizations become unofficial rulers of Chinatowns.

The era of Chinese exclusion lasted for a period of 61 years. During World War II, President Franklin D. Roosevelt's Executive Order 8802 in 1941 ended job discrimination in defense-related industries and federal government. This provided Chinese men and women with opportunities to work alongside other racial and ethnic groups and to join the U.S. military, which increased inter-group contacts and opened doors for GIs to become citizens. The Chinese Exclusion Act itself was not repealed until December 17, 1943, after China became a war ally of the United States. However, the Congressional hearings and Roosevelt's correspondence suggest that the repeal was more a measure of bolstering the image of United States and its strategic interests in war than it was motivated by justice for the Chinese. The Repeal Act repealed all exclusion acts against the Chinese passed in previous years and allowed Chinese immigrants to become naturalized citizens; it allowed an annual immigration quota of 105 to China, based on the 1924 Immigration Act, but limited those directly from China or born in China to less than 80. A total of 383 Chinese were admitted into the United States under this immigration category during 1944–1949. The War Brides Act on December 28, 1946 and the Fiancées Act of June 29, 1946 allowed Chinese wives and minor children of American Citizens to enter the United States on a non-quota basis. The two laws resulted in the entry of 5,687 Chinese and reduced the male to female ratio.

The establishment of the People's Republic of China in 1949 and the outbreak of the Korean War in the early 1950s reversed the geopolitical relations between the United States and China and the favorable attitude toward the Chinese in America. The Confession Program (1956–1966) was instituted to allow those Chinese who confessed to immigration authorities that they entered the United States under a fraudulent identity ("paper sons"), to adjust their immigration status and to bring their families to United States. A total of 13,897 Chinese confessed in the ten-year period under this program. This same program, a product of McCarthy era, was also used to tightly control the Chinese community through suspicion, stress, and anxiety, in an effort to expose so-called red agents and Red China sympathizers. Fueled by the anti-Communist fervor, the China Area Aid Act assisted the 3,610 Chinese students and scholars who were enrolled in the U.S. colleges and universities to establish residency after their graduation. Among the individuals who established residency under this program were Nobel Physics Laureates T.C.Lee (*Li, Zhengdao*) and C.N.Yang (*Yang, Zhenning*). Other Chinese immigrants, political refugees, merchants, professionals, and former diplomats, also found refuge in the United States. The influx of these highly educated and elite immigrants—the twentieth-century version of the Chinese "forty-niners"—altered the composition of the Chinese population in the United States. Unlike the nineteenth-century Chinese "forty-niners" who were largely laborers, these new immigrants were the elite of Chinese society and came to the United States to stay. They were the first generation of Chinese immigrants who brought fortunes with them and lived outside of Chinatowns, becoming the predecessors of contemporary suburban-bound immigrants. After World War II, both longtime Chinese immigrants with savings and new Chinese immigrants with financial resources could afford, and were allowed, to move to suburban areas previously almost exclusively reserved for white Americans. Chinatowns in large metropolitan areas experienced moderate growth primarily due to increasing native-born generations while the ones in smaller cities declined as a result of later generations moving out during the first two decades after WWII.

Contemporary Society (since 1965)

Immigration and Diversity

The Chinese-American community after 1965 exhibited pronounced ethnic and class distinctions that fragmented the population politically. The 1965 Immigration and Naturalization Law, which allocated 80 percent of all visas to family reunification, was a landmark for Chinese American society. For the first time in history, the Chinese were allowed to enter without the restrictions of the earlier quotas; however, there was a limitation of 170,000 immigration visas for people from the eastern hemisphere per year and a 20,000 per year limit per country. The end of the Vietnam War and the subsequent 1980 Refugee Act brought in large number of refugees from Vietnam, Laos, and Cambodia, many of whom were ethnic Chinese who had lived in Southeast Asia for generations. The Immigration and Nationality Act of 1990 tripled the ceiling on employment-based visas and created a new investor visa category (EB-5) which further prompted the unprecedented growth of highly skilled or wealthy immigrants from the Chinese diaspora countries (Indonesia, Malaysia, Myanmar, Philippines, Singapore, Thailand,

and Vietnam) to the United States. The 1992 Chinese Student Protection Act granted permanent residency for China nationals who resided in the United States from June 4, 1989 to July 11, 1990, in order to protect students from persecution in China following the student protests in Tiananmen Square and the subsequent government crackdown. Some 100,000 Chinese reportedly adjusted their legal status under this law, many of whom are a new generation of Chinese students and scholars enrolling in American universities and colleges on F-1 or J-1 visas at the time. Additionally, a number of Chinese hold H-1B non-immigrant visas, a program designed for those temporary workers employed in specialty occupations that require highly specialized knowledge and at least a bachelor's degree or its equivalent. H-1B visa holders are allowed to bring families and are eligible to adjust their legal status to permanent residents during their six-year maximum visa period. The number of people with these visas increased dramatically in the 1990s and early 2000s as the U. S. Congress repeatedly increased the quotas. Spurred by the increase in quotas, the numbers of Chinese immigrants have been consistently higher than those of native-born Chinese Americans in the last three decades. Three-quarters of the 1,825,285 foreign-born Chinese in 2000 came during last two decades—42 percent in the 1990s alone. The total Chinese population in the United States almost doubled in every decade from 1950 to 1990 and increased another 73.8 percent in the 1990s, while maintaining a relatively balanced sex ratio.

Although native-born Chinese Americans have traditionally enjoyed higher socio-economic profiles compared to either their foreign-born counterparts or U.S. population in general, the profiles of Chinese immigrants have changed drastically since 1965. Unlike the traditional, "old immigrants" who came primarily from Guangdong Province, the new immigrants come from various geographic areas, including mainland China, Hong Kong, Taiwan, Southeast Asia, and other parts of the world. They speak a wide range of dialects and possess an overall higher level of education, English language knowledge, and job skills. As a result, the current socio-economic diversity among Chinese Americans, regardless of place of birth, is unprecedented. Chinese have a high rate of self-employment; they own businesses ranging from restaurants or retail stores to large international trade corporations or professional services. Some Chinese, however, are trapped in the low-paying ethnic economy due to a lack of job skills or transferable human capital. Many undocumented immigrants are at the bottom of the socio-economic ladder. In 2000, 68 percent of all Chinese immigrants five years or older whose native language is not English reported a good command of spoken English. On the other hand, about one third of all 907,380 Chinese American households considered themselves linguistically isolated, with no one 14 years or older in the household speaking English only or fluently. While 22.2 percent of all Chinese Americans 25 years or older did not graduate from high school, another 22.7 percent possessed a professional or graduate degree, although women are less likely to gain an advanced degree, with only 18 percent in the same category having advanced degrees. Chinese Americans have higher income levels compared to the nation as a whole: $51,119 v $41,994 for household income and $22,519 v $21,587 for per capita income in 1999 respectively; though women again trail men in their annual income. Their overall high income level derives from multiple workers per household and high-paying occupations; more than half of all civilian Chinese American employees 16-year or older occupy management or professional positions. However, 13.2 percent of Chinese Americans live below the federal poverty line more than two thirds of whom are immigrants, and 3.5 percent receive some public assistance income. While 57.8 percent of Chinese American households have achieved their "American dream" by owning their homes, those who rent, in contrast, struggle economically. 21 percent of all renters spend more than half of their monthly household income on rent alone, compared to only 12 percent of owners who spend a similar percentage for housing, and renters cannot enjoy tax relief. Some suffer crowded living conditions as more than 60 percent of renter households live in an apartment with no bedroom at all or just one bedroom.

Settlement and Community

Chinese Americans are an urban-bound population: almost 98 percent of them live in urban areas in 2000, compared to 79 percent nationwide. They tend to concentrate in several states: California, New York, Hawaii, Illinois, Texas, and major metropolitan areas such as San Francisco, Los Angeles, New York, and Chicago, among others. However, the last decade has witnessed the increase of Chinese-Americans in non-traditional gateway cities such as Seattle, Atlanta, and Northern New Jersey, much of which relates to high-tech development. Chinese-Americans, both recent immigrants and native-born, are also highly mobile: 51 percent of them moved between 1995 and 2000.

One of the important changes in Chinese-American settlement patterns and community forms has been increasing suburbanization. While inner-city Chinatowns traditionally dominated Chinese settlement, the dramatic increase in immigration since 1965 means that congested, small, downtown Chinatowns are no longer able to house all the new immigrants. A smaller proportion of Chinese continue to live in Chinatowns, mainly the elderly and the poorer of the new immigrants. Many Chinatowns have been transformed from traditional ethnic ghettos or enclaves to sites for international investment and urban renewal efforts. In recent decades, many of the better-off Chinese move to suburbs for better housing and neighborhoods, some becoming spatially dispersed and socio-economically assimilated into the mainstream society. However, the Chinese communities in the suburbs of some large metropolitan areas, such as Los Angeles, Chicago, Houston, New York, San Francisco, and Washington D.C. have become more relatively concentrated. Increasingly, new immigrants directly settle in suburban areas and never experience living in an American urban center. This diverse mix of suburban-bound immigrants includes wealthy people bringing cash as well as poor, unskilled, or undocumented workers. As a result, a new form of ethnic settlement called the ethnoburb—multi-ethnic suburb—has arisen in some large metropolitan areas, especially in those global cities that have pre-existing ethnic concentrations. Contemporary Chinese settlements thus occupy a spectrum ranging from Chinatowns and ethnoburbs, along with other dispersed forms of Chinese communities linked primarily by socio-cultural activities and organizations. While some traditional Chinese community organizations remain active and strong, their impact diminishes rapidly beyond Chinatown boundaries, although some new city- or state-based organizations among recent immigrants have emerged in many large metropolitan areas. In the meantime, various forms of professional or service organizations have gained ground in community affairs.

Identity and Contribution

Chinese-Americans have been integral to the American national community. Even during the exclusion era, Chinese immigrants used legal tools to protect their rights. Chinese Americans joined the Civil Rights Movement in the 1960s, raising awareness about their identity as racialized minorities and seeking justice. Chinese American Studies has since become an important part of Ethnic Studies programs in universities and colleges, and some K–12 programs also incorporate the contributions of Chinese-Americans in their curricula. Prominent Chinese Americans figures, including Taiwanese Americans, are known to the country and abroad: in politics alone, noteworthy figures include Secretary of Labor Elaine Chao, the first Chinese American appointed to a cabinet level position; two-term Governor of Washington Gary Locke; and two-term Oregon Congressman David Wu. Other significant figures include I.M. Pei and Maya Lin (architecture); Nobel Laureates Steve Chu and Yuen T. Lee; Ang Lee, Bruce Lee, Yo Yo Ma, and Anna May Wong (arts); Maxine Hong Kingston, Ha Jin, and Amy Tan (literature); Michelle Kwan and Michael Chang (sports). Millions of Chinese-Americans contribute to the American economy and society as entrepreneurs, laborers, professionals, consumers, and taxpayers.

Despite their contributions, Chinese-Americans still face obstacles in American society. In particular, when the United States and China encounter conflicts of interests in the international arena regarding as trade or geopolitical alliances, Chinese-Americans face hostility or even violence, and their loyalty is often questioned—even though many are native-born or naturalized American citizens; 92 percent of all Chinese immigrants who arrived before 1980 were U.S. citizens by 2000, along with 69 percent of those who came during the 1980s and 18 percent of those who arrived in the 1990s. The 1982 beating death of U.S.-born citizen Vincent Chin and the 1999 wrongful charge of espionage against Taiwan-born nuclear scientist Wen Ho Lee are just two examples.

As in the case of some other ethnic groups, many Chinese-Americans actively seek to pass on their cultural traditions to later generations and promote their cultural heritage in American society by operating Chinese language schools, cultural lessons, Chinese newspapers, radio, and television stations, and by holding Chinese festivals. Some first-generation adult immigrants feel nostalgia toward their countries of origin and passionately care about the situations there. Such endeavors, however, should not undermine their contributions and commitments to the United States, although there is room for further mutual understanding and educational efforts. With the globalizing economy and society, increasing international flows of population, goods, financial resources and information, and the rise of China's stature in the global economy and world affairs, transnational connections and identities have become a way of life for many people, and they pose both opportunities and challenges in the era of globalization.

In summary, sixty years after the repeal of Chinese Exclusion laws, Chinese-Americans have made tremendous progress in gaining economic justice and political representation in the United States. However, there is still a long way to go before Chinese-Americans will be fully accepted as truly equal participants in American society. With increasing immigration and growing native-born generations, Chinese Americans will continue seeking equity and civil rights, while contributing to the peace and prosperity of the United States, their countries of origins and the rest of the world.

WEI LI

See also **Assimilation; China**

Further Reading

Chan, Sucheng, editor, *Entry Denied: Exclusion and the Chinese Community in America 1882–1943,* Philadelphia, Pennsylvania: Temple University Press, 1991

Dirlik, Arif, and Macolm Yeung, *Chinese in American Frontier,* Colorado Springs, Coloardo: Rowman and Littlefields, 2003

Fan, Cindy, "Chinese Americans: Immigration, Settlement, and Social Geography," in *The Chinese Diaspora, Space, Place, Mobility, and Identity,* edited by Laurence J.C. Ma and Carolyn Cartier, Lanham, Maryland: Rowman & Littlefield Publishers, 2002

Fong, Timonthy, *The First Suburban Chinatown: The Remaking of Monterey Park, California*, Philadelphia, Pennsylvania: Temple University Press, 1994

Kwong, Peter, *The New Chinatown,* Revised Edition, New York: Hill and Wang, 1996

Lee, Erika, *At America's Gates: Chinese Immigration during the Exclusion Era 1882–1943,* Chapel Hill: The University of North Carolina Press, 2003

Li, Wei, "Anatomy of a New Ethnic Settlement: The Chinese *Ethnoburb* in Los Angeles," *Urban Studies,* 35, no. 3, 1998

Lin, Jan, *Reconstructing Chinatown Ethnic Enclave, Global Change*, Minneapolis: University of Minnesota Press, 1998

Peffer, George Anthony, *If They Don't Bring Their Women Here: Chinese Female Immigration before Exclusion,* Urbana and Chicago: University of Illinois Press, 1999

Saito, Leland T., *Race and Politics: Asian Americans, Latinos, and Whites in a Los Angeles Suburb,* Urbana and Chicago: University of Illinois Press, 1998

Wong, Kevin Scott, and Sucheng Chan, editors, *Claiming America: Constructing Chinese American Identities during the Exclusion Era*, Philadelphia, Pennsylvania: Temple University Press, 1998

Yung, Judy, *Unbound Feet: A Social History of Chinese Women in San Francisco,* Berkeley: University of California Press, 1995

Zhao, Xiaojian, *Remaking Chinese America, Immigration, Family, and Community, 1940–1965,* New Brunswick, New Jersey: Rutgers University Press, 2002

Zhou, Min, *Chinatown: The Socioeconomic Potential of an Urban Enclave,* Philadelphia, Pennsylavania: Temple University Press, 1992

Zhou, Min, "Chinese: Once Excluded, Now Ascendant" in *New Face of Asian Pacific America,* San Francisco, California: Asian Week 2003

Chittagong Hill Tribes

Capsule Summary

Location: The Chittagong Hill Tracts in southeast Bangladesh.
Total Population: approximately 830,000 (0.6% of the country population).
Language: Chakma, Marma and other tribal languages.
Religion: Buddhist.

The Chittagong Hill Tracts (CHT) region spans 5,093 square miles (13,191 square kilometers) in southeast Bangladesh and borders tribal areas in neighboring India and Burma (Myanmar). This region comprises only 10 percent of resource-poor Bangladesh's territory, but it contains significant natural gas deposits, and its dense vegetation and tropical rainforests make up 60 percent of the country's reserve forests. The indigenous inhabitants are collectively referred to as the Chittagong Hill Tribes, Chakmas, or Jummas. The Chakmas are the largest of the 13 tribes, comprising almost half of the tribal population. The term *Jummas* refers to the tribals' historical occupation, slash and burn cultivation.

The Chittagong Hill Tribes entered Bangladesh from Burma in three waves beginning in the fiteenth century. Historically, the tribals have violently opposed encroachments on their territories. Following protracted warfare with the mid-seventeenth century Mughal empire, the Chittagong tribals were able to retain local autonomy in return for paying taxes. Incorporation in the British Indian Empire was resisted until 1860. When India and Pakistan became independent in 1947, the Chittagong Hill Tracts was included in Muslim-majority East Pakistan despite the residents' desire to establish a confederation of northeastern tribal states.

From 1900 to the late 1950s, enforced isolation through legislation which declared the CHT a protected and excluded area, coupled with the region's remote location, allowed the tribals to maintain their local customs with minimal external involvement. The early 1960s marked a turning point as the Pakistani government eliminated the region's special status, opening the door to immigration and economic exploitation.

The massive Kaptai hydroelectric project, completed in 1963 in the Chittagong Hill Tracts, generated much resentment among the tribals. Some 40 percent of the region's total arable land was lost and one-forth of the population, around 100,000 tribals, was displaced. Of these, some 60,000 received no compensation while the remainder crossed into India as they could no longer engage in agriculture, the source of their livelihood. The benefits of the Kaptai dam were primarily reaped by the plains-dwelling Bengalis.

Bangladesh is one of the world's most densely populated countries. Since the 1960s, successive administrations attempted to relieve this stress by promoting immigration to the sparsely occupied Chittagong Hill Tracts. Tribal fears of being overwhelmed by influxes of Bengali settlers appear to have been realized by the 1980s. In 1951, tribals constituted 91 percent of the CHT's population; by the mid-1980s, Bengalis were reportedly 50 percent or more of the hill tracts' population.

In 1972, a year after Bangladesh seceded from Pakistan, tribal leaders led by Manabendra Narayan Larma sought to obtain autonomy for the hill tracts. Their attempts were rejected by Prime Minister Sheikh Mujibur Rahman, the leader of Bangladesh's independence movement. Larma and his brother Shantu subsequently formed a political organization, the CHT United People's Party (the PCJSS), to press for tribal demands. An armed wing called the Shanti Bahini or Peace Force was also assembled, primarily as a self-defense organization in response to violent attacks and land expropriations by Bengali settlers.

Throughout the 1970s and 1980s, tribal grievances about immigration into the CHT, their limited access to the benefits of economic development, a desire to preserve tribal ways of life, and demands for autonomy were rejected by successive Bangladeshi military governments. Further, Bengali attacks against tribals were not addressed. In the mid-1970s, the Shanti Bahini responded by engaging in armed attacks against both Bengali settlers and state authorities. Other tribal organizations sought redress through demonstrations and strikes. In 1986, violence between tribals and Bengali settlers led some 50,000 Chakmas to flee to neighboring India and to the permanent deployment of the army in the CHT. Relations between India and Bangladesh also deteriorated due to the refugee situation and reciprocal accusations of support to each other's domestic insurgencies.

Bangladesh's military regime attempted to address some tribal grievances in 1989 by creating three semi-autonomous districts in the Hill Tracts. These districts were to be governed by tribal councils which would exercise control of the region's land and resources. Tribal leaders rejected these local councils, pressing for greater autonomy. Meanwhile, violent attacks by the Shanti Bahini, Bengali settlers, and the state's security forces continued. In April 1992, for instance, in what is referred to as the Logong Massacre, several hundred tribals were killed by Bengali settlers.

Periodic talks between the PCJSS and the government had occurred since the mid-1980s, but Bangladesh's return to democratic rule in 1992 helped provide the impetus for periodic cease-fires. The negotiations, however, continually stalled on the issues of limiting Bengali immigration to the hill tracts, the return of the Chakma refugees still residing in India, and the provision of autonomy.

In 1996, Sheikh Hasina, the daughter of the country's first leader, became Prime Minister, promising to end the continuing insurgency in the CHT. Following seven rounds of talks between government representatives and the PCJSS, a peace accord was signed in December of 1997. By this time, the Shanti Bahini was a depleted force and the region's population was weary of more than two decades of warfare that has claimed more than 25,000 lives.

The peace agreement provides for the Chittagong Hill Tracts to be governed by a regional council, two-thirds of which are tribal members. The council is to maintain responsibility for public administration, law and order, and promoting the region's development, including monitoring the sale of land to non-tribals. The accord allows Bengalis residing in the CHT to remain in the region. In early 1998, the Shanti Bahini disbanded and its political wing, the PCJSS, became a political party. Around 60,000 Chakmas returned from refugee camps in India and the withdrawal of the army and paramilitary forces from the CHT is underway.

Some Bangladeshi political parties oppose the peace agreement, arguing that it limits the country's sovereignty. A minority of tribal organizations also rejects the accord asserting that it does not provide genuine autonomy. Whether violent conflict erupts again will likely depend on whether the agreement is fully implemented, including the provision of economic benefits for the marginalized Chittagong Hill Tribes.

DEEPA KHOSLA

See also **Bangladesh; India**

Further Reading

Ali, S. Mahmud, *The Fearful State: Power, People and Internal War in South Asia,* London and New Jersey: Zed Books, 1993

Amnesty International, *Bangladesh: Human Rights in the Chittagong Hill Tracts,* London: Amnesty International, 2000

Anti-Slavery Society, *The Chittagong Hill Tracts, Militarization, Oppression and the Hill Tribes,* London: Anti-Slavery Society, 1984

Bhaumik, Subir, Meghna Guhathakurta, Sabyasachi Basu Ray Chaudhury, *Living on the Edge: Essays on the Chittagong Hill Tracts,* Calcutta: South Asia Forum for Human Rights, 1997

CHT Commission, *Life Is Not Ours': Land and Human Rights in the CHT Bangladesh,* Copenhagen and Amsterdam: Chittagong Hill Tracts Commission, 1991

Levene, Mark, "The Chittagong Hill Tracts: A Case Study in the Political Economy of 'Creeping' Genocide," *Third World Quarterly,* 20, no.2 (1999)

Minorities at Risk Project Web site, Center for International Development and Conflict Management, University of Maryland, <http://www.bsos.umd.edu/cidcm/mar>

Rashiduzzaman, M., "Bangladesh's Chittagong Hill Tracts Peace Accord," *Asian Survey,* 38, no. 7 (1998)

Talukdar, S. P., *Chakmas: An Embattled Tribe,* New Delhi: Uppal Publishing House, 1994

Christians: Overview

Capsule Summary

Location: Originated in the Middle East but spread around the globe.
Total Population: In excess of 400,000,000
Languages: Not confined to any in particular but in early developments Latin & Greek

Origins

Christian was the name first given to the followers of Jesus Christ, the founder of Christianity, and is recorded Acts of the Apostles (in the New Testament, xii, 26) as such at Antioch in the year 43 CE. In the Hebrew or Jewish Scriptures known as the Old Testament, the word Christ meant *the Messiah*, a meaning it shared in Greek; therefore the Jews did not refer to the early Christians as "the disciples of the Messiah," but to the "Nazarenes" or "Galileans." Indeed the word *Christian* was used in a derogatory way in early Roman writers such as Cornelius Tacitus (circa 56–120 CE). Throughout history the term *Christian* has been used generally to include those who follow the teachings of Jesus and profess faith in him, but in particular, the term encompasses those who have been baptized in the name of Jesus.

In his brief ministry, his execution on a cross, and reports of his resurrection from the dead, Jesus attracted little immediate attention outside the small troubled Roman province of Palestine where the events of his life took place. His original following of twelve apostles and their disciples traveled preaching his message and the four evangelists, Matthew, Mark, Luke, and John wrote of his life and teachings in their Gospels which became the basis of the New Testament. Therefore the sacred scriptures of the new religion grew naturally out of Judaism as the life and teachings of Jesus were seen to be the fulfillment of the Old Testament prophecies and Jesus as the Messiah sent by God as promised to Abraham. Others saw him as another Jewish Rabbi reinterpreting the traditions of the Jewish law and indeed, others saw him as a rebel leader in the fight against Rome. However, sects such as the Zealots were disappointed in Jesus as such a leader because of his teaching of non-resistance, while the Pharisees and Saducees rejected his teachings outright. The early Christians lived at a time and in a nation buoyed up with the hopes of a Messiah or Deliverer and into a world pervaded by supernatural beliefs. Jewish history after all provided much evidence of the power of the prophets to perform miracles as a manifestation of the divine will of God; both orthodox Judaism and the early Christians anchored their faith in the belief that God was related to his people by the covenant with Abraham.

The Rise of Christianity

During the first few centuries following the death of Jesus Christ, his followers spread his teaching with phenomenal rapidity throughout the Greco-Roman world. What had been a small local movement among other competing sects within Judaism now became a far- reaching group of communities among many different peoples of every social and intellectual class and well organized and with a distinctive worship of one God. In less than three centuries after Jesus's crucifixion, his followers, despite persecution, had established Christianity as the official religion of the Roman Empire. It is of interest that when Paul, the greatest of all Christian missionaries, first visited Rome he found a community of Christians. Several factors assisted the spread of the Christian communities. The synagogues throughout the Roman empire provided Paul and others with a port of entry to make converts among the Hellenized Jews; also Hellenistic Greek was the common language from Italy to India and was the language used by Paul in his letters which form part of the New Testament. Following Caesar and Octavian's conquests the vast Roman empire enjoyed a period of peace—the *pax romana*—which lasted for about three centuries. The ease with which Greek philosophical thought, especially Platonism, adapted to the new and powerfully ethical religion made a strong appeal to the intellectual leadership of the times. In time, Christians became distanced and distinct from the worlds of paganism and ritualistic Judaism. Paul spelled out the basis of a new world order : "There is neither Jew nor Greek, there is neither slave nor free, there is neither male or female, for you are all one in Christ Jesus."

Christians have sustained three characteristic beliefs for over two thousand years. These include the belief that Jesus gave a new law to fulfill the law of Moses; that his death was a redemptive sacrifice for all such that he was the universal savior atoning for the sins of mankind; and thirdly the belief in the union of the spirit and human in the person (embodiment) of Jesus Christ. In a slightly later theology, Christians commemorated Jesus's Last Supper, sufferings, and death in the *Eucharist*, referred to in the Mass as a repetition of the second of these, the original redemptive sacrifice.

The spread of Christianity throughout Europe became a cohesive force in the history of western culture and society, through the establishment of its churches, the founding of monastic orders, missionary activity based on Jesus's commission to his followers to "Go forth and teach all nations…,"and in the intellectual developments of the nascent universities—as well as periodic clashes with the secular authority. The experience of Christians left an indelible impression not only on purely religious developments but on virtually every endeavor in art, literature, science, law, politics, and economics; in a global sense it would be difficult to find minorities not touched in some way by the Christian cultural legacy.

John McGurk

***See also* Christians: Africa; Christians: Asia; Christians; Coptic Christians**

Further Reading

Ayerst, D., and A.S.T. Fisher, *Records of Christianity,* Oxford: B.Blackwell, 1977

Bainton, R.H., *A History of Christianity,* Reprint Society, 1966

Brownrigg, R., *Who's Who in the New Testament,* 1986

Cohn-Sherbok, L., *Who's Who in Christianity,* New York: Routledge, 1998

Livingstone, E.A., editor, *The Oxford Dictionary of the Christian Church,* revised edition 1997

McGrath, A.E., editor, *The Blackwell Encyclopaedia of Modern Christian Thought,* 1993

Walsh, M. ed. *A Dictionary of Christian Biography,* Oxford: Oxford University Press, forthcoming

Christians: Africa

Capsule Summary

Location: Africa
Total Population: 393 million as of 2000
Languages: African and European
Religion: Christianity

Christians is the general name for followers of the system of religious belief and practices taught by Jesus Christ. Christians declare a belief in Jesus as God incarnated and follow a faith based on Jesus' teachings. The early church experienced schisms and heresy due to doctrinal differences—that is, different interpretations of what Jesus' teaching really meant. As a result, several distinct groups of Christians developed within the first centuries of the religion. African voices were powerful in the formulation of the doctrines, policy, liturgy, and ethics of early Christianity.

The African Christian population grew from 10 million in 1900 to 393 million in 2000 (Isichei 1995, 1). It has been estimated that by the middle of the twenty-first century more than one-third of the world's Christians will live in Africa.

Egypt and North Africa

It is not certain when Christianity first made inroads into Egypt and the Maghreb. Northern Africa, however, provided some of the earliest intellectual framework of Christian theology. Egypt, particularly the city of Alexandria, was an important center of the new religion in the first century CE. According to traditions of the Coptic Orthodox church, the apostles Thomas and Mark the Evangelist were in Egypt during the persecution of the early church. The See of Alexandria was said to have been founded by Mark (Sundkler and Steed, 2000, 9). By this period, Egypt was acquainted with the events of Pentecost and Passover, the work of John the Baptist, and the life and work of Jesus (Youssef and Sawyer, 2004). Egypt and Cyrene are mentioned in the New Testament. The flow of faithful diasporic Jews provides one likely route of diffusion for the story of Jesus. There were a few Christians in Egypt around the year 239, and their numbers grew at a significant rate from 274 on (Kalu, 2004).

As noted above, the early church was divided in fundamental beliefs and concepts. Alexandria and Antioch constituted the dominant competing schools in Christian theological debates. The Alexandria school was very important and influential in early Christian thought; in particular, Gnosticism (from the Greek *gnosis*, knowledge), which emerged there, was an early challenge to orthodox Christianity. Gnostics drew extensively on Neoplatonism, and the Gnostic tradition is an indication of the diversity of voices in early Egyptian Christianity. Gnosticism was rooted in widely eclectic sources and many religious traditions. It was part of the Pauline polemic found in the New Testament and more broadly in many noncanonical sources (King, 2003). Various forms of Gnosticism and several Gnostic schools throve in Egypt and attracted followers. The Gnostics believed that there was no original sin but that the world was inherently evil, and that the secret knowledge passed down from Paul was the route to salvation. All Gnostic thought was rooted in a central dualism that questioned the goodness of material creation and the redemption of the material realm. Gnostics believed that material existence accounted for the fall of humanity from a spiritual realm into the bondage of substance, but humanity could return to the spiritual realm by receiving secret, esoteric knowledge. Gnostics believed that the "true interpretation of human identity and destiny was hidden from everyone except the Gnostics" (Youssef and Sawyer).

Not everyone accepted the Gnostics' interpretation of Christianity and the universe. Nevertheless, opponents of Gnosticism such as Irenaeus and Hippolytus preserved much of what was known of Gnostic groups until the relatively recent discoveries of ancient texts. The Gospel of the Egyptians, the Gospel of the Hebrews, and the Epistle of Barnabas indicate aspects of Gnostic Egyptian Christianity (Youssef and Sawyer). Alexandria's apologists such as Pantaneus, Origen, and Dionysius used both allegory and creative syncretism to interpret the Christian faith and to grapple with the fundamental discords that perplexed the Christian community.

Another major faction of early Christianity was centered in Rome. This faction was very much influenced by the apostle Paul, whose teachings became prominent in the fourth century when the Roman empire officially became Christian. The Roman faction, recognizing the importance of a sacred text, collected writings by early Christians that became the New Testament and were proclaimed to have been spiritually inspired by God. The Roman faction used the New Testament to solidify its control over Christianity and rejected as heresy all other writings about the life and teachings of Jesus, including those based on the Gnostic tradition.

From about the third century on, the divisions that developed in early Christianity gave the church in North Africa a distinctive character. The emergence of monasticism in Egypt was part of a larger process of developing identity and spirituality as Christianity gained prominence in the Mediterranean world. The Egyptian context was reinforced by social dislocation, particularly as Roman oppression intensified. Thus Egyptian belief became the religion of dissent against the expanding Roman empire. It was also used for social advancement as monasticism developed. In this milieu, Christianity became less interested in eschatology and more attentive to evangelism and faithfulness. The bishops of Alexandria forged alliances within monasticism, sometimes breaking with tradition.

This monasticism was nonecclesial or explicitly antiecclesial in outlook and organization. Saint Anthony of Egypt (circa 251–356) and many laypeople went to desolate places to seek God through individual piety. The "story of the unordained, unlettered, unsophisticated came to speak for generations of Egyptian Christians and all those who yearned for holiness" (Youssef and Sawyer). Communal monasticism, which was favored by Pachomius (circa 290–346), regulated the life of its adherents to guard against fraud, self-delusion, and dissipation. The holy men and women who went to the wilderness or sequestered themselves attracted pilgrims from Rome and beyond, and the monastic communities became deeply involved in the theological discourse of the time and shaped the theological debates that in turn shaped Egyptian Christianity. By the beginning of the fourth century, monastic groups had gained some degree of independence, although they remained under the influence of bishops.

From the third century on, the use of the Coptic language by most monastic communities and by many individuals in the faith also gave Egyptian Christianity a unique identity. The New Testament was translated into the four dialects of Coptic—Bohairic, Sahidic, Akhmimic, and Fayumic—and this vernacular aspect of the Egyptian monastic tradition helped to preserve it.

Despite the repression of the Gnostics by the Romans, Christianity continued to flourish throughout North Africa until the arrival of Islam in the seventh century. By then, the Coptic Orthodox church had lost touch with most of the Gnostic influence, although the Coptic faithful, like the Gnostics, placed a great deal of emphasis on contemplation and monastism. The Coptic church, headed by a patriarch in Alexandria, was similar to the church of Rome in that it had the same sacraments and was made up of priests and bishops. Coptic Christians continued a small but important segment of Egyptian society after the Arab Muslims took over. Today, Coptic Christians are approximately 15 percent of the Egyptian population.

Nubia

Historically, Nubia has roots in the era of the Egyptian pharaohs. Cultural interaction between Egypt and Nubia led to the introduction of Christianity. There is archaeological evidence that a church existed at Farah in the fourth century. The evangelistic bishops of Philae "must have introduced the Hebrew Bible and Christianity into Nubia and many who escaped from various persecutions took their Christianity down the Nile" (Kalu). By the seventh century, Christianity was entrenched in Nubia: the rulers of Nubia and most Nubians had converted to it.

In practice and structure, the Nubian church was similar to the Coptic Orthodox church in Egypt. Egyptian influence continued as the patriarch of Alexandria supplied the leadership and personnel: monks from Egypt and Syria (Kalu). Muslim Arab traders arrived in Nubia in the eighth century and lived in harmony with the Nubian Christians until the fifteenth century. Over time, though, the Nubian ruling class converted to Islam, and the Muslims gradually dismantled certain aspects of African Christianity. By the sixteenth century, the majority of Nubians were Muslims, and Christianity declined.

Aksum (Ethiopia)

Modern Ethiopia is historically connected to the kingdom of Aksum. Aksum became a predominately Christian nation about the same time that the Roman empire officially became Christian: in the fourth century, the rulers of Aksum converted to Christianity after Christian travelers and traders brought the religion into the area from Egypt and western Asia. Eventually a distinctly Ethiopian form of Christianity developed. By the time Islam was introduced into this region of northeast Africa in the eighth century, Christianity was embedded in the Ethiopian state and in Ethoipisn society and culture. While Nubia to the northwest of Aksum and the coastal areas to the east of Aksum gradually converted to Islam, Aksum remained Christian despite periodic attacks by Muslims from the twelth century to the sixteenth.

Structurally, the Ethiopian Orthodox church was similar to the Coptic Orthodox church in Egypt and to the Syrian Orthodox church in western Asia. The clergy included priests, bishops, nuns, and a patriarch as the head of the church. Contemplative orders of monks and nuns were an important feature of the Ethiopian church; monasteries were important centers of learning; and monks were important in writing down and consolidating the traditions of the Ethiopian kingdom. In this role, they helped develop a common identity among the peoples of Ethiopia. A strong identification with the church and the kingdom of Ethiopia shaped the history of both Ethiopia and Ethiopian Christianity. In this regard, the Aksumite court was a significant factor. Ethiopian rulers repelled periodic attacks by their Muslim neighbors, starting with the sultan of Shoa and culminating in a decisive victory over the Muslim king of Adal 1543. King Digna-Jan in the ninth century, Dilna'od in the tenth, and Amda-Siyan, who restructured the church extensively in the fourteenth, stamped the power of the state on the church.

Ethiopian Christianity survived the Islamic influence that reduced the fortunes of Christianity in Nubia and adjoining regions. This survival of Christianity was linked to Yohannes IV (r. 1872–1889) and Menelik II (r. 1889–1913). Yohannes and Menelik left an indelible imprint on the modern Ethiopian Orthodox faith, building churches and monasteries. Yohannes, with four Coptic bishops, revitalized the church and evangelized the Galla, who had clung tenaciously to traditional religion. Menelik, who warded off foreign influences including the Mahdists from Sudan in 1899, was in a sense a founder of the modern Ethiopia that was inherited and developed by Emperor Haile Selassie, who continued to maintain the influence of the church until the Marxist revolution.

The Coptic church in North Africa and the Ethiopian Orthodox church were early examples of Christian independence in Africa. These Christians had much in common with Christian groups in western Asia and in Europe in both teaching and beliefs, but they were also significantly different from Christian practice in other parts of the world. That difference gave their relgion an African flavor.

Portuguese Missionaries

In the fifteenth century, Portugal focused on Africa south of the Sahara. Earlier, the spread of Christianity to sub-Saharan Africa had been arrested by the spread of Islam. As Europeans began to search for a new sea trade route to Asia, Portugal sent ships down the west coast of Africa, thereby also cutting into the Arabs' trans-Saharan gold trade. Papal bulls "offered the *padroado* rights to the Portuguese monarch to appoint clerical orders for evangelization and to fend off competing European interests" (Kalu). The combined motives of gold, glory, and God accorded with the Christian rhetoric of the period, but commercial interests remained privileged; this may explain why there was so little mass conversion from the sixteenth century to the eighteenth.

The Portuguese supported Roman Catholic missionary priests who first attempted to work with the rulers of some African kingdoms. There was a hope that converting courts would lead to mass conversion of the people. Thus the Iberian Catholic presence in Africa was characterized by alliances with African courts and by the use of religion as an instrument of diplomacy and commerce. These Catholics established contacts in the Canary Islands, the Cape Verde Islands, the Guinea coast, the Kongo, Angola, Mozambique, and Kenya; they built offshoots of Lisbon and established churches and cathedrals on the islands of Cape Verde and São Tomé. They built trading forts on the Gold Coast on the Atlantic Ocean and at Kilwa on the Indian Ocean. Their evangelization, however, concentrated on the *mestizo* population.

Conversion among Africans achieved mixed success. Some African rulers rejected Christianity because it threatened their own spiritual and temporal authority. Attempts in the kingdoms of Benin and Warri soon failed, and the Portuguese in any case began to focus their search for pepper on India. The Portuguese missionaries had their greatest success in the Congo (Kongo) and Soyo kingdoms. The Portuguese came into contact with the Congo kingdom in 1483; by 1491 missionaries were sent to the Congo,, and soon afterward King Nzinga was baptized as a Christian. Nzinga's son Nzinga Mbembe was sent to Portugal for a Catholic education and on his return to the Congo replaced his father as king and changed his own name to Alfonso I. Missionaries opened schools across the kingdom, and many Congolese were converted to Christianity. But the evangelical movement often took second place to commerce, particularly after the introduction of the slave trade in the seventeenth century, and in time commercial interests compromised the missionary spirit.

Among the Soyo, Capuchin missionaries from Portugal established themselves as intermediaries between that kingdom and Europe. They were helped by local interpreters who translated during confession, prepared the altar, and taught converts. By the late seventeenth century the ruler of Soyo was attending mass three times a week and wearing a gold cross. As with the Kongo, conflict developed between the Capuchins and the Soyo over issues such as monogamy, traditional religious practices, and the slave trade. The Capuchins did not want the Soyo to sell baptized slaves to the English or other non-Catholic traders; they insisted that baptized slaves could be sold only to the Portuguese. As in the Kongo, the missionary effort was compromised by ambivalence.

The Portuguese missionary effort in inner Africa faced internal and external challenges. In Mashonaland in central Africa, missionaries were expelled for meddling in local politics and commerce. On the east African coast, missionaries faced increased competition from Indians and Arabs and persistent conflicts with the indigenous groups of Madagascar, and the Omani empire reestablished control over the northern part of the east coast. Competition from other European countries challenged Portuguese dominance of the lucrative trade in slaves, ivory, and other goods. Overall, the fleeting encounter with Christianity ended as the missionaries concentrated on enslaving prospective converts. Missions and mass conversions would not be revived until the nineteenth century.

Nineteenth-Century Evangelism

The Dutch settled in South Africa starting in 1652 and founded the beginnings of the Dutch Reformed church there, and in the eighteenth century South Africa was the site of considerable Christian missionary activity: the Moravian Brethren of eastern Europe established a mission in 1737, and in 1799 the London Missionary Society (LMS) followed. Elsewhere, however, there were only a few pockets of Christians, and throughout most of sub-Saharan Africa, Christianity made few inroads until the nineteenth century. The largest Christian community at this time was in Ethiopia. A small community of Coptic Christians remained in Egypt, and there were also small communities in the Cape region of South Africa and in the Portuguese colonies of Angola and Mozambique. The nineteenth century and the twentieth were to witness a rapid expansion of Christianity in Africa, so that by the beginning of the twenty-first century, more than 40 percent of the African population would identify themselves as Christian.

Many factors contributed to the growth of Christianity in Africa in this period, but the most important, historically, were undoubtedly the evangelical revival in Europe and the abolition of the Atlantic slave trade. Spiritual awakenings occurred in many European nations from the mid-eighteenth century through the nineteenth. These revivals were characterized by an emphasis on the Bible, the "conversion experience," and evangelism. The revivalist movement called on Christians to proselytize and spread the faith to all parts of the world, including Africa. European and North American missionary endeavors were directly tied to the nineteenth-century revivalist movement. Many Christian missionaries from Europe, North America, and the West Indies worked throughout the African continent to spread Christianity.

Abolitionism, promoted by a network of philanthropists and religious groups within and outside Europe, became a component of evangelicalism. The abolitionists proposed to stop the slave trade on the African side and establish "legitimate commerce." British philanthropists in particular were concerned about the poor conditions of liberated slaves. It was hoped that the mission to civilize could be achieved by introducing Christianity and commerce.

Missions were established by various Christian groups, including Roman Catholic orders and Protestant denominations. The missionaries came from different races and backgrounds, and not all of them represented predominantly white churches. As early as 1792, liberated Africans formed the core of the Sierra Leone mission, intending to build a new society based on the gospels. Liberated slaves associated the Enlightenment and Christianity with individual liberty and freedom, setting the cultural tone of industry and religion in Sierra Leone between 1807 and 1864; some of them became agents of the missionary enterprise throughout the west coast. Liberated slaves who returned to Yorubaland served as educators, interpreters, counselors to indigenous communities, negotiators with the new agents of change, preachers, traders, and leaders of public opinion in many west African communities. One example is Ajayi Crowther, who was made a bishop in 1864. The founding of Liberia in 1822 by the Colonization Society and the recruitment of African-American missionaries were significant factors in the missionary enterprise to Africa. The African Episcopal Methodists and National Baptist Convention, among other African-American churches, "created a form of appropriation of the gospel that endured" (Kalu).

The rapid expansion of Christianity in Africa also owed much not only to the large number of missionaries working in Africa but also to the support of colonial governments. Colonialists and missionaries established a hegemonic relationship that used Christianity as a civilizing agent. Colonial authorities provided a politically peaceful and supportive environment for the work of Christian missionaries, in the hope that Christianity would provide support for colonialism as Africans converts saw the value of colonial rule.

But the relationship between the colonial authorities and the missionaries was sometimes ambivalent. This relationship could be symbiotic, most strongly in colonies that did not have a large Muslim population. But in colonies such as Nigeria that did have a large Muslim population, colonial governments discouraged Christian missions, not wanting to jeopardize the collaborative arrangements that enabled the colonial state to function. Thus geography remained an important factor in African religious beliefs.

Moreover, "collusion with the civilizing project diminished the spiritual vigor of the missionary presence and turned it into cultural and power encounters" (Kalu). Often, the missionaries' strategies were contrary to their enlightened ideals. Missionaries often became part of colonial exploitation and expropriation. For instance, at Bagamoyo, off the coast of Zanzibar, the Holy Ghost Fathers turned their plantation into a lucrative site for the exploitation of young people; in South Africa, the Dutch Reformed Church was instrumental in formulating the ideology of apartheid; and in the Congo, Belgian Catholic missionaries acquiecsed in the brutal treatment of the local people by employees of Leopold II's Congo Free State. The situation in the Congo lasted until Leopold relinquished the colony to Belgium in 1908; and even then it was an international outcry, rather than any enlightened ideals on the part of the Belgian missionaries, that ameliorated the virtual enslavement of the Congolese.

Nevertheless, large-scale conversation did take place throughout most of sub-Saharan Africa as a result of Christian evangelization. Missionaries learned African languages and often translated portions of the Bible into local languages in order to facilitate conversion. They opened schools that focused on reading and religious instruction as means of conversion. Missionaries believed that the ability to read the Bible was vital in the conversion process. As colonialism became entrenched, colonial governments spent money on education, and mission schools expanded. It should be noted, though that many Africans accepted conversion and missionary education for utilitarian purposes.

Both the missionary and the civilizing endeavors of the colonialists were imbued with values and attitudes that reflected their understanding of Christianity and their view of African religions and cultures. To many missionaries, the Christianization and civilization of Africans involved adopting Euro-American culture and shedding African beliefs and cultures, which were regarded as inferior. This belief in the superiority of European culture became a lens through which many missionaries interpreted their experiences in Africa. The challenges mounted against this distorted image of African culture were important in the establishment of African-centered churches.

African Independent Churches

African independent churches are the fastest-growing Christian groups in many parts of Africa. Although numerous Africans embraced Christianity, they did not always embrace the messengers of the faith; and their Christianity evolved in its own way as people practiced an Africanized form of the religion.

African independent churches trace their origin to the eighteenth century, when Beatrice Kimpa Vita, a young Congolese woman from a noble Catholic family, broke away from the Catholic church and founded a syncretist movement in an attempt to revive the fortunes of the Congo kingdom. She claimed that Saint Anthony had appeared to her in a vision and encouraged her to do this; that Jesus was in the Congo; and that the Virgin Mary came from a neighboring area. In 1704 Beatrice led a crusade of a thousand followers to São Salvador. Although she did not denounce the pope or work openly against missionaries, she developed a priestly order and instituted practices influenced by Congolese culture, such as an Africanized liturgy that included indigenous music and dancing. Her crusade, known as the Antonine movement after Saint Anthony, grew rapidly; it reflected dissatisfaction with Portuguese rule and sought to establish a type of Christianity that would be independent of the European missionary church. Beatrice became so popular that she was seen as a threat to the Catholic church and to Portuguese control in the Congo; in 1706 she was burned at the stake for heresy.

By the late nineteenth century, some African Christians broke away from missionary churches. Thereafter a wide variety of African churches established autonomy and became independent of mission churches. Most of the expansion of Christianity in Africa during the second half of the twentieth century was a result of missionary efforts by the African independent churches. By 1980, there were an estimated 7,000 different independent groups in Africa with a combined membership of more than 12 million. By 1990, the number of African indigenous churches in South Africa had grown to more than 6,000, from only thirty in 1913 (Kalu).

Several interrelated factors gave rise to the Afrocentric Christian movements. One very important factor was the racist ideas held by colonial churches. The widespread notion of African cultural and intellectual inferiority frustrated attempts by African Christians to obtain positions of leadership in the mission churches; this situation led to the emergence of indigenous charismatic, prophetic figures. "Native agency" became a means of growth as some Africans "gave voice to the indigenous feeling against Western cultural iconoclasm and control of decision-making in the colonial churches" (Kalu).

The colonialists' dismissal of African cultural and religious beliefs turned the African Christian movements into a movement of cultural and religious protest and a form of cultural appreciation (Kalu). The characterization of African cultures and religions as primitive and pagan and the attempt to force African Christians to abandon most of their cultural and religious beliefs led them to reject mission dogma and to incoporate aspects of African cultural practice into Christianity.

One movement of cultural and religions protest, "Ethiopianism," was taken up by numerous educated Africans to create an African Christianity. Ethiopian independent churches, most of which are in western and southern Africa, are so called because Ethiopia is mentioned in the Bible. To the early leaders of African independent churches, the biblical representations of Ethiopia, such as a promise in Psalms that Ethiopia shall raise its hands to God, demonstrated God's enduring interest and involvement in Africa. Ethiopian churches differed from mission churches in leadership, and some leaders of the Ethiopian churches changed their English names to African names and wore African clothes; however, the basic teachings and worship remained essentially the same.

Two of the earliest Ethiopian independent churches were formed in the late nineteenth century in southern Nigeria, where missionaries had been working for nearly a century. In 1889 a Baptist minister named Vincent Mojola Agbebi, broke away from the mission Baptist church to form the Native Baptist church. In 1891, Samuel Ajayi Crowther, the first African-Anglican bishop, broke from the Anglican (Episcopalian) church in Nigeria to form the African Anglican Pastorate. From these roots in Nigeria, many such churches were formed in western, eastern, central, and southern Africa.

The second major division of African independent churches to emerge was the Zionist independent churches or Spirit churches. They are referred to as Zionists in southern Africa, Aladura in West Africa, and Roho in East Africa. These churches emphasized spiritual and physical healing through the intervention of the Holy Spirit. Their emphasis on healing, and their use of African symbols and African musical instruments, reflected the influence of indigenous religious belief and practices. Zionist worship is characterized by singing and dancing, possession by the Holy Spirit, and healing of illnesses. Zionist churches changed the face of Christianity in Africa by adapting to African cultural values, beliefs, and practices. Many Zionist groups follow the Old Testament Jewish tradition and observe Saturday as their holy day. While there has been considerable change in their practices, Zionist Christians can still be distinguished from the Ethiopian churches by their distinct attire and insignia.

Overall, the common elements found among the African independent churches include direct communication with God through prayer; dreams and possession by the Holy Spirit; adaptation of Christianity to indigenous beliefs and practices; and the emergence of strong charismatic leaders who claim a direct relationship with God. Also, the African independent churches have created more space for women. Some revivalist groups are nationalist apologists who feel that Africa knew and worshiped God. Kalu argues that groups such as the Godianists, Orunmila, and Afrikania have established links between Bible stories and African religions.

Neo-Pentecostal Christianity

Independent neo-Pentecostal churches—a significant new wave of Christian evangelization—have continued to transform African Christianity. During the 1930s, classical Pentecostal denominations related to western missions emerged; these included the Assemblies of God in Africa and indigenous Pentecostal churches such as the Christ Apostolic church. A core element of classical Pentecostal denominations is the doctrine of "new birth" followed by "speaking in tongues." In these Pentecostal churches, unlike the earlier independent movements, worship and liturgy are devoid of ritual symbolism. Classical Pentecostals encourage simplicity, modesty, and sacrifice as signs of holiness. They have an overwhelming sense of receiving power from the Holy Spirit—a power that enables believers to discard African traditions infused with Christian significance in the older independent churches.

The theology of neo-Pentecostalism is more immediate. God's kingdom is seen in earthly terms and is believed to be established through the power of prayer, positive thinking, and prosperity. The leaders are often well educated, and the congregations are liberal-minded and urban-centered. Neo-Pentecostals want to convey an international image, using modern mass media in the style of American "electronic churches" and televangelists such as Oral Roberts, Benny Hinn, T.L. Osborn, Morris Cerrullo, Kenneth Hagin, and Kenneth and Gloria Copeland. Groups such as Kingsway International Christian Center, Living Faith World Outreach, Christian Action Faith Ministries International, Global Revival Ministries, International Central Gospel Church, and Winners International have a broad international outreach that links them to an international network of churches. Nigeria is a major inspiration behind the formation of neo-Pentecostal churches throughout Africa and in African diaspora communities all over the world.

Chima J. Korieh

See also **Africans: Overview; Christians: Overview; Coptic Christians; Diaspora: African; Egypt; Ethiopia**

Further Reading

Allo, Elizabeth Isichei, *A History of Christianity in Africa: From Antiquity to the Presen,*. Grand Rapids, Michigan: W.B. Eerdmans Publishing Company, 1995

Anderson, Allan H., *African Reformation: African Initiated Christianity in the Twentieth Century*, Trenton, New Jersey: Africa World Press, 2001

Kalu, Ogbu U., editor. *African Christianity: An African Story*, Forthcoming

King, K., *What Is Gnosticism?* Cambridge, Massachusetts: Belknap Press of Harvard University Press, 2003

Miller, P., *Biography in Late Antiquity: A Quest for the Holy Man*. Berkeley: University of California Press, 1983

Pearson, B., *Gnosticism, Judaism, and Egyptian Christianity*, Minneapolis: Fortress, 1990

Sundkler, Bengt, and Christopher Steed, *A History of the Church in Africa*, Cambridge: Cambridge University Press, 2000

Ward, Benedicta, *The Sayings of the Desert Fathers*, London: A.R. Mowbray; Kalamazoo, Michigan: Cistercian Publications, 1975

Youssef, Youhana, and Ken Sawyer, "Early Christianity in North Africa," in *African Christianity: An African Story*, edited by Ogbu U. Kalu, Forthcoming

Chuvash

Capsule Summary

Location: Volga region of European Russia, mostly in the Chuvash Republic.
Total Population: 1.6 million.
Language: Chuvash, some Russian.
Religion: Russian Orthodox Christianity.

The Chuvash are an ethnic group living in the middle Volga region of European Russia. The present number of Chuvash amounts to 1.6 million, of whom fewer than 1 million live in the Chuvash Republic. There are large Chuvash settlements in the neighboring republics of Tatarstan and Bashkortostan and in regions of Russia, and there is some diaspora in the Ukraine and Kazakhstan. The Chuvash are the fourth largest minority group in Russia with 1.1 percent of the total population, after the Tatars, Ukrainians, and Bashkirs.

Almost 80 percent of the Chuvash regard Chuvash as their mother tongue; the rest speak mainly Russian. Chuvash is a Turkic language of the Bulgar subgroup. Other representatives of this branch include the already extinct Bulgar and Khazar languages. Chuvash has no close modern relatives. Chuvash has been influenced by Tatar, neighboring Finno-Ugric languages, and Russian. It is traditionally divided into two or three main dialects: northern, southern, and a mixed central dialect. The language borders also reflect ethnographic differences.

Most Chuvash speak Russian as their second language. The Chuvash are Russian Orthodox Christians, but there are some Muslims, as well as traces of folk religion.

The Chuvash Republic is a constituent republic and a member of the Russian Federation since 1992. It is one of the 21 national republics of Russia, which consists, all together, of 89 federal subjects.

The Chuvash Republic has an area of 18,301 square km and a population of 1.3 million. Approximately 70 percent are ethnic Chuvash, the others being Russians (26 percent, mostly urban) and Tatars (3 percent), with negligible percentages of other groups. Sixty percent of the inhabitants live in cities. In comparison to other republics in the Russian Federation, the percentage of Russians is relatively low in the Chuvash Republic. Its capital and largest city, Shupashkar, or Cheboksary in Russian, is one of the major ports on the Volga River and has a population of 446,000. The republic is rich in phosphates, gypsum, and forests; industry and agriculture are the main occupations.

The Chuvash are generally held to be descendants of the seminomadic Bulgars and Suvars, Turkic-speaking peoples that immigrated from the south to the middle Volga region around the eighth century. The ethnonym Chuvash is supposed to originate from the Suvars. The Bulgars and Suvars assimilated local Finno-Ugric peoples and created the multiethnic Volga-Bulgar state, which lasted until the Mongol conquest in 1236.

The Mongols ruled the area in the thirteenth and fourteenth centuries; this period is commonly known as the Golden Horde. In 1438, after the fall of the Golden Horde, the Tatars created the Kazan Khanate, which also included the Chuvash. The ethnonym Chuvash is mentioned for the first time at the beginning of the sixteenth century by Russian and foreign travelers. The Chuvash appear to have been known also by other names during this time.

In 1552, when the Russians conquered the Kazan Khanate, the areas inhabited by Chuvash were incorporated into Russia. In the next centuries the Chuvash were subjected to Christianization and Russification campaigns. A majority of the Chuvash were converted to Russian Orthodox Christianity, which is the main religion today. A small minority are Muslim. Apart from these religions, old traditions have persisted and there are some ancient religious beliefs among the Chuvash.

The eighteenth and nineteenth centuries marked a Chuvash cultural and linguistic revival. The first Chuvash grammar was published in 1769, and dictionaries, translations, prose, and poetry were published throughout the nineteenth century. More than 700 books in Chuvash appeared until Soviet times. A high school opened in Simbirsk, now Ulyanovsk in Russia, in 1868 and soon became the center of cultural activities and the Chuvash literary tradition. Some research on the Chuvash was done at Kazan University, now in Tatarstan. Some of the Chuvash books were published in Kazan.

The Chuvash language was taught at the end of the century in many local schools. I.Y. Yakovlev created a Chuvash alphabet in 1871, which provides the basis for the modern Chuvash script. This alphabet uses Russian Cyrillic letters and adds four letters for sounds specific to the Chuvash language.

The Chuvash Autonomous Region was established on June 24, 1920. It was converted into the Chuvash Autonomous Soviet Socialist Republic (Chuvash ASSR) on April 21, 1925. In the 1920s, strong Chuvash nationalism developed, based on an idea of the Chuvash as heirs to the Bulgar empire. The central government of the Soviet Union suppressed these nationalist movements and redesigned the borders of the republic so that many of the ethnic Chuvash found themselves living in the neighboring republics and Russian districts. Russian immigration was encouraged. Still, rural collectivization was long opposed by the Chuvash. The republic remained a primarily agricultural region until the beginning of the twentieth century, when it was heavily industrialized. Both agriculture (mainly grain production, but also hops), and industry (forestry, textile, mining) are important sectors today.

During the Soviet era, the Chuvash, as well as many other minorities, were subjected to Russification campaigns. The Chuvash language disappeared from schools and public use. In the wake of the changes in 1989, a new Chuvash revival movement started, which has led to the establishment of Chuvash educational, cultural, and political institutions. Chuvash language, history, culture, and traditions are now encouraged and revitalized in Chuvash regions.

In 1992, the republic signed the treaty of the Russian Federation and organized its first elections. In 1993, it joined the Unrepresented Nations and Peoples Organization (UNPO), and in 1994, the Constituent Assembly of the Volga-Ural region met in Shupashkar-Cheboksary. In 1995, the Chuvash took active part in the formation of the League of Nations of Russia. In the same year the 1,100th anniversary of the Volga-Bulgar state and the seventy-fifth anniversary of the Chuvash Republic were celebrated.

Today the Chuvash language is taught in the schools of the Chuvash Republic and in regions outside the republic with a compact Chuvash population. Apart from the Chuvash-language media within the republic, the Chuvash diaspora in Tatarstan and Russia has newspapers as well as television and radio in its own language. Representatives of the Chuvash diaspora held a meeting in Shupashkar in 1998.

Sabira Ståhlberg

See also **Bashkir; Kazakstan; Tatars; Ukraine**

Further Reading

Aygi, Gennady, editor, *An Anthology of Chuvash Poetry*, translated by Peter France, London: Unesco Library of World Poetry, Forest Books, 1991

Benzing, Johannes, *Bolgarisch-tschuwaschische Studien*, Wiesbaden: Harrassowitz, 1993

Ivanov, Vitalii P., *Chuvashskaia diaspora: Rasselenie i chislennost'. Etnogeograficheskii spravochni* [The Chuvash Diaspora: Population and Figures. An Ethnogeographical Reference Book], Cheboksary: 1999

Ivanov, Vitalii P., V. V. Nikolaev, and V. P. Dimitriev, *Chuvashi: Etnicheskaya istoriya i traditsionnaya kul'tura* (The Chuvash: Ethnic History and Traditional Culture), Moscow: DIK, 2000

Krueger, John R., *Chuvash Manual: Introduction, Grammar, Reader, and Vocabulary*, Bloomington, Indiana: Uralic and Altaic Series 7, 1961; Taylor and Francis, 1997

Róna-Tas, András, *Chuvash Studies*, Budapest: Ak. Kiadó; Wiesbaden: Harrassowitz, 1982

Tafaev, Gennadii I., *Bolgaro-chuvashskaya tsivilizatsiya* [The Bulgar-Chuvash Civilization], Cheboksary: Chuvashskii Gos. Pedagog. Universitet, 2002

Circassians

Capsule Summary:

Location: Northwest Caucasia mainly in three constituent republics (Georgia, Azerbaijan, Armenia) of the Russian Federation, including Turkey, Syria, Jordan, Israel, Egypt, Libya, Germany, United States, and the Netherlands
Total Population: 2–6 million (about 1 million in Caucasia).
Language: Kabardian (Circassian)
Religion: Sunni Islam (99%), Orthodox Christianity (1%).

The Circassians, together with the kindred Abkhaz-Abaza and the Ubykh, have formed the autochthonous population of Northwest (NW) Caucasia for thousands of years. The number of Circassians in Caucasia is approaching 1 million. The majority live in the following republics of the Russian Federation, in each of which they have a different nominal designation: the Kabardino-Balkarian Republic (Kabardians, 600,000), the Karachai-Cherkess Republic (Cherkess, 100,000) and the Republic of Adigea (Adigeans, 200,000). There are also Circassian communities that exist outside these republics but inside Russia, including the Shapsugh community of almost 20,000 in the Tuapsa and Lazareyvsky regions on the Black Sea coast, and the Christian Kabardian community in Mozdok, which numbers a few thousand. There are also significant Adigean and Kabardian communities in the Krasnodar and Stavropol Krays, respectively. In the Krasnodar Kray there are 60,000 Adigeans not contained within the borders of Adigea.

The Circassians constitute almost 0.7 percent of the population of Russia. There are Circassian diaspora communities in Turkey, Syria, Jordan, Israel, Egypt, Libya, Germany, the United States, and the Netherlands, but their precise numbers are not known, with estimates ranging between 1 and 5 million people. The Circassian community in Turkey is believed to be the largest in the world, with estimates numbering more than four million; however, they are scattered throughout the entire country, and many of their members have been assimilated.

Circassian is one of the three divisions of the NW group of Caucasian languages, which form a unique group distinct from the other major world language groups, the other two being Abkhaz-Abaza and the now extinct Ubykh. Though genetically related, the three languages are mutually unintelligible, the lexical differences among them being quite substantial. There are two official and literary languages: Kabardian in Kabardino-Balkaria and Karachai-Cherkessia and Adigean in the Adigean Republic. The two languages, or more accurately dialects, are mutually intelligible and use Cyrillic orthography. It is thought that Northeast Caucasian, which is spoken by about 3.5 million people in Chechnya, Ingushetia, and Dagestan, is genetically related to NW Caucasian. The third group in the Caucasian language family is South Caucasian or Kartvelian: Georgian, Mingrelian, Svan, Adjar, and Laz, all of which are spoken by about 4.5 million people in the TransCaucasia and Northeast Turkey. Some linguists dispute the existence of any genetic link between North and South Caucasian. During the Soviet period (1917–1991), Circassian was relegated to a secondary position as Russian was made the language of instruction at schools and universities. In consequence, Circassian had suffered tremendously by the end of Communist rule in 1991. The present challenge is to restore the native language to pre-eminence. There are TV and radio broadcasts in Circassian, which are also relayed to the diaspora in the Middle East.

The ancient Nart Epic of Abkhazia and the oral tales of the bards had formed the bulk of Circassian literature until the early part of the nineteenth century. The twentieth century witnessed a quantum leap in quantity and quality of literary output, despite being somewhat tainted by Communist ideology.

History

In the Bronze Age, the Maikop culture flourished in the valley of the Kuban in the NW Caucasia, from the Taman Peninsula to present-day Chechnya, almost five millennia ago. It was contiguous with the Kuro-Arax culture of the kindred Chechens and Dagestanis. There are extant monuments to the glory of this civilization, especially in Western Circassia. Some scholars believe that the people of the Maikop culture, together with a significant input from the Dolmen People who inhabited the coastal and highland regions, engendered the forebears of the Adiga or at least formed an important component of the proto-Circassians.

The Iron Age in the NW Caucasia began in the eighth century BCE. Pre-Kuban culture is attributed to the proto-Circassian Maeots who inhabited the NW Caucasia and the steppes north of the Black Sea. Their civilization lasted for some 1,200 years. The Maeot State was contemporaneous with the Greek colonies on the Eastern Black Sea coast, which were established in the seventh and sixth centuries BCE and lasted for almost a millennium. The Greeks set up trade relations with the Maeots. By the fifth century BCE, the Sinds, a people kindred to the Maeots, had set up the magnificent Sindika civilization, which spread over the lower reaches of the Kuban, the Black Sea coastal strip between Anapa and Taman Peninsula. The Romans occupied the Eastern Coast of the Black Sea in 64 BCE. It was Strabo in 26 CE who first mentioned the name Zyghoy for Circassians, which replaced the old appellation Kerket.

The Goths, who established a state north of the Black Sea in the third century CE, invaded the NW Caucasia and engaged in fierce battles with the Circassians. The marauding Huns, who had settled to the east, undid the Eastern Gothic State in 370 CE and invaded the NW Caucasia in 374 CE. The Byzantine Empire secured a foothold in the Western Caucasia in the fourth century CE, erecting fortresses on the Black Sea coast and the Taman Peninsula. Thenceforward the Roman scribes referred to the Maeots as Zikhis. Christianity was introduced gradually among the upper classes of the Circassians, the masses clinging to their ancient beliefs. The Byzantine presence lasted until they were replaced by the Venetians, who were themselves displaced by the Genoese in the thirteenth century.

By the tenth century, the Circassians had emerged as a cohesive ethnic and linguistic entity. At the time, Circassia stretched from the middle of the Caucasia to the Black Sea. In the hinterland lived the Circassian nations of the Papaghis and Kasakhs. To the east of the Kasakhs, modern-day Kabardians, lived the Alans, ancestors of the Ossetes. The Circassians had kept their independence until the thirteenth century, when part of their country and Abkhazia were subjected by the Georgians under Queen Tamara (1184–1213) and Christianized. Around 1424 CE, the Circassians threw off the Georgian yoke for good. Ghenghis Khan led his Mongol hordes across the Caucasia in the thirteenth century and laid waste to the North Caucasia. Batu, grandson of Ghenghis, established the Khanate of the Golden Horde in the North Caucasia in 1227. The Kipchak Khanate dominated the North Caucasia until the fifteenth century, when Tamerlane conquered the Caucasia and ended Mongol rule. In the thirteenth to fifteenth centuries, the Genoese constructed trading posts on the coastal regions of Circassia and Abkhazia. During their incessant wars with the Mongols and Tatars, the Circassians sought to forge closer relations with Russia, from whom they perceived no threat since it was relatively distant and of the same faith. Circassian Mamluks furnished medieval Egypt with an important element of her elite warrior caste for about six centuries and its reigning Sultans for 135 years.

The Russian-Circassian War

After destroying the Empires of the Golden Horde at the end of the sixteenth century, Russia began to push south towards the northern steppes of the Caucasia in a process of gradual encroachments. Russia began to meddle in the affairs of Circassia in 1736. The construction of the Caucasian Military Line hastened the first open conflict between the Circassians and Russians in 1771. A protracted and devastating war extended for decades, and the Russian juggernaut had ground all resistance by 1864.

On May 1, 1864, later dubbed the Circassian Day of Mourning and celebrated by all Circassian communities, Russia proclaimed the end of the Caucasian War. Covertly, the Russians pursued a policy of organized and systematic terror and thousands of people were massacred. Those horrific acts, together with the collusion of the Ottomans, resulted in a mass exodus and near-genocide. Only 10 percent of the Circassians, about 200,000, remained in their ancestral lands to face occupation and persecution first under the czars and later the Communists.

During the czarist period, Circassia remained desolate. There was an influx of Slav colonists, especially in the coastal regions. The Circassians joined the North Caucasian Mountain Republic in 1917. After victory of the Bolsheviks in the Russian Civil War, the Circassians were divided into four regions, which kept changing status and nominal designations until the early 1990s. The horrors of centralization, the purges, and World War II gave way to a long period of quiet and stagnation until the years of Glasnost and Perestroika. The demographic situation changed dramatically in the NW Caucasia, such that presently the Slavs constitute the overwhelming majority in the region.

Current Political Situation

After the demise of the Soviet Union in 1991, Circassian nationalists actively demanded autonomy and even independence. The International Circassian Association was established in 1991 and included organizations from the Caucasia and the diaspora. In 1993, it became a member of the Unrepresented Nations and Peoples Organisation (UNPO), which was created in 1991 in The Hague to represent those ethnic groups around the world that are barred from joining the United Nations for whatever reason. The secessionist tendencies reached fever pitch during the Georgian-Abkhaz war of 1992–93. Victory gave the nationalists overwhelming popular support, but collusion of the local and central authorities, together with the onset of the Chechen war in 1994, overturned the tables. Nowadays, the nationalists are on the defensive, being hounded by the local government. People are now more concerned with their material well being, and nationalism has taken a secondary place in their reckoning. The concept of a united Circassia is however still strong in the hearts and minds of all Circassian peoples. Some regard the re-creation of historical Circassia as inevitable, since Russia's colonial stance will have to ease for it to join the world comity. Ethnic tension is evident in all three republics: the Kabardians vs. the Balkars, the Cherkess-Abaza vs. the Karachai and the Adigeans vs. the militant Cossacks. Fortunately, no serious conflicts have thus far erupted.

The Circassian diaspora, which is as yet not very politicized, could play a decisive role in the demographic and political situations in the NW Caucasia, if the right conditions obtain. Already the 100 or so Kosovar Circassians have found refuge in their ancestral lands, causing trepidation among the local Cossacks, already wary of Adigean domination.

Society

The eastern Circassians, those living on the right-bank of the upper reaches of the Kuban, are composed of the Kabardians and Beslanay. The western Circassians are comprised of many tribes: Abzakh, Shapsugh, Temirgoi, and Bzhedugh, among others. Some tribes and clans have disappeared from the Caucasia as a result of the Russian-Circassian war. Historically, the social structure of Circassian society was extremely complex and was generally based on hierarchical feudalism. The main castes were princes, nobles, freemen, serfs, and slaves. A few egalitarian tribes existed in the mountainous regions of Western Circassia. The feudal system came to a tragic end in 1864 when Russia conquered Circassia.

Traditional Circassian society was martial in nature and the offspring of the upper-classes were required to go through a harsh training regime. The society cherished frugality and abstinence. The code of chivalry had respect for women, with elders, hospitality and blood-revenge as its trinity. Avoidance customs, as when husband and wife and siblings are proscribed from associating in public, were manifestations of the severity of social relations. Women, especially of the upper class, enjoyed a relatively high social status. The position of Circassian women remains significantly better in many respects than in Russia.

Traditional economy was agrarian and pastoral in nature. During the Soviet era centralization and industrialization transformed and modernized the economy. However, individualism and initiative were frowned upon, and after collapse of the Soviet Union, the economic situation in the Circassian republics took a nosedive. The two Chechen wars and political uncertainty and tensions have aggravated the situation.

The Circassians are nominally Sunni Muslims. There is a small Christian community in Mozdok in North Ossetia. The two most powerful formers of Circassian system of beliefs are the ancient animistic-pagan religion and the code of conduct, Adige Xabze, which also has regulated the mundane life. Religious persecution during the Soviet period and great attachment to traditions, a characteristic of the Circassians, have resulted in a superficial knowledge and practice of religion. There is no tradition of religious fanaticism.

AMJAD JAIMOUKHA

See also **Chechens; Kabardians, Jordan; Mongols; Turkey**

Further Reading

Bell, James Stanislaus, *Journal of Residence in Circassia during the Years 1837, 1838 and 1839*, 2 vols., London: Edward Moxon, 1840

Jaimoukha, Amjad, *The Circassians: A Handbook*, Richmond, Surrey: Curzon Press; New York: Palgrave, 2001

Khan-Girey, Sultan, *Zapiski o Cherkesii* [Studies on the Circassians], St Petersburg, 1836; Nalchik: Elbrus Book Press, 1978

Longworth, John Augustus, *A Year among the Circassians*, 2 vols., London: Henry Colburn, 1840

Nogmov, Sh. B., *Istoriya adigeiskogo naroda* [History of the Adigey People], Tiflis: Kavkazky kalendar, 1861; Nalchik, 1947

Traho, Ramazan, "Literature on Circassia and the Circassians," in *Caucasian Review*, Munich, no. 1, 1955, pp 145–62

Civil Rights, *See* **Equal Opportunity, Human and Minority Rights Organizations**

Civil War, United States

The American Civil War began on April 12, 1861, when Confederate forces opened fire on Fort Sumter in Charleston Harbor, South Carolina. It lasted until May 26, 1865. The war caused more than 600,000 deaths, destroyed over $5 billion in property, and brought freedom to four million African-American slaves. Some of the core issues raised by the war are still unresolved, meaning that the political and social legacies of the conflict have not been completely resolved over 140 years later.

Slavery was the main and immediate cause of the war. The southern states, particularly the eleven states of the Confederacy, depended on slavery to support their economy. Slave labor produced crops, particularly cotton and tobacco, maintained domestic households, and accounted for almost all manufacturing in the South. Southern slave-holding males also maintained a state of polygamy on their plantations, allowing them sexual dominance over African-American females and their own wives. Even though slavery was illegal in the Northern states, few Northerners actively opposed it. The political crisis of the 1850s centered on whether slavery should be allowed in the Western territories acquired during the Mexican War (1846–1848), including New Mexico, part of California, and Utah. Opponents of slavery were concerned about its expansion, in part because they did not want to compete against slave labor and they did not want the immigration of African-Americans into the Western territories.

In 1860, cotton was the chief crop of the South, representing 57 percent of all U.S. exports. Revenue derived from cotton completed the South's dependence on the plantation system, which relied heavily on chattel slavery. Alternatively, the North was an industrial society. The dominance of the plantation system in the South was an impediment to industrialization. Southerners had to import almost all manufactured goods. Thus, they opposed high tariffs, or taxes placed on imported goods that increased the price of manufactured articles. The manufacturing economy of the North, on the other hand, demanded high tariffs to protect its own products from cheap foreign competition, particularly that of Great Britain.

Before the Civil War, loyalty to one's state often took precedence over loyalty to the country. Many considered the Union a voluntary compact entered into by independent, sovereign states. In the nation's early years, neither North nor South had any strong sense that the Union was permanent. New Englanders considered seceding, or leaving the Union, when the War of 1812 cut off trade with England. As the slave system developed, the South became less dependent on the federal government than did other regions. Therefore, Southerners felt no need to strengthen it. Southern planters also feared that a strong central government might interfere with slavery.

The 1860 presidential campaign was one of the most bitterly fought in history. Lincoln received 180 electoral votes, a majority. John C. Breckinridge, who carried the entire Deep South, was second with 72. John Bell, from Tennessee and a member of the Constitutional Union Party, received 39 and Douglas 12. Thus, Lincoln won only 40 percent of the popular vote. Of the total votes cast, he won 1,865,593, Douglas 1,382,713, Breckinridge 848,356, and Bell 592,906. Lincoln failed to win a single electoral vote in ten Southern states.

Even before Election Day, Southern militants had threatened to secede from the Union upon the election of Lincoln. In December, with the Republican victory final, South Carolina seceded. By February, Mississippi, Florida, Alabama, Georgia, Louisiana, and Texas had followed. These states joined together to form the Confederate States of America, or Confederacy. President Buchanan did nothing to stop the secessionist movement, and President-elect Lincoln was powerless to intercede. Lincoln remained silent on the issue, hoping that Union sentiment might reassert itself in the South.

By Abraham Lincoln's first term in Congress, it had been clear that he was opposed to slavery. He supported the Wilmot Proviso, which proposed that slavery would be prohibited in any territory acquired from Mexico. He also put forward a program for the abolition of slavery in Washington, D.C. This proposal never came before Congress, but it exemplified his opposition to slavery. Lincoln did not believe that Congress had the power to abolish slavery in individual states. However, where Congress had the power, as in Washington, and where the electorate was agreeable, he thought that it should abolish slavery. He became an antislavery leader after the passage of the Kansas-Nebraska Act in 1854. The act created the territories of Kansas and Nebraska, and stated that each territory could be admitted as a state "with or without slavery, as their constitution may prescribe at the time of their admission." This program was referred to as *popular sovereignty* because it allowed the voters in these territories to decide for themselves whether slavery should be allowed. The Kansas-Nebraska Act repealed the old dividing line between free and slave states as set by the Missouri Compromise of 1820.

On March 4, 1861, Lincoln was sworn in as the 16th president of the United States. Lincoln attempted to allay Southern fears in his inaugural address. He said that he had no legal right to interfere with the institution of slavery in the states where it exists. However, he flatly rejected the right of any state to secede from the Union, and he announced that he would "hold, occupy, and possess" the property and places belonging to the Federal government. The rebellious states had already seized Federal forts, arsenals and customhouses within their boundaries.

Lincoln had attempted by all means to preserve the peace with the rebellious states. He feared that taking direct action against the Confederacy would lead to the secession of Virginia, North Carolina, Tennessee, and Arkansas. Lincoln reacted promptly to the Confederate firing at Fort Sumter. He asked the loyal states to provide 75,000 militia for three months' service. He also called a special session of Congress to convene on July 4, 1861.

On the surface, the war should have never lasted as long or caused as many casualties as it did. The Union had vastly superior war potential. For example, there were 23 states in the Union (3/4 of the territory) to 11 in the Confederacy (1/4 of the territory). The Union contained 23,000,000 people to 9,000,000 in the Confederacy—4,000,000 of which were slaves, many actively hostile to the Confederate cause. The Union army was able to muster 2,898,000 men to only 1,300,000 for the Confederacy. In addition, the Union Navy effectively blockaded the Southern ports and cut off support from Great Britain. Finally, the Union had 75 percent of the nation's banking and industrial capital, along with 85 percent of the manufacturing. In contrast, the Confederacy had the better army at the start of the war. Their officers were more experienced and the enlisted men better trained due to the South's need to be perpetually armed in order to suppress slave rebellion.

The years 1861 and 1862 were marked by a succession of Union military disasters, at First Bull Run, Shiloh, Seven Pines, Seven Days, Second Bull Run, Antietam (reputed as a Union victory, but the Union suffered greater casualties in the battle), and Fredericksburg. The failure of the Union to win quickly was the result of its weak military command and unclear political objectives. In particular, the war stagnated because outmoded Napoleanic military tactics were ineffective against the weaponry of that period. The Confederates maintained an advantage by fighting a defensive war. The Union suffered horrendous casualties due to its practice of marching masses of men into concentrated fire on the battlefield. As casualties mounted, political support for the war's aims faded in the North. Finally, Lincoln, in attempting to preserve the Union, did not effectively marshal the strategic requirements to win the war.

Slavery was the root cause of the war, and it was slavery and the action of African-Americans that was needed to bring it to a swift conclusion. African-American leaders made it clear that both the end of slavery and the raising of black units were needed to win the war. Karl Marx and Frederich Engels wrote in the *New York Herald Tribune* agreeing that ending slavery and raising Black units were necessary to win the war. Even members of his own party, called the radical Republicans, began to oppose Lincoln's policies. They wanted immediate action against the South, the freeing of the slaves, and punitive measures levied against Southern leaders.

However, Lincoln continued to pursue a cautious policy. Whenever possible he assured whites that slavery was not the key issue in the war. This policy was designed in part to stop the border states of Maryland, Delaware, and Kentucky from secession. Lincoln decided to issue the Emancipation Proclamation because the North was on the verge of a military defeat. Confederate Commander Robert E. Lee and the Army of Northern Virginia invaded Northern territory in July of 1863. Lee's aim was to destroy the Army of the Potomac, threaten Washington, D.C., and offer Lincoln terms for peace. These plans unraveled at a small town in Pennsylvania called Gettysburg. The Union victory here was made possible by the combination of tremendous heroism, such as that of Joshua Chamberlain and the 2nd Maine regiment at Little Round Top, along with colossal blunders by Lee and his staff. Chief among these errors were their failure to occupy the heights around the city and the ordering of an assault against a heavily defended Federal center (called Pickett's charge.) Simultaneously, on the western front, Ulysses S. Grant had captured Vicksburg, giving the Federals control of the Mississippi River and cutting the Confederacy in two.

At this point, the Confederacy was finished militarily. Yet it would require two more additional years of bloody conflict before the war was ended. Lincoln's decision early in 1864 to promote Grant to command of the entire Federal Army was crucial. Grant differed from his predecessors who feared confrontations with Lee. Instead, he realized that the key to victory was engaging Robert E. Lee and destroying the army of Northern Virginia. Grant understood that the superior industrial potential and population of the North would eventually wear down the South's ability to make war.

Lincoln also faced a serious re-election battle in 1864. The Democrats were running former Commanding General George McClellan. McClellan ran on the promise of ending the war by making peace with the Confederacy. Grant's successes in the field, along with the votes of Union soldiers, helped Lincoln win reelection.

The Emancipation Proclamation that freed slaves in territories in rebellion against the Union was a hollow act since it did not impair the Confederacy's economy; however, it did agree to raise Black regiments. The 54th Massachusetts Infantry was among the first organized. Their heroism at James Island and Fort Wagner, where the 54th lost 42 percent of its number in the assault, lead to the eventual raising of 178,975 African-Americans who served in the Union Army. Of these 37,635 were killed, about 25 percent mortality, mostly from disease. This figure was 35 percent greater than the Euro-American troops of the Union. This illustrates how badly African-American troops were mistreated, particularly if one recognizes that African-American units did not enter the war until 18 months after the fighting began. The Confederate government issued orders that any African-Americans in Federal uniform or officers in command of them would be executed upon capture. One example was at Fort Pillow. After the surrender of African- American troops, Confederate Major General Nathan Bedford Forrest ordered them massacred. Forrest would later be a founder of the Ku Klux Klan, a post-war terror organization designed to return political power to the former plantation owners.

Despite these deprivations, the contribution of African-American troops was indispensable to the final union victory. They took part in the final siege of Richmond and Lincoln made the symbolic act of being escorted into Richmond by African- American troops. Lincoln attributed much of the winning of the war to their efforts. The events of the war had taught Lincoln a great deal about African-Americans, and in part, he recanted his views about white superiority. He was the last casualty of this most important battle to prepare the ground for the equality of all people, assassinated by John Wilkes Booth in the Ford Theatre on April 14, 1865.

The Civil War completed the process that allowed for the creation of the United States as a modern industrial nation. Before the war, the South had sent a large fraction of its cotton exports to, and bought a great deal of its manufactured goods from, Great Britain. This had the impact of retarding the growth of American industrial power. The capital inflow from Southern agricultural production gave the slaveholders a great deal of political power, which they used to maintain the institution of slavery. The Civil War opened up new opportunities for industrial growth through the elimination of slavery and the end of England's control over southern agricultural produce. It brought about the opening of the South for potential industrial growth and prepared the nation for westward expansion.

JOSEPH L. GRAVES, JR.

See also **Africans: Overview; Slavery**

Further Reading

Angle, P., and E. Schenk Myers, *The Living Lincoln: The Man, His Times, and the War He Fought, Reconstructed from His Own Writings,* New York: Barnes and Noble, 1992

Aptheker, H., *The Negro in the Civil War,* New York, International Publishers, 1940

Cook, R., Civil War America: Making a Nation, 1848–1877, London/New York: Langdon Press, 2003

Douglas, F., "The Claims of the Negro Ethnologically Considered", in *The Life and Writings of Frederick Douglass, Vol. 2. Pre-Civil War Decade,* Lecture delivered at Western Reserve College, July 12, 1854, edited by P. Foner

Emilio, F., A *Brave Black Regiment: The History of the 54th Regiment of Massachusetts Volunteer Infantry, 1863–65,* New York: Da Capo Press, 1995

Graves, J.L., *The Emperor's New Clothes: Biological Theories of Race at the Millennium,* New Brunswick: Rutgers University Press, 2001

Helper, H.R., *The Impending Crisis of the South: How to Meet It,* New York: Collier Books, 1963

Parrish, W., editor, *The Civil War: A Second American Revolution,* New York: Holt, Rinehart and Wilson, 1970

Colombia

Capsule Summary

Country Name: Republic of Colombia
Location: Northern South America, bordering the Caribbean Sea, between Panama and Venezuela, and bordering the North Pacific Ocean, between Ecuador and Panama
Total Population: 41,662,073 (July 2003)
Minority Populations: Blacks (26%), Native Indians (2%), Mestizo (55%), White (17%)
Language: Spanish
Religion: Roman Catholic (90%)

The Republic of Colombia is the fourth largest Latin American country in area and the third in population. It borders Brazil, Ecuador, Panama, Peru, and Venezuela. The majority of the original indigenous groups belonged to the linguistic family of the Chibchas, whose most notable societies were the Taironas, who lived on the Caribbean coast, and the Muiscas, who lived in the interior mountains. The harsh climatic conditions of the Colombian lowlands led most of the indigenous population to settle in the mountain slopes. The Taironas settled in the lower slopes of the Sierra Nevada, a mountain range that rises abruptly from the Caribbean shores, where they developed a sophisticated society. The Muiscas, on the contrary, never developed any kind of long-lasting construction or engineering works like the Taironas. They were a mainly agrarian society that enjoyed internal peace and had good relations with their neighbors. Neither of these two societies developed empires comparable to those of the Aztecs or the Incas.

History

In the early sixteenth century, the first Spanish explorers, called *conquistadores*, arrived in Colombia, an event that caused abrupt and traumatic changes in the lives of indigenous peoples. The *conquistadores,* well-known for their gruesome cruelty to the natives, came searching for gold, slaves, and lands and conquered the main indigenous groups with relative ease. Once the chief resistance groups were defeated, the Spaniards organized a new society in which they occupied the upper layer and had the natives as their labor force. The most important institution of this new society was the *encomienda*, a system in which a group of Indians was entrusted to a Spaniard in charge of "civilizing" them—meaning conversion to Catholicism and the abandonment of their previous culture. In return the Spaniard received labor from the natives who worked in his fields.

During the seventeenth and eighteenth centuries, three processes took place that defined the country's ethnic composition. The first was the drastic decrease of the Indian population due to the harsh working conditions and disease. This was especially apparent in the Caribbean Coast, where the Indian population was reduced by around 95 percent from their pre-conquest level. The second was the growing interracial marriage between Spaniards and Indians creating the *mestizo* (mixed) population that eventually became the majority. The third was the arrival of thousands of African slaves brought to replenish the decreasing Indian labor force.

Columbia became independent of Spain in July 1810. By the nineteenth century the colonial society was clearly divided into five groups. In the upper layer were the Spanish officials, closely followed by the *criollos*, Latin American-born white people of Spanish descent. The third layer was occupied by the *mestizos* that represented a small but growing urban middle class and the growing peasant population. After the *mestizos* came the Indian population followed by the black slaves.

In the 1820s, the growing tensions between the *criollo* upper class and the Spanish government over economic policy and political freedom led to the Independence war, in which Indians and blacks were used by both sides to fight the enemy. After gaining its independence, the new government granted full citizenship to the Indians and attempted to abolish the *resguardos*, lands originally ceded by the Spanish crown to Indian communities to protect them from the abuse of the Spaniard landowners. With a booming agricultural export economy, the *criollo* elite needed to increase its landholdings and the *resguardos* stood in their way. Many *resguardos* were abolished and the lands appropriated by *criollo* landowners or occupied by *mestizo* colonists, leaving a floating population of landless Indians who had no choice but to work for the new owners of their former lands. However, an absolute formal abolition of the *resguardos* was not possible in part because of the strong resistance of some indigenous groups.

In 1851 the government abolished slavery. During colonial times, the authorities had dealt with numerous cases of slave rebellions and the existence of isolated communities of runaway slaves (*palenques*), some of which led a free, self-sufficient existence for the centuries to come. After the abolition of slavery, most of the black population remained working in domestic service, mines or plantations. Unlike the Indians, the blacks never organized themselves politically as an ethnic group.

The nineteenth century witnessed an uninterrupted reduction of indigenous lands. The surviving *resguardos* faced constant encroachments by large landowners as well as attacks by Liberal Party politicians who saw them as remnants of the colonial past and an obstacle for economic growth. Many *resguardo* lands were also lost when the government declared them unclaimed territory, subsequently granting them to large landowners. Additionally, the new political Constitution of 1886 withdrew full-citizenship from the Indians, permitting, however, the legal existence of the *resguardos*.

Between 1910 and 1918, 6,000 Paez Indians of the Cauca region led by Manuel Quintin Lame rose against the local landowners in what became the most serious indigenous rebellion in twentieth century Colombia. Lame was a Westernized Paez Indian who did not speak Paez but led the defense of the Paez *resguardos* against the large landowners and colonists. The Army eventually defeated the rebels and Lame spent the rest of his life in jail.

The Colombian indigenous movement had to wait several decades to reorganize after Lame's defeat. In 1971, some Indian communities organized themselves under the Cauca Indigenous Regional Council (CRIC) and the Colombian National Indigenous Organization (ONIC). These groups were viewed suspiciously by the government and some of their leaders were assassinated by right-wing paramilitary groups.

A dramatic change came in 1991 when a Constitutional Assembly wrote a new political constitution with the participation of indigenous representatives. This new constitution granted full-citizenship rights to the indigenous people, giving them the right to vote for the first time in the century, and also gave indigenous communities legal jurisdiction over their lands. The constitution additionally provided provisions for the black population to organize itself as an ethnic group. This political achievement was somewhat offset by the fact that in the following decade both blacks and Indians proved to be the most vulnerable victims of the war between the Colombian government, the left-wing guerrillas, and the drug Mafia. President Alvaro Uribe Velez has governed since August 7, 2002.

Society and Economy

Present day ethnic Colombian populations include 58 percent *mestizo* , 20 percent white, 14 percent mulatto, 4 percent black, 3 percent mixed black-Amerindian, and 1 percent Amerindian. Fifty-five percent of the population lived below poverty level, as of 2001. The population is variously employed in the following sectors: 46 percent in services, 30 percent in agriculture, and 24 percent in industry.

The country's GDP in 2002 was $251.6 billion with a per capita income of $6,100. The economy has struggled with low domestic and foreign demand, rigid government budgets, and serious internal armed conflict. President Uribe has been challenged to reform the country's pension system as well as reduce high unemployment and debt. Key export commodities include petroleum, coffee, coal, apparel, bananas, and cut flowers, although coffee and oil—the country's chief producers of income—have suffered in recent years due to depressed markets and the need for new exploration technology. Colombia is the supplier of about 90 percent of the cocaine to the U.S. market and the great majority of cocaine to other international drug markets.

MARCELO BUCHELI

See also **Latin Americans**

Further reading

Bushnell, David, *The Making of Modern Colombia: A Nation in Spite of Itself*, Berkeley: University of California Press, 1993

Rappaport, Joanne, *The Politics of Memory: Native Historical Interpretation in the Colombian Andes*, Cambridge: Cambridge University Press, 1990; Gutierrez, Ildefonso, *Historia del negro en Colombia*, Bogota: Nueva America, 1980

Colonialism

Colonialism can be generally defined as a type of domination by one country, the colonial power, over another, its colonies, for political, economic, religious, and or strategic purposes. By the end of World War II (1939–1945), "colonial territories" covered about one-third of the land surface of the globe. The origin of the word is the Latin *colonia,* historically signifying a plantation of people who emigrated and settled, and in the classical sense, tilled the soil. In the broadest sense, colonization can be partly understood as part and parcel of humankind's conquest of the earth's surface. But that is not the whole story, for a colony so planted became dependent on the "mother country" which the colonists had left voluntarily or involuntarily, for political or religious reasons, or simply as an outlet for over-population.

Some historians would claim that colonialism established a system of dependency in the colony, by which the administration served not the needs of the colonists but those of the colonial power and thus became a form of naked exploitation of the colony's resources for the benefit of the imperial power. In the history of colonies it could therefore be maintained that such dependency and exploitation made it difficult for the colony to develop on its own terms, and that even after decolonization dependent countries and peoples continued in a "backward" state as they comprised the under-developed Third World countries. In the context of minorities, colonies can be conceived to be originally smaller groups or minorities and part of a dependency culture until they became strong enough to assert their own political and economic independence. The subject can now be treated in a broad historical framework with appropriate sorties into colonial ideology.

Historical Framework

From the eighth to the sixth centuries BCE the Greeks and the Phoenicians established colonies from the Black Sea to the South of France and on the north African coast at Carthage; in the main they were peaceful enterprises and these colonies soon became independent city states. Greeks migrated too into the Persian Empire when it was conquered by Alexander the Great and these led to Hellenistic kingdoms rather than colonies in Egypt and Syria. The entire history of colonies and therefore of colonialism is the description of the ways in which the power, prestige, and profits of growing empires were enhanced, or so their leaders thought, by external dependencies of migrant settlers. It is useful to point out that not all migrants became colonists and not all colonists integrated with the native populations; some returned home.

In the expansion of the celebrated Roman Empire across Europe, Latin poets, philosophers, and statesmen made much of the mission of Rome to bring civility to barbarian peoples. Virgil (70–19BCE), the court poet of Augustus Caesar defines this mission with the following exhortation: "*Tu regere imperio Romano memento Hae tibi erunt artes, pacisque imponere morem, parcere subietis et debellare superbos"* [Remember Roman to rule firmly; these are to be your arts, to impose the ways of peace, to spare the downtrodden and put down the mighty] These sentiments would be echoed through the ages in justificatory statements in the cant of conquest and colonization, especially among the armchair philosophers and government officials often responsible for the undertaking of colonial enterprises.

Colonialism always requires justification. By the early modern period (i.e., the sixteenth century) the question of the appropriation of land and for surplus population looms large in the theory and practice of colonialism. In Thomas More's famous text of 1516, *Utopia*—that imaginary and ideal land—the author confronts the problem of overcrowding as he provides a justification for colonialism:

> "If the population (of Utopia) should happen to swell above the fixed quotas, they enroll citizens out of every city and, on the land nearest them, wherever the natives have much unoccupied and uncultivated land they found a colony under their own laws. They join with the natives, if they are willing, so that gradually the two parties merge and absorb the same way of life and the same customs to the advantage of both peoples....those who refuse to live according to their laws they drive from the territory which they carve out for themselves and if they resist they wage war against them...it is a just cause for war when a people which does not use

its soil but keeps it idle and waste yet forbids the use and possession of it to others who by the rule of nature ought to be maintained by it..." (More 1965, p.137).

More wrote as a lawyer and humanist; he knew of the Papal Bull of 1492 granting Ferdinand and Isabella of Spain dominion over all lands in the New World not already possessed by a Christian king. Henry VII of England granted John Cabot rights to possess for the King territories previously unknown to Christians. All the line of the Tudor monarchs became extensively and expensively engaged in an effort to take lands in Ireland and govern often using arguments that could have come out of More's *Utopia*. Beginning in the late fifteenth and lasting up until the seventeenth century, the preoccupation with trade routes and long-distance voyaging steadily increased. The English in particular became the significant presence in the North Atlantic, where their merchant slaver ships transported African slaves across the Atlantic. They also opened direct trade with Asia and eventually with India, where the Portuguese had preceded them. English seamen and merchants appeared indifferent to the explorations and colonization by other Europeans until they experienced competition from the burgeoning Dutch overseas activities; this competition began to expose many weaknesses in both English and French maritime enterprises. Many distinguished historians of the British Empire, for example, do not see a master plan or conscious development in its accumulation of colonies around the globe; instead they describe British colonization as the product of accident rather than design.

However, convictions of racial superiority undeniably shaped attitudes about how best remote places could be "civilized", how their unruly peoples could be reformed and their over-mighty chiefs tamed in an effort to impose western law and order in place of tribal feuds, and their native idleness turned into productive labor. According to such rhetoric, native peoples could theoretically inhabit an ordered polity regulated by the law and, above all, by Christian morality.

Methods of carrying out such a program of colonialism ranged from wholesale ethnic cleansing and destruction of native peoples to assimilation. Most colonies soon found that they needed to maintain a militarized frontier; examples of such multiplied in Ireland during the sixteenth century—Ireland being England's earliest colony and a prototype, or trial run as it were, for young Elizabethan adventurers on the make and on the move across the Atlantic to what became New England. Violence was justified not just on the basis of natural law, as More had argued, but also, according to theorists, churchmen and politicians, because the non-Christians such as the Indian and the African had to be evangelized: "brought to that knowledge (which the Romans could not give us) of that God who must save both them and us," as William Strachey preached in 1612 about the Indians of Virginia (cited in Canny, 1998, p.155).

Colonialism or Imperialism

By the nineteenth century the distinction between settling "colonia" and territorial aggrandizement or confiscation following on rebellion became blurred. France, for example, under the Third Republic embraced an imperial program second only to Britain's: Algeria had been occupied since the 1830s, and Tunis became a French protectorate in 1881. By 1912, the French had secured Morocco by ceding half of the Congo to Germany. French spheres of influence in Africa covered Senegal, parts of the Congo, the Sahara Desert extending from Somaliland towards the Sudan where they conflicted with Britain. The whole movement in the last decades of the nineteenth and early twentieth centuries became known as the Scramble for Africa, or the Partition of Africa. By means of the *Entente Cordiale* in 1904, France agreed to give Britain a free hand in Egypt in return for recognition of French interests in Morocco. And as the Entente merged into the Triple Entente of France, Britain, and Russia in 1907, France had ceded part of the Cameroons to Germany. Until about 1870, the greater part of the continent of Africa had been unknown to Europeans. The original settlements or colonies established by the Portuguese, Dutch, French and British had all been localized; no European power could claim an African "empire." But from 1875 until the outbreak of World War I in 1914, almost all of Africa and indeed a large portion of Asia and the Far East were occupied and parceled out among European nations in what became identified as an era of New Imperialism. This new wave of colonialism has often been explained by economic forces like industrialization that brought an increased demand for raw materials, a search for new markets for surplus manufactures, and an accumulation of capital that pursued profitable investment in the plantations, railways, mines, and rubber forests of both Africa and the Far East. Sometimes the old argument of population pressure surfaced as well, especially in Britain, Germany, France, and Italy. Economic and demographic forces can however be simplifications for the new wave of imperial colonization because nationalism, militarism, and patriotism also became conditioning factors in aggressive colonialism as the possession of a colonial empire conferred extra power and often, as in the case of Britain, brought strategic and military gains. British India became known as "The Jewel in the Crown." However, the impact of the West upon the East, especially in Asia, was very different from that of Africa.

Asia was densely populated and the home of older civilizations than the European, and colonization in Africa was speedier in comparison with Asiatic penetration where developments were gradual and continuous. In India, the British had reorganized the entire structure of a subcontinent, and despite mutual advantages the growth of nationalism and the inevitable anti-European reaction eventually led to British withdrawal. In 1892, Frederich Engels wrote: " ...colonies proper, that is, the countries occupied by a European population—Canada, the Cape, Australia—will all become independent; on the other hand countries inhabited by a native population which are simply subjugated—India, Algeria, the Dutch, Portuguese and Spanish possessions—must be taken over...by the proletariat and led as rapidly as possible to independence" (cited in Avineri, 1969, p.473).

The emergence of independent nation states in Asia and Africa after World War II raised many questions concerning the social and economic impact of colonialism and its enduring legacy as the period from 1947 to the 1970s can be seen as one of *decolonization.* Some writers see the continuing influences in trade and through cultural contacts with the indigenous elites as a form of "colonial nationalism"; others as the continuation of imperialism "by other means." In the same period the shift of global domination away from western Europe to that of the United States has been perceived by some commentators as inherently imperialist—from the Spanish-American war of 1898, no less an imperial one than the Boer War or the Russo-Japanese war, down to the Cold War politics of post-1945. Other historians and cultural critics even view in the global spread of contemporary mass culture from America a form of cultural colonialism or imperialism. Thematically then, colonialism can be studied from historical, economic, cultural, demographic, and political angles as part of humankind's conquest for territorial domination and confiscation.

JOHN MCGURK

See also **Assimilation; Imperialism; Nationalism; Self-determination**

Further Reading

Andrews, C.M., *The Colonial Period of American History,* New Haven: Publisher 1934

Andrews, Kenneth R., *Trade, Plunder and Settlement: Maritime Enterprise and the Genesis of the British Empire, 1480–1630,* Cambridge: Publisher, 1984

Avineri, Shlomo, editor, *Karl Marx on Colonialism and Modernization,* Garden City New York: Doubleday, 1969

Jennings, F., *The Invasion of America: Indians, Colonialism and the Cant of Conquest,* Chapel Hill: University of North Carolina Press, 1975

Canny, N., editor, *Europeans on the Move: Studies on European Migration 1500–1800,* Oxford: Oxford University Press, 1994

Canny, N., *The Origins of Empire,* Oxford: Oxford UP,1998

Canny, N., K.R. Andrews, and P.E.H. Hair, editors, *The Westward Enterprise,* Liverpool: Publisher, 1978

Grafton, Anthony *New Worlds, Ancient Texts: The Power of Tradition and the Shock of Discovery,* Cambridge, Massachusetts: Harvard University Press, 1992

Kiernan, V.G., *European Empires from Conquest to Collapse 1815–1960,* Fontana: Publisher, 1982

Kennedy, Paul, *The Rise and Fall of Great Empires,* New York: Publisher, 1987

More, Thomas, *Utopia,* edited by E. Surtz and J.H. Hexter, New Haven and London, 1965

Padgen, Anthony, *Lords of all the World: Ideologies of Empire in Spain, Britain, and France,* New Haven: Yale University Press, 1995

Parry, J.H, *The Age of Reconnaissance,* reprint, London, 1973

Comoros

Capsule Summary

Country Name: Islamic Federal Republic of the Comoros
Total Population: 632,948 (July 2003)
Minority Populations: French, Malagasy
Languages: Comorian (official), Arabic (official), French (official), Shikomoro (a blend of Swahili and Arabic), Shibushi
Religions: Sunni Muslim (98%), Roman Catholic (2%)

The four islands of the Comoro group, located in the western Indian Ocean, were settled early in the first millennium of the Christian era by African, Arab, and Austronesian immigrants. Comoros comprises three islands: Grande Comore (Njazidja), Anjouan (Nzwani), and Moheli (Mwali), in addition to four administrative municipalities named Domoni, Fomboni, Moroni, and Moutsamoudou. One of the poorest countries in the world, the islands suffer from a steadily increasing population, inadequate transportation, few natural resources, and ongoing political instability.

Long under Arab influence, the indigenous population includes Arabs, Asians, and peoples from the African mainland. Culturally the islands are Bantu and Islamic: Islamic influences may have been felt as early as the first century of the Hegira and today the population of 734,000 are almost entirely Sunni Muslem following the orthodox Shafiite rites. Independent from France since 1975, the islands form a federal republic with institutions based on the French model; however, the island of Mayotte (Maore), is occupied by France, while neighboring Ndzuani (Anjouan) declared its independence in August 1997. The independent but unstable republic has endured 19 coups or attempted coups since gaining independence from France in 1975. The 1996 Constitution established Comorian (of which there are four dialects), French, and Arabic as official languages; 30 percent of Comorians speak French, while approximately ten percent have knowledge of Arabic. Ethnic groups include Antalote, Cafre, Makoa, Oimatsaha, and Sakalava.

There are no significant cultural differences among the four islands, although perceived differences have on occasion, particularly since independence, had significant consequences. Historical writings that separated the population into Arab and Bushmen (*Wamatsaha*) components were based on physical characteristics more than on ethnic criteria, although there are families of Arab descent who practice endogamous marriage and claim descent from the Prophet, particularly in urban areas on the island of Ndzuani. Other groups referred to in the literature as Makwa and Cafres have no contemporary relevance: although many Comorians are descended from Makwa slaves, they in no sense form an ethnic group.

There are several small groups whose characteristics distinguish them from the general population. Most numerous are the Malagasy-speaking population of Mayotte, formerly referred to as Antalotes or Sakalava. Forming a third of the population of that island, they are descendants of eighteenth and nineteenth century immigrants from Madagascar and continue to speak Shibushi. However, they are now Muslem and are otherwise culturally assimilated to their Comorian speaking neighbors.

On Ngazidja, small group of Hadhramis continues to maintain a distinct identity and links both with Yemen and the East African coast, despite being socially well integrated. Several families of Gujerati origin, descendants of nineteenth century immigrants, live in urban areas on all four islands. A result of their Ismaili religious beliefs, they are less well integrated and form an endogamous group. Although they retain few contacts with India, many speak Gujerati as well as Comorian and French.

17,000 Comorian refugees, known as Sabenas, fled racial rioting in Mahajanga, Madagascar in 1976. Many live in and around the capital, Moroni, but although they continue to be distinguished from local-born Comorians, the basis for doing so is disappearing, and they are being absorbed into the local-born population. Other Madagascar-born Comorians, known as Zanatany, may also be identified as such but rarely suffer discrimination.

On Ngazidja (Grande Comore), there is a Malagasy community of recent origin, numbering several hundred and practicing the Christian (Protestant) faith. Approximately 2,500 ethnic French immigrants, mostly Catholic, who have established themselves as an economically dominant group inhabit Mayotte. While relations between Comorians and Malagasy are reasonably good, there are tensions between Comorians and French in Mayotte. Furthermore, since the declaration of independence of Ndzuani in 1997, a significant number of immigrants from that island have arrived in Mayotte. Subject to discriminatory treatment by the French administration as well as by the local population, they live in constant fear of deportation and enjoy few economic or political rights.

In 2002, the GDP per capita income in Comoros was only $700. Agriculture, including fishing, hunting, and forestry, contributes 40 percent to the GDP, and employs 80 percent of the labor force. While the government continues to attempt to increase education levels, technical training, health services and privatization, Comoros remains heavily dependent on decreasing sources of foreign aid.

Iain Walker

See also **Ismailis**

Further Reading

Chagnoux, Herv_, and Ali Haribou, *Les Comores,* Paris: Presses Universitaires de France, 1990

Lambek, Michael, *Human Spirits: A Cultural Account of Trance in Mayotte,* Cambridge: Cambridge University Press, 1981

Martin, Jean, *Comores: Quatre Iles Entre Pirates et Planteurs,* Paris: LÕHarmattan, 1983

Newitt, Malyn, *The Comoro Islands: Struggle Against Dependency in the Indian Ocean,* Boulder: Westview Press, 1984

Ottenheimer, Martin, and Harriet Ottenheimer, *Historical Dictionary of the Comoro Islands,* Metuchen, New Jersey: Scarecrow Press, 1994

Verin, Pierre, *Les Comores,* Paris: Karthala, 1994

Congo

Capsule Summary:

Country Name: Democratic Republic of Congo
Location: Central Africa, northeast of Angola
Total Population: 56,625,039 (July 2003)
Ethnic Populations: Central Bantu Type (Kongo, Kunda, Lala, Ndembu, Sakata, Yaka, Yanzi) (34%); Mongo Type (Kasai Luba, Mongo) (15%); Luba Type (Katanga Luba, Songye) (12%); Kivu Cluster (Furiiru, Havu, Hunde, Nyanga, Banyarwandan, Shi, Nande) (9%); Azande-Mangbetu Cluster (7%); Ngbandi-Ngbaka-Mbandja Type (6%)
Languages: French (official), Lingala (a lingua franca trade language), Kingwana (a dialect of Kiswahili or Swahili), Kikongo, Tshiluba
Religions: Roman Catholic (50%), Protestant (20%), Kimbanguist (10%), Muslim (10%), other syncretic sects and indigenous beliefs (10%)

The Democratic Republic of Congo (DRC), formerly Zaire, is the second largest country in Sub-Saharan Africa. It is bounded by nine different countries, the Central African Republic, Sudan, Uganda, Rwanda, Burundi, Tanzania, Zambia, Angola, and the Republic of Congo. With a total area of 905,356 square miles (2,344,872 square kilometers), it is home to some 200 ethnic groups. Most members of these diverse groups speak one or more of the four major African languages of the country: Lingala, Swahili, Kikongo, or Tshiluba. Its population of over 56,000,000 is effected in part by excess mortality due to AIDS, which can result in lower life expectancy, higher infant mortality, and death rates.

A governmental dictatorship since its 1960 independence from Belguim, Congo's central government has not had complete control over its territory. Relations between ethnic groups have been contentious at various periods of the country's history, most recently during the civil wars of 1996–97 and 1998–present.

History

Belgium colonized the present-day Congo in the nineteenth century. King Leopold II ruled the Congo Free State as his personal fiefdom following the Berlin Conference of 1884–85, using forced labor to extract rubber, ivory, and minerals. He was forced to turn over the administration of the colony to the Belgian government because of his excesses against the people. The colonial government continued to extract the resources of the vast, wealthy country without making any effort to develop it. Congo's abundant natural resources include minerals, timber, rubber, ores, and crude oil. The Belgian government also moved the *Banyarwandans*, ethnic Hutus or Tutsis of eastern Congo, into the two Kivu regions to work. The Belgians also relocated the ethnic *Luba* of the two Kasai provinces (south-central DRC) into the Katanga region (southeast DRC) to labor in the mines. Both of these moves increased ethnic tensions in these regions.

Calls for independence of the country began in the Katanga region, and political parties were formed, largely along ethnic lines. In the late 1950s, the separatist party Conakat (Confederation of Katangan Associations) was established by Moise Tshombe. Conakat drew support from the *Lunda* and *Yeke* ethnic groups. The Congolese National Movement also emerged as an important independence actor. It split into two camps in 1959. The ethnic *Lulua* of the Kasai provinces supported one faction, led by Patrice Lumumba. The *Luba* of Kasai supported the other faction led by Joseph Ileo, Cyrille Adoula, and Albert Kalonji.

Belgium granted the Congo independence on June 30, 1960, and Patrice Lumumba became prime minister. Five days later, the army mutinied. Belgium used the army mutiny to reestablish itself in the country, and United Nations troops were sent in to maintain order. In September 1960, President Joseph Kasavubu fired Lumumba. The military took over temporarily and Lumumba was arrested. Order was restored and power turned back over to Kasavubu in February 1961. Power struggles continued in the early 1960s between President Kasavubu and Katangan leader Moise Tshombe. In November 1965, the military took power again, and Mobutu Sese Seko became head of state. He renamed the state the Republic of Zaire in 1971 and ruled until 1997.

During the Cold War, the West used Mobutu in the fight to contain the spread of communism in southern Africa. He was able to hold onto power for so long first because of Western support and second because he systematically stole millions of dollars from state funds. Taking his cues from the Belgian colonial administration, Mobutu extracted resources from the country without building infrastructure or human capital. Lack of infrastructure, in turn, led to a lack of control by the central state over much of the country.

Politics

Several of Congo's ethnic groups have played a prominent role in its political development. The *Lunda* of Katanga Province were leaders in the secessionist attempts of that region just after independence and again in 1977 and 1978. The Katangans were aggrieved mainly because their region was plundered for its wealth by the central government without receiving any benefits. The Lunda also have a history of ethnic conflict with Congolese from other regions. For example, during the early 1990s, native Katangans drove out nearly all the Luba from the region, even those who had lived there for generations. The spark that ignited their expulsion from Katanga was the appointment of Etienne Tshisekedi, a Luba, as Prime Minister in 1992.

The Luba, originally of East and West Kasai provinces, became an indigenous elite under Belgian colonial rule. They took advantage of missionary education opportunities and became administrators in the colonial government. The *Banyarwandans* are people of Hutu and Tutsi ethnicity that were part of the greater Tutsi kingdoms of Rwanda and Burundi in pre-colonial times. They have long been resented by other ethnic groups in Congo, Rwanda, and Burundi because of their relative prosperity first under the Tutsi kingdoms and then under the colonial powers.

In 1996, a rebellion led by ethnic Tutsis broke out in eastern Congo. They had been subject to growing discrimination after the influx into Congo of approximately two million refugees, mostly Rwandan Hutus, following the 1994 Rwandan genocide. The Congolese Tutsis received support from their Rwandan brethren, Uganda, and other ethnic groups of eastern Zaire. Within less than a year, the rebels were able to overthrow Mobutu and installed Laurent Kabila, a Luba, as president. Kabila renamed the country the Democratic Republic of Congo and included many Rwandan and Congolese Tutsis in his administration. This led to resentment against the Tutsis by other Congolese who considered them foreigners. After a short time in power, Kabila felt secure enough to separate himself from his former allies, ordered all Rwandans out of the country, and allied himself with his former allies' enemies, the *Interahamwe*, the Rwandan Hutus responsible for the 1994 genocide. The Rwandan and Ugandan governments, mainly for security reasons, in turn launched a second rebellion in eastern Congo in late 1998. They nearly captured the country in a bold attack on Kinshasa, but were repelled by Angolan troops allied with Kabila. Kabila himself was assassinated on January 16, 2001 by one of his security guards. His son Joseph was installed as president shortly thereafter. The rebellion continues as of this writing with Ugandan and Rwandan troops and their Congolese allies controlling much of the east and north of the country and Kabila's government controlling much of the west and south.

The international community has attempted to broker a peace agreement since the second rebellion began. A cease-fire agreement, the Lusaka Peace Accords, was signed by all parties in July 1999. However, the Accords did little to end the fighting. In addition to Angola, Namibia and Zimbabwe are allies of the Congo government in the war. Aside from all the international actors in the war, there have also been numerous rebel groups from the region active in the DRC. Among the rebel groups that have launched raids from the DRC into their own countries are the *Interahamwe* from Rwanda, Hutu rebels from Burundi, members of the Allied Democratic Forces from Uganda, and UNITA rebels from Angola. The war in Congo has not been limited to its borders, and security in the entire region is precarious. Ethnic relations remain tense, and ethnic fighting over the past several years has taken place between the Hema and Lendu, among others, resulting in thousands of deaths. As many as 1.7 million people have died as a result of the wars in the DRC since 1996.

Society and Economy

It is estimated that the fighting between the Congolese government and the Uganda- and Rwanda-backed Congolese rebels resulted in 1.8 million Congolese who are internally displaced and 300,000 Congolese refugees who fled to surrounding countries. The civil war has dramatically reduced national output and government revenue, increased external debt, and has resulted in the deaths from war, famine, and disease of perhaps 3.5 million people. The republic has a literacy rate of just 65.5 percent and a GDP per capita income of only $600 as of 2002. Its export commodities include diamonds, copper, crude oil, coffee, and cobalt; key industries include the mining of diamonds, copper, and zinc, mineral processing, and the manufacture of consumer products including textiles, footwear, cigarettes, and processed foods. Despite the considerable economical potential, the Democratic Republic of Congo's economy has been greatly hampered by the effects of political instability, although conditions improved in late 2002 with the withdrawal of a large portion of the invading foreign troops.

Anne Pitsch

See also **Angola, Burundi, Rwanda, Tutsis, Uganda**

Further Reading

Ajulu, Rok, "Congo is Back! Congo is Gone! The Congo Crisis Again!" *Africa World Review,* February–April 1999

Amnesty International, *Zaire: Collapsing Under Crisis*, New York: Amnesty International, 1999

Meditz, Sandra W., and Tim Merrill, editors, *Zaire: A Country Study*, Washington, D.C.: Library of Congress, 1994

Prendergast, John, and David Smock, *Reconstructing Peace in the Congo*, Washington, D.C.: The United States Institute of Peace, August 1999

United Nations Office for the Coordination of Humanitarian Affairs, Integrated Regional Information Network (IRIN) daily reports Web site, <http://www.releifweb.int/IRIN>

Weiss, Herbert, *War and Peace in the Democratic Republic of the Congo,* Uppsala, Sweden: Nordiska Afrikaninstitutet, 2000

Young, Crawford, *Politics in the Congo: Decolonization and Independence*, Princeton: Princeton University Press, 1965

Congo Republic

Capsule Summary

Country Name: Republic of Congo
Location: West-Central Africa, on the right bank of the Congo River, neighboring former Zaire, Gabon, and Angola, and bordering the Atlantic Ocean
Total Population: 2,954,258 (July 2003)
Languages: French (official), Lingala and Monokutuba (lingua franca trade languages), many local languages and dialects (of which Kikongo has the most users),Teke, M'Bochi, Sangha
Religions: Christian (50%), animist (48%), Muslim (2%)

The Republic of Congo is a multi-ethnic country in West-Central Africa, independent from France since 1960. Its border countries include Cameroon, the Central African Republic, the Democratic Republic of Congo, the Cabinda exclave of Angola, and Gabon. With an area of 132,047 square miles (342,002 square kilometers), the Republic is composed of nine regions including its capital, Brazzaville, where 70 percent of the population lives.

History

The history of Congo has its roots in the thriving kingdoms of Kongo, Louango and Tio (or Teke), which included part of the country's present territory especially in the south and west. The Congo, then called the Kongo kingdom, was founded in the fourteenth century. The Portuguese first initiated slave trade in the coastal area in the fifteenth to the nineteenth centuries. In the age of imperialism and colonization in the late nineteenth century, the territory of what is now Congo was claimed by France. Pierre S. de Brazza, the French envoy in the area, negotiated a protectorate with the Teke king in the 1880s and established colonial posts to consolidate the French claims. French activities led to the final decline of the Teke and Louango kingdoms, already seriously weakened at the time of the arrival of the French. De Brazza was, however, opposed to the commercial exploitation of the region, which led to his replacement by the French government in 1886. Later Brazzaville became an important trading center and the capital of French Equatorial Africa.

The area became a territory of French Equatorial Africa in 1910; its status changed to that of French overseas territory in 1946. It became an autonomous republic within the French Community in 1958 and achieved full independence in 1960. The Republic of Congo has suffered political instability since that time with the government changing hands several times throughout the twentieth century.

After 1960, Congo's political system went though phases of multiparty democracy, one-party rule, and a military leadership to a presidential democracy in 1992. Congo's politics were always volatile and often accompanied by violence, playing upon ethnic animosities and rivalries. In 1968 a northern army officer, Marien Ngouabi, came to power in a *coup d'etat*, creating a socialist-Marxist regime under a unity party (the Congolese Workers' Party, PCT) and trying to do away with ethnic divisions. From 1977, when Ngouabi was assassinated, to 1979 a military junta ruled the country, and from 1979 to 1992, Colonel Denis Sassou-Nguesso, also a northerner, held power in a nominally Marxist one-party state (PCT).

In 1992, after a serious economic crisis and mass demonstrations of citizens and trade unions, a national conference of opposition groups forced the then-President Sassou to allow presidential elections. These yielded President Pascal Lissouba, a former prime minister. His rule was unsuccessful, and before the presidential elections of 1997, a civil war broke out, led by militias of various prominent political figures. The former President Sassou and the mayor of Brazzaville, Bernard Kolelas, had their own paramilitary forces recruited from certain ethnic groups. This led to devastating conflict in 1997 and also in 1998–1999, causing large-scale bloodshed, sexual violence, huge destruction of property including government offices and archives, displacement of hundreds of thousands of people, and looting of the premises of ex-patriots and foreign companies. In 1997, Sassou, who had ended the war in his favor with the help of Angola and former Rwandan Hutu troops, retook power, and the 1998–99 disturbances did not oust him from power. He is backed by the French and tries to consolidate his rule and expand his national support basis.

Society and Economy

Post-independence, Congo's economy, which was urbanized and relatively developed compared to other African countries, entered a phase of slow growth largely based on indigenous agriculture, fishing, export of primary agricultural products, manufacturing, mining, and logging. In the late 1970s oil was struck and oil revenues and oil refinery became the basis of accelerated growth and migration to the towns in the South. Oil has supplanted forestry as the mainstay of the economy; other exports include petroleum, lumber, sugar, cocoa, coffee, and diamonds. The port city Pointe-Noire became the economic hub of the country. Other manufacturing centers are Nyaki and Brazzaville. Outside the towns, most of the population still largely lives from subsistence agriculture, hunting, petty trade, fishing, and some cash crop production. In 2002, Congo had an estimated per capita GDP of only $900. Population growth was 1.53 percent in 2003 and remains affected by the excess mortality due to AIDS.

Congo contains various ethnic groups within its borders, many of which can also be found in the neighboring states of Gabon, Central African Republic, Cameroon, and the Democratic Republic of Congo. The country is marked by a high degree of urbanization, and virtually all of the ethnic groups are represented in the urban centers, though often living in segregated ethnic quarters. Despite this, the Congo population is mixed through intermarriages and has no solid ethnic polarization. This is also attested by the two important Creole trade languages, Lingala and Monokutuba.

Ethnicity

Congo has no clear majority group that has always held power, and consequently the problematic of minorities takes on a special from in the country. Ethnicity or "tribal" belonging, whether artificial or not, has always played a role in Congo's politics, but as a general background of competition for political access and economic resources. Identity struggles and persistent ethno-regional oppositions have determined much of the political rifts and recourse to violence that this country has seen since independence. This partly derives from the divergent political experiences and systems that the various ethno-regional groups have had: some were inheritors of a kingdom structure, but most, especially in the east, central and northern areas, were small-scale, non-centralized polities based of clan and lineage bonds and not sharing any overarching political culture.

The largest ethnic grouping, the BaKongo (about 50 percent of the population) never acted as a unit but was divided in many sub-groups with only a vague solidarity; among them, the Lari are one of the most important. The next largest groupings are the Sangha (some 18 percent), another diffuse group, and the M'Bochi (about 13 percent), also in the north. (The former ruler and current president Sassou originates from this group). The BaTeke, about 15–20 percent of the population, are an important group who live largely in the central Pool region. There is a long relationship of distrust and rivalry between the northerners and southerners in social life, business, and politics. Other groups—and as with the larger groups, it is not always clear what their boundaries are— include the Kota, the Maka, and Mbeti. The Binga pygmies are the only group who do not speak a Bantu language. As in many other African countries, scholarship on the nature and extent of cultural and social diversity of the various peoples of Congo is greatly lacking.

Congo's overarching state structure is inspired by French law and institutions, and its once-promising, urbanized economy did not preclude the recurrent political use of violence. Notably in the 1990s, the ethnic-based militias organized by elite politicians—not by army leaders—competed without a specific political program except looting and robbery, undermining the political and socio-economic fabric of the country in recurrent episodes of chaotic civil war. Congo's laws and constitutions, including the most recent approved by referendum on January 20, 2002, did not officially deal with ethno-cultural diversity and the social, economic, or cultural needs of minorities. Ethnicity was instrumentalized by power elites and not addressed within a political framework. Hence, the reconciling of concepts of democracy, ethno-cultural rights, and ethnic power-sharing have not found a promising solution.

Jon Abbink

See also **Angola; Congo; Rwanda**

Further Reading

Bazenguissa-Ganga, Remy, *Les Voies du Politique au Congo: Essai de Sociologie Historique*, Paris: Karthala, 1997

———, "The Spread of Political Violence in Congo-Brazzaville," *African Affairs* 98, no. 390, 1999, pp. 37–54.

———, "The Popularisation of Political Violence in Congo," *CODESRIA Bulletin* 1, 2000, pp. 55–59.

Clark, John F., "Congo: Transition and the Struggle to Consolidate," in *Political Reform in Francophone Africa*, edited by John F. Clark and David E. Gardinier, Boulder, Colorado: Westview Press, 1997

Decalo, Samuel, Virginia Thompson, and Richard Adloff, *Historical Dictionary of Congo*, Lanham, Maryland: Scarecrow Press, 1996

Ekholm Friedman, Kasja, and Anne Sundberg, "Ethnic War and Ethnic Cleansing in Brazzaville," in *From Post-traditional to Post-modern?: Interpreting the Meaning of Modernity in Third World Urban Societies*, edited by Preben Kaarsholm, Roskilde: International Development Studies, Roskilde University, 1995

Frank, Phillipe, "Ethnies et parties: le cas du Congo," *Afrique Contemporaine* 182, 1997, pp. 3–15

Sundberg, Anne, "Class and Ethnicity in the Struggle for Power–The Failure of Democratization in Congo-Brazzaville," *Africa Development,* 24, no. 1–2, 1999

Coptic Christians

Capsule Summary

Location: Egypt, with immigrant communities in various Western nations
Total Population: approximately 6–7 million
Language: Arabic
Religion: Christianity

The word *Coptic* is an anglicized form of the Arabic word *qibt*, which in turn is derived from the Greek *Agyptos/Agyptioi* meaning *Egypt/Egyptians*. Since the Arab conquest of Egypt in 641 CE, the term, originally a geographical and ethnic designation, has come to designate the Christians of Egypt who at that time constituted the absolute majority of the population. Today, Coptic Orthodox Christians are the largest single Christian population in Egypt and the entire Middle East region.

In the absence of reliable statistics, recent estimates as to the size of the community have ranged from five to ten million. They live throughout Egypt, but are found in greater concentrations in urban centers such as Cairo and Asyut. Since the mid 1970s, significant numbers of Copts have emigrated to western nations. Today, in addition to scattered Coptic parishes spanning Europe and Australia, major concentrations can be found in the United States on the East Coast and in Southern California. Still, the overwhelming majority of Copts reside in Egypt, where the dominant language of the Church is Arabic—and has been for the better part of the past millennium. The Coptic language, the last vestige of ancient Egyptian, is still retained to varying degrees as a liturgical language. Outside of Egypt, most parishes combine their country's vernacular with Coptic and Arabic to create a multilingual liturgical service.

History and Beliefs

The Coptic Orthodox Church traces its origins to the first century ministry of Saint Mark the Evangelist. Little is known of the Church's history until the end of the second century CE, at which time the School of Alexandria, the most prestigious theological institution of the time, came into its own under Origen, the protégée of Clement of Alexandria. Concurrently, during the long tenure of Patriarch Demetrius I (189–231 CE), the shroud that veiled the history of Christianity in Egypt lifted to reveal a vibrant Christian community. By the middle of the fifth century, Christians clearly constituted the majority of the populace in Egypt, though some regions retained a significant pagan presence.

The Great Persecution of Christians initiated by emperor Diocletian (284–305 CE) was especially harsh for those living in Egypt. Many heroic stories of martyrdom emerged from this period. This era was—and is—for the Copts an era of particular significance as both an historical and ideological Golden Age. This is best exemplified by the fact that in the Middle Ages while under Islamic rule, the dating system most often used in Egypt, the Era of Diocletian (beginning in 284 CE), was renamed the Era of the Martyrs. To this day, the liturgical calendar and consciousness of Coptic Christianity are inextricably bound to the Age of Martyrdom.

From the latter half of the second until the sixth century (roughly from the time of Clement of Alexandria to patriarch Theodosius), the See of Alexandria produced some of the greatest theological minds in all of Christendom. Two Alexandrian patriarchs, Saints Athanasius and Cyril, stand out not only as bulwarks of Alexandrian theology, but also as pillars of orthodox Christianity worldwide. The Copts also take pride in the fact that monasticism originated in Egypt during the fourth century with Saint Antony the Great. Later, those he influenced articulated various expressions of Christian monasticism. Among these were individuals such as Pachomius, Macarius the Great, and Shenoute of Atripe. Fourth and fifth century pilgrims, prominent among whom is John Cassian, were instrumental in recording and diffusing the monastic ideals of Egypt far into the West. The actions and words of these early Egyptian monks, as recorded in various hagiographic lives and the *Sayings of the Desert Fathers*, have persisted as the foundation of Christian monastic spirituality. Although Egyptian monasticism endured a number of fluctuations under Islamic rule, it eventually lost more than it had gained. Today, since the 1960s, the Coptic Orthodox Church has experienced an often-acclaimed monastic revival. Many monasteries, which were abandoned for centuries, have been repopulated, and the number of monks in many monasteries increased, sometimes as much as ten-fold. This monastic revival is likewise apparent in Egypt's convents.

The Coptic Church upholds the decisions of the first three Ecumenical Councils: Nicea (325 CE), Ephesus (381 CE), and Constantinople (431 CE). However, it has always rejected the decrees of the council of Chalcedon (451 CE), believing that it forwarded a heretical Nestorian Christology. Throughout the centuries this has caused a number of unfortunate incidents and severed communion between the anti-Chalcedonian Churches (which include the Coptic, Ethiopian, Syrian, Armenian, and Indian Orthodox) and those that accept the Council of Chalcedon—most notably the Roman Catholic, Greek, Russian, and Antiochian Orthodox Churches. In the centuries after Chalcedon, the Copts were accused of Monophysitism, the belief that Christ had only one divine nature and were thus labeled heretics. Recent scholarship, however, has cast serious doubts as to the accuracy of this label, which the Copts have always disavowed both doctrinally and liturgically. The Copts believe that Jesus Christ was perfect in his humanity as he was perfect in his divinity, the two natures uniting without mixing, confusion, alteration, or separation to forge one individual/person. Currently, scholars and theologians prefer to define the Coptic Orthodox Church as non-Chalcedonian, or anti-Chalcedonian. Although the rift born of Chalcedon persists into the present, great strides have recently been made toward its mending. In 1973, Shenouda III, 117th Pope and Patriarch of the See of St. Mark, together with the Roman Pontiff Pope Paul VI, signed a declaration in which the Christological controversies of the fifth century were put to rest. A similar agreement is all but signed between the Coptic and other Orthodox Churches.

Arab Muslims conquered Egypt in 641 CE. The Christian Egyptians (Copts) were able to retain their language and popular majority into the tenth century. But by that time Arabization and conversion to Islam were well underway and clearly visible. From the eleventh through the thirteenth centuries, the process of official (i.e., church-sponsored) Arabization was in full swing, its most notable signature being the translation of the liturgy into the Arabic language. In theory, the Copts, as a non-Muslim (*dhimmî*) community, were required to pay a poll tax (*jizya*) but otherwise allowed to govern their own affairs. Although it would not be difficult to cite many incidents of dysfunction in this idealistic arrangement, Coptic Christians—through their ecclesiastical hierarchy and influential notables—did, for the most part, govern much of their own affairs. This arrangement was further formalized under the Ottoman *millet* system.

Throughout the Middle Ages, the Christian population experienced steady numerical decline and was periodically the object of various discriminatory decrees and even persecutions by both the Islamic state and populace. Some of the most horrendous periods of persecution came from the hands of Caliph al-Hakim bi-Amr Allah (996–1021 CE) and during the turbulent period of the Crusades. But for the most part, Christians and Muslims coexisted peacefully. Today, this is still true, though a noticeable increase in Muslim fundamentalism has made the Copts increasingly vulnerable to various types of discrimination that has at times escalated into violence. Some of these incidents are quite serious. The Copts are a people easily identified by their Christian names, religious necklaces, and cross tattoos on the inside of the right wrist; as such, they are easy targets for fanatics. And indeed, a number of major incidents of violence against Christians occur every year, especially in Upper Egypt and rural towns—most recently at the village of al-Kosheh, although the grisly events of al-Zawya al-Hamra in 1981 must also be mentioned.

The Coptic Church, like all other Orthodox churches, holds to the seven sacraments of baptism by immersion, Chrismation, confession, communion/Eucharist, unction, matrimony, and holy orders. Its ecclesiastical structure, dogma, theology, and practices are closely aligned with the rest of Eastern Orthodoxy. Coptic priests are usually married while bishops and patriarchs are necessarily celibate, as they are chosen exclusively from monastic ranks. Within the last decade, many women have also been consecrated deaconesses; however, this is not a clerical rank in the Coptic Church.

Coptic Society

Officially, the Coptic hierarchy—which in recent decades has become the sole voice for the Copts in Egypt—refuses to be identified as a minority, religious or otherwise. They claim that as citizens who participate in all aspects of Egyptian society, the Copts cannot be a minority within their own country. Still, discrimination is visible and is perhaps most blatant in the current legislation which makes it necessary to obtain a presidential decree to simply repair a church, much less build a new one.

Coptic Christians contribute to their communities in all capacities as soldiers, doctors, teachers, etc. In recent decades, however, with the notable exception of Boutros Boutros Ghali, the former Egyptian Minister of State for Foreign Affairs and later United Nations Secretary General, they have been significantly underrepresented in the political establishment. Copts are almost always appointed to government positions, and very seldom elected to such posts.

The Copts are present in every economic stratum of society; some have successfully amassed exorbitant fortunes while the *zabaln* of Cairo, the garbage collectors who constitute the lowest socio-economic stratum, are disproportionately Christian. Higher education and secondary degrees are common among the Copts. Outside of Egypt, as is the pattern for many other first-generation immigrants, the Coptic community is saturated with medical doctors, engineers, and PhDs, almost always in the sciences.

The Coptic Church underwent an important period of "reform" under Patriarch Kyrillos IV from 1854–1861 and is currently (since the 1960s) experiencing a renaissance that is evident in many areas: monasticism, education (the Sunday school movement), iconography, social work, and women's roles, among others. It is difficult to overestimate the importance and extent of the current renewal; still, the results have been mixed. Perhaps most notable, due to its ramifications, are the new requirements instituted for the election and elevation of clergy. Currently, only college graduates are considered for ordination as bishops or priests. Even though this has been a vital step forward, the advancement is asymmetrical. The vast majority of ordained clergy hold degrees in the sciences, while very few hold degrees in theology, ecclesiastical history or the like. And while many have obtained secondary degrees from the Coptic Seminary, it must be admitted that the curriculum and level of study—while a great improvement over past centuries—cannot be compared to those of Western institutions. The current revival has also resulted in the shrinking of leadership roles for the laity in the Church, which was a natural consequence of the centralization of moral, religious, and political leadership into the hands of the hierarchy. Still, the role of the laity, both men and women, must not be underestimated. While the Church's hierarchy provides vision and motivation, the laity carry out the actual work.

Outside of Egypt, Coptic communities tend to cluster around their parish churches, the first seven of which were founded during the patriarchate of Kyrillos VI (1959–1971). The number of Copts who have emigrated to western nations (and consequently the number of Coptic Churches outside of Egypt) has increased exponentially during the current patriarchate of Shenouda III (1971 to present). There are currently over one hundred and seventy Coptic Churches in Western nations. These immigrant communities face new, yet similar challenges, and tend to follow one of two patterns. The first may be observed in regions such as Southern California where the bulk of the first generation immigrants were composed of nuclear families. Consequently, the first generation tends to be self-contained. The number of converts and incidents of intermarriage are negligible, and the Arabic and Coptic languages tend to monopolize the liturgical services. As second and third generations are born, however, these communities tend to face the same challenges with regard to language, identity, and intermarriage that communities who follow the second pattern of immigration face during their first generation. The second pattern is evident in countries such as the Netherlands, where a large segment, if not the majority of the first immigrants, was composed of single young men. In such communities, incidents of intermarriage with westerners are very common and consequently result in a greater rate of social and linguistic acculturation. The Coptic Church's hierarchy has been sensitive to these changes, encouraging the use of the vernacular in the liturgy and sponsoring youth-centered retreats and conferences. In the past eight years it has even taken the historical step of ordaining bishops for Western countries and regions in which there are sizeable Coptic populations.

Maged S.A. Mikhail

See also **Christians: Overview; Christians: Africa; Egypt; Pope Shenouda III (Coptic Christian)**

Further Reading

Atiya, Aziz S., editor, *The Coptic Encyclopedia*, 8 volumes, New York: Macmillan, 1991

Atiya, Aziz S., *A History of Eastern Christianity*, Indiana: University of Notre Dame Press, 1967; Rep., Krause Reprint, 1980

van Doorn-Harding, Nelly, and Kari Vogt, editors, *Between Desert and City: The Coptic Orthodox Church Today,* Oslo: Novus Forlag, 1997
Ibrahim, Saad Eddin, *The Copts of Egypt*, United Kingdom: Ibn Khaldoun Center, 1996
Malaty, Fr. Tadros Y., *Introduction to the Coptic Orthodox Church*, Ontario, Canada: Saint Mary Coptic Orthodox Church, 1987
Meinardus, Otto F. *Two Thousand Years of Egyptian Christianity*, Cairo: American University Press, 1999

Corsicans

Capsule Summary:

Location: Corsica, France, Western Mediterranean/Tyrrhenian Sea
Total Population: approximately 160,000
Language: Corsican (*corsu*), French
Religion: Christian

An island belonging to France and located southeast of that country, Corsica lies in the Tyrrhenian Sea, between northwestern Italy and Sardinia. Its position has been considered significant as a platform for military operations, which were violent and ongoing between Italy and France for centuries. Corsican (*corsu*) is a Romance language closely related to Italian, and in particular to some Tuscan dialects. The development of the language is largely due to the rule of Pisa (1077–1284), which was followed by Genoese domination of the island (1284–1768).

From time immemorial Corsican politics has been marked by rivalry among the clans, resulting in a social system similar to the one which developed in other Mediterranean islands, especially Sicily. According to this system, families play a leading role in social and political life, each one with her definite range of activities. Clanism, despite being opposed by many nationalist movements, has survived to the present day.

History

In 1755, while the island was still under Genoese rule, nationalist leader Pasquale Paoli proclaimed the independence of Northern Corsica. Paoli established the capital in Corte, where he also founded a university, and launched an economic policy based on traditional farming. The Corsican Consititution preceded both the French and the American consitutions. In later centuries Paoli would be remembered as Corsica's national hero, *u babbu di a patria* (Father of the Homeland). Although many politicians and scholars admired him, no European state recognized his independent Corsica.

In 1768, Genoa sold Corsica to France. One year later, at Pontenovu, Paoli was definitively defeated by the French army, marking the beginning of French rule of the island. On November 30, 1789, the National Assembly declared Corsica an integral part of France. With British support, Paoli expelled the French in 1793, and in 1794 Corsica voted its union with the British crown. The French under Napoleon Bonaparte recovered it in 1796, and French possession was guaranteed at the 1815 Congress of Vienna. French rule brought education and relative order to Corsica, but economic life remained agrarian and primitive. Since the French took control in 1768, Corsica has seen separatist movements, with repeated incidents of violence. In the 1800s, a group of Corsican intellectuals, led by Salvatore Viale, tried to promote Italian culture. They came in touch with several Italian writers and politicians, including Niccolò Tommaseo and revolutionary leader Giuseppe Mazzini. The French language, however, was already taking root in the island.

During World War II, Italian and German troops occupied Corsica, until late in 1943 the population revolted, and, joined by a Free French task force, drove the Axis forces out. A postwar population exodus spuured the French government to announce a program of economic development. In 1958 a right-wing coup, similar to that in French Algeria, contributed to the return to power in France of Charles de Gaulle.

After 1962 when Algeria won independence from France, all French Algerians were forced to leave the new African republic. The French government decided to resettle many of them in Corsica's eastern plain. The massive immigration of French Algerian refugees to Corsica, however, aroused widespread discontent among the Corsicans, because the government aid granted to newcomers damaged existing businesses. Moreover, other critics believed that France's loss of Algeria would be offset by a heavier *francisation* (frenchification) of Corsica.

Corsica's recent difficulties date from the 1960s, when France came to be perceived as pursuing a colonialist policy on the island. In response, Corsican movements for independence and autonomy began to take shape. In general the Corsican autonomist proposals have centered on the promotion of the Corsican language, increased power for local governments, and some supplementary tax relief. The French government has remained strongly opposed to the idea, fearing it would threaten the unity of France.

The autonomist movement gained headway in the late 1960s with Edmond and Max Simeoni, two brothers who founded the *Azzione pe a Rinascita Corsa* (Action for Corsican Renaissance, ARC). Their organization advocated an autonomy similar to that enjoyed by South Tyrol (an Italian region which was once part of the Austro-Hungarian empire) and refused violence, even though it was involved in a tragic event. In August 1975, in Aleria, a group of armed men led by the Simeoni brothers occupied the vineyard of Henri Depeille, who had been involved in a scandal of doctoring wine with excessive amounts of sugar. The French Government sent troops and gunfighting occurred, resulting in two men shot dead. Simeoni was jailed and tried; the Public Prosecutor invoked the death sentence although he was sentenced to life imprisonment. Thousands of Corsicans gathered in the streets showing their solidarity.

The ARC was banned but was soon revived by Max Simeoni as *Unione di u Populu Corsu* (Union of the Corsican People, UPC). Simeoni was pardoned and released in 1975. He and his brother began networking with several European autonomist movements, such as the Basque and the Welsh. Not all Corsicans, however, refused violence. In May 1976, some of those who had been involved in the Aleria affair, alongside with others from disbanded terrorist organizations, founded the Fronte Naziunale di Liberazione di a Corsica (Corsican National Liberation Front, FLNC). The new armed organization issued a manifesto declaring war on the French Government and advocating total independence.

The FLNC was given space in the press due to dynamite attacks in several French cities. For over a decade, however, the terrorists carefully avoided killing people.

In 1981, before being elected Prime Minister, Socialist leader François Mitterrand promised that Corsica would be granted a larger degree of autonomy. In the same year, the powers of the Corsican regional assembly became wider than those granted to other regions, including employment and broadcasting. Most Corsicans, however, were not satisfied with the French government's promises. Clan domination, meanwhile, remained strong. The French Government banned the FLNC in 1983, although this did little to stop the organization and caused the various separatist movements to go underground.

The 1990s were marked by several splits which weakened the separatist milieu. Many militants were killed by rival factions. In 1998, the newly elected Prefect of Corsica, Claude Erignac, was killed by a separatist commando in the centre of Ajaccio. This urged the French Government to find a way to settle the question.

In 2000 Prime Minister Lionel Jospin launched his proposal of autonomy for Corsica in exchange for a cessation of what was beginning to resemble gang violence. Jospin's plan provided greater local powers, including the teaching of the Corsican language within the educational system; France traditionally has discouraged the use of regional or minority languages. The Prime Minister was strongly opposed by the Jacobin (Gaullist) politicians in the French National Assembly who viewed autonomy as the first step towards the balkanisation of France. They feared, for example uprising autonomist movments in Brittany and elsewhere. One of the most fervent advocates of a "one and indivisible France", Minister of the Interior Jean-Pierre Chévenement, resigned as a gesture of protest against Jospin's proposals. In contrast, Jospin's viewpoints were welcomed by the other French minorities—Alsatians, Basques, Bretons, Catalans, Flemish, Occitans—which total several million people. In 2003, after constitutional amendments permitting greater local autonomy were approved, a referendum on autonomy was held, but Corsican voters narrowly defeated it.

ALESSANDRO MICHELUCCI

See also **Algeria; France; Italy**

Further Reading

Centre européen des questions de minorités (ECMI), *Autonomies insulaires: Vers une politique de la différence pour la Corse?*, Ajaccio: Albiana, 1999.

Culioli, Gabriel Xavier, *Le complexe corse*, Paris: Gallimard, 1990.

Jaffe, Alexandra, *Ideologies in Action: Language Politics on Corsica*, Berlin-New York: Mouton de Gruyter, 1999.

Poggioli, Pierre, *Journal de bord d'un nationaliste corse*, La Tour d'Aigues: Editions de l'Aube, 1996.

Ramsay, Robert, *The Corsican Time-bomb*, Manchester: Manchester University Press, 1984.

Renucci, Janine, *La Corse*, Paris: Presses Universitaires de France, 1982.

Saint-Blancat, Chantal (ed.), *La Corsica: identità etnico-linguistica e sviluppo*, Padua: CEDAM, 1993.

Simeoni, Edmond, *La volonté d'être*, Ajaccio: Albiana, 1995.

Costa Rica

Capsule Summary:

Location: Central America, bordering both the Caribbean Sea and the North Pacific Ocean, between Nicaragua and Panama
Total Population: 3,896,092 (July 2003)
Minority Populations: White (including *mestizo*) (94%), black (3%), Amerindian (1%), Chinese (1%), other (1%)
Languages: Spanish (official), Creole English (Southwestern Caribbean), Amerindian (Chibchan) languages (Bribri, Cabécar, Maléku Jaíka, Ngäbere), Chinese
Religions: Roman Catholic (76.3%), Evangelical (13.7%), Jehovah's Witnesses (1.3%), other Protestant (0.7%), other (4.8%), none (3.2%)

The population of the Republic of Costa Rica has historically been concentrated in the central highlands of the country. The country, with an area of 19,652 square miles (50,899 square kilometers), is slightly smaller than the state of West Virginia. It lies at the base of Central America, just above Panama, and stretches from the Pacific Ocean to the Caribbean Sea. It is bordered by Nicaragua and Panama. The development of Costa Rica's minorities is related to the growth of population centers beyond this historic axis of the highlands.

History

Spaniards first reached Costa Rica in the sixteenth century making it a province in 1540 and establishing a settlement in the 1560s. Unlike other areas of the Spanish empire that had been earlier occupied, Costa Rica had no mineral wealth and was sparsely inhabited by native Indians. The colonists who settled the area , therefore, concentrated in the rich agricultural land of the central valley highlands. The indigenous people were of only marginal interest to Spanish colonial officials.

Land was occupied in the form of both large and small farms so that, unique in Spanish America, Costa Rica had a sizable minority of small, independent farmers. The weight of this socioeconomic balance would go far in ultimately providing Costa Rica with a singularly stable, democratic, middle-class society. It enjoys the highest annual per capita income in the region. It maintains no army, an institution that has been the bane of so many other Latin American countries.

Costa Rica declared its independence from Spain in September 1821 and adopted a constitution in 1871. A democratic republic, the country has been relatively free of violence and conflict that could potentially mar its democratic development since the nineteenth century. The country's border disputes with Panama began in the turn of the last century and not settled until 1941. In 1962 Costa Rica joined the Central American Common Market, and in 1987 then-President Oscar Arias Sánchez was awarded the Nobel Peace Prize for his efforts in negotiating peace among El Salvador, Nicaragua, and Guatemala.

Society and Ethnicity

Never large, the native Indian population of Costa Rica today compromises less than one percent. They have settled almost entirely along the southern edge of the country. The principal native languages, in the Chibchan family and spoken by at most a few thousand, are Bribri, Cabécar, and Ngäbere. There remain only a few hundred speakers of Boruca and Teribe. In the north, a similar pocket of speakers of Maléku Jaíka exists. The native population was early evangelized into Roman Catholicism.

The population of Costa Rica has historically been white and Spanish-speaking. Indeed, much of this population has differentiated itself, if at all, in terms of its origins from provinces in Spain, such as Galicia, Castile, the Basque country, or Catalonia.

Africans were imported in colonial times to work on plantations along the Pacific coast. This population interbred with the white, producing a considerable *mestizo* (mixed race) element. They maintain no distinct black African cultural tradition, speaking Spanish and following the Catholic religion. Indeed, Costa Ricans present a singular level of national homogeneity and identity, and have a distinguishing name for themselves, *Ticos*. This Tico identity permeates much of the national popular legend, music, and culture.

Nevertheless, a second black population, along the Caribbean coast, remains distinctive. It originated from Jamaica and the West Indies, coming to Costa Rica in the late nineteenth century. These people came as labor for building a railroad from the capital in the central interior, San José, to the coastal city of Limón. They were distinct from the majority of the Tico population not only because of race but also because of language and religion. Their language was a Creole form of Caribbean English, and, since they had been Christianized from Africa in British colonies, they were Protestant. They settled in the Caribbean coast city of Limón, making it the major port of Costa Rica. However, they made that city an English-speaking, Protestant entity. Moreover, since they worked on the route of the railroad from San José and on the banana plantations along it, they gave their cultural characteristics to this corridor of territory.

The Ticos did not easily accept these alien characteristics. The railroad, the Limón port facilities, and the banana plantations and trade were owned or controlled by Americans. Their laborers were seen as part of a foreign economic interest, the United States, itself a Protestant, English-speaking country that was often at war with Catholic, Spanish-speaking countries. Well into the twentieth century, there was suspicion and hostility toward this minority. However, in 1949 they were awarded the right to Costa Rican citizenship and over the decades since have gradually been absorbed into Tico society.

The only exception to this integration has been the community of Afro-Costa Ricans that remain in or near Limón. Comprising now about two percent of the national population, they still retain their distinct cultural and religious orientation. Standard and Creole English are the dominant languages in the Limón area. However, these Afro-Costa Ricans suffer much less now from bias. They are important to the Caribbean tourist trade and their distinctiveness is now seen as a contribution to the cosmopolitan variety of Costa Rica in an age of globalization. Costa Rica prides itself on the sophisticated nature of the tourism to its tropical forest lands, which emphasizes—indeed pioneered—environmental or eco-tourism.

Another minority that arrived in Costa Rica with the building of railroads was the Chinese. A few thousand descendants of the original Chinese still speak Mandarin or Hakka forms of their ancestral language. They are concentrated mostly in San José and along the corridor to Limón and are bilingual in Spanish or English.

Costa Rica's basically stable economy depends on tourism, agriculture, and electronics exports. With a 2002 GDP per capita income of $8,300, the 1.9 million labor force is employed in the following sectors: agriculture (20 percent), industry (22 percent), and services (58 percent). Costa Rican industries include microprocessors, food processing, textiles and clothing, construction materials, and fertilizer. Although poverty has been substantially reduced in the last 15 years, a great disparity of wealth remains among the population.

EDWARD A. RIEDINGER

See also **Afro-Caribbeans**

Further Reading

Barry, Tom, *Costa Rica: A Country Guide*, 3rd edition, Albuquerque, New Mexico: Inter-Hemispheric Education Resource Center, 1991

Biesanz, Mavis Hiltunen, Richard Biesanz, Karen Zubris Biesanz, *The Ticos: Culture and Social Change in Costa Rica*, Boulder, Colorado: Lynne Rienner, 1999

Creedman, Theodore S., *Historical Dictionary of Costa Rica*, Latin American Historical Dictionaries, vol. 16, Methuen, New Jersey: Scarecrow Press, 2nd edition, 1991

Harpelle, Ronald, *The West Indians of Costa Rica*, Montreal: McGill-Queen's University Press, 2001

Sánchez, Margarita, and Michael J. Franklin, *Communities of African Ancestry in Costa Rica, Honduras, Nicaragua, Argentina, Colombia, Ecuador, Peru, Uruguay, Venezuela*, Washington, DC: Inter-American Development Bank, 1996

Stanisfer, Charles, compiler, *Costa Rica*, World Bibliographical Series, vol. 127, Oxford, England: Clio Press, 1991

Côte D'ivoire

Capsule Summary:

Country Name: République de la Côte d'Ivoire
Total Population: 16,962,491 (July 2003)
Minority Population: Baoule (23%), Bété (18%), Senufo (15%), Malinke (11%), Agni, Foreigners (35%)
Ethnic Groups: Akan (42.1%), Voltaiques or Gur (17.6%), Northern Mandes (16.5%), Krous (11%), Southern Mandes (10%), other (2.8%) (includes 130,000 Lebanese and 20,000 French) (1998)
Languages: French (official), 60 native dialects including Diola, Baule, Senufo
Religion: Christian (20–30%), Muslim (35–40%), indigenous (25–40%) (2001); the majority of foreigners (migratory workers) are Muslim (70%) and Christian (20%)

Côte d'Ivoire (Ivory Coast) is a nation of nearly 17 million inhabitants in western Africa, bordered by Liberia and Guinea in the west, Mali and Burkina Faso in the north, Ghana in the east, and the Gulf of Guinea in the south. Its political capital is Yamoussoukro; its administrative and commercial center remains Abidjan, the former capital, a city of nearly three million inhabitants. A republic, the Côte d'Ivoire established a multi-party presidential regime upon gaining independence from France in 1960.

The country is heavily dependent on agriculture and its economy is vulnerable to weather conditions and sensitive to fluctuations in prices of its main exports: coffee, cocoa, and palm oil. Estimated GDP per capita income was $1,400 in 2002.

Côte d'Ivoire is inhabited by about 60 peoples speaking different languages. They are usually classified into seven main groups: Akan, Kru, Senufo, Lobi, Lagoon, and both Nuclear and Peripheral Mande. The largest subgroups are the Akan Baule, who make up 23 percent of the population, and the Kru Bété who comprise 18 percent. Numerous are also Senufo, Malinké, and Agni. Ethnic groups overlap present-day frontiers. It is estimated that over one-third of the population consists of non-Ivoirian born Africans, mainly Burkinabe and Malians. The influx continues as Liberians flee civil war. The Ivory Coast has had a tradition of hospitality and tolerance, but in recent years politicians have institutionalized ethnic strife.

Estimates concerning the inhabitants' religion vary widely, because traditional beliefs survive among members of theistic religions. It appears that 30 to 40 percent of the population is Muslim, 20 to 30 percent Christian, and 25 to 40 percent indigenous or animist.

Côte d'Ivoire remained somewhat isolated for centuries. Islam made only minor inroads. The first Europeans to arrive were the Portuguese in the fifteenth century. French missionaries arrived in 1637. In the eighteenth century, the country was invaded by the Agni, who occupied the southeast, and the Baule, who settled in the central section bringing with them their culture and artifacts. An inhospitable coast and inadequate harbors delayed European exploration, although in the 1830s and 1840s the French did negotiate treaties with chiefs along the coast.

French explorers, missionaries, trading companies, and soldiers gradually penetrated into the interior. After the 1884–85 Berlin Conference, the French used these earlier contacts to claim ownership of the region. They developed plantations and factories; goods from French possessions on the Niger were shipped from the Ivoirian coast.

From 1904 to 1958, Côte d'Ivoire was a member of the Federation of French West Africa. From then to the 1990s, the evolution of the country was directed by one man, Félix Houphouët-Boigny, a Baule physician and wealthy coffee grower. He began his political career in defense of African planters protesting the French administration's race-based crop prices and the use of forced labor. He was elected Deputy to the French National Assembly in 1945 on the ticket of the Democratic Party of Ivory Coast (PDCI) which he founded. Upon Houphouët-Boigny's urging, the French Assembly outlawed forced labor in the colonies in 1946, making him a hero to West Africans.

Between 1946 and 1960 Houphouët-Boigny occupied a series of influential administrative posts. At the same time, he built up his party's strength and organization. When independence came in 1960, he was elected president, and for the next three decades he ruled Côte d'Ivoire and maintained the most stable government in West Africa. The country was technically a democratic republic; the one-party government held regular presidential and legislative elections. Under his leadership the country enjoyed a strong economy with free-enterprise policies that attracted foreign investments, in particular in close cooperation with France. The agricultural economy profited from stability in world market prices for its cash crops. By the early 1980s Côte d'Ivoire had the highest per capita income in sub-Saharan Africa except for the oil-producing states.

However, the situation deteriorated: a worldwide recession in the late 1970s and early 1980s weakened the economy and hence decreased Houphouët-Boigny's popularity. Ivoirians criticized him for spending billions unproductively to transform his native village of Yamoussoukro into a modern capital with a basilica as large as St. Peter's in Rome. Opposition leaders, who accused him of accepting French neocolonialism, and international donors concerned about possible governmental instability, pressured him to hold multiparty elections. Massive street protests forced him to legalize opposition parties and hold a presidential election in 1990. He received 81 percent of the vote.

After his death in 1993, Henri Konan Bédié, also a Baule, was elected president as PDCI candidate in a rigged election. Protests resumed in 1998 when he engineered a constitutional revision. Bédié promoted the concept of *ivoirité*—national pride according to supporters, and racism according to opponents. Specifically, the new laws barred anyone from running for president unless he or she, and both parents, were native Ivoirians. Bédié thus disqualified his main political rival, Alassane D. Ouattara, born in Burkina Faso. Fanned by the President and aided by the economic crisis, the exclusionary message struck a responsive chord in the population. The new laws have led to dangerous manifestations of xenophobia. Numerous Malians and Burkinabe have been victimized.

President Bédié was overthrown in the country's first ever military coup in December 1999. General Robert Guei assumed control, promising elections and a return to civilian government. Guei too drafted a new constitution tailor-made to keep Ouattara off the ballot. Opponents spoke of apartheid; the international community halted foreign aid. African leaders tried to mediate, but were accused by Guei of fomenting violence in Côte d'Ivoire. Guei ran for election in October 2000. Unexpectedly, the little known civilian opposition candidate Laurent Gbagbo, a socialist who had opposed Houphouët-Boigny in 1990, won the election. Both, Guei and Gbagbo declared victory. A major popular outcry forced Guei to leave the country. Gbagbo was installed as president with the help of the armed forces. The uprising that had toppled General Guei degenerated into tribal and religious violence. Followers of Ouattara were arrested, injured, or killed.

Gbagbo has been chief of state since October 26, 2000; he appointed Seydou Diarra as transitional prime minister in January 2003. Ouattara is in exile in Paris. Rebel forces claimed the northern half of the country and in January 2003 were granted ministerial positions in a unity government. However, tensions remain high between Gbagbo and rebel leaders. The traditional alliances on the basis of which Houphouët-Boigny governed are broken. Northern Muslims feel persecuted by long-ruling southern Christians, westerners feel left out, and Côte d'Ivoire risks further ethnic turmoil.

L. Natalie Sandomirsky

See also **Christians: Africa; French**

Further Reading

Amondji, Marcel, *Félix Houphouët et la Côte d'Ivoire* [Félix Houphouët-Boigny and the Ivory Coast], Paris: Karthala, 1984

Bernheim, Marc, *African Success Story: the Ivory Coast,* New York: Harcourt Brace, 1970

David, Philippe, *La Côte d'Ivoire* [The Ivory Coast], Paris: Karthala, 1986

Gaudio, Attilio et Patrick van Roekeghem, *Etonnante Côte d'Ivoire* [Amazing Ivory Coast], Paris: Karthala, 1984

Gora, Arsène Ouegui, *Côte d'Ivoire: quelle issue pour la transition* [Ivory Coast: what way out for the transition], Paris: L'Harmattan, 2000

Harshé, Rajen, *Pervasive Entente: France and Ivory Coast in African Affairs,* New Delhi: Arnold-Heinemann,1984

Mundt, Robert J., *Historical Dictionary of the Ivory Coast,* Lanham: Scarecrow Press, 1995

N'Da, Paul, *Le Drame démocratique africain sur la scène en Côte d'Ivoire* [The African democratic drama on stage in the Ivory Coast], Paris: L'Harmattan 1999

Creole (Mixed-Origin Minorities)

Given that race is socially constructed, various terms have come into and dropped out of use concerning specific groups around the world. Historically, the motivation for these changes has come from both those describing the groups and from within the groups themselves. In addition, the terms have also included both biological and social conceptions of race at the same time. Thus, people who were called Negro or Indian were identified as such by both observable physical features along with cultural and social characteristics.

Although these terms are socially constructed, they have historically taken on inferred biological meaning. "Indians" were people who had descended from the original inhabitants of the Western hemisphere, and "Negroes" had African ancestry. However, as the populations of the New World began to intermix, new terminology was invented to describe them, such as *mulatto*, *Mestizo*, *Creole*, or "half-breed." Mulattoes were the offspring of European slave masters and African slave women, while *Mestizo* referred to the offspring of Europeans and the natives of the Western hemisphere. *Creole* could refer to a variety of descendents of French, Spanish, or Portuguese settlers of North America and the Caribbean. The term "half-breed" was used to refer to any individual of any mixed blood.

The term *Creole* was first used in sixteenth century Latin America to distinguish the offspring of European settlers from American Indians, Africans, and later immigrant groups. In colonial America, the designation originally applied to the American-born descendants of European-born settlers. In the United States, Louisiana has a diverse Creole population. French-speaking descendants of early French or Spanish settlers were called *white Creoles*; black Creoles were generally the French-speaking descendants of slaves or free Africans, with varying amounts of European admixture. Before Louisiana became part of the United States, Creoles of color were French-speaking with mixed European and African ancestry and considered a separate group. However, they are now considered part of the black Creole population. The Creoles of Louisiana have their own culture and customs and a composite language derived from the French.

The development of Creole culture in Louisiana began after the French government neglected the territory, which had only about 10,000 colonists when it was transferred to Spain in 1763. At this point, American-born French speakers dominated the French community of the Louisiana colony. Louisiana quickly became a magnet for French-speaking refugees. From 1764 to 1788, 2500 to 3000 Acadian exiles established a new homeland in Louisiana, where they became known as Cajuns. From 1791 to 1809, more than 10,000 refugees from revolutionary conflicts in Haiti made their way to New Orleans. Between 1815 and 1914, tens of thousands of French people, driven from their homeland by successive political and economic upheavals, entered the United States through New Orleans. The Creoles and the Cajuns, who have partly merged, retain much of their original culture, including the French language and the Roman Catholic religion.

In Latin America, the term may refer to people of direct Spanish ancestry or just to members of families whose lineage goes back to the colonial period. In the West Indies, Creoles are descendants of any European settlers. Creoles were often considered intermediary classes between the social elites and the socially subordinated.

In nineteenth century Mexico, race was an indicator of social class. The highest social class was composed of people who were living in Mexico but had been born in Spain, called the *peninsulares*. They were sent from Spain to hold the highest colonial offices in both the civil and church administrations. The *peninsulares* never made up more than 1 percent of the population of the colony and they held themselves aloof from the *criollos* (Creoles), people of purportedly European descent but born in the Americas, who occupied the next step on the social ladder. *Criollos* were almost never given high office. The resentment of the *criollos* against the more privileged *peninsulares* became an influential force in the later movement for Mexican independence. Below the *criollos* were the *mestizos*. *Mestizos* were people of mixed American Indian and European descent. This group was followed in the social order by the Indians and finally by people of African descent. Gradually class became more important than race as a measure of social status in colonial Mexico. Wealthy and socially important individuals of mixed racial background often claimed *criollo* status. The Spanish monarchy established a legal device that allowed claimants to *criollo* status to pay a fee that established a person's legal whiteness. This can be compared to the racial caste system in the United States were individuals of any detectable African ancestry could never become white. However, depending upon the state, various racial admixtures of American Indians could be considered white.

Throughout most of the nineteenth and the early twentieth century, biologists argued that racial admixture resulted in degeneration. Around the turn of the twentieth century, several extended families were studied for many generations in an attempt to prove that criminality, insanity, and pauperism were genetic traits found in "bad stock." Eugenicists Arthur Estabrook and Ian McDougle studied the WIN tribe of rural Virginia with this in mind. The acronym WIN stood for an intermixture of white, Indian, and Negro. Eugenicists considered groups like the WIN tribe a great threat because many of their members could pass for white, hence pass inferior Indian and Negro genes into the white population.

In actuality, there is no scientific evidence to support the notion that the mixing of populations leads to biological decline. In fact, all available evidence suggests the opposite. Individuals whose parents come from similar genetic ancestry are more likely to suffer from rare genetic diseases and suffer overall fitness decline through inbreeding depression. Alternatively, the children of individuals who have more distinct genetic lineages are more likely to benefit from greater genetic diversity (heterozygosity).

The term *Creole* also denotes a language that has a complex grammar and vocabulary. The various Creole dialects result from native speakers that have developed it over the years in different regions. The French-based Haitian Creole and the English-based Krio, spoken in Sierra Leone, are examples.

JOSEPH L. GRAVES, JR.

See also **Haitians; Latin Americans; Mulattos (South Africa Coloureds)**

Further Reading

Bennet, H., *Africans in Colonial Mexico: Absolutism, Christianity, and the Afro-Creole consciousness, 1570–1640.* Bloomington: Indiana University Press, 2003

Bacigalupo, M., *A Changing Perspective: Attitudes toward Creole Society in New Spain (1521–1610)*, London: Tamesis Books, 1981

Brasseaux, C., *Acadian to Cajun: Transformation of a People, 1803–1877*, Jackson: University of Mississippi Press, 1992

Brynne, F., and J. Holm, editors, *Atlantic Meets Pacific: A Global View of Pidginization and Creolization; (selected papers from the society for Pidgin and Creole Linguistics)*, Amsterdam, Philadelphia: J. Benjamins, 1993

Estabrook, A., and I. McDougle, *Mongrel Virginians: The Win Tribe*, Baltimore: The Williams & Wilkins Company, 1926

Hall, G., *Africans in Colonial Louisiana: The Development of Afro-Creole Culture in the Eighteenth Century*, Baton Rouge: Louisiana State University Press, 1992

Critical Race Theory

Critical race theory emerged from United States law schools in the late 1980s and early 1990s. This movement was comprised primarily of legal scholars of color who sought to examine why the liberal strategies of reform advocated by the National Association for the Advancement of Colored People (NAACP) did not achieve a complete social and cultural reform in the United States. These legal scholars held yearly meetings at the convention of the Association of American Law Schools to develop a broad-based coalition of scholars who sought to transform how law understands race and to create a more sophisticated notion of race that could dismantle racial hierarchy. Critical race theory then migrated across the university and emerged in philosophy, literature, and other humanities departments in the early to mid-1990s. As critical race theory expanded beyond the law schools, its practice grew more and more varied.

The Critical Race Theory workshop began in 1989 as the idea of Kimberlé Crenshaw. Crenshaw convened the meeting to discuss how lawyers could continue the work of dismantling racial hierarchy. This meeting brought together scholars including Kendall Thomas, Neil Gotanda, Mari Matsuda, Richard Delgado, and Stephanie Phillips. At this meeting, these scholars organized around two common interests. First, they shared an understanding that white supremacy inhered in dominant and formally equal institutions as endemic features rather than as deviations. They argued that lofty legal ideals, while in theory neutral and fair, have relied on unstated and unconscious racial assumptions. Thus, they expressed a certain amount of shared skepticism that legal principles such as the rule of law, objectivity, and equal protection are necessarily neutral legal principles. Secondly, they shared a commitment to altering racial hierarchy as it existed in the United States. While not all attendees shared a common perspective on how to accomplish this change, all desired to use law to transform American culture.

The roots of critical race theory are varied. The movement responded to a series of social, legal, and intellectual trends. One primary factor in the genesis of critical race theory was that law, and the courts in particular, had become less hospitable for claims of racial justice. While the courts had proved very amenable to such claims in the 1950s and 1960s during the height of the Civil Rights Movement, courts in the 1970s and 1980s began backtracking from their earlier decisions. Moreover, economic crises in the United States during that same period diverted mainstream America's attention away from remedying racism to fixing the economy. Coupled with these social and legal trends, scholars and academics had begun using the theories of postmodernism and poststructuralism to explain the fragmentation of life and the inability of scholarly models to predict and direct social institutions. Critical legal studies, which argued that law is simply politics and that legal reasoning is just a form of power, became the dominant mode of intellectual inquiry in law schools. This critique adopted a skeptical attitude toward the litigation strategy of the NAACP and the use of law to change American culture. At the same time, life in urban areas with large minority populations became extremely violent due to chronic unemployment and underemployment, white flight to the suburbs, increasing drug use, and the growth of armed gangs.

In the 1970s and 1980s, the legal strategy of the NAACP and the tools of the analysis favored by scholars seemed inappropriate to deal with the problems faced by minority communities given the changes in the social and legal environments. Derrick Bell, then a professor of law at Harvard, began writing short stories that illustrated the limits of traditional legal analysis. Bell's stories, which were collected in his *And We Are Not Saved: The Elusive Quest for Racial Justice* (1987), demonstrated that law in the United States rested on a foundation built on race. Unlike their postmodern counterparts, Bell and other critical race theorists insisted that human beings have created the category of race to realize particular social and economic structures and that this category has real effects in people's personal lives. In a series of autobiographical essays that blurred the boundaries between self and society, Patricia Williams then illustrated how the social construction of race shapes identity. Their work and that of Charles Lawrence provided the impetus and direction for the Critical Race Theory workshop. Moreover, their work demonstrates how critical race theory challenged not only the content of legal and academic analysis but they way in which those analyses are completed and written.

Both the name and practice of critical race theory quickly spread across the academic landscape. By the mid-1990s, philosophers, sociologists, and literary scholars had begun using critical theory to examine how race unconsciously structured much academic and social thought.

Critical race theory thus merged with developments in ethnic studies, African American Studies, and postcolonial theory to demonstrate how supposedly neutral ideas in fact assume a racialized foundation. The example of Emanuel Eze's 1997 *Postcolonial African Philosophy* is instructive. Eze collected a series of essays that explore how eighteenth and nineteenth century German philosophy aided and abetted the colonization of Africa. Eze demonstrates how Immanuel Kant's theories of anthropology and geography structure his moral and epistemological writings, such as *The Critique of Pure Reason* (1781). Kant's work on the nature of reason in turn justified the colonization of Africa as Europeans saw Africa and its inhabitants as primitive and irrational and thus not worthy of the same moral consideration as Europeans. While Eze's scholarship may seem far removed from the original concerns of the Critical Race Theory workshop, it nonetheless shares the two common interests identified by workshop members: (1) it demonstrates how white supremacy is endemic to social institutions and academic thought and (2) it seeks to contest the forms that racial hierarchy has taken.

Most recently, critical race theory has been criticized by LatCrit, a group of Latino/a critical theorists. They have argued that critical race theory has focused almost exclusively on a binary, or black-white, conception of race. By looking to the complex racial and ethnic heritage of Latinos and Latinas, they have demonstrated the complexity of racial identification in America and furthered critical race theory's critique of American culture.

RICHARD SCHUR

See also **National Association for the Advancement of Colored People (NAACP); Race; Racism**

Further Reading

Bell, Derrick, *And We Are Not Saved: The Elusive Quest for Racial Justice*, New York: Basic Books, 1987

Crenshaw, Kimberlé, Neil Gotanda, Gary Peller, and Kendall Thomas, *Critical Race Theory: The Key Writings that Formed the Movement*, NewYork: New Press, 1995

Delgado, Richard, and Jean Stefancic, editors, *Critical Race Theory: The Cutting Edge*, Philadelphia: Temple University Press, 1995; 2nd Edition, 2000

Delgado, Richard, and Jean Stefancic, editors, *The Latino/a Condition*, New York: New York University Press, 1998

Eze, Emmanuel, editor, *Postcolonial African Philosophy*, New York and London: Blackwell, 1997

Matsuda, Mari, Charles R. Lawrence III, Richard Delgado, and Kimberlé Crenshaw, *Words that Wound: Critical Race Theory, Assaultive Speech, and the First Amendment*, Boulder and Oxford: Westview Press, 1993

Williams, Patricia, *The Alchemy of Race and Rights*, Cambridge and London: Harvard University Press, 1991

Croatia

Capsule Summary

Location: Southeast Europe
Total Population: 4,422,248 (July 2003)
Minority Populations: Serb (4.5%), Bosniak (0.5%), Hungarian (0.4%), Slovene (0.3%), Czech (0.2%), Roma (0.2%), Albanian (0.1%), Montenegrin (0.1%), Slovaks (0.11%), Macedonians (0.1%), Germans (0.07%), Ruthenians (0.05%), Ukrainians (0.04%), Jews (0.01%).
Languages: Croatian (96%), other (4%) (including Italian, Hungarian, Czech, Slovak, and German)
Religions: Roman Catholic (87.8%), Orthodox (4.4%), Muslim (1.3%), Protestant (0.3%), others and unknown (6.2%) [2001]

The Republic of Croatia is situated in Southeast Europe neighboring Slovenia, Hungary, Serbia-Montenegro, and Bosnia-Herzegovina. It has 1,777 kilometers (1,104 miles) of East Adriatic coastline and a total area of 21,829 square miles (56,537 square kilometers), although its borders have varied greatly at different periods. The Croatian language, belonging to the South Slavic subfamily of Slavic languages (Indo- European group) is spoken and Latin script used. Its capital is Zagreb with 779,145 inhabitants.

History

From the seventh century CE the region was inhabited by Croats, a south Slavic people who were eventually converted to Roman Catholicism. An independent Croatian medieval state was ruled by Croatian dynasties from the end of ninth century until 1102 when it joined with Hungary in dynastic union. Most of Croatia was taken by the Turks in 1526, and the remainder of the region fell under Hapsburg rule by 1527. Simultaneously, the western part of Croatia—Dalmatia, Istria and the islands—remained under Venetian control leaving the country disunited for 400 years.

In the sixteenth and seventeenth centuries a considerable number of the Croatian population fled north, away from the advance of the Ottoman empire to areas that are presently Austria, Hungary, and Slovakia. The Hapsburg Empire populated the emptied Croatian areas with refugees from Bosnia and Herzegovina, referred to at the time as Vlachs and Serbs; they were nomadic, mountain, and predominantly Orthodox Christian people. Under the *Vojna krajina* system of rule—which was legislatively exempted from the rest of the Croatia that enjoyed a certain level of self-governance—newcomers were offered a wide range of freedoms and property rights in exchange for military service.

The dual monarchy of Austria-Hungary, formed in 1867, created an empire that married the Austrian empire and the kingdom of Hungary, including what is present day Bosnia-Herzegovina, Croatia, and other Central European states. After the dissolution of Austria-Hungary in 1918, Croatian and Slovene parts of the monarchy, along with Bosnia and Herzegovina, united with the Kingdoms of Serbia and Montenegro to form a new country, from 1929 called the Kingdom of Yugoslavia. The new union, ruled by the Serbian dynasty, was less favorable towards the Croats than expected under the nineteenth century ideology of Yugoslavism, that is, a common independent state that would incorporate all South Slavs and their territories equally.

During World War II, a puppet-state called Ustashi, comprised of fascist, right-wing Yugoslav exiles dedicated to the overthrow of Communism in their homeland, committed violent crimes committed against Jews, Serbs, and Roma (Gypsies). In turn, the Serbian guerrilla Chetniks massacred Muslims and Croats. The Communists under the leadership of Josip Broz Tito organized a partisan resistance movement comprised of Croats, Serbs, and others. A large portion of the Jewish community (approximately 30,000) was annihilated during the Ustashi regime while most survivors left for the state of Israel.

After the war, Croatia became one of the constitutive republics of the Socialist Federative Republic of Yugoslavia and incorporated Istria, a northwestern region with a significant number of Italians. Except for one village in the West Slavonia region, Italians were an urban population who had lived along the Croatian coast since Roman times. About 250,000 Italians and Germans fled the country while their property was confiscated. Germans had historically inhabited continental and east Croatia along with a variety of other nationalities: Czechs, Slovaks, Ukrainians settled there under the Hapsburgs after 1750. By 2001, 19,631 Italians and 2,902 Germans remained in Croatia.

Croatia declared independence from Yugoslavia on June 25, 1991 and was recognized by the international community in 1992. After 1991 it took four years of sporadic, but often bitter, fighting before occupying Serb armies were mostly cleared from Croatian lands. Croatian Serbs who suddenly found themselves in a minority position with diminished status opposed Croatian independence. Serbian rebels occupied the third of Croatian territory that had suffered tremendous destruction; around 700,000 people were forced to flee their homes and 10,000 killed. The Croat-Serbian war lasted from 1991 until August 1995 when those territories were reincorporated to Croatia during a 36-hour-long military operation. The conflict provoked the largest single refugee flow of around 200,000 Serbs who left for the Republic Serbska (the Serb controlled portion of Bosnia and Herzegovina) and Yugoslavia (Serbia-Montenegro). Around 8,600 people, mostly elderly Serbs, remained in the area, and many were subsequently murdered, their property looted and burned despite late president Franjo Tuman's public calls for safety guarantees. Under United Nations (UN) supervision, the last Serb-held enclave in eastern Slavonia was returned to Croatia in 1998.

Society

Croatia's government is a presidential/parliamentary democracy. Legislative power resides in the hands of a unicameral parliament (*Sabor*), while the seat of Government holds executive power. The President—Stjepan Mesic since February 18 2000—is the head of state and is elected on a separate poll.

Croatia recognizes 22 ethnic and national minorities: Albanians, Austrians, Bosniacs, Bulgarians, Czechs, Germans, Hungarians, Italians, Jews, Macedonians, Montenegrins, Poles, Roma, Romanians, Russians, Ruthenians, Serbs, Slovaks, Slovenes, Turks, Ukrainians, and Vlachs. The percentage of minority groups in Croatia was 16.9 percent in 1991; it decreased significantly to 7.47 percent by 2001 primarily due to the war. The largest minority group is the Serbs, whose number decreased from 12.16 percent or 581,000 in 1991 to 4.54 percent or 201,631 in 2001. Though both Croats and Serbs speak basically the same language, Croats use Latin script while Serbs use Cyrillic in addition.

Before the dissolution of Yugoslavia, Croatia was the most prosperous and industrialized area after Slovenia, with a per capita output about one-third above the Yugoslav average. In 2002 the GDP per capita income was $9,800. Although tourism has emerged as a growing industry, Croatia's economy has been hampered by massive unemployment (21.7 percent in 2002) as well as the government's inability to institute economic reforms. Industries include chemicals and plastics, machine tools, electronics, aluminium, paper, textiles, shipbuilding, and petroleum and petroleum refining. Croatia is a transit point along the

Balkan route for the transport of Southwest Asian heroin to Western Europe and has been used as a transit point for maritime shipments of South American cocaine bound for Western Europe.

IVANA DURIĆ

See also **Bosnia; Croats; Serbs; Yugoslavs; Yugoslavia**

Further Reading

Banac, Ivo, *The National Question in Yugoslavia, Origins, History, Politics,* Ithaca: Cornell University Press, 1993

Crkvenčić, Ivan and Klemenčić, Mladen, *Agression Against Croatia - Geopolitical and Demographic Facts,* Zagreb: Državni zavod za statistiku, 1993

Goldstain, Ivo, *Croatia: A History,* Montreal: McGill-Queen's University Press, 1999

Katunarić, Vjeran, *Multicultural Reality and Perspectives in Croatia,* Zagreb: Interkultura, 1997

Report on the Implementation of the Framework Convention of Council of Europe on the Protection of Minorities in Republic of Croatia, Croatian Helsinki Committee, September 1999. http://www.riga.lv/minelres/reports/croatia/NGO/croatia_NGO.htm

Croats

Capsule Summary

Location: Southeastern Europe, Republic of Croatia
Total Population: 4,282,216
Language: Croatian
Religion: Roman Catholic (76.5%,) Orthodox (11.5%,) others (approximately 10%).

The Croats are the quintessential border people of Central Europe. They inhabit the crossroads of Europe and the Balkans, largely in the Republic of Croatia, straddling the fault line between Roman Catholicism and Russian Orthodoxy, east and west. As a small nation, Croatia had little chance of an independent existence as neighbor to the powerful Habsburg empire. They have lived as a minority in Hungary, Austria, Austria-Hungary and what was once the Kingdom of Yugoslavia and have fought tenaciously through the centuries to maintain a tradition of political and cultural autonomy, a fact that complicated efforts to maintain a viable south Slav state in the twentieth century.

Medieval Kingdom to Habsburg Subjects, 910–1683 CE

Like their future Serb countrymen, the Croats constituted a powerful medieval state between 910 and 1102CE. Known as the Triune Kingdom, this entity comprised all or part of modern Croatia and Bosnia-Herzegovina. Under King Zvonimir (1075–1089), the Croats accepted Roman Catholicism, a decision fateful for future relations with Orthodox South Slavs. Although the Croatian state was strong, it could not survive the king's death without heirs in 1089. In 1102, King Laszlo of neighboring Hungary took control of Croatia by virtue of his marriage into Croatia's royal family.

The Croats lived under Hungarian rule, with conditions. They viewed themselves as joined to the Hungarian king for matters of common import, but always insisted on the right to administer purely local affairs through their *sabor* (assembly). For his part, the Hungarian monarch appointed a *ban* (governor) to represent him in Croatia. While both sides sought changes in this arrangement from time to time, it remained in force until the 1918 collapse of the Habsburg Monarchy.

The twelfth through the sixteenth centuries saw mostly peace and prosperity in Croatia, notwithstanding the loss of Dalmatia to the Venetians. This peaceful interlude abruptly ended with the conquest of Hungary by the Ottoman Turks in 1526. The Hungarian and Croatian lands bore the brunt of the Ottoman occupation. When the Habsburg Monarchy defeated the Ottomans in 1683, Croats and Hungarians began a new era as subjects of Austria. Towards the end of the eighteenth century, they found common cause in opposition to Emperor Joseph II's campaign to streamline the cumbersome Austrian bureaucracy. This rapprochement would be tested by successive national revivals in the nineteenth century.

When Joseph II declared German the official language of the Habsburg empire, Hungarians launched the first phase of their national movement by declaring that Hungarian—not German—should become the official language of Hungary. Already influenced by the Romantic movement in Europe, some Croats responded in kind. Drawing inspiration from the Illyrians, ancient and illustrious predecessors of the South Slavs, the Croat intellectual Ljudevit Gaj began promoting the Croatian language and culture. As founders of what became the Illyrian movement, Gaj and his supporters wrote a Croatian national hymn, staged the first Croatian opera and founded the Croatian newspaper *Danica*. Gaj personally advocated broader South Slavic unity, cultivating ties with Serbs in Croatia and autonomous Serbia, despite the difficulties posed by the Serbs' use of the Cyrillic alphabet and Orthodox religious orientation. Although this passion for unity was not unanimous, the "Illyrians" had enough support by 1847 to convince the *sabor* to declare Croatian the official language of Croatia.

Before the Hungarians could react, the 1848 revolutions began, ushering in a difficult interval in Hungarian-Croat relations. Taking advantage of the chaos in the Austrian capital, Lajos Kossuth and his supporters proclaimed Hungarian autonomy in March 1848, establishing a liberal administration connected to Austria only for national interests, such as defense. The new Hungary had a strong nationalist emphasis as well, as it failed to affirm Croatia's special status in the Hungarian lands. The Croats responded by making the same demands of Hungary that Hungarians were making of Austria. Having received no response, Croat representatives in the *sabor* elected General Josip Jelacic as *ban*, or governor. Jelacic marked his appointment by volunteering his services in Austria's campaign against Hungary's subsequent bid for outright independence. Jelacic and his Croat forces contributed greatly to the defeat of the rebellion, helping to drive Kossuth and the rebels east to Debrecen, where Austrian forces eventually defeated them with Russian help.

After their meritorious service, Croats expected a measure of recompense, perhaps a resurrected Triune Kingdom. Instead, the young emperor Francis Joseph decided to administer the entire empire directly from Vienna, believing that a centralized Austria would be a strong Austria. A Hungarian official noted ironically that Croats had received as a reward what Hungary received as punishment. Events abroad, primarily the loss of the Monarchy's Italian possessions and its preeminent status in Germany, eventually forced changes in this policy. The Emperor concluded that he must accommodate the Hungarians or see his empire perish. The ensuing 1867 *Ausgleich* (compromise), divided the empire into two parts, joined in the person of the emperor and common ministries of national affairs. Hungary henceforth administered without interference the peoples of the Hungarian lands, which of course, included Croatia.

A Turbulent Era: Croats in Austria-Hungary, 1867–1914

The *Ausgleich* marked the beginning of a fractious chapter in Croat-Hungarian relations and in the life of the empire generally. The next year, the Croats had to negotiate their own arrangement with Hungary. In the 1868 *Nagodba*_(Hungaro-Croatian Compromise), Croatia was guaranteed its *sabor*, its national guard and the use of the Croatian language. However, Hungary reserved the right to appoint the *ban* and retained a greater share of revenue, an arrangement that seemed to threaten Croatia's cherished autonomy. Therefore some Croats now joined their other Habsburg minorities in seeking changes in their status within the empire. The Party of Right, led by former Illyrian Ante Starcevic, rejected both Austrian and Hungarian rule of Croatia and agitated for independence. The National Party, successor to the Illyrians, backed a Yugoslav program. Its members called for the unification of the Habsburg South Slav peoples and close contacts with the Serbian state.

In the first years after 1868, National Party members could not anticipate their future success. Led by Bishop Juraj Strossmayer, they advanced the cause of cultural unity in the founding of Zagreb University and the Yugoslav Academy of Arts and Sciences. They also sought cooperation with Serbs but encountered numerous obstacles. In Croatia, they faced divide-and-rule tactics from Ban Karoly Khuen-Hedervary, who did everything possible to inflame Serb-Croat relations during his tenure. In contacts with the leadership of independent Serbia, they disagreed about the basis of South Slav unity and the status of Bosnia-Herzegovina. Both Serbs and Croats claimed that territory as part of their heritage.

After 1903, the future looked brighter for pro-Yugoslav Croats. With the passing of the Khuen-Hedervary era, ambitious young politicians launched new political initiatives such as the Croato-Serb coalition. The Czech professor Thomas Masaryk inspired Croatian youth with visions of a South Slavic state. Meanwhile, Serbia had a new king, Peter Karadjordjevic, who signaled a dynamic new direction for his country. Even so, there remained formidable barriers to the achievement of a Yugoslav program. Supporters of Yugoslavism enjoyed increasing electoral success, yet lacked consensus on when and how unity might be achieved; they agreed only that Croats should somehow join other South Slavs on the basis of equality. It was unclear what role Serbia could play in any Yugoslav plans. Its leadership seemed focused on specifically Serbian goals such as the recovery of former Serbian territories Kosovo and Bosnia-Herzegovina. The fact remained, moreover, that only the disappearance of Austria-Hungary could make a Yugoslav state possible, and the Monarchy remained very much alive in the early 1900s.

World War and the First Yugoslavia, 1914–1940

The coming of World War I created the necessary conditions for South Slav unity. In 1915, two prominent Croats, Ante Trumbic and Franjo Supilo, sought support in Allied capitals for a South Slavic state. They initially envisioned an autonomous entity within Austria-Hungary, perhaps under terms similar to the *Ausgleich*, because few believed the Monarchy would fall. Subsequent events mandated the inclusion of the defeated Serbian state, whose representatives Trumbic met on Corfu in June 1917. These meetings produced the Corfu declaration, a blueprint for an independent postwar state that stipulated linguistic and religious equality under the leadership of the Karadjordjevic dynasty. Significantly, nothing was decided about the organization of the state. It had always been an article of faith among Croats that South Slav unity should be grounded in equality, while Serbs saw themselves as rightful leaders by virtue of their long period of independence.

When Austria-Hungary collapsed prior to the defeat of the Central powers in 1918, the way was cleared for the establishment of the first Yugoslavia. By terms of the postwar settlements, Croatia, Slovenia, and Bosnia-Herzegovina joined Serbia and Montenegro in this multinational entity, putting the concept of South Slavic unity to the test. From the beginning, crucial differences emerged between Croats and Serbs, the two largest groups. In the Constituent Assembly, a meeting charged with determining state organization, Trumbic and like-minded Croats insisted on a decentralized Yugoslavia. They wanted an arrangement approximating that which they had had previously with Hungary: cooperation on matters of national import but control over their own local institutions. But Serbian leaders believed in a centralized state administered directly from Belgrade, with no special arrangements for anyone. They stressed their leadership experience in resurrecting and governing independent Serbia, their pre-existing state apparatus and—less publicly—their concern for their fellow Serbs living in Croatia. Appalled at the prospect of direct rule by Serbs, Croat delegates boycotted the Assembly's final vote, insuring that the Serb vision prevailed in the so-called Vidovdan Constitution. The results nonetheless shocked Croats, who suffered the loss of their *sabor*, symbol of their traditional autonomy, and even the name of their nation on the maps of the new country.

Inspired by their charismatic political leader, Stephen Radic, Croats soon signaled that they would not accept the Vidovdan Constitution. They loudly proclaimed their disenchantment in interviews and speeches abroad, while alternately cooperating with and boycotting the Yugoslav *skupstina* (legislature). The Serb authorities attempted to neutralize them, using legislative and police tactics. The dispute escalated in June 1928 when Radic was shot in the *skupstina*. After Radic's death, King Aleksandar Karadjordjevic proclaimed a royal dictatorship. Intended as a cooling-off period, the dictatorship only added insult to injury for many Croats, who had hoped for redress of their grievances but saw their spokesmen silenced instead in the suspension of political life. Meanwhile, others concluded that only radical action could help Croatia. These Croats, whose leader was Ante Pavelic, called themselves *Ustase* (rebels) and intrigued with revanchist neighbors Italy, Bulgaria, and Hungary against Yugoslavia in order to destroy it and create an independent Croatia. They engaged in repeated acts of sabotage beginning in 1929. In 1934, *Ustase* masterminded the assassination of King Aleksandar and French foreign minister Louis Barthou in Marseilles. Although most Croats did not support the *Ustase*, their campaign of terror eventually impressed upon the Serbian government the dangers in Croat hostility to Yugoslavia. In the late 1930s, Yugoslav Prime Minister Dragisa Cvetkovic approached Radic's successor, Vladko Macek, for a resolution of the Croat-Serb dispute, despite Serb protests that such an agreement would again consign Croatia's Serbs to foreign rule. Signed in August 1939, the ensuing *Sporazum* (agreement) granted Croats what they had sought originally: a federal arrangement in which they regained local autonomy. Unfortunately, the *Sporazum* came only days before the outbreak of World War II, too late to save a fragile Yugoslavia from the Axis onslaught.

Independent Croatia and the Beginnings of the Second Yugoslavia, 1941–45

World War II came to Yugoslavia in April 1941, after a group of Serbian officers overthrew the government of Prince Paul for its pro-Nazi orientation. With the support of Nazi German and Italian invaders, Ante Pavelic and the *Ustase* triumphantly returned to Croatia. They realized their prewar objective in the proclamation on April 10 of a Croatian independent state, which in fact relied heavily on the patronage of Italy and Germany. Many Croats initially hailed this development, because of the protracted struggle with the Serbs. This enthusiasm cooled when it became apparent that one of the founders' chief goals was a purge of non-Croat minorities. Indeed, Pavelic and his lieutenants zealously persecuted Jews and Serbs in independent Croatian territory, via language restrictions, deportations, forced conversions to Catholicism, and outright annihilation in camps such as the notorious Jasenovac. Serbs and Jews in Bosnia-Herzegovina received special attention from the *Ustase*, since they believed that it had always belonged to Croatia.

As was the case elsewhere, *Ustase* excesses gave rise to spontaneous, then organized resistance. The veteran Yugoslav army officer, Draza Mihailovic, formed an organization known as the Chetniks, after the Serbian militias that helped destroy Turkish rule in Serbia. Another group, organized by the Croat Communist Josip Broz Tito, called itself the Partisans and operated on the basis of what they called brotherhood and unity. The two organizations cooperated briefly, but soon parted company over tactics and their views of the postwar future. It appeared that the multinational Partisans intended to create a different kind of Yugoslavia, one based on the equality of all national groups. An overwhelmingly Serbian group, the Chetniks promised more of the same *modus operandi* that had helped submarine the first Yugoslavia. By early 1945, the Partisans had triumphed, securing victory over both foreign and domestic enemies and the right to organize a second Yugoslavia. Although Pavelic himself fled the country, many of his *Ustase* supporters fell into Partisan hands and faced bloody reprisals.

Croats in Tito's Yugoslavia, 1945–1980

Their first period of independence having ended in infamy, Croats recognized that they would again become a minority in a multinational state. While certain aspects of the new regime were distressing, such as the persecution of the Catholic church, many saw immediately that their lives would change in this second Yugoslavia. The state's organization clearly reflected the Partisan ethos of brotherhood and unity. The capital remained Belgrade, but the 1946 constitution guaranteed all citizens equality, and the six constituent republics the same status and rights. Thus Croats' fundamental disagreement with the first Yugoslavia effectively evaporated.

The first two decades of this Yugoslavia, particularly after Marshall Josip Tito's 1948 defiance of Joseph Stalin, proved a heady interval for Croats and their countrymen. Having escaped Stalinism, they prospered economically and enjoyed a degree of freedom and autonomy denied their neighbors. It gradually became evident, however, that old grievances against Serb domination lurked just beneath the cheerful exterior. In 1967, Croat intellectuals protested perceived bias in a dictionary of the Serbo-Croatian language; Serbian examples predominated, to the near-exclusion of Croatian ones. This eventually led to demands that only Croatian be used in Croatia, to which Serbs responded by demanding accommodation for the thousands of Serbs in Croatia, whose language was written in the Cyrillic alphabet. Croats' complaints were not exclusively cultural in nature. Some politicians charged that Belgrade, the country's capital and financial center, made economic policy that shortchanged Croatia. Croatia provided the ports essential to the country's foreign trade and attracted tourists by the thousands to their Adriatic resorts. Yet Croats got no acknowledgment of their importance, it was alleged, since their hard-earned revenue went for political factories, Tito's white-elephant enterprises built for the benefit of less-developed areas in Serbia, Macedonia, and Kosovo.

Tito handled these challenges by purging the most outspoken activists and summoning the ghosts of ethnic strife past. His personal prestige, combined with his tangible achievements and mastery of the Yugoslav Communist Party enabled him to maintain an equilibrium among the aggrieved. As subsequent events were to demonstrate, his only flaw was his mortality.

An End and a Beginning, 1980–1991

Yugoslavia after Tito's death in 1980 was to continue as before, ruled by a Presidency rotated among the six republics. Instead, the state became a theater for nationalist posturing that eventually destroyed it. Anxious for a role as socialism declined, Slobodan Milosevic portrayed himself as chief defender of Serb interests in a staged 1987 dispute between Albanians and Serbs in Kosovo. His subsequent incorporation of two autonomous regions into Serbia and steady escalation of incendiary rhetoric spelled Serbian domination in Croatia and Slovenia. In their first free elections held in May 1990, Croat voters voted for Milosevic's Croat counterpart, the nationalist historian Franjo Tudjman. Tudjman engineered Croatia's independence from Yugoslavia, proclaimed the same day as Slovenia's on June 25, 1991.

Croatia's second independence, like its first, began inauspiciously. Milosevic decided to contest by force Croatia's departure, if only to capture some of the majority-Serb areas. The brief war that followed featured hair-raising episodes of ethnic cleansing, with neighbors killing and disenfranchising neighbors, and the deliberate resurrection of *Ustasa* imagery and tactics. In fact, when the war of Yugoslav succession spread to Bosnia in 1992, *Ustasa*-era maps of Croatia featuring pictures of Ante Pavelic circulated widely. Croat troops in Bosnia emulated their *Ustasa* predecessors—and their former Serb countrymen—in committing outrages there against Muslim citizens and Bosnia's Islamic past. After all, it was reasoned, Bosnia-Herzegovina was always part of independent Croatia.

Croatia's post-independence ordeal formally ended in the negotiation of the Dayton Accords, though Tudjman's rule continued to cause controversy until his death in December 1999. The millennium truly represented a new era for Croats. They had spent much of the previous thousand years attempting to preserve their identity as members of multinational states. Now they face the challenge of proving that the first two periods of Croatian independence were brutal anomalies, the product of war. They doubtless realize that their future in the new Europe depends on the degree to which they succeed in accomplishing this objective.

Brigit Farley

See also **Bosnia and Herzegovina; Croatia; Serbs; Serbia; Yugoslavia**

Further Reading

Banac, Ivo, *The National Question in Yugoslavia: History, Origins, Consequences*, New Haven: Yale University Press, 1984

Crampton, Ben, and Richard Crampton, *Atlas of Eastern Europe in the Twentieth Century*, London: Routledge, 1996

Jelavich, Charles, *South Slav Nationalisms: Textbooks and Yugoslav Union before 1914*, Columbus: Ohio State University Press, 1990

Judah, Tim, *The Serbs: History, Myth and the Destruction of Yugoslavia*, New Haven: Yale University Press, 1997

Lampe, John, *Yugoslavia as History: Twice There Was a Country*, Cambridge: Cambridge University Press, 1996

May, Arthur J., *The Habsburg Monarchy 1867–1914*, New York: Norton and Co., 1968

Tanner, Marcus, *Croatia: A Nation Forged in War*, New Haven: Yale University Press, 1997

Cuba

Capsule Summary

Name: Republic of Cuba (República de Cuba).
Location: Caribbean, island between the Caribbean Sea and the North Atlantic Ocean, 150 kilometers (93 miles) south of Key West, Florida
Total Population: 11,263,429 (July 2003)
Minority Population: mulatto (51%), white (37%), black (11%), Chinese (1%)
Language: Spanish (official); English and Haitian Creole.
Religions: nominally (85%) Roman Catholic prior to Castro assuming power; Protestants, Jehovah's Witnesses, Jews, and Santeria are also represented

Cuba is the largest island in the Caribbean and, with over 11 million inhabitants, the most populated country. Havana, the capital, is home to 2.2 million people; Santiago, the second city, has 400,000 inhabitants. By most estimates, Afro-Cubans comprise the majority of the population, but there is a substantial white minority. Spanish is universally spoken, but many descendants of the large West Indian and Haitian communities also speak English or Haitian Creole. The Cuban economy was severely shaken by the collapse of the Soviet bloc in the late 1980s and early 1990s and the tightening of U.S. sanctions, contributing to a per capita GDP of only $2,700 (2002).

History

Within decades of Christopher Columbus stepping ashore 1492, Cuba's indigenous Ciboney and Taino populations were largely absorbed or extinguished, victims of disease or forced labor. In eastern Cuba's mountainous Oriente region, however, Indian communities were noted as late as 1936, and Taino traditions still survive in isolated pockets. During the sixteenth century, Havana served as a base for Spanish colonization of the Americas, and over the next two centuries, tobacco and cattle emerged as the most important economic sectors. Although a substantial black population existed, the Cuban economy was not reliant on slave labor as in neighboring islands. From the mid-eighteenth century, however, Cuba was transformed into a wealthy sugar colony, dependent on large-scale import of African slaves. "Without blacks there is no sugar," went a Cuban maxim, and by the 1820s the Afro-Cuban population exceeded the white. With a booming economy based on tobacco, coffee and sugar, Spain jealously held onto Cuba as its empire collapsed in the early nineteenth century.

Although the slave trade had been declared illegal in 1817, it continued openly until 1835, not ceasing until 1860. Emancipation began in 1880, with abolition in 1886. Sugar planters sought alternative labor sources; Indians from Yucatan (Mexico) were imported between 1849 and 1861, but it was Chinese laborers, enduring slave-like conditions, who, from 1847, arrived in greatest numbers. Approximately 130,000 Chinese arrived between 1853 and 1872 alone. By 1945 approximately 300,000 Chinese had migrated to Cuba, with later arrivals destined for cities. Plantation mortality rates were high, and many survivors left the island. Moreover, as Chinese women were scarce, intermarriage between Chinese men and white and non-white Cubans was common, all helping to account for the low number of people who identify themselves as Chinese. Even so, a Chinatown emerged in Havana in the 1860s and even small provincial towns had a Chinese grocery store. By the 1960s, Cuban officials estimated there being 25,000–27,000 Chinese on the island, over half residing in Havana. Many later emigrated to Florida or New York.

Following the Spanish-American War (1898), Cuba gained independence, becoming a republic in 1902 after the withdrawal of the U.S. forces. At this time Cuba's population was estimated as 66 percent white, 33 percent black and 1 percent Chinese. Entrenched class and racial hierarchies stressed European culture and values and favored whites over non-whites, but did not altogether prohibit the latter from rising through the ranks. But the Little War of 1912, which pitted Afro-Cubans against the Cuban state, made it clear that the Creole conceptualization of the republic would not tolerate challenge. Integration was held out as the ideal for Afro-Cubans and non-white migrants alike. Spanish immigration was promoted, and by 1930 one million Spaniards (especially Galicians, Asturians and Canary Islanders) had migrated to Cuba.

With Spanish and native Cuban workers unwilling to work in cane fields, plantation owners (often U.S. companies) lobbied to import cheap workers. Between 1905 and 1916 2,000 East Indians were transported from Jamaica to Guantanamo, with some 600,000 Haitian and the British West Indian (especially Jamaican) laborers introduced between 1900 and 1930. Although Spanish immigrants outnumbered these Afro-Antilleans, during crises they served as useful scapegoats by the Cuban elite. Haitians in particular were targeted, experiencing brutal expulsions during the 1930s. Nevertheless, many laborers remained in Cuba, and while only faint traces of the East Indian presence are now noticeable, distinct Haitian Creole and English-speaking enclave communities remain in central and eastern provinces.

Between 1910 and 1930 Japanese farmers settled in Cuba, establishing successful agricultural communities producing for the home and U.S. markets. The most enduring colony was in the Isle of Youth (formerly the Isle of Pines), where a distinct Japanese community remains. U.S.-owned farms on the island also attracted several thousand workers from the Cayman Islands, the isolated south coast of Isle of Pines having long been settled by Caymanians.

In 1933, a coalition of students, intellectuals and right-wing politicians, joined forces to overthrow General Gerardo Machado, who had ruled as a virtual dictator since 1925. Between 1934 and 1939, Cuba experienced five changes of government, though Colonel Fulgencio Batista loomed behind the scenes. Cuba's 1940 constitution made the state the official sponsor of nationalism and rendered racial discrimination illegal. Batista's elected term lasted from 1940 to 1944 and he was succeeded by Grau San Martín (1944–1948) and Carlos Prío Socarrás (1948–1952). Both administrations failed, largely due to corruption, paving the way for Batista's 1952 coup. It was against Batista's dictatorship that Fidel Castro and the M-26 guerrillas waged war from 1953. On 1 January 1959, Castro and the rebels assumed power in Havana instituting a Communist regime.

Society

Although nominally Roman Catholic, Cubans of all walks of life practiced Santería, the Afro-Cuban religion that in recent years has undergone a resurgence as the Revolutionary government has become more tolerant of organized religion. Protestantism took root following the Spanish-American War, with over 40 denominations establishing churches, schools and hospitals, with U.S. financial support. Overall, relatively few converts were attracted, but the churches and schools played an important role in the maintenance of West Indian culture and language. After the Revolution, foreign missionaries were unable to work in Cuba and non-state schools were closed, contributing to a decline in West Indian group identity. In the 1990s, however, Protestant churches in towns and cities throughout Cuba attracted significant new following.

By 1959 the Jewish population in Cuba numbered 8,000 to 12,000. Sephardics from Turkey settled in the early twentieth century, with Ashkenazis fleeing Nazi-occupied Europe between 1933 and 1941. Initially generally supportive of the Revolution, most Jews emigrated in the 1960s to Florida (with others settling in Puerto Rico, Venezuela, Mexico and Israel) as the socialist state imposed restrictions on private enterprise upon which the majority were dependent on. Arab (Lebanese and Syrian) immigration had also been fairly important, with merchants scattered widely. Like the Jewish community their numbers fell due to the emigration and the gradual assimilation of those who remained.

Despite assimilation and emigration, cultural expressions of minorities persists. Since the economic crisis of the early 1990s, communities have renewed, or established, links abroad and business openings have been cautiously permitted. In Havana, previously decaying Arab, Chinese, Jewish, Galician, Canary Island and Andalucian community centers have been revitalized, with active welfare, social and cultural programs. Throughout Cuba, synagogues have reopened, with the number of people identifying themselves as Jewish increasing from a few hundred in 1990 to over 2,000 within a decade. Havana's Chinatown has also been renewed, with family and clan associations (representing over 3,000 members) allowed to run restaurants. In Guantanamo, the West Indian Welfare Center (founded in 1945) encourages maintenance of West Indian identity in Cuba, while the Tumba Francesa promotes the Haitian heritage.

Most of all, however, the strength of mainstream Afro-Cuban influences are vibrant and strong in Cuba today. The Revolution offered opportunities to the overwhelmingly poor Afro-Cuban population, though racist attitudes remain entrenched within Cuban society. Racism is particularly problematic in the Cuba's emerging tourist industry. Nevertheless, African influences are now celebrated as central to Cuban culture, especially in music, dance, and the visual arts.

The communist state continues to try to balance the need for economic growth with political control. Limited economic reforms have attempted to alleviate the shortage of food and improve enterprise efficiency. The loss of Soviet aid post-1990 created a severe economic depression, and the Cuban standard of living remains quite poor. The GDP per capita income in 2002 was just $2,700. Cuban industries include sugar, petroleum, tobacco, chemicals, construction, nickel, steel, cement, agricultural machinery, and biotechnology.

Darién J. Davis and Oliver Marshall

See also **Afro-Cubans; Asians in Latin America; Cuban Americans; Haitians**

Further Reading

Barreiro, José, "Indians in Cuba" *Cultural Survival Quarterly*, 13, no. 3 (1989)

Corbitt, Duvon Clough, A *Study of the Chinese in Cuba, 1847–1947*, Wilmore, Kentucky: Ashmore College, 1971

Fernández Robaina, Tomás, *El negro en Cuba, 1902–1958: Apuntes para la historia de la lucha contra la discriminación racial.* La Habana: Editorial de Ciencias Sociales, 1990

Levine, Robert M., *Tropical Diaspora: The Jewish Experience in Cuba*. Gainesville: University Press of Florida, 1993

McLeod, Marc C., "Undesirable Aliens: Race, Ethnicity, and Nationalism in the Comparison of Haitian and British West Indian Immigrant Workers in Cuba, 1912–1939," *Journal of Social History*, 31, no. 3 (1998)

Peréz Sarduy, Pedro, and Jead Stubbs, editors, *AfroCuba: An Anthology of Cuban Writing on Race, Politics and Culture*. Melbourne, London and New York: Ocean Press, Latin American Bureau, 1993

Cuban-Americans

Capsule Summary

Location: Miami, New York, Los Angeles, Chicago.
Total Population: 1.24 million (0.4 % of the total U.S. population).
Religions: Catholicism, Santería.
Languages: Spanish and English.

Cuban-American refers to people of Cuban descent living in the United States and is commonly associated with a community of exiles and refugees. This group includes people born in Cuba as well as later generations born in the United States who have been raised bilingually and bi-culturally. Cuba, the largest island in the West Indies, is located 90 miles (145 km) south of Key West, Florida. The estimated total population of Cuban-Americans is 1.24 million, with over 60 percent living in southern Florida and the city of Miami. Other communities live in New York, Los Angeles and Chicago. Cuban-Americans speak Spanish and English and have a strong commitment to their cultural heritage and political activism.

History

Cuban-Americans have a diverse ancestry of Spanish, West African, and indigenous Caribbean origin. The island of Cuba was originally inhabited by indigenous *Taino* peoples displaced and decimated by epidemics when the Spanish settled the island in the 1400s. West Africans were shipped to Cuba through the trans-Atlantic slave trade to work in the main industry of sugar cane, whose market became dominated by U.S. interests over the next four centuries.

People living in Cuba have had contact with the United States as early as the 1600s, when Havana was used as the administrative center for Spanish colonists conducting expeditions to Florida. Rum, cigar, and corn were traded between Spaniards in Florida and Cuba, establishing the first commercial interests between the future United States and Cuba. The first refugees from Cuba fled from The Ten Year's War (1868–1878) in which Cuba fought for independence from Spain. Cuba finally gained its independence in 1902 after its cause was championed by Jose Martí and supported by the United States. Having forged an alliance during the Cuban independence movement, there was a great deal of population movement between Cuba and the United States in the first half of the twentieth century. It was during this time that many Cuban cultural practices (such as the *cha cha cha* dance) became popular in the United States.

The Cuban Revolution

Despite the earlier existence of Cubans living in the United States, the creation of the substantial present-day Cuban-American community was set into motion in 1959, when the revolution of Fidel Castro and his 26th of July Movement ousted U.S. -backed President Batista from office. Castro installed a communist government and exiled sympathizers of the previous Batista government. They were offered asylum in the United States by President John F. Kennedy. The United States welcomed these Cubans, many of whom were educated white and professional elites.

In the subsequent 45 years that Castro has been in power, there have been three more major waves of Cubans arriving in the United States, the majority as refugees persecuted by the Castro government. A lesser number have immigrated to the United States from Havana, lack refugee status, and are free to return to their homeland. Migration has been precipitated by worsening economic conditions and the Cuban government's intolerance for dissent as well as by the United States' open door policy for Cuban asylum seekers. Between 1965 and 1973, an estimated 500,000 Cubans escaped in freedom flights, consisting of primarily upper classes. In 1980, Castro initiated the *marielitos* movement, in which more than 100,000 Cubans of disadvantaged and lower classes were shipped in small boats to the United States. The 1990s brought the collapse of the Soviet Union and their economic support of Cuba. Facing extreme economic hardship, in 1994 thousands more poor and disadvantaged Cubans went to the United States (many on rafts destined for Key West), but were eventually intercepted by U.S. Coast Guard and sent back to Cuba by orders of U.S. President Clinton. Following this unprecedented refusal of Cubans on U.S. territory, an agreement was made between the Cuban and U.S. government to admit 20,000 Cubans a year, half with the benefits and privileges of refugee status. This tougher stance on Cuban migration was further enforced in 2000 during the controversial Elian Gonzalez affair, in which a six-year-old survivor of a capsized raft bound for Florida was eventually sent back to his father's family in Cuba. The incident raised great protest from Cuban-Americans and defined them as a minority at odds with the U.S. government.

Political Involvement

While Cuban-American communities are made up of diverse groups of individuals, the ethos of exile is very prominent and has shaped political agendas and international relations between the United States and Cuba. Tension exists between Cuban-Americans, many of whom oppose Castro's communist regime, and island Cubans, who continue to live under the rule of Fidel Castro. Many Cuban-Americans have taken great interest in their homeland, apparent by a strong involvement in political efforts to oust Castro and the continued support of strict trade embargoes. Redistricting efforts in Florida after the 1990 census gave Cubans and other Latinos the power to vote for community representatives in the government; today Cuban-Americans enjoy a prominent place in state and local politics in Florida. The formation of the Cuban-American National Foundation in Florida (CANF) has used political and economic power to lobby anti-communist policy makers in the U.S. government, notably conservative Republicans. The CANF was instrumental in its lobbying efforts for the Helms-Burton Act of 1985, which allowed American citizens to file for financial compensation property confiscated in Cuba, limited movement of Cuban diplomats, and re-established anti-Cuban radio broadcasting.

Of all Latino groups in the United States, Cuban-Americans have the highest individual and family incomes, larger numbers of professionals, and more formal education. Cuban-American communities contrast greatly to other Caribbean and Latin American migrant groups who are among the lowest-earning populations in the United States. The overall greater success of Cuban-Americans is a result of multiple factors that include the elite status of the first exiles, who had considerable resources and were highly educated as doctors, lawyers, bankers, business owners, and college professors in Cuba. Cuban-Americans' relatively higher socioeconomic position has also been shaped by the strong unification of Florida communities. Cuban-Americans in Miami have employed family members in their businesses and consolidated financial and political interests. The economic strength and highly organized power of the Cuban-American community in Miami has given strength to lobbies such as the CANF.

The Miami Community

Most Cubans settled in Miami when they arrived and created Little Havana, which has long been the heart of the Cuban-American community. The population of Miami is 50 percent Latin American, while over half of Latin Americans there are Cuban. Many Cuban-Americans living there maintain a strong identification as Cuban, even if they have never visited the island. *Calle Ocho*, Spanish for "eighth street," is the main street of Little Havana, where business is conducted in Spanish and monthly outdoor festivals take place. Here, the many Cuban restaurants sell Cuban sandwiches (pork and cheese flattened between toasted bread), *café cubano* and *ropa vieja* ("old clothes;" a dish with beef and *chiles*). There are also Caribbean fruit markets, *botánicas* (stores selling herbal and magical remedies), Cuban butchers, several cigar factories, and parks where people play dominoes and *cubilete* (a game using colored dice). The community celebrates traditions such as *La Noche Buena*, a festival on New Year's Eve. Bilingual education efforts are strong and there is even a Spanish version of the *Miami Herald*. Miami, a city of high crime, experiences conflict between minority populations of Cubans and African Americans who occupy competing economic niches. As the Cuban-American population grows in size and economic strength, people are also moving out of urban centers in Miami, New York and Boston to other cities in the United States.

Religion

The colonial context of Cuba plays an important role in present-day Cuban-American religious practices. Cuban-Americans are predominately Catholic and celebrate the patron saint of Cuba, *Nuestra Senora de la Caridad de Cobre* (Our Lady of Charity of Copper), on September 8 every year. However, a substantial number of Cuban-Americans also practice *Santería*, a West African-derived religion. While Spanish colonizers made Catholicism the dominant religion of Cuba, West African slaves of Yoruban heritage continued to practice their religious traditions even though they were condemned by colonial law. Over time, these religious elements blended to form a popular religion commonly known today as *Santería*. *Santería* practitioners worship a Catholic God but also make petitions to the *Orishas,* a pantheon of saints with dual Catholic and Yoruban identities. The presence of *Santería* is evident by the proliferation of *botánicas*, stores selling spiritual goods, in New York City, Miami, and other locales. *Santería* has also gained some popularity with African American groups in the United States. The U.S. Supreme Court legalized animal sacrifices necessary for *Santería* practices in 1993.

Music

Cuban-Americans have made important contributions to music, art, and other cultural areas in the United States and throughout the world. In the early part of the twentieth century, Cuban musicians brought their homeland rhythms of *rumba* and *son* to New York, the world epicenter of Latin music. Before the revolution, Cuban music had become extremely popular in the United States through Cuban-Americans such as Desi Arnaz, who popularized *conga* dance music and was later well-known for his starring role on the 1950s sitcom *I Love Lucy.* During this time, Cuban music greatly influenced North American jazz, a legacy carried on by contemporary jazz great Paquito de Rivera. Following the revolution, Cuban-American singers such as Celia Cruz and Olga Guillot became famous for their nostalgic *sones*, *salsas*, and *rumbas* that evoked the sadness of never returning to the homeland. Cruz was particularly known as the salsa queen and popularized the Latin American genre in the early 1970s. Other famous Cuban-American musicians, such as Willie Chirino and Emilio and Gloria Estéfan of the successful band *Miami Sound Machine* developed "Miami Sound," a music style with bilingual lyrics, homeland nostalgia, and Anglo-American appeal.

HANNAH E. GILL

***See also* Cuba**

Further Reading

Boswell, Thomas D. *The Cuban-American experience: culture, images, and perspectives.* Totowa, NJ: Rowman & Allanheld, 1983

Cortés, Carlos E, editor, *The Cuban Experience in the United States.* New York : Arno Press, 1980

Gonzales-Pando, Miguel, *The Cuban-Americans*, Westport, Connecticut: Greenwood Press, 1998

Hijuelos, Oscar, *The Mambo Kings Play Songs of Love*, New York: Farrar, Straus, Giroux, 1989

Pérez Firmat, Gustavo, *Life on the Hyphen: The Cuban-American Way*, Austin: University of Texas Press, 1994

Pérez, Jr., Louis A., *On Becoming Cuban: Identity, Nationality, and Culture*, Chapel Hill: University of North Carolina Press, 1999

Cypriots, *See* **Cyprus**

See **Cyprus**

Cyprus

Capsule Summary

Location: Island of the Eastern Mediterranean, South of Turkey and West of Lebanon and Syria.
Total Population: 771,657 (July 2003)
Ethnic Population: Greek (85.2%), Turkish (11.6%), other (3.2%) (2000)
Languages: Greek, Turkish, English, Armenian, Cypriot Maronite Arabic.
Religions: Greek Orthodox (78%), Muslim (18%), Maronite, Armenian Apostolic, and other (4%); in the Southern sector, Cypriot Orthodox (92%); Maronite (1.3%); other (6.7%) (1995)

The island of Cyprus is divided into two de facto states reflecting the two main ethnic groups, the Republic of Cyprus—mostly peopled by Greek Cypriots—and the Turkish Republic of Northern Cyprus, currently gathering the Turkish minority. The Republic of Cypress, a presidential republic, is recognized by the international community as the legitimate government ruling the the whole island since independence from Great Britain on Aug 16, 1960. Its capital is Nicosia. The Northern republic is only recognized by Turkey. The Turkish army invaded the area on July 20, 1974 to protect the Turkish Cypriots, bringing in some 100,000 new immigrants from Anatolia. The unilateral proclamation of the new state followed in November 1983.

Evidence of inhabitation dates from circa 6000 BCE. During Antiquity the island was a bridge for neighboring powers. Since the end of the second millenium simultaneous Greek and Phoenician domination overlaped with previous Cypriot indigenous culture (possibly of Palestinian origin). Throughout the first millenium, the island was successively held by Assyrian, Egiptian, Persian and Hellenistic monarchs. In 58 BCE it was annexed to the Roman Empire. Cypress was included in the Eastern part of the Byzantium Empire when Emperor Teoudosius divided in two his dominions in 395 CE.

In the twelfth century, the island became independent but soon was seized by English and French crusaders who established a Latin kingdom whose rulers were also crowned as kings of Jerusalem. In the last centuries of the Medieval ages, the island was the site of confontation between maritime powers (Genoa, Venetia, Aragon), while local kings tried to revive Crusades againt the Muslims.Venetia finally inherited the country in 1489 and held it until the Ottoman Turkish invasion of 1570. The loss prompted a Christian coalition between Venetia, the Holy Siege and the Spanish crown, which defeated the Turks at Lepanto (Greece). But paradoxically, the peace treaty secured the island to the Turks. Thus Cyprus was subject to the Ottoman Empire until World War I. In 1925 it became Bristish colony. During the 1930s, increasing claims for union with Greece brought about the prohibition of teaching Greek history and the imprisonment or exile of political and religious leaders. In 1954, the EOKA movement (Ethnike Organosis Kypriakou Agonos) began a violent fight for the independence that was achieved six years later.

Today Cyprus is a multiethnic country marked by political separation between North and South along ethnic lines. People from both sides were forced to leave their homes in order to create ethnic homogenous areas. A part from Greek Cypriots (621,800 people; 83.9 percent of the total population) and the Turkish Cypriots (89,200 people; 12 percent, excluding settlers after 1974), there are other original ethnic groups in the island, that is Armenians, Maronites and Latins. Though the 1960 Constitution only recognized the Greek and Turkish communities, so other minorities were urged to decide within three months which of the two comunities to join. Sharing a common Christian religion, they opted overwhelmingly for the Greek community. The main communities had agreed to distribute power and political representation on the basis of 70 percent for the Greek Cypriot and 30 percent for the Turkish Cypriot. 6 districts were created.

Cypriot Maronites are about 4,500 (0.6 percent) according to the 1996 census. They lived in the north of the island since the Medieval Ages, altough some of them came as refugees from Lebanon during the century century. After the 1974 Turkish invasion, they were displaced to the south, where they mostly mixed with the Greek population. They are the only southeners allowed to cross the Green Line between the rival communities to visit their relatives in the north: about 200 Maronites remain in four Turkish-sector villages, namely Kormakitis, Karpasia, Asomatos and Santa Marina. Their original language, a hybrid Arabic with roots in both the Anatolia and the Levant, is currently dying out. Less than 1,300 speakers remain, being most of them bilingual in Greek.

Armenians number about 2,500, representing 0.4 percent of the population. They speak the Western Armenian dialect, and the older ones speak also Turkish. For centuries, Armenians used to live in Cyprus, but they mainly arrive to the island between 1915 and 1920, during and after the Turkish repression and massive killings in Armenia. During the 1974 Turkish invasion, the Armenian community lost monasteries in the North, as well as its main school, church, and prelature of Nicosia. They currently try to preserve their identity through their own newspapers published in Armenian and several associations and clubs.

Latins represent 700 (0.1 percent) and foreign nationals represent 22,300 (3 percent) of the population. Armenians, Maronites and Latins maintain their own schools, and the state subsidizes their religious practices. The Maronites' sense of common identity seems to be looser than that of the Armenians because of their integration in a Greek environment.

Overall, a solution to overcome the political fracturing of Cypress seems distant. Some progress however has been made: by reaching the 1977 Denktash-Makarios and the 1979 Denktash-Kyprianou High Level Agreements, both communities agreed on a federal system. Talks led by the United Nations between the two sides to reach a comprehensive settlement to the division of the island began in January 2002 but have since expired diminishing the chances of Turkish-Cypriot participation in EU membership in 2004.

Cypress's economy has been greatly affected by regional political turmoil and fluctuations in Western Europe. The Turkish Cypriot economy has roughly one-third of the per capita GDP of the south. Because it is recognized only by Turkey, it has had much difficulty arranging foreign financing and investment. The Greek Cypriot GDP per capita income was $15,000 compared to the Turkish Cypriot's per capita income $6,000 (2001 and 2002 estimates respectively). Agricultural products include potatoes, citrus, vegetables, barley, grapes, olives, and vegetables; industries include food, beverages, textiles, chemicals, metal products, tourism, and wood products.

Martí Grau

See also **Armenians; Greeks; Greece; Turks; Turkey**

Further Reading

Joseph, Joseph S., *Cyprus: Ethnic Conflict and International Politics: From Independence to the Threshold of the European Union*, Macmillan/St. Martin's press, 1999

McDonald, Robert, *The Problem of Cyprus*. (Adelphi Papers, No. 234.), London: Brassey's for the International Institute for Strategic Studies, 1989

Oakley, Robin, "The Turkish Peoples of Cyprus," in *The Turkic Peoples of the World*, edited by Margaret Bainbridge, New York: Kegan Paul, 1993

Panteli, Stavros, *The Making of Modern Cyprus*, Herts, United Kingdom: Interworld Publications, 1991

Panteli, Stavros, *A Historical Dictionary of Cyprus*. Lanham, Maryland: Scarecrow Press, 1995

Salem, Norma, editor, *Cyprus: A Regional Conflict and its Resolution,* New York: St. Martin's Press, 1992

Czech Republic

Capsule Summary

Total Population: 10,249,216 (July 2003)
Minority Populations: Moravian (13.2%), Slovak (3.1%), Polish (0.6%), German (0.5%), Silesian (0.4%), Roma (0.3%), Hungarian (0.2%), other (0.5%) (1991)
Languages: Czech (mother tongue), Slovak, Romanes, Polish, German
Religions: Roman Catholic (39.2%), Protestant (mainly Lutheran) (4.6%), Eastern Orthodox (3%), other (13.4%), Greek Catholic (0.1%); other Christian (0.3%); atheist (39.8%)

The Czech Republic is a landlocked country in central Europe, comprising the historic regions of Bohemia and Moravia, and part of Silesia. The republic borders

Poland to the north, Germany to the northwest and west, Austria to the south, and Slovakia to the east. It has an area of 30,450 square miles (78,864 square kilometers). The population of the Czech Republic totaling nearly 10.3 million people is ethnically rather homogenous, though recently more attention is being paid to its minorities. Approximately 70 percent of the population live in urban areas.

The Czech Republic is a parliamentary state with two legislative houses (the Chamber of Deputies and the Senate), the head of the state is the President (Vaclav Havel, since February 2 1993), the head of the government is the Prime Minister. The long awaited process of decentralization resulted in establishment of 14 new regions with regional governments led by elected executives (Hetmans) as of January 2001. Prague is the capital and largest city.

History

In the past the Czech lands were multiethnic. For nearly four centuries after 1527 the Czech territories were part of the Habsburg monarchy, later Austro-Hungarian Empire. Czech aspirations for greater autonomy in the Empire grew during the nineteenth century. The Czechoslovak Republic was proclaimed in October 1918. Its composition was multiethnic: 51 percent Czech, 23 percent German, 14 percent Slovak and 5.5 percent Hungarian, according to the 1921 census. The republic was broken up during World War II, but was re-established at the end of the war in 1945. From 1948 to 1989 it was ruled by a Communist regime. Historical development brought major changes in the ratio of minorities. However, even after the Second World War, despite the Nazi genocide directed at Jews and at Czech and Moravian Roma and despite the forced removal of Germans, Czechoslovakia remained an ethnically heterogeneous state with two distinct nations, Czechs and Slovaks. During the early 1990s, political and economic conflicts developed between the Czechs and Slovaks, and leaders of both groups decided to dissolve the federation. In January 1993 Czechoslovakia split into two independent states, the Czech Republic and Slovakia.

The fall of the Communist rule in 1989 brought the official recognition of the Roma as an ethnic minority group, but also lead to the growth of racism, racially motivated attacks against the Roma, and emergence of extreme right political parties which included anti-Roma measures in their political programs. The Roma have had to face high unemployment, inappropriate and ineffective education, hidden discrimination from the part of state and public administration, providers of public services and other institutions. Racism and discrimination have been among the main reasons behind the immigration of the Roma to Canada and the European Union (EU) countries since 1997.

The rights of national minorities are formally protected by the Constitution, the Charter of Fundamental Rights and Freedoms, and international commitments of the Czech Republic that, according to the Czech constitution, "take preference before the law". De facto protection against discrimination that would be ensured by law enforcement mechanisms, however does not exist.

Society

Czechs, descending from Slavic tribes who arrived in Bohemia and Moravia in the fifth century CE, are the country's dominant ethnic group, representing 94.8 percent of the population (1991 census). Moravians and Silesians consider themselves to be a distinct group within this majority. A Slovak minority of 3 percent remains from the federal period. A small Polish population (0.6 percent) lives in northeastern Moravia, where they have managed to keep Polish schools, a system from kindergartens and primary schools to several secondary schools. The Roma (previously referred to as Gypsies) constitute a distinct visible minority (around 2 percent). Other minorities are Germans (0.5 percent) Hungarians (0.2 percent), Ukrainians, Bulgarians, Ruthenians, Russians, Jews, Croats, and Greeks

The results of the 1991 census are considered accurate even in 2001, with the exception of the Romani minority that was substantially underrated. An official government report from 1999 estimates that about 200,000 Roma live in the Czech Republic. Of this number 10 percent are Vlach Roma whose culture and language are substantially different. More than 95 percent of Roma living in the Czech Republic have Slovak origin. According to the government report, the reason for the low number of persons who declared *romipen* (Romani national identity) was fear of possible consequences: Information collected in a 1930 public census, when all citizens were required to state national identity in a non- anonymous manner, was used in 1939 and thereafter to send the Roma into concentration camps and later to death transports. At present, negative attitudes of the majority towards Roma are very distinct.

In the 1991 census the Moravian and Silesian national identities were included for the first time in the history of the Czech Lands. The Moravian identity was declared by 13.2 percent and the Silesian identity by 0.4 percent. According to the government report (1999), this was a sign accompanying the search of identity in some areas of the Czech Republic during the process of social transformation following the change of regime in November 1989. The issue was politicized by leaders of Moravia-oriented movements during a discussion about the so far unresolved status of Moravia and Silesia in the territorial and administrative structure of the Czech Republic.

The majority of the population (95.8 percent) speaks Czech as their first language, while Slovak is the first language of the largest minority. These mutually intelligible languages belong to the West Slavic language group. Hungarian, Polish, German, Ukrainian, and Russian are among the other languages spoken in the republic. Romanes, the language of Romani minority has recently witnessed a certain revival, mainly due to the official policy of non-assimilative integration, declared in 1999.

Just over 39 percent of the population is Roman Catholic; other Christian churches include the Orthodox Church and Protestant denominations such as the Evangelical Church of Czech Brethren and the Czechoslovak Hussite church. Many of those who identify as members of religious organizations do not practice their religion actively.

Before World War II, the country had a large Jewish population; most of it was exterminated in the Holocaust. There are currently between 15,000 and 18,000 Jews living in the Czech Republic; the Jewish population is centered in Prague.

One of the most prosperous and stable of the post-Communist era states, the Czech Republic has sought to overcome an economic recession since late 1999. Recent growth in the twenty-first century has been stimulated by exports to the EU, especially to Germany but also Austria, Slovakia, and others, including machinery and transport equipment 44 percent, intermediate manufactures 25 percent, chemicals 7 percent, raw materials and fuel 7 percent, according to 2000 estimates. The GDP per capita income in the Czech Republic was $15,300 in 2002. In December 2002 the Czech Republic was invited to join the EU, and it is expected that it will accede in 2004.

LAURA LAUBEOVA

See also **Croats; Hungary; Hungarians; Germans; Poles; Poland; Roma (Gypsies); Slovakia; Slovaks; Ukraine; Ukranians**

Further Reading

Čanek, David, *Národ, národnost menšiny a rasismus*, Praha: ISE, 1996

Frištenská, Hana, and Andrej Sulitka, *Průvodce právy příslušníků národnostních menšin v ČR*, Praha: Demokratická aliance Slovákov v ČR, 1995

The Czech Republic, Information about Compliance with Principles Set Forth in the Framework Convention for the Protection of National Minorities, Prague: Office of the Government of the Czech Republic, 1999, Also available online at http://www.vlada.cz

Czech Statistical Office, <http://www.czso.cz/>

European Roma Rights Centre, ASpecial Remedy. Roma and Schools for the Mentally Handicapped in the Czech Republic, Country Report Series, No. 8. June 1999

Helsinki Watch, Struggling for Ethnic Identity. Czechoslovakia´s Endangered Gypsies, New York: Human Rights Watch, 1992

Socioklub, Romové v České republice, Praha: Socioklub, 1999

Dagestanis

Capsule Summary

Location: Northeastern Caucasus region of Europe, in the Dagestan Republic of the Russian Federation
Total Population: 2.5 million
Ethnic Population: Dagestanis (80%), Russians (9%), Chechens (3%), Other (8%)
Languages: Russian (official), also a wide collection of Caucasian and some Turkic languages
Religion: Sunni Islam with minority Shi'ite and Jewish communities

The Dagestanis form a kaleidoscope of mainly Caucasian ethnic groups with a couple of Turkic nationalities. There are some 2.5 million Dagestanis, most of whom live within the Russian Federation in the Dagestan Republic, with Makhachkala as the capital. Dagestan is situated in the northeast of the Caucasus and has an area of 50,300 square kilometers (19,617 square miles). It borders the Kalmuk Republic in the north, the Caspian Sea in the east, the Chechen Republic and Stavropol Territory in the west, and Azerbaijan and Georgia in the south. There is no single ethnic group with the name *Dagastani*. The largest ethnic group in Dagestan is the Avars (501,000), followed by the Karghins and Lezghins (over 200,000 each). There is a considerable Lezgin population just across the southern border in Azerbaijan.

The Caucasian languages of Dagestan belong to the northeastern Caucasian language group, together with Chechen, Ingush, and Bats. The size of these language communities ranges between a few hundred (Khunzal) to a few hundred thousand (Avars). Fifty-six percent of the Dagestani population lives in scattered villages. Many languages previously classified as separate in their own right are now grouped as dialects of other languages, thus reducing perceived linguistic diversity. There are two Turkic languages spoken by the Kumyks (300,000) and Nogai (40,000). The majority of Dagestanis are Sunni Muslims and, like their kin the Chechens, are followers of the Sufi tradition, which had kept the faith alive through the 70 years of religious and cultural persecution by the Communists. Additionally Mountain Jews (3,649), Tats (11,000), Jews (9,390), and Orthodox Russians and Ukrainians (165,940 and 9,000, respectively) are found in the area.

After the collapse of the Soviet Union in 1991, many latent ethnic tensions arose with the various groups jockeying for more political and economic control of republican resources. However, no serious conflicts have erupted since the early 1990s, largely because the various ethnic groups are unified by religious bonds and by a shared north Caucasian culture, including customs and traditions. The elders are also wary of a vortex of violence that could engulf the whole region, and are thus quick to resolve any destabilizing issues.

History

The most ancient civilization attributable to people ancestral to the Dagestanis (and Chechens) is the Kuro-Arax culture in the eastern Caucasus in the Early Bronze

Age, which was contiguous with the Maikop culture of the kindred Circassians. From the fifth century BCE Dagestan was part of Caucasian Albania. In the seventh century CE the Arabs occupied southern Dagestan and converted the people to Islam. The Arabs were replaced by the Seljuk Turks in the tenth century, who in turn were succeeded in the thirteenth century by the Mongols and the Golden Horde, ancestors of the Nogai. The Ottomans dominated the region in the sixteenth century, and the Persians in the eighteenth century.

In the sixteenth century, the Russians tried to co-opt the regional rulers, or *Shamkhals*, but their efforts proved in vain. The *Murid* Imams of the nineteenth century, especially the legendary Shamil, were a source of considerable resistance to Russian advances in the region that began in earnest in the eighteenth century. Shamil managed to unite not only the Dagestanis under his banner, but also the Chechens. He sought to unite both the northeastern and northwestern Caucasians, namely the Circassians, Abaza, and Ubykh, but was thwarted by apathy of the western Caucasians and the superior Russian forces. Shamil's resistance lasted until 1859 when the Russians captured him and the eastern Caucasus subsequently pacified. After occupation, the status of Shamil flitted frequently between a marauding bandit and an inspired freedom fighter. Presently he is regarded with extreme veneration not only by Dagestanis but also by the Chechens, many of whose leaders regard him as the paragon of the Caucasian hero.

The Dagestanis were never reconciled to Russian occupation and sought many times to oppose it. As the most religiously educated of all north Caucasian peoples, the Dagestanis often served as mullahs in the villages of their neighbors as late as the eve of the Bolshevik Revolution of 1917 and even during a few years after. They suffered severe religious persecution under Communism. In 1921 Dagestan became an autonomous republic in the Russian Soviet Republic. After the demise of the Soviet Union in 1991, Dagestan became a constituent republic of the Russian Federation. The preponderance of diverse ethnic nationalities has created many tensions, but at the same time has stiffened resolve of the various groups to keep the peace. There is a Russian streak of racism directed at the Dagestanis, who are still ingrained with the tragedies inflicted by the Russians. The Chechen War (1994–1996) failed to rouse the Dagestanis, as had been widely expected. Even the events of August and September 1999, which led to the second post-Soviet Chechen War, did not draw the Dagestanis into the fray, despite the popular sympathy with the Chechen cause and animosity toward the Russians. Nevertheless, there are still sore issues that need addressing. The Lezgins (270,000) adamantly claim that their land divided between southern Dagestan and northern Azerbaijan should be united. In addition, the Chechens in western Dagestan (75,000), who were exiled by Stalin after World War II, demand that their lands occupied by other groups be returned to them. Political and economic competition among the various groups is also a source of potential conflict. In the event of roll-back of Russian hegemony, it is not clear if Dagestan would survive as one country or be riven into myriad entities along ethnic lines. However, the wisdom of the various ethnic leaders that has been shown thus far bodes well for the future.

Dagestani Society

Dagestan (literally "mountain-country") is dominated by the eastern Caucasus Mountains in the south and east and by the Caspian steppes in the north. The mountains played a major role in the history of the region and certainly shaped the character and the customs and traditions of the people. Despite the ethnic, linguistic, and cultural diversities, Dagestani society is remarkably uniform in many aspects. Two factors have united to cancel out differences despite strong familial and tribal loyalties: religion and customary law, or *adat*. From Arabic meaning custom or habit, *adat* has come to signify customary law as it prevailed in the Caucasus. Its main tenets were hospitality, respect for elders, and blood revenge—the common north Caucasian code of chivalry. Caucasians have been known to go to extremes to ensure the safety and comfort of their guests. Dagestanis also revere their elders, who act as arbiters in mundane affairs. Women are expected to be and actually have acted as bastions of customs and traditions. Blood revenge has been largely supplanted by the laws of civil society. Bravery and physical strength are still characteristics valued and vigorously inculcated. There was no caste system, as there was among the Kabardians, all members of a clan being considered freemen with communal affairs regulated by an elected council of elders.

Religion plays an important role in Dagestani society and is firmly established. The overwhelming majority of the people are Sunni Muslims and generally they are pious believers. *Mullahs* are respected and their pronunciations are obeyed. During Communist years, those who survived the onslaught went underground and kept the religious lore alive. There are still vestiges of pagan beliefs and ceremonies, but these are certainly much less pronounced than among western north Caucasians.

Sheep breeding is the traditional economy in the mountainous regions, while cattle breeding is in the northern lowlands. Grain and other crops are cultivated in small terraces in the valleys. The economy has been on a downward slide since the collapse of the Soviet Union in 1991. It is presently one of the poorest and least urbanized regions of the Russian Federation, as it had been in the Soviet years.

AMJAD JAIMOUKHA

See also **Avars; Chechens; Circassians**

Further Reading

Adighe, R. [R. Traho pseud.], "Literature on Daghestan and Its People", *Caucasian Review*, Munich (CRM), no. 4 (1957)

Baddeley, J.F., *The Russian Conquest of the Caucasus*, London: Longmans, Green & Co., 1908; reprinted version, New York: Russell & Russell, 1969; reprinted version, Richmond, United Kingdom: Curzon Press, Paul & Co. Publishers, 1997

Chenciner, Robert, *Daghestan: Survival and Tradition*, Richmond, United Kingdom: Curzon Press, 1997

Curtis, William Eleroy, *Around the Black Sea: Asia Minor, Armenia, Caucasus, Circassia, Daghestan, the Crimea, Roumania*, New York: Hodder & Stoughton, George H. Doran Company, 1911 Gammer, Moshe, *Muslim Resistance to the Tsar: Shamil and the Conquest of Chechnia and Daghestan*, London: Frank Cass, 1994; Portland, Oregon: Frank Cass, 1994

Dai (Tai)

Capsule Summary

Location: Dehong and Xishuangbanna (Sipsong Panna) prefectures, Yunnan, southwest of China, northern Thailand, and Laos
Total Population: 1,025,128 in China
Languages: Four Dai/Tai languages
Religion: Buddhism

The Dai (Tai) have been officially recognized as one of 55 ethnic minorities by the People's Republic of China (PRC) government. The total population of the Dai based on the 1990 national census is 1,025,128, which represents 0.09 percent of Chinaís population. One of the largest Dai groups live in Xishuangbanna Dai autonomous prefecture in Yunnan on the border between Laos and China. Another large Dai group inhabits the Dehong Dai-Jingpo autonomous prefecture in Yunnan on the border between China and Myanmar (Burma). Dais also live in Thailand, Myanmar, and Laos.

The Dai speak four distinct, mutually unintelligible languages, each of which has its own completely different written scripts. These Dai languages belong to the Tibetan-Burmese branch in the Chinese-Tibetan language family. Among scholars, there is disagreement as to whether the various Dai groups should be categorized as one single Dai ethnic group. Apart from linguistic differences, historically and culturally these Dai people have little contact with each other and rarely share the same social systems, cultures, and customs.

History

The history of contact between the Dai and Han peoples dates back to 109 BCE when Emperor Wu Di of the Han Dynasty established the Yizhou prefecture in southwestern Yi (the name used to signify the minority areas of what are now Sichuan, Yunnan, and Guizhou provinces). In the twelfth century, the Dai (referred to as Dai-Lue or Tai-Lue) lived in Xishuangbanna (Sipsong Panna) under the rule of a king who established the "Jinghong Golden Hall Kingdom" with Jinghong as its capital. According to local records, the kingdom had a population of more than 1 million, and recognized the Chinese imperial court as its sovereign. The king wielded effective political and economic power, owned all the land, and controlled the water system. The kingdom had one unbroken royal family line until 1953. The last king was Chao Hmoam Gham Le, (Dao Shixun in Chinese), who is currently the deputy head of the Xishuangbanna prefecture. During the Yuan Dynasty (1271–1368), the Dai area was subordinate to Yunnan and a system of appointing hereditary rulers from among the ethnic minorities was instituted; this system was consolidated during the Ming Dynasty

(1368–1644). Under these feudal systems manorial lords established a set of political institutions and maintained their own troops, courts, and prisons to facilitate their plunder and strengthen their rule.

The historical conditions of the Dai communities were different, as were the stages of their social development. Each had its own characteristics as to the form of land ownership, class structure, and political system. The Dai who lived in Dehong had a different political system without a king. Since the Ming Dynasty eight Dai *tusi* (local chieftains) controlled the area. Each *tusi* ruled his own territory with political and economic power. The Qing Dynasty (1644–1911), on the whole, maintained the Yuan and Ming systems in the minority areas. However, it placed the Dai areas with more advanced economy under its jurisdiction and sent officials to practice direct control. This system was not replaced by the Chinese government in 1953.

Society

The religious beliefs of the Dai people were closely related to their economic development. Residents on the borders generally followed Hinayana, a sect of Buddhism, while retaining remnants of shamanism. There was a Buddhist temple in every village, with two to five temples in large villages. It was common practice that as a form of schooling, Dai parents sent their sons between the ages of 7 and 18 to the Buddhist temples for at least three years where they learned to read and write Dai script. Some Dai boys stayed in the temple for life, while most of them returned to secular life. The village bore all temple expenses. Today over 80 percent of male Dai are literate in Dai script because of this religious education. Since the Compulsory Education Law was issued in 1986 by the Chinese government, some Dai boys attend state schools during the day and go to the temple after school. In the past only males received education. Since the 1950s, however, Dai girls started attending state schools.

Since the 1980s, state government schools have been promoting bilingual education. The Dehong Dai script has been taught to children at the lower primary school level. The written language of the Dai-Lue underwent modification in the 1950s and is now referred to as "new script," while the original script is referred to as the "old script." The new Dai script is taught in some state primary schools while the old script is taught in temples for reading religious scriptures.

Historically the marriage of the Dais was characterized by intermarriage based strictly on equal social and economic status. Polygamy was common among chieftains. Today Dai youth generally have the freedom to choose their marriage partners. The patriarchal monogamous nuclear family, however, predominates in the countryside where Dai women have the lowest status. Young girls between the ages of seven and eight are responsible for domestic duties and childcare for their families. When they are older they work in the rice fields (weeding, planting, harvesting, etc.). Women do not have the right to inherit property. In the last 20 years with greater access to education, more and more women have undertaken professional careers, such teaching and medicine.

Traditional Dai villages are commonly found among clusters of bamboo on plains near rivers or streams. Their buildings are normally built on stilts. Some of the houses are square with two stories; the upper story serves as the living space, while the lower space (without walls) serves as a storehouse and for keeping livestock.

The Dai have a rich, colorful culture. They have their own calendar, which started in 638 CE. There are books in Dai script for calculating solar and lunar eclipses. Dai historical documents carry a rich variety of literary works covering poetry, legends, stories, fables, and children's tales.

The areas the Dais inhabit are subtropical with plentiful rainfall and fertile land. The chief products include rice, sugar, tea, coffee rubber, and a wide variety of tropical fruits. These tropical forests are the home of elephants, tigers, and peacocks. In China the Dai people have developed their handicraft industry (including weaving, winemaking, oil-pressing, and bamboo work) to commercial proportions. Since two airports were built in both Jinghong and Mangshi in the 1980s, the Xishuangbanna and Dehong autonomous regions have become the most popular tourist destinations in southern China for both Chinese and western tourists.

The provision of education, health facilities (including anti-malarial measures), and infrastructure have generally served to raise the living standards of Dai people over the past 40 years. These facilities have also enabled Dai people to assimilate into the mainstream Han economy more successfully than many other ethnic minorities.

LINDA TSUNG

Further Reading

Hsieh, S., On the Dynamics of Tai/Dai-Lue Ethnicity (An Ethnohistorical Analysis), in *Cultural Encounters on China's Ethnic Frontiers*, edited by S. Harrell, Hong Kong: Hong Kong University Press, 1994

Ma, Yin, *China's Minority Nationalities,* Beijing: Foreign Language Press, 1989

Dalai Lama (Tibetan)

His Holiness the 14th Dalai Lama Tenzin Gyatso is the head of state and spiritual leader of Tibetan people. He was born Lhamo Dhondrub to a peasant family on July 6, 1935, in a small village called Taktser. He was recognized at the age of two, in accordance with Tibetan tradition, as the reincarnation of his predecessor the 13th Dalai Lama, and thus an incarnation of Avalokitesvara, the Buddha of Compassion. Lhamo Dhondrub was, as Dalai Lama, renamed Jetsun Jamphel Ngawang Lobsang Yeshe Tenzin Gyatso–Holy Lord, Gentle Glory, Compassionate, Defender of the Faith, Ocean of Wisdom. The enthronement ceremony took place on February 22, 1940, in Lhasa, the capital of Tibet.

On November 17, 1950, the Dalai Lama was called upon in an extraordinary session of the National Assembly of Tibet to assume full political power after the Chinese Communist troops invaded Tibet. In 1954 he went to Beijing to hold peace talks with Mao Tse-tung and other Chinese leaders, including Chou En-lai and Deng Xiaoping. In 1956 he had a series of meetings with the Prime Minister of India Jawaharlal Nehru and the Premier of China Chou En-lai about deteriorating conditions in Tibet. His efforts to bring about a peaceful solution to the Sino-Tibetan conflict were thwarted by Beijing's ruthless policy in Eastern Tibet. In Lhasa on March 10, 1959, the massive protest demanding the independence of Tibet began but was cruelly suppressed by the Chinese occupational powers. The Dalai Lama escapted to India where he was given political asylum. Since 1960, the Dalai Lama has resided in Dharamsala (northern India), the seat of the Tibetan government-in-exile.

From the first years of his exile, the Dalai Lama drew the attention of the United Nations to the problem of Tibet. The results of his activities were three resolutions adopted by the General Assembly of the United Nations in 1959, 1961, and 1965, in which China was asked to observe the rights of Tibetan people including the right of self-determination.

The Dalai Lama, with the Tibetan government-in-exile, engaged in the problems of Tibetan refugees and of preserving the Tibetan culture. He organized the creation of 53 settlements for Tibetan refugees in India and in Nepal. After creating the necessary economic basis, he organized an autonomous educational system for the children of the refugees, which would give them the opportunity to get a complete education in the fields of language, history, culture, and religion of their own country. The Dalai Lama also created some institutions of culture with the purpose of protecting the Tibetan fine arts, sciences, and traditions, and took part in the restoration and re-establishment of more than 200 monasteries.

In 1963 the Dalai Lama proclaimed the democratic constitution, based on principles of Buddhist spirituality and the Universal Declaration of Human Rights, as a basis for the future state regime of the independent Tibet. In the constitutionís project, the Dalai Lama included a paragraph that would make his impeachment possible. Since that time the Dalai Lama has been defending the idea of the political self-formation of the Tibetan refugeesí community, confirming his decision to leave his political post after the liberation of Tibet.

In September 1987, Sino-Tibetan relations became aggravated. The result of the new protests and cruel repressions was the introduction of martial law in Lhasa. At that time the Dalai Lama organized the first conference in Dharamsala, and the United States Senate unanimously condemned the Chinese actions.

In spite of repressions, the marches and other protest actions of Tibetans did not stop. In a counterbalance to the political aggravation and hoping to stop the bloodshed, at the Congressional Human Rights Caucus in Washington, D.C., on September 21, 1987, the Dalai Lama proposed a Five-Point Peace Plan as a first step toward resolving the future status of Tibet. This plan provides: (1) the transformation of Tibetan plateau into a zone of Ahimsa (a state of peace and non-violence); (2) the cessation of the mass Chinese migration to Tibet, as a result of which the Tibetans become an insignificant minority in their own country; (3) the respecting of fundamental rights and democratic liberties of Tibetan people; (4) the restoration and protection of Tibetan natural environment, including the abolition of Chinese practice to use the territory of Tibet as the cemetery for its nuclear wastes; and (5) the beginning of peace negotiations about the future status of Tibet and about the establishment of peaceful relations between the Chinese and Tibetan population.

On June 15, 1988, the Dalai Lama elaborated on a developed variant of that plan in Strasbourg, France, at the European Parliament and proposed that Tibet become a completely autonomous democratic political entity "in association with the People's Republic of China." The Dalai Lama thought that his plan laid the groundwork for negotiations with China, but the Chinese government was not willing to enter into negotiations.

On September 2, 1991, the Tibetan government-in-exile declared the Strasbourg Proposal invalid because of the negative reaction of the Chinese leadership toward the ideas expressed in the document.

Since 1967 the Dalai Lama has visited all five continents. From the year 1970 he began to visit the countries of the West. He has visited more than 40 countries, meeting their political leaders, clergy, and leaders in culture and business. Everywhere the Dalai Lama gave conferences he addressed everyone's sense of responsibility for the destiny of the whole world. He declared that the best way to resolve problems was to develop the mutual understanding among the people and that only non-violence ensured security.

The Dalai Lama met with Pope Paul VI at the Vatican in 1973 and met with Pope John Paul II at the Vatican in 1980, 1982, 1986, 1988, and 1990.

The decision of the Nobel Committee of Norway to award the Dalai Lama the 1989 Nobel Peace Prize was approved by the international community, with the exception of China. The Committee emphasized that in his struggle for the liberation of Tibet, the Dalai Lama has consistently opposed the use of violence. Instead he has advocated peaceful solutions based upon tolerance and mutual respect in order to preserve the historical and cultural heritage of his people.

The Dalai Lama visited Washington, D.C. from April 21 to 24, 1997, to address a gathering of parliamentarians from around the world at the III World Parliamentarians Convention on Tibet.

On March 10, 1999, while the Tibetans celebrated the national day of Tibet and the 40th anniversary of their revolt against China, some mass demonstrations took place in India and Nepal. The young Tibetans who took part expressed a desire to pass from the "quiet" position to a more definitive struggle for independence. The same day, the Dalai Lama made a speech in which he declared that Chinese repression against the Tibetan people had become stronger. He assured his audience that he could maintain his control on the more radical Tibetans if China would agree to resolve the conflict in a fair and just manner. He promised to use all his authority to convince the Tibetans not to engage in violence in the struggle for a free and independent Tibet.

In December 2000, the Dalai Lama proclaimed the reanimation of non-official contacts between his administration and the Chinese government. His brother visited Peking by invitation of the Chinese authorities. The Dalai Lama informed the public about his plans to send an official delegation to China and Tibet after receiving the answer of the Chinese leaders to his offerings transmitted by his brother.

The Dalai Lama often says that he is just a simple Buddhist monk. Residing in a small cottage in Dharamsala, he arises at four in the morning, mediates, and reads prayers on the well-being of all living creatures. Most of his days pass in official meetings with the members of the Tibetan government-in-exile and the Assembly of Tibetan Peopleís Deputies.

Biography

Tenzin Gyatso. Born 6 July 1935 in Taktser, Amdo, in northeast Tibet. Studied according to traditional system (which includes ten sciences: poetry, music, drama, astrology, literature, logic, Tibetan fine arts and culture, Sanskrit language, medicine, Buddhist philosophy) at Potala and *Nor-bu-Lingkhe* Palaces (winter and summer residences of the Dalai Lama), Lhasa, 1941–1959: completed Geshe Lharampa Degree (Doctorate of Buddhist Philosophy), 1959; took preliminary examinations at each of the three monastic universities: Drepung, Sera, and Ganden; took final examination in Jokhang Temple. Head of state and government of Tibet, 1950–1959; escaped to India, 1959; head of Tibetan government-in-exile, since 1960. Author and co-author of more than 40 published works (including books on Buddhist philosophy, autobiographical essays, speeches, articles, interviews, and series of lectures given at Harvard University). Major awards: Ramon Magsaysay Award to Community Leadership, Philippines, 1959; Admiral Richard E. Byrd Memorial Award, United States, 1959; Lincoln Award, Research Institute of America, 1960; Special medal, Asian Buddhist Council for Peace, Mongolia, 1979; Liberty Torch, Gilbert di Lucia, New York, 1979; Albert Schweitzer Humanitarian Award, Human Behavioral Foundation, New York, 1987; Raoul Wallenberg Human Rights Awards, Congressional Rights Caucus Human Rights, Washington, D.C., 1989; Le Prix de Memorie, Foundation of France, Danielle Mitterrand, Paris, France, 1989; In Recognition of Perseverance of Times of Adversity, World Management Council, 1989; Nobel Peace Prize, Norwegian Nobel Committee, Oslo, Norway, 1989; Le Prix de la Memorie, Foundation, Danielle Mitterrand, Paris, France, 1989; Advancing Human Liberty, Freedom House, New York, 1991; Distinguished Peace Leadership Award for 1991, Nuclear Age Peace Foundation, Santa Barbara, California, 1991; Earth Prize, United Earth and United Nations. Environmental Program, New York, 1991; Wheel of Life Award, Temple of Understanding, New York, 1991; Peace and Unity Awards, National Peace Conference,

New Delhi, India, 1991; Shiromani Award, Shiromani Institute, Delhi, India, 1991; First Prize for Humanity, Sartorius Foundation, Germany, 1993; World Security Annual Peace Award, New York Lawyer's Alliance, New York, 1994; Roosevelt Four Freedoms Award, Franklin and Eleanor Roosevelt Institute, Middelburg, Holland, 1994; Spirit of the Dream, International House of Blues Foundation, Hollywood, California, 1996; Juliet Hollister Award, New York, 1998; Life Achievement Award, Hadassah Women's Zionist Organization, Jerusalem, Israel, 1999. Degrees: Doctor of Letters, Benares Hindu University, India, 1957; Doctor of Divinity, Carol College, Waukesha, Wisconsin, 1979; Doctor of Buddhist Philosophy, Oriental Studies, UCLA, California, 1979; Doctor of Humanities, Seattle University, Washington, 1979; Doctor Honoris Causa, University of Paris, France, 1984; Dr. Leopold Lucas Prize, University of Tubingen, Germany, 1988; Doctor of Divinity, Central Institute of High Tibetan Studies, Sarnath, India, 1990; Doctor of Education, Bologna University, Bologna, Italy, 1990; Degree of Doctorate Literature, Karnataka University, Dharwad, India, 1990; Honorary Doctorate of Laws, Melbourne University, Australia, 1992; Degree of Literature, Andra University, Visakapatnam, India, 1992; Degree of Doctor Honoris Causa, Pontifica Universidade Catolica de Dao Paulo, Brazil, 1992; Honorary Degree of Doctor of Laws, Aberdeen University, Aberdeen, United Kingdom, 1993; Honorary Degree of Doctor of Laws, St. Andrews University, St. Andrews, United Kingdom, 1993; Honorary Fellow, Hebrew University, Jerusalem, Israel, 1994; Doctor of Human Letters, Berea College, 1994; Doctor of Human Arts and Letters, Columbia University, New York, 1994; Honorary Doctorate of Philosophy, Sun Yat-sen University, Chungshan, Taiwan, 1997; Honorary Degree, Emory University, Atlanta, 1998; Honorary Degree, Brandeis University, Boston, Massachusetts, 1998. Citizenships: Honorary Citizenship, Mayor of Houston, Texas, 1979; Honorary Citizen, City of Wheaton, Illinois, 1981. At present lives in Dharamsala, India.

Selected Works

My Land and My People, 1962; 2nd edition,1977; reprint edition (My Land and My People: The Original Autobiography of His Holiness the Dalai Lama of Tibet), with a new introduction by the author, and a foreword by Melissa Mathison Ford, 1997

Universal Responsibility and the Good Heart, 1980

Kindness, Clarity, and Insight, translated and edited by Jeffrey Hopkins, co-edited by Elizabeth Napper, 1984

The Dalai Lama at Harvard: Lectures on the Buddhist Path to Peace, translated and edited by Jeffrey Hopkins, 1988

My Tibet, photographs and introduction by Galen Rowell, 1990

Freedom in Exile: The Autobiography of the Dalai Lama, 1st edition, 1990; reissue edition, 1991

Tibetan Portrait: The Power of Compassion, photographs by Phil Borges, Prologue by Jeffrey Hopkins, Epilogue by Elie Wiesel, 1996

Ethics for the New Millennium, 1999; 2nd edition, 2001

Live in a Better Way: Reflections on Truth, Love, and Happiness, Renuka Singh, compiler, Lama Rinpoche, contributor, 2001

Olga Kul'bachevskya

See also **Tibetans**

Further Reading

Avedon, John F., *In Exile from the Land of Snows: The Definitive Account of the Dalai Lama and Tibet since the Chinese Conquest,* New York: Harpercollins, 1998

Farrer-Halls, Gill, *The World of the Dalai Lama: An Inside Look at His Life, His People, and His Vision,* Theosophical Publishing House, 1998

Goldstein, Melvyn C., *The Snow Lion and the Dragon: China, Tibet, and the Dalai Lama,* Berkeley: University California Press, 1997, 1999

Harrer, Heinrich, preface to *Return to Tibet: After the Chinese Occupation,* translated by Ewald Osers, New York: J.P. Tarcher, 1998

Harrer, Heinrich, *Seven Years in Tibet,* translated from German by R. Graves, New York: J.P. Tarcher/Putnam, 1996

Piburn, Sidney, compiler and editor *The Dalai Lama, a Policy of Kindness: An Anthology of Writings by and about the Dalai Lama,* foreword by Claiborne Pell, Ithaca, New York: Snow Lion Publications, 1990; 2nd edition, 1993

Dalits, *see* **Untouchables (Harijans/Dalits/Scheduled Castes)**

Damara

Capsule Summary

Location: Namibia (southwestern Africa), principally the central and northwestern areas (southern Kunene and northern Erongo regions) and the former Township of Katatura, adjacent to the capital, Windhoek
Total Population: 134,921 (July 2003)
Language: Khoekhoegowab (spoken by Damara, Nama, and Hai||om)
Religion: Christian

Some historians assert that Damara people were among the first inhabitants of the territory presently known as Namibia. Damara, like the Nama and Hai||om ethnic groups, speak Khoekhoegowab. This is a language cluster associated with the Sn (Bushmen) languages under the broader grouping of Khoesān. Damara people distinguish themselves from other Khoe-speakers by the term *Nū Khoen*, literally translated as "black people" and affirming, lexically, their identity as "true people." The creation of the tribal category of the Damara required the melding of several smaller independent lineage-based groups called *!haoti* (sing. *!haos*), defined with further reference to geographic territory (*!hūs*). These Damara groups once extended throughout much of Namibia.

The first European encounters in the seventeenth century with people who became known as Damara (or Bergdama) were with small, dispersed groups of Khoe-speaking people retreating from a number of devastating pre-colonial historical processes. These economically and culturally impoverished bands, however, were treated as representative of a Damara tribe, leading to a rather negative stereotype typified by the German missionary Heinrich Vedder's assertions that they were primitive hunter-gatherers with no conception of property or fixed abode, and were persecuted by all who encountered them.

Flaws in these views have now been acknowledged. For example, although it was once believed that Damara people were subjugated by Nama herders, and through slavery lost their original language and acquired the Khoe-language of the Nama, it is presently considered erroneous. An alternative explanation is that Damara and Nama shared a similar ancestry, and that it is their historical separation that has led to contemporary physical and language differences between the two. Similarly, Damara people were classified as culturally hunter-gatherers who have acquired livestock only in very recent times. Historical sources (such as accounts by travelers, explorers, and traders) instead reveal considerable variation regarding subsistence practices among Damara people. In several eighteenth century observations, Damara people were described as residing in relatively large groups and engaging in a range of subsistence activities, including livestock herding and the specialist production of valued commodities (copper jewelry, tobacco, and soapstone pipes) for exchange purposes. In a pre-colonial context, therefore, it now appears that Damara people were linked within dynamic regional trade networks enabling accumulation of movable property, such as livestock and the replenishing of herds following drought periods. In today's context of overlapping claims to land by different groups, this revised history is important.

Current circumstances for Damara people, as well as for other Namibian groups, reflect the particular colonial imperative as it played out in Namibia. This amounted to the wholesale appropriation of land in the southern and central areas of the country to satisfy settler farming and mining agendas. Damara people were dispossessed of the majority of their territory in the creation of both Native Reserves and the 1970s Damaraland "homeland." Particular groups, or *!haoti*, lost all the land to which they traced their ancestry (e.g., |Khomani-, !Oe≠gā-, !Gaio-, Dani-, !Gowani-, Tsoaxau-, !Khuise- and ≠Ao-Daman). Like land-dispossessed Hai||om and Sān elsewhere in Namibia, many Damara remained in their ancestral areas as impoverished and generational farm laborers and domestic-workers, or left to be absorbed into the labor system which serviced urban areas and industry.

Damara people also have been dispossessed of land in the national interest of wildlife conservation. For example, in the 1950s Damara people were evicted from what became Daan Viljoen Game Reserve, established for the recreational benefit of Windhoek's white inhabitants by the South African administration of what was then South West Africa. Those evicted were relocated several hundred kilometers away to the farm Sores-Sores on the Ugab River. This is a less productive and very remote area, and promises of government assistance to become self-sufficient farmers remained largely unmet. Post-independence efforts to reclaim ancestral lands have been unsuccessful.

Many aspects of what might be termed Damara social relations facilitate flexibility in procuring livelihoods in an unpredictably productive arid environment. Damara people currently subsist through varying combinations of pastoralism, resource collecting, and horticulture, as well as cash incomes generated within the formal and informal economies. Flexibility in terms of accessing resources is facilitated by what anthropologists term "classificatory kinship," which allows reciprocal exchange relationships to be expanded and contracted as needed.

In terms of ritual and religion, the enormous social changes wrought by more than a century of missionary activity, colonial rule and apartheid administration have contributed to the assumption of Christianity and beliefs in God (*Elob*). These are combined and integrated with traditional beliefs and practices suffused with cultural and symbolic relationships with land, and formerly with the healing qualities of trance-dances.

Regarding leadership, again colonial and apartheid interactions have played a large role. The highest Damara leader is the "King," Justus ||Garoëb. This title harks back to the time that the German colonial governor Leutwein, on ceding the southern Native Reserve of Okombahe to the Damara in 1894, made the local Damara leader Cornelius Goroseb their king. Subsequently, the apartheid administration promoted a supposedly traditional system of male hereditary headmen as a means of enhancing control over indigenous populations. Coupled with other countrywide phenomena (particularly labor-migration by men), this had significant impacts on women through eroding their capacity as recognized leaders and heads of households. Today the positions of headmen are strongly defended in many places, against a legislative context wherein the power of traditional leaders *vis à vis* elected regional and local government is rather uncertain. Interactions between the traditional leadership and the state also are significant. Currently, for example, the Damara king is a member of parliament and is also leader of the United Democratic Front (UDF), a political party that has strong Damara support.

As elsewhere, Damara people today are grappling with a range of complex political, economic, and demographic dynamics. While some Damara individuals have been able to take advantage of the political and economic opportunities presented by independence, others have been impoverished. A particular problem is a current situation whereby the post-independence constitution enables Namibian citizens to move to wherever they choose on communal land. Without security of land tenure, or recognition of ancestral and familial linkages with land areas, an emerging outcome is marginalization in the face of incoming herders who frequently are wealthier in terms of livestock-holdings. Damara, and other groups unable to construct themselves as Bushmen, find themselves further disadvantaged by a current emphasis on Sān (Bushmen) in donors and institutional support for indigenous minorities, even though they may have experienced, and be undergoing, similar processes of dispossession.

SIAN SULLIVAN

See also **Namibia; San (Bushman); South Africa**

Further Reading

Haacke, Wilfred H.G., Eliphas Eiseb, and Levi Namaseb, "Internal and External Relations of Khoekhoe Dialects: A Preliminary Survey," in *Namibian Languages: Reports and Papers*, edited by Wilfred H.G. Haacke and Edward D. Elderkin, Köln: Rüdiger Köppe Verlag, 1997; Windhoek: Gamsberg Macmillan Publishers, 1997

Lau, Brigitte, *Southern and Central Namibia in Jonker Afrikaner's Time*, Windhoek: Windhoek Archives of Namibia, 1987

Rohde, Rick, *Afternoons in Damaraland: Common Land and Common Sense in One of Namibia's Former "Homelands,"* Edinburgh: University of Edinburgh, Centre of African Studies, 1993

Rohde, Rick, "How we see each other: Subjectivity, photography and ethnographic re/vision (including 'Matida sida ra mûgu: From an exhibition by rural Namibian photographers')," in *The Colonising Camera: Photographs in the Making of Namibian History*, edited by Wolfram Hartmann, Jeremy Silvester, and Patricia Hayes, Cape Town: University of Cape Town Press, Windhoek: Out of Africa, and Athens: Ohio University Press, 1998

Sullivan, Sian, "Folk and Formal, Local and National—Damara Knowledge and Community Conservation in Southern Kunene, Namibia," Cimbebasia, 15, (1999)

Sullivan, Sian, "Gender, Ethnographic Myths and Community Conservation in a Former Namibian 'Homeland,'" in *Rethinking Pastoralism: Gender, Culture and the Myth of the Patriarchal Pastoralist*, edited by Dorothy Hodgson, Oxford: James Currey, and Athens: Ohio University Press, 2000

Vedder, Heinrich, "The Berg Damara," in *The Native Tribes of South West Africa*, edited by Heinrich Vedder, Cape Town: Cape Times Ltd., 1928

Dayaks

Capsule Summary

Location: Borneo
Total Population: 1 million
Languages: Austronesian, Malayo-Polynesian
Religions: Mostly Animist and Christians

Dayaks, also spelled *Dyak*, or in the Dutch language *Dajak*, are the indigenous people of southern and western Borneo. Dayak means up-country or inland people. In Kalimantan (Indonesian Borneo) the Dutch referred to all pagan upriver people as Dajaks. In Sarawak (Malaysian Borneo) Dayak can mean Sea Dayak (Iban) or Land Dayak (Bidayuh). The former are a river people who used to go to sea as pirates with Malays. The latter live inland and seldom use boats. Both usually call themselves by the river or place where they lived. The term Dayak is now used as a collective political category for the native ethnic groups of Sarawak: the Iban, Bidayuh, Orang Ulu, and many more. Dayak is a generic term that has no precise ethnic or tribal significance, but today it is used for purposes of political unity due to the minority status of many of the Sarawakian tribes.

The word Dayak, Dyak, or Dajak has been widely used in particular by the Dutch colonial administration to signify non-Malay natives. James Brooke apparently originated the term Sea Dayak by which the Ibans first became generally known. Upon his arrival in Sarawak, the First White Rajah spoke of the Hill Dayaks (or sometimes the hill tribes) who lived around Kuching (sometimes on the tops of hills that offered them protection against the raids of the more aggressive sea tribes). Brooke first encountered the Land Dayaks and subsequently, in suppressing piracy, came across the Sea Dayaks because they frequented the ocean. The Ibans became known to the Europeans as the Sea Dayaks. It was sometime before Brooke clearly realized that the difference in political behavior was only part of a more basic difference in the culture of the two groups, extending to language, religion, house construction, and many other traits.

Ling Roth wrote that Dyak is used in its generally, but incorrectly, accepted application to all natives of Borneo. The Dutch in Indonesian Borneo employed the unmodified word Dayak as a collective term for all the tribal peoples; this practice continues in modern Indonesia. This manner of usage was never followed in Sarawak, where the Kenyahs and Kayans, for example, were never known as Dayaks. Despite its continued usage, the term Dayak is surrounded by confusion. It was used to designate two specific tribal groups, Sea Dayaks (Ibans) and Land Dayaks (Bidayuhs). When Sarawak administrators wrote of Dayaks, they were referring to Sea Dayaks or Ibans in most cases.

Until recently the Iban people were more generally known as Sea Dayaks, a term which is still widely used. However, there is a growing acceptance of Iban. Nevertheless, before the Ibans came into contact with Europeans they had no word that expressed their own relative cultural unity, nor did the members of the other tribal societies in Borneo. They identified themselves by the name of the river by which they lived—"We of the Skrang River" or "We of the Undup River," and the like.

For a long time Sea Dayak continued to be the preferred name of the sophisticated native who had received some Western education and commonly abandoned their traditional religious practices; on occasion they would refer disdainfully to the others as Ibans. In recent years, more especially with improved communications, Iban has come into general use not just as the only name for information, broadcasting, and other official services in the Iban language, but for the people as a whole. The Sea Dayaks (Ibans) are the largest native group in Sarawak.

Dayak Society

The Sea Dayaks (Ibans) make up one-half of the total number of natives in Sarawak and are predominantly found in Baleh, Saribas, Skrang, and Serian. The Ibans also live in the north bank of the Kapuas River in Kalimantan (Indonesian Borneo). The Land Dayaks (Bidayuhs) are the third largest native group. They live in four districts in Sarawak: Serian, Kuching, Bau, and Lundu.

Most of the ethnic groups that are collectively labeled Dayaks are riverine people who live in longhouses. The longhouse is a drawn-out structure supported on numerous hard-wood posts and stretches for 100 yards or more along the bank of a river. A longhouse is made up of a series of independently owned family apartments (bilek), which is longitudinally joined one to the other so as to produce a single attenuated structure. However, in Indonesian Borneo the government encouraged the Dayaks to live in separate houses within a village.

The Dayaks have a bilateral kinship system whereby they trace their descent through both the male and female lines. Children live with their parents until they marry. Marriage partners are often chosen from outside their own village or family room in the longhouse (bilek-family) among the Ibans. The Ibans are monogamous people and when they marry can choose to move and live in either the wife's natal bilek or the husband's natal bilek. According to Iban custom both forms of post-marital residence is permissible, but among other Dayak groups the dominant form of post-marital residence is marrying into the wife's natal village or bilek in the longhouse.

Among the Sea Dayaks (Ibans) and Land Dayaks (Bidayuhs), hereditary class distinction is absent. However, among the Orang Ulus (Kayans and Kenyahs), social stratification is an important aspect of social organization. The Ibans are known for their egalitarianism, but they also have a strong sense of achievement orientation and individualism.

The Dayak economy, or rather their subsistence, relies on the shifting cultivation of hill paddy with fishing, hunting, and foraging as the other main economic activities. Besides being engaged in dry paddy cultivation, they also have smallholdings of rubber and pepper. Furthermore, the Dayaks have been involved in gathering forest products, which they exchanged with and sell today to Chinese and Malay traders. Important items obtained from this trade include the enormous earthenware jars that are found as heirlooms in almost every longhouse. Rice cultivation is no longer the sole way of life; now they are also engaged in wage work. Today money is an important resource to be obtained. To a large extent their orientation to work is defined in terms of the cash economy.

Their religious beliefs are animistic and highly developed and complex. Farming is marked by a host of rituals among the Dayaks. The harvesting rituals among the Ibans have become a national festival, Gawai Dayak, which is celebrated by all Dayak groups. These rituals or festivals are practiced to a greater or lesser extent by all Dayak groups. Differences in the names of the rituals or pattern of rites indicate local adaptation. The Dayaks have spectacular myths that tell the stories of gods and spirits who brought the world and the lives within it into being. However, many of the Dayak subgroups have adopted Christianity, and to a lesser extent Islam, but they still are predominantly animistic.

Minority Status

Constitutionally, Dayak refers to two native groups in Sarawak, the Ibans and the Bidayuhs. However, the term Dayak cannot be used in an ethnic sense because most of the native ethnic groups in Borneo have their own term for describing their identity. There was resistance among most native groups in Sarawak to the application of the term Dayak because it was considered a label created by their colonizers. This was the moment in their history that required them to assert cultural distinctiveness. At that time they perceived these differences as important for identity formation. Even though the term Dayak exists in the constitution, it did not forge a common identity among the various groups. Nonetheless, the need to have a wider identity became imperative as the Dayaks realized their marginal status within the context of the modern nation state. The need to assert indigenousness is a response of political awareness. This awareness is related to the defense of their social, political, and economic interest.

In Sarawak the population strength of each ethnic group as recorded by the population census for the year 2000 is as follows: 22.2 percent Malays, 29.3 percent Ibans, 8.4 percent Bidayuhs, 5.7 percent Melanaus, and 6 percent other indigenous people (Orang Ulus). The

Chinese constitute 27.6 percent of the population and other Malaysian citizens are 0.9 percent of the population. There are about 3.1 percent non-Malaysian citizens in Sarawak. Ibans are the majority even though they are not much larger then the Chinese and the Malays in population size. However, they are not as strong as the Chinese and the Malay/Melanau groups in the political and economic spheres. In addition, the other indigenous groups can be considered to be minorities. Therefore, the need to have a larger sense of identity combined with the notion of indigenousness was important for political reasons. This led to the re-emergence of the term Dayak.

Toward mid-1987, the term Dayak started to gain wider usage again in Sarawak, particularly in the political domain. This time other groups besides the Ibans and the Bidayuhs were included in this category, such as the Kayans, Kenyahs, Kelabits, and Penans. This usage emerged for the purposes of acquiring political advantage in order to subvert the minority status of individual native groups. For political convenience it was also easier to categorize ethnic groups in three distinct political camps: the Dayaks, the Malays, and the Chinese. The emergence of the concept and sentiment of Dayakism was a reaction to the dominance of either Chinese- or Malay-led political parties in Sarawak. Dayakism was the foundation of the strength of the newly formed political party Parti Bansa Dayak Sarawak that accepted only Dayaks as its members. A group of Dayak leaders opposed to the leadership of Chinese politicians and businessmen formed the new party. In the 1987 elections this new party almost made a clean sweep of all the Dayak-dominated state constituencies.

However, it is important to emphasis that the Dayak category is also prone to internal divisions, especially along ethnic lines, although it is also considered as a unifying concept in certain circumstances. The process of integrating Sarawak or Kalimantan into a wider pan-Malaysian or pan-Indonesian political system involves the emphasis of local ethnic cleavages. The result of internal conditions, external impositions, and links has led to the marginalization of the Dayak population to a certain extent from the arena of decision-making both in Malaysian Sarawak and Indonesian Kalimantan. The need to emphasize commonality through the notion of indigenousness is only activated in certain instances, usually for political ends, but this does not necessarily give rise to a sense of common identity.

SHANTHI THAMBIAH

See also **Malays**

Further Reading

Freeman, Derek, *Report on the Iban,* Monographs on Social Anthropology No. 41, London School of Economics, London: The Athlone Press, 1970

Hose, Charles, and William McDougall, *The Pagan Tribes of Borneo*, Vol. I and II, London: Macmillan, 1st edition, 1915; reprinted, Singapore: Oxford University Press, Vol. I and II, 1993

Jawan, Jayum A., *The Sarawak State Election of 1987: The Dayakism Factor*, Kuala Lumpur: Maju Tulis, 1987

Leigh, Michael B., *The Rising Moon: Political Change in Sarawak,* Sydney: Sydney University Press, 1974

Pringle, R., *Rajahs and Rebels: The Ibans of Sarawak under Brooke Rule, 1841–1941,* London: Macmillan, 1970

Roth, Ling Henry, *The Natives of Sarawak and British North Borneo*, Vol. I and II, London: Truslove & Hanson, 1st edition, 1896; Kuala Lumpur: University of Malaya Press, 1980

De Klerk, F.W. (Afrikaner)

Frederick Willem de Klerk was the last apartheid-era president of South Africa, serving from 1989 to 1994. He was instrumental in dismantling apartheid, a universally reviled system of racial segregation, which had been enacted in 1948.

De Klerk was born in Johannesburg on March 18, 1936. His father, Senator Jan de Klerk, was an influential politician, and the family had been active in South African political circles for decades. De Klerk's grandfather and uncle had helped in founding the National Party, which championed the cause of the minority population of Afrikaners, or Boers. The Boers had held political power for over 300 years.

In 1958 de Klerk earned a law degree with honors from Potchefstroom University and went on to have a successful law practice in Vereeniging, in the Transvaal.

De Klerk quickly became involved in civic and political issues. In 1972 he was elected to Parliament as a National Party representative for Vereeniging. His legal talents and the respect he commanded won him a number of key ministerial portfolios under presidents B.J. Vorster and P.W. Botha. He was Minister of Mines and Energy Affairs from 1979 to 1982, Minister of Internal Affairs from 1982 to 1985, and Minister of National Education and Planning from 1984 to 1989.

During this early stage of his career, de Klerk adhered to an extremely conservative political ideology. He was a fervent believer in the Boer ideal of *kind, kerk, en keuken* (child, church, and kitchen). De Klerk's conservative tendencies were apparent when he upheld the stringent apartheid practices while serving as education minister, although he did equalize tuition rates for all students. He was ultimately responsible for administering the large and complex bureaucracy necessary for overseeing and maintaining apartheid. In his autobiography he explained his work in support of apartheid as a result of the political circumstances of the time, rather than the reflection of any deeply held personal beliefs. De Klerk also became a member of the Broederbond (Brotherbond) and the Ruiterweg, although he was not active on their committees. His efforts on the behalf of the National Party were recognized, and in 1986 de Klerk was elected leader of the House of Assembly. On September 14, 1989, he was elected president by South Africa's Parliament, with strong support in the heavily populated Transvaal.

Once he became president, de Klerk surprised observers with his accelerated reform program, given his reputation as a generally cautious politician. Most people in South Africa expected change to come slowly. However, de Klerk was aggressive in his reforms, and was eager to dismantle apartheid as quickly as possible. He held meetings with representatives of all South Africa's ethnic groups (white, black, colored, India/Asian) to draft a new constitution. He released political prisoners, including Nelson Mandela, and lifted the bans on the African National Congress (ANC) and the Pan-African Congress. By 1991 de Klerk's government had repealed the apartheid laws regarding residence, public amenities, education, and health care, and racial classification had ceased. He held a referendum in 1992; his reforms were approved by 69 percent of Africa's white voters.

Reform proved to be a complex and arduous process. The ANC and the Inkatha Freedom Party (IFP) were often hostile to the ongoing meetings and discussions, as well as each other, sometimes walking out in protest and at other times committing acts of violence. The IFP was responsible for the massacre of the residents of Boipatong Township, while blaming de Klerk for the act and the subsequent violence that ensued. ANC supporters were shot and killed, and the IFP fomented a propaganda campaign against de Klerk. He was unable to bring an end to the violence, and the United Nations Security Council ordered a hearing on the volatile situation in South Africa.

The numerous political parties agreed to help set up and defer to a commission that would study the situation and offer ways to bring an end to the violence. The Standing Commission of Inquiry Regarding the Prevention of Public Violence and Intimidation, better known as the Goldstone Commission, was established in 1991. Simultaneously an agreement of understanding was established between the government and the ANC. However, the leader of the IFP, Mangosuthu Buthelezi, left the talks in protest. Meanwhile, in response to the Goldstone reports, de Klerk purged the military of individuals who had been accused of killing South Africans. These people had not been charged officially with any crimes, however, so the military turned on de Klerk and he lost valuable political support from the military and its supporters.

In negotiations, de Klerk acquiesced to every ANC demand, which led to an agreement to make the unprecedented transition to black majority rule. A new National Assembly was created. White rule in South Africa ended on April 27, 1994. The ANC won the majority of the seats in Africa's first democratic election in 1994, and Nelson Mandela became the first democratically elected president. De Klerk joined Mandela's National Unity coalition government as deputy president. Together Mandela and de Klerk won the Nobel Peace Prize in 1993 for their efforts to establish majority rule and end apartheid in South Africa.

De Klerk resigned his position in April 1996, and the following year he made the surprising move of resigning from the National Party. He retired from South African politics in 1997 and currently devotes his time to international affairs and his W.F. de Klerk Foundation.

Capsule Biography

Frederick Willem de Klerk. Born 18 March 1936 in Johannesburg. Earned a law degree with honors, Potchefstroom University, 1958. Married Marike Willemse, 1960; had two sons and one daughter; divorced Marike Willemse, 1998; married Elita Georgiadis. Minister of Mines and Energy Affairs, 1979–1982;

Minister of Internal Affairs, 1982–1985; Minister of National Education and Planning, 1984–1989. Elected leader of the House of Assembly, 1986; elected president, 1989; worked to repeal apartheid throughout the early 1990s; awarded the Nobel Peace Prize with Nelson Mandela,1993; stepped down as president, 1994; joined Mandela's National Unity coalition government as deputy president; resigned, 1996; left the National Party, 1997; retired, 1997.

ANNETTE RICHARDSON

See also **Afrikaners; Apartheid; Mandela, Nelson (South African); South Africa**

Further Reading

Benson, Mary, *Nelson Mandela, the Man and the Movement*, Harmondsworth: Penguin, 1994de Klerk, Frederik Willem, *The Last Trek—A New Beginning: The Autobiography*, Basingstoke: Macmillan, 1998

de Klerk, Willem, *F. W. de Klerk: The Man in His Time*, Johannesburg: Jonathan Ball, 1991Ottaway, David, *Chained Together. Mandela, de Klerk, and the Struggle to Remake South Africa*, New York: Times Books, 1993

Schrire, Robert. *Edi Malan to De Klerk: Leadership in the Apartheid State*, St. Martins Press, 1994Sparks, Allister, *Tomorrow Is Another Country: The Inside Story of South Africa's Road to Change*, New York: Hill & Wang, 1995 Waldmeir, Patti, *Anatomy of a Miracle: The End of Apartheid and the Birth of a New South Africa*, London: Viking, 1997

Denmark

Capsule Summary

Location: Northern Europe, bordering the Baltic Sea and the North Sea, on a peninsula north of Germany (Jutland); also includes two major islands (Sjaelland and Fyn)
Total Population: 5,384,384 (July 2003)
Ethnic Population: Scandinavian, Inuit, Faroese, German, Greenlandic, Turkish, Iranian, Somali, settled guest workers, refugees
Languages: Danish, Faroese, Greenlandic (an Inuit dialect), German (small minority); English is the predominant second language
Religions: Evangelical Lutheran (95%), other Protestant and Roman Catholic (3%), Muslim (2%)

The Kingdom of Denmark, in northwest Europe, is bound on the north by the Skagerrak Sea, on the east by the Kattegat, Øresund, and Baltic seas, on the south by Germany, and on the west by the North Sea. It comprises most of Jutland Peninsula (projecting north of Germany) and a group of islands in the Baltic Sea. With an area of 16,629 square miles (43,069 square kilometers), Denmark is a modern and prosperous constitutional monarchy. Its capital is Copenhagen.

Partly because of its relatively small size, one of the most common images of Denmark (in the eyes of Danes and non-Danes alike) is of cultural homogeneity. By comparison with the United Kingdom or France, for example, today there are no enormous differences of language, education, life-style, or religion between ethnic Danes from Jutland or the eastern islands. However, today there are substantial numbers of people who are not ethnically Danish and are settled in Denmark. As the rump of a once extensive kingdom, Denmark has never –(without even taking account of once-marked regional differences) been wholly homogenous.

History

Danes, a Scandinavian branch of Teutons, settled the country in the sixth century CE and participated in Viking raids on England, France, and the Low Countries from the eighth to the tenth centuries. Denmark was Christianized in the tenth and eleventh centuries. By the eleventh century the united Danish kingdom included Schleswig, Sweden, England, and intermittently Norway. In 1523 Sweden became independent and threatened Danish supremacy. Under the influence of the Protestant Reformation, the Danish Lutheran Church was sanctioned. Evangelical Lutheranism remains the dominant religion today. The kingdom ceded Norway and Hegoland in 1814, sold the Danish West Indies to the United States in 1917, recognized Iceland as a sovereign state in 1918, and in 1933 was awarded East Greenland (occupied by Norway in 1931). While Greenland was made an integral part of Denmark in 1953, it received Home Rule status in 1979. Denmark joined the United Nations in 1945 and

NATO in 1949. The Faroese (Faroe Islands) are currently considering proposals for full independence from Denmark.

Minorities

The minorities settled in Denmark today fall into three categories: (1) historical minorities, (2) settled guest workers, and (3) refugees. (Although more than 100,000 European and North American nationals resided in Denmark in 2000, there is no way of knowing how settled they are—the Nordic nationals who have freedom of entry, the small Jewish community, and the descendents of Swedes, Poles, Russians, and Germans who immigrated either as workers or refugees between the end of the nineteenth century and the 1930s.)

Historical Minorities

Between the beginning of the seventeenth century and the middle of the twentieth century, Danish territory shrank from an empire that included Denmark, southern Sweden, Norway, Iceland, the Faeroes, Greenland, and parts of northern Germany to its present shape and size as a result of military failure, disastrous diplomacy, and isolation during World War II,. Consequently, there are a number of ethnically distinct indigenous minorities settled within Danish borders.

In the county of Southern Jutland, north of the border with Germany, live the *hjemmetysker* (literally "home Germans")—indigenous, native Danish citizens whose first language is German. Matched on the other side of the border by Danish-speaking German citizens, these populations are the human face of a cultural and political border zone –(Slesvig) that was fought over in 1848 and 1864 when the Germans took it, and partitioned by plebiscite in 1920 when the northern portion was re-united with Denmark. It is currently designated by the European Union (EU) since 1973 as a cultural region. North and south of the border, minority language newspapers, schools, and cultural organizations indicate substantial communities and continuing sensitivity.

The North Atlantic territories of Greenland, *Kalaallit Nunaat* (population 56,385 in 2003) and the Faroe Islands (population 46,345 in 2003) are integral, economically supported parts of Denmark, returning members to the national parliament in Copenhagen. However, their status is complex: they also have their own legislative assemblies, governing internally under conditions of limited Home Rule –(the Faroes since 1948, Greenland since 1979) and have elected not to join the EU. Ethnically and politically, Greenlanders identify with other Inuit peoples in the Inuit Circumpolar Conference, formed in 1977 and accorded nongovernmental organization (NGO) observer status at the United Nations (UN) in 1983. The Faroese are the descendents of Norse medieval colonists of the islands, speak their own language, and from time to time debate secession, an ambition which is limited by economic problems and emigration. As citizens, Greenlanders and Faroese have full rights of abode in Denmark. In the case of Greenlanders in Denmark, in particular, there is a long history of disadvantage and ethnic tensions.

Settled Guest Workers

As in many other European countries, the demand for labor seriously began to outstrip supply in Denmark in the early 1960s. In addition to increasing female economic participation, as elsewhere, the Danish response was to import temporary labor from the periphery. Guest workers came primarily from Turkey, then Yugoslavia and Pakistan. The late 1960s saw between 5,000 and 6,000 immigrants coming from Turkey and Yugoslavia to Denmark every year; the first available figures for Pakistani immigration, in the early 1970s, suggest an annual figure of 2,000 to 3,000.

From 1970 onward, however, in response to increasing numbers of migrant job-seekers, hostility in the popular press, fear of escalating chain migration, and the perception that there was an absence of policy, restrictions were imposed on the entry of migrant workers to Denmark. Even so, as a consequence of settlement of existing migrants and family reunion, the Turkish, Pakistani, and Yugoslavian minority populations continued to grow. In 1974 there were 8,138 resident Turkish nationals, in 2000 there were 36,569, while the equivalent statistics for Pakistani nationals were 3,733 and 7,115. These are concentrated in the large urban centers, disproportionately vulnerable to unemployment, but also disproportionately likely to be in self-employed small business.

Refugees

The reason why no statistics for Yugoslavian migrants were given in the preceding paragraph is that since the mid-1990s, in particular, their numbers have been augmented by refugees, particularly from Bosnia and

Herzegovina. In 1974 Yugoslavian nationals resident in Denmark numbered 6,779; in 2000 there were 33,931 nationals of the former Yugoslavia registered.

Denmark has always taken its obligations under the 1951 Geneva Convention more seriously than most signatories. Between 2,000 and 3,000 refugees a year were admitted from the 1950s to the early 1970s, largely from Eastern Europe. From the mid-1970s there were two main groups of refugees: Vietnamese "boat people" and Chileans. Subsequent refugee communities have included Palestinians, Tamils, Somalis, and tribal people from Iraq. The number of refugees being granted entry has risen since the mid-1980s. Between 1985 and 1989 the figure was 26,352; between 1990 and 1994 it was 17,191. In 1995 the figure was 20,402, of whom 16,185 were Bosnian. In response to popular political reaction since then, entrance requirements have been more restrictive and the number of refugees admitted have dropped.

The policy response to refugees has been twofold—dispersal and integration—and neither has proven particularly easy. The settlement in Denmark of significant Muslim communities, whether as guest workers or as refugees, has thrown the axiomatic Christianity of Danish society into sharp relief and led to tensions in schools and elsewhere. Dispersal has produced isolated refugee communities. A popular press-supported backlash and the political success of right-wing, anti-EU, and anti-immigrant parties, such as *Fremskridspartiet* (Progress Party) and its successor *Dansk Folkeparti* (Danish People's Party), have forced an awareness that the popular image of nonracist, tolerant Denmark needs at least some revision. All of this must be understood in the context of pressure on resources available for all welfare programs. The place in Danish society of second-generation migrants (New Danes) has yet to be settled, and multiculturalism remains a prospect with which Danish political culture is extremely uncomfortable. However, on the other hand, the absorption of relatively large numbers of refugees has been accomplished so far without the levels of violence and authoritarianism, which have been seen elsewhere, in some of Denmark's neighbors.

Denmark enjoys a modern market economy with well-developed agriculture, small and corporate industry, extensive government welfare measures, comfortable living standards, and a stable currency. In 2002, its GDP per capita income was $28,900. It is active in foreign trade, particular with Germany and Sweden but also the United Kingdom. Exports include machinery and instruments, meat and meat products, dairy products, fish, chemicals, furniture, and ships.

RICHARD JENKINS

Further Reading

Coleman, D., and E. Wadensjö, *Immigration to Denmark: International and National Perspectives*, Aarhus: Aarhus University Press, 1999

Enoch, Y., "The Intolerance of a Tolerant People: Ethnic Relations in Denmark", *Ethnic and Racial Studies*, 17 (1994) Mørck, Yvonne, *Bindestregs-Danskere: Fortællinger om køn, generationer og etnicitet*, Copenhagen: Forlaget Sociologi, 1998

Nauerby, Tom, *No Nation is an Island: Language, Culture and National Identity in the Faroe Islands*, Aarhus: Aarhus University Press, 1996

North Atlantic Studies, 1, no. 2 (1991), (special edition on Greenland)

Statistical Yearbook 2000, Copenhagen: Danmarks Statistik, 2000

Diaspora

The word *diaspora* derives from a Greek term meaning "dispersion." Diaspora originally referred to the status of the Jews during the Babylonian captivity of the sixth century, but it has also been used more generally to describe the history of that people who remained without a state until 1948.

In the contemporary world, however, dispersion is not unique to the Jews. Diaspora has therefore been applied to a whole range of refugees, expatriates, and resident aliens. The spread of the term's usage to an ever wider spectrum of displaced populations has generated debate about its meaning. Indeed one of the most interesting things about diaspora is the semantic malleability of the term. While a diaspora is most basically a people living outside its homeland, this definition would offer more conceptual clarity if given greater specificity. How best then to define a diaspora?

According to William Safran, for the members of a minority community to constitute a diaspora, they must share certain characteristics. They or their predecessors must have been dislocated from a homeland or original center to at least two peripheral areas. They retain a memory, vision, or myth about their previous homeland. They feel a lack of acceptance by their host society and therefore experience a sense of alienation from it. They believe their ancestral homeland to be their true or ideal homeland and hold a conviction that it is a place to which they must return. Barring their own return, their descendants should return. Related to this is a commitment to act as stewards or guardians and maintain or restore the homeland's well-being, prosperity, and sovereignty. According to Safran's definition, on a psychological level, they continue to relate to the homeland as an ongoing concern. Their ethnic consciousness, identity, and solidarity are therefore defined by their interpretation of their relationship to the historic homeland.

In light of this definition, it is possible to recognize that many groups meet some but not all of the criteria of diaspora. For example, the gypsies are undoubtedly a dispersed people, but not a diaspora per se because they have no plans to return to India where they are believed to have originated. While gypsies encounter discrimination and are sometimes forced to relocate, on the whole their dispersion and mobility is part of a chosen way of life. Similarly, the Turks living and working in Germany meet some but not all of the characteristics of a diaspora. On one hand they believe themselves to be temporary residents of Germany and point to an imminent return. On the other hand, their departure from their country of origin was largely voluntary and their home country has remained in existence, obviating a need to protect a threatened culture or even forcibly remain in exile. A third example is offered by African-Americans who speak of a black diaspora. While they were forcibly removed from the African continent and have in some cases constructed an idealized myth of that lost homeland, few blacks seriously consider a return to Africa as a viable solution to their contemporary problems.

The growing relevance of diaspora and the resultant proliferation of the term can be attributed to three factors. First, the marked increase of migration flows between states in the aftermath of radical changes in the political and economic structures of Eastern Europe, wars in Africa, and Third World poverty have created new diasporas. Of particular note are the new diasporas in the former Soviet Union (dissolved in 1991) that have been created as a result of political and economic upheaval and attendant "ethnic sorting." Second, a rise in political and social pluralism helps maintain the diasporas that have been created by offering opportunities to participate in politics in the host country, as well as ways to preserve communication links with the home country via modern transportation and telecommunications. Third, the rise of nationalism and ethnic politics throughout the world has increased the salience of diaspora—ethnicity has become an organizing principle and focus of political organizing. If these trends continue, scholars expect that rather than disappearing, modern ethnic diasporas will continue to emerge, increase in number, and develop greater political mobilization.

Aspects of the Jewish, Armenian, and Palestinian Diasporas

The Jews are one of the world's oldest diapsoras. They were exiled from their homeland first in 722 and 586 BCE and then in 70 CE. In Antiquity there was a thriving Jewish settlement in Alexandria, Egypt where a significant minority of the population was Jewish. By the first century CE, more Jews lived outside Palestine, primarily within the Roman Empire, than in the homeland, although Palestine was viewed as the core of their religious and cultural life. The diasporic centers of Judaism shifted over time, including Babylonia, Persia, Egypt, Spain, France, Germany, Poland, Russia, and the United States.

The various centers of Jewish diaspora have had remarkably different fates. Many of the Soviet Union's Jews migrated to Israel with the disintegration of the 15 constituent republics. The Jewish experience in Europe has been very troubled, whereas the Jews in the United States have enjoyed considerable political influence. According to Arnold Ages, Jews experienced initial acceptance in Europe and underwent considerable assimilation and even conversion. This was followed by a stage of heightened patriotism among Jews. In France, Germany, and Russia in particular, this was eventually followed by rampant anti-Semitism, sequestering of the Jewish population, and eventual destruction.

Jews hold divergent views about the diaspora and the desirability return. Most Orthodox Jews support the Zionist movement and the return of Jews to Israel, feeling that Jewish life and culture are threatened in the diaspora because of assimilation and acculturation. In contrast, Reform Jews hold that life in the United States and elsewhere is not antithetical to God's will. Some believe that dispersal was in fact arranged by God to foster monotheism throughout the world. There are also Jews who feel the diaspora came to an end with the establishment of Israel, although the physical dispersal of the Jews continues.

Dispersion has also been a recurrent phenomenon in Armenian history over the last one thousand years. But perhaps the greatest single disaster in the history of the Armenians occurred in 1915 with the outbreak of World War I, when the Young Turk government decided to deport the whole Armenian population. In what is known as the "first genocide" of the twentieth century, hundreds of thousands of Armenians were forced to flee their homes and were massacred and marched to death. The mass exodus from the homeland at this time created the modern Armenian diaspora. The territory where they had previously lived was depopulated of Armenians and the homeland was lost without any possibility of return.

This Armenian genocide coupled with the creation of an independent Armenian state in the Soviet Union in 1918 are the most significant factors shaping Armenian history. Even though the Armenian Soviet Socialist Republic only encompassed about one fifth of Greater Armenia, it was the most concrete homeland available. As Penossian has pointed out, although the diaspora's *original* homeland lay in western or Ottoman Armenia, the existence of this new republic shifted the focus of national consciousness to the new Soviet Armenia.

Ever since, the major divisions within the Armenian diaspora have been concerned with (and divided over) how to relate to this homeland. For example, while the Dashnak bloc was opposed to Armenia because of its Soviet regime, the Ramkavar-Hnchak bloc supported the homeland regardless of its politics, even through the Cold War. This demonstrates concretely how diasporas may circumvent bipolar politics on the way to becoming part of interstate relations. The increasingly direct contact between homeland and diaspora that occurred after the disintegration of the Soviet Union led to another adjustment in relations between the diaspora and the homeland and within the diaspora itself.

By the 1990s Armenian identity became increasingly independent of the homeland and the idea of return. The diasporic community had developed a unique, hyphenated identity. The majority of Armenians live outside the ancestral homeland and have developed new centers of religion and culture.

It was the partition of Palestine in 1948 that led to the displacement of as many as 770,000 Arab residents of Palestine, now known as the Palestinian diaspora. They fled their homes in the aftermath of military confrontation between the new state of Israel and neighboring Arab countries. In 1949 the United Nations General Assembly created the United Nations Relief and Works Agency (UNRWA) to deal with the crisis of the Palestinian refugees, inaugurating a phase in which international organization would formalize and enhance their involvement with refugee and diasporic populations. By 1950 they had established over 50 refugee camps in the East and West Banks of Jordan, the Gaza Strip, Lebanon, and Syria. Eventually, tents were replaced with concrete block houses. In spite of the UNRWA's efforts, poverty and unemployment remained intractable problems among camp residents. While upper and middle class Palestinians were able to find more permanent housing and jobs, many Palestinians remained alienated and disenfranchised from their host societies.

Palestinians in the camps remained unassimilated and developed a sense of identity based on pan-Arabism, an idealized memory of their lost homeland, and the emerging pan-Islamic movement. As a result of their experience, members of the Palestinian diaspora became a community defined by the experience of exile, and united by the goal of a physical return to Palestine. Palestinian identity itself developed in the camps. Residents who fled settled in the same areas, preserving their cohesion. Streets and markets were named for the villages and towns the residents came from. Families retained the keys to their homes as symbols of their commitment to return, displaying them long after their actual homes had been destroyed. It is important to recognize that their intense focus on the details of their remembered homeland is qualitatively different than the unreflective, more spontaneous attachment to home before exile. As a result of the exile experience, Palestinians constructed a more self-conscious identity and more intentional relation to place.

Diaspora Consciousness

As the examples show, the conditions of diaspora vary. A common development associated with the exilic experience regardless of the specific circumstances is the emergence of a complex of emotions and attitudes marked, in particular, by a tension between the advantages of staying and the dream of return. This has customarily been referred to as "*diaspora* consciousness." The imagined utopia of the homeland is made more vivid by the *dystopia* of exile with its material hardship, emotional stress, and social dislocation.

Diaspora consciousness challenges the traditional sociological distinction between being socially rooted and displaced because members tend to maintain a bifocality with regard to their allegiances. While members dream of returning, they are either unable or unwilling to actually go home. In some cases there is no homeland to return to. More often the homeland still exists but the material, social, and psychological costs of return seem to outweigh the benefits. In the meantime, the so-called myth of return serves to solidify ethnic consciousness. The return of most diasporas can be seen as an eschatological concept. It is used to make life more tolerable by creating a utopia that provides a necessary contrast to the dystopia in which life is actually lived.

In a *myth of return*, a concrete and familiar home is overlaid with an abstracted or idealized image of home. However, as Zetter has observed, the so-called myth of return that characterizes diaspora consciousness may be somewhat of a misnomer. What is mythologized is not *return* as much as *home*. It must also be highlighted that the myth of return is an external construct, not used self-referentially by exiles themselves, but employed by social scientists and other observers. Among diasporic populations, the myth of return home can vary from encompassing a mild remembrance of a distant homeland to a pathological condition characterized by anger and violence. Why variation occurs and the extent to which myths help exiles to adapt and survive or lead to dysfunctional responses are questions that are still inadequately understood. What *is* certain is that creating and maintaining a myth of return home is one of the most readily available means of re-establishing continuity with the past, no matter how inconsistent or unreal the myth may seem to the objective observer. Diaspora consciousness therefore disrupts conventional temporal experience. As James Clifford has observed, the present is shadowed by a past, which is strangely also the basis of a desired but unattainable future.

The commitment to the homeland's well-being, and in some cases plans for its liberation, distinguish diasporas from other types of displaced groups. This commitment sometimes leads to political complications because there is a simultaneous need to demonstrate political loyalty to the state in which they find themselves. Diasporas are motivated on one hand by strong sentiments of attachment with respect to the home country and on the other hand by concerns of survival in their host state.

Political Implications

Whenever a state chooses to forge a collective identity on the basis of race, religion, ethnic, or national affiliations, it produces minorities. A mono-national ideology of integration in a multi-ethnic setting invariably leads to disenfranchised groups that are subject to exclusion and prejudice if not outright expulsion.

Political scientists originally studied diasporas in terms of the dyadic relationship between the minority ethnic group and the host country. However, this does not allow for the international dimension of diasporas. Therefore, diasporas are increasingly conceived in terms of the triadic relationship between the minority ethnic group, the host country, and the country of origin. These relationships are now recognized as an integral part of foreign policy formation and international affairs. In fact the power and the prevalence of contemporary diasporas has called into question the traditional view of international relations theory that the most important actors in world politics are the nations-states. In light of modern developments, a consideration of so-called non-state actors has become imperative.

Just as diasporas can affect politics in their home and host countries, the members of diaspora groups receive a variety of treatment from the countries in which they live, ranging from being welcomed for the sake of the domestic and diplomatic interests of the host country to being viewed as strangers and shunned. So the political implications of a diaspora community can be located in two primary spheres. First, diasporas influence the host or the home state, and secondly, host or home states may use the diaspora in various ways in foreign relations with one another.

These two spheres can be further broken down into four principal dynamics:

1. *The diaspora influences on the host government.* With regard to the host state, the diaspora may advocate it and take a particular stance on an issue not concerning the home state, in which case they are acting like an interest group. But the diaspora may also advocate a particular foreign policy stance with respect to the home state.

For example, in the United States, the Jewish and Greek diasporas are well known to have shaped perceptions of U.S. national interest abroad. Scholars and lay persons alike have therefore questioned whether a diaspora's identification with a homeland threatens America's cohesion as a nation. The diaspora's effectiveness will largely depend on their level of mobilization, the material resources available to them, and the degree of openness of the host government. Internal divisions and cohesiveness also have critical importance with respect to the diaspora's ability to influence policy.

2. *The diaspora influences events in the home country.* A principle way in which diasporas may influence the home state is when members return to take up key political posts or advisory positions. For example, this occurred in Latvia and Armenia following the breakup of the Soviet Union. Scholarly and citizen exchanges can also affect significant influences on the host society.
3. *The home government attempts to use the diaspora to accomplish their goals.* The mere existence of a diaspora can shape foreign policy when the leadership of the home state finds it advantageous to advocate on behalf of co-ethnics in a different state, such as Hitler and the Sudenten Germans. Another example is provided by the Armenian diaspora when the Armenian leaders looked to the large diaspora to generate and organize foreign aid.
4. *The host government attempts to use the diaspora to accomplish their goals.* The U.S. government, for example, has attempted to use prominent members of various diasporas to influence the government in the home state. A related aspect of this is that the host and home states may use the diaspora as a source of political capital in relations with each other or third parties. This represents a variation of the above because the primary focus of foreign policy is not so much the diaspora itself as the potential benefits each party hopes to gain by strengthening ties with each other. For example, political leaders of host and home countries may find in the diaspora to be a common opponent and a point of departure for improved state relations.

Critical Reflections

There is a tendency in the postmodernist literature to assume that the globalization process, characterized by mobility of people, goods, capital, and ideas together with the subsequent erosion of spatially bounded social worlds, has led to a *de-territorialization* of identity. According to this view, regardless of their territorial origin people are in the process of becoming citizens of a world in which nation-state borders have less and less salience. The argument is that although people have always been mobile, as a result of changes in the world's political and economic structure, mobility has become the mode of human existence. However, in spite of our obvious global interconnectedness, the propensity to define ourselves on the basis of ethnic or national origin, as well as territorial location, has not necessarily decreased.

The postmodern or *anti-sedentarist* interpretation has a tendency to conflate two separate issues: the extent to which globalization has fundamentally changed the way we live, and the extent to which the problem of modernity and the nostalgia for place is an ontological condition as opposed to a sociological problem. Thus the plight of the refugee or exile comes to symbolize the modern condition to the extent that there is a profound sense of displacement in all of us. But the cosmopolitan effect of globalization is by no means all-encompassing and should not be transposed to exiles, refugees, or those living in diaspora. Their life histories attest to the physical, emotional, and psychological suffering of being displaced in a world in which citizenship, national allegiances and nation-state borders hold a surprising amount of significance.

This said, proponents of the anti-sedentarist position hold that embracing the reality and inevitability of a diasporic existence is actually a positive alternative to the modern nation state with its exclusionary politics. According to this view, diaspora identities are an antidote to the problems of exclusionary politics and exclusionist societies.

Greta Uehling

See also **Arabs: Palestinians; Armenians; Diaspora: African; Diaspora: Chinese; Diaspora: Indian; Diaspora: Jewish; Israel; Nationalism**

Further Reading

Ages, Arnold, *The Diaspora Dimension*, The Hague: Marinus Nijhoff, 1973

Al Rasheed, M., "The Myth of Return: Iraqi Arab and Assyrian Refugees in London," *Journal of Refugee Studies*, 7 no. 2/3 (1994) Bisharat, George, "Exile to Compatriot: Transformations in the Social Identity of Palestinian Refugees in the West Bank," *Culture, Power, Place,* edited by Akhil Gupta and James Ferguson, 1999 Clifford, James, "Diasporas," *Cultural Anthropology*, 9, no. 3 (1994)

Connor, Walker, "The Impact of Homelands Upon Diasporas," in *Modern Diasporas in International Politics*, edited by Gabriel Sheffer, New York: St. Martin's Press, 1986

Dubnow, Simon, "Diaspora," *Encyclopedia of the Social Sciences*, Vol. 5, New York: Macmillan, 1931

Gupta, Akhil, "The Song of the Nonaligned World: Transnational Identities and the Reinscription of Space in Late Capitalism," *Cultural Anthropology*, 7 no. 1 (1992)

Hall, Stuart, "Cultural Identity and Diaspora," in *Identity: Community, Culture, Difference*, edited by Jonathan Rutherford, 1990

Panossian, Razmik, "The Armenians: Conflicting Identities and the Politics of Division," in *Nations Abroad: Diaspora Politics and International Relations in the Former Soviet Union*, edited by Charles King and Neil Melvin, Boulder, Colorado: Westview, 1998

Platias, Athanassiios G., and Dimitri C. Constas, editors, *Diasporas in World Politics: The Greeks in Comparative Perspective*, London: Macmillan, 1993

Safran, William, "Diasporas in Modern Societies: Myths of Homeland and Return," *Diaspora*, 1, no. 1 (1991)

Zetter, Roger, "Reconceptualizing the Myth of Return: Continuity and Transition Amongst the Greek-Cypriot Refugees of 1974," *Journal of Refugee Studies*, 12, no. 1 (1999)

Diaspora: African

Capsule Summary

Location: Worldwide, especially Europe, the Caribbean, North America (including the United States and Canada), South America, and Central America
Total Population: Unknown
Language: Varies with place
Religion: Varies with place

Borrowed from the Greek *speiro* (to sow) and *dia* (over), the term African *diaspora* is conventionally applied to a description of the forced removal of continental Africans as part of the transatlantic slave trade, which began in the sixteenth century. During a process known as the Middle Passage, 10 million Africans were transported by ship across the Atlantic Ocean to the southern United States, the Caribbean, and Brazil. They were then sold as slaves, who would provide the plantation labor for the cultivation of commodities such as cotton and sugar. The greatest number of Africans were dispersed to these regions during slavery, which explains why this is the defining historical moment for the study of the African Diaspora. However in recent years their numbers include a rising number of voluntary emigrants and asylum-seekers.

Historical Antecedents of the African Diaspora of Slavery

There have been debates among historians, some of whom have challenged the widely held belief that it was the dispersal of continental Africans during the transatlantic slave trade which created the first and only significant African Diaspora. Although the most socially and culturally disruptive, it is argued that the forced migration of continental Africans for the purposes of labor exploitation was not the first African Diaspora. Scholars such as Ivan Van Sertima have provided historical and archaeological evidence that continental Africans circumnavigated the globe—the New World in general and the Americas in particular—centuries before the fifteenth century journey of Christopher Columbus, among other explorers. Ancient African migrations also led to a sustained African presence in Asia, the Middle East, and Europe.

The African Retentions and Survivals Debate

In 1968, historian George Shepperson is credited with drawing attention to the African Diaspora, as those cul-tures emerging from the dispersal of African people as a result of the transatlantic slave trade. Initial discussions of people of the African Diaspora as culture bearers and producers developed from a post-emancipation debate over the historical origins of African diasporic culture. *The Myth of the Negro Past,* written by anthropologist Melville Herskovits in 1941, was one of the first attempts to link the cultural and historical experiences of Africans within the Diaspora. In this publication, he challenged the claims made by African American sociologist E. Franklin Frazier.

While Herskovits devoted much of his research to proving that *Africanisms* (aspects of African cultures, such as religion, language, and family structure) existed in the New World in retained or modified forms, Frazier argued that no African residues existed and that African diasporic cultures developed as a direct result of slavery and in response to oppression.

Others claimed that Herskovits' generalizations about Africanisms and retentions without reference to either specific systems of slavery or plantation cultures (as both existed in the Americas and the Caribbean) called into question many of his findings. Sociologist W.E.B. DuBois provided a compromise perspective, which addressed both the existence of African survivals and the reality of cultural adaptation. Whether studying the African Diaspora of slavery, post-colonialism, or asylum and immigration, contemporary scholars tend to adopt an integrative approach, which incorporates one or both of two main themes. One refers to Africans as carriers of cultures—complex and varied traditions and practices—which are characteristic of Africa south of the Sahara and seem to persist in the Diaspora in spite of oppressive circumstances. The second acknowledges the important role racial hierarchies play in the African Diaspora as a means to organize groups on the basis of physical characteristics, which in turn determine one's access to privilege and opportunity in the case of those socially designated "white" and disadvantage and discrimination in the case of those categorized as "black." In the United States, during the Black Power Movement of the 1960s, black was reclaimed as a term signifying pride and defiance, as in "black is beautiful." This social movement influenced liberation struggles in other societies wherein blacks were victims of white supremacy, such as South Africa, the United Kingdom, and Brazil. As racism played such a key factor in the evolution of the African Diaspora, some refer instead to the Black Diaspora.

Slavery and Resistance

The most popular approach to the study of slavery in Brazil, the Caribbean, and the United States focused on the formation of plantation societies and cultures. Though the Caribbean differed from the United States and Latin America in its paucity of people indigenous to this region, forced enslavement and the structure and function of plantations united these regions. Plantations operated like societies. They were based on a single crop economy consisting of agricultural factories producing special crops (such as sugar or cotton) designed for an overseas market and consumption. There was social stratification consisting of dominant white plantation owners and subordinate black or *mulatto* workers. Where there was domination, there was also resistance in the form of slave revolts. Some historians argue that the political separatism, characteristic of the Black Nationalism in the 1960s, emerged from everyday forms of resistance and collective struggle during slavery. Garveyism, Pan-Africanism, and Rastafari in Jamaica are additional post-emancipation examples of resistance and revolution.

Race and Caste

The concept of race was a tool used to study cultural diversity among the many societies in the African Diaspora. Race was an idea that allowed for the social stratification of people based on skin color among other physical criteria. The caste system, which originated in India, is frequently used to describe the rigidity of racial structures in the United States. Within the caste system one's status is fixed at birth. Castes are hierarchically ranked, culturally distinct, and interdependent. Social mobility is available to those at the top of the caste system but denied to those at the bottom. Studies of race and caste in the African Diaspora looked at the social dimensions of racial discrimination as they were played out in plantation societies. Comparisons were made between the more fluid system of racial classification in Brazil, wherein anthropologist Marvin Harris identified 492 different categories for mulattoes and blacks, and the binary black/white scheme in the United States.

Comparisons were also made between North European and South European institutions of slavery. It was argued that a more oppressive racial regime existed in the United States because Northern Europeans who settled in the United States had less experience with miscegenation than their Southern European (Portuguese and Spanish) counterparts whose populations had been racially diversified as a result of 700 years of Moorish (North African) occupation. The counterclaim made is that such a distinction is of secondary significance when one focuses on the primary dehumanization and exploitation that existed in both contexts. Further debates address the questions: did slavery cause racism, did racism cause slavery, or are biology and ideology linked in justifications for the exploitation of cheap labor for the accumulation of capital?

Post-Emancipation Cultures and Family Organization

In addition to social stratification within the African Diaspora, researchers looked at social organization and social roles. The interrelatedness of class, gender, and culture in the organization of family life is one of the pivotal points around which competing formulations of the African Diaspora have been centered. After the emancipation of slaves at the end of the nineteenth century, in the various culture areas of the African Diaspora, economic and political structures impinged on populations and limited their range of life choices. Former slaves continued to suffer discrimination and lived in impoverished conditions. Post-emancipation cultures could be viewed as a frame of reference which was constantly changing in response to people's attempts to cope with their material circumstances. As was previously mentioned, one of the major intellectual disagreements was the extent to which Africans in the Diaspora have retained traditional African family forms and functions. Social scientists such as Nobles and Sudarkasa have adopted what is known as an Afro-centric or emergent framework, where one examines the influence of social conditions in the African Diaspora on the persistence of African retentions. Sudarkasa stressed the importance of blood relations (consanguinity) as opposed to marital ties (conjugality) when debating the relative stability of African-American family structures. These perspectives countered claims that the supposedly maladaptive African-American family with a matriarchal structure was the root cause of the discrepancies between black and white family life. Mothering was thought to involve the nurturing of the whole community, not just one's nuclear family or birth children.

Other African Diasporas

The other topical usage of the African Diaspora is to describe the post-colonial mass migration to Europe of African people from the Caribbean (such as Jamaica or Barbados) and West African countries (such as Ghana and Nigeria). This exodus took place after countries that were formerly under colonial rule (such as by Britain) gained independence in the late 1950s and 1960s. The same ideology of racism that was used to justify slavery was put forward to justify Imperial expansion. The Industrial Revolution happened as the result of profits from the slave trade.

In post-World War II Britain, for example, there were labor shortages in the public sector, such as transport and health care, which could be filled by employing migrants from the Caribbean. Recruitment campaigns encouraged people to settle in Britain. Caribbean economies suffered after the departure of the colonial authorities, who had deliberately underdeveloped industries in these territories. Poverty led African people in the Caribbean to seek an improved standard of living in Britain. Many West Africans migrated to Britain as students. Other European countries that had colonized parts of Africa and the Caribbean, such as France and the Netherlands, also had to contend with the influx of economic migrants.

Throughout Europe, immigration control remains an issue that polarizes political debates and public opinion. Since the 1990s, the waves of migrants from continental Africa to Europe and North America as a result of war, political, religious, and ethnic persecution (what are known as asylum-seekers and refugees), or poverty (economic migrants) have generated unresolved scholarly debates about whether these movements can be characterized as the latest type of African Diaspora. Through both voluntary migration and forced displacement, there are Sudanese in Minnesota, United States; Senegalese traders in Thessaloniki, Greece and Turin, Italy; Nigerians in Malaga, Spain; and Somalis in Ottawa, Canada. The existence and rapid growth of these new African communities pose particular intellectual challenges for scholars of the African Diaspora. Mapping specific African communities on to particular landscapes of slavery or post-colonialism does not work. More recent migrants and refugees from continental Africa have different shared narratives of home, community, and belonging than their predecessors. The myth of return is to a place they recently knew rather than to an *imaginary homeland*, as Africa is said to be described by descendants of African slaves.

The African Diaspora as a Concept

In addition to describing particular groups of African people now located in specific and different geographical areas outside the African continent, the African Diaspora is also a concept. That is, as a general idea that connects the conventional African Diaspora with the other two types of African Diaspora previously mentioned. As a concept the African Diaspora can be thought of as a political process, space, and condition. First, contemporary African diasporic processes extend the links of the migration chains that originated in the historical moments of the transatlantic slave trade and the rise of European Empires. Second, the African Diaspora is spatially constituted wherever

Africans find themselves, be that conventionally in the Caribbean, North and Latin Americas, or increasingly in Europe. Their similar histories of racial discrimination create the need for political activism and social solidarity, which in the past have taken the form of Garveyism, Pan-Africanism, the Black Power Movement, and other liberation struggles. Finally, African diasporic conditions persist and are transformed by the interaction of traditions of resistance, protest, and cultural innovation with economic and political hierarchies based on social inequalities. These are different outcomes to the similar economic and political legacies of slavery and colonialism, such as racism, sexism, and class discrimination. The seeds of contemporary African migrations were thought to have been sown as part of the same economic imperatives of transatlantic slavery and mercantile imperialism. It is said that global capitalism is the latest manifestation. Spanning five centuries and still unfolding, one could argue that the unique history of the African Diaspora is also in part a history of continental Africa.

JAYNE IFEKWUNIGWE

See also **Africans: Europe; Colonialism; Diaspora; Du Bois, W.E.B. (African-American); Garvey, Marcus (Jamaican); Nationalism; Race; Racism; Rastafari**

Further Reading

Essed, Philomena, *Understanding Everyday Racism*, London and Newbury Park, California: Sage, 1991

Forna, Aminatta, "Mothers of Africa and the Diaspora: Shared Maternal Values, " in *Black British Culture and Society*, edited by Kwesi Owusu, London and New York: Routledge, 2000

Gilroy, Paul, *The Black Atlantic*, Cambridge: Harvard University Press, 1993

Harding, Jeremy, *The Uninvited: Refugees at the Rich Man's Gate*, London: Profile and the London Review of Books, 2000

Hargreaves, Alec, and Mark McKinney, editors, *Post-Colonial Cultures in France*, London and New York: Routledge, 1997

Okpewho, Isidore, Carole Boyce Davies, and Ali Mazru, editors, *The African Diaspora: African Origins and New World Identities*, Bloomington and Indianapolis: Indiana University Press, 1999

Owusu, Kwesi, editor, *Black British Culture and Society*, London and New York: Routledge, 2000

Patterson, Tiffany Ruby, and Robin Kelley, "Unfinished Migrations: Reflections on the African Diaspora and the Making of the Modern World," *African Studies Review*, 43, no.1 (2000)

Segal, Ronald, *The Black Diaspora*, London and Boston: Faber and Faber, 1995

Van Sertima, Ivan, *They Came before Columbus: The African Presence in Ancient America*, New York: Random House, 1976

Diaspora: Chinese

Capsule Summary

Location: Worldwide, especially in Southeast Asia, North America, South America, Europe, Australia, and New Zealand
Total Population: 30 million
Languages: Chinese and local languages, with Putonghua (Mandarin) as the standard Chinese language
Religions: Mainly Chinese and Buddhism

People of Chinese origin are found all over the world. Calculations based largely on the censuses of the 1980s give a population figure of around 25 million, not including Taiwan, Hong Kong, and Macao. Thirty million is thus a reasonable estimate for the present population. They represent small minorities in their respective countries. Most of these Chinese are in Southeast Asia where they number close to only 5 percent of the total population. Singapore is an exception as they are the majority at about 78 percent. Malaysia is unique also as it has a high proportion of Chinese, about 28 percent. Some writers treat Chinese in Hong Kong, Macao, and Taiwan as *Overseas Chinese*, even though they really live in their Chinese homelands. Hong Kong and Macao are now part of China, albeit under the one country, two systems arrangement.

Definitions of the Diaspora

The Chinese in diaspora have been called Overseas Chinese in English. Those who are proud of their respective local identities reject this label as they feel that they are not overseas in the countries of their birth. The English term is perceived as equivalent to the Chinese label *huaqiao*, Chinese sojourners. As pointed out by Professor Wang Gungwu, the term *huaqiao* was first officially used in China in the nineteenth century and was later also adopted by the Chinese immigrants themselves. After World War II, colonial societies in Southeast Asia achieved independence. Most Chinese then realized that their home had to be in the new states; there was little choice anyway when the communist government took over China in 1949. With the growth of local consciousness of identity, the Chinese in Southeast Asia started to refer to themselves as *huaren*, Hua people, not *huaqiao*. Huaren is used in the ethnic sense, in contrast to the label *zhongguaren* (zhongguo, meaning China), which can also mean the nationality of China. Thus, the English term Chinese does not reflect the complex identities of all the Chinese.

With the establishment of diplomatic relations with different countries following President Richard Nixon's visit in 1972, China has reiterated its respect of the local status of Chinese who are citizens of local societies. Thus, China and its scholars have since adopted the label *huaqiao/huaren* to refer to all the Chinese in diaspora, both the Overseas Chinese (Chinese nationals) who are *huaqiao* and Chinese of other nationalities (*waiji huaren*) who are known as *huaren*. Alternatively, the term *haiwa huaren*, Chinese overseas, is also used. The English language lacks a neutral term to cover all the Chinese in diaspora. Hence the term Overseas Chinese remains popular. Ethnic Chinese scholars in Southeast Asia dislike the term diaspora because, as it has been historically used for the Jewish people, it implies longing for an original homeland. However, if it can be understood that there is no implication of China as homeland, then it is convenient and better as a general reference.

Migration and Settlement

Chinese had a long history of contacts with the coastal regions of Southeast Asia, then known to them as the South Seas, long before the arrival of the western powers in the sixteenth century. The early Chinese sojourners were traders, an important component of Chinese migrants to Southeast Asia. By the mid-nineteenth century, the expanding colonial economies and the hard times in China during the Taiping Rebellion had encouraged large-scale immigration of Chinese laborers to Southeast Asia, both skilled and unskilled. Most of them were from Fujian and Guangdong. At the same time this coincided with the end of African slave trade in the Americas in the 1860s, which created a huge demand for laborers there, hence the Chinese coolie trade. Chinese laborers were also recruited for the construction of railroads in the United States in the 1860s and in Canada in the 1880s. Another pull factor here and also to Australia and South Africa was the gold rush. But unlike the situation in Southeast Asia, Chinese migrants in North America encountered organized white labor and related racism. They had to live in ghettos for self protection and mutual support, and those who ventured into business opted for lines that did not have to compete with the whites, hence the Chinese specialization in laundry business. The emergence of Chinatowns and restaurants had to do with the constraints of the larger society. U.S. immigration laws, such as the Chinese Exclusion Act of 1882 and Canadian Immigration Act of 1923, discriminated against the Chinese. Australia, New Zealand, and South Africa also introduced laws to keep the countries white; the white policy in Australia was abolished only in 1973.

It was in the 1960s that the United States and Canada abolished racial immigration laws with the introduction of the New Immigrant Act in 1965 in the United States and the introduction of non-racial points-system in 1967 in Canada to screen immigrants. This makes it possible for more and continuous Chinese migration to this day. But today Chinese immigrants range from illegal migrants to students, professionals, transnational businessmen, and political exiles. In the past Chinese migrants to the United States and Canada were mainly from the Pearl River Delta of Guangdong. Today they come not only from Guangdong but also Fujian and elsewhere in Mainland China, Taiwan, as well as Chinese from Southeast Asia and other countries. Before the handover of Hong Kong to Mainland China in 1997, many people from Hong Kong migrated to North America, Australia, and Europe, and today their presence in the United States and Canada is very noticeable in such cities as Vancouver and San Francisco.

There was relatively less Chinese migration to Europe before World War II. Nevertheless, the Allied Forces in World War I recruited Chinese laborers. Most early migrants were from Guangdong as well as East and North China, including Zhejiang. Former colonial powers like the United Kingdom, France, and the Netherlands attracted Chinese from their former colonies after World War II. Thus, in the Netherlands today there are not only Chinese from Mainland China, but also those from Indonesia, Surinam, and other countries. As in North America, today there are Chinese migrants from different parts of China as well as from other countries.

Chinese migration today is very much linked to global capitalism, involving not only businessmen and professionals, but also legal and illegal Chinese workers. Opportunities to work as wage laborers encourage chain-migration, migration through the network of relatives and friends. Such opportunities for work and the dream of becoming rich have also been exploited by the Chinese underworld, which organizes complicated transnational human smuggling to North America and Europe. The continuous supplies of immigrants to western countries have continued to transform the diversities of the Chinese there. Unlike in Southeast Asia (except Singapore) where the governments have strictly restricted new Chinese immigration since independence, there are both Overseas Chinese who still regard China as the original home to return to and local-born Chinese who are citizens of their respective countries. There are also those who see themselves as having more than one home, such as one in Canada and one in Hong Kong, or one in the United States and one in Malaysia.

Socio-Cultural Life and Cultural Identities

The cultural identities of ethnic Chinese are very heterogeneous, even within one country. In Malaysia, for example, there are Chinese who emphasize Chinese literacy as crucial for Chinese identity. On the other hand there are creolized Chinese who speak a Malay creole as mother tongue but identify strongly as ethnic Chinese. These are the Babas, who also call themselves *Peranakan*. There are also many Chinese Malaysians who can express themselves better in English than in their own Chinese dialect. More and more young Chinese Malaysians now are more literate in Malay than in Chinese. In Indonesia, the local Chinese speak Indonesian fluently even among themselves. In the United States there are English-speaking Chinese-Americans on the one hand, and on the other hand there are recent Chinese immigrants who speak limited English. As for Chinese education, opportunity for learning to read and write Chinese differs from country to country. Ethnic Chinese in Malaysia have government-run Chinese-medium primary schools and 60 independent (i.e., privately managed) Chinese secondary schools. In Indonesia the (Mohamed) Suharto government banned not only Chinese education but also the display of Chinese characters, and today few Chinese-Indonesians can still read Chinese.

The lifestyles of ethnic Chinese are cosmopolitan, having incorporated modern and globalized lifestyle into their cultural life. Generally they still emphasize family as a value of mutual support and for organizing businesses. Surnames are passed down patrilineally (following the father's line) although many have adopted or added non-Chinese (e.g., English) personal names. Chinese cultural continuity is most visible in the celebration of festivals and life crisis occasions as well as in religious rites. Generally Chinese everywhere observe Chinese New Year, and basic Chinese symbols of blessings are observed or understood. While one can find representatives of all kinds of religions, especially Christianity and Buddhism, among the Chinese in diaspora, many still observe Chinese Religion—the worship of gods and ancestors and propitiating ghosts and spirits, as well as conducting Taoist or Buddhist rituals. Chinese temples are generally built in traditional Chinese architectural styles and stand out as an expression of Chinese identity.

Chinese as a Minority

Except in Singapore, Chinese in diaspora are minorities in their respective countries. In Malaysia, Chinese have their own political parties and are represented in the government, but in most countries they are still striving to be politically represented. Historically, Chinese in Southeast Asia have focused on economic activities, but they also realize the importance of political connection and representation. Chinese associations have always played an important part in the organizational life of the Chinese. Internal diversity is reflected in the types of Chinese voluntary organizations, which are based on regional and provincial origins in China, as well as speech groups and religious organizations. School alumni and recreational associations are also important, although younger Chinese today join a diverse range of clubs and professional organizations. In each state or country, the diverse Chinese organizations are usually united under one or two umbrella associations, which serve as a common mouthpiece of the Chinese.

Chinese minorities in many countries still encounter social and/or institutional discrimination. The situations in western countries have improved a lot since the 1960s, thanks to the civil rights movement and the discredit of racism as an ideology. But racial attitude toward Asians still remains. Often racial treatment of ethnic Chinese is linked to the politicization of the economic status of the Chinese. In Indonesia, for example, Chinese have always been portrayed both by indigenous nationalists and politicians as controlling the economy and are blamed for economic problems in the country as well as the poverty of the indigenous people. In actual fact Chinese make up only about 3 percent of the population, and most of them are small businessmen and wage earners, the visible rich is really small in number. Similarly, the "model minority" label in the west can have racial tone and may polarize ethnic Chinese and other minorities. Political and racial ideologies also play a part in discrimination against the Chinese. The *bumiputera* (sons of the soil) ideology is used by Malay nationalists and politicians to discriminate against non-Malays. The ideology of racial homogeneity and racial purity contributes much to the Japanese racial treatment of ethnic Chinese and Koreans as well as aboriginal Ainu. International conflict between a national government and China can result in government oppression of Chinese minority, as happened to the Chinese in India following Sino-Indian border conflict, and to the Chinese in Vietnam following the border war between Vietnam and China. Overall, depending on the nature of democracy and local politics, the status of Chinese as minority is volatile.

Transnationalism

The advance in information technology since the late twentieth century has allowed the Chinese in different countries to keep in touch with members of a family or an organization. The more affluent Chinese and professionals can travel easily worldwide, and migration and remigration have become common. Chinese businessmen have also kept up with global capitalism and transnational investment is common. They have extended their traditional regional network to more countries worldwide. The end of the Cold War has made it possible for uninhibited interactions between Chinese of different nationalities, including between Chinese of China and those in diaspora. There are also transnational networks between Chinese organizations. Indeed since the 1980s, various Chinese organizations have formed global associations and have organized international conventions in different countries, as well as in China. There are also various web sites that cater to the exchange of information between Chinese worldwide or between specific categories of Chinese. However, the Chinese worldwide do not form a nation, nor do they identify as one. They relate to each other as Chinese of different identities and political orientation. What they have in common is the identification as ethnic Chinese albeit perceived and expressed differently; as Chinese they are interested in things Chinese as well as opportunity for networking.

TAN CHEE-BENG

See also **Diaspora**

Further Reading

Benton, Gregor, and Frank N. Pieke, editors, *The Chinese in Europe*, London: MacMillan Press Ltd, 1998

Ong, Aihwa, and Donald Nonini, editors, *Ungrounded Empires: The Cultural Politics of Modern Chinese Transnationalism*, New York: Routledge, 1997

Pan, Lynn, editor, *The Encyclopedia of the Chinese Overseas*, Singapore: Landmark Books Pte Ltd, 1998

See, Teresita Ang, editor, *Intercultural Relations, Cultural Transformation, and Identity: The Ethnic Chinese*, Manila: Kaisa Para Sa Kaunlaran, Inc., 2000

Suryadinata, Leo, editor, *Ethnic Chinese as Southeast Asians*, Singapore: Institute of Southeast Asian Studies, 1997

Wang, Gungwu, *Community and Nations: Essays on Southeast Asia and the Chinese*, Singapore: Heinemann Educational Books (Asia) Ltd., 1981

Wang, Gungwu, *China and the Chinese Overseas*, Singapore: Times Academic Press, 1991

Wang, Ling-chi, and Wang Gungwu, editors, *The Chinese Diaspora: Selected Essays*, 2 vols., Singapore: Times Academic Press, 1998

Zhou, Nanjing, editor, *Encyclopedia of Chinese Overseas*, Beijing: Chinese Overseas Publishing House, 1999–2000

Diaspora: Indian

Capsule Summary

Location: Worldwide
Total Population: 10 million
Languages: Hindi, Tamil, Urdu, Gujarati, Bhojpuri, English, Creoles
Religions: Hindu, Muslim, Sikh

The Indian diaspora refers to the dispersal over the past century of substantial numbers of people from the Indian subcontinent (India, Pakistan, Sri Lanka, Bangladesh, Nepal, and Bhutan) to various western and non-western countries worldwide. Members of this diasporic population typically view themselves as ethnic others in their countries of settlement, reworking traditional forms of social custom, religious engagement, popular culture, and linguistic affiliation through collective interaction with their host societies. They also cultivate a shared sense of heritage and homeland through participation in community-based migrant organizations that facilitate the interactive flow of resources to and from their countries of origin. Although the origins of the Indian Diaspora may be traced to the colonial practices of the mid-nineteenth century, South Asian migration has reached unprecedented levels in the last few decades due to significant changes in the global political economy.

Indentured and Contract Labor, 1830–1920

The first phase of the Indian diaspora may be traced to the transcontinental movements of labor under the British colonial empire. The abolition of slavery in the European colonies during the nineteenth century prompted tropical plantation owners worldwide to seek new sources of affordable and efficient human labor. Beginning in 1834 the indentured labor system enabled plantation owners to procure cheap labor from the Indian subcontinent through arrangements with colonial authorities. According to this system, men and women recruited as laborers from the countryside would sign contracts of indenture to work for a certain number of years in one of the other colonial territories in return for basic pay, room, and board. Indentured laborers from India began to emigrate to cocoa and sugar plantations in Trinidad, Mauritius, Guyana in the 1840s, Natal (South Africa) in the 1860s, Surinam in the 1870s, and Fiji in the 1880s. By the time that the system was formally abolished in 1918, there were nearly half a million Indian immigrants in Mauritius, a quarter million in Guyana, over a hundred thousand in Natal and Trinidad, and significant numbers in Fiji, Guadeloupe, Reunion, Jamaica, and East Africa. Approximately two-thirds of the indentured workers remained in their host colony after the expiration of their contracts.

Most indentured workers were recruited from Hindi-speaking North India, especially Bihar and the Northwest Provinces (Uttar Pradesh), although smaller numbers were also recruited from the Tamil and Telugu districts of South India. Tamil-speaking South Indians were far more likely to migrate regionally to Ceylon (Sri Lanka), Burma, and Malaya, where their work on tea and rubber plantations continued until the 1930s. The great majority of the labor population was Hindu by religion, with significant numbers of Muslims as well. Punjabi Sikhs, rather than work as indentured servants, migrated to East and Central Africa in the 1890s to work as artisans and railway men.

As time progressed in the colonies, South Asian migrant populations began to emerge as distinct ethnic communities in each settlement site. Various factors contributed to these patterns of ethnic identification. Indentured laborers were largely unable to maintain close ties to their homeland because of their geographical distance from South Asia and their restricted movement while living under contract. At the same time, colonial management typically clustered all South Asians together in isolated rural enclaves under conditions that gradually disintegrated regional differences in dialect, caste, religious affiliation, and cultural tradition. Such groups thus experienced a high degree of linguistic creolization and cultural homogenization. The distinct economic niche of migrants in each location also played a role in forming ethnic communities. For example, plantation workers in Mauritius, South Africa, Fiji, and the Caribbean Islands became rural laborers and independent farmers in the sugar cane industries after the termination of their contracts. Migrants to East and Central Africa remained in the region as small shop owners *(dukawallahs)* and professionals, while Indians in Southeast Asia filled privileged positions in the civil service.

The decades immediately following the abolition of indentured servitude saw some degree of free movement of people from South Asia to other countries. For example, Gujaratis in search of trading opportunities freely migrated in large numbers to East Africa in the early part of the twentieth century. However, the patterns of the Indian diaspora changed considerably during the era of decolonization following World War II.

Migration to Great Britain

Prior to Indian Independence, small numbers of students, sailors, and emissaries migrated to the imperial capital by exercising the right of all colonial subjects to travel to and settle in Britain. New types of migration occurred, however, during the post-war period of decolonization, as the British government began recruiting labor from its former colonies to fill vacancies in its industrial sectors resulting from substantial losses of young male soldiers. These South Asian workers typically followed an arrangement known as *chain migration*, in which men from certain villages and districts (generally in Gujarat, Bengal, and the Punjab) would migrate to industrialized inner cities and share dormitory-style accommodations while searching for employment as semi-skilled laborers. As the national government began to restrict entry into Britain in the 1960s, many of these men decided to stay permanently in the country, sponsoring their immediate families and re-establishing their lives in this new context.

In the late 1960s and early 1970s, various nationalist leaders in East and Central Africa began to pressure and, in the case of Uganda, forcibly expel South Asian migrants from their countries. Although some of these formerly indentured families returned to their home countries, many resettled as *twice migrants* in Canada and especially Great Britain. By 1981 there were more than 150,000 South Asians of East African origin living in Britain. The public anxiety and fear prompted by this influx of immigrants found expression in the extreme right-wing discourse of the National Front Party, which found a certain degree of popularity in the 1970s. As Canada and the United States began to relax their immigration policies in the 1980s, Great Britain continued to tighten its entry permit procedures through the years of the Thatcher administration.

Migration to the Gulf States

The oil boom of the early 1970s prompted the large movement of South Asian workers to the Gulf States, where the six oil-exporting countries (Kuwait, Bahrain, Qatar, the United Arab Emirates, Oman, and Saudi Arabia) turned to contract migration to satisfy their rapidly increasing demand for expatriate labor. This movement occurred with little official coordination between the labor-sending and the labor-receiving nations, and official assessments of foreign immigration typically underestimate the actual numbers of workers. Unofficial estimates suggest that there were roughly 2 million Indians, 1.5 million Pakistanis, and 200,000 Bangladeshis in the Gulf States by the late 1980s. Given their access to substantially higher wages in the Gulf States, these South Asian laborers are able to remit much of their income to their families at home. However, their status on the margins of society makes them susceptible to legal abuses, particularly during times of social tension. This vulnerability is even higher for the tens of thousands of female domestic workers who have migrated from South Asia (Sri Lanka and Bangladesh) to the Gulf States, where their service is explicitly excluded from consideration by local labor laws.

Migration to the United States

The first phase of migration from South Asia to the United States occurred in the early part of the twentieth century as agriculturalists from Punjab, attracted by the possibility of labor in the lumber yards of the Pacific Northwest, began relocating to the American West. By 1914 there were approximately 10,000 migrants from South Asia working in California. Ultimately forced out of the labor markets, these predominantly Sikh workers pooled their resources and resumed their agricultural activities as landowning farmers in the valleys of California. Because U.S. immigration laws discouraged them from bringing families into the country, these men remained unmarried or settled with Mexican and Mexican-American women who labored in the California fields.

Due to increasingly restrictive immigration laws, the rate of South Asian immigration to the United States gradually declined after 1910, reaching very low levels during the 1930s and 1940s. Legislation passed in 1946 raised immigration quotas to the fixed rate of one hundred individuals annually from India and Pakistan combined. This modest pattern of immigration continued for the next several decades, such that the estimate of total Indian migration to the United States before 1964 is around 6,400.

A second phase of South Asian migration to the United States was prompted by the Immigration and Nationality Reform Act of 1965, legislation which facilitated the entrance of skilled professionals in search of educational and employment opportunities. Tightly screened for employability by immigration officials, these immigrants constitute part of a world-wide professional elite whose tendency to cluster in wealthy nations is commonly termed the *brain drain* of talent from developing countries such as India. These Indian-Americans are perceived as a model minority, one of the most economically successful Asian immigrant communities in the country. The 1990 Census suggests that Indian-Americans have very high levels of educational attainment, professional and managerial employment, household income, and family stability. Such socioeconomic measures suggest that these immigrants have secured financial prosperity and professional success.

The Immigration and Nationality Act of 1984 prompted a third phase of migration by eliminating the system of national origin quotas and establishing a system of preference based on the principles of family reunification. These changes enabled settled professionals to sponsor their family members through extensive use of preferential categories for independent relatives. Rates of immigration from South Asia accelerated, such that in 1991 nearly 80 percent of the 44,121 persons of Indian origin admitted into the United States were sponsored by family members. These sponsored relatives tend to find their first jobs in the unskilled manual categories of employment, although they exhibit a considerable degree of occupational diversification after several years in the country. According to the 2000 Census, the number of people identifying themselves as Asian-Indians or Indian-Americas in the United States has nearly doubled in the past decade to 1.7 million.

Migration to Canada

The first South Asians arrived on the western coast of Canada between 1900 and 1908, as several thousand predominantly Sikh agriculturalists from Punjab established a small but enduring migrant community amidst the lumberyards and farmlands of British Columbia. Subsequent legislative restrictions virtually eliminated the migration of South Asians into Canada for several decades. The rate of South Asian immigration drastically increased, however, in the 1960s with the implementation of immigration reforms giving preference to prosperous members of the professional classes. Substantial numbers of twice-migrants also entered Canada in the 1970s as political refugees from the former British colonies, particularly East Africa. The rate of immigration by South Asians and other visible minorities has continued to increase due to various changes in immigration policies since the 1980s, such that there are nearly half a million South Asians living in Canada according to the 1996 Census. These South Asian migrants and twice-migrants have typically clustered together in the three main ports of entry—Montreal, Toronto, and Vancouver.

National debates about immigration policy in Canada since the 1970s have revealed certain popular conceptions concerning the presence of South Asian and other immigrants in the country. Proponents of stricter immigration standards claim that immigrants are a burden on the national economy, draining the state's overburdened social security system and increasing unemployment among non-immigrant laborers. They also claim that the increased ethnic and religious diversity of the population will threaten Canadian national values. Immigration activists, however, highlight the economic and cultural contributions of immigrant communities. They point out that immigration encourages the growth of trade and industry, and many immigrants create economic opportunity through capital investment in land development and small business ownership. They also emphasize that tolerance for ethnic diversity is a fundamental characteristic of Canadian identity, as reflected by the official multiculturalism policy of the Canadian government. Despite the complexity of national attitudes towards ethnicity and diversity, South Asian immigrants have become a permanent part of the multicultural fabric of Canadian society.

HALEY DUSCHINSKI

See also **Diaspora; India; South Asian-Americans (India, Pakistan, Bangladesh); South Asians in Asia and the Pacific; South Asians in Europe; South Asians in the Americas (non-United States)**

Further Reading

Bates, Crispin, editor, *Community, Empire, and Migration: South Asians in Diaspora,* Hampshire and New York: Palgrave, 2001

Clarke, Colin, Ceri Peach, and Steven Vertovec, editors, *South Asians Overseas: Migration and Ethnicity,* Cambridge: Cambridge University Press, 1990

Coward, Harold, John R. Hinnells, and Raymond Brady Williams, editors, *The South Asian Religious Diaspora in Britain, Canada, and the United States,* Albany: State University of New York Press, 2000

Esses, Victoria M., and R.C. Gardner, "Multiculturalism in Canada: Context and Current Status," *Canadian Journal of Behavioral Science,* Special Issue on Ethnic Relations in a Multicultural Society, 28, no. 3 (1996)

Kumar, Amitava, *Passport Photos,* Berkeley: University of California Press, 2000

Lessinger, Johanna, *From the Ganges to the Hudson: Indian Immigrants in New York City,* Boston: Allen and Bacon, 1995

Northrup, David, *Indentured Labour in the Age of Imperialism, 1834–1922,* Cambridge: Cambridge University Press, 1995

Owen, Roger, *Migrant Workers in the Gulf,* London: Migrant Rights Group, 1986

Prashad, Vijay, *The Karma of Brown Folk,* Minneapolis: University of Minnesota Press, 2000

Tinker, Hugh, *A New System of Slavery: The Export of Indian Labor Overseas, 1830–1920,* London: Oxford University Press, 1974

Tinker, Hugh, *The Banyan Tree: Overseas Emigrants from India, Pakistan, and Bangladesh,* London: Oxford University Press, 1977

Van der Veer, Peter, editor, *Nation and Migration: The Politics of Space in the South Asian Diaspora,* Philadelphia: University of Pennsylvania Press, 1995

Diaspora: Irish

see **Ireland; Travelers (Irish Nomads)**

Diaspora: Jewish

Capsule Summary

Location: United States (5.8 million), France (600,000), Russia (550,000), Ukraine (500,000), Canada (360,000), United Kingdom (300,000), Argentina (250,000), Brazil (130,000), South Africa (106,000), Australia (100,000), and 78 other countries
Total Population: 13.5 million (8.7 million in Diaspora, 4.8 million in Israel, non-diasporic)
Language: Varies depending upon place (Hebrew in Israel)
Religion: Judaism

The Jewish Diaspora is the world's oldest Diaspora and as such is complex and ever changing. It continues to exist despite its fragmentation, its lack of cohesive identifying characteristics, and its persistent marginalization. Today the efficacy of the Diaspora is at once buoyed and undermined by the multitudinous, often tumultuous, relationships with the one Jewish state. Judaism is at another important crossroad. It, like so many nations, has been secularizing. Both within Israel and within the Diaspora more people identify with the ethno-national character of the Jewish identity than the religious character. Israelis hold on to their Jewishness through their socio-political identity—they are citizens of a Jewish state. The Diaspora is left with rituals softened by a reduced need to act nationalistically to seek or maintain a Jewish state, a dearth of religious proclivities, and intermarriage. In stark contrast to the rise of anti-Semitism witnessed in Europe and the United States half a century ago, the greatest threat to Diaspora today comes from within.

History

Jewish history traces its roots back to the birth of Adam and Eve in 3760 BCE. As such it is the world's oldest living religion. The Jewish belief in one true God forms the basis for both Christianity and Islam. The Jewish people are not identified historically until the Egyptian King Marniptah (approximately 1224–1211 BCE). Thus the history that precedes this, known as the Age of the Patriarchs, is reliant on an oral history written down more than a thousand years later. According to Jewish history, the first patriarch of Judaism was Abraham. A Semite, he was born in the city of Haran in northern Mesopotamia in 1813 BCE. His father, Terah, came from Ur in southern Mesopotamia. According to the Biblical text, God came to Abraham and told him to move his family (Genesis 12:4-7). Existing written historical records confirm that this was a time of strife in Mesopotamia. God wanted to chose the Hebrew people for a special relationship. He would protect them as long as they served him. Abraham was chosen by God as an obedient follower. God promised Abraham that if he helped him he would grant him the son he never had, and Isaac was born. In a famous biblical passage (Genesis 22:1-2), God then requested Abraham to demonstrate his faithfulness by asking him to kill his own son. Abraham consented, thereby proving his devotion, although God stopped him just before he committed the deed.

The Jewish people in Mesopotamia were nomadic—not landowners. As part of his covenant, God said he would give the Jewish people land and protect them if they would live in Palestine and listen to him. What the boundaries of Palestine were at the time is a subject of great debate. Many very religious Jews today cite Exodus 23:30, 31 and Joshua 1:4 to mark it from the Euphrates River to the Mediterranean and from the Red Sea to Lebanon. This is a point that has been very contentious in modern day Israel's negotiations with Palestinians and with its neighbors. It is from Abraham's covenant with God that the Jewish religion finds its basis in both family and devotion. It is from here that Abraham became the forefather of the Jewish religion. And, it is from here that the Jewish people established their tie to a particular geographic region along the Mediterranean Sea. While the Jewish people gave up much of their nomadic lifestyle during this period, they maintained many of the tribal norms and the hierarchical social organization.

Abraham had a grandson named Jacob, whom God renamed Israel. Israel had twelve sons: Reuven, Shimon, Levi, Judah, Issachar, Zevulun, Dan, Naphtali, Gad, Asher, Joseph, and Benjamin. Each of these sons became the leader of a different tribe. Of note, the modern word Israel is derived from Jacob's name and the word Jewish is derived from Judah (Yehuda), forming the linguistic connection of one people of one origin.

Many Jews were nonetheless driven from Palestine, mostly into Egypt. This came during a long, violent, chaotic period where foreigners, especially Jewish people, were enslaved and dealt with harshly. Foreigners in Egypt were called habiru; some scholars believe this is where the modern word Hebrew was derived. The habiru were to be routed from the land. In 1250 the second great patriarch of the Jewish people, Moses, was instructed by God to lead his people out of Egypt. This Exodus is the most important event in Jewish history; its recognition as a unifying moment transcends religious doctrine to become a defining cultural feature. Critical here is the deepening of God's bond with the Jewish people. God *chose* Moses as a leader. The centrality of his figure unites the tribes into a single, identifiable nation. Most importantly, the Jewish people did not practice the ritual of worshipping God. According to *Exodus* they were taught by Moses how to do this in a singular fashion during their migration. Here the central tenets of Judaism, still practiced today, became halakha, Jewish law. The process of this lawmaking, the historical uncertainty as to whether there were other slaves (not the descendants of Abraham) in the Exodus, and the uncertainty about whether there were significant populations of Abraham's descendents living in or assimilated in Palestine leads some (secular) scholars to question whether the genealogical roots of Judaism lie more in the Exodus than in the covenant.

The period that followed the Exodus and the years of wandering was one of great disorganization in the religion. The Jewish people attempted to take over Palestine. However, their marginal success led many of them to live under various Caananite lords; the chosen people were greatly divided. It appeared that Judaism might cease to exist, as intermarriage and the abandonment of Jewish ritual were common. There is a strong archeological record of the blending of Baal (the Caananite God) and Yahweh (the Jewish God) as the alters were disassembled and reassembled to shift representation.

In 1050 BCE the tribes united to form a single monarchy, ultimately conquering the Caananites and once again ruling Palestine. This is known in history as the rise of the First Temple. The great period lasted until King Solomon died (around 926 BCE). The 12 tribes would not unite under his son Rehoboam. The Kingdom was split in two: Israel in the north (with a capital in Samaria) and Judea in the south (with a capital in Jerusalem). This division of power would prove critical as Mesopotamian kingdoms to the northeast and Egypt to the south were at war. The two Jewish kingdoms held valuable real estate. In 722 BCE the Assyrians conquered Israel and the ten tribes of the state were exiled. They were lost to history. The tribes of Benjamin and Judah remained with Jerusalem as the capital and are thought to be the heritage from which modern Jews descend.

Judah was conquered by the Chaldeans ("New Babylonians," who had taken over Mesopotamia with the fall of the Assyrians) in 597 BCE. At first only higher castes—skilled craftspeople, large landholders, others of wealth—were forced into exile. These numbered about 10,000. Of historic note, in the short run it was welcomed by many Jewish people for instrumental reasons. The Chaldeans redistributed the lands among the poorer castes, particularly advantaging the landless. In 586 BCE Judah was assimilated and ceased to exist as an independent kingdom. The First Temple fell. The fate of the Jewish people living in Judah is unknown, but it is presumed that they themselves became assimilated. Those that were in exile, however, lived together in Babylon. They forged a strong sense of unity and an identification of Judaism under the *halakha*. It was a time of great pain, but also high productivity with this learned society forming bonds, planning for the future, and writing. It was during this Exile that the Torah, the first five books of the Jewish Bible, took shape. The common identity forged, and the writings that are still followed today were of a people in exile. Thus, a tremendous emphasis was placed on looking toward the future when there would be a re-establishment of a great Jewish state in Jerusalem.

The Chaldeans were conquered by the Persians in 538 BCE. The Persian King Cyrus is thought by many to be the first king to seek world expansion. While he was polytheistic, he also believed that the Jewish God was a good God and that the followers of Yahweh should return to Jerusalem to worship him. The children of the Exiles returned to form a quasi-independent theocratic state within the powerful Persian Empire. So began the rise of the Second Temple.

Alexander the Great of Rome conquered the Persians in 333 BCE. He split the empire into three regions, each controlled by one of his generals. Judea ultimately fell to the Seleucids, which was dominated by Greek culture. The rise of Greek influences in Judaism created rifts within the population between new Hellenic Jews and Traditionalists. Laws of occupation also stymied traditional practices, challenging the free worship under *halakha*. This lasted until 168 BCE when Judah Maccabee led the Hasmonean revolt. Hellenic Jews were defeated and enormous autonomy was granted to the Temple. The city grew rapidly. Under King Herod's reign (37–4 BCE), it saw its greatest period of expansion, growing strongly northward even while under Roman control. It is during this period that we saw the now-famed symbols of Jewish regional identity built—the Second Wall, the Citadel, Temple Mount, and the Tower of David.

To some Herod was seen as an appeaser. He accepted the quasi-independence afforded under the Roman yoke. After he died the Jewish people sought greater autonomy. This was met with strong-armed Roman tactics, followed by ever-increased Jewish revolt and ongoing escalation. Zealots entered the city in 66 CE, and Jerusalem fell to the Romans in 70 CE. Much of the city was destroyed and the Jewish people fled into exile. This began the first significant period of the Jewish living in Diaspora.

The Diaspora

The Diaspora really began with the expulsion of elites from Judea in 597 BCE. However, while this may have led to displacement and, ultimately, assimilation of a large percentage of the Jewish population, it did not drive them out of the region en masse. With the fall of Jerusalem to the Romans, the Jewish resistance took refuge in Masada. When Herod came under threat he took refuge in the small mountain top town south of Jerusalem. Between 37 and 31 BCE he had the town fortified in case of future threats to his people. In 70 CE it became the rebel base of operations. Roman governor Flavius Silva determined in 72 CE that it had to be destroyed. He sent between 10,000 and 15,000 troops to surround the mountain to assure no escape. Left only with the prospects of enslavement, the approximately 1000 fervent resistors joined their leader, Eleazar ben Yair, in committing mass suicide rather than being captured. This event became a sign of courage to the Jewish people; its importance as a symbol surged in the twentieth century as the Jewish people fought long odds to establish a new state. This event also symbolizes the last time for nearly 2000 years that the Jewish people would live in one central location. The Diaspora, the dispersion of Jews amongst other peoples of diverse heritage and religions, was complete.

During the early years of the Diaspora there was a precipitous decline in the number of Jewish people who were knowledgeable about their heritage. The death of Judaism by assimilation appeared imminent once again. In a watershed event the Roman Governor Tinneius Rufus banned circumcision (an act which is taken to be the ultimate symbol of the Jewish covenant with God). This led to the Bar Kochba Revolt in 135 CE. Rabbinic scholars sought once again to use common cultural bonds and writing as a means of assuring the persistence of beliefs. Rabbi Judah HaNasi (138–220 CE) became the first in a line of new patriarchs that sought to provide centrality. The Age of the Tannaim, as it came to be called, saw Rabbi Judah write the Mishna—a codification of critical oral laws given to Moses by God—into a complimentary reading to the Bible. There are a total of 63 tracts that still today are intended to serve as the basis for Jewish life. In the centuries that followed Rabbinical scholars studied the Mishna and wrote down comments and clarifications. By around 400 CE this collection of writings came together into a series of books called the Talmud (the Jerusalem Talmud). The discussions continued for another century. Edits and additions were made until a new Talmud emerged (the Babylonian Talmud).

The Babylonian Talmud is that which is read by practicing Jews today. It gives specific guidance on the *halakha.* In addition, it provides a way in which the Jewish people are intended to live, including social customs, historical information, folklore, and even medical advice. It is second only to the Torah in the holiness of scripture and is persistently controversial. Yet the writings are likely in large part responsible for the ability of Judaism to survive so many decades in the Diaspora.

The region changed forever in 324 CE. Emperor Constantine was the first Christian to ascend to the throne. During this Byzantine period Christianity became the official religion and life for the Jewish population became more unbearable. Among the various edicts, Jews were banned from Jerusalem. A spate of church building was hallmarked by the 326 CE building of the Church of the Holy Sepulcher. The Jewish people migrated further, populating modern day Europe. Large Jewish populations emerged in Brittany (France) in 465 CE, Valence in 524 CE, and Orleans in 533 CE. A large Jewish community in Paris erected a (short-lived) synagogue in Ile de la Cite. Anti-Jewish sentiment was unusual in France during this period and it thus became a common destination for immigrants. By the eighth Century CE, the Jewish population became a powerful force in commerce and high trades such as law and medicine. This was a critical moment in the development of the Jewish Diaspora. For the first time a sizeable Jewish population in Europe was concurrently more free and wealthy than the Jewish population in the homeland, and much of this population pined in vain to return.

Meanwhile, in early seventh century Palestine there was a rise of anti-Jewish sentiment and violent attackers challenged religious practices and dealt with those who practiced Jewish rituals harshly. Some Jewish people fled to Russia, China, India, and elsewhere. Others retaliated by supporting the Persian army. In 614 CE the region fell to the Persians. For a very brief spate the Jewish people were granted leadership of the city of Jerusalem in gratitude for their assistance against the Byzantines. However, in 629 CE Byzantine Emperor Heraclius recaptured Jerusalem and the Jewish people were punished with even more vehemence. Jerusalem fell once again to conquest in 638 CE, this time to Arab conquest. Islam quickly rose throughout the region and Jerusalem became the third holiest Muslim site. Arab leadership was more genial than its Byzantine predecessors. Christians and Jews were allowed to live and worship in Jerusalem in a fragile peace.

On July 15, 1099, Christian Crusaders sacked Jerusalem, massacring both Jews and Muslims in the name of the Holy Father. Pope Urban II had beseeched now more powerful European states to launch a holy war against the infidels in the sacred land of Jesus Christ. The Jewish quarter of Jerusalem was burned. Where the residents sought refuge in synagogues, they died in the fires. The rest either were taken into slavery or fled. In the decades that followed, the Christian rulers opened trade routes between Europe and Palestine. Some Jewish families that had fled to Europe used this as an opportunity to return, settling quietly in the northern cities of Acre and Jerusalem. However, the majority remained in Europe.

Hasdai Ibn Shaprut (915–970 CE) became the first Jewish dignitary under Arab rule. He established a Jewish center for Talmudic study in Cordoba, Spain. A small but important Jewish population continued to develop the *halakha.* Some of the Jewish population fleeing Jerusalem during the First Crusades came to Cordoba. It remained a central focus for Jewish thought until it also was conquered by Christians in 1236. The population fled to Granada, Malaga, and Seville, only to be turned away thereafter by Christian conquerors.

France continued to be the primary destination, though William the Conqueror established a Jewish population to England for the first time. England quickly became a safe haven with new laws created for Jewish protection. This was maintained until Richard the Lion-Hearted rose to the throne in 1189, when Jewish massacres began. As an exchequer—a ministerial account for the Jews—was created in 1194 it started to become clear that Jewish life in England would come at an economic price. King John wrote a charter for Jews that required regularized payment to the crown and arbitrary taxes were levied. When the Magna Carta was signed in 1215, it placed limitations on the power of the monarchy, but it also codified many of the economic burdens specific to the Jewish population. Jews were ultimately expelled from England in 1290.

The French Jewish population was fairing no better. They were expelled from Brittany in 1240. The Talmud was burned in Paris in 1242. Jews were banished from France in 1254. While they were readmitted a couple years later, in 1305 Phillip IV launched a mission to imprison all Jews and confiscated all Jewish goods and lands. Louis X released the Jews and allowed the remainder to return in 1315. Hardly a respite, their presence in society led to mass killings in Alsace, Paris, Nantes, and throughout the eastern part of the country. Some fled to Palestine, but found that the Mameluke rulers (Muslim Egyptians of Asian descent) took control of Jerusalem in 1260. Newcomers were treated just as the existing Jewish population—ruled under violent repression. Once again Judaism seemed it would cease to exist.

Times continued to become worse in the Diaspora. Pope Innocent III (1198–1216 CE) had set the Inquisition in motion, and in 1233 Pope Gregory IX set it in full force. The original efforts were to combat Christian heresy. It quickly spread throughout central and eastern Europe. The punishment for heresy was an Act of Faith where a priest would carry out the sentencing. These punishments could include imprisonment, torture, or death. If one confessed to heresy and reasserted his faith in the church then he was flogged, removed from public life, and had his property confiscated. If one did not confess, he would be burned at the stake. Those who confessed but did not repent were shown the mercy of being strangled, then burned at the stake. All of these were public spectacles.

1288 CE marked the first mass burning of Jews, but the precipitous event came with the Inquisition in Spain in 1481 CE. Thirteen thousand Jews were burned in Spain during the first dozen years. The remaining Jewish population of Spain, about 200,000, was expelled by King Ferdinand in 1492 CE. When Ferdinand's daughter Isabella married King Manuel of Portugal four years later, all Jews were expelled from there as well. The Spanish Inquisition continued well into the eighteenth century; it is estimated that during this period nearly 50,000 Jews were burned at the stake and nearly 340,000 recanted Judaism and made penance. Of note, both Spanish and Portuguese Jewish communities were affluent and at one time influential. The Jewish population landed in Turkey, North Africa, the Middle East, and elsewhere. Ultimately these populations became known as Sephardim (Sefarad being the Hebrew word for Spain). Their geographic separation, intermarriage, and varied history led to marked ethnic and ritualistic differences. Others fled to Belgium, Hungary, Germany, Austria, and elsewhere.

The Ottoman Turks sacked the Mameluke in 1517 CE. Sultan Suleiman allowed Judaism to flourish once again, but not the city of Jerusalem. The Jewish population increased as European, and particularly Sephardic, Jews sought its protections. In the four centuries that followed persecution was not high, but Jerusalem stagnated. It was unimportant and provincial to the Ottoman Empire.

Russia marginally allowed Jewish settlement during this period. Officially it was banned, but unofficially the role the Jewish community played in commerce entitled them to middle class lifestyles. It was a time of Jewish expansion and great division. Israel Ba'al Shem Tov (1698 CE–1760 CE) founded Hassidic Judaism. Hassidim believed that Judaism should be led by the heart. This manifested into a following of the doctrine of the *Tzaddikim* (a religious leader), that is, the Jewish population should follow the teachings as interpreted by their Rabbis. Where the Rabbi could establish a dynasty, his family became wealthy, powerful, and influential. Elsewhere the sect would die with the Rabbi. By the time of Israel Ba'al Shem Tov's death, there were an estimated 10,000 Hassidim in Russia, Poland, and Eastern Europe. It grew to encompass a significant portion of European Jewry. For their part Orthodox Jews, *Mitnagdim*, saw Hassidism as a vulgarization of Judaism. Deep rifts between communities emerged and Jewish unity waned. In 1791 a Russian decree mandated that all Jews were to be expelled from Moscow. They were allowed to move to Poland, which was Russian controlled. Hassidic and Orthodox Jewry came together out of need to form single court systems, legal, and social practices, even if religious differences continued to proliferate. Their numbers proliferated beyond the Pale, particularly in Germany, Austria, Belgium, Hungary, and the United States.

In 1800 CE the Jewish population of the United States was about 2,000. By 1840 it was 15,000; by 1850, 50,000; by 1860, 200,000; and by the turn of the century, 3 million. Deep divisions persisted between Jewish sects. Starting in the end of the eighteenth century, Berlin saw a growth in a particularistic Jewish population that believed in Jewish Enlightenment, *Haskalah*. The belief is that the Jewish people should study not just the Torah but secular subjects, the arts and sciences in particular. Moses Mendelssohn (1726–1789) was a German-Jewish community leader who is considered the father of *Haskalah* and of a Reform movement limiting the religiosity of Jewish worship. He won the favor of gentile leaders such as Frederick the Great and Joseph II who wanted to normalize Jewish education. It was revolutionary in that *Haskalah* schools offered education in Jewish thought and Talmud, but also in math, science, and letters. For the first time it also opened equal education to girls. To date, girls were barred from education as education was based on the Talmud and Talmud was a male study. By the middle of the nineteenth century, Jewish literature, poetry, music, art, and science were making their mark on society in Vienna, Prague, and Berlin. Most importantly a Jewish professional class began to emerge. The *Haskalah* reached Russia in the 1840s, but never in the great wave that took over Europe.

In 1881 Alexander II of Russia began passing edicts against the Jewish people. A series of 200 pogroms—systematic, organized attacks—were launched against them in that year alone. Alexander III expanded these edicts and the pogroms were stepped up. Under Czar Nicholas II the pogroms reached a climax. In 1903 the Jewish people were accused of aligning with Japan in the Russo-Japanese wars, and the killings, rapes, and evacuations of Jews reached a frenzy. Those that came to Europe found a tremendous challenge to their religious beliefs and that which they thought they had fought for. Both Hassidim and Orthodox Jewry took the *Haskalah* as an affront. Their fears were, to some degree, well founded. Having given up Judaism's religious traits, many followers of the *Haskalah* ultimately abandoned the customs and rituals as well, assimilating into European society. It was this assimilation, not persecution, that ended the particularism of Jewish Enlightenment.

The *Haskalah* shaped the Jewish Diaspora and how it grew as a political force. One of the most fundamental advocates was the Budapest-born Theodor Herzl (1860 CE–1904 CE). When he went to the university in Vienna, the Jewish population of the city was approximately 200,000. About 1.2 million Jews lived in Austria as a whole. Five million Jews lived under the Russian Czar, 850,000 in Hungary, and 560,000 in Germany. Only about 100,000 remained in France, and half that in Spain and Italy combined. Herzl's beliefs in the *Haskalah* were hardly representative of the majority of even the Europe-based Diaspora. Yet Hertzl's vision of a new Zion for the Jewish people—a Zionism—took hold with the powerful Jewish business class. Famed elites such as Baron Hirsch and Baron Rothschild backed his call. They believed that this, not Hassidism or Orthodoxy, was the best way to stem the tide of assimilation while protecting the Jewish population from anti-Semitism.

One of the great determinants of the course of Zionism was the Dreyfus Affair of 1894. Captain Alfred Dreyfus, of French Jewish extraction, was accused of spying for Germany. Despite protests of his innocence, he was convicted in a court that defied the due process guaranteed him under French law. He was stripped of his rank and sentenced to spend the rest of his life in a penal colony. He ultimately was acquitted and restored to rank in 1906. French novelist Émile Zola famously wrote of this in "*J'accuse!*" and Hertzl wrote of it in *Der Judenstaat* (The Jewish State, published in 1896). These textual accounts widely spread the Dreyfus story. Hertzl demonstrated that this affair was evidence that even in free France anti-Semitism abounds; something had to be done he argued to secure the future of the Jewish people free from such arbitrariness and persecution. Hertzl started a worldwide movement, the Zionist Organization, to collect funds to support the Jewish Return.

In this way Zionism became a political and social movement—as opposed to a religious movement—seeking statehood. Its appeal to large groups in Europe led to the First Zionist Congress in 1897. The movement met in Basle annually thereafter until it moved to Jerusalem in 1936.

The Rise of Jerusalem

At the end of World War I the Ottoman Turks surrendered Jerusalem to the British. General Allenby triumphantly made the city the capital of Palestine for the first time in 400 years. The three decades that followed were a time of great expansion. The Jewish population in Palestine grew into the 1920s. The Hebrew University was formed; new Jewish communities rose beyond the city gates; hotels, services, and business all benefited from newfound global connections. There were two problems. The first was that many Jewish immigrants were relatively wealthy new Zionists—largely secular in view and at odds with the existing Orthodox population. The second was that there was a large Arab, and particularly Palestinian, population as well who claimed an equal tie to the land. The Jewish expansion came at their expense. Tensions heightened until an Arab-Jewish war erupted in 1936. It came to a halt only to make room for World War II in 1939.

Where Hertzl left off at his death, it appeared a new European Enlightened leader emerged. In 1904

David Ben Gurion, then only 18 years old, wrote from Germany:

> Let us not delude ourselves with empty phrases. Our situation is so terrible, so fearsome. This is the most dangerous epoch in our history. Here in the Diaspora there is nothing for us young people to do. The general flood will sweep us away against our will. If we do not work there, in Zion, with dedication, then we are lost!

This view, written in a letter to a friend by the man who would one day be Israel's first prime minister, resonates the tone he followed for the rest of his life. Life in the Diaspora corrupts the Jewish people, warping their beliefs. Israel must exist. It must be a Jewish state. It must be a Jewish state in Palestine. On this there can be no compromise. The view from this portion of the Diaspora was that only the relationship with the state could provide Jewish salvation. Gurion rightly feared the challenging views stemming from such eminent Russian and European Jewish leaders as Trotzky, Zinoviev, Kaminiev, Radek, and Rosa Luxembourg who saw Judaism as needing to flourish despite a state not because of it. Gurion moved to Palestine, fought in the Arab wars, and became leader of the *Histadrut* (the very powerful workers' fund).

World War II and the rise of the Third Reich brought out a quandary. Of course no one in the Jewish world supported Adolph Hitler. However, Gurion appeared to view German actions as a *fait accompli*. It was a horrible crime against the Jewish people, against humanity, but not one unforeseen. Its latent potential was, after all, what Hertzl argued out of the Dreyfus affair. Gurion later argued that if a Zionist Jewish state had risen earlier, even under the sort of partition plan that he supported in the 1920s, then there would have been a place for European Jewry to escape. This was a fundamental argument used by Zionists for the formation of a post-World War II state.

The New State

The State of Israel would not have come into existence were it not for two factors: the enormous Jewish refugee crisis in the aftermath of World War II and the tremendous support from the Diaspora as political forces within their own countries (primarily the United States, Britain, and France). The great world powers did very little to assist the Jewish refugee population in the period prior to and during the war. Indeed they made it deeply challenging for Jewish populations to immigrate, even while Britain froze large-scale immigration to Palestine. The Jewish population quickly equated this lack of refuge with the many of times in history persecution followed them.

Britain made its desire to withdraw from Palestine in 1946 after negotiations with the United States and particularly President Harry Truman. On October 4, 1946, Truman agreed that the future of the Jewish people was dependent on a "viable Jewish state." On February 7, 1947, Britain announced it would terminate its mandate. The United States supported the whole area becoming a Jewish state; Britain and in November the United Nations supported a partition to make two states—one for the Jewish people, one for the Palestinian people.

A clear edict from the combined powers never came to fruition. The British Mandate expired on May 14, 1948, and Gurion declared Israel a non-partioned, independent state. The United States recognized Israel the same day, and Egypt, Syria, Jordan, Lebanon, and Iraq attacked Israel the next day.

While the strife of war is always tremendous, it did serve to at least temporarily unify the new Israeli population. It also served to forge an early bond between European and American Jewry living in Diaspora and the Jewish population of the new state. The support of American Jewry in particular for the United States stance was critical to the strong line American policy position. On July 20, 1949, an armistice was reached between Israel and Egypt, Lebanon, Jordan, and Syria.

Diaspora and Difference

The first population of the new Israel was comprised of three populations: those whose families had managed to stay through the long and difficult times of Diaspora in the homeland, those that came under Zionist pretensions in the nineteenth and early twentieth century, and those that came as refugees after World War II. From a religious perspective there were deep divides. Many did not share the secular socialism of the Zionist powers that orchestrated the rise of the state, meaning there was a secular-religious divide. There was also a divide that persisted amongst intra-religious factions, including Hassidic and Orthodox sects. For the state to succeed, a careful balance had to be created between a secular, enlightened, democratic government and a powerful Rabbinate, married through a Ministry of Religious Affairs and a number of religious political parties. The Rabbinate formed is particularly Orthodox. It maintains a religious court system established during the years of Ottoman rule.

It also is responsible for social services that take on a political flavor—burials (the nature of the service), granting marriage licenses (only Orthodox may be married), *Mikves* (religious bath houses necessary by law for a woman to marry), *kashruth* supervision (which grants restaurant permits), and so forth.

The 1950s brought a wave of immigration to Israel of Jewish people from North Africa and Middle Eastern countries. These were the descendants of the Sephardim, those that fled the Spanish Inquisition. They differed linguistically, socially, culturally, and ritually. The essence of Judaism may have remained the same over the centuries, but the details of how it was practiced did not. An important ethnic divide marred the Israeli socio-political landscape.

Beyond this divide within the new state, a divide was emerging between the direction of the Jewish state and Jewish leadership in the Diaspora. The question revolved around whether the state of Israel had the right—even obligation—to lead global Judaic pretensions. Gurion and American Jewish leader Jacob Blaustein signed an accord in 1950 that in essence tried to minimize Israel's role in diasporadic Jewish affairs. This is an ongoing problem illustrated by the Jonathan Pollard affair of 1985. Pollard was a Jewish-American Naval Intelligence Officer. He was accused of spying on the United States for Israel. In his defense he argued that he did share information with Israel, but not anything classified or that would endanger the United States. Israel said that he did not have a relationship with Israeli intelligence and that he should be freed. The American Jewish community was split on their allegiances. Israel has been unable to encourage enough American Jewish action to bring about his release and he remains in prison. To be clear, this sort of divide that exists between Israel and the United States exists between many countries with a Jewish population. The people of the Diaspora are not monolithic in their view toward Israel or each other. Loyalties are as vacillating as identities.

The nature of Jewish identity in the Diaspora has been complicated in recent years. Most notable is the rise of Ethiopian Jewry. Some Jewish scholars believe that this particular group is descendant from the lost tribe of Dan. As such they hold a very different history since the Assyrians conquered Jerusalem in 722 BCE. While rituals have shared notable similarities, they of course have not been followers of the Talmud. Slow immigration of Ethiopian Jewry to Israel began in 1974, but it accelerated in two airlifts by Israel in 1984 and 1991 to bring the population in Israel to around 65,000. In the two decades that have followed, Ethiopian Jewry has transformed from a diasporadic community noted for their difference as Jews living among gentiles to a racial community of Black Israelis.

Lemba people in modern day Zimbabwe are thought by many to be displaced Jews (Sephardim who migrated from Yemen). Some scholars point to the 15 million Pashtuns (Pathans) living in Pakistan and Afghanistan and note the great similarity to Judaic practices. Khazars of the great Khazar Empire of the eighth to tenth century CE are thought by some scholars to be the ancestors of many European Jews. The belief is that some of the lost tribes journeyed north to Khazar before immigrating to Europe.

Modern Institutions

The great diversity of Judaism is reflected in the institutions that support it. United Jewish Communities is a North American organization that represents the particular views of 156 American Jewish Federations and 400 communities. Their mission is philanthropic; that is, to bring money to the Jewish population in need, whether in Israel or North America. While an important lobby for Israel, it is far from a united force. The Religious Action Center of Reform Judaism (RAC) introduces another quandary. The largest group of American Jews, 35 percent, are Reform (founded by Moses Mendelssohn, it trades many of the Orthodox tenets for enlightened secular visions). The RAC is their political lobby in Washington. Israel, however, does not recognize Reform or Conservatives who make up another 26 percent of the American Jewish population as Judaism. It recognizes only Orthodoxy—a scant 10 percent of American Jewry and a minority in much of Europe today.

Other groups are even more divisive. The late Rabbi Meir Kahane formed two groups. The first, the Jewish Defense League (JDL), is a U.S. militant organization aimed at protecting Jewish populations against perceived threats no matter where they are and at any cost. In Israel he formed the Kach party. After he was assassinated in 1990, his son formed Kahane Chai (Kahane Lives), which has since made the U.S. Foreign Terrorist Organizations list. The former has served to separate not only American Jews from Israeli Jews, but American Jews from each other along lines of militancy. The latter continues to divide an already fractious Israeli religious culture within the political sphere. Other groups in the United States (Jewish Council for Public Affairs, Hadassah, B'nai B'rith

International, American Jewish Committee, Conference of Presidents of Major American Jewish Organizations), France (Paris Consistoire, Mouvement Juif Libéral de France, l'Union des Etudiants Juifs de France), Germany (Einheitsgemeinde, Palestine Treuhand-Stelle der Juden in Deutschland), Russia (Congress of Jewish Religious Communities and Organizations), India (Central Jewish Board), South Africa (South African Jewish Board), and around the world hold different mandates for their very diverse diasporadic communities.

Identities

One of Israel's Basic Laws is the Right to Return. It says that anyone who is Jewish, anywhere in the world, can move to Israel. The State of Israel necessarily assists this process through social programs and economic assistance packages. Yet, the Jewish population of New York, 1.75 million, exceeds that of Tel Aviv and Jerusalem combined. Indeed, of the 13.5 million Jews in the world today, only 4.8 million live in Israel; 5.8 million live in the United States; 600,000 in France; 550,000 in Russia and 86 other countries around the world. This is indicative of the unusual blend of Jewish identity. In some ways it is primordial. How Judaism is defined, the right to be considered a Jew, and the practices undertaken in Judaism have roots millennia long. Clearly Jewish identity is inextricably linked to its history of being oppressed. The Jewish Diaspora did manage to survive despite cultural, geographic, socio-economic, and political divides.

Yet, the resurrection of the Jewish state after more than 2,000 years did not bring the majority back to the homeland. This is an indication that Jewish identity is equally instrumental. It is more cost-effective, economically beneficial, or socially gratifying to remain in Diaspora. Put another way, the majority of the Jewish nation is *choosing* to live among gentiles, even when they can live in their own state. In contrast to the Jewish people living in Babylon who wrote the Torah, this would suggest that they do not feel like they are in exile and do not feel overly oppressed.

Critical also is that religion is not the driving source of Jewish identity for the majority of people living in Diaspora. Most are secular, and very few who are religious are Orthodox. Jewish nationalism exists in duality—it is both cultural and religious. Survey data and policy actions indicate that Jewish population throughout Europe and North America identify in the main more with cultural aspects of Judaism than religious ones.

The great fear is the same as the one expressed by Hertzl, and lurks in the shadows of Spain, Rome, Canaan, and Judea. A Jewish population living a secular life in Diaspora has little to link it to its Jewishness. Populations intermarry and assimilate. Some scholars estimate that of the 8.6 million Jews living in Diaspora today nearly half will be assimilated out of the Jewish nation in the next generation alone. Furthering this challenge the *halakha* defines a Jew as either being the child of a Jewish mother or a person who converts to Judaism under Jewish law. In the United States intermarriage is rampant. Twenty-four percent of Jewish households have non-Jews living in them. This means that if a Jewish man marries a gentile woman, as is commonly the case while living in a Christian society, his children cannot be Jewish. By this definition there are far fewer Jews left in the United States or the world, and the numbers are ever dwindling.

Of even greater concern is that this is reflected in Israel itself. The *halakha* that defines the Orthodoxy is maintained, via the Rabbinate, by the secular Israeli state. Many people in Israel today do not identify with this Orthodoxy. One million of the brightest and wealthiest Israelis have emigrated from Israel to other countries, mostly the United States. While economics is perhaps the precipitating factor, the religious or ethno-national bonds are not strong enough. The state of Israel, it appears, cannot hold on to its own children let alone assure the perpetuation of Judaism abroad.

Conclusion

Zionism as a particular form of nationalism calling for the rise of a Jewish state for all of the Jewish people was not representative of the whole of the Jewish nation in Hertzl's day. While it is critically important, it is no more representative today. Israeli leaders, bred in the Zionist tradition, have called for the return of all Jewish people to the Land of Israel. It is a divine providence for which the nation waited through extended eras of persecution. As anti-Semitism rises once again in Europe, and assimilation grows in Diaspora, there is once again the specter of state need to assure it can never happen again. In the future these calls will likely diminish. Despite the assimilation of the Jewish Diaspora and threats from anti-Semites that rise, there does exist a content core. The future is likely to change the debate from Gurion's time. It will not be a question of whether and how the Jewish people in Diaspora should be led by the Israeli state, but rather whether and how the Diaspora will shape the Israeli state. The Israeli state continues to suffer under its deep internal ethnic and religious cleavages. These are dynamically linked to the relationship between Israel and the Diaspora. If such great divides are not mended, it is likely to lead to a deeply fractured society exacerbated by a systemic national divide between those who live in the Promised Land and those who choose not to.

RICHARD R. MARCUS

See also **Anti-Semitism; Arabs: Palestinians; Assimilation; Assyrians; Diaspora; Ethiopian Jewry (Falasha); Genocide; Israel; Nationalism; Pashtuns (Pathans); Refugees**

Further Reading

Ben-Sasson, H.H., editor, *A History of the Jewish People*, Cambridge: Harvard University Press, 1976

Brenner, Frederic, *Diaspora: Homelands in Exile*, New York: Harper Collins, 2003

Gerber, Jane, *The Jews of Spain: A History of the Sephardic Experience,* New York: The Free Press, 1992

Hoffman, L.A., editor, *Jewish Perspectives,* Chicago: University of Notre Dame Press, 1986

Horowitz, Irving Louis, *Israel Ecstasies/Jewish Agonies,* New York: Oxford University Press, 1974

Israel, Jonathan Irvine, *Diasporas Within a Diaspora: Jews, Crypto-Jews and the World Maritime Empires (1540–1740)*, Leiden, Boston: Brill, 2002

Lasry, Jean-Claude, and Claude Tapia, *Les Juifs du Maghreb: Diasporas Contemporaines,* Paris: Editions l'Harmattan, 1989

Marcus, Jacob R., *The Jew in the Medieval World*, Cincinnati: Hebrew Union College Press, 1990

Safrai, Shemuel, and M. Stern, *The Jewish People in the First Century: Historical Geography, Political History, Social, Cultural and Religious Life and Institutions*, Philadelphia: Fortress Press, 1976.

Sheffer, Gabriel, *Diaspora Politics: At Home Abroad,* New York: Cambridge University Press, 2003.

Diola (Joola)

Capsule Summary

Location: Senegal, The Gambia, and Guinea-Bissau
Total Population: Senegal, 500,000; Gambia, 57,000; Guinea-Bissau, 15,000
Language: Joola (also known as Diola, Jola, Dyola, etc.)
Religions: Muslims, Christians, and Animists

The Diola (Joola, Jola, or Jolas, according to a new orthography) people are found in three different countries. Their history is marked by the heritage of mainly the British, French, and Portuguese colonial empires. The majority of them live in Senegal, in the Casamance Region, in the south of that country where they make up 9 percent of that population. In The Gambia they inhabit the Combo and Foni districts. In Guinea-Bissau they are located in the northwest. The Diola language is a member of the West Atlantic branch of the Niger-Kordofan language phylum. Independent from France in 1960, Senegal joined with The Gambia to form the nominal confederation of Senegambia in 1982. However, the envisaged integration of the two countries was never carried out, and the union was dissolved in 1989. Despite peace talks, a southern separatist group sporadically has clashed with government forces since 1982.

History

Diola (Joola) are believed to have lived in the aforementioned areas as early as the first millennium BCE. Some oral sources contend that the Diola (Joola) originated in Egypt and traveled across North Africa in the tenth century BCE, settling in the Niger wetlands. Drought and wars later forced them south. As a vulnerable minority group, they fled to the marshes and swamps of the Casamance region during the slave trade era to become the earliest likely settlers south of the Gambia River. The dissolution of the Ghana Empire in the eleventh century and that of the Mali Empire in the middle of the fifteenth century brought about an important movement of Mande-speaking Muslim populations into the Senegambian region, a former confederation combining Senegal and The Gambia. The newcomers forced indigenous groups such as the Baynunk, Joola, Manjak, and Mankaañ to flee and to take refuge in the forest or the coastal areas. Furthermore, linguistic evidence places the center of ancient Joola dispersion around Kerouhaye, a village northwest of Guinea-Bissau. This claim is also based on the fact that the Diola *Boekin* (shrine) is located in Kerouhaye. The Diola people considered it to be the most potent shrine in the Joola world.

The Venetians were the first Westerners to have entered the south of The Gambia in 1456, followed by the Portuguese in 1570, and the French in 1837, who purchased land in order to build the fortress of Seju *(Sédhiou)*. A second important incursion in Diola land by Mandinka Muslims occurred at the end of the nineteenth century. With the help of some of small bands of Mandinka already based in The Gambia, Fode Kaba (the son of Fode Bakan Dumbuya, a Diaxanke Muslim priest from Gumbel, a small village in the northeast of Senegal) invaded the north bank of the Casamance River in southwest Senegal from 1878 to 1880 and imposed Islam and the Mandinka culture on the Diola living there. In 1886 the capital city of Ziguinchor cedes to the French according to signed convention between France and Portugal.

The colonial occupation of the Diola territories lasted about 315 years (1645–1960 CE). The Portuguese and finally the French tried unsuccessfully to subjugate the Diola, who have historically resisted their foreign domination. The French general governor Van Vollenhoven, in Casamance with the purpose of military recruitment during World War I, pronounced the Diola as hostile. He stated on November 17, 1917, "We are not the masters of Lower Casamance. We are only tolerated. The Casamance must not be some kind of worm in the colony in which she ought to be the jewel" (Diatta 1998, 41). Diola vigorously opposed the forced recruitment of their youth by France for the two World Wars (1914–1918 and 1939–1945). The French had to quell rebellious movements throughout the Casamance bases. The Diola refused to pay taxes, resisted conscription in the French army, and tried to withhold rice and cattle requisitions that were to be war supplies. Their stance led the French authorities to use violence, repression, and banishment as a method of governance. Such policies led to serious military confrontations among the Effock (1909), Youtou (1909), and Bayotte (1920). The French responded with violence and sent many indigenous leaders into exile. King Sihalebe Diatta of Oussouye was arrested in 1903 and died in prison. A priestess, Aline Sitoe Diatta, was arrested in 1943 and sent into exile. She died in detention.

After World War II, about 100 intellectuals and leaders led by two primary schoolteachers, one a Catholic Diola, Emile Badiane, the other a Muslim Peul, Ibou Diallo, along with Edouard Diatta and Dembo Coly founded the rebel Mouvement Des Forces Démocratiques de Casamance (MFDC, or Casamance Movement of Democratic Forces), on March 4, 1947, in Sédhiou, Moyenne Casamance. The objective of the regionalist- and ethnic-based organization was to defend indigenous interests throughout the region and oppose centralization. Initially MFDC was eager to free itself from the control of French overcentralization.

When the Bloc Démocratique Sénégalais (BDS, later renamed Parti Socialiste), a socialist party run by the president of Senegal, Leopold S. Senghor, was formed, MFDC joined it and became one of its regional branches. At the 1954 party congress in the city of Ziguinchor, when BDS decided to abolish regional branches and introduce a system of individual applications for membership, one group from Casamance broke away and formed the Casamance Autonomous Movement (MAC). MAC demanded autonomy just as MFDC had done 10 years earlier. Independence from Senghor's party was the chief concern of MAC's founders, who were Casamance Wolof from the region (Djbril Sarr, and later Assane Seck).

Postindependence

Despite peace talks, the MFDC separatists have sporadically clashed with government forces since 1982, often involving violent and bloody confrontations. The southern separatist movement in Casamance, however, is not based upon ethnic differences; the Diola are not persecuted, for example, and no apparent ethnic conflicts seem to exist among the different groups. Rather the conflicts seem to have stemmed from the region's belief that its physical geography, culture, and relative isolation from the rest of Senegal (it is sandwiched between The Gambia and Guinea-Bissau) separate it from the rest of Senegal.

To this end on December 26, 1982, the MFDC reformed under the leadership of a Diola Catholic priest, Abbé Diamacoune Senghor. Two major events triggered the revival of the MFDC. On January 11, 1980, the police killed a young schoolboy during a student demonstration in Ziguinchor. In December 26, 1982, in the same city the security forces fired on a demonstration led by men and women with sticks, arrows, and machetes. A year later six paramilitary were killed by members of the new MFDC, which included this time the issue of independence on its platform. The armed wing of MFDC known as *Atika* ("fighter" in Diola) was formed in 1985, and the party fought for the creation of a separatist state with autonomy from Senegal. The armed struggle started in earnest in 1990 as the Senegalese government refused to discuss the independence issue arguing that national integrity was non-negotiable. Since then the Senegalese government and the MFDC have signed several peace agreements, all of which were immediately broken.

Displacement of civilians caused by intermittent clashes between government forces and MFDC rebels continued to be reported in 2002 and 2003. Most people fleeing the violence have sought refuge in neighboring Gambia and Guinea-Bissau; however, at the close of 2002, an estimated 5,000 people remained internally displaced, according to the U.S. Committee for Refugees. Both the Senegalese government and the separatists have been accused of human rights abuses against civilians, including extra judicial executions, torture, and forced displacement. A situation of no war, but no peace still prevails in the region.

Diola Society

The principal economic activity of the Diola has been the farming of wet rice, a form of labor that is dominated by females. They also practice river fishing and those in the north bank grow groundnut and millet. South of the River, they are Christians but over 20 percent of the population remains animists, with a Muslim minority. North of the river most Diola are Muslims, but there are also some Christians and a few animists. Compared with other ethnic groups, Diola society is non-hierarchical and egalitarian. The society does not have hereditary leaders, slaves, or servants. At the village level a council of elders makes all the daily decisions, and although it lacks ultimate political clout the councils still exercise a great deal of influence.

The elders are believed to possess occult powers and the guard societal traditions. Although the Diola society is patriarchal, women occupy important positions in its organization as members of village councils, religious leaders, and landowners. Polygamy and sexual mutilation are not practiced south of the river but these practices do occur in certain villages in the north due to Mandinka influence.

Like most African traditional societies, the Diola people are finding it difficult to deal with modernity and the encroachment of urbanization and globalization. The government developed opportunities for tourism in Cap Skiring on the Atlantic coast of Casamance in the early 1960s. The creation of hotels and other sectors of the tourist industry introduced some drug trafficking as well as prostitution, presenting the Joola with new challenges. The greatest difficulty facing the Diolas today is their survival as a group in Senegal. Recent events tend to indicate that their way of life, language, religion, and identity are threatened. The spread of Islam (over 90 percent of Senegal is Muslim) presents another encroachment to the Joola way of life.

Abdoulaye Barry

See also **Senegal; Senghor, Leopold (Senegalese)**

Further Reading

Barbier-Wiesser, François George, editor, *Comprendre la Casamance: Chronique d'une intégration contrastée*, Paris: Karthala, 1994

Diatta, Christian Sina, *Parlons Jola: Langue et culture des Diolas*, Paris: L'Harmattan, 1998

Girard, Jean, *Genèse du pouvoir charismatique en Basse Casamance*, Dakar: IFAN, 1969

Pélissier, P., *Les paysans du Sénégal: Les civilisations agraires du Cayor à la Casamance*, Saint-Yrieix (France): Imprimerie Fabregue, 1966

Roche, Christian, *Histoire de la Casamance: Conquête et résistance: 1850–1920*, Paris: Karthala, 1985

Sapir, David, *A Grammar of Diola-Fogny: A Language Spoken in the Basse-Casamance Region of Senegal*, Cambridge: Cambridge University Press, 1965

Thomas, L-V, *Les Diola: Essai d'analyse fonctionnelle sur une population de Basse-Casamance*, Paris: Larose and Dakar: IFAN, 1959

Djibouti

Capsule Summary

Location: Horn of Africa
Total Population: 457,130 (July 2003)
Ethnic Population: Somali (60%), Afar (35%), French, Arab, Ethiopian, Italian (5%)
Languages: Somali, 'Afar-af, French, Amharic, Arabic
Religions: Muslim (94%), Christian (6%)

The state of Djibouti is a former French colony on the Red Sea coast near Eritrea, Ethiopia, and Somaliland. Its land surface is not more than 23,200 square kilometers (9,048 square miles), but the tiny country lying between Somaliland, Ethiopia, and Eritrea, opposite Yemen, has a key strategic position at the entrance of the Red Sea. The country became independent in 1977 after about a century of French protectorate rule. Its main economic lifeline is Djibouti port, the major seaport in the Horn of Africa, connected by railroad to Addis Ababa in Ethiopia. Before 1859 when the French first appeared and concluded a treaty with the local Afar sultan of Obock, the area was inhabited by Afar nomadic pastoralists and had no political or territorial identity.

Djibouti's population is ethnically diverse. The two main ethnic groups in Djibouti are the majority Issa Somali and the Afar. There are also Gadabursi and Isaaq Somali, as well as migrant minorities from the Arabian peninsula (mostly Yemeni), from Europe (mainly French, including a few thousand military personnel) and Ethiopia. The latter Ethiopians in particular—among them many port workers, laborers, cleaners, and women working in bars—are vulnerable to state suppression and campaigns of expulsion (one such campaign occurred in 2003). Of the total population, an unknown number are refugees from Ethiopia, Eritrea, and Somalia. Movement across the boundary is relatively easy, and exact figures for the fluctuating number of refuges and occasional migrants are difficult to obtain. More than 65 percent of the Djiboutians reside in the capital, Djibouti city. The rate of population growth is about 2.5 to 3 percent. Djibouti's economy is very weak, and under- or unemployment is estimated to be between 40 and 50 percent. Because there is little in the way of natural resources or agricultural potential, the country is precariously dependent on the port revenue (mostly from Ethiopia) and on outside assistance, now growing because of campaigns against international terrorism. Per capita GDP was $1,300 (2002 estimate).

About two-thirds of Djibouti territory traditionally belonged to Afar sultanates; the southern part, below the Gulf of Tadjourah was inhabited or used by Issa herders. Both Afar and Somalis are originally nomadic pastoralists in the surrounding semiarid plains, speaking related languages of the Cushitic family. However, French and Arabic are Djibouti's official languages. The Afar and Issa kept livestock such as camels, cattle, goats, and sheep. Fishing and regional trade (mostly done by Arabs, Greeks, and Indians) were also sources of income. Many features of social organization and community life are similar (clan organization, elders' councils, ritual chiefs, and also marriage customs). French rule yielded a joint political and economic structure affecting the two groups. The French followed a divide-and-rule policy before independence—now supporting the Issa, then the Afar. This has tended to create tensions between the two groups. In fact, pre-independence history of Djibouti was marked by often violent rivalry between the political leaders of both groups. The Issa (and Gadabursi) Somali also gradually bypassed the Afar in numbers, mainly owing to immigration from Somalia. The Afar and Issa thus have had tense and competitive relations in Djibouti, with phases of armed conflict in the last quarter of the twentieth century, but there is also a minimal shared national identity and consciousness among the country's citizens that distinguishes them from neighboring countries (all population groups in Djibouti also live in these countries). After independence in 1977, the president was an Issa Somali, Hassan Gouled Aptidon, succeeded in 1999 by Ismail Omar Guelleh of the same group. After independence the arrangement made was that the prime minister would always be an Afar. A careful division of political and public functions between Afar and Issa—in fact an ethnic quota system—extends into many other domains.

Before the colonial era, the Afar and Issa had their indigenous political organization based on clan identity, clan territories, and local chiefs, but they had no states. Until today neither Afar nor Issa pastoralists have cared much about national state boundaries. The Afar were more hierarchically organized than the Issa. Some of the Afar had chiefdoms—for example, the sultanates of Raheita, Goubaad, Aussa, and Tadjourah. The Issa had a more decentralized clan organization with only the ruler of Zeila, a trading center on the nearby Somali coast, as a powerful figure. Both are strongly patrilineal societies in which men have more rights and higher status than women. Afar-Issa intermarriage is not frequent. In the rural areas, both the Issa and Afar communities follow customary law for most of their life-cycle rituals, for family matters, and for resolving disputes.

The rural sector in Djibouti is quite marginal and neglected. Economic problems of pastoralists, who have been reduced to some 20 percent of the population, are increasing because of persistent droughts and population growth, and the government does not invest significantly in either agriculture or the pastoral sector. Traditional minorities within Djibouti's two dominant ethnic groups are the occupational castes, such as blacksmiths or tanners. A distinction of major significance is that of indigenous people (*autochtons*) and foreigners (*allogènes*). The latter, as non-natives, are always vulnerable to expulsion in times of crisis or criminal offense. A minority with a particularly precarious position in Djibouti are the refugees from neighboring countries as well as the semi-legal or illegal labor migrants in Djibouti city.

Since their unsuccessful armed rebellions in the 1980s and 1990s, the Afar (especially the youth) have increasingly felt themselves to be a minority of second-class status (they comprise about 35 percent of the population) unduly dominated by the Issa, who as Somalis are mostly supported by Gadabursi and Isaaq. But there have also been some armed clashes between Issa and Gadabursi. The dominance of the Issa is also notable in the economic sphere and in politics. As of this writing a civil war between Afar and Issa had been averted, but there was growing concern about ethnic-based competition for resources in the country as well as political rivalry.

Jon G. Abbink

See also **Afar; Ethiopia; Eritrea; Somalia; Somalis**

Further Reading

Aboubaker, Daoud Alwan, *Historical Dictionary of Djibouti*, Metuchen, New Jersey: Scarecrow Press, 2000

Chiré, A.S., "Djibouti: Migrations de populations et insertion urbaine des femmes," in *L'Afrique Politique*, 1996

Coubba, Ali, *Le Mal Djiboutien: Rivalités Ethniques et Enjeux Politiques*, Paris: L'Harmattan, 1996

Oberle, Philippe, and Pierre Hugot, *Histoire de Djibouti, des Origines à la République*, Paris and Dakar: Présence Africaine, 1985

Pérouse de Montclos, Marc-Antoine, "L'œil du cyclone: Djibouti, une cité-état entre guerre et paix," *Afrique Contemporaine*, 198 (2001)

Rouaud, Alain, "Pour une histoire des Arabes de Djibouti, 1896–1977," *Cahiers d'Études Africaines*, 37 (1997)

Schraeder, Peter J., "Ethnic Politics in Djibouti: From 'Eye of the Hurricane' to 'Boiling Cauldron,'" *African Affairs*, 92 (1993)

Dogri

Capsule Summary

Location: State of Jammu and Kashmir, India
Total Population: 2.1 million
Language: Dogri
Religion: Hindu

The Dogri community is concentrated in the region of Jammu in the state of Jammu and Kashmir, India. They are referred to collectively as Dogras, their language is Dogri, and like the majority of Indians they are Hindus. But within the predominantly Muslim state of Jammu and Kashmir, as Hindus speaking a distinct language, they are a minority community. Once powerful in the region when the minority Dogras ruled over the majority Muslim population in British India, their political status has shifted since Indian independence in 1947. Since then the Dogri community constantly has had to negotiate to improve its political and economic status with the elected governments in the state of Jammu and Kashmir, which largely represent the majority interests of the Muslim population.

Prior to the British withdrawal from the Indian subcontinent and their granting independence to India and Pakistan, the state of Jammu and Kashmir were ruled by the Dogra Maharaja Hari Singh. His ancestor Raja Gulab Singh had acquired the principality of Jammu (with its majority Dogra Hindu population) in 1820, annexed the kingdom of (largely Buddhist) Ladakh in 1834, and for a price of 7.5 million rupees in 1846 received from the British the (overwhelmingly Muslim) Valley of Kashmir. Once the British had established their control over the Indian subcontinent, this state became a part of the British Empire's princely India. While the British ruled directly 60 percent of the territory of India, they allowed more than 500 princely states in India to have internal autonomy while controlling the areas of foreign affairs, defense, and communication. Jammu and Kashmir was one of these princely states with a Hindu Dogra king ruling over a majority Muslim population.

During the Dogra rule all administrative and political positions were held by Hindus, either the Dogras of Jammu or the Kashmiri Pandits of the Kashmir Valley. The Hindu community was also the major beneficiary of the standardized English education in government-run schools and colleges. Jammu's educated Dogras and the Kashmiri Pandits, who had earlier campaigned for the reservation of administrative positions for the people of the state, were the major beneficiaries of the new state-subject ordinance (1927) which restricted government employment exclusively to the citizens of the state. Consequently in 1931 under the leadership of a Kashmiri Muslim, Sheikh Mohammad Abdullah, a nationalist movement against the Dogra rule emerged. The movement was deeply rooted in the Muslim Valley of Kashmir and sought the overthrow of the Dogra rule and the creation of a socialist democratic republic.

After the British granted independence to India in August 1947, Jammu and Kashmir was one of the princely states not to accede to either India or Pakistan. In October 1947 the tribesmen of the North-West Frontier Province of Pakistan took upon themselves to liberate Muslim Kashmir. Unable to defend the state, on October 26, 1947, the Maharaja of the state, Hari Singh, signed the Instrument of Accession with India. In accepting the offer of accession, the Indian government agreed to put the question of accession to the will of the people of Kashmir through a referendum once law and order had been restored. Meanwhile Sheikh Abdullah formed the first democratic government in the state of Jammu and Kashmir. While the Kashmir issue became embroiled in the geopolitics and India-Pakistan relations, India established its constitutional relationship with the state whereby it granted a special status to Jammu and Kashmir. Under this arrangement, while restricting the Central government's legislative power to the areas of foreign affairs, defense, and communication, it allowed the state government complete internal autonomy. It was to be the only state in the Indian federation which would write its own constitution and have a separate state flag.

In the Jammu region the Dogra population aligned itself with a nationalist Hindu party, the Praja Parishad, which began an agitation in 1952 for complete accession and full integration of the state of Jammu and Kashmir into the Indian federation. The Parishad party was also resentful of the 1951 Big Landed Estates Act because it abolished the large landholdings without compensation and adversely affected the economic power of the Dogra landlords. This agitation was supported by the Hindu nationalist parties and groups operating in India, such as the Bhartiya Jan Sanghm Hindu Mahasabha, Ram Rajya Parishad, and Punjab Arya Samaj. While the Praja Parishad party mobilized the Dogra urban population of Jammu city, particularly the students, batches of Hindu volunteers from the northern and central parts of India traveled to Jammu to participate in the agitation. In 1953 the agitation suffered a serious blow with the death of Shyam Prasad Mookherjee, the leader of the Hindu nationalist party who had come to the state to provide support to the Praja Parishad agitation and was arrested and died during his house arrest. The impact of this agitation was quite negative for Jammu's Hindu population. Both the Indian and Kashmir governments (the latter dominated by the Valley's Muslim population) came to equate Jammu and its Dogra population with Hindu communalism. This negative perception of Jammu has effectively marginalized the region's political role and its legitimate demands of an equal and fair representation in the state's political and administrative apparatus.

A general consensus prevails among the Dogra population in the Jammu region that the state government has consistently discriminated against Jammu's Hindus in favor of the Kashmir's Muslim population. The state government is taken to task for discriminating in its hiring policies in the state bureaucracy, the police, the revenue department, and its making of political appointments. The Chief Minister of the state has always been a Muslim from the Valley. At the Cabinet level, Jammu's Hindus appear to have not received their fair share. Jammu contains almost half of the state's population and has an area of 26,293 square kilometers (10,254 square miles) to Kashmir's 15,948 square kilometers (6,220 square miles). But Jammu's Hindus grieve that they have only 37 members in the state legislative assembly as opposed to 46 for the Kashmir region. While Kashmir returns one member for every 1,942 inhabitants, Jammu returns one member for every 2,584 people. The same scenario applies to the Parliamentary elections. Jammu's Dogra population claims that the recruitment pattern of the state civil service confirms its discrimination. Indeed, during the last five decades there has been a conscious attempt on the part of the state government to reduce the dominance of the Hindu population in the state bureaucracy. Attrition in the upper ranks and the preponderance of Muslim as new entrants in the lower ranks of the civil service reflect this policy and effort. Moreover, almost all professional and technical institutions are located in the Kashmir Valley. Jammu's share in these Valley-based institutes is less than 40 percent. Similarly, Jammu's Hindus note that, until 1989 (before a mass-based political insurgency began in the Valley, resulting in a shift of resources to contain the insurgency) all major industrial plants (such as the Hindustan Machine tools factory, the telephone and television industries, and the cement factory) were all located in the Kashmir Valley. It is claimed that the Jammu youth found virtually no employment in the 12 corporations whose headquarters were based in the Valley. Jammu's Dogras also point out that Jammu contributes more than 70 percent of the revenues to the state's treasury, but the developmental allocations made to Jammu are less than 30 percent.

While both the state and the Indian government have duly noted Jammu's grievances over a 40-year period, neither government has been able or willing to take concrete measures to redress them. The Gajendragadkar Commission was appointed in 1967 to inquire into the complaints of regional imbalance in development programs and recruitment policies. The Commission acknowledged Jammu's Hindus complaints of an unequal share of civil service job allocations and rejected the governmental policies of distributing jobs on a communal basis—50 percent for the Muslims and 40 percent for the Hindus. Except the Commission's recommendation for the establishment of a Medical College and Jammu University in Jammu city, none of its other recommendations (such as parity in ministerial positions and an equitable civil service) were implemented. Several other commissions and enquires appointed later to review Jammu's Dogras demands have met a similar fate.

Presently two organized civil society organizations, the Jammu Mukhti Morcaha (JMM) and the Jammu Autonomy Forum (JAF), are at the forefront in articulating Jammu's grievances and have suggested different solutions to the Jammu and Kashmir government and to the Indian state. The JMM envisions a separate state for Jammu by partitioning the existing state of Jammu and Kashmir. On the other hand the JAF seeks a constitutional provision of devolution of power within the state of Jammu and Kashmir.

REETA CHOWDHARI TREMBLAY

See also **India**

Further Readings

Behera, Navnita Chadha, *State, Identity & Violence: Jammu, Kashmir & Ladakh*, New Delhi: Manohar Publishers, 2000

Chowdhari Tremblay, Reeta, "Jammu: Autonomy within an Autonomous Kashmir?" in *Perspectives on Kashmir: The Roots of Conflict in South Asia*, edited by Raju Thomas, Boulder, Colorado: Westview Press, 1992

Puri, Balra, *Simmering Volcano: Study of Jammu's Relations with Kashmir*, New Delhi: Sterling Publishers, 1983

Dominica

Capsule Summary

Location: Caribbean, island between the Caribbean Sea and the North Atlantic Ocean, about one-half of the way from Puerto Rico to Trinidad and Tobago
Total Population: 71,000 (2004)
Ethnic Population: Black, white, mulatto, Carib Indian (also Kalinago), Arab
Languages: English, Kweyol (French Creole)
Religions: Roman Catholic (77%), Protestant (15%) [Methodist (5%), Pentecostal (3%), Seventh-Day Adventist (3%), Baptist (2%), other (2%)], none (2%), other (6%)

Dominica lies midway in the arc of islands known as the Lesser Antilles along their windward curve, facing eastward to the Atlantic Ocean and westward to the Caribbean Sea. It lies between two French-speaking islands, Guadeloupe to the north and Martinique to the south. The island has a tropical climate and is most singular for its rugged terrain. The island comprises the peaks of former volcanoes and rises along much of the coast abruptly and starkly from the sea. Steep mountains reaching heights over 4,000 feet (1219 meters), narrow valleys, gorges, and cliffs mark the landscape, which is also dotted with thermal lakes. The size of the island is about half that of New York City.

The challenging physical dimensions of the island have directly affected its social and cultural character. Christopher Columbus stopped at the island in 1493 and named it "Dominica," having discovered it on a Sunday. Unlike other parts of the West Indies, Dominica was not conquered and occupied by the Spanish. It was of relatively less importance in relation to the major islands Spain occupied.

Moreover, the Carib Indians on the island offered fierce resistance. They had reacted with equal force against the Spanish elsewhere but had been defeated. On Dominica, however, they had the advantage of a uniquely mountainous and forested terrain that offered them abundant favorable locations for attack and defense. The abundance of tropical vegetation, rising and falling over Dominica's rich volcanic soil, has earned it the title of "nature island of the Caribbean." The native name for Dominica was *Waitukubuli*, a comparison of the island to the body of a tall woman. The native name that the Caribs had for themselves was the *Kalinago*. They originated from the valley of the Orinoco River in Venezuela following a previous migration of natives from this region, the Arawak, who earlier settled the Caribbean.

For nearly two centuries no European power controlled Dominica so that it preserved a surviving remnant of the original Carib, or *Kalinago*, inhabitants of the Caribbean. Some mulattos (or mixed blood), refugees, and fugitive slaves from other islands were able to settle on plots of coastal land, practicing subsistence farming and engaging in small trading activities with nearby islands. Dominica thereby began to have a small peasant class. By the seventeenth century, however, due to repeated foreign incursions and diseases that devastated the indigenous population, the French and English could compete to settle on Dominica. Initially the French dominated and established sugar cultivation, bringing in black African slaves as labor. The island did not, however, have extensive plains for plantation agriculture.

By the end of the eighteenth century, Britain had become dominant. Under both the French and British the island's economy was based on agricultural exports from plantations using black African slave labor. The most lasting consequence of French influence was the Roman Catholic religion to which most Dominicans still adhere. The French language has survived on Dominica until today in a patois or Creole form known as *Kweyol*. English spoken in a local dialect form is the official language of the country. Nonetheless, two-thirds of the population, especially in rural and remote village areas, use Kweyol.

Britain abolished slavery in the early nineteenth century. In subsequent decades Dominica acquired the cultural mosaic that characterizes it today. It has a rare minority of Carib Indians, who have otherwise disappeared in the Caribbean. About 3,000 in number (four percent of the population), they engage in small-scale farming. Their native language is extinct. The dominant racial character of the island is black and mulatto. The island had sufficient market activity historically that some slaves had been able to obtain income from small-scale agricultural marketing. Accumulating sufficient funds to buy their freedom, some of these freedmen acquired plantations and slaves themselves. The white population is a tiny minority yet is economically significant. A very small Arab minority engages in urban commercial activities.

Seventy-seven percent of the population is Roman Catholic and 15 percent is Protestant. The largest Protestant religion is the Methodist sect, representing approximately five percent of the population. Other sects each have adherents from about two to three percent of the population. These groups include primarily the Pentecostals, Seventh-Day Adventists, and Baptists. Since the middle of the twentieth century, much Protestant evangelization in the Caribbean has originated from U.S.-based sects.

Obtaining independence in 1978, Dominica has had an unsteady economic and political course. It did, however, obtain some measure of stability during the long prime ministry of Eugenia Charles, the first woman ever elected prime minister of a Caribbean country. In 1940 Dominica had also been the first in the Caribbean to elect a woman to its local legislature. It is a member of the British Commonwealth of Nations.

Dominica's population is overwhelmingly literate. It has substantial food resources for its population from fishing and ample arable land. However, its main export crop, bananas, is subject to extensive international market and diplomatic fluctuations. The economy remains highly vulnerable to climatic conditions as well. It does not offer foreign tourists the allure of idyllic beaches or an international airport, as do other Caribbean islands; however, it is developing a niche market for ecological tourism. The per capita GDP was $5,400 in 2002. Mostly rural, the national population has declined over the past decade as many Dominicans emigrate to obtain employment. The main urban area is the capital, the port of Roseau, with slightly more than one-fourth of the country's population.

EDWARD A. RIEDINGER

Further Reading

Allaire, Louis, "On the Historicity of Carib Migrations in the Lesser Antilles," *American Antiquity*, 45, no. 2 (April 1980)

Amastae, Jon Edward, "Dominican Creole Phonology I," *Georgetown University Papers on Languages and Linguistics*, 15 (1979)

———, "Dominican Creole Phonology II," *Georgetown University Papers on Languages and Linguistics*, 16 (1979)

Baker, Patrick L., *Centering the Periphery: Chaos, Order, and the Ethnohistory of Dominica*, Jamaica: The Press, University of the West Indies, 1994

Craig, Susan, editor, *Contemporary Caribbean: A Sociological Reader*, 2 vols., Port of Spain, Trinidad: College Press, 1981–1982

"Dominica," in *Islands of the Commonwealth Caribbean: A Regional Study*, edited by Sandra W. Meditz and Dennis M. Hanratty, Area Handbook Series, Washington, DC: Federal Research Division, Library of Congress, 1989

Fontaine, Marcel, and Peter A. Roberts, *Dominica's Diksyonnè: Kwéyòl-Annglé/Dominica's English-Creole Dictionary*, Roseau, Dominica: Folk Research Institute, Konmite Pou Etid Kweyol (KEK), Department of Use of English and Linguistics, University of the West Indies, 1991

Honychurch, Lennox, *The Dominica Story: A History of the Island*, London: Macmillan, 1995

Myers, Robert A., *Dominica*, World Bibliographical Series, 82, Oxford, England: ABC-Clio Press, 1987

Pezeron, Simone Maguy, *The Carib Indians of Dominica Island in the West Indies: Five Hundred Years after Columbus*, New York: Vantage Press, 1993

Trouillot, Michel-Rolph, *Peasants and Capital: Dominica in the World Economy*, Johns Hopkins Studies in Atlantic History and Culture, Baltimore, Maryland: Johns Hopkins University Press, 1988

Dominican Republic

Capsule Summary

Location: Caribbean, between the Caribbean Sea and the North Atlantic Ocean, east of Haiti
Total Population: 8,715,602 (July 2003)
Ethnic Population: Haitian, Chinese, Jewish
Language: Spanish
Religion: Roman Catholic (95%)

The Dominican Republic shares the island of Hispaniola with the Republic of Haiti. It is one of three Spanish speaking islands in the Caribbean located between Puerto Rico and Cuba.The state sanctioned religion in the Dominican Republic is Catholic. An agreement with the international community with regard to Jewish holocaust refugees in the 1930s also established a small Jewish community on the island. Dominicans consider themselves to be a mix of Spanish, Taino, and African cultures. *Indios* are the ethnic majority. Sugar plantations import workers from Haiti each year. Haitian refugees, Dominicans of Haitian descent, and Chinese also live in the Dominican Republic. The major issues facing the country include political conflict and rising inflation. Although the Dominican Republic officially became a democracy in 1961, it has had many problems with election fraud.

History

The island of Hispaniola was the first colony of the so-called New World. As early as 3000 BCE it was subject to several waves of migration from the South American Native Nations of Ciboneys, Igneri, and various Arawaks. By 700 BCE these immigrants became a cohesive culture known as the Taino who dominated the island until 1492.

The Tainos' contribution to Dominican culture was primarily linguistic and agricultural. Many of the non-Spanish words in the Dominican lexicon have Taino origin. They also introduced the main staple in Dominican diets—yucca. National interest in the Tainos began in the nineteenth century with the *indigenismo* movement. Artists, historians, and politicians turned to Taino culture as the basis for Dominican identity.

Between 1493 and 1495 Columbus campaigned to enslave Tainos, supplant their religion with Catholicism, and extract gold. An uprising in 1496 killed half of the colonizing population and emptied the city. This rebellion led to the redistribution of wealth amongst Spaniards, the founding of what would become the capital city of Santo Domingo, and the command to marry Indian women living as concubines. The 1502 mandate to intermarry was used to deprive those made wealthy from the rebellion of their land and riches. It also established the first legal intermixing of ethnic groups on the island. Despite these changes most Tainos were forced into labor in the gold mines where they died of starvation and overwork or committed mass suicides. As a result there were only 500 Tainos left by 1519. Gold mines were depleted the same year.

Colonials turned to sugar and cattle, and imported the first African slaves in 1520. Remaining Tainos periodically attacked plantations and freed slaves. By 1542 between 2,000 and 3,000 *cimmarrones* (escaped slaves) lived in their own communities on the island. Though they were tortured and killed under the leadership of Alonzo López de Cerrato between 1543 and 1546, slaves continued to escape into the mountains. Escapes and the rise of piracy effectively put an end to Spanish slavery and sugar mills in the Dominican Republic until the late 1700s.

Conflicts with the French over sovereignty on the island led to the establishment of Haiti and Dominican aid to escaped slaves.

Independence

In 1801 Haitian leader François Dominique Toussaint (also known as Toussaint L'Ouverture) declared independence for the entire island. He abolished slavery and attempted to reorganize Dominican labor from subsistence agriculture and livestock to export farming but was ousted by a joint Dominican-French effort a year later. After 20 years of fighting, Haitians regained control. Besides labor redistribution they attempted to improve infrastructure including offering land to escaped slaves from North America. Their descendants speak a mix of Spanish and English and are primarily Protestant. However, the Dominican *Trinitarios*—Duarte, Sanchez, and Santana—fought and won independence on February 27, 1844.

After a series of conflicts and failed governments, the Dominican Republic had a national treasury balance of zero. As a result, Americans officially took over the government from 1916 to 1924. During that time they created a national mail service and police force and improved roadways and education. By encouraging foreign investment and sugar production, Americans created dependence on sugar and Haitian labor that continues to this day. Finally, occupation led to the rise of Raphael Trujillo.

On August 16, 1930, Trujillo took over the government with support gained under US occupation. During his 31-year regime the state funded highways, bridges, irrigation canals, and agricultural settlements throughout the country. It also cultivated new and fortified existing industries. Trujillo also paid off foreign debt and forced all but two foreign sugar plantation owners out of business.

In 1961 elections were once again held. Joaquin Balaguer took office after a U.S.-backed coup against elected president Juan Bosch. Like his predecessor, Balaguer maintained the spectre of Haiti while emphasizing the Taino and Spanish roots of Dominican society. Despite some economic gains under Balaguer, foreign debt and International Monetary Fund (IMF) programs led to massive Dominican migration to the United States from 1965 onward.

However, under Trujillo many disappeared or were imprisoned. He was known to summon and abduct women from schools and homes without consent. His racial policies led to the erasure of African/blackness in Dominicaness. His racial purity program led to the killing of 15,000 to 35,000 Haitians and dark-skinned Dominicans on October 4, 1937. This was followed by the relocation of Dominicans along the border to prevent Haitian settlement.

Thirteen years later newly elected president Osiris Guzman revitalized democratic rule. Constitutional reform led to an end of presidential consecutive terms until it was reversed in 2003. Economic booms in the late 1980s and early 1990s also increased confidence. Dominican-Americans aided the building of schools, churches, and roads through sister city programs, direct investment, and remittances. This period also saw an attempt to include African heritage along side Taino and Spanish.

Despite widespread opposition of strikes and protests, President Rafael Hipolito Mejia intends to run again leading to a split in his cabinet (May 2004); such political conflicts are exacerbated by domestic and economic concerns. Changes in 2000 to 2003 led to a loss of confidence in the Dominican government and economy. The number of Dominican migrants has increased steadily during these years while the peso fell from an exchange of 16-1 in 2000 to 50-1 in 2004. The country suffers from marked income inequality; the poorest half of the population receives less than one-fifth of GNP (per capita income was $6,300 in 2002) while the richest 10 percent enjoy nearly 40 percent of national income. The electricity remains out regularly. Despite recent and dramatic growth, the Dominican Republic's economy was made vulnerable by Hurricane Georges in 1998. While major exports still include sugar, coffee, and tobacco, the service sector has recently surpassed agriculture as the economy's largest employer due to growth in tourism and free trade zones. Eighty-five percent of its exports go to the United States.

Ime Kerlee

Further Reading

Moya Pons, Frank, *The Dominican Republic: A National History*, New Jersey: Marcus Wiener Publishers, 1998

Sagas, Ernesto, *Race and Politics in the Dominican Republic,* Florida: University Press Florida, 2000

Wucker, Michele, *Why the Cocks Fight: Haitians and the Struggle for Hispaniola,* New York: Hill and Wang, 1999

Dong

Capsule Summary

Location: Southeast of the Popular Republic of China, mainly in the eastern part of Guizhou province, but also in the northeast of Guangxi, and southwest of Hunan
Total Population: 3,356,250 (2003)
Language: Kam
Religion: Animist

The Dong are an ethnic group living in the southeastern part of the People's Republic of China, more precisely in a mountainous area straddling the three provinces of Guizhou, Guangxi, and Hunan. Half the Dong population lives in Guizhou. Dong (or Kam) are one of the 55 officially recognized Chinese minority ethnic groups (nationalities or *minzu*). Dong is a Chinese name derived from a Kam term referring to narrow valleys, which typically constitute their natural environment. The members of this group call themselves either *Kam*, *Geml*, *Jeml*, or *Gaelm*. Of the 2.5 million Kam people of China (known inside China as Northern Dong and Southern Dong) about 40 percent speak only Kam, 32 percent speak only Chinese, and 28 percent speak both languages. In the 1990 census there were 2.5 million Dong, 3 million in 1995, and about 3.5 million in 2000. In 2003 population figures were 1,275,500 Northern Dong and 2,081,250 Southern Dong.

Their language (Kam) is a tonal language—eight tones—of the Austro-Thai branch of the Thai-Kadai family in addition to Zhuang and Shui. It has two dialects: the northern and southern, the former integrating more loan words from Chinese than the latter. This language has no script of its own.

Between 1951 and 1953 several autonomous counties whose populations were mainly constituted by Dong were created. Among the most important of these are Sanjiang in the Guangxi province, Tongdao in Southeastern Guizhou, and Xinhuang in the Hunan province. In these counties, as well as in other areas, Dong cohabit with the Han and with other Thai minorities such as the Zhuang, Shui, and Buyi. The Miao (Hmong) and Yao are other neighbors with whom conflicts occurred in the past.

The Dong's economy is partly based upon the logging and trading of fir trees, which are grown extensively. Agriculture is another important source of income with rice, wheat, millet, maize, sweet potatoes, and various cash crops (cotton, tea, oil-producing tea, colza). Crops are cultivated on lowland or within terraces extending to higher slopes of mountains. Dong live in villages of 20 to 40 households located near streams. Covered bridges and drum towers are the most typical buildings in these villages. The latter serve as rallying points for public meetings and festivals. The houses are usually built of fir wood. Dong are animist but their religious beliefs and practices have been influenced by the Chinese *san jiao* ("Three doctrines," namely Buddhism,Taoism, and Confucianism). This influence is deepest in relation to ancestors' worship, funeral ceremonies, and some calendar festivals (i.e., the Spring Festival and the Dragon Boat Festival).

History

The first mention of the Dong in Chinese chronicles dates back to the Ming Dynasty (1368–1644). Various hypotheses have been put forward concerning their origin. Some Chinese historians consider that they are aborigines of Guangxi, and toponymy (place-name) research as well as Dong mythology suggest they could have come more specifically from the region of Wuzhou. Other scholars suggest that they were expelled by the Han from the lowlands they populated in Guangdong, Jiangxi, Fujian, or Zhejiang and were driven to the remote mountainous region they now inhabit. Others believe that they stem from the intermixing of conquerors and natives. Whatever the hypothesis, Chinese scholars believe that Dong form a branch of the Bai Yue—people who inhabited the basin of theYangze River during the first centuries of the Christian era after the splitting of the Yue kingdom into a vast number of small chiefdoms.

During the Qing Dynasty (1644–1911) agriculture developed rapidly in southeast Guizhou and southwest Hunan, provinces that Dong populated. Irrigation infrastructures were extended and rice production increased significantly, but these improvements mainly benefited feudal landlords. After the first Opium War, 1840 to 1842, most of the Dong were further impoverished because of a harsher exploitation by foreign capitalists, Qing officials, landlords, and usurers. As a consequence, a large number of peasants of this ethnic group joined or helped the Communist Party after its founding in 1921. They supplied food to the Chinese Red Army when it went through Guangxi during its Long March in the mid-1930s. They also organized guerilla units fighting side by side with People's Liberation Army against the forces of Tchiang Kai-shek. After 1949, as a reward for this active support, roads were rapidly built to make the area less isolated, primary schools were opened in the remote areas, many small-scale factories were established locally, and a large number of militants (men and women) became communist cadres. In the 1990s about 6,500 Dong held government posts in Guangxi. Up to now these signs of recognition by the central authority have been emphatic enough to prevent the rise of ethno-nationalist movements among this minority.

Bernard Formoso

See also China

Further Reading

Beauclair, Inez de, *Ethnographic Studies, the Collected Papers of Inez de Beauclair*, Taipei: Southern Material Center, 1986

Ma, Yin, *China's Minority Nationalities*, Beijing: Foreign Language Press, 1994

Druze

Capsule Summary

Location: Lebanon, Syria, Israel; very small population in Jordan
Total Population: 800,000
Language: Arabic
Religion: Druze

Few minorities live in such vastly different political settings, account for such small percentages of the general population, and possess such divergent political levels of political influence, as do the Druze minorities in the contiguous states of Lebanon, Israel, and Syria. In Lebanon, a state where the high political positions (and frequently the bureaucratic as well) are allotted according to a confessional key, the Druze are approximately 200,000-strong, accounting for seven percent of the population. Most Druze concentrate in a semi-autonomous territorial base in the Shuf Mountains south of Beirut in which Walid Jumblat, the paramount leader (za'im), and his party, the Progressive Socialist Party, enjoy as his father Kamal before him, considerable if not overwhelming influence. The Druze therefore posses a high degree of unity and political power in their relationship to the state, and perhaps more importantly in respect to the other often rival communities.

Though their importance in the predominantly Jewish state of Israel is by no means comparable to the situation prevailing in Lebanon, it certainly exceeds what one would expect from a minority of 100,000 that accounts for less than two percent of the population. The reason has much to do with Israel's political isolation in the predominantly Arab and Muslim surroundings and the inherent hostility the states and their populations harbor against the state for failing in their view to satisfactorily solve the Palestinian problem. The Jewish establishment and majority perceived the Druze as a non-Muslim, non-Arab minority (though they speak Arabic exclusively) and thus as welcome allies. The Druze are the only minority who serve on the basis of mandatory conscription in the Israel Defense Forces. Many choose to become career soldiers and officers upon completion of mandatory service or to join the other security branches such as the Border Police and the regular police force. The Druze, in participating in these policing functions in the West Bank and Gaza, have frequently generated the anger of the Palestinian national movement and the official institutions it has spawned.

Ironically, least known and least felt are the Druze minority in Syria today, who form the largest concentration of Druze in the world with an approximate population of 300,000, or 3 percent of the population. Like the Druze in Lebanon, they are concentrated in a mountainous area known to this day as Jebel Druze, or the Druze Mountain. Whereas the Druze might be said to have maintained power in Lebanon, to have increased their influence in Israel relative to pre-State times, in Syria their stature has declined considerably since the early stage of the evolution of the Syrian state under the French Mandate (1920–1945). The emergence of a highly centralized one party and highly repressive state presumably ruled by an elite emanating from a rival confession, the Alawites, might explain their radical decline in stature. One of the major problems, however, is ascertaining this decline since there is so little information on the Druze in Syria—itself probably a reflection of the repressive policies toward the Druze by the regime. The Syrian regime, committed to the pan-Arab ideology of the Ba'th, does not provide or facilitate information on a confessional group, which the Syrian or Arab nationalism it espouses is supposed to have effaced. Thus, while there are numerous academic articles and news reports on the Druze in Lebanon and in Israel, few can be found on Druze society in Syria.

Despite these notable differences, it is clear that for many of the Druze in Israel and Syria, the Druze area in the Shuf Mountains is regarded as the spiritual center of the Druze community, or nation at least to some in both communities. A discussion on the origins and development of the Druze religion and practices can explain in what sense the Druze are a confession, a community, or a nation.

The Religion of the Druze

The Druze religion may be regarded as an offshoot of Isma'ili Islam, itself one of the branches of Shi'ite Islam. Many scholars attribute its beginnings to the

Fatimid caliph of Egypt, Hakim (996–1021 CE), who considered himself the final incarnation of God. His close associates and followers Hamza and Darazi (hence the name Druze) spread the new doctrine among the inhabitants of southern Lebanon, and founded among them a sect that non-Druzes called Druze, understood to mean those who follow *unitarianism*. The Druzes believe that Hakim is absent rather than dead and will reappear to his people. Like their Shi'ite neighbors they believe in emanations of the deity, supernatural hierarchies, and the transmigration of souls. Such beliefs have aroused the hostility of the Sunnis, who compromise the vast majority of Muslims. By professing and practicing rites that conform to the practice of the majority, a practice known as *taqiyya*, they have been able to reduce hostility toward the community while at the same time preserving their cohesiveness. Such behavior has been facilitated by the fact that the Druzes are religiously divided into two groups: the *uqqal* (the mature) who master the secrets and teaching of the sect and practice its dictates in their daily life, and the far larger percentage of *juhhal* (the ignorant) who are not entitled to know the inner secrets of the religion and its true practices.

Nevertheless, the Druze have historically encountered opposition from the surrounding religious communities, forcing them to seek refuge in inhospitable, relatively secluded mountainous regions. The sense of threat also explains why the Druze, in an age of rising state and pan-Arab nationalism and the emergence of ideologically committed states, have never demanded a state of their own. Though the Druze in Lebanon have sometimes used the word nation to describe the Druze, their identification with the term confession *(ta'ifa)* is far more common. Even more common is to identify with the most powerful ideological currents of the day.

This is not to say that the Druze have shied away from confrontation. The Druze have rebelled against centralized authority under the Ottomans in 1834, fought the Christians in internecine war in the 1840s and again in 1860 in Mount Lebanon, and participated in rebellions against centralized authority in Syria under the Mandate in the 1925–1927 revolt. These rebellions ceased as centralized authority emerged under the Ba'th in Syria. In a weaker state based on confessional lines such as Lebanon, the Druze have allied with other groups against their Maronite Christian nemesis. With the division of the eastern Mediterranean littoral into three distinctive independent states, the differences between the Druze communities in the three states have grown to the point that they best be described according to the state in which they reside.

The Druze Community in Lebanon

Two factions have traditionally vied over leadership of the Druze community in Lebanon: the Jumblat (also spelled Jumblatt) and the Yazbak (Arslan) family confederations. The Druze in turn have traditionally challenged the Maronite community, and in the twentieth century its more modern political expressions, the *Kata'ib* (Phalangists) and the Lebanese forces, in order to preserve their autonomy. Though the Druze retained their autonomy with the emergence of the modern State of Lebanon in 1920, they were not accorded major political positions according to a confessional key, as were the Maronites, the Sunnis, and the Shi'ites.

In the early 1970s just before the outbreak of Lebanon's civil war in 1975, the major figure in Druze politics, Kamal Jumblat, allied with forces on the left to champion a secular Lebanon in a bid to attain a position of leadership denied him under the existing order. When civil war broke out in April 1975 between the Phalangists and the Palestine Liberation Organization (PLO) forces, Jumblat allied with forces on the left and the PLO to fight the Maronites. Their overwhelming military success, however, proved to be their undoing. Interested in maintaining a balanced and therefore weak Lebanese arena in 1976, Syrian President Hafiz al-Asad demanded of the PLO and of Jumblat and his allies to cease hostilities against the Maronite forces. Jumblat's refusal to do so might have cost him his life; he was assassinated in 1977. Within seven years his son and successor, Walid Jumblat, was ordering his adherents to fight the very same Palestinian factions with whom his father allied in what became known as "the war of the [refugee] camps." Allied with him was the Shi'ite *Hizbullah* whose theocratic aspirations painted a sharp contrast to his father's former allies.

Hizbullah's ascent reflected yet another cost of prolonged civil war for the Druze. The religious radicalization of the formerly quiescent Shi'ites, the largest communal group in Lebanon, meant a diminution in stature for the Druze even though it was partially offset by the subsequent political fragmentation and weakening of the Maronite political community. The Druze therefore naturally supported Arab efforts to bring an end to the Lebanese civil war in 1989. Even though the Druze failed to prove their official standing in the

Ta'if agreement of that year, they have by and large supported the Syrian-dictated status quo, including the presence of Syrian forces on Lebanese soil and the Syrian-backed government, not least because the present government allows the Druze to preserve considerable political and bureaucratic autonomy. In the fall of 2000 when he called for the withdrawal of Syrian forces, Walid Jumblat's temporary deviation from a pro-Syrian stance prompted an assassination threat against him.

The Druze in Syria

Though by far the largest community, little can be said about the Druze under the present Syrian regime. Disturbances in southern Syria in November 2000, ostensibly over grazing rights between the mostly Druze inhabitants of Swaida and Bedouins living on the city's outskirts, were also attributed to the tensions between the Syrian leadership and Lebanese Druze leader Walid Jumblat. This suggests that the Druze remain a cohesive community that identify with their brethren in Lebanon.

Thirty thousand Druze also live in the Golan Heights, which Israel, defying the international community, formally annexed in 1980—thirteen years after it occupied it during the June 1967 war. The Druze in the Golan Heights are divided between those who support continued Israeli rule and those who oppose it. The former worry over the economic effects of reintegration into the Syrian state given the notable difference in economic levels between the two countries; the latter worry over the political consequences of taking an anti-Syrian stance should such reintegration take place.

Israel's Druze Community

Israel's Druze community, unlike the Druze communities in the Shuf Mountains or in Jebel Druze, hardly had a leadership of its own in pre-State days. To settle disputes amongst the Druze or with the Muslim majority in Mandate Palestine, local Druze often used Druze intermediaries from Lebanon and Syria. The Muslim majority thwarted attempts by the Druze to achieve the status of a recognized confession during Mandate times—something they only achieved within the State of Israel in 1958.

The Druzes' position changed radically in the early years of Israeli statehood when Amin Tarif became both a spiritual and political leader of the local Druze. Israel's political and strategic isolation was partially responsible for the change. No less important were deliberate attempts by the State to accentuate the uniqueness of the Druze in an attempt to thwart the forging of a common Arab identity to the Arabic-speaking, non-Jewish population of the State. Transforming the Shu'aib tomb into the swearing-in ceremony for Druze recruits into the Israeli army and the establishment in 1975 of a joint Druze-Israeli committee to design a curriculum that would cement Druzes' feelings of pride about their uniqueness and traditions has been perceived as deliberate attempts to create a wedge between the Druze and fellow Arab citizens.

Nevertheless the position of Israel's Druze in Israeli society and politics is fraught with tension. On the one hand, they take an active part in Israeli politics, are amply represented in the Israeli parliament (two members represented the right-wing Likud in Israel's Keneset in 2003), and have risen in the ranks in the army and security forces. On the other hand, the Druze complain of discrimination in government allocations and excessive land-use restrictions. Ironically they have been adversely affected by Israel's peace agreement with Jordan in 1994, which led to the relocation of Israeli textile workshops and factories there, and subsequently to the loss of employment for (mostly) Druze women.

HILLEL FRISCH

See also **Israel; Lebanese; Muslims: Shi'a in Sunni Countries; Syria**

Further Reading

Atashe, Zeidan, *Druze and Jews in Israel: A Shared Dlestiny?* Brighton, United Kingdom: Sussex Academic Press, 1995

Betts, Robert Brenton, *The Druze,* New Haven : Yale University Press, 1988

Dana, Nissim, *The Druze in the Middle East: Their Faith, Leadership, Identity and Status*, Portland, Oregon: Sussex Academic Press, 2003

Frisch, Hillel, "State Ethnicization and the Crisis of Leadership Succession Among Israel's Druze," in *Ethnic and Racial Studies*, 20, no. 2 (1997)

Gelber, Yoav, "Antecedents of the Jewish-Druze Alliance in Palestine," in *Middle Eastern Studies*, 28, no. 2 (1992)

Harik, Judith P., "Change and Continuity Among the Lebanese Druze Community: The Civil Administration of the Mountains, 1983-90," in *Middle Eastern Studies*, 29, no. 3 (1993)

Hitti, Philip Khuri, *The Origins of the Druze People and Religion*, New York: AMS Press, 1966

Du Bois, W.E.B. (African-American)

W.E.B. Du Bois was one of the most important American intellectuals of the twentieth century. Du Bois was an activist, sociologist, historian, essayist, critic, and promoter of the arts. He spent the majority of his life fighting racial inequality and imperialism and promoting Pan-Africanism. His approaches and ideas often were out of step with prevailing civil rights orthodoxy, especially in the latter portion of his life; but upon his death on the eve of the March on Washington in 1963, Du Bois was still regarded as one of the preeminent figures in the struggle for black equality.

Du Bois first made his mark on American intellectual life when he received his doctorate from Harvard in 1895, becoming the first African-American to receive a Ph.D. from that university. After graduating from Fisk University, he took a Master's degree at Harvard in 1891. He had hoped to receive his Ph.D. from Friedrich Wilhelm University in Berlin where he studied from 1892 to 1894, but when they refused to grant him a third year of funding due to residency requirements, he returned to Harvard. His dissertation on the slave trade would become the first volume of the Harvard Historical Monograph series just one year later. This sort of accomplishment would undoubtedly have earned a white scholar a position at one of America's elite institutions. The racism of the academy, however, forced Du Bois to take a position at all-black colleges, first at Wilberforce University in Ohio where he began teaching before receiving the Ph.D., and then at Atlanta University with a brief stint at the University of Pennsylvania where he had been hired to study Philadelphia's black community. The result of his year at Penn was his monumental study *The Philadelphia Negro*, the first sociological study of its kind in the United States.

Even these early successes gave no indication as to the status Du Bois would garner as a consequence of the publication of his collection of essays *The Souls of Black Folk* in 1903. Included in these essays was Du Bois' famous assertion that "the problem of the twentieth century is the problem of the color line," his rebuke of and public squabble with the accommodationist philosophy of Booker T. Washington, and his exposition of his belief in the need for "The Talented Tenth," the elite among the African-American population, to integrate themselves into American society. *The Souls of Black Folk* stands as one of the monumental works in American intellectual life.

The Souls of Black Folk established Du Bois as a sort of counterbalance to the black leadership of the Tuskegee Institute's Washington. Where Du Bois was born after the Civil War in rural western Massachusetts, Washington had been born into slavery and had experienced the emergence of Jim Crow in the South firsthand. Washington's accommodationism thus arose from lived experience in the South. However, Du Bois had a vision for America's black population that envisioned and demanded full acceptance in an integrated America. He believed that Washington's insistence on vocational education and economic advancement failed to provide Americans of African descent their full rights and opportunities. He noted that African-Americans faced a double consciousness in which they were aware of their status as being blacks in a racist society, while at the same time they were also Americans who desired everything that American citizenship was supposed to mean.

Du Bois' belief in integration led him to be one of the founders of the Niagara Movement at a meeting in 1905 of 29 black leaders in Fort Erie, Ontario—it was held in Canada because of segregation in accommodations on the American side of the Falls. The Niagara Movement was intended to advance the cause of black civil rights through protest and organization. The Niagara Movement did not prove to have much success, but soon after Du Bois would be integral to the founding of the National Association for the Advancement of Colored People (NAACP). Du Bois would serve that organization as its director of publications and research, and he was elected as the organization's only black member of the NAACP Board of Directors. Chief amongst his responsibilities for the organization was his stewardship of the NAACP's publication *The Crisis*. He edited, wrote for, and oversaw the operations of the journal from 1910 until 1934, when he resigned from the organization after a disagreement with the NAACP's leadership over the approach African-Americans should take in dealing with the Great Depression. During his tenure as editor, *The Crisis* was a voice of political, economic, and cultural concerns for the black community. In addition to Du Bois' often probing essays, the journal also included poetry and prose from leading African-Americans, including figures from the Harlem Renaissance, a movement to which Du Bois gave his support, although he believed that artists needed to become more actively involved in the political, social, and economic struggles of the era. In 1928 his daughter married the poet Countee Cullen in Harlem to much fanfare, although the marriage lasted only a year, and ultimately was a sham as Cullen was gay and Yolande Du Bois admired but never truly loved him.

The schism between Du Bois and Washington, and Du Bois and the NAACP, as well as public disagreements between Du Bois and the black nationalist leader Marcus Garvey reveals much about Du Bois' approach to the race question. Although he was the preeminent African-American figure in the first third of the twentieth century, he often found himself at odds with other figures in the black community over matters of philosophy and tactics. He was an iconoclastic thinker whose far-ranging writings and speeches changed over time, and he was always willing to challenge the status quo. As he grew older Du Bois also became more doctrinaire, which often served to alienate himself from other thinkers and activists on the race issue.

By 1920 Du Bois had begun to examine Marxist thought. His relationship with Marxism, Socialism, and Communism is often murky, but it is clear that he took a materialist approach to American society. This rings especially true in the most important work of the latter half of his career, which he wrote after resigning from the NAACP and returning to Atlanta University. In *Black Reconstruction in America* (1935) he challenged the prevailing historiography that depicted a white South beset by carpetbaggers and scalawags who propped up corrupt and invidious regimes of ignorant blacks. Although the historical profession did not give the book the attention that it merited, this revisionist view did gain some acclaim in newspapers and magazines as well as within the black intellectual community, and would find voice in subsequent depictions of Reconstruction, including works by Kenneth Stampp, C. Vann Woodward, Leon Litwack, and Eric Foner. However, if Du Bois often drew on Marxist theory in his scholarship and other writings, he did not do so uncritically. Du Bois believed that most Marxists ignored the race question in deference to class critiques, even when racial tensions often proved to be a barrier to the improvement of the plights of the working classes. It is this intellectual break that separated Du Bois from much of the Marxists left.

Nonetheless, Du Bois sympathized with much of the Communist cause. Although he did not join the Communist Party until 1961, he was a vocal supporter of Stalinism, a support he unfortunately clung to even after its excesses were revealed. Part of his romance with Communism undoubtedly springs from his ardent opposition to colonialism. He believed that imperialism was fundamentally a problem of race and class with wealthy white nations asserting their domination over poor regions of people of color. Du Bois was an avowed Pan-Africanist who called for decolonization of that continent. After World War II he opposed much of American Cold War foreign policy as he believed it was a part of this colonial endeavor. He had rejoined the NAACP in 1944, but broke with that organization again in 1948 after his radicalism alienated many in the organization's upper ranks. In that year he broke with most major black leaders in supporting Henry Wallace's insurgent challenge to Harry S. Truman. This would mark the beginning of a period in which Du Bois was beset with personal and public difficulties.

Du Bois' outspokenness and increasing radicalism in the 1950s led to the State Department and others labeling him a subversive. In 1952 the State Department refused to issue him a passport, declaring that Du Bois traveling abroad was not in the national interest. They further tried to force him to sign a statement saying that he was not a member of the Communist Party. Although he was not, Du Bois refused to sign. After a Supreme Court decision in 1958 allowed him issuance of his passport, Du Bois traveled widely throughout the world. In 1961 at the invitation of Ghana's President Kwame Nkrumeh, Du Bois moved to that country and two years later became a citizen. At Nkrumeh's behest Du Bois took on the project of editing the *Encyclopedia Africana*, which he never completed, and where he functioned as an honored citizen and elder statesman until his death at the age of 95 in August 1963.

Biography

William Edward Burghardt Du Bois. Born 23 February 1868 in Great Barrington, Massachusetts, United States. Studied at public schools in Great Barrington; Fisk University, Nashville, Tennessee, A.B., 1888; Harvard University, Cambridge, Massachusetts, A.M., 1891, Ph.D., 1895; Friedrich Wilhelm University, Berlin, 1892–1894. Taught at Wilberforce University, Xenia,

Ohio, 1894–1896; University of Pennsylvania, Philadelphia, 1896–1897; Atlanta Univercity, Atlanta, Georgia, 1897–1910 and 1934–1944. Founder, Pan-African Congress, 1900; Niagara Movement, 1904. Editor, *Moon Illustrated Weekly*, Memphis, Tennessee, 1906–1907; *Horizon*, Washington, D.C., 1907–1910. Cofounder, National Association for Advancement of Colored People, 1910. Director of publicity and research and editor of *The Crisis*, 1910–1934; Director of Special Research, 1944–1948. Editor, with A.G. Dill, *Brownie's Book*, 1920–1921; columnist for Pittsburgh *Courier*, 1936–1938; *Amsterdam News*, New York, 1938–1944; Chicago *Defender*, 1944–1948; *People's Voice*, 1947–1948; also wrote for *Current History, Journal of Negro Education, Foreign Affairs,* and *American Scholar*; founder and editor, *Phylon*, Atlanta, 1940–1944; editor, *Encyclopedia Africana*, 1961–1963 (never completed). Vice Chair, Council on African Affairs, 1949–1954; candidate for U.S. Senate for New York, 1950. Immigrated to Ghana, 1961; became citizen, 1963. Awards: Spingarn Medal, 1920; International Peace Prize, 1952; Lenin Peace Prize, 1959. Knight Commander, Liberian Order of National Redemption; Fellow, American Association for the Advancement of Science; Member, American Academy. Died in Accra, Ghana, 27 August, 1963.

Selected Works

The Suppression of the African Slave Trade to the United States of America, 1638–1870, 1896
The Souls Of Black Folk: Essays and Sketches, 1903; revised editions, 1953, 1997
The Quest of the Silver Fleece, 1911
Darkwater: Voices From Within the Veil, 1920
The Gift of Black Folk: The Negroes and the Making of America, 1924
Dark Princess, 1928
Black Reconstruction in America: An Essay Toward a History of the Part Which Black Folk Played in the Attempt to Reconstruct Democracy in America, 1860–1880, 1935
Black Folk, Then and Now: An Essay in the History and Sociology of the Negro Race, 1939
Dusk of Dawn: An Essay Toward an Autobiography of the Race Concept, 1940
The Black Flame (trilogy), 1957–1961
An ABC of Color: Selections From Over a Half Century of Writings, 1964
The Autobiography of W.E.B. Du Bois: A Soliloquy on Viewing My Life From the Last Decade of its First Century, edited by Herbert Aptheker, 1968
Selected Writings, edited by Walter Wilson, 1970
W.E.B. DuBois: A Reader, edited by Meyer Weinberg, 1970
W.E.B. DuBois Speaks: Speeches and Addresses, 1890–1963, edited by Philip Foner, 2 vols., 1970
A W.E.B. Du Bois Reader, edited by Andrew D. Paschal, 1971
The Seventh Son: The Thought and Writings of W.E.B. DuBois, edited by Julius Lester, 2 vols., 1971
The Crisis Writings, edited by Daniel Walden, 1972
The Education of Black People: 10 Critiques, 1906–1960, edited by Herbert Aptheker, 1973
The Complete Published Works, edited by Herbert Aptheker, 20 vols., 1973–1986
The Correspondence of W.E.B. Du Bois, edited by Herbert Aptheker, 3 vols., 1973–1978
The Writings of W.E.B. DuBois (selection), edited by Virginia Hamilton, 1975
Against Racism: Unpublished Essays, Papers, Addresses, 1887–1961, edited by Herbert Aptheker, 1985
W.E.B. Du Bois: Writings, edited by Nathan Irving Huggins, 1986
W.E.B. Du Bois: A Reader, edited by David Levering Lewis, 1995
The Oxford W.E.B. Du Bois Reader, edited by Eric J. Sundquist, 1996

Derek Catsam

See also **National Association for the Advancement of Colored People (NAACP); Washington, Booker T. (African-American)**

Further Reading

Aptheker, Herbert, *The Literary Legacy of W.E.B. Du Bois*, White Plains, New York: Krauss International, 1989
Bell, Bernard, Emily Grosholtz, and James Stewart, editors, *W.E.B. Du Bois on Race and Culture: Philosophy, Politics, and Poetics*, New York: Routledge, Chapman, and Hall, 1996
Frederickson, George M., *The Black Image in the White Mind: The Debate on Afro-American Character and Identity, 1817–1914*, New York: Harper and Row, 1971
Lewis, David Levering, *W.E.B. Du Bois: The Biography of a Race, 1868–1919*, New York: Henry Holt, 1993
Lewis, David Levering, *W.E.B. Du Bois: The Fight For Equality and the American Century, 1919–1963*, New York: Henry Holt, 2000
Marable, Manning, *W.E.B. Du Bois: Black Radical Democrat*, Boston: Twayne, 1986
Posnock, Ross, *Color and Culture: Black Writers and the Making of the Modern Intellectual*, Cambridge, Massachusetts: Harvard University Press, 1998
Zamir, Shamoon, *Dark Voices: W.E.B. Du Bois and American Thought, 1888–1903*, Chicago: University of Chicago Press, 1995

Dukhobors

Capsule Summary

Location: Canada (mostly British Columbia and Saskatchewan), United States, Russia (Tambov, Rostov, Tula, and Orenburg Regions, Krasnodar Area, Far East), Georgia, Azerbaijan, Ukraine, Central Asia
Total Population: 90,000
Language: Russian
Religion: Christian

The Dukhobors ("Spirit Wrestlers") are a religious group living in Canada, the United States, Russia, Azerbaijan, Georgia, Ukraine, Central-Asian Republics, and some other countries. There are approximately 90,000 Dukhobors. They speak mainly Russian.

Dukhobors are one of the groups of Spiritual Christians. (Spiritual Christians is a common name for religious sects that split with the Russian Orthodox Church in the seventeenth and eighteenth centuries, probably under the influence of Protestantism-penetrated Russia.) The sect of Dukhobors arose among the Russian peasants. The exact time of the appearing of the Dukhobors is unknown, but they were completely formed in the second part of the eighteenth century. The first promoter of Dukhobor ideas was Siluan Kolesnikov from Ekaterinoslav Province; his successors were Illarion Pobirokhin and Saveliy Kapustin, preaching in the Central Russia.

Dukhobors do not recognize Bible, but they have their own oral tradition called *Zhivotnaya Kniga Dukhobortsev* (Dukhobor Book of Life), which allegorically interprets Bible and Christian dogmas. It consists of questions and answers concerning dogmas and psalms. *Zhivotnaya Kniga* contains so many psalms that one person cannot recall them. It is in the common memory of the whole community. Parents teach *Zhivotnaya Kniga*, which is considered to be baptism, to their children between the ages of 6 and 15. *Zhivotnaya Kniga* was first published only in 1909.

Dukhobors believe that God is not separated from the human being. Trinity in their understanding is Light (Father), Life (Son), and Peace (Holy Spirit) with which every man may be linked by Memory, Understanding, and Will. According to Dukhobors, Jesus Christ was simply a man, though possessing the Divine Reason in the highest degree. They think that every generation of people has its own mortal Christ who is their moral teacher. Dukhobors do not believe in life after death and suppose that only memory remains after death. At the same time they believe that the soul undergoes metempsychosis. According to them the souls existed already before the creation of the world, but then they fell together with angels. As a punishment they are being sent on earth and incarnated in bodies. After the death the soul of a righteous man transmigrates into the body of another righteous man (or newborn); as to the soul of a sinner, it transmigrates into an animal. According to Dukhobors, the Kingdom of Heaven will be on earth for the living, the world will never end, and the end of the world will be limited by the extermination of the sinners. Dukhobors do not admit original sin.

The state power is considered by Dukhobors as an instrument against robbers and villains only. Hence they rejected state taxation, public education, and censuses. Taking an oath and swearing are not allowed to them. Under the influence of Leo Tolstoy they refused to serve in the army, burned their weapons, and became pacifists. The Dukhobors symbols are bread, salt, and a water jug. They put them on the table during their divine services. The services are held either in the special rooms or outside. The Dukhobors do not have clergy—all the believers consider themselves to be priests. They do not recognize the church holidays, though they time their prayer services for the Orthodox holidays. Dukhobors are agrarian and hold property in common. They are vegetarians.

Because of their non-recognition of the state power, the Dukhobors were often subjected to persecutions and deportations. In the late eighteenth century they were exiled to Siberia. In the early nineteenth century they were settled in Taurida (northern coast of the Black Sea) as an agrarian community, but in 1841 they were banished again, this time to Georgia. In 1898 and 1899 with the assistance of Quakers (whose teaching has something in common with that of Dukhobors) and Leo Tolstoy, 7,400 Dukhobors migrated to Canada. There the conflict with authorities also arose because Dukhobors did not want to register births, marriages, and deaths, as well as to owe lands in private. In protest an extremist group of Dukhobors called Sons of Freedom appeared in the early twentieth century. They opposed the attempts of the Canadian government to integrate Dukhobors into the larger society. They paraded naked and committed 800 acts of violence, including bombings and arsons. The Sons of Freedom actually broke with the larger Dukhobor community in 1933. The majority of Dukhobors were more loyal and came to compromise with the Canadian authorities. They formed the Union of Spiritual Communities of Christ (Orthodox Dukhobors in Canada), which is the oldest group of Dukhobors in Canada. They consider God as an eternal spiritual being who frequently chooses to speak through the mouths of chosen men, usually Dukhobors' leaders. The members of the Union soon became prosperous but they were often dissatisfied with their leaders. In 1924 their leader Peter Verigin who claimed that Christ was reincarnated in him was killed. Under the leadership of his son, some 18,000 Dukhobors (mostly residents of Saskatchewan) formed the Society of Independent Dukhobors. They rejected the original communal ideals and communal lifestyle.

From Canada Dukhobors migrated to the United States and later to some other countries. The Union of Spiritual Communities of Christ is the largest group of Dukhobors in North America now.

Those Dukhobors remaining in Russia established relations with the Communist authorities in 1921, but under the Stalin regime many of them were liquidated, though some Dukhobor villages remained in Trans-Caucasus. In the late 1980s and early 1990s many Dukhobors moved from the Trans-Caucasus Republics to the Central Russia. In June 1991 "Religious Association of Spiritual Fighters of Christ—Dukhobors of the USSR" was formed (after the collapse of the USSR renamed into "Religious Association of Spiritual Fighters of Christ—Dukhobors of the NIS").

The Dukhobors preserved their traditions, customs, psalms, stories, and the co-operative ethics.

Olga Kazmina

Further Reading

Crim, Keith, editor, *Abingdon Dictionary of Living Religions,* Nashville, Tennessee: Abingdon, 1981

Douglas, J.D., editor, *The New International Dictionary of the Christian Church,* Grand Rapids, Michigan: Exeter; The Paternoster Press, 1974

Elkington, J., *The Doukhobors. Their History in Russia. Their Migration to Canada,* Philadelphia, 1903

Inikova, Svetlana, *Doukhobor Incantations Through the Centuries, Volume II,* New York, Ottawa, Toronto: LEGAS, 1999

Inikova, Svetlana, *History of the Doukhobors in V.D. Bonch-Bruevich's Archives (1886–1950s),Volume I,* New York, Ottawa, Toronto: LEGAS, 1999

Meagher, Paul K., Thomas C. O'Brien, and Sister Consuelo Maria Aherne, *Encyclopedic Dictionary of Religion,* Washington, DC: Corpus Publications, 1978

Mealing, F.M., *Doukhobor Life,* Castlegar, British Columbia: Cotinneh Books, 1975

Melton, Gordon J., editor, *Encyclopedia of American Religions,* Detroit, Washington, DC, London: Gale Research Inc., 1993

The Oxford Dictionary of the Christian Church, Oxford, 1974

Каблиц, И.И., *Русские диссиденты. Староверы и духовные христиане* [Russian Dissidents. Old Ritualists and Spiritual Christians], St. Petersburg, 1881

E

East Timor

Capsule Summary

Country Name: Democratic Republic of Timor-Leste, or East Timor

Location: South-central Indonesian archipelago

Total Population: 997,853 (July 2003)

Minority Populations: *Mestiço* (Portuguese, Timorese, African), Tetum (Belu), Mambai, Tocodote, Kemak (Ema), Galoli, Makassae, Idate, Chinese, Arabs, Malays

Languages: Tetum (official), Portuguese (official), Indonesian, English, and about 16 indigenous languages (Tetum, Galole, Mambae, Bahasa, and Kemak)

Religions: Roman Catholic (90%), Muslim (4%), Protestant (3%), Hindu (0.5%), Buddhist, animist (1992)

Stretching for over 3,000 miles (4,827 kilometers) across Southeast Asia, Indonesia is a country of mammoth ethnic, linguistic, geographic, and religious complexity. Its population of over 200 million is the fourth largest in the world. It is divided into a multitude of hundreds of ethnic groups, speaking an even greater multitude of languages. These people live on more than 13,000 major and minor islands. Although the country is overwhelmingly Moslem, and is the largest Moslem country in the world, there are also significant minorities of Hindus, Buddhists, Christians, and spiritists.

East Timor is located in Southeastern Asia, northwest of Australia in the Lesser Sunda Islands at the eastern end of the Indonesian archipelago. It includes the eastern half of the island of Timor, the Oecussi (Ambeno) region on the northwest portion of the island of Timor, and the islands of Pulau Atauro and Pulau Jaco. The great struggles of Indonesia in this century have been to free itself first from the Japanese occupation of its islands during World War II and, after the war, to free itself from its colonial ruler, The Netherlands. To achieve national liberation and unity, an authoritarian government controlling powerful military forces developed. This power was used not only to consolidate the Indonesian nation but also to suppress any dissent. It has been most brutally applied to East Timor, which is surrounded by Indonesia, and to the Timorese people.

History

The Portuguese colonized East Timor in the fifteenth century, seeking its rich resources of sandalwood. Portugal brought the Catholic religion, together with the Portuguese language, to the Timorese. Having been a Portuguese possession for over four centuries, East Timor is distinctly different from Indonesia in terms of language, religion, cultural heritage, and ethnic composition. The Portuguese interbred with the native Timorese, creating a *mestiço* population. From their colonies in Africa, the Portuguese also brought Africans who mixed with the population. The largest native ethnic group in East Timor was the Tetum or Belu. Other groups, however, included the Mambai, Tocodote, Kemak (Ema), Galoli, Makassae, and ldate. From other countries came the Chinese, Arab, and Malay minorities. The term used by the East Timorese to describe themselves as a people was "Maubere."

In 1974 a revolution in Portugal resulted in the granting of independence on November 28, 1975, to East Timor as well as its other remaining African colonies. The tiny archipelago was ill-prepared for independence. It was a poor agricultural economy, producing mainly rice, corn, and other subsistence crops. East Timor's main income came from the export of coffee, as the sandalwood trees had been exhausted. Some potential for riches, however, was estimated to exist in the oil and gas deposits off the coast of the island in the Timor Sea.

Indonesia alleged that an entity as poor as East Timor, left to itself, would become Communist. On this pretext, and with American and other foreign support, Indonesian forces invaded East Timor 9 days post-independence in November 1975, and within a few months had brutally absorbed it as a new province. They quickly prohibited the Portuguese language, imposed the Indonesian national language, Bahasa, and repressed any expression of Maubere nationalism or identity. Indonesians from the most densely populated parts of the country were transferred to East Timor. Indonesia invested extensively in infrastructure and education as a means of further persuading the Timorese to accept absorption. The archipelago was incorporated into Indonesia in July 1976 as the province of East Timor.

Timorese resistance was adamant, however. Fervently Catholic and culturally distinct, they would not accept the imposition of the Indonesian language or religious and ethnic dominance. Moreover, despite the new skills the Timorese acquired, they were often unemployed, losing jobs, land, and economic opportunities to the newly settled Indonesians. Their resistance spurred an Indonesian military reaction of extraordinary and almost unprecedented violence and brutality. During the Indonesian occupation, from an original Timorese population of almost 700,000 people, nearly 200,000 of its people were slaughtered. Many were tortured, raped, and maimed.

Poor and ignored by the rest of the world, the Timorese continued in the face of nightmarish force to push for their independence. They were organized by an ecclesiastical leader, Bishop Felipe Carlos Ximenes Belo, and a civilian leader, José Ramos-Horta, who jointly received the Nobel Prize for Peace in 1996 for their efforts to obtain a peaceful transition to Timorese nationhood and independence from Indonesia.

With the fall of the authoritarian and corrupt government of Indonesian President Mohamed Suharto in 1998, the way was open for East Timor to obtain independence. After a United Nations (UN)-supervised popular referendum among the Timorese on August 30, 1999, they overwhelmingly voted for and obtained independence. However, this was not before the last, and possibly the most savage, assault by Indonesian forces on the Timorese. From 1999 to 2001, pro-integrationist militias—supported by Indonesia—conducted indiscriminate violence, slaughtering thousands as the troops retreated.

A constitutional assembly met at the end of 2001, and on May 20, 2002, East Timor was internationally recognized as an independent state and the world's newest democracy. However, democracy is a fragile concept in the native culture. East Timor is a country that can barely sustain itself. Until a constitution was written and national elections were conducted, it was under UN administration. For centuries, the Timorese had been under authoritarian rule, and they were accustomed to elders within the ethnic groups making determining group decisions.

About 70 percent of the economic infrastructure of East Timor was destroyed by Indonesian troops and anti-independence militias after the final attacks in 1991, causing about 260,000 people to flee westward. East Timor survived because of international aid from the UN, Portugal, the European Union, and Australia. In 2001 it reached an agreement with Australia to receive a major portion of the prospective royalties obtained from oil and gas extracted from the Timor Gap hydrocarbon reserves. By mid-2002, all but about 50,000 of the refugees had returned. The GDP per capita income was only $500 in 2001, one of the lowest in the world, although the prospect of drilling for oil in nearby waters has looked promising. The unemployment rate (including underemployment) is 50 percent. Massive rebuilding of the domestic infrastructure and strengthening of the republic's administration is planned. At publication, the East Timor-Indonesia Boundary Committee meets regularly to survey and delimit the land boundaries, and some East Timorese refugees have delayed their return from camps in Indonesia.

EDWARD A. RIEDINGER

Further Reading

Carey, Peter, and G. Carter Bentley, editors, *East Timor at the Crossroads: The Forging of a Nation*, New York: University of Hawaii Press and Social Science Research Council, 1995
Hainsworth, Paul, and Stephen McCloskey, editors, *The East Timor Question: The Struggle for Independence from Indonesia*, London: I.B. Tauris, 2000
Imbaraj, Sonny, *East Timor: Blood and Tears in ASEAN*, Chiang Mai, Thailand: Silkworm Books, 1995
Jardine, Matthew, *East Timor: Genocide in Paradise*, 2nd edition, Odonian Press, 1999
McGuinn, Taro, *East Timor: Island in Conflict*, Minneapolis, Minnesota: Lerner Publications, 1998

Ecuador

Capsule Summary

Location: Western South America, bordering the Pacific Ocean at the Equator, between Colombia and Peru

Total Population: 13,710,234 (July 2003)

Ethnic Groups: *Mestizo* (55–65%), indigenous (25%), Caucasian and others (7–10%), African (3–10%)

Languages: Spanish (official), Amerindian languages (especially Quechua)

Religions: Roman Catholic (95%), often mingled with indigenous beliefs in practice

The Republic of Ecuador is located in western South America and borders Colombia to the north, Peru to the south and east, and the Pacific Ocean to the west. The size of the nation is approximately 109,483 square miles (283,561 square kilometers), slightly smaller than the state of Nevada. Quito is the capital, as well as the ancient name of Ecuador, and was once a center of the Inca Empire (circa 1438–1527). Some of its well-preserved early colonial architecture presently remains in the city.

Ecuador is divided into three regions: the Costa (coastal lowlands and mountains between the Pacific Ocean and the Andes Mountains); the Sierra (which includes two major chains of the Andes, the Cordillera Occidental and Cordillera Oriental, and a plateau in between); and the Oriente (Andean piedmont and eastern lowlands). Ecuador also has possession of the Galápagos Islands (population 9,785) located about 600 miles (965 kilometers) off the coast.

History

Ecuador, with a 5,000-year history, was conquered by the Incas in the fifteenth century, about 100 years before the arrival and subsequent conquest by the Spanish in 1534. Ecuador was a Spanish colony for the following 300 years until 1822. During this period, the Spanish introduced cattle ranching and banana and cocoa cultivation. The indigenous peoples, who had long enjoyed a high level of social organization and mutual assistance (*ayllus*), were enslaved and cruelly exploited under Spanish rule.

In 1809, a local movement toward independence began. Independent forces led by Simon Bolivar defeated the Spanish at the Battle of Mt. Pichincha on May 24, 1822. Ecuador, together with Colombia, Panama, and Venezuela, formed the Republic of Greater Colombia, or Gran Colombia, from which it seceded to become a separate republic in 1830. The remainder of the nineteenth century was characterized by ongoing political and economic instability, especially due to conflicts over political and financial influence that arose among a conservative group in the highlands area of Quito, supported by the Catholic Church and liberal groups in the city of Guayaquil (on the Pacific). Tensions tended to emerge between coastal and highlands regional groups. Ecuador experienced ongoing political and territorial tensions with Peru and Colombia in the nineteenth and twentieth centuries: A boundary dispute with Colombia was settled in 1916, but the one with Peru remained unsettled until 1942. (In the early 1940s, Peru had seized a contested area around the Amazon River, claiming its political rights to the territory.)

Ecuador experienced severe economic deterioration because of a collapse in the cocoa market in the 1920s and the Great Depression in the 1930s. However, from 1948 to 1960, the country enjoyed a stable rule as a result of the growing banana industry. Social unrest occurred in the 1960s, and the country fell under an anticommunist military government that ruled without a constitution. The discovery of oil reserves in the early 1970s marked the beginning of economic modernization and state-led industrialization in Ecuador. Increasing numbers of people from rural areas moved to the cities, and the gap between the rich and the poor widened. In 1979 the nation returned to democracy when a new constitution was adopted. In the 1990s, Ecuador encountered a series of political and economic challenges as indigenous populations began to appeal for greater human and political rights. A border war with Peru reignited in 1995, but after armed struggles that caused dozens of causalities, both sides finally reached an agreement in 1999.

In the midst of economic crisis, President Janil Mahuad was toppled by a January 2000 coup and replaced by Vice President Gustavo Noboa. President Lucio Gutierrez subsequently took office in January 2003, with the support of the Pachakutik Movement (led by Miguel Lluco), a party formed by Indian groups and left-wing parties.

Ethnicity and Society

The population of Ecuador is ethnically mixed: *Mestizos* represent 55–65 percent of the population, indigenous groups represent 25 percent, Caucasians and others, 7–10 percent, and Africans, 3–10 percent. Spanish is the official language of Ecuador. A majority of the indigenous population speaks Quechua as their first language and Spanish as their second. Twenty-four ethnic groups live in Ecuador, scattered throughout four distinct regions: the coastal areas, the highlands, the Amazon, and the Galápagos.

The chief ethnic groups in Ecuador descended from South American Indians and Spanish colonizers. The mixed people of these two groups—*mestizos* or *cholos*—make up today's major population group. Another group consists of descendants of African slaves who were forced in slavery on coastal plantations during the sixteenth century.

However, Ecuadorian ethnic identity involves not only descent and race, but is also deeply related to and connected to social status. Status criteria include one's dress, language, and community membership. Indigenous groups also self-identify based on the aforementioned criteria, and a group may constantly seek to improve its status over another (*mestizos* vs. Caucasians, for example). Ecuadorian social hierarchy undisputedly still exists, with ethnic diversity used to rank various groups: The highest are Caucasians, followed by *mestizos*, then Africans, and finally Indians as the lowest rank.

Traditionally, the Caucasian population lived in the more urban areas, whereas other groups resided in smaller towns and villages throughout the rural areas. The geographical divisions among ethnicities began to shift significantly as migration to the cities surged in the 1950s. Today, only 3 percent of the total Ecuadorian population lives in the mountain or highland regions previously inhabited by indigenous populations.

In the early 1990s, several large-scale political protests among the indigenous peoples occurred as they fought for the rights to own land, to gain amnesty, and in general to increase governmental attention to racism and inequality. These political pressure groups included the Confederation of Indigenous Nationalities of Ecuador (CONAIE), the Federation of Indigenous Evangelists of Ecuador (FEINE), the National Federation of Indigenous Afro-Ecuatorianos and Peasants (FENOCIN), and the Popular Front (FP).

Ecuador obtained its independence from Spain on May 24, 1822. Since achieving independence in 1830, Ecuador has had 17 constitutions, only one of which (1906–1929) has lasted over 20 years. The current constitution took effect on August 11, 1998. The president (Lucio Gutierrez since January 15, 2003) is the head of the executive branch, which also includes 15 cabinet ministers. A unicameral Congress is the legislature, and the judicial branch consists of the Supreme Court and Provincial Courts. More than a dozen political parties exist, although none in particular predominates.

Ecuadorís indigenous population has historically tended to avoid the official political system. However, indigenous groups began to participate actively in the 1996 election and established themselves as a significant force, resulting in the gaining of several cabinet positions.

Economy

Ecuador is substantially rich in oil resources and agricultural areas. Because the country exports primary products such as oil, bananas, and shrimp, fluctuations in world market prices influence the domestic markets. Ecuador's economy is dependent on exports of petroleum (40 percent of export earnings, mostly to the United States) and agricultural products such as bananas (of which they are the world's largest exporter), shrimp, and, more recently, canned seafood and flowers.

Economic conditions deteriorated in the late 1990s, in part due to the El Niño phenomenon in 1997 as well as a depressed oil market, culminating in financial crisis in 1999. More than 600,000 Ecuadorians subsequently left the country for the United States or Europe in the following 2 years. Then-President Noboa anaged to pass substantial economic reforms and mend relations with international financial institutions. In 2001 the nation adopted the U.S. dollar as its official currency as a tool for economic recovery, although some critics have worried that "dollarization" might increase illegal money-laundering activity, especially along the border with Colombia. This successful strategy stabilized the Ecuadorian economy quickly, contributing to higher oil prices, accelerated GDP real-growth rates (2.3 percent in 2000, 5.6 percent in 2001, 3.4 percent in 2002), and decreased inflation. In 2002 the nation's GDP was $42.65 billion and the per capita income was $3,200. Nonetheless, in 2001 70 percent of the population lived below the poverty line, a rate double that of 5 years ago. Ecuador joined the World Trade Organization in 1996 but has failed to comply with many of its accession commitments.

Ai Hattori

Further Reading

Handelsman, Michael, *Culture and Customs of Ecuador*, Westport, Connecticut: Greenwood Publishing Group, 2000

MacDonald, Theodore, Jr., *Ethnicity and Culture amidst New "Neighbors": The Runa of Ecuador's Amazon Region*, Upper Saddle River, New Jersey: Pearson Education, 1998

Roos, Wilma, and Omar Van Rentergham, *In Focus Ecuador: A Guide to the People, Politics, and Culture*, Portland, Oregon: Interlink Pub. Group, 2000

Selverston-Scher, Melina, *Ethnopolitics in Ecuador: Indigenous Rights and the Strengthening of Democracy*, Miami, Florida: North-South Center Press, 2001

Williams, Colleen Madonna Flood, and James D. Henderson, editors, *Ecuador*, Broomall, Pennsylvania: Mason Crest Publishers, 2003

Education Rights

Achievement of education rights has been one of the cornerstones on the path to democracy and equality among people. The fundamental right to education is a main principle of nondiscriminatory treatment and a most important means of ensuring this treatment by empowering all categories of people, including minorities, to improve their personal and social status. A proper education enables self-reliance on all levels as well as the realization of other human rights. The general right to education is a basic human right formally acknowledged by national and international law. On a national level, the state should fulfill its obligation to provide the appropriate access to and conditions for education. According to international standards, this implies observing several levels of state obligations (see references in the Further Reading section to some basic international legislative instruments). On the international level, these principles guarantee the right to education on a nondiscriminatory basis, which implies *respect* for individual rights, the *protection* of those rights, and the *fulfillment* of this obligation by facilitating and providing general equitable access (in his analysis, Fons Coomans includes here minorities, migrants, refugees, and the socially vulnerable); by adopting positive measures of promoting intercultural education; and by eliminating passive discrimination. On a practical level, this takes the form of (1) *positive* and (2) *negative* state obligations; these correspond to (1) a social aspect of *availability* and *accessibility* to education, and (2) a political aspect of the granting of personal freedoms and a policy of noninterference in private matters based on *acceptability*, *adaptability*, and *flexibility* of the education provided. The latter can also be referred to as the right to educational freedom, which translates into nondiscrimination and equal treatment, and also includes minimal standards of relevant cultural and religious or moral appropriateness as well as the special rights of minorities. The World Declaration on Education for All, adopted in 1990 in Jomtien and confirmed by the Framework for Action adopted during the World Education Forum in Dakar in 2000, reasserted the necessity of giving substance to the right to education by generalizing access to it in practice. However, it was also noted that this was far from being a fact, as millions of people, both children and adults, still lacked access to a basic education. Article 14 in the Charter of Fundamental Rights of the EU (2000/C 364/01) states the right and freedom to exercise one's right to education "with due respect for democratic principles," and is to be related to the principles of equality in chapter III, including nondiscrimination (art. 21); cultural, religious, and linguistic diversity (art. 22); and other aspects. However, there is a discrepancy between these general principles and their actual application in practice, depending on the social, political, and economic factors of development, and even equity relations among states and zones of the world. Millions of children and adults continue to be deprived of their education rights, either by lack of appropriate forms and/or levels of education or by inadequate access to them. Violations occur with respect to the implementation of due education rights, for example, among nonrecognized but also official minorities.

The Original and Evolution of Education Rights

Access to education has always been related to sociopolitical and economic factors.

In the context of international migration and regarding the rights of minorities, education rights should be regarded both as a general human right equally applicable to all persons, irrespective of their origin, ethnic background, or social status, and as a particular subject within this general framework. The latter raises additional issues, sometimes regarded as below or exceeding the basic level included in the human rights definition of the concept of educational rights. Factual access to education is conditioned by availability and the practical capabilities of ensuring conditions—institutions and an educational process—that can put a theoretical principle into practice. The freedom aspect is thus related to the possibility of benefiting from an educational process of one's own choice and gaining due recognition for the completed studies. The specificity of minorities' access to education relies, in particular aspects, on their demands for a certain educational process, such as enhancing mother-tongue education, bilingual education, or other specific issues. Achievement of such a goal presupposes political will, economic capabilities, and the availability of specialized personnel who are able to cover such instructional needs—mainly teachers with special knowledge who can satisfy the requirements of the envisaged educational process. The limitations of entitlement often remain a debatable issue—for example, the possibility of following a special educational program organized or reserved for members of a certain community. The main issues regard the availability of resources, the question of what can reasonably be included in the concept of educational human rights, and the acceptable limitations and imposable conditions between the rights of individuals and the obligations of the state.

Historical and Political Aspects

Education rights have historically been related to power relationships within and outside the society, which have traditionally embodied the quest to preserve power among the dominant social classes. The lower classes, as social outcasts, have often been denied access to education as a means of control, for instance, by precluding access to education for slaves or discriminated minorities. Education rights are regarded as an individual or a group right within a general framework related to the rights of individuals, as granted by international law, within the obligations of the state, and assumed under the provisions of national and international law.

In the course of history, access to education rights has been closely related to the social and economic development of human societies, with connotations and limitations following the power-class divisions as well as politicized spheres of influence within a society. For the influential classes in more advanced societies, it has become obvious that the level of knowledge may be a decisive factor in the capacity to preserve power. Limiting access to education has explicitly been used throughout history as a deliberate instrument of control and for imposing subservience. An extreme example is the traditional Indian social system, which is keen on observing the direct relationship between knowledge, power, and control by instrumentally preserving a strict stratification of the society into *castes*, as reflected in an imposed, correspondingly strict proportional access to education. A unique expression of this awareness is the placement of the teacher caste—the *Brahmins*—at the top of the social pyramid (with the highest level of knowledge equated with the top of the social pyramid) while placing the cast of political rulers—the *Ksatriya*, the kings (representing the supreme power almost everywhere else)—on the second level of both formally acknowledged power and access to knowledge, and otherwise gradually decreasing to none for the outcasts—the *Pariah*—situated beyond the very class system. Some patriarchal religious societies, such as the Taliban regime in Afghanistan, precluded women's access to education as a means of perpetuating their subordination. Similarly, historical ethnic minorities, such as the Saami in Northern Europe or the Roma throughout Europe, have long been confronted with inadequate education rights that should take into consideration their cultural specificity, a situation that has bettered only during the last decades. Finding adequate solutions and levels of guarantees to ensure equal education rights for immigrant populations, whose numbers formed increasingly multicultural societies after World War II, is still an ongoing process.

ELENA DINGU-KYRKLUND

Further Reading

African Charter on Human Rights and Peoples' Rights (art. 17)

Arnove, R.F., and A. Torres, *Comparative Education: The Dialectic of the Global and the Local*, 2nd edition, Lanham, Maryland: Rowman & Littlefield, 2003

Charter of Fundamental Rights of the EU (2000/C 364/01) (art. 14)

Convention on the Elimination of All Forms of Discrimination against Women (art. 10)

Convention on the Rights of the Child (arts. 28 and 29)

Declaration on the Rights of Persons Belonging to National or Ethnic, Religious, and Linguistic Minorities (art. 4)

Document of the Copenhagen Meeting of the Conference on the Human Dimension of the CSCE (1990), (paras. 32–34)

European Charter for Regional or Minority Languages (1992), Council of Europe (art. 8)

European Convention on Human Rights and Fundamental Freedoms (art. 2 of Protocol No. 1)

Framework Convention for the Protection of National Minorities (1994) (arts. 12–14)

International Convention on the Elimination of All Forms of Racial Discrimination (arts. 5e and v)

International Covenant on Civil and Political Rights (art. 27)

Office of the High Commissioner for Human Rights, CESCR, General Discussion on the Right to Education (arts. 13 and 14 of the Covenant); Fons Coomans—Background paper: "The Right to Education as a Human Right" (Nov. 1998)

Office of the High Commissioner for Human Rights, CESCR, Implementation of the International Covenant of Economic, Social, and Cultural Rights (General Comment No. 13). The Right to Education (arts. 13 and 14 of the Covenant); State Obligations, Indicators, Benchmarks, and the Right to Education (Nov. 1998)

Protocol of San Salvador to the American Convention on Human Rights (art. 13)

UNESCO Convention against Discrimination in Education (1960)

United Nations International Covenant on Economic, Social, and Cultural Rights—ICESCR (arts. 13 and 14)

United Nations Economic and Social Council, CESCR, The Right to Education (art. 13): .08/12/99. E/C.12/1999/10, CESCR General Comment 13. (General Comments), Implementation of the International Covenant of Economic, Social, and Cultural Rights: Art. 13—The Right to Education.

United Nations Resolution A/RES/53/202, adopted by the Millennium Assembly of the United Nations (1999)

Universal Declaration on Human Rights (art. 26)

Egypt

Capsule Summary

Country Name: Arab Republic of Egypt

Location: Northern Africa, sandwiched by Libya and the Gaza Strip, bordering the Mediterranean Sea and the Red Sea north of Sudan

Total Population: 74,718,797 (July 2003)

Minority and Ethnic Populations: Eastern Hamitic stock (Egyptians, Bedouins, and Berbers) 99%, Greek, Nubian, Armenian, other European (primarily Italian and French) 1%

Languages: Arabic (official); English and French widely understood by educated classes

Religions: Muslim (mostly Sunni) (94%), Coptic Christian, other (6%)

The Arab Republic of Egypt (formerly United Arab Republic) is located in Northeast Africa with an area of 386,900 square miles (1,002,071 square kilometers). As a time-honored bridge state between Africa and Asia, Egypt is one of the oldest world civilizations (approximately 6,000 years). Despite a paucity of arable land (less than three percent) and vast deserts, the annual flooding of the Nile River permitted a number of conquering forces to rule the country throughout the centuries. Strategically situated, Egypt was ruled by the Persians, Greeks, Romans, Byzantines, the French, and various Muslim powers. The Arabs introduced Islam and the Arabic language to the country in the seventh century CE. Subsequently, Egypt was ruled by the Mamluks, Ottoman Turks, and Muhammad Ali (1805–1848). Britain seized control of the Egyptian government and the Suez Canal in 1882. Egypt gained limited autonomy from Britain in 1922, followed by the Free Officers' Revolution in 1952. At the present time, the government of Egypt is a republic, with President Hosni Mubarak as the chief of state. Egypt's GDP (2002 estimate) is $289.8 billion with a per capita income of $4,000 (2002 estimate).

Ethnicities and Minorities

The population of modern Egypt reflects the country's ancestral roots and features Africans, Arabs, Jews, Greeks, Berbers, Persians, Turks, Romans, and other minority groups. Linguistic minorities include communities of Greeks, Armenians, Italians, and other European groups. In addition, Egyptians of Berber origin inhabit the oases of the Western Desert. The largest Berber community is found in the Siwa Oasis. The Berbers are Muslim, with their own language (numerous dialects) and distinctive cultural practices. They are working to foster greater affirmation of their own identity, culture, and language in Egypt.

Nubians live in metropolitan areas such as Cairo and Alexandria in Lower Egypt, and in village locations along the Suez Canal and the Nile River in Upper Egypt. Prior to the construction of the Aswan High Dam (completed in 1970), thousands of Nubians were forced to resettle as a result of the planned flooding of the Nubian Valley. Nubians were unsatisfied with the Egyptian governmental resettlement arrangements, which involved the disruption of familial ties and relocation into government-built housing. As a result, many Nubians migrated to large cities. Some Nubians have elected to receive university training, whereas others have returned to the Lake Nasser area to construct small villages.

The Bedouin form the largest cultural minority in Egypt. They live in the Western and Eastern Deserts and the Sinai Peninsula. Although these Bedouin tribes speak various Arabic dialects, they have their own specific cultural practices. Historically, the Bedouin were nomads who wandered in particular territories in search of water and grazing land for their sheep, goats, and camels. A traditional tribal structure and patrilineage (descent thorough the male line) are key factors in their kinship and marital arrangements, territorial resources, and inheritance practices. At present, most Bedouin tribes have adopted sedentary agricultural lifestyles (acting on government incentives), and others have chosen the route of urban migration. The Bedouin continue to face many cultural, environmental, and social changes, which include some of their youth pursuing college degrees. They are addressing challenges such as poverty-level subsistence, water scarcity, and land degradation.

The Copts are the largest religious minority in Egypt and claim direct lineage from the ancient Egyptians. The present use of the word "Coptic" refers to the Coptic Christians, who believe their church was founded by Saint Mark in Alexandria during the first century CE. The Coptic Church teaches that the Bible was translated into the Coptic language in the second century CE. The Coptic script was developed from the written language of the ancient Egyptians. The Coptic alphabet is based on the Greek alphabet and is still used in the liturgy of the Coptic Church. During the next several centuries, the Coptic Orthodox Church developed its own creeds and religious rituals.

Coptic religious traditions were significantly different from other Eastern churches by the time Constantine made Christianity the official religion of the Roman Empire in the fourth century CE. Desert monasticism became an important expression of the Coptic faith in the third and fourth centuries. Exemplars of the early Coptic Church, including Saint Anthony of Upper Egypt and other desert fathers, helped to spur on the practice of leading spiritual, disciplined lives in hundreds of monasteries, cells, and caves in the Egyptian environs. As a part of the Ottoman Empire millet (religious community) system, the Copts of Egypt experienced a mixture of tolerance and persecution. In the tenth century CE, Coptic was supplanted by Arabic as the principal spoken language. The demise of the millet system in the nineteenth century CE allowed Copts to fill positions as civil servants. Today, urban Copts serve as doctors, lawyers, politicians, professors, and employees in the service industry, hold factory jobs, and work in other professions.

Islamic resurgence in the 1970s in Egypt came coupled with anti-Coptic sentiments that resulted in Coptic churches being burned during clashes between Copts and Muslims. Copts make up the majority of the *zabbaleen*, the traditional rag and bone collectors of garbage in Cairo. The *zabbaleen* began migrating to Cairo in the 1930s and 1940s. Today, these "invisible" members of the Egyptian society use donkey carts (motorized trucks since the early 1990s) to haul back and sort through the refuse in their garbage settlements in the Mokkatam hills on the outskirts of Cairo. The *zabal* face pressure to relocate outside of Cairo and have their livelihood taken over by private-sector companies. Younger *zabbaleen* are pressing the Egyptian government to help increase the number of *zabal* children (especially females) enrolled in schools, establish more effective health care, and enable the *zabal* to manage their own assets.

Religious minorities in Egypt also include the Greek, Armenian, and Syrian Orthodox Eastern Rite churches, Latin Rite and Eastern Catholics, Protestant churches, and a small Jewish population. The linguistic, cultural, and religious minorities of Egypt are an integral part of the changing Egyptian culture. Each minority group seeks to articulate and preserve its own cultural heritage, history, and language.

JEFF BURKE

Further Reading

Ahmed, Leila, *Women and Gender in Islam: Historical Roots of a Modern Debate*, New Haven, Connecticut: Yale University Press, 1992

Atiya, Aziz Suryal, *The Coptic Encyclopedia*, New York: Macmillan, 1991

Bestavros, Azer, *Encyclopedia Coptica: The Christian Coptic Orthodox Church of Egypt*, 2001. http://www.copticnet/cn/Home.html, *Egypt: A Country Study, Library of Congress Country Studies Series*, Washington, DC: U.S. Government Printing Office, 1990

Esposito, John L., *The Oxford Encyclopedia of the Modern Islamic World*, New York: Oxford University Press, 1995

_______, *Unholy War: Terror in the Name of Islam*, New York: Oxford University Press, 2002

Nisan, Mordechai, *Minorities in the Middle East: A History of Struggle and Self-Expression*, Jefferson, North Carolina: McFarland and Company, 1991

El Salvador

Capsule Summary

Country Name: Republic of El Salvador

Location: Middle America, bordering the North Pacific Ocean, between Guatemala and Honduras

Total Population: 6,470,379 (July 2003)

Minority Populations: Amerindian (1%), white (9%)

Languages: Spanish, Nahua (among some Amerindians)

Religions: Roman Catholic (83%) (There is extensive activity by Protestant groups throughout the country; by the end of 1992, an estimated 1 million Protestant evangelicals resided in El Salvador.)

The Republic of El Salvador (República de El Salvador) is the smallest and most densely populated of the seven Central American countries and has a total area of 8,260 square miles (21,476 square kilometers), or about the size of Massachusetts. Its territory is situated entirely on the western side of the isthmus, and it is therefore the only Central American nation that lacks a Caribbean coast. El Salvador is bounded to the south by the Pacific Ocean, to the northwest by Guatemala, and to the north and east by Honduras. Mountains separate the country into three distinct regions: the Pacific Coastal Lowlands, the Central Region (central valleys and plateaus), and the Interior Highlands. Today, the Central Region, with its cattle ranches and coffee plantations, is home to about 75 percent of the population, while the Interior Highlands are thinly populated. Politically, El Salvador is divided into 14 departments and 261 *municipios*.

Before the Spanish Conquest, Salvadoran territory was occupied in the sixteenth century by a number of Amerindian cultures. Of these, the Pocomam, Chortí, and Lenca (all related to the Maya) are more ancient, but the Pipíl were predominant demographically. El Salvador was initially explored by Pedro de Alvarado in 1524 and became a Spanish colony, achieving its independence from Spain in 1821 and from the Central American Federation in 1839. Historically, El Salvador was home to a culturally diverse mix of peoples including blacks, Amerindians, Hispanics, and Northern Europeans. The abandonment of Indian languages and customs was hastened by political repression following an abortive peasant Indian uprising in 1932. By the 1980s the population had become homogeneous in terms of ethnicity and cultural identity. The civil war (1979–1992) between the government and leftist rebels cost about 75,000 lives. About 20 percent of the population is estimated to have left the country, departing in about equal numbers for neighboring countries and the United States. The massive population displacement has been characterized by a general movement of people from the areas of conflict in the north and east to cities in the Central Region.

El Salvador's population numbers about 6,479,379 (July 2003 estimate); almost 92 percent are *mestizo* (of mixed Indian and Spanish extraction), also called *ladino*, a term more commonly used in Central America. *Ladino* denotes individuals who are Spanish speakers and follow Spanish-American lifeways regarding clothing, housing, and food consumption. In addition, the term covers those Indians who have adopted Spanish-American culture. Hence, the term is indicative of cultural rather than biological traits, since indigenous peoples are often categorized as *ladino* for social or political reasons. Approximately five percent of the population is of European origin. Extreme variations in wealth, abject poverty, and contrasting lifestyles have created serious rifts in Salvadoran society that have effectively divided the population into distinctive subcultural groups.

Spanish, the official language, is spoken by virtually all Salvadorans. About three percent of the population is indigenous, but very few Indians have retained their customs and traditions (however, some estimates run to ten percent based on physical or biological—that is, "racial"—parameters). The native communities of Pipíl and Lenca constituted about 60 percent of the Amerindian population throughout the colonial era and into the early decades of independence. The current number of natives is uncertain, but the general estimation counts approximately 60,000 individuals. The Pipíl (also called Pancho Indians) are the most numerous and are located mainly in the southwestern part of the country, clustered near the village of Panchimalco. An estimated 40,000 aborigines speak Pipíl, a dialect of Nahua, and are the descendants of an Aztec Nahua migration from central Mexico at the time of the Spanish Conquest. The Lenca of eastern El Salvador are also defined on linguistic grounds, although nearly all Pipíl, Lenca, and Izalco Indians also speak Spanish. Other aboriginal languages are found only as traces, yet no segment of the population is linguistically distinct. Much of the Salvadoran population has an Indian racial background, but culturally there is no significant aboriginal ethnic sector in the country. Nonetheless, Indian ethnicity is still a rallying point, as evidenced by the popular support of the National Association of Salvadoran Indians (Asociación Nacional Indigena Salvadorena, or ANIS).

Salvadorans are largely Roman Catholic (about 85 percent), although Protestant missionary groups, especially evangelicals, are active and continue to make a significant number of converts among urban *ladinos*.

El Salvador's demographic growth rate during the 1980s was about 2.3 percent per annum but is now estimated at 2.7 percent. Demographic calculations are potentially misleading because an estimated 2 million other Salvadorans live in the United States and are an ever-growing presence and economic force in their homeland, sending back about $2 billion a year (the equivalent of 15 percent of the nation's GDP). Approxi-mately 400,000 Salvadorans live in the Washington, DC, area. The capital city of San Salvador has about 1.7 million people, and an estimated 42 percent of El Salvador's population live in rural areas. Seventeen cities have more than 20,0000 inhabitants, mostly *mestizo/ladino*. Among these are Chalchuapa, Cascatancingo, Delgado, San Marco, San Miguel, Santa Ana, San Miguel, Soyapango, La Unión, Usulután, and Zacatecoluca. In 1985 San Salvador had 395,000 inhabitants, and the dynamic growth of the capital is indicative of massive rural-to-urban migration.

El Salvador's economy has suffered in recent years not only from factory closings but also from natural disasters since 1998, including hurricanes and earthquakes. The GDP per capita income in 2002 was $4,600, and in 1999, 48 percent of the population lived below the poverty line. Industries include food processing, beverages, petroleum, chemicals, fertilizer, textiles, furniture, and light metals, and important exports such as coffee, sugar, corn, rice, beans, and cotton have grown substantially in recent years. The U.S. dollar is the legal tender.

CHARLES C. KOLB

Further Reading

Blutstein, Howard I., Elinor C. Betters, John Cobb, Jr., Jonathan A. Leonard, and Charles M. Townsend, *Area Handbook for El Salvador*, Washington, DC: U.S. Government Printing Office, 1971

Dow, James W., editor, *Encyclopedia of World Cultures, Volume VIII: Middle America and the Caribbean*, Boston: G.K. Hall & Company, 1995

Ember, Melvin, and Carol Ember, editors, *Countries and Their Cultures*, New York: Macmillan Reference, under the auspices of the Human Relations Area Files (Yale University), 2001

Flemion, Philip F., *Historical Dictionary of El Salvador*, Metuchen, New Jersey: Scarecrow Press, 1972

Jackson, Robert H., *Race, Caste, and Status: Indians in Colonial Spanish America*, Albuquerque: University of New Mexico Press, 1999

Lungo, Mario, Economía y sostenibilidad en las zonas exconflictivas en El Salvador, San Salvador: FUNDASAL, 1997

Martínez Peñate, Oscar, *El Salvador diccionario*, San Salvador: Editorial Nuevo Enfoque, 2000

Minority Rights Group, *No Longer Invisible: Afro-Latin Americans Today*, London: Minority Rights Group, 1995

Nickles, Greg, *El Salvador: The People and Culture*, New York: Crabtree, 2002

Zárate Martín, Antonio, *El Salvador*, Anaya, 1988

English

Capsule Summary

Location: England, part of the British Isles adjoining Scotland and Wales; also in diaspora worldwide, but especially Australia

Population: 43,600,000 (2001 in the United Kingdom)

Language: English

Religions: The State religion is the Church of England (Protestant Christian), but people of many different faiths and also atheists are part of the population

The English live in a heavily populated island state, Great Britain or the United Kingdom, of which England is one internal area. The most densely populated area is London, with 4,611 people per square kilometer. There are also 16,500 rural towns and hamlets with a population of less than 10,000. Although many people use the terms England and Britain indiscriminately, Britain consists of Scotland, Wales, England, and Northern Ireland. England has been the dominant political presence in this arrangement, however, and this has led to confusion, particularly in international attitudes. Since the election of Prime Minister Tony Blair and a Labor government in 1997, Scotland, Wales, and Northern Ireland have established separate parliamentary assemblies in an effort to recognize regional differences, national aspirations, and local interests. England has nine government offices attending to its internal regional needs. It also elects 529 representatives to the House of Commons in Westminster and 71 Members of the European Parliament (MEP).

Northern Ireland is the most hotly disputed territory within the United Kingdom, however, and one where two religious populations—Protestant and Catholic—are divided on sectarian principles. England itself has an established church—the Protestant Church of England—dating from the sixteenth century, but its population is not necessarily deeply religious, comparatively speaking (although the minority groups of Catholics, Muslims, and those of other faiths maintain a high level of devotion). Northern Ireland, as both a religious area and one broiling with division, continues to represent the defining symptom of England's colonial past and stands as a reminder of the uneasy relationship that exists between all constituent members of the United Kingdom.

To describe the English as an ethnic minority is surprising, especially to the English themselves. English ethnicity is firmly bound up with myths of world status, which have created the illusion that "Englishness" is a state of origin from whence other histories and national entities grow, usually to overtake their erstwhile homeland (the United States is the penultimate example). The degree to which the English themselves notice these now centuries-old conundrums is best measured by their attitudes on foreign policy issues as well as on customs and cross-cultural matters. The question of the intimate relationships of the English with members of other nations continues to emerge as problematic and often controversial for them. Conflicts between the English and other nations or nationalities often result in a tendency to make strategic alliances with English-speaking countries before neighbors, a fact that underlines the significance of linguistic and cultural ties over geographical ones.

At least since the time of the records of the Alexandrian mathematician Ptolemy (87–150 CE), England, or an inexact approximation of the defined area, was known as Albion. The name still lingers in French slang (*la perfide Albion*) and in the names of football teams (West Bromwich Albion). The English derived their present name from the migration of Angles, who came, roughly, from the area of central Europe presently known as Germany to the British Isles in the fifth century CE (after the withdrawal of the Romans). They joined, and were joined by, a diverse population, which included Frisians and Jutes from Northern Europe and indigenous Celts and Picts. Recent DNA tests have indicated that the west coast of England is still mainly populated by people of Celtic origin. The kingdom of England, which covered a large proportion of the South and West of the present territory, was established in 954 CE. It centered around the royal house of Wessex, and the current royal family honored this historical marker by naming the youngest son Edward, Earl of Wessex on his marriage in 2000. Wessex, however, no longer exists. It is memorialized in the nostalgic novels of Thomas Hardy but has no formal status on the political map. The last successful invasion of England took place in 1066, when William, Duke of Normandy took power. He changed the state language to French and instituted a law of "Englishry." This decreed that if a slain man were found, he must be proven to be English. If he were not, he would be presumed a Norman and the slayer would be required to pay blood money. This decree was repealed in the fourteenth century, no doubt after causing years of ill feeling between English and Norman-French cohabitants. The subsequent period saw a high level of territorial coordination between the emerging powers, but French and English relations ultimately turned to great conflict. A famous citation of belligerent Englishness occurs in *Henry the Fifth,* a play substantially about Englishness in old wars against France, written by the national poet, William Shakespeare.

The English are therefore a highly hybridized people. After William's Norman invasion, immigration continued by other means. England became a seafaring country through necessity of position and climate. The English engaged in the wars against France, the Crusades in the Levant, and from the eighteenth century, multiple colonial campaigns. These activities brought prisoners, migrants, and refugees into England, but they also left English foot soldiers, and later civil servants, to make new lives elsewhere. The slave trade (and indenture system, which was a close approximation) brought Africans and Asians through Liverpool, London, and Bristol. Some of those people traveled on to the Americas, and others stayed, giving yet more diversity and depth to the English profile. In recent years, reverse migration from former colonies has again challenged fixed notions of Englishness as an Anglo-Saxon preserve. The result is contradictory. England has an enviable civility in its political culture. It also has tendencies toward growing prejudice, historical amnesia, and dangerous self-deprecation.

Speaking is perhaps the best clue to how the English divide themselves into factions. This small landmass has an astounding number of regional accents, all of which are inflected by urban and rural distinctions, class differences, and generational shifts. Speaking "posh," talking "scouse," or having a southern burr on one's vowels makes one English, but it also defines one's cultural status. In the 1990s actors would do well to cultivate a slight apparently working class northern voice (not a rural southern accent), whereas Londoners have all recently taken to talking with a strange Estuary twang that is neither Cockney nor Prince Charles. In 2001 a controversy broke out over the popular BBC radio soap opera *The Archers*, when a character on the show was only identified as black by his voice. Questions of political correctness surfaced when listeners were forced to surmise race through the means of speech, as nothing about the character's race was explicitly stated. This local emphasis is the underpinning of football fandom in England. At home, team rivalry is intense; abroad, local differences are forgotten, and a small but significant group of young men define Englishness in the worst possible manner. According to one commentator, Bill Buford, on watching his fellow Englishmen riot at an Italian football ground:

> Someone shouted that we were all English. Why were we running? The English don't run. . . . And so it went on. Having fled in panic, some of the supporters would remember that they were English and this was important and they would remind others that they too were English, and this was also important, and with renewed sense of national identity, they would come abruptly to a halt, turn around, and charge the Italian police. (Paxman, 1999, 247)

STEPHANIE DONALD

See also **Catholics in Northern Ireland; Ireland; Northern Ireland**

Further Reading

Cannadine, David, *Class in Britain*, Penguin Books, 2000

Jack, Ian Robert James, and *Granta*, editors, *London: The Lives of the City (Granta: The Magazine of New Writing, 65, Spring 1999)*, London: Penguin, 1999

Keiller, Patrick, *Robinson in Space and a Conversation with Patrick White*, London: Reaktion Books, 1999
Lawson, Mark, "The Plot Thickens," *The Guardian*, 16 February 2001
Paxman, Jeremy, *The English: A Portrait of a People*, London: Penguin Books, 1999
Runnymede Trust Commission on the Future of Multi-Ethnic Britain and Bhikhu C. Parekh, *The Future of Multi-ethnic Britain: Report of the Commission on the Future of Multi-Ethnic Britain*, London: Profile Books, 2000

Environmental Racism

The Reverend Ben Chavis originated the phrase "environmental racism" in 1982, during his tenure as director of the United Church of Christ's Commission for Racial Justice (CRJ). He was referring to Warren County, North Carolina, and the location of a toxic waste landfill in a county whose residents were predominantly of African-American descent. He argued that Warren County was selected as the site of the toxic waste landfill because its residents were poor and black. In 1987 the CRJ published a report entitled "Toxic Wastes and Race in the United States," which examined the location of hazardous waste sites by race and income. The report concluded that the most important factor in determining where to place these facilities was race.

Subsequent studies have questioned whether race or minority status really is the best predictor of the location for hazardous waste facilities in the United States. A Scripps Howard News Service study of facilities listed on the web site of the U.S. Environmental Protection Agency (EPA) in 13 industrial states did not find a disproportionate number of polluting facilities in minority areas. In Louisiana, which is 31 percent African American, only 18 percent of its industrial plants are located in African-American areas. A recent study of the Boston area found basic differences in how toxic risks were assessed between regions with different racial compositions, distributions of income, and industrial histories. It showed that the Toxic Release Inventory (TRI) was an inappropriate indicator of toxic hazards in deindustrialized urban areas (with higher minority populations). In these communities, the legacy of past industrial activity is best understood in the form of unlicensed abandoned waste sites, which constitute the most prominent toxic hazard. Ironically, since these communities are unable to attract new industries, they face comparatively smaller risks from TRI releases.

Nevertheless, the problem of toxic materials and race in the United States is daunting in scope. For example, the nation's largest landfill, which receives toxic materials from 45 states and several foreign countries, is located in Sumter County, predominantly inhabited by poor African Americans. The primarily African-American and Hispanic Southside neighborhood of Chicago has the greatest concentration of hazardous wastes in the nation. In Houston, Texas, six of eight municipal landfills are in predominantly African-American neighborhoods. In West Dallas, Texas, children residing in one African-American neighborhood suffered irreversible brain damage from exposure to lead at a nearby smelter. Chronic lead exposure is related to a number of disease conditions, including hypertension and a predisposition for violence. Data from the Third National Health and Nutrition survey showed that, out of a representative sample of 14,952 African-American and European-American men and women over the age of 18, the former had between 22 and 13 percent higher blood levels of lead. The blood lead levels were further shown to increase blood pressure in predictable ways. Other studies have validated the generally higher blood lead content of African Americans at all ages compared with both Mexican Americans and European Americans. Pesticide exposure among Hispanic farm workers causes more than 300,000 illnesses a year. A large percentage of these illnesses befall women of childbearing age and children.

Social structures, therefore, can be responsible for the higher lead exposure suffered by African Americans and other minorities. Social structure determines where one lives and the quality of the environment in that location. For example, most children poisoned by lead are exposed in and around their home, with this exposure originating from harmful levels of lead-contaminated dust, deteriorated lead-based paint, and lead-contaminated soil. The two key risk factors linked to elevated blood lead levels in children are living in older housing and living in a low-income household. In addition, the widespread use of silicofluoride additives in drinking water has disproportionately affected African Americans. The role of silicofluorides in transporting heavy metals such as lead and mercury was not tested before their introduction into drinking water in the 1950s. Now over 140 million Americans are exposed to this chemical, which ferries lead into the blood stream from drinking water. The U.S. Centers for Disease Control and Prevention (CDC) considers lead poisoning the foremost environmental health threat to American children. Almost 1 million children (4.4 percent of all preschoolers) have enough lead in their blood to reduce intelligence and attention span, and to cause learning disabilities (and potentially permanent damage) to a child's brain and nervous system. The EPA monitors more than 40 compounds present in pollutants that contain lead.

The test of the environmental racism hypothesis revolves around the question of whether toxic exposure is strongly linked to socially constructed race. Over 53 percent of the toxic waste sites across the country are located within 1 mile (1.6 kilometers) of housing projects that have a minority occupancy over 75 percent.

Proponents of environmental racism charge that minority communities bear greater environmental and health risks than society at large, and that this results from intentional action on the part of the socially dominant group. Before President Bill Clinton's administration (1992–2000), litigants had to prove a hazardous waste site or pollution source was deliberately located in an area because of that area's racial composition and was thus the result of discriminatory intent. In 1992 the Clinton administration allowed arguments of "disparate impact," which only required evidence that the facility had the "effect" of discriminating by differentially exposing minority communities to the environmental hazard. The EPA's Title VI rule applied a disparate impact standard to all permits issued by state and local agencies that received federal funding. Opponents argued that the policy would vastly increase the number of suits brought by environmental activists to halt industrial development. In 1998 the Japanese corporation Shintech abandoned plans to build a polyvinyl chloride production plant in Convent, Louisiana. Some called this a major victory against environmental racism, whereas others—including many of the African-American community leaders in this parish—felt that the failure to build the plant amounted to economic racism against their underemployed constituents.

It seems clear that the meaning and detection of environmental racism remains elusive. Patterns of morbidity and mortality in minority communities are consistent with the idea that these communities are differentially exposed to hazardous wastes. Yet scholarly research is equivocal concerning exactly how socially defined race and social dominance combine to produce this disparate impact.

JOSEPH L. GRAVES, JR.

Further Reading

Bryant, B., and P. Mohai, editors, *Race and the Incidence of Environmental Hazards: A Time for Discourse*, Boulder, Colorado: Westview Press, 1992

Bullard, R., "Dismantling Environmental Racism in the USA," *Local Environment*, 4, no. 1 (1999)

Cole, L., *From the Ground Up: Environmental Racism and the Rise of the Environmental Justice Movement*, New York: New York University Press, 2001

Krieg, E., "Methodological Considerations in the Study of Toxic Waste," *Social Science Journal*, 35, no. 2 (1998)

Nordquist, J., *Environmental Racism and the Environmental Justice Movement: A Bibliography,* Santa Cruz, California: Reference and Research Services, 1995

Payne, H., "Green Redlining," *Reason*, 30, no. 5 (1998)

Equal Opportunity

This complex and contested concept often assumes shared meaning that, on further exploration, proves to be superficial or erroneous. Often, its meaning is reduced only to "avoiding unjust discrimination and prejudice" or "treating everybody the same." A broader meaning entails that all individuals have an equal opportunity to reach their potential by developing their particular talents. In this sense, it is also related to the debate over positive action. Equal opportunity can be analyzed on both a societal and an organizational level.

To understand the concept, it is useful to distinguish at least four types of equality.

The first of these, formal equality, refers to equality under the law (everyone is equal and entitled to equal treatment under the law). The second, equality of opportunity is the provision of equal access to institutions and social positions among relevant social groups. Third, equality of condition is a variable that actually allows for equal access through securing equal circumstances of life for different social groups. The argument here is that inequalities of condition obstruct real equality of opportunity because all those who are competing do not start from the same point (leveling the playing field). Fourth, equality of outcome refers to the application of different policies or processes to different social groups in order to transform inequalities of condition at the beginning into equalities at the end. This is often viewed as a radical approach to equal opportunity and is linked to positive action that aims to compensate for the disadvantages that restrict equal opportunities. Proponents of this concept claim that the idea of preferential treatment for disadvantaged groups is, despite its limitations, one of the few policy tools capable of breaking through the self-perpetuating cycle of deeply embedded inequalities. Critics argue that this approach requires considerable intrusion on individual liberties and the family, and that it is both unrealistic and impossible to enforce.

However, this categorization is regarded as problematic, as it may seem that formal equality, equal opportunity, and equality of outcome are mutually incompatible.

The Affirmative Action Plans required of federal contractors in the United States can serve as a useful example: The composition of the workforce of a business ought to reasonably reflect the ethnic makeup of the local population, both in the numbers employed and their positions within the business hierarchy. However, there is a major problem: The proportion of minorities that contractors must endeavor to replicate in their workforce is a measure of the current situation, which is itself the result of past discrimination. There is a difference between the concept of equality of opportunity as applied to individuals and to groups of people, identifiable by their color, culture, or ethnicity.

Most academic debate about the concept of justice starts with John Rawls's famous difference principle, which asserts that inequalities in the distribution of scarce goods (power, money, access to health care) are justified only if they serve to increase the advantage of the least-favored groups in society. The difference principle in Rawls's theory of justice and fairness has lower priority than the principle of greatest equal liberty and the principle of equality of fair opportunity (Marshall 1996).

Bhikhu Parekh argues that

> equal treatment involves [the] absence of direct or indirect and institutionalised discrimination. The law should require all public institutions periodically to examine the hidden biases of their rules and procedures, and should set up appropriate bodies such as the Commission for Racial Equality in the UK and the Equal Employment Opportunity agency in the USA.

Moreover, he claims that "positive equality requires equality of rights and opportunities," including cultural rights, as ensured by the politics of recognition. Parekh further notes that "all citizens should enjoy equal opportunities to acquire the capacities and skills needed to function in society and to pursue their self-chosen goals equally effectively," and that additional help or "equalising measures are justified on [the] grounds of justice as well as social integration and harmony" (Parekh 2000, 210–211).

According to Parekh,

> A theory of equality grounded in human uniformity is both philosophically incoherent and morally problematic. Equality involves equal freedom or opportunity to be different, and treating human beings equally requires us to take into account both their similarities and differences. (p. 240)

In other words, equality requires differential treatment. Parekh also notes that "Equality before the law and equal protection of the law, too, need to be defined in a culturally sensitive manner" (p. 241).

Many policy makers argue that the principle of equal opportunity, in its broadest sense, enshrines the principle of merit. Thus, in recruitment, when positive action is either taken in the form of advertising or training, the final selection for posts must be made according to the principle of "the best person for the job." In other words, positive action should not be committed to a preference for a less-qualified candidate.

Very often, equal opportunity is used in its narrow sense as equality of access. According to Ellis Cashmore (1996), the principle of equal opportunity was appropriated by the conservatives in the late 1970s and used as an alternative to policies that emphasized equality of results, as opposed to equality of opportunities. He argues that it was a

> perfect complement to the conservative egalitarianism that was preeminent in the US and Britain through the 1980s and 1990s. The appeal to market

forces, absence of government in the expansion of opportunities, and the opposition to the granting of special privileges or rights made it a successful weapon with which to challenge some forms of modern liberalism. In contrast to policies that urged an active role for government in the advancement of disadvantaged groups, conservative egalitarianism emphasised laissez-faire and "supply-side" economic theory as the way to correct the glaring inequalities in the distribution of resources.

Apart from the societal level of theory and practice, equal opportunity policies can be analyzed on the organizational level. Barbara Bagilhole (1997) provides the following categorization of different approaches to equal opportunity in organizations (pp. 183–184, 37–39): (1) The minimalist position reflects a colorblind approach while complying with antidiscrimination legislation; (2) the liberal perspective (also referred to as the short agenda) focuses on the equality of treatment, assuming that a level playing ground will ensure equal opportunities, and recognizing that institutional discrimination may exist in the form of unfair procedures and practices; and (3) the radical perspective (referred to as the long agenda) focuses on the equality of outcomes, as opposed to procedures, and rejects the individualistic conceptions of fairness and promoting positive action. Equal opportunity programs, as a part of general organizational change theory for managing diversity approaches, aims to increase productivity and meet employee needs through challenging the cultures of organizations.

LAURA LAUBEOVA

Further Reading

Bagilhole, Barbara, *Equal Opportunities and Social Policy: Issues of Gender, Race, and Disability*, London: Longman, 1997

Blakemore, K., and R.F. Drake, *Understanding Equal Opportunity Policies*, London: Prentice Hall, 1996

Cashmore, Ellis, *Dictionary of Race and Ethnic Relations*, London: Routledge, 1996

Howe, Kenneth R., *Understanding Equal Educational Opportunity (Social Justice, Democracy, and Schooling)*, Advances in Contemporary Educational Thought Series, New York: Teachers College Press, 1997

Marshall, Gordon, editor, *The Concise Oxford Dictionary of Sociology*, Oxford and New York: Oxford University Press, 1996

Mithaug, Dennis E., *Equal Opportunity Theory (Fairness in Liberty for All)*, Thousand Oaks, California: Sage Publications, 1996

Parekh, Bhikhu, *Rethinking Multiculturalism: Cultural Diversity and Political Theory*, London: Macmillan Press, 2000

Roemer, John E., *Equality of Opportunity*, Cambridge, Massachusetts: Harvard University Press, 2000

Eritrea

Capsule Summary

Location: Eastern Africa, bordering the Red Sea, between Djibouti and Sudan

Total Population: 4,362,254 (July 2003)

Ethnic Populations: Ethnic Tigrinya (50%), Tigre and Kunama (40%), Afar (4%), Saho (Red Sea coast dwellers) (3%), other (3%)

Languages: Tigrinya, Tigre, To-Bedawi, Kunama, Nara, Afar, Bilen, Saho, Arabic, English

Religions: Orthodox Christianity, Islam, Protestantism, Catholicism, traditional religion

Eritrea is a recent country in the Horn of Africa, located on the shore of the Red Sea and bordering Ethiopia, Sudan, and Djibouti. It was officially founded as an independent state in May 1993 (de facto in May 1991) after an almost 30-year armed nationalist struggle against a repressive Ethiopian regime (imperial rule up to 1974, and a military-Marxist dictatorship from 1974 to 1991). The country is currently a one-party republic. The total population is about 4.3 million, with about 300,000 refugees in Sudan and about 400,000 people living in other countries, mainly in the West. At least 12 languages are spoken in Eritrea, not counting dialectical differences. The dominant ones are Tigrinya and Tigre (of the Semitic language family). Others belong to the Cushitic and Nilo-Saharan language families. English is used in secondary and higher education, and Arabic by traders and for Islamic religious purposes. In 2002 the GDP per capita income was $700.

Eritrea was created in 1890 as an Italian colony in a region that had been linked to Ethiopia for about 2000 years. In 1941 Italy lost World War II and had to give up Eritrea. Britain became the mandatory power under a United Nations (UN) arrangement, pending the final status of the territory. This lasted until 1952 when, after a UN report and vote, and with the formal consent of the Eritrean Assembly, the country was federated with Ethiopia, a move strongly contested by most of Eritrea's Muslim population. The federation was abrogated in 1962, when Eritrea was included in Ethiopia. After 29 years of resistance and armed struggle, the country became independent in 1993 (de facto in 1991, when in Ethiopia another guerrilla movement took over state power).

The current Eritrean government is led by a unity party (People's Front for Democracy and Justice) that emanated from the guerrilla movement, the Eritrean Peoples' Liberation Front (EPLF). Although of mixed composition, the EPLF found its basis of support mainly among the Tigrinya speakers of the central highlands, the dominant population group in the country, which makes up about 55 percent of the total population of about 4 million.

Eritrea is a multiethnic country with at least nine ethnolinguistic groups, the borders of which are, however, difficult to draw. The nine officially designated groups, or "nationalities," as they are called in state parlance, are, in the order of their numerical strength, the Tigrinya, Tigre, Hidarib (Beni Amer), Afar, Kunama, Saho, Bilen, Nara, and Rashaida. All of them are indigenous groups except for the Rashaida, who are relatively recent (early nineteenth century) Arabic-speaking migrants from the Arabian peninsula. The Hidarib and Rashaida have sections in Sudan, and the Tigrinya, Afar, and Kunama also live in Ethiopia. Slightly more than half of the Eritrean population are (nominal) Christians of Orthodox faith, with minorities of Catholics and Protestants (the Tigrinya, Bilen, and part of the Kunama), whereas the rest are Muslims (the Afar, Hidarib, Tigre, Rashaida, Nara, Saho, and part of the Kunama) or adhere to traditional religions (e.g., a large part of the Kunama). In a political and cultural sense, one might consider the eight non-Tigrinya-speaking groups as "minority" groups because of their rather different sociocultural and religious characteristics and their relatively marginal position vis-à-vis the central state elite.

There is a significant diversity in the lifestyles and economic activities of these groups, and cultural and religious pluralism has been a characteristic of Eritrean society for ages. Nor is one language common to all groups, although most people are at least bilingual. This diversity had its effect in the liberation struggle, as the initial revolt against Ethiopia rule was started by Muslims (mainly Beni Amer) in the lowlands. They had founded the Eritrean Liberation Movement (ELM) in 1960. Later, it spread to the Tigrinya highlanders, who became dominant in the movement when internal dissent led to the emergence of the EPLF. Tension between the lowlanders and the highlanders that was based on a history of armed conflict and raiding still persists, although much effort has been made to defuse it within the framework of "nation-building."

Eritrean society was traditionally a complex mix of groups tied into hierarchical relationships, especially in the Tigre lowlands, where a quasi-feudal lord–vassal system existed. Significant animosity between some of these groups also existed, such as the Tigrinya with the Afar, the Tigre with the Kunama the Beni Amer with the Kunama and Nara, and the Nara with the Kunama. Conflicts over cattle (raiding), pasture, and land were not rare. The British Mandate period did not improve things and even led to an aggravation of conflict between various groups. Nor could the British protect vulnerable minorities such as the Kunama against the predations of others.

Under Ethiopian rule and after independence, the smaller minorities such as the Afar, Kunama, Saho, Rashaida, and Bilen remained marginal politically, although they produced highly influential individuals, both in the period of imperial rule and in the ELM.

In independent Eritrea, the aim is to forge one nation-state while respecting the existence of ethnocultural differences. The current government has tried to work with traditional leaders of the various groups to translate its policy and command support from them. The expression of language, culture, and folklore of the various "nationalities," including the Tigre group, is officially stimulated. Local languages are used in primary education and literacy programs. Literature in the native languages is encouraged and frequent "cultural shows" and performances of music, plays, songs, and dances are staged. Teams of researchers from the Ministry of Information and Culture also carry out "ethnographic surveys" of the various groups, to be used in policy preparation.

Any *political* expression of ethnic identity, such as in political parties or associations, is not condoned. However, beyond the rhetorical level, exactly what the policy of the new Eritrean government is toward ethnic groups and how it turns out in practice are not clear because of a lack of independent research in the country. The news reported from opposition movements and other observers suggests that minorities such as the Beni Amer, Tigre, Kunama, and Afar are unsatisfied with national policy. The Kunama, who live in the large western plains, which are very suitable for agriculture, have seen massive settlement of Tigrinya highlanders on their land because of land scarcity and exhausted soils in their home areas. They receive land from the government (as by law all land in Eritrea is state land), and this has led to the Kunama becoming a minority even in their own ancestral region. Furthermore, because the agricultural systems of the two groups differ widely, the Kunama complain that the newcomers do not "respect the land." Several local clashes have been reported. Among pastoralists such as the Tigre, Saho, and Afar, there is dissent over the lack of protection of pastoral land rights in the Eritrean Land Proclamation (1995), sedentarization plans, and religious policies. In sum, there seems to be no accepted national policy or effective formula to handle the socioeconomic, religious, and cultural rights of minorities apart from the national integration ideology. This may create more problems in the future, especially with regard to the religious cleavage between Christian and Muslims and the land question.

In 1998 a two-and-a-half-year border war with Ethiopia erupted and was ended under the auspices of the UN in 2000. Although the two nations have agreed to abide by a 2002 independent boundary commission delimitation decision, demarcation, which is scheduled to begin in 2003, has been hampered by technical delays and postponed indefinitely. Eritrea currently hosts a UN peacekeeping operation that is monitoring the border region.

JON ABBINK

See also **Ethiopia**

Further Reading

Joireman, Sandra F., "The Minefield of Land Reform: Comments on the Eritrean Land Proclamation," *Journal of Modern African Studies*, 95, 1996

Killion, Tom, *Historical Dictionary of Eritrea*, Lanham, Maryland, and London: Scarecrow Press, 1998

Naty, Alexander, "Linguistic Diversity in Eritrea," *Africa* (Roma), 55, no. 2 (1999)

Pool, David, *Eritrea: Toward Unity in Diversity*, London: Minority Rights Group, 1997

Taddia, Irma, "Post-Twentieth-Century Eritrea," *Northeast African Studies*, 5, no. 1 (New Series) (1998)

Tekle, M. Woldemikael, "The Cultural Construction of Eritrean Nationalist Movements," in *The Rising Tide of Cultural Pluralism*, edited by Crawford Young, Madison: University of Wisconsin Press, 1993

Eskimo, *See* **Inuit**

Estonia

Capsule Summary

Country Name: Republic of Estonia

Location: Eastern Europe, bordering the Baltic Sea and Gulf of Finland, between Latvia and Russia

Total Population: 1,408,556 (July 2003)

Language: Estonian (official), Russian, Ukrainian, Finnish, other

Religions: Evangelical Lutheran, Russian Orthodox, Estonian Orthodox, Baptist, Methodist, Seventh-Day Adventist, Roman Catholic, Pentecostal, Word of Life, Jewish

Estonia is located in Northeastern Europe, bordering Russia in the east, Latvia in the south, and Finland in the north (divided by the narrow Gulf of Finland). The country has a land area of 45,227 square kilometers (17,462 square miles), and it is one of the smallest in the former Soviet Union. The strategic importance of Estonia is in its location on a major sea route connecting Russia with Western Europe.

In 2003 the population of Estonia was estimated at over 1.4 million. It is predominantly urban, with around 74 percent of the people living in cities and towns. The country's capital city, Tallinn, is home to 408,329 people (2000), or 35 percent of the population. Estonia has a negative population growth rate of –0.49 percent (2003 estimate), and its population is expected to decline to 1,350,000 by 2010. Estonia has one of the highest population densities in the former Soviet Union, standing at around 31 people per square kilometer (82 people per square mile).

Estonia is a parliamentary democracy. It is the legal successor of the independent government that existed from 1918, after independence was gained from the Russian Empire (Russia acquired Estonia from Sweden in 1721), until 1940, when it was annexed by the Soviet Union. The country declared its independence from the Soviet Union in 1991 and introduced a new constitution in 1992. The *Riigikogu,* the Parliament, is a unicameral 101-member national legislative body. The president is the head of state, with limited executive authority, and is elected by a two-thirds majority of the *Riigikogu.* The president nominates the prime minister, who selects a cabinet of ministers and heads the executive branch. Since independence, all political parties, including opposition organizations and radical nationalists groups, have been functioning freely in the country, although they are required to pass the barrier of having five percent of the total votes to gain representation in the *Riigikogu.* Voters' preferences are not necessarily divided according to the ethnic makeup of the country, despite its multiethnic composition. For example, over a third of the ethnic Russians in Estonia supported secession from the Soviet Union in a March 1991 Referendum on Independence, even though the pro-Moscow Interfront movement, which was very active in the early 1990s, recruited its supporters largely among the ethnic Russians. Despite some existing tensions between the Estonians and the ethnic minorities, who are predominantly of Russian origin, there have never been militant conflicts or confrontations in the country.

Estonia is a multiethnic country with a diverse population. Ethnic Estonians, who are ethnically and linguistically close to the Finns, make up 64 percent of the country's population. Ethnic Russians make up the largest minority, around 28 percent of the population. Additionally, ethnic Ukrainians make up 2.5 percent, Belarusians make up 1.5 percent, Finns make up 1.0 percent, and various other groups together make up the remaining 3 percent of the population. The current ethnic structure was formed after World War II, when the Soviet government encouraged migration from various parts of the Russian Federation and forcibly deported a significant number of ethnic Estonians to other parts of the Soviet Union. This policy led to an increase in the proportion of ethnic minorities in the Estonian population, from 10 percent in 1940 to 39.5 percent in 1989 (based on the last Soviet census). Many migrants settled in Narva, an industrial center located in the northeast of the country on the border with Russia, and in Tallinn. After independence in 1991, 2.9 percent, or around 41,700 residents, opted to leave the country, mainly for Russia. In the 1990s there were reports that illegal migrants from South Asia and the Middle East had begun to arrive to Estonia and other Baltic republics, aiming to migrate further to Western Europe. Their numbers, however, still constitute an insignificant proportion of the Estonian population, although they may become a new source of migration into the country.

The Estonian language, which is distinct from both Russian and Latvian, was made the official language of the country in 1989. This represented a dramatic reversal from the policy of the previous government, which encouraged the speaking of Russian. According to the 1989 census, approximately 80 percent of ethnic Russians in Estonia did not speak Estonian because the Russian language was widely used in education, mass media, and everyday life. Moreover, ethnic Russians occupied important social and economic niches, where they were employed chiefly in the large industrial enterprises and in the defense sector. In postindependence Estonia, the language policy has been at the center of political debates and of disagreements between the Estonian government and ethnic minorities. This is mainly because the Law on Citizenship, which was adopted in 1992, automatically granted citizenship to all people who had lived in the country before 1940 and to their descendants, and it required all people who arrived after 1940 to be "competent" in the Estonian language in order to obtain Estonian citizenship. Under this criterion, most of the representatives of the Russian-speaking minority (Belarusians, Russians, and the Ukrainians) became "noncitizens," even though many of them had lived and worked in the country for decades. Additionally, the existing regulation requires knowledge of the Estonian language in some categories of civil service, defense, and security services. The introduction of Estonian as the state's official language, and especially the citizenship legislation, led to a rise in tensions between the Estonian majority and ethnic minorities, and in the case of Russian-dominated Narva, there were demands for secession or at least regional autonomy. In the wake of such confrontation, and based on criticism from the Conference on Security and Cooperation in Europe (CSCE), the Estonian government revised its position on citizenship considerably. In 1992 it granted citizenship to several hundred non-Estonians for "special services"; in 1993 it amended the Law on Aliens, abandoning the requirement for all noncitizens to obtain residence and work permits within 2 years; in 1994 it reduced the qualification for residence from 16 to 10 years; and in 1998 it allowed the children of "stateless" residents to become citizens.

As in all countries of the former Soviet Union where religious activities were strongly discouraged, after independence, the people of Estonia experienced growing interest in religion, largely as it related to the process of strengthening national identity. The majority of ethnic Estonians (80 percent) practice Lutheranism, whereas most of the ethnic minorities (more than 90 percent) belong to the Russian Orthodox church. There are also many other small religious communities where individuals are allowed to practice their beliefs without restriction. However, the churches have largely been kept outside political life, and despite growing religious practice and the growing influence of the churches, religion does not play an important role in Estonian political affairs.

Since the last Russian troops left in 1994, Estonia has been free to promote economic and political ties with Western Europe. Rapid economic transformation after 1991 largely contributed to political stability in the country. The Estonian government was quickly able to privatize most of the enterprises in the industrial and agricultural sectors, to establish one of the most stable currency systems in the former Soviet Union (the Estonian krooni was pegged to the German mark), and to achieve one of the highest GDP per capita among the former Soviet countries. Estonia's GDP per capita income in 2002 was $11,000. Estonia joined the World Trade Organization in November 1999 and was invited to join the European Union in 2002. Services and manufacturing are the two main pillars of the Estonian economy, contributing 69.7 and 30.7 percent, respectively, to the GDP. Nevertheless, despite the macroeconomic stability and success in structural changes, these economic changes led to a steady decline in the living standards among pensioners, the rural population, and women with children. In 1998 the United Nations Development Programme's Human Development Index ranked Estonia 46th, behind Hungary, Poland, and the United Arab Emirates but ahead of Costa Rica and Croatia.

Rafis Abazov

Further Reading

Chinn, Jeff, and Robert Kaiser, *Russians as the New Minority: Ethnicity and Nationalism in the Soviet Successor States*, New York: Westview Press, 1996

Kask, P., "National Radicalization in Estonia: Legislation on Citizenship and Related Issues," *Nationalities Papers*, 22, no. 2 (1994)

Narodnyi Kongress: Sbornik Materialov Kongressa Narodnogo Fronta Estonii, Tallinn, Kongress, 1–2 Okt. 1988 (in Russian)

Raun, U. Tolvo, *Estonia and Estonians*, Stanford, California: Hoover Institution, Stanford University, 2001

Smith, Graham, editor, *The Baltic States: The National Self-Determination of Estonia, Latvia, and Lithuania*, New York: St. Martin's Press, 1996

Spilling, Michael, *Estonia*, Tarrytown, New York: Marshall Cavendish, 1999

Taagepera, Rein, *Estonia: Return to Independence*, New York: Westview Press, 1993

Ethiopia

Capsule Summary

Location: Horn of Africa, bordering Eritrea, Djibouti, Somalia, and Sudan

Total Population: 66,557,553 (July 2003)

Ethnic Populations: Oromo (40%), Amhara and Tigre (32%), Sidamo (9%), Shankella (6%), Somali (6%), Afar (4%), Gurage (2%), other (1%)

Languages: Amharic, Oromiffa, Tigrinya, Gurage, Sidama, Wolayta, Somali, English, and about 50 minority languages

Religions: Orthodox Christianity (52%), Islam (38%), Evangelical Christianity (5%), animist (12%), other (3%–8%)

The Federal Democratic Republic of Ethiopia, the dominant country in the Horn of Africa with nearly 66 million people, is an exceedingly complex state, with dozens of linguistic and ethnic groups within its borders. Contrary to a common perception, however, these groups can only with great difficulty be identified as separate units. The conventional view of Ethiopia's ethnic groups always refers to the following groups: the Oromo, Amhara, and Tigray as the three largest communities, followed by the Sidama, Somali, Gurage, Wolayta, and Kafa.

Ethiopia's languages number more than 50 and belong to several linguistic families: Ethio-Semitic (e.g., Amharic, Tigrinya, Gurage, Adere), Cushitic (Oromiffa, Somali, Sidama, Konso), Omotic (Wolayta, Maale, Aari, Dizi), and Nilo-Saharan (Mursi, Majang, Me'en, Bertha). In the last two families, one often finds smaller minorities numbering no more than 10 to 20,000 people. Amharic is the language with the largest number of mother-tongue speakers, even though the Oromo are most likely the largest ethnic group. It is the oldest independent country in Africa and one of the oldest in the world—at least 2,000 years.

History

Historically, one could say that minority status of the diverse ethnic groups in Ethiopia has been related to their relative position with regard to the centers of power. In this respect, the Oromo, who entered the Ethiopian highland domain in a large migration movement in the mid-sixteenth century, have been a minority group for most of their history. The same goes for the Afar, the Somali, or the Agaw, an indigenous, Cushitic-speaking population of the central highlands.

Ethiopia, which had its own peculiar traditions of state formation in both the northern and southern highlands as well as in the eastern lowland plains, was historically the scene of constant interaction and mixing of populations. Many of the groups, including the formerly dominant Amhara and the Oromo, are themselves the product of the mixing and assimilation of traditions, of intermarriage, and of creolization of language, customary law traditions, and world views. However, a prestige hierarchy of ethnolinguistic groups has existed according to their place and role in the national state structure, certainly until 1974, when the imperial state collapsed. In this hierarchical, feudalist structure, the Amhara from the region of Shoa have largely been dominant since the late thirteenth century, together with sections of the Tigray, Eritrean, and Shoan Oromo people who spoke Amharic. The resulting "civilizational model"—associated with the state and with the Christian faith as the ideology of royal legitimacy—tended to generate disdain for the minority groups excluded from power. These minority groups (basically a politicocultural and not a numerical concept) were defined based on a mixture of ethnocultural and regional criteria: A neat overlap among regions, languages, and ethnic identities never existed. There were also traditional oppositions between groups living as pastoralists in the lowlands and peasants and landed aristocrats in the highlands. Such an opposition could be crosscut by religious differences (e.g., the Orthodox Christians and the Muslims).

Ethiopia was never colonized, except for Eritrea from 1890 to 1941 (which previously was part of the Ethiopian cultural and political domain) and 5 years of Fascist Italian occupation of the country in 1936–1941. The Ethiopian highland state dates back to the heritage of the Aksum Empire (first to ninth century CE), but was redefined in the thirteenth century when a Christian dynastic ("Solomonic") tradition was reestablished with reference to the Aksum state. In the course of its political evolution, Ethiopia was also influenced by state formation processes in neighboring areas, such as the sultanates of the Afar and Somali in the eastern lowlands (Adal, Harar); the Kafa, Hadiya, and Wolayta kingdoms; and the Oromo states of the late eighteenth and nineteenth centuries. The political elite of the highland state, although dominated by Amharic speakers, was not a closed set but incorporated elite groups from the Gurage, Tigray, and Oromo communities over the past centuries. Furthermore, although an ideology of political and religious unity was often proclaimed by the emperors, the reality was that the state was more of a regional federation than an uncontested unit, with local rulers claiming autonomy while paying tribute. Even under the Shoan Amhara emperor Menelik II (reigned 1889–1913), who conquered large territories along the highland state in the 1880s and 1890s, a system of regional autonomy and continuity of local authority structures was maintained.

Only under Emperor Haile Selassie I (1930–1974) did the central state powerfully affirm itself (with a strong program of modernization of bureaucratic institutions, the army, and the educational system). This state reached its demise in the totalitarian and bloody regime led by the army officer Mengistu Haile-Mariam (1977–1991), a Marxist-inspired dictator whose regime provoked economic crisis, societal havoc, and persistent armed rebellion in many areas. Haile-Mariam's regime was chased out by a coalition of ethnoregional rebel forces in May 1991.

The present Ethiopian state—since that year led by the former insurgent movement, the Ethiopian Peoples' Revolutionary Democratic Front, or EPRDF (with, at its core, the Tigray Peoples' Liberation Front, or TPLF)—has followed an "ethnofederal" political model based on prescriptive ethnic identities for Ethiopia's citizens. The ideology is based on the self-determination of nationalities (ethnic groups), with an ultimate possibility of secession. The TPLF emerged as a rebel movement aimed at political autonomy for its home base, the northern Tigray region, then later extended its model—apparent devolution, but keeping control at the center—to the whole country. In practice, the Tigray minority (some nine percent of the population) largely held the reins of power and installed parallel parties in the various regions drawn from the majority groups in that region. These parties were not fully representative grassroots organizations but stood under the patronage of the EPRDF-TPLF. This model of ethnicized politics has led to a significant overhaul of the state structure and the political system of Ethiopia, ostensibly giving vent to ethnocultural feelings and long-suppressed rights, but also evoking violent new oppositions. Diversity of identity is emphasized over and above unity and shared characteristics. Ethnic identity became an ideological mechanism for claiming resources in the widest sense. In this new order, ethnoregional conflicts between disadvantaged groups have, unfortunately, not diminished but increased. Often, any group conflict is now formulated (by those involved) much more in ethnic than in other terms, thus setting up alleged ethnic groups, such as the Gedeo and the Guji, or the Amhara and the Oromo, or the Afar and the Tigray, against each other. Numerous local clashes have occurred between groups in a idiom that used to be rare in Ethiopia. Another result of this model is the perception that democratic rights have to be defined *through* ethnicity instead of on a pragmatic, problem-oriented basis, and this is controversial for many. It may even solidify a new ethnic inequality structure.

It is true that the Ethiopian ethnic mosaic, as a favorite metaphor goes, has indeed received breathing space under the new political dispensation, as evident in language, cultural, and education policies: People are not penalized or publicly looked down upon if they speak their mother tongue. However, Ethiopia has not yet found a good solution to the challenge of what is socially and economically an interconnected, multiethnic society in which ethnic identities are nested and not mutually exclusive.

Ethiopia's poverty-stricken economy is based on agriculture, which accounts for half of its GDP, 85 percent of exports, and 80 percent of total employment. However, agricultural production (of cereals, oilseed, sugar cane, potatoes, cattle, and sheep) suffers from frequent drought and poor cultivation practices. Ethiopia's war with Eritrea in 1999–2000 and recurrent drought have buffeted the economy, in particular coffee production. In 2002 the GDP per capita income was only $700. Ethiopia is landlocked and, by agreement with Eritrea, was using the ports of Assab and Massawa; however, since the border dispute with Eritrea flared, Ethiopia has used the port of Djibouti for nearly all of its imports.

Jon Abbink

See also **Eritrea**

Further Reading

Abbink, Jon, "Ethnicity and Constitutionalism in Contemporary Ethiopia," *Journal of African Law*, 41, no. 2 (1997)

Assefa, Hizkias, "Crucible of Civilization and Conflict: Ethiopia," in *Arms and Daggers in the Heart of Africa: Studies on Internal Conflicts*, edited by P. Anyang'Nyong'o, Nairobi: Academy Science Publishers, 1993

Clapham, Christopher, "Boundary and Territory in the Horn of Africa," in *African Boundaries: Barriers, Conduits, and Opportunities*, edited by P. Nugent and A.I. Asiwaju, London: Pinter, 1996

Donham, Donald L., and Wendy James, editors, *The Southern Marches of Imperial Ethiopia: Essays in History and Social Anthropology*, New York: Cambridge University Press, 2001; 1st edition, 1986

James, Wendy, Donald L. Donham, Eisei Kurimoto, and Alessandro Triulzi, editors, *Remapping Ethiopia: Socialism and After*, Oxford: James Currey, 2002

Olmstead, Judith, *Woman between Two Worlds: Portrait of an Ethiopian Rural Leader*, Urbana and Chicago: University of Illinois Press, 1997

Zewde, Bahru, *A History of Modern Ethiopia, 1855–1991*, Oxford: James Currey; Athens, Ohio: Ohio University Press; Addis Ababa: Addis Ababa University Press, 2nd edition, 2001

Ethiopian Jewry (Falasha)

Capsule Summary

Location: Israel, Ethiopia (mostly Northwestern)
Total Population: 70,000–95,000
Language: Hebrew, Amharic
Religion: Jewish

The most widely used term to signify the group of people of Jewish heritage coming from Ethiopia is "Falasha." However, this is a derogatory term meaning "the wandering ones" in the Ethiopian language of Amharic, but also referring to them as "exiles" or "strangers." Some scholars prefer "Beta Israel," meaning "House of Israel," but "Ethiopian Jewry" is the most neutral term.

Ethiopian Jews come predominantly from the Tigrean plateau, the surrounds of Lake Tana, and the town of Gondar in northwestern Ethiopia. Ethiopian Jews have always been a minority in Ethiopia. Today, approximately 26,000 people in Ethiopia claim to be of Ethiopian-Jewish heritage. The majority of the population, about 70,000, presently lives in Israel.

Israeli recognition of Ethiopian-Jewish identity came in 1975. The basis of Israeli recognition lies in the possibility that Ethiopian Jews are the descendants of the lost tribe of Dan, one of the ten Hebrew tribes carried away by Assyrians in 722 BCE. This, however, is far from certain. Ethiopian Jews have commonly seen themselves as the progeny of King Solomon and the Queen of Sheba or her handmaiden. Other accounts link Ethiopian Jews to exiles from the Assyrian conquest; the offspring of those who fled Israel after the Babylonians destroyed the First Temple in 586 BCE, or to the Agau tribes, who are thought to be Ethiopia's indigenous people.

Most common among scholars, however, is the belief that Ethiopian Judaism is rooted in the political processes that took place in Ethiopia between the fourteenth and sixteenth centuries CE. Disparate groups living around Lake Tana were brought together through a gradual process of economic and land disenfranchisement within a Christian Amharic context. This distinction of nonreligious identification recognizes that Ethiopian-Jewish identity has changed over time among ethnic, caste, and clan identities. As a minority culture, Ethiopian Jews have had to adapt as a group to changes in and challenges from the Amharic monarchy and other exogenous forces. Following this view, not only has Ethiopian-Jewish identity been constructed over several centuries, but the religious system of Ethiopian Jews itself is actually a growth of the Christian-Ethiopian tradition.

Although there is reason to doubt the connection of Ethiopian Jewry to the lost tribe of Dan or King Solomon, there is no doubt that today they stand as devout Jews. Certain Ethiopian-Jewish rituals and customs are distinct from Western and Eastern Judaism, but the basic practices are unequivocally the same. Their oppression over the centuries is hallmarked by the religious persecution they faced in Ethiopia in the twentieth century. With their recognition of Ethiopian-Jewish religious claims, the state of Israel obligated itself to protect them. Under the Law of Return, Israel must assist anyone who is Jewish. (The Israel Knesset, or Parliament, in 1950 passed the Law of Return, which states that "every Jew has a right to immigrate to this country," thereby ending 2,000 years of wandering.)

The first challenge to the state of Israel came in 1984 as the suffering of Ethiopian Jews mounted under Ethiopian strongman, Mengistu Haile-Mariam. In a breathtaking show of organization called Operation Moses, Israel airlifted approximately 12,000 Ethiopian Jews to Israel in 1984 and 1985.

In May of 1991 the Mengistu regime was in a state of collapse, and the minority Ethiopian Jewish population faced the significant possibility of persecution under a new rebel government. Israel launched a second campaign, Operation Solomon, which brought an estimated 15,000 Ethiopian Jews to Israel in a 21-hour period. With concomitant immigration and population growth, the number of Ethiopian Jews in Israel reached nearly 40,000 by 1992 and nearly 70,000 in 2000.

A great deal of controversy faces those who claim to be Ethiopian Jews left behind in Ethiopia. Called "Falasha Mura," these are people who claim to be Ethiopian Jews who officially converted to Christianity to avoid persecution but who maintain their Jewish identity. There is little intermarriage with Christians, and few families go to church. However, skeptics argue that their claim to Jewish identity is a ploy to better their lot through state-assisted immigration to Israel. Of the estimated 26,000 Falasha Mura, the state of Israel has recognized the claims of about 2,500.

Life for Ethiopian Jews in the Promised Land has not been easy. Operation Moses proved to be a successful airlift, but subsequent relocation camps were often poor in quality, offering few opportunities for advancement. Integration was slow and tedious. Although those who came under Operation Solomon faced a significantly better Israeli immigration system, they competed for resources with the new immigrant Russian population. Many Ethiopian Jews felt that they were treated as second-class citizens by comparison. Further, social recognition was slower in coming. Many Ethiopian-Jewish rabbis were not recognized, and synagogues often wanted Ethiopian Jews to go through conversion rituals.

From a practical position, Russian Jews came with much higher skill levels and resources than Ethiopian Jews. As a result, Ethiopian Jews quickly became an underclass. Although careful urban planning avoided the creation of ghettos, Ethiopian Jews have continued to rank as the country's poorest Jewish population subset.

Israeli skepticism led to the marginalization of Ethiopian Jewry from much of society. Over the past decade, however, there have been substantial improvements. Particularly helpful has been the integration of men into Israel's mandatory conscription (compulsory military service for all Israeli boys and girls after secondary school). Differences between other Israeli groups and Ethiopian Jews over education, culture, language, and religious practices have decreased with the generational shift. Ethiopian Jews are increasingly accepted into Israeli society, as evidenced by the willingness of Israelis to have an Ethiopian Jew as a boss, the willingness of Israelis to socialize with Ethiopian Jews, and the willingness to have Ethiopian Jews in need access state resources. However, more persistent in Israeli society has been the fear that Ethiopian Jewry will bring cultural divergence. A large part of the Israeli population remains unwilling to support romantic relationships with Ethiopian Jews. This, many Ethiopian Jews purport, is a product of racial conflict, not religious conflict.

With the first generation of Ethiopian Jews born in Israel now coming of age and having children of their own, it is becoming clear that Ethiopian-Jewish identity is in a period of dramatic flux. Many Ethiopian Jews are raised speaking only Hebrew, not Amharic, and most Ethiopian Jews look upon their suffering in Ethiopia as something of the distant past. As they transform from an immigrant society of Ethiopian Jews to a minority culture of Black Israelis, they are facing many of the same obstacles minorities face in other countries, including racial, economic, and civil rights inequalities. In a society replete with divisions along religious, ethnic, and cultural lines, racial identity is proving to mount its own unique challenges.

RICHARD R. MARCUS

See also **Diaspora: Jewish; Ethiopia**

Further Reading

Kaplan, Steven, *The Beta Israel (Falasha) in Ethiopia: From the Earliest Times to the Twentieth Century*, New York: New York University Press, 1992

Kaplan, Steven, and Hagar Salamon, *Ethiopian Jewry: An Annotated Bibliography.* Jerusalem: Ben Zvi Institute, 1998

Kessler, David. *The Falashas: A Short History of the Ethiopian Jews*, London: Frank Cass, 1996

Quirin, James, *The Evolution of Ethiopian Jews: A History of Beta Israel,* Philadelphia: University of Pennsylvania Press, 1992

Rapoport, Louis, *The Lost Jews: Last of the Ethiopian Falashas*, New York: Stein and Day, 1981

Shelemay, Kay Kaufman, *Music, Ritual, and Falasha History*, 2nd edition, East Lansing: Michigan State University Press, 1989

Westheimer, Ruth, and Steven Kaplan, *Surviving Salvation: The Ethiopian Jewish Family in Transition*, New York: New York University Press, 1993

Ethnic Conflict

The vast majority of violent conflicts in the world since the end of World War II have occurred within states rather than between countries. Most of these involve a minority population that has taken up arms against the state, although in some exceptional cases—such as apartheid in South Africa—members of the majority may revert to violence against the national government to assert political and other claims.

Contrary to popular opinion, ethnic conflicts are not a phenomenon now reaching plague-like proportions. Despite the tens of thousands of ethnic groups that coexist around the world, relatively few situations of actual violent conflict exist. In other words, the general rule would seem to be that most ethnic groups live in relative harmony with their neighbors. Events in Chechnya, Sri Lanka, Turkey, Sudan, and Yugoslavia are conflicts that attract widespread media attention, but these constitute only a few exceptions in relation to the vast numbers of minority groups peacefully integrated in most societies.

Also contrary to popular perceptions, most so-called ethnic conflicts do not involve a direct conflict between two ethnic populations. Violent ethnic conflicts usually manifest themselves as armed insurrections by more militant or extreme segments of a minority population against the state and its apparatus rather than in "sectarian" attacks against members of the ethnic majority. Although there are exceptions, most targets of the Kurdish (Turkey and Iraq), Achenese (Indonesia), Basque (Spain), Irish Catholic (Northern Ireland), Muslim (Philippines and Thailand), Tamil (Sri Lanka), and other minorities are against the military, police, and other institutions of the state, not civilians from other ethnic groups. The designation of these conflicts as "ethnic" is therefore not without controversy, since minorities are more directly in conflict with the state than with other ethnic groups in most cases.

Most examples of ethnic conflict involve situations in which the state is not ethnically neutral. In democracies and nondemocracies alike, most functions of the state tend to be dominated by one ethnic group (usually the majority). Often, the consequence is that the language, culture, or religion of the majority tends to be imprinted on the activities, symbols, and favors of the government in most societies.

Ethnic conflicts are sometimes portrayed as irrational affairs, connected to feelings of tribalism and extreme nationalism. Yet not only do they still occur in all parts of the world, but they also occur in well-developed democracies, as well as in Asia or Africa. Detailed empirical studies over long periods of time seem to confirm that democracies are still subject to violent ethnic conflicts (United Kingdom, Spain, France), although in most cases the intensity of these conflicts seems to diminish. Emerging democracies actually seem to be more prone to the eruption of ethnic conflicts until some kind of modus vivendi is in place, usually through granting of territorial autonomy or enshrining legal protection for the minorities.

Preconditions for Conflict

Some commonalities also seem to appear in most situations of ethnic conflict. Rather than simply involving "irrational tribalism," most conflicts tend to occur in specific contexts in which situations gradually spiral from increased tension to actual violence. Once again, empirical studies suggest that the typical situation of conflict emerges when certain preconditions are encountered. Conflicts are more likely to occur: (1) when one ethnic minority is fairly large or constitutes a substantial percentage of the population; (2) when an ethnic group is concentrated in a specific territory that is considered "traditional"; (3) when an ethnic group is an indigenous people or a national minority; (4) when an ethnic group has some demographic strength, has strong attachments to the language, religion, or culture, or exercises some form of control in law or in fact over a territory, and when the central authorities disregard or undermine these factors; and (5) when a government, through its laws and policies, is prone to favor identification with the ethnic majority and their interests, which causes the counterreaction to risk being more violent, especially from a large indigenous people or national minority.

State Neutrality and Ethnicity

Where there is a community, its members will have interests that they will seek to promote, partly because it helps them survive as a community and preserve what are deemed to be important, and partly for the self-interest of its individual members.

The relationship between government and individuals within a modern state is often posited very differently, especially in relation to democracies. Representative government in a democratic state is said to represent all of the people since all individuals are entitled to participate in the formation of government, whether by direct free elections or some other mechanism, and they can freely voice their concerns and dissatisfactions. Since all individuals participate in this sense regardless of their ethnic backgrounds, the state itself is seen as neutral and universal, with its laws and policies applying to everyone in the same way.

This view of individuals within a modern state has little connection with how individuals actually interact with their governments. This has been pointed by a number of scholars, who have noted that there is really no way of avoiding, at least indirectly, the identification of the state, its institutions, and its laws with the collective interests of whatever group controls the state machinery.

"Government by the majority" in most countries often equates with government by an ethnic majority. Political control by an ethnic group is important because the state is not neutral. Perhaps even more so in a democratic setting, governments will generally be more favorable to the interests of the majority that has much greater electoral clout, and may directly or indirectly disadvantage the minorities through favoring the ethnic majority directly or indirectly, especially with language or even religious preferences. The culture, language, religion, or other preferences of the group in a majority that governs a state's political and legal institutions will always be replicated or favored to some degree within the state's political and legal institutions. This is clearly what occurs in states where a particular religion, language, or culture has official or national status. Many European states have close identification, for example, with a particular religion in more or less constitutional form (Ireland, United Kingdom, Armenia), as do states in the Middle East (Israel, Iran) and other parts of the world.

The Objects of Conflict

Ethnic conflicts usually have as their subject a minority against the state. But what are they fighting over, what is the object of these conflicts? Again, contrary to some widely held views, poverty does not appear to be the main cause of conflict: Ethnic conflicts occur in developed countries (France, United Kingdom) as well as in underdeveloped countries (Indonesia, India).

Ethnic conflicts tend to occur where the state has contributed to an unfair allocation of resources and where a substantial minority sees itself excluded or disadvantaged in terms of land rights or economic and educational opportunities. In most countries where conflicts have erupted, minorities have claimed that the state had actually discriminated against members of their group (Irish Catholics in the United Kingdom; Tamils in Sri Lanka, Muslims in the Philippines) while members of the ethnic majority have unfairly benefited from the state's largesse.

Another common factor in conflicts is that minorities, or sometimes indigenous peoples, claim that their rights, especially in relation to the use of a minority language or to freedom of religion, have been violated (the Kurds in Turkey, the Mayas in Mexico). This is also often couched in terms of a struggle for self-determination, although strictly speaking, ethnic minorities do not have the right to self-determination under international law. The right is limited to a "people," generally understood not as a social or a political construct but as a much more restricted "legal category," that is, the entire population of an existing state or colony.

The objects involved in ethnic conflicts therefore tend to be either a struggle over allocation of resources, or a struggle for rights that minorities feel are being denied them. This is once again a consistent occurrence in conflicts worldwide.

The Eruption of Ethnic Conflicts

Government by the people can often lead to government that tends to reflect the cultural, linguistic, and religious preferences of the ethnic majority. Eventually, at one point or another, an ethnic minority is bound to suffer some disadvantages, either directly or indirectly, because of the ethnic preferences in the structures or operations of even a supposedly neutral ethnic state.

A pattern tends to occur in terms of the use of violence involving minorities. Before the actual eruption of an ethnic conflict, there is a lead-up period during which anger and frustration increase the polarization of views and attitudes. During this period, there is generally either a misallocation of resources and opportunities between a substantial minority and the majority-controlled state, or a failure to respect the human rights of minorities as now increasingly understood under international law. The failure to respect these rights in matters of language, religion, or culture very often inflames the climate between the state and the members of a minority. Failure to respect the use of the main minority language in Spain during the Franco era, in Corsica, France, in East Pakistan, and in Sri Lanka all involved state linguistic preferences that today could be seen as violating rules of international law. These were the immediate sparks for the conflicts still plaguing these countries today.

Most studies tend to agree that when substantial, traditional, or territorially concentrated minorities are subjected to discrimination, denied freedom of expression, are unable to use their language, practice their religion, enjoy their culture, or obtain a proportionate allocation of resources and opportunities from the state, a situation of ethnic conflict may eventually develop.

Ethnic Conflicts and Their Prevention

International organizations involved in conflict prevention, especially the Organisation for Security and Cooperation in Europe (OSCE) and the United Nations (UN), have in recent years recognized this linkage. For this reason, they have developed various documents and recommendations to address ethnic conflict issues from a minority perspective. This can be seen in the conclusions of UN experts and the Secretary-General, the latter identifying "group inequalities" between ethnic groups as a root cause of conflict. Even clearer is the UN Commission on Human Rights, which acknowledges the link between the promotion and protection of minority rights as an essential aspect of conflict prevention.

The OSCE has essentially arrived at similar conclusions, and it has been instrumental in assisting in the development of a series of expert "recommendations" for the prevention of conflict in Eastern Europe and Central Asia, including the *Oslo Recommendations on the Linguistic Rights of National Minorities* and the *Lund Recommendations on the Effective Participation of National Minorities in Public Life*. They broadly agree that the denial of these various rights serves as one of the causal factors in conflicts where power and resources are unevenly distributed along ethnic lines.

FERNAND DE VARENNES

Further Reading

de Varennes, Fernand, *Language, Minorities and Human Rights*, Dordrecht: Martinus Nijhoff, 1996

de Varennes, Fernand, "The Protection of Linguistic Minorities in Europe and Human Rights: Possible Solutions to Ethnic Conflicts," *Columbia Journal of European Law*, 2, no. 1 (1995/1996)

Gurr, Ted Robert, *Minorities at Risk: A Global View of Ethnopolitical Conflicts*, Washington, DC: U.S. Institute of Peace, 1993

Horowitz, Donald L., *Ethnic Groups in Conflict*, Berkeley: University of California Press, 1985

Wippman, David, editor, *International Law and Ethnic Conflict*, Ithaca: Cornell University Press, 1998

Euronesians

Capsule Summary

Location: Polynesia, Micronesia, Melanesia
Total Population: 170,000–180,000
Languages: Various Austronesian languages, English, French
Religions: Christians (Catholics, Congregationalists, Reformed, Methodists, and others)

Euronesians are the result of marital and extramarital relations between European men and either Polynesian, Micronesian, or Melanesian women. In the nineteenth and twentieth centuries, many European men who were settling in Oceania for some time established extramarital (more seldom, marital) relations with local women. As a result, significant groups of European-Oceanian *mestizos* appeared in Oceania.

The process of mixing was the most extensive on the Polynesian Islands. It was connected with the fact that European men found Polynesian women more attractive in terms of their somatic characteristics. In different ethnogeographic regions of Oceania (Polynesia, Micronesia, Melanesia), as well as on different archipelagos, the populations constituting Euronesian communities, the proportions of these communities in the total population of a certain country, and also their status in local societies were quite different.

Hawaiians (168,000 people, or 14 percent of the population of the state of Hawaii) are not considered Euronesians because they have not only European-Polynesian but also Asian-Polynesian blood. Nor are persons of European-Maori origin considered Euronesians, because, both socially and culturally, they are tightly integrated with the pure Maoris (the combined number of pure and mixed Maoris makes up 340,000, or nine percent of the total population of New Zealand). Excluding these two groups, Euronesians number approximately 170,000–180,000 people. They are located in three regions of Oceania: Polynesia, Micronesia, and Melanesia. The Euronesians who settled in Polynesia (more than 70,000) are the most commonly known, and the term Euronesians is most often associated with them.

Samoa (former Western Samoa) has a population of 13,000 Euronesians (seven percent of the total population). Samoa's Euronesians, one of the most well-formed groups among the *mestizo* populations of Oceania, have a strong group self-consciousness. In the period of New Zealand's control over Western Samoa, *mestizos* were in a privileged position. On Upolu Island, a special settlement called Aleisa was even built for a large group of Euronesians. This settlement was given some economic privileges and soon became prosperous. After 1962, when the independence of Western Samoa was proclaimed, the constitution provided for equal rights for Samoans and Euronesians.

Euronesians also live in neighboring American or Eastern Samoa (4,000 people, or six percent of the population of the country). In comparison with Western Samoa's Euronesians, this group blends in more with the major population. Admittedly, Eastern Samoa's Euronesians are also a little more prosperous and have more European and American borrowings in their culture and everyday life.

Tokelau Islands, located to the north of Samoa archipelago, also have a *mestizo* population. They live mostly on the Fakaofo Atoll and are the descendants of Portuguese men and Polynesian women. This group numbers several hundred people.

Euronesians are also found on the Tuvalu Islands, now an independent state, where they number 600 persons (5.4 percent of the population).

In Tonga, a kingdom in Oceania, a *mestizo* group of European-Polynesian origin consists of approximately 700 persons (0.7 percent of the total population). In both cultural and linguistic terms, they are close to the Tongans.

A group of about 200 Euronesians (nine percent of the total population) also lives on Niue Island, which belongs to New Zealand. This group is close to the Niueans in their culture, lifestyle, and ethnic self-consciousness.

On the Cook Islands, also a subject of New Zealand, there are 1,600 Euronesians (eight percent of the total population). Most have no tendency to form an ethnosocial group distinguished from the major population of the islands, although the population of Palmerston Atoll is distinctive within *mestizos* of the Cook Islands. Palmerston Atoll was uninhabited until 1862 when William Marsters, an Englishman, settled there with two Polynesian women from Penrhyn Atoll. Then one more Polynesian woman joined them, and this harem produced numerous Anglo-Polynesian progeny.

The population of Pitcairn Island (some 50 people), which belongs to Britain, are descendants of the rebelled *Bounty* team and the Polynesian women captured by this team. A part of the population of Norfolk Island (located to the east from Australia) is a branch of Pitcairn Islanders that moved there. They number more than 600.A large group of European-Polynesian *mestizos* lives in French Polynesia, an overseas territory of France. It embraces the Society, Austral, Tuamotu, Gambier, and Marquesas Islands. *Mestizos* number not less than 50,000 (one-fifth of the total population) and are mostly concentrated on Tahiti Island, the largest of the Society Islands. They are called *demis* and, unlike the aforementioned European-Polynesian groups, are closer to Europeans than to Polynesians in their ethnic self-consciousness, language, and mode of life.

Many people of mixed European-Polynesian origin reside on Easter Island (approximately 1,500, or two-thirds of the total population), which belongs to Chile.

In Micronesia, European-Micronesian *mestizos* number some 90,000. These are, first of all, Chamorro, who settled in Guam (73,000 people, or 47 percent of the population) and on the Northern Mariana Islands (15,000 people, or 21 percent of the population). Both of these territories are controlled by the United States. A *mestizo* group was formed there after Spaniards exterminated practically the entire male population of the Marianas during a cruel colonial war in the seventeenth century. The present population consists of descendants of the local women and Spanish soldiers.

A small group of Euronesians live in Kiribati, now an independent state in Micronesia. They number more than 1,000 (1.3 percent of the total population). Numerically small groups of *mestizos* also reside on other Micronesian islands.

In Melanesia, significant groups of European-Melanesian *mestizos* live only in Fiji (11,000 people, a little more than one percent of the total population), New Caledonia, and Papua New Guinea (some 1,000 in each group).

In their religious affiliation, Euronesians usually do not differ from the majority of the local population. They are divided into Catholics (Guam, Northern Mariana Islands, Kiribati, New Caledonia, Easter Island), Congregationalists (Samoa, American Samoa, Tokelau, Tuvalu, Niue, Cook Islands, Kiribati), Reformed (French Polynesia), Methodists (Fiji, Tonga), Anglicans (Norfolk), Seventh-Day Adventists (Pitcairn), and others.

PAVEL PUCHKOV

See also **Micronesia; Melanesians**

Further Reading

Beaglehole, Ernest, "The Mixed Blood in Polynesia," *The Journal of the Polynesian Society*, 58, no. 2 (1949)

Bourgeau, Jan, *La France du Pacifique. Nouvelle-Calédonie et Dépendances. Wallis et Futuna. Nouvelles-Hébrides. Etablissements Français de llissements Français de l*Paris: Editions maritimes et coloniales, 2nd edition, 1955

Пучков, Павел Иванович, *Население Океании: Этногеографический обзор,* Москва: Издательство "Наука," 1967 (Puchkov, Pavel Ivanovich, *Population of Oceania: Ethnogeografic Survey,* Moscow: Nauka Press, 1967)

Пучков, Павел Иванович, *Формирование населения Меланезии,* Москва: Издательство "Наука", 1968 (Puchkov, Pavel Ivanovich, *The Forming of the Population of Melanesia,* Moscow: Nauka Press, 1968)

Пучков, Павел Иванович, *Этническая ситуация в Океании,* Москва: Издательство "Наука", 1983 (Puchkov, Pavel Ivanovich, *Ethnic Situation in Oceania,* Moscow: Nauka Press, 1983)

Europeans: Overview

Capsule Summary

Location: *Europeans* is the generic name given to people living on or descending from the European continent, situated in the Nordic hemisphere between 71° 8'–36° latitude N and 9° 31–67° 20' longitude E, occupying a total surface of 10,050,000 square kilometers (3,863,220 square miles) between the Atlantic Ocean in the west, the Arctic Ocean in the north, the Ural Mountains, the Caspian Sea, and the Caucasus Mountains in the east, and the Mediterranean Sea and the Black Sea in the south.

Total Population: 727.3 million, of which 56.1 million (7.7 percent) are migrants (International Organization for Migration, 2003 estimate)

Languages: Numerous languages belonging mostly to the Indo-European group and to the Finno-Ugric group, but due to migration, an increasing proportion of the population has a mother tongue or ethnic origin different from the majority population of their country of residence

Religions: Roman Catholic, Protestant (several), Orthodox Christian, Muslim, Jewish

The history and development of the Europeans as a group is that of their migration and settlement. Their forefathers came to Europe from Africa in approximately 700,000 BCE, as *Homo erectus*. Later, *Homo sapiens* entered Europe from the Near East, between 35,000 and 10,000 BCE. The migrant populations gradually became sedentary as agriculture was introduced and adopted around 8,000 BCE.

Invading migratory movements of groups (e.g., Germans, Celts) relocated between 800 and 400 BCE, and new groups from the steppes moved in from Asia. The period of Greek colonization (2000 to 400 BCE) led to emigration to the Middle East and later Egypt, whereas the Roman expansion (400 to 500 BCE) caused migration not only throughout Europe but also to Northern Africa and the Near East. The period between 400 and 1000 CE is recognized as an era of migration between nations, characterized by invasions and movements of ethnic groups from within and outside the continent, leading to the building of Europe. Most tribes finally settled, and those settlements were the foundations of future European states. Migratory movements, some leading to permanent settlement, continued during the age of Viking expeditions (700–1000 CE) and during the Crusades (1000–1500 CE). The three centuries from 1450 to 1750 CE witnessed mass migrations as a result of religious wars on the European continent. From 1650 to 1900 CE, the majority of mass migration was due to economic factors.

Europeans expanded their holdings beyond the limits of the continent for several centuries, between 1500 and 1950, colonizing overseas territories in North America, South America, Asia, and Africa. Colonization led to both emigration and immigration, and peoples moved from one territory to another.

The period between 1750 and 1914 witnessed industrial development and change, as well as demographic upheavals and political revolutions, all of which were interrelated. Improved medical care and better living conditions prolonged average lifespans, while higher birthrates resulted in a demographic explosion. Technical development and a turn toward industrialization led to migratory movements from rural to expanding urban areas. Colonial wealth accelerated the industrialization process, stimulating labor-oriented migration within and beyond Europe. As the nation-state strengthened, the regulatory role of the state increased, also affecting migration.

Numerous European emigrants returned home during and after World War I, which caused economic stagnation and an overall reduction in international labor migration to Europe. Political tensions and the war led states to impose strict border control. European nations increasingly institutionalized and monitored immigration through a system of visas, as labor and residence permit requirements replaced rather liberal and unexamined immigration circulation. The decolonization period between 1922 and 1975, when European nations divested themselves of their colonial holdings, also intensified migration flows.

Historical transformations were reflected in patterns of migration. Between 1945 and 1973, there was a significant amount of immigration to a Western Europe that was rebuilding itself. Immigrants were workers from the European periphery, returnees from former colonies, intra-European refugees, and asylum-seekers from Asia and the Middle East.

From the mid-1970s, the character of immigration changed. Fewer immigrants were driven by a search for economic opportunity, while more were led to immigrate to Europe for personal or family reasons and to seek political asylum. The immigrant population consolidated, despite socioeconomic exclusion and xenophobic manifestations.

By the mid-1990s, the levels of immigrant populations stabilized, despite numerous ethnic conflicts in regions of the world such as the Balkans, the Middle East, and Africa, due to increasingly restrictive immigration legislation. From 2000, migration continued under circumstances marked by global unrest. After the terrorist attacks on the United States on September 11, 2001, suspicion toward potential immigrants (especially from Arab countries) increased in both the United States and Europe.

Most migratory movement has created culturally diverse "pockets" within national borders of states with distinct ethnic, cultural-linguistic, or religious features. These are either indigenous populations that survived the initial occupation of a newly migrated group that became a majority in time (the Saami in Northern Europe, Alsatians or Corsicans in France, Irish Catholics in Great Britain, Basques in Spain) or groups that settled on territories they migrated to under various historical pressures (Hungarians in Central and Eastern Europe, Albanians in the former Yugoslavia, Russians in the Baltic region). Long-standing historical minorities with distinct features in Europe include the Jews and the Roma (gypsies). Switzerland, Spain, Great Britain, and Cyprus are characterized by an acknowledged historic and multilingual diversity. Some minorities were created as the result of programmatic political action, as in the former Soviet Union and the former Yugoslavia. There is also the case of minorities who are barely acknowledged or recognized even in their original territories, such as the Kurds and the Palestinians. More recent migrant groups to Western Europe—the Turks, Asians, and Africans—are not legally considered minorities in the European nations where they reside.

ELENA DINGU-KYRKLUND

Further Reading

Alcock, Antony, *A History of the Protection of Regional Cultural Minorities in Europe: From the Edict of Nantes to the Present Day*, New York: St. Martin's Press, 2000

Castles, S., and M.J. Miller, *The Age of Migration: International Population Migrations in the Modern World*, New York: The Guilford Press, 1993

Collinson, Sarah, *Europe and International Migration*, London and New York: Pinter Publishers, 1994

Sassen, Saskia, *Guests and Aliens*, New York: New Press, 2000

Ewe

Capsule Summary

Location: Coastal strip and inland to about 250 kilometers (155 miles) in West Africa, mostly in southern Togo, southeastern Ghana, and with small populations in southwestern Benin and along the Route Nationale in Togo

Total Population: Approximately 2–2.5 million

Language: Ewe and related dialects

Religions: Traditional animist voodoo and/or Christian

The Ewe (pronounced Ev'he using a bilabial fricative) are an ethnic group living along the coastal strip and inland to a depth of about 250 kilometers (155 miles) in southern Togo (where they are approximately 35–40 percent of the population), southeastern Ghana (18 percent), and with small populations in southwestern Benin (fewer than 10 percent) and along the Route Nationale in Togo. Their language and the various related and mutually intelligible dialects are part of the Kwa branch of the Niger-Congo family (Greenberg, 1970). Besides language, Ewe unity is based on a number of mutable variables, including religious practices, state formation, gender roles, heredity and lineage patterns, and migration narratives from the ancestral homelands of Notsé (Nuatja in central Togo) and Oyo (in western Nigeria).

In retrospect, one can assert that the difficulty in establishing the "essence" of modern "Ewe-ness" arose during the colonial period, with its partitions and repartitions of the Volta basin. Within the Ewe family, there are many subgroups, and within each there are separatist generational and political factions that would have outsiders view them as ethnically distinct from the Ewe. People in the Peki district of Ghana and north of Hohoe are more closely allied with the Twi people, and many speak dialects of both languages. The Ouatchi plateau, north of Anécho in Togo, is home to another subgroup. Although they reside around Anécho, the Ga or Guin subgroup trace their ancestry to those who fled Ga-speaking territory near El Mina in Ghana. The Buem and Akposso subgroups in the mountainous cocoa zone have long opposed each another because of perceived ethnic subgroup allegiances, whereas the Anlo, although ethnic kin, are considered traitors for aiding the Ashanti during the invasion of Ewe-land (circa 1850s–1870s).

Many Ewe speakers throughout the region consider that those from the Ho-Kpalime border region speak the "purest" Ewe, yet all would identify Notsé as the "spiritual home" of their people. Differences in traditions are also important, for although patrilineage is generally the most common kinship unit, among the Anlo, dispersed segmentary clans are the norm (Greene 1996). Finally, the most contentious contemporary issue is the place of the Mina speakers. Mina as a dialect originated in the Anécho region (El Mina = Mina), although it has quickly spread along the coast to become the quasi-official language of the Togolese capital, Lomé. Although some speakers self-identify as Mina and cannot speak the standardized form of Ewe, most who speak it consider their ethnicity to be Ewe. Moreover, Mina, unlike Ewe, remains an unwritten language, which curiously has currency beyond ethnic boundaries. Many of Togo's other minorities (Kabiyé, Kotokoli, etc.) who reside in Lomé use it to communicate with the Ewe people.

Despite these divergences, Ewe has a discernible culture, history, and personhood. The familial homes of Oyo and Notsé remain the most important. Notsé, a premodern walled city characteristic of the region (circa 1700 CE), was ruled by a cruel king by the name of Agokoli. According to oral traditions (Gayibor, 1975), the population was held hostage until one day the womenfolk hatched a plan to weaken the walls. When the walls were broken, the Ewe fled in several directions south and west, founding new settlements in the Volta River basin. The Ewe never lived within one state, but rather in a series of discontiguous microstates in which clans (*dou*), governed by religious officials and lineage heads, curtailed the authority of the chief (*fia*). Sandwiched between two powerful kingdoms, Ashanti and Dahomey, the Ewe were preyed upon and participated in the transatlantic slave trade.

It was not until German and Swiss Protestant missionaries arrived in the mid 1850s that the many Ewe dialects were transcribed, and the process of standardization and orthographic representation began. Missionary involvement in education and pedagogy led to the flourishing of the Ewe language in a standardized form (Lawrance, 2000). Scholars also produced an extraordinary corpus of ethnographic data (Spieth, 1906, 1911; Westermann, 1935). During the German colonial period (1884–1914), a large proportion of Ewe territory (up to 70 percent) was united under one colonial administration. Although Catholic missions were also extensive, the lasting legacy of Protestant activity was the first independent African church in West Africa, the Ewe Presbyterian Church (Debrunner, 1965; Schöck-Quinteros and Lenz, 1986).

After the redivision of the German colony into two mandate territories, British (1914–1957) and French (1914–1960) calls for the reunification of the Ewe homeland grew louder. Many Ewe intellectuals identify the German colonial experience as fundamental in the establishment of a coherent Ewe ethnic identity (Mamattah 1976). Throughout the German, British, and French colonial periods, however, primary education was conducted in Ewe, marking a significant departure from the colonial experience in many other regions of Africa. Because of their outstanding educational achievements, Ewe men and women established leadership positions in all walks of colonial and post-colonial life, especially commerce.

The termination of the United Nations (UN) trusteeships and the wider process of decolonization (1945–1960) brought the "Ewe question" before the UN as a test case for ethnic self-determination (Amenumey 1989; Coleman 1956). In a hard-fought plebiscite campaign over whether British Togoland should join Ghana in independence or remain under UN trusteeship until the independence of French Togoland, the Ewe political leadership was split into many factions. The decision to join Ghana went against the wishes of the majority of Ewe speakers, who instead sought a reunified Ewe homeland. This issue contributed to much political instability between Ghana and Togo during the 1960s and 1970s.

From a modern political standpoint, the Ewe are very influential in contemporary Ghanaian culture and politics, although not so in Togo. The northern-led dictatorship of Eyadema has constructed itself in opposition to the first Togolese president, the Ewe-speaker Sylvanus Olympio. Although Ewes control southern commerce and local power networks, they constitute only ten percent of the military leadership. Just as political power remains a chimera to the Togolese Ewe elite, a coherent ethnic identity applicable to all class divisions seems a conundrum. Christianity is all-pervasive, yet the majority of Ewes still follow animist cults to some degree. Traditional chiefly offices (Verdon 1983); marriage, lineage, and heredity laws (Nukunya 1968); voodoo cults (Rosenthal 1998); and general patterns of naming, authority, and respect remain very powerful. Most Ewe are peasant farmers, with maize and yams being the staple crops, although fishing, coffee-farming, and cocoa farming are also important. Perhaps the beautifully colored woven cloth called Kente is the Ewe peoples' most unifying cultural product.

Benjamin Nicholas Lawrance

See also **Togo**

Further Reading

Amenumey, D.E.K., *The Ewe Unification Movement*, Accra: Ghana Universities Press, 1989

Coleman, James S., *Togoland: International Conciliation No. 509*, New York: Carnegie Endowment for International Peace, 1956

Debrunner, Hans W., *A Church between Colonial Powers: A Study of the Church in Togo*, London, 1965

Gayibor, N.L., *Migrations, Société, Civilisation. Les Ewe du Sud-Togo*, 2 volumes, Paris: Thèse de 3e cycle, 1975

Greenberg, Joseph, *The Languages of Africa*, 3rd edition Bloomington: Indiana University, 1970

Greene, Sandra E., *Gender, Ethnicity, and Social Change on the Upper Slave Coast*, Portsmouth, New Hampshire: Heinemann, 1996

Lawrance, Benjamin N., "Most Obedient Servants: The Politics of Language in German Colonial Togo," *Cahiers d'Etudes Africaines*, 157, no. XL-3 (2000)

Mamattah, Charles M.K., editor, *The Ewes of West Africa Oral Traditions Vol. 1: The Anglo-Ewes and Their Immediate Neighbours*, Accra: The Advent Press, 1976.

Nukunya, G.K., *Kinship and Marriage among the Anlo Ewe*, London: Althone Press, 1969

Rosenthal, Judy, *Possession, Ecstasy and Law in Ewe Voodoo*, Charlottesville: University of Virginia Press, 1998

Schöck-Quinteros, Eva, and Dieter Lenz, editors, *150 Jahre Norddeutsche Mission 1836–1986*, Bremen: NDMG, 1986

Spieth, J., *Die Ewe Stämme: Material zur Kunde des Ewe Volkes in Deutsch-Togo*, Berlin: 1906

Spieth, J., *Die Religion der Eweer in Süd-Togo*, Leipzig: Vandenhoeck & Ruprecht, 1911

Verdon, Michel, *The Abutia Ewe of West Africa: A Chiefdom That Never Was*, Berlin: Mouton, 1983

Westermann, D., *Die Glidyi-Ewe in Togo*, Berlin: 1935

Exchange of Population

International population exchanges have been suggested as a possible solution to minority issues. This political solution was much discussed in the first half of the twentieth century, although it was largely abandoned in the second half of the century. During the last decade of the twentieth century, the practice of population transfers by force gained notoriety as "ethnic cleansing" and has been universally condemned by the international community.

Population Exchanges Before and After Nationalism

The transfer of peoples from one place into another is a practice that long predates the modern world. Imperial rulers frequently used such a policy to remove a politically unreliable population from a region and replace them with more reliable subjects. Furthermore, military considerations played an important role in such transfers. In many premodern empires, tribes and military units were settled into specific regions with the express purpose of securing the territory for the empire.

In the modern period, political considerations continued to play an important role. The famous Soviet deportations of various minority groups are a prime example of minority persecution as a result of their actual or imagined lack of loyalty to the state. Whereas the Soviet deportations were a continuation and extension of earlier imperial policies, the modern nationalists of the nineteenth and twentieth centuries further expanded the scope of population transfers and applied them to entire groups of people who happened to find themselves on the "wrong side of the border."

It was after World War I and the subsequent collapse of the Russian, Hapsburg, and Ottoman empires that population exchanges were seriously considered as a potential solution to the infamous "nationality question" in Eastern Europe. In a nutshell, the war led to the construction of new nation-states (Poland, Yugoslavia, Hungary, Romania, Czechoslovakia), all of which included sizeable minority populations. One of the possible solutions to this problem was simply to move the ethnic minorities to their respective national homelands. The most well-known application of this strategy is the Greek–Turkish population exchange (1923).

The Greek–Turkish Population Exchange

The Lausanne Treaty of 1923 sanctioned this exchange. In 1920, following the Treaty of Serves, Greece was awarded a considerable portion of Western Anatolia, including Smyrna (Izmir) and its adjunct territory. From that point on, the Greek army began a military campaign aimed at increasing Greece's territorial gains. This was the high point of the Greek irredentism of the nineteenth and early twentieth centuries.

Unfortunately, domestic political changes, international geopolitical alliances, and most important, the military and political mobilization of the Turkish peasantry under Kemal Ataturk brought the campaign to a halt and eventually led to a devastating military defeat. As the military front collapsed and Turkish forces began their march toward the Aegean Sea, both military personnel and Anatolian Greeks fled for their lives.

The Lausanne Treaty sought to establish a permanent solution to the de facto "ethnic cleansing" of Anatolian Greeks. Moreover, the Turkish side was committed to the principle of a territorial state centered on Anatolia and did not want to extend its reach to the various Ottoman Muslim communities of the Balkan nation-states. Consequently, the two sides agreed that the Ottoman Muslims and Turks of Greek Macedonia would be deported to Anatolia while all Anatolian Greeks would be deported to the Greek nation-state. Close to 2 million people were involved in this population exchange. For the next 30 years, both states had to deal with considerable problems stemming from the need to acculturate and integrate the newcomers into their respective national societies.

During the interwar period, similar population exchanges (but quite smaller in size) were carried out between Greece, Turkey, and Bulgaria. The ultimate goal was the ethnic homogenization of these states. A similar strategy was applied in Kosovo and Macedonia by the Serb authorities, where some 90,000 to 300,000 Albanians, Turks, and Muslims were deported to Turkey.

In the aftermath of World War II, similar strategies were applied throughout Eastern Europe against the various German minority communities of Hungary, Czechoslovakia, Romania, and Poland. Furthermore, the same policy led to the ethnic homogenization of Poland. The population exchanges failed to solve completely the minority question in Eastern Europe, and minorities continued to live in many states throughout the region.

Population Exchanges Today

The legacy of these population exchanges reveals the reasons that led the international community to gradually abandon this practice during the second half of the twentieth century. This has been a slow and relatively uncertain trend, however. In the post–World War II period, the principle of population exchange was exported from Eastern Europe to the Third World. The most well-known example is the case of India and Pakistan. When the two states became independent, they agreed to move the Hindu and Muslim groups along the newly established national boundaries between the two states. The goal of the exchange was to provide for stable and uncontested boundaries, thereby reducing the likelihood of future political revisionism.

The growth of a new international human rights regime in the last 30 years has greatly delegitimized such practices today. But such forceful population transfers continue to occur wherever one side is successful in obtaining the power and legitimacy to do so. Although the 1999 Kosovo Crisis might signify the beginnings of a new regime with regard to population exchanges, it would be premature to argue that this practice belongs squarely to humanity's past.

VICTOR ROUDOMETOF

Further Reading

Ergil, D., "A Reassessment: The Young Turks, Their Politics, and Anti-colonial Struggle," *Balkan Studies*, 16, no. 2 (1975)

Human Rights Quarterly, various issues

Kitromilides, Paschalis M., and A. Alexandris, "Ethnic Survival, Nationalism and Forced Migration: The Historical Demography of the Greek Community of Asia Minor at the Close of the Ottoman Era," *Review of the Center for Asia Minor Studies*, 5 (1984/1985)

McCarthy, J., *Muslims and Minorities, The Population of Ottoman Anatolia and the End of the Empire*, New York: New York University Press, 1983

Nations and Nationalism, The Official Journal of the Association for the Study of Ethnicity and Nationalism (London School of Economics, United Kingdom), various issues

Pearson, Raymond, *National Minorities in Eastern Europe 1848–1945*, New York: St. Martin's Press, 1983

Pentzopoulos, D., *The Balkan Exchange of Minorities and Its Impact upon Greece*, Paris: Mouton, 1962

Roudometof, Victor, "The Consolidation of National Minorities in Southeastern Europe," *Journal of Political and Military Sociology*, 24, no. 2 (1996)

Thornberry, Patrick, *International Law and the Rights of Minorities*, Oxford: Clarendon Press, 1991

F

Fanon, Frantz Omar (Algerian)

French psychoanalyst and revolutionary activist, Frantz Omar Fanon, whose writings had deep influence on the radical movements of the 1960s, both in the Western world and the Third World countries, was born in 1925 in Fort-de-France, Martinique, in the French West Indies. He left Martinique in 1944, when he volunteered at the age of 19, to fight with the Free French in North Africa as part of the effort to rid Europe of German fascism. After World War II, he studied medicine and psychiatry in France. Seared as a youth by racism and strongly influenced by Jean-Paul Sartre's philosophical and political ideas, Fanon analyzed the impact of colonialism and its consequences.

In 1952 Fanon began to practice psychiatry in the French colony of Algeria. Before he left France in 1953, he married Jose Duble, a French woman. At the same time, he was appointed director of the psychiatric department at the Blida-Joinville Hospital, where he instituted reforms in patient care and desegregated the wards.

In 1956 he associated himself with the Algerian *Front de Libération Nationale* (FLN) that rebelled to throw off French colonial rule in Algeria. Fanon then worked briefly for the provisional Algerian government as an ambassador to Ghana; he also edited the FLN's newspaper *al-Moudjahid* in Tunisia. Some of his work from this period was collected and published in 1964 as *Towards the African Revolution.*

Fanon survived several political murder attempts in Algeria and Morocco, but finally contracted leukemia and died on December 12, 1961 at the National Institute of Health in Bethesda, Maryland, where he had sought treatment for his cancer. At his request, his body was returned to Algeria and buried with honors by the Algerian National Army of Liberation.

His two major works *Black Skin, White Masks* (1952), written as a doctoral thesis, and *The Wretched of the Earth* (1961) have made Fanon a prominent contributor to postcolonial studies as well as an influence in both radical and antiracist social and political movements. *The Wretched of the Earth* was completed in 10 months and published by Jean-Paul Sartre in the year of Fanon's death. This book was based on Fanon's terrible experiences in Algeria during its war of independence.

A collection of his essays was published in two books, *A Dying Colonialism* (1959) and *Towards the African Revolution* (1964), the latter published posthumously. In these two books Fanon focused on the interpretation of the individual and the non-neutrality of medicine and technology in environmental and social life. In his psychiatric practices it was characteristic of Fanon to insist on recognizing the social origins of an individual's problems. His approaches had important prognostics with respect to the conventional view of psychiatry and psychoanalytic theory. His examinations in themselves could become a tool of socialization—a means of legitimizing power and control.

All of Fanon's works were translated into English and other Asian and African languages in the decade following his death. They stand as an important influence for current postcolonial social theorists, for example Edward Said (Middle Eastern writer) and Ali Shari'ati (one of the main progressive theorists and leading intellectuals of the Iranian Revolution of 1979 in Iran). Both Paris-educated Shari'ati and Said were grave about cultural imperialism. They tried to conceptualize and describe cultural imperialism as part and parcel of the European expansion and domination around the globe—especially in the Third World—and its reaction to the rise of the anticolonial nationalistic movements with strong emphasis on their national cultural identity.

Colonialism, according to Fanon, not only physically disarmed the colonized subject but also robbed her of a traditional cultural heritage. Fanon was alert to emphasize that these challenges at recovering national continuity throughout history are often contrived and eventually self-defeating. As he stated:

> I am ready to concede, that on the plane of factual being, the past existence of an Aztec civilization does not change anything very much in the diet of the Mexican peasant of today.... A national culture is not a folklore, not an abstract populism that believes it can discover the people's true nature. It is not made up of the (concentrated, intense) dregs of gratuitous actions, that is to say actions that are less and less attached to the ever-present reality of the people. A national culture is the whole body of efforts made by a people in the sphere of thought to describe, justify, and praise the action (through) which that people has created itself and keeps itself in existence. (Fanon, *The Wretched of the Earth*, 1966, p. 233)

This idea had a great influence on Shari'ati's works, who was trying to reconstruct a radical Islamic political ideology based on some Islamic Shi'ism symbols to describe the contemporary sociopolitical, cultural, and economic problems of both Iranian and Islamic societies in the 1960s and 1970s. *The Wretched of the Earth* has been translated by Shari'ati and had a major influence on the Iranian Revolution. The book could also be seen as a manifesto of the black liberation movement, especially of the 1960s and 1970s.

One of the main themes of *The Wretched of the Earth* is the analysis of decolonization and its endorsement of violence (the "question of violence"). It is not the critique of violence that is the principal contribution of the work. It is the analysis of political development in the Third World, specifically Algeria and Africa, in which the question of violence plays an important role. Fanon used the concept of violence in different contexts and to describe different phases. He specifically used the term *decolonization process*. The entire colonial enterprise was built on a foundation of force and conquest, hence, the whole background of violence. He tried to demonstrate that the implications of this situation affected human relations and the self-image of both colonizer and colonized. According to Fanon, decolonization would occur only through violent means. The reasons for this were implicit in the nature of colonialism and the vested interests of the colonial country and in the relationship of the colonizer to the colonized. Decolonization means the destruction of the colonial system. It also implies the possibility of reconstructing human relations and so producing a new society. Decolonization, achieved through the use of violence and armed struggle, would give birth to the new man.

Black Skin, White Masks was published when Fanon was 27 years old. The book had a great influence on anticolonial, black consciousness around the world. Part of the book was based on his lectures and experiences in Lyon. In this work, Fanon argued that white colonialism forced an existentially false and humiliating existence upon its black subjects to the point that it commanded their conformity to its distorted values. He demonstrated how the problem of race and color, united with a whole range of words and images, came primarily from the dark side of the soul. Here, Fanon's personal experiences as a black intellectual in a whitened world elaborated the ways in which the colonizer/colonized relationship was constructed as a psychology.

Fanon emphasized the fact that "white" depends for its stability on its negation, "black." He saw the two as a totality, both of which were the product of imperial conquest. Fanon situated the historical point at which certain psychological configurations turned into existence. He presented a vital study of how historically bound cultural systems could continue as psychology.

Fanon concluded his testament, as he was to conclude his life, with words of unwavering hope: "For Europe, for ourselves and for humanity, we must turn over a new leaf, we must work out new concepts, and try to set afoot a new man." The work remains to be done.

Mehdi Parvizi Amineh

Biography

Frantz Omar Fanon. Born 1925 in Martinique, the French West Indies. Served in the French army (the Free French in North

Africa) during World War II, then completed his studied in medicine and psychiatry, University of Lyon. Served as head of the psychiatry department of Blida-Joinville Hospital in Algeria (1953-56), then a part of France. Joined the Algerian Front de Libération Nationale (FLN), 1954; became an editor of its newspaper, *El Moudjahid*, published in Tunis (1954); appointed ambassador to Ghana by the rebel Provisional Government (1960). Contracted leukemia, died at National Institute of Health in Bethesda, Maryland after treatment for cancer, on December 12, 1961.

Selected Works

Peau noire, masques blancs, 1952; as *Black Skin, White Mosks*, translated by Charles L. Markmann, 1967

L'An V de la révolution algérienne, 1959; as *A Dying Colonialism*, translated by Haakon Chevalier, 1967

Pour la révolution africaine, 1964; as *Towards the African Revolution*, translated by Haakon Chevalier, 1968

Les Damnés de la terre, 1961; as *The Wretched of the Earth*, translated by Constance Farrington, 1966

MEHDI PARVIZI AMINEH

Further Reading

de Beauvoir, Simone, *Force of Circumstance*, New York: Putnam, 1964

Bouvier, Pierre, *Fanon*, Paris: Editions universitaires, 1971

Caute, David, *Frantz Fanon*, London: Collins, Fontana, 1970

Geismar, Peter, *Fanon*, New York: The Dial Press, 1971

Gendzier, Irene L., *Frantz Fanon: A Critical Study*, New York: Pantheon Books-Random House, 1973

Gordon, Lewis R., *Fanon and the Crisis of European Man*, New York: Routledge, 1995

Lucas, Phillippe, *Sociologie de Frantz Fanon*, Alger: SEED, Societe nationale d'edition et de diffusion, 1971

Said, Edward, *Culture and Imperialism*, New York: Vintage Books-Random House, 1993

Farrakhan, Louis (African-American)

Born Louis Eugene Walcott in the Bronx, New York, Louis Farrakhan is the son of West Indian immigrants. Never knowing his father, Farrakhan credits his mother, Mae Clark (Farrakhan), a follower of Marcus Garvey, with instilling in him racial pride and a love for music. Farrakhan spent much of his childhood performing as a concert violinist with the Boston Civic Symphony and the Boston College Orchestra, winning numerous competitions, becoming one of the first African Americans to appear on television.

As his mother profoundly influenced his racial and cultural ethos, so did Reverend Nathan Wright. Wright emphasized the importance of black self-sufficiency, encouraging young Louis to embrace the teachings of Black Nationalism. Whereas other community leaders pushed blacks to integrate through dominant (white) institutions, Mae Clark and Nathan Wright schooled Louis in the importance of creating black-owned, controlled and operated businesses and institutions.

After graduating from high school, Walcott earned an athletic scholarship to Winston-Salem State Teachers College in North Carolina. Upon graduation with a degree in English and following marriage to his childhood sweetheart, Louis Walcott returned to Boston in pursuit of a career as a calypso singer.

In 1955, while performing at a Chicago nightclub, Walcott encountered a friend who was a member of the Nation of Islam. Having already rebuffed several invitations to attend NOI events, Walcott relented, agreeing to accompany his friend to the Muslim's annual Savior's Day Convention that following day in Chicago. As he sat listening to Elijah Muhammad, the self-proclaimed messenger of Allah, Walcott faced a truth not yet heard about the black man and the "white devil." Shortly thereafter, Walcott enrolled in Temple No. 7, the New York Mosque, changing his name to Louis X, as a loyal follower of Elijah Muhammad.

Louis X's belief in the teachings of Elijah Muhammad did not lead to a career change, despite the strict demands from the Nation. Though Elijah Muhammad excoriated the overemphasis of sports and entertainment within the black community as reflective of their slave mentality of pleasing the white man instead of working toward racial empowerment, Louis X still had dreams of stardom. Not concerned with his personal dreams, Malcolm X, then minister at Mosque No. 7, demanded that Louis make a choice between the Nation and the stage. Louis X's choice was put to the test when a manager offered him a lucrative contract. Tempted, Louis saw a vision as he slept that night.

> And in the vision I saw two doors. Over one door was written "success." I could look into that door and I saw an amount of gold and diamonds, which represent, of course, riches that would accrue. But there was another door, and over that door was the word "Islam." And in the vision I chose the door of Islam. (Gardell, *In the Name of Elijah Muhammad: Louis Farrakhan and the Nation of Islam,* 1996, pp. 120–121)

Walking through that door, Louis X gave his life to the Nation of Islam.

While dedicated to overseeing the growth of the Nation through serving as assistant minister for the Harlem and Boston Mosques, Louis utilized his artistic talents as well. He wrote and directed two plays, *Oregena, A Negro Spelled Backwards* and *The Trial*, in which the black man tries and convicts the white man of evil deeds against humanity. The power of his oratory skills and the impact of his creative works pushed Louis X into the forefront of the Nation's organizing efforts throughout black America.

In 1965, having broken from the Nation of Islam, three unidentified gunmen assassinated Malcolm X during a speech at the Audubon Ballroom. Given the tense relations between Malcolm and the Nation, many blamed the Nation and Louis X specifically for his murder. This anger and constant accusations contributed to a waning support for the NOI within the black community. Able to withstand opposition against the Nation and the personal attacks against himself, Louis X emerged from the rubble to rebuild the Harlem Mosque in his own image. Successfully reviving the largest Mosque in the country, Elijah Muhammad named him its national representative in 1967, replacing his "X" with the name of Farrakhan.

Despite declining support and shrinking visibility compared to the Black Panther Party during the late 1960s, Louis X and NOI maintained its presence within the black community, focusing on reforming individuals through race pride, personal responsibility, economic empowerment, and historical consciousness.

In 1974, upon the death of Elijah Muhammad, his son, Wallace D. Muhammad seized control of the Nation of Islam, creating an organization grounded in the teachings of Sunni Islam. Wallace quickly eliminated gender-segregated training classes, challenging the patriarchal orientation of his father's teachings while not abandoning the longstanding privileges of fathers and husbands in providing for their families economically, spiritually, and socially.

Although these changes proved acceptable to a majority of black Muslims, who remained loyal to the Messenger's son, Louis Farrakhan reclaimed control of the organization in 1978 and successfully restored the original teachings by reinstating gendered-based classes to teach proper male and female conduct and by reemphasizing racial purity, domestic leadership, self-defense, economic independence, and the cultivation of black self-esteem. He also introduced *The Final Call*, an internationally circulated newspaper similar to *The Muhammad Speaks*.

In 1984, Louis Farrakhan reestablished himself and the Nation of Islam as a force within the black community. Through his relationship with Jesse Jackson and the presence of the Fruit of Islam as Jackson's security detail, Farrakhan transformed himself into a household name. With this increased visibility, Farrakhan faced an increased amount of scrutiny, withstanding accusations of anti-Semitism and anti-white hatred. Unfazed by the constant protest against him, Farrakhan remained dedicated to teaching black America about the program of Elijah Muhammad, spreading the Nation to over 80 cities in the United States and Great Britain.

In 1986, Farrakhan introduced a program of economic development, emphasizing the importance of black economic power. The Nation initiated a line of personal hair products and, under Farrakhan's leadership, expanded its business base. In 1988, the Nation of Islam repurchased its Mosque in Chicago, renaming it the Mosque Maryam: the National Center. The National Center offers "Re-training and Re-education of the Black Man and Woman" and includes a preschool and K-12 University of Islam.

While his popularity increased throughout the 1990s, 1995 proved to be the most successful year for Louis Farrakhan and the Nation of Islam. He purchased hundreds of acres of Georgia farmland, opened the $5 million dollar Salaam Restaurant, and took a well-publicized tour of Africa. Most importantly, Farrakhan initiated the 1995 Million Man March, in which he brought together almost one million African American men in a symbolic affirmation of a responsible black masculinity that included sobriety, empowerment, and racial pride. Demanding that black men reassert their responsibility as the leaders of family and community, he called upon his brothers to fight drugs, violence, and unemployment.

While shifting his emphasis toward mainstream politics and the vote (long forbidden to NOI members, Farrakhan registered to vote in 1986,), Farrakhan continues to push the NOI membership toward securing alternative visions of masculinity, family, and community as a response to systematic oppression and bigotry. Although he has ushered in change under his leaderships, the continued media scrutiny, the magnitude of the Million Man March and his popularity within the black community, demonstrates the persistent power of the teachings of the Honorable Elijah Muhammad and the leadership of Louis Farrakhan.

Biography

Louis Farrakhan. Born Louis Eugene Walcott on May 11, 1933 in Roxbury, Massachusetts. Studied at public schools in Roxbury, Massachusetts; Winston-Salem State Teachers College, 1950-1954. Assistant Minister of Temple No. 11, Boston, 1956-1965; Assistant Minister of Temple No. 7, New York, 1965-1975; National Minister, Nation of Islam, 1975-. Founder of the *Final Call*, National Center, Salaam Restaurant, and principal organizer of Million Man March. Currently resides in Chicago, Illinois.

DAVID LEONARD

See also **Malcolm X (African-American); Muhammad, Elijah (American-American); African-American Nationalism and Separatism**

Further Reading

Gardell, Mattias, *In the Name of Elijah Muhammad: Louis Farrakhan and the Nation of Islam*, Durham: Duke University Press, 1996

Lincoln, C. Eric, *The Black Muslims in America*, 3rd edition, Trenton: Africa World Press, 1994

Magida, Arthur, *Prophet of Rage: A Life of Louis Farrakhan and His Nation*, New York: Harper Collins, 1996

Federalism

Federalism is a political philosophy that recommends combining "shared rule," in a federal government and "self-rule" in regional, provincial, cantonal, or state governments. It is a philosophy for cooperation that includes respect for differences. Political institutions inspired by federal political philosophy include confederations, federations, "federacies," leagues, functional organizations, and condominiums. Many maintain that federalist philosophy and its various institutional arrangements are especially helpful for ensuring the protection and freedom of minorities (Elazar 1987; Watts 1998). As of this writing there were 23 federations in the world (with Iraq scheduled to join the list).

Confederations originate as leagues of member states that agree to share a limited number of governmental functions, such as defense or a customs union, while permitting each member state to retain its sovereignty. In confederations the member states are sovereign; the confederation itself is not—its authority is delegated from the member states. The world's most famous confederation is the European Union, though some insist it is becoming a federation. Confederations may be constructed for defensive purposes, but the units of union regard themselves as majorities, not minorities.

In federations sovereignty and authority are shared and divided between the federal government and the federated units, that is, the regional governments. In federations, then, at least two units of government have direct authority over each territory and its citizens. They are co-sovereign. In the federal government there is normally a federal assembly of the citizens as a whole, the house of representatives, that makes laws and public policy jointly with a second legislative chamber, the house of the regions (or nations), the senate. Federations may be created as voluntary unions of existing states; they may be created by a centralized unitary state as the best way to hold together diverse peoples; or they may be coercively put together (Stepan 1999). The origins of federation matter: minorities who believe they were coerced into membership may well be disposed toward secession. Voluntary unions are more likely to be lasting.

Federations typically spell out divisions of "competencies" between the different layers of government, allocating some functions to the federal government, others to regional governments, and establishing shared competencies in some domains. This "horizontal" division of powers is the hallmark of all federations. But federations vary extensively in the organization of their executives, legislatures, and judiciaries. Some, like the United States, separate them, having an executive president, a congress, and a supreme court. Others, such as Canada and India, have parliamentary governments in which the legislature controls the executive. Switzerland has an indirectly elected collective presidency. In the German model of federation the federal government makes general law and policy, whereas the regional governments, *Länder*, execute policy and enjoy significant discretion in how they implement the law. Most federations have supreme courts or constitutional courts to police the division of powers; the exception is Switzerland, which leaves federal governmental authority checked by the device of the popular referendum. In all federations, courts play crucial roles that affect the lives of minorities, especially when they regulate the interpretation of bills of rights.

Federations vary in the following five structural respects. First, in some, "residual powers" are held by the federal government, in others by the regional governments. Second, in most the federal supreme court or the constitutional court determines whether a matter is within the competence of the federal government, but there is no reason why joint courts might not decide jurisdiction. Third, in some federations the senate is coequal in power and authority with the house of representatives; in others the senate is much the weaker chamber. Fourth, in centralized federations the federal government has established fiscal and monetary superiority and control over natural resources and is able to use these capacities extensively to steer public policy throughout the regions. In others, such as Canada, Switzerland, and Belgium, the regions have extensive fiscal autonomy and are never less than full partners in making federal public policy. Fifth, federations are of two generic types: symmetrical federations insist that each region enjoys identical status, powers, and capacities; asymmetrical federations, by contrast, enable at least one regional unit to be distinctive, either culturally or in its powers and capacities.

All these structural variations may have implications for how minorities are treated by federal institutions. One should not assume, however, that either centralized or decentralized federations are necessarily better for minorities: context matters. Perhaps the most crucial factor for minorities is how the federation is nationally or ethnically conceived. Some federations are national federations, such as the United States, Germany, Austria, and Argentina. In a national federation there is presumptively one nation, and one public language and culture; the expressions "national government" and "federal government" are used interchangeably; and, typically, mino-rities are not majorities in any of the regional governments. Such federations may grant human rights to minorities, but as individuals. Typically they grant neither territorial nor cultural rights to minorities. If they do, this is explicitly conceived of as exceptional (e.g., the reservations of the indigenous Indians of the United States). Champions of national federations call them "territorial" or nonethnic federations. Their exponents claim that what matters for good relations with minorities is proper protection of human rights by both the federal and the regional governments, and the creation of federation-wide party and electoral systems that encourage cooperation across communities' ethnic origins. Typically these federations appear to work best in assimilationist settler societies where the immigrant populations are initially fairly homogeneous, such as Australia and the United States. It is not clear that they are appropriate models for peoples living in their own homelands, for example, the peoples of contemporary Iraq.

By contrast, multinational or ethnic federalists explicitly conceive of a federation as a voluntary union of peoples who retain their distinctiveness. They expect that functioning multinational federations will create dual or multiple identities among citizens: one based on federal citizenship, the other based on community of origin. They argue that one benefit of federation is that in at least some regions, nations that are minorities within the federation as a whole will be majorities who enjoy national self-government and national self-determination. Multinational or ethnic federalists believe that undue efforts to homogenize or centralize the federation will produce conflict, and they recommend pluralism and multiculturalism in public policy. They expect and are relaxed about the fact that a multinational federation will produce regional political parties. They are inclined to argue that asymmetry and tolerance are better insurance against secession than national federation—which in their view is more likely to create secessionist pressures. Examples of multinational federations include Canada and Belgium (which are both basically binational) and Switzerland. Multinational federations will usually seek to grant self-government both to territorially concentrated minorities, by entrenching regions where they are electoral majorities; and to territorially dispersed minorities, by guaranteeing them cultural rights. The more they grant the latter rights, the more the federation may be said to have a corporate or consociational as well as a territorial character.

National and multinational federations may be conceived of as polar types. Some federations hover in between these categories. India insists that it is one nation. Its federal government enjoys the right to create new regions, and it refuses to create religiously defined states, such as Khalistan for Sikhs. In these respects it behaves like a national federation. But India has also recognized nearly 30 official languages and has reconstructed its regions around these linguistic clusters. It has protected the multiple religions in the federation and permitted plural legal systems, notably in its marital laws. In these respects India is a multilingual, multireligious, and multicultural federation. The new South Africa likewise insists that it is one nation, and it has created a highly centralized federation. But it has recognized eleven official languages and has special provisions regarding traditional rulers, Zulus, and Afrikaners. In these respects it resembles a multinational or plurinational federation.

Federations have been created, broken down, and reemerged throughout the last two centuries. Though widely predicted to decay in the 1940s and 1950s federations in fact appear to be harbingers of the future. Though they number less than one in nine of the world's states, they include many of the world's geographically largest states (e.g., Russia, Canada, the United States, and Brazil) and some of the most populous states (e.g., India, the United States, Russia, and Nigeria). Indeed, it is difficult to see how some of the world's largest states and multiethnic states could be democratically governed without being federations. If the European Union becomes a federation, half the planet and a majority of the planet's minorities will then live within federations. The federation is therefore a political institution that is here to stay: the key question for minorities will be to ensure that it works in their interests. In the twenty-first century we can expect democratic federations to be encouraged for a range of multiethnic states, for example, Iraq (O'Leary, McGarry, and Salih 2004) and Indonesia.

Several factors appear to facilitate the stability of federations. Federations which have been brought into being through voluntary union and which have had a durably democratic character appear to have better prospects of enduring. Federations in which centralizers do not push their ambitions to the point of civil war are more likely to function. Arguably Czech, Serbian, and Soviet recentralizers provoked the breakdowns of Czechoslovakia, Yugoslavia, and the Soviet Union (though all these federations also had coercive origins and authoritarian pasts). Federations with a *Staatsvolk*, a dominant people, appear to have better prospects of enduring—whether because a secure majority can afford to be reasonable and generous toward minorities, or just because it can enforce its will (O'Leary 2001). Federations without such a dominant people are not doomed, however. To maintain themselves they need to adopt some of the following consociational practices: (1) executive power-sharing at the federal level which is inclusive of the key minorities in the federation; (2) proportional representation of linguistic, ethnic, and religious minorities in the federal institutions, including its bureaucracies; (3) granting cultural government to dispersed minorities and territorial government to concentrated minorities; and (4) granting minorities veto powers over major constitutional or legislative changes that might endanger their interests or identity. This is an elaborate way of saying that multiethnic societies are best advised to adopt multinational rather than national federal practices.

Federacies are singular units of government that enjoy extensive autonomy. They may be units within an otherwise unitary and centralized state that enjoy a special status. That special status makes the relationship with the central government federal or covenantal in character: the central government cannot unilaterally alter the constitutional powers and competencies of the autonomous government. The most celebrated example of a federacy is the relationship of the Swedish-speaking Aaland Islands with the Federal Republic of Finland. The idea of a federacy is a useful device to assist territorially concentrated minorities that may accept a political status which falls short of independence, but agreement on a federacy requires a partnership with the host state, a partnership in which the dominant people must accept asymmetrical institutional arrangements. Minorities throughout the world can be expected to advance both federal and federacy arrangements to enable them to recover self-government without divorcing themselves from the states within which they have found themselves entrapped.

BRENDAN O'LEARY

Further Reading

Elazer, Daniel, *Exploring Federalism*, Tuscaloosa: University of Alabama, 1987

O'Leary, Brendan, "An Iron Law of Federations? A (Neo-Diceyian) Theory of the Necessity of a Federal Staatsvolk, and of Consociational Rescue. The 5th Ernest Gellner Memorial Lecture," *Nations and Nationalism*, 7, no. 3 (2001)

O'Leary Brendan, John McGarry, and Khaled Salih, editors, *The Future of Kurdistan in Iraq*, Philadelphia: University of Pennsylvania Press, 2004

Stepan, Alfred, "Federalism and Democracy: Beyond the U.S. Model" *Journal of Democracy*, 10, no. 4 (1999)

Watts, Ronald A., "Federalism, Federal Political Systems, and Federations," *Annual Review of Political Science*, 1, (1998)

Fiji

Capsule Summary:

Country Name: Republic of the Fiji Islands

Location: Oceania, island group in the South Pacific Ocean, about two-thirds of the way from Hawaii to New Zealand

Total Population: 868,531 (2003)

Languages: English (official), Fijian, Hindustani

Religions: Christian (52% [Methodist 37%, Roman Catholic 9%]), Hindu (38%), Muslim (8%), other (2%)

Fiji comprises two large, and several hundred small, islands that together have a land area of 18,270 square kilometers (7,125 square miles). It is a slow growing, lower middle income country with a per capita GDP in 2002 of US$2,160. The economy is heavily dependent on the sugar industry, tourism, and garment manufacturing. Although generally peaceful, Fiji is one of the world's most ethnically polarized nations, and ethnic competition for political power and state resources has been present, most notably in the overthrow of Indian dominated governments in 1987 and 2000. According to 1998 estimates Fiji's ethnic groups include the Fijian (51 percent of the population, predominantly Melanesian with a Polynesian admixture), Indian (44 percent), European, other Pacific Islanders, overseas Chinese, and other (5 percent).

The indigenous Fijians, racially and culturally, have Melanesian and Polynesian roots. They first discovered and settled the country 3,500 years ago. As their population grew it coalesced into various chiefdoms between which there was some trade, blood ties, a generally common culture, and languages. Though similar, the languages nonetheless admitted of some significant regional variation. These chiefdoms frequently competed for power and were often engaged in low-level skirmishes.

European settlement began in the nineteenth century, and the superior weaponry they introduced intensified existing inter-chiefdom rivalries and permitted one chief, Cakobau, to achieve dominion over all others. It was under Cakobau's influence that Fijians abandoned their traditional religion and adopted Christianity. However, incursions and demands by American, French, German, and Tongan traders so constrained his ability to govern that he sought help from the British and ceded the country to Britain as a colony in 1874.

To make its colony profitable, the British introduced plantation sugar cane production using land leased from the native owners who managed to retain traditional communal ownership. Due to imported diseases, the Fijian population fell from a quarter million at the time of European contact, to 84,000 after the 1918 flu pandemic. Accordingly the colonial authorities turned to India for labor. Between 1879 and 1916 60,000 workers were imported under five-year contracts of indenture. Most of them chose to remain in Fiji at the end of their contracts. By 1946, Indians became a majority, numbering 130,000 to 119,000 Fijians.

While Indian settlement was concentrated in a narrow sugar-growing area and in the towns, Fijians remained largely dispersed and rural. This geographic separation, the emergence of separate schools, the colonial policy of divide and rule, and mutual antipathy between the two races, meant there was little interaction or assimilation between the two populations. Furthermore, while Indians quickly moved from sugar into other economic sectors, colonial policies limited both the spatial and occupational mobility of Fijians and prevented any significant involvement in the economy. A critical exception, however, was the army.

During World War II, while many Fijians volunteered and fought in the Solomons, virtually no Indians enlisted, being unenthusiastic for British colonial rule in Fiji and India and not being prepared to fight unless receiving the same rate of pay as European Fijians. Since then the army has remained almost totally Fijian.

In the 1950s, Indian political leaders enjoined Fijian leaders to pressure the British to end colonial control. The prospect of independence, however, did not sit well with Fijians, who feared the removal of the colonial power would lead to the takeover of their country by the Indian settlers. This fear was rooted not just in demography but also in the fact that the Indian community was playing an increasingly dominant role in small-scale retailing, small business, transportation, and the professions, as well as dominating employment in the all-important sugar industry.

Since Britain was actively committed to getting out of the colony business, the desire of Fijians for the country to remain a part of Britain was hopeless. Accordingly, Fijian and Indian delegates sat down with the colonial authorities to work out a post-independence constitution and a system of parliamentary democracy which paved the way for independence in 1970.

From 1970 to 1987 Fijians, working with other ethnic groups and Indian business interests, managed to retain political control of the country. However, in 1987 an Indian- dominated party won a general election only to be overthrown by the Fijian-dominated army. The army's claimed objectives were not simply to restore Fijian control but also to prevent Malaysia-style ethnic bloodletting. While civilian government was quickly restored, Indian representation therein was reduced and a heavy-handed system of affirmative action for Fijians was introduced. This led to widespread Indian emigration which, by 1996, led to Indians being a minority.

A new, progressive constitution in 1997 brought renewed hopes for stability. In 1999 Mahendra Chaudhry become the country's first Indian Prime Minister. One year later, however, he was overthrown in a civilian insurrection backed by some elements of the army and the Fijian establishment. Fresh elections in 2002 were won by a nationalist Fijian political party.

This recent political history shows the strong desire among Fijians for the country they discovered to remain a Fijian, Pacific state over which they can exercise self-determination, rather than have its defining character give way to a plural democracy in which Fijian claims of primacy may be reduced. However, this infringes upon the equality and political rights of Fiji's Indians. Although Fijians are now a slim majority, they perceive themselves to be a tiny minority on the world's stage, unlike Fiji's Indians who are the heirs of a culture adhered to by over one billion people. The political fault lines, therefore, include not just ethnicity and demography but also a tiny island/local community sharing the same space and political jurisdiction with an essentially continental/ global community. Adding further strains are chronic Fijian under-representation in higher education, the professions, and business; a land tenure system that hugely limits the opportunities of Indians to own land; increasing urbanization that is eroding the traditional value systems and discipline of Fijians and Indians alike; and the emergence of a Fijian middle class uncomfortable with traditional ascribed authority. The limited employment opportunities of a slow-growing economy add further strains. The main task for the future is to minimize ethnic competition for political power and to forge a more unified, national identity.

JOHN DAVIES

See also **Pacific Islanders**

Further Reading

Davies J., "On the Sources of Inter-Ethnic Conflict in Fiji," *Peace Initiatives*, vol. VI, no. 1-3 (2000)

Derrick, R.A., *A History of Fiji, Suva*, Fiji: Government Press, 1946

Fraenkel, J., "The Triumph of the Non-Idealist Intellectuals? An Investigation of Fiji's 1999 Election Results," *Australian Journal of Politics & History*, 46, no. 1 (March 2000)

Lal, Brij, *Broken Waves: A History of the Fiji Islands in the Twentieth Century*, Honolulu: University of Hawaii Press, 1992

Mara, K., *The Pacific Way: A Memoir*, Honolulu: University of Hawaii Press, 1997

Filipinos, *See* Philippines

Finland

Capsule Summary:

Location: Northern Europe, bordering the Baltic Sea, Gulf of Bothnia, and Gulf of Finland, between Sweden and Russia
Total Population: 5,190,785 (July 2003)
Ethnic Populations: Finn (93%), Swede (6%), Saami (0.11%), Roma (Gypsies [0.12%]), Tatar (0.02%)
Languages: Finnish (93.4% [official]), Swedish (5.9% [official]), small Saami- and Russian-speaking minorities
Religions: Evangelical Lutheran (89%), Russian Orthodox (1%), none (9%), other (1%)

The Republic of Finland is located in Northern Europe, bounded by Russia in the east, Sweden in the west, and Norway in the north. The country has a population of nearly 5.2 million people (2003). Most of the population lives in the southern parts of the country, concentrated mostly in the capital region of Helsinki. The Greater Helsinki metropolitan area has a population of 1.2 million people. The population is made up of two main ethno-linguistic groups, composed of the Finns (93 percent) and Finland-Swedes (6 percent). Other notable ethnic minorities include the Saami, the Roma (Gypsies), and Russians. Finland is officially a bilingual country using Finnish and Swedish. Evangelical Lutheranism dominates, although the Russian Orthodox faith is observed in small numbers.

The earliest history of settlement in Finland is traced to the Stone Age habitations dating to 8000 BCE in the eastern part of Finland. Stable settlements were concentrated chiefly on the western coast during the Iron Age (circa 400 BCE). In the ninth century, Vikings introduced settlements along the southern coast of Finland, when the Gulf of Finland became the main trade route that led to Russia and the Black Sea. The country did not evolve appreciably until the twelfth century, when the first Swedish crusade led by King Erik IX brought Finland into the Western cultural sphere and introduced Christianity to the population.

The history of Finland can be summarized as including three major periods of development. The initial crusades by the Swedes brought the country under Swedish rule and incorporated the realm of Finland into the Swedish Kingdom from the twelfth century until 1809. During this period, the Finns were an important part of the growing economy of the Swedish kingdom. They provided peasants, soldiers for armed conflicts, and settlers who developed the interior of Sweden (Värmland), as well as provided colonizers for New Sweden in North America. During the Russian period from 1809 until 1917, the Finns were able to maintain a semi-autonomous existence under the governance of the Russian czarist regime. The Swedish language remained the cornerstone of the Finnish educated class, and the minority Finland-Swedes were assured their position in the country. By the 1850s, growing nationalism among the Finnish majority led to friction with the Finland-Swedes. The Finns desired to gain linguistic rights while the Finland-Swedes sought to maintain their centuries-old position within the country. Language conflicts arose, which led to bitter struggles between the two linguistic groups. By the end of the 1910s, this language struggle had reached its peak and also became part of the initial struggles of an independent Finland. Today there are approximately 300,000 Finland-Swedes who use Swedish as their primary language. Finland gained independence from Russia in December 1917, ushering in a third historical period.

The indigenous Saami population in Finland number almost 6,000. The majority of them still live in their native area, called Sápmi, in the Province of Lapland in northern Finland. Although the Finnish government initially referred to the Saami as *Lapps*, this term has since been rejected as pejorative and the group adopted the name Saami as the preferred indigenous term. Finnish legislation has introduced a definition of Saami, which is primarily based on linguistic criteria such that a Saami is a person who identifies him or herself as a Saami; moreover, this individual, or at least one of his or her parents or grandparents, learned Saami as their first language. In 1995 the Saami definition was broadened to cover descendants of a person who had been entered in a land, taxation or population register as a mountain, forest, or fishing Lapp. The broadening of the definition has been opposed by the Saami Parliament, which alleges that it opens the door to the Saami community for persons whose forefathers had long ago been assimilated into the Finnish population.

The Roma Gypsies of Finland first arrived in the kingdom of Sweden-Finland in the sixteenth century. In spite of repressive legislation the Roma remained in Sweden. Roma joined the Swedish Army and fought in the Thirty Years War. In the seventeenth century the Roma were ordered to settle in the eastern part of the realm, Finland. At the end of the eighteenth century and the beginning of the nineteenth, the official policy was to assimilate the Roma into the Finnish population. Since the 1960s the goal has been to integrate the Roma into Finnish society, while at the same time respecting their need to maintain a distinct identity. The Roma population is presently about 10,000. Most of them live in southern Finland close to urban areas.

The Russian, or Russian-speaking, population of Finland are divided between Old Russians and New Russians. The ancestors of the Old Russians came to Finland throughout the history of Finland up until the Russian Revolution. The number of Old Russians reached its peak of 19,000 in 1921. It is difficult to estimate their present number as they have largely been assimilated into the Finnish-speaking majority or (to a lesser extent) into the Swedish-speaking minority. The number of Old Russians has been estimated as between 3,000 and 5,000. The Old Russian communities are in the urban areas around Helsinki, Turku, and Tampere. The New Russians are made up of the recent post-Soviet immigrants. It is estimated that some 20,000 Russian speakers live in Finland today, and include many Ingrians (Russian ethnic Finns), who spoke only Russian when they arrived in Finland.

At present, Finland is changing from one of the most homogenous populations to a land with increasing numbers of immigrants. Some of the most newly arriving minorities have faced struggles of acceptance. Some of these immigrant populations include Estonians (10,500), Somalis (4,800), former Yugoslavs (3,300), and Iraqis (2,800). The challenge to Finland is to adjust its attitude and welcome its new immigrants.

Finland is a well-developed, post-industrialized nation with a thriving free market economy. The Gross Domestic Product (GDP) per capita income was $25,800 in 2002, ranking with that of much of Western Europe. Its key economic sector is manufacturing, principally the wood, metals, engineering, telecommunications, and electronics industries. Trade is important, with exports such as machinery and equipment, chemicals, metals; timber, paper and pulp equalling almost one-third of the GDP.

In politics, Finland has maintained a carefully neutral position. Since World War II, the republic has steadily increased its trading and cultural relations with other countries. Finland was admitted to the United Nations in 1955, and it joined the European Union in 1995. It was the only Nordic state to join the Euro system at its initiation in January 1999. Finland maintains close ties with the other Scandinavian countries, sharing a free labor market and participating in various economic, cultural, and scientific projects. Finland elected its first female president, Tarja Halonen, in 2000.

MIKA ROINILA

See also **Finns; Roma (Gypsies); Saami**

Further Reading

Beijar, Kristina, Henrik Ekberg, Susanne Eriksson, and Marika Tandefelt, *Life in Two Languages—the Finnish Experience*, Espoo, Finland: Schildts Publishing, 1997

Horn, Frank, "National Minorities of Finland," Rovaniemi, Finland: The Northern Institute for Environmental and Minority Law, University of Lapland, 2000. http://virtual.finland.fi/finfo/english/minorit.html

Jutikkala, Eino, and Kauko Pirinen, *A History of Finland*, Porvoo, Finland: Werner Söderström Osakeyhtiö, 5th edition, 1996

McRae, Kenneth D., *Conflict and Compromise in Multilingual Societies, Vol. 3—Finland*, Waterloo, Canada: Wilfrid Laurier University Press, 1997

Zetterberg, Seppo, *Finland After 1917*, Keuruu, Finland: Otava Publishing, 2nd edition, 1995

Finns

Capsule Summary:

Location: Northern Europe, mostly in the country of Finland.
Total Population: 4,827,430 (July 2003)
Languages: Finnish (93.4% [official]), Swedish (5.9% [official]), small Saami- and Russian-speaking minorities
Religion: Evangelical Lutheran (89%), Russian Orthodox (1%), none (9%), other (1%)

The Finns are an ethnic group found in Northern Europe with a 2003 population of just over 4.8 million, the large majority of whom live within the country of Finland. The dominant language of the country is Finnish, spoken by nearly 5 million people. The Finnish language belongs to the Finno-Ugric branch of the Uralic language family. Finnish is linguistically different from other Indo-European languages found in Scandinavia to the west and the Slavic languages in Russia to the east; only the nearby Estonians across the Gulf of Finland (1 million speakers) and the Hungarians in Central Europe (10 million speakers) are linguistically related to the Finns.

The Finnish language is also found in a number of minor areas outside the country. A large contingent of Finnish speakers are found in Northern Sweden, which owe their existence to the boundaries drawn after the Finnish War against Russia in 1809. As the Torniojoki/Torneå River became the boundary between Russia (Finland) and Sweden, thousands of Finns remained in the western side of the valley, which is part of Sweden. In the northern province of Norrbotten, the Swedish and Finnish governments recognize some 20,000-35,000 Finnish speakers.

Finns settled around St. Petersburg Russia since the 1600s and are known as Ingrian Finns. During the 1930s and 40s up to 100,000 Ingrians lived along the southern shores of the Gulf of Finland. Joseph Stalin's purges sent thousands to the gulags (labor camps) of Siberia, while World War II also caused thousands to flee from the region. Over 20,000 have immigrated to Finland following the collapse of the Soviet Union in 1991. Karelian Finns in Russia also are included as Finnish speakers who have maintained an existence in the former Soviet Union, along with Finnish speakers known as Kveens, who have lived along the Arctic Ocean in northern Norway. Their numbers are smaller in comparison to the historically documented Finnish speakers in Sweden and Ingria.

The Finns also comprise a second distinct ethnolinguistic minority – the Finland-Swedes, who are natives of Finland but speak Swedish as their mother tongue. The Finland-Swedes have occupied coastal areas in Finland since the twelfth century and have developed a distinct dialect and culture, which is neither Sweden Swedish, nor Finland Finnish. Approximately 260,000 Finland-Swedes compose only 5 percent of the country's population, and are concentrated along the southern and western coasts of the country, along with the Åland Islands, located between southwestern Finland and Sweden. For centuries, the Finland-Swedish distribution has maintained itself on a narrow strip of coastland, perhaps 20 miles (32 kilometers) wide on average. Beyond this strip the Finnish speakers dominate. Most Finns (including Finland-Swedes) are Christians, belonging to the State Church, which is Lutheran. Finland has been independent from Russia since 1917, but has a history that dates well into the past.

History

The Finno-Ugric language family, which represents the dominant language of the Finnish people, has roots dating circa 7,000 BCE on the western flanks of the Ural Mountains in Siberia. From this linguistic hearth, tribal invasion and movement to the west ensued over thousands of years and led to the Finno-Ugric tribes travelling towards Finland. The movement of these early peoples split into three general directions, leading to the present day Hungarians, found in southeastern Europe; the Estonians on the southern shores of the Gulf of Finland; and the Finns in Finland proper.

Prior to settlement in Finland, the indigenous Saami (originally called Lapps under Finland domination) were encountered in the southern parts of the country. Over time, the Finns pushed the Saami further north; they now reside in the northern parts of the country. Germanic peoples from Scandinavia and Central Europe moved into the Finnish coastal areas between

1500 BCE and 800 CE, during which time many Baltic and Germanic words made their way into the Finnish language. Indeed, linguists consider present day Finns to be best identified as Indo-Europeanized Finno-Ugrians. Prior to and during the period of the Swedish Crusades, 1050 to 1150 CE, Swedes settled in the uninhabited coastlands of western and southern Finland, and brought with them their Germanic language and different cultural makeup.

Beginning in the 1150s, Sweden sought to gain control over Finland, and for the next 6 centuries, the Swedish language, society, and culture dominated the Finnish-speaking majority. The influence of Swedish language and culture in Finland was at its peak in the eighteenth century when Finnish language and culture were extant principally among the peasantry. After Sweden lost the so-called Finnish War against Russia (1808–09), Finland became an autonomous Grand Duchy within the Russian Empire. Swedish remained the official language in Finland, but by the middle of the nineteenth century, the Finnish language and Finnish nationalism was being promoted and fostered by the Finns.

Conflicts of interest and differences in ethnic attitudes and intergroup relations between the Finnish-speaking majority and Swedish-speaking minority have a long history. With the Swedish superiority and control of over six hundred years, the Finnish population and its culture were considered inferior. Without a written language, the culture of the Finns as well as any linguistic rights of the Finns were not recognized by the Swedes.

During the Russian period (1809–1917), a Finnish literature emerged, galvanizing the Finnish-speaking majority to seek more control of the country's political, social, economic, and educational elite. The formation of political parties holding a platform on Finnish linguistic rights led to eventual change. In the early 1900s, two big waves of "surname change" led thousands of Finns holding Swedish surnames to change into Finnish surnames. Street signs and other signs were made Finnish, and Swedish was abhorred by the Finnish nationalists. The Finland-Swedes in turn established a Swedish People's Party, which sought to maintain and protect the Finland-Swedish position within the society of Finland. While no armed conflicts existed between the two ethno-linguistic groups, the Finnish Civil War of 1917-1918 has left many bitter memories amongst the combatants. The War has been labeled as a class battle between the bourgeoisie and the working class—it has been shown that the winning White Guard sided with the Finland-Swedes while the Red Guard was almost exclusively a Finnish-speaking working class front. The end of the war led to atrocities by the whites, and hundreds of Reds fled abroad. In North America, many immigrants from these two factions still remain at odds and hold animosities toward one another.

Finland was the first nation in the world to embrace universal and equal suffrage, and women's right to vote was achieved in 1906. The formation of Finnish- and Swedish-leaning political parties ensured a just treatment of linguistic issues in the newly formed Finland after the Civil War. Legislation of bilingualism and equal rights to the Finnish- and Swedish-speaking populations was achieved in 1919, and the autonomy of the Åland Islands was guaranteed in 1921 as a result of the edicts declared by the League of Nations. This island is part of the island archipelago on the southwest corner of Finland, which, since the twelfth century, has had a Swedish-speaking population. Many historians and linguists consider the Åland Islands as the best example of solving the difficult autonomy and identity questions that plague many nations today. As the Finnish-speaking majority has achieved high positions and is no longer are at a disadvantage compared to the past, attitudinal differences between the coastal Finland-Swedes and the Finns persist. According to Marika Tandefelt, the "Finn still thinks that the typical Finland-Swede is a man of means" (Tandefelt, "The Finland-Swedes—The Most Privileged Minority in Europe?" 1992).

Society

The society in Finland has traditionally involved an agrarian population, with the Finnish speakers working small subsistence farms along with lumbering. The Finland-Swedes along the coast were also small-scale farmers as well as fishermen. As late as 1950, 46 percent of the population was involved in primary industries, with 27% in manufacturing industries and 27 percent in service-sector positions. Since the 1950s, Finland has changed dramatically, developing into a highly industrialized and urbanized free-market economy. In the 1990s, only some 8 percent of the workforce was engaged in primary activities, while 30% were involved in manufacturing industries and 60 percent in service-sector positions. Led by the telecommunications giant Nokia, Finland has achieved worldwide acclaim in the high-tech industries.

For centuries the educational system exclusively used the Swedish language, curtailing a Finnish educational background. The rise of the Finnish language and creation of a Finnish literature was formed during the mid-1800s as a number of well-known Finland-Swedes fought for the use of the Finnish language. These included the epic saga *Kalevala* by Elias Lönnrot (1802–84), and the patriotic poetry of Johan Ludvig Runeberg (1804–77). Another influential statesman and thinker was Johan Vilhelm Snellman (1806–81), who fought for equality between the Finnish and Swedish languages, and helped establish Finnish-speaking grammar schools. As the Finnish language became formalized in schools across the country, over time, the largest university in Scandinavia, the University of Helsinki, also began to teach classes in Finnish rather than Swedish. In the Finland-Swedish areas of the country, the 1921 legislation has guaranteed that in unilingual Swedish-language communities, Swedish language is used in education. In the Åland Islands, the Swedish language enjoys more autonomous rights, along with privileges for their own stamps and flag.

Due to the rise in economic prosperity, the Finns have been able to maintain an excellent healthcare system and social infrastructure. A national health insurance scheme provides all residents with equal access to healthcare facilities, medical attention, and drug benefits. Many of these are provided free of charge for chronically ill patients, while others pay minimal fees. The Finns are proud of their egalitarian system which has allowed women to move up the socioeconomic ladder. In fact, maternity/paternity leave which is generously supported by employers and the government is allowed for both mothers and fathers. A growing number of fathers elect to stay home with their newborn babies.

Mika Roinila

See also **Finland; Saami; Sweden; Swedish-Speakers**

Further Reading

Allardt, Erik, and K.J. Miemois, "A Minority in Both Centre and the Periphery: The Swedish-Speaking Population in Finland," *European Journal of Political Research*, 10, (1982)

Beijar, Kristina, Henrik Ekberg, Susanne Eriksson, and Marika Tandefelt, *Life in Two Languages—the Finnish Experience*, Espoo, Finland: Schildts Publishing, 1997

Blom, G., et al., editors, *Minority Languages—The Scandinavian Experience*, Oslo, Norway: Nordic Language Secreteriat, 1992

Facts about Finland, Keuruu: Otava, 1999

Jakobson, Max, *Finland in the New Europe*, Westport, Connecticut: Praeger, 1998

Jutikkala, Eino, and Kauko Pirinen, *A History of Finland*, Porvoo, Finland: Werner Söderström Osakeyhtiö, 5th edition, 1996

McRae, Kenneth D., *Conflict and Compromise in Multilingual Societies, Vol. 3—Finland*, Waterloo, Canada: Wilfrid Laurier University Press, 1997

Roinila, Mika, *Finland-Swedes in Canada: Migration, Settlement and Ethnic Relations*, Turku, Finland: Institute of Migration, 2000

Tandefelt, Marika, "The Finland-Swedes—The Most Privileged Minority in Europe?" in Zetterberg, Seppo, *Finland After 1917* (2nd edition), Keuruu, Finland: Otava Publishing, 1995

France

Capsule Summary

Country Name: French Republic
Population: 60,180,529 (2003)
Religion: Roman Catholicism; Islam; Protestantism
Language: French

France is a territory of 212,918 square miles (551,500 square kilometers), which is divided administratively into 96 departments. The national territory also comprises four overseas departments (Guadeloupe, Martinique, French Guyana, and Reunion, which are all former colonies), three overseas territories (New Caledonia, French Polynesia, and Wallis and Futuna) and two territorial collectivities (Mayotte, Saint-Pierre and Miquelon). The overseas territories and the territorial collectivities have a different status and are not a part of the European Union, as is the rest of the nation.

France is the highest producer of agricultural goods in the European Union, and the second-highest in the world, after the United States. France ranks fifth in the world in terms of production and foreign exchanges. Since the 1990s, France has been the number one tourist destination in the world. In 2002, the Gross Domestic Product (GDP) per capita was $26,000. France has been a presidential democracy since 1958 and the signing of the constitution of the Fifth Republic. The President is directly elected for five years.

As of 2003, France had a population of 60,180,529. The French people are mostly Catholic (90 percent), but there are also Muslim (4 percent), Protestant (2 percent) and Jewish (1 percent) populations. The ethnic composition of France is varied, a consequence of the historical formation of the territory and the history of colonization and immigration.

The Roman region of Gaul was the first variation of modern day France. It was mostly peopled by Celts and Romans after the conquest of Gaul by Rome. French history is generally traced back to when the Francs settled the region, at the time of the great invasions in the fifth century. The arrival (or invasion) of the Barbarians from the east and the north contributed to the collapse of the Roman Empire, and the ethnic formation of the different people of present day Europe, including France.

The French population today is the result of the mixing of early Celt, Latin, and German peoples. The Francs Saliens and the dynasty of the Merovingians (481-751) played a leading part in the religious formation of the future France with the baptism of the king Clovis, between 496 and 506. Roman Christianity was primarily spread, however, by the dynasty of the Carolingians (751-987), who included such leaders as Charles Martel and Charlemagne. It also was under this dynasty that the *Occidental Francie*, future kingdom of France, was born, when the empire of Charlemagne was being divided up at Verdun in 843.

The long reign of the Capetians (987-1792) brought unity to the kingdom of France, with a central power in the king of France. The authority of the king was strengthened by the prestige attached to the divine character of the monarchy. There was an alliance between the king and the Catholic Church, symbolized by the crowning of the King. The Capetians expended the crown lands and reduced feudal power. That dynasty included the direct Capetians (987-1328), the branch of the Valois (1328-1589) founded by Philip VI, and the branch of the Bourbons (1589-1792) founded by Henry IV.

During the Capetian era, the edict of Villers-Cotterêts was issued, which imposed the use of the French language instead of Latin in official governmental and administrative documents. The Capetian era saw the end of the wars between the Catholics and the Protestants (under the reign of Henry IV) that began in the second half of the sixteenth century, which paved the way for the legal recognition of Protestantism in France. Roman Catholicism remained the official religion of the French state until the law decreeing the separation of the church and the state on December 9, 1905.

The French Revolution was triggered by a serious financial and political crisis, as well as the philosophical ideas which gained currency during the Enlightenment. The French Revolution resisted royal absolutism, abolished feudal rights, and established equality in society, as guaranteed by the Declaration of the Rights of Man and of the Citizen of 1789.

A mass immigration began in the second half of the nineteenth century. The first census of 1851 revealed that 380,000 foreigners lived in France. Thirty years later, they numbered one million. Until World War I, their number had steadily grown. The migrants mainly came to work in the mining, textile, and metallurgic industries. Most of them came from neighboring states. Until the end of the nineteenth century, the majority were Belgian. The Belgian people represented 38 to 46 percent of the foreign population in France. At the beginning of the twentieth century, they were outnumbered by the Italians. In 1911, the Italians composed 36 percent of the foreign population and the Belgians 25 percent; the foreign population estimation was at that time 1,160,000 persons (i.e., 2.6 percent of the total of the French population).

This mass immigration continued during World War I. Approximately 342,000 workers arrived in France during the course of the war. After the war, with the reconstruction of the country underway, France needed foreign manpower. A new wave of migrants settled in the country up to the beginning of the 1930s. In 1921, the recent immigrants represented 3.9 percent of the total population; by 1931, that number had risen to 7 percent. In addition to the border states which had supplied the previous generation of immigrants, this next wave of individuals seeking work also came from Eastern Europe. The Polish were the largest Eastern European immigrant population, numbering 406,000 in 1921, and 508,000 in 1931.

The economic depression of the 1930s brought about the introduction of new legal measures with regard to immigration. A law passed on August 10, 1932 limited the number of immigrants who could legally work in France. Any potential immigrant seeking to work in France had to obtain a ministerial authorization to enter the French territory, and would be legally permitted to work only in a specific industry where workers were needed. The policy became more restrictive with the law of February 6, 1935 that obliged migrants to have an identity card in order to work. In the inter-war years, a high unemployment rate coupled with a mass of political refugee immigrants (primarily Armenians, Jews, and Russians) contributed to an increase in xenophobia in France.

After World War II, France once again found itself faced with a shortage of workers. A policy was officially put forward for the recruitment of immigrant workers. The edict of November 2, 1945 created the National Office of Immigration (ONI) which became the Office of International Migrations (OMI) in 1987. It was set up expressly to assist in the immigration process and oversee immigration to France.

Up to the end of the 1950s, the foreign population in France was small, only representing 4 percent of the total population in 1946, and 3.6 percent in 1954. However, the rapid economic growth of the next twenty-odd years witnessed a simultaneous rise in immigration. From the middle of the 1950s until the official end of immigration in 1974, foreign-born individuals arrived in continuous waves. In 1947, an edict allowed for the free circulation of residents between Algeria and France. Since 1975, Algerians have formed the second-highest immigrant community, behind the Portuguese. The census of 1999 revealed that 3,260,000 foreigners were resident in France, composing 5.6 percent of the total population.

Since the 1950s, the countries of origin of immigrants have become more varied. Immigrants from Asia and especially sub-Saharan Africa have steadily increased in steadily since the 1990s. The integration of these newcomers is based on the principles of the French Republic, meaning that ethnic particularities are overlooked, while allegiance to the customs and law of secular France is encouraged. The ideal goal is the integration of every immigrant into French society. Assimilation into the French society is mainly carried out via the educational system. The recognition of regional languages has been at the center of heated debates in France. Some regional languages are now taught at schools, but French is still the only official language. The success and usefulness of the French system of immigrant assimilation is currently a matter of debate.

MONIQUE MILLIA-MARIE-LUCE

See also: **Africans: Europe; Algeria; French**

Further Reading

Braudel, Fernand, *L'identité de la France*, édition Arthaud-Flammarion, 1986

Brubacker, Rogers, *Citoyenneté et nationalité en France et en Allemagne*, édition Belin, 1997

Horowitz, Donald, and Gérard Noiriel, *Immigrants in Two Democraties, French and American Experience*, New York University Press, 1992

Lebecq, Stéphane, *Les origines franques (5e-11e siècle)*, édition du Seuil, 1990

Noiriel, Gérard, *Le Creuset français, histoire de l'immigration 19e-20e siècle*, édition du Seuil, 1988

French

Capsule Summary

Location: France; Europe; Africa; North America
Total Population: 60,180,529 (2003.), plus approx.2 million living abroad
Languages: French; English
Religion: Primarily Roman Catholic

Approximately two million French speakers and citizens live outside the national borders of France. They may be more numerous than that, given that available statistical sources only cover French individuals that have registered with the consulates in question. The French living abroad represent a heterogeneous group. Not only does this expatriate community include those who live abroad for only a short period of time, it also includes those who left France permanently. It also comprises people of French nationality, or those who have a double nationality, as citizens of both France and another nation. The French living abroad may be civil servants temporarily living abroad, or students. Though the French living abroad constitute a significant numerical group today, a look at the history of expatriation reveals that moving abroad generally has not been an especially appealing option for the French population.

Unlike many countries in recent centuries, France did not experience large waves of emigration as a result of economic factors, war, or demographic pressures. Nevertheless, France does have a long history of emigration. The emigration of the French in any significant numbers began at the time of the Crusades and also surged during the great maritime expeditions of the sixteenth and seventeenth centuries. Several Europeans expeditions, including that of the French Jacques Cartier, explored the American and Asian continents at that time. The discovery of new sea routes contributed to the history of navigation techniques and a better knowledge of the world. It also led to the establishment of European colonies all around the world. The history of the French living abroad can thus be linked with French colonial history.

The development of the colonies required manpower and a labor force. In addition to the use of the local population and the introduction of slaves, the French government encouraged the emigration of settlers by paying their passage, and sometimes by giving them land. The government also made use of foreign immigration (such as Chinese and Indian immigration to the French West Indies after the abolition of slavery) and the French penitentiary population. The prisons of French Guyana and New Caledonia initially provided a significant labor force to assist in the exploitation of the colonies.

Between the seventeenth and the nineteenth centuries France claimed territories all around the globe, but few French people expatriated themselves to these colonies. Before the resumption of the colonial expansion at the beginning of the nineteenth century, French émigrés were present primarily in the Caribbean territories. Santo Domingo had approximately 10,500 residents, Guadeloupe had 13,500, and Martinique had 10,500. In the first quarter of the twentieth century, French émigrés were numerous in the colonies of North Africa. Algeria had a population of 690,132 French nationals in 1926, Morocco had 74,558, and Tunisia had 71,090 in 1926.

For a long time the French living abroad were settled in former French colonies, particularly in Africa, the Near East, and the Middle East. Since the 1990s, however, there has been a shift in destinations. The directive that citizens of European Union (EU) member states can migrate easily across those states' borders led some French residents of France to move to other EU nations, such as Germany or Switzerland. There is also a notable emigration to Eastern European countries; the number of French expatriates to Poland and the Czech Republic doubled between 1991 and 1995. French emigration is supported by extensive institutional and private networks and organizations, such as the Center for the French Living Abroad, a division of the Ministry of Foreign Affairs.

The French-speaking communities of the world are referred to as *la francophonie,* a term created in 1880 by Onésime Reclus to describe the linguistic and cultural community composed of France and its colonies. For a long time it referred pejoratively to the French colonial enterprise. However, the term has been reclaimed for more positive use, and today it valorizes French culture and has two different meanings. With a capital letter, *Francophonie* refers to the governments of countries that have in common the use of French in their work and their exchanges. They have regularly met in summits since the Convention of Niamey in 1976, which also created the *Agence de coppération culturelle et technique* (it became the *Agence de la francophonie* in 1997). When spelled with a lowercase initial letter, *francophonie,* the term refers to the body of peoples or groups of speakers that partly or entirely use the French language in their daily life. Today, the French language is present on every continent and is spoken by approximately170 million people.

Naturally, the greatest number of French-speakers are found in France and the bordering nations of Belgium, Luxembourg, and Switzerland. But to a large extent, the former French colonies have contributed to the perpetuation of the French language. The history of the French living abroad and the history of French-speaking communities are linked to French colonial history.

MONIQUE MILIA-MARIE-LUCE

See also: **Colonialism; France**

Further Reading

Gentil, Bernard, *La population française immatriculée à l'étranger est en forte hausse*, INSEE, no. 919, août 2003

Rossillon, Philippe, *Atlas de la langue française*, Bordas, 1995

Tétu, Michel, *Qu'est-ce que la francophonie*?, Hachette-Edice, 1997

Frisians

Capsule Summary

Location: Along Dutch and German North Sea Coast
Total Population: approximately 1 million
Language: Frisian
Religion: Protestant

The Frisians are linguistically a quite heterogenic group living in four different areas along the North Sea Coast and on the offshore islands in the Netherlands and Germany. The origin of the name (Frisians, Friesen, Fresken, and several other variants) remains unclear. There are different hypotheses based on derivations from certain proto-languages such as Indo-European and Germanic and from Old Frisian. Among the possible meanings are "the ones from the edge (i.e. coast)" and "the loved ones (i.e. friends)" (Indo-European), "the free ones" (Germanic), and "those with curly (frizzy) hair" (Old Frisian).

The three areas populated by Frisians today are the Dutch province of Frisia (West-Frisia), the German landscape East-Frisia stretching from the Dutch border to the Jade Bay, and the German district North-Frisia stretching from the City of Husum up to the Danish Border. One Frisian-speaking group resides in neither of the areas mentioned above but in a landscape called Saterland not far from the city of Oldenburg.

An exact figure of the number of Frisians presently living in Germany and the Netherlands is difficult to ascertain. Approximately 1 million people inhabit Frisian territory: 600,000 in West-Frisia, 350,000 in East-Frisia, and 50,000 in North-Frisia. However, there is neither legal status granted to Frisians nor any objective criteria making a person a Frisian. Frisian ethnicity is achieved through a mixture of criteria ranging from language, birth, marriage, residence, or just a sympathy and identity with Frisianity. The Frisian language is the most outstanding feature of Frisian ethnicity, however, not all people regarding themselves as Frisians actually speak the language.

Frisian belongs to the West Germanic branch of the Indo-European language family and is thus a close relative of English. There are three major dialect groups, West-, East-, and North-Frisian, which correspond with the aforementioned geographic areas.

West-Frisian has the greatest number of speakers, approximately 400,000, while North-Frisian is spoken by approximately 10,000 persons. East-Frisian is not spoken in East-Frisia anymore but by roughly 1,500 persons in the aforementioned Saterland which was settled by East-Frisians in the thirteenth century.

Frisians were first mentioned by Pliny the Elder (23-79 CE) as a Germanic group to have settled around the mouth of the river Rhine. According to the Alexandrian astronomer and geographer Ptolemy (circa. 85-160 CE), the easternmost boundary of the territory inhabited by Frisians was the river Ems. Around the year 800 CE Frisians settled as far north as the mouth of the river Elbe. While under Frankish rule, the Frisian area was divided into West, Middle, and East Frisia. In 1289, West Frisia (today the northern part of the modern Dutch province of North-Holland) came under the dominion of the Counts of Holland while East-Frisia remained part of the East-Frankish empire. Middle Frisia, which comprised modern West-Frisia and the northern part of the province of Groningen, gained political independence during the thirteenth and fourteenth centuries.

In contrast, the history of North-Frisia remains somewhat unclear. However, most scholars agree that the islands were settled first while the mainland was settled from either the islands or from the southern parts of Frisia. The time of settlement is highly disputed, ranging from 500 to 1000 CE for the mainland and sometime well before the year 0 to 700 CE for the islands. Except from the short period when historical Middle Frisia was politically independent, the Frisias were incorporated into the state territories of The Netherlands, Denmark, and several German counties and kingdoms that became the German Reich and modern Germany successively. Today Germany and the Netherlands remain the two states incorporating Frisian territory.

Frisians do not experience ethnic discrimination in the Netherlands or Germany by the respective majorities, and German and Dutch Frisians are not denied any rights other citizens enjoy. In Germany, Frisians were even regarded as particularly Germanic since the beginnings of the Romantic Movement in the late eighteenth and early nineteenth centuries. However, since the early twentieth century, Frisian discomfort against a supposed German or Dutch influence grew steadily, leading to a strong Frisian movement which gained power throughout the century. The idea of a Frisian identity apart from a Dutch or German identity is quite common among Frisians today. In 1925 the first supraregional Congress of Frisians was held, and in 1930 the Frisian Council with delegates from the three regions was formed. In West-Frisia, the *Fryske Akademy*, a scientific center for research and education concerning West-Frisia and its people, language, and culture, was founded in 1938 in the city of Leeuwarden, and the University of Groningen offers study programs in Frisian language and literature. In 1985 the provincial council declared Frisian a second official language. However, this legislation was turned down by the central government and resulted in a compromise which in turn was rejected by the highest court of the Netherlands. After years of negotiation, Frisian became a fully accepted language, even permissible for use in court since an appropriate law became effective in 1997.

The history of German Frisians differs remarkably. From the 1940s until the 1970s the Frisian language was regarded as anti-modern—even among Frisians. This attitude, combined with the fact that many inhabitants left for the cities, caused a sharp decline in the numbers of Frisian-speakers. Only in the last 20 to 30 years has Frisian culture and language regained prestige. Today there are two university chairs for Frisian language and literature in Kiel and Flensburg, respectively, and a *Nordfriisk Instituut* (founded in 1948/1949 in Bredstedt), which is dedicated to the cultivation, promotion, and study of Frisian language, history, and culture. However, the general knowledge about Frisian is still extremely limited. The legal status of Frisian in both The Netherlands and Germany improved through the European *Charter for Regional or Minority Languages* which was ratified in 1995 by the Dutch and in 1998 by the German parliament.

LARS KARSTEDT

See also **Germany; Netherlands**

Further Reading

Borchling, Conrad, and Rudolf Muus, editors, *Die Friesen,* Breslau, 1931

Gorter, Durk, "A Frisian Update of Reversing Language Shif," in *Can Threatened Languages Be Saved*? edited by Joshua A. Fishman, Clevedon: Multilingual Matters Ltd, 2001

Markey, Thomas L., *Frisian,* The Hague, Paris, New York: Mouton, 1981

Ramat, Paolo, *Das Friesische: Eine sprachliche und kulturgeschichtliche Einführung*, Universität Innsbruck, Institut für Sprachwissenschaft, 1976

Friulians

Capsule Summary

Location: Northeast Italy (Friuli-Venezia Giulia region)
Total Population: 1,000,000
Language: Friulian

Friulian is the native Romance language of Friuli (or *Friûl*), presently part of the Autonomous Region of Friuli-Venezia Giulia. In the extreme northeast of the present territory of Italy, it shares political and administrative borders with the Veneto Region (Italy) to the west, Austria to the north, and Slovenia to the east, and linguistic borders with the Venetian dialect of North Italian, German, and Slovene. The region's geographic limits are the Dolomite Alps, the Carnic Alps, the Julian Alps, and to the south, the Adriatic Sea. With the capital in Trieste, Friuli-Venezia Giulia measures 3,028 square miles (7,842 square kilometers).

Friulians speak a Romance language that some linguists connect with the Rhaeto-romance (Romansh) language in Switzerland and Ladin in the Italian Alps. Others consider it a North Italian dialect, although as a sister dialect, it is not directly subordinated to standard Italian. Standard Italian is in itself a recent phenomenon, since it existed only as a written variety since Dante used it in the fourteenth century, and it was only in the nineteenth century that a standard norm was created and slowly introduced.

Friulian is spoken in the region north of Venice toward the Austrian and Slovene borders, surrounding the city of Udine. It is not officially recognized as a language but enjoys considerable unofficial support from the Friulian-speaking community. It is also spoken in two neighboring provinces of the Veneto region in the southwest. Trieste is situated in the east, close to the Slovene border, but the more centrally located town of Udine is the cultural center of Friulian culture.

After the collapse of the Roman empire the Friuli-Venezia Giulia region was taken by different Germanic tribes (mainly Langobards) while the Byzantine Empire (i.e. Eastern Roman Empire) conquered the coast. Later on, after some centuries of Venetian dominance, Trieste and the northern part of the region was taken by Austria. Austria conquered the rest during the Napoleonic wars, at the beginning of the nineteenth century.

In 1866 Udine and most of the region joined the recently unified Italy, while the north was not returned from Austria until 1918. Trieste remained a disputed territory between Yugoslavia and Italy until it was finally given to Italy in 1954. It became a semi-autonomous region in 1963.

Approximately 700,000 people speak Friulian (or Furlan) in the region today, and Friulian-speakers outside Italy (mainly in Australia, North America, South Africa, and Romania) number some 300,000, which makes it one of the largest minorities in Italy. According to the UNESCO evaluation it is an endangered language, and due to strong Italian influence, it is sometimes difficult to ascertain if a person speaks Friulian and not Friulian-flavored Italian. Up until World War II different dialects were predominantly used by the majority of the Italians, and although standard Italian has increasingly dominated in most parts of the country, this is also the case in Friuli. Differences among dialects remain noticeably bigger in Italy than in other European countries.

There are three dialects of Friulian: a conservative northern variety (Carnic Friulian with two subvarieties), the most commonly used central-eastern one, spoken in Udine and in the southeast of the region (with three subvarieties), and, finally, the more Italianized and innovative western variety, influenced by the Veneto dialects close to Venetia. There is a high degree of mutual understanding and recognition among speakers of all the dialects, so most speakers of each are easily understood throughout the region. No religious or political obstacles impede this intercommunication.

Although there are some phonetic and morphologic differences among the dialects, these do not constitute a linguistic or communicative hindrance. Remnants of the long contact with German and Slovene languages remain in Friulian vocabulary. Presently the central dialect is gaining terrain and is generally used for both literary and official purposes.

Friulian experienced a high point in its sense of linguistic identity in the 1950s, when two new grammar books, a description of the dialects, and a history of the Friulian language were published. After gaining status as a semi-autonomous region in 1963, Friuli-Venezia Giulia was able to increase the usage of Friulian in mass media and consider its introduction into the schools. The administrative unification of the Friulian-speaking areas in 1961 led, however, to the emergence of organizations and movements such as *Moviment Autonomist Furlan, Int Furlan,* and *Scuele libare furlane*, dedicated to the preservation of Friulian language and culture.

More recently, the economic differences between Southern and Northern Italy have led to a political split in the 1990s, and most of the independence movements in Northern Italy have been drawn into the *Lega Nord* party in its aspiration to create more autonomy or even a new country—Padania. The Friulians still have a linguistic problem with this because they want to maintain their own language and culture. As recently as 1996 a regional law was passed that promoted the Friulian language and finally, after long discussions, a unified orthography was chosen. The chief cultural society, *Società Filologica Friulana,* was responsible for this and used it in the influential dictionary *Nuovo Pirona.*

The promotion of Friulian has lagged behind the dominance of the so-called colonial Venetian dialect, which was the official language from the fifteenth to the eighteenth centuries. More than half the population uses Friulian at home (55 percent) and 46 percent use it among friends. However, it is true that its speakers are growing older and that Italian is spreading among younger people. On the other hand, there is a recent interest in Friulian even among the youth, which might change the situation. The relatively high degree of bilingualism and Italian lexical interference do not bode well for the future of Friulian, however, since it is always difficult to fight against a prestigious majority language. Nevertheless, the still widespread use of Friulian in most daily situations is a promising sign for the survival of Friulian and the diversified linguistic situation of Italy may also help Friulian survive.

INGMAR SÖHRMAN

See also **Italians**

Further Reading

Francescato, Giuseppe, "A Sociolinguistic Survey of Friulian as a Minor Language," *International Journal of the Sociology of Language*, no. 9 (1976)
Frau, Giovanni, *Friuli*, Pisa: Pacini, 1984
Gregor, Douglas Bartlett, *Friulian Language and Literature*, New York and Cambridge: Oleander Press, 1975
Hearder, Harry, *Italy. A Short History*, London: Cambridge University Press, 1990
Holtus, Michael Günter, Michael Metzeltin, and Christian Schmitt, editors, "Friaulisch," in *Lexikon der romanistischen Sprachwissenschaft* [in Italian], Vol. 3, Tübingen, 1989

Fulani

Capsule Summary

Location: West Africa, mostly in the Sahel region
Total Population: approximately 11 to 12 million
Language: Fulfulde (Fulani or Fulbe)
Religion: Muslim

The Fulani, also known as the Fulbe, Fula, and Peul, are one of the most widespread ethnic groups in West Africa. Known primarily for their expertise as cattle pastoralists, many Fulani today practice other occupations such as farming, commerce, and Islamic education. The Fulani are spread across two thousand miles of savanna, from Senegambia on the Atlantic coast in the west to Cameroon and the Central African Republic in the east. They are easily the most significant pastoralist group in West Africa, and one of the most important and widespread pastoral groups in Africa in general. They were also the single most instrumental black African group in spreading Islam, the dominant religion, throughout much of the savanna region of West Africa.

Presently Fulani number between approximately 11 and 12 million in many different countries, primarily Mauritania, Senegal, the Gambia, Guinea-Conakry, Mali, Niger, and Nigeria, with smaller numbers in neighboring countries. However, they are not the majority in any West African nation. Their dispersion across the Sahel region and intermarriage with other ethnic groups makes it virtually impossible to count their population accurately in any single country. Their language is part of the West Atlantic group of Niger-Congo languages and is closely related to Wolof and Sereer, languages spoken originally in Senegambia. Because of their widespread geographic distribution, there are numerous dialects of Fulfulde, the language of the Fulani.

Because of this broad dispersion across Anglophone and Francophone countries, the Fulani have been known by a variety of names in the literature. Arbitrary distinctions between Muslim and non-Muslim and between nomadic and sedentary Fulani have caused variations in terminology. Even today there is considerable confusion about what term to use and who is actually Fulani. All Fulani speak the language of Fulfulde, which has numerous dialects, depending on location. The Fulani of Senegambia call themselves *Haalpulaar'en* (speakers of Pulaar, the local dialect of Fulfulde). In addition, Fulani in Futa Toro are often called *Futankobe* or *Futanke*, while those of Futa Bundu are known as *Bundunkobe*. During the colonial period, the French divided the *Haalpulaar'en* of Senegal into *Toucouleur* or *Tukolor*, whom they considered primarily agricultural and centered in Futa Toro, and *Peul* or *Peuhl*, using the Wolof term for primarily pastoral peoples inhabiting the upper river region and the Casamance. The French also mistakenly labeled the so-called Tukolor as radical anti-French Muslims, and considered the Peuls as docile non-Muslims. The government of Senegal, many Senegalese, and some scholars continue to differentiate between Tukolor and Peul to the present, inaccurately treating them as separate ethnic and linguistic groups. Many Senegalese, especially the Wolof, refer to the dialects of the Fulfulde language spoken in Senegal and the Gambia as *Tukolor*. Guinea Fulani are often called *Pula Fuuta*, after their center of concentration in Futa Djallon. In Sierra Leone and the Gambia, the Malinke term, *Fula*, is most often used to refer to local Fulani. In Niger, the Fulani are labeled *Woodabe*, or "red Fulani," because of their apparently lighter complexion than other groups. In northern Nigeria, the Fulani are actually called the *Fulani*, borrowing the Hausa term. Others refer to both the Hausa and the Fulani as the *Hausa-Fulani*, combining the two closely related and mixed ethnicities into one large group. In Cameroon, the Fulani are called the *Adamawa Fulbe* as their concentration in that area is greatest in the Adamawa region of northern Cameroon.

Some Europeans, especially in Anglophone regions, divided the Fulani into town Fulani, who mostly farmed, and cattle Fulani, who were more pastoralist and usually non-Muslim. Hence, a people with an essentially similar language, culture, and identity are found in the literature under a confusing variety of names. Recent scholarship confirms that all these groups are essentially Fulani. The language of the Fulani is Fulfulde with numerous dialects.

Origins

The origins of the Fulani have caused considerable speculation among early European ethnographers and have continued to puzzle later Western anthropologists, linguists, and historians. Fulani oral traditions suggest an origin in Egypt or the Middle East, a common theme in West African Muslim traditions. According to these origin myths, the Fulani then migrated westward until they reached the Atlantic Ocean. They then moved south into the highlands of central Guinea. Based on these traditions, some early ethnographers ascribed an Egyptian, Arab, or even Jewish origin to the Fulani who appeared to be lighter-skinned, taller, and more Caucasoid than other West African groups. Some commentators claimed that the Fulani were not African at all but a Semitic people. These ethnographers also concluded that the Fulani spread from North Africa and then east to west, finally drifting southward in a deliberate and calculated pattern. In all these accounts, the Fulani were associated with pastoralism and some Fulani groups were also accredited with a devout adherence to Islam.

Linguistic evidence suggests that the Fulfulde language belongs to the West Atlantic subgroup and is closely related to Wolof and Serer, both spoken originally in western Senegambia. Therefore, the modern Fulani and their language, Fulfulde, originated in Senegambia, probably in the northern river area of Futa Toro. The original Fulani may have descended from a pastoral group inhabiting the Western Sahara in the Chadian wet phase 5,000 to 10,000 years ago, before moving into the Mauritanian Adrar as the Sahara dried up. Later they may have gradually filtered down to the lower and middle Senegal River Valley, the area known as Futa Toro, and intermarried with local groups. From Futa Toro, the Fulani most likely spread into the Sahel zone along the Senegal and Niger Rivers, and then further east. They also migrated south from Futa Toro into the upper Senegal River valley, the upper Casamance region, and eventually into the Futa Djallon highlands of Guinea. Existing landowners throughout West Africa had no reason to treat the pastoralists as competitors for resources and did not hinder their spread. Occasionally clashes did occur between the migratory Fulani and settled farmers, but more often the interaction was peaceful cooperation. It is also likely that the Fulani migrated to areas that were suited to cattle herding and that did not require considerable defense from farmers. The migratory process was not a single set mass movement but a series of short and long distance moves, sometimes temporary and sometimes permanent, occurring at various intervals over hundreds of years.

Society

The Fulani have always maintained a strong sense of identity separate from other West African groups. They have consistently been aware of their occupational specialty and distinctive appearance. In fact, many Fulani may feel racially superior to their agricultural neighbors and have incorporated some of the early European ideas about a North African or Middle Eastern origin into their traditions. Traditionally, the Fulani have always emphasized their independence and freedom of mobility in comparison to their settled neighbors. The Fulani note that they follow the *pulaaku*, or traditional Fulani way of life, which includes certain standards of behavior, language, and ideology.

The Fulani, like many neighboring West African groups, have also maintained a strong caste system. The free-born consist of Fulani-origin nobles, and the majority, non-noble "pure" Fulani. Artisans have traditionally belonged to specialized, hereditary, endogamous occupational groups, including ironworkers, silver and goldsmiths, woodworkers, leatherworkers, and entertainers, or *griots*. Among most Fulani, descendants of former slaves, often called *maccube*, form a distinctive, endogamous strata. The *maccube* perform certain tasks, such as well and grave digging, that free-born Fulani consider beneath their status.

History

The Fulani dominated several states in precolonial West Africa. The earliest known state in Senegambia, Tekrur, which flourished in the central Senegal River valley from the tenth through the thirteenth centuries, was dominated by predecessors of the Fulani. Tekrur, which also included minority populations of Wolof, Berber, and Soninke, was succeeded by Futa Toro, which stretched along the Senegal River for approximately 250 miles (402.3 kilometers) from north to south, but only about 15 miles (24 kilometers) on either side of the river. In the period from 1490 until 1776, Futa Toro was ruled by a Muslim dynasty. From Futa Toro and its environs, a Fulani clerical diaspora helped spread Islam throughout West Africa. It was also during this period that other Fulani from Futa Toro began to migrate permanently to the south and to the east, eventually spreading the Fulani way of life across the Sahelian belt to the Central Sudan and northern Cameroon.

In 1776, the Muslim Fulani clerics of Futa Toro overthrew the ruling dynasty and established a clerical oligarchy or *almamate*. The Fulani of Futa Toro engaged in agricultural and pastoral activities as well as extensive river and desert trade. They ruled over minority populations of Soninke, Wolof, and Berber. A group of Fulani from Futa Toro established a clerical oligarchy in Bundu to the south of Futa Toro on the upper Senegal River. In addition to the Muslim Fulbe, Bundu also included non-Muslim pastoral Fulbe, Mandinka, and Soninke populations. By the 1880s, both Futa Toro and Bundu were conquered and colonized by the French and incorporated into their colony of Senegal.

In the highlands of Guinea, the Fulani dominated the state of Futa Djallon, a kingdom founded in approximately 1725 where the Senegal, Niger, and Gambia Rivers originate. The Muslim Fulani of Futa Djallon, also closely related to the Fulani of Futa Toro and Bundu, established a Muslim state that dominated the region until the French conquest of the late nineteenth century. Another Muslim Fulani state was Futa Masina, centered on the Niger River in modern day Mali. Like other Fulani states in the Western Sudan, Futa Masina was dominated by the clerical Muslim Fulani who ruled over several different ethnic groups and practiced a combination of farming and herding. All the Fulani states in West Africa had a strong Islamic identity.

In addition to forming their own states, the Fulani played critical roles in pastoralism and trade in most centralized precolonial West African states and kingdoms, including the ancient Western Sudanic kingdoms of Ghana, Mali, and Songhay. The rulers of these states (the Soninke, the Mande, and the Songhay peoples respectively), exacted tributes and taxes from both the Fulani herdsmen and the Fulani town merchants. In general, relations between sedentary agricultural peoples and the Fulani were based on mutual cooperation and trade, although periodic clashes erupted over water and pastureland. The Fulani also became renowned for their Islamic learning. Beginning in the sixteenth century, the Fulani began increasingly to adopt Sufi brotherhoods, especially the Qadirayah and Tijanniyah branches, carried across the Sahara Desert from North Africa by Tuareg and Berber traders. By the late eighteenth century, many devout Muslim Fulani were rejecting the leadership of non-Muslim leaders, non-Fulani rulers, and even some Muslim leaders they considered insufficiently Islamic.

Two major Islamic reform movements in nineteenth century West Africa were led by the Fulani. Usman dan Fodio, a Fulani from northern Nigeria, led a reform movement beginning in 1802 against the numerically dominant Hausa. The movement established the Sokoto Caliphate which included part of modern day southern Niger and much of northern Nigeria. By the 1840s, the caliphate was one of the dominant states of West Africa and was unrivaled in its size, military power, and economic strength. The Fulani of the Sokoto Caliphate incorporated numerous Muslim and non-Muslim groups into their vast empire. In 1903, the caliphate fell to the British and most of it was eventually incorporated into the colony of Nigeria. A small northern section of the caliphate was incorporated into the Federation of French West Africa. Another Fulani Muslim cleric, al-Hajj Umar Tal who was born in Futa Toro in 1794, led a reform movement in the Western Sudan that created the so-called Toucouleur Empire. This large empire controlled most of modern day Mali. As in their other states, the Fulani minority ruled over numerous other ethnic groups until the European conquests of the late nineteenth century.

Several smaller Fulbe-dominated *almamates* emerged in the late nineteenth century in the Gambia region. The most important of these was Fuladu, led by Alfa Molo Balda who subdued three small Mandinka states on the south bank of the Gambia River. The French took over control in 1903.

Under colonial rule in the late nineteenth and early twentieth centuries, most nomadic Fulani abandoned the purely pastoral life and adopted agriculture and trading as their primary occupations, although they kept their traditional attachment to cattle and herding. According to colonial officials, the Fulani were noted for their herding skills as well as their Islamic learning. In northern Nigeria, the administration began to refer to both the Hausa and the Fulani as the Hausa-Fulani, reflecting the increasing mixture of Hausa and Fulani groups in the region.

When most countries where the Fulani lived in West Africa became independent in 1960, they formed a significant minority in numerous nations but did not constitute a majority anywhere. Some Fulani did hold important government positions and rose to prominence. Many Fulani in the rural areas refused to send their children to government schools, preferring Islamic education. In addition, government schools were presumed to corrupt young Fulani by teaching them French and removing them from traditional Fulani beliefs. Fulani maintained their reputation for Islamic scholarship and cattle-herding skills, even though the vast majority did not practice pastoralism as their primary or even secondary occupation. The Fulfulde language is not the most important national language in any country, although it is one of the most widely spoken languages, both by Fulani and others, in numerous nations.

Ethnic Conflicts

Because of their minority status, the Fulani suffered considerable persecution under the regime of Sekou Toure in Guinea-Conakry who accused them of plotting to overthrow his regime, dominated by the Susu and the Mande. Many Fulani fled into exile in neighboring Senegal, Guinea-Bissau, and Sierra Leone. With the death of Sekou Toure in 1984, many Fulani returned to Guinea-Conakry, but a large number remained in their adopted countries, further contributing to the Fulani diaspora in West Africa.

In Mauritania, dominated by Maures of Arab-Berber descent, the Fulani, as well as other African groups, have been persecuted by the military regime. Large numbers of Fulani exiles fled across the Senegal River into neighboring Senegal. In 1994, border clashes erupted between Senegal and Mauritania, and thousands of people were displaced on both sides, with large numbers of Fulani being forced to leave Mauritania to take up permanent residence in Senegal. The situation between the two countries has stabilized although many of the Fulani have remained in Senegal.

Today there are certain areas within the Sahelian nations of West Africa where the Fulani are numerically dominant. These include the Senegal river valley in both Mauritania and Senegal, the upper Gambia region, Futa Djallon in central Guinea, the Kayes-Nioro region of western Mali, northern Burkia Faso, central Niger, northern Nigeria, and northern Cameroon. However, because of their minority status, the Fulani have often been assimilated into the dominant ethnic group of the country or region. This is especially true in Senegal, where many Fulani now speak Wolof as their primary language and frequently intermarry with Wolof and Serer. In northern Nigeria, the Fulani and the Hausa have become so intertwined as to be referred to as the Hausa-Fulani. In some cases, for example, the Woodabe of Niger, the Fulani have remained quite distinct from their neighbors. It remains to be seen, however, how long the Fulani will be able to maintain their separate identity, language, and traditions in the twenty-first century.

Andrew F. Clark

See also **Mali, Mauritania, Nigeria, Senegal**

Further Reading

Azarya, Victor, *Aristocrats Facing Change*, London: Sage, 1978

Clark, Andrew F., "The Fulbe of Bundu (Senegambia): From Theocracy to Secularization," *International Journal of African History Studies,* 29, no. 1 (1996)

Curtin, Philip, *Economic Change in Precolonial Africa: Senegambia in the Era of the Slave Trade,* Madison: University of Wisconsin Press, 1975

Dupire, Marguerite, *Organisation sociale des Peul*, Paris: Plon, 1962

Hanson, John, *Migration, Jihad, and Muslim Authority in West Africa: The Futanke Colonies in Karta*, Bloomington: Indiana University Press, 1996

Kane, Moustapha, and David Robinson, *The Islamic Regime of Fuuta Tooro*, East Lansing: Michigan State University Press, 1984

Last, Murray, *The Sokoto Caliphate*, London: Longman, 1977

Robinson, David, *The Holy War of Umar Tal*, Oxford: Clarendon Press, 1985

Stenning, Derrick, *Savannah Nomads,* London: Oxford University Press, 1959

Webster, J.B., et al., *The Revolutionary Wars: West Africa since 1800*, London: Longman, 1980